Broken Eagles

Volume 2:
WÜRTTEMBERG, BADEN, HESSE-DARMSTADT,
WESTPHALIA, AND THE SMALLER STATES

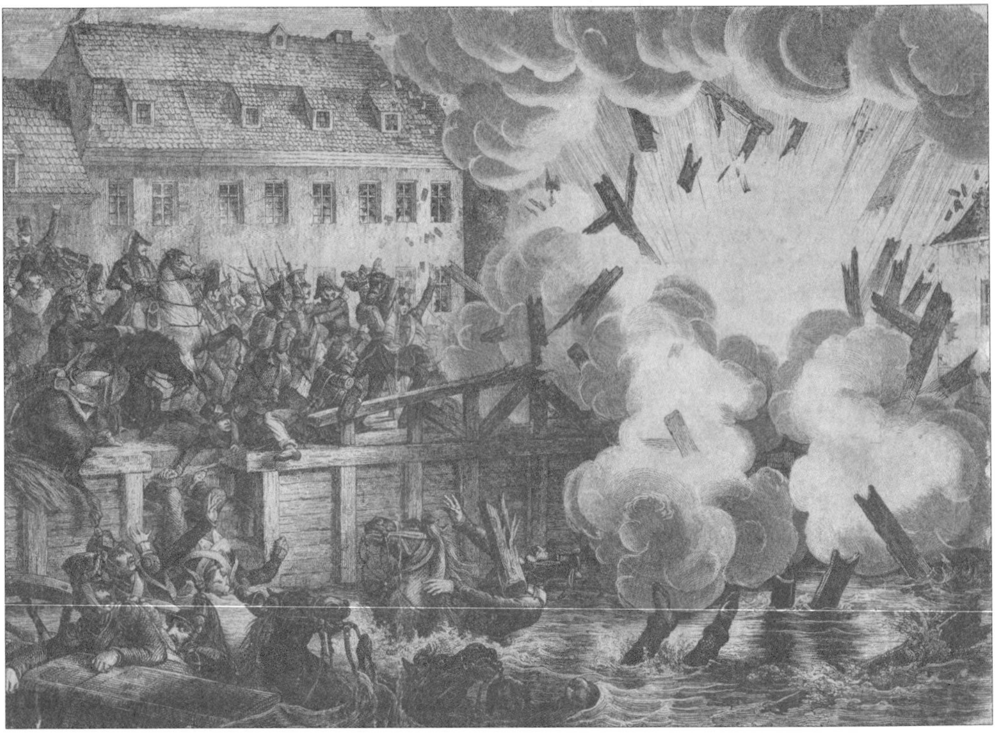

Broken Eagles

Napoleon's German Allies *and the* Campaigns of 1813

Volume 2:
WÜRTTEMBERG, BADEN, HESSE-DARMSTADT, WESTPHALIA, AND THE SMALLER STATES

John H. Gill

Greenhill Books

Broken Eagles
First published in 2025 by
Greenhill Books,
c/o Pen & Sword Books Ltd,
George House, Unit 12 & 13,
Beevor Street, Off Pontefract Road,
Barnsley, South Yorkshire S71 1HN

www.greenhillbooks.com
contact@greenhillbooks.com

ISBN: 978-1-80500-176-8
ePub ISBN 978-1-80500-177-5
pdf ISBN 978-1-80500-178-2

All rights reserved. No part of this book may be reproduced, transmitted, downloaded, decompiled or reverse engineered in any form or by any means, electronic or mechanical including photocopying, recording or by any information storage and retrieval system, without permission from the Publisher in writing. NO AI TRAINING: Without in any way limiting the Author's and Publisher's exclusive rights under copyright, any use of this publication to 'train' generative artificial intelligence (AI) technologies to generate text is expressly prohibited. The Author and Publisher reserve all rights to license uses of this work for generative AI training and development of machine learning language models.

© John H. Gill, 2025

The right of John H. Gill to be identified as author of this work
has been asserted in accordance with Section 77
of the Copyrights, Designs and Patents Act 1988.

CIP data records for this title are available from the British Library

The Publisher's authorised representative in the EU
for product safety is Authorised Rep Compliance Ltd.,
Ground Floor, 71 Lower Baggot Street, Dublin D02 P593, Ireland.
www.arccompliance.com

Edited and designed by Donald Sommerville
Typeset in 10.8/13.8 pt. Arno Pro Small Text

Printed and bound in the UK by CPI Group (UK) Ltd,
Croydon, CR0 4YY

Frontispiece: The premature detonation of the bridge over the Elster River west of Leipzig on 19 October stranded thousands of French and Rheinbund troops in the doomed city, most notably the Baden and Hessian contingents as well as the Berg Lancers of the Imperial Guard.

These volumes are dedicated to
Gregory James Gill
(1956–2022)
Best of Brothers.

Contents

Lists of Maps, Charts and Schematics — ix
List of Illustrations and Credits — xiii

Introduction to Volume 2 — 3

CHAPTER 4 **Württemberg: Unconditional Obedience** — 7
König Friedrich: Generals are not Permitted to Challenge Decisions 9; Your Majesty No Longer Has an Army 16; Uniformed Farm Boys 20; Injunctions, Marches and Secret Instructions 26; Across the Elbe 34; Exhausting Pursuit: We Faced the Enemy Rear Guards Daily 44; The Armistice: Cantonments, Controversies and Condemnations 47; The 38th Division: Autumn Actions East of the Elbe 62; Normann's Brigade: Innumerable Small Engagements 84; Grim October: From Wartenburg to Leipzig and Home 90

CHAPTER 5 **Baden and Hesse-Darmstadt: Fighting to the Last** — 119
Baden: 'Current Circumstances Require Efficacious Measures' 119; Hesse-Darmstadt: Remnants, Recruits and Remounts 126; The Spring Campaign: Glories, Privations and Long Marches 133; The Armistice Period: Reviews, Replacements and Repose 153; The Autumn Campaigns: 'Marches in the Most Dreadful Rain' 158; Leipzig: The Great Drama 174; From France to the Coalition: A Capitulation not a Convention 196

CHAPTER 6 **Westphalia: Kingdom's End** — 205
The Moral Conquest of a Model State 207; 1809–1813: The Evolution of an Army 210; The Spring Campaign: Inundated with Enemy Bands 224; Armistice Arrangements 237; Autumn: A Mixed Record on the Road to Leipzig 241; September: The Porous Kingdom 258; Leipzig: Encircled by Every Nation! 281; Last Days of the Kingdom and an Unroyal Dismissal 284

| CHAPTER 7 | The Miniature Monarchies: A Spectrum of Soldiers | 290 |

1812: Small State Contingents to Russia and Back 290; Würzburg: A Habsburg in the Rheinbund 294; Frankfurt: The Prince-Primate's State 304; Berg: Cudgel Russians and Loyal Lancers 308; The Saxon Duchies: 'Where is your Contingent?' 317; The Anhalt Duchies: In Battle for Both Sides 332; The Lippe Principalities: Lost in Magdeburg 337; Reuß, Schwarzburg, and Waldeck: Bound for Magdeburg 341

| CHAPTER 8 | The Fortress War: The Iron Yoke of Fate | 345 |

Defence, Defiance, Disease: Rheinbund Fortress Garrisons 346; Danzig: A Community of Perils and Courage 348; Vistula, Oder and Elbe: The Rheinbund under Siege 370

	Epilogue	397
	Notes	417
APPENDIX 1	Synoptic Tables of Battles and Sieges/Blockades	507
APPENDIX 2	Draft Evasion, Desertion and Defection	510
	Bibliography	518
	Index	569
	Gazetteer	576

In the first part of this study:

Broken Eagles
Volume 1:
THE CONTINGENTS OF SAXONY AND BAVARIA

CHAPTER 1	A War to the Death
CHAPTER 2	Saxony: The Price of Loyalty
CHAPTER 3	Bavaria: The First to Fall

Maps, Charts and Schematics

Maps

All maps © John H. Gill 2025. All rights reserved.

33. Württemberg Marches and Actions, April–June 1813	page 29
34. The Württemberg Division at Bautzen, 20–21 May 1813	37
35. Groß-Rosen, 31 May 1813	46
36. Württemberg Marches and Actions, August–September 1813	65
37. Thießen and Euper, 3–4 September 1813	68
38. Operational Area, September–October 1813	87
39. Engagement at Wartenburg, 3 October 1813	93
40. Operational Area North of Leipzig, 16 October 1813	101
41. 39th Division Marches and Baden/Hessian Actions, April–October 1813	135
42. The 39th Division at Lützen, 2 May 1813	138
43. Baden & Hesse at Leipzig, 19 October 1813	176
44. Locations of Major Westphalian Formations on Resumption of Hostilities, 16 August 1813	245
45. Area of Allied Raids into Westphalia and Thuringia, April and September–October 1813	255
46. Chernishev's Raid into Westphalia, September–October 1813	264
47. Chernishev's Attack, 28–30 September 1813	267
48. The Fortress War Overview: Places Blockaded and/or Besieged	347
49. Blockade & Siege of Danzig, January–December 1813	355

Charts

27.	Württemberg Units, February–October 1813	page 19
28.	Initial Württemberg Contingent, April–May 1813	25
29.	Württemberg Reinforcements, late May 1813	51
30.	Württemberg Contingent, August 1813	63
31.	Reorganised Württemberg Contingent, September–October 1813	82
32.	Renumbered and Renamed Württemberg Cavalry, 1813	111
33.	Baden Units, 1813	122
34.	Hessian Units and Organisation, 1808–1813	128
35.	Rheinbund Troops in 3rd Corps, mid-April 1813	132
36.	The Glogau Garrison, Spring Campaign	151
37.	Rheinbund Troops in 3rd Corps, August 1813	159
38.	The Baden 2nd Brigade, 14 August 1813	167
39A.	The Leipzig Garrison, 30 September 1813	170
39B.	Wilhelm von Hochberg's Command, Late September 1813	171
40.	Baden and Hessian Troops at Leipzig, 16–19 October 1813	178
41.	The Westphalian Army, 1812–1813	211
42.	Westphalian Troops in Germany, mid-to-late April 1813	222
43.	Westphalian Field Forces, mid-August 1813	246
44.	Girard's Command, mid-August 1813	252
45.	Westphalian Home Defence Forces, September 1813	259
46.	Select Allied Raiding Detachments, mid-September 1813	263
47.	Dispositions of Minor State Contingents, 1812	291
48.	Dispositions of Minor State Contingents in the Theatre of War, 1813	293
49.	Microstate Monarchs, 1813	318
50.	Forces at Magdeburg, 15 September 1813	328
51.	The Danzig Garrison (10th Corps), 21 January 1813	350
52.	Rheinbund Troops of the 34th Division at Danzig, early 1813	352
53.	The Modlin Garrison, 1 February 1813	371
54.	The Küstrin Garrison, 21 February 1813	375
55A.	The Torgau Garrison, 21 October 1813	382
55B.	The Torgau Garrison, 11 November 1813	383
56.	The Dresden Garrison, 10–11 October 1813	390

Schematics

2.	Baden Contingent Deployments, January–November 1813	123
3.	Hessian Contingent Deployments, January–November 1813	130

Key to Map Symbols

Countries are plain text: Bavaria   Regions/provinces are italics: *Silesia*
International border: ————————   Internal border: ....

Primary road: ══════   Secondary road: — — — — —

Forests/large gardens: Marsh/water meadows: Windmills:

Outlines for towns/villages include gardens as well as structures as these contributed to the defensive value of the buildings.

Fortresses or forts: ★   Battles and engagements:

Units types are indicated by the following symbols with nationality shown by colour: white for Allied, black for French and grey for Napoleon's Rheinbund allies.

    Allied: **French:**   **Rheinbund:**
Cavalry units:
Infantry and mixed units:
Artillery (all sides): ▯▯▯   **Cavalry outposts:**

Examples:
Bavarian 29th Division = 29   **Allied III Corps =** III

Allied movements (advance and retreat) are shown with dashed lines, while those of the French and Rheinbund troops are solid.

Allied movement = ·····►   **French/Rheinbund movement =** ——►

Date format: day/month so that 19/6 = 19 June

Notes on Charts & Schematics

Unless otherwise specified, all strength figures are for those officers and men (combined) 'present under arms' (*présens sous les armes, rücken aus*, etc.), that is, those who were available for combat at any particular moment. These figures also include some (such as drummers) who were not always considered 'combatants'. In French and in most German strength reports, 'present under arms' was *not* the same as 'effectives'. The term 'effectives' would usually be much larger as it included those detached, sick, prisoners of war or otherwise absent in addition to those immediately at hand. Note that the number detached could be half or more of a unit's strength, especially in the case of light cavalry which were favoured as scouts, escorts for senior officers and staff orderlies; furthermore, all cavalry units often had large numbers of dismounted men 'detached' in depots along the line of communications awaiting fresh horses.

The following abbreviations are used:
  Bde = brigade
  Bns = battalions
  Div = division
  Sqdns = squadrons
  Pdr = pounder (as in 6-pounder)

Format: where multiple battalions of a regiment are present, an entry such as 'Würzburg Regiment (II, III)' shows that the Würzburg Infantry Regiment was assigned with its 2nd and 3rd Battalions. If only one battalion is present, the entry will read 'V/Würzburg' (5th Battalion of the Würzburg Infantry Regiment).

Illustrations and Credits

Frontispiece

Destruction of the Elster bridge at the end of the Battle of Leipzig, 19 October 1813 (*Leipzig, VS000765*).

Plates

1. Three phases of an officer's life in 1812–13: self-portraits by Württemberg Leutnant Christian von Martens (*all LABWHStA*).
2. Uniforms. a) Württemberg line infantry; b) Württemberg light infantry; c) Württemberg Leib-Chevauleger (*all Napoleonic Uniforms, vol. III*); the Engagement at Euper, 3–4 September (*LABWHStA*).
3. Uniforms. a) Baden light dragoon (*Napoleonic Uniforms, vol. III*); b) Bavarian lieutenant serving as common soldier (*ASKB*); c) Anhalt Jäger-zu-Pferd; d) Saxon-Gotha line infantry; e) Saxe-Weimar light infantry; f) Berg lancer (*all Napoleonic Uniforms, vol. III*).
4. Hessian encampment during the armistice (*HStAD*); Hessian infantry; Hessian Garde-Chevauleger (*both Napoleonic Uniforms, vol. III*).
5. Uniforms. a) Westphalian line infantry; b) Westphalian light infantry; c) Westphalian Garde-Fusilier; d) Westphalian Chevaulegers-Garde; e) Westphalian hussar; f) Westphalian cuirassier (*all Napoleonic Uniforms, vol. III*).
6. Uniforms. a) Würzburg infantry; b) Würzburg chevauleger; c) Frankfurt infantry; d) Lippe infantry; e) Reuß infantry; f) Schwarzburg infantry (*all Napoleonic Uniforms, vol. III*).
7. Battle of Dennewitz, 6 September; Battle of Wartenburg, 3 October (*both LABWHStA*).
8. Leipzig: the Grimma Gate after the battle (*Leipzig, GR17151*); Corvée labour outside a fortress (*ASKB*).
9. French leadership: Ney (*ASKB*); Marmont (*Author*); Bertrand (*ASKB*); MacDonald (*Author*).

10. Württemberg leadership: König Friedrich (*Author*); GM Karl Graf von Normann-Ehrenfels (*Wikimedia*); GM Ludwig Friedrich von Stockmayer (*LABWHStA*); GL Friedrich von Franquemont (*Wikimedia*).
11. Württemberg Jägers at Bautzen (*Stein*); Prinz Emil of Hesse-Darmstadt (*HStAD*).
12. GM von Normann's Württemberg cavalry attacks Lützow at Kitzen (*Author*); Württemberg troops escort Lützow prisoners (*LABWHStA*).
13. Graf Wilhelm von Hochberg; GD Jean Rapp; Jérôme Bonaparte; GM Karl Freiherr Stockhorner von Starein (*all Author*).
14. Bridge and fortress at Würzburg (*LABWHStA*); Bombardment of Würzburg (*Author*).
15. Soldiers improving defences (*ASKB*); Bread riot in Dresden (*Leipzig, VS000988*); Firewood Shortage (*ASKB*).
16. The final assault on Leipzig (*Leipzig, GR009959*); Allied monarchs enter Leipzig (*Leipzig, GR009899*).

Illustration Acknowledgements and Abbreviations

ASKB = Anne S. K. Brown Collection where the former curator, Mr Peter Harrington, repeatedly earned my special appreciation for his courtesy, knowledge and helpfulness.

HStAD = Hessisches Staatsarchiv, Darmstadt. The sketches of the armistice encampment are from Best. G 61 N2. 26/4, Rußland–Feldzug 1812–1813, Band 3: Tagebuch des Garde Füsiliers Regiments in der Campagne 1812 u. 1813 von GM Schmidt (special thanks to Dipl.-Ing. Nasser Amini)

LABWHStA = Landesarchiv Baden-Württemberg, Hauptstaatsarchiv, Stuttgart: J 56 Bü 4, 5 and 52,'Tagebuch meines Feldzuges', Christian von Martens; and M 703 R195N1, Karl Stockmayer, Generalmajor.

Leipzig = Stadtgeschichtliches Museum Leipzig (thanks to Dr Poser and Herr Brandt).

Napoleonic Uniforms, vol. III = John R. Elting, *Napoleonic Uniforms*, vol. III, Rosemont: Emperor's Press, 2000 (with special thanks to Mr Todd Fisher).

Stein = Herr Markus Stein (with warm thanks).

The curators and staffs at the following museums and archives have all been remarkably prompt and helpful in providing images and valuable suggestions: Hessisches Staatsarchiv, Landesarchiv Baden-Württemberg Hauptstaatsarchiv, Museum Bautzen, Militärhistorisches Museum der Bundeswehr, Stadtgeschichtliches Museum Leipzig, Städtische Galerie Dresden.

Broken Eagles

Volume 2:
WÜRTTEMBERG, BADEN, HESSE-DARMSTADT,
WESTPHALIA, AND THE SMALLER STATES

Introduction
to Volume 2

WELCOME TO VOLUME 2 of this study of the Confederation of the Rhine (Rheinbund) armies in 1813, the year that broke Napoleon's German alliance. As explained at the end of Volume 1, this account has been divided into two parts in order to present the readership with a manageable work without compromising on detail or analysis.

The first volume opened with an overview of the Rheinbund as an institution and a brief review of its history before turning to a tight summary of the complex conflict that stained the lands between the Vistula and the Rhine with blood in 1813 (Chapter 1). These elements set the context for the participation of the various Rheinbund contingents in the battles, blockades, sieges and marches that comprised the spring and autumn phases of the war. The next two chapters examined in detail the roles of the Saxon and Bavarian contingents within the historical and political framework of each state.

The war presented Saxony with an existential crisis. Exasperated by the French alliance, fearful of the Russo-Prussian bloc and seeing their land devastated by the armies of both sides, the king's advisors persuaded him to sign a convention with Austria that they hoped would assure neutrality. The court, however, quickly discovered that neutrality was a delusion. König Friedrich August therefore abrogated the agreement with Austria after little more than three weeks and reaffirmed his fealty to the French emperor. He remained true to this decision for the remainder of the brutal contest, a loyalty that left him a prisoner of war after the Battle of Leipzig and cost him half his kingdom at the Congress of Vienna. In the meantime, his army fought across the length and breadth of his realm, generally serving well but suffering especially at Großbeeren (23 August) and Dennewitz (6 September) before most of its remaining troops defected to the Coalition during the fighting at Leipzig on 18 October. The Saxon heavy cavalry was an exception, gaining glory for its actions at the Battle of Dresden (26–27 August) and earning honest praise until formally released from service after Leipzig.

In addition to describing these famous battles, the narrative also gave particular attention to the Engagement at Kalisch in Poland on 13 February as this prominent piece of the Saxon Army's history has never received a detailed treatment in English.

Bavaria's leaders also perceived an existential threat in 1813. Like Saxony's monarch, Bavaria's König Max Joseph turned to Austria as the least bad option in this crisis, but he only agreed to an alliance treaty with the Habsburg crown on 8 October (the Treaty of Ried) after months of hoping for some sort of neutral outcome. He thereby preserved his state and dynasty (albeit as a decidedly junior ally) and eventually received some compensation for territories lost to Austria after the war. In interactions with the French, on the other hand, the Bavarian regime cleverly used the threat of Austrian invasion to limit the number of troops committed to the Grande Armée. Although the Rheinbund treaty obligated Bavaria to provide 30,000 men for the 'common defence', the kingdom sent only one division of fewer than 8,000 men to the war front along the Elbe, citing its need to protect its long border with Austria and Bohemia to restrict its contribution. Though neglected by Munich once it was dispatched, the division served satisfactorily until after Leipzig, only returning home on receiving permission from its French commanders. As this division's remnants were marching back to Bavaria, however, General von Wrede, formerly one of Napoleon's favourites, was leading a combined Austro-Bavarian army to intercept the tattered Grande Armée as it retreated to the Rhine. Napoleon repulsed Wrede in the two-day Battle of Hanau at the end of October, but the French defeat at Leipzig and Bavaria's defection cued the rapid collapse of the entire Confederation.

Saxony and Bavaria will feature conspicuously in this present volume as well. The former because so much of the war was fought inside Saxony's borders, the latter because Wrede's march was a critical factor in coercing other Rheinbund monarchies to capitulate quickly. Indeed, the Kingdom of Württemberg, the Grand Duchy of Baden and the Grand Duchy of Hesse-Darmstadt all received dire and direct threats from Wrede as he advanced towards the confluence of the Main and Rhine Rivers in late October. All would likely have left the Rheinbund in any case, but Wrede's haughty ultimatums accelerated the process.

This volume begins with these three states. Chapter 4 discusses Württemberg and its corpulent König Friedrich, a ruler of iron will and high intelligence who insisted on absolute obedience to his royal commands. The bulk of the Württemberg contingent served with great distinction throughout the war, piercing the Allied centre on the second day at Bautzen (21 May), conducting stout rear-guard actions in August after Großbeeren and resisting to the last in the bitter fighting at Dennewitz (6 September) and Wartenburg

(3 October). One cavalry brigade, however, operated separately, participating in the controversial crushing of a Prussian raiding detachment in June and then defecting to the Allies on 18 October at Leipzig to Friedrich's intense disapproval.

From Württemberg, the focus shifts to Baden and Hesse-Darmstadt in Chapter 5. Most of the troops from these two contingents served together in the 39th Division during the entire war, conducting independent patrols and fighting tenaciously at the centre of the French line at Leipzig. The Baden contribution to the defence of Glogau during the spring was another example of competence, courage and loyalty. Notably, though trapped in Leipzig by the premature destruction of the lone bridge leading out of the city, the two young princes who commanded these contingents insisted on being taken prisoner so as not to attract the dishonour of changing sides without the approval of their monarchs.

The short-lived Kingdom of Westphalia is the subject of Chapter 6. Under Jérôme Bonaparte, Napoleon's youngest brother, Westphalia was supposed to be a Confederation 'model state', but it was already unsteady when 1813 began and suffered repeated shocks during the war as Allied raiding parties penetrated its borders and even captured its capital Kassel for a few days. The crowd of central German microstates examined in Chapter 7 were also subject to Allied raids and propaganda. The quality of the contingents from these different states varied widely. Some Westphalian units performed adequately when properly led. Others, under the command of weak officers or the often-feckless Jérôme, disintegrated under pressure. Most of the tiny microstate contingents were even less reliable. Assigned to the garrison of Magdeburg, some crumbled in their lone open battle (Hagelberg, 27 August) and all became such a nuisance to the fortress governor that he released them rather than expend scarce resources on troops noted for desertion. In contrast, Würzburg contributed a generally well-regarded contingent and Berg, the other 'model state', supplied a fine regiment of lancers that was brigaded with the Imperial Guard.

This volume's final chapter (8) covers fortress warfare in 1813. Rheinbund troops comprised parts of the garrisons of many of the fortresses the French continued to hold along the Vistula, Oder and Elbe Rivers during both the spring and autumn phases of the conflict. Some, such as the Bavarian and Westphalian regiments in Danzig, were considered exemplary by their French commanders. Some began to diminish through desertion over time, especially after Leipzig, but others served with honour and skill until the end. The details highlight the importance of distinguishing among units within a contingent as well as between contingents, such as the excellent reputation enjoyed by the 1st Westphalian Infantry Regiment in Danzig and the scepticism with which the French viewed the kingdom's troops elsewhere in the theatre of war. The different fortress experiences also illustrate the need to assess the various contingents over time as troops that had been reliable enough during the spring or early in the autumn might become increasingly unsteady and even eager to depart or desert after Napoleon's cataclysmic defeat at Leipzig. Combining this chapter with the account of the Bavarian defence of Thorn described in Volume 1 thus provides a synoptic history of all the sieges and blockades involving Rheinbund troops during 1813.

An epilogue and two appendices conclude this volume. The epilogue analyses the Rheinbund experiences in 1813 in broad terms, offering general observations about these armies and their states within the political context of the time and within the historiography of the era. Appendix 1 consists of two matrices showing when and where each contingent served, whether in the open field and/or as part of a fortress garrison. Finally, Appendix 2 provides a discussion and assessment of the challenging topics of draft evasion, desertion and defection, highlighting the problems of data in understanding these issues and suggesting possible avenues for future research.

I am pleased to offer this completed work to the reading public. Founded on years of research in archives across Germany as well as France, it is unprecedented and as comprehensive as possible within reasonable limits of time and space. As the author, it is my hope that you will enjoy reading it as much as I have enjoyed writing it.

Chapter 4
Württemberg: Unconditional Obedience

'His Royal Majesty has been most displeased to learn that some officers of His army have taken the liberty of making unacceptable remarks about military affairs, politics and relations with other powers. The Most High hereby again forbids such most earnestly and adjures each and every officer to unconditional and silent obedience to the orders of His Royal Majesty as those are made known to them by their superiors.'

Royal order read to the army, 16 April 1813[1]

WÜRTTEMBERG'S HISTORY WITH NAPOLEON resembled that of its neighbour Bavaria in many respects. Both southwestern German states had allied themselves with France as Napoleon drove towards Ulm in 1805 (Württemberg sent a brigade to perform line of communication duties), both joined the Rheinbund as founding members in 1806, both participated on the margins of the 1806–7 campaigns and both played significant roles in 1809. In recompense for their allegiance, Napoleon greatly expanded both states, thereby justifying the elevation of the two monarchs to royal status. The stern Kurfürst Friedrich thus became the first König von Württemberg just as Max Joseph became Bavaria's first king. Moreover, the French emperor, satisfied with the manner in which the two new kings managed their states, did not meddle in their internal affairs. Friedrich, like Max Joseph, was able to avoid dispatching troops to Spain, but neither could evade the imperial summons to participate in the invasion of Russia in 1812. Indeed, Württemberg eventually committed 15,800 men to the Russian expedition, well above its 12,000-man obligation under the Rheinbund treaty. As with Bavaria and all the other Rheinbund contingents, however, the fine Württemberg army that crossed the Niemen was consumed in the ensuing months and images composed by Württemberg artillery Leutnant Christian Wilhelm von Faber du Faur have become emblematic of the campaign's many miseries.[2] In early 1813, therefore, König Friedrich, in common with his fellow

Rheinbund rulers, was faced with the daunting task of creating an entirely new army under the hideous shadow of the Russian debacle.

The political circumstances of the two states were also similar. Both Friedrich and Max Joseph feared revolution and found the proclamations issued by the Russians and Prussians threatening rather than promising. Neither trusted Prussia and both were wary of Russia's intentions despite close family connections (Friedrich was Tsar Alexander's uncle and a brother and a nephew of his were serving Russian generals). 'These middle states', Friedrich would tell one of his diplomats in 1814, 'will be the victims of both powers as they were the victims of Napoleon'.[3] Nor did either have any desire to see Germany return to its dispensation under the defunct Holy Roman Empire. Appalled by the outcome of the Russian war, sceptical about Napoleon's ability to recover, suspicious of one another and fearful of losing all that they had gained thanks to their alliances with France, each viewed Austria as a determining factor for his own future. Both Munich and Stuttgart were thus trying to gain time in desperately uncertain circumstances: exerting themselves to placate Napoleon and urging him to make peace, while limiting their commitments to the rebuilding Grande Armée and hoping for Habsburg help to attain and maintain some form of neutrality.[4] Neither court, however, regarded Vienna with unalloyed trust. As Franz Binder von Krieglstein, the Austrian ambassador in Stuttgart, reported on 13 January 'They are disproportionately afraid of us and are worried beyond words about the role we will play after the French are defeated.'[5]

Another shared concern was domestic stability. Although both kings worried that anti-French sentiment and Coalition propaganda would generate disturbances internally, Württemberg had less to fear from the sort of irredentist movements that burned in Bavaria's Tyrol and Vorarlberg. Friedrich, however, was not without his concerns, as he outlined to his foreign minister in a 23 February letter:

> Furthermore, I cannot hide from you that dissatisfaction with everything French is escalating daily in Stuttgart and in the lowlands. The return of the officers, many of them sick, crippled and unfit for duty so that they must be discharged, who unambiguously attribute all the hardships suffered and all the horrors endured to the mistakes and obstinacy of one man, is daily giving rise to a mood, which does not actually cause me to fear anything in respect to loyalty and devotion towards me and my house, but whose influence on officers and soldiers must arouse no little concern… The court and my table are perhaps the only places where these sentiments are not openly expressed. But even the most moderate, driven to exasperation, seem to renounce their previous views. Proclamations to the public are

beginning to be posted in various places across the country... which speak of liberation from the oppressive yoke with the assistance of Austria.

He concluded this missive with the ominous observation that 'The mine is growing bigger and bigger; God protect us it if explodes.' Friedrich's concerns were excessive, but rumours, satiric verses and forbidden pamphlets were certainly in circulation and the returning soldiers made an appalling impression. Nonetheless, tight controls on the press and strict policing would preclude any premature detonation through to the end of the alliance.[6]

König Friedrich: Generals are not Permitted to Challenge Decisions

If they shared many fears and hopes, however, Bavaria and Württemberg were starkly different in the nature of their monarchs. Unlike the amiable and anxious Max Joseph who appended his signature to Montgelas's memoranda without changes, Friedrich was every inch the king and allowed neither subject nor foreigner to forget whose hand held the royal sceptre in Stuttgart. Friedrich, like Max Joseph, had considerable military experience. He had spent 1774 to 1781 as a Prussian officer under Frederick the Great, going on campaign during the War of Bavarian Succession but seeing little combat before resigning as a major general to take service in Catherine the Great's Russia. Here he served in both military and administrative positions (though again seeing little combat) before returning to Württemberg where he became *Herzog* (duke) upon his father's death in 1797 and *Kurfürst* (prince elector) in 1803. His time in Prussia and Russia imbued him with their sense of enlightened absolutism and he quarrelled incessantly with the old estates on assuming his birth right, chafing under the restrictions they imposed on his rule. In addition to a dramatic increase in territory and the royal title, therefore, one of the most important benefits of the Rheinbund for the newly-minted König Friedrich was the ability to sweep away an encumbrance he regarded as a 'relic of the Middle Ages' and to reign unhindered according to his own lights.[7] He pursued an intensive programme of reforms across the affairs of his kingdom, providing his ministers with concept outlines for most edicts in his own hand and carefully editing the resulting drafts before approving them for dispatch or publication. He applied the same personal attention to his correspondence and especially to matters relating to the army. He neither sought nor desired initiative from his cabinet and was thus, as one historian notes, 'his own chief minister'.[8]

Nor did Friedrich look for advice from his son and heir, Kronprinz Friedrich Wilhelm (known as 'Fritz' to his family at the time, he ruled as König Wilhelm). Indeed, the gruff and overbearing Friedrich kept all authority in his own hands, tightly controlling his son's life and purposefully excluding him from state business. Friedrich Wilhelm, 32, deeply resented his domineering father and, like his counterpart Ludwig in Bavaria, he openly detested Napoleon. His frustration with both was evident in a comment he made to the Austrian ambassador that spring: 'Despot by principle as he is, he has a natural penchant for the Tyrant of Europe.'[9] The crown prince was thus a source of potential embarrassment for the kingdom, causing Friedrich to remind him that 'our political existence depends entirely upon the emperor; only through him have I been in a position to found that state whose ruler you shall one day become'. Such cautions notwithstanding, Friedrich Wilhelm had no compunction about expressing his passionate bitterness to the Austrian ambassador and others, but his influence on his father's policies was even less than that of Bavaria's Ludwig.[10]

As his son experienced, Friedrich as a person was daunting in all respects. He combined an iron will and adamantine conviction of his right to rule with great energy, a sharp intellect and keen political insight. He placed an inviolable premium on loyalty, most particularly on the oaths his officers had taken and on the strict obedience they owed to him. In historian Paul Sauer's words 'the king regarded the officer corps very much as his personal retinue who had to subordinate themselves unconditionally to his will'.[11] In August 1812, for example, on learning that some of his officers had indulged in nearly seditious liberties when discussing the invasion of Russia, Friedrich wrote: 'if the lord and sovereign has taken a side in any matter, generals are not permitted to challenge those governing decisions; their sole purpose is to execute them, to obey and above all not to allow themselves any impertinent judgements'.[12] He applied his severe conception of duty and loyalty to himself as well, and breaking his pledges to Napoleon would not be an easy decision. Beyond his colossal personality, Friedrich was also physically imposing, uncommonly tall and growing to weigh an estimated 200 kilograms (440 pounds) by the time he was king (a notch was reportedly carved in his dining table to accommodate his prodigious girth). Napoleon respected him and frequently confided details of his plans and opinions that he shared with no other German ruler; the emperor even tolerated Friedrich's often brusque queries and criticism in their correspondence. His Baden and Bavarian neighbours may have respected him, but they also feared his acquisitive instincts, always apprehensive that he might find means to enlarge his dominion at their expense. Friedrich and his court fully returned the scepticism, reserving a special suspicion for Montgelas.[13]

Powerful personality and intra-Rheinbund mistrust notwithstanding, Württemberg's situation in early 1813 led Friedrich to adopt a hedging policy similar to Bavaria's. Among other considerations, he initially believed that 'France will find itself deserted by its larger allies [Prussia and Austria] and be forced to peace' thus leaving its Confederation partners vulnerable to Napoleon's adversaries.[14] His concerns prompted him to open covert contact with Austria while maintaining his alliance with France and working to re-create a viable army. Metternich, hoping to deny Napoleon Württemberg's support as a step towards detaching the kingdom from the Rheinbund, responded by instructing Ambassador Binder to insinuate that Württemberg could assume 'a more independent stance' (in other words neutrality). 'Without being untrue to his obligations to France', wrote Metternich, Friedrich could best help restore peace 'if he just pursues the equipping of his contingent slowly'. 'The king', he urged, 'can only gain if he observes a wise temporisation in his arming.'[15] Passing through Stuttgart on 2 April, Schwarzenberg endeavoured to reinforce the image of Austria as moderate and obliging by offering vague guarantees of Württemberg's safety and sovereignty on Metternich's behalf. Friedrich replied that Württemberg would change sides once it could do so without endangering its own security, adding that 'the engagements of the Confederation sovereigns were only obligatory insofar as France could accord them the protection it had promised'.[16] All was very preliminary from Friedrich's point of view, but Metternich, encouraged by Binder's reports, reiterated Austria's interest in 'the independence and well-being of the second and third order powers' and invited Friedrich to send an envoy to Vienna for further discussion. Time and Napoleon, however, were conspiring against Metternich's hopes.[17] Friedrich duly dispatched a colonel in disguise as his representative, but the Grande Armée's rapid progress and the victory at Lüzten rendered this clandestine mission otiose. As the first tranche of Württemberg's contingent marched off to join the French, Binder concluded that his utility in Stuttgart had come to an end; negotiations could only resume when an Austrian army actually entered southern Germany.[18] Friedrich's envoy thus returned to Stuttgart and Württemberg's contacts with Austria and the Coalition powers lapsed into dormancy for the next several months.

As these tentative contacts with Austria wandered from budding to wilting, Württemberg's relations with France were in crisis. The proximate causes were actions Friedrich took in late December 1812 and early January 1813, but some of the points of irritation stemmed from the Russian campaign and it is necessary to review those before proceeding. Commanded by Kronprinz Friedrich Wilhelm, the Württemberg contingent was in superb form when it arrived in Poland as the 25th Division of Marshal Ney's 3rd Corps in May 1812. Even before the invasion, however, strident complaints arose alleging that the four Württemberg cavalry regiments were guilty of rampant 'pillage and brigandage'. In part as an apparent punishment for these infractions and in part owing to his organisational preferences, Napoleon separated the four mounted regiments from the rest of the contingent. This move alone angered Friedrich who, like every other Rheinbund monarch, tried to insist that his contingent remain united under national command. The removal of the cavalry generated additional indignation among the contingent's officers, already incensed by what they perceived as unfair accusations of poor discipline. Worse was to come.

As noted earlier in this chapter, word reached Napoleon in July that some of the Württemberg officers had freely expressed their condemnation of the French, of the Rheinbund alliance and of the conduct of the invasion. They thus displayed insubordination towards their own uncompromising king, disrespect towards their French allies and a general attitude of defeatism. Napoleon was incensed. In a stern and menacing letter to Friedrich Wilhelm, he specifically cited GM Ludwig Joachim Friedrich von Walsleben and one of the cavalry regimental commanders as the offending parties, while GL August Friedrich Wilhelm von Wöllwarth was already under a cloud for allegedly licensing the plundering in Poland prior to the invasion. In typical fashion, the emperor mixed censure with praise, writing that, 'The soldiers and the core of the officers are very good,' but the dark warning was very clear and both generals were sent back to Stuttgart to be investigated by military tribunals (and to be unavailable for any French retribution). Friedrich Wilhelm, desperately ill, also returned home during the summer and the scandal was subsumed in the urgency of military operations and pressing affairs of state.

Napoleon retained a generally favourable opinion of the Württemberg troops and treated the division with earnest solicitousness during a review at Moscow in October, generously distributing crosses of the Legion of Honour and words of praise to officers and men alike. At the Berezina, observing that a hardy knot of 50 Württembergers still had all their flags and maintained a steady appearance, he was prompted to remark that 'even in these circumstances they distinguish themselves'.[19] He did not, however, forget the allegedly errant generals, and their fates became one of his concerns in dealing with Friedrich in the opening months of 1813.[20]

Against this background, several of Friedrich's actions in the wake of the Russian disaster erupted as the immediate causes for the Franco-Württemberg crisis in early 1813.[21] The catalogue of measures Napoleon found objectionable was long, but most prominent were Friedrich's decision to publish lists of officers killed or missing in Russia, the cancellation of almost all commemorations of the king's coronation on 1 January (normally a festive occasion)[22] and the wording used to announce a special tax imposed at the beginning of the year to cover new military expenditures. The emperor, who wanted to turn attention away from the unprecedented cost in lives and treasure caused by the invasion of Russia, may not have been pleased that Württemberg's public notice opened with a sentence that described the new taxes as necessary 'to meet the great expenses which have been caused by the considerable loss suffered as a result of the latest war events'; this was honest but perhaps blunter than Napoleon may have wished. What roused his ire was the next sentence: 'When, as a result, We are forced to impose new burdens on our good and faithful subjects through no fault of their own, We feel very keenly how difficult these sacrifices must be for them under the present circumstances.'[23] The inclusion of the phrase 'through no fault of their own' seemed to Napoleon a direct and intentional attack on France, designed to absolve Württemberg of any responsibility and rile the populace against their French ally.

Other measures compounded his imperial anger: several courtiers known to be friendly towards France were ostentatiously denied access to the king and excluded from court affairs, the French ambassador, Clément Édouard, comte de Moustier, was deliberately ostracised, and the two generals dismissed in 1812 were reinstated with their full ranks and all their privileges. Furthermore, these measures, so contrary to his conception of the alliance and his personal respect for Friedrich, awakened new doubts in Napoleon's mind about the familial connections between Württemberg and Russia, especially as Empress Dowager Maria Feodorovna, the tsar's mother and Friedrich's sister, was, as he described her, 'my most cruel enemy'.[24]

Napoleon first conveyed his discontent in an 18 January letter. Most of this lengthy missive mirrored the messages sent to the principal Rheinbund monarchs on the same date: recounting the events of 1812, condemning Yorck's treason, emphasising the danger of 'revolt and anarchy' in the current circumstances, renewing his guarantees to his German allies and calling on them to fulfil their military obligations. A long paragraph inserted towards the end of the letter to Friedrich, however, was specific to Württemberg, 'completely confidential between you and me' in Napoleon's words; none of the other 18 January letters contained such a specific paragraph. Here the emperor expressed his surprise and displeasure at Friedrich 'throwing the blame on France'. 'The danger which it is most important to forestall is the agitation of the people,' he wrote, 'But how can we hope to prevent this if the sovereigns themselves adopt a language which is designed to excite it?' Such language and such actions would only redound to the detriment of the German princes as the Coalition aimed to create 'something called a Germany' through violent upheaval that would 'desolate the various states'. He urged Friedrich 'for his present interests, to break off all communication between his subjects and Russia, to disperse those associations which have only disorder as their object, and to inspire his subjects with sentiments of friendship towards my people'. The king attempted to defuse these imperial allegations point for point in a detailed reply, but his counter-arguments were not convincing, and he seemed to denigrate Napoleon's new dynasty by mentioning that most of the German princely houses had histories dating back 800 years or more.[25]

Given the strategic context in January 1813, Napoleon's dissatisfaction is hardly surprising: with the remnants of the 1812 army reeling back towards the Vistula, Yorck's defection and Schwarzenberg's dubious dealings with the Russians called all French alliances into question, while violent unrest in Berg provided evidence of the anti-French ferment brewing in Germany. He, not unlike the Rheinbund rulers, needed to gain time, to hold off the encroaching Allied armies and to contain German discontent while he rebuilt his strength. To him, Friedrich's actions deliberately highlighted the dire situation, promoting popular disaffection and calling the alliance itself into question. He thus vented his imperial anger in a heated 3 February audience with the Württemberg ambassador, Carl Friedrich Heinrich Levin von Wintzingerode. Napoleon's demeanour, recorded the distressed ambassador, 'was initially cold, then increasingly biting, until finally all expressions of anger and the foulest mood were brought forth'. Accusing Friedrich of 'stirring up the country and arousing it against me', Napoleon evinced a sense of personal betrayal by a trusted ally whose intelligence and ability he respected. He found Friedrich's actions inexplicable: 'Does he want to become an ally of the British, of the Russians, of this Herr von Stein, of all these turbulent heads that want to plunge Germany into revolution?' Friedrich, he claimed, was the only ally who had abandoned him, the only one who had failed to offer condolences and reaffirm loyalty after the retreat from Russia. He was especially irritated by the timing of king's actions. 'Is this the moment to embarrass himself and create a public uproar?' he asked, 'Is the present the moment to have disagreements with the French ambassador? . . . Does the king, in declaring himself against me in such a public fashion, wish to arouse his people and gather all the malcontents around himself?' He reviewed all the king's disturbing measures and, in typically Napoleonic fashion, mixed admiration and good will with baleful threats. In addition to comparing Friedrich unfavourably with Bavaria's Max Joseph, he told Wintzingerode that he could reestablish Württemberg's estates, restore the rights of the old imperial knights and publish negative stories about the kingdom in French periodicals.

Though well chosen to strike at Friedrich's deepest fears (such as competition with his neighbours and internal sovereignty), Napoleon had no intention of implementing these threats; he needed the full support of all his allies and these menacing statements were uttered as a means to bring the wayward king back into line.[26] As Maret explained to Wintzingerode during an interview later that evening:

The emperor harbours no suspicion concerning the king's loyalty, that is not possible; but he cannot but conclude that the discontented across Germany will grow in numbers and boldness if they see that France is publicly insulted by a prince of the Rheinbund as has occurred with the steps taken against Monsieur de Moustier, with the reactivation of the two generals who the emperor himself had dismissed and with all these public announcements.[27]

Maret's comments may have helped soften the impact of Napoleon's pungent discourse, but they did not address the foundations of the emperor's unhappiness with his ally's behaviour and Friedrich hastened to respond when Wintzingerode's report arrived in Stuttgart. 'I search in vain for words to express the deep pain I feel when I see that your feelings of friendship for me have been changed to the point that you believe me to be at odds with you and even to have intentions contrary to my character, to my loyalty and to my invariable desire to prove my sincere attachment to Your Imperial Majesty on all occasions', he wrote in a conciliatory letter five days after Wintzingerode's stormy audience.[28] To reinforce his message of fealty and avoid any further misunderstanding, he entrusted this letter to his foreign minister, Ferdinand Ludwig Graf von Zeppelin, for personal delivery to Napoleon. The speed with which Friedrich reacted indicates the urgency he assigned to achieving reconciliation with his powerful ally and 'protector'. Zeppelin reached Paris late on 12 February, met with Maret the following day and had a long audience with Napoleon on the 15th. Although the atmosphere was generally cordial, the emperor repeated his litany of complaints in very sharp terms, stressing the infelicitous timing even as he expressed his desire to move beyond these aggravations. 'Let us pass over this, but I would have liked it better, if you had done it a month from now, when I would have 400,000 men on the Oder and when all the sensation that such publications could produce in Germany would have done nothing to me.' Coming to the reinstatement of Wöllwarth and Walsleben, he grabbed the button of Zeppelin's coat to underscore his frustration over the bad timing: 'I do not wish to make them miserable; what use is that? If only the king had not chosen the present moment to return them to active service; later, and I would have said nothing.'[29] His point made and compliance restored, however, Napoleon accepted Friedrich's contrite explanations and allowed his anger to recede. Despite some tense minutes in his audience, therefore, Friedrich's letter and Zeppelin's personal skill succeeded in restoring Franco-Württemberg relations. The minister returned to Stuttgart several days later bearing a brief but extraordinarily friendly reply from Napoleon, assuring the king that 'my dispositions towards you and your house will always be the same' and that Zeppelin would communicate 'my esteem and my sentiments for you'. Knowing Friedrich's concerns about command of his troops, Napoleon would later offer to have a royal prince command the Württemberg contingent directly subordinate to a French marshal; the king, with the 1812 fiasco in mind, politely declined this special concession.[30]

The crisis in relations thus passed. The emperor and the king quickly returned to the depth, candour and frequency of correspondence that had characterised their previous exchanges and Napoleon quietly replaced the objectionable de Moustier with Just Pons Florimond de Fay de la Latour-Maubourg in April.[31] Despite the reconciliation with France, Friedrich continued his covert contacts with Austria until mid-May and the arrival of a substantial Austrian army in southern Germany might have persuaded him to change policy as the Prussian ambassador believed.[32] Barring such a dramatic alteration in the political–military environment, however, his course was set according to the French compass. Indeed, Friedrich's letters to Napoleon were soon packed with intelligence concerning Austria's behaviour and hints that Vienna might turn towards the Allies.[33] As winter warmed into spring, therefore, his formidable attention and that of his imperial ally focused on preparing the Württemberg contingent for war and it is that contingent that now becomes the focus of this narrative.

Your Majesty No Longer Has an Army

Under Friedrich's careful eye, the Württemberg army had expanded considerably from the time the new kingdom joined the Rheinbund in 1806. It had also adopted numerous reforms, aiming, among other things, to achieve Friedrich's desire for a more 'national' army composed primarily of his own subjects rather than the semi-mercenary, multi-national military of the past. In the process, the Württembergers learned from the French but carved their own path to modernisation rather than simply imitating their large ally.[34] This updated army quickly proved its worth, particularly during 1809, and by the time of the invasion of Russia, Württemberg could field a competent, experienced force consisting of eight line infantry regiments numbered 1 through 8, two battalions each of Jägers and light infantry, five line cavalry regiments and seven or eight artillery batteries. Additionally, Friedrich maintained a regiment of Horse Guards (Garde-Regiment zu Pferd) and a battalion of Foot Guards (Garde zu Fuß) and a Guard Horse Artillery Battery but these remained inside his realm and were not involved in Russia or in the 1813 campaigns under consideration here.[35] The army also carried a 9th Infantry Regiment on its rolls in 1812, but this was a garrison unit of battalion strength. It would be dissolved in January 1813 to rebuild the 7th Infantry and its number would be assigned to a new formation as described below.[36]

Each of the Württemberg line infantry regiments was authorised a strength of 1,434 officers and men organised into two battalions of four companies, each of 173 men. Each regiment also maintained a depot company within the kingdom. The 1st Company of each 1st Battalion was designated as grenadiers, but these were not picked elite soldiers as in other armies, rather they bore this title as an honorific, similar to the 'Leib' companies of other German militaries. The men wore white breeches and dark blue jackets with regimental distinctions shown on the collars, cuffs, shoulder straps and turnbacks of their jackets as well as on the piping around their lapels. In a change from the past, the infantry was issued black shakos as headgear in 1813 rather than the two styles of crested helmets that had been standard from 1799 to 1812.[37] Unlike the French and many of their Rheinbund comrades, the Württemberg infantry fought in a two-rank line but the units were capable of performing manoeuvres in three-rank formations if called upon to do so.[38]

The Jägers and light infantry battalions each had four field companies for a theoretical campaign strength of 686 officers and men in addition to its depot company at home. These units had worn earlier styles of black shakos since 1802 and 1808 respectively but received new ones on the same pattern as the line infantry when they were being re-equipped after Russia. Jackets were dark green for both, but the Jägers were distinguished by green breeches, black distinctions and black leatherwork, while the light infantry had white breeches, light blue distinctions and buff leather equipment. Furthermore, the Jägers were armed with rifled muskets and carbines equipped with special sword-bayonets. The light battalions, on the other hand, carried French infantry muskets with ordinary bayonets.[39]

Numbered as the 1st through 5th Cavalry Regiments, Württemberg's mounted arm consisted of two regiments of chevaulegers, two of Jäger-zu-Pferd and a lone dragoon regiment. The chevaulegers wore dark blue jackets while the Jäger-zu-Pferd were dressed in dark green, regimental distinctions being shown on collars, cuffs and coat turnbacks like the infantry. All four of these older regiments had worn black leather helmets through the Russian campaign, but the two Jäger-zu-Pferd Regiments (3rd and 4th Cavalry Regiments) were issued with black shakos when they were re-established in 1813. The *Prinz Adam* Chevaulegers and the Leib-Chevaulegers (1st and 2nd Cavalry Regiments), on the other hand, retained their leather helmets surmounted by flowing horsehair crests similar to those sported by French cuirassiers. The *Kronprinz* Dragoons (5th Cavalry), the newest of the five regiments, had only been formed in 1809 and had yet to see combat. Its troopers wore shakos to accompany their dark green coats with white regimental distinctions trimmed in red. Regardless of title, there was no difference in tactical employment of the various regiments and for 1813 all five had a planned strength of 580 officers and men organised into four field squadrons.[40]

Like the infantry, the artillery shifted from helmets to shakos in 1813. Mounted and foot gunners alike wore light blue or bluish-grey (sometimes termed cornflower blue) coats and breeches featuring black collars, cuffs and shoulder straps with yellow piping around the lapels. The principal difference in the dress of the two brands of artillerymen was that the foot soldiers had plain black turnbacks on their coats, while those of the horse artillery were yellow trimmed in black.[41] The artillery train wore a simpler single-breasted coat in light blue with black trim while the drivers assigned to equipment wagons, as in many armies, wore a simple grey jacket also trimmed in black.

In contrast with Bavaria and most of the other Rheinbund states, Württemberg had retained a substantial military force at home during the invasion of Russia: three of its eight line infantry regiments, the dragoon regiment, two artillery batteries, the garrison 'regiment' and the Royal Guard. The bulk of the army, however, was committed across the Niemen. Commanded by the crown prince until illness forced him to stay behind, the contingent consisted of four infantry regiments, all four Jäger/light battalions, four cavalry regiments and 32 artillery pieces. In another similarity to Bavaria, Württemberg had also been required to provide a regiment and two guns for the Danzig garrison in 1811. Where the Bavarian 13th Infantry survived its experience largely intact, however, the Württemberg regiment, the 7th Infantry, marched for Russia in October 1812 with its two attached guns, only to be destroyed in heavy fighting between Minsk and the Berezina River in November. A 1,300-man replacement detachment dispatched in August also met an evil fate, evaporating after a few days in the unforgiving cold outside Vilna in December. It 'only served to increase our losses', recorded Faber du Faur.[42] The rest of the division was already in a state of disintegration. 'Our cavalry had already completely dissolved at Smolensk, our artillery at Krasnoi,' wrote Leutnant Christian von Martens of the 6th Infantry, 'our infantry, only 57 men strong under Hauptmann [Friedrich August] von Koseritz, formed the escort for our headquarters, which it did not leave until it was gradually swept away by cold and want.' GL Johann Georg von Scheler, who had taken Friedrich Wilhelm's place in command of the contingent, thus reported in late December that, 'The lack of provisions and the rigours of the season have led to the complete dissolution of the army corps and were the reason that each individual could only be concerned with his own self-preservation.'[43] These sad remnants, collecting themselves in Poland in early January, numbered only some 800–900 men. Perhaps another 400–500 later returned from captivity or their own personal odysseys. In all, this amounted to no more than 10 per cent of the original contingent. The

Chart 27: Württemberg Units, February–October 1813

Unit	Jacket colour	Distinctive colour (lapel piping)
1st Infantry *Prinz Paul*	dark blue	yellow (white)
2nd Infantry *Herzog Wilhelm*	dark blue	orange (white)
3rd Infantry	dark blue	grass green (white)
4th Infantry	dark blue	rose (white)
5th Infantry	dark blue	light blue (white)
6th Infantry *Kronprinz*	dark blue	white (red)
7th Infantry	dark blue	black (white)
8th Infantry	dark blue	straw yellow (yellow)
9th Infantry (*Fuß-Jäger König*)	dark green	black (white)
10th Light Infantry	dark green	light blue (white)
1st Cavalry, *Prinz Adam* Chevaulegers	dark blue	yellow
2nd Cavalry, Leib-Chevaulegers	dark blue	scarlet
3rd Cavalry, Jäger-zu-Pferd *Herzog Louis*	dark green	yellow
4th Cavalry, Jäger-zu-Pferd *König*	dark green	rose
5th Cavalry, *Kronprinz* Dragoons	dark green	white (red)

rest – 14,000 men and 4,000 horses with all their guns and equipment – were gone. To convey the extent of the tragedy, Scheler sent his chief of staff, GM Karl August Freiherr von Kerner, to Stuttgart to render a personal account to the king. Friedrich had already sent out a second replacement column of 2,200 men to reconstitute his division, but Kerner, in the course of a tense interview, told his royal master that 'Your Majesty no longer has an army.'[44] Shocked and angry, the king immediately cancelled all preparations to rebuild his forces in the field and issued Scheler new orders to return at once with as many of his officers and men as possible. News of the disaster was soon public: on 24 December, the *Stuttgarter Zeitung* published the French 29th Bulletin announcing the defeat and retreat of the Grande Armée, leaving Friedrich's stunned subjects to wonder how their fine army could have vanished with such terrifying suddenness.[45]

Kerner's verbal report to the king almost did not occur and his experience affords another example of Friedrich's severe personality and his expectations of his officers. Kerner entered the kingdom on 24 December and halted for the night some 100 kilometres from Stuttgart. The king, however, thoroughly disapproved of senior officers leaving their posts without his express consent. Apprised of Kerner's mission but unaware of his proximity, Friedrich sent couriers to intercept the approaching general and communicate his censure in the sternest terms:

> As His Majesty regards the dispatch of the chief of staff and his removal from the army corps as inappropriate, disadvantageous and outside the authority of the lieutenant general [Scheler] and must therefore disapprove, in view of this, His Majesty thus orders General von Kerner, wherever this order should reach him and whosoever should deliver it, to return to Danzig and send in the dispatches and reports he has with him.

To ensure his wishes were understood, he added that 'General von Kerner is charged with the most exact compliance with this all-highest order on his special responsibility'. Luckily, Kerner did not have to make the 900-kilometre return trip to Danzig. He had dutifully reported his arrival and Friedrich, learning that his general was already within the bounds of his realm, allowed him to continue to the capital. Kerner could thus deliver his grim report in person as intended, but this little incident once again highlights the strict obedience Friedrich demanded of his subordinates and the lengths to which he was prepared to go to enforce his will.[46]

While Kerner was making his way from Danzig to Württemberg, the remains of the contingent collected themselves at Inowrazlaw (Inowrocław)[47] southwest of Thorn under GD Andoche Junot, the unreliable commander of the Westphalian 8th Corps. Scheler and his command had arrived in the town on 30 December and soon received the urgent orders from Friedrich to return home. Junot was initially reluctant to release them, but cadres began to head west on 6, 7 and 8 January, and by the 12th, Scheler had departed for Württemberg with most of his officers, NCOs and men.[48] He was required to leave behind a small 'battalion' of 182 relatively fit men organised into two companies under Major Carl Friedrich von Gaupp. Originally destined to garrison Posen, this battalion soon found itself packed off to Küstrin with the Westphalians; Gaupp and his steadily diminishing little command would thus see out the remainder of the war in this blockaded fortress.[49] Also trapped in a fortress were two officers with 96 men who had been left behind in Danzig.[50] This tiny detachment would remain part of the city's garrison under French 10th Corps even when the kingdom later switched sides to join the Coalition.

Uniformed Farm Boys

Friedrich immediately began to rebuild his army after the Russian catastrophe. A respectable army was important for his own purposes to give him weight in the Rheinbund and larger European affairs, but a serviceable contingent, of course, was also one of his principal obligations under the Confederation treaty. He took the first steps in late December: recalling all his troops from Poland, ordering the re-establishment of the ruined regiments and releasing the first of four conscription edicts. Two more rounds of conscription would be declared in January 1813 and a final one in February resulting in the induction of 13,000 men, approximately 1 per cent of the kingdom's population, by the end of the latter month.[51] The replacement column that was supposed to reinforce the division in Poland was also recalled. The column had reached Leipzig, where GM von Walsleben, freed from arrest, had gone to purchase the necessary horses.[52] The return of these men and mounts would benefit the army's rebuilding, but arms and equipment were in short supply, and both the new conscripts and the fresh horses were entirely untrained. Furthermore, as with all the other Rheinbund states and the French themselves, finding suitable officers and NCOs presented a major challenge. Despite the horrors of the Russian ordeal, a relatively large number of officers had survived, as many as 40 to 50 per cent in some regiments (as compared to near-total destruction of the other ranks); these men were immediately put to work in their home garrisons, but as Friedrich had written, many were not fit for duty.[53] Hauptmann Heinrich von Arlt, whose wife had not recognised him on his return from Russia, was 'hardly recovered' from his wounds when he departed to join the 7th Infantry and Leutnant Heinrich August von Vossler of the 3rd Jäger-zu-Pferd *Herzog Louis*, renowned in the army as the '*Louis-Jäger*', was so incapacitated that he had to travel in a carriage for the first several weeks. He summed up the situation of many: 'so recently and painfully returned from Russia, so obviously unfit, and yet on my way to new battles'.[54] Individual officers were permitted to refuse, but that would entail being placed on half-pay at their units' depots or in the kingdom's depot regiment. There was thus a strong financial incentive to remain with their field formations. Nonetheless, even employing such semi-decrepit returnees from Russia, leadership positions could only be filled by pulling cadets from the officers' academy near Stuttgart, assigning pages from court and promoting select sergeants to lieutenant. As Leutnant von Martens recalled, therefore, 'the wounds in our frozen limbs were not yet fully healed when we and our as yet unknown comrades began exercising the young, newly conscripted troops'.[55]

Foreign officers might have filled some of the gaps, but Friedrich limited the number of acceptable candidates by placing constraints on the admission of non-Württembergers into his service: those who were not from noble families or who had no prior service were deemed unacceptable. Moreover, the army lost a few serving officers when former Prussians who had taken the king's oath after Prussia's defeat in 1806 requested release to avoid fighting against their countrymen. Friedrich had no sympathy for such persons. At best they were permitted to depart unhindered, but they went without honourable discharges and those who had received the kingdom's service awards had their names stricken from the list of recipients. Only four or five officers seem to have sought release under these conditions.[56] One officer was publicly humiliated and threatened with dire punishment: Prussian-born Major August Friedrich de la Chevallerie of the 7th Infantry. When Chevallerie refused to serve, Friedrich ordered a court martial and, upon conviction, directed that his sword be taken, his officer's patent torn up and that he be escorted over the border by gendarmes with the warning that he would be shot should he ever set foot in Württemberg again. Commanders in the field and all garrisons were to publicise de la Chevallerie's sentence as a caution to others.[57]

Problems with foreign officers notwithstanding, Württemberg managed to place men in most of the essential slots during the first few months of the year. The result, however, was often that freshly minted officers and NCOs who knew little of their new military duties were required to drill and indoctrinate equally ignorant new conscripts. As Martens noted, 'In the entire regiment [6th Infantry], only a few of the officers were familiar with field duties.'[58] Furthermore, the youth and inexperience of the troops left them vulnerable to the rigours of active campaigning, and the exigencies of the moment left no time for measured acquisition of routine soldiery skills. It is also worth noting that the new troops did not have the experience of multiple victorious campaigns under French banners as a bedrock for their own morale and for trust in their allies. For the cavalry regiments the difficulties were compounded by the need to train brand-new horses when many of the men of all ranks were ignorant of individual equitation, leave alone organised cavalry manoeuvres. These manifold problems notwithstanding, the army's mobilisation proceeded with surprising speed. By drawing on the untouched dragoon regiment and depots established prior to the Russian campaign, for instance, the cavalry regiments were able to fill their ranks with men and horses by mid-February. Similarly, the infantry regiments inducted drafts from their depots and non-deploying units to march for Saxony with their full establishments. 'The necessary NCOs and 30 old soldiers were taken for each company from the regiments that remained at home,' wrote the newly promoted Hauptmann Ernst Wilhelm von Baumbach of the 1st Infantry, 'whereas the rest of the men consisted entirely of recruits who had been given some superficial training in February and March.'[59] Training and equipment remained serious deficiencies, but the rapid re-creation of the army was no mean accomplishment.

Napoleon's insistence on the swift replacement of the armies lost across the Niemen added urgency to Württemberg's mobilisation. Military affairs were thus a central feature of the king's correspondence with the emperor even as the two monarchs dealt with the political crisis outlined above. The emperor understood that his allies would need time to rebuild their armies, but he was also coping with a desperate military situation and expected the Rheinbund to help. Among his top priorities early in 1813 was the protection of key points along his lines of communication, a mission to which Württemberg was to contribute by sending two battalions and a battery to Würzburg. Friedrich, however, worried that dispatching ill-prepared troops would only redound to his detriment. He described his kingdom's losses in detail in his 26 January letter to Napoleon: assuring the emperor of 'his zeal for the common cause', he recounted that, 'I wasted no time in remedying my losses and in reorganising, as well as my means permit, the contingent to which the Confederation treaty obligates me'. At the same time, he pointed out that the men he could raise on short notice would all be conscripts and that he was experiencing tremendous difficulties in acquiring horses, arms and all manner of equipment. 'Above all, it is the lack of officers that retards the formations and to which I see no remedy, at least for the moment.'[60]

As with all the Rheinbund contingents, Napoleon especially stressed the importance of cavalry in his letters to Friedrich. Indeed, the question of mounted troops was a dominant theme in their correspondence through the end of April, Napoleon repeatedly insisting and Friedrich firmly demurring. 'I have an indispensable need for Your Majesty's two thousand horse ... my operations will not be hindered by the delay of a few battalions, but they will be by the delay of your cavalry,' wrote Napoleon on 8 April, elaborating eight days later that the 'two thousand horse that will be very precious to me at the present moment, will not be useful to me in a month'. Friedrich, exasperated that the emperor persisted on this point, refused to budge. The Dragoon Regiment or 5th Cavalry was nothing but a 'depot regiment' he wrote and as for the others, 'these are recruits mounted on new horses, who have difficulty holding themselves in the saddle and who have no idea of evolutions or movements; I pity the officers who will expose their honour and reputation with such a troop, and I repeat to Your Imperial Majesty that you can expect no service from them'.[61] Despite the imperial pressure, Friedrich's stubbornness was largely successful. Although he reluctantly released two regiments (approximately 1,000 troopers) at the end of April, he would not send the remaining two (to make up the desired 2,000) until late May.

As direct as he was with Napoleon, Friedrich was even more blunt with his subordinates, relaying his fears and suspicions in very clear language. Although he was prepared to send the two battalions to avoid criticism for being unsupportive, he was deeply worried that his men would not meet Napoleon's expectations and that he would be blamed for their poor performance should they encounter the enemy. He thus instructed Zeppelin in Paris to stress the deficiencies of the troops he could be expected to provide in the near term as most had only been under arms for four weeks or less and their equipment consisted of old muskets only suitable for drill and training. 'In a word, the numbers can depart, but they are not soldiers, not a one has fired a single shot; most of the officers have not held their rank for more than fifteen days,' he wrote on 18 February, 'That is the truth'. Two days later, having received the formal troop request from the despised de Moustier, he wrote again to Zeppelin: 'these two battalions are not soldiers, rather still completely raw, untrained recruits, commanded by entirely new NCOs and officers who are at least half new ... As regards the artillery, it is utterly impossible to send off even a single cannon before the end of March.' He foresaw embarrassment and dishonour because 'half of the uniformed farm boys I dispatch will desert before they arrive at their destination as these men will have no proper notion of their duty'. The grim news from the east, especially the fall of Warsaw to the Russians, only accentuated his fears. He expected 'a new violent explosion' from Napoleon and demands that 'cavalry, artillery and infantry that have only existed for few days march off at once ... I cannot expose myself to the danger of seeing my troops throw down their weapons in order to go over to the enemy like the Italian, Westphalian and lower Rhine cohorts, as will inevitably be the case if we are not left enough time to instil military spirit and discipline in these new formations'.[62]

These royal anxieties notwithstanding, two battalions (but no artillery or cavalry) duly marched for Würzburg on 4 March to arrive on the 7th. Curiously, Friedrich selected the freshly reconstructed 7th Infantry for this assignment rather than one of the intact regiments that had not participated in the Russian campaign. Württemberg would fulfil its treaty obligations dutifully, and these three regiments, the 3rd, 5th and 8th Infantry, would be depleted to provide replacements and cadres for the field contingent but all three would remain inside Württemberg during 1813 as they had in 1812. Friedrich, however, always precise about his commitments, deducted the men besieged in Danzig and Küstrin (most of whom were from the 7th Infantry) from the number provided to Würzburg. Commanded by Oberst Franz Xaver von Spitzemberg, the regiment thus departed with 1,174 men and 29 officers rather than the 1,434 it would have had at full strength.[63]

As the 7th Infantry took up its duties in and around Würzburg, Württemberg was preparing the rest of its required contingent for war. This would mirror the configuration established for the invasion of Russia with some organisational modifications. That is, the 3rd, 5th and 8th Infantry Regiments, the dragoon regiment and the Guard would stay in Württemberg while the bulk

Chart 28: Initial Württemberg Contingent, April–May 1813

38th Division: *GL von Franquemont*

		bns/sqdns	present under arms as of 1 May	at Bautzen c. 20 May
Division staff			57	57
Cavalry Brigade	*GM von Jett*			
Staff			7	7
1st Cavalry, *Prinz Adam* Chevaulegers		4	527	397
3rd Cavalry, *Herzog Louis* Jäger-zu-Pferd		4	526	412
3rd Horse Battery		4 × 6-pdr, 2 × howitzer	131	120
1st Infantry Brigade	*GM von Neuffer*			
Staff			7	7
1st Infantry Regiment, *Prinz Paul*		2	1,354	1,202
2nd Infantry Regiment, *Herzog Wilhelm*		2	1,332	1,224
3rd Infantry Brigade (or Light Brigade)	*GM von Stockmayer*			
Staff			7	7
7th Infantry Regiment		2	1,150	1,040
9th Light Infantry Regiment, *König Jäger*		1	698	625
10th Light Infantry Regiment		1	720	673
3rd Foot Artillery Battery		5 × 6-pdr, 1 × howitzer	121	115
Total			6,637	5,886

Notes: (1) an additional 499 men were listed as 'not fit for duty' ('*rücken nicht aus*') on 1 May; (2) some of the regimental histories assign each foot battery four guns and two howitzers; (3) the staff numbers at Bautzen are simply carried ahead from 1 May; and (4) the numbering of the infantry brigades in inconsistent, but this is the most common. The figures for Bautzen do not include detached troops or staff.

Source: 'Rapport auf den 1sten May 1813', LABWHStA, E 270a Bü 227 and Major von Bangold's account of Bautzen, LABWHStA, E 284g Bü 94.

---

of the army marched off to join the Grande Armée in Saxony. The contingent was to consist of 4 cavalry regiments, 12 infantry battalions and 24 guns for a total paper strength of 11,336 officers and men when assembled together.[64] The army introduced an organisational change, however, by amalgamating the remnants of the Jäger and light battalions into two new regiments. The Jägers took over the number of the old garrison unit to become the new 9th Light Infantry while the combined light battalions would now be known as the 10th Light Infantry. The men of the 9th adopted the uniform of the former 1st König Jägers and were considered part of the king's household troops. Furthermore, they were quite proud that the army still referred to them as 'Jägers' both on- and off-duty despite their official title as a light regiment. In similar fashion, the new 10th Light Regiment was issued the same uniform coat as the former 1st Light Battalion. Both new regiments retained the arms of their predecessors, thus rifles and muskets respectively, but in both cases, numbers were too few to form two battalions, so each regiment would field only one battalion during the coming campaigns.[65]

Injunctions, Marches and Secret Instructions

Neither Napoleon's desires nor Friedrich's energy, however, could conjure troops out of thin air. Württemberg would thus have to dispatch its contingent in two separate combined arms detachments. The first of these left the kingdom on 19 April. Commanded by GL Friedrich von Franquemont, it consisted of two infantry brigades each of four battalions, a foot artillery battery, and a cavalry brigade of two regiments with a mounted battery for a nominal total of 6,850 men and 12 guns. Franquemont was a skilled and experienced officer who enjoyed the king's favour and the respect of his men. He was 'highly esteemed and admired by all of us', wrote one of his junior officers, 'a man of rare character, firm, earnest and of cold-blooded determination who instilled courage and confidence in every subordinate'.[66]

Friedrich paid close personal attention to the detachment's preparations and drafted two sets of orders for Franquemont. The first reflected the negative experiences from 1812. They were to be read out to the officer corps to apprise them in no uncertain terms of their royal master's expectations concerning their comportment during the coming campaign.

> His Royal Majesty has been most displeased to learn that some officers of His army have taken the liberty of making unacceptable remarks about military affairs, politics and relations with other powers. The Most High hereby again forbids such most earnestly and adjures each and every officer to unconditional and silent obedience to the orders of His Royal Majesty as those are made known to them by their superiors. Should one or another nonetheless permit himself remarks which run counter to the respect due the powers allied with His Royal Majesty, the brigade generals and commanders are instructed that it is their gravest responsibility to report such persons immediately to the division commander, who is instructed to treat such persons as traitors to the state and to send them back to His Royal Majesty in chains, who will have them punished with well-deserved life sentences according to the laws of war.[67]

Furthermore, strict censorship of communications to and from the contingent was introduced 'to preclude the disorder and disadvantages which arose during the previous campaign through the exaggerated and often highly inappropriate correspondence of officers and other ranks in the field army and which even reached into the state itself'.[68]

Friedrich's second set of instructions were secret. Given the uncertainties of the political–military situation that spring and considering Yorck's defection, these orders were intended to ensure that Franquemont had detailed royal guidance to cover a number of potential eventualities. The king foresaw four possible situations in which his general might have to act without the benefit of specific royal direction. First, if the French corps to which the Württemberg contingent was attached suffered a defeat and was forced to retreat towards the borders of the kingdom or even further, Franquemont was to try to separate his division from the French and withdraw into Württemberg. If this proved impossible, he was to continue with the French to the Rhine but not to cross the river under any circumstances. Second, should the French insist, Franquemont was to reveal these instructions to his officers and warn them that any who failed to obey their king's orders would be punished for insubordination. Third, in the extreme case that the French tried to force the Württemberg division to cross the Rhine, Franquemont and all his officers were to declare themselves prisoners of war. The NCOs and soldiers, on the other hand, were to consider themselves released from their duties; however, they were to be sharply warned against taking service with another country on pain of being labelled 'disobedient subjects' and treated as such on their return to Württemberg. Finally, if any of these cases allowed Franquemont to separate his men from French command, he was to make his way back to the kingdom 'by any way free of the enemy, but under no circumstances enter into negotiations with the army or the corps of the Russo-Prussian allied armies, rather to regard and treat them as enemies until the arrival of other orders'. Should the Russo-Prussian forces block his path, he was to force his way through or, if they were overwhelmingly strong, he should attempt to return through a ceasefire agreement, 'but in no circumstances, enter into any commitment to the benefit of the enemy army and, in the worst case, to give himself up as a prisoner of war'. Considering past experience, Friedrich foresaw that GM Karl August Maximilian von Jett's cavalry might be detached from the division and therefore authorised Franquemont to inform Jett of these secret instructions if necessary.[69]

In summary, then, Friedrich warned his commanders to obey the French honourably, but neither to cross the Rhine out of Germany under French control nor to enter into any arrangements with the Coalition unless specifically instructed to do so. Although Franquemont would not need to make use of these conditional orders, they shed light on Friedrich's concerns and, along with the public warning to his officers, they illustrate the challenges he and his fellow Rheinbund monarchs faced as they tried to preserve their states while navigating between the French and the Coalition in a period of great internal and international turmoil.

With his master's injunctions very much in mind, Franquemont headed for Würzburg, endeavouring to move by easy marches to avoid exhausting his raw troops. He was pleased with his men, but his early reports painted a disturbing picture of some of Napoleon's other troops and the overall situation. Local people told him that the attitude of the other Rheinbund soldiers 'was not very favourable towards France' and that desertion was rife among the Frankfurt and Hessian units. The Hessians, he wrote, 'even make remarks in public places that are a disgrace to them, for example: we are only waiting for the moment when we see the enemy to throw away our muskets,' and 'The Hessian officers say they would be happy if their men desert.' The first French companies he had seen were 'very wretched' and, once he joined Bertrand's corps, he also reported that the Italian 15th Division 'is very ill-disciplined and has a great deal of desertion'. Logistics were a major problem at this early stage in the war as the French had not yet established magazines. 'One is forced to live from what one finds', he wrote, but assured Friedrich that, 'This takes place with us in the greatest order and through proper commissaries ... Your Majesty's troops are still the most sparing in employing this cruel but necessary measure.' The threat posed by the ubiquitous enemy light troops was another frequent theme in his reports. He recounted stories of the capture of couriers and staff officers, the raid on Rechberg's Bavarians in Langensalza, and the surrender of a ducal Saxon battalion to a small band of Prussian hussars. Such disturbing details, delivered in the driest, most matter-of-fact manner, could hardly inspire confidence in the attentive Friedrich.[70]

Friedrich was also annoyed by the subordination of his troops to a French general rather than a marshal. Napoleon's organisational plan designated the Württemberg contingent as the Grande Armée's 38th Division, while the Baden, Hesse-Darmstadt and Frankfurt contingents constituted the 39th. Together, the two divisions were placed initially under the command of GD Marchand as a separate German 'sub-corps' within Ney's large 3$^\text{e}$ Corps d'Armée along with the Bavarian 29th Division. Although Marchand had earned the respect and affection of the Württemberg troops while commanding them in Russia during most of 1812, Friedrich found the arrangement demeaning and wanted Franquemont to request a different dispensation. Franquemont had apprehensions of his own, worrying that he and his men were victims of 'the mistrust of the French'. Repeated visits by staff officers who asked about the division's strength, the status of its equipment, how long the men had served, and other details excited his suspicions. Though such queries were routine matters in the Grande Armée as officers tried to slake Napoleon's insatiable thirst for military

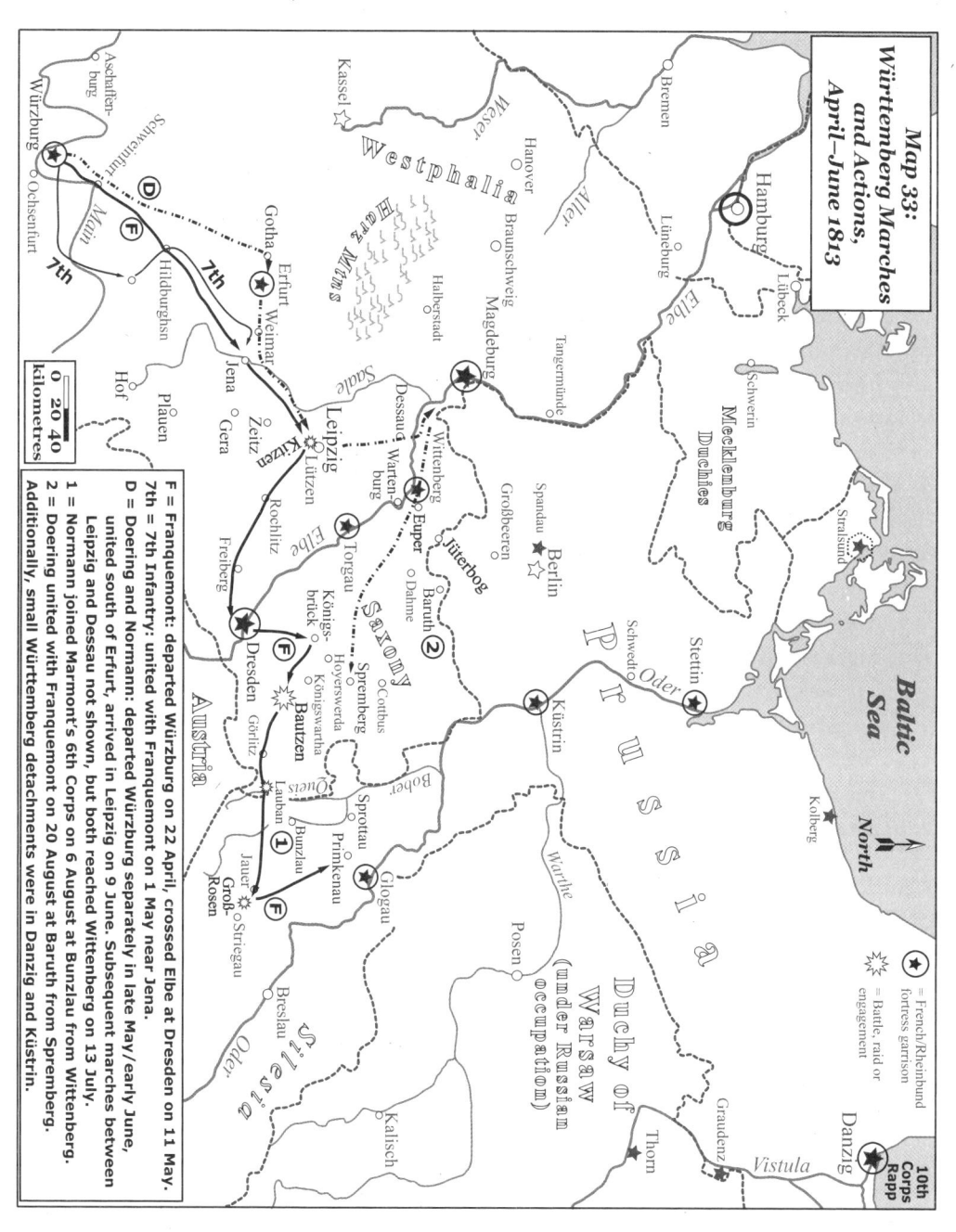

Injunctions, Marches and Secret Instructions 29

detail, Franquemont fretted that he was being subjected to special scrutiny and decided to report through private channels safe from interception by the French authorities.[71]

Fortunately for Franquemont, he did not have to plead this case before his French superiors.[72] By the time, Friedrich's order arrived, command relationships had changed. Leaving the 7th Infantry behind (another point of temporary irritation for Friedrich) under Ney's command, the division set out from Würzburg for Saxony on 22 April. Only five days later, however, Franquemont received new orders assigning the contingent to GD Bertrand's 4th Corps. He thus turned the division northeast to reach Jena on 1 May. Other than the loss of a handful of rather incautious Jägers from the 9th Infantry who were captured by Cossacks on 30 April, this march proceeded without incident. Furthermore, Franquemont was pleased to be reunited with the 7th Infantry, which had been assigned a different route to the Jena area from Würzburg. Endeavouring to find his new corps, he continued northeast, and the men arrived at Lützen on 3 May to bivouac near Kaja on the corpse-strewn field only one day after the sanguinary battle. 'The view of the battlefield just where we were to bivouac was not at all one to please our young troops as it was so strewn with corpses that we had to clear them away just to find space to lie down,' wrote Baumbach of the 1st Infantry. Two wounded Prussian corporals retrieved from among the survivors during the night received all the medical care the Württemberg surgeons could offer but 'left us in no doubt as to their disgust at Germans who were still fighting on the French side', remembered Leutnant Vossler: 'Dawn revealed to us a ghastly sight of the bloody execution done so recently in this place ... A great mass of corpses, some of them terribly maimed, weapons and equipment of every kind, smashed wagons and shattered guns littered the ground all around us, and many a young recruit no doubt wished himself safely back home beside his parents' hearth.'[73] Relieved to march on, the division caught up with 4th Corps over the next several days on the road to Dresden.

After his earlier apprehensions, Franquemont found Bertrand courteous and respectful of Württemberg's interests. The corps headquarters was 'somewhat disorderly', but the Württemberg troops 'are not disregarded in any respect or assigned harder marches than the other divisions; I am treated exactly like any French division commander, and no one meddles in our internal affairs.' Although Bertrand had placed Jett and his brigade under GB André Louis Briche to comprise the corps' light cavalry along with 2nd Neapolitan Chasseurs, Franquemont was acutely relieved to report that the brigade remained under his orders for administrative matters. The Württemberg mounted regiments and their attached horse battery would frequently be sent on reconnaissance missions, but they remained closely associated with Franquemont's command. As usual, the French valued the German light cavalry and Bertrand offered special praise for the Württemberg horse battery whose horses outshone the pathetic nags pulling the French guns.[74]

Now integrated into their new corps, the Württembergers arrived in Dresden on the morning of 11 May after an arduous but largely uneventful

Injunctions, Marches and Secret Instructions

march shadowed by Allied cavalry and Cossacks. Franquemont described the situation for the king:

> The extended marches thus far, the bivouacs in the worst weather, the precautions against attacks and ambushes, the dreadful roads, the shortages that have occurred now and again, have greatly diminished the infantry and cavalry. Many infantry stragglers have remained behind. Not ill will, but total exhaustion is the reason. The complete absence of civilian horse teams, which the enemy have taken with them, hinders me from collecting wagons to bring along those who have fallen behind.[75]

Bertrand's corps was now to pass over the Elbe under Napoleon's eye and the Württembergers, adversities notwithstanding, put on 'the best appearance possible' as they paraded across on the damaged stone bridge in Dresden with the emperor watching from the side. Napoleon did not speak to Franquemont directly but seems to have been satisfied with what he saw. Indeed, for the Württembergers he was in one respect too satisfied. As the 38th Division's baggage was approaching the bridge under escort of a 7th Infantry company commanded by Hauptmann Karl von Suckow, the emperor suddenly asked, 'whose horses are those?' Suckow suspected what might happen next but dutifully reported their ownership only to hear Napoleon announce, 'they will be taken for the artillery!' Suckow was forced to turn over fourteen of his fine draft horses but boldly took himself to Berthier and managed to negotiate their replacement with a like number of oxen. Returning to the division that night after experiencing no little frustration with the refractory oxen, he presented himself to Franquemont expecting a reprimand and was relieved when the general answered: 'Ah, well, Suckow, that is also good; at least we can eat them.'[76]

While Suckow replaced his horses with oxen, the bulk of the division passed to the east bank of the river to halt 15 kilometres northeast of Dresden on the road to Königsbrück with the corps cavalry posted ahead as an advance guard under Briche's overall command. Logistics remained Franquemont's chief complaint. Although the corps received bread and flour from French magazines for the first time on 13 May, supplies were generally irregular and insufficient. The general could report, however, that the Württemberg troops were treated equally as far as distribution was concerned and that Bertrand was particularly 'courteous and friendly' after Napoleon's review.[77]

Despite the enervating marches, poor weather and numerous privations, Franquemont told Friedrich that his men displayed good spirits; none of his characteristically candid correspondence with his king makes mention of disruptive behaviour or negative expressions in the division at this stage in the war. There was doubtless grumbling beyond that common to all armies and presumably some degree of discontent with their French ally as Leutnant von Martens recalled when the men began their march for Würzburg: 'The horrible events of the just-completed campaign in Russia, had made such a deep impression on all of the others that our young troops – almost all newly raised – did not depart our homeland with the cheery courage that our experienced soldiers used to display.' As the weather improved, however, 'so too did the mood of our soldiers, they sang their songs and thus we reached, after a very easy march with a wide view into the Main valley, the pleasantly situated Würzburg'.[78] Hauptmann von Baumbach likewise 'went towards the new dangers in good spirits' despite 'an oppressive feeling to have to fight against Germany's interests and against Germans'. 'No one, however, dared to express such ideas out loud', he continued, 'The king demanded unconditional obedience and would have severely punished any utterances that stood in contradiction to his will.' Some others also had misgivings. Ludwig von Schlaich, an *Unterleutnant* in the 3rd Jäger-zu-Pferd *Herzog Louis*, hoped at this early stage of the war that his regiment's march would not be in support of 'the Corsican world-destroyer', but this feeling would in no way inhibit him in the performance of his duties.[79] Desertion was not a serious problem and the general sentiment, instilled by the officer corps, seems to have been one of sturdy professionalism in obedience to their monarch's commands even among those who were just learning their duties as soldiers. One subsequent Württemberg military historian described the common attitude as 'a kind of defiant stubbornness'.[80]

An incident that occurred just before Bautzen perhaps serves to illustrate this mood. An *Unteroffizier* (NCO) of the 1st Chevaulegers *Prinz Adam* named Lorenz Buck was charged with taking a detachment of ten troopers to escort a captain from Königsbrück to imperial headquarters in Dresden on 16 May. Mission accomplished, they were returning to the Württemberg division the following day with orders and dispatches but discovered on reaching Königsbrück that their division had departed, and Cossack quartering parties had arrived in the town. Buck suggested that they attempt to escape cross-country and took possession of the various messages from the captain reasoning that, if they were captured as seemed possible, the enemy would be less likely to suspect an NCO of carrying important papers than an officer. Chased and briefly surrounded by Cossacks, they were able to break away and seek refuge in a nearby town, Buck and his troopers hiding in a manor house with the help of the local villagers. The captain eventually escaped by doffing his uniform and disguising himself as a farmer. Buck and most of his men also avoided capture but they became separated in the confusion, and he decided to return to Dresden on foot and alone. Arriving at 3:00 a.m. on 18 May, he found the remaining men of his little detachment and sent them to join the regimental depot in the city. Buck, however, having held on to the dispatch case and having even recovered the officer's discarded uniform, was resolved to resume his place with his regiment. Hitching a ride with French and Bavarian staff officers, he began his return journey that very day, bivouacked with the French overnight, and cadged another ride with a French artillery battery the next day to report to Franquemont at his headquarters near Bautzen on 19 May. In recognition of his presence of mind, leadership, courage and determination, he would be promoted to *Unterleutnant* during the armistice in June.[81]

Buck's story is illuminating in several respects: in addition to serving as an example of individual resolution and bravery, it sheds light on how affairs were conducted in the Grande Armée (and likely in any army of the era) and highlights the pervasive threat posed by Allied light troops in the French rear in 1813. What is especially noteworthy, however, is what did not happen: neither the captain, nor Buck nor any of the troopers surrendered or deserted. Instead, they made every effort to evade their pursuers and carry out their assigned tasks. Part of the reluctance to surrender is explained by watching the Cossacks beat and rob one of their number after he recklessly stepped from hiding, but their sense of duty, honour and loyalty to country and comrades were the paramount factors. This instance from the lower ranks is consistent with the views of senior officers such as the observations of GM Ludwig Friedrich von Stockmayer, one of the brigade commanders:

> I have never served under one of the various allies by my own inclination or choice or to the achievement of some personal advantage. In dealing with the French, I always remained German, mainly, however, in all circumstances a Württemberger in the strictest sense, cherished the old slogan 'God bless Württemberg first and always!' in my loyal breast and comforted myself with the total confidence in the distant help of He who had guided my fate thus far, who had never yet abandoned me. I was always bound by duty and sense of honour towards the interests of my king and fatherland as well as towards my subordinates and the honour of our arms.[82]

That sense of duty and honour would soon be tested. Writing to Friedrich on 14 May, Franquemont reported that the Allies were ensconced near Bautzen, but he did not believe they would stand 'because the position at Bautzen can be out-flanked and substantial numbers of [French and Rheinbund] troops have already passed over the Elbe'. He concluded his report, however, by noting that 'If the Russians hold themselves at Bautzen, then it will come to an affair tomorrow or the day after'.[83] He was premature in his guess as to the date of battle, but he was precisely prophetic in observing that the Bautzen position could and would be out-flanked.

Across the Elbe

As detailed earlier, the Württemberg 38th Division and the rest of 4th Corps were on the road to Königsbrück on the evening of 11/12 May. The next several days would bring them to the Spree River to form the left wing of Napoleon's main army for the looming struggle at Bautzen. The infantry saw almost no action on this march, but the corps advance guard – the Württemberg cavalry and horse battery along with the Neapolitan chasseurs – were engaged in minor skirmishes with Prussian troops and Cossacks almost every day. Clashes began on the very night of 11/12 May when Württemberg troopers surprised and captured a number of Prussians southwest of Königsbrück. They exploited this miniature achievement the following day by seizing Königsbrück itself to bring their total of prisoners to about four dozen. The shine of these successes was blotched by ambushes sustained on the 13th. Although their reconnaissance patrols yielded valuable information, engagements with Major General Vasily Ilovaysky's Cossacks cost the Württemberg regiments 10–20 men along with more numerous casualties among the Neapolitan chasseurs and their infantry supports (two companies of the 2nd Provisional Croatian Regiment who apparently surrendered at once). Among those captured was Leutnant Vossler of the *Louis-Jäger*, who made every effort to escape 'a shameful surrender', even abandoning his horse to hide in a dense thicket overnight, only to be taken the next day when he attempted to rejoin his regiment.[84] Similar small advance-guard clashes occurred over the next several days as the corps pressed east to reach its assigned position at Cölln 5 kilometres northwest of Bautzen on 17 May. The cavalry incurred additional losses that afternoon while reconnoitring Allied positions towards the Spree. The division shifted to the area around Großwelka and Kleinwelka the following day to be closer to the main army.[85]

In addition to these reconnaissance missions, the Württemberg cavalry was also involved in another crucial task in the lead-up to Bautzen: courier escort. In this case, ensuring that Chef d'Escadron Alphonse Frédéric Emmanuel Grouchy, one of Berthier's staff officers and son of the future marshal, safely delivered orders to Ney outlining the role his army was to play in the coming battle. Reflecting the significance of the orders and the insecurity of the French rear area, 2½ squadrons of the *Herzog Louis* Jäger-zu-Pferd under Major Friedrich August von Seebach were dedicated to this mission. As noted in the introductory chapter, GD Peiri's Italian 15th Division was ordered to Königswartha on 18 May to serve as a link to Ney's approaching forces. Furthermore, the Württemberg 7th Infantry and forty chevaulegers from *Prinz Adam* were stationed at Luga on the left (northern) flank to protect communications with the Italian division. Departing on the 18th, Seebach's squadrons followed the lead elements of the 15th Division to Königswartha before continuing on to reach Hoyerswerda. Though badgered by Cossacks en route, they reached their destination at 2 o'clock on the morning of the 19th and Grouchy was able to deliver his messages to Ney. Seebach turned about almost at once and made his way back to gain Königswartha around 1:00 p.m. Here he stopped to feed his horses. He was planning to ride on, but the Italians had no cavalry and GB Pietro Sant'Andrea, one of Peiri's brigade commanders, either asked or ordered him to remain. The Württembergers thus became involved in the defeat of the Italian division when Barclay's Russians attacked later that afternoon. Utterly surprised owing to the Italians' poor positioning and lax field security, Seebach rallied his men in the confusion and attempted a countercharge but was quickly forced to retreat with Sant'Andrea's fleeing men. Unexpected reinforcements from Ney's command restored the situation late in the day and Seebach was fortunate to have lost only six men killed and five wounded despite the heavy Russian artillery fire. He and his troopers rejoined the rest of 4th Corps the next day along with the 15th Division.[86]

While Seebach was coping with the surprise attack at Königswartha, the rest of the contingent experienced short, sharp skirmishes with the enemy. Though hearing the 'strong cannonade in the direction of Königswartha', Franquemont was ordered to undertake a reconnaissance towards Klix on the Spree. The division soon encountered enemy outposts, however, and had pushed no further than Quatitz when Franquemont and Bertrand cautiously elected to halt. The division returned to its bivouacs around the Welka villages that evening having lost two cavalrymen in the skirmishing. At the same time, the 7th Infantry repelled persistent Cossack raids in their interim position at Luga.[87] Other than these actions, however, the bulk of the 38th Division and the cavalry brigade spent most of their time during 17–19 May resting, repairing their equipment and waiting to see what the coming days would bring.

First Day at Bautzen, 20 May: Like Veteran Soldiers

The morning of 20 May found the Württemberg division awake and under arms around the two Welkas by 3:00 a.m. News of the Italian division's disaster had left Bertrand understandably embarrassed and led him to order the Württembergers back to Cölln to guard the corps' northern flank. He and Franquemont had just sent the 9th Light Infantry to reconnoitre towards Luga when, around nine o'clock, Marshal Soult arrived. Soult, appointed to oversee operations on the army's left, apparently treated Bertrand quite rudely but became alarmed on spying a column approaching from the north. 'Now everything was in an uproar!' wrote Franquemont, as Soult, fearing an attack from Königswartha, sent adjutants flying in all directions to call for assistance in countering the supposed threat.[88] The Württemberg 7th Infantry was recalled from Luga and nine regiments of the 1st Cavalry Corps hastened to support 4th Corps, but scouts soon discovered that the mysterious column was the shaken remnants of the Italian division re-joining the army and the marshal could return his attention to the business of the day: preparing for the decisive engagement Napoleon hoped would occur on 21 May.

The 20th of May was indeed a day of preparation. As Napoleon wanted to hold the Allies in place to allow Ney's out-flanking move to evolve, he focused on clearing the Russians out of Bautzen and establishing his right wing firmly on the eastern side of the Spree. These tasks fell to the 6th, 11th and 12th Corps, while the 4th Corps, under Soult's overall command, was to secure crossings opposite the Kreckwitz heights. The marshal thus shifted Bertrand's corps and the cavalry back to Quatitz and arrayed them facing east towards the little river. The 1st Cavalry Corps and Briche's brigade with the two Württemberg regiments opened Soult's advance, pushing towards the Spree to force Allied cavalry out of the low ground along the river with lively skirmishing and artillery fire. This was accomplished without any sabre-to-sabre action, and the French regiments soon trotted off to post themselves with the Imperial Guard near Bautzen. Briche's regiments remained with Bertrand.

With the enemy cavalry out of the picture, Soult opened his main attack around noon with Morand's 12th Division in the lead. As the French moved on Briesing and Niedergurig, Franquemont's 38th Division followed in support while the battered Italian 15th remained in reserve. The Württemberg infantry moved up to the river between the Gottlobsberg and Niedergurig around 3:00 p.m. with the 9th and 7th Infantry Regiments of Stockmayer's brigade in front and the 10th Infantry and II/2 detached to the left to cover the division's northern flank. The division had to cross an open area of a kilometre or so under the punishing crossfire of several enemy batteries, what Suckow recalled as 'a treeless plain of soft earth, perhaps 1,200 paces long, and, in a circle before us, the nearby hills truly lined with enemy artillery pieces of every sort ... It was a difficult half hour for us', he wrote, but the young troops marched 'with the calm and composure of veteran soldiers' despite losing 16 men killed and 24 wounded as they advanced.[89] Most of the division was able to find cover behind the Gottlobsberg, but the 10th Infantry was drawn into the fight for Niedergurig, successfully storming the village late in the day to allow the 23ᵉ Ligne of GB Joseph Victorien Sicard's French brigade to push east across the Spree. To the north, the French occupied Briesing and pressed towards Pließkowitz, while seizing the Bölauberg just across from the Gottlobsberg in the south. Franquemont posted the 9th Infantry and I/7 near Niedergurig to support Sicard's men, but his other five battalions remained in the lee

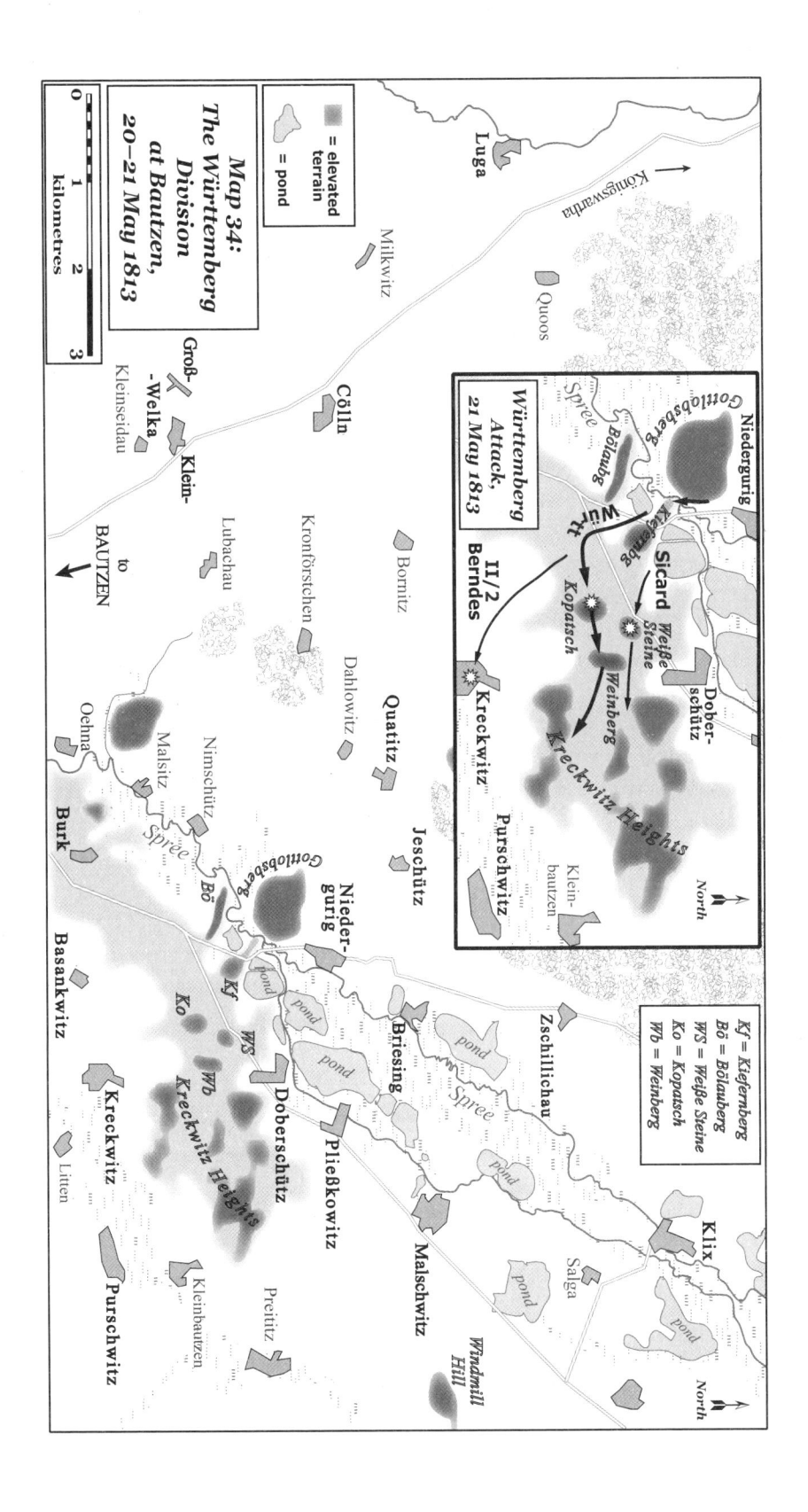

Map 34: The Württemberg Division at Bautzen, 20–21 May 1813

of the Gottlobsberg.[90] Here the soldiers 'were allowed to make themselves comfortable and lie on the ground', as Surgeon Christoph Heinrich Groß of the 2nd Infantry recorded. Danger arrived even in this protected position, however, especially for the thoughtless and inexperienced. Groß recalled 'how cannon balls would come over the hill and roll down; thus we stood for a time together and avoided a rolling ball which a soldier lying on the ground struck with his foot as it rolled past near him and was thereby seriously wounded'.[91]

After helping to chase off the enemy horse, the two cavalry regiments and the horse battery had remained near Jeschütz during the afternoon, but the two howitzers from the Württemberg foot battery unlimbered on the Gottlobsberg to support a dozen French 12-pounders that were engaged in an artillery duel with the Russian and Prussian guns across the Spree. Two of the men were killed when Allied shot disabled one of the howitzers. As his gunners sweated over their pieces and his infantrymen moved into their allotted positions sheltered from the enemy's guns, Franquemont mounted the Gottlobsberg. Although he did not wax lyrical as Bavarian GL von Raglovich did away on the right flank (*see* Chapter 3), the little hill offered a spectacular view and he reported that 'one could very clearly follow the battle' from this vantage point. He mistakenly concluded, however, that 'one could clearly observe that nothing had been won on the 20th'.[92] From Napoleon's broader viewpoint, of course, the day had proceeded more or less as he had desired, and the stage was set for a potentially conclusive battle on the morrow.

Second Day at Bautzen, 21 May: 'We Gained a Great Victory'

The Württembergers had played a supporting role on the first day of the battle, but they would take centre stage on the second, 21 May. Moreover, on this occasion, though they did not know it at the time, they would be under the eyes of the emperor as well.[93]

Marshal Soult appeared on the Gottlobsberg shortly after sunrise. Sending for Franquemont, he outlined Napoleon's overall plan and pointed to two hills the Württemberg division was to seize as soon as Ney and Marmont made sufficient progress on the northern and southern flanks. The nearest of these low hills, the Kopatschberg (or Kopatche), and its more distant companion, the Weinberg, were both crowned with Allied artillery. Other enemy batteries loomed to the flanks and Franquemont quickly discerned that his division would come under 'multiple crossfires' on its way to its objectives. He raised his concerns to Soult, noting as well that 'the division was too weak for such an undertaking'. 'I was not at all comfortable with this', he would later write, but Soult promised strong artillery support and the assistance of the other two divisions of the corps. Franquemont was hardly reassured and when the marshal returned sometime around 10:00 a.m., he repeated his objections, adding 'I also told him that I only had recruits and that the mission assigned to me truly required good veteran soldiers.'[94] Soult was unmoved, but delayed giving the attack order, apparently hoping that Ney's progress would force the enemy to retreat without a direct assault by 4th Corps.

Despite Franquemont's apprehensions, the morning passed in relative quiet on the 4th Corps' front. The senior Württemberg officers used the opportunity to observe the enemy positions and plan their approach. At Stockmayer's suggestion, they decided on a narrow column of companies, a formation that would allow them to traverse the constrained terrain but swiftly form squares should they come under attack by the superior Coalition cavalry. The three infantry battalions near Niedergurig were recalled during the morning and the division passed over the Spree on a newly constructed bridge around 1:00 p.m. Briche's cavalry, crossing first, deployed on the right with the Württemberg infantry compressed in the confined ground below the Kiefernberg and Sicard's French brigade on their left. Russian and Prussian artillery attempted to disturb this movement, but they could not see their targets and their shot and shell flew harmlessly overhead. For the untested young troopers standing by their mounts that afternoon, this was a terrifying new experience and the commander of the *Louis Jäger*, Oberst Ludwig von Gaisberg, chastised them with 'sharp words' for ducking and hunching as the enemy's iron hurtled by above. Gaisberg himself, however, would later be thankful for bending down, albeit involuntarily. Having injured his knee, he could not sit his horse properly and had to lean far forward in an awkward posture. Had he not sat so low in the saddle, he would likely have been decapitated when a Prussian ball tore through the air above his mount at normal head height later that afternoon.[95]

While the infantry and cavalry waited in the lee of the Kiefernberg, their artillery support was trundling over the bridge. Just as Soult had promised, some 30 guns (including the 11 remaining Württemberg pieces) unlimbered on the Kiefernberg itself and in the low ground nearby to supplement the battery on the Gottlobsberg. The French and Württemberg pieces at first held their fire to encourage the enemy to exhaust his ammunition while conserving their own, but they opened up with full fury when Franquemont's infantry stepped off at approximately 2 o'clock, Stockmayer's 3rd Brigade in the lead. Although their initial objective, the Kopatschberg, lay almost due east, the Württemberg generals initially angled their column to the right so as not to mask their own batteries and to give their men some protection from the enemy's guns. Indeed, those Allied guns immediately pummelled the Württembergers just as Franquemont had feared. 'At every step we became aware of new enemy batteries, that fired so fiercely that very many men were laid low, some dead, some wounded. Nonetheless, this caused no faltering, no wavering in the column'. By swinging to their right, however, the Württemberg battalions were headed almost directly for Kreckwitz from where an additional Prussian battery took them under fire. 'Our appearance on the low ground in the open was the signal for the enemy batteries to concentrate their fire on us; we were fired upon from the front and both flanks at the same time,' remembered Baumbach, 'It was especially a battery in the direction of Kreckwitz that caused us great harm.' As he pivoted his column back to the left towards the Kopatschberg, therefore, Franquemont detached II/2nd Infantry as a feint to 'amuse' or distract the Prussian gunners while the rest of the division ploughed ahead.[96]

The attackers were now closing on their first objective and Allied artillery fire intensified. GM Carl von Neuffer, one of the brigade commanders, noted that the enemy gunners tended to fire too high so that their shot and shell flew over the leading battalions of Stockmayer's brigade to fall amongst his own men causing many casualties. Of his experiences at the head of the column Stockmayer later recalled:

> As we were only some 300 paces or so from the enemy batteries and exposed to their effective canister fire that raged dreadfully through our ranks, the cries of Forward! Forward! grew ever louder but the steps became ever smaller, and the column began to waver. In this moment, I saw on the right wing of the enemy's main battery the first cannon fire and then pull back. Familiar with this artillery manoeuvre as the beginning of a retreat, I quickly looked to the left wing and as I observed that the last cannon and thus in sequence the other pieces fired and drew back, I turned to my men and shouted: 'Look, boys, they are falling back – Allons! Allons, now forwards!' at which the entire column doubled its pace with the greatest enthusiasm.[97]

Stockmayer's encouragement had the desired effect. 'General von Stockmayer's voice, so well-known to us, echoed loudly,' recalled Suckow, 'at which the entire column, as if electrified, dashed up the deadly slope with a loud hurrah and successfully mastered it despite all the canister being thrown against us.'[98]

Mounting the crest of the hill, Stockmayer's men deftly deployed in line to the right while Neuffer's brigade did the same on the left. Swiftly aligned, the two brigades 'greeted the fleeing enemy with well-directed musketry' while the 10th Light Infantry and I/2nd Infantry were held in column on either flank as reserves. Under heavy fire, the Württembergers had to repel several Prussian counterattacks and were fortunate to receive reinforcement when their own two batteries pounded up to add their weight to the defence. They had only been on the hilltop for perhaps thirty minutes, however, when Major Josef

Konrad von Bangold, the division's deputy chief of staff, rode up with tears in his eyes to tell Stockmayer that Franquemont had been seriously wounded. Stockmayer replied that Neuffer should take over as the most senior general, but Bangold relayed that Neuffer had also taken a bad wound and been forced to remove himself from the battlefield. 'Very well', rejoined Stockmayer, 'then stay by me until I too am wounded.'[99]

Neuffer had been wounded while positioning I/2nd Infantry on his left as Prussian guns on the Weiße Steine hill were perfectly placed to enfilade the Württemberg line and he feared a flank attack. Sicard's brigade, however, which had initially held back in the low ground under punishing fire, now advanced, cleared the Weiße Steine position and removed the threat to the Württemberg left. Additionally, an Italian battery joined the line on the right to contribute to the repulse of another Prussian counterattack. Though its arrival was timely, Stockmayer considered this battery dilatory in the execution of its duties. Finding the guns still limbered up at the bottom of the hill, he demanded to know why it had not joined the firing line despite the urgency of the situation. The horses were exhausted, the battery commander replied and needed to rest before climbing the slope. 'I told him I would show him how the task can be best and most swiftly accomplished in such a situation. I thereupon ordered my adjutant to smack not the horses, but the train soldiers with the flat of his sword and, if that did not work, to chop away with the sharp edge of his blade, at which suggestion the battery reached the heights in a flash and went into position.'[100]

The Württembergers held on, but intense enemy fire knocked men out of the ranks with terrifying frequency, and at one point, bold Prussian Jägers crept on hands and knees to within sixty paces of Stockmayer's line before being driven off. 'I lost six men, some dead, some wounded, and many horses from the crew and team of my cannon,' wrote Unteroffizier Johann Gottlob Heere of the horse battery, 'Balls from the Prussian Jägers frequently rattled off the metal of the cannon, but I was not wounded.'[101] Heere's gun would exhaust its basic load of 160 rounds during the afternoon and Stockmayer had to resupply his infantrymen with ammunition before they could consider assaulting their next objective.

Among those observing the assault was Chef de Bataillon Jules Antoine Paulin, one of Bertrand's staff officers. He recorded that,

> The honour of seizing the principal hill was assigned to the Württemberg division, supported by the French infantry and cavalry. After a half an hour of very lively fire, General Franquemont charged towards the redoubt at the head of the Württemberg regiments who in an instant covered the slopes and summit of the hill with their masses dark and compact. The Russian [sic] lines were thrown back and the hills from which a hellish fire had come

suddenly became silent; the attackers, after having reached the summit of the position, returned to the attack with a new impetuosity and pushed the disconcerted enemy, bayonets in their backs.[102]

It was now between 3:00 and 4:00 p.m., and Soult, who had just come from Napoleon, rode up to lavish praise on the Württemberg division. While he and Stockmayer conversed, imperial staff officers dashed along the battleline to announce that the battle was won. Cheers of '"*Vive l'Empereur!*" echoed from many thousands of tongues even more and courage rose even higher because earlier we had not been entirely sure of victory.' recorded Stockmayer. Soult now attached additional artillery to Stockmayer and ordered him to resume his advance towards the next set of hills. With 40–42 pieces at his command and Sicard's men driving forward on his left, Stockmayer pressed on, but found that the enemy was already withdrawing. He was thus able to occupy the Weinberg and push on to master the sets of hills overlooking Kreckwitz and Purschwitz without serious resistance. Here he granted his weary infantrymen a well-deserved rest and called for his pipe and a glass of wine as he used his riding crop to direct the fire of his numerous artillery at the retreating foe. 'Finally, the enemy fled in all directions and victory was ours!' exclaimed Leutnant von Schlaich in a letter the following day, 'We had suffered on this day a very great loss, but we also gained a great victory.'[103]

The Württemberg 38th Division thus accomplished its missions at Bautzen in spectacular fashion, earning plaudits not only from Soult and Bertrand but from the emperor as well. Their attack was easily visible from Napoleon's position and as they advanced onto the Kopatschberg, he turned to his entourage and exclaimed: 'Look, gentlemen! My cousin, the King of Württemberg, made excuses that after the preceding campaign most of what he was able to send me were conscripts; well, gentlemen, look and say if those are conscripts!' Bertrand was likewise pleased, using his immediate after-action report to credit 'the success of the day' to 'the intrepidity of the 23rd Regiment and the Württemberg division and to the good dispositions of General Comte Morand'.[104] Composed later, the 4th Corps 'Journal Historique' also acclaimed the 38th Division's performance:

> It took the plateau with the greatest possible resolution, without hesitation or wavering, and when it reached the highest point of the plateau, this division had to withstand an attack from the enemy second line, flanked by formidable artillery; it held firm and was unshakeable in the position it had valiantly taken... The Württemberg division, which had already made a name for itself with its exact manner of service, earned the esteem of officers and soldiers alike witnessing the valour it deployed in this battle.[105]

Stockmayer, of course, paid warm tribute to the men and the wounded Franquemont reported to Friedrich that, 'I cannot praise the courage and dedication of the royal troops enough, all arms, officers and men fought with the same distinction.' Junior officers were also impressed with their men. 'This was a rough start for the young soldiers', wrote Hauptmann von Baumbach, 'They had conducted themselves very well and deserved the praise they received from all sides.'[106]

Briche's cavalry brigade had accompanied the Württemberg division's attack, serving as a shield on its right flank. The first across the Spree, the horsemen initially deployed between the Bölauberg and Basankwitz. They suffered from enemy fire and took part in some mounted skirmishing but saw no hand-to-hand combat as they followed the infantry's advance past the Kopatschberg and east towards Purschwitz. Their presence, however, sufficed to chase off an enemy battery and deter attacks by Prussian cavalry. These minor encounters included one with what was almost certainly the Silesian Uhlan Regiment with which the Württemberg *Herzog Louis* Jäger had been brigaded during the invasion of Russia a year earlier. The Württemberg troopers thus found themselves fending off men with whom, in the words of their regimental history, they had 'fought, starved, frozen, in short, with whom they had shared the whole bitter fate of the history of the previous campaign'.[107] The Prussians withdrew according to orders and the two regiments did not come to blows, but neither side's ardour was dimmed by the prior experience together, another instance of former allies on opposite sides in 1813. The intensity of emotion, however, was evident in the attitude of some ultra-German patriots (*'ultra-Deutsche'*) on the Prussian side who advocated shooting south German prisoners 'to make them aware of their crime' and thereby induce their comrades to join the Allies. The Prussian leaders wisely rejected this atrocious step but the prevalence of these suggestions caused Blücher's chief of staff Gneisenau to worry that such horrors could arise if the war went on too long. 'God knows what would become of us,' he told a colleague after interviewing an artless young Württemberg captive, 'the blood of the men of the Thirty Years War still flows in us and a long nurtured bitterness would then give rise to savagery and through this to mutual destruction, but our hereditary enemy, as back then, would rejoice.'[108]

No prisoners were shot, but the Württemberg division's success at Bautzen came at high cost. The total bill for the two days was 1,431 men killed, wounded, captured or missing, some 25 per cent of the total under arms at the start of the battle. At least 240 of the casualties came from II/2nd Infantry. This battalion had been the last in line when the division began its advance from the Spree, but it only consisted of three companies as one had been assigned to guard the contingent's trains. As previously mentioned, Franquemont detached II/2 early in the attack to distract and contain the Prussian battery that was firing on the main column from near Kreckwitz. Franquemont reported that this was to be a feint, a false attack, but instead the battalion charged straight at the village. It is unclear whether Franquemont was dissembling in his account, or if his orders were misunderstood or if the battalion commander, Oberstleutnant Ludwig Friedrich von Berndes, simply decided that a full-on attack was safer and wiser than standing in the open under fire. Whatever the answer, the Württembergers successfully evicted the Prussian defenders from Kreckwitz but soon found themselves nearly surrounded and under heavy pressure. Berndes sent the battalion's standard away with a party of thirty men to save it from capture, but he was wounded and taken prisoner along with almost all his command after a desperate defence. Owing to the regiment's heavy losses, its five remaining companies would be combined and considered as a single battalion for the remainder of the war.[109]

Casualties among the Württemberg senior leaders were especially notable. Franquemont would be out of action for several weeks, and Neuffer's wound required a return home and reassignment to convalesce. The division chief of staff and the commanders of the 1st, 2nd, 9th and 10th Infantry Regiments were also wounded (as was French GB Sicard, who would succumb to his injuries within the month). These losses resulted in some changes to the command hierarchy: Jett assumed command of the division, Stockmayer became the senior infantry commander, his place at the head of the 3rd Brigade filled by Oberst von Spitzemberg of the 7th Infantry, while Oberst Fidelis Baur von Breitenfeld, commander of the 2nd Infantry, took Neuffer's post in command of the 1st Brigade. Additionally, for the French at least, the absence of Franquemont meant that the reduced Württemberg contingent came under Morand's orders, an arrangement that would remain in effect until Franquemont's return during the armistice.

Exhausting Pursuit:
We Faced the Enemy Rear Guards Daily

The exhausted but proud Württemberg division bivouacked near Hochkirch on the night of 21/22 May, marching on the next morning to participate in the painful pursuit of the retreating Allies. Bertrand's 4th Corps followed the Saxons at first but was diverted to the right and crossed the Neisse River on 23 May south of Görlitz (*see* Map 21, in Vol. 1). Along with MacDonald's 11th Corps, it thus formed the right wing of Napoleon's drive into Silesia. Reaching Lauban on the 24th, the corps found the town unoccupied, but the Russian rear guard resisted efforts to cross the Queis (Kwisa) River until II/7th Infantry, followed by the 9th and the cavalry, located a ford and out-flanked the enemy position. The *Prinz Adam* Chevaulegers gave the Cossacks a lesson in the value of formed regular cavalry the following day when they supported MacDonald's cavalry in a fight just 8 kilometres east of Lauban. The Cossacks were driving the French squadrons, but the Württemberg regiment, thanks to cool leadership from its experienced commander, Oberstleutnant Friedrich Wilhelm von Bismarck, was able to cover the disorderly flight and counter-charge to punish the pursuing Cossacks. The French thus gained time to re-form and return to the attack as well. Though Bismarck was wounded in the skirmish, he and his men earned the marshal's gratitude: 'I must offer you my compliments, it is thanks to you that we have had a fortunate issue from this affair.' Bismarck would be elevated to officer rank in the Legion of Honour during the armistice at MacDonald's recommendation.[110]

Each ensuing day offered similarly fatiguing and repetitive scenes: clouds of Cossacks, wearying marches and tough little actions against Russian rear guards who ably exploited the terrain. 'Night-time disturbances by the Cossacks occurred often,' wrote Surgeon Groß, 'Thus it could come to pass that the night-time peace and calm of the camp would be suddenly interrupted by a charge of Cossacks riding at the gallop past our lines and firing their pistols.'[111] On the 28th, the Württembergers took the unusual step of assigning a cannon to the outposts to discourage the pestilential Cossacks. GM von Jett described these enervating actions in a summary report to his king:

> We faced the enemy rear guards daily, skirmishing with the Cossacks and with other enemy light cavalry occurred constantly; often it came to cannonades and musketry. The marches were not long, but the great caution with which we marched, the many reconnaissance patrols, the manner of always marching cross country from hilltop to hilltop without regard for the roads, and the constant presence of the enemy made the marches extremely tiring and meant that the entire day from early morning into the late night was required to cover a few hours distance and that our end position was only occupied at 9:00 or 10:00 in the evening.[112]

As the army's right wing, Bertrand and MacDonald pivoted to the southeast as the Allies, hugging the Austrian border, withdrew towards Striegau (Strzegom) at the end of the month. This move resulted in a sharp battle with Lt. Gen. Emmanuel St Priest's Russian rear guard around the village of Groß-Rosen (Rogoźnica) on 31 May. The two French corps pushed cautiously south from around Jauer between 9:00 and 10:00 that morning, MacDonald on the right, Bertrand on the left. They encountered Russian outposts only 4 or 5 kilometres southeast of the town and MacDonald, fearing for his right flank in the face of what he believed were superior enemy forces, decided to

Map 35: Groß-Rosen, 31 May 1813

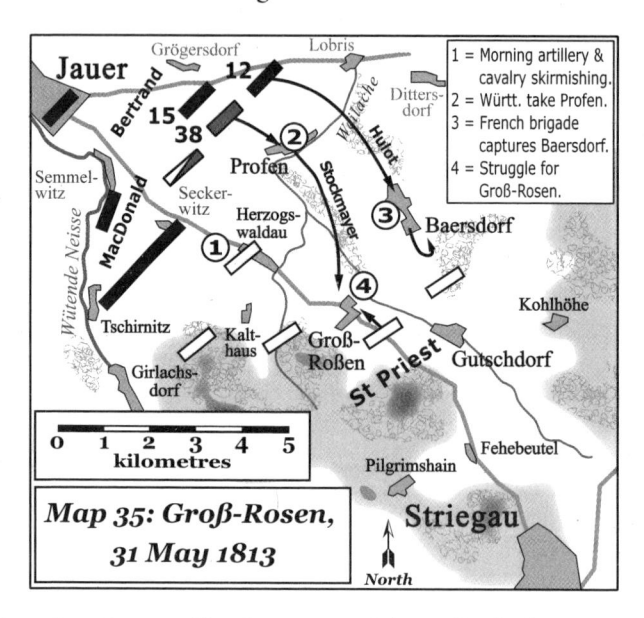

1 = Morning artillery & cavalry skirmishing.
2 = Württ. take Profen.
3 = French brigade captures Baersdorf.
4 = Struggle for Groß-Rosen.

halt, hoping that Bertrand's advance would out-flank the Russian position and permit him to continue. Bertrand was indeed making progress. On the left, GB Étienne Hulot's brigade of the 12th Division pressed forward towards Baersdorf (Targoszyn) while the Württemberg cavalry drove off the Russian horse near Herzogswaldau (Niedaszów) and Württemberg artillery silenced the opposing Russian guns. This allowed Spitzemberg's infantry to capture Profen (Mściwojów) against light resistance. Bertrand, however, became apprehensive that he was outnumbered and called off his attack. Thus far the combat had consisted of lively skirmishing spiced with some cannon fire but MacDonald, thinking Bertrand too timorous, rode over and persuaded his compatriot to test the enemy's strength with a more vigorous reconnaissance in force. Hulot's men had by this time taken Baersdorf to clear the Württemberg left flank, so Bertrand sent the French and Württemberg infantry forward again at 4:30 p.m. to probe the Russian positions, hoping that seizure of Groß-Rosen would cut off the Russians in Herzogswaldau. The French were soon brought to a halt between Baersdorf and Gutschdorf (Goczałków), but Stockmayer drove for Groß-Rosen with the 'Light Brigade' of 7th, 9th and 10th Infantry. The Württemberg 1st Brigade remained in close support. What had begun as a fairly desultory engagement that morning thus escalated into a surprisingly bitter struggle for possession of the village as the afternoon darkened towards evening. The Württemberg infantry were able to eject the tenacious Russian defenders late in the day but were themselves evicted in fierce fighting that flared on until late that night with Groß-Rosen changing hands several times. Concluding that they could not retain their grip on the village with the enemy dominating the heights beyond, the Württemberg light infantrymen set fire to the buildings and withdrew around 10:00 p.m., their retreat covered by parts of the 1st and 2nd Infantry. The determined defence and what seemed large numbers of enemy troops on the far side of the village convinced MacDonald and Bertrand that the Russians here were too strong to dislodge. They decided to retire on Jauer, a destination the weary Württemberg units only attained around 1:00 a.m. that night.

Though minor in the context of the larger campaign, the combat at Groß-Rosen was costly for the Württemberg contingent: 359 officers and men dead or wounded and another 132 missing or captured for a total loss of almost 500 from the small division. The 7th Infantry alone suffered 177 casualties. Stockmayer had 'covered himself in glory' during the engagement in the words of the 4th Corps journal, but he was wounded in the process, leaving Jett as the only untouched Württemberg general in the field; Oberst von Spitzemberg was elevated to commander of the contingent's infantry.[113] The troops had again displayed dogged courage and tactical skill, garnering praise from both Bertrand and Morand. Like the rest of the army, however, the men were exhausted and in dire need of a break to rest and recover. When they learned that a temporary ceasefire had been declared starting on 1 June, the men thus greeted this utterly unexpected news with great relief. 'We turned about by platoons and went into our comfortable bivouacs near Jauer with bands playing,' wrote Leutnant von Schlaich to a friend that day, 'Like us, the enemy went into his old camp. We live in complete peace!' The sudden shift in circumstances left him and many others reflective as well as thankful: 'How quickly the iron game of the soldier twists and turns, how uncertain and unsteady is its dangerous course!'[114]

The Armistice: Cantonments, Controversies and Condemnations

Following the ceasefire announced on 1 June and the formal armistice three days later, the Württemberg division and the rest of 4th Corps initially remained in and around Jauer. Combat and sickness had reduced the number of infantrymen fit for duty to a mere 2,400 (with an additional 109 for the foot artillery battery) compared to more than 4,700 at Bautzen. The cavalry, on the other hand, had deployed 809 at Bautzen and still had 749 officers and men in the saddle (plus 103 gunners) despite the daily grind of the pursuit, a condition Jett attributed to the attention GB Briche paid to the mounted regiments.[115] The contingent regained some of its strength through the return of convalescents and detachments during the armistice, but König Friedrich did not send any replacements, so the 38th Division and its associated cavalry brigade remained well below authorised manpower levels when the war resumed in August.[116]

The 38th Division: 'Time Passed in a Comfortable Fashion'

The corps left Jauer on 6 June to take up its assigned cantonment area southwest of Glogau. For the Württembergers, this meant moving into billets around Primkenau (Przemków) where they arrived on the 10th. The armistice of course brought a reprieve from intense battles and endless marches as well as a chance to repair or replace equipment and clothing. It also meant, in theory at least, a more regular, varied and generous supply of food provided by the local inhabitants. As far as victuals were concerned, however, the men were often disappointed in the early weeks of the summer. The region was impoverished and had already been raked over by both armies, leaving the Württemberg troops, in the words of one regimental history, to starve along with the Silesian villagers. Regimental commanders were instructed to have their men grind their own meal and bake their own bread at the local level while the contingent established a brandy distillery to provide this vital item.[117] A supply convoy sent from Württemberg helped alleviate some deficiencies and the situation improved for the soldiers over time. Like Surgeon Groß, therefore, most memoirists would record that 'the time passed in a comfortable fashion'.[118]

As with other contingents, the summer was spent in solidifying discipline and executing a rigorous training regime. Three topics received special attention on the infantry's drill schedules: repelling cavalry, marksmanship and skirmishing. The first, a consequence of the qualitative and quantitative superiority of the Allied mounted arm, had been stressed in ad hoc practice on the march since early May after the French experience at Lützen. The second aimed at improving infantry fire at both the individual and unit levels with target practice taking place at distances of 100, 150 and 200 paces. Each man was allotted 10 to 15 rounds of live ammunition for this purpose and shooting competitions for the entire corps were held at Bertrand's headquarters in Sprottau. The benefits of this focused training would be evident in the autumn campaign. Overall, then, Franquemont's men made a favourable impression on their allies, with a French inspection report concluding that, 'The Württemberg division is animated by a good spirit and is well commanded.'[119] Though not yet combined with the division, a new infantry brigade led by GM Christoph Friedrich David von Doering was en route from Württemberg, and these regiments likewise drilled on a daily basis, stressing the formation of columns and squares as well as skirmishing tactics.

The cavalry also engaged in strenuous and, at least in the case of the *Prinz Adam* Chevaulegers, rather innovative training that the regimental commander, Oberstleutnant von Bismarck, termed his 'Schützen-System'. He selected men from the regiment who had some familiarity with firearms and trained them to skirmish aggressively with the enemy's irregular cavalry.

He could not achieve much in the opening campaign, 'as the regiment was composed of recruits who had a lot to learn,' but by the autumn 'the regiment was never again troubled by the increasingly bold Cossacks'. 'For their part,' he proudly recorded, 'these Schützen soon became so bold and had so much faith in their firearms, especially their carbines, that they behaved with the greatest confidence when skirmishing. The enemy's irregular cavalry found themselves at a disadvantage and lost the reputation they had gained when we did not dare to use the recruits against them in single combat at the beginning of this campaign.' Their effectiveness was such that his regiment would often remain dismounted while its Schützen skirmished away with the Cossacks.[120]

Several changes in the contingent's hierarchy occurred while the men drilled, restored their equipment and recovered from the exertions of the spring campaign. At the higher level, Friedrich decided to attach a general to Imperial Headquarters to represent his interests and report on political–military developments far from the knowledge of his combat commanders. This assignment fell to GM Joseph Graf von Beroldingen, a close royal confidant who had held a similar position during the Russian campaign.[121] Internal to the contingent, Franquemont's wounding led the king to dispatch newly promoted GL Christian Johann Gottgetreu von Koch to serve as the contingent's interim commander until Franquemont recovered. Koch arrived in early June and held this temporary position until Franquemont's return on 10 July, whereupon he was assigned as the commander of all the Württemberg infantry. Stockmayer likewise resumed his place at the head of the 3rd or Light Brigade in July and Spitzemberg, promoted to *General-Major*, was appointed to command the 1st Brigade. The troops under Doering – two regiments and a battery – become the 2nd Brigade when they joined the division after the expiry of the armistice. With Koch's arrival, Jett returned to command the two cavalry regiments and their attached light battery, newly designated as the 24th Light Cavalry Brigade. The brigade was still under GB Briche, but by the time hostilities resumed, the 2nd Neapolitan Regiment had been removed from 4th Corps and allocated to MacDonald's 11th Corps. As with Beaumont and Wolff in 12th Corps, therefore, the rearrangements during the armistice left 4th Corps with the anomaly of having two generals, one French and one German, in charge of a pair of light cavalry regiments and a horse battery, fewer than 1,000 men in all. Franquemont, however, was pleased with Briche: 'If indeed the royal cavalry must be given a French general, then Briche is my choice, in that he does not meddle in internal matters, cares for the men and the horses, and does not sacrifice or fatigue them unnecessarily.'[122]

In addition to reshuffling the existing leadership and adding some new senior officers, the division was showered with awards in recognition of its achievements during the fighting in May. Friedrich, who personally pored over every incoming report and personally edited every outgoing order, was exceptionally proud of his army's performance.[123] He was thus lavish in promotions as well as in the distribution of gold and silver service medals (Verdienstmedaille) and in inducting officers into his Chivalric Order of the Golden Eagle (Ritterorden vom Goldenen Adler). He was especially pleased with Franquemont and sent the general a personal letter expressing his extreme satisfaction with the role the Württemberg troops played in the victory and his regrets at Franquemont's wounding. Furthermore, he made Franquemont a *Graf* (count) and accorded him a substantial annual income. At the same time, he was peevishly furious that Napoleon only elevated Franquemont to 'officer' status in the Legion of Honour rather than as a 'commander', the next higher rank. His efforts to enhance Franquemont's status having failed, he wrote to his imperial liaison officer Beroldingen in disgust that 'lickspittles and such persons who say "yes" to everything' had been favoured ahead of an officer 'who honours every decoration more than they honour him'.[124]

While generous with rewards for those he deemed deserving, Friedrich visited his implacable wrath upon those suspected of failing to do their duty. Officers and men who returned to Württemberg without proper documents, even escaped prisoners of war, were subjected to detailed examination and might be incarcerated in a fortress until their cases were adjudicated. Even harsher was the punishment meted out to a lieutenant and his detachment of 20–25 NCOs and men who were captured by Prussian Major von Colomb's raiders in western Saxony. In response to Franquemont's complaints about the lack of logistical support in the Grande Armée in late April and early May, Friedrich had directed that a supply convoy of 12 wagons loaded with biscuit (*Zwieback*) and rice be sent under escort of a small detachment from the 8th Infantry.[125] Unfortunately for the lieutenant and his soldiers, Colomb trapped them in a clever ambush southeast of Jena on 25 May, capturing the entire detachment and seizing all their wagons. Owing to surprise and ineptitude, the Württembergers offered no resistance and the lieutenant, trying to flee on horseback, was collared by a Prussian hussar and dragged back to Colomb in disgrace. A number of orders for the field troops were also included in Colomb's haul. Friedrich was wroth. For not attempting to defend themselves, he ordered the lieutenant and his NCOs reduced to the rank of private and all members of the detachment condemned to ten years in the depot regiment. In addition to doling out salutary penalties, however, the Württemberg leadership learned a valuable lesson about the insecurity prevalent in the army's rear areas. A second supply convoy, the one that reached the contingent during the armistice, was to be accompanied by a much stronger escort under command of a major and supported by a 3-pounder cannon. Additionally, the two brigades sent to Saxony in late May were directed to march together in tactical order taking all precautions against surprise.[126]

Kitzen: 'In a Moment We were Sabre to Sabre'[127]

The two new Württemberg brigades on the road for Saxony were intended to complete the kingdom's Rheinbund contingent obligations. Friedrich and his officers considered them the third tranche of troops committed to the Grande Armée, the 7th Infantry and Franquemont's division having been the first and second respectively. Regardless of how they were counted, Napoleon was pleased and specifically praised the kingdom for its exertions. 'His Majesty is extremely satisfied with the kings and grand dukes of the Confederation,' proclaimed the official French press, 'The King of Württemberg has particularly distinguished himself. He has made efforts proportionally equal to those of France; and his army, cavalry, infantry and artillery, has been brought to full strength.'[128]

The infantry element of this new contribution was commanded by GM von Doering and consisted of the 4th and 6th Regiments supported by the 2nd Foot Artillery Battery. The cavalry component under GM Karl Graf von Normann-

---

Chart 29: Württemberg Reinforcements, late May 1813

	bns/sqdns	Present under arms as of 25/26 May
Light Cavalry Brigade — GM *von Normann*		
Staff		7
2nd Cavalry, Leib-Chevaulegers	4	580
4th Cavalry, *König* Jäger-zu-Pferd	4	580
2nd Horse Battery	4 × 6-pdr, 2 × howitzer	154
2nd Infantry Brigade — GM *von Doering*		
Staff		7
4th Infantry Regiment	2	1,434
6th Infantry Regiment, *Kronprinz*	2	1,434
2nd Foot Artillery Battery	4 × 6-pdr, 2 × howitzer	167
Artillery staff		15
Total		4,378

Notes: Normann's brigade would be designated the 25th Light Cavalry Brigade during the armistice.

Source: 'Ausweis des am 25ten und 26ten May 1813 ausmarschierenden Theile des König. Contingents', LABWHStA, E 270a Bü 224.

Ehrenfels was comprised of royal household troops: the Leib-Chevaulegers (2nd Cavalry Regiment) and the *König* Jäger-zu-Pferd (4th Cavalry Regiment) with the 2nd or Maison du Roi Horse Battery. It would soon be designated the 25th Light Cavalry Brigade in the French organisational system. Leaving Württemberg soil on 25 and 26 May the two brigades were united south of Gotha under Doering's overall command. Along the way, they received Friedrich's warning about the danger of enemy raiding detachments and instructions to march with all appropriate security measures. Furthermore, the king specifically directed Normann to seek out and eliminate Prussian raiders if he could do so without deviating too far from the proscribed route of march.[129] The king had expected that his two brigades would proceed to Dresden and move from thence to Silesia to join Koch and Franquemont. This had indeed been the original plan, but Doering and Normann received orders from the French command diverting them northeast to Leipzig, in which city they arrived on 9 June.[130]

The halt in Leipzig was appreciated, but Leutnant von Martens, who had passed through the city on his way to and from Russia, immediately detected troubling changes. Not only were the streets empty and unwelcoming, but the population seemed distant and suspicious: 'it was easy to mark the adverse feeling in the faces of the inhabitants standing around us to see us Germans still with the French'.[131] The anti-French sentiments of some of city's residents would soon be expressed in action and prompt a sharp reprimand from Napoleon.

At this point in the war, GD Arrighi was responsible for Leipzig in addition to commanding the half-formed 3rd Cavalry Corps. He was thus in charge of an ad hoc collection of troops in and around the city with the mission of securing the army's rear area and purging it of the various Allied raiding parties. 'His Majesty's intention is that you command a reserve to sweep and assure the entire left bank of the Elbe,' Berthier told him on 3 June, writing four days later that he was to 'send parties everywhere to sabre and destroy the partisans who, despite the armistice, remain on the left bank of the Elbe ... if any are found, treat them like brigands'.[132] The two Württemberg brigades were placed at his disposal for these purposes. Reaching Leipzig, Doering and Normann thus found themselves assigned to Arrighi and immediately tasked with all manner of onerous security duties that dispersed their men across the map. One detachment, composed of I/4 Infantry and two squadrons of Leib-Chevaulegers, was sent to Dessau to ensure Russian adherence to the stipulations of the armistice, especially concerning a Westphalian enclave on the right bank of the Elbe between Magdeburg and Dessau. Additionally, four small mobile columns, each comprised of 100 cavalry (each actually amounted to a squadron of 115–120 troopers) and 200 infantry were to scour the area around Leipzig. Arrighi, pleased that the Württemberg column commanders 'seem animated by the best will', assigned each a quadrant (northwest and so on) to search, and provided them with detailed instructions: 'If he finds any armed enemy parties that will not surrender, he will have them sabred and have all the others disarmed and taken prisoner.'[133]

The mobile columns all set out from the Leipzig area on the morning of 15 June. The three that were directed to the northwest, northeast and southeast aroused local ire with their insensitive requisitions but discovered little to report as far as the enemy was concerned. The story of the column assigned to the southwest, however, was different. Commanded by Oberstleutnant Johann Karl Christoph von Kechler of II/4th infantry, this column became involved in the controversial fate of Prussian Major von Lützow's Freikorps.

The history of the 17 June attack on Lützow's band is a Gordian knot of contention and contradiction surrounded by a near-impenetrable aura of nationalistic German legendry.[134] It is not the purpose of this study to recount the various claims, counter-claims and lacunae associated with this incident, but the basic positions are clear. From the Prussian perspective and for many other Germans both at the time and subsequently, the attack was a dastardly breach of military honour and the norms of civilised conflict as they were understood in 1813. Frequently described as having been intentionally plotted by Napoleon himself because of his 'vengefulness and hatred for everything that is called a Freikorps,' it was alleged to have involved disgraceful deception to entrap and cruelly destroy a chivalrously noble representative of German national resistance to foreign oppression. The French official view, on the other hand, was that the incident, while perhaps unfortunate, was largely the result of misunderstanding. In any case, Lützow and his men had transgressed by refusing to acknowledge the armistice and were thus, like others of their ilk, little better than bandits. In the past, Napoleon would write, it had been customary in war to hang such persons.[135] Considerations of honour and legality aside, both sides, of course, sought to portray and exploit the action for their own benefit. Caught in the middle were the Württembergers. Rather than delve into the details of irresolvable accusations and allegations, therefore, the following will offer a concise outline of the attack and its antecedents to provide the context for the subsequent evolution of the kingdom's contingent.

The armistice found Lützow's Freikorps split into two pieces. His infantry component had retired east of the Elbe after participating in the attack on Leipzig under Vorontsov and Chernishev on 7 June. The major himself, however, was in Plauen with some 400 volunteer cavalrymen, 50 Russians (Cossacks and a few hussars) as well as approximately 300 men in an ad hoc infantry formation composed of captured Rheinbund militia and deserters.[136] Having received unofficial notice of the halt in hostilities from the local Saxon magistrate and from the detachment that had made the abortive raid on Hof as recounted in Chapter 3, he decided to await formal confirmation before making any other moves. Several days passed before a message from Saxon GL von Gersdorff convinced him that an armistice had indeed been concluded. He would now have either to slip into 'neutral' but friendly Austria or return to Prussian territory on the eastern side of the Elbe. He elected the latter course and, accompanied by a Saxon commissary, headed north on 15 June intending to cross the river near Dessau with all his men, horses and arms as well as the booty his volunteers had collected during their two-week foray.[137] He halted for the night south of Gera, negotiated with and even dined with senior French officers in Gera, and marched for Zeitz the following day.

Württemberg's Oberstleutnant von Kechler now enters the picture. Arriving in Zeitz on the evening of the 15th, he learned of Lützow's proximity and immediately announced his presence to the French in Gera, offering to combine with the French troops during the night for an attack on the partisan band. The French, however, were confused and uncertain, with different officers voicing different opinions on how to treat Lützow. Their replies to Kechler's repeated queries were correspondingly vague and ambivalent. Conscious of his instructions, Kechler nonetheless tracked Lützow's march during the 16th with patrols, reported the situation to Arrighi and followed his quarry north towards Leipzig on the 17th. As their two columns approached Kitzen that evening, Kechler had a lengthy discussion with Lützow, assuring the Prussian on his word of honour that he had no knowledge of hostile intentions towards the partisans. Otherwise, he said, he would have already attacked. Though Lützow was deeply suspicious of French intentions, he parted amicably from Kechler and rode off to settle his band around Kitzen for the night.

Returning to his own little force, however, Kechler encountered GM von Normann and French GD Fournier, one of Arrighi's division commanders. Fournier, renowned throughout the army as reckless and hot-headed, was initially furious with Kechler for parleying rather than attacking at once, but he quickly calmed and praised Kechler's decisions. With no further orders, Kechler sent a sergeant to inform Lützow that he had to retract his promise about the state of hostilities and rode into the gathering darkness to re-join his men. Night had fallen by the time he got his column moving to unite with Fournier and Normann so he and his men 'followed the noise and a few shots in the distance' but played no further part in the episode.[138]

As Kechler rode off-stage, Normann rode on. The departure of the various mobile columns on 15 June had left Doering and Normann at Leipzig with the remaining elements of their respective brigades: two squadrons, two infantry battalions and the artillery batteries. On receiving Kechler's warning of Lützow's approach, Arrighi created an ad hoc combined force under Fournier's command and sent it south on the shortest route 'in such a way as to cut off the enemy's retreat'. Fournier's column consisted of two squadrons of French dragoons, an infantry battalion of the French 3rd Naval Artillery Regiment and Normann's troops: one squadron each of Leib-Chevaulegers and *König* Jägers, three infantry companies (two from the 4th, one from the 6th Infantry) and three pieces from his horse battery. In total, the force likely numbered some 1,100 infantry and 360 cavalry plus the three guns. Looking to his flanks, Arrighi also dispatched the other three pieces from the horse battery to the northwest with 100 French dragoons to intercept any scouts or stragglers from Lützow's band.[139] He held Doering and the few remaining Württemberg troops in Leipzig (five infantry companies and the foot battery).

Fournier's column, Württembergers in the lead, closed on Lützow's bivouac at Kitzen sometime around 8:00 p.m. as the sun was setting. Ordered to occupy Kitzen but not to be the first to open fire, Normann deployed his men, unlimbered his three guns and slowly advanced as Lützow approached from the village with a trumpeter. 'To show him straightaway that we were serious,' wrote Normann later, 'I had my men draw their sabres and rode towards him myself with my sabre in hand.'[140] The alarmed Lützow asked what Normann intended and was told to confer with Fournier but received Normann's word of honour that the Württemberg troops would not attack while the two negotiated. The discussion with Fournier, of course, quickly reached an impasse, with the Frenchman insisting that Lützow halt and accept instructions and the Prussian determined to choose his own path and surrender nothing.

Before long, therefore, Lützow swept past Normann at the gallop and the Prussian squadrons turned north on the road to Leipzig. 'It became very dark, and I had to ride very close in order not to lose sight of them,' Normann told Friedrich in his initial report, 'The Prussians thereupon rode ever faster, and I was forced to command my men to gallop. Now a shot was loosed against us, and they began to ride all out.' 'There could no longer be any thought of negotiations', he would write somewhat later, 'In a moment we were sabre to sabre.'[141] Lützow had issued strict orders for his men not to open fire but the Freikorps' discipline was weak, and it is easy to credit the French and Württemberg claims that the Prussians fired first. In the darkness and confusion, the outcome was perhaps inevitable: the Württembergers demanded that the Prussians dismount and surrender, the Prussians, still shooting, refused, and Normann's men, supported by the French dragoons, charged. The French and Württemberg infantry were not involved, the Württemberg gunners fired not a shot and Lützow's infantry, mostly comprised of barely trained Rheinbund militia deserters, disintegrated at the first blow. It was thus largely a cavalry fight in the darkness with approximately equal numbers on each side (if not a slight advantage to Lützow), but the Prussians were swiftly overwhelmed. Although only a few of the partisans were killed (Coalition claims of a 'massacre' notwithstanding), almost half were taken prisoner, and many fled into the protective obscurity never to be seen again. Total casualties came to an estimated 325–350 of Lützow's men dead, wounded and captured, plus almost all of the 'infantry' detachment who just vanished into the countryside.[142] Lützow himself was lucky to escape, and his young adjutant, a romantic poet patriot of subsequent fame named Theodor Körner, was rescued by local people after collapsing in the underbrush with a severe sabre wound to the head. French and Württemberg losses amounted to 5 killed and 25 wounded.[143]

Kitzen spelt the temporary end of Lützow's Freikorps.[144] One squadron and the Cossacks escaped across the Elbe on 18 June, but the major had to conceal himself in Westphalia for a week before slipping across the river on the 23rd. Other fugitives managed to make their way to Prussia over the coming weeks and the Freikorps would be rebuilt to a larger but even more cumbersome size during the armistice. Though it would attain a glorified prominence in later years, its actual combat contribution was marginal, and its notoriety would owe much to the passionate and often bloodthirsty 'liberation poetry' of the 21-year-old Körner whose death in the autumn campaigns only amplified the band's nimbus of romantic heroism. Saxon General Ferdinand von Funck, who knew Körner and his family, would mordantly observe that, 'The fame of this young man actually made the entire renown of Lützow's corps.'[145]

The incident at Kitzen had significant repercussions for the Württemberg contingent on several levels. In the first place, Allied propaganda was successful in creating the image of an irresistibly powerful force in the service of the oppressive French emperor overwhelming a small but doughty band of self-sacrificing patriotic volunteers through treachery and deceit. Prussian writers then and later were especially offended by claims that Normann or his men had shouted 'Surrender, Prussian dogs!' or some similar imprecation during the brief fight.[146] That much of this depiction was badly canted if not outright false made no difference. It quickly became the dominant narrative in contemporary journals, leaving an indelible impression for years to come. Expressly alarming for Württemberg was the claim that Berthier had purportedly labelled the Württemberg troops as 'the aggressors' in a conversation with a Prussian major sent to locate Lützow and guide him back across the Elbe. Berthier scoffed at the notion that he would have made such a statement 'to some wretch of a Prussian' when Friedrich's liaison officer pressed for an answer on this alleged remark, but the comment remained embedded in common perceptions.[147] Similarly, Württemberg's efforts to counter these stories by publishing Normann's report in Stuttgart's paper did not resonate. Friedrich even received anonymous correspondence, supposedly from an 'eyewitness', that condemned the behaviour of his troops. The allegation that Württemberg officers had broken their words of honour was especially galling to a king who so closely identified the arms of the state with his own person.[148] An insult to the army's honour was an attack on his personal prestige.

Just as important for Friedrich was his conviction that his troops had been misused. In his mind, Württemberg involvement in this dubious affair would never have occurred had his two brigades not been detained, dispersed and dispatched into combat by second-rate French generals. He was less concerned initially with the Kitzen fight, but his royal rage boiled over when he learned that his men were still being employed in mobile columns after the repulse of Lützow and Colomb. Incensed, he sent a stinging set of instructions to GM von Beroldingen at imperial headquarters on 12 July, decrying the employment of his men in such demeaning missions as an unprecedented interference in the internal affairs of the Württemberg brigades and the cause of present and future problems. 'As there are no more raiding parties about, these columns must chase after individual marauders and actually perform the duties of gendarmes,' he fumed. Given that most of his officers were new and inexperienced, he feared that 'excesses will arise and all order and discipline cease'. Beroldingen was instructed to demand that Arrighi be admonished for his 'outrageous' actions and that the two brigades be reunited, preferably with Franquemont's division. Doering and Normann were not spared Friedrich's royal wrath: 'His Majesty has made clear to the two Generals Doering and Normann his very great displeasure with their weak behaviour,' he told Beroldingen. Indeed, he had.

On the same day that he signed the letter to Beroldingen, the king sent the two generals 'a very stern reprimand' for obeying French orders that 'could never be permitted whatever the pretext'. The king, they were bluntly informed, was not inclined to tolerate 'such high-handedness from French generals on the one side' or 'irresponsible pliancy from royal brigade commanders on the other side'.[149] Friedrich, in other words, was not troubled by the attack on Lützow as an alleged crime against supposed exponents of some nebulously envisaged German nationhood, rather his eye was focused on the honour, integrity and independence of his army as a reflection of his kingdom's status and his personal rights as its sovereign ruler.

It is not difficult to imagine the cruel dilemma in which officers such as Doering and Normann found themselves. On the one hand, they were called on to carry out instructions on the spot from French generals who were their seniors in rank. Moreover, most of these instructions were not, as Friedrich often thought, arbitrary, but derived from Napoleon's orders as communicated from imperial headquarters. If some tasks seemed beneath the dignity of regular combat units, most made military sense: hunting down partisan bands or occupying Confederation territory on both sides of the Elbe near Dessau, for instance. On the other hand, the two Württemberg generals also had to contend with the punctilious demands of their dread sovereign. Rather than 'irresponsible pliancy', he expected that they seek Beroldingen's help to have what he considered inappropriate orders retracted. At the very least they should 'thoroughly consider' any such orders before complying. Left unspecified was how they were to accomplish this as relatively small fish in a very large pond without compromising themselves, their troops or their king.

Even Beroldingen feared he would lose respect and effectiveness in Napoleon's headquarters. Berthier always treated him with great courtesy and repeatedly expressed his admiration for Friedrich and the Württemberg soldiers, but as Beroldingen earnestly attempted to press his king's cases, he began to acquire the reputation as the Rheinbund representative who incessantly carped, often over matters that seemed transitory or insignificant to French staff officers.[150] As one example, Napoleon had every intention of uniting Doering's brigade with Franquemont as soon as the partisan emergency was resolved; he initially planned the same for Normann's troopers.[151] For Friedrich, however, the separation of his army into several sub-elements was an affront to his sovereignty that contained within it the danger of indiscipline and dissolution through attrition. Beroldingen was thus wedged in the impossible vice of trying to convey his master's insistent demands to the French while simultaneously communicating Berthier's assurances to his doubting king and not complaining himself into irrelevance in the process.

With these competing pressures and within the context of growing scepticism about the French alliance, it is hardly surprising that the Kitzen episode also had an effect at the level of the individual officer. This was most pointedly the case with Normann. His actions during the autumn campaign will be scrutinised later in this narrative, but at this stage it is useful to note that the seeds of his defection to the Allies at Leipzig were likely sown on the fields around Kitzen. In his thorough post-war research, Major von Bangold observed that Normann 'possessed the characteristics of a good, practical soldier . . . 'He was active, courageous, decisive; he had a proper sense of the use of terrain and the employment of the different arms [and] retained his presence of mind in combat.' Nonetheless, Bangold concluded that Kitzen, the subsequent portrayals of that affair and especially the harsh admonishments he received from his king left Normann feeling 'that he had to make good on something', that he had something to redeem.[152] Several months would elapse, however, before the evolution of his thinking coincided with operational exigencies and opportunity to result in his fateful decision to defect on the battlefield.

Before turning to the autumn, it is important to remind ourselves that neither Normann, nor Kechler, nor their men exhibited any hesitation about engaging Lützow over those several days in mid-June. The two officers seem to have regarded Fournier with distaste, viewing him as impulsive, dangerously impetuous and potentially dishonourable, and they found ways to reject or circumvent his orders when they deemed these inconsistent with their models of dignity and honour. Normann, in particular, grew to believe that the French wanted to heap all the blame for Lützow's escape on him. When it came time to attack, however, they showed no reluctance. Kechler twice offered to do so and was surprised at the indecision evident in the replies he received from the French in Gera and Zeitz; Normann's squadrons charged with vigour once they believed they had been fired upon. Indeed, convinced that a clash was likely and that he was outnumbered, Normann concluded that surprise offered his only hope for success. 'I was therefore not entirely displeased that the Prussians fired first,' he told Franquemont in a 14 August report.[153] Furthermore, Normann and his troopers garnered praise from their French commanders, Fournier specifically citing the 'brilliant bravery' displayed by 21-year-old Oberst Prinz Friedrich von Oettingen-Wallerstein of the Leib-Chevaulegers.[154] Subsequent recriminations notwithstanding, the leading Württemberg officers were thus prepared to execute their orders, and their actions, along with those of the French dragoons, contributed directly to the incapacitation of Lützow's Freikorps and nearly led to the capture of Lützow himself. 'That night', wrote Normann later in the year, 'I made a report that was purely military as it never occurred to me that this attack could be considered unjust.'[155]

A view from the lower officer ranks comes from Leutnant von Martens whose company of the 6th Infantry had been assigned to Normann for the expedition against Lützow. He and his comrades encountered difficulties in trying to follow the cavalry in the darkness as they trotted after the retreating Prussians. In his published memoir, he wrote: 'We advanced in a skirmish line through the thick field of grain, stumbled over saddles, haversacks and other objects, but also over a few dead and badly wounded, the second of whom our company doctors wanted to help, but the Prussians were so aroused against us that most of them would not accept it.' His original manuscript, however, is slightly different, offering an example of how a veteran might attune his published recollections to the more pan-German spirit of a later era. Describing the Prussian officers that they captured as being so outraged that they would hardly speak to Martens and his comrades, he added that, 'Their defiance went so far that one of the wounded among them who was about to be treated by one of our doctors, announced that he refused to be bandaged by any Württemberg dog.' Martens, a thoughtful and experienced officer, may not have had a strategic or legalistic perspective, but he, like his king, manifested little sympathy for Lützow's band. He was dismissive in both his manuscript and in the published version of his recollections. 'Unjustly, a cry of indignation went through the whole of Germany over this tragic incident, everyone took the side of this "corps of vengeance" whose defeat was regarded as a victory,' he wrote in his published account, 'It was not up to us to decide who was right and who was wrong but Major von Lützow had only himself to blame for this hard outcome.' 'The greater part of these Prussian heroes', he scoffed in his unpublished journal, 'left their weapons, haversacks and suchlike behind and sought to save themselves through flight.'[156]

Training, Theatrics and Trepidation

As the partisan threat evaporated and the situation around Leipzig calmed, Doering and Normann were reassigned. Doering, who had gone to the area around Dessau to ensure compliance with the terms of the armistice, shifted first to Wittenberg and then across the Elbe to Spremberg in north-central Saxony. His brigade remained there until linking up with Franquemont's division once hostilities resumed. Normann and his brigade, on the other hand, were transferred to Bunzlau to serve as the light cavalry for Marshal Marmont's 6th Corps. This move was entirely logical from a military perspective as Marmont's large corps had no cavalry whatsoever, but it became another cause for disgruntlement for König Friedrich who always wanted to see all his regiments united under one Württemberg commander.[157]

Beyond separation from his countrymen, Normann's woes multiplied as the armistice proceeded. Grievances from a Westphalian official who claimed some of the Württemberg cavalry officers had insulted and mistreated him during their patrolling operations came to Friedrich's attention when the Westphalian government complained to imperial headquarters. On top of this, the king heard new accusations of misbehaviour when Normann's brigade rode off to join Marmont. The result was another scathing admonition from the king on 18 August.

> His Royal Majesty has learned with the greatest indignation that his cavalry brigade has allowed itself to commit exactions, violence, slanders and all manner of licentiousness in all the places it has been stationed or through which it has marched, that all military order and discipline has vanished and this has become a band of freebooters rather than a regular military unit. His Majesty cannot attribute this breakdown to anything but the weakness and negligence of the general, who, rather than reprimanding this shameful conduct, has instead reinforced it by unheard-of leniency.

Normann, he threatened, would be arrested and brought back to the kingdom for judgment at the first complaint while the officers and men of 'the bandit hordes' were liable to be cashiered and distributed to other regiments. Normann was to acknowledge receipt to this severe note and publish it for his men. In his reply, Normann blamed Arrighi's arrangements for the misconduct ascribed to the mobile columns around Leipzig and assured his monarch that no such infractions had occurred since his return to full command. He and his men had been received 'with joy' in every town through which they passed, he wrote, pledging that any future delinquency would be notified to Friedrich and punished appropriately.[158] These accusations from afar, however, could hardly fail to cause dismay to a professional of Normann's experience, looming in the background of all his future actions and causing him to second-guess himself at every moment of doubt in the coming campaign.

Franquemont did not have to suffer these royal slings and arrows. The division's cantonments around Primkenau may have been deficient in many ways, but training marched along well and there were no major problems with discipline or desertion. Major von Bangold bemoaned the challenges of being a staff officer in an international setting, echoing the griefs of staff officers across the centuries and up to the present day: 'I cannot repress the remark that it is sad to serve on our general staff. One must fight with the enemy, with the French, with our own faulty organisation and with biases.' Beyond drill, target practice and tedious staff duties, however, the officers found little to occupy their time in this remote and impoverished region. 'The period of the armistice passed rather monotonously,' wrote Baumbach. The local people were friendly, and Hauptmann von Suckow found everything in the best of order as in peacetime, but he, too, recalled the time as one of extended boredom passed in visits to an improvised but poorly supplied coffee house when not on duty. To relieve some of this tedium, newly promoted GM von Spitzemberg sent Suckow to Glogau to hire a theatrical troupe. Suckow succeeded in this peculiar mission: with little difficulty, he persuaded a small band of unemployed thespians to relocate to Primkenau and had the division's sappers transform a farm building into a 'field theatre' including something that was to pass as a Grecian temple. The poetically inclined Leutnant von Schlaich could not contain his disdain for the players whose music abused his ears and whose performances led him to lament 'Poor Schiller!' but the actors, though an odd assortment of humanity, provided a welcome diversion – intentionally and unintentionally – for the Württemberg officer corps during the ensuing weeks.[159]

Owing to the general destitution of the region in which they were billeted, the events associated with the advance celebration of Napoleon's birthday seem to have been rather more modest in the Württemberg contingent as compared to other Rheinbund armies. Nonetheless, Franquemont reported favourably on the day's activities:

> The soldiers entertained themselves after their fashion; there were amusements of all sorts: races, masquerades, rural dances with village girls and more. The area surrounding the banquet was decorated in an especially festive manner with garlands and wreaths, inscriptions and allegorical figures. In the evening, the town of Primkenau even prepared an illumination. Monograms appropriate to the celebration were to be seen; a prologue appropriate to the day was spoken in the theatre [this was delivered by the impresario of Suckow's small troupe].
>
> The limited venues and the lack of time, of course, did not permit the sort of arrangements that would have been appropriate to the significance of the day; but the general cheerfulness may have compensated for the lack of grandeur.[160]

For Hauptmann von Baumbach, however, the merriment was lacking, 'as no one doubted the imminent resumption of hostilities'. Schlaich also looked to the autumn with foreboding: 'War again all around! and the hope for peace has vanished like a smiling meteor that lovingly lights the dark night for a few minutes. We have war once again! and a war that cannot possibly have a happy ending for the Gauls.'[161]

Equally anxious about the future was Suckow's theatrical troupe. Having spent weeks entertaining 'the enemy', they feared reprisals from the Prussians once the Württembergers marched off. They turned to their intermediary, Suckow, for help. Advised to follow the Württemberg column, their leader readily agreed 'and thus on the day of our departure, one saw in the train of the royal Württemberg ammunition- and bread-wagons, the driver of this thespian-wain rolling behind, the latter loaded with the previously mentioned Grecian temple, graceful forests, cool waterfalls and peaceful peasants' huts'. Suckow could not recall the troupe's fate but excused himself by noting that 'for us it was again a matter of accustoming ourselves to a different proscenium than that of the sheep shed in Primkenau – that of the bloodiest battles and skirmishes!'[162]

The 38th Division: Autumn Actions East of the Elbe

Along with the rest of 4th Corps, the Württemberg 38th Division was ordered to Baruth as the armistice came to an end. The division arrived on 19 August and was joined by Doering's brigade the following day. As Bertrand marched off with the rest of Oudinot's Army of Berlin, however, the Württembergers stayed behind to guard the army's flank. 'The greatest vigilance was required',

Chart 30: Württemberg Contingent, August 1813

		bns/sqdns	Present under arms as of 1 August
38th Division, 4th Corps	GL von Franquemont		
1st Infantry Brigade	GM von Spitzemberg		
1st Infantry Regiment, *Prinz Paul*		2	917
2nd Infantry Regiment, *Herzog Wilhelm*		5 companies	760
2nd Infantry Brigade	GM von Doering		
4th Infantry Regiment		2	1,057
6th Infantry Regiment, *Kronprinz*		2	1,286
3rd Infantry Brigade (or Light Brigade)	GM von Stockmayer		
7th Infantry Regiment		2	728
9th Light Infantry Regiment, *König Jäger*		1	509
10th Light Infantry Regiment		1	533
2nd Foot Artillery Battery		4 × 6-pdr, 2 × howitzer	114
3rd Foot Artillery Battery		5 × 6-pdr, 1 × howitzer	116
24th Light Cavalry Brigade, 4th Corps	GB Briche and GM von Jett		
1st Cavalry, *Prinz Adam* Chevaulegers		4	398
3rd Cavalry, *Herzog Louis* Jäger-zu-Pferd		4	350
3rd Horse Battery		4 × 6-pdr, 2 × howitzer	117
Division total			6,885
Detached to 6th Corps			
25th Light Cavalry Brigade	GM von Normann		
2nd Cavalry, Leib-Chevaulegers		4	551
4th Cavalry, *König* Jäger-zu-Pferd		4	381
2nd Horse Battery		4 × 6-pdr, 2 × howitzer	136
Brigade total			1,068
Division and brigade staffs			117
Württemberg total fit for duty			8,070

Note: not included above are 2,996 unfit for duty for a total of 11,066.

Source for 1 August present under arms: 'Rapport des auf den 1sten August 1813', LABWHStA, E 270a Bü 227. Additionally, the 1st and 3rd Brigades had 642 men detached, 1,094 in hospital, and 416 prisoners of war – 284 of these from the 2nd Infantry's loss at Bautzen (4th Corps 'Situation' of 16 August, SHD, 2C539).

wrote Franquemont, 'as the division was separated from the other divisions of the army corps, was surrounded by considerable enemy forces and left to fend for itself.' Fortunately, Bertrand placed Briche, Jett and the Württemberg cavalry brigade under Franquemont's orders for this rather isolated mission. Bertrand called the division to join the rest of the corps when Oudinot's army pivoted towards Berlin and the Württembergers made an agonisingly slow slog to Werben on the 23rd on 'bottomless roads under persistent rain', their march badly impeded by a cumbersome French supply train. They arrived 'very exhausted and soaked to the skin' to establish a miserable bivouac 'where everything was in short supply'.[163] Franquemont was supposed to attack Mittenwalde the next day, but with the defeat at Großbeeren Oudinot abandoned his tentative offensive towards Berlin and ordered a general retreat. The Württemberg division thus found itself trudging back to Baruth on 24 August to reclaim its old bivouacs around the town.

Holbeck, Jüterbog and Euper: 'Another Report of the Good Behaviour of his Troops'

The next several days saw the 38th Division engaged in a series of sharp rearguard actions as Oudinot turned his army towards Wittenberg. The division thus shifted west on 25 August, enemy light troops harassing Stockmayer's rear guard near Baruth as he covered this movement and Cossacks launching an abortive attack on the Württemberg advance guard while it approached Holbeck that afternoon. The Cossacks and a Russian Jäger battalion renewed the attack at Holbeck on the 26th, reigniting a combat in and around this little hamlet that would cost the Württembergers 132 casualties before they were able to continue towards Jüterbog. Despite the losses, Franquemont was satisfied to note that his men were learning that they could face the dreaded Cossacks if they remained calm and steady. He issued a laudatory order of the day and Spitzemberg wrote in his report that the men of the 1st Infantry 'commenced a well-aimed fire by battalion with a calm that is usually particular to veteran soldiers'.[164]

Retaining its role as the 4th Corps rear guard, the division endured more skirmishing to reach the eastern outskirts of Jüterbog on the evening of the 27th. Allied infantry and cavalry were clearly visible to the north and Oudinot, fearing an attack, had Franquemont move the 38th Division through the town on 28 August to assume an extended defensive position on low hills just to the north, the men of the 10th Light Infantry occupying a wood north of Kappan after chasing off 'Cossacks and Bashkirs' who 'fired their pistols and arrows' before departing.[165] Oudinot deployed the rest of 4th Corps, the cavalry corps and 12th Corps to Franquemont's left (west) and rear. Most of the day passed without incident and Reynier's 7th corps began its withdrawal towards Wittenberg. Around 6:00 o'clock that afternoon, however, the Württemberg division came under attack. The initial assailants, several regiments of Cossacks, clashed with the Württemberg horse but, as on 25 May east of Lauban, the formed Württemberg squadrons dominated the field, withdrawing

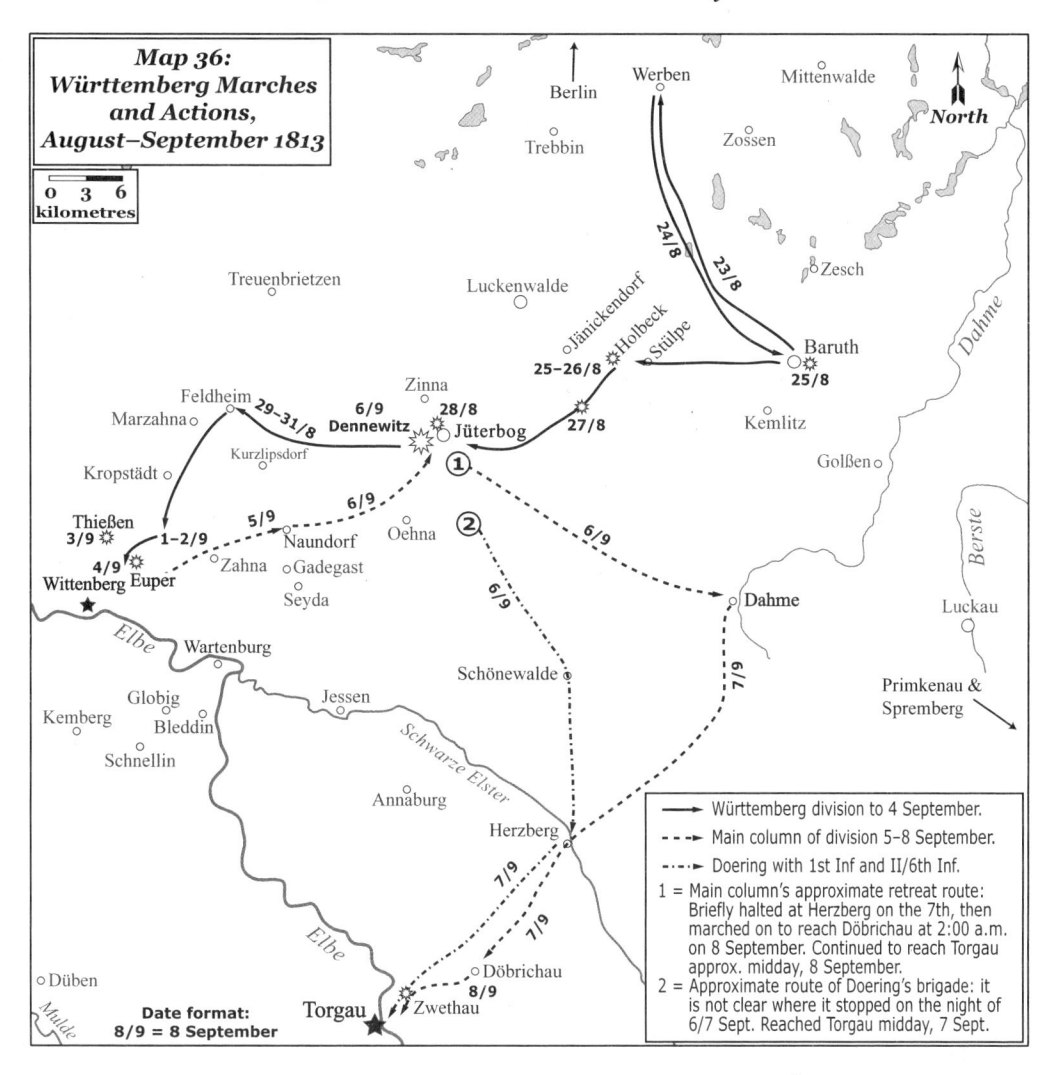

Map 36: Württemberg Marches and Actions, August–September 1813

Legend:
- → Württemberg division to 4 September.
- --→ Main column of division 5–8 September.
- ·-·→ Doering with 1st Inf and II/6th Inf.
- 1 = Main column's approximate retreat route: Briefly halted at Herzberg on the 7th, then marched on to reach Döbrichau at 2:00 a.m. on 8 September. Continued to reach Torgau approx. midday, 8 September.
- 2 = Approximate route of Doering's brigade: it is not clear where it stopped on the night of 6/7 Sept. Reached Torgau midday, 7 Sept.

Date format: 8/9 = 8 September

in exemplary fashion only when Russian infantry and artillery (four battalions and eight guns) appeared. The Russians pressed towards the town and made some gains at first, but found their efforts foiled by the Württemberg infantry with efficacious support from their three batteries. The firing died away as darkness descended around 8:00 p.m.

Though more a determined probe by a small Russian advance guard than a true attack, the combat had lasted approximately two hours and cost the division 97 casualties, but the division had again displayed calm competence under fire. Franquemont proudly reported that his men had fought the battle entirely on their own: 'this affair has increased the fame of the royal troops before the eyes of a large army that was no more than a spectator'. Oudinot and Bertrand, who had observed the entire engagement, were especially impressed by the two light horse regiments for their stalwart performance against the far more numerous Cossacks. 'This combat does the Württemberg division great credit, above all the cavalry which charged both to its front and to its flanks,' Bertrand told Berthier, 'It showed itself not just equal to but far superior to that of the enemy.'[166] For his part, Franquemont heaped particular praise on Briche and Jett, requesting Friedrich reward both for their skilful leadership during the action. König Friedrich, delighted at 'another report of the good behaviour of his troops', was happy to grant awards to the list of officers Franquemont submitted, including Jett and Briche as well as Briche's adjutant.[167] This relatively minor affray at Jüterbog thus helped validate the favourable impression of Franquemont and his men in the minds of their French allies as well as their sharp-eyed king. Unfortunately for the men of the division, they would soon acquire a much grimmer acquaintance with Jüterbog.

Several days of retreat now ensued as the anxious Oudinot slowly retired on Wittenberg. Cossacks continued to pester the Army of Berlin and the need to be constantly alert made the marches enervating, but there were no serious clashes, and the army was able to enjoy a relatively untroubled rest day on 2 September. Here the men were informed of Napoleon's victory at Dresden. The ranks complied when told to cheer, 'but this did not come from the heart and was therefore very feeble'. At least one private of the 7th Infantry muttered half-loud 'it's all lies' in his thick Swabian accent.[168] Enthused or not, the army resumed its withdrawal, and, by the morning of 3 September, its component corps occupied a semi-circular defensive position east of Wittenberg with both flanks anchored on obstructive terrain towards the Elbe. Dąbrowski held the left side of the position with Polish troops from the Wittenberg garrison, followed in order by Reynier's 7th Corps, 12th Corps in the centre and 4th Corps on the right or southeastern end of the line. Arrighi's largely ineffectual cavalry were placed in reserve and some effort was expended to begin field defensive works. Advance elements of Bernadotte's Army of the North came up against Oudinot's position that very day, Russians probing the Saxon line on the left while Borstell's Prussians initiated a sanguinary struggle with the Italian 15th Division near Thießen. This last combat soon widened to encompass parts of the Württemberg 38th Division as well.

Bertrand had deployed his corps with the Italians on the left at Thießen, a brigade of Morand's division in Euper on the right and the Württembergers in the centre between the two villages. There was no pressure on the corps' right flank, so when the Italians were attacked, Bertrand ordered Franquemont to advance part of his division in support. Franquemont chose Spitzemberg's 1st Brigade which deployed and moved towards the woods to their front while the Württemberg artillery played havoc with the Prussian infantry by firing at them from an angle. The fight was brief but intense. 'We had hardly deployed into line when the Prussians broke out of the woods in mass,' recorded the 1st Infantry's Baumbach, 'a well-sustained fire by files, however, forced them to pull back hurriedly leaving behind their many wounded ... The usefulness of the target practice that we had conducted many times during the armistice proved itself fully in this engagement, never did I see such decisive effect from infantry fire.' The musketry diminished around 1:00 p.m., by which time casualties for the 1st and 2nd Regiments came to 153 officers and men killed or wounded plus 6 captured. The 6th Infantry had pushed forward on Spitzemberg's right to cover his flank and came under Prussian artillery fire but was not heavily engaged. As the regiment entered a wood, the men encountered numerous Prussian Jägers, 'some dead, some still breathing' all dressed in what Leutnant von Martens described as 'English dress' with 'shakos that had been manufactured in London'. One of the wounded sparked considerable mirth among Martens and his comrades by lamenting that he had been made 'a defender of the fatherland' against his will and asking artlessly to be sent back to Berlin as soon as possible.[169]

That evening, Bertrand sent his chief of staff, GB Marie Joseph Raymond Delort, to Franquemont with orders to replace Morand's brigade in Euper during the night. Franquemont complained that his men always seemed to get the most dangerous tasks, but after some discussion with Delort he gave this assignment to the Light Brigade and Stockmayer's men marched off into the closing darkness. For his part, Stockmayer placed the 7th Infantry in Euper itself and in the woodline to the northeast towards Woltersdorf, posted the 9th Infantry atop a knoll on his right and kept the 10th in reserve. Additionally, he had been reinforced with a squadron of *Herzog Louis* Jäger-zu-Pferd and a mixed detachment of fifty troopers from the Rheinbund regiments of GB Wolff's 29th Light Cavalry Brigade (12th Corps); these he used to patrol and cover his flanks. With woods on both wings and the village as a central strongpoint, Stockmayer felt shielded from the superior Allied cavalry. He emphasised this advantage to his men, pointing out that they would be vulnerable to being ridden down if they had to retreat across the open ground to their rear. 'This observation as to our situation had the most advantageous effect on my brave subordinates,' he later wrote.[170]

Ney now arrived to take command of the Army of Berlin, a welcome change as far as most of the troops were concerned. Coming under the orders of one of Napoleon's most renowned marshals 'made the best impression on all of us', commented Martens. Moreover, the logistical situation improved as well, and the men happily received bread, rice and brandy 'which was particularly good for us given our strenuous exertions and the prevailing bad weather'. Ney's

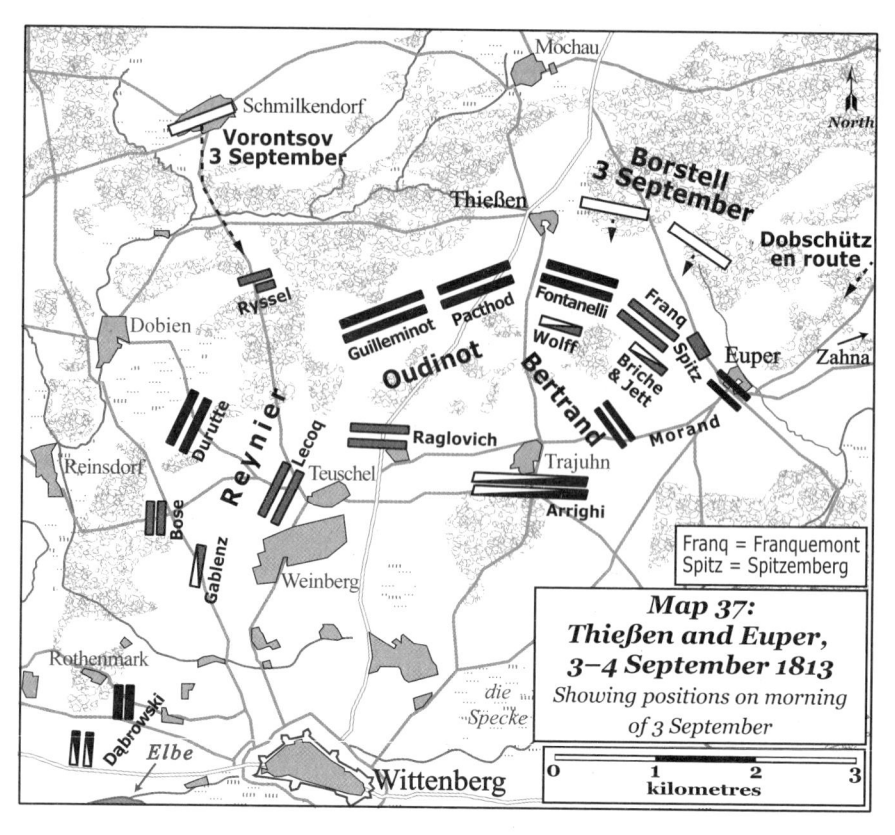

**Map 37:
Thießen and Euper,
3–4 September 1813**
*Showing positions on morning
of 3 September*

planned inspection of the Württemberg division on 4 September, however, was interrupted by a costly struggle that evolved around Euper that morning. As Martens would write: 'Now things became serious for us too, as up to now we had only skirmished and manoeuvred.'[171] This time, the Württemberg division's opponents were Prussians from Dobschütz's command which had moved up on Borstell's left on the 3rd during the fighting around Thießen. It is not clear that Dobschütz intended an attack, but the outpost lines were as close as 50 paces from one another and skirmishing began to crackle between 7:00 and 8:00 that morning. The firing grew rapidly as the Prussian commanders fed more men into a fight that soon absorbed Stockmayer's entire brigade. Not long after the engagement opened, Stockmayer received a surprise visitor.

> Marshal Ney, who had been named commander-in-chief of the army, came to me shortly after the first attack, greeted me in the most cordial and complimentary fashion amidst the musketry as he had not seen me since the Russian campaign, expressed his satisfaction with my deployment and with the bravery of the troops and, leaving adjutants and entourage behind, proceeded with me alone to the most forward line to determine if the enemy would receive more reinforcements and therefore a general attack

was to be expected, or if they only had in mind pushing the rear guard back as much as possible as had occurred on a daily basis during our withdrawal. After the passage of an hour, during which he was extremely exposed to the small arms fire, he returned and, as the enemy had not deployed any larger forces, he gave me the order to hold as long as possible but to inform him at once if the Allies received any further reinforcements.[172]

Stockmayer's men stoutly maintained their positions under 'damnable fire' as the fighting swayed back and forth.[173] 'No soldier of the regiment left the ranks,' reported Oberstleutnant von Kechler that night. Kechler, who had been transferred from Doering's brigade during the armistice to take command of the 7th Infantry, was full of praise for 'the courage and zeal' of his men, noting that 'the engagement lasted many hours and every soldier fired off 150–200 cartridges'.[174] Some units thus expended all their ammunition three times and companies had to be switched out repeatedly to allow for replenishment as Suckow experienced:

> We had fired off almost all of our rounds when we were relieved by other companies of the regiment which, as mentioned, had been standing in reserve. Many of our numerous shots could have been spared but we had many young, newly recruited men and certainly, as all my veteran comrades would agree, there is nothing more difficult for an officer than to keep recruits from *firing too much* during an engagement.

Stockmayer several times asked for reinforcements but was refused and had to rely on his own brigade alone, as Suckow, to his dismay, soon learned:

> I had hardly returned to the main reserve with my three much-reduced companies when Oberst [*sic*] von Kechler, tapping me on the shoulder in a friendly manner, said to me in his laconic way of speaking: 'Excellent, excellent, dear Suckow, now grab more cartridges quickly and get back to the line soon!' I must admit that I was not at all keen on gaining more laurels on this day after the heavy losses suffered, especially as I, probably like all Germans who were still tied to French banners by the orders of the princes, would gladly have forgone any further glory under them.[175]

For the moment, however, it was back to the heat of the action. Stockmayer, denied reinforcements, grew concerned that the fighting would go on into the night eviscerating his little brigade. He asked Franquemont once more for at least a horse artillery battery to finish off the engagement for the day.

> My request was not only fulfilled but the 4th Infantry Regiment under Oberst Prinz Hohenlohe was also sent over which, however, I placed in

the village of Euper as reserve and did not employ it as my men wanted to keep the triumph of the engagement for themselves and did not want to be relieved. As soon as the battery arrived, I placed myself at its head and hurried with it at the gallop to the extreme right wing of my position whence I could flank the entire left wing of the enemy before the battery that the enemy had placed in his centre could work against mine. No sooner arrived at this point, the guns were unlimbered and several seconds later the six guns blasted out their canister along the enemy's ranks, which thereby suffered significant losses as we ourselves could see as their wounded fell in heaps.[176]

To Stockmayer's great relief and satisfaction, the Prussians indeed withdrew, and the combat came to a close around 3:00 p.m. Though small in scale, the engagement at Euper had been long and relentless for the men of Stockmayer's brigade. 'I have been in many a battle, many an engagement during six campaigns,' wrote Suckow, 'but none of them were fiercer, even though it was confined to a small space.' The cost was correspondingly heavy: 318 officers and men dead or wounded during the seven or eight hours of fighting. The brigade had performed extremely well and received due acknowledgement from its comrades, as Stockmayer recorded: 'Toward evening Doering's brigade relieved me in the Euper position and I marched back to the main position to the accompaniment of the horns of the Jägers and light infantry and the band of the 7th Infantry Regiment as well as the cheers of the entire division which had been witness to the affair through the entire day.' Franquemont was equally pleased, reporting to Friedrich that 'General von Stockmayer has done the impossible with his brigade today,' and that all the troops who had been under fire during the two days had 'surpassed everything'. Doering's brigade, having replaced Stockmayer's near Euper, took a few casualties but did not come under attack.[177]

The 4th of September also brought news that the army would cease retreating and return to the offensive. Leutnant von Schlaich likely expressed the sentiments of many when writing to a friend that day: 'Tomorrow we will again take the offensive under Ney's orders. Thank God! I have had enough of defensive fighting.'[178] Indeed, the 38th Division was granted no time to recuperate from its exertions at Thießen and Euper as Ney had the entire army up and moving early on 5 September on his ill-fated march to meet the emperor at Luckau. The Württembergers were not involved in the fighting at Zahna on the 5th, but Stockmayer was present for a brief exchange between Ney and Bertrand in which Ney expressed his satisfaction with the 12th Corps for its actions during the day. 'Now, tomorrow it will be your turn,' he said when he told Bertrand that 4th Corps would lead the next day's advance. Stockmayer would later conclude that Bertrand's eagerness to meet Ney's expectations would contribute to the disaster at Dennewitz.[179]

In addition to intense and costly combat, the brief sojourn before the walls of Wittenberg brought another incident of Franco-Württemberg friction, but one that subsequently became the subject of frequent exaggeration. When GB Delort, Bertrand's chief of staff, delivered the order for Württemberg troops to replace Morand's men in Euper on the evening of 3 September, Franquemont, as noted above, took the opportunity to express his frustration with what he perceived as unfair treatment, telling Delort 'that I was extremely displeased that the royal troops were always placed at the most dangerous points while Morand's division was always lodged comfortably in villages and kept away from the enemy.' 'After several evasions', Franquemont reported, Delort 'admitted that the current policy seemed to be to spare the French troops especially.' Franquemont then complained about the supply of rations, to which Delort replied that 'the Württembergers were the best provisioned and that the French often had nothing but the potatoes they found in the fields'. That was the sum total of Franquemont's account of this exchange as taken from his 4 September report to his king.[180]

This conversation is of interest in two respects in terms of this study. First is how it was transformed into a vicious condemnation of the French. Bernadotte's 20 September bulletin and later accounts published in Germany claimed that Delort had used the phrase 'It is in our interest that you all be killed, otherwise you will soon be against us!' Bernadotte's bulletin was hardly an unbiased or first-hand account but with each retelling Delort became more derisive and arrogant. He was soon sneering at Franquemont 'in proper French tone' and angrily proclaiming this phrase or some similar formulation.[181] Though Delort's words as reported by Franquemont clearly and understandably left a negative impression with the Württemberg general (he wrote the single word 'Delort' next to the 3 September entry in a chronology he prepared for Bangold in 1816), there is no indication in his reporting at the time that Delort employed the inflammatory and jeering language as specified in Bernadotte's bulletin or later renditions.[182] Many French officers, including Napoleon, harboured doubts about the loyalty of some of the German contingents in 1813, but there is no evidence that Rheinbund troops were singled out for the most arduous and perilous missions. Even if such had been the case, it is highly unlikely that an officer of Delort's experience (he had been in service since 1792) would have been so careless and irresponsible as to treat a key subordinate with such casual contempt. Second, while Franquemont's pique is certainly comprehensible, particularly after the Württemberg division had been serving as rear guard for several days and everyone was weary and edgy, his statement was simply inaccurate as far as Morand's men were concerned. The French division had suffered heavy casualties while playing a central role on both days at Bautzen and had advanced alongside the Württemberg troops in the engagement at Groß-Rosen. Similarly, though the Württemberg 38th Division was in the lead for much of the post-Bautzen pursuit, the Italian 15th had formed the van on the way to Großbeeren/Blankenfelde and would be in that position again when the army marched for Dennewitz. Nor does this assertion apply to other major German formations: witness the second-line role of the Bavarian division in most cases and the equal distribution of tasks in Reynier's 7th Corps. Furthermore, Delort signed and perhaps drafted the 4th Corps 'Journal Historique' that was replete with effusive praise for the Württemberg Division.[183] The claim that Delort made such foolish and erroneous remarks thus seems more likely to have been a useful propaganda ploy by opponents of Napoleon and the Rheinbund than an instance of ill-tempered scorn on the part of the French general. Franco-German discord was one of the themes of 1813, but the Franquemont–Delort exchange on 3 September was at most a minor manifestation of the problems within the alliance.

Dennewitz: Our Unparalleled Defeat[184]

Ney may have been pleased with the performance of 12th Corps on 5 September, but the following day brought a completely different result. The Army of Berlin lurched forward on the morning of the 6th in a clumsy and uncoordinated fashion with little knowledge of the enemy and with its columns too widely separated to provide mutual support. Bertrand's 4th Corps led the march with the Italian 15th Division in front followed by Morand's 12th, Lorge's attached 5th Light Cavalry Division and the Württemberg 38th bringing up the rear with responsibility for the safety of the corps baggage train and artillery park. 'To the front we were thus secure from enemy surprises,' wrote Oberleutnant Leo Ignaz von Stadlinger of the 2nd Infantry, but the distance between the corps and the ubiquity of the Allied cavalry meant that 'great vigilance was required on both sides and to the rear'. Indeed, Briche had to throw the Württemberg cavalry regiments at the cocky Allied squadrons to protect the baggage train. The pernicious and pervasive dust made matters worse, obscuring vision and making it difficult to distinguish friend from foe. The lack of food and clean drinking water intensified the debilitating effects of the oppressive heat and choking dust that day. Stadlinger lamented the lack of rations and grimly recalled soldiers trying to filter murky water from puddles and fens through cloth sacks and neck stocks in an effort to achieve something remotely potable. His own morning meal consisted of a spoonful of chocolate purchased from a sutler that he dissolved in swampy water, 'and that was my nourishment until

The 38th Division: Autumn Actions East of the Elbe

Potsdam where I came three days later as a prisoner'. Nonetheless, Martens wrote that the division set off that morning towards Jüterbog and Berlin 'in good spirits, confident in our strength'. 'Bright rose the sun in the cloudless sky', he recalled, 'but not to illuminate our triumphal march to Berlin, it rose to be witness to our unparalleled defeat.'[185]

The route of march took the corps cross-country east of Gölsdorf and over the Ahe-Bach at Dennewitz, but on cresting the low rise north of the village, the column discovered Tauentzien's troops moving west from Jüterbog. Fontanelli's Italians in the lead immediately deployed to attack while Morand's and Lorge's divisions angled off to their left in support. The Italian infantry and Lorge's horsemen were soon heavily engaged with Tauentzien while Morand turned west to face Thümen's 4th Prussian Brigade approaching from Kaltenborn.

The Württemberg 38th Division numbered some 6,600 officers and men present under arms on 6 September, but they were distributed on different parts of the battlefield.[186] Bertrand initially held six of the Württemberg battalions in reserve south of the stream and village while leaving Doering with the other five battalions in the rear to guard the corps' trains. As the fighting against Tauentzien intensified, however, Ney arrived. Essentially assuming the role of corps commander, he encountered Stockmayer around noon and expressed his frustration that Bertrand was 'making a mess' (*cochonnerie*) of things by entering into a serious engagement. He then ordered the Württembergers north of the Ahe-Bach. This small force consisted of the one combined battalion of the 2nd Infantry, II/4th Infantry and Stockmayer's four battalions (7th, 9th and 10th Infantry Regiments), supported by the horse guns and two foot batteries.[187] Forming up north of the village, they were just in time to stave off the Prussian cavalry that had overthrown Lorge's men and charged through the Italians in Tauentzien's desperate but successful strike to save his infantry. As the Prussian horse retreated and the French troopers pelted pell-mell to the rear, Ney ordered Franquemont to occupy the western portion of the pine copse north of Dennewitz on the right flank of the Italian division. Franquemont sent Spitzemberg towards the trees with II/4th, the 2nd Infantry battalion and five guns. He also advanced the 7th Infantry into the open ground to the west as a link to his two remaining battalions, the 9th and 10th Light Regiments under Stockmayer. These two remained in position just north of Dennewitz with the four guns of the horse battery. Spitzemberg placed some of his troops in the woods as skirmishers but formed most of the 2nd Infantry and all of the 7th in squares in the open ground. He was uncomfortable in his assigned position: 'The large extent of the woods, the distance [from friendly troops] and its location, in that the town of Jüterbog was occupied by the enemy, made the execution of this order extremely questionable without a larger number of troops,' he would later report.[188]

A tense lull descended on this portion of the battlefield for a time as Tauentzien and Thümen rallied their disordered infantry battalions and the bitter struggle swirled around Gölsdorf. Near 2:00 p.m., however, the fighting resumed with great ferocity when Thümen, reinforced by some of Hessen-Homburg's battalions, attacked the pine woods in an attempt to out-flank the solid position Morand's men occupied between the trees and the Ahe-Bach. Thümen's men forced the Italians out of the western portion of the pine copse and fell upon the now exposed left flank of the Württemberg position. Spitzemberg requested reinforcement and tried to withdraw his men from their perilous situation. 'The enemy batteries that fired on us with canister, did murderous damage to the squares and made any further occupation of the little woods impossible,' he wrote in his report, 'I therefore gave the order to pull the skirmishers out of the woods.'[189] It was too late. Most of II/4th Infantry was able to retreat towards Morand's ranks, but a company that had been dispersed among the trees as skirmishers were taken prisoner almost to a man while they tried to reassemble. The artillery battery and Spitzemberg himself were also able to escape, but a very different fate awaited the men of the 2nd and 7th Infantry Regiments.

Unable to advance against Morand's ranks, Thümen's troops paused briefly in the narrow gaps between the two sets of woods to collect themselves and then drove into the eastern copse which the Württemberg 2nd Infantry had just evacuated. By now, Tauentzien's revived command was approaching from the north as well and Spitzemberg's men found themselves trapped between the two converging Prussian forces. Formed into square to protect themselves from Tauentzien's cavalry, the 2nd Infantry fell back behind the shield of Kechler's 7th. The 7th repelled initial thrusts by Prussian skirmishers from the woods and Tauentzien's squadrons, but both Württemberg units soon found themselves in impossible situations as they were under heavy artillery fire and pressed by combined infantry and cavalry attacks in the open ground east of the woods. 'From minute to minute the situation became more critical,' recalled Suckow. The Prussian cavalry, though repulsed by fire from the Württemberg squares, had ridden between the two regiments. Gathering themselves to the left of the squares, the Prussian horsemen charged the 7th Infantry just as Kechler's men were themselves trying to deploy into line to face Prussian infantry emerging from the woods. 'We pulled back a bit and formed or, more accurately, wanted to form square,' Suckow wrote, 'but this unfortunate formation came about very imperfectly.' Stadlinger watched in horror from the 2nd Infantry's square as Prussian horse closed in on the 7th Infantry from front and flank.

Pressed from all sides and defenceless as it changed formation, the regiment dropped back and sought succour in the nearby square of the *Herzog Wilhelm* Regiment [2nd Infantry]. The latter, in the dreadful situation of having to fire on its own comrades or being unable to hold off the pursuing enemy, shouted out to the men of the 7th Regiment to throw themselves down or duck, at which most of them lay down in front of the square. As one Prussian infantry column continued its unstoppable march towards the flank of the square, a second advanced against the front from the little wood and the cavalry simultaneously began its attack, the 7th Regiment, incapable of defending itself, thus blocked the defence of the square completely. With the greatest sacrifice, the officers and NCOs of *Herzog Wilhelm* sought to maintain order; although already badly wounded by a ball, Oberst von Baur ceaselessly tried to encourage his men to brave resistance. But a Prussian 6-pounder battery opened a lively canister fire. The Prussian infantry drove at the square over the men of the 7th Regiment and their cavalry renewed its attack. Now disorder erupted here as well, individual enemies sprang into the square, the colonel was stabbed and cut up by Prussian cavalry; his last words were: 'Battalion, fire!' The regiment kept up the fight man-to-man and eventually in individual clumps until, surrounded on all sides, the remainder were taken prisoner sometime after 5:00 o'clock in the evening.[190]

Stadlinger, now a prisoner himself, was mistaken about the timing of his regiment's demise, which likely occurred between 3:30 and 4:00 p.m., but there was no doubt about the destruction of the 2nd Infantry's remaining five companies as well as both battalions of the 7th Infantry. The highly respected Oberst von Baur of the 2nd was killed, Oberstleutnant von Kechler of the 7th captured and, as the regiment's history grimly concluded, 'The 7th Regiment no longer existed.'[191]

By approximately 4:00 p.m., Prussian pressure had forced the 12th and 15th Divisions to retreat towards Rohrbeck and Bertrand turned to his last remaining troops to restore his situation. These were Stockmayer's two battalions with the horse battery, still holding just north of Dennewitz. 'At this moment, General Bertrand dashed up to me like one who had lost his senses, ordered the horse battery to follow him forward and gave me the order to follow the battery with the rest of the 9th and 10th Regiments at the double and support it.' It seemed to Stockmayer that 'Bertrand wanted to risk the utmost with the last troops available to him to restore or to seek death himself in his desperation.' The outcome of such a mad advance was clear to Stockmayer and he held his infantry back. Franquemont would later report that little would have been left of the division 'if I had followed all the orders that Gen. Bertrand gave me'.

Under Bertrand's direct orders, however, the horse battery had no choice and it hurried forward at the gallop into a maelstrom of enemy fire with predictable results. Twenty-four horses were killed, and one of the 6-pounders was disabled before the guns could even be unlimbered and the battery soon came bouncing back towards the stream in confusion. Unteroffizier Heere was with the guns: 'The fire grew more and more violent and so intense that all would be destroyed if we stayed, the call rang out: "all retreat!"' One of his gunners had had both ankles smashed by a ricocheting ball and had to be left behind. 'We laid him atop one of the cannons that could not be drawn away for lack of horses, gave him a shot of schnapps at his request which he drank down in haste,' remembered Heere, 'Thus he and the cannon fell into enemy captivity.' 'Death raged in my two battalion columns as the enemy's shells, canister and balls slammed into them', wrote Stockmayer, 'Despite being under continuous artillery fire for 8 hours in the Battle of Mojaisk [Borodino], this was the heaviest I had ever been exposed to in such a short space of time.' He quickly retired south of Dennewitz to reorder his two weakened battalions and the battery.[192]

Stockmayer, however, was soon back in action. Joined by II/4th and the foot artillery, he was ordered to a coppice north of Rohrbeck in Ney's final attempt to reinvigorate his army's offensive. This proved a very brief foray. Bertrand's renewed attack soon collapsed and the Württembergers covered the increasingly disorderly retreat across the stream. The 10th Infantry held the village of Rohrbeck until a Prussian shell set it on fire and forced the battered regiment to withdraw to a low hill south of the village where it joined the rest of Stockmayer's men. From this vantage the general observed 'with great sadness the fine advance of the enemy on the one side and the disorganised flight on our side'. Stockmayer soon joined the retreat but, forming his men into a square, he managed to hold them together while chaos roiled on all sides. 'The army was now beaten at all points,' reported Franquemont.

> Panic gripped the troops; the retreat devolved into a general flight. The infantry ran at the trot, the cavalry sought safety with the infantry and shoved into the jumbles of men; equipment, artillery, ammunition wagons sped off in different directions, the drivers cut the traces and left their wagons, caissons, cannons behind, everyone sought salvation in flight.

Ney, Bertrand and the 4th Corps staff rode alongside or sheltered within the Württemberg square as it made its slow way through this pandemonium towards the woods under constant attack. Somewhere along the way, the square met up with I/4th and I/6th Infantry which Franquemont incorporated into the retreating column as the park they had been protecting had long since dispersed in panic. These two battalions had also withdrawn through the confusion in squares. 'The tumult was so great that one no longer heeded the thunder of the guns and only heard the cannon balls as they hissed through the air,' remembered Martens, 'I might compare this horrible situation with that on the Berezina where the enemy shells likewise fell into the tangled and tightly packed masses of men and caused frightful destruction.' 'The retreat', recalled Bismarck, 'became a storm that carried everything away with it'.[193] One of the artillery histories notes that the disorder of the retreat was such that many guns became separated from their batteries and struggled back alone – remarkably, none were lost. Darkness and Prussian exhaustion finally brought an end to the pursuit and the French generals rode off after expressing their gratitude to Stockmayer for the protection his troops had afforded them. Leaving a trail of exhausted stragglers, the weary remnants of the division trudged through the darkness to reach Dahme at 3:00 a.m. on 7 September where a small band of Württemberg troopers helped the Bavarians storm the town.[194]

The *Herzog Louis* Jägers also joined Franquemont's main column on the retreat. The two cavalry regiments had remained south of the Ahe-Bach during the battle, but now gave 'new proofs of their valour' according to Bertrand as they helped to hold off the Prussian pursuit for a time. GB Jett was almost captured at one point and a number of men and horses were lost when the troopers unexpectedly came to a ditch that some of their tired mounts could not jump. While the *Louis-Jägers* eventually moved with Franquemont, the *Prinz Adam* Chevaulegers became separated in the swirling dust and confusion.[195] They would find their own way to Torgau over the next two days.

Also separated from the bulk of the contingent were the other three battalions of Doering's brigade: 1st Infantry and II/6th Infantry. Like every other infantry unit that maintained some semblance of order, Doering's men marched in squares. They suffered losses from enemy artillery fire but do not seem to have been set upon by pursuing cavalry. With no instructions, this part of the Württemberg division took a route through Schönewalde rather than Dahme and from thence to Herzberg to reach Torgau around midday on 7 September. Along the way, the Württembergers encountered some unidentified Saxon infantry and seem to have helped them recover two Saxon guns that had been temporarily commandeered by Prussian raiders.[196]

Franquemont and the bulk of the division departed Dahme on the morning of the 7th with the rest of 4th Corps, crossed the Schwarze Elster at Herzberg that day and halted near Döbrichau at 2:00 a.m. on 8 September. Remarkably, an officer of the French 5th Chasseurs commented that 'only the Württemberg division', despite its heavy losses, remained 'animated by a very good spirit'.[197] They marched on to Zwethau outside Torgau after several hours' rest and Franquemont loaned Fontanelli two guns to chase off several hundred

Cossacks who had appeared on the army's left flank. Most of the Army of Berlin was arranging itself around Zwethau when more Cossacks arrived with some Prussian cavalry and several Russian horse batteries. While the Russian and Württemberg guns were exchanging fire, however, enemy infantry appeared in the distance and the Russian horsemen threatened the bridge that crossed an old dead arm of the Elbe at Zwethau. Panic ensued. The disheartened men of Ney's army, fearing they would be cut off, fled towards Torgau in disorder as Russian shot and shell crashed into the packed crowd of fugitives. The 4th Corps managed to pull itself out of the tangle and establish a position around the Torgau bridgehead on the east bank of the Elbe as the rest of the mob shoved its way towards the fortress. The threat subsided, some order was restored, and the shattered Army of Berlin spent the night in and around Torgau before retiring across the river on the 9th.

Dennewitz was devastating for the Württemberg division. 'It is with the greatest displeasure that I report the loss of a part of the army corps that has been placed most graciously under my command,' Franquemont told Friedrich in his formal report on 10 September.[198] Total casualties came to at least 2,304 dead, wounded, captured or missing, approximately a third of the entire division. As might be expected, more than a thousand of these were from the 2nd and 7th Regiments destroyed in the fighting in and around the little pine wood; only some 70 from the former and 82 from the latter escaped their debacle. Similarly, II/4th Infantry likely lost as many as 200 in this part of the battle and its subsequent employment north of Rohrbeck. These four battalions thus accounted for half of the contingent's losses that day. 'The scythe of death has swept dreadfully through our ranks, my dear friend!' wrote Leutnant von Schlaich two days later, 'and only a few small remnants are left of the fine, courageous army that trod upon the battlefield of Jüterbog.' Historian Pfister would later remark that no battlefield from the Rheinbund era was as firmly lodged in local memory as 'the blood-soaked sand of Dennewitz'.[199]

Two aspects of the casualty figures, however, are surprising. First is that the 9th and 10th Light Infantry Regiments suffered relatively minor losses despite being involved in much of the action. The second is that the 1st and 6th Infantry each lost heavily. As 37 officers and other ranks from these regiments were killed or wounded, the two clearly came under artillery fire as Martens described, but each also lost a large number of men either captured or missing: 160–175 for the 1st and 360–390 for the 6th. The 1st Battalion of the 4th Infantry also seems to have lost more than 200 men.[200] These anomalous losses caught the attention of the alert Friedrich and he asked for an explanation.[201] By the time the king's missive reached Saxony, however, the events at Dennewitz had been overtaken by other actions and Franquemont never answered this particular query.

Like much else associated with the rout from Dennewitz, therefore, the cause behind these units in the rear losing so many soldiers is unclear. It is impossible to determine how many might have been captured after resistance, how many fell out from exhaustion to be picked up by Allied cavalry and how many may have availed themselves of the opportunity to desert in the confusion. The number of men who returned to their regiments in the ensuing days is known, but in the immediate aftermath of the battle Bertrand reported that a large number of fugitives from the Württemberg and Italian divisions had 'dispersed into the night'. Both contingents needed a morale boost in his view. In contrast, Franquemont's initial report described the exertions and privations the men had undergone over the preceding several days but pronounced himself 'entirely satisfied with the behaviour of the royal troops' and made no mention of desertion as problem. Although he may have been protecting his division's reputation in the king's eyes, given his usual frank style, it seems unlikely that he would dissemble on this point. Franquemont did note that a number of officers and men from the 2nd and 7th Regiments had eluded their captors and returned to the division unanimously complaining about the 'horrible mistreatment' they had received at the hands of the Prussians.[202]

Among those who escaped was Unteroffizier Heere of the horse battery. Ordered with twenty-four of the battery's mounted men to hold off Prussian hussars during the retreat south of Dennewitz as improvised cavalry, he had been overwhelmed, wounded, captured and robbed. While being transported towards Berlin, however, he slipped into a forest and, in the company of a Bavarian soldier and Saxon lieutenant who also freed themselves, made his way to Leipzig. Here he was re-united with his battery some weeks later, his comrades pleasantly surprised to see someone they had given up for dead.[203]

Curiously, the contingent had lost only one 6-pounder despite the intensity of the combat and the chaotic retreat; this was the piece that had been disabled and subsequently captured in the wake of Bertrand's abortive 'artillery charge' with the horse battery. Five or six other pieces, however, had been damaged or become so worn as to be unserviceable. As outlined below, they would be sent back to Württemberg with several other guns, leading to a drastic reduction in the division's firepower.

September: Reports, Reorganisations and Recriminations

The psychological impact of Dennewitz was also significant. The shock was accentuated because of the bright optimism generated by Ney's assumption of command. As Bismarck observed, 'The troops placed great confidence in the prince [Ney], and surrounded him with their affection, whose brave, glorious name inspired a devotion that seemed to deserve a better fate.' Similarly, Schlaich told his correspondent on 8 September that 'the almost unparalleled defeat' had robbed Ney of 'the finest blossoms in his crown of laurels'. In a postscript two days later, he added: 'The army strides rapidly towards its dissolution! Those Germans who can, evade the fight and hundreds go home as sick almost daily! We are not pressed by the enemy, but our situation seems highly precarious to me, and a complete defeat is no longer a distant prospect!'[204] Franquemont's concerns paralleled these impressions from his senior officer's vantage point. He was similarly distressed by the length of the sick lists, reporting on 12 September that, 'The soldiers generally show the best will, conceal their ailments until they collapse and look like corpses.' The general blamed the extent of sickness on constant bivouacking under foul weather with no straw to sleep on, lack of bread and especially the shortage of brandy. Likewise, his 10 September report acquainted the king with 'the shameful flight' on 6 September and 'the great demoralisation of the army'. 'It seems to me', he wrote, 'that the French generals and officers are tired of war and the soldiers can only be enlivened by the presence of the emperor.' He further observed that, 'The mistrust of the French towards the German troops shows itself more than ever. Since MacDonald's, Vandamme's and Ney's defeats, they believe they will only find shelter from the Cossacks behind the Rhine. They complain to me about the Bavarians, the Hessians and Saxons; behind the scenes we will not be spared either.'[205] There is no evidence that senior French commanders specifically cast aspersions on the Württemberg contingent – quite the contrary – but the fact that they disparaged other Germans in conversations with Franquemont and that he assumed he and his men were also targets of obloquy were manifestations of the growing tension in Franco-Rheinbund relations. In order to demonstrate loyalty and deflect distrust, Franquemont took the unusual step of having 400 men from the sick lists stand with their formations when Bertrand reviewed the division on 14 September. Providing palpable proof that his command was enfeebled by sickness and casualties rather than dereliction of duty seemed all the more important to him as by this point the Westphalian hussar regiments (Chapter 6) and Major von Bünau's Saxon battalion (Chapter 2) had joined the Allies: 'As the distrust of the French towards the Germans . . . has become daily more tangible to me, to which, of course, the defection of the Westphalian and Saxon troops to the enemy has provided occasion, I had these 400 sick men brought up behind their companies so that General Bertrand could convince himself of the condition of these people.'[206]

Friedrich, disturbed by the alarming details in Franquemont's almost clinical reports, hastened to assure the general of his steadfast support. In a series of private letters written during September and October, he was happy to express his 'satisfaction with your performance in the unparalleled and undeserved misfortunes of my army corps'. Exonerating his general for the 'losses and sad condition of the royal army corps', he blamed 'circumstances' and the French. 'You would be very wrong, my dear general, to reproach yourself because of the misfortunes on the 6th and 7th, as the smaller party must follow the fate of the larger and the enormous military mistakes Marshal Ney made are no fault of yours,' he told Franquemont after receiving the report on Dennewitz. He regretted that he could proffer little assistance and trusted Franquemont's intelligence and energy to address the contingent's immediate problems but offered surprisingly warm personal encouragement at the end of one letter: 'Do not lose faith in yourself or in your king.'[207]

Among the immediate problems facing Franquemont was the restructuring of the division as the losses inflicted at Dennewitz and rampant illness necessitated a drastic reorganisation. From eleven battalions, the 'division' was now reduced to four composite battalions by integrating the remnants of the 2nd and 7th Regiments with the less battered units. The infantry was thus organised into two small 'brigades' as shown in Chart 31 under '21 September'. Although the cavalry had not suffered many casualties at Dennewitz, each of the two regiments was consolidated into a single squadron with some additional number remaining detached to the division headquarters and other elements of the 4th Corps (such as orderlies for Bertrand). Similarly, a shortage of suitable horses and intact equipment led Franquemont to combine his remaining artillery assets into a lone horse battery of four 6-pounders and two howitzers: one column of 36 men, 19 horses and 5 guns left for home on 10 September; a second similar convoy departed on the 13th, apparently at Ney's direction. All these changes left the Württemberg contingent a 'division' in name only with a mere 2,879 men present under arms. The rest, probably close to 2,000 men and a large number of horses, were sent back to Württemberg in small detachments over a period of several weeks. Those returning home included many now excess officers and NCOs along with all the transportable sick and wounded. Not all made it safely back as Allied raiders intercepted at least one detachment as it passed through Saxony.[208] Of the men and horses who did reach the kingdom's borders, some would be invalided out of service on their arrival, but others would help rebuild the army for the campaign against France in 1814. Curiously, Generals von Koch and von Spitzemberg remained with the division through the Battle of Wartenburg on 3 October even though there was surely no need for so many generals with the tiny remains of the contingent.

Several facets of the repatriation process are noteworthy. First is the size: nearly a third of the contingent was headed back to Württemberg by the beginning of October; more would follow. The division's artillery provides an example: in the wake of Dennewitz a lieutenant led 35 men with 6 damaged

Chart 31: Reorganised Württemberg Contingent, September–October 1813

As of 1 September (prior to Dennewitz)

		bns/sqdns	Present under arms
38th Division, 4th Corps	GL von Franquemont		
1st Infantry Brigade	GM von Doering		
4th Infantry Regiment		2	1,260
6th Infantry Regiment, *Kronprinz*		2	1,261
2nd Infantry Brigade	GM von Spitzemberg		
1st Infantry Regiment, *Prinz Paul*		2	878
2nd Infantry Regiment, *Herzog Wilhelm*		5 companies	819
3rd Infantry Brigade (or Light Brigade)	GM von Stockmayer		
7th Infantry Regiment		2	796
9th Light Infantry Regiment, *König Jäger*		1	434
10th Light Infantry Regiment		1	533
2nd Foot Artillery Battery		4 × 6-pdr, 2 × howitzer	114
3rd Foot Artillery Battery		5 × 6-pdr, 1 × howitzer	114
24th Light Cavalry Brigade, 4th Corps	GB Briche and GM von Jett		
1st Cavalry, *Prinz Adam* Chevaulegers		4	356
3rd Cavalry, *Herzog Louis* Jäger-zu-Pferd		4	344
3rd Horse Battery		4 × 6-pdr, 2 × howitzer	113
Division total			7,022

As of 21 September (prior to Wartenburg)

			Present under arms
38th Division, 4th Corps	GL von Franquemont		
1st Infantry Brigade	GM von Stockmayer		
Combined Light Battalion			473
(9th and 10th Infantry plus remnants of 7th Infantry)			
1st Combined Battalion (based on 1st Infantry Regiment *Prinz Paul*)			528
2nd Infantry Brigade	GM von Doering		
2nd Combined Battalion			439
(based on 4th Infantry Regiment)			
3rd Combined Battalion			395
(based on 6th Infantry Regiment, *Kronprinz*)			
Horse Artillery Battery		4 × 6-pdr, 2 × howitzer	179

or burnt-out guns back to the kingdom on 10 September; three days later, the artillery was further consolidated and a second convoy marched for home with 5 other pieces and 90–100 men. These moves left the division with only its horse battery, albeit with an over-large complement of soldiers and the best horses and equipment available.[209] Second is that this Württemberg decision

24th Light Cavalry Brigade, 4th Corps *GB Briche and GM von Jett*
1st Cavalry, *Prinz Adam* Chevaulegers	1	175
3rd Cavalry, *Herzog Louis* Jäger-zu-Pferd	1	134
Division total		2,323

In October

	bns/sqdns	as of 6 Oct.	at Leipzig 19 Oct.
38th Division, 4th Corps *GL von Franquemont*			
1st Combined Light Battalion (light infantry)	1	247	213
1st Combined Battalion (line infantry)	1	305	325
2nd Combined Battalion (line infantry)	1	234	251
3rd Combined Battalion (line infantry)	1	169	142
Horse Artillery Battery	1 × 6-pdr?	109	109
24th Light Cavalry Brigade, 4th Corps *GB Briche and GM von Jett*		160 (total)	
1st Cavalry, *Prinz Adam* Chevaulegers	1		58
3rd Cavalry, *Herzog Louis* Jäger-zu-Pferd	1		70
Division total		1,224	1,168

Note: Bangold omits the 1st Combined Line Battalion and supplies smaller numbers for the others; he thus gives the total for the division as 945 (LABWHStA, E 284 g Bü 102); but this seems to be an oversight in his draft notes. Additionally, five of the horse battery's pieces were captured at Wartenburg on 3 October, leaving the division in possession of only one damaged 6-pdr. It is not clear if the contingent had any usable guns thereafter. Bangold recorded that there were four, so it is possible that the battery was able to field some of the previously damaged pieces.

25th Light Cavalry Brigade, 6th Corps *GM von Normann*

		Strength as of 1 Oct.
2nd Cavalry, Leib-Chevaulegers	4	469
4th Cavalry, *König* Jäger-zu-Pferd	4	466
2nd Horse Battery	4 × 6-pdr, 2 × howitzer	121
Brigade total		1,056

Sources: Bangold's papers, LABWHStA, E 284 g Bü 101 and Bü 102; 4th Corps 'Situations' for 1 and 21 September (SHD, 2C539); and Juhel, 'Automne 1813', pp. 60–2, for Normann, citing the 6th Corps' 'Situation' of 1 October.

occurred without specific prior permission from imperial headquarters. Friedrich's orders to Franquemont and to all the rear-area depot, hospital and convoy commanders were sent on 18 September, the same day that a request for release was sent to Berthier.[210] Indeed, the first news Napoleon and Berthier had of one Württemberg column was a message from the King of Westphalia stating that the arrival of an all-arms convoy near Kassel was spreading alarm through the Harz region with tales of defeat and disaster. Under the command of Oberst Friedrich Christian von Bieberstein, this column was on its way back to Württemberg from the theatre of war and first came to Jérôme's notice as it arrived unannounced on his borders. When queried, Franquemont explained in his matter-of-fact fashion that the men were all wounded or ill, the horses crippled and the guns in need of reboring. Other than the bland note sent to Berthier from Stuttgart on the 18th, however, there is no indication that Franquemont or any other Württemberg authority sought formal imperial approval for this convoy (which had departed just after the 4 September engagement at Euper) or for any of the others. Moreover, in contrast to the Bavarian case, the repatriation of Württemberg men, horses and equipment seems to have excited little attention and no special suspicion from the French after the initial flurry of exaggerated excitement about the column in Westphalia.[211]

Finally, the return of so many men and horses was a deliberate effort on König Friedrich's part to preserve as much of his army as possible. He remained true to the alliance with France, but the war was clearly going badly, and he had no desire to see his army sacrificed to the ineptitude of French generals who, as far as Franquemont had come to believe, were themselves only half-committed to their emperor's cause. He thus instructed Franquemont in a private letter 'to save what can be saved' and thanked him later for rescuing 'at least a portion of my troops' from what he conceived to be otherwise certain destruction. Similar instructions were issued to Normann but in typical fashion, his were stern and cold in tone: 'With the circumstances that have arisen, His Royal Majesty recommends to the General-Major that he take the utmost care of the troops, above all not to sacrifice [them], to manage all responsibly and to set himself in communication with General-Leutnant Graf Franquemont and follow his orders to the letter.' There is no little irony in the timing of these orders. As they were making their way to Saxony, Normann was approaching Leipzig where his notion of preserving his brigade would clash with his king's conception of obedience.[212]

Normann's Brigade: Innumerable Small Engagements

Franquemont's diminished 'division' and the rest of Bertrand's 4th Corps spent the remainder of September marching and counter-marching along the west bank of the Elbe as part of a generally fruitless series of French operations. 'We have been going about the world in a strange way; and I almost want to say – without plan and without purpose!' wrote Schlaich on 22 September, 'We were in Torgau and Schildau; then in Torgau again, then again in Schildau, and so it goes always here and there, and there and here in this poor exhausted region.'[213]

This relative lull in combat, though enervating for the poorly provisioned men endlessly slogging along under wretched weather, allows us an opportunity to return to mid-August and account for the actions of Normann's brigade with Marmont's 6th Corps.

Wallerstein to Dresden: Marching with Marmont

Marmont expressed his satisfaction with the appearance of Normann's brigade when he reviewed it on 9 August and the Württembergers spent the first ten days after the renewal of hostilities conducting scouting and liaison missions to keep 6th Corps connected with other French corps during operations against Blücher in Silesia. Their only combat action during this brief period was a small skirmish on the Bober southwest of Bunzlau on 21 August. When Napoleon turned towards Dresden to counter the Army of Bohemia's advance, however, the brigade was split up. The young Oberst Prinz von Wallerstein, commander of the Leib-Chevaulegers, marched to Dresden with 6th Corps leading two squadrons of his own regiment and one of *König* Jägers supported by three of the horse battery's guns (approximately 400 men total). Normann, on the other hand, was detached towards Kamenz with the rest of his brigade and two French battalions on an independent mission.

Wallerstein was thus present at the centre of the French line for the second day of the Battle of Dresden. The three Württemberg guns were actively involved in the day's cannonade, but the horsemen remained in support and took no part in the combat. Similarly, the detachment participated in the pursuit following the battle, pushing almost to Teplitz with the rest of 6th Corps. Other than a few advance and rearguard skirmishes, however, it saw little action and returned to Dresden on 4 September while the army recoiled following Vandamme's defeat at Kulm. After several days of fruitless marching towards Kamenz and Hoyerswerda, Wallerstein's little command once again found itself bivouacked east of Dresden on the 10th. It remained with the rest of the corps on the right bank of the Elbe between Dresden and Meissen until it crossed to the western bank on 27 September and reunited with Normann. Marmont pronounced himself very pleased with the detachment and offered special praise for its youthful commander.[214]

Normann at Hoyerswerda and Kamenz: Another Royal Reproach

While Wallerstein marched with Marmont, Normann commanded an independent force based around Hoyerswerda and Kamenz. Napoleon had ordered Marmont to post a 'mobile column' in this area to shield the main army's flank as it headed for Dresden and to serve as a link to Oudinot's army as it embarked on its abortive strike for Berlin. Marmont selected Normann for this mission and gave him a task force consisting of the remaining five Württemberg squadrons (two of Leib-Chevaulegers, three of *König* Jägers), three of the Württemberg horse battery's guns and a battalion each of French light infantry and naval artillerymen from 6th Corps. Although there is no written evidence to suggest that Napoleon personally selected Normann for this task, no one questioned Marmont's decision to appoint him, and he was not replaced or subordinated to a French general.[215] Indeed, Normann would hold this combined Franco-Württemberg command for a month. Moreover, in what was regarded as a sign of special privilege and honour, he routinely reported directly to Berthier, not through any lower headquarters. Though not unique (*see* Chapter 5), Normann's position as commander of an independent, multi-national force was rare and suggests that Napoleon and the senior French generals regarded him as an individual and the Württemberg army in general as broadly reliable and competent.

This extended period in this position was, in Normann's words, one of 'innumerable small engagements'. 'Enemy partisans swarmed around me the entire time', he reported on 11 September, writing later that 'we fought the enemy's light cavalry daily such that we were often left no time to cook'. For one of his NCOs, on the other hand, these weeks were not without their benefits. Wachtmeister Benedikt Peter of the *König* Jägers recalled that 'this detached duty was not uncomfortable for us; we had daily scuffles but in recompense always had a surfeit of food and fodder in this time'.[216]

The only skirmish of any significance occurred on 11 September when a large band of Cossacks and possibly Prussian hussars attacked Normann's outpost line near Kamenz. The Württemberg troopers were initially victorious, so much so that their excitable commander, Major Eduard von Miller of the Leib-Chevaulegers, became 'hotheaded' as the Cossacks withdrew into a marshy wood in seeming disarray. Miller accepted the bait and launched his squadron in a rash pursuit despite Normann's efforts to call him back. He rode into a trap. Surrounded and outnumbered, his squadron was soon in a desperate fight. Normann called up his infantry and threw two other squadrons into the fray to extricate Miller, first one from the *König* Jägers, then another. In the latter was Wachtmeister Peter: 'I rode into the woods with my platoon … and soon came upon Cossacks who were plundering the captured Chevaulegers and Jägers; their horses were already gone!' Peter and his men freed some of the captives, but Normann's piecemeal attempt to recover from Miller's imprudent advance was only partially successful and the cost was high. The enemy withdrew when Normann's two French battalions appeared on the scene, but the affair had been a decided defeat for the courageous but ineptly employed Württemberg squadrons. Total casualties in this unfortunate affray came to 138, of whom 49

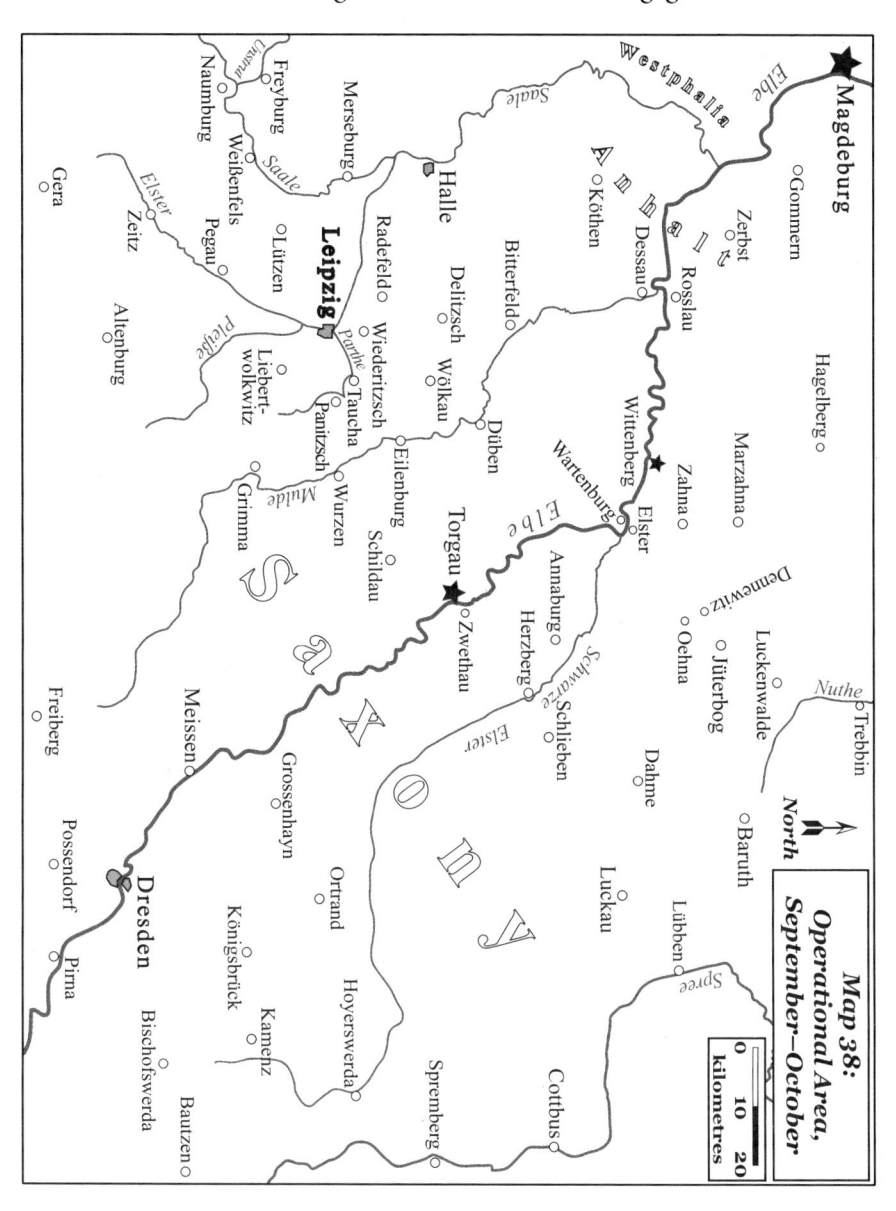

Normann's Brigade: Innumerable Small Engagements 87

Map 38: Operational Area, September–October

were killed, including the reckless Miller, and 55 captured (most of whom were wounded) as well as another 34 wounded who remained with the brigade.[217]

The French seem to have regarded the Kamenz affair as just another small setback in the incessant struggle against the ubiquitous enemy light troops and the skirmish hardly registers in Allied accounts, but Friedrich was furious, and another scathing letter was on its way to Normann as soon as his report reached Stuttgart. The king, ran the text, could not refrain from expressing 'his complete dissatisfaction' with Normann's 'military dispositions during the engagement on the 11th'. In the king's eyes, Normann had 'not only sacrificed the men under Major von Miller's command, but involved 2 other squadrons, and those one after the other, whereby he obviously repeated Major von Miller's mistake ... This entire heavy loss is therefore to be ascribed to the faulty and incomprehensible actions of the General-Major which clearly shows that he acted without thinking [ohne Kopf].' This harsh missive went on to criticise Normann for imprecise reporting and for the manner in which he had divided the brigade between his detachment and Wallerstein's. The substantive portion concluded with a reiterated reproach: 'His Majesty therefore sternly reprimands the General-Major for all this with the very serious reminder not to be guilty of such totally unforgivable mistakes in his future military dispositions.'[218] Normann's brigade thus passed over the Elbe on 27 September with its commander under a royal cloud for perceived poor judgement.

Once across the river, the brigade spent the next several days switching back and forth on the western bank of the Elbe in response to the slowly closing circle of Allied armies. Normann again had two French battalions attached to his command as he directed reconnaissance patrols to deter or destroy Allied raiding parties. These missions, conducted under ugly weather, imposed a heavy burden on the troopers, but the logistics situation improved, and the brigade did not suffer the health problems that debilitated Franquemont's command. The regiments and battery maintained their strength, the horses remained in good condition and none of the senior officers mentioned any problems with morale or anti-French sentiment in their reports.

As October began, the brigade was drawn back towards Leipzig and for a time operated more or less on its own north of the city while Marmont led the rest of 6th Corps further east along the Mulde as part of Napoleon's futile attempts to bring on a battle with Blücher. The brigade re-joined Marmont (now reinforced with Lorge's 5th Light Cavalry Division) near Delitzsch on 8 October and participated in the manoeuvring between that town and Düben before returning towards Leipzig on the 13th. Most of Marmont's corps shifted south of the Parthe by forced marches, to support Murat if necessary, but the cavalry and some infantry remained in a position near Möckern where the Württemberg horse battery helped to drive off probes by Blücher's advance guard that day. The 14th of October saw a more serious skirmish flare further to the northwest near Radefeld as Marmont's corps came back across the Parthe and pushed elements north. The action was largely confined to a cannonade, but the Württemberg battery was involved, and the fire was sufficiently intense that three of its pieces were temporarily disabled. The remaining three guns were again engaged in outpost skirmishing on 15 October while workmen tried to repair the previously damaged pieces in Leipzig. The two cavalry regiments were present during these minor affairs, but they do not seem to have been directly engaged.[219] The evening of 15 October, the eve of the Battle of Leipzig, thus found Normann's brigade north of the city with the rest of 6th Corps and Lorge's squadrons to shield Napoleon's flank from Blücher's Army of Silesia around Halle.

This brings Normann's brigade to the edge of the Battle of Nations, but some discussion of officer and other rank loyalties is necessary before returning to Franquemont's diminished division. During one of the skirmishes north of Leipzig, Rittmeister Emanuel Graf von Leutrum of the Leib-Chevaulegers turned to his squadron and called on the men to defect to the enemy with him. A trumpeter, a trooper and an assistant surgeon moved to join him, but one of the squadron's senior NCOs, a *Wachtmeister* named Böhm, turned about, drew one of his pistols and shouted: 'I will shoot down whoever rides out!' Leutrum dashed off, but Böhm's decisive action sufficed to hold the squadron in place. Over the following two days, two lieutenants, one each from the Leib-Chevaulegers and the *König* Jägers, also took advantage of the enemy's proximity to change sides and induced some 30 troopers to desert with them.

Wachtmeister Peter of the *König* Jägers could not contain his disgust for these individuals or his scorn for the other officers who sat 'like lumps on a log' and did not intervene to arrest Leutrum. 'After the Rittmeister of the Leib-Chevaulegers, two other officers went over to the enemy under fire – foreigners naturally!' he wrote, 'One of these heroes defected while the brave squadron was giving the Cossacks a proper lesson,' and the other, from his own regiment, 'left his platoon in the lurch' to desert during a reconnaissance. 'Later, when all of us Germans marched against Napoleon, we Württembergers happily pitched into the French, and we Jägers always in the advance guard – but what happens to discipline when the brigade is under fire and every individual decides for himself: now we will ride over here or over there, when the soldier is duty-bound to his king and his flag!'[220] Leutrum would be dismissed for 'dishonourable behaviour' but it is not clear that Böhm was ever rewarded for his bold act of loyalty.

What is clear is that the number of officers who changed sides prior to Normann's defection on 18 October was very small: two captains and a lieutenant in October along with a lieutenant of Mecklenburg origin who seriously wounded a fellow officer in a duel during August and fled to the Allies fearing punishment. All of these men were discharged for 'dishonourable behaviour'. Normann later stated that only two officers left, but that thirty troopers also slipped away to the enemy during these few days. Approximately seven other officers in the field army accepted the king's offer and submitted proper letters asking to leave Württemberg service during September and October. All were originally from Mecklenburg or Prussia and all requested release after Dennewitz as Napoleon's prospects were darkening precipitously. Although they lost their previous privileges and were not granted a formal *Abschied* (discharge), most of these departures seem to have occurred with royal permission and the men were not cashiered as Major de la Chevallerie had been in April. Nor does it seem that any of these men changed sides on the battlefield as Leutrum and the other two officers did. The Mecklenburg-origin officers seem to have decided that they wanted to avoid fighting against their former countrymen that autumn (even though they had voiced no objections during the spring); while the former Prussians (three brothers) were understandably alarmed at an edict issued by the Prussian king that threatened his former subjects with property confiscation and other dire consequences if they did not return to Prussian service.[221]

Grim October: From Wartenburg to Leipzig and Home

While Normann was shifting across the Elbe and towards Leipzig, Ney had sent 4th Corps to Wartenburg to block an attempt by Bülow's Prussians to bridge the river at Elster. Morand's 12th Division and the Westphalian Chevaulegers skirmished with a small Prussian detachment there on 23 and 24 September. The rest of the corps joined the following day with the Württembergers posted near the village of Bleddin. Bernadotte, however, had ordered Bülow to abandon the nascent bridgehead, so the Prussians withdrew, breaking up the bridge as they crossed back to the east. With the threat at Wartenburg eliminated, Ney feared that Bernadotte might attempt a passage near Dessau. On 26 September, therefore, the Württembergers, along with the rest of 4th Corps hurried west to support Reynier's 7th Corps facing Dessau. Left behind at Wartenburg was a chain of outposts manned by the *Herzog Louis* Jägers.

The Prussians, however, soon returned to Elster. Crossing in boats, Prussian infantry from Borstel's brigade chased off the Württemberg cavalry patrols, restored the bridge and began work on a bridgehead on the left bank. When the report from the *Herzog Louis* outposts reached Ney, he ordered Bertrand 'to attack the enemy infantry that has passed to this bank' because 'it is extremely important to prevent the enemy from re-establishing his bridge over the Elbe vis-à-vis Wartenburg'. Bertrand chose his nearest troops for this mission, the 38th Division, but he correctly recognised the Prussian effort as a diversion and told Franquemont that 'one brigade is more than sufficient' to repel the enemy. Doering's tiny 'brigade' and the Württemberg cavalry were thus soon on their way back to Wartenburg. Arriving late on the 30th, Franquemont occupied the town and ordered a night advance by a company of the 3rd Combined Battalion to probe the Prussian position. At the cost of two men killed and two wounded, this brief foray drove the Prussians out of what Doering derisively termed their 'so-called bridgehead, really just an abatis' and back across the river. The Prussians broke up their bridge as they withdrew, but the Württembergers did not occupy the partly constructed bridgehead owing to the danger of being smothered by artillery crossfire from the dominant bank on the far side of the river.

As Bertrand had correctly deduced, the enemy activity on 29 and 30 September had been a diversion ordered by Bernadotte. This feint was thus easily repulsed, but Blücher was now approaching with his Army of Silesia, intent on carrying his command across the Elbe. On 1 October, therefore, Prussians from Yorck's I Corps paddled over, re-occupied the dilapidated bridgehead, and began work on a new crossing. Progressing steadily but, to Blücher's mind far too slowly, Prussian and Russian engineers managed to construct two bridges during the night of 2/3 October. The rest of Franquemont's division arrived on 1 October, but Ney, alarmed at the reports from Wartenburg, sent the rest of 4th Corps to reinforce the small Württemberg force. As the Allied engineers were labouring to complete their spans, therefore, Morand, Fontanelli and Beaumont arrived to take up defensive positions around the town.[222]

Wartenburg, 3 October: An Unequal Combat[223]

The Elbe makes a sharp bend between Wartenburg and Elster, creating a narrow peninsula with Wartenburg at its western base. The terrain in 1813 was flat and marshy, cut up by numerous watercourses, divided by dykes and covered by patches of fen, forest, scrub and heavy underbrush. All these factors made a direct assault on Wartenburg very chancy and likely to involve high casualties. Towards the village of Bleddin on the southern outlet from the peninsula, however, the landscape is more open. Here, where deployment, manoeuvre and artillery employment are easier, is where Yorck would decide to out-flank the daunting defensive position at Wartenburg itself, and here is where the Württemberg division found itself posted when the Prussians advanced early on the morning of 3 October.

On reaching Wartenburg the previous day, Bertrand had arrayed his corps with Morand on the left in and north of the town, Fontanelli around Globig and Franquemont on the right at Bleddin. As the battle evolved on the 3rd, he would bring the Italians forward to the centre just south of town, leaving only the Rheinbund cavalry brigade (Beaumont and Wolff) in reserve just east of the village of Globig. Bertrand was rightly confident in the strength of the position, but his arrangements had at least two major flaws: they left a gap between Fontanelli and Franquemont in the right-centre and they placed the weakest of the corps' subordinate elements, the Württemberg contingent, in the most vulnerable portion of the line where the terrain afforded the best opportunities for attack. Furthermore, the position was too extensive, especially for the much-weakened 4th Corps. As many commentators note, a wiser deployment would have been to fill the woods around the Moyenhainichtgraben with skirmishers supported by formed troops in the open plot to the south (the 'Schützberg'). The Moyenhainichtgraben (a deep, water-filled ditch) was a serious obstacle in itself, impassable to cavalry and artillery, while the wooded zone would have allowed the skilful French and Württemberg light troops to engage in a prolonged skirmish battle, trapping their attackers in the marshy low ground towards the river.[224] The corps' late arrival on 2 October may have left Bertrand few options and little time to redeploy before Yorck attacked, but he would pay heavily for these errors.

On the right flank of the defensive line, Franquemont's tiny 'division' numbered perhaps 1,800 infantry and something over 100 cavalry along with its six artillery pieces. He stationed the 2nd and 3rd Combined Battalions (essentially the remnants of the 4th and 6th Infantry Regiments respectively) approximately 700 to 800 metres forward of Bleddin with four of his six guns unlimbered in front of them and skirmishers pushed up to the Moyenhainichtgraben. An outpost was placed 300 metres ahead of the two battalions on the Landdamm, a dyke that fringed the small western arm of the Elbe, as this area permitted the only relatively easy egress from the peninsula to the north. The remaining two battalions were posted on the northern side of Bleddin while the rump cavalry brigade, still commanded jointly by Briche and Jett, and the other two guns were held southwest of the village. Franquemont was just completing a report to König Friedrich 'when the enemy crossed the bridge and attacked'.[225]

The Prussians did not expect much resistance and GM Prinz Carl von Mecklenburg-Strelitz, leading the advance with only three battalions, was simply told to cross over and take the town at which point the rest of the corps would follow. Mecklenburg's men succeeded in clearing the French skirmishers from the woods immediately outside the bridgehead but found the terrain baffling and enemy opposition anything but light. He received reinforcements, but rather than drive straight at Wartenburg, he left part of his force to screen the town and swung south towards the Moyenhainichtgraben with the rest. After considerable delay and confusion, his men pushed back the Württemberg 3rd Battalion's outpost along the dyke to emerge into the open ground south of the woods around 9:00 a.m. Here he encountered Doering's two battalions, 2nd (4th Infantry) on the left, 3rd (6th Infantry) on the right, supported by four of the horse battery's guns. Mindful of his instructions, Mecklenburg endeavoured to slide to his right so as to out-flank the town, but the terrain was

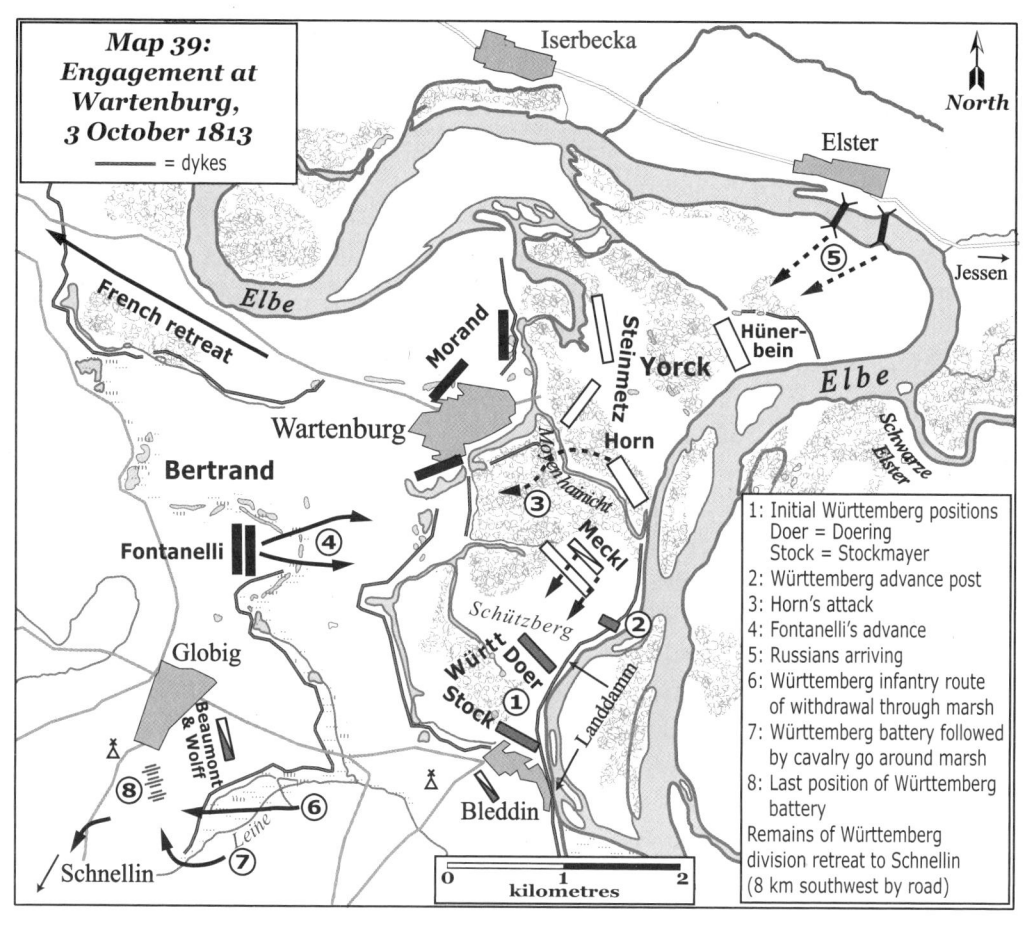

Map 39: Engagement at Wartenburg, 3 October 1813
— = dykes

1: Initial Württemberg positions
  Doer = Doering
  Stock = Stockmayer
2: Württemberg advance post
3: Horn's attack
4: Fontanelli's advance
5: Russians arriving
6: Württemberg infantry route of withdrawal through marsh
7: Württemberg battery followed by cavalry go around marsh
8: Last position of Württemberg battery
Remains of Württemberg division retreat to Schnellin (8 km southwest by road)

impossible, and his men came under effective fire from the Italian division that Bertrand had brought up south of Wartenburg as well as from the Württemberg guns north of Bleddin. 'All his attempts failed under the fire of our artillery', reported Franquemont, 'as soon as his columns appeared they were dispersed before being able to form in the open terrain.'[226] Unable to turn the town and unwilling to risk his small force with neither artillery nor cavalry in an advance across the open ground against Doering, Mecklenburg halted to await further reinforcement.

A lively, lengthy and enervating skirmish thus developed between Doering's two battalions and the four that Mecklenburg had been able to bring forward. The combat near the Landdamm was especially costly and bitter. Franquemont first ordered the 3rd Battalion forward on the right to bolster its forward outpost and skirmish line. As the struggle dragged on and ammunition began to run low, he then sent the Light Battalion forward from Bleddin to support Doering's men. Meanwhile, he dispatched repeated requests for reinforcement to Bertrand. Bertrand offered no further troops but did announce rather hopefully that the Italian 15th Division would advance to take the pressure off the Württembergers. The 4th Corps 'Journal Historique' would later claim that Hulot's brigade (that is, the 23^e Ligne) and the Italian division had been sent to occupy the gap between Bleddin and Wartenburg to support Franquemont. The Italians, however, quickly stalled and Hulot's brigade, if actually sent, was far too late to restore the situation on the corps' right flank. The 2,000 or so men of the 38th Division would be on their own.[227]

While skirmishing rolled back and forth in the fields north of Bleddin, the Prussians in front of Wartenburg were suffering under galling fire. Commanded by Oberst Carl von Steinmetz, the best they could do was hold their ground; advancing against Morand's defences was out of the question. When he arrived on the scene that morning, it was thus immediately evident to Yorck that the only prospect for success lay in attacking Bleddin to out-flank Bertrand's centre and right. Yorck's other brigades were making their way over the two bridges, and he slotted GM Heinrich Wilhelm von Horn's 7th Brigade into the centre between Steinmetz and Mecklenburg while placing GM Friedrich Heinrich Carl von Hünerbein's 8th in reserve. All of this took some time, especially improvising crossings over the Moyenhainichtgraben to get artillery and cavalry over the ditch and through the tangled undergrowth to Mecklenburg's position. By midday, however, most of Yorck's corps was on hand and Russian infantry was also beginning to arrive on the western shore. Mecklenburg now had 6 battalions, 7 squadrons and 13 guns across the ditch. Although several of his battalions were severely depleted from their protracted duel with Doering's brigade, he was ready to advance. At 1:00 p.m. Yorck ordered him to attack.[228]

By this time, Franquemont had thrown two of his remaining four companies from the 1st Battalion (1st Infantry) into the exhausting exchange with Mecklenburg's men. His position was critical. He had only two companies left in reserve, his requests for reinforcement had been denied, enemy pressure was building to his front, now with artillery and cavalry in support, his troops were running out of ammunition, and he could see Horn's brigade advancing into the gap between his division and the rest of the corps. The Italians had not been able to advance, he knew nothing of the supposed move by Hulot's brigade, and the Prussians were continuing to press forward as far as he could see. It was clearly time to withdraw. Around 2:00 p.m., he therefore gave the order to pull back to a new position near a windmill on slight rise some 700–800 metres behind Bleddin. Stockmayer would hold the village as long as possible to protect the withdrawal. Despite their weariness and Prussian pressure, the engaged battalions retired coolly and in good order, established themselves on the low hill and replenished their ammunition. His division thus posted, Franquemont recalled Stockmayer's companies, placed his artillery on the left of his line to dominate the exits from Bleddin and repelled several Prussian attempts to dislodge him. He now faced the question of what to do next. Bertrand had instructed him to join Morand at Wartenburg, but the direct road was already blocked by the advancing Prussians. Baumbach, for example, tasked with carrying the message to inform Bertrand of the withdrawal, considered himself most fortunate to complete his mission in one piece.[229] Franquemont therefore took his little command towards Globig, marching at double time in closed battalion columns and hoping that Beaumont's cavalry would shield him long enough to reach the village.

Franquemont's hopes were not fulfilled. Coming upon a boggy area along the Leine stream, he ordered his infantry to slog through the marsh so they would not be vulnerable to the Prussian squadrons looming on his flank. He sent the battery at the gallop south (left) of the marsh covered by his small cavalry force, intending that the entire division would re-unite on the far side of the stream south of Globig. Unfortunately, this was not to be. Instead of protection from Beaumont, 'the enemy cavalry turned the marsh by the right [north], put General Beaumont's cavalry to flight and charged on the royal battery that had already taken position and commenced firing'. With the Württemberg infantry still wading through the marsh and the few Württemberg troopers not yet on hand, the battery was alone on the barren hill. In a trice, it was overrun and captured entire by a squadron of the Prussian 2nd Leib-Hussars. One cannon, previously sent to the park for repairs, escaped, but the other five pieces fell into Prussian hands along with four caissons and forty-four men.[230]

There was now no possibility of reaching the rest of 4th Corps. The cavalry and three of the combined battalions, still south of the swamp, thus angled off to the left more or less unmolested and made for Schnellin, 4 kilometres southwest of Globig 'to escape the unequal combat'. The combined Light Battalion, on the other hand, had already passed through the marsh and was approaching the lost battery's position. Some 30 mounted Württemberg officers from the division staff and the battalion made a desperate attempt to rescue the guns. Forming themselves into an ad hoc troop, they charged out only to be repulsed by the Prussian horsemen.[231] Not only was the battalion too late to save the guns, but it was also instantly attacked from all sides by the elated Prussian hussars and had to focus on saving itself. Franquemont, at its head, was in danger of capture as were Generals Koch, Stockmayer and Spitzemberg along with the entire division staff. 'I owe it solely to its composure that I was not taken prisoner,' Franquemont told the king in acknowledgement of the Light Battalion's steadfastness, 'hornists and other individuals who were not within the ranks of the column were cut to pieces alongside it.' 'The conduct of the enemy battalion commander on this occasion must be praised for keeping his troops intact despite being subjected to the attacks of a victory-drunk cavalry mass of several squadrons,' wrote one of the attacking Prussian hussar officers later, 'His attitude was so impressive that the weak attempt to attack him with partly reorganised squadrons was soon abandoned and he reached untroubled a small stand of brush which put an end to any further pursuit by cavalry.' Franquemont drily recounted that 'We carved our way through the swarms of enemy cavalry towards Schnellin where I reformed and deployed the royal army corps.'[232]

Before reaching Schnellin, however, the battalion had to undergo a further trial: being shelled by one of its own guns. A lieutenant of the 2nd Leib-Hussars thought to have the Württemberg gunners fire on the retreating Light Battalion and halted the first gun as the drivers attempted to gallop away. Cursing and waving his sabre, he threatened to cut the gunners down if they did not open fire. Their excuses only roused him to greater fury, and he forced them to loose at least two rounds, both of which missed as the artillerymen deliberately shot too long or too short. Other Prussian officers, disgusted by this antic, persuaded their colleague to end the farce and the battery trundled off into captivity without further disturbance.[233]

With the Württembergers in retreat and Beaumont's cavalry driven from the field, Prince Carl of Mecklenburg deposited a small force to watch his left flank and turned north to participate in the final defeat of Bertrand's corps. His brigade pivoted to the right to come behind the Italian division while Horn's men surged forward from the front. The entire French position thus came unhinged. The 15th Division broke and fled to the rear, Morand's men withdrew in better order, but the superb position was lost, and the conglomeration retreated hastily north towards Wittenberg in no little confusion. Bertrand was fortunate that additional Allied cavalry had not crossed over the Elbe in time to cause still more damage to his corps. The Prussians, having taken heavy losses (some 1,600 dead and wounded) encamped southwest of the town to celebrate their victory. The success was a major step towards the coming encirclement of the Grande Armée and Yorck would be granted the title 'von Wartenburg' in recognition of his role just as Bülow had been honoured with 'von Dennewitz' after his triumph on 6 September.

As for the Württembergers, their odyssey had not yet concluded. Completely cut off from the rest of the corps, Franquemont decided on further retreat when enemy forces neared Schnellin late in the day. He thus fell back another 23 kilometres to take shelter behind the Mulde River at Düben. Here the division counted its losses. These came to 7 officers and 500 other ranks or approximately a third of the division's infantry as well as five of its six artillery pieces. The 3rd Combined Battalion (former 6th Infantry) seems to have suffered the heaviest casualties, accounting for 5 officers and 300 men. This is consistent with its role on the right of the skirmish line and in the contest for the area along the Landdamm.[234] This heavy toll left the division, already a pale shadow of its former self, no stronger than a weak regiment. The four combined infantry battalions were thus further consolidated into three, one for each of the former brigades: the 1st or Light Battalion, 2nd (former 1st Infantry) and 3rd (formerly Doering's brigade). 'What the Battle of Jüterbog had left of our corps', lamented Schlaich, 'was entirely destroyed in the very unfortunate engagement at Wartenburg.'[235]

The division's performance, on the other hand, had once again been excellent. It had held on for six hours or so in a disadvantageous position, had only yielded to superior numbers when ordered to retire and had withdrawn in good order to earn the honest respect of its opponents.[236] There were no defections, no desertions and men who were captured almost invariably sought to escape to return to the regiments. Franquemont, though dismayed by the losses, proudly told the king that the men 'were animated by the best of spirits' and once again lauded their 'courage and endurance'. He made a special point to attach no blame to the artillery for the loss of the guns, attributing the calamity rather to 'the unpredictable concatenation of unfortunate circumstances'. Indeed, he offered particular praise for the officers and men of the artillery arm: 'I have rather every reason to be satisfied with the artillery which ... did good service and caused the enemy much loss on this day as in all previous opportunities.'

Bertrand, on the other hand, offered a mixed review. Though no great tactician himself, he was displeased as far as tactics were concerned. He told Napoleon the outcome might have been different if the Württemberg division had conducted its defence more artfully by placing its artillery behind dykes and its infantry in houses rather than advancing. He also lamented that he did not have 'a fine regiment to send' to assist. This criticism was not entirely unfair, but Bertrand understated the sector Franquemont had to cover, claiming its front was 400 metres in length when it was actually close to a kilometre with an additional kilometre separating it from the nearest 4th Corps troops. Nor did Bertrand explain why he had left this tiny 'division' so far from the rest of his corps and unsupported. At the same time, he respected the courage and fidelity of the Württemberg troops. Indeed, he attributed what he considered the division's ill-advised deployment to be the result of 'an excess of ardour' and sent a heartfelt letter to Franquemont when they were reunited several days later: 'No one, I dare say, has felt such a lively joy as me at the news that you with your generals and your brave troops have eluded such a great danger.'[237]

Württemberg veterans of the campaign were understandably outraged years later when French General Pelet wrote that 'the Württembergers hardly defended Bleddin' which he described as almost as strong a position as Wartenburg itself. Pelet had many fine qualities as a soldier and as a historian, but he was fundamentally suspicious of all Rheinbund contingents – especially in his writings after Napoleon's defeat and exile – and his characterisation of the Württemberg role at Wartenburg was patently unfair and inaccurate. Unfair in that the Württemberg troops had conducted themselves competently and courageously for many hours and at heavy cost; inaccurate because Bleddin was not nearly as defensible as Wartenburg.[238] Even if some French thought Franquemont should have displayed more caution in his tactical dispositions, there could be no question regarding the courage, skill and dedication of the Württemberg division at Wartenburg. The defeat stemmed from a general insufficiency of forces and Bertrand's faulty deployment rather than failures on the part of Franquemont or his troops.

Save What Can be Saved

Wartenburg sparked another explosion of royal rage in Stuttgart. 'If the disgraceful behaviour of the French commanders towards the German troops needed any other proof, it is provided by the affair of 3 October . . . at Jüterbog bad dispositions and disgraceful negligence were the cause of such large losses, at Wartenburg, there seems to have been just as much ill will as incompetence,' Friedrich wrote in a 7 October reply to Franquemont's report. His assumption of ill will was misplaced in this instance, but it reflected his exasperation after the heavy losses his army had suffered in its latest two battles. Angered that his contingent could no longer even be considered a 'division', he was determined to withdraw it from Saxony: 'I therefore order you, wherever this letter may find you, to submit a detailed report on this most recent affair and the condition of the army corps to the Major General Prince of Neuchâtel [Berthier] and depict for him the impossibility of taking any further active part in the campaign with this small band which furthermore lacks everything.' Whatever Berthier's reply, the king expected Franquemont to 'insist firmly on your orders and not permit any further misuse of the troops'. Two days later, apparently prompted by news that Bavarian GL von Raglovich had been recalled, the king issued additional instructions. If the French would not release the entire contingent, Franquemont, Stockmayer and all excess officers were to return home, using their wounds as an excuse. Jett and Doering were to be left in command. Anticipating a French retreat over the Rhine via Frankfurt, he concluded with 'Save Normann's brigade if you can.' Another royal letter, drafted on 18 October sharpened these sentiments: 'The collapse of everything can be foreseen', wrote Friedrich, 'save therefore what can still be saved and if a total retreat takes place, try to take the direction here.' Validating the king's grim forebodings, of course, was the fact that by this time the Battle of Leipzig was reaching its brutal climax.[239]

In his 7 October letter, Friedrich also told Franquemont that he had written directly to Napoleon on 19 September requesting release of 'the sad debris' of his contingent 'in order not to lose at least the cadres, without which it will be impossible to re-form a corps that has suffered so much'. He repeated his appeal in a second missive dated 3 October. It seems, however, that neither of these messages reached the emperor. In addition to the enormous delays imposed by Allied raiding parties in the French rear, GM von Beroldingen, Friedrich's liaison at imperial headquarters, decided not to hand Napoleon the king's 19 September letter during a long audience with the emperor on 5 October. Beroldingen had returned to Württemberg in mid-September to report to the king, but it had taken him nearly three weeks to make the normally relatively straightforward journey from Stuttgart back to Dresden owing to the insecurity of the rear areas. When he met the emperor, however, he judged the timing unpropitious to deliver his monarch's request and chose to wait for a more apposite moment. That moment never seems to have arrived. In contrast to the turmoil associated with the Bavarian request, there is thus no evidence of Napoleon or Berthier addressing the question of releasing the Württemberg troops until well after Leipzig. All the emperor received from Beroldingen during their meeting was a letter from early September offering congratulations for the victory at Dresden in August.[240]

Furthermore, Friedrich's 3 October letter conveyed his anxiety that Bavaria's impending defection and the likely approach of a Coalition army would 'submerge my lands'. Such an eventuality, explained Friedrich, could force him 'to make declarations contrary to my way of thinking' so as not to 'deliver my country to devastations and the fury of the enemy'.[241] This was a back-handed way of returning to the notion that he, as a Rheinbund prince, was only bound to the treaty so long as France was able to serve as Württemberg's protector. If Napoleon could not shield his state from external enemies, he would have to find other means to safeguard his interests. The implications were clear, but, again, there is no evidence that Napoleon ever saw this letter; its fate is unknown. Instead, the emperor demonstrated his 'great trust' in Friedrich during his wide-ranging discussion of political affairs and military details with Beroldingen in the 5 October audience. Beroldingen was as yet unaware of the warnings in Friedrich's 3 October letter, so when Napoleon asked if Friedrich had any security concerns, Beroldingen merely replied that his king was disturbed by the heavy losses his troops had sustained but was capable of protecting himself from threats out of the Tyrol and Vorarlberg. As events slid towards the denouement at Leipzig, therefore, Napoleon had no reason to think that Friedrich urgently desired the return of his contingent or that the king was seriously considering a future alignment with the Allies.[242]

That Noble Confraternity: Franquemont from Leipzig to Württemberg

The impediments to communications meant that release of the Württemberg contingent would not even be considered prior to Leipzig. Imperial approval would have been unlikely in any event. As a result, the enfeebled division would remain a constituent part of the Grande Armée until several days after the great battle.

The first half of October was spent in seemingly endless marches in poor weather. Franquemont rejoined 4th Corps west of the Mulde on 5 October (prompting the note from Bertrand cited above) and for the next ten days they trudged back and forth on both banks of that river between Düben, Wurzen, Schildau and, once again, Wartenburg, a 'repugnant locale' that Schlaich and his comrades had hoped never to see again. 'The current operations are inexplicable,' complained Schlaich, 'The continual marching back and forth through this pitiable region has so exhausted it that potatoes we dig from the fields are our only nourishment. Most villages stand empty as the poor inhabitants have nothing left from which they can live; and the entire area between Schildau, Torgau, Dessau and Düben resembles a giant bivouac.' The men had no option but to sleep in the open 'under heavy rain without wood and without straw' on the night of the 13th, for example, and under 'the same adverse conditions' the next night as well.[243] These peregrinations brought Franquemont and his men to the twin Wiederitzsch villages, 6 kilometres north of Leipzig, on the night of 15/16 October. The next day, while fighting raged north and south of the city, the division marched south to take up a position outside the Outer Halle Gate (also known as the Gerbertor or Gerber Gate) while the rest of 4th Corps continued on to Lindenau on the western side of the Elster–Pleiße river complex.

Franquemont's division played a useful but marginal role at Leipzig. On the 16th, while Normann's brigade was heavily engaged to the north, it held its position at the Outer Halle Gate until late in the day when Marmont personally arrived and requested support to cover the retreat of his defeated corps. The 3rd Combined Battalion thus advanced to the bridge over the Rietzschke stream but was not involved in the combat. The following day, Franquemont, fearing for the security of his position at the gate, sent two companies from the 1st Battalion to secure Gohlis on the left of the battalion at the bridge. The companies at Gohlis had seven men wounded in skirmishing with Blücher's troops, but Ney relieved the Württembergers with Poles of Dąbrowski's

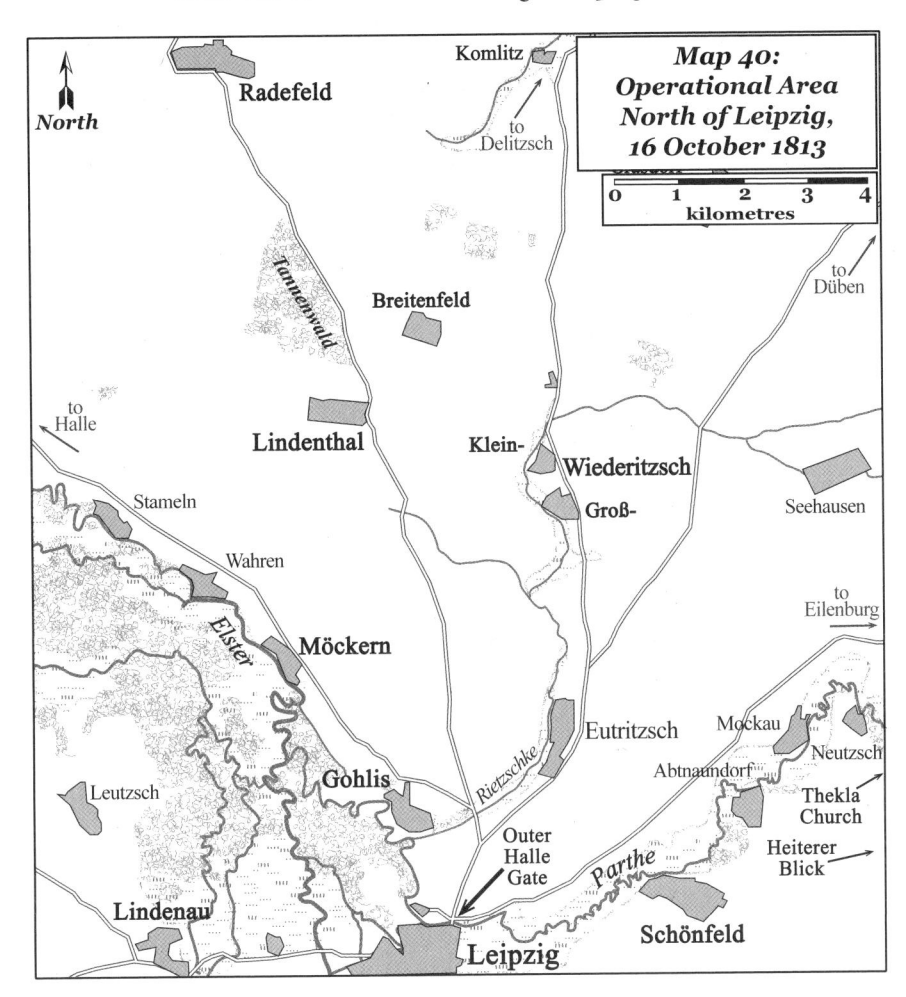

Grim October: From Wartenburg to Leipzig and Home 101

Map 40: Operational Area North of Leipzig, 16 October 1813

division and Franquemont withdrew to fortify the houses around the gate. Other than some incoming artillery fire, however, his defences were not tested and he turned the position over to Dąbrowski's men just after midnight to rejoin 4th Corps around Lindenau early on the morning of 18 October.

When Bertrand began his march towards Markranstädt, therefore, the Württembergers advanced as well. As a prelude, a small detachment of twenty-five Württemberg cavalrymen supported the French 13ᵉ Ligne in capturing Kleinzschocher to clear the corps' left flank, assisting thereby in the capture of some 600 Austrian defenders.[244] Later, as the advance progressed, Franquemont was assigned three French dragoon regiments to constitute the corps' rear guard. Despite the presence of substantial Austrian forces, the march was only troubled by some ineffective artillery fire and the Württembergers reached their bivouac site southwest of Lützen late that night without loss. Their repose was brief. They were on the road again at 1:30 a.m. on 19 October and later that morning, as doom was descending on much of the battered Grande Armée at Leipzig, the remnants of the Württemberg 38th Division crossed the Saale at Weißenfels to take up a defensive position on the western bank. This night march to Weißenfels 'surpassed all capacity', wrote Martens, 'drunk with sleep, some fell into the roadside ditches, the French dragoons, wrapped in their white mantels, swayed ghostlike to and fro on their mounts, our soldiers bumped groggily into one another'. On reaching their destination 'everyone collapsed as if on command and suddenly fell into the deepest slumber, fortunately we were not at first exposed to any enemy attack, no one could have defended himself, no picket could have been set'.[245]

The next several days were consumed in the confusion of the army's retreat. Other than brief brushes with Cossacks on the 20th and 21st, the Württemberg troops were spectators rather than participants in these actions. Passing over the Unstrut in the chaos at Freyburg, they had a final glimpse of Napoleon as Martens recalled:

> With the greatest perception and remarkable calmness Napoleon later directed this important crossing himself, in fortune and misfortune he was always the same, he mastered every emotion marvellously, the only difference was that in the first instance he dealt with his commanders in a friendly manner and in the other case in the rudest way ... It was the last time we were under his supervision.[246]

The ragged retreat rolled westward, the Württembergers guarding the corps' baggage train through Erfurt on 23 October to stop that night just east of Gotha. Here Franquemont sent a letter to Berthier formally asking permission to return to Württemberg. 'Guided by the intentions of my sovereign and considering that the debris of my division are more embarrassing than useful to the army, I believe it is my duty to request permission to take myself to the Kingdom of Württemberg where we have every reason to fear an incursion on the part of the enemy,' he wrote. In addition to these reasons, Franquemont believed himself under a shadow of French mistrust and, with the army on the edge of dissolution and Cossacks everywhere, he seems to have been motivated by rampant rumours not only that Normann had defected, but that his king had decided to align with the Coalition. Nonetheless, he closed with great courtesy: 'My regret at seeing myself obliged to separate from the French army for a time is softened by the conviction that the Württemberg division has performed its duties scrupulously during the course of the entire campaign and that it has found occasion during many combats to prove its devotion to HM the Emperor and King and its attachment to the French nation.' Even French general and historian Pelet, often suspicious of the Rheinbund troops, referred to the relationship with the Württemberg contingent as 'that noble confraternity sealed by the blood of the brave'.[247]

Franquemont's letter proved prescient. That very evening he finally received Friedrich's instructions to seek release from French service. Awaiting an answer from imperial headquarters, however, he held to his duty, escorting the cumbersome baggage column and halting just east of Fulda on the evening of 26/27 October. It was apparently here that a reply from Bertrand arrived. Bertrand did not specifically grant approval, but his chivalrous words implied an end to the alliance: 'Whatever may eventuate, I will keep good memories of the relationship I had with you, I hope that you will do justice to the feelings which have always guided me.' Bertrand also sent back all the Württemberg officers and soldiers who had served in his headquarters as guides, orderlies and couriers for the past several months.[248] Franquemont thus understandably concluded that he was free to leave. Reaching Fulda on 27 October, he passed responsibility for the baggage train to a French detachment and turned south for home.

The troops were naturally overjoyed at their release, but their separation from the French also had its sentimental aspects. 'We parted from the Italian and French officers, as good comrades, without rancour,' wrote Martens, 'we had, after all, shared joys and sorrows and all manner of hardships with one another for so long'. It was also a poignant moment for Amédée Massé, one of Bertrand's secretaries. After spending the campaign with the corps, Massé was travelling back to France in the company of the Württemberg contingent. 'We said a most heartfelt farewell,' he recorded, 'The Württembergers had conducted themselves so well with us, they had gained so much esteem and consideration from the whole French division that we parted from them as true brothers in arms'.[249]

Berthier had also replied to Franquemont's 23 October letter. His message expressed surprise at Normann's defection and stated that there was no news of Württemberg having changed sides. Regardless, he wrote, 'His Majesty does not wish to see the troops under His orders suffer for the conduct of their governments.' Franquemont was therefore to draw four days' worth of rations and march for Württemberg, 'but the sentiments of honour and loyalty require that you and your officers give your word on behalf of yourselves and your soldiers not to serve against France from now until one year hence'.[250] It is not clear that this letter ever made its way to Franquemont's hands, but whatever the case, within two months, he and many of his men would cross the Rhine to embark on a new campaign against their former French allies.

Of the nearly 11,000 officers and men who had set out from Württemberg only six months earlier, Franquemont brought back only some 1,300 fit for duty from the original division. A lone damaged 6-pounder cannon remained from the 18 he had had at the end of the armistice; 6 had been captured and the other 11 had been sent back as unserviceable or for lack of horses to pull them. His column also included a little over a hundred detached men from Normann's brigade who had joined him during the retreat (previously assigned to 6th Corps staff, for instance). It is impossible to track gains and losses with satisfactory accuracy (such as accounting for wounded men returned to duty or the sick who may have been evacuated to Württemberg), but Württemberg's case is notable for the lack of replacements and for the large number recalled during the autumn campaign. Friedrich claimed that he had withdrawn 3,000 men from the field and the figure may have been as high as 4,000. Battle casualties and losses to sickness, however, were high, coming to at least 5,200 of the division's men dead, wounded, captured, or missing from May to October. Although some doubtless deserted, a substantial number of those initially listed as captured or missing managed to escape and, like Unteroffizier Heere, made their way back to their units. Bertrand, for example, reported that some 500 had already returned in the first weeks following Dennewitz.[251] Nonetheless, the overall losses in men, horses, vehicles, guns, muskets and all manner of equipment had been significant. Württemberg would thus face serious challenges raising yet another army at the end of the year as demanded by the Coalition authorities.

Indeed, the kingdom's situation was changing rapidly as, simultaneously with Franquemont's actions, other momentous developments were taking place in Württemberg. On the same day that Franquemont sent his request to Berthier, Friedrich's foreign minister, Graf Zeppelin, concluded a military convention with Bavarian GL von Wrede who was marching north at the head of an Austro-Bavarian army to intercept Napoleon's retreat. Zeppelin hurried east the next day to find Metternich in hopes of arranging a pact that would bring Württemberg formally into the Coalition. Furthermore, on the 26th, when Franquemont was reading Bertrand's warmly courteous letter, GM von Walsleben – the same one who had roused Napoleon's ire in Russia in 1812 – set out from Württemberg for Aschaffenburg on the Main River in support of Wrede's army. Before outlining these events, however, the fate of GM von Normann and his brigade must be addressed.[252]

Soldiers who have Forgotten their Duty: Normann's Brigade at Leipzig and Beyond

'Nothing reliable is known about Normann's brigade', reported Franquemont on 23 October from his halt near Fulda, 'it is rumoured that they were captured, and that this may have been intentional'.[253] He was, of course, correct in his guess and the consequences for Normann would be severe.

Normann's 25th Light Cavalry Brigade was north of Leipzig with Marmont's 6th Corps in early October. Here they were heavily engaged on 16 October in the Battle of Möckern, a hard-fought subset of the larger Battle of Nations in which Blücher's Army of Silesia overcame Marmont's defences to press up to the very gates of the city. Although three of the Württemberg battery's guns had been disabled during skirmishing over the preceding days, these had been repaired and his brigade was at nearly full strength as far as its cavalry regiments were concerned with more than 900 officers and men on hand.

On the morning of the 16th, Normann was posted towards Radefeld with his brigade and GB Louis Jacques Coëhorn's brigade of the French 22nd Division, well forward of Marmont's main position between Möckern and Lindenthal. When Blücher's advance began around midday on the 16th, therefore, Normann was confronted by Langeron's Russian corps as it debouched through Radefeld, while Yorck's Prussians moved on Möckern and Lindenthal. Commanded by Oberleutnant Wilhelm August Fleischmann, the Württemberg battery opened up on the Russian columns, but counter-battery fire from Langeron's artillery soon forced it to retire. Indeed, as more and more Russians emerged from Radefeld, Coëhorn and Normann recognised that they were heavily outnumbered and would have to withdraw. However, they seem to have delayed the enemy until approximately 11:00 a.m., the Württemberg battery moving back by prolong (that is, the men pulling the guns with special harnesses) so as to keep up a steady fire. The withdrawal was made 'slowly and in good order' as Marmont later recorded, adding that the 'brigade of Württemberg light cavalry... also conducted itself with valour and courage' as it retired.

Under pressure, the brigade had several clashes with its pursuers as it fell back west of the Tannenwald (pine forest) towards Lindenthal. In one case, Normann's regiments repulsed an attack by Prussian cavalry by drawing aside at the last moment to unmask an infantry square that opened a heavy fire on the attackers; skirmishers in the woods and a nearby artillery battery (likely the Württemberg horse battery) joined in the discomfiture of the Prussians. 'This lesson served us well', wrote Wachtmeister Peter, 'the enemy now became more cautious and circumspect'. Somewhat later, Cossacks fell upon Fleischmann's battery when it was momentarily without protection. The gunners discharged a last salvo, but the battery seemed lost. Desperate but determined, Fleischmann galloped to a nearby battalion of French naval artillerymen and asked their commander to open fire on the battery's position. The unexpected volley scattered the Cossacks and the Württemberg gunners quickly returned to their pieces to chase off their attackers with canister fire. Its mission skilfully accomplished, the brigade re-joined the corps around 3:00 p.m. to take up a position behind Marmont's left wing southeast of Möckern. Lorge's 5th Light

Cavalry Division was deployed to their right, the French and Württemberg cavalry 'distributed by regiment along the entire line, 200 paces behind the battalions opposite the intervals, ready to throw themselves forward to profit from a success or to remedy some setback'.[254]

What happened next became controversial. Although Marmont was pleased with his Württembergers for their steady performance during the covering action from Radefeld to the Tannenwald in the morning, he later tried to blame them for the defeat he suffered that afternoon. In his memoirs many years later he described this withdrawal as 'the last movement of honour and fidelity of General Normann and his soldiers'. The time would have been around 4.00 p.m., before the Prussian cavalry attack that decided the battle. The vicious struggle for Möckern was at its height and Prussian infantry were stumbling back in disarray after their latest failed effort to capture the town. Perceiving this tempting but temporary target, Marmont claimed in his memoirs that Normann had refused an order to charge the fleeing Prussian foot soldiers. He thus depicted an evanescent moment of opportunity that passed owing to Normann's obstinancy. The marshal wrote that he then repeated the order, but 'instead the Württembergers charged a battalion of the French 1st Naval Artillery Regiment, throwing it into confusion. 'If the Württembergers had done their duty,' he concluded, 'a complete success would have been the reward for our efforts'.[255] Instead of emerging victorious, his corps was temporarily shattered and forced to retreat south of the Parthe that evening in great disorder.

There are several problems with Marmont's portrayal of the situation at Möckern. In the first place, his description of the sequence of events is inconsistent with all other histories and there are discrepancies between the memoir account and the report he submitted to Napoleon that night. In the 16 October report, he acknowledged that much of his own infantry was disordered and stated that it was being threatened by Prussian horse. To gain time for his troops to rally, 'I ordered my cavalry to charge that enemy cavalry to disengage the dispersed troops, but that cavalry, instead of going straight at the enemy, turned about and threw itself onto the ordered battalions so that they were overthrown.' His initial account thus describes an enemy cavalry threat, not an opportunity to destroy disordered enemy infantry. Furthermore, Marmont made no mention of dereliction of duty by the Württemberg brigade in the longer after-action report he submitted on 19 October or his summary account later that year.[256] Beyond the incongruities of Marmont's various accounts, a refusal to obey orders seems entirely contrary to Normann's personality and the previous performance of his brigade. Mounted combat was 'Normann's actual, natural element', recounted then Oberleutnant (later General) Franz Karl von Troyff of the Leib-Chevaulegers, 'He was a born cavalry general.'[257]

Troyff provided an alternative, and probably more likely, explanation. He recalled that the brigade became engulfed in a crowd of fleeing French infantry and swung about with their sabres to clear a path out of the tangle. There can be no certainty at this great remove, but it seems at least possible, perhaps probable, that this was the moment when Marmont sent his order to attack and that he misrepresented the jumbled mass of Württemberg cavalry and French infantry as a refusal to obey orders and a fatally false attack.[258] The officers and men of 6th Corps, including Marmont, had displayed tremendous gallantry, tenacity and skill during the battle on 16 October, but they occupied a second-best position and were outnumbered by an equally brave and competent adversary. Moreover, they suffered from several instances of extraordinarily bad luck (several ammunition caissons exploding simultaneously, for one) and from a recklessly bold but successful Prussian cavalry charge. Marmont's defeat can thus be attributed to these factors, not to the alleged failings of a single 900-man brigade.[259]

Whatever the case, Normann's men were soon in action again. When Yorck launched his desperate cavalry attack around 5:00 p.m., the Württemberg brigade charged into the vulnerable left flank of the lead echelon (Brandenburg Hussars). 'The enemy cavalry attacked us with great determination', wrote Major Friedrich Georg von Sohr, the hussars' commander, but were then taken in the flank themselves by the onrushing Brandenburg Uhlans forced back and 'thrown upon their own infantry and artillery'.[260] The Württemberg regiments were overthrown and caught up in the mass of men fleeing towards the bridge north of Gohlis in the general rout of 6th Corps. Pursuing Prussians were intermingled with the fugitives, riding alongside and between the guns of the Württemberg battery and even grabbing hold of Oberleutnant Fleischmann's coat. Fleischmann managed to free himself by striking his assailant with his knout and, astonishingly, the battery escaped with all its guns. As Peter remembered, the troopers were edging their way past a marshy spot outside Gohlis when 'the Prussian hussars partly caught up with us and demanded that we surrender, which we did not do; instead we dealt out some solid blows and, as they became convinced that we would answer their demand with sabre strokes rather than give in, they backed off from further pursuit'.[261] Collecting itself outside the Grimma Gate that evening, the brigade counted casualties of fifty-two men killed or wounded, while Fleischmann reported that his battery had once again suffered significant loss as two of its 6-pounders had been damaged and the howitzers had exhausted their ammunition.[262]

At some point early that afternoon before the devastating Prussian cavalry attack, Normann had a brief meeting with Franquemont near the Outer Halle Gate 'for the first and only time during this campaign'. Franquemont showed him the secret royal instructions from April and outlined the king's intention that the troops should return to the kingdom rather than crossing the Rhine if the French were defeated. In the self-justification he later composed, Normann dismissed these instructions as out of date and not applicable to him as he had not personally received a copy. At the time, however, 'this information left General Graf Normann visibly flustered and confused' according to Bangold, who seems to have been present at the meeting. Normann barely had time to scan the king's order or discuss their respective situations before events on the battlefront near Möckern called him away. He never saw Franquemont again. Normann would thus be on his own in determining how to handle his brigade over the coming days, but comments he made at dinner that evening suggest what he was thinking. A Württemberg-born merchant who was living in Leipzig joined Normann and his officers as they dined at an inn in the city that night. Despite the presence of numerous French officers in the dining room, Normann spoke 'loudly and blatantly' about the poor performance of the French during the day's battle and opined that 'it was no longer an honour to fight at their side'. He then whispered to the merchant that 'I would soon hear something extraordinary about him'.[263] If this account is correct, Normann had already made up his mind to defect before the combat was renewed on 18 October.

If, as it seems, Normann was indeed inclined to defect, there was no opportunity to do so the next day. Other than a brief cannonade in the morning, 17 October passed quietly for the brigade. Owing to the damage incurred on the 16th and the lack of howitzer ammunition, only two of Fleischmann's guns took part in the artillery exchange and one of these was disabled in the process. With three of the 6-pounders now out of action and the howitzer caissons empty, Normann ordered Fleischmann back to Leipzig with these five pieces to repair and replenish as best he could. The brigade thus remained between Schönfeld and the Thekla Church with a lone 6-pounder, while Fleischmann assembled the rest of his battered battery on the esplanade outside the Grimma Gate to await developments. This battery will appear again in the discussion of the Hessian defence of the Grimma Gate in Chapter 5.[264]

While checking his outpost line on the morning of 18 October, Marmont visited Normann's position northeast of Schönfeld. The battlefield was largely quiet, and the marshal instructed Normann to pull back slowly to the main defensive line if he came under pressure. Marmont also told him that the corps likely would withdraw through Leipzig to the west if the enemy had not attacked by noon. The Allied general assault that morning, of course, soon erased this option but opened the possibility for defection that Normann seems to have at least entertained already. In his subsequent declaration, he depicted his situation as dire. Influenced by Coalition leaflets that claimed

Bavaria had already left Napoleon and that Württemberg and Baden were in negotiations to do likewise, he averred that his officers had been badgering him for days to change sides. Having not heard from their king for six weeks, they concluded that their royal master had no means to recall them so they would have to act on their own 'to avoid more Württemberg blood flowing for a cause that had become foreign' to them. Added to this background was the grim military situation that morning. From his perch on the St Thekla knoll, he could see Allied columns forming up 'all around the city' and he conveniently interpreted Marmont's words about withdrawal as meaning that there would be no halting before the Rhine. 'The officers urged me anew, even the soldiers surrounded me with pleading faces,' he stated in his explanation later that year, 'The moment had thus come when we should leave the French.' The corps was attacked 'with overwhelming strength, and I with the entire brigade was cut off,' he told Friedrich that night. 'The victorious Allied forces advanced from all sides, and I could only save the rest of the brigade by going over.' He did send an officer to Franquemont to ask for guidance, but the latter general was already in Lindenau and too far away to offer cogent advice. Moreover, Normann did not wait for his officer's return before leading his men across to the enemy.[265]

Normann, however, does not seem to have told his men before defecting. As Wachtmeister Peter described the scene 'all the officers of the brigade were standing together as if they were receiving orders from the general; the brigade stood in platoon columns, the two regiments next to one another. All were still dismounted; I leaned on my sabre and watched the discussion among the officers and thought to myself: something important is being debated.' Marmont arrived and spoke with Normann, on which the brigade advanced towards a height 'crowned with cannons' and 'black with Cossacks'. Peter, preparing to charge the guns, issued careful instructions to his platoon, but instead of attacking, Normann raised a white sack and the brigade dashed forward to be received 'with open arms' by the enemy. 'I must frankly confess it was frightening for me; I thought everyone will accuse us of cowardice.' One of Marmont's adjutants, sent to recall the brigade, had been caught up in the false charge and was now considered a prisoner. Peter observed as 'he dismounted and stood next to his horse, one hand resting on the saddle, the other laid across his forehead, awaiting his fate'. Fortunately for the unnamed adjutant, Russian Lieutenant General Matei Ivanovich Platov, commanding the Cossacks in this sector, allowed him to keep his sabre and return to French ranks, telling him cheerfully 'I will let you cross over the lines – I will have you by this evening anyway!'[266]

In the same general area as the Saxon cavalry, but not in coordination with them, the Württembergers thus rode across to the opposing Cossacks around

10:00 a.m. and turned themselves over in Wallerstein's words 'not as enemies, not as friends, but as neutrals'. Greeted with schnapps and cheers, Normann was taken directly to Tsar Alexander and Kaiser Franz where he was granted permission to remain 'passive and armed behind the Allied armies' until he received instructions from Friedrich. Franz went so far as to tell Normann that he would be his advocate and protect him from negative repercussions. Normann rode into Leipzig with the tsar on the 19th, where he and Fleischmann somehow managed to find one another in the moil of men, horses and vehicles. After much exertion and tribulation, the lieutenant was thus able to re-unite the remains of the battery with the brigade outside the city that night.[267] With his command once again assembled, Normann headed for home, corresponding with Schwarzenberg and, minimally, with his king en route.

Normann was convinced that he had saved his brigade for the king. Others were not persuaded. Franquemont, for one, seems to have been unsympathetic, finding Normann's rationale weak, especially as his military situation was not as desperate as Normann later claimed. Chief among those disapproving of the defection, however, was König Friedrich. He condemned Normann's action as the worst sort of insubordination and had no interest in excuses or extenuations. 'The honour of the service must be preserved,' Friedrich told Zeppelin on 26 October, and any sacrifice was preferable to his perception of dishonour.[268] He then sent GL von Wöllwarth to arrest Normann along with the two regimental commanders and bring the brigade to Ludwigsburg just north of Stuttgart for public punishment. Arriving in Ochsenfurt on 12 November, the last stop before re-entering the kingdom, Normann thus found Wöllwarth but also a clandestine letter from his brother warning him that he could hope for no clemency from his king: 'Your safety lies in flight,' it concluded.[269] Following a stiff exchange with Wöllwarth, therefore, Normann called his officers together for what became an emotional scene with extravagant pronouncements verging on rebellion, penned a farewell to his men and fled for Saxony during the night. Proceeding with their journey, but now under a pall of doubt, the other officers and men were halted outside Ludwigsburg on 17 November. Arrayed on a parade ground surrounded by ranks of infantry with bayonets fixed and muskets loaded, the troopers dismounted to listen as a senior official read a proclamation personally drafted by the king.

> Soldiers who have forgotten their duty! His Royal Majesty has had to learn with deep dismay, as well as with the most righteous indignation, of the disgrace which you have brought upon the hitherto unsullied honour of His army by your shamefully leaving the ranks of the army in which you were ordered to serve to go over to the former enemy. You have been encouraged to this outrageous perfidy and breach of oath by your shameful

Chart 32: Renumbered and Renamed Württemberg Cavalry, 1813

Number/Name in March	Number/Name as of November
1st Cavalry, *Prinz Adam* Chevaulegers	1st Cavalry, Leib-Chevaulegers
2nd Cavalry, Leib-Chevaulegers	4th Cavalry, *Prinz Adam*
3rd Cavalry, *Herzog Louis* Jäger-zu-Pferd	2nd Cavalry, *Herzog Louis* Jäger-zu-Pferd
4th Cavalry, *König* Jäger-zu-Pferd	5th Cavalry
5th Cavalry, *Kronprinz* Dragoons	3rd Cavalry, *Kronprinz* Dragoons

leader and brigade commander, who misused the authority entrusted to him to bring you to an act whose consequences you did not know and who has compounded his crime by furtively fleeing.

There was more. In addition to forfeiting all awards and decorations they had won in the 1813 campaigns, the men were told that they were not worthy to serve in regiments that bore the king's name and that they would therefore be distributed to other regiments where they might endeavour 'to erase this shameful blot with your blood and again earn the honour to be called Württembergers'.[270] Disarmed and deprived of their mounts, they were then marched off to arrest in their quarters until further notice. Wachtmeister Peter and many of his comrades were incensed by this treatment, blaming the bureaucrats and rear-area officers of the court martial for the proclamation and protesting that it was unfair to impugn soldiers who were simply obeying the orders of their officers on the battlefield. Normann had only communicated his intentions to the officers, he objected; for all the soldiers knew, their general could have had instructions from the king in his pocket directing him to go over to the Allies. The episode thus left him, and likely many others, bitterly angry at the 'everyday king and despot' who tossed the loyal soldier 'here and there like a billiard ball'.[271]

For most, however, these penalties did not long endure. As a member of the anti-French Coalition, Württemberg soon discovered that its new allies demanded as much or more than Napoleon had in terms of men, horses and munitions. It thus proved impossible to dissolve and disperse the two offending regiments. Instead, they retained their basic structures and were simply degraded in status and deprived of their royal affiliations. The 2nd Cavalry, Leib-Chevaulegers thus became the 4th Cavalry, *Prinz Adam*, while the former 4th Cavalry, *König* Jägers, became the 5th Cavalry with no associated patron. The other three mounted regiments each moved up one or two numbers as shown in Chart 32. Friedrich would eventually restore awards and medals to their recipients, but Oberstleutnant Carl Friedrich von Moltke, the interim commander of the *König* Jägers, received the same punishment as Normann, and Prinz von Wallerstein of the Leib-Chevaulegers was only spared harsher treatment because of his family connection to the king. Both these young men, along with several others, soon left Friedrich's service to seek new careers elsewhere. Fleischmann, judged guilty of lesser forms of insubordination, was removed from command and installed as the most junior lieutenant in a different battery. Meanwhile, Wachtmeister Peter and his fellows of the new 4th Cavalry marched off for France four weeks later.

Normann eventually made his way to Vienna, but even the intercession of Kaiser Franz did not suffice to change the king's mind and the disgraced general lived a distraught and penurious existence in the Habsburg capital until Friedrich's death in late 1816. Kronprinz Friedrich Wilhelm, now König Wilhelm, permitted his return the following year but still denied him access to the court and a proper profession. He married and fathered two children before turning once again to a military life. Volunteering for the Greek War of Independence, he departed in January 1822 and died of typhus in November that year in western Greece at the age of 38.

Normann has been reviled as a villain for Kitzen and acclaimed as a hero for his decision to align himself with 'the good cause'. The Württemberg historians who have studied him most closely concede that his defection at Leipzig was a case of disobedience, a transgression in a strictly military sense. At the same time, they follow Bangold to stress his crisis of conscience and concur that Normann felt he had 'something to make good', that he knew he had angered his king by being too submissive to the French, especially in the case of Kitzen. Indeed, in a letter to his father in December after arriving in Vienna, Normann wrote that he had defected 'at least to show the world that under the changed circumstances I dared to answer for the Lützow affair, which would never have been possible for me while on the French side'. His sense of personal desperation and confusion was also evident in this letter: having fallen from the king's grace, 'I thus had nothing more to lose,' he wrote. At the same time, it is not amiss to ask if Normann was insufficiently firm in command. He was very protective of his soldiers ('they love me as a father') and he may have indulgently allowed a negative atmosphere to fester among his officers so that he was swayed by their importunities when the moment of decision came. The same letter to his father offers hints in this direction ('I gave in to the pleas of the officers . . .') and offers some corroboration of the merchant's recollection that Normann was already leaning towards defection on the night of 16/17 October: 'The officers and men became dissatisfied and no longer wished to be sacrificed in a cause that they would leave this very day.'[272] Indeed, the wording of Normann's justification memorandum suggests that he had decided to defect no later than the evening of 17 October, well before his battlefield meeting with Marmont on the 18th.

Whatever conclusion one reaches regarding Normann's motivations, the impact of his defection was local and tactical. Marmont had to adjust suddenly to the loss of his cavalry screen by calling his infantry to arms in haste and the lack of mounted troops deprived him of some tactical flexibility. 'I took up a new line ... and, after arranging my masses in chessboard fashion and lining their front with all my artillery, I waited for the enemy without anxiety,' he wrote in the 6th Corps journal.[273] Furthermore, the Württemberg brigade's desertion did not incite the sort of opprobrium that French memoirists and historians piled on the Saxons. Marmont, for example, did not even mention the incident in his report immediately after the battle and Napoleon later cited the king's condemnation of the brigade as evidence of Friedrich being 'an honourable exception' amidst 'the general disloyalty' of his Rheinbund allies.[274] Rather, Normann's action became an addendum to the larger Saxon treachery and stood in contrast to Franquemont's loyalty just as the fealty of the Saxon cuirassiers was juxtaposed with the 'treachery' of their countrymen.

The return of Franquemont's and Normann's troops did not mean that all of Württemberg's soldiers had come home. The tiny detachments in Danzig and Küstrin were still serving under French banners even as their compatriots were marching for the Rhine as members of the anti-Napoleon Coalition. They would remain in place until December 1813 and March 1814 respectively and their stories will be covered in Chapter 8 on the fortress war.

Wrede and Württemberg: Forcing an End of Alliance[275]

As Franquemont and Normann were marching for home, Württemberg was in the process of joining the Coalition. This transition would occur in a surprisingly short period of time, essentially from 17 October, while the principal armies were still grappling with one another at Leipzig, to 23 October and then to its conclusion on 2 November.

Friedrich had already attempted to establish tentative contacts with the Allies, specifically Metternich. Faced with growing evidence that his untrusted neighbour Bavaria would ally itself with Austria, he feared – quite presciently as events soon proved – that such an alliance would present a direct threat to his state. Friedrich's diplomatic strategy in late September and early October thus had two principal components. First, in his relations with Napoleon, he not only sought the return of his troops from Saxony but also indicated that he would have to turn away from France should an Austro-Bavarian army advance against his borders. This concern was very clear in the 3 October letter discussed above, the wording of which set the stage for his renunciation of the

Rheinbund. Second, he sought to re-establish ties with Austria through covert messages passed to Binder, the former Habsburg ambassador in Stuttgart. When letters, first from a prominent publisher and then from Zeppelin, failed to reach their destination, he sent the court's banker to Saxony in person under the pretext of arranging army contracts. In reality, this individual was carrying an unsigned letter from Foreign Minster Zeppelin to the Austrian government suggesting the renewal of ties. The banker departed on 11 October but was repeatedly delayed by Bavarian authorities and eventually forced to journey via Linz and Prague to reach Leipzig. He did not see Binder until 20 October, by which time his mission had been obviated by developments along the Bavaria–Württemberg border.[276]

Württemberg's speedy shift was accelerated by the march of events and especially by the march of General von Wrede. Appointed to command a combined Austro-Bavarian army of 55,000 men after the Treaty of Ried as recounted in Volume 1, Wrede received instructions from Schwarzenberg to march for the Main River, seize Würzburg and intercept Napoleon's retreat from Leipzig. Wrede, however, had grandiose ideas of his own. He saw himself called to raise Bavaria into the ranks of the first powers of Europe and imagined a league of south German states over which Bavaria would exercise hegemonic leadership. Against this backdrop, he would also use his army's advance to demonstrate Bavaria's value and sincerity to the Coalition while clearing away even the most remote military threat to his strategic rear. On his own initiative, he thus undertook to force his erstwhile Rheinbund allies in the southwest to join the Coalition. Württemberg would only be the first state subjected to the pressure he planned to exert.

What followed was a blatant exercise in coercion backed by military power in which the long-standing enmity and envy between Bavaria and Württemberg came to the fore. As his army neared Württemberg's borders on 17 October, Wrede wrote to Zeppelin telling the minister of the army's approach and asking whether the Württemberg troops would oppose or facilitate his further progress. This letter, presumptuous in tone, could only be seen as a challenge in Stuttgart and immediately aroused Friedrich's anger. Furthermore, messages from Württemberg's ambassador in Munich had come in earlier the same day relaying alarming hints from his recent interviews with Montgelas and Max Joseph. The kingdom's situation was desperate: with only some 9,500 recruits on hand, it could not defend itself, it could expect no succour from French forces or Rheinbund allies, and it had no diplomatic links to seek assistance from the major Coalition powers. Friedrich, however, who did not yet know the results of Leipzig, held out some small hope that his kingdom could adopt a stance of armed neutrality. He thus sought to gain time and Zeppelin's answer to Wrede was full of innocent evasions and equivocations. The letter found Wrede adamant and his reply to Zeppelin was framed as an ultimatum: his army would occupy and administer Württemberg like enemy territory if he did not receive a satisfactory answer by the evening of 23 October. In essence this meant that Württemberg must join the Coalition at once and would be allowed no time to consider this drastic change.

While Wrede's threats were making their way to Stuttgart, Friedrich sent GM von Neuffer, recovered from his wound at Bautzen, to Wrede's army with instructions to negotiate with the senior Austrian general but to avoid Wrede. On arrival, however, he was quickly delivered to Bavarian headquarters where Wrede brusquely dismissed him with further threats. This attempt to bypass Wrede thus only succeeded in exciting his disdainful determination. A Württemberg colonel who appeared shortly after Neuffer's departure received similarly harsh treatment. Wrede, who was prepared 'to obtain by force that which the Württemberg government may not wish to grant willingly', repeated the threat of 'sequestration and administration' of Württemberg as a conquered land and told the colonel that an Austro-Bavarian force could be in Stuttgart in three days to enforce his demands.[277] The curt conversations with these two officers therefore produced further ultimatums from Wrede. Meanwhile, tough exchanges with the Bavarian ambassador at court yielded neither relief nor even an extension of the deadline. Friedrich, sensitive to any perceived slight or intimation of subordination, was furious. Wrede's use of terms such as 'sequestration and administration' was especially galling. 'Even in the rawest days of the French Revolution, the commanders of the armies and the agents of the government did not allow themselves such speech', he told Zeppelin. Fulminations, however, would not solve Württemberg's security crisis.

Although outraged by what was perceived in Stuttgart as Wrede's peremptory, even insulting, demeanour, Friedrich soon concluded that he had no choice but to abandon all hopes of neutrality. The weakness of his own resources and the lack of reliable allies left him no recourse but humiliating submission. He therefore equipped Zeppelin with plenipotentiary powers and sent him hastening to Wrede's headquarters where the minister signed a military convention with the Bavarian general on the night of 23/24 October. By the terms of this agreement Württemberg immediately renounced its former relationship with France, withdrew from the Rheinbund and committed to attach a force of 3,000 infantry, 500 cavalry and a battery to Wrede's army. These troops were to arrive in Aschaffenburg no later than 30 October and thus marched on the 26th under Walsleben's command as noted above.[278]

It is not clear when Napoleon learned that Württemberg had fallen away. Zeppelin had presented a long note to Latour-Maubourg, the French ambassador, on 19 October and met him again on the 22nd before departing to see Wrede. Latour-Maubourg protested in vain, but his passports had already been prepared and he soon departed for France. At the same time, Friedrich recalled his ambassador, Wintzingerode, from Paris in a long letter full of complaints about the manipulative Montgelas, the 'naturally vacillating' Max Joseph and the haughty Wrede.[279] As for Napoleon, Friedrich had requested the return of his troops on 19 September, had outlined the possibility of leaving the Rheinbund on 3 October, and on 14 October had stated frankly that the moment had arrived when he would have to break with the Confederation 'to save my kingdom from certain destruction'.[280] As discussed earlier, however, Beroldingen does not seem to have found the appropriate time to deliver the 19 September letter, the fate of the 3 October missive is unknown, and that of 14 October seems to have been intercepted by the Allies. It seems that the emperor did eventually read the 3 October letter since he referred to it on St Helena; perhaps it was in the stack of delayed correspondence he received while in Erfurt on 23 and 24 October, perhaps even later.[281] For Napoleon and Berthier at the time, however, Franquemont's 23 October request for release thus constituted the first serious evidence that Friedrich had left the alliance (even though Franquemont himself did not have certain knowledge of the impending change at the time). It is an irony of history that Franquemont submitted his request on the same day that Zeppelin was meeting Wrede.

Württemberg thus shifted from an ally to an enemy of Napoleon in a series of hasty transactions the speed of which had been determined largely by Wrede's high-handed demands. König Max Joseph seems to have given little attention to relations with Württemberg until after the fact, but he and Montgelas approved, the king observing laconically that, 'My big neighbour only got what he deserved.'[282] Friedrich, on the other hand, was thrown into anxious despair, describing himself as only a 'titular king' after such ill-treatment by what he saw as the brash and pushy general of an overweening equal.[283] He would never forgive Wrede, and Württemberg–Bavaria relations would simmer with suspicions for years to come.

Friedrich, furious as he was at what he perceived to be arrogant Bavarian pretensions, now had to hope for support from the major Allied powers, especially Austria. The military convention was to serve as the foundation for a comprehensive pact with the Coalition and he had instructed Zeppelin to seek out Metternich and negotiate a treaty with Austria as soon as he was finished with Wrede.[284] Zeppelin left for Saxony on 24 October, only hours after signing the convention with Wrede, but armies and imperial courts were on the move in the aftermath of Leipzig, and he only caught up with his quarry on 1 November. Fortunately for Zeppelin and his country, Metternich proved amenable and the

Grim October: From Wartenburg to Leipzig and Home

two concluded a formal treaty of alliance on the 2nd in Fulda. Modelled on the Austro-Bavarian Treaty of Ried but not as liberal in its concessions, this document guaranteed Friedrich's sovereignty, promised compensation for any territorial losses, and allowed him the freedom to maintain his uncompromising autocracy at home. Agreements with Friedrich's nephew the tsar and the rather more sceptical King of Prussia followed later in the month so that Württemberg and its stern monarch were able to emerge from this tumultuous period with the territory, population, royal status and internal sovereignty granted by Napoleon more or less intact.

*

In reviewing Württemberg's military experience as a Napoleonic ally during 1813, the most prominent feature is the overriding importance of König Friedrich. Intelligent, observant and with a capacity for work that seems to have matched his enormous girth, Friedrich was closely involved in all military matters from promotions, assignments and the distribution of awards to scrutinising reports from the field for discrepancies. As such, he could be a generous benefactor as Franquemont experienced or an unforgiving taskmaster as Normann discovered. Just as he demanded unconditional obedience from his soldiers, Friedrich tolerated no disloyalty from his subjects. He abhorred anything that resonated of 'revolution' and had no interest in pan-German visions that threatened to infringe on his independence and sovereign prerogatives. Stein and his affiliates were anathema to Württemberg's monarch and the manifesto he issued to explain his detachment from Napoleon was entirely focused on the French emperor's alleged failure to protect his kingdom. He expressed a desire for peace which did not rely on 'the despotism of any single state' but had nothing to say about Germanness or a unified, federated German nation.[285] In many respects, Friedrich thus stands as the very archetype of the absolutist, particularist prince. Obstinate, touchy and prideful, however, his difficult personality and his unwavering insistence on his rightful place in the constellation of European powers left him few, perhaps no, friends among his fellow monarchs as the Rheinbund came to an end. He was able to reconcile with his nephew the tsar and Metternich found value in maintaining his state, but all hopes for aggrandisement in the post-war order were dashed and he was fortunate to retain what he had.[286]

Friedrich's army stands out for its professionalism and tactical competence despite being composed mostly of raw recruits and untested officers. The division brilliantly executed a crucial attack on the second day at Bautzen, excelled in myriad small engagements during late August and early September and fought well under trying circumstances at Dennewitz and Wartenburg. Dennewitz, however, was a special case. The division put up a stalwart defence north of the stream and conducted itself well during the initial stages of the retreat, but some units seem to have fallen apart as the afternoon merged into night. The same, of course, could be said of all the elements of Ney's army that day, French, Italian and German alike, with only the Poles as a possible exception. Most of the credit for the battlefield accomplishments and for restoring order and utility after the Dennewitz disaster almost certainly belongs to key senior leaders, Franquemont and Stockmayer above all. Jett, Spitzemberg and some of the regimental commanders such as Bismarck and Baur also distinguished themselves, but Doering's qualities are harder to gauge (some of the junior officers regarded him as mediocre which may be why Franquemont assigned him baggage-guard duties at Dennewitz).

Desertion does not seem to have been a major problem. Soldier attitudes ranged from anger at their French allies (some of which in the memoir literature may have been *ex-post-facto* colouration) to exaltation at victories and sorrow at defeats. Leutnant von Schlaich, for example, exhibited both regret at having to fight on behalf of a foreign power and exhilaration at battlefield success such as his 'victory was ours!' outburst in describing Bautzen. Nonetheless, except for a handful of former Mecklenburg and Prussian officers, few men left the ranks to join the Allies. Even among the small number of officers who did change sides, most had made formal applications for release. What Pfister termed 'rising doubt' was unmistakable, but from his review of 'all records and diaries' he concluded that this was held in check by 'a sense of duty and loyal adherence to the king's cause'.[287]

In this sense Normann's brigade represents an aberration, but the details are important. Other than its poor showing at Kamenz, the brigade had garnered praise for its actions and Normann was repeatedly entrusted with independent missions with attached French infantry under his command. The brigade had done especially well in the withdrawal under pressure on 16 October. The defection on the 18th seems to have been the result of the personal stress Normann felt under the perceived shadow of Kitzen: the biting criticisms from his king and the urgings of his young officers (the regimental commanders were 21 and 26 years old). If Wachtmeister Peter's depiction is accurate, the NCOs and soldiers were unaware of his plan when he led them towards the enemy that morning. The brigade was thus not representative of the rest of the contingent and the defection may not have occurred at all had a different general been in command. Other than Marmont's understandable resentment at Normann's final act, therefore, French commanders and comrades regularly found the Württemberg units to be competent and reliable assets.

Chapter 5

Baden and Hesse-Darmstadt: Fighting to the Last

'I completely understand the necessity to do everything I possibly can that might be required in the circumstances.'

Großherzog Carl to Napoleon, 10 February 1813[1]

THE RHEINBUND TREATY OBLIGATED the Grand Duchies of Baden and Hesse-Darmstadt to contribute a brigade each to the Grande Armée, 8,000 and 4,000 men respectively. In 1813, Napoleon placed both brigades in the 39th Division, initially a component of Marshal Ney's 3rd Corps under GD Marchand.[2] A volunteer of 1791, Marchand had served in Italy, Austria, Germany, Poland and Spain before being recalled from Iberia to participate in the Russian campaign, first as Jérôme's chief of staff and later as commander of the Württemberg contingent (25th Division). A competent veteran, he had gained the trust of the Württemberg officers and men during 1812 for his tactical ability, the consideration with which he treated the troops and, most importantly for not interfering in the contingent's internal affairs (promotions, discipline, and so on). The Badeners and Hessians would likewise feel fortunate to have Marchand as their commander in 1813.[3] As shall be seen, parts of both contingents would end up posted elsewhere, but the joint assignment to Marchand's 39th Division makes it convenient to address both armies in the same chapter.

Baden: 'Current Circumstances Require Efficacious Measures'

Baden proved to be one of Napoleon's most loyal allies. As with Bavaria and Württemberg, its ruler, Kurfürst Carl Friedrich, had concluded a treaty of alliance with the French emperor in 1805 and its troops had participated on the margins of the Austerlitz campaign. The dramatic expansion in territory (from 4,904 to 17,724 square kilometres) and population (from 200,000 to 920,000 subjects) that it received as compensation for its alignment with France that year sufficed to justify an elevation in status, and it entered the Rheinbund as a founding member in 1806 as a grand duchy. Some at court in Karlsruhe were disappointed that Napoleon had not made Baden a kingdom by adding parts of

Switzerland or other territory, but even the increase in size deemed necessary to justify a grand duchy would pose a daunting administrative challenge to Karlsruhe's small and outdated bureaucracy for years to come.[4] These challenges of governance were compounded by complex and bitter family politics within the ruling Zähringen dynasty and by the accession of Großherzog (grand duke) Carl to the throne when the octogenarian Carl Friedrich died in 1811. Carl, only 27 in 1813, was dissolute, detached and ineffectual, but some degree of personal admiration for Napoleon and practical fear of French power would keep him remarkably faithful to the alliance until well after Leipzig. Marriage to Stephanie de Beauharnais, Napoleon's adopted daughter, created another important link to France and to the emperor personally. Napoleon was fond of Stephanie and, though this union was far from happy, consideration for the grand duchess was a factor in the Baden government's decisions.[5]

Given the administrative confusion and the unseemly family squabbling in Karlsruhe, it is hardly surprising that Napoleon judged his new ally to be mismanaged and inefficient. Desiring a stable and reliable partner, especially in military matters, he thus interfered repeatedly in Baden's domestic affairs. Baden, with powerful France just across the Rhine, was in no position to resist. Moreover, like Montgelas and his protégés in Bavaria, a cadre of reform-minded statesmen in Karlsruhe, most notably Sigismund Freiherr von Reitzenstein, saw the French alliance as an opportunity to raise Baden to the status of a middle power, to overhaul the state's institutions, and to unify the disparate elements of the greatly expanded realm. Reitzenstein, for example, was convinced that the state was in danger of terminal decline and that the government therefore had to 'reconstruct the entire edifice on entirely new foundations'. Otherwise, he warned, Carl would become 'the last reigning prince of the House of Baden'. In some respects, reformers such as Reitzenstein *desired* Napoleon's irresistible intervention as the only way to overcome the labyrinth of impasses, intrigues and indolence in Karlsruhe.[6] Among other effects, French pressure and internal momentum led Baden to adopt much of the *Code Napoléon* as the basis for its legal system in 1810, a foundation that would remain in place until new reforms were enacted in 1899.[7]

The emperor, of course, paid the closest attention to Baden's military. He found the army's administrative apparatus decrepit and its field performance during the 1806–7 campaigns unsatisfactory. Thereafter the army underwent a dramatic increase in size from 3,000 to more than 8,000 men and was entirely remodelled with new conscription ordinances and French organisation, drill and rank insignia replacing its old Prussian routines.[8] In line with their French allies, therefore, each Baden infantry battalion came to consist of six companies: two elite (grenadiers and voltigeurs) and four line (fusiliers). The first units to be deployed in this new structure were two infantry battalions and an artillery battery that Baden was forced to send to Spain in 1808; unlike Saxony, Bavaria and Württemberg, Baden was not considered a buffer state against Austria and was too weak politically to resist Napoleon's unwelcome demand. Closer to home, the bulk of the army (the 1st, 2nd and 3rd Infantry Regiments, its one light battalion, a light dragoon regiment and one and a half batteries) performed with distinction during the 1809 war against Austria. In a similar configuration, this splendid veteran army gained renown in Russia (the duchy's hussar regiment replacing the light dragoons as the mounted component), especially for its role in defending the crossing at the Berezina. Russia, of course, destroyed the army. Of the more than 7,600 men sent east that summer only 425 effectives were on hand when the brigade collected itself in Prussia on 30 December 1812 (a loss of well over 90 per cent). The wretched survivors were 'weary, half-frozen, starving wanderers', recalled Stabs-Hauptmann Karl Friedrich Pfnor, 'it is impossible to say what we actually lived on in those last days'.[9] The contingent managed to preserve its flags, but beyond the appalling human casualties, it lost all its guns, most of its horses and much of its other gear as well. As a specific example of the material cost, the Baden brigade left behind 10 artillery pieces, 48 artillery and infantry caissons, 40 supply wagons (*fourgons*), and 3 field forges, not to mention more than a thousand horses.

Baden's field contingent for 1813 would be constructed out of the remnants of the Russian disaster, a large replacement detachment that had been marching east, and the depot units left behind when the brigade departed in 1812. It would be organised according to the same formula used since 1809: three infantry regiments, a light battalion, a light cavalry regiment and supporting artillery. The enormous difficulties in raising and equipping the requisite men and horses, however, meant that Baden, like Württemberg, would send its troops to the Grande Armée in two tranches. Though small, each of these was termed a 'brigade' at the time and it is convenient to retain this designation even though the larger, combined contingents of 1809 and 1812 were also described as brigades. The 1st Brigade and the cavalry regiment would depart in April and participate in the battles of the spring campaign. The 2nd Brigade would not march until August and would perform rear-area security duties until the two were finally united during the Battle of Leipzig in October (*see* Schematic 2).

With one regiment still in Spain, the Baden line infantry available for duty in Germany in 1813 was organised into three regiments, each of two battalions, each battalion composed of the six companies standard in the French system for a nominal field strength of 1,716 officers and men per regiment. In addition to white breeches or pantaloons and a white leather strap for the cartridge box, the men wore dark blue coats with regimental distinctions shown on collars,

Chart 33: Baden Units, 1813

Unit	Jacket colour	Distinctive colour
1st Infantry *Stockhorn*	dark blue	crimson
2nd Infantry *Graf Hochberg*	dark blue	yellow
3rd Infantry *Großherzog*	dark blue	rose
4th Infantry *Neuenstein* (in Spain)	dark blue	white
Light Infantry	dark green	black
1st Light Dragoons, *Freystedt*	azure blue	red

cuffs and, for the 1st Infantry, on the cuff flaps as well. All had scarlet coat turnbacks. The Light Infantry Battalion also consisted of six companies with a planned strength of 858 officers and men. Its uniform was similar to that of its line counterparts, but with the coat in the traditional dark, hunter green of light infantry trimmed with black distinctions, scarlet coat turnbacks and black leather gear. Like Württemberg, Baden discarded helmets for its infantry in 1813; all were equipped with black shakos instead of the Bavarian-style Raupenhelms they had worn during their previous campaigns with the French. The men of the replacement detachment, however, were still wearing the old helmets and would thus pose a vexing sartorial problem for the 1st Brigade commander during the armistice. In addition to its infantry component, Baden also contributed two half-batteries of foot artillery to the Grande Armée in 1813, but, unlike the infantry, the gunners seem to have kept their Raupenhelms. In most other respects, the uniforms of the artillerymen resembled those of the line infantry: dark blue coats with red turnbacks and black facings on collars and cuffs along with white leather gear and either dark blue trousers or breeches in grey or white. Train troops, on the other hand, received shakos but had grey breeches and similar dark blue coats faced with light blue. The only other unit to retain its helmets in 1813 was the light dragoon regiment. In addition to this distinctive headgear, the cavalrymen wore azure blue coats decorated in red at the collars, cuffs and turnbacks with white leather equipment and either white breeches or blue riding trousers with red stripes on the outside and black leather inserts. Organised into four squadrons, the regiment had an authorised strength of 549 officers and men.[10]

The units mentioned above constituted almost the entirety of Baden's army in 1813 and all participated in the campaigns that year. The only troops left behind in the grand duchy were regimental depots, the Leib-Garde-Grenadier Battalion, the largely ceremonial Garde-du-Corps and a new cavalry regiment, the 2nd Light Dragoons *von Geusau*. Having been destroyed in Russia, the

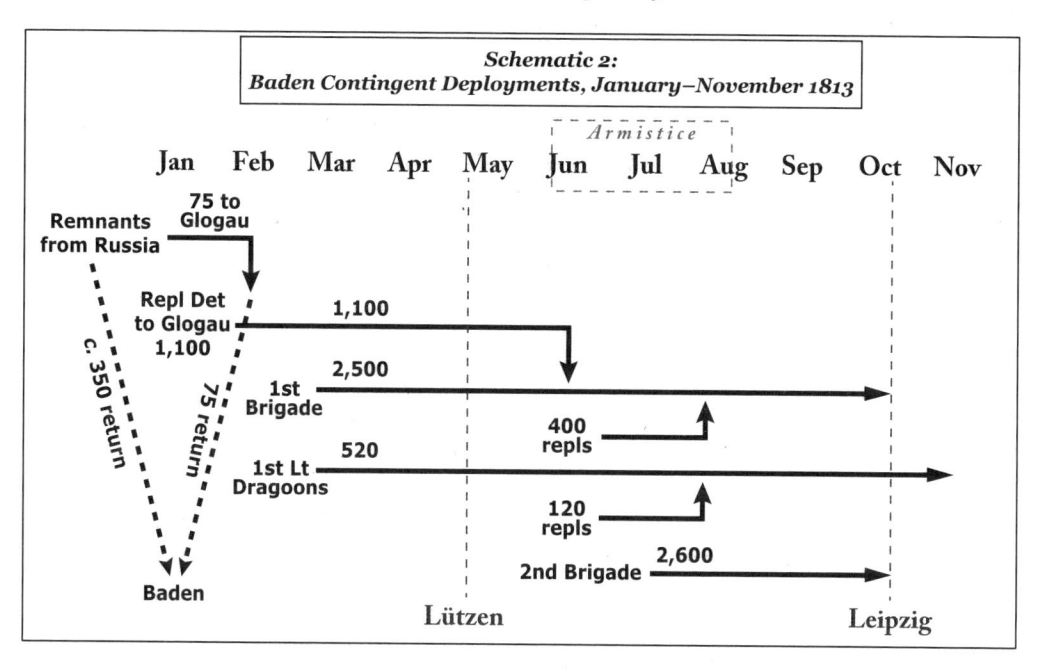

Schematic 2:
Baden Contingent Deployments, January–November 1813

[Figure: Timeline January–November 1813 showing Baden troop movements. Armistice spans Jun–Aug. Key movements: Remnants from Russia (c. 350 return to Baden); 75 to Glogau in February (75 return); Replacement Detachment of 1,100 to Glogau in February (1,100 return); 1st Brigade 2,500 from March through November (via Lützen to Leipzig); 1st Lt Dragoons 520 from March onward; 400 replacements in June/July; 120 replacements in June/July; 2nd Brigade 2,600 from August to Leipzig in October/November.]

valiant Hussar Regiment was disbanded in February 1813 to be replaced by the 2nd Light Dragoons but retaining General Karl Freiherr von Geusau as its proprietor. Its troopers were issued uniforms nearly identical to those of its sister regiment, but it would be repeatedly stripped of men to supply new squadrons and replacements to the 1st Regiment and thus did not represent a viable combat unit in Baden's last year as a Napoleonic ally.

As 1813 began, Baden's troops were scattered in several different locations. First were the ragged remnants from Russia collecting themselves in Marienwerder (Kwidzyn) on the Vistula. Most of these (approximately 350) soon headed back to Baden, many experiencing abuses from the locals in the Prussian towns through which they passed. 'As soon as we arrived in the place, the street boys chased after us and threw mud and snowballs at us as a welcome,' recorded the wounded Hauptmann Wilhelm von Cloßmann, 'The adults cursed and threatened us. We were received in a similarly friendly manner at the quartering office.'[11] As these survivors struggled homewards, some 75 relatively 'combat effective' souls under Hauptmann von Pfnor escorted Viceroy Eugène and a number of senior officers to Posen before marching on to Glogau. The men were then sent home, but Pfnor stayed on to make arrangements for a replacement detachment that had set out from Baden on 23 December.

This replacement detachment, the second group of Baden soldiers, numbered some 1,100 men and was originally intended to provide replacements for the three line regiments and the light battalion that had been sent to Russia in 1812. The destruction of the grand duchy's brigade in Russia and the return of its few survivors to Baden, however, had rendered the detachment's mission pointless. When the men arrived in Glogau on 7 February, therefore, they were immediately incorporated into the polyglot collection of French, Italian, Saxon, Croat and Spanish troops who comprised the city's garrison. As the troops were settling in their Glogau assignment, they received word that the War Ministry in Karlsruhe had decided to designate the replacement column as the new 1st Infantry Regiment *Stockhorn*. Confronted with the daunting task of rebuilding the army from scratch, the ministry reasoned that consolidating all the replacements as a single regiment made more sense than any other option. While the 2nd and 3rd Infantry Regiments were reconstructed in Baden, a new 1st Infantry thus came into existence in Glogau under Oberstleutnant Karl Freiherr von Brandt (or Brand). There were not enough men to fill out an entire regiment, so it was decided that this new 1st Infantry would temporarily consist of eight rather than twelve companies: all six companies of the 1st Battalion along with the grenadier and voltigeur companies of the 2nd Battalion. The four fusilier companies of the 2nd Battalion would be re-established in Baden and dispatched to complete the regiment later.[12]

The third group of Baden's troops were those in the grand duchy. The Garde-Grenadiers, Garde-du-Corps and 2nd Light Dragoons were considered outside Baden's Rheinbund commitment and thus did not participate in the 1813 campaigns. Its treaty obligations, however, still had to be met. Fortunately, each of the three line infantry regiments had formed a third battalion as a depot before deploying to Russia. These battalions were combined with whatever returnees from Russia were still fit for service plus a crowd of conscripts to rebuild Baden's infantry. Along with the partly mounted 1st Light Dragoon Regiment *Freystedt* and the 2nd Artillery Battery, they would become the foundation for the contingent Baden would commit to the Grande Armée for its last campaigns as a French ally.

They did not have long to wait. Napoleon's summons to action came in a 16 January 1813 letter to Großherzog Carl, emphasising cavalry as he did with his other German allies:

> The current circumstances demand that you take the most efficacious measures to re-form your contingent, reorganise your artillery, equip it and remount your cavalry. It will not be sufficient to have a regiment of infantry in the month of March if you do not include well-equipped artillery and a regiment of cavalry.

The emperor followed this brief personal note two days later with the lengthy 18 January epistle that went to all the major Rheinbund monarchs highlighting his concerns about domestic unrest and the 'evils without number and without measure' posed by Stein for the sitting German princes as well as the approach of enemy armies and his own preparations. Napoleon wanted the Baden infantry, cavalry and artillery in Würzburg as soon as possible. 'This is important', he told Carl, 'to protect the heart of the Confederation of the Rhine from Cossack patrols.'[13]

Despite the horrendous cost of the Russian campaign, Baden responded with alacrity to Napoleon's request. "I completely understand the necessity to do everything I possibly can that might be required in the circumstances and beg Your Majesty to be assured that I will not for a moment cease to direct my actions according to this principle,' Carl wrote in reply. 'As regards the reorganisation of my contingent,' he informed the emperor that he had enacted 'an extraordinary conscription' as soon as he received the first reports of his army's 'almost complete dissolution' and asserted that Baden would supply a cavalry regiment, four guns, and the 3rd Infantry Regiment 'no later than the first days of April' along with 'a reinforcement battalion to complete the 1st Regiment already in garrison in Glogau'.[14] Baden wrestled with all the shortages of men, horses and equipment that plagued the other Rheinbund states and France itself, but in Baden's case these challenges were compounded by the continuing presence of an artillery battery and its 4th Infantry Regiment in Spain (1,297 men). The return of this detachment was an important issue for Karlsruhe, and it would be a prominent topic when GM von Schäffer arrived in imperial headquarters as Baden's representative.[15] Unfortunately for the grand duchy, its efforts came to naught and the detachment with the Army of Spain would remain on the Iberian frontier until interned by the French in late 1813. Despite all the difficulties, Carl reiterated his commitment to the alliance in a 6 March letter announcing the imminent departure of his troops: 'Having nothing more at heart than to anticipate Your Majesty's desires in all things, I beg you to measure my zeal and my devotion for Your Majesty and for the good cause you deign to protect.'[16]

By dint of great effort, Baden was able to dispatch the first elements of its new contingent in late March. With four squadrons of 130 officers and men each, the 1st Light Dragoons set out for Aschaffenburg on the 23rd under the command of Oberst Friedrich Freiherr von Heimrodt,[17] and spent several days in that city before riding to Würzburg where they arrived on 3 April. Here they were matched with the French 10th Hussars to become the 3rd Corps' light cavalry brigade under GB François Garnier, Baron de Laboissière. The infantry and artillery headed for Würzburg several days later under GM Karl Freiherr Stockhorner von Starein, a well-regarded officer with twenty-five years of service who had distinguished himself in combat during the 1807 and 1809 wars.[18] Stockhorn's command, titled the 1st Baden Brigade, included the 3rd

Infantry Regiment *Großherzog* of two battalions and the four fusilier or centre companies of his own regiment, the 1st Infantry; these four companies were intended to complete the 1st Infantry, temporarily ensconced in Glogau, as noted earlier. Adding in a half-battery of guns from the 2nd Foot battery (four 6-pounders), the brigade amounted to 2,505 officers and men plus brigade staff.

Like Württemberg's GL von Franquemont, Stockhorn received a lengthy set of instructions when he set out. In contrast to Franquemont, however, Stockhorn was not issued secret orders on how to act if the French seemed about to drag his brigade across the Rhine or otherwise compromise them vis-à-vis the Coalition. Instead, his instructions stressed promoting the 'honour and advantages' of the grand duke and his house as well as the army, maintaining order and discipline, preserving the health of his men, and commanding his brigade in such a way as to earn the respect of the French, the other Rheinbund contingents, the local inhabitants and even the enemy. He was generally to obey orders from his French superiors but to object respectfully if he believed his troops were being misused and to try to keep the contingent together as far as possible.[19] For an officer of Stockhorn's experience, such instructions likely seemed routine and unremarkable, perhaps even mundane.

Whatever his thoughts on his orders, Stockhorn and his brigade left Baden on 29 March to reach Würzburg by relatively easy marches on 3 April with little to report. Here he found a Frankfurt battalion (*see* Chapter 7) and the lead elements of the Hessian brigade that were to be the other components of Marchand's 39th Division. Stockhorn's arrival in Würzburg thus makes a convenient point to pause and bring the Grand Duchy of Hesse-Darmstadt and its troops into the narrative.

Hesse-Darmstadt: Remnants, Recruits and Remounts

Großherzog Ludwig I of Hesse-Darmstadt was another of the Rheinbund's enlightened absolutists at the head of a bureaucratically modernising state. As Landgraf (Landgrave) Ludwig X, he had kept his lands neutral in 1805 but Napoleon's victory that year left him fearing for the existence of his monarchy and he joined the Confederation in July 1806 along with the other founding members. In addition to preserving his state, this move brought a tremendous expansion in land and population as well as his elevation to the rank of grand duke with the right to use the term 'royal' in matters of protocol (like Carl in Baden, he would thus be addressed as 'Your Royal Majesty' even though neither attained the rank of king). As the Hessian ambassador in Paris wrote, the monarchy had 'emerged happily from this crisis not only without loss, but with increased dignity and puissance'.[20] In the process, Ludwig transformed from a firm advocate of neutrality to one of Napoleon's staunchest allies.

One manifestation of Ludwig's loyalty to the French alliance was that the Hessian contingents sent off to the wars under the empire almost always exceeded the 4,000 men stipulated in the Rheinbund treaty.[21] These supplemental soldiers were dispatched not because of French demands but voluntarily because Ludwig believed that being forthcoming in military affairs served the interests of his state. 'The attitude at court during this period, that of his Royal Highness the Grand Duke and also the personal views of his ministers, was to want to be at the emperor's beck and call in all matters, to tie themselves to him as closely as possible,' recalled a former Hessian official.[22] Hesse-Darmstadt contributed its required contingent to the war against Prussia and Russia in 1806–7 and, like Baden, sent a regiment (*Groß- und Erbprinz*) and a half-battery to Spain in 1808. In 1809, however, the contingent that fought in Austria numbered 4,700, well over his treaty obligation despite the continued presence of the detachment in Spain. Similarly, some 5,000 men marched to Russia in 1812 under the command of Ludwig's fourth son, the 21-year-old Prinz Emil: the Leib-Garde and Leib Infantry Regiments along with a Provisional Light Infantry Regiment, the Garde-Chevaulegers and an artillery component. French commanders from Napoleon on down held the Hessians in high regard for their appearance, discipline and tactical competence; complaints about their performance or infractions were considered aberrations and not blamed on men who the emperor deemed 'brave and good soldiers'.[23]

Complimenting his favourable opinion of Hessian troops, Napoleon valued Ludwig as a monarch. Ludwig returned the sentiment, and the two men shared a degree of personal friendship reinforced by Napoleon's admiration of the intelligent and charming Großherzogin Louise, elder sister of Bavaria's Königin Auguste Wilhelmine and one of Ludwig's closest advisors. Ludwig 'impressed the emperor and instilled in him a high esteem', wrote one of Ludwig's officials, 'The grand duke, for his part, admired and revered in that person the greatest commander of the age.' Although Ludwig, like Carl, was disappointed not to have become a king, the personal relationship between the two men stood independent of politics. Ludwig, Louise and Emil would retain this friendly attitude and commitment through 1813 and beyond.[24]

As he considered Hesse-Darmstadt to be a reliable, well-managed state, Napoleon saw little need to meddle in the grand duchy's internal affairs as he and his representatives did in Baden. The army did learn French drill and adopted French rank insignia in 1810, but it retained a unique infantry structure through the 1809 war with Austria. In the Hessian system up to that time, the functional equivalent of a regiment was called a 'brigade' and consisted of two musketeer battalions uniformed in dark blue along with a single fusilier battalion in hunter green, each of these battalions consisting of four companies (*see* Chart 34). The

Chart 34: Hessian Units and Organisation, 1808–1813

'Brigade' Organisation to 1809

'Brigade'	Constituent units	Jacket colour	Distinctive colour(s)
Leib-Garde Brigade	Leib-Garde Regiment	dark blue	red
	Leib-Garde Fusilier Battalion*	dark green	red
Leib Brigade	Leib Regiment	dark blue	light blue
	1st Leib Fusilier Battalion*	dark green	light blue
Groß- und Erbprinz Brigade (sent to Spain in 1808)	Groß- und Erbprinz Regiment	dark blue	yellow
	2nd Leib Fusilier Battalion	dark green	yellow
Garde-Chevaulegers		green	black and red

Regimental Organisation in 1813

Unit	Jacket colour	Distinctive colour(s)
Leib-Garde Infantry Regiment	dark blue	poppy-red
Leib Infantry Regiment	dark blue	light blue
Provisional Light Infantry > Garde Fusilier Regiment	dark blue	red and light blue† > red
Garde-Chevaulegers	green	black and red

* These two battalions were combined to form the Provisional Light Infantry Regiment in February 1812.

† As the light regiment was still provisional at the start of 1813, its two battalions seem to have initially worn the facing colours of their former 'brigades': red and light blue respectively for the Leib-Garde and Leib Fusiliers. As the Garde-Fusiliers, the regiment's distinctive colour was to be red, but whether this change could actually be implemented is unclear.

Groß- und Erbprinz Brigade was restructured along French lines when it was sent to Spain, but the rest of the army only transitioned to a more conventional organisation in the 1810–12 period. This change, however, was occasioned by the exigencies of preparing for Russia and by decisions in Darmstadt, not by French pressure.[25] Furthermore, the army retained its tradition of four companies per battalion (not six as in the French system adopted by Baden). As a result, the Hessian infantry committed in 1813 would be comprised of three regiments (not the former 'brigades') each of two four-company battalions with an authorised strength of 166 officers and men per company. Two of these regiments were the reconstructed Leib-Garde and Leib Regiments, but the third was a relatively new creation titled the 'Provisional Light Infantry Regiment'. This had been formed in February 1812 by combining the two fusilier (light infantry) battalions formerly included in the Leib-Garde and Leib 'Brigades'.

Regardless of their origins, all three of the new regiments wore dark blue coats with red turnbacks and regimental facing colours on the collars, lapels and cuffs.[26] Breeches or trousers were to be white for summer and dark blue for winter with a stripe on the outside in the regimental colour and black gaiters, but it is not clear that all these niceties could be observed in 1813. Coats and legwear of the artillery and train troops were similarly dark blue but with black facings trimmed in red; additionally, the train soldiers wore coats of a simpler style. Infantry, artillery and train alike were issued black shakos for headgear. The men of the lone cavalry regiment, the Garde-Chevaulegers, on the other hand, had black leather Raupenhelms to accompany green coats with black lapels and collar fronts, red collars, red turnbacks and white decorative lace at the buttonholes. As was often the case with light cavalry, the troopers also had green or grey overalls with red stripes down the sides and leather inserts.[27]

The army's situation in late 1812 and early 1813 was not unlike that of its ally Baden: a replacement detachment was marching east; a small band of survivors from the Russian campaign was heading west; and the authorities in the grand duchy were scrambling to re-create an army in haste with inadequate resources. A major difference in Hesse's case was that 1812 represented a double disaster as its detachment in Spain, the *Groß- und Erbprinz* Regiment and a half-battery, had been captured in the fall of Badajoz in July that year; a mere 220 returned to Darmstadt in October. As for the troops in Russia, the Garde-Chevaulegers Regiment, after a gallantly self-sacrificing performance at the Berezina, retreated to Marienwerder with 2nd Corps. Its 88 survivors were released to return to Darmstadt on 10 January.[28] Most of the artillery battery was sent to Danzig while the remnants of the infantry and one gun withdrew to Königsberg on 30 December 1812 and left that city for Elbing on 1 January 1813. After several days in Elbing, they were ordered to Sommerau (Ząbrowo) as a flank guard (*see* Map 26). Here they were attached to the remains of the Imperial Guard and marched off with the French to Dirschau (Tczew) where their commander, Prinz Emil, and all excess officers and NCOs received orders to return to Darmstadt.

Remaining behind as part of GD Roguet's French Guard Division were 512 Hessians, all that were left fit for duty from the brigade of 4,500 or so infantry and artillery soldiers who had begun the war. Formed into a Provisional Battalion under Oberst Ernst Ludwig von Schönberg, they would march with Roguet's guardsmen for the next two months. The five guns and tiny residue of the artillery battery likewise left Danzig for home. To their everlasting pride, the gunners had managed to bring all six guns (including the one left behind with the Provisional Battalion) out of the chaos and misery of the Russian war.

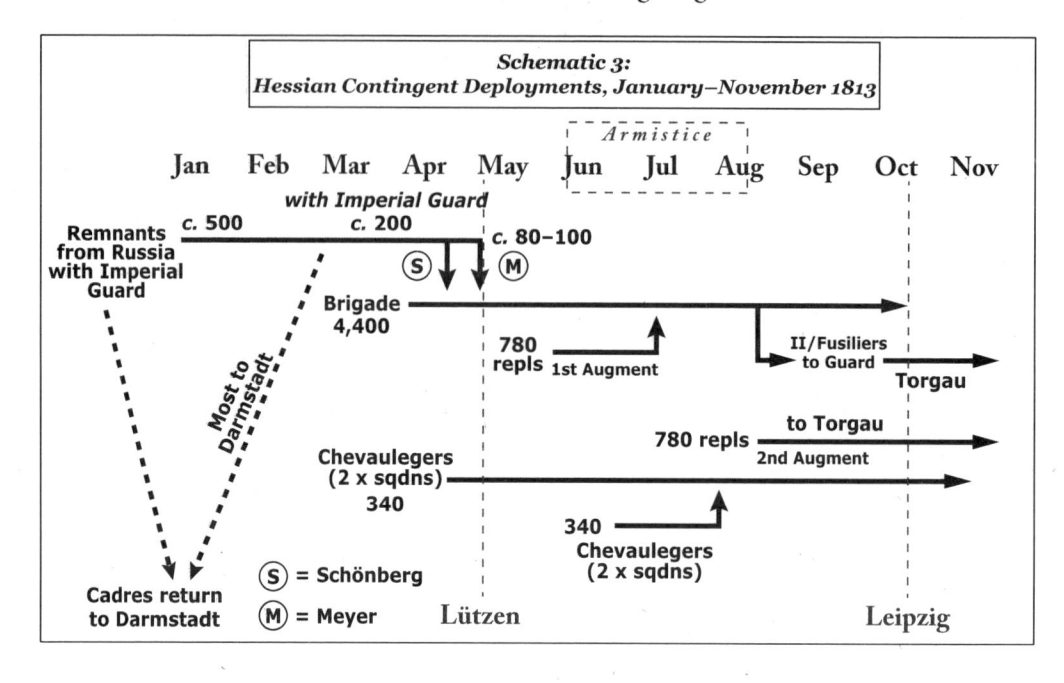

Schematic 3: Hessian Contingent Deployments, January–November 1813

Armistice

| | Jan | Feb | Mar | Apr | May | Jun | Jul | Aug | Sep | Oct | Nov |

- **Remnants from Russia with Imperial Guard** — c. 500 — with Imperial Guard — c. 200 — c. 80–100
- (S) = Schönberg
- (M) = Meyer
- Most to Darmstadt
- Cadres return to Darmstadt
- Brigade 4,400
- 780 repls 1st Augment
- II/Fusiliers to Guard → Torgau
- Chevaulegers (2 x sqdns) 340
- 780 repls 2nd Augment → to Torgau
- 340 Chevaulegers (2 x sqdns)
- Lützen
- Leipzig

When the Provisional Battalion set out from Dirschau with the Guard Division on 13 January as part of Viceroy Eugène's retreat to Posen, the task of rear guard was allotted to Hauptmann Karl Bernhard Meyer with 100 men from the Provisional Light Infantry Regiment. It was hoped he could also serve to escort the artillery from Danzig. With masses of Russians approaching, however, Meyer could not think of extended resistance and marched out of the town around midday in closed columns to follow the main body. He soon found himself forced to halt and fire repeatedly to hold off the Cossacks swarming about his little command. His pursuers called out to the Hessians to surrender and even sent a local civilian to convey a promise of lenient treatment if they gave up. Meyer and his men, however, were not persuaded. Indeed, at one stage late in the day, when the Cossacks had shied away from charging, he had his men stand with their muskets at their feet and urged them to mock their foes with laughter and insults. The Cossacks returned to the attack one last time but were met with a firm blast of musketry and finally abandoned the chase. Meyer's company thus continued on its way unmolested having refused to surrender even though temporarily surrounded and cut off from their comrades. Other examples of this sort of determination will emerge as the narrative proceeds.

The Hessian Provisional Battalion remained with the Imperial Guard Division during the painful withdrawal west of the Elbe. Arriving in Leipzig in early March, the Leib-Garde and Leib elements were sent home under Oberst von Schönberg, leaving only the troops from the Provisional Light Infantry

Regiment, perhaps 200 officers and men organised into two companies. Still known as 'the Hessian Battalion', these two companies were present at the Battle of Möckern east of Magdeburg on 3–5 April but remained in reserve with the Guard and were not engaged. Another reduction occurred on 10 April when the miniature 'battalion' shifted back across the river to a position between Magdeburg and Leipzig: most of the remaining troops and the lone cannon were called west to join a light infantry replacement detachment that had been sent from Darmstadt along with the rest of the resurrected Hessian contingent. Left behind with the Guard was a company of some 80–100 men under Hauptmann Meyer. This tiny remnant will re-enter the story on the eve of Lützen.[29]

In the meantime, the grand duchy was hastening to respond to Napoleon's demand for troops. Motivated by alliance loyalty, faith in Napoleon's genius and a determination that the grand duchy's sacrifices of 1812 not be forgotten in the new crisis, there was no question or hesitation.[30] 'It is my greatest ambition to gain Your Majesty's approval through my zeal and invariable devotion, and I flatter myself that Your Majesty is satisfied with the behaviour of my troops,' Ludwig wrote on 4 January.[31] He had already issued an order to rebuild his army on 1 January even before Napoleon's call to arms and the first new troops – the replacement detachment of two battalions for the Provisional Light Infantry Regiment and three guns – were thus able to depart on 26 February. They reached Würzburg in early March and remained there for nearly a month before shifting northeast to Königshofen (now Bad Königshofen) to make space for more units arriving around Würzburg. As the first units to depart, these two light battalions had drawn on the best of the men in the depots and included a significant number who had volunteered for field service. In addition to 500 men supplied by the depot of the captured *Groß- und Erbprinz* Regiment, each of the other two regimental depots had provided 125.[32] This measure, while useful as a means to generate new field troops quickly, meant that the manpower reserves of the Leib and Leib-Garde Regiments were seriously depleted just when they too would need to refill their ranks with men who had at least a modicum of familiarity with soldierly duties.

Ludwig wanted the rest of his troops to be ready by 26 March, but the other two regiments experienced severe difficulties preparing for the new campaign. The commander of the Leib-Garde Regiment, overwhelmed by the challenges of getting his men in shape within the stipulated time period, wrote to the war ministry to request a delay. 'Military history will be hard pressed to provide an example of a regiment being constructed from scratch in such haste with raw troops and led against the enemy,' he wrote. The grand duke, however, was not interested in the colonel's troubles: 'All that is contained in the report is well known to me. All obstacles will be overcome through tireless energy

Chart 35: Rheinbund Troops in 3rd Corps, mid-April 1813

		Bns/sqdns	Present under arms
39th Division	*GD Marchand*		
1st Brigade (Baden)	*GM von Stockhorn*		
1st Infantry, *Stockhorn*		4 companies	684
3rd Infantry, *Großherzog*		2	1,692
Foot Artillery Half-Battery		4 × 6-pdr	129
Attached:			
2nd Frankfurt Battalion	*Maj. Unkelhäuser*	1	692
2nd Brigade (Hessian)	*GL Prinz Emil*		
Leib Infantry Regiment		2	1,312
Leib-Garde Infantry Regiment		2	1,524
Provisional Light Infantry Regiment		2	1,427
Foot Artillery Battery		6 × 6-pdr, 2 × howitzer	149
Total Baden			2,505
Total Frankfurt			692
Total Hessian			4,412
Division total			7,609

Notes: Baden brigade staff not included; Hessian figures include 183 regimental staff. In the Provisional Light Infantry Regiment the 1st Battalion was derived from the former Leib-Garde Fusiliers, the 2nd from the former Leib Fusiliers.

3rd Corps Light Cavalry Brigade *GD Kellermann, GB Laboissière*

	Bns/sqdns	Present under arms
10th French Hussars	3	717
1st Baden Light Dragoons, *Freystedt*	4	c. 520
Brigade total		c. 1,237

Note: An additonal 569 French hussars were listed as en route in the 4th and 5th Squadrons. The 15 April French 'Situation' included the Hessian Garde-Chevaulegers with the corps' light cavalry, indicating a planned but not realised concept.

Sources: GLK, 8/4336; HStAD Best. G 61 N2. 28/3, Feldzug 1813, Band 2; SHD, 2C706; Bray, p. 35.

---

and exertion in service, and this is certainly what I expect from all my officers. The departure remains set for 26 March.'[33] Several expedients were employed to speed training and mobilisation. Privates were pulled from the *Groß- und Erbprinz* Regiment's depot, for instance, given promotions to corporal and assigned to new units, while older drill sergeants, who might not be fully fit for campaigning, were temporarily detailed to accompany their battalions for the first few weeks to ensure proper instruction of the fresh recruits. In some cases, teenage boys were appointed as new officers. One such was Christian Conrad Frey, a cadet in the Leib-Garde Regiment who became an instant lieutenant though not yet fifteen years old. A degree of delay was inevitable, but these measures sufficed to put the other two infantry regiments, four more guns and the requisite transport on the road to Würzburg between 2 and 7 April. The light infantry having shifted northeast to Königshofen in late March, the rest of the Hessian infantry and artillery was assembled around Würzburg by 11 April.[34] Here they were duly incorporated into Marchand's 39th Division as its 2nd Brigade.[35] The French ambassador in Darmstadt could thus report with some satisfaction that 'the Hessian contingent has been made ready with a speed that is truly prodigious'.[36]

Including the Provisional Light Infantry Regiment along with the men and one gun of Schönberg's Provisional Battalion returning from Russia, Hesse's contingent in Ney's 3rd Corps numbered nearly 4,500 combatants in three infantry regiments, an artillery battery of eight pieces (six 6-pounders and two howitzers) plus Hauptmann Meyer's company with the Imperial Guard. The Garde-Chevaulegers Regiment, however, was experiencing enormous difficulties in mobilising. Napoleon, as he had in 1812, offered to fund the doubling of the regiment to 1,000 troopers, but there were simply not enough suitable horses or qualified officers and men. Indeed, progress was so slow that the regiment would have to be sent out in two batches. The first two squadrons would not leave the grand duchy until 23 April and would serve separately from the rest of the contingent, initially with Marmont's 6th Corps. The second two squadrons would not reach the theatre of war until the summer. The specifics of the regiment's history will be examined later, but it is useful to note at this point that when the cavalry is added to the total Hessian contribution, the grand duchy had once again exceeded its commitment to Napoleon by approximately 25 per cent, that is, by an extra 1,000 men under arms.[37] As in the past, this was a voluntary initiative by Ludwig rather than a demand from the French.

The Spring Campaign: Glories, Privations and Long Marches

By the time the Hessians reached Würzburg, the Baden brigade had already departed for Saxony, and, after a few days, the Hessians moved on as well, picking up the Light Regiment at Königshofen as they slowly made their way eastwards. The young Baden and Hessian troops trained and organised as they moved. They not only practised basic drill, but such small unit tactics as passing defiles, forming advance and rear guards, march discipline and outpost duties. The Hessian drillmasters departed on 18 April before their contingent moved on from Würzburg, so these training tasks fell to the regular officers and

NCOs assigned to the contingent's battalions. As they cautiously shifted east into the unknown, the Hessians met up with Oberst von Schönberg and the light infantry elements of the Provisional Battalion that had survived Russia (not including Meyer's company). Schönberg thus assumed his proper role as commander of the Provisional Light Infantry Regiment at Meiningen on 23 April. At Ilmenau the next day, undeterred by snow squalls and the travails his other men had experienced, Schönberg formed the entire regiment up on parade, incorporated the returnees from Russia into the ranks, and continued the march east.[38] Taking various routes, all the 39th Division's components – Baden, Hessian and Frankfurt – were finally united at Jena on the 27th.

During the march to Jena, the Hessian units had been, technically at least, under Baden GM von Stockhorn's orders. At Hessian request, however, Berthier instructed Marchand to place all the Hessians under Prinz Emil as 'These troops will serve better, and the prince will be more satisfied.' These same orders assigned the Frankfurt battalion to Stockhorn's brigade.[39] When Emil arrived in Jena on the evening of 26 April, therefore, he was installed as the contingent's commander. Not yet 23 years old, Emil was Ludwig's fourth son. He had already led the Hessian troops through the horrors of the Russian campaign, earning the respect and affection of his men for his courage, stamina and willingness to share their hardships. Napoleon had come to know and respect Emil when he was attached to imperial headquarters during the 1809 war and his paternal fondness for the young prince only increased during 1812. As Maret informed the court in Darmstadt in November: 'the emperor, satisfied with the fine conduct of the Hessian troops and perfectly content with that of Prince Emil, has decided to unite these six battalions under His Grace's command and place them in the Imperial Guard'. In addition to praise from the French and his own troops, Emil's father rewarded him with a promotion to *General-Leutnant*. Despite the Russian experience and in contrast to other young scions of Rheinbund ruling families such as Bavaria's Ludwig, Württemberg's Friedrich Wilhelm or his own eldest brother Ludwig, Emil remained an admirer of Napoleon and, like his father, stood high in the emperor's favour.[40]

Though perhaps not as dire as suggested by Franquemont's disparaging remarks (*see* Chapter 4), desertion nagged at all three German contingents in the 39th Division. Worst was the Frankfurt battalion (*see* Chapter 7), but at least 50 men were absent from the ranks of the Hessian Leib Regiment by mid-April and even the relatively select Hessian light infantry lost 32 as it moved northeast from Würzburg in late March. Although losses to desertion may have been lower in the Baden continent, Stockhorn reported that 'the number of missing in general is significantly higher than I had expected'. He hoped, however, that the situation would soon improve.[41] Comprehensive and consistent figures are

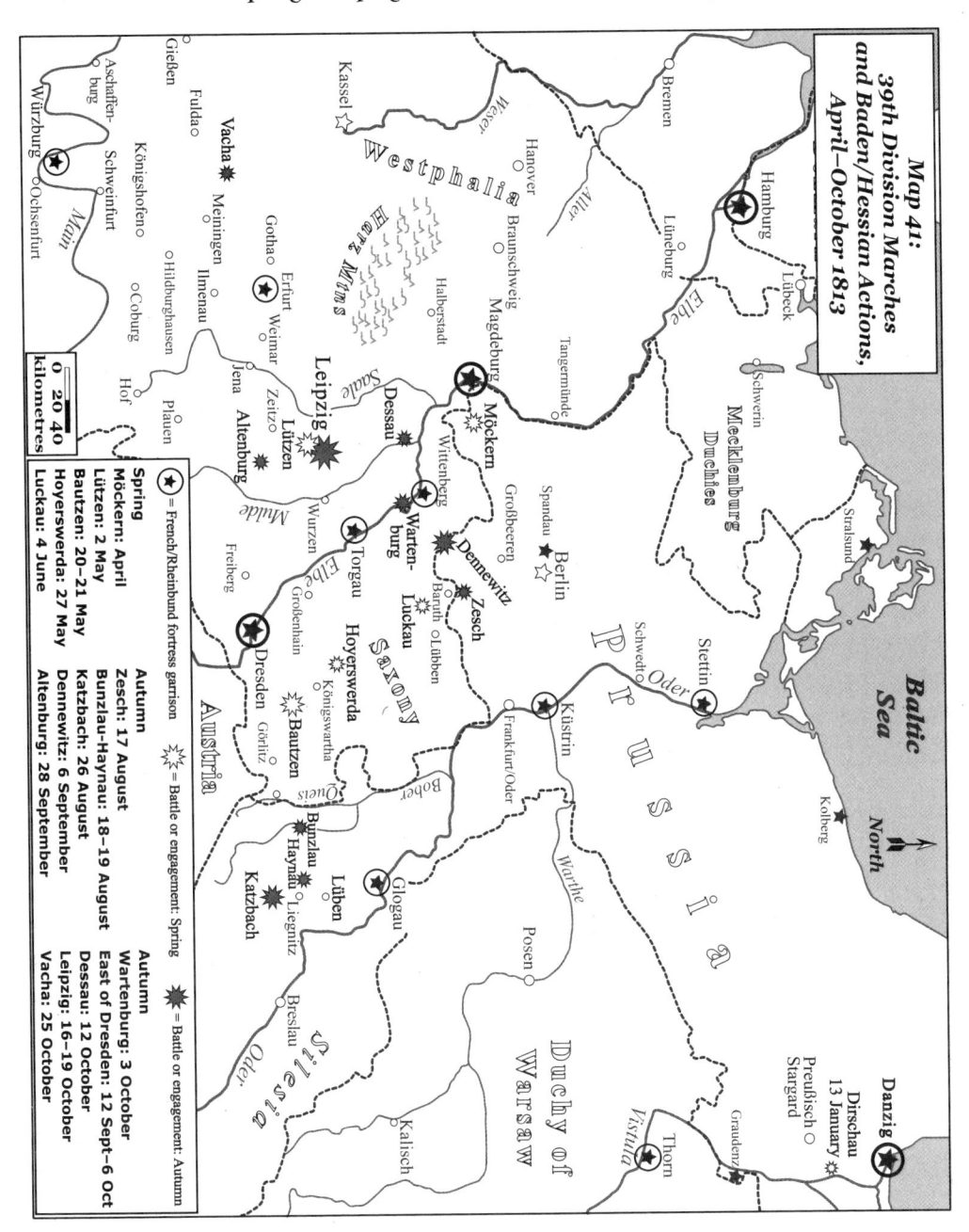

The Spring Campaign: Glories, Privations and Long Marches 135

not available to track desertion over time, but the patchy data suggest that the desertion rate for the Baden and Hessian troops ranged between 2 and 5 per cent of total strength at any particular point in time, hardly debilitating numbers. As discussed below, the number of missing (and thus likely deserting) would spike at Lützen but would then settle back to single-digit percentages for these two contingents until the very end of the autumn campaign. Stockhorn's hope would thus prove an accurate prediction and the following observations from Martin Carl Ignaz Kösterus of the Hessian II/Leib-Garde help illuminate the rise and decline of this phenomenon:

> As was later the case with the other troops, so earlier with these two battalions [the light infantry], the negative impression created by the gloomy rumours spread by the local inhabitants regarding the state of affairs gradually became widely felt and serious desertion occurred. Later, when marching into Saxony, the soldiers were practically harangued about whether they were not ashamed to be fighting against Germans, the Prussians are Germans too, etc., which, however, one must admit, made little impression as political views no longer thinned our ranks once those despicables who had deserted out of fear were gone.[42]

If some took opportunities to desert, others were already in action. Along with GD Souham's 8th Infantry Division, Laboissière's light cavalry brigade formed the 3rd Corps' advance guard. The Baden Light Dragoons thus scuffled with Prussian cavalry as the lead elements of the corps approached Weimar on the afternoon of 19 April. Their opponents were a squadron of the 1st Silesian Hussars who withdrew after a brief but intense clash in which both sides (unsurprisingly) claimed to have held the upper hand. Other than being the first engagement for the Baden horsemen, this episode was notable for Major Franz von Blücher, the general's son, taking a sabre wound to the face during the fighting.[43] As Napoleon's offensive gathered momentum, the 1st Light Dragoon Regiment was involved in skirmishing when Souham pushed into Weißenfels on 30 April and it came under artillery fire but was not engaged when the French pressed west towards Lützen and Leipzig on 1 May. Coming up, the 39th Division was harassed by Cossacks as it moved in battalion squares to a supporting position under Napoleon's direction but was not otherwise involved in the combat. The Hessians, however, had the pleasant surprise of coming upon Hauptmann Meyer's company of the Light Infantry Regiment as they passed near the Imperial Guard. This meeting seems to have provided an opportunity for Prinz Emil to renew an earlier request to have the company returned to his command, a request that would be granted the following day.

With the engagement over, Marchand's division was establishing itself east of Weißenfels when new orders arrived at 9:00 p.m. Given the uncertainty of the enemy situation, the division was to protect a bridge on the highway to Leipzig not quite 3 kilometres northeast of Lützen. This move entailed a 15-kilometre night march after which elements of the Hessian Light Infantry Regiment conducted a foot reconnaissance to the northeast and east to locate enemy outposts; these men only returned to their campfires in the earliest hours of the morning. Ney's four French divisions, on the other hand, settled in around Kaja, Rahna, Großgörschen and Kleingörschen, the area around this last village also serving as the bivouac for the French hussars and Baden Light Dragoons. Unaware that the Allied army was within striking distance, 3rd Corps took a casual approach to security and would suffer an unpleasant surprise as a result.

Combat and Confusion at Lützen

The morning of 2 May thus found the 39th Division at their post northeast of Lützen on the road to Leipzig. Around 10 o'clock, Napoleon, Ney and a large entourage appeared from Lützen, riding towards Leipzig escorted by the Guard cavalry. Napoleon was in an upbeat mood. He exchanged a few friendly words with Stockhorn, asked his typically detailed questions about the men and 'seemed very satisfied' when he rode on a short time later.[44] As the emperor's cavalcade moved on, Marchand's Germans set about preparing their midday meals. Around noon, however, the rumble of artillery fire began to roll up from the southeast, first a few individual shots then entire salvos. Urgent orders soon called the division to battle, the sudden rattle of drums and blare of signal horns surprising the soldiers so that 'a dreadful confusion developed in the bivouacs and on the highway' as the men hastened to empty their kettles, gather their gear and join the columns forming on the road. Many who had been out foraging or who took too long to ready themselves were left behind as Marchand set the division marching as soon as it was more or less assembled.[45]

The division's destination was the small village of Meuchen, about 2.5 kilometres north of Kleingörschen, the heart of the brutal struggle that was just opening. Passing the encampments of the Imperial Guard as they marched, the Hessians again encountered Meyer's company and this time the men were released to Emil's control. 'The division had just marched off as we reached it in a forced march and received the order to join our companies,' wrote Leutnant Georg Franz Schmidt of Meyer's company, 'this took place during the march' just before the division swung to its left off the highway. These 80 or so sunburned veterans of Russia were rapidly distributed among the Light Infantry Regiment's companies, creating a stark contrast with the hundreds of fresh-faced young recruits of the rebuilt contingent but providing a solid core of experience that would serve the unit well. While his men were welcomed, Meyer himself was under a cloud. He seems to have been rather a volatile individual and had been deprived of his sword as punishment for threatening his battalion commander with his pistol in an altercation over an incident that had occurred months earlier during the Russian campaign. He remained with

Map 42: The 39th Division at Lützen, 2 May 1813

1: First failed attack.
2: Hessian Light Infantry covers artillery.
3: Frankfurt battalion with two guns.

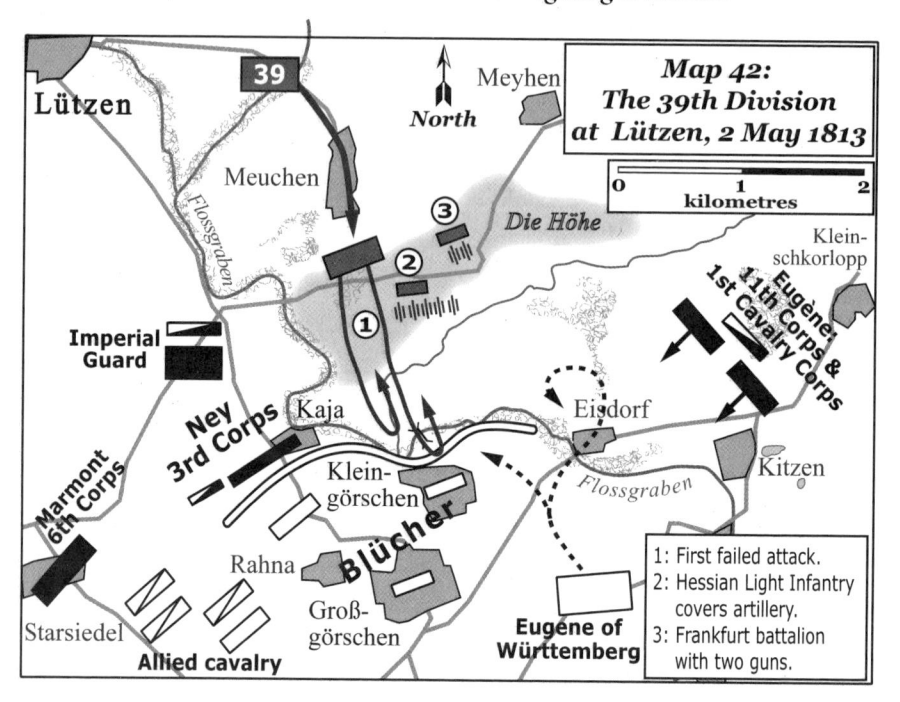

the regiment, however, and would serve as a 'volunteer' during the coming battle.[46]

The division rapidly reached Meuchen, its arrival heralded by 'an army of ravens who ... greeted us with a dreadful cackling'.[47] Such omens notwithstanding, Marchand deployed his infantry on the southern side of the village and sent the artillery to the east to chase off roving Cossacks and protect his open left flank. The Frankfurt battalion, his least reliable component, was allotted to cover the guns and remained on the left flank with two of the Hessian pieces when the rest of the artillery moved forward later in the afternoon. Otherwise, the division stood unengaged for several hours. As the day wore on, however, the Germans were launched into the fight. It is unclear whether Ney ordered this advance or whether Marchand acted independently on seeing that Russian troops were seeking to out-flank the French position at Kaja. Whatever the case, its intervention proved timely, as Viceroy Eugène's command, coming from around Leipzig to the north, was now rolling towards the Allied right flank. The movements of these two forces would thus put the Allied position at Kleingörschen under threat from two directions.[48]

Shortly after 5:00 p.m., the 39th Division advanced 'at the quick march [*Sturmschritt*] *in a single closed division column* towards Kleingörschen', with the Badeners on the left and Hessians on the right.[49] The combined artillery kept pace on the left, occupying a low rise (simply called 'die Höhe' or the heights) to engage the enemy guns around Kleingörschen.[50] The attack, however, seems to

The Spring Campaign: Glories, Privations and Long Marches 139

have been hastily conceived and ordered without proper preparation. The initial obstacle was the tree-lined Flossgraben, where Prussian Jägers had nestled in and kept up a damaging fire, but, as the frustrated Baden Hauptmann von Beck of the 3rd Infantry related, no one seemed to know what to do when the column advanced. The men were first ordered to charge too soon and had to halt out of breath after a few hundred paces. Then the order to open fire came while the battalions were still in column, but fire discipline among the inexperienced troops was almost nil and exasperating confusion ensued. Beck's company in the lead found that the companies behind him started shooting at once even though they were six to nine ranks in the rear. 'In this fatal situation', he wrote, many in the front ranks threw themselves to the ground to avoid being shot by their own men. Fortunately, most of the young recruits loosed their muskets into the air and there were few casualties to friendly fire. Beck was grateful that the enemy 'did not serve us with canister fire' during this confusion, but order was soon restored, the pointless and dangerous firing ceased, and the battalions deployed to continue towards the Flossgraben.[51]

Most of the Baden troops of the 3rd Infantry *Großherzog* managed to get across the Flossgraben, either over a small bridge or by scrambling down one of the steep banks, wading (the water was only up to their knees) through the stream and then clambering up the other side. Though the companies had been considerably disordered crossing this obstacle, they now engaged in a lively firefight with the Prussian and Russian defenders in the gardens around Kleingörschen. The men fired rapidly, but many of their musket balls still flew off uselessly into the sky and ammunition began to run low. As Württemberg Hauptmann von Suckow would note at Euper, new soldiers often fired off their ammunition too fast and to no useful effect, but unlike Suckow's situation, here there was no chance for a regular, organised relief of the engaged units. Nevertheless, the officers held their men in position across the stream for 30–45 minutes until they learned to their dismay that their supports were retreating.

Indeed, the lead Hessian unit, the Leib-Garde Regiment, had been rushing towards the little bridge when it suddenly lost all cohesion and routed to the rear. The appearance of 'a black cloud of enemy cavalry beyond the stream' was one reason for the regiment's rapid disintegration, but it seems that its commander wanted to fall back and deploy his column out of enemy musket range. He had just ordered the men to turn about when he fell from his horse wounded. Under heavy fire, feeling threatened by cavalry, their commander down, and orders unclear, 'the young soldiers halted, toppled back and their lines began to come apart'.[52] As the disgusted Prinz Emil would later report:

> The column went towards that narrow bridge at double-time but a group of cavalry that showed itself on the left caused a sort of panicked terror all at

once, namely in Your Royal Majesty's [Leib-] Garde Regiment. It is painful for me to say, but in fact all my efforts to lead them back against the enemy in good order were fruitless.

Emil praised the officers for doing their best 'to return the frightened soldiers to their duty' with exhortations about 'the sanctity of their flags', their own honour and that of their regiment, but even his 'most decisive measures' failed.[53] 'I saw … our Garde running away,' wrote Surgeon Wilhelm Jacob Schimpf of the Leib Regiment as he rode out of Meuchen, 'they hurried to the rear and said all is lost, all is broken.'[54] In the absence of its wounded colonel, a major led the Leib-Garde out of range and spent the evening gathering fugitives and restoring order.

A similar disorder afflicted the 3rd Baden Infantry so that it tumbled back over the Flossgraben in fear of enemy cavalry looming to its left. Although the four companies of the 1st Infantry retired in good order (they do not seem to have crossed the stream), the 3rd's companies were badly intermingled, and the men ran to the rear in disarray. The officers exerted themselves to gain control of the situation, but 'all pleas, threats and blows were useless', stated Beck. He even alluded to the officers firing on some of their own men, which may have been what Emil was suggesting with his phrase about his 'most decisive measures'. Nonetheless, Emil observed a contrast: 'The Badeners also fell back in disorder, but only part of the regiment continued its retreat beyond the brush, the larger group soon ordered itself again and only retired back to the line of our fusiliers owing to the enemy's superior numbers.'[55]

Although the Hessian Leib-Garde and most of the Baden brigade were now at least temporarily out of action, the division would soon renew its attack with the two remaining Hessian regiments. Fortunately, the Leib Regiment had been left near Meuchen in reserve when the advance began while the Light Infantry had been detached to the left to protect the artillery. As the division moved forward for the first time, so did the guns and the Light Infantry, but what one officer recalled as 'a strong column of infantry' loomed up in the open to the east off the division's left flank. When the attack collapsed, therefore, the light infantrymen and the artillery they were covering fell back toward Meuchen in a slow and orderly fashion. Hauptmann Meyer, impatient with the uncertainty over the identity of the approaching troops, rode out alone, armed only with a cudgel, and returned with a captured Cossack. His bold foray earned him the return of his sword,[56] but his prisoner proved a somewhat misleading find as the troops in the distance were neither Russian nor Prussian but units of MacDonald's 11th Corps from Eugène's army. An imperial adjutant who arrived around this time confirmed the identity of the friendly columns and announced that the battle was won. He may also have brought oral orders for the 39th Division to attack as it launched a new push towards Kleingörschen almost at once.

The Hessian Light Infantry Regiment led the revived attack as night came on, 1st Battalion on the left, 2nd on the right. The tenacious Prussian Jägers along the Flossgraben initially stymied the Hessian skirmishers even though two additional companies reinforced the firing line. Standing in the open, the Hessians were taking heavy casualties, including the wounding of Meyer and several other officers. Bold independent decisions by two of the company commanders, however, reversed the situation. Rousing their wavering men, they charged directly at the Prussians along the Flossgraben, threw them back and pressed on towards the village. 'A murderous business developed around Kleingörschen,' wrote Leutnant Schmidt, one of the remaining officers from Meyer's company. The two leading Light Infantry companies each took casualties of 25 per cent or more and Schmidt, wounded twice, had to limp to the rear.[57] Though losses were high, their efforts were not in vain. Whether before the Hessians stormed Kleingörschen or, as the Hessians maintained, after they had charged, elements of the French 36th Division were also involved in the attack on Kleingörschen and the two allies combined to evict the Prussian and Russian defenders.[58] While the 1st Battalion was conducting this attack on the left, the Light Regiment's 2nd Battalion, assisted by II/Leib, was pushing across the stream on the right. As night fell, these two battalions contributed to the recapture of Großgörschen but darkness and the firm countenance of the Prussians precluded any further advance. The Hessian I/Leib had been left behind to guard the artillery just north of the Flossgraben when the attack was renewed, but some guns made their way over the bridge to join the close-quarters fighting around the villages that evening. The 1st Battalion of the Leib Regiment also joined, its commander relieved that his partially trained young soldiers executed the crossing in good order so they could participate in the action.[59] Likewise, the re-formed Baden infantry followed in support. The Badeners took some additional casualties but details of their involvement in the evening's fighting are unclear. 'The fire suddenly died away', wrote the Hessian soldier Kösterus, 'and the cheers from more than 10,000 throats of the Young Guard nearby us on our right convinced us that the victory was ours.'[60] The division was assigned the area around Kleingörschen for its bivouac that night, the men seeking repose and some minimal sustenance on the blasted field among the dead and the dying.

Also near Kleingörschen that night were the Baden 1st Light Dragoons. Ney's light cavalry had camped around the village on the night of 1/2 May but the general neglect of security in 3rd Corps meant that the mood around campfires on the morning of the 2nd was relaxed with no sense of urgency or imminent danger. The Baden regiment, for instance, was only ordered to saddle up half the men while a lieutenant and some troopers were sent off on a rather casual reconnaissance. The alarm was instant when this lieutenant hurried back to report that 'the enemy is advancing in strength', but his message arrived at the same time as the Prussians, leaving the regiment only enough time to mount up and dash off in haste and confusion. Oberst von Heimrodt was able to rally his men near Kaja, however, and was soon ordered to the western side of the village where Ney, just arrived on the battlefield, found them sometime shortly after 1:00 o'clock that afternoon.

With Kaja under threat and the other three villages temporarily lost, Ney needed time to allow his infantry to recover its composure. Riding up to Heimrodt, he thus ordered the Badeners to charge the Prussians pressing from Großgörschen towards Kaja. Heimrodt initially intended to array and instruct his men before attacking, but the marshal wanted immediate action and personally guided them to the desired position. The Badeners charged, Ney accompanying the regiment 'almost up to the enemy's bayonets' until he suffered a slight wound and had his horse shot out from under him. The light dragoons charged on, scattering the lead Prussian battalion whose fugitives sought shelter in a culvert and a nearby coppice. As the Baden horsemen leapt over the ditch, some of the Prussians jumped up to engage them with bayonets. The cavalry prevailed and surged ahead, but quickly found themselves in trouble. As Heimrodt would later recount: 'Now it was time to turn around as not only were we greeted by the infantry in the woods, but squares that flanked us and canister fire sent a rain of balls [at the regiment]. I therefore ordered a retreat, which of course did not occur in as orderly a fashion as on the parade field and led us back to the side of our infantry which had once again collected itself.'

Mission accomplished, the Baden light dragoons once more joined the French 10th Hussars, the two regiments suffering terribly from Allied shot and shell as they held themselves in readiness for further employment. The dreadful struggle for the villages was mainly an infantry and artillery affair, however, and the light cavalry was not further engaged. Their torment under artillery fire eased as the Allies withdrew. 'The enemy fire grew ever weaker,' reported Heimrodt, noting that the Grande Armée not only regained its previous positions but that the enemy had been driven off with heavy losses. As darkness closed over the field, the regiment returned to the bivouacs it had occupied near Kleingörschen the previous night.[61]

The Battle of Lützen was the only major engagement for the Baden and Hessian contingents during the spring campaign and each paid a heavy price for its involvement. The 3rd Baden Infantry, as the lead regiment in Marchand's initial attack, suffered 137 killed or wounded, while the four companies of the 1st Infantry lost 74 in these categories for a Baden total of 211; the men of the 1st Infantry, though barely mentioned in the extant accounts, must have therefore had some involvement in the fighting even if only to have come under substantial artillery fire. Additionally, the two regiments lost a combined total of more than 300 missing in action. The artillery, on the other hand, had 'the rare good fortune not to lose a single man'. As for the light dragoons, their loss in killed and wounded came to 70 officers and men along with 6 taken prisoner and approximately 50 missing.[62] The toll of Hessian dead and wounded was considerably higher, coming to a total of 512. As would be expected given the central role played by the Provisional Light Infantry, this regiment suffered the most, losing 324 officers and men, for more than 60 per cent of the contingent's total casualties. Furthermore, 846 men were initially listed as 'missing' from the brigade. This surprisingly high figure equated to approximately 20 per cent of the Hessians present under arms at the start of the battle and brought the total Hessians losses to 1,358.[63]

The debut of these two Rheinbund contingents at Lützen thus presents conflicting images of fortitude and flight. On the negative side of the ledger, there were two major problems: apparent desertion and tactical ineptitude. The alarmingly high number of missing was the first serious issue. Many of the absent men were simply prisoners of war or dead who had not been recovered, including some who had fallen into the ditch formed by the Flossgraben as Stockhorn reported.[64] Many others, however, perhaps most, were almost certainly individuals who exploited the confusion of combat to take to their heels. Some may have returned to the ranks voluntarily after the battle and others were doubtless rounded up by cavalry and gendarmes, but many were gone for good. As Stockhorn would report three weeks later: none of the missing from Lützen had returned to the ranks and 'I must therefore assume with reason that some were taken prisoner but that the greater part was shameless enough to run off to Karlsruhe.'[65]

'Political' considerations may provide part of the explanation for the desertion – temporary or permanent – witnessed on 2 May. That is, some percentage may have been motivated by pan-German sentiments, and some number likely blamed the French for their being conscripted and placed in danger against their will, but it seems probable that most of the men fled owing to the terror they experienced in this, their first frightening taste of combat. With only a few weeks to train and socialise the 'raw recruit boys', units had not had time to develop the bonds of comradeship and leadership that create coherent, resilient military organisations.[66] In a letter penned five days after the battle, Major Christian Zimmermann of the Hessian I/Leib thus wrote that he would be happy to stay in the Leipzig area for an extended period 'to exercise our still all too raw men daily and make them more apt to their duties'.[67] In other words, the absence of so many soldiers at Lützen indicates the sort of discipline and cohesion problems that so worried Friedrich of Württemberg should his men be thrown into combat before their units had solidified. The deficiencies and desertions apparent in the two contingents on 2 May were thus evidence of collections of raw, untrained troops experiencing combat for first time rather than expressions of some nascent pan-German nationalism.

Inexperience, lack of training and weak cohesion combined with what seems poor orchestration by the senior officers also explain the tactical ineptitude evident in the first attack as recounted so vividly by Baden Hauptmann Beck. Most of the troops were entirely innocent of any campaign experience and even fewer had ever seen actual combat. The Baden light dragoons had been involved in the brief skirmish at Weimar on 19 April, but 'our division remained a mere spectator' during the fighting on 1 May, so the infantry had had no opportunity to acquaint itself with combat before being hurled into a major battle at Lützen.[68] The initial advance thus saw the Hessian Leib-Garde dissolve and flee, while the Baden 3rd Infantry, though it managed to get across the Flossgraben, also retired in disorder after experiencing nearly debilitating confusion. At the same time, the second attack was executed with vigour and valour, leading to a successful crossing of the stream and direct contributions to the capture of both Klein- and Großgörschen. The Hessian Light Infantry was especially notable. It benefited from a higher proportion of veterans and volunteers led by officers and NCOs who conducted themselves with particular energy and resolve. Many Hessian accounts specifically credit the regiment's good performance to the incorporation of Meyer's company of Russian veterans, 'a core that distinguished itself throughout the campaign' by providing an example of discipline, courage and endurance to the young recruits.[69] The light infantry thus held together and accomplished its missions despite difficulties of terrain and enemy resistance. The Leib Regiment also performed well, perhaps incentivised to avoid disgrace after watching the rout of the Leib-Garde. Major Zimmermann quoted above wrote that he was able to lead his battalion as a 'closed mass' across the narrow bridge 'with the greatest order' despite being 'under the heaviest small arms fire'.[70] In the Baden contingent, the infantry reordered itself and supported the second attack towards Kleingörschen late in the day, while the light dragoons burnished the fine record they had acquired during 1809 by charging with conspicuous gallantry under Ney's personal direction.

The actions of the officers and NCOs are especially noteworthy as they consistently endeavoured to encourage, organise and inspire their men. There are no cases of officers undermining morale or attempting to change sides (again, contrary to Franquemont's deprecatory observations). Both Emil and Stockhorn thus praised their officers in their official reports, the prince highlighting the disgrace the Leib-Garde officers felt following their regiment's rout. 'I once again take the liberty of praising to Your Royal Highness the conduct of the Leib Regiment and especially of the Fusilier Battalions,' Emil told his father, 'they did as old Hessian soldiers are accustomed to do and made us forget the misfortune that had occurred with the [Leib-] Garde to the deep distress of the so very good officer corps of the same.' Indeed, he appealed to the grand duke to grant the Leib-Garde officers his grace as they had done their best to restore order and lead the regiment back against the enemy. Stockhorn's report was likewise full of accolades for the 'zeal and enthusiasm' of his infantry officers. He acknowledged that his men had had to fall back several hundred paces in the first attack but also commented on the composure of the troops and opined that 'the position might have been forced if the Hessian Garde-Regiment, composed entirely of very young recruits, had not become somewhat disconcerted'. Using almost exactly the same phrasing, each commander also asserted that the artillery component of his contingent 'had maintained its old reputation'.[71]

The French were also generous with their praise. Although the division's performance had been decidedly uneven, its combat debut generally left a favourable impression on their powerful ally. The 3rd Corps operations journal recorded that the attack on the Flossgraben (clearly the second one) 'was conducted with vigour' and that 'the allies rivalled the French in courage'.[72] Napoleon personally praised Emil in early June during the armistice, instructing him to 'write to the grand duke to tell him how pleased I am with you'. He received further warm acclaim in the official press the next month. 'Prince Emil of Hesse-Darmstadt, who commands the Hesse-Darmstadt contingent, has constantly distinguished himself in the previous campaign [1812] and in this one by great composure and great intrepidity,' the *Journal de l'Empire* told its readers, 'He is a young prince of great potential of whom the emperor is very fond.' Even before learning of Napoleon's words, however, Ludwig had already expressed his pride in his young son. Emil had 'my paternal and friendly thanks' for his performance on 2 May, Ludwig wrote in a tender letter on 9 June, 'You have especially distinguished yourself on this occasion and completely lived up to all that I have come, with every certainty, to expect from you.'[73]

The Baden 1st Light Dragoons earned particular recognition. Not only was Heimrodt very satisfied with his regiment's performance, reporting that 'the behaviour of all officers and NCOs during this battle was exemplary', but

Ney gave him 'the most flattering praise'. The marshal reinforced his plaudits when he reviewed the regiment on 5 May. Laboissière had directed Heimrodt to prepare a list of men to recommend for the Legion of Honour and the colonel handed over ten names during the review. Ney, however, thought this far too few for a unit that had so distinguished itself. The emperor wanted to demonstrate his extreme satisfaction with the regiment, he said, and told Heimrodt to add fourteen more names. Somewhat nonplussed by this demand, Heimrodt hastened to expand his list of recommendations, and these were duly presented to the regiment during the armistice. Additionally, several officers were granted other honours from the French or entry into Baden's own Military Service Order.[74] Despite the problems with desertion, therefore, the Baden and Hessian troops left Lützen with the good opinion of their French allies. Beyond that, the men began to feel greater confidence in themselves after their participation in a victorious grand battle.

From Lützen to Lüben

For the Baden and Hessian contingents, the remainder of May passed with a great deal of marching, but very little fighting. The two weeks after Lützen were spent west of the Elbe, first around Leipzig, then by careful moves over the Mulde towards the great river as Ney pushed the enemy east, forced the Allies to lift their blockade of Wittenberg, and secured Torgau from the obstinate Thielmann (*see* Chapter 2). With Torgau open, Ney could begin moving his ad hoc army (3rd, 5th and 7th Corps followed by 2nd Corps and 2nd Cavalry Corps) across the Elbe. Leaving the Frankfurt troops behind in the fortress, the 39th Division made its passage on 14 May. Ney's initial instructions were to strike for Berlin, but on reaching Luckau he was redirected to the southeast where Napoleon had located the main enemy army. This change caused considerable regret within the ranks as Kösterus explains: 'The assumption that we were going to Berlin was so widespread that the time of day in which we would enter was being calculated, and the disappointment of the men was loud when we left the road that led there.'

The army was now aimed at the Russo-Prussian right flank at Bautzen. Marching through Hoyerswerda, Ney's command reached Klix on the Spree on the 20th, forced a passage and threw itself into the enormous battle on the 21st. The Baden and Hessian troops had a splendid view of the struggle from the heights upon which they were posted, but, held in reserve, they 'were simply spectators to the grand drama'. Part of this drama was Marshal Ney, sitting on a drum and wearing a big boot on one foot and a shoe with a white silk stocking on the other owing to his wound from Lützen. 'Ney did not lose his composure for an instant,' wrote one admiring Hessian, even when a French attack failed, and the soldiers could be seen fleeing their Russian pursuers in the low ground below. As the enemy came in range, the heavy French guns on the hill began to roar and the astonished Russians 'flew apart', opening the way for a renewed French advance. 'In our position atop a hill we watched the decision of the battle and the retreat of the Russians', wrote Hessian Leutnant Schmidt, 'The air was filled with cheers of *Vive l'Empereur!*'[75]

A poignant scene played itself out during this waiting period. GB Charles Henry Guillaume Anthing, who had commanded the Hessians along the Baltic coast prior to their departure for Russia in 1812, now led a brigade in the 9th Division of Ney's corps. He had been wounded and was being carried off the field when he recognised the Hessian troops, gave them as hearty a greeting as possible and asked to have a Hessian surgeon he remembered bind his wounds. More prosaically, the Hessians of the Leib Regiment joked cheerfully with French artillerymen they had come to know in Russia, and no one paid attention to a French drummer busily stripping a dead Russian in a ditch not far from Ney.[76]

Along with the rest of 3rd Corps, the 39th Division marched east the following day, passing through Görlitz, Bunzlau, and Haynau to reach Liegnitz on 31 May. The Baden light dragoons had a minor role in the fighting on 22 May but other than this and one or two inconsequential scuffles with Cossacks, they and the division were not involved in further combat.[77] Detachments became a constant burden, however, with Hessian battalions left behind to garrison Bunzlau (II/Leib) and Haynau (II/Light) while a captain and 300 men of the Leib Regiment were detailed to escort the remains of Napoleon's friend GD Duroc (killed on 22 May) to Dresden. In one case, the men of I/Light (the former Leib-Garde Fusiliers) received an unanticipated imperial visit. Napoleon was returning to Dresden just after the declaration of the armistice and came upon the battalion unexpectedly. The men were gathered around a barn outside Liegnitz cleaning their muskets and did not have time to render the proper honours to the emperor. Napoleon, however, master of interacting with common soldiers, took no notice of the protocol infraction. Instead, he asked the men – in his awkward German – how they were doing and complimented them on their dutiful attention to their weapons before riding on past the doubtless astonished troops.[78]

The Baden brigade also contributed detachments. One battalion was held in Görlitz for two days before re-joining the division, men were assigned to escort Napoleon's foreign minister Maret, and the brigade sent detachments of up to battalion size on various other brief escort duties almost daily. Though not a detachment per se, Laboissière provided an example of the value the French placed on German light cavalry for their ability to interact with local populations. During the move from Leipzig to the Elbe, he had sent a Baden NCO in civilian disguise to determine the state of the bridge over the Mulde at Eilenburg. Thanks to the sergeant's dedication and observational skills, he was able to determine that the bridge had been dismantled but that there were few enemy troops in the area.[79]

With the announcement of the armistice in early June, however, all the various detachments were recalled to join the division around Liegnitz. From here they marched north to the small town of Lüben (now Lubin in Poland, not to be confused with Lübben in Saxony) where they would spend the next two months resting, training and reorganising.

As with the rest of the army, logistics proved a tremendous problem during the spring campaign as recorded in the Hessian brigade's journal:

> The supply of the troops was again done in a unique fashion. Every regiment baked its own bread in the villages where it was quartered from the flour which the division had requisitioned for this purpose. Meat was obtained in just the same way. Plundering and devastation were therefore routine.[80]

Stockhorn reported similar challenges. He had ordered four wagons to carry food, but they had not yet arrived. 'No bread is to be had', he complained, 'and the soldiers, where they find the opportunity, must bake it themselves during the night.' He also asked the War Ministry in Karlsruhe for a supply of sleeping bags 'as straw for the bivouacs is often absent and the men must spend the night on the bare earth'. Nonetheless, 'The morale of Your Royal Majesty's troops is very good despite the many fatigues and the rare distribution of victuals.'[81]

A vignette from Hessian soldier Kösterus illustrates the importance of straw as well as the quotidian campaign life of the soldier and the burdens inflicted on local populations in the armies' paths:

> To get an idea of a soldier's existence in the field, one must see such a bivouac. The soldier, exhausted from the fatigues of a difficult march, forgets all the hardship as soon as he has stacked his musket in the pyramid and tossed off his knapsack. If foraging is permitted, he hurries on his sore feet to the nearest village to seize something for his needs and, as strict as the orders against such actions may be, what always happens is that he will strive to find more than his needs demand. He greedily grabs some object that he throws away in the next moment and he often comes back more tired and hungry than when he left the bivouac. Those from every squad who remained behind will have sought out the most useful bits of the collected wood to put together the frame of the barracks, others cover it with straw and in moments small huts arise which replicate themselves and soon become a small village. Still others go for water and, if meat is

distributed, it is soon in the kettle over the fire. But things do not always go so well with the meals; very often there is nothing but flour to be had and then the hungry soldier must satisfy himself with a flour soup of water and bread flour without salt, flavoured with gunpowder, often, however, also do without any hot nourishment at all and only maintain the fire for its warmth.[82]

Unlike the infantry and artillery, the Baden Light Dragoon Regiment saw some combat. As part of the corps' advance guard, it arrived towards the end of the action at Königswartha on 19 May but was not engaged. The next day, it participated in the forcing of the Spree crossing near Klix, a fight that left GB Laboissière mortally wounded. Colonel François Monnier of the 10th Hussars, a veteran with thirty-two years of military service, thus assumed command of the 3rd Corps light cavalry even though he had already been wounded at Lützen. The French and Baden regiments supported the attack on Preititz on 21 May and were then shifted to Ney's left flank where they clashed with Prussian cavalry and took losses from Allied artillery fire. They were again present but not engaged during the ferocious combat at Reichenbach but were involved in no further actions up to the announcement of the armistice.[83]

The Hessian Garde-Chevaulegers

Missing from the 3rd Corps order of battle that spring was the Hessian Garde-Chevaulegers Regiment. Despite earnest effort, the difficulties involved in re-creating the regiment after Russia were such that only two squadrons could be made ready in April, and these did not leave for Saxony until the 23rd. Designated the '1st Division' (two squadrons, like two companies were termed a 'division'), they numbered 338 officers and men on departure under the newly promoted Oberst Carl von Münchingen. They reached Dresden on 9 May but the haste with which the regiment had been organised, the inexperience of the troopers and the newness of their mounts meant that only 173 horses were fit for service on arrival. Initially assigned to GD Beaumont's ad hoc division and brigaded with GB Wolff's Westphalian cavalry, Münchingen's men operated north of Dresden as part of Marmont's 6th Corps. As Marmont headed for Bautzen, however, Beaumont was shifted east to cover the army's northern flank and purge the area of Cossacks and other Allied raiding parties. Beaumont was attached to Oudinot's 12th Corps after Bautzen, so the Hessians (approximately 160 strong) and Westphalians skirmished with Prussians beyond Hoyerswerda on 27 May and were present but seemingly not engaged the following day. They likewise seem to have had no significant role at Luckau on 4 June and retired to the Schwarze Elster with the rest of the corps where they learned of the armistice on the 8th.[84]

Baden at Glogau

In addition to its troops in the field under Stockhorn, a significant proportion of Baden's troops spent the spring campaign in the fortress of Glogau. This was typical of Napoleon's desperate efforts to retain control of key fortresses with hastily assembled garrisons of new recruits and weary survivors of the Russian catastrophe. The Baden troops came from Oberstleutnant von Brandt's large, 1,186-man detachment originally intended to provide replacements for the brigade in Russia. As such, it was composed of men from all regiments, each in his future unit's distinctive uniform, including the prominent Raupenhelm. The detachment, however, was diverted to Glogau when it became clear that the entire contingent would have to be rebuilt. It arrived in the city on 7 February and was redesignated as the 1st Infantry Regiment *Stockhorn* as part of Baden's post-Russia reorganisation. These men would become the first of the grand duchy's troops to engage in combat in 1813.[85]

Glogau, a city of some 8,300 inhabitants, sat on the left (west) bank of the Oder guarding a key passage over the river. It had many deficiencies as a fortress in 1813, but the French leadership team was superb. Overall responsibility was entrusted to the energetic and determined GB Jean Grégoire Barthélmy Rouger, comte de Laplane as governor. He was assisted by two extremely talented officers: Colonel Pierre Michel Nempde-Dupoyet as chief engineer and Adjutant-Commandant Antoine-Simon Durrieu (whose role as a *général de brigade* interacting with the Bavarians was described in Chapter 3). As noted earlier, the garrison of approximately 4,000 officers and men was a colourful collection of French, Italian, Saxon, Croatian and Spanish troops. The arrival of Brandt's Badeners thus added yet more variety to this mix. Thanks to good planning and vigorous leadership on the part of Laplane, Nempde and Durrieu, however, the Glogau garrison cohered into an effective force and conducted a lively defence during the spring blockade despite its variegated composition.

Laplane's opponents during the first few weeks were Russians pressing west from the Vistula. The first Cossacks began to appear outside the fortress between 18 and 20 February and by 1 March the garrison and residents considered themselves cut off from the outside world. It was a blockade rather than a proper siege, however, so the city only had to endure minor shelling and the few batteries and trenches laid in by the attackers were shoddy and swiftly destroyed by the active garrison. Moreover, the Allies were hesitant to bombard a Prussian city, especially once Prussians assumed primary responsibility for the blockade in late March. Lacking men, tools, siege guns and trained engineers, the attackers could only hope to intimidate the garrison into surrender, but this effort failed in the face of the stalwart and aggressive defence mounted by Laplane and his subordinates. Repeated sorties and superior artillery fire

Chart 36: The Glogau Garrison, Spring Campaign

Governor: *GB Laplane* **Commandant:** *Chef de Bataillon de la Roche*

Strength figures for 1 June 1813

		bns/sqdns	present under arms	hospital
French/Italian infantry (former 4th Corps):			1,529	219
13th Division				
8e Léger, 84e, 92e and 106e Ligne		1		
14th Division				
18th Léger, 9e, 35e and 53e Ligne		1		
15th Division (Italian)				
3rd Light, 2nd and 3rd Line, Dalmatian Regiment		1		
1st Baden Infantry	*Oberstleutnant von Brandt*	8 companies	1,095	17
1st Provisional Croatian Infantry		1	1,029	125
Spanish infantry company		1 company	132	17
French sappers		–	51	
French artillery and artillery artisans		–	368	65
Saxon 9th Artillery Company	–		114	
Total			4,318	443

Note: the French and Italian troops were the remnants of the 4th Corps of 1812, each former division organised into a single battalion. The original French sapper company was 51 strong as shown above, but in practice this total was almost doubled by seconded infantrymen.

Sources: Brun, pp. 98–9, 120, 167; Grande Armée, 'Situations', 15 March 1813, SHD, 2C705.

'destroyed the enemy's illusions about our weakness and our impending capitulation' wrote Durrieu.[86] Napoleon's victory at Bautzen, as already noted, spelt the end of the blockade. The garrison awoke on the morning of 27 May to find that the enemy had vanished and a patrol of the 7th Chasseurs from Sebastiani's cavalry corps soon arrived to confirm the French success. Laplane sent Durrieu to report to imperial headquarters where Napoleon, thoroughly pleased with the conduct of the defence, instantly promoted both Durrieu and Nempde to generals of brigade and Laplane to general of division.

The Baden regiment was an essential part of the successful defence. Like the Bavarians at Thorn, they participated in numerous forays from the fortress to disrupt enemy siege works and gather supplies from the countryside. These expeditions would range from forty to several hundred men depending on their assigned missions and sometimes included one or two cannons as well.[87] The Badeners were involved in many of these activities, sometimes on their own, other times as part of a larger group. Furthermore, Baden officers often either led these detachments or held important subordinate leadership positions. On 17 February, for example, two of the regiment's lieutenants led 140 men

13 kilometres east of Glogau to cover the withdrawal of Reynier's baggage train while 7th Corps made its way to Saxony after the Battle of Kalisch. More typical was a sortie launched on 6 April to gather fresh meat. While two Croatian companies (1st Provisional Croatian Regiment) targeted one village and two Baden companies waited in reserve, Hauptmann Pfnor led two Baden companies towards a different hamlet to collect a dozen oxen and 200 sheep despite the enemy's efforts to intercept his detachment. Pfnor was prominent again on 7 May when Durrieu conducted a major sortie to destroy enemy trenches. Baden troops under Pfnor made up 200 of the 600-man force and he was praised for his 'rare intrepidity' in leading a successful counterattack that Durrieu ordered to cover their withdrawal. The other Baden officers were also lauded for their 'good performance' and the men for their 'good will'. The cost was fairly high, however, as 24 of the 96 casualties in this bold raid came from Pfnor's detachment. Although most of the sorties were remarkably successful, a patrol of 12 Baden infantry and 10 Saxon artillerymen was captured on 28 February when they sought information about the enemy while protecting a wood-cutting party 5 or 6 kilometres south of the fortress. Ten of the Badeners, however, managed to escape and make their way back to Glogau.[88]

The French repeatedly praised their Baden allies for their behaviour in the garrison's sorties. Durrieu reported, for example, that 'no one would have thought the Badeners were coming under fire for the first time' when they participated in a 19 March reconnaissance in force to probe the enemy's strength. Similarly, Nempde recorded that, 'The Badeners made many bayonet charges with as much aplomb as if on manoeuvre' during the 7 May sortie. 'I could not be more content with the four battalion commanders of the 4th Corps [French and Italian] and with the major [sic] commanding the 1st Baden Regiment,' concluded Durrieu in his summary. Laplane also erred in titling Oberstleutnant Brandt as a major, but he used similar terms to express his satisfaction: 'I could not be more pleased with the conduct of Major Brandt, the manner in which he disposed the troops of his detachment convinces me that this senior officer possesses great talents.'[89] For his part, Brandt valued the 'fatherly care' shown towards his regiment by Laplane and asked Großherzog Carl to grant the French general an award as recognition for his strong leadership.[90]

These repeated activities outside the fortress and long, lonely stints of guard duty at night afforded the troops numerous opportunities to desert, but few from the Baden regiment availed themselves of these chances. The regiment's meticulous journal recorded only 31 desertions during the four months of the blockade, or approximately 2 per cent of its manpower. The number was so low that the Baden scribe could note individual details about most of the men, many of whom came from one company (5th Fusiliers) where discipline seems to have lapsed owing to weak leadership and a toxic command climate.[91] The loss of men to desertion clearly troubled and embarrassed Brandt and he took steps to stem a practice that he and his officers found abhorrent. Although it is not clear that this case arose from regimental orders, in at least one situation, a Baden soldier fired on a countryman fleeing their outpost at night. Brandt's concerns notwithstanding, the overall number of desertions remained small. This was despite propaganda efforts by the Russians and Prussians as well as the coaxing of Glogau's pro-Prussian inhabitants. Indeed, Allied propaganda targeted the city's population as well as the garrison, leading to strict measures restricting fraternisation between civilians and soldiers. The news spread by the inhabitants 'tended to discourage the allied troops, and to lead them to desertion', wrote Nempde, therefore, 'The soldiers were further isolated from the burghers; one of the suborners was arrested and shot; and thereafter everyone kept to themselves.'[92] Although there were serious desertion problems with some of the other non-French units (especially the Croats and Spanish as Brandt took pains to highlight in his report), few of the men of the 1st Baden were deceived by the false stories of Allied victories or tempted by the offers of free passage.[93]

The Armistice Period: Reviews, Replacements and Repose

The Baden infantrymen remained in Glogau for several weeks after the declaration of the armistice. Their immediate fate was uncertain. The Grande Armée's approach towards the fortress and the impending suspension of hostilities had led Stockhorn to hope that he could unite all twelve companies of his regiment (as he almost always referred to it) to complete his brigade. He thus sent an appropriate request to Berthier and went to review the regiment in Glogau while awaiting a reply. Laplane, on the other hand, impressed with Brandt and his soldiers, wanted to retain them as part of his garrison. Fortunately for Stockhorn, his appeal to Berthier to bore fruit. Replaced by the Frankfurt contingent, whose story is addressed in Chapters 7 and 8, the Baden 1st Infantry, some 1,000 strong, joined its compatriots in late June.[94]

In the meantime, the 39th Division had moved from Liegnitz to Lüben, its designated cantonment area during the armistice. The artillery was quartered in the villages around Lüben and the 1st Light Dragoons near Liegnitz, but one of the first tasks facing the commanders was the construction of lodgings for their infantrymen. This process took two weeks, but by late June a small town had arisen outside Lüben entirely inhabited by German soldiers, their accompanying non-combatants and various civilian camp followers. Neatly ordered wooden huts with thatched roofs each housed two NCOs and twenty men while officers enjoyed larger buildings with multiple interior rooms (*see illustrations*). Beyond the living quarters and protected structures for arms, there were tidy streets, vegetable plots and even flower gardens for decoration and relaxation. 'Everything possible was done for the comfort of the soldiers, for proper order and for beauty,' recorded the Baden brigade's journal. It was 'an imposing sight', wrote Kösterus, 'and anyone who visited after the usual drill period had the true picture of a soldiers' colony':

> Market, dance area, physical exercise, taverns, barbershops, tailors and shoemaker-boutiques, in short everything that promoted interaction among a large number of persons and built a community was to be found here, and the greatest cleanliness heightened the appeal of this show to which many curious from the nearby town daily found their way ... Thus we lived in our soldier's style, unconcerned with what was to come.

The curious certainly would have been intrigued by this 'new city' in their neighbourhood, but the Badeners also noted that, '[E]ven the construction of the camp caused great damage to the local inhabitants, but the requirements of self-preservation forced us to still harder measures, the demand for vegetables and meat was so great that normal requisitioning would not have sufficed, and we often had to resort to the hardest measures.'[95]

In most respects, the activities of the Baden and Hessian soldiers during the armistice resembled those of the Rheinbund contingents discussed in earlier chapters. Both brigades drilled almost every morning, as Stockhorn reported: 'I try to conduct drill twice a day, one day with the brigade on line, the next at battalion and regimental level, and afternoons with the maladroit.'[96] Reviews were another common feature of the armistice period. Ney reviewed the division on 30 June, including a march at double-time, awarded thirty crosses of the Legion of Honour and praised the men for their appearance and 'the precision of their manoeuvres' in a 1 July order of the day.[97] Prinz Emil had held a review and hosted a breakfast on 14 June in honour of his father's birthday (curiously, Stockhorn does not seem to have done so for Großherzog Carl's 11 June birthday), and congratulated the troops on their progress in training after another review on 11 July. Marchand took Ney's place at the 30 July monthly review and Emil proudly reported that 'the foreigners are unanimous in considering the *Division alliée* as good as the finest divisions of the army'. Stockhorn was also pleased, expressing his particular appreciation for the care and consideration Marchand displayed towards his German subordinates. Target practice and competition shooting also received close attention. This had clear benefits as training for combat but also paid off during the armistice when Baden and Hessian marksmen came away with six of thirteen prizes awarded at a 3rd Corps musketry contest overseen by Marshal Ney. Despite the drill, reviews, target practice and camp amusements, 'we soon began to feel the deadly boredom of our inactivity,' wrote Kösterus. This tedium may explain the rise in frictions between the two German brigades that eventually led to a soldiers' brawl towards the end of the armistice in which a Baden infantryman was badly injured. Emil and Stockhorn thus welcomed the celebration of Napoleon's birthday on 10 August as an opportunity to quash indiscipline and restore good will. In addition to the diversions attendant upon the reviews, religious services, games, music and fireworks, they had their men invite one another as guests at the festival meal so that 'the Baden and Hessian soldiers were together at every table' as evening came on.[98]

Other aspects of the Baden and Hessian armistice experiences contrasted with those of their Rheinbund confreres. In the first place, unlike the Bavarian and Württemberg contingents, the Baden and Hessian brigades both received replacements. Second, both brigades underwent changes in organisation. In the Hessian case, what was termed the '1st Augmentation Battalion' departed Darmstadt on 28 June to arrive in Lüben on 26 July after having been subjected to an imperial inspection as it passed through Dresden on the 18th. Having lost 90 men to desertion en route (as Emil 'painfully' reported), the battalion numbered 745 officers and men along with 30 horses when it reached Lüben to be incorporated into the brigade. Großherzog Ludwig, who had personally reviewed the battalion before its departure, was very pleased with these men. Though young, 'they are fully drilled and have fired live rounds at targets as well as blanks and may therefore be employed immediately,' he told Emil, lamenting that the Leib-Garde would not have disgraced itself at Lützen had it been as well prepared. On the organisational side, Ludwig honoured Schönberg's Provisional Light Infantry Regiment by decreeing that its two battalions would henceforth be permanently combined as the 'Garde-Fusiliers Regiment'.[99] These changes left Emil with three integrated infantry regiments, each of two battalions with a total of roughly 1,100 officers and men present under arms after deducting the sizeable numbers in hospital. Adding his artillery, the prince thus commanded a brigade with a field strength of approximately 3,500 when the armistice came to an end.

Stockhorn also received a substantial number of reinforcements and replacements. He was especially pleased when the eight companies of his regiment arrived from Glogau on 27 June (154 men under Hauptmann Pfnor, having been left behind to await the Frankfurt troops, did not reach Lüben until the 29th). One month later, GM Ludwig Johann Brückner arrived leading a replacement detachment from Karlsruhe with an additional 402 officers and men for the infantry and train along with 16 horses and the requested sleeping bags. These, combined with the 1,000 from Glogau, brought the brigade to near full strength. Deducting those in hospital, however, meant that he would embark on the autumn campaign with 2,400 officers and men fit for duty.

Uniforming his men posed a frustrating problem for Stockhorn. The troops from Glogau had originally marched out of the grand duchy as a replacement detachment for the brigade in Russia. As such, the light infantry replacements were dressed in dark green coats, their line counterparts in dark blue, and all of the men were wearing the then-standard Raupenhelm. Although the eight companies from Glogau and the four new ones from Baden were amalgamated into the 1st Infantry, the result was a jarring mismatch in dress. Stockhorn was able to procure enough dark blue cloth to put all the men in his regiment in the proper coats, but the problem of headgear remained. This seems to have been insurmountable. Not only was there the awkward admixture of shakos and Raupenhelms, but Ney had remarked that the contingent's shakos were unsuitable and the French general who had inspected the replacement detachment in Dresden made similar comments (by striking coincidence, this was the now promoted GB Durrieu).

Stockhorn was not even sure which model shako to use. He had ordered some from Dresden, but now, with war imminent, the contractor told him he was overwhelmed with orders from the French, the Poles and the Saxons; the required quantity could not be provided for weeks. An alternative manufacturer in Dresden wanted twice as much per hat and could not promise timely delivery, nor could a dealer in Glogau. Stockhorn's only recourse was to source them from home, but the autumn campaign was already under way by the time this request reached Karlsruhe. It thus seems highly likely that the Baden brigade marched out to its last combat as a French ally with its soldiers wearing an unsightly mix of shakos, helmets and perhaps even simple cloth fatigue caps rather than some sturdy and uniform headgear.[100]

As for the men themselves, both contingents suffered significant desertion at Lützen as described earlier. Although the incidence of men leaving the colours had tapered off dramatically after that initial battle, the gaps in the ranks remained until the summer. The Hessian and Baden replacement battalions both included some number of former deserters and these men received special attention when they reached the encampment at Lüben. 'I gave them to their commanders for their own punishment,' wrote Stockhorn in reference to 'the cowardly deserters of 2 May'. He told his officers that returned deserters could be struck twice with a shoe by each of their comrades and could be forced to wear their uniform coats reversed for three days as a sign of shame. They would also, of course, be singled out for the most onerous camp duties. Such punishments, he believed, would have a salutary effect on the miscreants and provide additional incentive for others to remain with the colours. The deserters and stragglers returning to duty in the Hessian brigade were likewise greeted with 'exemplary punishments' in which 'some of the company commanders distinguished themselves by their talents for invention', as Leutnant Schmidt of the Light Infantry, now Garde-Fusiliers, described:

> ... the Augmentation Battalion arrived and among them were many deserters who had run off during the Battle of Lützen and returned to their home districts. The soldiers in camp had been preparing to receive them for some days. The arrival of these men brought a general punishment in the Baden camp as well as ours. The soldiers had free play with these cowards, every company took some in and found inventive ways to show their scorn towards the deserters. They had to wear their clothes reversed and stand guard at the latrines in fatigue caps with brooms, take on all the unpleasant chores, all while they were being industriously sabotaged by their comrades ... Eight days passed before a general amnesty was declared.

Kösterus was not convinced that such treatment would suffice to reawaken the 'lost sense of honour' of these men but he mused that 'there were many among them who had left their banners simply from inexperience or foolishness'.[101]

Light Cavalry Overture

The two cavalry regiments also received reinforcements over the summer armistice. The Baden 1st Light Dragoons, quartered near Liegnitz, welcomed the arrival of the regiment's 5th Squadron on 15 July with 122 officers and men as well as some replacement horses. All assembled, they made a good impression as noted in a 16 July French inspection: 'This regiment is well trained and very fine.'[102] Also welcome was the promotion of Heimrodt to *General-Major* and his advancement to command the 3rd Corps light cavalry brigade when the wounded Colonel Monnier returned to France to convalesce on 9 August. Decidedly unwelcome in the regiment, however, was Heimrodt's ensuing transfer. Napoleon, impressed with Heimrodt's abilities, appointed him to command the 3rd Brigade (5th and 8th French Lancers, 1st Italian Chasseurs-à-Cheval) in GD Jean-Baptiste Juvénal, comte de Corbineau's 1st Light Cavalry Division of the 1st Cavalry Corps. The regiment's officers sent a letter of protest to Ney, asking that their former colonel be allowed to remain as commander of the 3rd Corps' light cavalry. Their objections were in vain, but Ney replied with great courtesy, telling them that if peace came and they led their regiment home, they would do so with 'the respect of the French army'. If, on the other hand, the war resumed, 'then you will be able to win new laurels, as you are brave men and have demonstrated your courage at every opportunity'. The officers had to content themselves with these generous words as Rittmeister Franz Speck assumed interim command of the regiment.[103] The Badeners and their partners in the French 10th Hussars continued as the mounted component of 3rd Corps, but they were redesignated as the 23rd Light Cavalry Brigade and placed under French GB Frédéric Auguste Beurmann.

The Hessian Garde-Chevaulegers (approximately 260 men, see Chart 43) remained with 12th Corps with the Westphalian Chevaulegers-Garde and the Bavarian Combined Chevaulegers Regiment in what was now the 29th Light Cavalry Brigade under the odd dual command of GD Beaumont and GB Wolff. The first two squadrons were quartered near Lübben where they were joined by the two squadrons of the 2nd Division on 13 August. The reinforcement squadrons had set out from Darmstadt on 21 July with 338 officers and men but in the words of the regimental history, this 2nd Division 'even more than the first, consisted mostly of very young men who, owing to lack of time, were very incompletely trained and of remount horses whose training could in no way be considered finished'.[104]

Another Marengo or Friedland?

A few comments on the outlooks from Karlsruhe and Darmstadt are necessary before concluding this section on the armistice period. Großherzog Ludwig's attitude was evident in his 9 June letter to Prinz Emil. Unaware that the armistice had already gone into effect, Ludwig wrote his son to expect another Marengo or Friedland on the joint anniversary of those two battles (14 June) if the rumoured armistice did not come about. 'God preserve him', he told Emil, referring to Napoleon. Not all in his government would have agreed with his assessment of Napoleon's prospects or his pro-French predilections, but Ludwig remained in awe of the French emperor and his military genius. His sovereign will would thus continue to guide the grand duchy's policies towards loyal adherence to the French alliance until well after Leipzig. A similar approach prevailed in Baden where 'the German cause' aroused very little interest among the populace or at court. Despite some discontent with conscription and taxes commonly associated with France, Karlsruhe, too, would thus remain attached to Napoleon until his dramatic defeat at Leipzig.[105]

The Autumn Campaigns: 'Marches in the Most Dreadful Rain'

Almost all the Baden and Hessian troops would end up at the Battle of Leipzig in October. In the preceding weeks, however, they were more scattered than they had been during the spring campaign and thus fought in multiple parts of the war's main theatre. The 39th Division was transferred from the 3rd Corps

Chart 37: Rheinbund Troops in 3rd Corps, August 1813

	Bns/sqdns	Present under arms	Detached	Hospital
39th Division	**GD Marchand**			
1st Brigade (Baden)	**GM von Stockhorn**			
1st Infantry, *Stockhorn*	2	1,428	2	177
3rd Infantry, *Großherzog*	2	1,292	2	330
Half of 2nd Foot Battery	4 × 6-pdr	123	–	4
2nd Brigade (Hessian)	**GL Prinz Emil**			
Leib Infantry Regiment	2	1,066	15	389
Leib-Garde Infantry Regiment	2	1,038	35	282
Garde-Fusilier Regiment	2	1,037	56	442
Foot Artillery Battery	6 × 6-pdr, 2 × howitzer	232	11	15
Total Baden		2,843	4	511
Total Hessian		3,373	117	1,128
Division totals		6,216	121	1,639
10th Light Cavalry Brigade	**GB Beurmann**			
10th French Hussars	6	1,072	76	153
1st Baden Light Dragoons, *Freystedt*	5	521	9	31
Brigade totals		1,593	85	184

Note: An additional 128 officers and men were to join the 10th Hussars.

Sources: 3rd Corps 'Situation Sommaire' for 5 August (SHD, 2C539) with artillery numbers taken from the 'Livret de Situation', 1 August 1813 (SHD, 2C708). The 'Livret' gives substantially lower numbers for the Baden infantry regiments: 1,286 and 1,002 present for duty respectively. Figures for the other regiments, however, are roughly similar to those above and the corps' report, likely being more accurate, is cited here.

---

to the 11th but missed the defeat on the Katzbach and saw no major combat before Leipzig. The Baden light dragoons, on the other hand, remained with 3rd Corps to be caught up in the Katzbach debacle and the subsequent retreat. The Hessian Garde-Chevaulegers were likewise swept up in a disaster – Dennewitz – and participated in the defeat at Wartenburg as well. Finally, additional forces from both grand duchies would arrive in Saxony. The 2nd Hessian Augmentation Battalion and one of the battalions from the 39th Division were assigned to the Torgau garrison, while the 2nd Baden Brigade appeared and became involved in a number of small rear-area security actions as part of the French force based at Leipzig. Given this dispersal, these various elements will be examined separately until most of them come together in mid-October for the climactic clash in the Battle of Nations.

The 39th Division: Confusion, Honour and Duty

Looking first at the 39th Division, the period from mid-August to mid-October was one of minor skirmishes, constant alerts, repeated reconnaissance missions, exhausting marches and seemingly unremitting privation under execrable weather. Although the division was not involved in any major engagements, its strength steadily eroded from sickness, straggling and clashes with Cossacks. The division departed its comfortable encampment on 15 August and operated generally between Bunzlau and Liegnitz for the next ten days along with the rest of 3rd Corps. Though not directly engaged, the Baden and Hessian battalions supported the French divisions in several combats and provided garrisons to cover the lines of communication. For the men, this to and fro marching was disturbingly perplexing, indicative of uncertainty in the higher command. 'Our division wanders alone in this confusion,' wrote Kösterus, 'hears cannon fire now left, now right and soon to our front and does not know where it should turn.'[106]

The Hessians of II/Garde-Fusiliers missed some of this misery and befuddlement. The battalion was attached to the Imperial Guard on 22 August as a special honour for the Hessians but also a practical means of providing security for the Guard's wagons without committing French Guardsmen. The battalion was thus present at the Battle of Dresden on 26 and 27 August but was not engaged. Assigned as part of the escort for the Guard's baggage, it would remain separated from the Hessian brigade for the remainder of the war and would end its time as a French ally as part of the Torgau garrison.

The rest of the 39th Division was marching between Haynau and Liegnitz on 26 August when MacDonald and Blücher collided along the Katzbach. Though spared that catastrophe, the Baden and Hessian brigades were bundled up in the chaotic, dispiriting rout as MacDonald's defeated Army of the Bober fell back to the west in utter disarray. The Hessian II/Leib-Garde, for instance, had been sent ahead of the division to garrison Liegnitz. Having marched through that day's drenching rain, the men were just settling into quarters and beginning to dry their clothes when the drums called them back into the street to withdraw to the west. As recorded in the history of the Baden 1st Brigade, it was a wretched retreat 'through a region entirely denuded of everything, one slept on the bare earth with no cover, the rain fell in rivers, the numerous baggage wagons made the roads bottomless, the enemy light cavalry swarmed around our infantry columns, he who could not follow from exhaustion was captured'.[107]

As a relatively intact formation, the 39th Division was employed to cover the army's passage over the many watercourses that hindered its retreat. These, swollen to raging torrents by the incessant rain, posed serious obstacles and many men were swept away to drown as they struggled through surging water up to their chests. Confusion reigned at crossing points such as Bunzlau. In Stockhorn's words: 'Fragments of all arms piled up at the Bober and we had a small replica of the Berezina.' Left in Bunzlau to protect the crossing, Oberstleutnant von Brandt and I/1st Infantry had to fight their way through 'constantly surrounded and in combat with the enemy's advance guard' to rejoin the brigade on 30 August west of the river.[108] Although some weary stragglers fell into the hands of the inevitable Cossacks, desertion was not widespread and many of the men who were captured attempted to escape, sometimes risking drowning to make their way back to their units. Having spent two weeks marching back and forth over the same roads east of Bunzlau, Marchand's men were now called on to send individual battalions off on independent missions to hold towns, secure crossings or destroy bridges while the desperate straggle of MacDonald's army stumbled westward. By 2 September, the Badeners and Hessians had retreated to Bautzen as the demoralised Army of the Bober attempted to re-order itself behind the Spree. 'The recent marches and countermarches in the most dreadful rain and usually in the presence of the enemy have exhausted the troops,' reported Stockhorn. Prinz Emil offered similar observations in his reports, noting that more than a hundred men had been left behind during the rain-soaked marches, most of whom had likely been captured.[109]

Nonetheless, on arriving at Bautzen, Emil commented that the troops were holding up well despite the enormous exertions of the preceding eighteen days. Indeed, defiance was common. On 26 August, for example, I/Leib-Garde had been left behind to hold Haynau while the division marched on Liegnitz. Two regiments of Cossacks surrounded the town and a *parlementaire* delivered a formal surrender demand to the battalion commander, Oberstleutnant August Ludwig Prinz von Wittgenstein. Wittgenstein, however, gave what Emil termed 'the appropriate response': if the enemy wanted his battalion, they could come and try to take it. Unwilling to risk an attack, the Cossacks vanished, and Wittgenstein was able to rejoin the division.

A similar situation arose on 4 September near Bautzen. The 2nd Battalion of the Leib-Garde had been sent towards Klix to gather intelligence, food and fodder when it learned that the town was occupied by Prussian cavalry with artillery. Major Karl von Stosch und Siegroth, the battalion commander, posted his men in a walled farmstead and soon received a written summons to defect. 'Knowing that the garrison [of the farmstead] were Hessians', wrote the Prussian commander, he expected that 'they would join the common cause of Germans'. If not, they would be destroyed. Stosch, like Wittgenstein, wrote back that 'if the enemy commander knows that Hessians are here, he should also know that they are not defectors,' and that the enemy 'would be received according to honour and duty'. The Hessians prepared to defend themselves, but it soon became clear that the Prussian force was nothing more than cavalry who rapidly withdrew on the appearance of Wittgenstein with a company of I/Leib-Garde and a cannon. Moreover, as Emil would report the next day, Napoleon was approaching from Dresden with the Guard and a large mass of cavalry.

Although not formally surrounded and summoned as in these two cases, I/Garde-Fusiliers had evaded encirclement during the retreat from Görlitz to Bautzen and the French, as mentioned above, had no reservations about sending Baden and Hessian troops on distant independent missions.[110] Despite the miseries of the wretched withdrawal from Silesia and despite the poor example set by most soldiers in the disheartened Army of the Bober and its mobs of marauders, the officers and men of the Baden and Hessian contingents stayed with their colours and did not avail themselves of the repeated opportunities to defect or desert.

The 39th Division was transferred to MacDonald's 11th Corps on 8 September, Stockhorn reporting that he had been well received by the marshal and once again expressing his appreciation for Marchand's solicitude. Under the new corps headquarters, the division remained around Bautzen for several more days, the final troops pulling out on the 12th covered by a rear guard composed of the Baden I/3 Infantry and Hessian I/Leib Regiment. Similar circumstances and similar employment prevailed as it withdrew towards Dresden. That is, endless soaking rain, illness and deprivation characterised daily existence while constant small actions enervated the men and wild speculation of another armistice floated through the ranks. 'One still hopes for peace and peace soon!' wrote Major Zimmermann of the Leib-Garde as he recounted the flurry of rumours in a 7 September letter.[111]

The Baden and Hessian troops now served as part of the shield east of Dresden, escorting convoys, protecting key towns and conducting numerous independent reconnaissance missions. As the division had no cavalry, these probes were carried out by mixed detachments of German foot soldiers and French horse, usually under German command. On 2 October, for instance, Stockhorn took the four elite companies of his regiment and twenty French lancers to scout the area northeast of Dresden. Finding nothing but Cossack outposts, he felt comfortable enough to send foraging parties out the next day covered by a battalion. Oberstleutnant Brandt led a more ambitious reconnaissance on 4 October, pushing towards Großenhain with two battalions (I/3, II/1) and fifty French cavalry. This well-conducted operation brought on a sharp encounter with Prussian hussars and Landwehr cavalry, but the detachment returned with few losses. Most of these missions lasted only one day, but in a least one case, a Baden captain led his company and thirty Würzburg light cavalry on an extended patrol from 27 September through 1 October. Finally, Marchand took the entire division on a probe north on 6 October that helped uncover Blücher's flank march to Wartenburg. This, however, was the division's last action east of the Elbe. It crossed the great river that day at Meissen amidst scenes of confusion and spent the following week manoeuvring between the Elbe and the Mulde along with the rest of 11th Corps, marching as far as Wittenberg before turning towards Leipzig on 13 October.[112]

Before passing over the Elbe, the troops underwent their final imperial review on 28 September. Napoleon inspected the troops carefully, distributed twenty crosses of the Legion of Honour to each contingent and expressed himself, according to Stockhorn, 'very satisfied with their appearance'.[113]

This was not, however, the last time the Hessians and Badeners would see the emperor. Indeed, they were able to observe him quite closely on 7 October as they marched from Meissen towards Wurzen after crossing the Elbe as Kösterus described:

> The emperor had preceded us and bivouacked in a straw hut ... He sat on a camp stool as we marched past and seemed absorbed in a large map on the table before him; many other maps lay on the ground around him. His entourage stood in groups around the blazing fire. The encircling guards did not prevent close approach and one could thus see the emperor very clearly. He held his left index finger on the map, supporting his head with his right hand. He suddenly stood up from the stool and called '*Mon cheval!*' at which everyone instantly jumped up and, after the emperor's horse had been led over, the entire entourage also mounted and dashed away with him.[114]

Light Cavalry Interlude

Like their infantry counterparts, the Baden and Hessian light cavalry regiments were badly afflicted by attrition during the autumn campaign owing to foul weather, illness, exhaustion and incessant skirmishing with enemy horse. Each of the two, however, also suffered severe depletion from its involvement in one or more major actions.

In addition to the casualties in the 1st Light Dragoons, Baden also lost the newly promoted GM von Heimrodt during the autumn fighting. Having only received his appointment as a brigade commander in the 1st Cavalry Corps at the beginning of August, he had barely had time to acquaint himself with his three regiments when they were thrust into combat at Kulm on the 30th. Badly wounded and captured during the battle, he died in Teplitz on 3 September, an unusual case of a Rheinbund officer being placed in command of a major French formation.

As for the regiment, while the 39th Division was held in a supporting role in the weeks immediately after the resumption of hostilities, the dragoons were entangled in serious fighting from the very beginning, losing 54 men in engagements between Haynau and Bunzlau on 18 and 19 August. GB Beurmann was wounded in the latter action but remained in command of the brigade. The Baden 2nd Squadron and two infantry battalions chased the Russian garrison out of Liegnitz on the 24th. The 1st Squadron replaced the 2nd in Liegnitz on 26 August, but the regiment's other four squadrons were overwhelmed in the rout at the Katzbach that day. Swept away by fleeing troopers of Sebastiani's 2nd Cavalry Corps, the Badeners were 'broken apart, separated from the 10th Hussars and almost totally dispersed' in the words of the regimental account. Finally re-united with the French Hussars and the 1st Squadron in Bunzlau on the 28th, the squadrons were parcelled out to the infantry divisions for the retreat back to Görlitz. Here they were re-assembled, and Oberstleutnant Friedrich Freiherr von Degenfeld, recovered from an injury received at Lützen, arrived to assume command of the regiment.

For the next four weeks, the light dragoons participated in the back-and-forth actions that flared as Napoleon engaged in his abortive attempts to bring either the Army of Silesia or the Army of Bohemia to battle. With both evading his thrusts and with Blücher marching north towards Wartenburg, however, Napoleon began the process of withdrawing across the Elbe. The 23rd Light Cavalry Brigade and the 8th Division thus crossed at Dresden on 30 September to occupy new positions on the western bank of the river near Meissen. The French and Baden troopers were employed continually in reconnaissance and advance guard roles with French light infantry as 3rd Corps marched north over the ensuing two weeks. The French and Baden cavalry also played a major role in the brilliant capture of Dessau on 12 October, but this was to be their last success.[115] Napoleon had decided to abandon his thrust north and the corps headed southeast towards Düben on the 14th.

The autumn campaigns began with a serious setback for the Hessian Garde-Chevaulegers. Like their Bavarian and Westphalian allies, the Hessians (approximately 260 officers and men) were part of the Beaumont/Wolff 29th Light Cavalry Brigade assigned to the 12th Corps. As discussed in Chapter 3, the three regiments were deployed to form a screen north of Baruth for Oudinot's Army of Berlin when the armistice ended on the night of 16/17 August. The Hessians, in the centre of this array near Zesch, were the most vulnerable of the three (*see* Map 31). 'We all knew the sort of military position in which we found ourselves,' wrote Joseph Freiherr Warisch von Bubna, then a teenage lieutenant, 'in the middle of a forest whose trails we did not know and with the nearest infantry outpost of approximately 12 men over an hour away from us.'

Surprised and scattered when the Prussians attacked just after midnight, some of the men did not even have time to mount and the inexperienced regiment did not rally until it reached the infantry outpost line just north of Baruth. This miniature misfortune cost the regiment 13 men wounded and 62 missing as well as 83 horses. 'The colonel was beside himself,' recalled Bubna, observing that this 'sad beginning to hostilities had an especially disadvantageous effect on such young soldiers'.[116]

A few days later, the Beaumont/Wolff brigade was attached to Bertrand's 4th Corps for the advance on Berlin. The Hessians were present for the fighting at Jühnsdorf and Blankenfelde on 22 and 23 August but their involvement was limited to some skirmishing and a few losses to artillery fire. Like the rest of Oudinot's army, they retreated to Wittenberg in the wake of the Groß-beeren defeat. Several of the regiment's junior officers earned acclaim for their conduct during this withdrawal. Charged with guarding the stream running between Woltersdorf and Zahna (Map 32), they handily repelled an attack on their outpost line on the morning of 2 September, in part by dismounting most of their troopers to sustain aimed carbine fire. One lieutenant even led a charge to retrieve a man who had fallen into the hands of the Cossacks. Wolff was so pleased that he praised them to Beaumont and cited them as models for the rest of the brigade.

The regiment was not engaged on 3 or 4 September but it lost its colonel when Oberst von Münchingen was decapitated by a cannon ball on the 5th near Zahna as he reconnoitred the Prussian position. Nearby officers watched in horror as his trunk remained erect in the saddle for a few moments before toppling from his plunging, frightened mount.[117] An attempted advance shortly thereafter was thrown back in disorder by well-aimed Prussian artillery fire. The actions on 5 September thus proved discouraging for the Hessians, but disaster struck the next day at Dennewitz. Riding through the near-impenetrable dust clouds, the Garde-Chevaulegers arrived south of Gölsdorf with the rest of 12th Corps during the mid-afternoon of 6 September. The story here is unclear, but it seems that the squadrons had barely deployed when they were ordered to withdraw. As they pivoted about by platoons to do so, however, they were charged by Russian dragoons who emerged from the swirling murk with terrifying suddenness. The Hessians broke and fled. Thanks to great exertions, the officers managed to rally some 120 men during the night and passed through Herzberg to cross the Elbe at Torgau the following day. Painfully collecting themselves west of the fortress, the officers had managed to assemble to 190 men by the 8th. Wolff led the rallied Hessians and Westphalians to Zwethau that day, but the brigade retired west of the river on 9 September with the rest of Ney's shattered army.

With the dissolution of 12th Corps after Dennewitz, the much weakened 29th Light Cavalry Brigade (minus the Bavarian regiment) was transferred to Bertrand's 4th Corps and operated west of the Elbe under its command for the next several weeks until the Battle of Wartenburg on 3 October. As with Dennewitz, the actions of the Garde-Chevaulegers at Wartenburg are unclear. There were approximately 531 officers and men in the Beaumont/Wolff brigade that day, 350 Westphalians and 181 Hessians.[118] As detailed in Chapter 4, they were posted near Globig to support Bertrand's right flank and were charged by Prussian hussars as the remains of the Württemberg 38th Division drew off to the southwest. According to Prussian accounts, the brigade was discomfited by artillery fire, then struck by the hussars' charge as it attempted to turn to its left to withdraw. Receiving the attack at a standstill, a cardinal error, the Westphalian regiment in the first line broke and the entire brigade, crushed against Globig with no room to manoeuvre, fled in panic to be chased like rabbits by the exultant Prussian horsemen. The Hessian regimental history also states that the Westphalians broke and threw the Hessian squadrons into disorder as they tumbled back towards the village. The Hessians, however, claim to have launched at least a partial counterattack to deter the Prussian hussars before retreating to the northwest. Whatever the details, the Garde-Chevaulegers lost at least 50 men captured as well as a number of dead and wounded in this new calamity. Some redemption was found on another part of the field where 30 chevaulegers attached to Fontanelli's Italian division rescued two guns from Prussian capture. Nonetheless, the casualties suffered at Dennewitz and Wartenburg ruined the regiment. Combined with sickness and lack of horses (so that many troopers were sent home), these losses meant that the Garde-Chevaulegers were reduced to less than a single squadron when they rode into Düben on 13 October.

The Burdens of Rear-Area Security

Baden and Hessian troops were also committed to rear-area security tasks. The 2nd Hessian Augmentation Battalion left Darmstadt on 5 August with 722 officers and men destined as replacements for the three infantry regiments. Losing 100 men to desertion en route (*c.* 14 per cent of its starting strength), it passed through Leipzig to reach Torgau on 23 August where it was assigned to the bridgehead on the right bank of the Elbe as part of the fortress garrison. As noted above, II/Garde-Fusiliers was also added to the Torgau garrison. With its assignment to the Imperial Guard, the battalion had accompanied Napoleon's headquarters during its movements in the first half of September before returning to Dresden. When the emperor moved north on 7 October, the fusiliers, 450 strong, marched as well, providing part of the escort for the

Chart 38: The Baden 2nd Brigade, 14 August 1813

GL Graf Wilhelm von Hochberg

		Bns/sqdns	Present under arms	Detached	Sick
2nd Baden Brigade	GM von Brückner	–	25	–	–
2nd Infantry, *Hochberg*		2	1,676	5	1
Light Infantry Battalion		1	871	3	2
Half of 2nd Foot Battery		2 × 6-pdr, 2 × howitzer	114	–	–
Total			2,686	8	3

Notes: Brückner departed on 18 September owing to ill health. In addition to the above, the brigade had lost 30 deserters (*c.* 1 per cent of total strength on departing Baden).

Guard's baggage train under GB Durrieu. They reached Eilenburg on the 13th after a brief reunion with the rest of the Hessian brigade along the way. Here they remained until the night of 18/19 October when Durrieu managed to slip away from Allied forces to gain Torgau on the 19th as discussed in Chapter 3. Another month would pass before the survivors of the siege were released to return home (*see* Chapter 8).[119]

While these two Hessian battalions marched into Torgau, the second half of the Baden contingent was arriving to join the French forces around Leipzig. Titled the 2nd Baden Brigade, this small formation was slow to assemble and its quality, in the view of its youthful but experienced commander, was dubious. Graf Wilhelm von Hochberg, the second son of Großherzog Carl Friedrich's second marriage, was barely 21, but he had campaigned in 1809 as one of Marshal André Masséna's staff officers and had led the Baden brigade with skill and determination through the horrors of the Russian war. Having recovered from the rigours of Russia, by the summer of 1813 he was eager to return to the army and asked the grand duke for a posting. He was thus named to command the entire Baden contingent with the rank, like Emil of Hesse-Darmstadt, of *General-Leutnant* while GM Brückner, though in poor health, was placed at the head of the 2nd Brigade. On reviewing the brigade on 8 August, however, Wilhelm had concerns:

> The impression I was left with was not the most favourable. The three battalions were entirely composed of young soldiers who had barely three months in uniform; there was a great shortage of officers as well as NCOs. Most of the lieutenants had only joined in March and had received only the most minimal military instruction from Major von Kalenberg: most came from school or clerking careers, possessed neither sufficient military education nor prior knowledge for their new profession. With the great

shortage of officers, one could not proceed very selectively with their enrolment; thus it came that the performance of many of these improvised officers did not bring honour to the Baden corps and a spirit of crudeness crept in that had been previously unknown.[120]

Misgivings notwithstanding, Wilhelm and the brigade departed Baden on 9 August and passed through Würzburg to reach Erfurt on the 24th. 'Our young soldiers cheered,' on encountering large numbers of Austrian prisoners, remembered Leutnant Ferdinand Wolff of the 2nd Infantry, but he and the other veterans knew this was just the result of the first battle of the autumn campaigns.[121] Both Wilhelm and Großherzog Carl hoped and expected that the two Baden brigades would soon be united under Wilhelm's orders. Napoleon, however, was troubled by the seemingly intractable threats to his lines of communication and allotted this new tranche of Baden troops to the force he was assembling at Leipzig under GD Margaron. Indeed, the Badeners would constitute a significant proportion of Margaron's force: 37 per cent in late August, declining to approximately 28 per cent in September as additional French troops arrived.[122] Rather than marching for Dresden and the 39th Division, therefore, Wilhelm found himself on the road to Leipzig.

Margaron's mission in the autumn was similar to Arrighi's during the summer. 'The intention of the emperor', Berthier had told him, 'is that your column defend Leipzig and march against the partisans that trouble the countryside,'[123] Most of the units that were to comprise his command, however, were still en route when the Badeners reached Erfurt. These French columns were composed of green conscripts packed into provisional regiments, replacement detachments or newly constructed battalions, and Napoleon worried that they would be set upon and dispersed by Allied raiding parties if they marched in small numbers. Beginning what would soon become commonplace, therefore, some 1,050 French reinforcement and replacement troops were placed under Wilhelm's command for their march from Erfurt to Leipzig. Combined with his own brigade, this gave him a force of nearly 4,000, strong enough to deter Allied raiders. These raw French soldiers, however, made a poor impression on Wilhelm. The cavalrymen, for example, who had just been issued their horses and who could hardly keep themselves in the saddle 'presented a pitiful picture' and he recounted that a number of the French intentionally wounded themselves in the hand so as to be sent home.[124] Overall, he wrote, 'the haste with which these conscripts had been armed and sent to the army did not bode well, and there was in general a visible lack of that confidence which had previously been so predominant in the French army'.[125]

Wilhelm and his ad hoc command reached Leipzig on 26 August. For the next six weeks, the Badeners performed a multitude of unglamorous but essential rear-area tasks: assuring the safe transit of replacement columns and convoys of wounded, escorting prisoners, and collecting crucial supplies of food and fodder. They also responded to incessant alarms, often false or exaggerated, that sapped both physical and mental strength. 'An anxious, eerie restlessness ruled the city,' wrote Wilhelm Meier, a surgeon in the Baden brigade, 'uncertainty and indecision manifested themselves in all orders and movements; we were as if in a besieged fortress, were alarmed night after night by enemy patrols, and kept under arms for hours at a time.'[126] The ubiquity and boldness of the Allied raiders infused the entire rear area with an inescapable sense of anxiety and Margaron, newly promoted to general of division, seems to have been especially jittery. 'Much fear, but little resolution', observed Wilhelm shortly after his arrival in Leipzig, 'All that was needed was a couple of hundred Cossacks to gallop up in front of the gates to bring the confusion to the highest pitch.'[127]

As for his own position, Wilhelm felt somewhat superfluous as there was no prospect for uniting the two Baden brigades into a combined contingent under his command. It was soon apparent, however, that GM Brückner, who had complained of multiple infirmities while leading the replacement battalion to Lüben during the summer, was not fit for field service. He received permission to return home in early September and Wilhelm was left to command the small brigade. Competent, intelligent, energetic and enjoying Napoleon's favour, he quickly gained the confidence of his French superiors and was repeatedly entrusted with independent missions during the ensuing weeks. Though technically too senior in rank to command a simple brigade, he was keen to maintain the honour of Baden's arms, approached his manifold tasks in a calm professional manner and accomplished them with considerable skill.

The nature of their duties meant that the Baden troops and their French allies were usually scattered along the lines of communications leading north, west and south from Leipzig. On 4 September, for instance, the Baden Light Infantry Battalion, the I/132e Ligne and 200 French cavalry were assigned to escort 12,000 prisoners to Erfurt, while the IV/35e Léger and 180 French cavalry were at Dessau. In another case, Wilhelm commanded a mixed detachment that included his regiment (the 2nd Baden Infantry *Hochberg*), four French guns and 150 French cavalry on an expedition to clear the road to Erfurt for a large French convoy on 18–19 September.[128] This mission took Wilhelm to Weißenfels where he spent several days coordinating with GD Lefebvre-Desnouettes. Assigned a substantial body of cavalry, Lefebvre-Desnouettes was to suppress the pestilential Allied raiding detachments in the French rear area south of Leipzig. His instructions were succinct: 'take yourself in partisan fashion wherever you hear there are Cossacks or enemy bands'. In response

Chart 39A: The Leipzig Garrison, 30 September 1813

Governor: *GD Arrighi*

	Bns/sqdns	Present under arms
French troops *GD Margaron, GB Bertrand*		
Gendarmes (French and Saxon)	–	11
IV/35e Léger (in Pegau)	1	605
I/36e Léger	1	492
II/96e Ligne	1	717
II/103e Ligne	1	669
I/132e Ligne (in Merseburg)	1	730
1st Provisional Cavalry Regiment	?	644
2nd Provisional Cavalry Regiment	?	679
3rd Provisional Cavalry Regiment	?	919
4th Provisional Cavalry Regiment	?	1,106
Horse artillery, train and artisans	–	358
2nd Baden Brigade *GL Graf Wilhelm von Hochberg*		36
2nd Infantry, *Hochberg*	2	1,591
Light Infantry Battalion	1	803
Half of 2nd Foot Battery	2 × 6-pdr, 2 × howitzer	114
March company for 1st Brigade	–	49
Total		**9,523**

Notes: II/54e Ligne (634) would arrive on 12 October to join the garrison. Many troops passed through Leipzig on a daily basis en route to other destinations.

Sources: SHD, 2C546 and Lystrac, XP3.

---

to Lefebvre-Desnouettes's request for infantry and artillery support, Wilhelm handed over two of the French cannons and four companies of I/2nd Infantry under Major Franz Jagemann.[129] These departed with the French general on 23 September as will be discussed below. For himself, Wilhelm returned to Leipzig on the 24th, but he was back in Weißenfels three days later, now placed in charge of the area stretching from Naumburg (where Leutnant Wolff was installed as commandant because he spoke French) through Weißenfels and Lützen to Merseburg (*see* Chart 39). His command, he reported, was not large but was important owing to the criticality of maintaining communications with Erfurt. Wilhelm exercised his authority in full to include the enforcement of discipline among the French troops in his area of responsibility. Finding the behaviour of Lefebvre-Desnouettes's troopers in Weißenfels repugnant, for example, he administered pitiless corporal punishment. When one of the Frenchmen indignantly objected that he was 'from Versailles' (that is, a member of the Guard), 'I had him given twice as many blows.'[130] The French, of course,

Chart 39B: Wilhelm von Hochberg's Command, Late September 1813

Location	Unit
Weißenfels	Headquarters, *GL Wilhelm von Hochberg*
	4 companies, 2nd Baden Infantry
	129 French cavalry
Naumburg	3 companies, 2nd Baden Infantry
Lützen	1 company, 2nd Baden Infantry
	25 French cavalry
Merseburg	I/132^e Ligne
	300 French cavalry
	2 French guns
Detached to Lefebvre-Desnouettes	4 companies, 2nd Baden Infantry (*Major Jagemann*)
In Leipzig	Baden Light Infantry Battalion
	Baden half-battery

Source: Hochberg, *Denkwürdigkeiten*, p. 241/Note 2.

were not the only soldiers to treat the locals poorly as evidenced by orders of the day admonishing the Baden troops for making excessive demands on the families providing their quarters. Nevertheless, local authorities were sad to see the Baden brigade leave when it was called back to Leipzig on 6 October.[131]

Wilhelm and his men would remain in and around Leipzig for the next two weeks, up to and through the coming great battle. Now under the overall command of Arrighi, who had been installed as the city's governor again on 21 September, they performed guard duties, sent frequent foraging parties into the countryside and generally endeavoured to prepare the city and its suburbs for defence. As a further sign of the confidence the French invested in Wilhelm, he was appointed commandant in Leipzig on 14 October, an unusual responsibility for a Rheinbund officer and one that would test his sense of duty and honour during the closing days of the battle.

Indeed, Wilhelm provides another example of the interior conflict experienced by many Rheinbund officers at the individual level as well as a barometer of the tensions inherent in the relationships between France and its various German allies in 1813. Respected and trusted by the French and loyal to the grand duchy and its monarch, Wilhelm dutifully attended to his responsibilities with energy and determination. He was especially resolute in his efforts to mitigate plundering by the desperate and disorderly soldiery, a bane he largely attributed to a disorganised and undisciplined French army he could no longer admire. At the same time, he was disgusted by the rosy but manifestly false reports of success he received from the French and took a sort of juvenile pleasure in baiting a French diplomat and intelligence agent in Leipzig named Theobald Bacher.[132] He and Württemberg legate Kölle exchanged news from Prussian papers and other sources 'which was of high value to me as the French authorities always sought to hide the truth about the unfortunate turn that the campaign took and described everything as if victories were being won everywhere'. In their memoirs, Wilhelm and Kölle depict 'the mood among the German officers' at this stage of the war as 'retaining their German hearts' alongside their 'sense of duty'. 'This brought all of us to the greatest struggle with our feelings,' wrote Wilhelm, 'May such a time never return!' In a practical expression of this emotional dilemma, Wilhelm evaded instructions to arrest Bavarian GL von Raglovich who, as previously mentioned in Chapter 2, had turned over his command and had arrived in Leipzig as he attempted to make his way back to Bavaria. Although Maret, the French foreign minister, had directed him to detain Raglovich now that Bavaria had switched sides, Wilhelm avoided this unpleasant task by the simple expedient of ensuring that he did not encounter the Bavarian general 'as I foresaw that we would be in the same situation in a very short time'. Managing these contending impulses, Wilhelm and his men would soon find themselves engulfed in the greatest battle of the entire Napoleonic epoch.[133]

Unfortunately for Wilhelm, his brigade would face the trial of battle minus the four companies of the 2nd Infantry that had been detached to Lefebvre-Desnouettes on 23 September. The French general had moved most of his command to Altenburg but he lingered in the town too long and his faulty dispositions left him vulnerable to the many Allied raiding detachments in the area. Thielmann, Mensdorff, and the Cossack Platov thus plotted a surprise attack for 28 September. With support from a detachment of Klenau's Austrian corps under Oberst Alexander von Illesy, their bold attack was completely successful. In a series of clashes that lasted from morning till after dark, the mix of Allied troops drove Lefebvre-Desnouettes's division out of Altenburg and back to Zeitz, inflicting heavy casualties along the way. Among the losses were the four Baden companies and a French battalion (III/35e Léger) who were wrapped up and captured after stiff if confused resistance during the long retreat. Of the 417 Badeners taken, most, including Jagemann, were transported to Hungary as prisoners.[134] The Allies may have attempted to persuade the Badeners to change sides by quartering the officers and treating the men relatively well, but there is no indication that any defected.[135] A few managed to escape their captors, such as a Hauptmann Georg Möller who requested and received the Legion of Honour by claiming that his voltigeur company's defence of a bridge just west of Altenburg had allowed the French cavalry to escape.[136] Lefebvre-Desnouettes retreated all the way to Weißenfels that night, nearly 50 kilometres from his starting point. Fortunately for the French, the approach of Augereau, Poniatowski and other French forces compelled Thielmann to temporary caution, and he withdrew to the southeast for the time being. His victory at Altenburg, however, accentuated the threat to the French rear areas, rousing Napoleon's ire, humiliating Lefebvre-Desnouettes, causing his command 1,421 casualties (including the 417 Badeners) against Allied losses of approximately 300, and depriving the Baden brigade of four of its 18 companies.[137] The loss of these companies, combined with those on the sick list and other deductions, left the Baden 2nd Brigade with slightly more than 2,000 officers and men fit for duty as the armies converged on Leipzig in mid-October. This minor disaster also led Wilhelm to reorganise his regiment so that each battalion would consist of four companies for the remainder of the campaign.[138]

Furthermore, the defeat left Franco-Baden recriminations in its wake. Baden accounts accused the French of abandoning Jagemann's battalion and claimed that the men only capitulated 'after a long and valiant resistance'. French veterans of the engagement disparaged Lefebvre-Desnouettes's dispositions but stated that the Baden troops gave up too readily. 'Staying in the rear at that moment to try to rally our hussars,' asserted an anonymous former officer of chasseurs in a letter to the *Spectateur Militaire*, 'I distinctly saw the Baden battalion fire a hasty volley at the enemy cavalry and then lay down its arms almost at once.'

'This battalion did not fulfil its mission,' wrote GB Hippolyte Marie Guillaume de Rosnyvinen, Comte de Piré, who had commanded the nearest French brigade. He also disapproved of the French deployment and acknowledged that the battalion had been disadvantageously placed but, in his mind, this did not permit 'Baden panegyrists' to blame their loss on abandonment by the French cavalry. He concluded his brief observation, however, with praise for France's Baden allies: 'Nonetheless, I am persuaded that this was pure inadvertence; I often served with Baden troops in the Grande Armée, I do them justice by avowing that they conducted themselves in all circumstances with as much bravery as zeal and loyalty.' For the experienced Piré, therefore, the poor showing at Altenburg was a deviation from the usual performance of the Baden troops. The staff at the *Spectateur Militaire*, veterans themselves, largely agreed with Piré, adding this note when they published these two letters and an account from Wilhelm: 'Most of the editors have often applauded the courage shown by the Badeners on the battlefields and remember with great satisfaction the confraternity that reigned for so long between these troops and ours. It must be said, however, that French historians have been misled by the writers of the Coalition.'[139]

Leipzig: The Fate of Europe

Much reduced, the various elements of the Baden and Hessian contingents now bent their paths towards Leipzig: the Hessian chevaulegers with 4th Corps, the Baden light dragoons with 3rd Corps, and the infantry and artillery of the 39th Division under MacDonald's 11th Corps. Graf Wilhelm's 2nd Baden Brigade was already in and around the city but it would not be united with its countrymen until the very last act of the sanguinary struggle that was about to unfold, what he called 'the great drama that would decide the fate of Europe'.[140]

2nd Baden Brigade, 16–18 October: 'The Circle was Closing ever Tighter'

The first troops of the two contingents to engage at Leipzig were the men of I/2nd Baden Infantry *Hochberg*. While the principal action on 16 October occurred south of the city along the Wachau–Liebertwolkwitz front and Blücher attacked Marmont near Möckern in the north, the Austrian III Corps advanced against Lindenau to the west. Most of the defending units under GD Margaron consisted of French troops, but the four companies of I/2nd Baden and the 2nd Brigade's half-battery were also part of Margaron's command. Initially held in reserve southeast of Lindenau, the battalion and half-battery were committed to the counterattack by Bertrand's 4th Corps during the afternoon. Embroiled in the effort to recapture Plagwitz and Kleinzschocher, the battalion was decimated, losing 246 dead and wounded. Although Baden accounts proudly state that none of the men were taken prisoner, the battalion's involvement in that afternoon's combat left it with only two officers and some 80–100 men fit for duty. It was, wrote Wilhelm, 'the greatest loss that a Baden regiment had ever suffered'.[141]

The rest of Graf Wilhelm's little brigade (II/2nd Baden and the Light Battalion) comprised the city garrison along with an Italian Milan Guard battalion and, at least nominally, the Saxon Royal Guards. The four line companies and half of the Light Battalion were posted in Leipzig's market square, while three of the light infantry companies were distributed to the Ranstädt and inner and outer Halle gates ('A', 'B', and 'a' on Map 43).[142] These men saw no action on the 16th or 18th, but 50 light infantrymen at the Halle Gate charged out of the gate in a sudden foray on 17 October to drive off a Russian effort to capture it. The major commanding this little attack killed a Russian officer and brought his enemy's sash to Wilhelm as a prize, one that the *Graf* preserved for many years. As the combat ebbed away that day, Wilhelm returned to the city and climbed one of its many towers from which he could see 'how the circle that the enemy armies were drawing around Leipzig was closing ever tighter'.[143]

The 39th Division, 14–18 October: 'Balls Rained on us from All Sides'[144]

The 39th Division began its shift to Leipzig on 14 October, marching from the area south of Wittenberg through Düben to Wölkau, the distant growl of artillery from the fighting around Liebertwolkwitz clearly audible as they drew closer to the battlefield. The men bivouacked around Panitzsch the following day where, for once, they found adequate victuals, but they broke camp early the next morning to head for Holzhausen as 11th Corps moved to take its place on Napoleon's left flank for what became known as the Battle of Wachau. 'The 16th of October stepped from the darkness clad in a thick cloak of fog,' wrote Kösterus, 'It was drear and cold, and no sun shone.'[145]

A subset of the grand Battle of Nations, the Battle of Wachau raged between Connewitz on the Pleiße and Klein-Pösna throughout 16 October. MacDonald, as the French left wing, advanced from Holzhausen towards the Kolmberg late in the morning with the 2nd Cavalry Corps in support to his left. The marshal arrayed his corps with the 31st and 35th Divisions on his left and the 36th Division in the lead on his right followed by the 39th. His opponent was Klenau's Austrian IV Corps and, as the French 31st and 35th angled off to attack Klein-Pösna and Seifertshain, the 36th drove straight ahead to shove Klenau's men off the Kolmberg. The French then pushed into the Niederholz, beginning an extended struggle for this wood, while Marchand's Germans took position on the Kolmberg, where they 'could watch the course of the battle peacefully until near evening' as Leutnant Schmidt recalled.[146] With the assistance of French sappers, the men hastily threw up earthworks around an old Swedish redoubt (*Schweden-Schanze*) in anticipation of a counterattack, but no attack came and the infantry of the 39th retired for the night without participating in the combat. Other than providing MacDonald's reserve, the only Baden and Hessian involvement was apparently to support the French towards Liebertwolkwitz with artillery fire. Although some Allied shot and shell fell amongst their ranks as they occupied the Kolmberg, the only reported casualty was a lone Baden draft horse and a Hessian officer whose cloak had been grazed by a bullet. The men spent a miserable night on their hilltop in close proximity to the enemy and to Marshal MacDonald, who had chosen the Kolmberg for his headquarters. It was 'such a bivouac as we had not experienced even in this campaign, which says a lot', remembered Kösterus, 'On the barren sand hill without straw or firewood, without food other than the little biscuit that was found in the rucksacks of dead or captured Austrians, the dead tired soldier had

Baden and Hesse-Darmstadt: Fighting to the Last

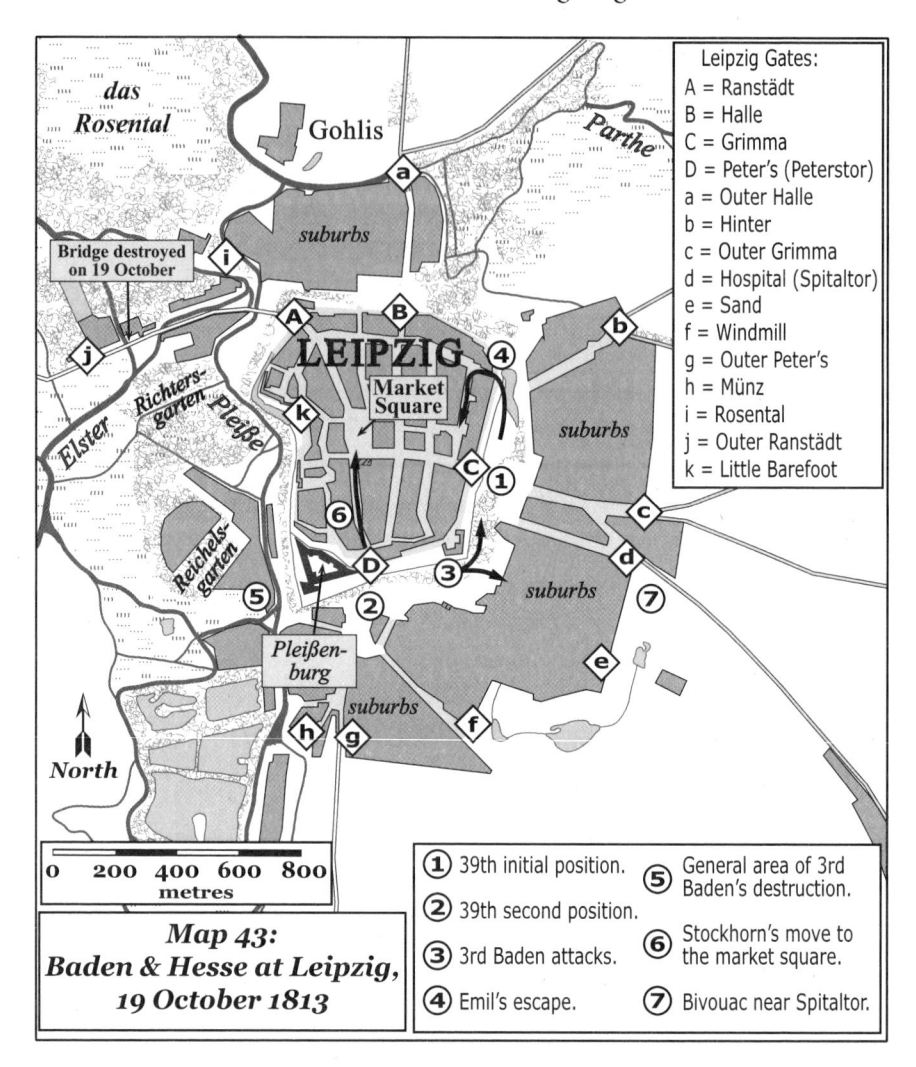

Leipzig Gates:
A = Ranstädt
B = Halle
C = Grimma
D = Peter's (Peterstor)
a = Outer Halle
b = Hinter
c = Outer Grimma
d = Hospital (Spitaltor)
e = Sand
f = Windmill
g = Outer Peter's
h = Münz
i = Rosental
j = Outer Ranstädt
k = Little Barefoot

Map 43: Baden & Hesse at Leipzig, 19 October 1813

① 39th initial position.
② 39th second position.
③ 3rd Baden attacks.
④ Emil's escape.
⑤ General area of 3rd Baden's destruction.
⑥ Stockhorn's move to the market square.
⑦ Bivouac near Spitaltor.

to lay himself down, and did not even have the possibility of warming himself in the cold, damp weather.' Kösterus was not alone in his recollection of the miserable night. Fourrier Wilhelm Diehl of the Garde-Fusiliers remembered it as one of the most unpleasant nights of the entire campaign and for Leutnant Frey the lack of wood meant that 'The few meagrely maintained fires were thus partly and sometimes wholly nourished by the saddles and pistol holsters from the dead horses lying about.'[147]

As on the rest of the field, Sunday 17 October, passed quietly for the Badeners and Hessians: 'other than light skirmishing and a few cannon shots, nothing happened'. There was a brief alarm in the late afternoon when loud cheers were heard from the enemy's lines. The men rushed to arms, but it was soon clear that the acclamations had arisen during the course of a review and did not presage an attack. Despite the strange quiet of the 17th, however, no one was in doubt about the near-term future as recorded in the Baden brigade's journal: 'One anticipated with certainty a second battle on the coming morning.'[148]

As part of the general French withdrawal, the division retired to Zuckelhausen early on the morning of 18 October. To its left, the French 36th Division occupied Holzhausen, the 31st was in Baalsdorf and the 35th was held in reserve along with the squadrons of the 2nd Cavalry Corps. Marchand placed his two brigades with the Badeners generally on the left and the Hessians on the right: the 3rd Baden, two companies of I/1st Baden, I/Leib-Garde and I/Garde-Fusiliers in the village, II/Leib-Garde protecting the right flank and 1st Baden connecting the defence to the French in Holzhausen on the left with its two voltigeur companies supported by two additional companies. The artillery unlimbered in front of the village covered by skirmishers (in Baden's case, the two voltigeur companies of 3rd Baden), while II/1st Baden and the Hessian Leib Regiment were in reserve on a low rise to the rear behind their respective brigades.

The Baden and Hessian battalions had hardly reached their assigned locations when they were attacked around 10:00 a.m. 'in a lively manner' by Austrians of Klenau's IV Corps from the southeast and Prussians of GM Hans Ernst Karl von Zieten's 11th Brigade from the southwest.[149] 'Before long,' recorded Emil, 'the most intense battle raged anew on all sides.' Kösterus recounted the scene in typically vivid imagery:

> There began a fire from the unlimbered guns such as the oldest veterans had never heard, such as was unknown in the annals of history; now in intervals of seconds, now in terrifying crashes following hard upon one another like nearby thunder, the machines of death spat forth. It seemed as if the elements were fighting alongside murderous mankind; the earth was shaken, and the ground rocked under the dreadful din. Grey, impenetrable clouds of smoke rose up by the hundreds, spread over the broad plain and cloaked the individual scenes of combat.[150]

The wrath of war notwithstanding, the Germans were not easily dislodged. French sappers coolly cut down willows along the road under fire to create an abatis, the bulk of the defenders found shelter behind a wall that surrounded Zuckelhausen, and the skirmishers cleverly used ditches for cover to creep near the advancing enemy and suddenly loose volleys into their dense columns as Hessian Leutnant Schmidt described:

> [A]n Austrian battalion came towards Zuckelhausen in masses at the charge. We kept ourselves under cover and calm to receive it at close range and more certainly. Up ahead, our skirmishers lay in a ditch, and they began

Chart 40: Baden and Hessian Troops at Leipzig, 16–19 October 1813

	Bns/sqdns	Present under arms

11th Corps

39th Division — GD Marchand

1st Brigade (Baden) — GM von Stockhorn

1st Infantry Regiment, *Stockhorn*	2	1,502
3rd Infantry Regiment, *Großherzog*	2	1,108
Half of 2nd Foot Battery	4 × 6-pdr	140

2nd Brigade (Hessian) — GL Prinz Emil

Leib Infantry Regiment	2	573
Leib-Garde Infantry Regiment	2	668
I/Garde-Fusilier Regiment	1	324
Foot Artillery Battery	6 × 6-pdr, 2 × howitzer	219
Total Baden		2,750
Total Hessian		1,784
Division total		4,534

Sources: Baden figures from the brigade's 7 October report (GLAK, 48/4336); Hessians from the 16 October morning report in HStAD Best. E 8 B3.10.3, Nr. 128/6128/6. Juhel gives a total of 4,602 for Marchand's 39th Division with no further detail ('Automne 1813', pp. 59–65).

3rd Corps

10th Light Cavalry Brigade — GB Beurmann

10th French Hussars	6	c. 750
1st Baden Light Dragoons, *Freystedt*	5	c. 320
Brigade total		1,065

Source: Brigade total as of 1 October from a summary situation of Ney's command, SHD, 2C539 (printed in Koch, *Journal des Opérations du IIIe Corps*, p. 123); detached troops *not* included. Estimates based on strengths from the 10 September summary situation showing the 10th Hussars as 754 present with 285 detached, 369 sick; and the Baden Light Dragoons as 334 present, 111 detached, 67 in hospital and 12 prisoners of war.

---

to fire. Straight away the Austrian battalion halted, perhaps 100 paces from the skirmishers, but soon turned around again and returned to its previous line. It seemed as if it felt itself too isolated from its fellows to attack.[151]

After several hours, however, the Allies succeeded in seizing Holzhausen to the left of the 39th Division and the French forces to the right had also fallen

Ausmarsch von Heilbronn 1812.

Auf dem Rückzug.

Three phases in the life of an officer in 1812–13: Württemberg Leutnant Christian von Martens of the 6th Infantry *Kronprinz* composed these naïve images of himself over the period of slightly more than a year. First, departing Württemberg as a proud, well-dressed infantry officer with the helmet Württemberg troops wore up to 1812 (*above left*). Second in the misery of the retreat from Russia with scenes of horror in the background (*above right*). Third, embarking on campaign in 1813, now in a shako instead of a helmet and generally more modestly and practically dressed as compared to 1812 (*left*). Many of the images that follow come from Martens's (previously unpublished) drawings and paintings made at the time.

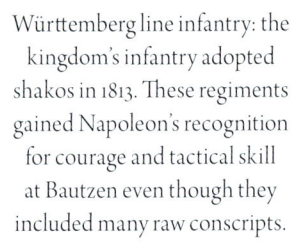

Württemberg line infantry: the kingdom's infantry adopted shakos in 1813. These regiments gained Napoleon's recognition for courage and tactical skill at Bautzen even though they included many raw conscripts.

Württemberg light infantry: in the typical dark green of the era's light troops, Württemberg's Jägers and light infantry were considered an elite. Leaders of the assault at Bautzen, they maintained a fine reputation during the trials of 1813.

Württemberg Leib-Chevauleger: the two chevaulegers regiments retained their traditional helmets in 1813. Part of the royal household troops, the Leib-Chevaulegers fought at Kitzen and defected with Normann's brigade at Leipzig.

The Engagement at Euper, 3–4 September: Württemberg infantry are arrayed in three formations in Leutnant von Martens's watercolour: skirmishers on the left in a treeline, in column in the centre flanked by a battery, and in line on the right engaging in a firefight with their Prussian opponents in the distance. In the lower left corner, surgeons render emergency assistance to the wounded.

Baden light dragoon: the grand duchy's hussar regiment having been destroyed in Russia, its light dragoons were assigned to the contingent in 1813, serving with the French 10th Hussars in 3rd Corps through the spring and autumn campaigns.

A lieutenant of the 13th Bavarian Infantry serving as in the ranks of the 'King of Rome Regiment' in Danzig. Rapp organised excess officers and NCOs into battalions to perform security duties. This lieutenant thus wears his officer's sash but carries a soldier's musket.

Anhalt Jäger zu Pferd: in its handsome uniform of dark green trimmed in dark rose, this new regiment was one of the most ephemeral of the era – formed in July, it was destroyed in Vandamme's calamitous defeat at Kulm in late August.

Saxon-Gotha line infantry: Gotha provided one of the five contingents from the 'Saxon Duchies' that comprised the 4th Rheinbund Regiment in 1812. The regiment's remnants did well in the siege of Danzig in 1813, but the re-formed contingent was prone to desertion and performed poorly at Hagelberg and Magdeburg.

Saxe-Weimar light infantry: in contrast to the blue-clad contingents of the combined Saxon Duchies regiment, Weimar's men and Coburg's were dressed in dark green jackets. Weimar formed the regiment's light battalion while Coburg's two companies served in the two line battalions.

Berg lancer: assigned to the cavalry of the Imperial Guard, this fine regiment was dressed in a Polish-style uniform of dark green with dark rose trim. It received accolades from its French commanders, especially after being joined by veterans with years of experience in Spain.

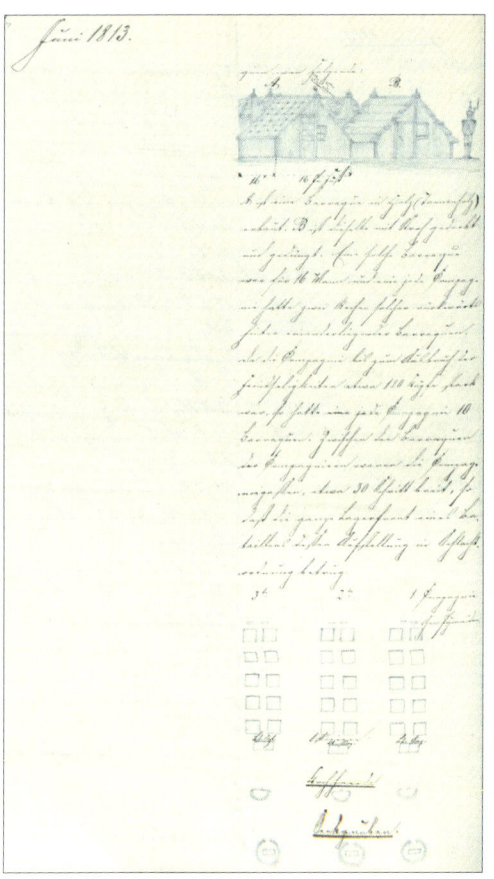

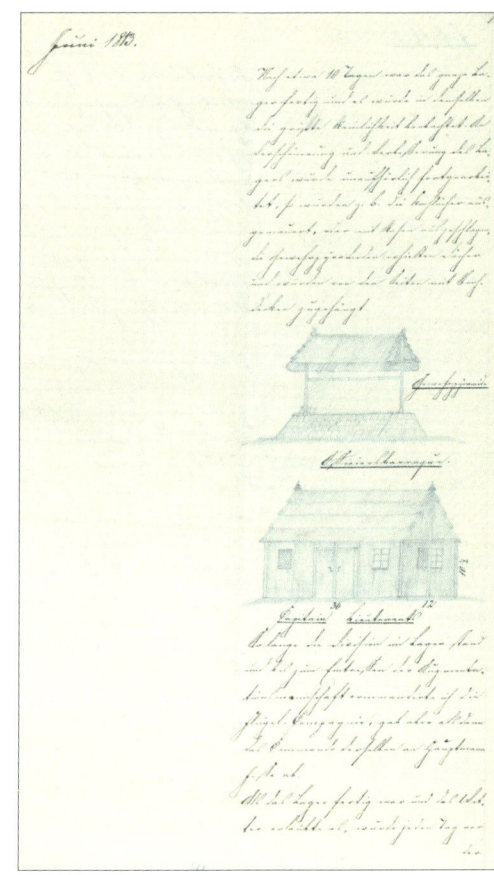

The men of the Grande Armée constructed elaborate camps during the armistice as shown by these pages from the journal of Hessian Leutnant Georg Franz Schmidt. *Above, at top*, are barracks for common soldiers with a figure to indicate the scale; each was intended for 16 men. The sketches at the bottom of the page show the arrangement of huts in camp: ten per company for enlisted men with musket shelters in front and officers' quarters at the rear. Below the officers' barracks are cooking pits and latrines are at the very bottom. *Above right* are sketches of a musket shelter ('*Gewehrpyramid*' or 'musket pyramid') and an officers' hut.

Hessian infantry: after initial problems with desertion, the three Hessian regiments gave a good account of themselves as part of Marchand's 39th Division.

Hessian Garde-Chevauleger: this regiment served with the Westphalian Chevaulegers-Garde, first with 12th Corps and then the 4th Corps light cavalry brigade.

Westphalian line infantry: the kingdom's line infantry were dressed in simple white uniforms, the only regimental distinctions being numbers on their buttons and shako plates. Combat performance was spotty, and the regiments experienced serious desertion problems.

Westphalian light infantry: like with rest of Westphalia's troops, the green-clad light infantry could be an asset when well-led, but the French generally regarded them as unreliable, and the battalions could disintegrate if their commanders were timid or indecisive.

Westphalian Garde-Fusilier: formed in 1812 as the Queen's Regiment, the Garde-Fusiliers missed the horrors of Russia. Initially assigned to 11th Corps in 1813, the reduced regiment was transferred to the Imperial Guard in the autumn and ended its brief existence at Leipzig.

Westphalian Chevaulegers-Garde: poor leadership and lax security led to an embarrassing defeat by Cossacks in this regiment's first action in April, but it recovered and seems to have performed adequately in most cases despite a poor showing at Wartenburg in October.

Westphalian hussar: the image shows the 2nd Regiment in full dress regalia; the 1st Regiment wore a similar uniform in dark green. Colonel von Hammerstein led four squadrons to defection in August, but the other two served faithfully until surprised and captured in September at Freiberg.

Westphalian cuirassier: brigaded under GM von Bastineller, the men of these two regiments wore body armour and helmets similar to their French counterparts. Chernishev worried that the brigade might interfere with his Kassel raid, but it disintegrated without any real combat.

Würzburg infantry: the image shows one of the Würzburg Regiment's voltigeurs in his simple white uniform. Despite the stress of the times and increasing disaffection regarding the French alliance, the grand duchy continued to provide soldiers, exceeding its treaty commitments.

Würzburg chevauleger: though lacking combat experience, this squadron of long-service troopers acquired a fine reputation for its actions in 1813. The amount of attention this small unit received is another indicator of Napoleon's desperation for reliable cavalry in these gruelling campaigns.

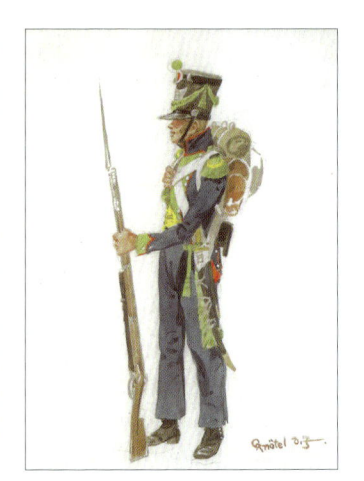

Frankfurt infantry: although the remnants of the regiment committed to Russia fought well in Danzig, the two new battalions formed in 1813 suffered heavily from desertion before being consigned to the garrison in Glogau. The soldier shown here is a voltigeur.

Lippe infantry: like the other microstate contingents, the Lippe troops in Danzig were considered reliable assets, but the two companies sent to Magdeburg diminished rapidly from desertion and the third company never left its homeland.

Reuß infantry: the five Reuß principalities contributed a combined contingent dressed in white coats with blue breeches featuring 'Hungarian knots' on the fronts. The new companies sent to Magdeburg in 1813 proved to be unreliable.

Schwarzburg infantry: the two Schwarzburg principalities uniformed their troops in similar fashion with dark green jackets trimmed in red, but they proved no more trustworthy or combat capable than the contingents of the other microstates.

The Battle of Dennewitz, 6 September: The time is early afternoon and Württemberg cannons deployed in the middle distance create huge billows of smoke while engaged with Prussians on the crest of the rise in the background in Martens's painting. The Württemberg caissons wait in front of two infantry columns. A third infantry unit is formed in square owing to the enemy cavalry on the right. The spires of Jüterbog appear in the distance on the far right.

The Battle of Wartenburg, 3 October: here Martens depicts Württemberg skirmishers and artillery defending the thin line of trees in the centre while Prussian infantry advance from the marshy woods to their front and Prussian cavalry manoeuvre on their left flank.

Contemporary Leipzig artist Christian Gottfried Heinrich Geißler's painting of the Grimma Gate on 20 October depicts the human, animal and material wreckage after the battle but also shows how the city could only be entered through its gates (in the centre with raised barrier pole). The Hessian brigade and some of the Baden infantry fought in this area, and it was here that Fleischmann's Württemberg battery had been left.

Corvée labour: civilians were often forced to work on the fortifications around besieged or blockaded cities. This was a detested imposition (in part because wealthier residents had to participate, as here). This image is from the siege of Hamburg but is representative of the demands on citizens in Danzig, Küstrin and elsewhere.

	Bns/sqdns	Present under arms

4th Corps

29th Light Cavalry Brigade   GD Beaumont/GB Wolff

Westphalian Chevaulegers-Garde	–	155
Hessian Garde-Chevaulegers	–	64
Brigade total		219

Source: Hessian numbers from the 4th Corps summary situations of 6 and 19 October; Zimmermann (*1. Großherzoglich Hessischen Dragoner-Regiments*, vol. I, p. 198) credits the regiment with some 150 men fit for duty (perhaps including detached troops not present with the regiment).

Leipzig Garrison

2nd Baden Brigade   GL Wilhelm von Hochberg

Staff and light dragoons	–	68
2nd Infantry Regiment, *Hochberg*	8 companies	1,030
Light Infantry Battalion	1	828
Half of 2nd Foot Battery	2 × 6-pdr, 2 × howitzer	105
Brigade total		2,031

Source: 'Situation de la Place de Leipzig', 14 October 1813, SHD 2C546.

Baden Strength/Losses after Leipzig

	Present	Dead	Wounded	Missing
1st Infantry Regiment, *Stockhorn*	884	25	44	211
2nd Infantry Regiment, *Hochberg*	587	104	108	206
3rd Infantry Regiment, *Großherzog*	523	72	56	205
Light Infantry Battalion	403	2	9	211
Totals (whole table 3,650)	2,397	203	217	833

Source: GLAK, 48/4351, Hochberg's 20 October 1813 report. 'Present' shows the number of Baden troops who were captured at Leipzig. The 'missing' figure, of course, could include unknown dead or wounded as well as stragglers and deserters. The table does not include the men who escaped as part of formed units (e.g., infantry detached to escort wagons and artillery pieces) or on their own (e.g., those who swam to safety on 19 October).

back. In danger of being cut off, Marchand received orders to withdraw. 'A hail of musket balls from our village' forced the Austrian troops on the left to recoil, but the Hessians were shocked to encounter Prussians behind Zuckelhausen as they moved to retire. 'The infantry opposite us had proceeded to the northern side of the village and seemed as surprised at our appearance as we were to see them on our retreat route,' wrote Frey. The Hessian officers reacted with admirable celerity, slowing the pace of their column and sending skirmishers to chase off their Prussian foes. 'The greater part of the battalion [I/Leib-Garde] would have been laid low had the enemy infantry not been hindered in firing by their surprise and by the number of their ordered and dispersed troops,' observed Frey, 'The enemy now found it appropriate to make room for us and the battalion was soon united with the rest of the brigade that was in the process of retreating to the village of Stötteritz east of Leipzig.' With this fortunate escape from its near isolation, the division pulled out of Zuckelhausen in good order and retired towards Stötteritz in 'masses' owing to the threat of Allied cavalry, frequently halting to deter pursuit and occasionally even conducting brief local counterattacks as it withdrew.[152] The Hessians were unanimous in their admiration for their commander's calm demeanour during the retreat: 'Prince Emil, at the head of the column, led it out of this dangerous situation back to the line of the main army with cool composure and without forcing the march,' noted the admiring Schmidt.[153]

The firm defence of Zuckelhausen and the orderly, measured withdrawal to Stötteritz showed how much the two contingents had matured since their initial trial by fire at Lützen. The training imparted at Lüben during the armistice combined with solid leadership to hammer the Baden and Hessian units into resilient military formations that held together and performed admirably in this fiery crucible despite the potentially debilitating rigours and privations of the preceding weeks.

The division reached its new position south and east of Stötteritz at approximately 2:00 p.m., the Baden brigade deployed in line on the right towards Probstheida and the Hessians on the left with their backs to the village.[154] Prince Emil was pleased and proud that 'only our German division of the 11th Corps had behaved coolly and calmly' during the withdrawal, but he was unhappy with the new location. 'The position was unfortunate,' he recorded, 'Balls rained on us from all sides and caused me to fear considerable loss even though most luckily landed before or behind the line.' To minimise casualties, he and Stockhorn thus shifted their men to take advantage of the numerous ditches, dips and folds afforded by the terrain. 'Much was gained by this,' he concluded, 'as the spot where we had stood was thoroughly dug up by shot and shell from all directions.' Regrettably, noted Emil, the number of 'dead and mangled' mounted despite this careful deployment. Sitting on their packs or on the ground, men were repeatedly struck by the incessant Allied bombardment. Of a group gathered near the prince, shots decapitated one officer, struck another fatally in the head and tore the arm from a third in such quick succession that it seemed as if one ball had caused all the dreadful damage.[155] Moreover, the troops had to suffer the particular agony of enduring the enemy's shot and shell without being able to reply. Reprieve only came when 'night, so silently desired, finally fell' and 'the enemy's destructive endeavours' came to an end.[156]

As usual, the division's artillery, supplemented by at least one battery of French 12-pounders, was deployed in front of the infantry at Stötteritz and supported by skirmishers (the Baden 1st Infantry's 1st Voltigeur Company in the case of the French guns). The Baden guns may have supported the French moves to cover the gap left by the defecting Saxons. As recalled by French Sous-Lieutenant Rilliet: 'a Baden battery arrived at the gallop; these brave Germans seemed to resent the ignominy that the perfidy of the Saxons was heaping on their country'.[157] Late in the afternoon, Russian skirmishers were pestering the gunners and threatening to ensconce themselves in advantageous positions near the batteries. The light infantrymen of I/Garde-Fusiliers were ordered to drive them off in conjunction with the French 8th Hussars. Despite the danger, this was a welcome relief for men who had been sitting under fearful cannon fire for hours. The Hessian skirmishers first redoubled then ceased their fire when the hussars charged followed by the Garde-Fusiliers at the run. 'The soldier awakened anew to life even though death threatened at every moment,' recalled Diehl. Surprised, most of the Russians threw themselves to the ground where they were safe from the hussars' short sabres and where the horses were reluctant to tread on them. Some leaped up to fire at the cavalrymen as soon as they had ridden past. The Hessian fusiliers, however, soon arrived and snatched up some 30–40 of the Russians who they turned over to the 8th Hussars as prisoners; another 20 captured somewhat later they escorted to the rear themselves.[158]

Though relieved of the bothersome Russian skirmishers, the busy Hessian gunners encountered a frustrating problem of a different sort: ammunition. Having exhausted their own caissons, they had resupplied from French stocks only to discover to their chagrin that the French 6-pounder balls were slightly larger than their own. All six of the battery's cannon were thus soon out of action with outsized balls lodged in their barrels. Four of the cannon and (apparently) the two howitzers were sent across the Elster and would thus be saved from the coming debacle, but an enterprising lieutenant and his men managed to restore two of the 6-pounders to serviceability and these remained with the brigade for the remainder of the battle.[159]

It had been a grim and trying day, but the men of the Baden and Hessian contingents had turned in a solid, professional performance. The move to Zuckelhausen had been executed smoothly and the 39th Division had held on to the village, only retreating under orders when nearly isolated. The withdrawal to their new position between Probstheida and Stötteritz had also been conducted with great skill and composure. Enemy pressure eased once the division was deployed in its new location as the Allies did not believe they could launch a full assault on Stötteritz without first capturing Probstheida which the French were defending with great tenacity. Nonetheless, the Baden and Hessian troops held on stoutly under heavy fire, made small but effective local counterattacks and employed their artillery to good effect. Indeed, both contingents exhausted their artillery ammunition, the eight Hessian pieces alone firing 855 rounds of various types during the day. Both also paid a price for their actions. According to his first reports, Emil counted 217 dead, wounded or captured and 162 missing for a total of 379 or approximately 21 per cent of his strength on 16 October.[160] As a specific example, Diehl's company (as *Fourrier* he was responsible for the muster lists) had numbered 79 men on 17 October but lost 38 during the following day to count only 41 men in the ranks that night.[161] Stockhorn's journal noted a comparatively light initial estimate of 136 dead or wounded (with no figure for missing).[162] Adding some missing to the Baden figure and deducting several hundred sent west across the Elster during the night to escort guns and baggage, it seems likely that the 39th Division still counted 3,400–3,500 officers and men present under arms on the morning of 19 October.

'The brigade spent the night in this position,' recorded the Baden journal, 'The vehicles of the train with 100 men as escort, then the reserve park and two cannon as well as the artillery ambulance were sent back towards Lindenau on the road to Lützen.'[163] The Hessians likewise directed most of their wagons across the tangled waterways to the west of Leipzig in addition to all but two of their guns. These measures, while prudent, were clear indications that the next day would bring a general retreat.

'This Memorable Catastrophe': 19 October

The 19th of October was indeed a day of retreat, as well as one of confusion, conflicting orders and bitter fighting. Most of the Baden troops would finally be united under Wilhelm's command, but only just in time to surrender, and both he and Emil would confront the challenge of discerning the path of honour in the chaos during the final moments of what a Baden account termed 'this memorable catastrophe'.[164]

The day began with withdrawal for the 39th Division. Ordered to the Grimma Gate, the men were shocked at the chaotic scene revealed by the rising sun. 'All the roads were covered with columns of all arms and equipment trains,' wrote Emil, 'One could not contemplate without astonishment how one would be able to withdraw in such disorder under the eyes of a powerful and [illegible] enemy, how one could dare to leave one's position in the full light of day when all entrances to the city, only an hour distant, were clogged with baggage, artillery and sutlers' wagons.' Nonetheless, 'Leipzig had to be defended to prevent annihilation', and the division slowly rammed its way through the jumbled mass of men, women, horses and vehicles to take up a position along the esplanade on both side of the inner gate by around 8:00 a.m., Hessians on the left with their two remaining guns, Badeners on the right.[165] Behind them, a detachment of fifty or so Baden light infantry from the 2nd Brigade was posted inside the gate, denying passage to all but imperial adjutants and the seriously wounded. Similar small detachments of the Baden Light Battalion guarded the Peterstor, the Halle Gate and apparently other gates and portals as well.[166]

Napoleon, in his last meeting with his allies, paused by the brigades as he entered the city at approximately 9:30 that morning. He exchanged a few words with Stockhorn and the Hessians, asking his usual questions about their condition and their losses the previous day, pronouncing 'all good, all good' before riding on. Most of the men never saw him again.

Also in front of the Grimma Gate were the five remaining pieces of Leutnant Fleischmann's Württemberg light battery from Normann's brigade. As Normann had already defected and none of the Württemberg officers in Leipzig had offered guidance, Fleischmann decided to save as many of his men and horses as possible. When the Allied attack intensified, therefore, he abandoned his guns and somehow withdrew into the city through the crush of men and vehicles. He managed to salvage 41 men and 22 horses by this timely move, but the rest were captured or temporarily lost in the confusion of the battle. At least two of his guns were still serviceable and loaded with canister; these the Hessians used to stave off Prussian attacks during the coming fight until they were overpowered by Russian and Swedish guns.[167]

Prinz Emil sent his two cannons to the rear in hopes of preserving them from capture, but the Hessian infantry remained in this position outside the Grimma Gate throughout the morning as the Allies rather belatedly opened their assault. A soldier of I/Leib Regiment named A. Bieler and his comrades were searching the abandoned Württemberg caissons for food outside the gate when the attack began. 'While we were busily plundering away, a number of balls flew overhead to slam into the walls around the gate,' he wrote, 'The rain of balls came nearer and nearer and increased significantly; the crashing of the explosions in the suburbs caused a dreadful din and the constant booming and reverberations deafened the ear.'[168] Shifting their attention to defence, Bieler and his compatriots stoutly helped hold off growing numbers of Allied attackers and launched periodic counterthrusts to drive back their assailants. The I/Garde-Fusiliers, for example, reinforced the French at the Outer Grimma Gate for a time and charged forward again later to gain a brief respite. Similarly, Emil, worried about enemy approaching from the Hintertor to his left, dispatched II/Leib to protect this flank. In the end, however, all was for naught. Retreating in desperation, Emil found a portal in the north-eastern corner of the old city walls and led some of his troops through to temporary safety. The way was too narrow for most of his remaining men, however, and the space atop the wall did not permit him to deploy, so he raced down to the interior streets. In the confusion along the esplanade, some of the battalions did not get the word to withdraw or were unable to disentangle themselves from combat. As a result, the bulk of Emil's brigade and hundreds of French were stymied outside the Grimma Gate, as Kösterus noted:

> Ordered action now ceased. A horrible shouting, cursing and raging filled the air before the blocked gate, while those still fighting outside, posted behind trees, in doorways, in shopkeepers' stalls, etc., exerted themselves to hold back the enemies who were in a position to break through to the plaza from the nearby streets of the suburbs.[169]

The Baden light infantry detachment charged with guarding the gate had been ordered to allow only imperial couriers and select others to enter. In perhaps overzealous interpretation of their instructions, they refused to open the gate despite the desperate situation on the outer side. A furious exchange between Baden and Hessian officers ensued as the fighting raged. Speaking through a firing slit in the wall, the Badener threatened to shoot anyone who tried to enter. The Hessian responded with a like warning while ordering two of his sappers to smash the gate with their axes. The rotten old gate soon gave way and, fortunately, the Baden light infantrymen did not fire on their allies when the Hessians forced their way in.[170] The angry Hessians were thus able to collect themselves to resume their defence while the Baden soldiers hastily tried to restore the barricade behind the broken gate.

Having descended from the wall, Emil's band was re-united with most of the rest of his men inside the walls north of the Grimma Gate. Several officers who had fallen into enemy hands freed themselves to join the group here. 'With the gate once again barricaded, a few Hessian officers, namely Major Königer of the Leib Regiment, came inside, they had already been captured and were without hat or epaulettes, but were able to escape again owing to the disorder prevalent among the enemy.'[171] The prince and his officers, however, soon found their situation impossible. The enemy had already broken into the city at multiple points and the Hessians, desperately seeking escape, found all routes of egress cut off. 'We, too, hoped to make it out of the [Ranstädt] gate and over the bridge to avoid capture,' wrote Diehl, but it was too late. As Bieler remembered: 'We had only just gained sight of the first street that led away from the Grimma

Gate when a rain of balls from a Prussian column came at us ... Meanwhile, the danger grew with every moment ... From this point on everything dissolved.' 'The matter was decided,' the prince reported and, though his men were more than loyal, 'Captivity was their fate and mine as well.' Hiding their regimental standards, most of the brigade's sad remnants submitted to their captors and were led to the city's market square. Sergeant C. G. Roller of the Prussian 2nd Reserve Infantry Regiment had the honour of capturing Emil and claimed to have protected him from fellow Prussians who had hoped to rob the prince and his officers, but the prince apparently ended up 'thoroughly robbed' anyway.[172]

Several officers, however, managed to escape before giving their words of honour not to serve against the Allies. Many soldiers also eluded the enemy. Bieler was one of these: 'As I had no desire to share captivity with my *Hauptmann* and was also not interested in blows from Prussian musket butts or other mistreatment, I betook myself to retreat further surrounded by the most imminent threat of death.' He would make a narrow escape through the chaotic city to gain Lindenau, where he had a brief glimpse of Napoleon before joining the crowd of fugitives struggling westward. Baden Leutnant Wolff had a similar experience, lucky to have a reason to leave the falling city as he struggled through the crowds to escort Arrighi's baggage to the rear. 'It was an indescribable crush,' he recalled, 'This retreat had much in common with that from Russia.' Reporting to his French superior in Weißenfels, he was simply told: 'Farewell, save yourself!'[173]

Also joining the swarm of retreating men, horses and vehicles were the Hessian artillerymen who had manned the two pieces left with the brigade. Instructed to seek safety west of the city, they were still wending their way through the confused crush towards the causeway bridge to Lindenau when it was prematurely destroyed. Unable to save their guns and horses, they rendered the cannons unusable, left their horses behind, and swam or waded to the far side of the Elster to camp in no little misery near Lützen that night. As the journal of the Garde-Fusiliers recorded, the Hessian prisoners remaining in Leipzig 'experienced the pain of seeing among the trophies of the enemy two Hessian pieces that had to be left behind owing to the destruction of the Pleiße [sic] bridge and could not watch without anger as enemy officers made use of Prinz Emil's horses and equipment as well as those of many staff officers.' Emil's presence, however, inspired his men, as Major Zimmermann wrote on 20 October: 'We had to bear our further fate all the more courageously as our beloved prince shared it with us.'[174]

The story of the Baden 1st Brigade was more complex but reached a similar conclusion. Around 10:00, that is shortly after his brief exchange with Napoleon and before the Grimma Gate came under attack, Stockhorn was ordered to the

Peterstor (Peter's Gate) where he was to come under the command of Marshal Augereau.[175] No sooner had the brigade reached its new destination when Marchand galloped up and ordered the 3rd Infantry back to the Grimma Gate at the double to throw back Allied troops that were threatening to overwhelm the gate's defenders. Heading directly for the gate, the 2nd Battalion quickly found itself in combat with Prussians on the esplanade, while Stockhorn, following with the 1st Battalion, a squadron of cuirassiers and some Polish lancers, swung to the right to repulse Russians who were emerging from the suburbs south of the Spitaltor.[176] Having succeeded in pushing back the attackers, at least for a short time, Stockhorn returned to the 1st Infantry at the Peterstor. Here he received instructions from Graf Wilhelm to bring his brigade to the city's market square. After consulting with Adjutant-Commandant Pierre Joseph Richard, the 39th Division's chief of staff, Stockhorn rode to recall the 3rd Regiment but was unable to reach them and returned to join the 1st Infantry as it made its way into the city. Richard rode with them. Like Emil, however, Stockhorn found the streets already teeming with Allied soldiers. Though taken under fire almost at once, he and his men managed to reach the square only to find it already occupied by the enemy. Just as a Russian officer demanded his surrender, two Baden majors appeared to inform him that Wilhelm had already capitulated and that he was to bring his men to the square to join the remains of the 2nd Brigade. Disconsolate, he dutifully marched the reduced regiment to the square and formed it next to the Saxon Guard Grenadiers to await events. As he would write in his report, therefore, 'The results of 18 and 19 October brought about the catastrophe which united the rest of the troops with the Second Brigade at the moment when both would have to surrender in Leipzig.'[177]

The 3rd Baden Infantry was unable to enter the city at all. Disordered by friendly fire from the walls and ditch after repelling the Russians south of the Spitaltor, it was still near the city's south-eastern corner when Stockhorn tried but failed to reach it with the order to retire to the market square. Precise details of its subsequent travails are unclear, but it seems to have swung around the outside of the city walls to struggle over the Pleiße near the Pleißenburg only to be scattered and destroyed between the Pleiße and the Elster along with many French and Polish units. In Wilhelm's words: 'only a few could still come into the city; all the rest were wounded, killed, or sprang into the water and were captured'.[178]

As for Wilhelm and the remains of his 2nd Brigade, most were distributed to the various city gates in small detachments: a hundred to the Halle Gate and fifty each to the Grimma, Peter's and Ranstädt Gates. A few guards seem to have been placed at several of the smaller portals as well. He posted others in the Pleißenburg and in the gardens outside the walls and held the rest in reserve in the market square.[179] In the increasingly chaotic and desperate circumstances, he tried to maintain a strictly correct stance so as not to compromise his personal sense of honour or the honour of the army and the grand duchy. When Napoleon appeared for his farewell meeting with Saxon King Friedrich August, for example, Wilhelm deliberately stepped aside to avoid speaking with the emperor. He feared Napoleon would make him promise to defend the city at all costs and he did not want to consider himself bound to an order that would result in 'the certain destruction of a German city to spare the French army a few casualties while losing all the rest of our troops'.[180] Disdainful of Arrighi, who he believed had fled dishonourably, he was determined to remain to the last: 'I regarded it as my duty to stay at the post that had been entrusted to me,' he would write. The end of this duty, however, was not long in coming. As Allied troops swarmed into the market square around midday, the various Baden light infantry detachments fell back to the square as well while a Russian officer hailed Wilhelm and called upon him to surrender:

> Cut off by the destruction of the Elster bridge and entirely surrounded by superior numbers of Allied troops, no choice remained to me but to comply with the request made to me and thereby at least save what little remained of the Baden troops, whose preservation was of the highest importance to the grand duke in the anticipated political shift.[181]

Surrender rather than Defection

By the time the Allied monarchs and their glittering suites rode into Leipzig sometime before one o'clock that afternoon, all the Baden and Hessian troops still in the city had surrendered. The sudden transformation from Napoleon's departure to the arrival of his opponents left many observers staring in wonder. It was 'a surprising, unforgettable scene', remembered Baden surgeon Meier, in which 'enemies became friends'.[182] Or so he hoped. In actuality, the transition from foes to friends would be neither simple nor rapid for the troops of the two grand duchies.

'To Your Royal Majesty I humbly report that yesterday was remarkable and tragic for Your Majesty's contingent, as it resulted in our complete dissolution and brought us into the hands of the Coalition powers.' Thus Wilhelm began his report of the events of 19 October. Though finally united, the status of his command was unclear. They had surrendered but had not been disarmed: 'All that came into the city and to the market square have till now retained their muskets and their personal possessions and have been treated till now with care and courtesy,' he wrote on the 20th.[183] Emil's few remaining Hessians found themselves in a similar situation. From the first, the Allies acted as if both contingents had switched sides, an assumption both Wilhelm and Emil rejected. Indeed, in this awkward situation, they were determined to demonstrate the opposite: that they had remained loyal to their instructions and had *not* defected. Wilhelm, for example, was embarrassed when some Baden soldiers recruited from formerly Austrian regions gave a cheer on the arrival of Kaiser Franz in the square, and he was appalled during a call with Bernadotte when the former French marshal asked if he could not have captured Napoleon while the emperor was in Leipzig. Comments from two of Bernadotte's staff officers only heightened his concerns: 'Both believed that we had changed sides, which was very uncomfortable for me.' 'I assured them', he wrote later, 'that this was not the case and that I would not serve again until I had received the order to do so from the grand duke, whose situation so close to the French border was very difficult.'[184]

Stockhorn, troubled that his men were conducted to the market square 'as if we had gone over to the Allied armies', took particular pains to avoid any misapprehension. On receiving Wilhelm's order to come to the marketplace, he attempted to secure approval from his proper chain of command. As noted above, he consulted the 39th Division's chief of staff, Adjutant-Commandant Richard after failing to locate Augereau, Poniatowski or Marchand. He took care to be very precise in his report to Carl:

> I asked him [Richard] for his opinion, and he told to me to obey this order [from Wilhelm] as I could not get any orders from the division commander at that moment. He himself rode in with the regiment. I humbly hold myself duty-bound to make special mention of this circumstance in order to pre-empt any possible rumours that this regiment had gone over because the appearance could be given credence easily as we are not yet disarmed.
>
> I had come thus far in this most humble report when I received the attached newspaper and the army report, wherein mention is made of a Baden regiment changing sides. As this statement is utterly groundless and could be particularly disadvantageous, in part for Your Royal Majesty's realm and also in relation to the order that I obeyed from Graf von Hochberg, thus do I humbly submit these pieces as well so that Your Majesty may initiate whatever steps you deem appropriate.
>
> I learn just now that we will be disarmed tomorrow and sent to Berlin; I would have wished that we had been disarmed at once to avoid any misperception.[185]

Assigned a bivouac area near the Spitaltor, the Baden and Hessian troops numbered 2,397 and approximately 245 respectively.[186] They were indeed disarmed on 21 October, turning in their weapons against receipts for later recovery. There was some initial theft and abuse by their captors, but they were generally treated well as the Allies were interested in 'possession of the German troops' and hoped to cajole or bully Wilhelm and Emil into changing sides.[187] As part of this effort to bring the Baden and Hessian troops to the Allied side, Wilhelm was received with great courtesy in his audiences with Bernadotte, Tsar Alexander and King Friedrich Wilhelm III. At the same time, he detected darker undercurrents. The Allies had given Prussia authority over the Baden and Hessian prisoners and after his meeting with the king on the 21st, Wilhelm commented that 'the well-meaning and simple comportment of the king did me a lot of good and contrasted favourably with the arrogance and the contempt that manifested itself in the attitude of so many Prussian officers who could not conceal their hatred for the "*Rheinbündler*" [Confederation of the Rhine troops]'. Despite repeated royal inducements, pressing invitations to take Prussian service and the looming threat of transportation to Siberia, both Wilhelm and Emil were committed to waiting for instructions from their monarchs and refused to defect on their own initiative. When they marched off to captivity in Prussia on 22 October, Wilhelm even insisted on an escort 'in order to show that we had not changed sides'.[188] Although Wilhelm and Emil rejected the Allied offers, the Prussians permitted them to send officers to their respective capitals to learn the intentions of their sovereigns: GM von Schäffer (who had remained behind when imperial headquarters departed) and a major to Karlsruhe and one of Emil's adjutants to Darmstadt. The Prussians had granted three weeks to receive replies before the prisoners would be transported to Russia, but answers were a long time coming. As the weeks passed, the Baden and Hessian officers had to fend off increasing Prussian pressure and simultaneously dissuade their men from accepting offers from British agents attempting to recruit them into the Russo-German Legion. Only at the end of November did the two princes receive word that their rulers had joined the Allies and that they were free to head home. Another month would elapse before the former prisoners of war reached their garrisons, but by the end of December, they had all returned, just in time to participate in preparations for the 1814 campaign in France as members of the Coalition forces.

Countering Calumnies:
'Strict Obedience to the Orders of their Royal Sovereign'

Long before they marched to a welcome reception in Karlsruhe, the Badeners were engaged in defending their honour against charges of disloyalty and defection. The initial assertions and insinuations came not from the French but from Allied battle reports published immediately after Leipzig. No such allegations were made against the Hessians, but these charges against Baden later gained purchase in French histories and Baden veterans thus found themselves contending with inaccurate accusations that persisted for many years after the Napoleonic Wars had concluded.

The first point of contention arose while the Badeners were still in Leipzig. Released under Schwarzenberg's name, the Austrian official bulletin on the just concluded battle included a statement that a Baden infantry regiment had followed the example of the Saxons and 'turned its weapons against the French'. Wilhelm was incensed. He complained directly to Bernadotte during their conversation on the 20th and immediately wrote a dignified but firm letter to Schwarzenberg to request a retraction. As the Austrian report had been released to the public and soon appeared in various newspapers, Wilhelm also had his 'correction' (*Berichtigung*) published. GM von Schäffer, en route to Karlsruhe to seek the grand duke's orders for the contingent, delivered the 'correction' to a journal in Nuremberg where it was included in the 27 October edition. It was also carried in the Baden official paper, stressing that the troops 'had again on this occasion honourably distinguished themselves by strict and meticulous obedience to the orders of their royal sovereign'.[189] Austria never issued a retraction, but Wilhelm and his officers at least had the satisfaction of seeing their more accurate account in print.[190]

In addition to the vague assertion that a Baden regiment had fired on the French, some accounts specifically stated that Baden troops had shot at the French and German defenders outside the Grimma Gate. Although there is no indication that a Baden unit intentionally opened fire on their French allies, it is entirely possible that one or more 'friendly fire' incidents occurred in the bitter and confused fighting along the esplanade between the city walls and the suburbs on the morning of the 19th as the Baden II/3rd Infantry counter-attacked towards the gate. Rather than the Badeners firing on the French, it was they who were disordered by musketry from the ditch and possibly from the walls. In an article published anonymously in the French *Spectateur Militaire* in 1828, Wilhelm offered the following detail:

> During this affair, the Baden battalion, which was advancing along the esplanade, came under fire from outside the town's moat; this fusillade, about which the French also complained, was undoubtedly caused by isolated individuals, who, separated from the columns of their units, had put themselves in a place of safety in order not to be surprised, or by some hotheads who did not belong to the army and were not recognised owing to the disorder that existed among the troops.

Wilhelm's description of a regrettable friendly fire situation is reasonable and represents the most likely explanation, but some of this firing may have originated with soldiers of the Baden Light Battalion as assumed by some historians. It is also possible, as stated in some accounts, that local inhabitants contributed to the confusion by loosing a few shots against the French and their German allies from the city's walls.[191]

The second point of contention concerned allegations by Allied writers that Baden troops had turned over the Peterstor to the enemy without a fight. This claim seems to have originated in a memoir published by Dmitry Petrovich Buturlin, one of the tsar's adjutants, in 1817. In the grand square, wrote Buturlin, 'the victorious Russians and Prussians [met] an Austrian column to which a Baden company that was guarding the Peterstor had allowed free entry'. This statement was problematic for at least two reasons. A minor discrepancy was that there were no Austrians involved in storming Leipzig on 19 October (other than a few Jägers supporting with skirmish fire); there was certainly no 'Austrian column'. More significant was that the Peterstor was opened *from the inside* by attacking Prussians. These exuberant attackers (I/Pomeranian Infantry Regiment, Fusiliers/2nd Reserve Regiment and Pomeranian Grenadiers) were pursuing French fugitives from the city's centre towards the Peterstor and, pushing through the gate from the inside out to the esplanade, they then proceeded to engage with enemy troops – including the 3rd Baden Infantry – who were trying to escape *outside* the city walls. There was thus no question of assaulting the gate from the exterior. The fate of the fifty or so Baden light infantrymen assigned to the Peterstor, however, is unclear. Most likely, as Aster records, they marched to the market square and joined their countrymen.[192] Stockhorn, Adjutant-Commandant Richard and the 1st Baden Infantry had already passed on to the market square. Perhaps the light infantrymen joined Stockhorn's regiment? They may simply have fled. Attacked from the rear in a period of great confusion, they would have been surprised and overwhelmed by the jubilant Prussians if they had remained at their post in any case, and Prussian accounts make no mention of either resistance or capitulation when they approached the gate from the city's streets.[193] A similar scene seems to have played out at the Barfußpförtchen where a city resident watched the small Baden guard detachment lay down its muskets on the approach of Prussians (Fusiliers/2nd Reserve Regiment) from inside the city's walls.[194]

Picked up by prominent French historians and memoirists in the ensuing years, however, Buturlin's remark persisted. These publications prompted Wilhelm to submit rebuttals to widely read military journals in Germany and France in the 1820s. In his efforts to correct the record, he cited Stockhorn's report quoted above and the absence of an actual Allied assault on the Peterstor to demonstrate that 'there was nothing to reproach in the conduct of the Baden general and that he had scrupulously fulfilled his duties vis-à-vis his ally'.[195]

The various accusations levelled against the Baden contingent for its actions at Leipzig on 19 October were thus largely hollow. One or more friendly fire incidents likely occurred along the esplanade that morning in which the 3rd infantry and possibly some French troops were the victims and in which some Baden light infantrymen may have been among the perpetrators. This, however, was the product of combat confusion on the part of what seems to have been a fairly small number of individuals, not an intentional attack on the French by outraged Badeners as some sort of vengeful act of rebellion. The claim that Baden troops handed the Peterstor over to Allied troops, on the other hand, was a clear canard as the gate fell to Prussians attacking from inside the city. 'Baden veterans later always rejected every other characterisation of their behaviour as an insult,' wrote the 3rd Infantry's regimental historian, 'At that time, they proved their convictions by freely choosing captivity to remain true to the orders of the sovereign lord.'[196]

Finally, despite easy assumptions on the part of the Allies, neither the Baden nor the Hessian contingent switched sides. Instead, both very deliberately surrendered. Rather than defecting, even in that desperate hour, they consigned their contingents to captivity, hiding their flags and taking receipts for their weapons while awaiting word from their monarchs. Though separated from the rest and unaware of the surrender, even the Baden 3rd Infantry did not defect. Its officers and men tried to escape over the Elster (many drowning in the attempt) and only capitulated when no other option remained. There is no indication that officers or men of either contingent objected to the choice of surrender over defection as the honourable course. Indeed, a minority (Stockhorn and a few others) worried that perhaps they should have fought longer or been disarmed immediately to avoid being branded as oath-breakers. For the two commanders, however, their path was clear. Despite Wilhelm's internal conflict between his sense of duty and his 'German heart', and despite Allied threats to transport their men to Siberia if they did not change sides, both he and Emil adhered to their conception of loyalty to their rulers and their two contingents marched off to Prussia as prisoners of war.[197]

Remnants in Retreat

While most of the Baden and Hessian infantry headed off to Prussian captivity, parts of both contingents were slogging westwards in the jumbled stream of the retreating Grande Armée. The remaining elements of the Baden contingent retreated in two fairly coherent detachments – artillery and cavalry – while the Hessians were dispersed in mostly ad hoc groupings that only gradually and adventitiously came together.

The Hessian Garde-Chevaulegers, for example, were already west of the Elster on 19 October. Numbering only 64 officers and men fit for duty, the regiment had taken part in some minor skirmishing on 16 October when 4th Corps crossed over to Lindenau. Along with the remains of the Westphalian Chevaulegers-Garde and Franquemont's two Württemberg cavalry regiments, they then participated in Bertrand's successful attack on Plagwitz on the 18th that netted several hundred Austrian prisoners and helped to open the army's route of retreat. It is not clear, however, that the Hessian and Westphalian regiments of the Beaumont/Wolff brigade (barely more than 200 men in total) contributed to this small victory in any significant manner.[198] Retreating with the army on the 19th, the regiment returned to Darmstadt on 30 October.

Along the way, the Garde-Chevaulegers met up with the remaining six guns of the Hessian artillery battery, most of the gunners and a detachment of 100 or so infantrymen under the ailing Oberst von Schönberg who had left Leipzig on the night of 18/19 October to escort the contingent's baggage. Passing through Erfurt, most of this extemporaneous grouping reached Vacha on 25 October. Here they saw their last action of the campaign, coming under fire from the Baden battery, which mistook them for the enemy, with the Hessians then firing a few of their remaining rounds to chase off Mensdorff's raiding detachment of Cossacks and Austrian hussars. Unfortunately, the Hessian intervention was too late to save the Baden battery from being overrun and mostly captured. Although they were involved in no further combat action after this brief clash, details of the Hessian march home are cloudy. Schönberg seems to have received permission to leave the Grande Armée at some point, so that the various elements of the contingent set off towards the Main River more or less independently. Through a combination of cleverness, brazen bluffing and good luck the Hessian groups carefully skirted through and around Hanau just before the battle there began, some of them even negotiating with Bavarian GL von Rechberg to allow safe passage. By these boldly adventurous means, the remaining components of the contingent returned to their garrisons between 30 October and 3 November, just as the grand duchy was changing sides to join the Allies.[199] Emil and his detachment of prisoners, of course, were on their way to Prussia, but also left behind and still fighting under French eagles were the two Hessian battalions besieged in Torgau. Their story will be told in Chapter 8.

The Baden experience was more straightforward, but its artillery less fortunate. Although Stockhorn had sent back all four of his guns before the 19th, three of these were ensnared in the disorder of the retreat east of the Elster and fell into Allied hands. Wilhelm had also dispatched his four pieces across the Elster and all four safely reached Erfurt along with the contingent's reserve artillery park. Joined by Stockhorn's lone remaining cannon, the combined remnants of the two Baden half-batteries headed west only to be engulfed by Cossacks on 25 October near Vacha between Gotha and Fulda as noted above. The nearby Hessian guns helped drive off the attackers, but Mensdorff's Cossacks and hussars had already devastated the remains of the Baden artillery component, capturing four of the five pieces, almost all the other vehicles and many of the men. The surviving 6-pounder would become something of an icon for the Baden artillery for participating in six campaigns between 1805 and 1815, but that was small consolation to the gunners who had lost all their other pieces between Leipzig and their return to garrison on 3 November.[200]

The Baden 1st Light Dragoons, on the other hand, concluded their time as French allies with some ceremony and considerable honour. Despite the ferocity of the fighting at Leipzig, the light dragoons were not engaged during the battle and crossed the Elster on 19 October having lost only one man during the four days of fury – a trooper who had been attached to one of the French division commanders as a courier. The regiment marched through Weißenfels and Freyburg in the company of the French 10th Hussars to reach Erfurt on 23 October before continuing on to have its final skirmish with Allied cavalry near Gotha on the 25th. Arriving in Eisenach the following day, the Baden dragoons were assigned to escort Napoleon to Vacha that evening. At some point during this mission, Oberstleutnant von Degenfeld apparently sought permission to leave the Grande Armée for home, a request Napoleon granted with warm compliments to the regiment. On 27 October, therefore, the Badeners took their leave of their French comrades-in-arms in what became an emotional exchange. GB Beurmann praised the light dragoons for their courage and loyalty in a brief speech and Colonel Jean Nicolas Curély of the 10th Hussars, surrounded by his officers, likewise paid tribute to the Badeners, closing with: 'Although we will soon encounter one another as enemies, as long as I am commander of the 10th Hussar Regiment, not a man will draw his sabre against a Baden dragoon!' The men of the two regiments mingled for a time to pay each other 'a hearty farewell' and the Badeners departed to return to their garrison on 3 November with approximately 280 officers and men still fit for duty.[201]

A Different Fate: Prussia or Siberia?

Both contingents left behind many sick soldiers whose fates are unknown. Georg Klein, a common soldier of the Hessian Leib-Garde, however, composed a short summary of his service during 1813 in a simple, guileless style. It is likely that his experience echoed that of many Badeners and Hessians who fell ill and were lost to their regiments during these difficult campaigns.[202]

Conscripted in June 1812, Klein was assigned to the Leib-Garde depot when the army was re-formed in 1813 and thus marched out with his regiment in early

April. He was present at Lützen, where he saw a man ahead of him lose a leg, and then at Bautzen where 'we had our position on a height and could oversee the battlefield ... Twenty-one villages were on fire,' he noted, and continued, 'We were victorious and marched through Görlitz and Bunzlau over the border into Schlesing [Schlesien, Silesia].' After the armistice, he fell seriously ill with an unspecified ailment sometime in late September or early October while 11th Corps was east of Dresden: 'Owing to the continuous marching back and forth, the lack of food, exertions day and night, and no shelter, my health declined.' The army was now in retreat but there was no transport for the sick.

> No wagon was to be had. So me and many other sick were told we should drag ourselves along as far as possible. The retreat went towards Wittenberg. Now, when one is sick and needs rest but should carry a musket that weighs 12 pounds, a cartridge box with 50 rounds, a pack of 30 pounds, then everyone must see that this is impossible. To make myself lighter, I threw my musket away, my cartridge box too. When I had marched for a quarter of an hour, however, I had to sit myself down. Thus I lost the division as is easy to understand. Cossacks took me prisoner many times, but God protected me, and I came away with my life, although many sick French were stabbed to death at my side. When a German said '*Sachs*' [Saxon], then they let you through. I finally reached Wittenberg after many tribulations as it was autumn and cold and poor clothing and, as already said, sick. I was so full of vermin that I could not rest in a warm room.

Somewhat recovered, Klein left Wittenberg after several days to seek his regiment and, after more escapes from Cossacks, came upon three fellow ailing Hessians who had also been left behind owing to the lack of transport. It was now mid-October. They heard the guns at Leipzig and learned from the locals that there was 'a dreadful battle'. Although the villagers had sheltered and fed Klein and his compatriots for some days, they were now nervous to have French allies in their midst and the Hessians were forced to leave once they were 'somewhat on their feet again'. They headed directly towards Leipzig but encountered Prussian military police who directed them to Halle where they could receive passes to return home.

> We went to Halle but unfortunately instead of passes we were taken prisoner. We were given the option of taking service [with Prussia] or going to Siberia as prisoners. We took service, received quarters, and began once again to live like humans.

Sadly, nothing more is known about Klein, his service in Prussian uniform or his subsequent fate. His pithy, naïve memoir, however, not only illustrates a common soldier's miseries when taken ill, it also shows that he and his compatriots were principally interested in re-joining their units and eventually returning home. They displayed no interest in being taken prisoner or changing sides and only took service in the Prussian army at the last extremity when presented with the prospect of consignment to the imagined horrors of Siberia. It seems likely that most men in the Baden and Hessian contingents, and likely many others, shared this attitude.

From France to the Coalition: A Capitulation not a Convention

Moving from the micro-history of one common soldier, the narrative now returns to the higher plane of international politics. With their contingents captured, Napoleon defeated and Allied troops on the borders of their realms, Baden and Hesse faced existential crises. Moreover, Bavaria's defection and Wrede's march had shaken both states: Baden as an immediate neighbour and Hesse as a dynasty related to the Bavarian Wittelsbachs by marriage. As the Bavarian ambassador in Darmstadt reported: 'It would be as difficult as superfluous to depict the deep impression that the change of system attributed to the court in Munich has produced here as in all states of the Rheinbund.'[203] Nor were there pre-existing covert contacts to exploit. Unlike Saxony, Bavaria and Württemberg, neither of the states had been approached by the Coalition partners prior to Leipzig. Karlsruhe and Darmstadt would thus be surprised by the turn of events in late October and, like Stuttgart, would have to take crucial decisions along very short timelines.

Baden: 'My Country is Defenceless'[204]

In Baden's case, its propinquity to France was an extenuating factor and its leaders tried to use their location 'under the cannons of Strasbourg' to solicit leniency in their dealings with the Coalition powers.[205] Graf Wilhelm had mentioned Baden's fear of its powerful French neighbour in his audience with Friedrich Wilhelm III in Leipzig and Großherzog Carl echoed this theme when he sent Schäffer to the Prussian king with a letter requesting an extension of the three-week deadline concerning the future of his captive contingent. The grand duke hoped for full acknowledgement of Baden's neutrality given 'the topographic situation of the land with a border of more than 30 [German] miles[206] vulnerable to the incursions of the French' as well as the steps he had already taken in Paris to secure neutral status for his state. At the same time, Reitzenstein wrote to the Prussian foreign minister to reinforce the request.[207] Friedrich Wilhelm seemed sympathetic, but his vague sympathy did not translate into acceptance of Baden neutrality.

Baden also appealed to Napoleon: Carl's mention of 'steps taken in Paris' referred to a request that the French ambassador solicit Napoleon's approval of Baden's neutrality after a cabinet meeting in Karlsruhe on 25 October. No immediate reply was forthcoming, but pressure on the government increased as a 27 October letter from Wrede arrived peremptorily demanding that the French ambassador be expelled and that Baden's troops be rapidly assembled 'for the general purpose of the good cause of the Allies'. In addition to Wrede's Austro-Bavarian army, Mensdorff's raiding detachment was probing towards the grand duchy's northern frontiers and the authorities in Karlsruhe worried about informal pillage as well as formal exactions. With Allied troops encroaching on his realm and time running out, Carl sent a personal letter to the emperor on 3 November with an urgent entreaty. 'Since the change in policy by the courts of Munich and Stuttgart, my country is defenceless on a long, extended border vulnerable to incursions, and its situation has become a most perilous one,' he wrote, a state of neutrality like Switzerland's was 'the only way to save my land from total ruin'. Napoleon's answer came in a note from the French ambassador on 5 November. It was a complete rejection of the request for neutrality. Napoleon offered asylum in France and recommended that Baden's troops evacuate to the left bank of the Rhine, but the emperor, wrote the ambassador, could only have 'friends or foes' on his borders. The grand duke, therefore, 'cannot be in doubt about the side he must chose'.[208]

The appeals to Napoleon having failed, Baden hastened to send an emissary to the Allies, already in Frankfurt. Carl himself would have preferred to stay with France – if only because he was loath to take any difficult decision – but he seemed disconnected from the urgent events, like 'a sleepwalker who strolled along the edge of an abyss' in the words of one historian.[209] His advisors thus prevailed in a cabinet meeting on the evening of 5 November. The meeting's lengthy minutes outlined the rationale for joining the Coalition. 'Given the rejection of neutrality by the French side . . . no further hope can be placed in her, rather a side must inevitably be chosen,' the councillors concluded, but this could not be France as its victory seemed unlikely and thus it would not be able to help or protect Baden. A 'declaration on the Allied side', however, would preserve the existence of the state and ruling house while also positioning Baden favourably should the Coalition succeed in establishing some kind of 'German independence'. Other practical concerns contributed to Baden's decision to join the Allies as rapidly as possible. Carl's cabinet hoped that siding with the Allies would both prevent loss of territory to Bavaria or Württemberg and forestall 'revolutionary' interventions or sequestration by Stein who Reitzenstein characterised as 'this violent and vicious Stein, so well made to be the instrument of hateful passions'.[210] Furthermore, with Wrede's army on Baden's soil and threatening to treat it as an enemy territory, there was an immediate need to protect people and property from unrestricted requisition and plundering by Allied soldiers. The rationale was thus entirely founded on the realpolitik of self-preservation rather than on any notions of pan-German patriotism. The decision taken, Reitzenstein left for Frankfurt on the 6th with hopes of negotiating a treaty similar to those granted to Bavaria and Württemberg. The French ambassador departed the same day, but he was treated with every mark of regret and courtesy, not like the representative of a hostile power.

In Frankfurt, Reitzenstein tried to promote the notion of Baden's neutrality but immediately encountered an adamantine wall of refusal. Indeed, Württemberg's envoy, Zeppelin, reported that the Allies 'laughed at' the Baden proposal.[211] Like their counterparts in Saxony, Bavaria and Württemberg before them, the authorities in Baden discovered that the neutrality option was a chimera and Reitzenstein resorted to hopes that his grand duke's personal intervention might help to mitigate the conditions the Allies planned to impose. Responding to his minister's urgings, Carl thus travelled to Frankfurt on 11 November and, with the help of family connections (Tsarina Elizabeth Alexeievna was his sister), he succeeded in at least partly mollifying the Allied monarchs. Nonetheless, the Allies dictated the treaties that Reitzenstein signed with the three major powers on 20 November, a process he regarded as more a capitulation than a series of conventions among equals.[212] Baden thus joined the Coalition, committing itself by a separate instrument to provide a military contingent 2½ times larger than that demanded by Napoleon: 10,000 regulars and 10,000 Landwehr, 8,000 of whom were to be considered field troops.

Meeting the Coalition's demands presented Baden's bureaucracy with a difficult task. Although Badeners were eager to see an end to the burdens of war, conscription, quartering and supplementary taxes that they associated with Napoleon, there was little enthusiasm for the pan-German cause among the populace and even less at court. Opposition to new conscription measures remained, desertion was a problem for the forces eventually sent west into France and raising even a lone volunteer cavalry regiment proved slow and unsatisfactory.[213] Even the literature produced in the southwestern German states was 'narrow' and 'remarkably moderate' as compared to that in Prussia. What most common people noticed was not the change in enemies and allies, but the simple fact that war and its afflictions persisted. As one pastor remarked, 'Germany was freed from the French yoke in the wake of the victory at Leipzig, but the victors, Austrians as well as Russians and Prussians, with whom the Bavarians, Württembergers and Badeners had allied themselves, filled the German regions along the Rhine like a flood,' bringing disease and consuming everything in their path. 'No one was master in his own house,' commented a local official.[214] Baden soldiers such as Stockhorn who had served under Napoleon and imbibed 'the magic of his genius' harboured lingering admiration for his skills and thought that he might yet succeed against the combined Coalition armies and return across the Rhine.[215] The decision to turn to the Allies was thus taken for pragmatic reasons of state, not pan-German idealism, and not without a degree of ambivalence. The circular Carl sent to the Coalition monarchs on 20 November, for example, made no mention of 'German liberation' and the proclamation released to his subjects that same day was 'lame and feeble' in its brief mentions of 'German freedom and independence'.[216] When Wilhelm returned to Karlsruhe on 9 December, therefore, he described the atmosphere as 'unique': 'On the whole, people were averse to all things French, but they did not quite trust themselves to express their attitudes out loud, in part because of respect for the grand duchess. Thus all that could not be avoided was done, but without enthusiasm for the so-called German cause.'[217]

Hesse-Darmstadt: 'It was a Matter of Life or Death'[218]

Hesse-Darmstadt's experience was similar to Württemberg's: sudden, hasty, and heavily influenced by Bavarian General Wrede. There were also similarities to Baden's situation in that not all members of the grand duchy's cabinet were convinced that changing sides was the right policy and some, including Ludwig, were not even persuaded that Napoleon was irrevocably defeated.

The first tremor of change hit Darmstadt on 24 October in the form of a letter from Wrede. Approaching Würzburg and anticipating that his army would soon enter Hessian territory, the Bavarian general sent his adjutant, Prinz Thurn und Taxis, to Darmstadt with a letter for Großherzog Ludwig. In his typically imperious style, Wrede demanded that Hesse immediately expel the French ambassador and that all Hessian troops must assemble to join his army by the 28th. Furthermore, in their conversations with the Hessians, including the grand duke, Thurn und Taxis and the Bavarian ambassador informed their hosts that failure to accede to Wrede's demands would mean that Hesse-Darmstadt would be treated as enemy territory and would be administered by the allies at Hessian expense. This was all shocking enough – 'the court is beside itself' wrote the Bavarian ambassador – worse was that the prince had appeared in public at the theatre while in full uniform. Wrede's demand, reported the ambassador, 'was generally condemned in form and substance, and even the numerous anti-French party saw nothing in it but a continuation from the other side of the despotism from which one wished to be liberated'.[219]

As news of Leipzig had not yet arrived in Darmstadt and the grand duchy was still an unquestioned French ally, Großherzog Ludwig's advisors concluded that Wrede intended to compromise their sovereign in front of the vigilant French ambassador, Denis Simon Caroillon de Vandeul. Regarding the method of delivery and the presumptuous tone of Wrede's letter as inconsistent with dignity of their grand duke and their country, the Hessians gently rebuffed Wrede's ultimatum and asked Thurn und Taxis to leave at once to avoid exciting French suspicions. The Hessians did tell the prince that they would send a representative to his general, but this was initially planned as an exploratory contact to learn what Wrede intended and to gather basic impressions. Karl Wilhelm Heinrich du Bos du Thil, an intelligent and observant but relatively low-level official, was selected for this mission.

The arrival of a captain who had escaped the Leipzig debacle brought a change in Hessian attitudes and du Thil's mission. 'My son and my troops have been captured,' Ludwig told du Thil on 26 October, 'Now I am determined to do what my brother-in-law [Bavaria's Max Joseph] has done.'[220] Du Thil departed that very day but as he was laboriously making his way to the Austro-Bavarian army, Wrede dispatched a second and more threatening letter. This contained notification that Walsleben's Württemberg brigade was en route to Frankfurt via Darmstadt and a reinforced demand that all Hessian armed personnel – including gendarmes intended for internal policing – join the Württemberg force immediately.[221] Unaware of this new menace, du Thil reached Wrede's headquarters in Aschaffenburg and was able to persuade the general to issue an order of the day for the army to treat Hesse as friendly territory. Back in Darmstadt, however, Ludwig now felt compromised vis-à-vis both belligerent sides. In fear of the Allies as well as Napoleon, he tilted back towards the French alliance and, on the urging of the French ambassador, decided to move to the relative safety of Mannheim in Baden with his family. Ambassador Vandeul had suggested Mainz, but Ludwig chose Mannheim as it took him out of the path of the Allied armies without crossing the Rhine into French territory. His place of refuge thus represented a middle way that avoided definitive commitment to either of the warring parties.[222]

Du Thil, having pledged on his word of honour that Hesse would side with the Coalition, was horrified to learn of Ludwig's seeming policy shift when he reported to his sovereign in Mannheim on 28 October. Further deliberations ensued along lines similar to those in other Rheinbund courts. Some of Ludwig's advisors argued for joining the Coalition as Napoleon could no longer protect their state, while others advocated adherence to the French alliance 'as much might still be expected from this extraordinary man who seems to be defeated at present'. 'There were many persons', noted du Thil, 'who could not detach themselves from the belief in Napoleon's invincibility.'[223] The conference did not reach a firm conclusion, but Ludwig, retiring to consider on his own, eventually decided on the Allies. Du Thil thus returned to Wrede, arriving in Hanau on 30 October just before the opening of the battle. As he and Wrede were beginning their discussion, however, the rumble of cannon fire outside grew to a steady roar and Wrede rode off never to return. The battle thus interrupted their negotiations before they even began and du Thil, trapped in Hanau when the French occupied it, burned his papers to avoid being arrested as a traitor to the Rheinbund.

Talks only resumed late on the 31st when Napoleon and his army continued west towards the Rhine. Wrede having been severely wounded, du Thil's counterparts were now the Austrian diplomat Hruby (the former envoy to Bavaria) and the senior Austrian general, FML Johann Karl Peter Ferdinand Graf Hennequin de Fresnel et Curel, who had taken Wrede's place as army commander. As with Württemberg, these negotiations produced an initial military convention on 2 November, stipulating that Hesse would provide as many troops as possible as quickly as possible and would increase their number as an integral part of the Allied armies. Most important, however, was that this document stressed Hesse-Darmstadt's separation from the Rheinbund 'to join the holy cause of the Allied powers'.[224] In another similarity with Württemberg, this military convention became the basis for the definitive treaties of alliance Hesse-Darmstadt would sign with Austria, Prussia and Russia on 23 November in Frankfurt. Ludwig's realm became thereby the last Rheinbund state to abandon Napoleon.

A last act remained to be played out before the final treaties were signed. 'It was', du Thil would later write, 'a matter of life or death.' Ambassador Vandeul, having left Darmstadt shortly after Ludwig and his family, met Napoleon in Mainz on 3 November and arrived in Mannheim the following day bearing the emperor's recommendations for Ludwig. The result was a tempestuous audience with the grand duke and duchess. Napoleon would return across the Rhine next spring, Vandeul told Ludwig, in the meantime, the grand ducal family and court could accept a brief period of comfortable asylum in either France or Switzerland at French expense. Ludwig politely declined these offers, however, explaining that he had already joined the Coalition and would soon return to his capital. This was entirely a matter of state policy, he said, and had nothing do with his personal friendship towards the emperor. Courtesies having failed, Vandeul then threatened Hesse-Darmstadt with ruination when Napoleon marched back across the Rhine, reputedly saying that no stone would be left atop another. 'Then I will go down to destruction with my subjects', replied Ludwig, and what du Thil termed 'this remarkable audience' came to an angry, awkward end with Vandeul storming out to board his carriage for France. Ludwig returned to Darmstadt on 5 November, but his admixture of awe and admiration towards Napoleon remained strong. Napoleon would soon throw the Allies back over the Rhine, he told du Thil in late November after the formal treaties had been inked. 'He will defeat them,' he continued, 'None of them is even close to being a match for him.'[225]

*

Baden and Hesse-Darmstadt stand out for their remarkable loyalty to Napoleon and the Rheinbund in both the political and military arenas. Politically, they were not unlike many of the other Confederation princes, fearing they would lose all they had gained as French allies should the Coalition prevail, while simultaneously worrying about the punishments Napoleon might inflict for disloyalty if they changed sides. The latter concern was especially acute for these two states owing to their proximity to France, 'under the guns', so to speak, of Strasbourg and Mainz respectively. At the same time, senior leaders in both capitals evinced a persistent belief in Napoleon's abilities as a commander. Baden's Stockhorn and Ludwig of Hesse were only two of the central individuals who thought that the emperor might recuperate and return. Prinz Emil was another. Although he composed his report on Leipzig in late December, he described his 'trust in the victory-bringing presence of the emperor' during the grim fighting on 18 October.[226] There were also human angles to consider for both states. Großherzog Carl's indecisive, indolent nature was one factor delaying a decision in Karlsruhe, but more important was his marriage to Stephanie de Beauharnais, while Ludwig and other members of his family maintained a personal attachment to Napoleon (notably not Ludwig's heir who would become Ludwig II). What was not present as a factor in either state was enthusiasm for pan-German or Prusso-German nationalism, 'the good cause' as its advocates termed it. Each of these two governments took its decision to abandon Napoleon on the basis of realpolitik, that is, preserving the state and dynasty, not on emotion or idealism. Baden's public proclamation of its switch to the Allies was thus vapid and uninspired, and Ludwig of Hesse confined himself to a cursory, matter-of-fact announcement of the blandest possible nature with no reference to German unity or 'the French yoke'. He merely enjoined his civil servants and subjects 'to regard all the troops of the Allied powers entering the grand ducal lands as their loyal friends, to receive them in the best possible manner, and to expect from them a treatment entirely appropriate to these circumstances'.[227] These political considerations help explain the thinking in the two grand duchies during 1813 as well as the opprobrium piled upon the two courts by subsequent German historians for being insufficiently zealous about throwing the French across the Rhine.

Turning to the ways in which these political decisions manifested themselves in the field, several points are worth highlighting. First, there are many reasons to be surprised not only by Baden's and Hesse-Darmstadt's political allegiance to Napoleon but also by the steadfast behaviour their soldiers displayed during this brutal, inglorious campaign. As already outlined, both had to contend with many disadvantages in simply mobilising their contingents and new problems arose when the men reached the theatre of war. Anti-French sentiment and a simple desire for peace were increasing among the populations against the backdrop of the unending war in Spain in Baden's case and the dark pall cast by the Russian disaster for both. The armies hastily knocked together in the emergency atmosphere that year consisted largely of brand-new conscripts and inexperienced junior officers with only tiny cadres of veterans. They thus resembled the new Grande Armée Napoleon was constructing in many respects; indeed, the debilities of the French contributed to the challenges the German contingents faced on campaign. The old admiration of the French as the pinnacle of military professionalism, competence and confidence declined dramatically when confronted with the indiscipline of the young French soldiers, the chaos along the lines of communication and the seemingly ubiquitous raiding columns of Allied light troops.

The two contingents thus took the field in 1813 with throngs of disincentives shadowing their marches. Unlike several other Rheinbund armies, however, there were no unit defections and few desertions despite innumerable opportunities.[228] This outcome may be attributed to several factors. Loyalty to their sovereigns, the culture of military obedience and a conception of honour that placed a premium on adhering to one's oaths are the strongest explanations. These, however, could only be encouraged and enforced by excellent leadership. Wilhelm von Hochberg, General von Stockhorn, Prinz Emil and most of the regimental and battalion commanders provided this critical leadership component, earning the admiration of their men and the respect of their French allies. There were certainly those, Wilhelm among them, who were conscious of their 'German hearts', but there was no sense of a grand confraternity with the Prussians, let alone the Russians, in pursuit of some larger, unified 'German' state.[229] There were also practical, 'realist' interests in being on the winning side and a professional desire to serve under Napoleon as part of *la Grande Armée*. Here the precipitous erosion of French discipline, the evident energy of the Allies and the steady drumbeat of defeats in the autumn could understandably be expected to undermine the ardour of officers and men alike. Yet they stayed with their colours and fought steadily until the very closing moments at Leipzig and strove afterwards to defend their loyalty against both Allied and French accusations of betrayal. Baden in particular actively repudiated post-war allegations that its troops had fired on the French or defected to the Allies, but Hessians were also keen to be remembered for dutiful and competent service under Napoleon even after his defeat. This determined attachment to notions of military honour and parochial loyalty to their monarchs was thus maintained both in the days just after the Battle of Nations when pressure to defect was high and subsequently when the tide of Prusso-German nationalism was on the rise. Writing about 1814, for example, Kösterus observed that the Hessian regiments that had called the French 'comrades-in-arms' only a few months earlier were in a 'unique situation' when they entered France as enemies.

> But the Hessian warriors could advance on their former comrades-in-arms with open visors. They had held out to the last with them, they had sealed their loyalty and honour with their blood even to the very end in the fields and streets of Leipzig! Thus, they could consider their account with their former commander [Napoleon] honourably closed and happily follow the call and altered policy of their prince.[230]

Baden surgeon Meier, who in his memoirs professed himself elated at Napoleon's defeat as 'a second Teutoburger Wald', praised Graf Wilhelm's decision to surrender at Leipzig as honourable. He perhaps captures the conflicts experienced by many of the troops in observing that the Badeners as Prussian prisoners of war were still 'subject to a foreign will and this in the German fatherland! ... This was terribly painful for us,' he continued, 'we who had been accustomed, if often with sighs, to always pull the chariot of victory.'[231]

Chapter 6
Westphalia: Kingdom's End

'If he had stayed in Kassel, his troops would not have disbanded, and he would have remained master of his kingdom.'

Napoleon to Cambacérès, 9 October 1813[1]

THE KINGDOM OF WESTPHALIA was a particular target of the Coalition in 1813.[2] No other member of the Rheinbund attracted as much hatred or inspired as much hope in the Allied camp as the realm of König Hieronymus Napoleon – that is, King Jérôme Bonaparte – Napoleon's youngest brother. Westphalia acquired this unique level of attention in part because it was an artificial state that violated all the legitimist principles the Allies supposedly espoused and, more importantly, because much of its territory had been carved away from Prussia when Napoleon created the kingdom in 1807 following his triumph at Jena-Auerstedt and the Treaties of Tilsit. Unsurprisingly, the antipathy towards Westphalia was strongest in Prussian circles. Prussia's leadership was keen to regain the lost lands, including the great fortress of Magdeburg, for reasons of national security as well as national pride. Prussia would always be vulnerable, a 'weak bulwark' in the words of Karl August von Hardenberg, Prussia's chancellor, 'if Napoleon remains master of the Elbe and the mouths of the Weser and the Kingdom of Westphalia endures'. As early as January 1813, therefore, when Prussia was still formally allied to France, the secret Prussian envoy sent to Vienna told Metternich that from Berlin's perspective the other Rheinbund princes could keep their thrones, but Westphalia would have to be eradicated.[3]

There was also a strong emotional component in Prussian thinking, a powerful desire for vengeance after the humiliations it had suffered since 1806. Blücher, for instance, reacted with disgust when presented with two Westphalian officers who defected after being surprised and captured in mid-April. They had deserted 'not out of good will but out of necessity', the old general told his wife, 'I despise these fellows with all my heart.'[4]

At the same time, the Allies saw Westphalia as a great opportunity. They correctly perceived Jérôme's state to be frail and hoped that the appearance of even a small number of Allied troops would cause it to collapse. This was not a new idea in 1813. Since its inception, anti-French, pan-German activists such as Stein had considered the new kingdom as a weak point in Napoleon's presence in Germany. The eviction of French power from German lands, for example, was a major aim of a quasi-secret association called the *Tugendbund* ('League of Virtue'). Founded in Prussia in 1808, the Tugendbund included a number of Westphalian officers among its members and its activities were partly responsible for a series of abortive raids and uprisings against Jérôme's regime in 1809. This perception of Westphalian vulnerability did not abate after these failed efforts. After corresponding with Wallmoden and Tettenborn, for instance, Chernishev reported to the tsar in the summer of 1811 that northern Germany seethed with discontent; should war break out, he perceived bright prospects for a 'German legion' 'composed of Germans, commanded by German officers and with a name well-known in Germany at their head'. Similarly, Stein, reporting for service with the tsar in June 1812, drafted a memorandum specifically referring to the kingdom as a target for raiding parties and propaganda.[5] In their enthusiasm, these men and their collaborators exaggerated the degree of fermentation, but they and their ideas would play significant roles during 1813.

When drafting an outline for the upcoming campaign in February 1813, therefore, it is hardly surprising that Scharnhorst envisaged three raiding columns of light troops flooding the regions west of the Elbe to converge on Kassel, Westphalia's capital and, in his words, 'the most important point, the centre of the enemy's military power'. Although many of the troops would be Russian, the officers leading these detachments would be German: Tettenborn in the north and Oberst von Dörnberg, brother of a former officer of the Westphalian Guard, in the centre. The third column was to consist of the Russo-German Legion (a band similar to that envisaged by Chernishev), but that organisation was only beginning to limp into existence and its place was taken by Lützow's Freikorps. While the raiding detachments sowed confusion in Napoleon's rear areas and incited rebellion from the Elbe to the Rhine, the Allies would depose Jérôme, install a regency and immediately begin to raise troops. Scharnhorst expected to gain at least 24,000 infantry and 4,000 cavalry from the conquered kingdom in addition to a sizable body of Landwehr and a force of home guards (Landsturm). These physical actions would be preceded and accompanied by what one scholar calls 'a gigantic wave of pamphlets, caricatures and other publications' as part of an intensive propaganda campaign designed to undermine the legitimacy of Jérôme's government, foment internal unrest in the kingdom and encourage defection by its soldiers.[6] From the very beginning, then, Westphalia was the centrepiece of the Allied efforts to ignite German national sentiment, to undermine Napoleonic hegemony as represented by the Rheinbund and to reorganise Germany after the French had been pushed west of the Rhine.[7] If Coalition expectations proved excessive, even the passive resistance or neutrality of Westphalia's civil servants, soldiers and civilians would prove crippling to its viability as a kingdom and, in a larger sense, to Napoleon's prospects in 1813.[8]

The Moral Conquest of a Model State

Westphalia was indeed considered an 'artificial' state in the context of the 19th century.[9] Napoleon established it in late 1807 in the wake of Tilsit by nailing together the old Electorate of Hesse-Kassel, the Duchy of Braunschweig (Brunswick), the British crown lands of Hanover, former Prussian territories west of the Elbe and a number of smaller entities. Combining this 'mosaic of territories' into a single, compact entity, the emperor hoped to assure his dominance in north-central Germany with two basic purposes. First, it was to serve as a defensive barrier against Prussia, hemming in and monitoring a potential foe. The fortress of Magdeburg was especially important in this regard.[10] Second, the emperor intended Westphalia to be a 'model state' within the Confederation.[11] Where Napoleon could ally with monarchies of southern Germany such as Bavaria or Württemberg to contain Austria, the two principal states of the fragmented north, Hesse-Kassel and Braunschweig had been his enemies in 1806 (the senior Prussian commander had been Braunschweig's reigning duke) and the other major territory, Hanover, was joined to the British royal house by personal union.[12] With no ruling family with which he could reliably ally and only thin legitimacy appertaining to his own dynasty, Napoleon needed to lay a new foundation for popular acceptability. This local support was to derive from the 'moral conquest' of the new lands that would build upon his military success to consolidate his hegemony on an enduring basis through a modern, centralised government rooted in a constitution (the first in Germany) that included the Napoleonic Code and other French concepts such as equality before the law, the abolition of serfdom, emancipation of the Jews and many other advanced ideas. In some cases, the reforms were more progressive than those in France itself.[13] Opportunities would expand, the quality of life for people at all levels of society would improve and the population would soon grow to appreciate the new government.

The Kingdom of Westphalia was to be the vehicle through which this 'moral conquest' would be achieved.[14] 'I rely more on their effects for the extension and consolidation of your monarchy than on the results of the greatest victories,' Napoleon wrote Jérôme at the kingdom's founding: 'What people would want to return to the arbitrary Prussian government when it has enjoyed the benefits of a wise and liberal administration?' Furthermore, Napoleon hoped that Westphalia would inspire changes in other members of the Rheinbund as well, solidifying their regimes (many of which were also struggling to incorporate disparate populations and multiple political heritages into homogeneous monarchies) and attaching them more closely to France. 'Be a constitutional king', the emperor adjured his brother, 'You will find that you have a strength of opinion and a natural ascendancy over your neighbours who are absolute monarchs.'[15] This was not simply propaganda, it was practical, far-sighted policy to ensure continued French supremacy in a critical region.

Unfortunately for Westphalia's stability and for Napoleon's longer-term goals, the emperor began undermining his own vision almost at once. The task of erecting a new state would have been a major project under any circumstances. The heterogeneous nature of the new kingdom militated against centralisation, while the differences between French institutional practices and the various political, judicial, social and economic systems within Westphalia's borders made implementation of reforms based on the French model a daunting prospect. Moreover, unlike other Confederation states, Westphalia had no dynastic or state history, no 'fatherland' to sustain the loyalty of its new subjects as they experienced all the dislocations associated with the era in general and their transition to an utterly new regime in specific. The sudden introduction of French practices, persons and language also hampered the promotion of a Westphalian identity worthy of a German population's allegiance. The official paper, *Le Moniteur Westphalien* or *Westphälische Moniteur*, was published with side-by-side columns in French and German, much official business was transacted in French, the language of command in some Royal Guard units was French, and King Jérôme, a few lackadaisical forays notwithstanding, never invested in learning German.[16]

Indeed, Jérôme Bonaparte was another obstacle to the formation of a coherent, viable state. Although he was not lacking in good qualities (he was amiable, charming and could be loyal, generous and forgiving towards subordinates almost to a fault), Jérôme was ill-suited to oversee a brand-new monarchy facing so many challenges. Only twenty-three when he assumed the throne, he was utterly inexperienced, having never governed anything and having grown up under his elder brother's sheltering shadow. He showed little interest in actually ruling his new realm, tending instead towards indolence and indulgence in personal pleasures, and his court, once installed in Kassel, quickly became infamous for expensive and fatuous extravagance, 'Asiatic pomp' as a confidant described it to Charles Frédéric Reinhard, Napoleon's representative.[17] His passion for women (other than his devoted queen, the King of Württemberg's daughter Katherine) and what the Germans regarded as scandalous modern theatre imported from France only served to entrench an image of debauchery and spendthrift frivolity. 'The king raises too many troops, spends too much, and changes his principles of administration too often,' wrote Napoleon in 1811.[18] Jérôme possessed considerable personal courage and could display grace under pressure, but he was feckless as a field commander and had a history of exaggerating both successes and threats. Additionally, his personality and his prodigal behaviour made him easy to caricature. He quickly acquired derogatory nicknames such as 'König Lustig' ('King Jolly', the 'Merry Monarch' or the 'Pleasure King') and outrageous stories circulated of his bathing in red wine or indulging in other lavish, lascivious and costly excesses.[19] Even if many people recognised these tales as fabrications spread by his foreign enemies and domestic detractors, the court's evident decadence, and the suspicion that there was more, damaged his personal reputation and his government's respectability in the eyes of Westphalia's rather staid and conservative populace.

Most of Westphalia's problems were not insurmountable given time, competent administration and a modicum of good luck. The greatest obstacle to the kingdom's success, however, was Napoleon himself.[20] The exactions and restrictions imposed by his policies and priorities rendered the establishment of a viable economy almost impossible, while the burdens of conscription, special taxes and distant wars left the common people angry and anxious. The exploitation of Westphalian estates to serve as endowments for French officers and officials was especially onerous. Many of Jérôme's ministers were experienced and talented, some had even been appointed by Napoleon personally to oversee the creation of the kingdom, but neither they nor Jérôme could defy their imperial overlord. Some of Jérôme's disinterest in governing can perhaps be explained by his brother's overbearing interference, usually delivered in a scolding, annoyed tone. Jérôme, observes one historian, was 'alternately protesting and servile' in his responses to Napoleon's demands, occasionally successful in fending off an imposition but more often helpless and obviously so.[21] The emperor's intrusions, the presence of senior French officials in the government and the humiliations inflicted by French generals led many citizens to credit rumours that Napoleon intended to annex Westphalia as he had other German territories. Even if not directly annexed, some concluded early on that the kingdom was 'no more than a province of France'.[22] Westphalia thus became a source of soldiers, domains and revenue in support of Napoleon's plans to the detriment of the initial concept behind the state's creation. It was not a cartoon kingdom as so often superficially portrayed, but the moral conquest lacked a moral compass as, in the words of one prominent historian, 'the emperor himself had deprived it of all its assets'.[23]

1809–1813: The Evolution of an Army

Like the state, Westphalia's army was a new creation, glued together from disparate parts when the kingdom was established in December 1807.[24] The Westphalian constitution stipulated that the kingdom would maintain an army of 25,000 men and formation began in early 1808. It was only beginning to come together, however, when it was forced into action both in Spain and in Germany. The 1st Chevaulegers Regiment, Westphalia's only light cavalry unit at that early stage, was dispatched across the Pyrenees in September 1808 and would remain in Iberia until disarmed by the French in December 1813. More significant was a full division of 7,500 sent to Catalonia in early 1809. This represented approximately half of the available Westphalian troops at the time, but they were soon ground to dust in the dreadful siege of Gerona compounded by countless actions against Spanish insurgents and, most of all, by pervasive illness.[25] In Westphalia, as in many other Rheinbund states, and indeed in France itself, Spain thus became synonymous with deprivation, disease and gruelling, inglorious combat far from local interests and unlikely to foster career advancement.

1809–1812: *Creation and First Encounters*

Meanwhile, Austria launched a war against Napoleon and his Rheinbund allies by invading Bavaria in April 1809. In addition to incursions by Habsburg regulars, the Austrian offensive inspired small uprisings inside Westphalia and prompted raids into the kingdom by a renegade Prussian major named Ferdinand von Schill and the dispossessed Duke of Brunswick. The half-baked Westphalian army was involved in countering all these threats. Most of the internal disturbances were quickly quashed and Schill was seen off after a bloody skirmish south of Magdeburg (in which the 1st Westphalian Infantry performed poorly) to be chased down and destroyed at Stralsund by Dutch and Danish troops. The most serious rebellion involved some units of the army and was led by an officer of the Royal Guard, Wilhelm von Dörnberg (the same who commanded at Lüneburg in April 1813 as a Coalition general – *see* Chapter 2), but this too was dispersed after a few days of tension. As commander of 10th Corps, Jérôme later oversaw a hesitant, bumbling campaign against intruding Austrian forces in Saxony that featured a great deal of plundering and pompous posturing but very little fighting. When the armistice was declared in July, however, the Duke of Brunswick refused to recognise it and successfully led a small band of adherents called the 'Black Corps' (so named because of their black uniforms) across Westphalia from Saxony to the North Sea and evacuation in British ships, wrecking the partly formed 5th Westphalian Infantry in the

Chart 41: The Westphalian Army, 1812–1813

Unit	Assignment in 1812	Assignment in 1813
Garde-du-Corps	8th Corps > Westphalia	Westphalia
Grenadier Guard Battalion	8th Corps	Westphalia
Jäger-Garde Battalion	8th Corps	Westphalia
Jäger-Carabiniers Battalion	8th Corps	Westphalia
Füsilier-Garde (Queen's Rgt)	Forming in Westphalia	11th Corps > Imperial Guard
1st Infantry Regiment	Danzig > 10th Corps	10th Corps in Danzig
2nd Infantry Regiment	8th Corps	Dresden garrison > grenadiers to Imperial Guard
3rd Infantry Regiment	8th Corps	Dresden garrison > grenadiers to Imperial Guard
4th Infantry Regiment	Swedish Pomerania > Russia	Küstrin garrison
5th Infantry Regiment	8th Corps	Küstrin garrison
6th Infantry Regiment	*8th Corps*	*Not re-raised*
7th Infantry Regiment	8th Corps	Westphalia
8th Infantry Regiment	Danzig > 8th Corps	11th Corps
9th Infantry Regiment	Forming in Westphalia	Magdeburg
1st Light Infantry Battalion	8th Corps	Meißen and Dresden garrison
2nd Light Infantry Battalion	8th Corps	11th Corps > cadres to Westphalia to re-form
3rd Light Infantry Battalion	8th Corps	Re-raised in Westphalia with returnees from Spain
4th Light Infantry Battalion	Forming in Westphalia	Re-raised from old 3rd Battalion > 11th Corps
Chevaulegers-Garde	8th Corps	12th Corps > 4th Corps
1st Hussars	8th Corps	2nd Corps > part defected in August
2nd Hussars	8th Corps	2nd Corps > part defected in August
Jérôme Napoleon Hussars	–	Formed in August 1813 in Westphalia
1st Cuirassiers	8th Corps > 4th Cav Corps	Re-formed mid-1813 in Westphalia
2nd Cuirassiers	8th Corps > 4th Cav Corps	Re-formed mid-1813 in Westphalia
1st Chevaulegers	Spain	Spain
2nd Chevaulegers	Forming in Westphalia	Incorporated into the Chevaulegers-Garde
Westphalian Battalion	Returned from Spain	Re-formed as new 3rd Light Infantry Btn.
Mobile column	Hamburg	Merged with 1812 survivors > 4th and 5th Infantry

Note: this chart is a general outline, see text for unit details.

process. These episodes thus had both worrisome and encouraging aspects for Westphalia and its army. On the one hand, many citizens and some local officials had welcomed and abetted the various raiders and insurgents, while several hundred soldiers took the opportunity to simply desert or to join Schill or Brunswick. On the other hand, despite his panic over the Schill raid and his timorous ineptitude at the head of 10th Corps, Jérôme displayed considerable composure and aplomb in coping with Dörnberg and the other uprisings. Moreover, the army, some desertions and waverings aside, did not disintegrate and few of the new kingdom's subjects signed on with either Schill or the duke. These were favourable signs that the army, given time and proper leadership, could cohere into a reliable military institution.[26]

By 1812, the losses of 1809 and Spain had been replaced and Westphalia's army had grown to nearly 30,000, well beyond the 25,000 specified by the constitution and its membership in the Rheinbund. In common with most other monarchies, the army was divided into line and Royal Guard units. The line infantry consisted of eight regiments, each of two battalions organised according to French norms with six companies per battalion, including a company each of grenadiers and voltigeurs (the 2nd and 7th Infantry Regiments, having three battalions each, were exceptions in 1812). All infantry regiments wore black shakos, white trousers or breeches and simple white coats with dark blue collars, cuffs, lapels and turnbacks; regimental numbers only appeared on shako plates, uniform buttons and in embroidery on the turnbacks. Although all infantry units were expected to be able to skirmish, there were also three independent light infantry battalions dressed in black shakos with breeches and coats in traditional dark green, the coats highlighted by light blue facings. This 1812 organisation would be the template for the Westphalian infantry as it was resurrected after Russia.

Two other types of Westphalian foot soldiers played a role in 1813: veterans companies and departmental companies. A veterans company of 80–90 officers and men was established in each of the kingdom's eight departments to provide a reinforcement for national defence in case of emergency. Composed of former soldiers who were no longer fit for field service, they were uniformed in simple dark blue coats and trousers with red trim and black shakos. Each department also had a company of 50 soldiers as a form of home guard to supplement the gendarmes, guard public buildings and perform other internal duties. They wore plain grey coats and trousers with red trim, white cross belts and black bicorne hats. When put to the test at several points during 1813, however, neither of these institutions performed well. The men tended to flee or surrender when faced with Allied raiding parties as will be described in the strikes on Halberstadt and Braunschweig during the spring and autumn campaign respectively.

The other force for internal security was the Royal Gendarmerie Legion. They would likely be considered a 'paramilitary' establishment today but in contrast to the veterans and departmental companies, they proved themselves both dedicated and competent in the trying circumstances of 1813, their mounted component even capable of performing as cavalry if needed. They were few in number, however, less than 1,000 in the entire kingdom, and their duties principally involved the maintenance of public order, including the enforcement of conscription and occasional support to the High Police in the detection and arrest of allegedly seditious persons. Carrying out these unpopular tasks with considerable zeal, they were feared and hated by the populace, and many were murdered or forced into hiding when the kingdom collapsed. Uniformed like the French gendarmes upon which they were modelled, both foot and mounted gendarmes wore dark blue coats with red trim, black bearskin caps in the grenadier style and distinctive buff breeches with buff leather gear.[27]

For regular cavalry, Westphalia formed both light and heavy regiments. The light cavalry included the 1st Chevaulegers who had been dispatched across the Pyrenees in 1808 and were still there in 1813, albeit much diminished. They were dressed in dark green coats with orange distinctions, dark green breeches and crested black leather helmets. There were also two regiments of hussars which will feature prominently in this narrative. Both regiments sported typical hussar-style uniforms, the base colour for the 1st Regiment being dark green, that of the 2nd sky blue; both had red distinctions and black shakos with fur busbies for the elite companies. The kingdom also raised two regiments of cuirassiers, a decision Napoleon considered both expensive and unnecessary.[28] Equipped with full steel cuirasses and steel helmets with black caterpillar crests, they wore comparatively simple white uniforms with red facings for the 1st Regiment and orange for the 2nd up to 1812. When rebuilt in 1813, however, unlike other elements of the army, the cuirassiers would experience a major change in appearance as both regiments were issued dark blue coats with orange distinctions along with their steel helmets and cuirasses. All of the cavalry regiments had four field squadrons for an authorised strength of 644 for the hussars and 652 for the cuirassiers not including the depot companies kept at home for each regiment.

If the uniforms of the line troops were handsome but rather modest, those of the Royal Guard were more elaborate, distinguished by distinctive lace across the fronts of their coats and by special shoulder cords (aiguillettes). The Guard was composed of a mounted personal bodyguard company for Jérôme called the Garde-du-Corps, the Chevaulegers-Garde light cavalry regiment, three infantry battalions and a horse artillery battery. The small Garde-du-

Corps, only 206 strong at most, was intended for ceremony rather than combat, performing palace duties and escorting the royal couple as required. The Chevaulegers-Garde, on the other hand, saw considerable action. Dressed in dark green coats and breeches or riding trousers with red distinctions, yellow lace and crested helmets of black leather, they made an impressive showing. Lances had been issued in 1811, at least to the 1st Squadron, and it is possible that at least some element of the regiment continued to carry these in 1813. The foot soldiers of the Guard infantry consisted of a battalion each of grenadiers and Jägers, the grenadiers in white coats with red facings, the Jäger-Garde wearing dark green trimmed in pale yellow. Both battalions also displayed the distinctive lace on their coats, gold or yellow for the grenadiers, silver or white for the Jägers. The grenadiers had tall bearskin caps like their French counterparts and were organised into six companies making a strength of 843, but actual numbers seem to have fluctuated between 800 and 1,000. The Jäger-Garde Battalion also had six companies for a total of 975 officers and men, but topped their uniforms with black shakos, rather than the grenadiers' bearskins. Though his accoutrements were costly, newly appointed Lieutenant Meibom of the Jäger-Garde was thoroughly pleased with the battalion's appearance, remarking that 'we rivalled the splendid Guard Grenadier Battalion'.[29]

Habitually attached to the Guard was the small battalion of Jäger-Carabiniers. With 424 men in four companies, it was supposed to be recruited from foresters and huntsmen, but this proved an unrealistic aspiration, and the battalion was recruited normally despite its designated elite status. Whatever their origins, the men wore an understated but attractive uniform of dark hunter green with black facings trimmed in red, accompanied by black leather gear and black shakos.

A new Guard unit was added in August 1812. Called the Queen's Regiment and later the Füsilier-Garde, the new entity was initially organised like the line infantry with two battalions of six companies each. Its uniform was also similar to the line: shakos and white coats with dark blue facings but decorated with elaborate Guard lacing on the collars and lapels in silver or white. In early 1813, however, it gave up both grenadier companies to rebuild the Guard Grenadiers and both voltigeur companies to the Jäger-Garde. The regiment thus took the field with twelve fusilier companies composed of conscripts.

The kingdom's artillery was divided between horse and foot companies. The lone horse artillery company was permanently organised as a battery with its own pieces and attached to the Guard (like the Jäger-Carabiniers), while the foot artillery was established as four foot companies which were assigned guns as circumstances demanded. Two of these companies, though badly understrength, were still in Spain in 1812 but returned to Westphalia in

1809–1813: The Evolution of an Army

April 1813 to participate in the fighting around Kassel that autumn. The horse artillery wore light cavalry style uniforms of dark blue with red facings and red lace across the chest for dress parades. The foot gunners dressed in the sober colours typical of the era's artillerymen: dark blue breeches and dark blue coats with black facings trimmed in red. The train troops were likewise typical: iron grey jackets and breeches or riding pants with red collars, cuffs and piping. Artillery and train alike were issued black shakos and, rather unusually, with light brown leather gear.[30]

1812: The 8th Corps is Virtually Non-Existent

Thus accoutred, by the time of the invasion of Russia, the army, though it lacked the experience and heritage accrued by most of its Rheinbund allies, had developed into a respectable fighting force with considerable potential.[31] Napoleon, reviewing a battalion of the 1st Infantry in Königsberg in June remarked to one of Jérôme's officers: 'tell your master that I am very pleased with his army and if all are as well instructed as this battalion, he will be able to do much with them, all that is lacking now is that they fight well and that they will certainly do'.[32] The Russian war, of course, ruined this army. The 1st Chevaulegers (236 officers and men) as well as a small battalion of approximately 400 with a few gunners (the remnants of the division sent to Catalonia in 1809) remained in Spain and depots were left behind in the kingdom, but the rest of the army was committed to the invasion of Russia. Most Westphalian units were united as the 8th Corps of the Grande Armée, but two regiments (1st and 8th) were initially assigned to Danzig, while the 4th infantry was posted in Swedish Pomerania (Chart 47). Like the rest of the Grande Armée, the 8th Corps suffered catastrophic losses from combat, march attrition and illness across the Niemen. The 4th and 8th Infantry Regiments, arriving separately late in the campaign, were likewise consumed in the frightful retreat. Only the 1st Infantry, attached to MacDonald's 10th Corps on the strategic left flank, was spared the unspeakable experiences its compatriots endured (*see below*). Sent to Russia by Jérôme to distribute awards and provide an update on his army, Major Friedrich von Bodenhausen reported that 'The 8th Corps was virtually non-existent' and barely escaped himself to return to Kassel on 4 January alive but ill and exhausted.[33]

Its potential notwithstanding, the army's performance in Russia was hobbled by serious problems in its top leadership. Napoleon gave Jérôme responsibility for the army's right wing, including his own contingent, but the king and the 8th Corps' commander, the difficult but highly competent General Vandamme, quarrelled bitterly, creating a toxic climate in headquarters. Rather to everyone's surprise, Napoleon relieved Vandamme at his brother's request, but Jérôme then found himself placed under the orders of Marshal Davout, another senior French officer with whom he had a disputatious relationship. It was only July and the campaign had barely begun, but Jérôme, offended by this perceived affront, departed for Kassel accompanied by his Garde-du-Corps. Napoleon let him go and, after a period under an interim commander, allotted the 'irresponsible and erratic' GD Junot to command 8th Corps. This disastrous choice meant that the Westphalians not only laboured against the enemy, the weather and the manifold privations attendant upon this campaign but also had to contend with a commanding general whose ineptitude and mercurial behaviour tainted their every action.[34]

The Westphalians were still under Junot's inconsistent command as December ground to its icy close and the survivors staggered back to their assembly point at Thorn in small bands or simply as haggard individuals. Despite the best efforts of some senior officers, 'it was not possible to form an orderly force,' recalled Meibom, now a major in the 8th Infantry; most of the remaining men, he noted, 'acted according to their own needs and whims'.[35] Collecting in Thorn during the last days of December and the beginning of January, the Westphalians had no guns and numbered at best 867 officers and men from the contingent's infantry and artillery. They were in a wretched state, 'wandering shadows' as Lieutenant Johann Friedrich Gieße of the 5th Infantry described himself and his countrymen. GD Hans Georg von Hammerstein-Equord led one of the few organised groupings, 155 officers and men constituting the remnants of the three light cavalry regiments plus 44 infantry stragglers he had picked up along the way. Hammerstein was a hellrake, personally ill-disciplined and devil-may-care with a distinctly chequered past, but Jérôme had favoured him, and he proved the right leader to hold his men together during the harrowing retreat. To the great delight of the returnees, on reaching Thorn they found a fresh 'mobile column' of some 1,300 fellow Westphalians. Among the newly arrived officers was one of Gieße's old friends who was 'full of mute astonishment at seeing me in such garb, and seized with pity and grief at my appearance, which had changed beyond recognition'.[36] This mobile column, composed of all regiments and including two guns, had been formed in June and had spent most of 1812 in Hamburg but was called to the east late in the year. Originally intended to provide replacements for the contingent, it now formed the bulk of what was – for lack of a better designation – still being listed as '8th Corps'. The cavalry (including the 129 troopers who had ridden with the mobile column) and remnants of the Guard soon departed for Westphalia, but the line infantry remained to be organised into their old regiments even though each only numbered some 200 men. In this configuration, the Westphalian infantry marched for Posen on 8 January accompanied by its artillery and under the command of the well-regarded GB Friedrich Wilhelm von Füllgraff. Major Gaupp's tiny Württemberg 'battalion' of 184 officers and men, the other component of '8th Corps', marched with them.

Reaching Posen on the 14th, the Westphalian contingent was restructured into two 'march regiments' (numbered 1st and 2nd), each organised into two battalions with four companies per battalion. With this change, 510 officers and men who were excess or unfit 'received the enviable task of leaving for the dear beloved fatherland Westphalia'.[37] Junot, his mental state visibly deteriorating, also departed, turning over command of '8th Corps' to Füllgraff, issuing his last order of the day, and heading for France on 22 January.[38] The Westphalians and Gaupp's Württembergers remained in Posen until early February, now assigned to GD Girard's division of the observation corps that Viceroy Eugène was assembling east of the Oder. Here, at the end of the month, it underwent a final reorganisation. According to a 16 January order from Kassel that arrived on the last day of the month, the 1st and 2nd March Regiments were redesignated respectively as the new 4th and 5th Infantry Regiments. The excess officers and men gratefully travelled west to return to the kingdom.[39]

The sojourn near Posen, however, was coming to an end. As the Russians pressed west, Eugène became concerned about his left flank and shifted Girard's division to shield the northern and northeastern approaches to the town. Füllgraff's brigade, approximately 1,680 strong, thus moved to Obornik (Oborniki) on the Warthe River on 4 February (*see* Map 28). The Westphalians remained around Obornik for several days, resting and completing their organisation. Russian movements on the 10th, however, prompted Girard to withdraw to the west on 11 February. The enemy advance cut off II/5th Infantry for two days, but the battalion forced its way through bands of harassing Cossacks to re-join its comrades and the entire division retired slowly towards the Oder to arrive in Küstrin on 20 February. 'We marched into Küstrin on full parade', wrote Gieße, 'and, as the barracks were already occupied, we were quartered among the inhabitants.'[40] Girard's Polish brigade continued on to Berlin, but Füllgraff's two regiments (numbering approximately 1,100 with the artillery) and Gaupp's handful of Württembergers thus became part of the Küstrin garrison, an assignment they would endure until the fortress capitulated in March 1814 (*see* Chapter 8).

While the former 'mobile column' and some of the survivors of what Meibom called the 'shipwreck' across the Niemen made their way safely to Küstrin, another Westphalian force was not so fortunate.[41] A replacement detachment of some 468 new conscripts was on its way to join Füllgraff when it was attacked by Cossacks in the predawn hours of 16 February in the village of Wriezen west of the Oder (*see* Map 28), apparently with the eager connivance of the villagers.

The Westphalian colonel refused to surrender, but his little command of green recruits gradually disintegrated despite the best efforts of its officers, and the entire detachment went into Russian captivity.[42]

The 1st Infantry: The Regiment is to be Commended

The Westphalian 1st Infantry that had so impressed Napoleon in June, had been assigned to GD Grandjean's 7th Division of Marshal MacDonald's 10th Corps for the invasion of Russia. It had thus operated on the Grande Armée's strategic left flank and was largely intact when the great retreat began. 'This exhausting march will always remain unforgettable for me,' recalled Major Johann Philipp Bauer as the regiment retired from Tilsit, 'and with what hopes had we passed through here in the summer of the previous year.'[43] Brigaded with the Bavarian 13th Infantry under GB Bachelu, it formed part of the division's rear guard during the withdrawal from Königsberg to Danzig in the wake of Prussian General Yorck's defection (*see* Chapter 3 and Map 26). As such, it participated in many of the small engagements that punctuated this arduous march. Most notable was a combat between Rosenberg (Różyny) and Langenau astride the road to Dirschau 15 kilometres south of Danzig on 14 January 1813. The regiment and its two guns were posted in Rosenberg as the outermost rear guard with the Bavarians behind them at Langenau and the Polish regiments further to the north towards Danzig. Here they were attacked by 'a swarm of Cossacks' accompanied by six guns. The Russian howitzers soon set the village afire, forcing the Westphalians to withdraw covered by their two voltigeur companies who deterred the enemy cavalry with 'a lively fusillade'.[44] This move was conducted in some confusion initially, but the officers restored order and formed the regiment into line as Bavarian Oberst von Butler arrived with I/13th Infantry and a Polish horse battery. While II/13th Infantry held Langenau to the rear, the Polish guns silenced the Russian pieces allowing the two regiments and the Polish gunners to hold off their pursuers for the remainder of the day. This little action cost the Westphalians 34 dead and wounded but earned the regiment and its Bavarian allies effusive praise from GD Rapp, the governor of Danzig. In his account to Berthier later that month, Rapp wrote that 'The 1st Westphalian Regiment is to be commended; it made its retreat from the village of Rosenberg in good order and held its second position with great steadiness.' He also lauded the 13th Bavarian Infantry and specifically named that regiment's Oberst von Butler along with Oberst Georg Ferdinand von Plessmann and Major Bauer of the 1st Westphalian Infantry for awards.[45] The regiment marched into Danzig several days later, Bauer proudly recording that the people 'were most astonished to see once again a properly armed unit in such fine condition'.[46] Like the Bavarians, therefore, the Westphalians had already established a good reputation before entering the fortress where the regiment would see out the remainder of its existence (*see* Chapter 8).

1813: Everything that is Humanly Possible

Back in Kassel, Jérôme knew little other than that the Grande Armée was conducting a successful withdrawal from Moscow. The news that Napoleon had passed through Dresden in a sleigh and nearly alone thus came as a shock and he wrote to his brother requesting permission to come to Paris. Napoleon, however, considered Jérôme's presence 'more useful in your kingdom than in Paris' and his reply set the stage for the coming campaign:

> There is nothing left of the Westphalian army in the Grande Armée and everything announces a crisis in the coming spring. Let me know what you can send to re-form your cadres; what you can do to complete your artillery and your cavalry; and finally, what you are able to do to supply and arm the position of Magdeburg against any eventuality.

Jérôme hastened to provide an appropriate response, assuring Napoleon that 'it is especially in this circumstance that I will do everything *that it is humanly possible to do* and make all necessary sacrifices to success'. At the same time, he highlighted the kingdom's severe deficiencies. He was confident that he did not lack manpower 'because the conscription of 1812 is far from being exhausted', but he explained, like every other Rheinbund monarch, that 'it is money, material and officers that I lack'.[47] Shortages notwithstanding, Jérôme and his government, appalled by the calamitous news from Russia, immediately set about supporting the survivors with money and material.[48] They also began to rebuild Westphalia's army, drawing on the 7,000 or so soldiers of the depots and incomplete regiments within the kingdom.

While Westphalia made earnest efforts to meet Napoleon's expectations as far as the army was concerned, the emperor had his doubts. He was worried about the security and reliability of the kingdom. He viewed Westphalia as a crucial bulwark for the defence of Germany and attached particular importance to the great fortress of Magdeburg, Westphalia's key bastion on the Elbe. In late December, he thus directed his trusted soldier-diplomat GD Narbonne to halt in Magdeburg on his return from a mission to Berlin. 'Examine the place with care to give me a good account,' he told the general. Narbonne was then to stop in Kassel for several days to 'observe the spirit, what's being done there, and whether there's any serious thought of reorganising the Westphalian army and defending Magdeburg properly'. In his conversations with Jérôme, Narbonne was to underscore that the king and his kingdom would be 'in the vanguard' should war come to central Germany.[49]

Given its centrality to Napoleon's strategic thinking, Magdeburg soon featured as the focal point of a lengthy and acrimonious correspondence between the two brothers over the kingdom's distressed finances in general and the fortress in particular. The emperor insisted that Westphalia bear all the costs of provisioning the huge fortress, while Jérôme countered that his impecunious kingdom could not afford the expense of supplying Magdeburg while simultaneously supporting thousands of French troops and re-raising his own army. 'One can gather food by treating Westphalia as an enemy country and by levying requisitions,' he warned in January, 'but then the contributions will not come in any more, the army cannot be reorganised and the public spirit, which gives me so much trouble to maintain, will be lost entirely.' Jérôme was especially distraught about not being able to pay his army.[50] These disputes were partly resolved in March, but food stocks in Magdeburg could only be filled by imposing severe requisitioning on the nearby Westphalian districts and the kingdom's financial situation would remain desperate for the rest of its brief existence.

Beyond Magdeburg, Napoleon's chief interest that spring was the army Jérôme could put in the field. Westphalia would resurrect most of its old formations and add several new ones during the year. Some units, however, disappeared from the kingdom's previous order of battle. The 6th Infantry was not rebuilt, and the half-formed 2nd Chevaulegers Regiment was dissolved, its troopers absorbed into the reconstructed Chevaulegers-Garde.[51] On the other hand, the 9th Line Infantry, the 4th Light Battalion, and the Füsilier-Garde that had all been under construction in 1812 would take their places in combat during 1813. Calling up conscripts, incorporating the few infantrymen and artillerymen returned from Spain, mobilising depot troops, and drawing on whatever fit officers and soldiers had survived Russia, the new army soon began to take shape. The process of re-creating the army was progressing at a fairly satisfactory pace in early March when Viceroy Eugène's withdrawal from Berlin brought the enemy to the Elbe and added fresh urgency to the project. The emperor, given the revised situation, wanted as many men as fast as possible, stressing to his brother that 'it is your kingdom the enemy most desires'.

Jérôme, however, feared that haste would merely result in delivering his unprepared units to the enemy. 'These new troops are neither clothed, nor organised, nor armed, the horses do not even have harnesses,' he wrote, 'I thus have neither a single battalion nor a single squadron that I can allow to march without fearing that it will do more harm than good.'[52] Napoleon relented on sending untrained conscripts to Eugène along the middle Elbe, but Jérôme acted to placate his elder brother by declaring that he would send the 9th

Infantry to reinforce the 3rd Infantry and III/4th Infantry (that regiment's depot) that were already stationed in Magdeburg.[53]

If Napoleon and Jérôme disagreed on finances and the kingdom's ability to sustain the costs of war, a subject upon which they agreed was distrust of the Westphalian public in general and of the army in particular. 'Of all the allied troops, yours are those I am bound to distrust most,' Napoleon had written in a letter to his brother in 1810 and he had specified that the Royal Guard should include a French element from the very beginning to provide for the king's safety. He modified his opinion to an extent in 1812, telling a Westphalian general that the men were 'very brave fellows and I am very pleased with them' (indeed the problem was 8th Corps' leadership not the soldiery), but his doubts persisted, reinforced by Jérôme's unauthorised departure from the army in Russia.[54] The events of 1813 would only deepen Napoleon's distrust and revive his insistence that Jérôme provide himself with French guards as Joseph had done in Spain and Murat in Naples: 'You must well perceive, at this moment, what I always told you, the disadvantage of not having at Kassel a guard of 4,000 Frenchmen, which it would have been so easy for you to form.'[55] Napoleon's representative Reinhard expressed his assessment of the mood of the kingdom's citizens in a January report, noting that 'in the current circumstances, it is only a step from desperation to revolution'.[56]

As for King Jérôme, he had communicated his concerns about the reliability of the army and the state of popular frustration almost from the time he assumed the throne. His worries only grew more acute in 1813. Violent protests in neighbouring Berg in late January, for example, led the nervous king to send a regiment to the border lest the discontent spread into his realm.[57] Fortunately, the unrest quickly subsided (see Chapter 7), and the troops returned to Kassel, but in a letter that April, Jérôme told Napoleon that 'Your Majesty can hardly imagine the agitation and fermentation that prevails in all heads'. Reinhard reported no 'anxiety' in Kassel, rather 'a menacing calm', but that was hardly a reassuring appraisal.[58]

The Westphalian army, of course, was not impervious to these pervasive sentiments of discontent and insecurity. The challenges of recruiting, training, inexperience, and leadership that plagued almost all elements of Napoleon's 1813 Grande Armée were thus compounded in Westphalia's case by grave doubts about the new army's morale and loyalty. These suspicions were not unwarranted. Draft evasion and desertion soon became widespread, the palpable manifestation of resentment against five years of essentially French rule including taxation, conscription, humiliations real and perceived, along with the disastrous campaigns in Spain and Russia.[59] Allied propaganda – 'almost as redoubtable for the new monarchy as the regular armies' of the

Chart 42: Westphalian Troops in Germany, mid-to-late April 1813

	Bns/sqdns	Present under arms
37th Division — GD von Hammerstein		
Infantry — GB Lageon		
Füsilier-Garde Regiment	2	1,073
8th Infantry Regiment	2	1,192
2nd and 4th Light Battalions	2	924
Cavalry — GB Wolff		
Chevaulegers-Garde	4	694
1st and 2nd Hussar Regiments (two sqdns each)	4	480
Artillery: 8 × 6-pdr (two foot batteries)	–	156
Total	–	4,519
Magdeburg garrison		
3rd Infantry Regiment	2	1,525
III/4th Infantry Regiment	depot	88
9th Infantry Regiment	2	698
Küstrin garrison		
4th and 5th Infantry Regiments	4	1,000
Danzig garrison		
1st Infantry Regiment	2	1,128

Notes: Figures for the 37th Division are from Berthier to Napoleon, 29 April 1813, Berthier, *Rapports*, vol. I, p. 79; SHD, 13C85; garrisons from Nafziger, *Lützen & Bautzen*.

enemy in the words of one historian – exacerbated local dissatisfaction, building on the prevailing uncertainty about the kingdom's future so that unrest burgeoned whenever Allied troops approached, or the French suffered a reverse.[60] Cossacks were welcomed in Halle, for example, and excited students at the university there were enthused about joining the Prussians. The morale of the Westphalian soldiers was 'very poor' reported the Hessian ambassador from his vantage point in Kassel, and the public mood was 'not good although the king himself is well-loved'.[61] As Jérôme would write to Napoleon on 18 April: 'Your Majesty will undoubtedly appreciate that I should not entrust myself entirely in this pressing moment to all the new troops that, despite all my care, are surrounded by every possible seduction.'[62]

The kingdom's manifold problems notwithstanding, the army assembled with commendable speed. Major Johann Ludwig Boedicker (or Bödicker), still

Forming near Kassel

Garde-du-Corps	2 companies	141
Grenadier Guards Battalion	1	798
Jäger-Garde Battalion	1	813
Jäger-Carabinier Battalion	1	236
2nd Infantry Regiment	2	1,379
I/7th Infantry Regiment	1	893
1st Light Battalion	1	763
3rd Light Battalion	1	448
Chevaulegers-Garde	1	c. 200?
1st Cuirassiers	4	527
2nd Cuirassiers	4	550
1st Hussar Regiment	2	c. 400?
2nd Hussar Regiment	2	c. 400?
One horse battery and one foot battery	–	?

Other Depots

1st Infantry	–	216
4th Infantry	–	208
5th Infantry	–	495

Notes: The 7th Infantry never formed a second battalion.

Figures for the units forming in and around Kassel are shown in *italics* because they include depots, sick, detached and others not considered 'present under arms'. These are drawn from 'Situation des Troupes Westphaliennes dans l'Intérieur', 15 April 1813 submitted by the Westphalian War Mininstry, SHD 2C542. The figures for the light cavalry are author's estimates.

---

recovering from severe wounds received in Russia, was sceptical and reluctant when Jérôme personally appointed him to command the new Jäger-Garde Battalion but exuded satisfaction when he recorded that 'the organisation proceeded so rapidly that very soon the battalion numbered over 900 men who were fully equipped, armed and exercised'. He was even more pleased when he led his brand-new battalion through its first review: 'it turned out so well that after its completion not only was an order given about the good conduct of the battalion, but I also received a patent as a baron that same evening.'[63] Capitaine Borcke concurred: 'The reorganisation of the Westphalian army proceeded with zeal and activity during the spring of 1813, so that a relatively large part of it was already back on its feet in March.' Borcke, however, also detected grave deficiencies 'Despite all exertions and expenses, the new army lacked good will and spirit, training and combat readiness'. In his view, 'The same factors that hindered Napoleon in creating anew troops such as those lost in Spain and Russia, were also at work here and even though they fought bravely everywhere, it proved far more difficult to instil in the Germans the spirit that in 1813 still inspired the new French regiments ... with us desertion was the order of the day'. Friedrich Christian Karl Graf Luxburg, the Bavarian ambassador and an admirer of Napoleon, related to Max Joseph that the kingdom was investing extraordinary efforts in reconstructing the army. 'One can hardly imagine more splendid troops, better uniformed, better trained and more adroit in their skills than those here,' he told his king, concluding with perhaps unintended irony that 'It would only be desirable that desertion were not so frequent.'[64]

Not all were shrouded in such hesitant gloom. Newly minted artillery Lieutenant Christian Normann and his fellow officers, for instance, fresh from the artillery school, were full of youthful enthusiasm when their battery was sent to Braunschweig and disappointed when they were ordered back to Kassel. They set off at once but were 'very displeased as we saw ourselves betrayed in our hopes of making use of what we had learned, distinguishing ourselves in our profession and, enriched with experiences, returning with honours like the older officers'.[65]

By late March, five of the kingdom's line infantry regiments and a depot battalion were already committed to fortress garrisons: 1st in Danzig, 4th and 5th in Küstrin, 3rd and 9th in Magdeburg with III/4th Infantry. Napoleon initially intended that the remaining Westphalian troops be employed in the field as the 37th Division of the new Grande Armée. These units were being organised around Kassel under GD von Hammerstein and by the beginning of April consisted of six infantry battalions and eight cavalry squadrons supported by eight guns in two foot artillery batteries: the Füsilier-Garde, 8th Infantry, 2nd and 4th Light Infantry, Chevaulegers-Garde, and both hussar regiments. Hammerstein's division departed Kassel on 1 April and marched off to take up positions east of the capital: the 8th Infantry at Münden with an advance guard in Göttingen, the 2nd Light in Eschwege with a company in Wanfried, and the remaining infantry, most of the cavalry and the two batteries in Heiligenstadt with Hammerstein and GB Wolff (*see* 'Westphalian outpost line' on Maps 4 and 45). The arrival of these troops, green as they were, proved timely since Allied forces were already beginning to encroach upon Westphalia's borders.

The Spring Campaign: Inundated with Enemy Bands

The strategic situation, of course, was unfolding while Westphalia mobilised. The King of Saxony's flight from Dresden in late February and the enemy's entry into Berlin a few days later prompted Jérôme to send Queen Katherine to France. Not a moment too soon in his mind, as major Allied forces were soon crossing the Elbe preceded by swarms of Cossacks and regular light cavalry. With Eugène's command established from Magdeburg southwest towards the Harz Mountains, the Allied advances across the Elbe posed threats to Westphalia from two directions: raiding parties from the north represented one danger, highlighted by Tettenborn's capture of Hamburg and the success Dörnberg had achieved at Lüneburg; more serious was the possibility of a direct enemy thrust towards Kassel from the area between Leipzig and Altenburg to the east. Ney's 3rd Corps, the lead element of Napoleon's Army of the Main, was approaching Eisenach and Erfurt from Schweinfurt to the south, followed by the Guard, Marmont, Bertrand and numerous other formations, but for a brief time in mid-April a wide gap yawned between these forces and Eugène's divisions further north. Allied raiding detachments exploited this gap, seeking not only to scoop up intelligence and disrupt French communications, but specifically aiming for Kassel as the capital of Jérôme's realm. As Reinhard observed: 'until the Prince of the Moskova [Ney] has passed Eisenach and Gotha, there is still a big gap to fill'.[66]

April Crisis: A Squadron of my Guard was Destroyed

Hammerstein's division was intended to fill the gap and shield Kassel from Allied raiders, but few in the kingdom's capital had much faith in the untried Westphalian troops, especially as unsubstantiated reports inflated Allied strength so that Hammerstein seemed outnumbered by hordes of bloodthirsty Cossacks. Between 11 and 21 April, Westphalia thus experienced a period of crisis, fuelled by wild rumours and the small but painful and embarrassing setbacks inflicted on French and Rheinbund troops by audacious Allied cavalry detachments. Prussian hussars almost captured the French ambassador to the Saxon Duchies, Nicolas Auguste Marie Rousseau de Saint-Aignan, in Gotha on 12 April and a newly formed battalion from those states surrendered without a fight in the villages around Ruhla on the 13th (Chapter 7), the same day that the Bavarians suffered the embarrassing loss of their guns to Hellwig's men at Langensalza (Chapter 2).

Two days later, disaster befell the Westphalians when two squadrons of the Chevaulegers-Garde were sent to reconnoitre east of Heiligenstadt. Riding towards Nordhausen on the night of the 15th with no flank security, the lead squadron was set upon by Cossacks and destroyed. These were two Cossack regiments that had been scouting in and around Nordhausen under the command of Major Vladimir Ivanovich von Löwenstern. Warned of the enemy's approach by a Westphalian forester, Löwenstern immediately deployed his men to trap the unwary Chevaulegers. 'By the clear light of the moon I saw the enemy coming towards me in complete security without perceiving me,' Löwenstern would later write. Westphalian Lieutenant Colonel von Göcking was riding carelessly at the head of his squadron when he was shocked to see the Cossacks only twenty paces away in the gloom. Löwenstern recalled with no little satisfaction that Göcking fired his pistol 'but did not have time to order his soldiers to form up, as I was already attacking him and in the twinkling of an eye he and his whole command were overwhelmed and enveloped'. Göcking, at the head of the surprised column, was helpless, and one of his captains chose to hide under a bridge rather than attempt to rally the troopers. Most of the men were thus killed or captured, but the well-mounted ones were able to escape into the darkness. The captain sneaked off safely from under the bridge and Göcking, to Löwenstern's regret, was saved by the speed of his exceptionally fine horse. Löwenstern need not have worried. The Westphalian colonel, taking shelter in a village, at first attempted to disguise himself by shaving his moustache and donning peasant's clothes, but he reconsidered and presented himself to Löwenstern the next day in Ellrich. 'Being the only one of my detachment to escape, I do not wish to return alone,' he told the Russian, 'I prefer to be your prisoner than to be shot back there.' Göcking was one of the Westphalian officers Blücher met and, as Löwenstern noted, 'he was very poorly received by General Blücher and by the Prussians generally'. The reaction in Westphalia to the embarrassing episode was dismay and discouragement. 'Although General von Hammerstein's corps was supposed to defend the homeland's soil, no one showed a great inclination for this and desertion remained a strong as before,' wrote Borcke, 'Every officer who held firm to duty and honour was thus in a most onerous situation, but even more regrettable were those who, carried away by patriotism, forgot their duty and went over [to the enemy].' Jérôme could only dejectedly report to Napoleon that, 'A squadron of my Guard that was on reconnaissance was overwhelmed by superior numbers and almost entirely destroyed.'[67]

The army suffered another setback on 17 April when Hellwig's Prussian hussar squadron surprised a company of the 2nd Light Battalion and a squadron of the 2nd Hussars in Wanfried east of Eschwege. Guided by a former Hessian officer, Hellwig's men approached the village at night and attacked from two sides just as a Westphalian patrol was riding back into town. Rapidly overpowering the Westphalian defenders, the Prussians captured two hussar officers, 80 troopers, 100 horses and some 50 light infantrymen, a substantial number of whom seem to have volunteered to join Hellwig's band.[68] It was a small defeat, but enough for Hammerstein to report that the peril to the kingdom was imminent as the enemy could effect a passage of the Werra River to march on Kassel from the vicinity of Eschwege. Feeling out-flanked in his position at Heiligenstadt, he said he would withdraw across the river to Witzenhausen, only 24 kilometres east of the capital; he later recanted and remained in Heiligenstadt, but the news of his contemplated departure heightened apprehension in Kassel. At the same time, bold patrols and cocksure proclamations issued by Dörnberg in Celle on the 17th and Cossack probes towards Hanover and Braunschweig ignited additional anxiety.[69]

Kassel was already in a state of nervous uncertainty as these events unfolded with news of disturbances in the countryside, fears of insurrection and rumours that Jérôme was packing for Paris.[70] The anxious city thus burst into alarm at the proximity of the exaggerated Allied raiding detachments, their boldness, their speed and their seeming invincibility. Dread was especially prevalent among the French residents, many of whom shipped their families and personal property off to safety across the Rhine. Jérôme feared a *coup de main* – a sudden surprise attack – but refused to leave despite the urgings of his advisors. In such moments, as in 1809, he seemed to rise above the frivolity and unconcern that were often the norm in his court and capital. Instead, he calmly walked the streets of Kassel, showing himself to the population to demonstrate his determination to stay. At the same time, he wrote directly to GD Teste at Gießen requesting the immediate dispatch of six French battalions. The letter to Teste was a risky step as Jérôme knew very well how angry Napoleon became when others gave orders to French troops without imperial authorisation. He thus sent simultaneous letters to Berthier and Napoleon, informing his brother of the loss at Wanfried and requesting urgent assistance:

> ...my troops are so young that it is almost impossible to undertake anything with them by themselves. The soldiers have only been formed for two months and the NCOs are not much more experienced, which is why I desire Your Majesty to send me six battalions of French troops, and I will at once place at your disposal six of our battalions; without this indispensable precaution, I cannot foresee what will happen if a small corps of the enemy appears.[71]

Reinhard likewise took the unusual step of writing directly to Napoleon to report that Hammerstein claimed the enemy's strength exceeded 10,000 men and that he believed the raiders were trying to cut communications between Kassel and Frankfurt. The envoy also reiterated concerns about the Westphalian army: 'It is only the chevaulegers of the Guard who hold; the other troops keep to the rear or disband.'[72]

To Jérôme's great relief, Teste marched on his own initiative and Napoleon approved Jérôme's decision to make a direct appeal for help. He cautioned that Teste only had two battalions but instructed his brother to complete the division with Westphalian troops until the rest of the French battalions arrived in May. The emperor also sought to allay Jérôme's fears by citing reports he had received from Ney's divisions at Gotha and Eisenach. 'The opinion of these generals is that there is nothing but partisans on their left [thus Jérôme's right],' he wrote, 'I fear that General Hammerstein sees phantoms and allows his spies to mislead him.' To further reassure the king, Napoleon explained that 'the entire army is on the move' towards Saxony and noted that he himself would soon head for Eisenach. He had Berthier respond to the king as well to reinforce the news about the Army of the Main's advances. The emperor, however, was hardly complacent. Ney had already been informed of the possible threat to Kassel by what was most likely a detachment of partisan raiders and warned that a similar group was reportedly heading for Nordhausen so that the area west of the Saale River was 'inundated with enemy bands'.[73] Ney should therefore be on his guard but was directed to cut off these bands and throw them across the Saale. At the same time, Napoleon asked Jérôme whether the reports of serious desertion problems in the Westphalian army were true and, if so, what the causes were. While these two letters to his brother were measured, the emperor was more pointed in his reply to Reinhard, telling his ambassador: 'I cannot comprehend how the enemy can make a serious move on Kassel; it must be phantoms or partisans.' He seemed exasperated by the reported incapacity and dubious loyalty of the Westphalian troops and asserted that he had repeatedly advised Jérôme to have French units in the Royal Guard, but the king had not taken this advice. 'And this is the result: with an army of 15 to 20,000 men, he is about to be driven out of his capital, probably by two or three squadrons of bad troops!' he fumed.[74] If partly accurate, in other respects this was an unfair judgment of both the Westphalian troops and their king, but it illuminates Napoleon's views of the Westphalian army and helps explain the manner in which it was distributed and employed during the remainder of the war.

The emperor's choler did not detain Teste and he duly arrived in Kassel with his two battalions (IV/36^e and IV/51^e Ligne) and four guns. Determined to make an impression on the population as well as on the enemy, at every stop he announced that he was coming with a division of 10,000 infantry and doubled the number of rations requisitioned for his troops. Although he only had some 1,200 to 1,300 men and his conscripts were as green as any in Westphalia, he marched them about so they would seem more numerous, and their presence contributed greatly to assuaging Kassel's concerns. 'Jérôme received me like a liberator,' Teste would recall, 'and I arranged with him to have six battalions of his infantry camp with mine'. From Teste's perspective, however, the Westphalian soldiers, though splendid, had little loyalty. He was convinced that even 'Jerome's faithful soldiers (with the exception of some praetorians fattened on his favours), believing the debacle to be imminent, will abandon him to his evil star.' Nonetheless, he focused on training his men – eventually joined by two more battalions, one per regiment – and soon declared that he was 'so pleased with their progress that I would not have exchanged my conscripts for old soldiers'.[75] With Ney's advances and Teste's arrival, the crisis passed, and Berthier could inform Ney on 23 April that:

> ... the news from Kassel as of the 22nd is that the King of Westphalia is entirely reassured about the movements of the enemy. General Teste has arrived in Kassel with two French battalions; the king will complete with his troops a fine division of infantry and artillery.[76]

The situation in the north also improved as Davout, Vandamme and Sebastiani were pressing towards the Elbe from the Weser, pushing Dörnberg back in the process. On 18 April, the day after he had announced himself as the herald of Britain's prince regent, Dörnberg was forced to evacuate Celle and slowly retire to the east. By the 27th, he was back on the right bank of the Elbe.[77] Indeed, despite bright successes such as the victory at Lüneburg, Benckendorff was dissatisfied with the response of the local population in northern Westphalia. 'Supporters are only the result of a victorious battle', he reported on 9 April, 'News travels very fast in the country and will be consolidated by a success, will disappear at a failure; one cannot therefore be too careful with this core of German patriotism ... the disorder, the fear of the enemy will cease, the ardour of the Germans will diminish with the torpor of our movements.'[78]

April to Armistice

Napoleon's advance towards the Saale and the push towards Hamburg by Davout and Vandamme in the north relieved the pressure on Westphalia. Hammerstein's division, thereby released for offensive operations, was immediately directed to Nordhausen and Sondershausen. The division, however, only totalled 4,500 officers and men with eight guns and Hammerstein complained that it lacked medical support and a proper staff.[79] Moreover, it was afflicted by considerable desertion. It lost approximately 250 men in the encounters with Löwenstern and Hellwig (mostly as prisoners), but historian Albert du Casse states that it lost as many as 2,000 men to desertion during the eight days it had been deployed east of Kassel. Most of these men, he asserts, did not go over to the enemy, but 'returned furtively to their villages'.[80] If correct, this figure would represent roughly a third of Hammerstein's entire force. Even if the 2,000 number is exaggerated (the extant archival reports do not permit comprehensive assessment), the kingdom clearly suffered a staggering level of both draft evasion and desertion in 1813. The increasingly harsh penalties imposed for men seeking to escape service or any who assisted them testify to the regime's view of these debilitating phenomena. Strict limits on soldiers' activities in garrison provide further evidence. In the Artillery Regiment, for example, the officer of the watch was to read out the edict announcing the death penalty for desertion at evening roll call three times a week.[81] Indeed, Reinhard reported that a key reason for calling on Teste's French troops was 'to stop the ravages of desertion among the Westphalian troops'.[82] This is why the report caught the emperor's eye and led him to ask Jérôme for explanations.

The causes behind these instances of draft evasion and desertion were many and overlapping: the anti-French mood prevalent in much of the population, the absence of a national history or tradition as a foundation for loyalty, the regime's dubious legitimacy, and the terrors evoked by the army's experiences in Spain and Russia. Allied propaganda and the general atmosphere of intense insecurity also played a role. Jérôme specifically cited his inability to pay his soldiers as a key factor and begged Napoleon for an infusion of cash to allow salaries to be distributed. Whether such funds were ever transferred is unclear (du Casse says they were not). Whether they would have made any difference is unanswerable. In addition to the threat of severe punishments, Jérôme, prompted by his clement instincts, proclaimed amnesties for deserters on several occasions but neither punitive nor merciful measures seemed to have anything but a transitory effect. The problems did not abate to any significant degree, and they would continue to attract unwanted attention from Napoleon for the remaining months of the kingdom's existence.[83]

The limited number of available Westphalian troops and the scepticism about their loyalty meant that there was no question of forming a separate Westphalian corps as in 1812 (unlike the Bavarian contingent which Napoleon at first had wished to form as the new Grande Armée's 9th Corps). One scholar suggests that the French may have hoped that distributing the Westphalians to fortress garrisons or among French divisions would make desertion more difficult and less damaging should troops leave the ranks anyway.[84] There was also the very pragmatic requirement for garrison troops in numerous locations and Napoleon preferred to leave such tasks to second-line forces or allies. As a result, Hammerstein's 37th Division would be broken up very early in the spring campaign.[85] For the moment, however, the division was placed under Marmont's command as part of 6th Corps and incorporated into the Army of the Main's eastward advance. The Westphalian infantry had only reached Naumburg by 2 May and thus missed the Battle of Lützen 'even though the thunder of the cannons clearly resounded to us' as Capitaine von Borcke noted. The cavalry, on the other hand, moving by forced marches, arrived on the battlefield at some point during the afternoon 'where the dreadful sight of dead men and horses was not very encouraging to our virgin military eyes' in the words of a young chevaulegers officer named Karl August Unico von Lehsten.

Their horses were exhausted from the strenuous march, however, and the squadrons were held behind the lines on the French right to rest and feed their mounts. They were soon ordered forward but were unable to manage more than a brief trot and were quickly recalled without taking any part in the combat. They witnessed the chaotic drama of the evening attack by the Allied cavalry but were not engaged and spent the night, like most of the army, on the field. 'We had to rest amidst the dead and many a corpse served as the pillow for the living,' recalled Lehsten. 'This night made a deep impression on me', he continued, 'I cannot say that it discouraged me. Rather it steeled my valour with the example of so many manly deeds and sacrifices.'[86]

In the wake of the victory at Lützen, the Westphalians made up part of the great army now bearing down on Dresden. The local civilians, of course, paid the price of its passage. 'The burden of the troops took a heavy toll on the poor Saxons,' wrote Lehsten, 'It was as if we were not in friendly territory ... Unfortunately, the German troops were often the roughest, Württemberger and Bavarian, Hessian and Westphalian did not leave a good reputation in the local area.'[87] As the 6th Corps reached Dresden, however, Hammerstein's division was split up. Lehsten and his comrades in the chevaulegers and hussars, eight squadrons strong and constituting a brigade under GB Wolff (who has figured in several previous chapters), continued with Marmont to serve as his light cavalry. Placed under GD Beaumont (who has also been discussed earlier), they crossed the Elbe on 10 May and skirmished successfully with Cossacks and Prussian light horse several days later during an extended probe towards Großenhain on the east bank of the river. As was often the case, Marmont sent one of his personal aides-de-camp along on this expedition; he concluded his report by noting that, 'The Westphalian hussars display great ardour.'[88] Marmont attached two of his naval artillery battalions and four guns to Beaumont, but Beaumont's entire division was placed briefly under Marshal Mortier on 16 May before being transferred to GD Durosnel on the 18th. Durosnel, elaborately titled as 'Commandant of the French Troops and Garrisons in Saxony', was based in Dresden and entrusted with wide-ranging responsibilities to include protecting the city from Allied troops to the north. Beaumont's division with the Westphalian cavalry thus operated in the general area between Dresden and Großenhain under Durosnel's orders until assigned to 12th Corps a week later. Shifting east, the German horsemen, the two French battalions and their four guns caught up with Oudinot on 27 May, joining him in time to participate in the engagements at Hoyerswerda (28 May) and Luckau (4 June) as described in Chapter 3.[89]

While Beaumont and Wolff rode off to join Oudinot, the rest of Hammerstein's former division went elsewhere. Marmont retained the services of the two Westphalian artillery batteries and these likely participated at Bautzen, but details are lacking.[90] The six infantry battalions, on the other hand, came under Durosnel's command in Dresden: 8th Infantry, 2nd Light, 4th Light and the Fusilier-Garde Regiment. Hammerstein, with no division to command, returned to Kassel, leaving GB Louis Bonaventure Lageon as the senior Westphalian officer. Lageon's command constituted a portion of the Dresden garrison and contributed to securing the army's lines of communication while Napoleon pressed east towards Silesia. A detachment of 100 men from the 4th Light Battalion relieved the Bavarian battalion (II/10) in Schmiedefeld, for example, and the 8th Infantry along with two Saxon cannons replaced the two Bavarian battalions in Bautzen so the Bavarians could re-join their division with Oudinot. The Westphalians were not employed to escort the large convoys Durosnel dispatched to the army every day, but in late May, Chef de Bataillon Emil Wilhelm von Lepel and 110 men of the 2nd Light were part of the detachment assigned to protect an element of imperial headquarters that was making its way east. Unfortunately, Cossacks ambushed the convoy on the 24th at Markersdorf leading to minor loss but major embarrassment as the wagons belonged to imperial headquarters and included a large shipment of specie (none of which was taken). Napoleon ordered a court of inquiry which exonerated most of the French but placed Lepel under arrest for several days for making faulty dispositions during the attack. The emperor, however, was displeased with the judgment and directed punishments for several of the French officers involved as well. The little Westphalian detachment – and presumably Lepel – would remain with imperial headquarters until some point in June.[91]

Humiliation in Halberstadt

As Napoleon and the Grande Armée pursued the Allies into Silesia after Bautzen, Westphalia suffered another embarrassing blow at the hands of Allied raiders. This time the perpetrator was Chernishev, who had dreamed of fomenting insurrection in 1811 and would inflict several painful humiliations on the kingdom during 1813.[92]

By mid-May most French regular forces were east of the Elbe, leaving little to cover Napoleon's strategic left flank, more or less from Torgau north. With few French troops available outside of major fortress garrisons and with the situation in this area very much in flux, Allied raiding detachments had considerable latitude to operate. Chernishev in particular took full advantage of this opportunity, launching frequent reconnaissance patrols and small raids from his base on the east bank of the Elbe. 'They continue to infest the countryside', wrote GD Nicholas Haxo, military governor in Magdeburg, on

30 May, 'and it is a great good fortune if a courier can pass without encountering them.' Haxo's garrison was constantly annoyed by Cossack patrols. He used two of his Westphalian battalions to drive off pestering raiders on 29 May and thought it likely that two French artillery convoys destined for his fortress would be in danger when they reached Halberstadt because a large enemy band had been reported crossing the Elbe with two cannons. He concluded, however, that the convoys should be safe in the walled town.[93] Haxo was right about the enemy's intentions, as Chernishev, having learned from his scouts that French artillery was trundling towards Halberstadt on the way to Magdeburg, had indeed decided to attack. The French general, however, would prove wrong about the safety afforded by Halberstadt.

Halberstadt was the temporary headquarters of GD Adam Ludwig von Ochs, commander of Westphalia's 3rd Military Division, an administrative entity embracing the kingdom's two eastern departments. Ochs was a competent and respected veteran and Jérôme had wanted to place him in command of operational troops, but his health had not recovered from the debilitating effects of the Russian campaign, and he was assigned this administrative post to recuperate. Unfortunately, his recovery would have to take place in Allied captivity.

Halberstadt was only 50–70 kilometres from the Elbe and its garrison consisted of a mere 80 Westphalian veterans and 30 mounted gendarmes. The arrival of the first of the two French artillery convoys on 28 May with 14 guns, 30 caissons, a large number of other vehicles, and an escort of 240 men was thus a considerable boost to the number of troops available to Ochs. This increase in force was deceptive, however, as the escort detachment was composed of untested conscripts and there were only enough more or less trained artillery personnel to man two or three of the guns. Two or three hundred sick, wounded or convalescent individuals (what the French called *isolées*) were also in Halberstadt, but they were unarmed and in no position to contribute to its defence. Moreover, the presence of the convoy represented a lucrative target for the brash Allied raiders. Ochs, keenly aware of the town's vulnerability, had requested reinforcements previously only to be denied. He had been informed that GD Teste had orders to march to Halberstadt with his command, now grown to four French battalions, but learned to his dismay that the first two battalions would not arrive on 29 May as promised, rather on the 30th at the earliest. Based on reports from informants and his own judgement, he feared an attack before the French appeared. He thus wrote an urgent note to Teste, posted the veterans at the town's gates, and deployed his gendarmes in an outpost line that night as improvised cavalry to at least give some advance warning.

Around 4:30 on the morning of 30 May, that early warning arrived when a gendarme dashed back to town and fired his pistol in the pre-arranged signal alerting the garrison to the enemy's approach. On hearing the alarm, Ochs hastened to position his men. The day before, he had assembled the guns, caissons and other vehicles in a *'Wagenburg'* or wagon fort on a slight rise outside town that was partly protected by forests and folds in the terrain. He now left the town in the hands of the departmental colonel with the veterans and rushed to the *Wagenburg*. The enemy, of course, were the outriders of Chernishev's force and Ochs had the three French guns open fire to gauge the enemy's mettle and to let Teste (whom he presumed to be nearby) know that a fight was imminent. The Cossacks kept coming, however, and from their boldness Ochs recognised at once that this was not a scouting patrol or foraging party. Indeed, they were the advance guard of at least 1,200 and possibly as many as 2,350 mounted men in five Cossack regiments along with Finland Dragoons, Riga Dragoons and Izum Hussars under Chernishev's command. The raiders may have numbered even more (sources vary) and, though they were tired from their long ride in the darkness, they dramatically outnumbered the 350 or so combatants available to Ochs.[94] Significantly, Chernishev also brought along two guns, about the same number that Ochs could employ. With no chance to drag the numerous vehicles off in the face of a mobile foe, Ochs decided to fight it out where he was and deployed some of the French infantry as skirmishers while keeping others in small squares in support. He also had all the spare train personnel mount up and deployed them alongside his mounted gendarmes to give the appearance of having cavalry at his disposal. Thus arrayed, he awaited the Russian attack, hoping that Teste and his battalions would soon appear on the highway from Braunschweig.

Teste was indeed on the way, but, sadly for Ochs, Chernishev struck first. While some of his men skirmished with Ochs and a detachment watched the road to Braunschweig, the rest of his band stormed Halberstadt. To Ochs's disgust, the veterans 'did not offer the least resistance', throwing down their muskets and fleeing to leave the Russians masters of the town.[95] Chernishev now turned all his attention to the *Wagenburg* on the rise. Despite their numerical inferiority, the Frenchmen and the Westphalian gendarmes were well placed and showed no signs of giving up. After about an hour of skirmishing peppered with artillery fire, however, a lucky Russian shot struck one of the ammunition caissons sparking a chain reaction of terrifying and damaging explosions. Capitalising on the sudden bloodshed and disorder, Chernishev charged and the defence collapsed, almost all the French troops being cut down or taken prisoner. Ochs managed to escape the chaos with some of the gendarmes and galloped through the town hoping to escape, but with Cossacks in pursuit his flight was hopeless. Seriously wounded by a lance blow and his gendarmes scattered, he too became a prisoner.

The entire engagement lasted only two or three hours, but Chernishev did not have time to linger. Around midday, as the Russians were resting, refreshing themselves and cataloguing the spoils of their victory, Teste's column finally put in an appearance on the Braunschweig road to the west. Chernishev, however, had enough advance notice to loot the Halberstadt treasury, burn the supply magazines in the town and slip away unhindered, taking with him 14 guns (12 of which seem to have been 12-pounders), 14 caissons, a number of other vehicles, 600 to 800 horses, and approximately 550 prisoners. Roughly 100 of these captives were Westphalian, the remainder were French from the escort detachment or the sick and wounded *isolées* in the town. Despite the nationality of most of the troops involved, the Halberstadt episode is often depicted as a signature *Westphalian* defeat. The Westphalian army certainly suffered from many crucial weaknesses and the behaviour of the veteran company in this instance was undoubtedly disgraceful, but Halberstadt is hardly evidence of the flaws in the army overall. On the other hand, news of Chernishev's success was discouraging and, for Napoleon, infuriating, especially given the loss of a prominent and well-regarded senior general. It handed the Allies more propaganda ammunition and was yet another indicator of the debilitating degree of insecurity in the French rear areas.

At the same time, Ochs represents another example of the manner in which many Rheinbund officers resolved the dilemma they faced in 1813, even in the 'artificial' state of Westphalia. Chernishev treated Ochs with careful consideration, had his wounds bound and provided a wagon to carry him to captivity in Berlin where Ochs had many acquaintances. When advised or urged to change sides, however, the general refused. In the words of his biographer, working from his private papers: 'Ochs, however, gave his explanation to the effect that he was far from being a friend of the French system, and had only had to give in to the demands of circumstances, nonetheless, he had given his oath of loyalty to his present national sovereign and would not break it'. He would thus rather 'endure the yoke of captivity' than break with his conception of duty.[96]

What of General Teste? His experience offers another instance of the prevalent sense of anxiety in the French strategic rear, especially in Westphalia. Before Teste left Kassel, Jérôme had tried to persuade him to remain. 'He feared, no doubt, that my departure would attract another visit to his capital by the Cossacks,' the general wrote in his memoirs. He proceeded towards Magdeburg as ordered anyway and his four battalions did reach Halberstadt on the afternoon of 30 May, but he retired half-way to Braunschweig that same night and to Braunschweig itself the following day. He thereby saved, in his view, the second artillery and supply convoy that had been headed to Magdeburg via Halberstadt. Choosing an alternative and, he hoped, safer route to the fortress, he marched again on 2 June. Along the way, he received an order from Jérôme directing him to return to Braunschweig, combine with the Westphalian forces there and, in case of danger, to then retire to Göttingen where the king promised to send additional troops. Teste, however, believed his route to Magdeburg was now clear 'and any hesitation or retrograde step must influence the soldier's morale and the spirit of the country, spirit already so poor'. To Haxo's happy surprise, Teste and his small division reached Magdeburg safely on 4 June. Here Teste received a congratulatory note from the Westphalian minister of war for completing what should have been a routine and unremarkable march: 'I felicitate you, general for the success of your good dispositions by means of which you have arrived in Magdeburg.'[97]

Chernishev's encounter with the Westphalians concluded before the armistice, but one more incident between Jérôme's men and Allied raiders took place towards the end of June near Köthen, some 65 kilometres south-east of Halberstadt. Like Lützow, Prussian Rittmeister Colomb was operating in southern Saxony west of the Elbe when the armistice went into effect and, again like Lützow, he headed back to Prussian territory at a very leisurely pace, organising food and accommodations with local authorities as he did so. Fortunate not to have been discovered by any of the roving patrols Arrighi was sending out of Leipzig, he was still west of Halle on 21 June when he learned to his great indignation of the destruction of Lützow's band five days earlier.[98] Somehow managing to elude detection, he had reached a village southwest of Köthen on the evening of the 22nd when a breathless civilian came to tell him that a Westphalian detachment was in pursuit. This was GB Karl Gottlob von Bastineller at the head of three squadrons of cuirassiers and the 3rd Light Infantry Battalion. Colomb arranged a parlay with one of the senior Westphalian officers and made excuses for his delayed departure, but the Westphalian found these unconvincing and told Colomb his band would have to lay down its arms until the general arrived. Incensed, Colomb replied: 'Whatever we have to negotiate we will do with sabre in hand!' Very well, said the Westphalian, 'then I will take you'. Colomb could see that the cuirassier squadrons were deploying to out-flank him on both sides and that infantry were hurrying up from the rear. He turned about, dashed away and gathered up his troopers to escape into the growing darkness chased by a few pistol and carbine shots from the Westphalians. A dozen or so of Colomb's men were captured, but the rest rode through the night to reach the Elbe and cross by boat on the morning of 23 June. The Westphalians, whose heavy cavalry horses were visibly weary from riding hard to catch up with the Prussians in the first place, were too tired to pursue.[99]

Several other Westphalian 'mobile columns' of cavalry and infantry were also active from late April through June as part of the effort to destroy or deter partisan bands, but Bastineller's detachment was the only one to encounter the enemy. These columns also had the onerous task of repressing desertion, as Major Meibom discovered when he was assigned to command one 'partly to track down the large number of men who had deserted from the corps that had marched to Saxony, partly to quell the disturbances caused by these deserters'.[100] After Halberstadt, however, Jérôme's concerns led him to make another appeal for external assistance. This time he turned to GD Dąbrowski in Gießen, telling him that he should march via Hersfeld to Eschwege and implying that he was relaying instructions directly from Napoleon. Dąbrowski met with Jérôme but the danger subsided, and his small Polish division continued through Eisenach and Naumburg to Leipzig. Although Dąbrowski's division was not diverted, the episode earned Jérôme another rebuke from his imperial brother, not because Jérôme had sent orders to a division commander as he had with Teste under emergency circumstances, but because he had done so in the emperor's name. Such actions confuse the generals and 'derange the march of my armies' he told Jérôme, threatening to issue an order of the day for officers to ignore Jérôme's messages if something similar happened again.[101] The incident not only provides another example of fraternal friction, it also illuminates Jérôme's anxieties about the security of his kingdom and his doubts about the loyalty of his subjects and soldiers.

Armistice Arrangements

Westphalia's troops were scattered, and their future status was uncertain as the armistice began. Napoleon remained deeply suspicious about Westphalian reliability, his negative impressions reinforced by reports from Reinhard, Jérôme's complaints and other inputs. Issuing orders to 'surround the partisans and purge the rear areas' around Dresden on 3 June, for example, he instructed Durosnel to form three or four mixed infantry/cavalry columns commanded by 'good Saxon officers' but warned that 'care should be taken not to employ Westphalians, unless one could be assured that they will not desert'.[102] His scepticism notwithstanding, summer saw the emperor contemplating the re-establishment of the Westphalian 37th Division to augment MacDonald's 11th Corps. The basic concept was that the 2nd and 3rd Infantry Regiments and the 1st Light Battalion would form a new brigade under GB Jacques Bernard. Along with two foot artillery batteries, the brigade then would be sent to Dresden where it would join Lageon's troops to create a revived division commanded by

GD Louis Danloup-Verdun, another Frenchman in Westphalian service and one of Jérôme's royal adjutants.[103] Jérôme embraced the idea – as long as his kingdom was adequately protected. The anxious king was torn between a desire to see his army united in the field and fear that sending the necessary units would denude his vulnerable realm of troops in the face of foreign invasion and internal unrest. As he told Berthier on 1 June, 'You will admit, my cousin, that it is distressing to see my country ravaged and traversed in all directions by enemy parties when five of my battalions and eight of my squadrons are guarding the King of Saxony's capital.' In the event, the plan quickly evaporated. In addition to Napoleon's doubts about Westphalian loyalty, the exigencies of the operational situation – the requirement to maintain a large field force while simultaneously garrisoning key fortresses – meant that Westphalian formations with the field army during the autumn campaigns would be no larger than brigades in size and much of the infantry would be assigned to fortress garrisons or retained to secure the kingdom itself.[104] Partly by accident (such as the 1st Infantry in Danzig) and partly by design, therefore, no other Rheinbund army would be as dispersed across the vast field of combat that autumn as was the Kingdom of Westphalia's contingent.

For the field army, most of the Westphalian infantry in and around Dresden went to 11th Corps as Napoleon had planned. Rather than a division, however, MacDonald only received five battalions which were incorporated into the 31st Division as its 2nd Brigade under French GB François Nivard Charles Joseph d'Henin along with a foot artillery battery: the Füsilier-Garde, 8th Infantry and 4th Light. GB Lageon remained as the senior Westphalian officer. The 2nd Light Battalion that had marched to the Elbe in May, however, had been greatly diminished by the time of the armistice and was disbanded, some of its men being absorbed into the 4th Light while the remainder returned to Westphalia to re-form.

The light cavalry was distributed between the 2nd and 12th Corps. Although all three Westphalian regiments (eight squadrons) had been under Beaumont's command in the spring, that ad hoc division was drastically reduced in late May and during the armistice. First, its naval artillery battalions and its four guns returned to Marmont's 6th Corps in May after Bautzen. Second, the two Westphalian hussar regiments were assigned to Victor's 2nd Corps as the 22nd Light Cavalry Brigade under GB Adrien François Bruno over the summer. A third squadron was also added to each regiment bringing the total to six and Colonel William von Hammerstein, commander of the 1st Hussars and younger brother of GD von Hammerstein, served as the senior Westphalian officer in the brigade. The junior Hammerstein, while militarily competent, seems to have been as unruly and impetuous as his elder sibling, perhaps even to the point of hot-headedness. Regardless of Hammerstein's qualities, according to an inspection report of the 1st Hussars, 'The uniforms, arms and equipment of the regiment are in good condition and complete, the horses are fine but appear a bit fatigued.' The report described the 2nd Regiment in similar terms, concluding that, 'The type of men in the two regiments is good, the dress is passably maintained and their instruction advanced.'[105] The departure of the naval artillery battalions and the Westphalian hussars, however, left GD Beaumont with only three Rheinbund light cavalry regiments, one each from Bavaria, Hesse-Darmstadt and Westphalia. These were now designated as the 29th Light Cavalry Brigade. Beaumont was technically too senior to command such a small force but remained in this position as did GB von Wolff even though only one Westphalian regiment was present in the brigade, his own former regiment the Chevaulegers-Garde. As noted earlier, the 29th Light Cavalry Brigade – or what was left of it – would be transferred to 4th Corps after Dennewitz.

Six of the Westphalian infantry regiments and one of the light battalions served in fortress garrisons. The 1st Infantry was in Danzig, the 4th and 5th in Küstrin and the 9th in Magdeburg; the last would also take part in the brief but disastrous foray to Hagelberg in August. Rather than forming a new division as proposed during the armistice, the 2nd and 3rd Infantry along with the 1st Light Battalion soon found themselves consigned to fortress duty as well: the 3rd Infantry moved from Magdeburg to become part of the Dresden garrison (joining the foot battery that was already there), while Bernard was assigned to Torgau with the 1st Light, the 2nd Infantry, a foot battery and the army's lone horse battery. This column reached the fortress on 25 July accompanied by a 600-man march battalion destined for the brigade in the 31st Division and 50 hussars to bolster the brigade in 2nd Corps. This too soon changed. The horse guns went first, rolling off to be incorporated into the 1st Cavalry Corps in time for the Battle of Dresden, 26–27 August. The infantry and the foot artillery shifted to Dresden in September after the great battle with the 1st Light Battalion serving for a time as the garrison of Meissen.[106] These five infantry battalions (2nd and 3rd Infantry, 1st Light) and the foot battery remained in and around Dresden for the remainder of the war under GB Bernard's command. GD Danloup-Verdun, like GD Hammerstein earlier, thus found himself without an appropriate command and returned to Kassel in late August after the Battle of Dresden.

The army's field and garrison deployments left most of the Royal Guard, the two cuirassier regiments and the 3rd Light Battalion in Westphalia, the bulk of these units encamped around Kassel and to the south (*see* Map 45).[107] A foot battery was established for the Guard in August and Jérôme intended to form a Guard horse battery as well, but the kingdom disappeared before this could be accomplished. Another new 'unit' of sorts was the Corps of Public Workers, basically a disciplinary organisation established in June 1813 to accommodate the growing number of draft evaders, deserters, and others who had committed grave violations against army regulations.

Finally, Napoleon's concerns about Westphalian loyalty convinced him that a force of French guards was 'indispensable' for Jérôme's security.[108] This was to consist of two battalions of light infantry, an artillery battery and a light horse regiment of 1,000 men. The only element to achieve formation, however, was the light cavalry regiment, albeit with 600 rather than 1,000 troopers. Designated the 'Jérôme Napoléon Hussars', this unit was to have four squadrons formed from French conscripts and convalescents, most of whom had no military experience and no notion of equitation. Their uniform was to be a handsome hussar ensemble with red dolman, blue pelisse and blue breeches topped by a red shako, all with yellow or gold trim and all paid for by Westphalia (along with their horses, saddles, harness and arms). They arrived on foot and had to be supplied with mounts from the depots of the Westphalian Chevaulegers-Garde and hussars. Borcke, who often saw them in Kassel in the few weeks of their ephemeral existence, remarked that, 'They remained under construction till the very end, incomplete and unequipped … splendidly but only partly uniformed, only half were mounted and those poorly, without saddles, just blankets and snaffles, the men were pitiful riders as they had been mashed together from all arms and mixed with convalescents and hired vagabonds.' The citizens called them 'crabs' owing to the red uniforms, noted Wilhelm Grimm, who was working in Kassel's library, adding sarcastically that, as far as their clumsy movements were concerned, 'they did not disgrace that name'.[109]

Jérôme held numerous reviews and distributed awards and promotions lavishly to encourage loyalty while his officers kept the troops as busy as possible in their encampments to make desertion more difficult and gendarmes scoured the countryside seeking draft evaders. The king also toured the most afflicted portions of his realm in mid-June to rally his officials and subjects, even visiting Halberstadt and the truculently unreceptive town of Halle where most of the university students and faculty had fled to volunteer for the Prussian army. His well-intentioned efforts did little to reassure a populace whose most earnest wish was that the armistice would lead to peace and an end to conscription, unbearable taxation and the depredations inflicted by both sides. He concluded his circuit with a lengthy stop in Dresden, arriving on 22 June and remaining until 1 July.[110] During this visit to his imperial brother, the young king expressed a lively interest in commanding a major force in the field himself, a plea he reiterated through Berthier some weeks later.[111] His hopes would not be realised. After the experience of 1812, Napoleon would not grant his brother a field command unless Jérôme agreed to subordinate himself to a marshal, if necessary, a stipulation the king would not accept.[112]

Though perhaps disappointed at being denied field command, Jérôme returned to Kassel buoyed by Napoleon's energy and his favourable impression of the Grande Armée but distressed by his kingdom's impossible financial situation and continuing exactions by French officers (such as the demands made by the new governor of Magdeburg, GD Jean Léonor François Le Marois).[113] Despite the assertions of fidelity he had received while travelling through the countryside, he also remained anxious about the popular mood. His concerns were certainly warranted given the levels of draft evasion and desertion in the army and the tacit cooperation if not always warm welcome most towns and villages had afforded the Allied raiders during the spring campaign. The French, and presumably the Westphalian authorities, were aware of Coalition efforts to raise combat units 'composed of Westphalians, Saxons and other subjects of the Confederation of the Rhine'. Intelligence reports specifically suggested that talented Westphalian officers received especially solicitous treatment to induce them to defect.[114] Jérôme and his government could take solace in the fact that there had been no widespread insurrection during the spring (much to the disappointment of the Allied leadership), but there was no guarantee that serious French setbacks or the reappearance of multiple Allied raiding detachments would not ignite a fire of rebellion if hostilities resumed.[115]

Autumn: A Mixed Record on the Road to Leipzig

Given the dispersal of its units, the Westphalian army's involvement in the autumn campaigns falls into three broad categories: troops with the field forces, those committed to the defence of the realm, and those assigned to fortress garrisons. Bearing in mind that actions were taking place simultaneously across the theatre of war, the following will intersperse actions in the field and in Westphalia to carry events to the kingdom's end in October. The fortress war will then be addressed in Chapter 8.

The Hussars: Infamous Treachery

The autumn phase of the war began with a disheartening episode: the defection of most of the Westphalian hussar brigade (that is, the Grande Armée's 22nd Light Cavalry Brigade under French GB Bruno). Although two of the squadrons (I/1 and II/2) were detached when hostilities began, the other four were posted at Reichenberg (Liberec) southeast of Zittau on the Bohemian border with Saxony. With Habsburg cavalry outposts only a few kilometres away, Colonel William von Hammerstein of the 1st Hussars and Major Ernst

Pentz of the 2nd decided to defect with their regiments. Beyond a general anger at French domination and depredations, their specific motivations are unclear. The regiments had been forced to move out of quarters in Görlitz several days earlier to make room for French Imperial Guardsmen, but this unwelcome aggravation would hardly seem to warrant defecting to the enemy. Whatever Hammerstein's and Pentz's motivations, the junior officers and men had no idea at the outset that their commanders were leading them to the enemy. They thought they were marching to attack a nearby Austrian hussar camp.

On the night of 22/23 August, the men were assembled in great silence and secrecy. No trumpets were sounded, and orders were only given in subdued voices. Hammerstein and Pentz then led the four squadrons (II and III/1 and I and III/2) off into the darkness over narrow mountain trails to Bohemia. The following morning, the two regimental commanders gathered their troopers in a small open area and announced their intention to defect to the Allies, specifically to the Austrians. According to Hammerstein family lore, William's address was laden with fiery references to 'breaking the yoke about our necks', the 'evil deeds' of the French and the 'shame and slavery' of foreign rule. These may have been subsequent embellishments, but when offered the choice to remain with their regiments in Habsburg service or return to the French lines unobstructed, only one officer, a Pole by origin, elected to ride away. This individual, Major Joseph von Czernitzky, who had lost a leg at Borodino, saluted, took his leave, and made his way back to the French army unmolested. 'Some of the non-commissioned officers and hussars returned during the day, and all agreed that they had been led to believe that they were mounting to surprise the enemy, and that after riding for a few leagues on almost impassable roads, they had been surrounded by Cossacks and Austrian cavalry, with whose leaders it seems that Westphalian colonel had agreed on this defection.'[116] Though some returned, most of the officers and enlisted men abandoned their allegiance to Westphalia, took new oaths to Kaiser Franz (who granted Hammerstein a personal audience) and eventually became the cavalry component of the Austro-German Legion that Vienna was organising as a repository for German deserters. In all, approximately 400 to 600 Westphalian hussars thus changed sides, boosting Allied morale while spreading suspicion in the ranks of the Grande Armée.[117]

GB Bruno reported that the Westphalians had planned their defection in great secrecy, arousing no suspicion and leaving all their equipment behind when they rode off. '*Voilà*, the 2nd Corps is without cavalry,' reported Victor, 'but this inconvenience would be much better than having traitors in our ranks who could compromise us.' He added the returning hussars to the two squadrons that had remained loyal and had them march with the headquarters, but he also took the opportunity to ask for French cavalry to replace the absconding Westphalians.[118]

Napoleon reacted to the defection with understandable anger, declaring he would dismount all the Westphalian cavalry regiments and turn their horses over to the large French cavalry depot at Magdeburg. In the event, however, this idea was not implemented: the Westphalian mounted units continued to serve until the end of the kingdom, and the only Westphalian horses turned over to the French were those delivered to the new Jérôme Hussars from the depots of the Chevaulegers-Garde and the two now disbanded hussar regiments. At the same time, the defection confirmed in the emperor's mind the impression that the Westphalian troops were fundamentally unreliable and reinforced his determination to see Jérôme guarded by French soldiers. 'This example proves that you cannot trust anyone in Westphalia,' he told his brother, 'Buy mounts promptly for the regiment of French hussars that I have granted you.' He sent similar instructions to his foreign minister: 'It is important that the king give all the horses of his cavalry to the regiment of French hussars and that he cease to raise troops: that it is only to give them to the enemy,' but here again, these instructions were executed at most in part when it came to turning over horses to the new hussars.[119]

Jérôme was shocked as well as angry. He initially feared that the hussars' defection signalled a wider conspiracy connected to the advances of Thielmann, Mensdorff and other raiders through Chemnitz towards Leipzig 'only six or eight marches from Kassel'. He thus had Reinhard send a letter to GD Louis Lemoine at Minden on the Weser 'inviting' him to march to the supposedly endangered Westphalian capital. Lemoine wisely demurred and Berthier tartly informed Reinhard that the ambassador should limit his correspondence with the general to intelligence updates and general reports on the state of affairs.[120] In the wake of the victory at Dresden, Jérôme's initial anxiety about a larger plot dissipated, but the defection of his two regiments hurt him personally as he had trusted the Hammerstein brothers, taking them into his confidence and showering them with awards, promotions, titles and positions. Indeed, William had just been nominated for the Legion of Honour during the armistice.[121] The younger Hammerstein being out of reach, Jérôme now had the elder brother, Hans, arrested and imprisoned, first in Westphalia, later in France where he was finally freed by the Allied victory in 1814. Hans returned to the new Germany, but the Prussians regarded him as a traitor, and he could find no further military employment. He would die in penury, while William remained a loyal Habsburg subject and rose to the rank of *General der Kavallerie*.[122]

The status of the two regiments, of course, was now in question. A Westphalian order of the day issued on 31 August pronounced the hussar brigade dissolved, adding that the regimental standards were to be publicly burned and that any remaining men were to be distributed to other regiments.[123] None of these measures seem to have affected the other two hussar squadrons (I/1 and II/2). They had been guarding corps headquarters when their compatriots defected, and they were still mounted and operating as Victor's light cavalry under GB Bruno nearly a month later. Indeed, Bruno seems to have employed the Westphalians in a completely routine fashion for normal scouting, outpost and courier duties even though his 'brigade' now consisted of only these two squadrons with at most 200–300 officers and men 'who rode with the headquarters'.[124]

Bruno worried that the two squadrons were 'extremely feeble' and had lost many horses, but loyalty does not seem to have been a major concern. Victor, for example, had no qualms about detailing the brigade to occupy Freiberg in mid-September as part of Napoleon's effort to protect his Bohemian flank and curb the activities of Allied raiding parties. An officer and four troopers who individually made their ways back to Freiberg on foot after being ambushed by Austrians seem to have been indicative of the attitude in these two squadrons.[125] Bruno, however, failed to observe elementary security precautions and was taken completely by surprise when attacked in the pre-dawn hours of 18 September by an Austrian raiding detachment under GM Georg Heinrich von Scheither. Although the Westphalians resisted, the guards at the town's main gate were quickly overwhelmed by the well-prepared Austrians and Bruno along with his entire command fell into Scheither's hands.[126] Interestingly, two officers and 14 troopers from the two hussar squadrons escaped their captors and reported to Durosnel in Dresden several days later.[127] This indicator and the behaviour of the squadrons while at Freiberg suggests that the Westphalian leadership in these units was of a different calibre than that evident under Hammerstein and Pentz. The available data does not support a definitive answer, but perhaps the officers in the two remaining squadrons held their men to their sworn duty where the tempestuous Hammerstein, disdaining his previous oath, grabbed what he perceived to be an opportunity to craft a new future for himself.

Napoleon was furious at yet another loss to Allied raiders, but his wrath was directed not at the Westphalians but at Bruno for the lapses in security and at Victor for not ensuring that his subordinate adhered to the necessary precautions. In fact, the official correspondence relating to the surprise at Freiberg only mentions the Westphalians in passing as the victims of the attack; there is none of the disparagement that surfaces in other situations. Instead, the emperor issued an order of the day to the army stressing vigilance and the procedures required of light troops. Victor, exasperated at the censure both public and private, wrote to Napoleon directly asking to be relieved from

Autumn: A Mixed Record on the Road to Leipzig   245

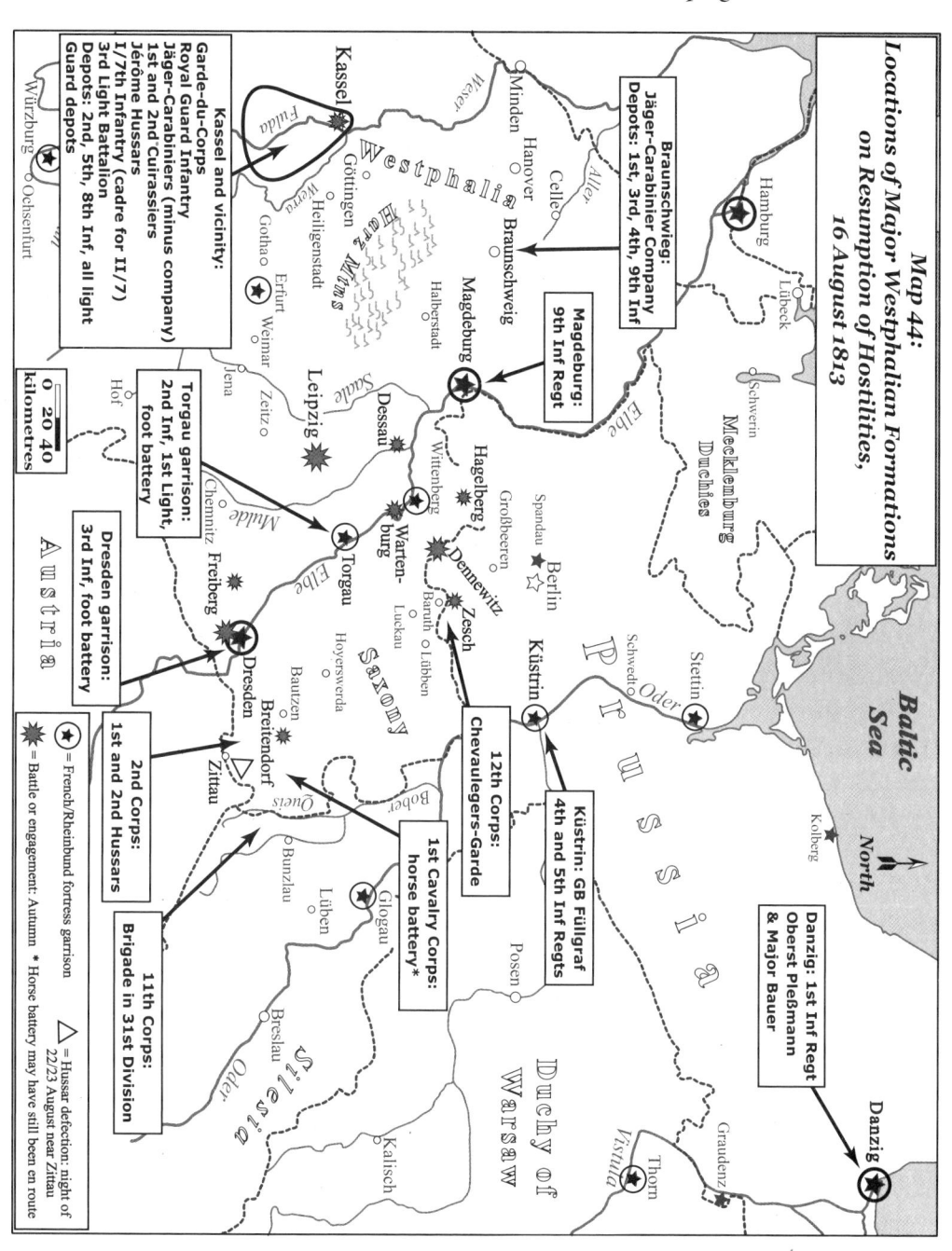

Map 44: Locations of Major Westphalian Formations on Resumption of Hostilities, 16 August 1813

command for failing to meet the emperor's expectations.[128] Victor's request was ignored (as he likely expected) but the hussars disappeared from the army's order of battle and 2nd Corps would operate without a light cavalry brigade for the remainder of the war.

Chart 43: Westphalian Field Forces, mid-August 1813

		Bns/sqdns	Present under arms
With 2nd Corps			
22nd Light Cavalry Brigade	GB Bruno, Oberst von Hammerstein		
1st Hussar Regiment		3	419
2nd Hussar Regiment		3	362
With 11th Corps, 31st Division			
2nd Brigade	GB d'Henin, GB Lageon		
Füsilier-Garde Regiment		2	925
8th Infantry Regiment		2	929
4th Light Battalion		1	704
Westphalian artillery and train		–	276
With 12th Corps			
29th Light Cavalry Brigade	GD Beaumont, GB Wolff		
Westphalian Chevaulegers-Garde		4	522
Bavarian Chevaulegers		3	410
Hessian Garde-Chevaulegers		3	260
With 1st Cavalry Corps			
Horse artillery battery		4 × 6-pdr, 2 × howitzer	142
With Magdeburg Division (or 1st Madgeburg Division)	GD Lanusse		
I/9th Infantry Regiment		1	817
Total Westphalian (only)		–	5,766

Notes: the cadres of the 2nd Light Battalion had been sent to Westphalia to re-form the unit; other men were incorporated into the 4th Light. II/9th Westphalian (*c.* 800 officers/men) is not included here; it was part of the Magdeburg garrison, and thus not a field force.

Sources: Livret de Situation, 15 August 1813, SHD, 2C708; 2nd Corps Situation, 16 August 1813, 2C538; Girard table of losses, 6 September 1813, 2C155 Quistorp, *Nordarmee*, vol. III, pp. 72–3. The 12th Corps 'Situation Sommaire' for 10 August 1813 gives slightly different figures for the 29th Light Cavalry Brigade: Westphalians 489 present, 37 detached, 7 sick; Bavarians 392 present, 223 detached, 65 sick; and Hessians 254 present, 29 detached, 6 sick. The other two Hessian squadrons had left Darmstadt on 21 July, but had not yet arrived.

Back in Westphalia, other regiments hastened to reaffirm their oaths with extravagant expressions of fealty in the wake of what the artillery regiment denounced as the 'infamous treachery' of the hussars. These public pronouncements may be viewed with some scepticism, but private disapprobation of the defection was common as well. 'We all condemned the desertion of our two hussar regiments in the strongest terms,' wrote Major von Morgenstern of the 2nd Infantry, especially as Hammerstein and Pentz had run no personal risk and had dragged their men along on their 'disgraceful felony'. He could understand, if not approve, of *individual* soldiers who changed sides because they were 'excited by the patriotic uprising of a great German people, [and] inflamed in their deepest souls by the wish to help shake off the foreign yoke'. 'Let each battle that out with his *own* conscience,' he would write. Conspiring with others, leading others to break their oaths 'or even luring entire regiments into a trap', however, was for him 'black treachery, showing contempt for every military and moral principal'. Morgenstern may have been especially ardent in his views, but many other officers shared his conception of military honour and looked askance at the hussars' defection. Whatever the public promises of the regiments or the private sentiments within the officer corps, the army was also determined to deal fairly with those innocent hussars who had not been party to the 'shameful treachery'. Punishment having been administered and the two regiments having been expunged from the rolls, the remaining men were to be treated with proper respect. Several weeks later, therefore, when the military command in Kassel observed that other soldiers were insulting the men of the former hussar regiments, strict instructions were issued that such behaviour was 'impermissible and punishable'.[129]

In the 31st Division: 'Rivalling my French Brigade in Courage'

Though it only totalled 2,834 officers and men present under arms, the 2nd Brigade of François Roch, Baron Ledru des Essarts's 31st Division in 11th Corps was the largest Westphalian contribution to the field army that autumn. A soldier since 1792, Ledru was an experienced officer who had participated in most of the great battles in central Europe and Russia. On adding the Westphalians to his division over the summer he expressed no concerns, writing to his brother that the Royal Guard (Füsilier-Garde) in particular was 'admirable for the appearance and the dress of the men'. The 31st Division encountered plenty of privation, sickness and hard marching in execrable weather, but MacDonald detached it to cover his flank as he advanced towards the Katzbach in late August, so the Westphalians missed that disaster and indeed saw little combat until early the following month.[130] On 4 September, however, the 31st Division was thrown into battle. With the discouraged MacDonald reeling back towards Bautzen in confusion after the Katzbach defeat, Napoleon rushed east from Dresden to restore the situation. Arriving at Bautzen on the 4th, the emperor immediately turned the army around and attacked along the highway running through Hochkirch and Wurzen towards Silesia (*see* Map 21). The 31st Division played an important role in this counter-offensive, pushing the enemy out of Breitendorf and charging up the slopes to seize the Wohlaer Berg just beyond. Details are lacking, but the division earned praise for its performance. MacDonald noted that it had achieved its mission after 'great efforts of courage' and Ledru, conscious of the emperor's and the army's eyes upon him and his men, proudly related the attack to his sister, highlighting that 'the Westphalian brigade and the Neapolitan brigade rivalled my French brigade in courage'.[131]

Lieutenant Normann's battery of four guns also spent part of September east of Dresden. It marched with the Guard after the Battle of Dresden, was dispatched to Meissen and then recalled to Bautzen where Normann was delighted 'to meet my comrades again and spend a few happy hours with them'. These included one officer whose 'servant' was a pretty, young lass ('similar situations were not uncommon', noted Normann). He accompanied the 31st Division into Silesia before returning to Dresden to assume a place as part of the Dresden Neustadt's defences. Along the way, he witnessed all the devastation inflicted by the foraging troops, including his own, who brought back 'items other than victuals' from the abandoned villages. 'The manner of sustaining the troops', he observed, 'ruined the region terribly, and exhausted and demoralised the troops'.[132]

Constant marching, abominable weather, poor provisions and desertion eroded the strength of the Westphalian brigade as 11th Corps roamed back and forth, first on the eastern side of the Elbe and later on the western shore. They also suffered combat losses in occasional skirmishes and minor clashes. The only serious engagement during this period occurred on 23 September when MacDonald tried to push Blücher's army back from Dresden. That day saw a series of tough actions between Bischofswerda and Bautzen during which Prussian and Russian cavalry captured approximately 350 men from 11th Corps, most of them from the Westphalian Füsilier-Garde.[133] The Westphalian contingent was further diminished in early October at Dresden as Napoleon pulled away the remnants of the Füsilier-Garde (now consolidated as a single battalion), combined it with the four grenadier companies of the 2nd and 3rd Infantry Regiments of the Dresden garrison and incorporated the resulting composite battalion and a battery of Westphalian foot artillery into the Imperial Guard.[134] It was thus a much reduced 'brigade' that marched with Ledru towards the culminating battle at Leipzig.

The Dresden Garrison: Awe, Confidence and Desertion

The departure of Lageon's brigade left the 3rd Infantry, the 1st Light and a foot battery in and around Dresden, while the lone Westphalian horse battery was assigned to Latour-Maubourg's 1st Cavalry Corps. Details of their roles in the great battle there on 26 and 27 August are sketchy, but the Westphalian foot artillery participated in the defence of Lunettes III and IV, while the 3rd

Infantry contributed part of the garrison in Lunette IV. French infantry held Lunette III with Westphalians manning some of the guns supported, as in all the lunettes, by a few Saxon engineer officers and sappers. The bulk of the 3rd Infantry was held inside the city's walls in reserve and the 1st Light had been detached to garrison Meissen. The command structure is obscure. GB Bernard was considered the Westphalian brigade commander but is seldom mentioned in the accounts as having any tactical role. On the other hand, Colonel von Pfuhl, the senior Westphalian artillery officer, seems to have had significant responsibilities for that arm including non-Westphalian men and guns.[135]

Indeed, the Westphalian artillery, ensconced in the lunettes outside Dresden's walls, received considerable praise for its performance. These lunettes were small fortifications hastily constructed during the armistice (*see* Map 10). They had earthen walls on their flanks and on the sides towards the enemy and each was closed at the back (or 'throat') by a wooden palisade with a locked gate. Austrian elements of the Army of Bohemia attacked both with vigour on 26 August. The Westphalian and French conscripts in Lunette IV, in combat for the first time, were jittery. They held out until nearly surrounded, but when a lucky Austrian shot smashed the gate in the palisade, the troops panicked to the rear despite the best efforts of their officers. Only the officers, some senior NCOs and the gunners remained behind. Fortunately, the 2nd Chasseurs of the Old Guard were near at hand in reserve. These veterans swept the Austrians from around the lunette and chivvied the frightened conscripts back to their places. Three even paraded up and down along the earthen walls for a few moments to encourage their young comrades. According to Leutnant Normann, the Westphalian horse battery and a French horse battery also unlimbered to drive off the supporting Austrian guns.

Although Lunette IV did not fall, the Habsburg attackers succeeded in capturing Lunette III after a bitter struggle, killing or wounding many of the Westphalian artillerymen in the process. Here again, however, French reserves were on hand and a counterattack regained the little fort before nightfall. Human and material losses were heavy among the Westphalian gunners, leaving the 19-year-old Leutnant Normann as the only remaining officer of his battery and only four of the eight pieces serviceable.

The Westphalians were 'peaceful observers' of the fighting on 27 August, but Normann had his first opportunity to see the emperor. 'The impression he made on me, evoked in me the greatest awe and confidence,' Normann would later write, 'so that I regarded the consequences of the battle that had begun with the greatest calm.' Napoleon, well pleased with the performance of the Westphalian artillery, granted the Legion of Honour to Normann and to Pfuhl, who had overseen much of the action during the first day, while Jérôme publicly lauded Pfuhl and made him a baron of the kingdom (Pfuhl would become one of the few Germans to follow his former monarch into exile in October).[136]

Other Westphalian units assigned to Dresden earned a very different reputation. GB Jean Lauer reported from Torgau in late August that the Westphalian soldiers sent to guard the line of the Elbe under a French officer 'have not shown themselves well'. 'Many have decamped', he complained, including some fifty who 'to all appearances have allowed themselves to be taken prisoner voluntarily or have gone over to the enemy'. These were likely men from the 2nd Infantry which was then in Torgau. Transferred to Dresden in mid-September, the regiment arrived with approximately 1,100 in its ranks but again occasioned worrisome reports. 'There is starting to be a lot of desertion in the Westphalian regiments garrisoned in Dresden,' Durosnel told Berthier on 20 September, 'The 2nd Regiment of the Line has lost 72 since its departure from Torgau and during the last two days the 3rd has lost 22 and the 1st Light Infantry Battalion six.'[137] Although these numbers were not large (72 deserters was only 6.5 per cent of the 2nd Infantry's 1,100) and the losses in these instances did not involve unit defections, French commanders were clearly concerned by the constant seepage of deserters over what they considered to be very brief periods of time. The drain of desertion continued throughout September. A particularly egregious incident occurred late in the month when Major Ludwig von Brethauer, a battalion commander in the 3rd Infantry, marched his men out into the countryside on the pretext of foraging only to defect to the Allies.[138]

The autumn campaign was now lurching towards Leipzig and, as noted above, the four grenadier companies of the 2nd and 3rd Infantry Regiments (roughly 300 men) were combined with the remnants of the Füsilier-Garde from Ledru's 31st Division in early October. This made a composite battalion of some 800 officers and men which was attached to the 2nd Old Guard Division along with a Westphalian foot battery of approximately 120 artillery and train personnel. These new honorary imperial guardsmen soon marched off to accompany the emperor on the road to Leipzig. The 2nd and 3rd Infantry Regiments as well as the 1st Light Battalion were left behind in Dresden as part of the city's garrison. Also included in the garrison were young Leutnant Normann and his battery, totalling approximately a hundred artillery and train personnel. They had returned from their marches with the Guard and 11th Corps towards Silesia and were now left to endure the rigours of the coming blockade.[139]

The 9th Infantry: From Magdeburg to Hagelberg and Back

Further north along the Elbe, the new 9th Westphalian Infantry was consigned to the Magdeburg garrison. Arriving early in the spring campaign, it was combined with the 3rd Infantry and placed under the command of

Westphalian GB Georg Julius von Langenschwarz to form a small Westphalian brigade. Langenschwarz found the 9th incomplete, not fully armed and 'very behind' in discipline, but earnest effort on the part of the regimental officers brought the regiment to 'fit for duty' status as far as training was concerned, at least in Langenschwarz's eyes. GD Haxo evidently felt sufficiently confident in the 9th's condition to use it in chasing off probing Cossacks in May, but the armistice brought changes in command and organisation. In command, Haxo set out for Hamburg to be replaced as the fortress governor by GD Le Marois. Organisationally, the 3rd Westphalian Line left for Dresden, while large numbers of additional French troops arrived along with Rheinbund contingents from the Thuringian states (*see* Chapter 7).[140] With these additional forces, Le Marois was directed to divide his command into two components: a field division under GD Lanusse that could operate beyond the fortress under the overall command of GD Jean-Baptiste Girard and a formal garrison to hold the city. These were titled the 1st and 2nd Divisions of the Government of Magdeburg respectively. Curiously, Le Marois was instructed to divide the 9th Westphalians as well, selecting six companies to serve with the field formation (the French would record this as the 1st Battalion or the 'elite battalion') and leaving the other six companies (2nd Battalion) in the garrison.[141] As discussed in Chapter 7, he would also split the Ducal Saxon Regiment between Lanusse and the fortress garrison when it arrived in the second half of August. He planned to do the same with the other microstate contingents (Lippe, Reuß, and so on) but the sad state of these units and their disordered and delayed appearance rendered this concept moot.

It will be remembered that Girard was to advance east from Magdeburg in support of Oudinot's offensive towards Berlin in late August (*see* Chart 44). For this task he had been placed in command of two formations: the Magdeburg field division of French, Westphalian, Thuringian and Croatian troops under GD Lanusse and GD Dąbrowski's Polish division from Wittenberg. Designed to serve as the link between the simultaneous advances of Davout and Oudinot for the offensive towards Berlin, Girard headed off on 21 August. Nothing, however, went as intended. Effective communication across unfriendly terrain infested by Cossacks proved impossible and 27 August found Girard still at Hagelberg, well east of Magdeburg and dangerously isolated. He had no information from Dąbrowski and was unaware that Oudinot was retiring towards Wittenberg after his chastening at Großbeeren. Surprised by Hirschfeld's Prussian division and the ubiquitous Chernishev's Cossacks, Girard and his untried division of conscripts suffered a devastating defeat. 'He departed with 8,000 men and he is returned with 3,300,' wrote Le Marois from Magdeburg when the division straggled back to the fortress. There are

Chart 44: Girard's Command, mid-August 1813

		Bns/sqdns	Present under arms
Polish Division	GD Dąbrowski (Wittenberg)		
Infantry Brigade	GB Żółtowski		
2nd Infantry Regiment		2	
4th Infantry Regiment		2	
Cavalry Brigade	GB Krukowiecki		
2nd Uhlans Regiment		4	
4th Uhlans Regiment		4	
Artillery, train and sappers		–	8 guns
Total		–	c. 3,800
Magdeburg Division (or 1st Magdeburg Division)	GD Lanusse		
Brigade	Colonel Joly		
III/24e Léger		1	1,002
III/26e Léger		1	903
III/18e Ligne		1	942
III/19e Ligne		1	1,006
I/9th Westphalian Infantry Regiment		1	817
Detachment II/1st Provisional Croatian Regiment		–	517
Brigade	GB Baville		
III/56e Ligne		1	961
III/72e Ligne		1	922
Ducal Saxon Regiment (I, II)		2	1,234
Cavalry (13th Hussars and two march squadrons)		5	591
Artillery and train		–	335
Total		–	9,230 with 15 guns

Sources: État de Situation de la 1er Division de Magdebourg, 6 September 1813, SHD, 2C155; Le Marois to Napoleon, 5 September 1813, AN/AF/IV/1662B Plaquette 8; and Lystrac, XP3.

Quistorp (*Nordarmee*, vol. I, p. 169, vol. III, pp. 72–3) correctly identifies the cavalry as three squadrons (I, III, IV) of the 13th Hussars plus a composite March Regiment of two squadrons. However, he is mistaken on two counts: (1) he inaccurately includes two battalions (III, VI) of the 134e Ligne and (2) erroneously places Col. Paul Noël Jules Senegon-Lasgonnière in command of the first brigade. Three battalions of the 134e were present at Magdeburg, but they did not participate in the Hagelberg expedition. Senegon-Lasgonnière was commanding the 155e Ligne in 5th Corps and thus was not in Magdeburg, nor was it GB Georges Hippolyte Le Sénécal who served briefly in Magdeburg during the autumn. Instead, Col. Étienne Joly of the Provisional Croatian Regiment commanded the brigade as shown.

no specific details on the 9th Infantry's role in the engagement, but Girard reported that 'the German battalions scattered at the first cannon shot,' their flight spreading confusion among the other troops. His account may have been slanted to divert blame from his French foot soldiers (although he scathingly described his French cavalry countrymen as 'more harmful than useful'), but it is clear that many men from the Westphalian and Thuringian battalions fled during the action. 'The Westphalians had almost no one left as they had lost 190 men as deserters or left in the rear since the 22nd,' he wrote in his after-action report. He praised the Westphalian battalion commander as a 'brave man and devoted' but concluded that 'The Germans not only displayed cowardice, but also a very bad spirit, despite their officers.' The 9th Infantry's battalion had departed with 817 officers and men, but it returned to Magdeburg after this dubious debut with only 121, having lost 242 killed or wounded, 203 taken prisoner and 251 simply missing. Some of the missing seem to have made their way back to Magdeburg because the regiment counted 399 fit for duty after a short time, but this was still a devastating defeat.[142]

Steadily dwindling, the two parts of the 9th Infantry would see out the remainder of their brief existence in and around the fortress. Command arrangements in these weeks shifted repeatedly as forces were allotted depending on missions and circumstances. Langenschwarz seems to have held a command position while also being responsible for administrative matters associated with the other Rheinbund units assigned to the fortress (the two Ducal Saxon battalions and the other Thuringian troops).[143] All the Rheinbund troops were occupied with constant drill and defensive fortress duties, especially construction and repair labour, but they do not seem to have had any role in the sorties conducted by the garrison during the autumn. As the weeks wore on, however, rates of desertion among these contingents soared. 'The frequent rumours of victories by the German [Coalition] armies, often true, often untrue, and sometimes even intentionally propagated, seduced many soldiers of my brigade, even officers, to desertion,' lamented Langenschwarz, 'and when the certain news of the victories of the German armies on 17, 18, 19 October at Leipzig finally arrived, desertion increased to such a degree that the German troops in Magdeburg could no longer be relied on.' Having observed the inexperienced Rheinbund troops – especially the calamity at Hagelberg – Le Marois may have come to doubt their loyalty and tactical competence, but the tipping point for him seems to have been the desertion of 500 men from a work party outside the fortress on 11 November. He thus decided 'to dissolve the entire German brigade' and ordered all the Rheinbund troops to assemble on the glacis on the afternoon of 12 November.[144]

The men were instructed to appear in their overcoats and present themselves without weapons or other equipment. Addressing the formation, Le Marois announced his decision and offered the assembled soldiers the choice of either departing for their respective homelands at once or staying on in Magdeburg and taking service in the French army. To no one's surprise, the brigade unanimously decided to head for home and the men marched off without further ceremony, leaving arms and all personal effects behind. The officers were given two days (three days for the Westphalians) to consider but they all chose to leave as well; unlike the enlisted men, they were permitted to take their personal belongings and were granted a half-month's pay.[145] By 16 November, therefore, the only Westphalian soldiers left at Magdeburg were those too ill or injured to move. As a result, although the French continued to pretend that the city was still part of the Kingdom of Westphalia, none of the kingdom's troops were there to defend it.

The Chevaulegers-Garde: Where my Honour is Pledged

The Westphalian Chevaulegers-Garde Regiment's engagements during the autumn fighting have been covered in Chapters 3 and 5 in the discussion of the 29th Light Cavalry Brigade under Generals Beaumont and Wolff. The qualities of the regiment, however, are difficult to assess, especially as young Lieutenant Lehsten's memoirs are almost the only source for details of the regiment's actions and attitudes.

Like the Bavarians and Hessians, the regiment came under attack north of Baruth on the night of 16/17 August when hostilities recommenced. Posted near Mückendorf, however, the Westphalians were prepared, placing outposts and keeping half the regiment in the saddle at all times. As a result, they repulsed their attackers and do not seem to have suffered as much as their comrades in the other two regiments. The Westphalians were not engaged at Großbeeren, but they had near daily skirmishes with Cossacks and Prussian hussars during Oudinot's abortive offensive and gained plaudits from Bertrand: 'General Beaumont with the Bavarian Chevaulegers Regiment and the Westphalians has consistently held the enemy one *lieue* [approximately 4 kilometres] from our infantry, often charging the cavalry that he had in front of him,' even when the enemy was more numerous.[146] The regiment held firm at Zahna on 5 September under such persistent artillery fire that Lehsten recalled 'the balls running about in the grass like rabbits' and attacked two Prussian batteries causing them to displace.[147]

Its performance at Dennewitz on 6 September, on the other hand, is lost in the obscurity of dust and confusion that characterised that battle. It seems to have delivered several charges while the French commanders attempted to stave off the Prussian assault, but it may have overrun some of the friendly infantry in its retreats. Like the rest of the army, it shattered into multiple pieces during the rout and individual elements struggled back to Torgau over the next few days to reassemble west of the Elbe. Stragglers gradually returned,

Autumn: A Mixed Record on the Road to Leipzig 255

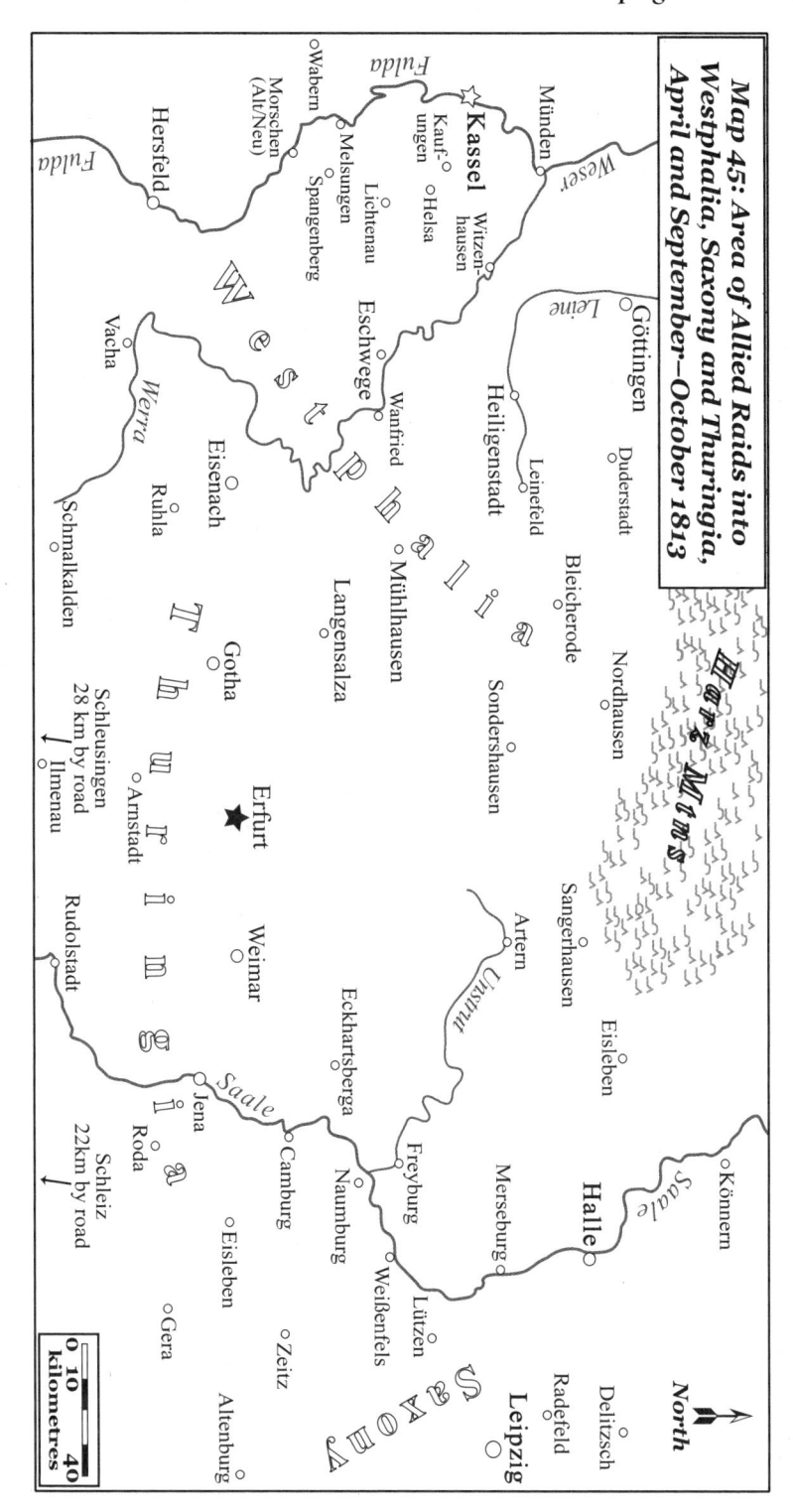

Map 45: Area of Allied Raids into Westphalia, Saxony and Thuringia, April and September–October 1813

and the Chevaulegers-Garde were once again fit for combat after several days of welcome rest.[148] Indeed, Oudinot wrote to Jérôme on 14 September to commend the regiment and GB Wolff:

> Sire, the Chevaulegers of Your Majesty's Guard have thus far fully justified my confidence in their bravery, their conduct has not ceased to be laudable for an instant, a small number of soldiers have left their colours, but having had no imitators for the entire campaign, I like to think that they have committed their crimes without complicity.
>
> I cannot praise General Wolff enough according to the reports of his attachment to the person of Your Majesty and his exactitude in fulfilling his duties, his high intelligence and his military qualities leave nothing to be desired.[149]

Other contemporaries also held Wolff in high regard. For Westphalian Colonel Friedrich Wilhelm von Mauvillon, Wolff was 'a very brave and capable cavalry officer' who 'always led his regiment exceptionally well' as commander of the Chevaulegers-Garde. From the junior perspective, Lehsten thought him sometimes too cautious in action when no senior officers were present but respected his 'great bravery'. 'I saw him halt calmly under fire,' he wrote, 'No hint of fear could be read in his features.'[150]

The regiment's next action came at Wartenburg on 3 October, but whether Wolff, or Beaumont or the regimental commander was responsible for the clumsy tactics deployed that day is impossible to ascertain. Perhaps it was simply bad luck to be caught unprepared when the Prussian hussars attacked the Westphalian and Hessian horsemen outside Globig that afternoon. Whatever the cause, the small brigade (531 officers and men) was badly knocked about in the course of the action.[151] Lieutenant Karl Philipp von Ochs, the general's son, complained in his diary that, 'Our men will not hold firm, they do not want to fight against the Prussians and prefer to be taken prisoner than to risk fighting, and then most change sides.'[152] Whatever the explanation, the regiment, forced back on the Hessians and jammed into the village, quickly dissolved into a crowd of fugitives fleeing the jubilant Prussians. Lehsten, riding back from delivering a message to Fontanelli, was horrified to see 'the cavalry brigade overthrown'. 'Intermingled with the black hussars, the mass rushes towards me', he remembered, 'There rode General Wolff and his escort,' but on the far side of a stream that Lehsten could not cross. He soon found himself a prisoner of the Prussian hussars, a sergeant smacking him across the back with his sabre and shouting 'You damned Germans, we want to show you how we deal with you!' Fortunately, the wrathful sergeant departed, and Lehsten was able to escape when the two troopers escorting him fell to quarrelling over his watch and other valuables. Collecting a small knot of men from his regiment and other elements of 4th Corps, Lehsten rode for Düben, joined the remnants of Franquemont's Württemberg division, and was delighted to find the much-reduced Chevaulegers-Garde Regiment when he arrived in Leipzig.[153]

Lehsten's sense of honour and duty led him to return to his post on this and other occasions, but that was not the case with all members of the regiment. Though few officers left the ranks, Lehsten was present when a captain allowed himself to be 'captured' by a Prussian outpost just before Dennewitz. This was a practice favoured by those who wished to change sides without the odium of obviously deserting. Comprehensive data is lacking, but if Lehsten's observations are correct, desertion in the regiment seems to have been in the 5–6 per cent range during the spring. He showed sympathy for those who fled and would have let four troopers slip away when they tried to desert during the armistice; he then defended the culprits during their court martial after they were captured by a fellow officer with a different conception of their crime. In his recollection, however, the entire regiment, including GB Wolff, felt grim and depressed when the men were convicted and executed. Afflicted by compassion for 'the poor devil', Lehsten also provided an opportunity for a wounded Prussian artilleryman to escape after being captured at Zahna.

At the same time, the young lieutenant is another example of the conflicting emotions among Rheinbund officers. His pride was touched when Wolff worried he would not return if permitted to visit his family in Silesia during the armistice, but Lehsten reassured the general: 'I have pledged the oath of allegiance to the King of Westphalia,' he told Wolff, 'and I will keep it'. 'It was painful for us all' when the 'trumpet of war called me back to my duty from the arms of my kin,' he would write, but his father, a former Hesse-Kassel and Westphalian general, 'could not hold me back where my honour was pledged'. He described Dennewitz as 'the so tragically lost battle' and was bitter at the confusion and paralysis that seemed to grip the senior commanders that day. He and Wolff and their fellow officers believed they had done their best at Dennewitz and were outraged when an inebriated Polish general (likely Krukowiecki) disparaged the regiment several days later at Torgau, claiming that all would have been lost had the Poles not covered the retreat. Several of the officers grabbed the Pole and made as if to throw him into the Elbe when Wolff called 'To horse!' and challenged their antagonist to a duel. Fortunately for all concerned, the Polish general eventually apologised and the regiment's officers, honour assuaged, returned to the business of preparing their men for the coming struggles.[154]

Even in fragile Westphalia's case, therefore, where many soldiers were former Prussian, Hesse-Kassel, Braunschweig or Hanoverian subjects, the code of personal and professional honour kept most officers at their posts through the trials of 1813. What was different in Jérôme's kingdom was that the army was more brittle, more likely to unravel as officers and men felt the pull of previous loyalties, especially when the Allies gained ascendancy and the kingdom itself seemed to be sliding towards dissolution.

September: The Porous Kingdom

Having brought the Westphalian field forces and fortress garrisons to the eve of Leipzig, the narrative now steps back several weeks to recount the Allied strikes against Braunschweig and Kassel in late September. Other Allied detachments were also active, 'perforating' Jérôme's realm in the words of one recent scholar.[155] Thielmann, for example, occupied Merseburg and Halle in mid-September and Wallmoden's corps threatened Westphalia from the north. The raids against the kingdom's two largest cities, however, though small and brief, highlighted Westphalia's fragility and had consequences beyond their scale.

Westphalia was vulnerable to such raiding detachments. The sprawling nature of this war, the paucity of reliable French cavalry, the Allied superiority in the mounted arm and Napoleon's logical focus on the main Allied armies meant that it was nearly impossible to protect every town and village in the eastern districts of Jérôme's kingdom. Westphalia was not entirely denuded of troops, but shielding Kassel was given priority with only a very small force designated to garrison Braunschweig, the kingdom's largest city (c. 31,700). Along with the capital's garrison of 4,300, GB Bastineller was thus posted around Heiligenstadt with a brigade consisting of the two cuirassier regiments, the 3rd Light Battalion and two guns (foot artillery) for a total of roughly 2,270 men. Similarly, Oberst Florentin Erbprinz zu Salm-Salm had been sent towards Hanover earlier in the month with some 380 infantry and cavalry to deter forays by Wallmoden's corps. The Chevaulegers-Garde in this detachment had gained a small success against a minor band of Cossacks and newly raised volunteer German units in Celle on 20 September, evicting the 80 or so enemy from the town and capturing several in the process.[156] Called back to the Harz Mountain region and placed under the command of GB Friedrich von Zandt, this detachment included 150 chevaulegers, 150 Jérôme Hussars and 80 infantrymen of the Jäger-Carabiniers. Zandt was soon ordered to Göttingen to guard the approaches to Kassel. The I/7th Infantry was initially posted at Münden in support, but Zandt called it to Göttingen as well (albeit without informing Major Meibom, the regimental commander).[157]

Chart 45: Westphalian Home Defence Forces, September 1813

		Bns/sqdns	27 September approx. strength	30 September approx. strength
Göttingen	*GB von Zandt*			
Chevaulegers-Garde		½ squadron	150	(see below*)
Jérôme Hussars		½ squadron	150	(see below*)
Jäger-Carabiniers		1 company	80	(see below*)
I/7th Infantry Regiment		1	816	(see below*)
Heiligenstadt	*GB von Bastineller*			
3rd Light Battalion		1	1,000	dissolved
1st Cuirassiers		4	600	dissolved
2nd Cuirassiers		4	600	dissolved
2 guns		–	70	captured
Kassel and vicinity	*GD Allix*			
Garde-du-Corps		2 companies	286	40?/Wetzlar
Jérôme Hussars		4	450	250*
Depot, Chevaulegers-Garde		–	140	100*
Grenadier Guards Battalion		1	1,000	110/Wetzlar
Jäger-Garde Battalion		1	840	100
Jäger-Carabinier Battalion (minus 1 company)		1	160	100*
Depot, Füsiliers-Garde		–	160	40
Depot, 2nd Infantry		–	150	40
Depot, 5th Infantry		–	150	40
Depot, 8th Infantry		–	150	40
Cadre, II/7th Infantry		–	150	100*
Depot, Light Infantry (all battalions)		–	300	40
Guard foot battery		–	209	?
Artillery Regimental Depot and artisans		–	127	?
Gendarmes		–	30	?
Veteran Company		1 company	?	?
Departmental Company		1 company	?	?

34 guns including 6 in the Guard battery and 6 at the training range

Braunschweig	*GB von Klösterlein*			
Jäger-Carabiniers		1 company	70	dissolved
Depot, 1st Infantry		–	150	dissolved
Depot, 3rd Infantry		–	150	dissolved
Depot, 4th Infantry		–	150	dissolved
Depot, 9th Infantry		–	150	dissolved
Gendarmes		–	16 (mounted)	?
Veteran Company		1 company	?	?
Departmental Company		1 company	40	?
Waldeck replacement detachment		–	250–300? (unarmed)	dissolved

Note: only about 300–400 of the Jérôme Hussars were mounted. Unit strengths marked by asterisks (*) are the totals remaining for these units after the fall of Kassel; the figures combine Zandt's troops and those that had been in Kassel.

Source: Specht, *Westphalen und seine Armee*, pp. 98–100, 137–8, 207–8.

Breakdown in Braunschweig

The raid on Braunschweig was conducted by Prussian Oberstleutant von der Marwitz, who commanded a small Landwehr brigade of one infantry and one cavalry regiment with two guns under Bernadotte's Army of the North. Leaving behind his infantry and cannons, Marwitz crossed the Elbe north of Magdeburg on 18 September with just his 3rd Kurmark Landwehr Cavalry, approximately 400 officers and men. His broad instructions were 'to remove the Westphalian authorities, cut the communications between Hamburg, where Marshal Davout stands, and the fortress of Magdeburg where possible, and impose contributions of all kinds'.[158] Marwitz at first spent several days collecting tribute, seizing Westphalian officials and causing general alarm in the area northwest of Magdeburg, but he was not entirely satisfied with the attitude of the local population:

> Here, beyond the Elbe, the people love us immensely; they are, however, without enthusiasm for the great cause. Should it [the cause] come to pass, they would enjoy it, but they will do nothing to further it. They are intimidated and fearful of their government and the gendarmes. Absolutely nothing is to be expected from them unless we occupy the country militarily and can then command it. They are therefore like children. The people of Braunschweig are still better than those of Magdeburg: the first view themselves as 'subjugated', the second believe, however, that they are 'separated' from our king [Friedrich Wilhelm III] and therefore proper Westphalian citizens.[159]

Nonetheless, he decided that he had an opportunity to surprise and overrun Braunschweig. This adventurous move succeeded beyond all reasonable expectation.

Braunschweig was the headquarters of the 2nd Westphalian Military Division under GB Karl Friedrich Adolph von Klösterlein. The troops available to defend the city, however, were few: four regimental depots totalling perhaps 600 men, a lone company of Jäger-Carabiniers, a veteran company, a departmental company and 16 mounted gendarmes (the only truly reliable element). Klösterlein, moreover, though only 57, was considered 'an aged and anxious man', hardly the officer to stand firm against a daring raider like Marwitz or to inspire reluctant conscripts who were likely 'to run off at the first shot'.[160] Two companies of 250–300 green Waldeck recruits were also in the city, but these were as yet unarmed and could barely be considered soldiers.[161] Additionally, Braunschweig in 1813 was a large and open city with no defensible walls. The extent of the city and the lack of protection, the dubious qualities of the troops and his own nervous nature thus led Klösterlein to accept advice from subordinates to withdraw to the town of Wolfenbüttel when he learned of Marwitz's approach. He hoped that Wolfenbüttel's smaller size and walls would offer better prospects for a successful defence with raw and shaky soldiers. By 25 September, he had packed off all the war material to towns further west and removed almost all his troops from Braunschweig, only leaving behind the Jäger-Carabiniers company as a rear guard and some men to stand watch at the city's entrances.

When Marwitz arrived outside Braunschweig around 9:00 a.m. on 25 September, therefore, the city was essentially undefended. The Prussian Landwehr cavalrymen quickly swarmed in, dispersing most of the Westphalians without a fight and overwhelming the Jäger-Carabiniers company after brief resistance. Learning that Klösterlein and the garrison had shifted to Wolfenbüttel, Marwitz detached a lieutenant and 50 troopers in pursuit. Why he did not send more and go himself is a mystery, but the small band sufficed as Klösterlein, giving in to his fears, decided to abandon Wolfenbüttel and retire further south. The Prussian horsemen thus caught the Westphalian column on the march just 2 kilometres outside Wolfenbüttel. Klösterlein's officers, hastening to the tail of the column, tried to organise a defence, but the men threw down their muskets and scattered to the four winds. Klösterlein and most of his officers escaped thanks to the speed of their horses, but the Prussians captured several hundred (estimates range from 376 to more than 600) Westphalian and Waldeck troops, armed and unarmed, during the day. Most of these men were released, but some joined Marwitz and eventually formed a volunteer Jäger squadron for the 3rd Kurmark Landwehr cavalry. Klösterlein's little detachment had thus ceased to exist.

'The joy of the Braunschweigers at our entry was tremendous', reported Marwitz, but he knew his lone regiment could not remain. He used 26 September as a rest day for his weary troopers, collecting papers, cash, horses and as many prisoners as he could before departing on the 27th, much to the disappointment of the city's residents.[162] At the cost of only two horses killed, Marwitz had achieved an astonishing success with significant psychological impact, causing such alarm in Kassel that Jérôme sent to Marshal François Étienne Christophe Kellermann in Mainz requesting the diversion of the 54th March Column, a replacement detachment that was on its way to the Grande Armée under GB Antoine Rigau. He also wrote to Berthier asking for instructions on where he was to go if he had to evacuate his capital.[163] The king's question was unconsciously prescient as the loss of Braunschweig was only the prelude to an even more devastating raid that would strike Kassel itself just two days later.

28 September: Crisis in Kassel[164]

The late September raid on Kassel brings Chernishev, Westphalia's veritable nemesis, back into this narrative. Attached to the Army of the North, Chernishev crossed the Elbe north of Dessau on the night of 14/15 September with a force of approximately 2,500 cavalry (Cossacks, dragoons and hussars) and a battery of four guns. Operating between Dessau, Köthen and Bernburg while pushing patrols as far as Halle, he conceived the idea of descending on Kassel after learning of a captured letter from Reinhard in which the French ambassador described the Westphalian capital's vulnerability and Jérôme's fears of a surprise attack. Long convinced that northern Germany was ripe for rebellion, Chernishev believed he had an opportunity to strike a telling blow by sowing confusion in the French rear areas, fomenting insurrection and undermining the Westphalian state. Although his objective was more than 230 kilometres away and behind enemy lines, he quickly gained Bernadotte's approval and struck off on his audacious enterprise on 24 September.[165]

Chernishev was relying on secrecy and speed to achieve surprise and thus led his men on a rapid and punishing march over rough mountain paths and then through Mühlhausen to avoid Bastineller's brigade around Heiligenstadt. Arriving near Kaufungen east of Kassel around 5:30 on the fog-enshrouded morning of 28 September, however, he soon discovered that the authorities in Kassel had been warned of his approach. Indeed, Jérôme had received general intelligence several days earlier that Allied raiders had crossed the Elbe near Magdeburg and posed a threat to the kingdom's interior.[166] Strangely, Chernishev himself sent the king a letter promising that Jérôme could retain his throne if he abandoned his brother's cause and sided with the Allies. This letter was almost certainly not authorised by the Allied leadership, simply an impudent ploy on Chernishev's part to instil uncertainty in his intended target. Jérôme, of course, promptly rejected any notion of defection, but the letter, coming in the wake of the alarming raid on Braunschweig, likely accentuated his accumulated apprehensions.[167] In part thanks to Chernishev's ruses, in part thanks to his own predisposition to exaggeration, for example, Jérôme had already fallen into the assumption that the Russian detachment numbered 4,000 or even 8–10,000 cavalry supported by artillery. Some of the reports emanating from Kassel credited Chernishev with as many as 15,000 men, including infantry, and all asserted that he was only the advance guard for an even larger enemy force. These rumours also swirled in the public sphere, generating uneasiness and uncertainty.

Curiously, despite these general warnings of an impending threat to the capital, the king and his officers failed to take even rudimentary steps to prepare the city for defence. This was especially puzzling as the senior French general,

September: The Porous Kingdom

> **Chart 46: Select Allied Raiding Detachments, mid-September 1813**
>
> | | Bns/sqdns | Approx. strength |
> |---|---|---|
> | **Attacking Braunschweig** — *Oberstleutnant von der Marwitz* | | |
> | 3rd Kurmark Landwehr Cavalry | 4 | c. 400 |
> | **Attacking Kassel** — *Major General Chernishev* | | |
> | Riga Dragoons | 2 | 176 |
> | Finland Dragoons | 2 | 169 |
> | Izum Hussars | 2 | 270 |
> | Sysoev III Cossack Regiment | – | 460 |
> | Grekov XVIII Cossack Regiment | – | 349 |
> | Vlasov III Cossack Regiment | – | 332 |
> | Ilovaysky XI Cossack Regiment | – | 402 |
> | Zhirov Cossack Regiment | – | 307 |
> | 1st Horse Battery | 4 guns | ? |
> | Total | | 2,465 + artillery/train |
> | **Arriving in Kassel on 3 October** — *Rittmeister von Rohr* | | |
> | Volunteer Jäger Sqdn., Prussian Neumark Dragoons | 1 | c. 150 |
>
> Source: Quistorp, *Nordarmee*, vol. II, pp. 71–4.

GD Allix de Vaux, was a hard-nosed, experienced and intelligent artilleryman who had been in Westphalian service since 1808. If local defensive measures were neglected, however, Jérôme did not delay in recalling Bastineller and Zandt from their covering positions. He was also hoping that Rigau's 54th March Column, already requested from Kellermann, would soon appear. Furthermore, the chief of the High Police, GD Jean François Marie Bongars, sent a message to Erfurt requesting help from the French commandant, GD Alexander Dalton.[168] The responses to these orders and requests would be key factors in determining Jérôme's actions on the 28th.

This general intelligence of a threat to the capital was confirmed by specific information that arrived during the night of 27/28 September from Bastineller and local Westphalian officials. As a result, Kassel's defenders were alerted in the early hours of the morning and Jérôme sent a platoon of his French Hussars (25–30 men) to reconnoitre, supported by the 2nd and 6th Companies of the Jäger-Garde. They were soon followed by the other four companies of the Jäger-Garde, the light infantry depot troops and two guns, all under the command of GD Danloup-Verdun. Meanwhile, Chernishev, as part of his attack plan, sent Benckendorff south to ford the Fulda near the Neue Mühle

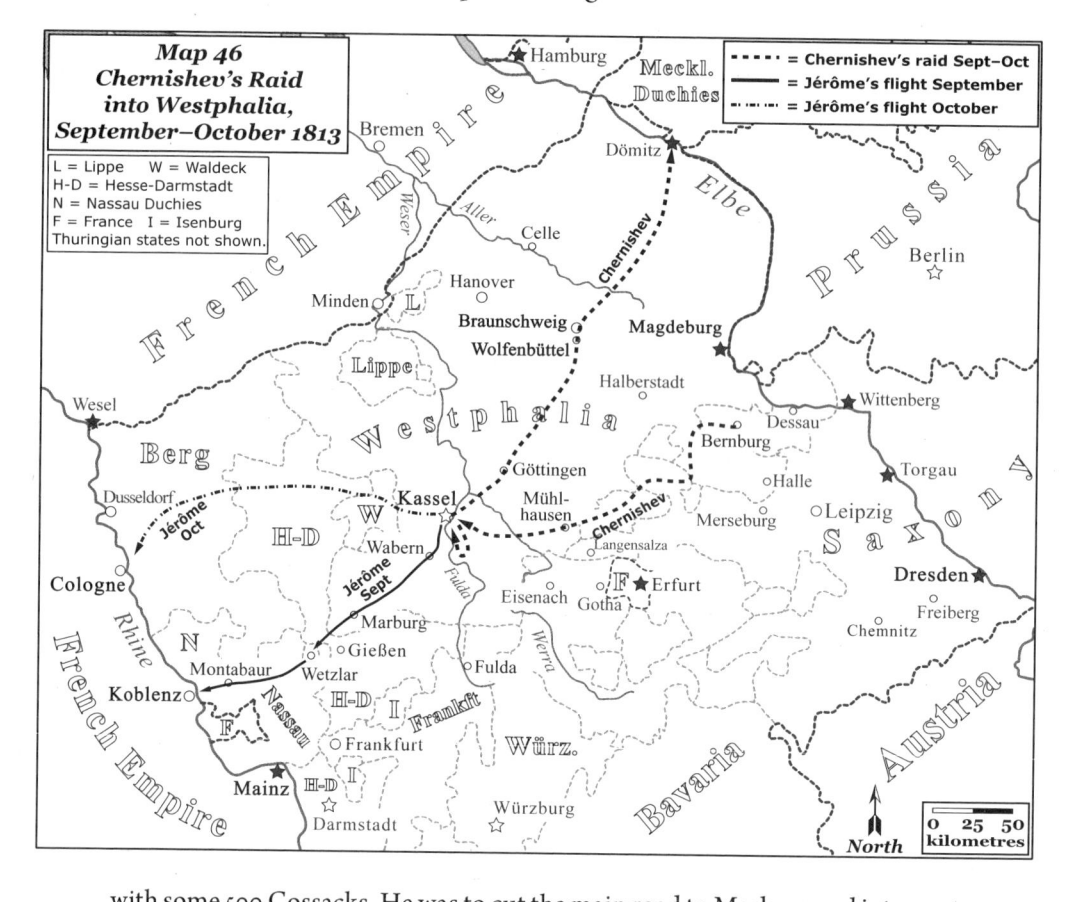

Map 46
Chernishev's Raid into Westphalia, September–October 1813

L = Lippe   W = Waldeck
H-D = Hesse-Darmstadt
N = Nassau Duchies
F = France   I = Isenburg
Thuringian states not shown.

- - - - = Chernishev's raid Sept–Oct
———— = Jérôme's flight September
— · — · — = Jérôme's flight October

with some 500 Cossacks. He was to cut the main road to Marburg and intercept Jérôme should he attempt to escape. Another 50 Cossacks were to splash over the river at Wolfsanger north of the city, apparently as a diversion. Leaving a small detachment at Kaufungen to watch for Bastineller, Chernishev advanced directly towards the Unterneustadt suburb with his main body, something less than 2,000 mounted men with his four guns.

There was widespread anxiety in Westphalia at this point in late September, many of its citizens convinced that the kingdom 'was facing a great and decisive catastrophe'.[169] Kassel, in particular, was already in a state of alarm after the sudden fall of Braunschweig and tensions were high on the morning of the 28th as the sounds of combat echoed through the fog from the east. 'Thus, many Kassel residents may have been awakened from their sleep by cannon shots!' remembered young artillery cadet Eduard August Oppermann.[170] Confusion and wild rumours were rife. Nevertheless, the assembled garrison greeted Jérôme with an appropriate *'Vive le roi!'* when he rode into the central plaza and the citizens, while worried, were relatively calm.[171] Indecision reigned, however, and the king, his court, his ministers and many of his generals seemed unnerved. The soldiers, roused from their beds with no time to eat, were hungry as well as anxious. Many 'were not animated by courage for their king' and some in the square apparently passed their live ammunition to teenage boys standing around trying to inhale all the excitement.[172] 'The panic', wrote Reinhard's wife, 'was general'.[173] Trepidation and vacillation notwithstanding, the Westphalians deployed athwart the main road leading into the Unterneustadt suburb: the 6th Jäger-Garde Company in a skirmish line southeast of Bettenhausen backed by the 2nd Company just outside the village; the rest of the battalion, the light infantry and the two guns behind the tree-lined Wahlebach near Siechenhof closer to the suburb. The officers rode and strolled among their men, offering encouragement and practical advice to relieve the mounting tension. Capitaine Otto von Hugo of the 6th Company, for one, called over a trembling new recruit and patiently walked him through the basic manual of arms to show that the procedures in battle were the same as on the drill field, an example that helped calm the entire company.[174]

As Danloup-Verdun was deploying his men, the patrol of Jérôme Hussars was probing east through the crepuscular murk. The troopers collided with Chernishev's advance guard near Kupferhammer around 7:00 o'clock but fell back rapidly and in some confusion when 200 Cossacks loomed up out of the fog. Although any hope of surprising the garrison had thus vanished, Chernishev's determination did not flag. With surprise lost, he now had to trust in his own boldness and the energy of his weary detachment, hoping that the shaky loyalty of Westphalia's soldiery and the latent anger of its citizens would undermine the defence of the city. In this he was assisted by the dense fog. It was 'such a fog as I had never seen before', he wrote, 'it was impossible to see anything two steps ahead of me,' but it obscured his numerical weakness and allowed rumour to exaggerate his strength well beyond reality.[175] The fog also hid his opponents, of course, but his veteran Cossacks and regulars were better equipped to cope with the unfolding uncertainty than the partly trained Westphalian conscripts. As the Westphalian hussar patrol retreated from its encounter at Kupferhammer and the fighting shifted west to Bettenhausen, therefore, Chernishev's detachment surged forward, driving back Hugo's skirmishers and bringing up two guns to blast the 2nd Company formed up near the road. In their first combat, the Jägers of the 2nd Company threw themselves to the ground as the canister flew and, despite the 'mighty curses and threats' of their officers, they scattered when the Russians charged. Although the 6th Company held together, many of the 2nd were captured and the remainder fled back through Bettenhausen towards the Wahlebach in disorder. The Cossacks also captured several hundred sick and wounded French in a hospital between Bettenhausen and Siechenhof as well as six untended guns at a practice firing range south of Bettenhausen that the Westphalians had neglected to withdraw.[176]

The Russians now pressed towards the Bettelbrücke or Beggar's Bridge over the Wahlebach, but their efforts to continue their advance were repulsed and an extended pause ensued. The Westphalians, however, failed to take advantage of the opportunity thus afforded to strengthen their defences either along the little Wahlebach, at Siechenhof or in the suburb. This lackadaisical attitude likely had its origins in complacency. If some officers and many in Jérôme's court were fretful, others like Danloup-Verdun dismissed the threat. 'Oh, it is nothing, it will soon pass,' he told his aide-de-camp, 'it is just an errant patrol that has arrived with the fog and will vanish with it.'[177]

Danloup-Verdun was soon disabused of his illusions when a bullet tore one of the buttons from his sleeve as the Russians renewed their attack around 9:30 a.m. Exclaiming 'Those fellows shoot damn well!' he turned about and rode back into the city leaving Major von Boedicker of the Jäger-Garde in command. The Westphalians resisted stoutly for a short time, but the Russian guns dismounted one of the Westphalian pieces, the crew for the other fled and Chernishev's men surged over the little stream on both sides of the road. The lieutenant in command of the two guns tried to save one by dragging it away with the help of some NCOs, but they were overtaken by Cossacks and the piece was lost. At least one Jäger-Garde officer allowed his detachment of twenty to be captured or simply defected, but others did their best to hold off the Russians. They were overwhelmed, however, and fled back to the Leipzig Gate at the Unterneustadt suburb, leaving many prisoners and both guns in the hands of the Russians.

The walled suburb should have offered a perfect strongpoint for the Westphalians. The retreating troops did close and barricade the lone gate, but all was in haste and the lack of preparation became painfully evident. As officer-historian Specht would later write: 'Given how well the 6th Company fought against the Russians, the other companies would have fought just as well under the eyes of their officers, especially if they could have done so from behind walls and hedges where the cavalry could not get at them.'[178] It was not to be. Having learned from Benckendorff that a substantial part of the garrison, led by Jérôme himself, had moved south of the city, Chernishev correctly concluded that the suburb's defenders were likely few and nervous. He had no infantry, but, not wanting to grant the Westphalians time to recover their composure, he ordered an attack. This was astonishingly successful, in part because of Major von Boedicker, the Jäger-Garde commander. Boedicker, who had been so proud of the speed with which his battalion had formed back in March and of the skill it had displayed on the drill field, now yielded to anger and frustration. He would

September: The Porous Kingdom

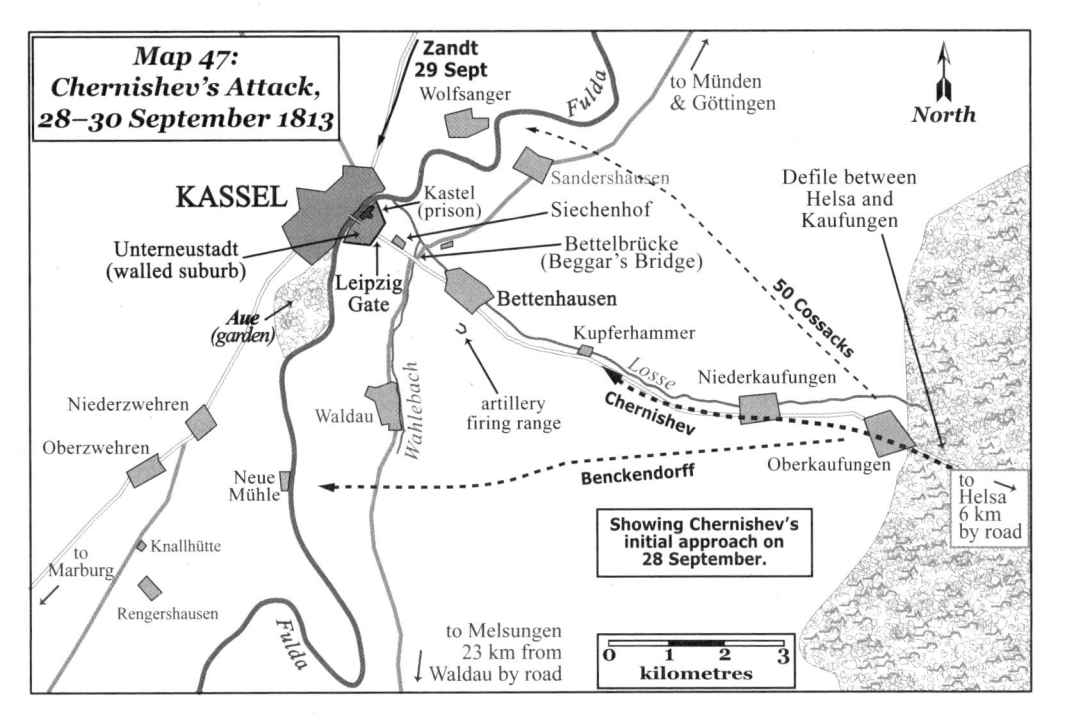

Map 47: Chernishev's Attack, 28–30 September 1813

Showing Chernishev's initial approach on 28 September.

later write that he had repeatedly requested reinforcements and guidance during the fight in the fog but had received no reply from his superiors. Already exasperated at the lack of support, he became furiously indignant on hearing of Jérôme's departure. He could not comprehend how

> The king dragged along all the generals, staff officers and the numerous infantry and cavalry on his rapid flight without employing these, or at least some of them, at the Leipzig Gate where the Cossack general would certainly have come off badly as his plan was not feasible! ... Embittered by this and by the conviction that I had done my duty the entire day even though left to my own devices, I sheathed my sword and declared to the nearby officers that I would never again fight for the French ... We took ourselves back to the city and the chasseurs [Jäger-Garde] scattered.

With the defenders in confused flight, the gate was opened with the help of local citizens after a few shots from Chernishev's guns, and the Russians stormed in, quickly capturing the state prison (the Kastel), freeing the inmates and charging towards the bridge over the Fulda that led into the city proper. Here the attackers were blocked by a barricade of wagons and sharp fire from dismounted Jérôme Hussars and Westphalian infantry behind this ad hoc fortification and in the neighbouring structures. Though the Russians were at least temporarily stopped, the morning thus far had cost Westphalia four companies of the Jäger-Garde, half of the light infantry depot and two guns. The struggle for Kassel was by no means over, but this was hardly an auspicious beginning.

While Chernishev's main body was trying to break into the city's centre, Benckendorff had forded the Fulda as instructed and encountered the king with much of Kassel's garrison. Jérôme had vacillated between staying or leaving that morning. With little faith in his army and fearful of being captured if the Russians took the city, he eventually succumbed to the councils of the anxious. He appointed Allix to hold the city, telling the French general that he needed to secure the road south where he expected the French reinforcements to arrive. He did not offer an explanation of why this task could not have been assigned to a subordinate when his royal presence in the city was of paramount importance. He then rode out on the main road towards Marburg with his Guard Hussars (about 400, 'all who could hold themselves in the saddle and strike a blow with a sabre' he told Napoleon), the Garde-du-Corps, the Garde-Grenadiers and the Guard foot battery with eight guns.[179] Jérôme planned to halt on a hill south of Niederzwehren to await the arrival of Bastineller or Rigau or both. Probing ahead through the dense fog, the Jérôme Hussars and Garde-du-Corps bumped into Benckendorff's Cossacks west of the river. Each side claimed success in the ensuing clash, but with the Westphalian Garde-Grenadiers advancing on the Neue Mühle Benckendorff became concerned that he would be trapped on the western shore. He decided that he had accomplished his mission by locating the king and retired to the eastern bank. This initial skirmish thus came to an end. Unfortunately, the inexperienced Jérôme Hussars were apparently so encouraged by the Cossack withdrawal that they forded to the far side in pursuit. This proved a grave error as the Cossacks, in typical fashion, turned about, charged, and cut down or captured many of Jérôme's Frenchman as they tried to flee across the ford.[180] Each commander drew his own implications from these minor clashes. For Jérôme, the presence of the Cossacks on the road to Marburg was confirmation of his fears of being out-flanked, out-run and captured. For Chernishev, Benckendorff's withdrawal meant that the king had escaped and that his own left flank was in danger of being turned.

It was now late morning and the fog had burned off. Benckendorff and Jérôme were south of Kassel, engaged in desultory skirmishing with the Cossacks occasionally crossing over the Fulda, but Chernishev's men in the Unterneustadt were embroiled in an intense fight with the French and Westphalian defenders at the barricaded bridge. Furthermore, Chernishev had decided to increase the pressure on Jérôme's government by opening a bombardment with his artillery. The shot and shell did little physical damage, but the residents became increasingly distraught and increasingly unruly. A crowd gathered and people began harassing, even threatening the soldiers, spreading exaggerated stories of the enemy's strength and encouraging disobedience. Other civilians exploited the chaos to loot the barracks while the soldiers were absent or distracted, shouting 'Fire!' to clear the buildings.[181] Though many soldiers fought resolutely, the Westphalian officers had to exert themselves to bring some of the conscripts up to the firing line at the bridge, trying two or three times before the men were properly placed.[182]

Then, around 11:00 a.m., the firing suddenly abated. The surprising lull was occasioned by reports from Chernishev's outposts that Bastineller was approaching Kaufungen in his rear. With Jérôme on his left flank, the fortified city to his front and Bastineller behind him, he worried that his little detachment might become surrounded and destroyed if the Westphalians took concerted action. So far, in fact, his adventurous advance looked like a risky failure: Kassel had not capitulated, the king had not been captured and his command, exhausted by the strenuous march, was well beyond any possible friendly assistance. He thus decided to break off the combat and, gathering up his numerous prisoners and the eight captured guns, he retired south to Melsungen to rest his men and await developments.[183] Along the way, however, he learned that Bastineller's brigade was smaller than initially reported and in very poor condition. Buoyed by this encouraging intelligence, he sent off some 100 Cossacks the following morning (29 September) to chase down the Westphalians and was delighted when they returned to Melsungen with a number of prisoners, Bastineller's two guns and confirmation that the enemy force was in a state of dissolution. He also learned that Jérôme had fled and could thus entertain every expectation that Kassel would surrender if again put to the test.

Jérôme also left the area of his capital that afternoon, but in his case, it was a flight rather than a withdrawal. Around midday, with no news of Bastineller, Zandt or Rigau, he gave in to his fears and headed west at speed. 'Instead of the eagerly awaited order to start the march to Kassel', therefore, his escort received 'the completely unexpected' order to turn south away from the capital. Having marched 12 kilometres, however, Jérôme seems to have reconsidered his flight but the column again reversed direction after only 15 or 20 minutes because of reports that 6,000 Cossacks were threatening the escape route. Jérôme, alarmed by these wild stories and baffled by the absence of reinforcements, thus decided to keep moving.[184] This decision would cost him most of his men.

The men in the ranks were already sceptical. Not only were their king and his commanders enmeshed in anxiety, confusion and indecision, but their trudge south and west led them to fear that they were being marched to France, a destination that was not only far from home but was also widely associated with the evil fate of the Westphalians who had been sent to Spain in 1808. Then, when the weary column finally stopped late in the evening, they were infuriated at being ordered to break camp hastily while in the midst of preparing their first meal of the day. Throwing their half-cooked food on their fires, the men were angry, apprehensive, hungry and disillusioned. Morale sank lower when the annoyed Jérôme rode ahead with his cavalry elements after telling the grenadiers and artillery that they were marching too slowly. Whatever sense of mission and duty the men had had in the morning drained away. All seemed lost and they deserted in droves, an action made all the easier because many of the grenadiers had been conscripted from the region through which they were passing (formerly Hesse-Kassel). Halting in Wabern as darkness fell, most of the companies had already lost a third of their members. The situation grew worse when the column was to proceed through the night after a meal and liberal applications of brandy. Some of the troops became mutinous, refusing to move and even threatening their officers. 'We will serve the French no more!' proclaimed one sergeant as he pointed his musket at a captain who was trying to threaten or cajole a group of soldiers out of a tavern. Most of the remaining grenadiers and artillery vanished during the ensuing night march and only some 180 men were still with the column when it reached Marburg near the kingdom's western frontier at 5:00 p.m. on 29 September. 'How much better it would have been for Jérôme if he had at least left this force in Kassel!' lamented Sergeant Justus Süstermann of the Garde-Grenadiers.

> Desertion would have been common here too without a doubt, but it would have been unlikely to come to a complete dissolution. The desertions would also have ceased as soon as Kassel was held and the Russians had to withdraw, and Kassel could have held with such a strong garrison. But Jérôme did not think about that; he was too occupied with his flight.[185]

What was left of the grenadiers continued on the following day, caught up with the Garde-du-Corps, whom Jérôme had also left behind, and finally arrived in Wetzlar on 2 October, beyond Westphalia's borders and more than 120 kilometres from Kassel. The majority of the grenadier officers and NCOs were still present, but there were at most 100–110 soldiers (out of 1,000 just days before) and the Garde-du-Corps, officers included, had largely disappeared. He still had many of the Jérôme Hussars, but their inexperience made these men problematic for different reasons. 'My regiment of French hussars conducted itself with great valour all day yesterday,' Jérôme told Napoleon, 'Unfortunately, I lost many who, not being used to riding, fell while charging the enemy.' These sad remnants would be quartered in Wetzlar, the designated rallying point for the army, until 6 October but without their putative monarch. Jérôme had spent the night of 29/30 September in Wetzlar, from whence he sent his imperial brother a lengthy message citing the lack of French troops as the cause of his defeat and flight.[186] In his mind, however, even Wetzlar was insecure as a refuge and he travelled on to Montabaur in Nassau, putting another 60 kilometres between himself and possible capture by Cossacks. A few days later, he would shift his court (still swathed in royal etiquette) yet further west to Koblenz on the Rhine. The king had abandoned his kingdom.

28–29 September: The Fate of the Kingdom

What of Bastineller and Zandt? On 26 September, news of the Russian march through Mühlhausen had led Bastineller to retire from Heiligenstsadt to Witzenhausen where he arrived on the 27th to report the enemy's presence. That night he received Jérôme's order to march to Kassel and he duly set out on the 28th after some delay owing to the fog. The farther he marched, however, the more hesitant and uncomfortable he became. Reaching Helsa, he learned of Chernishev's rear guard outpost near Kaufungen and feared he might be blocked or defeated while trying to pass through the narrow mountain defile that connected the two villages. He imagined the Russians opposing him with infantry and artillery (they had none of either) and concluded that it was safer to slip away to the south and try to meet the king outside Kassel. Although his troops were calling out 'Forward! Forward!', Bastineller yielded to his fantasies and turned his brigade towards Lichtenau. This proved a disaster. With the execution of these orders, noted Specht, 'the fate of the kingdom and of these fine troops was pronounced'. Marching over bad tracks through the gathering darkness led to disorder, exhaustion, discouragement and, eventually, desertion. Small detachments did not return, and the brigade was well on its way to dissolution as it passed through Lichtenau and Spangenberg to arrive at Morschen on the Fulda near midnight of 28/29 September. The lack of men and the fatigue of the draft horses meant that the guns could go no further, so Bastineller had them thrown into the Fulda in a futile effort to keep them out of Russian hands. Compounding the ignominy, the 100 Cossacks Chernishev had sent in pursuit of Bastineller on the morning of the 29th caught up with the Westphalians near Morschen. This bold band not only induced panic in the few remaining Westphalian troops but managed to drag both guns out the river to add to the impressive Russian haul of artillery trophies. Bastineller's wretched flight continued that day, the cavalry finally attaining Friedberg with a strength of only 40 men under arms, officers included, and the infantry arriving in Wetzlar with a similar number of drained and disheartened soldiers. Over the course of two days, the brigade of more than 2,200 men in which Jérôme had invested so much hope had thus shrunk to only 100 or so fit for any kind of duty and had lost both of its guns to boot.[187]

Zandt's story was sadly similar. Another agonisingly cautious officer tormented by doubts, he indulged in irresolution for much of 28 September and only reached Münden on the Fulda late in the afternoon. Meibom of the 7th Infantry pressed him to march at once along the eastern (right) bank of the river to Kassel: the king needed support urgently, he argued, the roads were better, the terrain better, and the Russians would be nonplussed by the sudden appearance of their enemy on their flank. 'Beyond this, given the generally negative attitude, one needed to be conscious of keeping the troops well in hand, under constant supervision,' wrote Meibom later, 'That would be impossible on a night march over poor paths on the left bank of the Fulda.' The converse was also true as Specht observed: 'In particular a decisive advance would evoke a good impression on the young, inexperienced troops.' Zandt, however, saw only risks and could not make up his mind. Twice he started ferrying his men over the river only to call them back for a direct march on the city. The negative impact this dithering had on the conscripts is not hard to imagine. Moreover, Zandt permitted the men an extended rest in Münden, opening the opportunity for local civilians to ply them with rumours, lies and half-truths as well as food and drink. 'On entry into Münden one could read a secret joy on the faces of the inhabitants,' recalled Meibom, 'the soldiers were advised to leave their duties and go home ... The people of Münden cleverly used this halt to work on our men.' Having absorbed this public mood and having watched their vacillating commander waste hours and effort wavering from one course of action to another, the men were finally boated across the Fulda as darkness was falling. The outcome Meibom had warned against, of course, eventuated. With and without weapons, men vanished into the forest during the difficult night march and when Zandt's little brigade reached Kassel around 10:00 a.m. on 29 September, the I/7th Infantry numbered only 200 out of 816 soldiers and many of the cavalrymen had fled as well.[188]

The stories of Jérôme, Bastineller and Zandt are miniature case studies in military leadership under trying circumstances. Assured, attentive and resolute leadership would have likely kept these various commands together despite the inexperience of the troops, the boldness of the Russians, the context of anti-French resentments and the incentives to desert proffered by many of the local civilians. Instead, all three commanders systematically contributed to the disintegration of their forces by their obvious indecision and lack of self-confidence and by their contradictory impulses either to ignore the physical needs of their men or to countenance excessive fraternisation with the restive civilian population. Under such circumstances, it was easy for the soldiers to believe for the first time that the kingdom was truly foredoomed. Repressed feelings thus emerged and many would express their distaste through

September: The Porous Kingdom

desertion.[189] Mired in fear and doubt, none of the three commanders proved equal to coping with these challenges. Different leadership, on the other hand, might have provided a different outcome. In other words, the fall of Kassel to Chernishev's brash band in late September 1813 was not inevitable. This is not to deny that Westphalia was facing potentially irremediable problems or that all would have been well in the kingdom had Chernishev been repelled. Rather, it is to note that the situation need not have been so dire, nor the humiliation as penetrating as it became when the city indeed capitulated to the Russian general on 30 September.

Before turning to the next act in the Kassel drama a few words addressing Jérôme's other hope are necessary: rescue by French troops. In addition to castigating his own army ('If my troops had been loyal, Chernishev would not have escaped,' he told his queen), Jérôme repeatedly blamed the defeat on the absence of an adequate French force.[190] This claim constituted an indirect attack on his elder brother for supposedly refusing to send French reinforcements, but was it realistic?[191] The presence of French troops in some numbers would certainly have bolstered the garrison materially and psychologically, reassuring the king's supporters, intimidating the malcontents and affording greater flexibility in deployment when attacked. Moreover, Jérôme likely would have remained in his capital and thus one of the most important effects would have been to counter the burgeoning conviction that the kingdom was spiralling to its doom. Distance, however, militated against timely French intervention in Kassel's crisis.

Jérôme's first request to Kellermann for reinforcements seems to have arrived in the marshal's headquarters in Mainz on the night of 26/27 September some hours before the particular object of the king's attention, Rigau's 54th March Column, was scheduled to depart the city. The king's second letter reached Mainz around 3:00 p.m. on the 27th, well after Rigau's departure. Kellermann might have dispatched Rigau earlier on 27 September or he might have sent him emergency instructions that afternoon, but Kassel was 200 kilometres from Mainz, a good five to six days' march even if Rigau had 'burned up the roads' (as the idiom went). The column, therefore, could hardly be expected to arrive in Kassel before 2 October, by which time Jérôme was in Montabaur and Chernishev was well ensconced in the Westphalian capital. As Kellermann explained to Napoleon, therefore, 'I would not have had any possibility of succouring the King of Westphalia.'[192]

Another march column, the 53rd under GB Étienne Jacques Travers (3,800 men), was approaching Erfurt from Eisenach via Gotha. Bongars had written directly to Travers on the 27th 'inviting' him to march on Mühlhausen because of the reports that Russian troops had appeared there. Travers would have needed authorisation first, but his cautious superior in Erfurt, GD Dalton, was worried about what might befall a group of raw conscripts if confronted with what had been reported as superior numbers of Coalition cavalry.[193] Assuming Travers could have gained permission or had acted on his own initiative, hard marching might have brought him to Mühlhausen from Eisenach late on 28 September or, more likely, on the 29th, but Chernishev's men were long gone by then, already knocking on Kassel's gates. Travers might have headed for Kassel instead, but the capital lay 80 kilometres away from Eisenach, a march of at least two days and probably more, meaning that he would have arrived when Jérôme was already in flight to Wetzlar. Given that Chernishev had only left the Bernburg area on 24 September and marched with extraordinary speed, time and distance factors thus made rapid French reinforcement of the Kassel garrison nearly impossible.

There were other considerations as well. In the first place, Chernishev was not the only Allied raiding detachment and Kassel was not the only locale in jeopardy; the French had to protect many other towns that held depots, hospitals and magazines. Kellermann was particularly worried about the Grande Armée's principal line of communications from Mainz to Erfurt should the raiders turn south from Kassel. Second, the march columns en route to the army were tasked to escort convoys of munitions as well as deliver replacements. Rigau's 54th March Column, for instance, had to guard 21 guns, 21 caissons, a large treasury consignment and a number of other supply wagons during its march; these would have to be deposited somewhere safe before the infantry and cavalry could divert to Kassel or anywhere else. Third, the march columns were mostly composed of conscripts supplemented by returned deserters and convalescents from a variety of units; as such they had to be employed with care and could not be thrown into combat like cohesive veteran formations. Finally, Jérôme's tendency to exaggerate worked against him. Whether genuine or contrived (to attract attention and thus reinforcements), the reports from Kassel crediting Chernishev with a strength of 4,000, 6,000, 8–10,000 or even more instilled caution in French rear-area commanders. As Dalton's case illustrates, these commanders were chary of risking march columns of 3,000 or so untrained conscripts against such large enemy forces, especially given the dominance of the Allied cavalry. Such uncritical reporting of inflated numbers, of course, also roused Napoleon's ire and vitiated Jérôme's credibility. In this instance, the emperor instructed Berthier to respond to a 24 September note from the king 'that Chernishev, far from having 17,000 men, has only 3,600; that Wallmoden has only a third of what he assumes; that all the information he has received is exaggerated'.[194]

Kellermann was also wary of Jérôme's reputation for hyperbole (he had witnessed several instances of the king's anxiety and exaggeration during the 1809 war). Nonetheless, as he told Berthier, 'I cannot totally abandon the king of Westphalia, in spite of the fact that I am on guard against alarms taken too easily.' In the course of the hectic days between 27 and 30 September, he informed Rigau of the situation and ordered him to halt at Fulda, dispatched two battalions (II/51e and II/55e Ligne) to reinforce Rigau at Fulda, and sent parts of two other battalions (III/127e and IV/128e Ligne) along with two companies of chasseurs-à-cheval to Marburg 'to receive the King of Westphalia or to support him in case he is obliged by the presence of the enemy to quit his capital and retire towards me'. As the situation evolved, all four of these battalions plus some additional infantry, several hundred cavalry and a battery would be re-routed to Wetzlar to join Jérôme.[195] They would form the basis for the French force that would recapture Kassel on Jérôme's behalf several days later.

29 September–4 October: Chernishev in Kassel

Jérôme's flight and the disintegration of Bastineller's and Zandt's brigades left Kassel's garrison severely undermanned. The best estimate gives Allix only some 1,000 men fit for duty: 350 cavalry, 500 infantry and perhaps another 150 artillerymen and gendarmes. Most of these soldiers were discouraged and the most recent arrivals, the remnants of Zandt's little brigade, had been misused by the commander and decimated by desertion on the 28th. Nevertheless, Allix placed his assets as best he could, blocking the Fulda bridge and posting the Jäger-Carabiniers from Zandt's brigade at the re-barricaded Leipzig Gate into Unterneustadt as they were rated the most reliable of the available men.[196] With an inadequate garrison of dubious troops and a population inclined towards insurrection, however, the outlook for the city's defence was grim.

Chernishev, on the other hand, regarded his prospects as bright. In addition to resting his men and horses, he had used 29 September to organise an ad hoc 'infantry battalion' of 300 men from Westphalian prisoners and deserters to compensate for his lack of foot soldiers. Additionally, he had incorporated the captured guns and howitzers into his command to give himself a battery of 13 pieces for his renewed assault on the city. Morale was good and he moved in from Melsungen on the morning of the 30th with every expectation of success.

The Russians hove into view in the open ground southeast of the Unterneustadt suburb around one o'clock on the afternoon of 30 September. Chernishev sent one Cossack regiment across the Fulda to cut the main road south, but the bulk of his force advanced on the eastern bank of the river as before. As his horsemen and the new 'infantry battalion' deployed, his augmented artillery unlimbered and opened a bombardment of the city at around 3:00 p.m. Four Westphalian pieces replied from the western side of the Fulda and a lively exchange was soon in progress. The Russian fire did little physical harm and only a handful of civilians were killed or injured, but the shelling excited acute alarm among Kassel's residents. The population, previously tense but generally tranquil, exploded with emotion, fearing that their city would be destroyed but also perceiving an opportunity to rid themselves of the French. Angry mobs jammed the streets demanding immediate capitulation and hurling insults and stones at Allix. Some armed themselves with axes and farm implements, and a furious woman attempted to grab the reins of the general's horse. Impeding movement, abusing, assaulting and even disarming some of the soldiers, they created the sort of turmoil that Allix had sought to preclude and Chernishev had hoped to incite. Many soldiers, of course, exploited the confusion to slip away.

With disorder erupting in the city, the Russians attacked the Leipzig Gate. The Jäger-Carabiniers, rather than showing themselves dependable, defected to the enemy, thereby allowing the new 'infantry battalion' and a squadron of dismounted dragoons to swarm into the suburb and assault the barrier at the bridge as they had on the 28th. Allix, unwilling simply to surrender, ordered a counterattack by the remnants of Meibom's 7th Infantry and a small group of Jäger-Garde. Remarkably, this gained a momentary success. Most of the Jägers soon took off, but 'the men of the 7th Regiment stayed by me and were animated by a good spirit,' wrote Meibom. 'People and Cossacks blocked the street before me ... and sought to move me to go over to the enemy.' The citizens moved aside and the Cossacks fled when Meibom threatened to use force and his soldiers shoved their way through the crowd, stormed over the bridge and into the suburb, overthrowing the Russian dragoons and the ad hoc battalion to gain the Leipzig Gate. Their surprising success, however, was short-lived. Bombarded by two Russian cannon and threatened by a surly mob in the suburb, the Westphalians fell back to the bridge, restored the barrier and readied themselves for a renewed assault.[197]

Rather than a new attack, the bitter fighting transitioned to negotiations. The combat that afternoon, though brief, had been intense and both sides had good reasons to compromise. With weak and unreliable troops, a riotous urban populace and no prospect of outside help, Allix had no incentive to prolong the defence. The best he could hope to achieve was an honourable capitulation that would allow Kassel's French citizens and officials along with his few remaining French and Westphalian troops to escape captivity or death at the hands of the Russians or the mob. Chernishev, too, was pleased to enter into negotiations.

The defence had proven stouter than he had expected, he had no real infantry, he was far from any reinforcements, and he had no desire to subject Kassel to the devastation that was likely to follow an unremitting assault. He thus sent Lieutenant Colonel Alexander Antonovich Balmain (who would later become the Russian representative on St Helena during Napoleon's second exile) with a letter demanding immediate capitulation.

Led blindfolded through the streets, Balmain's arrival ignited an uproar among the city's previously reticent civilians, leading many burghers to fear that 'it was the beginning of a general uprising' that would threaten order, life and property. While the crowd 'shouted and raged' outside, Allix agreed to a meeting and when Balmain emerged without the blindfold, Kassel's citizens knew that a capitulation was at hand. Chernishev designated Benckendorff as his plenipotentiary and the population, thrilled at the cessation of fighting and the likely end of French rule, welcomed Benckendorff with cheers for the tsar and their old prince-elector. The garrison, alert to the turn of events, began to melt away, so many soldiers leaving their posts that 50 Cossacks were able to ride into the city from the south unhindered. Allix threatened to break off discussions when the Cossacks pranced up outside his headquarters in violation of the truce, but Benckendorff sent the offending riders away and the two generals concluded an agreement as the sun was setting.[198] The capitulation required the French and Westphalians to leave their artillery pieces behind but allowed the soldiers to depart with their personal weapons and possessions under Russian escort along with the diplomatic corps, bureaucrats, French civilians and anyone else who wished to go. Allix, the few remaining French troops, and a convoy of French civilians thus left the city at 7:00 that evening. He had offered the Westphalian officers and men the choice of staying behind or accompanying him on the road to the Rhine. To no one's surprise, very few elected to join him on the retreat.

Chernishev's victory was thus complete. At the cost of only some 70 men killed or wounded, he had captured approximately 30 guns, 2,000 prisoners (although this number included the 600 or so French invalids taken at the hospital) and large quantities of weapons, munitions and military stores.[199] The most curious acquisitions to be taken away were a half dozen tame deer that Jérôme had maintained, though sources are divided on whether these ended up in the tsar's menagerie or the Cossack cookpots. Furthermore, roughly 1,000 men volunteered for a battalion being formed by Oberst Friedrich von Dörnberg for service with Wallmoden's corps. Chernishev and the Coalition leadership had hoped more would 'want to participate in the liberation of their fatherland', but most of the enlisted soldiers simply vanished and very few officers accepted positions with the Allied armies.[200]

Chernishev entered Kassel on 1 October to a tumultuous welcome – even more rapturous because many citizens at first mistook him for their 'own' Kurprinz Wilhelm, the heir to the Hesse-Kassel crown – and issued a proclamation announcing that the Kingdom of Westphalia had ceased to exist. To the great relief of the citizenry, the Russian occupation was generally mild and the Cossacks, their savage reputation notwithstanding, were simply objects of curiosity rather than barbaric terrors. Westphalian officials were harassed, roughed up, humiliated and worse, but otherwise the only victim of Russian presence was the marble statue of Napoleon that had been installed in the central square. This suffered the loss of its nose (allegedly to Cossacks through arrows or musket balls) and one arm (to vandalising local boys) before being placed under guard. Chernishev knew he could not stay. He was too far from the main Allied armies and vulnerable to the French forces he knew to be gathering to retake the city. The Volunteer Jäger Squadron of the Prussian Neumark Dragoons from Thielmann's corps arrived on 2 October seeking refuge after being cut off in Halle, but this accidental reinforcement was hardly sufficient to alter his parlous situation. While a small rear guard remained in the city, Chernishev thus departed on 3 October, heading east for the Elbe via Göttingen and Braunschweig. The treasury, of course, was confiscated before the Russians departed, and a number of Westphalian officials were arrested and deported to be imprisoned in Allied territory. His rear guard followed the next day, leaving behind a volunteer commission of local notables to manage the city. Also left behind were thousands of fearful citizens. 'Loaded down with the booty he had obtained and laughing at his successful deed of daring, he left us on 3 October disconsolate and unprotected against the return of those he had driven away,' wrote Ludwig Völkel, describing Chernishev as both the city's liberator and its destroyer: 'He may have shaken the kingdom, but he did not knock it down.' Capitaine Borcke agreed, writing later that the raid, 'so brilliant in its execution' was actually harmful to the country and its people because the state remained and would remain until Napoleon's fall; the raid only generated misery and further sacrifices by the exhausted land. The population was certainly apprehensive about French retribution, but they also feared mob violence, robbery and unrest perpetrated by their own countrymen, urban and rural alike. Some looting did occur (apparently more by Westphalian deserters and former soldiers than by Cossacks, a French observer called them a 'pillaging militia'), but a citizens' watch organised by the administrative commission was able to restore order fairy quickly.[201]

With Chernishev's triumphant return to the Army of the North, Bernadotte released a justly laudatory bulletin praising the audacious general's 'most brilliant success' and crowing that, 'The joy of the inhabitants was beyond all expression.' The counterpart French bulletin stated that the Westphalian troops had 'disbanded themselves' allowing the 'partisans' to enter Kassel and claimed that the Russians had 'pillaged everything that fell into their hands'. It concluded by blandly commenting that 'The King of Westphalia has retired towards the Rhine.'[202] Among the fugitives was Bavarian Ambassador Graf Luxburg, who reported back to Munich that, 'Westphalia is over and done, left to its own devices in insurrection and anarchy.'[203]

Kassel's fall also created new tensions between the emperor and his brother. Napoleon found the situation deplorable and confounding. 'In general, I am humiliated by the ridiculous role played by this prince who has neither administrative skills nor common sense,' he told his arch-chancellor, 'If he had stayed in Kassel, his troops would not have disbanded, and he would have remained master of his kingdom.' (Ironically, Chernishev unwittingly concurred with the emperor's judgment, telling the tsar that, 'As long as the king was in the city, his forces fought bravely'). Napoleon had not communicated directly with his brother since late August when the two hussar regiments had defected, nor would he do so through the remainder of 1813 or during the final months of his reign in early 1814. Instead, all his instructions and observations passed through Berthier or Maret or occasionally through other senior marshals and generals.[204] Napoleon's attitude is probably explained by the general distrust and disdain he had exhibited towards Westphalia over the years and by the need to focus his formidable attention on his increasingly desperate operational situation. In that larger context, Westphalia was a marginal concern. Its fate, as contemporaries noted, would be decided in Saxony.[205] If the emperor could defeat the Allied armies in the field, the kingdom would be preserved while its momentary loss or discomfiture would be a setback but not a crucial one.[206] Nonetheless, this lack of imperial correspondence left Jérôme feeling distressed and abandoned. With neither news nor orders from his brother, he often lapsed into apathy, telling Reinhard and other confidants that he did not know what to do, did not know what Napoleon expected of him. He seems to have alternated between thinking of himself as merely another French general and revelling in the thin façade of his lingering royal prerogatives. At times, he even seemed despondent, overwhelmed by circumstances as he depicted his situation during the flight from Kassel: 'my army has almost completely deserted,' he wrote in a letter to Napoleon's Minister of War, 'insurrectionary movements propagate themselves within the kingdom'.[207] 'The royal sun was shining ever duller and weaker,' noted Borcke, whose experience with the court at Koblenz conveyed the prevailing 'taint of unreality'.[208]

In addition to the heavy blow administered to the faltering kingdom, an increase in fraternal frictions and the production of another Allied propaganda coup, Chernishev's raid induced the shattering of the Westphalian army. Several thousand men still operated with the Grande Armée in the field or served in fortress garrisons, but by 30 September, with the exception of Magdeburg, there was not a single formed regular company within the confines of the kingdom. The recapture of Kassel would thus be accomplished by Allix at the head of the French troops Kellermann had collected on Westphalia's western border. Entering Kassel on 7 October, the general immediately set about restoring the government, reinstating officials and arresting those suspected of assisting or applauding Chernishev and his men during the Russian occupation or the local commission's interregnum.

The capitulation of Kassel, Chernishev's brief rule and Allix's re-occupation of the city as Westphalia's titular capital presented the army's officer corps with difficult choices. Although the army inside the kingdom had disintegrated, reactions among its officers varied. Some simply hid or attempted to hide. Young cadet Oppermann, for example, sneaked away to doff his uniform, don civilian clothes and leave the city before the capitulation was concluded. Boedicker, on the other hand, was boldly unrepentant. While preparing to leave on the 30th, Allix announced that the soldiers could go home but the officers should follow the king to the Rhine. Boedicker refused. 'Many officers asked me what they should do, to which I answered: since the king had left, and in the present circumstances I belonged only to the fatherland, I was released from my duties to the former [Jérôme], as not my rightful lord, and would remain in Kassel.' He claimed that none of the Jäger-Garde officers elected to ride with Allix. When Chernishev took control of the city the next day, he gave officers the choice of either joining the Allies or signing a parole pledging not to serve against them for a year. Boedicker would not volunteer for Russian or Prussian service, but he had no compunction about signing the parole and soon became a key figure in the city's temporary administration. Borcke and Meibom represented different points on the opposite side of the spectrum. Borcke, serving as Danloup-Verdun's aide-de-camp, remained with the general all the way to Koblenz even though 'my desire to fight for the tottering Westphalian throne was not great at a time when everyone was filled with the premonition of its near demise'. Sergeant Süstermann of the Grenadier-Garde also recorded that the soldiers had little interest in fighting for their king, but he considered it 'beneath my dignity to leave the flags to which I had sworn'. He likewise served until released in early November. Moreover, his comments about the lack of enthusiasm for his monarch notwithstanding, Süstermann expatiated in great detail on how the Westphalians could have been successful in opposing Chernishev's audacious assault. Meibom provides another example. He attempted to save himself and the remnants of his regiment by retreating with Allix but found his earnest efforts thwarted and was trapped in Kassel. Detained by the Russians when he declined to sign the parole, he was then imprisoned when the vengeful Allix returned. Though rudely jailed by the French general, he regretted that he had had no opportunity to 'convince the king that I did not deserve the poor treatment I received from General Allix, that I appreciated the benevolence bestowed upon me by the king and that I had served him truly and dutifully to the last moment'.[209]

As for Jérôme, he departed Koblenz on 13 October and returned to his putative capital on the 16th after a brief halt in Marburg. He found the army's collapse personally painful, especially as he believed he had lavished it with attention, praise, honours and awards.[210] His stay in Kassel would be brief, but fortunately for those such as Meibom and Boedicker incarcerated in the Kastel, his mere presence and reputation for clemency, along with persistent and effective intervention by Reinhard, helped to moderate some of Allix's harsh measures, commuting sentences, releasing prisoners, and delaying executions so that many of the condemned survived to outlive the kingdom.[211] Coinciding with the beginning of the Battle of Nations, Jérôme's re-appearance in Kassel provides an apposite moment to rejoin those Westphalian units still marching with the Grande Armée.

Leipzig: Encircled by Every Nation!

The Westphalian troops in the field in mid-October were divided among the Imperial Guard, Bertrand's 4th Corps and MacDonald's 11th. All were well below authorised strength, and all would be diminished further in the coming combat and retreat. Unfortunately, their small size and the lack of Westphalian records leaves us with little detail regarding their specific roles in the grand battle in which they were consumed.

Although one of Napoleon's personal staff officers reported that 'three strong battalions' remained with 31st Division after the Füsilier-Garde had been reassigned to the Imperial Guard, MacDonald claimed in a 12 October letter that the 8th Infantry and 4th Light together totalled only 300 men plus enough gunners and train personnel for their battery.[212] Nothing is known of this tiny detachment's fate. There are no reports of unit defections, and it may be presumed that they marched and fought alongside the other members of the 31st Division through the Battle of Leipzig (where the battery commander was badly wounded) to be released or to disperse on their own thereafter to return to their homes in the eroding kingdom.[213]

The same applies to the reinforced Füsilier-Garde battalion and battery attached to the Imperial Guard. They were present at Leipzig, were engaged in skirmishing southeast of Connewitz on 18 October, suffered some losses, and retreated through the city with the rest of the Guard on 19 October. 'The battalion of Westphalian fusiliers had already deserted by the hundreds over the previous two days,' reported GD Curial, the division commander, in recounting their last hours with the Grande Armée. Near Markranstädt on the 19th, Curial offered the remaining officers and men the choice of accompanying the army to the Rhine or of returning home.[214] As far as is known, all chose the latter option, and the Füsilier-Garde Regiment/Battalion thus vanished only fourteen months after being established.

The Chevaulegers-Garde also fought at Leipzig. Numbering 155 men in the saddle, the regiment was united into a single squadron and rode south through Leipzig on the morning of 16 October.[215] Initially directed towards Liebertwolkwitz, the guardsmen were diverted to Connewitz where they supported the defenders and at least once helped chase the attacking Austrians back into the village when they threatened to advance. Called back by Bertrand, the regiment crossed the Elster to join the rest of 4th Corps in its new position at Lindenau. The regimental officers took advantage of the unexpected lull on the 17th to dine – paying high prices for small portions – in the city. Here they met Colonel Frédéric Mathieu Benoît Lallemant of the 1st Westphalian Cuirassiers who had been sent by Jérôme to convey the grim account of Chernishev's raid to Napoleon. That night, the Westphalians had a brief interaction with the emperor as he stopped by the regiment after talking with Bertrand. 'He said farewell to us with great courtesy,' recalled Lehsten, 'It was the last time I saw this most eminent man, who, though he subjugated and tyrannised us Germans, nevertheless inspired respect and admiration.'[216] When combat resumed on 18 October, the Westphalians participated in the defence of Lindenau and then in the advance to Weißenfels the following day to clear the army's line of retreat. It would be their final combat under French eagles.

Lieutenant Lehsten again offers insights at the personal level. His challenge of coping with a disobedient soldier, for example, likely stands for the experiences of many Rheinbund officers that year. As mentioned previously, Lehsten had been separated from his regiment at Wartenburg but had collected up a band of stragglers and led them to Leipzig in the company of Franquemont's Württembergers. When he started off to rejoin the regiment, however, his trumpeter refused and began to ride away. When Lehsten confronted him, the trumpeter explained that nearby civilians had persuaded him to ride peacefully home because 'it was all over with Napoleon and the French, no honourable German should fight for them any more, etc.' The locals tried to take the soldier's side, but the rest of his men held firm and the trumpeter became rueful as Lehsten reminded him of his duty. Extracting a pledge of obedience, Lehsten rode off to locate the regiment, his little group intact. He was pleased to record that the trumpeter 'kept his word and remained with us to the end'. Other officers exhibited less confidence, as Lieutenant von Ochs wrote: 'We Westphalians are in the worst position, first because we may not leave our king to whom we have sworn an oath of loyalty, but on the other side where is one to go if one no longer has a country? And who will pay us? And all our people run away!!!!!'[217]

Lehsten seems to have missed most of the regiment's fighting on 18 October as he and an orderly had been sent to retrieve Colonel Lallemant who was still in the city awaiting a reply to take back to Jérôme on the Rhine. The colonel was not ready, so Lehsten and his orderly climbed a tower to see what they could discern of the battle.

> What a view for miles around! With Leipzig in the centre, there stood the French army, encircled by every nation! One no longer heard individual cannon shots, no, a continuous roll of cannon thunder. The earth shook. Musketry was even less distinguishable. With intense anticipation, we sought, now here, now there, to capture a moment. Everything blurred in the constantly renewing sea of fire.[218]

Returning to the colonel, they found Lallemant ready to depart and threaded their way through a chaos of crowds and occasional musket balls to return to the regiment. Although it is not clear that the Chevaulegers-Garde and the Hessian Garde-Chevaulegers contributed to the breakthrough on 18 October, they were present for the action and went west with 4th Corps on the 19th. On reaching Erfurt, Wolff was instructed to carry dispatches to Jérôme in Kassel, but the need for an escort in the Cossack-infested countryside led the general to ask that he take along 'the debris of his regiment'. Lieutenant Ochs expressed relief when permission was granted as 'the spirit of the men has sunk so low that they will no longer fight ... after the recent affair at Leipzig some twenty men deserted or stayed behind, including six NCOs and an orderly'. Wolff thus led the remaining Westphalian and Hessian horsemen away on 22 October, the two regiments parting as 'dear comrades', in Eisenach to take their separate roads home. Despite close scrapes with Cossacks, Wolff and his men returned to Kassel on 26 October, the same day that the king was leaving for the last time. On arrival, the Chevaulegers-Garde consisted of approximately 10 officers and 40 troopers out of the more than 500 who had begun the campaign in August. At Jérôme's request, Wolff gave the officers and the men the option of either following the king to the Rhine (on the promise of receiving their backpay) or 'retiring to their homes until further orders'. The regimental commander, a Frenchman named Berger, declared that he would never leave his king, but the rest elected to stay and, taking horses in compensation for their missing pay, rode off to their respective families. 'I took a touching farewell from General

Wolff that evening.' wrote Lieutenant von Ochs, 'I was really astonishingly sorry to have to part with him.'[219] Like the rest of the kingdom's field forces, the Chevaulegers-Garde thus came to an end.

Last Days of the Kingdom and an Unroyal Dismissal

The disbanding of Wolff's remnants meant that the only troops still in Westphalian uniforms were those in fortress garrisons and a few hundred guardsmen with Jérôme. These remaining guards, however, included Frenchmen of the Jérôme Hussars; only 100 or so Germans were still present under arms, almost all from the Garde-du-Corps and grenadiers. Most of these men returned to Kassel on 7 and 8 October along with several thousand French troops under Allix's overall command. Although the general, designated 'the king's lieutenant', issued orders in Jérôme's name to re-form the army, the entire kingdom was unravelling, and nothing came of these.[220] Much of the regime's administrative apparatus had broken down, incidents of uncoordinated unrest flared across the countryside and passive resistance was common.

Reactions to the kingdom's frailties and Allied successes varied across Westphalia depending largely on each region's historical background (whether Hanover, Braunschweig or Hesse-Kassel), and many of the disturbances – frequently led by former soldiers – were little more than opportunistic village vigilantism. These local outbursts were inspired by a fluctuating mixture of attachment to former princely houses, opposition to the exactions of Jérôme's government and fear of conscription, often combined with hatred of the foreign conquerors and a degree of antisemitism. They were also, of course, usually fuelled by alcohol. These acts of violent resistance did not represent a national uprising. Indeed, Allix reported that 'the Westphalian people are perfectly tranquil' and that troubles were limited to a few individuals.[221] Nonetheless, such incidents demonstrated that the government's writ was curtailed and crumbling.[222] For citizens at the time, the only thing that seemed certain was that Westphalia's days were numbered. As Wilhelm Grimm would write a few months later, 'Despite all the proclamations the predominant sense was that the kingdom no longer existed.'[223] Additionally, officials and citizens alike were anxiously ignorant of what was happening beyond their immediate cities, towns and villages. Jérôme re-entered his capital on 16 October, the day the Battle of Leipzig began, but efficient censorship and the dangers associated with conducting any communications across Cossack-infested territory deprived the citizenry of news from the theatre of war. All these cascading concerns left the population watchfully waiting in a state of tense insecurity.

The situation began to clarify when Colonel Lallemant arrived on 23 October to report that Napoleon had left Leipzig on the 18th. Lallemant did not know the extent of the Grande Armée's defeat, but his news was enough to set the court planning a second evacuation of Kassel. The intelligence that came in over the following days only confirmed the need for a rapid departure. Jérôme thus left his palace outside Kassel for the last time on 26 October, Wolff having one of the final royal audiences before the royal cavalcade trundled off. Unlike the flight in September, fear of Allied advances led the king and his escort (almost all French) to take a northerly route to arrive in Cologne on 1 November. Allix, Rigau and the last French troops left Kassel on 27 October to reach Cologne on the 3rd. The loyal Wolff went with them. The first Russian patrols arrived the following day.

The remaining Westphalian guardsmen were dismissed in Cologne on 4 November with rather perfunctory thanks offered not by Jérôme but by one of his court generals. The men were provided no funds for travel back to the former kingdom and, in a particularly miserly move, they were required to turn in their uniforms and equipment. Many were thus left nearly destitute. It was, as Süstermann noted, a most 'unroyal' farewell.[224] As the German members of the Westphalian Guard headed home to seek posts with the new rulers of Hesse-Kassel, Braunschweig, Hanover and other principalities, the Frenchmen turned west. Officers such as Wolff, Lageon, Berger, Pfuhl and Lallemant passed into French service as individuals (sometimes at a reduction in rank), while the officers and men of the Jérôme Hussars were simply redesignated as the 13th Hussars and incorporated into Napoleon's final Grande Armée for the 1814 campaign in France.[225] Jérôme's departure and the disbanding of his guard, however, did not mean the final end of the army. As Magdeburg remained in French hands, a tiny corner of Westphalia still existed, albeit as a sort of chimera kingdom. Furthermore, several thousand Westphalian soldiers were still serving under French banners in other fortresses on the Vistula, Oder and Elbe. Their fates will be addressed in Chapter 8.

*

Westphalia's situation was unsurprisingly similar in many ways to that of its Rheinbund allies in 1813, but it also differed in significant respects. Among the common characteristics were economic hardship, exhausted treasuries, the burdens imposed by the passing armies, popular disquiet (if not active unrest), prevailing uncertainty and, most prominently for this study, the utter destruction of its army in Russia and thus the need to create a new one rapidly under extremely trying circumstances. Westphalia's case, however, was distinct in critical ways that help understand its military history in its final year. One distinct factor was economic. Although all of the German states found their finances stressed, Westphalia was essentially bankrupt, its economy in such a shambles that Jérôme despaired of simply paying the army even as the court's voluptuous lifestyle seemed to proceed unhampered. Reinhard had provided a gloomy summary of Jérôme and his kingdom in the summer of 1812: 'His treasure is exhausted, his subjects depressed, his ministers despairing, his reputation damaged, his credit destroyed, his provision for the future eaten up in advance.'[226] By 1813, of course, Westphalia's situation had deteriorated yet further.

Westphalia's vulnerable northern and eastern borders presented another major problem. With all the main armies concentrated in Saxony, Jérôme's kingdom was painfully accessible to daring raids by the likes of Chernishev, Benckendorff, von der Marwitz, Hellwig and others. Although prostrate Saxony also endured Allied raiders, its larger misery was serving as the principal theatre of war to be trampled and devastated by the armies of both sides. Westphalia saw little of the vast contending hosts until the very end, but the seeming impunity with which raiding detachments penetrated its borders to inflict small but humiliating defeats, incite the restive population and undermine the state was only matched by the susceptibility of the far less significant Thuringian states. Despite the frequent intrusions by Prussian and Russian raiding detachments, however, the national uprising the Coalition had hoped to incite never occurred. Governance collapsed in some areas, passive resistance increased, and disturbances – though often little more than village-level banditry and anti-French vigilantism – erupted in places, but widespread popular insurrection remained conspicuous by its absence.

From a military standpoint, however, the most consequential of Westphalia's distinctive features were its 'artificial' nature and its foreign origin. Hammered together by imperial fiat from a multitude of previously existing states, it lacked historical foundations. There was no traditional dynasty or 'fatherland' to provide a mantle of legitimacy or serve as an anchor for popular loyalty. Though other Rheinbund states were also struggling to incorporate new territories and peoples, their dynasties and histories persisted as perdurable pillars of stability and security. The fact that the Kingdom of Westphalia owed its existence to the French emperor and that its appointed monarch was a Frenchmen – and a rather dissolute one at that – only accentuated the absence of these cohering factors. The Allies, of course, compounded the kingdom's problems by intentionally targeting it for disruption and destruction.

For Westphalia's army, the lack of a long-established ruling house with an associated homeland or nation placed acute pressure on the oaths sworn by soldiers and on their conceptions of professional honour. In an atmosphere of defeat, uncertainty and strident calls for German unity, some officers and many men in 1813 decided that Jérôme and Westphalia no longer had a claim on their loyalty. There were only two notable unit defections (the hussars and

Brethauer's battalion of the 3rd Infantry at Dresden) but draft evasion was clearly rampant and even in the absence of precise data, it seems evident that the Westphalia's army suffered more individual desertions than any other major Rheinbund state. More of the officers in the Russo-German Legion, for example, came from Westphalia than from all other Rheinbund states combined (*see* Appendix 2).[227] A number of common soldiers also ended up in Allied ranks, but the majority of the young conscripts who slipped away were men who had little interest in risking their lives for the foreign – and apparently failing – Napoleonic cause; they seem to have wanted nothing more than to return home.[228]

These examples of disloyalty, defection and desertion notwithstanding, there is also a need for nuance. The Westphalian officer corps, for instance, was afflicted by the same problems that hobbled the reconstitution of the officer establishments of the French army and other Rheinbund contingents: the physical and mental enervation of officers who survived Russia, the lack of qualified replacements, and the hasty promotion of numerous inexperienced, untrained young men. 'There was a great lack of capable officers, such that anybody and everybody had been appointed to the lower grades,' wrote Borcke.[229] Such new officers may have been less concerned with, or capable of, holding their men to their duty and may have been more inclined to desert or defect themselves. Furthermore, it is not unreasonable to speculate that many of the old officers who might have developed a sense of loyalty to their new king and nascent fatherland either lost that sentiment after the Russian 'shipwreck', died as a result of the campaign, or were left behind as prisoners. On the very pragmatic side, some individuals simply worried about their livelihoods and joined the other side in the hopes of regular pay rather than for political reasons.[230]

A different sort of anxiety plagued those captured by the Russians and urged to join the Russo-German Legion. After being robbed, starved and abused, many signed on with the legion simply in hopes of escaping their brutal captivity. Others, however, refused despite their miseries and the looming terror of Siberia. 'I still held myself bound by my oath to the Kingdom of Westphalia,' wrote Major Ludwig Wilhelm von Conrady of the 6th Infantry, a sentiment echoed by common soldiers who sought to escape or rejected appeals to join the legion. 'None of us had a desire to enter Russian service,' explained a captured Westphalian artilleryman when a former Westphalian officer who had changed sides approached a group of German prisoners. Threatened with transportation deeper into Russia, the group's spokesman replied, 'It is by no means our intention to champion Napoleon's cause, but we wish to remain true to our oaths and *only* take up arms for our fatherland.'[231] Even officers who might have shown pity at times for individual deserters or who felt the gravitational pull of a nebulous German identity condemned the hussars' defection and stayed at their posts until the very end as seen in the cases of Borcke, Lehsten, Meibom, Morgenstern, and others. The Westphalian army of 1813, then, was not without valour and utility, but neither was it the cohesive, competent force it had been a year earlier.[232]

The number of desertions and occasional defections, however, reveal that oaths did not prove sufficiently potent to keep the army intact as a fighting force. As Meibom stressed, resolute and aggressive leadership was necessary to keep the men in the ranks and focused on their missions. When this was provided, they could fight courageously and effectively as demonstrated in many instances: Füllgraf during the retreat from Posen, the artillery at Dresden, Ledru's Westphalian brigade near Bautzen and Wolff with the Chevaulegers-Garde on several occasions. The other side of the coin was that officers who wished to change sides could pull their men along into desertion or defection. The hussar regiments supply evidence of both betrayal and loyalty: Hammerstein and Pentz leading their four squadrons to the Austrians on the one hand, while the other two squadrons continued to serve dutifully until their French commander neglected his brigade's security. Unfortunately for Westphalia, such determined, energetic leadership was in short supply. Those charged with the defence of the kingdom seem to have been especially deficient. Commanders such as Klösterlein, Bastineller, Zandt and Jérôme himself proved timid and hesitant when the circumstances called for decision and forceful action. Their querulous behaviour sapped morale and led to the diffusion and eventual dissolution of the available troops. Specht's summary of the collapse of Zandt's brigade offers a tidy capsule illustration of the debilitating impact of such fumbling leadership. Zandt, in his view, 'promoted the malign seed' of disobedience and desertion 'by his dithering in the resolution to be taken ... [J]ust like Bastineller, he systematically persuaded the men to give up the cause of the French and of the kingdom as completely lost.' Surrounded by rumours of French defeats, Allied victories and Jérôme's desperate situation, the 'previously repressed bitterness' against the French awoke and the soldiers became convinced that the Kingdom of Westphalia was over. 'Only the accustomed obedience and the attention of their officers', Specht concluded, 'still held the men together and allowed ... at least a portion to reach Kassel.[233]

All of this meant that Jérôme's army was more brittle, more likely to unravel when officers and men felt the pull of previous loyalties, especially as the Allies gained ascendancy and the kingdom itself seemed to be sliding towards collapse. Better senior leadership would not have saved the kingdom. Its fate, as already noted, would be decided in Saxony, but Westphalia's end could have been less ignominious and its army's reputation less tarnished, had Jérôme and his officers demonstrated greater perseverance and resolve in coping with the daunting challenges they faced.

Major von Morgenstern's memoir offers an apt conclusion to this review of the Westphalian army in the last year of its existence. He served with the 2nd Infantry Regiment in Dresden up to the garrison's capitulation in November and penned the following as a retrospective.

> Thus, this final year of my military career was lacking in combat action. A genuinely German-patriotic assessment from the point of view of the accomplished facts [i.e., in hindsight] may perhaps count me fortunate that a miraculous coincidence of circumstances spared me the fratricidal battle against the liberators of the common German fatherland. Our feeling at that time – I may boldly assert this about the great majority of the officers – did not correspond to such a view at all. Only in the course of initially lost and bloody battles had a single great German race been given the impetus to throw off the unbearably burdensome fetters of foreign rule. In the further course of the changing fortunes of war, the time had not yet appeared to forget that disunity had prevailed for centuries and had recently led to foreign domination [*Fremdherrschaft*]. The lingering after-effects of the ideas of battle and victory, which had become second nature to us in the Napoleonic wars, were still too powerful, even apart from the oath of allegiance and the soldier's honour, to steer our minds, which were entangled in mistrust and doubtfulness and shrouded in thirst for action and glory, in the opposite direction.[234]

Chapter 7

The Miniature Monarchies: A Spectrum of Soldiers

'Where is your contingent?'
Napoleon to Friedrich von Müller, Weimar, 26 April 1813[1]

IN ADDITION TO THOSE MONARCHIES LARGE ENOUGH to form substantial contingents of all arms, the Rheinbund included a congeries of smaller states whose troops took the field as individual units or as components of amalgamated formations. Each contingent had its own individual history, but several general points are worth highlighting at the outset of this chapter. First, only one of these states supplied artillery in 1813 – the Grand Duchy of Berg – and only three contributed cavalry. The majority would thus be infantry units of varying sizes and reliability. Second, as with the contingents already covered, the armies of these microstates proved difficult to reconstruct after Russia and would be sent to the front in dribs and drabs as soon as they acquired even the most rudimentary sort of organisation. Third, the organisation and assignment of these contingents would differ considerably from past French practice, but the legacy of their involvement in the 1812 Russian campaign meant that almost all these small states would see their troop contributions divided in 1813. Notably, with the exception of Würzburg and Berg, all the contingents under consideration in this chapter had been assigned to the Grande Armée's 34th Division in 1812. Understanding the context for these miniature armies thus requires a review of that division's actions during the concluding weeks of the Russian campaign.

1812: Small State Contingents to Russia and Back

Prior to the invasion of Russia, the 34th Division had been stationed in and around Stralsund under GD Joseph Morand who was commanding the ad hoc force based around the Saxon *Prinz Maximilian* Infantry Regiment (*see* Chapter 2). In addition to the Saxon regiment, the division in early 1812 included the 4th Westphalian Infantry, Hesse-Darmstadt's Provisional Light Infantry Regiment and a French brigade. At the same time, the Frankfurt and Würzburg regiments as well as the three combined Rheinbund regiments were posted along the

Chart 47: Dispositions of Minor State Contingents, 1812
Showing the shift from coastal defence to active campaigning in western Russia

Unit	Summer: Coastal defence, Germany	Autumn/Winter: Western Russia
Würzburg Infantry Regiment	Division Princière	32nd Division/7th Corps
Frankfurt Infantry Regiment	Division Princière	34th Division/11th Corps
4th Rheinbund Regiment (Saxon Duchies)	Division Princière	34th Division/11th Corps
5th Rheinbund Regiment (Anhalt, Lippe)	Division Princière	34th Division/11th Corps
6th Rheinbund Regiment (Schwarzburg, Reuß, Waldeck)	Division Princière	34th Division/11th Corps
French Brigade (3e, 29e, 105e, 113e Ligne)	34th Division	34th Division/11th Corps
Saxon *Prinz Maximilian* Infantry Regiment	34th Division	(Stralsund/GD Morand)
4th Westphalian Infantry Regiment	34th Division	Independent/GL Wrede
Hessian Provisional Light Infantry Regiment	34th Division	Independent/GL Wrede

Note: during the summer of 1812, the so-called *Division Princière* was stationed along the North Sea coast from Bremen to Hamburg while GD Joseph Morand's 34th Division was posted in and around Stralsund. With the exception of the Würzburg Regiment, all of the *Division Princière*'s French and German infantry components were transferred to what may be described as a 'new' 34th Division under GD Louis Henri Loison at Königsberg in the autumn; most of these were committed to costly, but vain efforts to cover the retreat out of Russia; their remnants were assigned to the Danzig garrison. The 4th Westphalian and the Hessian Light Infantry were also called to Russia as a brigade and ended up (more by accident than design) coming under the command of Bavarian GL von Wrede with the remnants of 6th Corps. Morand remained at Stralsund, but with the gradual detachment of almost all his units, his 'old' or original 34th Division lost its title, and he was left with only the Saxon *Prinz Maximilian* Infantry (*see* Chapter 2).

Sources: regimental and contingent histories; Gill, 'Wrede in Russia'; plus François Houdecek, 'La Grande Armée de 1812: Organisation à l'Entrée en Campagne', CG, vol. XII.

North Sea coast as the so-called '*Division Princière*'. These allocations, however, soon changed and, by the autumn of 1812, the 34th Division had been completely restructured and the *Division Princière* had vanished from the French order of battle. Placed under GD Louis Henri Loison and assembled in Königsberg as a reserve formation, the new 34th Division included the Frankfurt Regiment and the three composite Rheinbund regiments (4th, 5th, and 6th) containing the microstate contingents as well as its original French brigade (*see* Chart 47).[2] The elements of the division were committed to cover the retreat of the ruined Grande Armée in late 1812 but soon succumbed to cold, sickness, combat and confusion. Despair induced by witnessing the wandering wreckage of Napoleon's once splendid host exacerbated these manifold miseries. 'Towards midday, the first fugitives of the French army arrived; wildly thrown together; only a few armed,' wrote Schaumburg-Lippe Hauptmann Johann Otto Georg Wilhelm von Düring in his diary on 10 December, 'Without order, the mob rolls through the streets like a stream ... nothing was to be heard but the question "which is the gate for the road to France?".'[3]

The 34th Division, much reduced and now under GD Marchand in place of Loison, reassembled in Königsberg, where the soldiers noted that 'the attitude towards everything French was very bad' among the local Prussians.[4] From here it was ordered to Danzig in early January, taking the same route through Elbing that the Bavarians, Westphalians and Poles in the rear guard would cover under Grandjean's 7th Division (*see* Map 26). This was a painful march that would cost it still more men, as a major from the Meiningen contingent described in a letter to his wife on arriving in Danzig:

> From Königsberg to here we have persistently had the Russians next to and behind us, marched nearly all day and night, seldom came under a roof, often had to stay under the open sky which, as you can imagine, was horrible in this bitter cold, every moment in danger of being taken prisoner and our few troops completely unable to fight as most had frozen hands or feet and many have dropped behind from exhaustion to fall into the hands of the Cossacks.[5]

The men certainly had to remain vigilant as they dragged themselves along – posting strong pickets and constantly patrolling – but with the 7th Division protecting their rear, they did not have any serious engagements with the Russians who shadowed them.[6] Nonetheless, all accounts agree on the suffering endured on this retreat and the division reached Danzig in a woeful state. 'Over time, our soldiers were so exhausted that they were reduced to speaking in single syllables,' recalled Sergeant Johann Friedrich Wilhelm Dornheim of Lippe-Detmold, 'loud talk among them ceased almost entirely, only a muffled murmuring was still to be heard here and there.'[7]

The many misfortunes notwithstanding, the Meiningen major may have painted an excessively negative picture in denigrating the fighting spirit of the men. On the contrary, they seem to have been gaining confidence against their pursuers. 'The Cossacks follow at our heels', commented an anonymous Schaumburg-Lippe officer in a letter to his wife on 12 January, 'But as they are not strong, we should amuse them a bit along the Vistula.'[8] An opportunity to 'amuse' the enemy arose east of the Vistula near Dirschau on 13 January when the Germans were forced to turn back and face a probing band of aggressive Cossacks. The men of the 34th Division not only chased off their pursuers but displayed determination and a surprising degree of vitality when officers called for volunteers to attack an enemy-occupied village that afternoon. Some fifty men from the ruins of the 4th Rheinbund responded and advanced. 'Under shouts of *"Es lebe der Kaiser!"* ["*Vive l'Empereur!*"] and with lowered bayonets,

Chart 48: Dispositions of Minor State Contingents in the Theatre of War, 1813

State/Unit(s)	Bns/sqdns	Spring	Autumn
Würzburg			
Infantry Regiment (II, III)	2	32nd Div/7th Corps	32nd Div/7th Corps
IV/Infantry Regiment	1	Modlin	Modlin
V/Infantry Regiment	1	–	Torgau
Chevaulegers	1	11th Corps	11th Corps
Frankfurt			
1812 remnants	–	Danzig	Danzig
Infantry Regiment (II, III)	2	39th Div/3rd Corps	Glogau
'Depot'	–	–	Torgau
Berg			
Lancers Regiment	1–6	Imperial Guard	Imperial Guard
Horse artillery battery	–	–	Imperial Guard
Saxon Duchies			
1812 remnants (4th Rheinbund)	–	Danzig	Danzig
Infantry Battalion (*Maj. Linker*)	1	defected	(with Allies)
Infantry Regiment	3	–	Magdeburg
Anhalt			
1812 Remnants (5th Rheinbund)	–	Danzig	Danzig
Jäger-zu-Pferd Regiment	2	–	1st Corps
Lippe			
1812 remnants (5th Rheinbund)	–	Danzig	Danzig
2 new companies	–	–	Magdeburg
Reuß and Schwarzburg			
1812 remnants (6th Rheinbund)	–	Danzig	Danzig
New companies	–	–	Magdeburg
Waldeck			
1812 remnants (6th Rheinbund)	–	Danzig	Danzig
2 new companies	–	–	Captured at Braunschweig

Notes: The Würzburg Chevaulegers consisted of three companies for a single large squadron. The 1st Battalions of the Würzburg and Frankfurt Regiments were in Spain; the rebuilt Berg 1st Infantry was assigned to Cherbourg and a new I/2nd Berg Infantry went to Montmédy in France with the depots late in the autumn.

the enemy, foot and horse, hidden behind hedges, fences and in houses were flushed out and driven from the village ... by and by the whole division took part in this Cossack chase.' The impetuous voltigeurs, carried away by their momentum, kept pushing ahead and Oberst August Christoph Karl Friedrich von und zu Egloffstein, the regimental commander, had to recall them personally for fear that they would fall into an ambush. Günther Schumann, an officer in the Schwarzburg contingent thus downplayed the Cossack threat: 'The enemy annoyed us anew, but the earlier fear of the Cossacks had vanished; we had become accustomed to them.'[9] 'Overall, the success of this little skirmish ... made a good impression on our men', noted one of the regiment's surgeons, and the troops retired for the night with considerable satisfaction.[10]

Though confident in their ability to see off the Cossacks, the Schaumburg-Lippe officer worried about the future: 'I only fear that we will be thrown into Danzig in the end and that the Russians will blockade it ... The only thing is that communications will be cut off.'[11] His letter proved prophetic. The 34th reached Danzig only two days later, on 14 January, where GB Jean Baptiste Marie Franceschi replaced Marchand at the head of the division with GB Claude Germain Louis Devilliers (who had a good command of German) as brigade commander.[12]

The remnants of the four German regiments thus came to be trapped in Danzig for the remainder of the war (*see* Chart 48). The various home governments, quite understandably, continued to regard these survivors as part of their Rheinbund requirements, especially as so many of their veteran officers were now confined within the fortress's walls. Napoleon's perspective was different. He discounted the men in Danzig and expected each Confederation member to supply a fresh contingent at full strength. The small states, with varying degrees of commitment, struggled to comply, but the results were often understrength units of raw recruits led by equally raw officers and NCOs, most of which also ended up in fortress garrisons. Their histories will therefore be recounted both in this chapter and in the next according to their respective fates.

Before turning to those that fought in Germany, however, the contingents that were not present deserve mention. These were two infantry regiments and two cavalry squadrons serving in Spain under the aegis of the two Nassau duchies. In accordance with an arrangement made at the Rheinbund's founding, the infantry regiments included the contingents from the principalities of Hohenzollern-Hechingen, Hohenzollern-Sigmaringen, Isenburg, Liechtenstein and Leyen/Hohengeroldseck, who either supplied soldiers or paid for substitutes to be recruited by Nassau. The 2nd Nassau Infantry and a light cavalry squadron crossed the Pyrenees in 1808, the 1st Infantry followed in 1810, and a second cavalry squadron in the summer of 1813. They remained with the French armies in Spain or southern France until they defected or were disarmed in late 1813.

Würzburg: A Habsburg in the Rheinbund

Being ruled by a senior member of the Habsburg House made the Grand Duchy of Würzburg one of the oddest members of the Confederation.[13] Ferdinand, both an *Erzherzog* (archduke) and a *Großherzog* (grand duke), was

Austrian Kaiser Franz's next youngest brother and had inherited the Grand Duchy of Tuscany when their father Leopold became Holy Roman Emperor in 1792. Losing Tuscany in the Treaty of Lunéville in 1797, he was transferred to Salzburg as Prince Elector, but lost that seat when the Treaty of Preßburg assigned Salzburg to the Austrian Empire in 1805. The Principality of Würzburg, formerly part of Bavaria, became Ferdinand's compensation for this latest forfeiture and with it the title of 'grand duke' to suit his status.[14] Although his reign was complicated by Habsburg dynastic pressures and persistent meddling from the court in Vienna, Ferdinand, his officials and his little army remained loyal to their Confederation commitments to the point of sending a 'division' (two companies totalling 210 men) of troops to serve as sappers with Napoleon's Army of Germany in the 1809 war against Austria.[15] In 1813, therefore, Ferdinand once again responded favourably to Napoleon's call to arms, as he wrote on 27 January:

> March companies that are designated to reinforce my contingent only await the orders giving their destinations and always stand at Your Majesty's disposal. I will also do everything possible to create a chevaulegers company of 90 men that matches the two companies that already find themselves with the army, and no sacrifice will be spared, Sire, to assure you of my unchanging zeal to fulfil your wishes, even in cases where the difficulties are almost insurmountable.[16]

A 15 March letter repeated these avowals: 'Please be persuaded, Sire, that I will always do all that depends on me to prove my devotion to you.'[17] Despite rising popular discontent, he would stay faithful to these pledges until Wrede's Austro-Bavarian army approached his capital in mid-October. At the same time, he was in constant communication with his elder brother and the Habsburg court through fraternal letters and interactions with the Austrian ambassador in Würzburg. Indeed, as war surged towards his borders in April 1813, Ferdinand fled to Prague with his family and his most precious possessions, using the routine of his annual visit to his estates in Bohemia as a pretext. He remained in Habsburg territory through most of the summer, only returning to Würzburg at the beginning of August. The brothers engaged in frequent correspondence and met several times while Ferdinand was in Bohemia, but details of their conversations – specifically what Kaiser Franz may have said or hinted about Austria's imminent adherence to the Coalition – are unknown. As will be seen below, however, regardless of what Ferdinand may have learned or surmised from his meetings with his brother, he continued to supply troops to the Grande Armée until the end of the armistice period. The French ambassador (who was aware of the contacts between the Habsburg brothers), could thus report with satisfaction that Würzburg would 'take the most prompt measures to fulfil the intentions of the emperor'.[18]

The army that would fulfil Napoleon's imperial wishes consisted of an infantry regiment, an artillery company and a squadron of Chevaulegers. The infantry and artillery, likely reflecting the Austrian heritage of their grand duke, were dressed in simple coats of white and brown respectively, with white breeches, red distinctions and black shakos. The light horsemen also had black shakos, topping dark green jackets trimmed in red along with grey riding trousers with red stripes and buttons down the sides. Ferdinand, a man of the arts who missed the luxuries of his native Florence, showed little interest in military matters, but his state would be a reliable troop contributor, going well beyond its nominal obligation of 2,000 men during this cruel year.

Würzburg's strategic importance, however, meant that French troops would also be stationed in the city and its great fortress, the Marienberg, perched high on the bluffs south of the Main River, throughout 1813. A major node for highways and a key station on the principal French lines of communication from Saxony to both France and Italy, Würzburg was also a crucial observation post to watch for and deter incursions from Bohemia and Thuringia. The city's central location and its relative proximity to the Bohemian border, of course, made it an important base for Austrian espionage, activities that were facilitated by the presence of a legation that was to conduct the Viennese court's diplomatic and dynastic affairs.[19]

The Würzburg Infantry Regiment: A Day of Honour

The Würzburg infantry and cavalry were involved in blockading Prussian fortresses and performing coastal defence duties during 1806–7, and the infantry regiment was sent to Catalonia in 1808 where it took part in the costly siege of Gerona the following year. The siege, skirmishes, disease and privations had reduced the regiment's three battalions to one (381 officers and men present under arms) by 1812, so three new battalions were formed when Napoleon called on the Rheinbund to provide troops for Russia.[20] The troops remaining in Spain were designated the 1st Battalion while the 2nd, 3rd and 4th Battalions marched off to Berlin. Organised according to the French pattern and drilled to French regulations, they joined 7th Corps as part of Durutte's 32nd Division in late 1812. Though inexperienced, the Würzburg 2nd and 3rd Battalions earned Durutte's warm praise for their performance in their inaugural engagement in November, but they suffered all the miseries of the retreat to Poland and their numbers steadily diminished.[21] With the 4th Battalion (the least experienced element of the contingent) deposited in Modlin as part of the garrison during the withdrawal from Warsaw, the remaining two battalions totalled only 605 men still in the ranks by the time they reached Kalisch on 12 February. The Würzburgers took part in the fighting at the end of the day and retreated with the rest of the corps thereafter, first to the Oder, then to the Elbe at Dresden. As Durutte withdrew towards the Harz Mountains in March to reform the skeleton remains of his division, the Würzburg battalions, numbering at best between 120 and 150 men fit for duty, were released to retire and rebuild: II/Würzburg escorting Durutte's artillery and baggage to Erfurt and III/Würzburg heading directly for home.[22]

The reconstruction of the two battalions proceeded with remarkable speed.[23] Würzburg had already prepared a replacement detachment of 733 officers and men which united with the remnants of II/Würzburg in Thuringia in mid-April to refill that battalion's ranks. The restored battalion then came temporarily under Marmont's command in the 21st Division of 6th Corps along with French replacements for Durutte's division before joining the reconstituted 7th Corps at Merseburg on 2 May. At the same time, the 3rd Battalion was rebuilt in Würzburg with raw recruits and departed for Saxony at near full strength on 24 April; it, too, was assigned to the 21st Division but it is not clear that it ever linked up with the division. Although both battalions benefited from a cadre of experienced officers and NCOs, the young men in these resurrected units were similar to those being raised all across the Confederation: utterly green, only partly trained and lacking the enthusiasm that had inspired earlier contingents.[24] Nonetheless, the two battalions came together as a regiment and joined Reynier's 7th Corps in Torgau, resuming their place in Durutte's division 1,179 strong and heading for Bautzen along with the rest of Ney's huge sub-army. Reynier's men were not involved in the great battle on 20 and 21 May, but they were in the lead during the subsequent pursuit, the Würzburgers exciting Napoleon's admiration when they advanced past him near Weißenberg on the 22nd.[25] Charged with attacking a Russian battery, they lost 18 men dead and wounded on 22 May and another 17 the following day as skirmishers from the regiment and their Saxon allies clashed with the Russian rear guard between Leopoldshain and Troitschendorf across the Neisse (see Map 21).

Although they continued east into Silesia, the actions on 22 and 23 May were the last engagements for the Würzburg Regiment during the spring campaign. The armistice saw 7th Corps shift to encampments around Görlitz where the welcome pause allowed the men to focus on training, repairing equipment and incorporating two replacement companies sent from the grand duchy. In addition to these replacements, Würzburg sent out an entirely new battalion during the armistice at Napoleon's request. Designated the 5th Battalion, it arrived in Torgau to become part of that city's garrison with 1,004 officers and men, another case of the least ready troops being assigned to fortress duty.[26] When hostilities resumed in mid-August, therefore, Würzburg had five battalions in the field in addition to its cavalry squadron: the 1st in Spain, the 2nd and 3rd with the 32nd Division in 7th Corps, the 4th in Modlin and the 5th in Torgau.[27]

The two battalions of the Würzburg Regiment assigned to Durutte's 32nd Division began the autumn campaign with 961 officers and men on hand and another 93 detached, but the fighting at Großbeeren and Dennewitz, combined with sickness and march attrition, soon reduced their numbers. They found themselves caught in the maelstrom at Großbeeren on 23 August, for example, as an unnamed officer recounted:

> We had to stand in squares because of the superior enemy cavalry and thus cannons were fired in volleys. Owing to the strong and steady rain, we could not fire a single shot with our muskets. Thus, the cannon fire continued from 4:00 until 7:30 with eight to ten guns at once. We lost many men to the shells until we were finally out-flanked and had to pull back in squares. The disorder was so great that nearly all the troops became mixed up... On this day we had 200 men killed or wounded as well as those who scattered and became lost in the swamps.[28]

Even if Oberst Gottfried Wilhelm Freiherr Moser von Filseck, the regimental commander, was accurate in reporting that the troops had 'behaved extremely well during the very violent cannonade and retired in good order', the loss of 245 men was a serious blow.[29]

Worse was to come at Dennewitz on 6 September.[30] Owing to the steadfast performance of the 2nd Battalion, however, Würzburg military history considers that battle a 'day of honour' despite the defeat of Ney's army.[31] The 3rd Battalion having been detached to guard the corps' baggage, only the 2nd took part in Durutte's advance and defence on the low slopes west of Dennewitz. According to Würzburg accounts, the troops retained their composure and maintained a steady musketry until forced to withdraw. As one of the regiment's members noted, the men could still be proud of their achievement 'even if such behaviour is not mentioned because of the small number of the combatants and because they were not crowned with success owing to the general disaster'. Its courage in action notwithstanding, the battalion was disordered and overrun by friendly fugitives and the pursuing enemy as it tried to withdraw (Durutte blamed the Württemberg cavalry, but this seems unlikely owing to their location on the field). The 3rd Battalion, too, seems to have been engulfed in the overall flight and the regiment suffered a total of 433 casualties, 370 of these being prisoners of war. These losses left only 273 officers and men available when the regiment mustered on 14 September, but 114 soldiers who had escaped captivity and fled to Leipzig soon re-joined to bring the strength to 387.³² Though few seem to have defected, others who freed themselves returned to Würzburg where they spread defeatist rumours that aroused the indignation of the French ambassador. Overall numbers of deserters seem to have been low (perhaps 100 in the city by mid-October), but a senior Würzburg official later asserted that the government attempted to provide returning deserters and stragglers with civilian clothes so they would not be detected by the French and forced back into service.³³

The Würzburgers participated in the fruitless manoeuvring of late September and early October to reach the Leipzig battlefield on 17 October with approximately 200 men in the ranks.³⁴ They were held in reserve during the brutal fighting on the 18th but were deployed as skirmishers in the Rosental woods and gardens on the 19th and heavily engaged. Only about a hundred managed to escape when the bridge was blown prematurely; the majority were killed, wounded or captured in the consuming chaos. This tiny band fled west with the rest of the army to reach the Unstrut River at Freyburg on 21 October. Here they had their last encounter with the emperor and their last action as a French ally. Trying to secure a crossing over the difficult defile presented by the river, Napoleon saw the Würzburg troops marching up and called out 'Soldiers of Würzburg, forward and chase off those buggers over there!'³⁵ Having helped protect the passage of the Grande Armée's pathetic remnants, the 'regiment' proceeded through Erfurt to reach Eisenach on 24 October. With the Rheinbund in a state of collapse and his little command slowly eroding, Oberst von Filseck persuaded Berthier to obtain Napoleon's permission to return home, ironically on the same day that Wrede opened a bombardment on Würzburg and the grand duchy changed sides to join the Coalition. The regiment's travails, however, were not over as the men were threatened by angry local villagers and then taken prisoner by roving Cossacks. After several days of confused captivity, they were allowed to proceed and finally arrived in Würzburg on 3 November with only 40–50 men under arms.

In addition to the five battalions of its regiment, Würzburg seems to have organised and sent off several other replacement detachments in accordance with Ferdinand's instructions to meet Napoleon's expectations. The two replacement companies that arrived during the armistice have already been mentioned, but another pair of companies (234 men) passed through Torgau in late August, presumably to join the regiment. Finally, some 301 men and two officers arrived at the great French depot in Dresden at some time in August, but their later history is unknown. Although they may have stayed to endure the privations of the siege, there is no mention of them in the garrison reports.³⁶

Back in Würzburg, however, French authorities became more and more concerned as summer waxed into autumn. They noticed increasing numbers of deserters and malingerers, claiming that most were from Rheinbund contingents, while the Würzburg government, in their eyes, was inert. The Austrian war manifesto made a particularly vivid impression given the Würzburg court's ties with Vienna. Moreover, Ferdinand seemed personally demoralised on his return from Bohemia in early August. In a distinctly unusual move, he had taken not only his family but his most valued possessions such as rare furniture and heirloom silver on his sojourn in Bohemia in April in case the Allies marched into Würzburg in his absence. Now, as autumn advanced, he kept all these valuables packed, loaded and ready for a rapid departure.[37] As for the general populace: 'It is difficult to express, how far the joy of the inhabitants goes, who wait impatiently for the approach of our enemies,' wrote the French ambassador on 15 October, 'It makes them forget the danger which can result for them from the defence of the city and the citadel.'[38] Before continuing to that defence and the final weeks of the grand duchy as a French ally, however, it is important to catch up with the other portion of its contingent: the Würzburg Chevaulegers.

The Würzburg Chevaulegers: 'The Cavalry is very Good'

The Würzburg Chevaulegers consisted of one squadron organised into two companies for an authorised total of 161 officers and men. Despite its small size, the dearth of reliable cavalry in the Grande Armée overall meant that this lone squadron would play an outsized role in the early weeks of the spring campaign.[39]

The squadron had been assigned rear-area security duties in 1812 and did not participate in the invasion of Russia. February 1813 thus found the Würzburg Chevaulegers concentrated in Berlin just as Allied raiding detachments were beginning to cross the Oder to threaten the Prussian capital. Supporting a battalion of the 112^e Ligne, part of the squadron had its first skirmish with Cossacks on the 17th (Benckendorff's men had overrun the Westphalian replacement battalion in Wriezen the previous day). The Würzburgers had the better of this initial encounter and likewise showed themselves unintimidated by their fearsome foes in small scuffles northeast of Berlin over the following several days. The rest of the squadron earned the gratitude of Marshal Augereau, the French commandant in Berlin, when they were instrumental in repelling a bold Cossack raid into the city itself on 20 February. This miniature success notwithstanding, Viceroy Eugène was convinced he had to seek safety behind the Elbe and the squadron, now attached to Grenier's 11th Corps, thus withdrew to Wittenberg under constant harassment by Cossacks. As part of 11th Corps, the Würzburgers participated in the clashes around Möckern during Eugène's tentative foray across the Elbe in early April with 139 men, a handful of whom helped to drive off Cossacks who came close to capturing the viceroy on the foggy morning of 5 April.[40] Along with the remnants of the 4th Italian Chasseurs, they formed the rear guard when the French withdrew across the Elbe that night. For the next several weeks, the squadron found itself repeatedly transferred among the divisions of 11th Corps as Eugène established himself between Magdeburg and the Harz Mountains to await the emperor's arrival. Here they conducted daily patrols and escort missions for the remainder of April until Eugène pushed south to meet Napoleon's advance from the Main.

The Würzburgers next came into action when Eugène moved to join the emperor. Seven troopers attached to MacDonald's staff captured 30 Prussians who had taken the marshal and his entourage under fire on 30 April and the squadron executed a splendid little attack against superior numbers of Cossacks on 1 May. Eugène, who had personally ordered the attack, was very pleased and conveyed his appreciation to Rittmeister Michael Hemmerth, the squadron commander, as Hemmerth noted in his report to the grand duke: 'His Imperial and Royal Highness the Viceroy publicly expressed his complete satisfaction regarding the demonstrated bravery of the troops.' Attached to GD Philibert Fressinet's 31st Division, the squadron was also involved at Lützen the following day when MacDonald's corps attacked the Allied right flank. Hemmerth reported laconically that:

> The cannonade on the right wing of the army [that is, near the quadrilateral of villages] was dreadful. It came ever closer. Finally, our division was required to attack the enemy in the flank. We covered the cannons, the enemy let all his guns play against us; drums beat the charge, the enemy was overthrown.

Hemmerth seems to have been overly modest, as Fressinet lauded the squadron's courage and skill in a personal letter to Hemmerth and recommended a number of officers and men for the Legion of Honour.[41]

Also at Lützen was a new 3rd Company of chevaulegers with 84 officers and men. Called into existence in February as Ferdinand had intimated to Napoleon in his 27 January letter, the company had ridden east with the Würzburg replacement detachment that became the rebuilt II/Würzburg Infantry and, like the infantry battalion, came under the temporary command of Marshal Marmont. A dozen of the men were scattered about as orderlies to French generals or staff officers and another dozen were detached elsewhere, but their commander reported of the remainder that, 'The men who came under fire behaved very well,' even though they do not seem have been involved in any actual combat. The company stayed with Marmont for another week before being transferred to 11th Corps to join its squadron.[42]

The ensuing drive to Dresden brought several clashes with Cossacks, the capture of a bridge by swimming a small river with a company of French voltigeurs and an encounter with the emperor. Near Colditz on 5 May, reported Hemmerth, 'The emperor himself came up in great haste; no sooner had His Majesty seen us, but he had me summoned, informed himself about strength and losses, both men and officers, and had as well the grace to tell me that the 3rd Company would soon join us.' The arrival of the new company brought the squadron to a strength of 212 as it passed Dresden and pushed east towards Bautzen, skirmishing with the enemy, screening the corps' advance, and conducting its own reconnaissance patrols all the while. The squadron was detached from the 31st Division on 19 May and combined with the 4th Italian Chasseurs directly under the corps chief of staff, but while Hemmerth witnessed the 'terrible' fire on both days of the Battle of Bautzen, his men were not engaged.

The Würzburgers were assigned to the advance guard for the pursuit after Bautzen, a period marked by wearing marches, poor logistical support and daily engagements with the Allied rear guards. Although each of these skirmishes cost the squadron a few troopers wounded, the only major loss was the capture of 36 men who had been left behind to tend sick horses and collect supplies. It was yet another instance of Cossacks plaguing the army's lines of communication, but in this case, 19 of the men were able to escape and return to their comrades. Present for the engagement at Groß-Rosen on 30 May, the chevaulegers gratefully welcomed the armistice and a chance to recover from the strains of the preceding several weeks.[43]

The Würzburg squadron received 16 replacements during the armistice and began the autumn campaign with 215 officers and men (169 present under arms, 25 detached and 21 sick).[44] Owing to the army's reorganisation, it was now part of the 28th Light Cavalry Brigade under GB Alexander Montbrun with the 4th Italian Chasseurs and 2nd Neapolitan Chasseurs. Unfortunately, sources for its actions between August and October are frustratingly sparse. The squadron remained with MacDonald's 11th Corps with 194 officers and men, fighting in the debacle on the Katzbach and being the first to cross that fateful stream on 26 August.[45] It later participated in the many small engagements east of Dresden during September before crossing the Elbe in early October. It is not even clear, however, that it was present at Leipzig nor how the men returned home after the Battle of Nations. Losses are also unknown as is the fate of a replacement company of 73 officers and men that departed Würzburg on 10 August.[46]

What is clear is that the French valued this valiant and capable squadron. Napoleon, for example, instructed Maret on 7 June to 'Write to my minister with the Grand Duke of Würzburg that I prefer cavalry to infantry: the cavalry is very good; I prefer therefore that Würzburg furnish me with fewer infantry and furnish me instead another squadron of cavalry.' He reiterated this request on 13 June not only because he was desperate for light cavalry but because he held the Würzburg troopers specifically in high regard.[47] Unfortunately for the emperor, Würzburg was unable to comply. Even if the grand duchy could have provided additional mounted men, it seems unlikely that they would have matched the quality of the existing squadron. Major Hermann Helmes, the unit's historian, argues persuasively that the two original companies and the third added in early 1813 were largely composed of veteran officers and long-service soldiers. Many might have been innocent of combat experience, but they were well-trained, comfortable on horseback, and integrated as a cohesive unit. Helmes disparages the replacement company sent in August and laments that it did not set out earlier to grant time for its young recruits to be incorporated into the squadron and learn from the veterans. Though small in size within such a vast arena of conflict, the Würzburg Chevaulegers thus earned a favourable reputation with their French commanders and created a proud history that they carried along when they were absorbed into the Bavarian army in 1814.[48]

The End of the Grand Duchy[49]

Wrede and his Austro-Bavarian army now return to the stage. The Bavarian general, again acting on his own initiative, was determined to capture Würzburg on the way to intercepting Napoleon's retreat from Leipzig. He hoped to accomplish this task quickly and, as he had with Friedrich of Württemberg and other Rheinbund monarchs, he sent a threatening and haughty letter to His Imperial and Royal Highness Großherzog Ferdinand demanding that Würzburg join the Allied powers at once.[50] Without waiting for a reply, Wrede marched on Würzburg to arrive outside the city's walls north of the Main on 24 October (the same day that Oberst Moser von Filseck was making his appeal for release to Berthier). He immediately summoned the French commandant to surrender. The French general, an old warhorse named Louis Marie Turreau de Garambouville, Baron de Linières, refused and Wrede opened fire on the city twice that night to the great outrage of the inhabitants who held unhappy recollections of their previous years as Bavarian subjects. The French defenders repulsed a poorly prepared attempt to storm the walls during the second bombardment, but GD Turreau knew he could not hold the entire city: the garrison was too small (*c.* 3,000 French), his Würzburg troops were on the verge of mutiny, some of the French units were unreliable and the population was in a state of great agitation. He thus negotiated an agreement that allowed him to abandon the portion of the city on the northern bank of the Main and withdraw across the river into the smaller southern precincts, including the Marienberg fortress.

Bavarians and Austrians occupied the city's gates on the evening of the 26th as the garrison began to pull out, but when Turreau ordered the 373 Würzburg infantrymen and gunners to the south bank, some of them rebelled and a firefight with the French troops ensued as the Würzburg soldiers tried to break out of the city. Quelling the attempted mutiny, the French disarmed the Würzburgers and corralled them in the fortress for the night, but Turreau permitted them to leave on the 27th despite the likelihood that they would join the enemy.[51] As indeed they did. Two ad hoc companies accompanied Wrede when he marched off on his ill-fated attempt to intercept Napoleon's retreat. The rest became part of the small force Wrede left behind to blockade the Marienberg where Turreau and his French garrison would hold out until May 1814.

By the time Wrede reached Würzburg, however, Ferdinand had gone. Departing on 17 October with a large convoy of wagons loaded with his most prized belongings, he had shifted his seat to Württemberg territory, appointing a council of notables to govern in his absence.[52] After being subjected to rude treatment from Wrede, these men agreed to the Bavarian general's demand that the grand duchy switch sides and issued a brief proclamation to this effect on 24 October. Ferdinand had already sent orders that his troops should no longer obey the French and he did not hesitate to concur with his council members. On 26 October, he thus signed a lengthy and rather turgid declaration renouncing his adherence to the Rheinbund after courteously informing Napoleon of his decision. Troops were soon being raised (more than Napoleon had required) to march with the Allied armies and, fortunately for the grand duchy, Ferdinand's family connections protected Würzburg from coming under the authority of Stein's commission. On the other hand, Austrian Kaiser Franz and his court were determined to treat Würzburg as if it were a Habsburg crown land and, unknown to Ferdinand, Vienna had already decided to transfer the grand duchy to Bavaria in partial compensation for Munich's loss of the Tyrol and other regions. Ferdinand, of course, also required compensation, By the summer of 1814, therefore, he had been transferred yet again, this time to his considerable satisfaction, back to Florence on the throne of the restored Grand Duchy of Tuscany. Bavaria, meanwhile, once again acquired Würzburg, an arrangement that would be formalised by the Congress of Vienna over the next several years.

Frankfurt: The Prince-Primate's State

Straddling the Main River west of Würzburg was the Grand Duchy of Frankfurt. This was another Napoleonic creation intended to secure control of critical territory and provide a domain for Carl Theodor von Dalberg, the Prince-Primate of the Confederation. Dalberg, the Archbishop of Regensburg, Bishop of Constance, and former Archbishop-Elector of Mainz, was an intellectual ecclesiastic with reformist ideas who believed Germany needed some form of federative structure. With the destruction of the old *Reich*, he saw Napoleon as the pole around which this structure could be formed. The emperor, respecting his intellect and influence, appointed him prince-primate when the Rheinbund was established and granted him a small state at the confluence of the Main and Rhine to rule. As prince-primate, Dalberg was to preside over meetings of the Rheinbund's college of princes and develop a federal constitution. Much to his disappointment, however, these notions foundered on opposition from key Confederation members and Napoleon's unwillingness to impose them by force or fiat. Although his Rheinbund office was thus something of a hollow sinecure, Napoleon expanded Dalberg's realm in 1810, elevating it to the status of a grand duchy with 300,000 souls in nearly contiguous territory and with Eugène de Beauharnais designated to inherit it on Dalberg's death.

The expansion in Frankfurt's size and prestige brought with it a requirement for more troops to meet its obligations as a member of the Rheinbund.[53] As the 'State of the Prince-Primate', Frankfurt had been required to supply a single battalion for the common defence and this unit had duly marched off to Spain in 1808. With its increase in population, however, Frankfurt was to contribute a full regiment and two new battalions were thus formed prior to the invasion of Russia. Designated the grand duchy's 2nd and 3rd Battalions – like Würzburg, the battalion still in Spain was considered the 1st – these were filled by the introduction of conscription and, though only raised with considerable difficulty, the men gradually acquired soldierly qualities. The regiment entered Russia in November 1812 as part of the 34th Division but was quickly consumed in combat and misery, a mere 209 officers and men reaching Danzig by way of Königsberg on 14 January 1813.[54] This tattered remnant, as with the survivors of many other Rheinbund armies, would remain to endure the coming siege while a new contingent was raised back home.

As with the units sent to Russia, the new battalions were considered the 2nd and 3rd Battalions of the Grand Duchy's regiment and were organised according to the French pattern with six companies per battalion including one each of grenadiers and voltigeurs.[55] They wore dark blue coats with red trim, dark blue trousers, black shakos and white leather gear; grenadiers and voltigeurs were identified respectively by typical red and green distinctions. The problems experienced with conscripting, arming and equipping the contingent the previous year were multiplied in 1813 and unrest – especially opposition to conscription – flared in and around Hanau in January. Calm was restored after a few days of isolated disturbances and a few spasms of violence, but these incidents were indicative of the widespread popular discontent. Though mobilisation continued, the grand duchy's authorities despaired of meeting their commitments under the prevailing circumstances as they saw no means of conjuring up suitable officers, sergeants, soldiers, muskets and other necessities.[56] The 2nd Battalion was in a poor state and the 3rd Battalion, unsurprisingly, received the dregs of the grand duchy's manpower: many of its officers were superannuated men drawn from the national militia and Dalberg lamented that a 'malicious spirit has embedded itself in the NCOs', many of whom would soon be sent to the field army.[57] Leadership in the hastily formed regimental depot was no better: only three of the thirteen officers were considered fit for field duty.[58] Curiously, Dalberg, not known as a forceful personality, was adamant that at least one battalion depart on 1 April as he had pledged that date to Napoleon:

> I have given my word that the grand duchy's battalion will march off to Würzburg on 1 April without fail. My royal word is thus given. As Prince-Primate, I am obligated to the Confederation and under this grave responsibility, I must insist on compliance. Old or new muskets is irrelevant; they must go. I demand it as a duty; the old ones [muskets] will also hit and if they do not hit, then the men can plant their bayonets on them and attack the enemy. I declare to you most earnestly that you both [his responsible ministers] will have to deal with Napoleon and me if the battalion does not march off on 1 April.[59]

Details regarding the Frankfurt Regiment's actions are scanty, but the 2nd Battalion duly set out on 1 April. The 3rd followed eleven days later and by 21 April, the 2nd was in Würzburg and the 3rd in Coburg numbering 847 and 713 officers and men present for duty respectively, but both were seriously deficient in officer strength.[60] As shown in Chapter 5, II/Frankfurt marched with Marchand's 39th Division of 3rd Corps and was present at Weißenfels and Lützen but was not significantly engaged in either battle.[61] There followed a pause in Leipzig before 3rd Corps crossed the Elbe at Torgau, but the Frankfurt battalion was left behind as part of the fortress garrison when Ney marched on towards Bautzen. It thus missed the second major battle of the spring campaign and only moved east to become part of the Glogau garrison sometime during the armistice. The battalion swiftly eroded owing to desertion, however, and only numbered 320–350 men fit for duty by mid-May. The 3rd Battalion had similar problems. It saw no combat but suffered so heavily from desertion that by the time of the armistice it was reduced to a mere 335 men present under arms, less than half its nominal strength.[62] Its peregrinations from Coburg took it across the Elbe where it was supposed to meet Oudinot's corps at Hoyerswerda after Bautzen, but it allowed itself to be surrounded by 200 Cossacks much to the astonishment and irritation of Dalberg and the military authorities back in Frankfurt. 'It was chased by the enemy and retreated up the road towards Torgau,' according to the 12th Corps operations journal. It apparently escaped without significant loss and joined the corps on 27 May in the company of GD Beaumont's little division. Oudinot, however, immediately sent it to Torgau to escort a convoy and here it remained with its sister battalion until both departed for Glogau in mid-June. A French inspection report in mid-July thus commented that 'The two battalions of the Grand Duchy of Frankfurt are well-uniformed and equipped but very weak.'[63] Fortunately, a reinforcement detachment of four officers and 326 green recruits arrived in Glogau just as the armistice was ending to bring the regiment to a more respectable strength of about 1,000 officers and men.[64] As there were no significant detachments and the regiment had seen almost no combat, this means its strength had been whittled down by half through desertion and sickness alone in the period from early April to mid-August despite the arrival of the large replacement detachment. A separate detachment of 190 men led by a lieutenant was also destined for Glogau, but the progress of the fighting made its march impossible, and it was assigned to the Torgau garrison as the Frankfurt 'depot' instead.[65]

The Frankfurt Regiment's involvement in the defence of Glogau is addressed in the next chapter, but the officers and men would end up serving as French allies for almost three months after the Grand Duchy of Frankfurt had ceased to exist. In the end, Dalberg's state simply deliquesced. He had no interest in approaching the Allies, and they had no intention of seeing his state survive. Well before the Coalition armies had neared his borders, even before Bavaria's defection through the Treaty of Ried, Dalberg decided to absent himself from the scene. His tenacious loyalty to Napoleon notwithstanding, he departed for his bishopric in Constance on 1 October, ostensibly to see to his ecclesiastical responsibilities there. He left behind a council of ministers to govern with the vaguest guidance on how to cope with the mounting military–political crisis. He never returned. He sent a letter to Bavaria's Max Joseph in an attempt to abdicate in favour of Eugène de Beauharnais as had been envisaged when the grand duchy was established in 1810, but this was, in the words of one biographer, simply 'an unnecessary, senseless demonstration' that only made him look ridiculous in the eyes of the Allied powers.[66] It predictably came to naught. Napoleon passed through the city after his victory at Hanau, but he was soon followed by Allied troops, the Allied monarchs and an Allied military government under Stein's supervision.[67] The Allies immediately set about organising a contingent to fight against France: three infantry battalions, three Landwehr battalions, a company of Jäger-zu-Pferd and two companies of Jägers-zu-Fuß, far beyond what Napoleon had required. The Grand Duchy of Frankfurt thus faded away, much of its territory going to the revived state of Hesse-Kassel and Frankfurt itself becoming a free city under the post-1815 political dispensation in Germany, much as it had been under the Holy Roman Empire. As for the remains of the Frankfurt battalion facing Wellington's army in southern France, they defected to the British along with the 2nd Nassau Regiment on 10 December and finally returned to their homes in July 1814.

Berg: Cudgel Russians and Loyal Lancers

In some respects, Frankfurt was as much a Napoleonic 'model state' as Westphalia. Dalberg, for instance, had introduced a version of the *Code Napoléon* as his legal system and many considered the grand duchy little more than another province of France owing to Dalberg's admiration for and subservience to the emperor. The other state that was actually intended to serve as model, however, and was also ruled by a Bonaparte, was the Grand Duchy of Berg. Berg's territorial composition changed considerably over the course of its brief existence, but the foundational elements were the former Prussian Duchy of Cleves (Kleve) and the former Bavarian Duchy of Berg (the grand duchy is thus sometimes known as 'Cleves-Berg'). Napoleon glued these two entities together along with some other minor lands to form the new grand duchy in 1806 and installed his brother-in-law, Joachim Murat, as its ruler. This arrangement only lasted until 1808, when he appointed Murat as King of Naples, replacing a brother-in-law with a nephew by naming Napoleon Louis, the second son of his brother Louis Bonaparte (then the King of Holland), as Berg's new grand duke. As Napoleon Louis was only four years old at the time, however, his uncle ruled as regent. Real power thus lay in Napoleon's hands, but day-to-day administration was carried out by bureaucrats in Paris and in Düsseldorf, the grand duchy's capital. Chief among these was Jean Claude Beugnot, a well-respected administrator who had been serving as Westphalia's minister of finance.

Napoleon's initial intention was that Berg should serve as a model state like Westphalia, a vehicle to introduce French political, social and legal concepts into Germany and inspire emulation among the other members of the Rheinbund.[68] As in Westphalia, however, the new government failed to fulfil this promise while Berg's prosperous economy fell into ruins owing to French policies associated with the Continental Blockade. Over time, these conditions resulted in an exodus of business, widespread unemployment, a flourishing smuggling scene and deep, if mostly repressed, popular frustration with the new regime. The government monopoly on salt and tobacco contributed to the growing resentment. This economic dislocation would be a major factor in the violent unrest that erupted in parts of the grand duchy in early 1813.

In addition to dismay at joblessness, loss of trade and increased taxation, subjects of the fledgling grand duchy detested conscription, a new phenomenon for at least some of its districts.[69] Nonetheless, Berg, like every other member of the Confederation, was required to supply a contingent for Napoleon's military enterprises. Two infantry regiments, an artillery component and a cavalry regiment (the later 1st Lancers) thus departed for Spain in 1808 where combat and disease would whittle the infantry down to a battalion in Catalonia while the cavalry acquired an excellent reputation in hard and costly service elsewhere in Iberia. A third infantry regiment campaigned in Germany under King Jérôme in 1809 and a fourth regiment was raised prior to 1812. Combined with returnees from Spain, these new units (minus II/3rd Infantry still in France and Spain) would constitute a brigade for the invasion of Russia along with a second cavalry regiment (2nd Lancers) and a rebuilt artillery company. The brigade's infantry and artillery were destroyed in Russia, especially in fighting at the Berezina. Of nearly 6,000 men who had marched east, only some 205 ragged survivors were on hand as they regrouped to head home on 21 January.[70] The cavalry was in an equally dire state. 'The debris of the 2nd Lancer Regiment cannot be mounted, armed or equipped where it is and most of the men who remain are so ill or so weakened that they are incapable of field service,' reported Hauptmann Carl von Reck, the senior remaining officer, on 5 January, 'We have lost all our horses and our effects, while the wagons with the officers' equipment, the regiment's cash box and all the records were taken by the enemy in the battle on the Berezina.'[71]

Other than the shattered remnants from Russia, therefore, at the beginning of 1813, Berg's military consisted of a lone infantry battalion (II/3, with 767 officers/men) and a depleted cavalry regiment (194 officers/men, approximately one squadron) in Spain as well as depot troops (501 officers/men) at home and a peripatetic cavalry squadron in central Germany.[72] This last unit, considered the 4th Squadron of the 1st Lancers, was under the command of Major August von Witzleben and had been sent east to reinforce the troops in Russia. Witzleben, with 203 officers and men fit for duty, reached the Oder by 24 December 1812, but does not seem to have crossed the river and had marched back across the Elbe by 1 February 1813. Napoleon, eager for cavalry, had wanted the squadron to join Eugène, but through confusion or perhaps ill will on Witzleben's part, it remained near Braunschweig for several weeks before returning to Berg in March.[73]

Indeed, all the Berg troops were recalled in 1813, but unlike other Rheinbund members, the grand duchy's contingent was not rebuilt to its pre-1812 size or configuration. The initial plan was to create a brigade of cavalry consisting of 2,500 men in ten squadrons, one infantry regiment and a battery of six guns. The task, however, was daunting as only 1,282 of the planned 4,360 men and less than half of the required 2,862 horses were available in the first months of the year. The situation with artillery pieces and vehicles was no better.[74] A new 1st Infantry Regiment was indeed formed by combining depot troops with the battalion returned from Spain (II/3), but this was immediately dispatched to Cherbourg in France where it arrived on 29 May with 1,468 effectives. Here it was accused of mistreating the city's inhabitants and French troops of the garrison over the summer. Tensions mounted, several unseemly incidents occurred and, more importantly, unsubstantiated rumours flew about, prompting a detailed investigation by GB Marie Charles César Florimond de Fay, comte de Latour-Maubourg (elder brother of the famed cavalry commander). The French reports on these frictions, however, not only exonerated the Berg regiment but heaped praise on the troops and officers 'of this fine unit' for their discipline and their 'severe exactitude' in the performance of their duties. The regiment, concluded Latour-Maubourg, 'is worthy of the complete confidence of the Emperor and King'.[75] By early August, these problems had been resolved ('The quarrel has been entirely calmed ... and seems to have been forgotten by both sides,' reported the regimental commander), and the regiment continued to serve to the satisfaction of its French superiors until it was disarmed and interned in December.[76] The 2nd Battalion was even credited with rounding up 500 French deserters and draft dodgers in Normandy. Curiously, therefore, troops who had been relegated to garrison duty in France for fear they would desert, earned an enviable reputation in their final months of French service.[77] A third infantry battalion (I/2nd Infantry) was created in mid-August 1813, but it and the depot were marched off to Montmédy in eastern France in November. They too were disarmed by the French late in the year after the Allies had occupied Berg. As a result, no Berg infantry took part in the 1813 campaigns in Germany.[78]

A key reason for the unusual treatment of the Berg contingent when Napoleon was desperately seeking soldiers lay in mistrust of Berg following a series of violent protests in early 1813. These disturbances had their roots in the economic distress and the rapid socio-political change associated with the French-installed government, but conscription was the catalyst.[79] With Napoleon's power seemingly broken across the Niemen and exaggerated rumours circulating of Russian victories, an expectation grew among the disadvantaged that the tsar's troops would soon be marching into the grand duchy. Jobless men and other angry souls began to gather secretly in forests, some using for themselves the sobriquet of 'Russian headquarters'. When violence erupted these bands of men thus acquired the nickname 'Knüppelrussen' ('cudgel Russians' or 'truncheon Russians') because they were mostly armed with sticks, iron rods and similar bludgeons, or 'Speckrussen' ('bacon Russians') because they were believed to dine principally on *Sauerkraut* and German bacon (*Speck*).[80]

Protests broke out more or less spontaneously in late January when Berg officials attempted to conduct the latest conscription drive. The unrest spread quickly with mobs of hungry, unemployed men threatening local officials, vandalising public and private property, attacking tobacco and salt magazines, attempting to destroy conscription records, and often simply indulging in opportunistic looting. Deserters and conscripts were frequently prominent among the rioters and inebriation was a common feature in many instances. In the words of one early twentieth-century historian of these riots, 'they arose in only a very few cases from feelings of love for the [pan-German] fatherland; most participants were driven by desperation and the hope that, having nothing to lose, they might have something to gain in the confusion or at least to eat their fill in the looted bakeries and butcher shops'.[81] 'Political convictions or motives, on the other hand, usually did not inspire the riots,' writes 21st-century scholar Bettina Severn-Barboutie, 'The idea of the nation does not appear anywhere.'[82]

One magistrate called the rioters 'a ragtag gang of true riffraff without a proper leader', but their rampages were also expressions of genuine discontent among some elements of the populace. As in Westphalia, there were distinct regional variations in the disturbances: while districts of the former Prussian Duchy of Berg were sorely afflicted, other portions of the grand duchy were untouched and government affairs (including conscription), though deeply unpopular, proceeded as usual. Moreover, many social strata were appalled by the chaos and destruction even if they had their own reasons to be unhappy with the French regime; many simply wanted a rapid return to peace and order. Overall, the danger to the state from unrest was likely exaggerated by officials who had not previously met such troubles. Beugnot, for one, remained agonisingly nervous until news of Lützen allowed him to put aside his fears about the stability of Berg and neighbouring Westphalia.[83] Though violence quickly exploded in many towns and villages, there was no coordination among the various groups of rioters, no sign of a widespread conspiracy.[84]

Whatever the inherent level of threat, however, the riots and protests generated alarm among the Berg authorities and quickly came to the emperor's attention.[85] Napoleon was furious and immediately sent GD Le Marois (the future governor of Magdeburg) to the grand duchy with 4,000–5,000 French troops and orders to 'Have all those who have been arrested brought before military commissions or special courts. Have five or six of the ringleaders shot, take hostages and, in short, halt this movement.'[86] On arriving in Berg on 3 February, Le Marois reported that the public mood was not good: 'HM is feared here but they completely detest everything that is French.'[87] He was not, however, overly concerned with 'these barely armed brigands who have neither chiefs nor organisation and do not defend themselves', and he executed his orders with what many in Berg considered pitiless precision.[88] Numerous arrests and a few executions swiftly put an end to the nascent insurrection. Beyond instilling distrust in Napoleon's mind, the chief consequence of this brief spasm of violence was the disruption of routine government business, especially conscription, and, as Beugnot noted, a gradual destabilisation and loss of state authority.[89] As one cavalry officer returning from Spain recalled: 'We had hardly arrived in Düsseldorf when recruiting began again, but this time under far more trying circumstances than before as unrest had broken out in a number of places in the land of Berg.'[90] Draft evasion and desertion notwithstanding, the grand duchy would continue to supply its quota of cavalrymen and gunners until late October.

Although the grand duchy's infantry was stationed in France in 1813 owing to concerns about its reliability, Berg contributed a horse artillery battery and a large cavalry regiment to the Grande Armée in Germany.[91] There were 18 officers and 177 men in the artillery depot in April, and these were formed into a horse battery that took to the field during the summer armistice. The gunners were dressed in typical artillery fashion with dark blue jackets featuring red collars and red trim around their dark blue lapels, along with black shakos and either grey riding trousers or dark blue breeches tucked into black, Hungarian-style boots with red tassels. Their comrades in the train were likewise typical of the era: light grey jackets with light blue trim, black shakos and grey riding trousers with black leather inserts. With six guns (four 6-pounders and two howitzers) and 219 officers and men, the battery passed through Leipzig to reach Dresden on 19 July. Here it was assigned to the Imperial Guard artillery under GD Charles Antoine Dulauloy and served in that capacity throughout the autumn campaigns, sometimes detached to the Guard cavalry, but suffering significant losses in draft horses. There were still 168 men present under arms in October when the battery rolled towards Leipzig, but the subsequent fate of the gunners and their guns is unknown.[92] The few remaining troops and much of the equipment back in the depot were evacuated to Montmédy in November when the French withdrew across the Rhine. This handful of men was disarmed in December and the equipment was transferred to the French artillery.[93]

The renowned Berg cavalry was also assigned to the Imperial Guard in 1813, upholding a reputation for courage and competence acquired over many years of imperial service.[94] Formed in 1807 as 'Chevaulegers du Grande Duc de Berg' under Murat, the initial regiment became the 'Chasseurs-à-Cheval du Grande Duché de Berg' in 1808 before being equipped with lances and rebranded as the 'Lanciers du Grande Duché de Berg' in 1809.[95] As lancers, the men were dressed in a handsome Polish-style uniform typical of that arm across Europe featuring dark green coats with amaranth or rose lapels, collars and cuffs, dark green or grey riding trousers and a rose-topped Polish czapka of black leather. They fought with distinction in Spain, becoming the 1st Berg Lancers when a second regiment was formed for the attack on Russia. Wearing identical uniforms to their compatriots, the 2nd Lancers also earned the respect of their French commanders during their bitter sojourn across the Niemen.

In addition to doubts about the reliability of the Berg troops, the other reason for the contingent's unusual employment in 1813 was the Grande Armée's urgent need for cavalry. Given his weakness in this arm and his favourable impression of the Berg Lancers, it is not surprising that Napoleon called for the grand duchy to produce a new unit of ten squadrons of 250 men each, to be commanded by GB Travers. The French referred to this unit as 'the Brigade of Berg Lancers' in the early weeks of 1813 because there were still nominally two Berg lancer regiments. The 'brigade' designation remained in official documents until the Berg troops were disarmed in December, but the unit was known as and functioned as a regiment when its constituent elements joined the Grande Armée. Whatever title was applied to these squadrons, Berg focused on meeting the emperor's extensive expectations for mounted troops for employment in Germany while its lone infantry regiment was shunted off to distant Cherbourg.

Major von Witzleben's squadron formed the nucleus of the new regiment. All the typical impediments hindered progress. A 10 March report, for example, noted that, 'The need for officers and NCOs is keenly felt,' and expressed concerns about the lack of experience, deficiencies in training and low morale among the recruits. A month later, the war minister complained about the poor horses he had received from the contracted broker and warned that the available men were 'far from being in a state to face the enemy'.[96] Nonetheless, although the total desired by Napoleon was never attained, a provisional squadron of 254 officers and men was assembled in the depot under Witzleben. Having annoyed Napoleon by not joining Eugène in February, it met up with his Army of the Main near Weimar in late April instead.[97] Partly in acknowledgement of their bravery in previous conflicts and partly because he was the regent of Berg, Napoleon brigaded the Berg Lancers with the Imperial Guard, an honour that would remain theirs throughout 1813.[98]

This initial unit became known as the 1st Squadron and had its first engagements on 29 April and 1 May near Weißenfels, taking 31 casualties from artillery fire as it manoeuvred with Souham's division and being close enough to Marshal Bessières to see him killed by a Russian cannon ball on the latter day. It suffered additional losses but performed well at Lützen the following day even though Witzleben defected to the Allies just before the battle.[99] The lancers escorted Napoleon during the pursuit to Dresden, paraded with the rest of the Guard to welcome the return of Saxony's king on 12 May, and accompanied the emperor when he travelled to Bautzen several days later. The Berg troopers were not engaged at Bautzen but participated in the lively cavalry combat around Reichenbach on 22 May, losing 19 men in the process but gaining commendations along with six awards of the Legion of Honour from Napoleon.[100] This would be the squadron's last battle during the spring campaign. By this time, losses in men and horses had reduced it to approximately 150 present under arms, in part because the squadron, above and beyond its losses to fatigue and combat, had had to give up more than 170 horses to the Polish Lancers of the Guard.[101] In this diminished state, it participated in the pursuit into Silesia without further action and went into cantonments near Görlitz with the rest of the Guard when the armistice was declared.

Desertion had proven a problem during the first weeks of the regiment's existence. It lost 210 men to this cause from early March to early May, approximately 14 per cent of an overall strength of some 1,500 as of 22 May. The timing of the desertions, however, is notable. Over half of these men fled before the regiment left its depot in late April, followed by nearly 100 more up to 8 May. Thereafter the problem quickly subsided, and the lancers only reported six deserters for the second half of May up to the armistice. The 1st Berg Infantry had a similar experience with desertion as it marched through Belgium towards Cherbourg: first losing a substantial number of men but then settling into a steady, reliable performance. This is hardly a conclusive data set, but it lends solidity to the comments Kösterus made about the Hessian troops early in the war: that the ranks were no longer thinned once 'those despicables who deserted out of fear were gone'.[102]

The regiment was rebuilt during the armistice with the arrival of the 3rd and 4th Squadrons from home. Reaching Dresden by 1 June, these two squadrons numbered 458 officers and men including 176 who had returned from Spain. The presence of these veterans from Spain and a number who had survived the Russian campaign meant that the regiment had something of an advantage in training and experience as compared to many of the other Guard regiments. These men proved invaluable, for example, in instructing the new recruits in combat manoeuvres, target practice, fieldcraft and the difficult art of employing the lance. Major Ludwig von Toll, who had replaced the absconding Witzleben in command, expressed concern at the condition of the exhausted 1st Squadron, but was very pleased with the other two. 'The officers continue to perfect themselves in their duties, they display great activity and conduct themselves well,' he reported, while the troops, 'though not as good as those I commanded in Spain,' were animated by 'good spirit and they comport themselves well'.[103] These reinforcements meant that there were 586 officers and men present in three squadrons (1st, 3rd and 4th) when Napoleon inspected them on 10 August. The emperor accorded them the signal honour of a placing on the right of the line during the review and congratulated the regiment for its valorous behaviour in Spain.[104] An additional squadron (the 5th) soon arrived so that four were present at the Battle of Dresden. By this time, Napoleon had reduced the 'brigade' from ten to six field squadrons plus a depot, but he wanted the remaining two (2nd and 6th) dispatched as soon as possible along with a replacement detachment to bring the existing squadrons up to strength. The 6th was thus en route when hostilities resumed to bring the total number of lancers in the theatre of war to more than 1,000.[105]

The Berg Lancers remained an integral element of the Guard cavalry for the rest of the war. They came under the command of GB Édouard Colbert who told Napoleon that he considered them 'an elite unit, men and horses know how to make war'.[106] Spectators at the Battle of Dresden on 26–27 August in a strength of four squadrons, the regiment was caught in an ambush by Prussian and Austrian cavalry at Possendorf 9 kilometres south of the city during the pursuit on the 28th. The morning was foggy, and the lancers may have advanced too impetuously. They were taken by surprise when they were suddenly fired upon by Austrian Jägers then charged and completely overthrown by the enemy horse. The regiment lost 169 killed or wounded and 112 taken prisoner in this disheartening episode as against very limited Allied casualties.[107] On the other hand, the regiment did well in clashes along the Bohemian frontier and east of Dresden during September as Napoleon sought vainly to bring one of the Allied armies to battle.[108]

The Berg Lancers, 448 strong, arrived at Leipzig on 14 October with the rest of the Guard and bivouacked near Probstheida that night. The next day passed quietly, but the regiment was heavily engaged on the 16th, losing 60 men in the great cavalry charges that marked the sub-battle of Wachau that day. That very evening, however, a fresh squadron of new recruits arrived to bring the regiment back to more than 500 officers and men in the saddle.[109] There was only some desultory artillery fire to mark the lull on the 17th and the regiment spent most of 18 October south of Connewitz, skirmishing with Austrian hussars and watching spent cannon balls knock the heads off cabbages as they rolled through nearby gardens. The Austrians were making occasional attempts to push north and apparently endeavoured to persuade the lancers to change sides but received only negative replies.[110] GB Travers praised the regiment for its 'bravery and devotion' in his report, asserting that it had fought stoutly and 'performed great services for the infantry during the retreat'.[111] That evening, however, the lancers suffered badly when it came their turn to join the army's general withdrawal towards Leipzig. They were riding north on the lone street through Connewitz around 8:00 p.m., when a flurry of musket shots rang out – Austrian infantry had crept into the village after the Poles occupying it had retreated. With the regiment confined in the narrow street, all order was lost and the men, many of them brand new recruits, rode madly north to escape the galling gauntlet of fire. At least 16 officers were killed or wounded, and approximately 160 troopers lost before the regiment was able to reassemble itself just outside the Leipzig suburbs.

After a grim night with little sustenance for man or horse, the regiment was arrayed near the Pleißenburg bastion as part of Poniatowski's command for the defence of the city on 19 October. The prince himself twice led them against the approaching Allies but these charges brought only temporary relief and, as the morning edged towards midday, the lancers found themselves near the Reichelsgarten with their backs to the Elster River (Map 43). Poniatowski had ordered another desperate charge when a thunderous detonation announced the destruction of the Elster bridge. Chaos ensued as the Berg troopers sought to escape over the flooded river alongside the Poles. All could have been saved, reported Travers, if the bridges had not been cut and the retreat intercepted by a column of Prussian infantry. After arriving at the banks of the river, some succeeded in crossing over, but many, not knowing how to swim, could not bring themselves to leap in, others drowned in the attempt, and those left behind were taken prisoner or 'killed by the bayonets of the enemy infantry'.[112]

The disaster at Leipzig was not quite the end of the Berg Lancers. Roughly 100 had escaped the defeat and officers collected another 130 or so who had been serving as orderlies and couriers for French generals (most with Marshal Marmont). These made their way through Thuringia as part of the Grande Armée's dolorous retreat, losing some of their number to angry villagers, roving Cossacks, and desertion as they headed west. A few officers and men were thus still loyally riding with the emperor as the army struggled towards the Rhine and these fought in the Battle of Hanau. When the army retreated across the Rhine in the wake of that battle, however, many deserted or fell into Allied hands (arousing disgust among those who stayed loyal).[113] Nonetheless, some 64 officers and men ended up in the garrison of Mainz where they served faithfully until the fortress surrendered in April 1814. Curiously, in this case the Berg troopers were opposed by their former countrymen as the Allies had committed freshly organised Berg troops to the Coalition's blockade force. The other remnants of the regiment continued into France where they were united with the regimental depot and the infantry depot, both of which had also shifted to Montmédy. A total of 386 cavalrymen were assembled here by mid-November, but the horses were all in poor condition and fewer than 100 of the men were armed and fit for service. Moreover, Travers recommended that they should be sent to Spain as they would desert 'all at once' if employed near the Rhine.[114] All were disarmed at the end of December and held as prisoners of war until Napoleon's abdication in 1814. While thoroughly understandable from the French point of view, this treatment left many of the Berg officers bitterly indignant after years of loyal service to the emperor.[115]

If piqued by the treatment they had received from the French, the officers found the reaction back in Berg little better when they returned in May 1814:

> The land of Berg was provisionally administered by a civil governor, Justus Gruner, in the name of the high Allies. Everything here had changed so much that we were seen as foreigners in our own fatherland, even cursed as traitors. Many civilian officials who had earlier praised the French regime to the heavens, were now suddenly disgusted with all things French and were denouncing us poor fellows as arch-French. In short, we were quite poorly received and miserably treated *because we had served France*, even though this rationale seemed utterly ridiculous since we were really as innocent as children in this transfer to France. We had only done our duty, but these Sir Bureaucrats did not want to recognise that faithful performance of duty under all circumstances is a virtue of the soldier.[116]

Thus ended the army of the Grand Duchy of Berg. Though the French mistrusted the infantry regiment and relegated it to garrison duty far away, the artillery battery seems to have served faithfully and the attitude towards the Berg cavalry was entirely different. Despite unrest at home, the lancer regiment was regarded as reliable and the grand duchy's bureaucracy kept producing new troopers through late October while the squadrons in the field, attached to the Imperial Guard, served with distinction until the end and beyond.

The Saxon Duchies: 'Where is your Contingent?'

Among the mélange of microstates nestled within the hills and forests of Thuringia were five small monarchies known collectively as the 'Saxon Duchies'. Where Friedrich August of Saxony was descended from Albertine branch of the Wettins, these five were ruled by offshoots of the family's Ernestine branch: Sachsen-Weimar-Eisenach, Sachsen-Gotha-Altenburg, Sachsen-Meiningen, Sachsen-Hildburghausen, and Sachsen-Coburg-Saalfeld. Each of these miniature monarchies was distinct, each sought to assert its rights or even primacy within the Ernestine branch of the family, and each of the rulers had his own history and interests.[117] While some, such as August of Sachsen-Gotha-Altenburg, admired Napoleon, others had fought against him. Carl August of Sachsen-Weimar who had led a division of the Prussian army during the 1806 campaign as a *General-Leutnant* was one of the latter, as was Ernst I of Sachsen-

Chart 49: Microstate Monarchs, 1813

State	Ruler
Duchy of Sachsen-Weimar-Eisenach	Herzog Carl August
Duchy of Sachsen-Gotha-Altenburg	Herzog Emil Leopold August
Duchy of Sachsen-Meiningen	Herzogin Louise Eleonore (regent)
Duchy of Sachsen-Hildburghausen	Herzog Friedrich
Duchy of Sachsen-Coburg-Saalfeld	Herzog Ernst Anton Karl Ludwig (Ernst I)
Duchy of Anhalt-Bernburg	Herzog Alexius Friedrich Christian
Duchy of Anhalt-Dessau	Herzog Leopold III
Duchy of Anhalt-Köthen	Herzog Ludwig Augustus (Leopold III regent)
Principality of Schwarzburg-Rudolstadt	Fürstin Caroline Louise (regent)
Principality of Schwarzburg-Sondershausen	Fürst Günther Friedrich Carl I
Principality of Waldeck	Fürst Georg I, died 9 Sept. 1813, then Georg II
Principality of Lippe-Detmold	Fürstin Pauline Christine (regent)
Principality of Schaumburg-Lippe	Fürst Georg Wilhelm
Principality of Reuß-Greiz (senior line)	Fürst Heinrich XIII
Principality of Reuß-Ebersdorf (junior line)	Fürst Heinrich LI
Principality of Reuß-Lobenstein (junior line)	Fürst Heinrich LIV
Principality of Reuß-Schleiz (junior line)	Fürst Heinrich XLII

Note: all male members of the House of Reuß (senior and junior) were named 'Heinrich', in honour of Holy Roman Emperor Heinrich VI (1165–1197), who had assisted the family during his reign.

Coburg who had been a supernumerary at Prussian headquarters as that year.[118] All, however, saw no option but to preserve their thrones and possessions by joining the Rheinbund through the Treaty of Posen in December 1806.[119]

Adherence to Napoleon's Germanic alliance, of course, meant all five of the duchies were obligated to provide soldiers. Each duchy was responsible for raising and equipping its own small contingent, but these were then combined into a single regiment of three battalions designated the 4th Rheinbund. Overall organisational direction of military affairs resided with either Weimar or Gotha on a rotating basis (in 1813, it was Gotha's turn), and the regiment developed as one of the best of the German formations despite the diversity of its composition. It saw its debut as a French ally at the Siege of Kolberg in the spring of 1807, fought in the vicious insurgency in the Tyrol in 1809 and, as with all the other units sent to Spain, suffered heavy losses in Catalonia from 1810 to early 1811. Re-formed for the invasion of Russia, it was committed to the campaign in December as part of the 34th Division and saw only limited combat, but enemy action, cold and sickness reduced it to a fraction of its initial strength. Like the rest of that ill-starred division, its remnants (349 officers and men) were allotted to the garrison of Danzig and would see out their time as French allies in the gruelling siege of the city.

Through these many campaigns, the 4th Rheinbund acquired a reputation for professionalism, courage and competence, in no small part thanks to the qualities of the regimental commander, Oberst von Egloffstein. Differences among the five duchies notwithstanding, the regiment was also a cohesive combat organisation. At the same time, the officers and men were intimately conscious of their origins: such as the home state of each officer or how many soldiers were contributed by one duchy versus another. The variety of uniforms within the regiment was emblematic of this persistent differentiation. The contingents of Weimar and Hildburghausen, for example, wore dark blue coats with red collars, cuffs and lapels over dark blue pantaloons. The coat colour of the other three duchies was dark green, but there were variations here as well. While Weimar and Hildburghausen featured yellow collar patches and coat turnbacks with grey trousers, Coburg was unique in having yellow collars and cuffs on their dark green coats and light blue breeches of a tight, Hungarian cut with decorative yellow knots sewn on the fronts. Furthermore, the leather equipment for Weimar and Hildburghausen was black while the others were issued white crossbelts for their cartridge boxes and bayonets. In part to account for these uniform variations, the regiment was organised into three battalions for the invasion of Russia: a light battalion composed of men from Weimar and Hildburghausen, and two line battalions (1st and 2nd) made up of men from the other three duchies. The Light (or 3rd) Battalion was thus at least consistent in the dark green colour of its coats, but the other two battalions each had a company of green-jacketed soldiers from Coburg along with the blue-uniformed troops from Gotha and Meiningen. These Coburg contingents were designated as the voltigeur or light infantry companies of their respective battalions. Although most of the men had black shakos, the two grenadier companies (one for each line battalion) and the carabinier company of the Light Battalion wore tall bearskin caps to signify their elite status. These, at least, were the prescribed uniforms for 1812; how far such niceties could be observed in the turmoil and urgency of 1813, however, is unclear.

They Allowed their Contingent to be Taken[120]

With the remnants of the 4th Rheinbund behind the walls of distant Danzig, the five duchies struggled to respond to Napoleon's demand for new contingents. As with all the other Confederation states, the challenge of finding adequate officers was especially daunting. 'We have raised successively a number of conscripts who can be trained by the small number of officers and NCOs who find themselves at the depot in Weimar,' wrote one of Carl August's officials to the French ambassador on 30 March.[121] These men were hardly ready to take the field, but Major Johann August Ludwig von Linker (or Lynker) of Weimar was designated to form a new battalion (termed a *bataillon de marche* or 'march battalion') as an initial measure to placate the emperor.[122] By 3 April, Linker had assembled four companies with 428 officers and men in and around the village of Ruhla, 10 kilometres southeast of Eisenach. These represented the first contributions from Gotha, Weimar, Meiningen and Hildburghausen with more to come, especially the Coburg contingent. The organising, training and equipping of these green recruits, however, would soon be interrupted.

As described earlier, the Allies pushed multiple cavalry and Cossack forces into Westphalia and Thuringia after crossing the Elbe in late March. 'General Blücher had advanced up to Altenburg and small detachments of his light cavalry were already swarming as far as the Thuringian Forest [Thüringerwald],' recalled Friedrich von Müller, a privy councillor in Weimar, 'It seemed as if a great part of Blücher's army corps would arrive in Jena and the Saale valley in the next few days.'[123] Müller's recollections reflected the prevailing anxieties at the time, but Blücher was not on the verge of an immediate drive westward with his main body. The many scouting detachments that he and Wittgenstein sent out, however, inflicted many ignominies on the half-formed Rheinbund troops in the region in mid-April: Hellwig snatched most of Bavarian General von Rechberg's guns at Langensalza on the 13th (Chapter 3) and dispersed Westphalian units at Wanfried four days later, while Löwenstern's Cossacks broke a Westphalian squadron near Nordhausen on the 15th as related in Chapter 6. The Saxon Duchies suffered similar embarrassments. Saint-Aignan, Napoleon's ambassador to the five dukes, barely escaped capture when Prussian hussars raided Gotha on the night of 11/12 April, for example, but the hussars seized his secretary and most of his embassy's papers.[124] Worse was to come the next day.

Among the Prussian units operating in Thuringia that April were the Brandenburg and 1st Silesian Hussars. It was a patrol of Brandenburg troopers that almost captured Saint-Aignan at Gotha, while a detachment of the 1st Silesians probed further west under Leutnant Friedrich Graf von Pinto.[125] Major Franz von Blücher, Pinto's commander, comfortably ensconced at Weimar, sent the lieutenant to reconnoitre towards Eisenach on 12 April with a detachment of between 20 and 50 hussars and mounted Jägers. With information provided by eager villagers and details garnered from several ducal soldiers he had been lucky enough to capture, Pinto learned that Linker was forming his new battalion around Ruhla. He decided to disrupt the proceedings. Thanks to local guides, he and his tiny detachment were able to sneak to within striking distance of Ruhla by late afternoon of 13 April.[126] The Prussians waited till near dusk, then dashed into the little town just as the unarmed ducal troops were returning to their billets from their evening rollcall. Linker had established no local security, claiming later that he believed himself safe given the French garrison in Erfurt, Bavarian troops on his right and the French army approaching from the Rhine.[127] The result was total surprise.[128] The shocked and weaponless soldiers offered no resistance and Pinto, hurrying to Linker's quarters, quickly concluded an agreement with the Weimar major whereby the entire battalion would be disarmed and treated as prisoners of war pending Herzog Carl August's approval.[129] With the troops in Ruhla neutralised, Pinto and Linker rode to two other nearby villages to convey the capitulation to the rest of the battalion, apparently telling the other officers that a Russian advance guard of 1,600 men was only 40 kilometres off to the east.[130] After some doubts and debate, the other officers accepted Linker's lead and the entire battalion marched off to putative captivity escorted by the Prussian hussars. The Military Commission in Gotha, alarmed by the raid on their city and reports of additional enemy cavalry in the vicinity, had tried to warn Linker, but the courier arrived an hour after Pinto. 'Now it is too late,' remarked Pinto when Linker handed him the commission's message.[131]

Rather than remain prisoners of war, the captives were easily persuaded to take Prussian service and they continued to Altenburg where General Blücher heartily urged them to 'help us whip the French'.[132] Illustrating the importance of leadership, the soldiers apparently replied 'If our officers have taken service, then we will also stay with them and serve with the Prussians', when Blücher asked if they wished to enter Prussian service or continue as prisoners.[133] A review by Tsar Alexander and König Friedrich Wilhelm III followed several days later as what became known as the 'Thuringian Battalion' passed through Dresden en route to Glogau where it was assigned to the Prussian blockade force. Incorporated into Yorck's I Prussian Corps during the armistice, the battalion fought at the Katzbach, Wartenburg and Möckern, its surviving members finally returning home late in the year when Weimar changed sides.[134]

Linker's defection placed Carl August in an awkward position, but it also highlighted his ambiguous attitude. On the one hand, Linker was a Weimar officer and the battalion had been quartered in Weimar territory, so Napoleon's attention naturally focused on Weimar's duke, who had, after all, served as a senior Prussian general against the French in 1806 and whose pro-Prussian outlook was well known.[135] Moreover, as unwanted as Linker's defection was, Carl August had elected not to evacuate his capital when the Allies advanced; instead, the enemy had been welcomed in his lands. One resident of Weimar, for example, wrote how the Prussians 'were entertained to the uttermost' and the population 'energetically danced and drank through the afternoon and evening until late in the night' with them. Major von Blücher himself was wont to dine at the ducal palace in Weimar and apparently paid a visit to the pro-Napoleon Herzog August in Gotha as well.[136] Indeed, he was seated at lunch in Weimar's palace on 18 April and had to hasten away when a rider galloped up to report that GD Souham's advance guard (the French 10th Hussars and Baden Light Dragoons) was approaching. Similarly, Pinto rode to Weimar on 14 April and met the duke to ask that he approve the capitulation Linker had signed. Carl August refused and simply told Pinto to handle the captives according to the rules of war, but his behaviour and the easy access the Prussians enjoyed validated French preconceptions regarding his loyalty to the Confederation.[137]

French mistrust deepened when Karl Freiherr von Müffling, one of Carl August's closest advisors, fled the Weimar court in mid-April after attending the meeting with Pinto. Müffling, a well-known former Prussian officer who had served under Carl August in 1806, resumed his place in the Prussian army as an *Oberstleutnant* and prominent voice on Blücher's staff.[138] From Napoleon's perspective, such developments were hardly consistent with the stance to be expected of a Rheinbund ally. Reading Saint-Aignan's report of events, he told his ambassador on 20 April to return to Gotha and Weimar as soon as possible and inform the respective dukes that he 'was surprised that they allowed their contingent to be taken and that they stayed in their countries while they were occupied by the Russians'.[139]

The emperor's choler was in full evidence when he met Friedrich von Müller and Christian Friedrich Carl von Wolfskeel, Carl August's emissaries, in Erfurt on the 26th. Müller had gained an audience in an effort to secure the release of two senior Weimar officials whom Souham had arrested on suspicion of espionage, but he knew that the subject of the surrendered battalion and doubts of Weimar's loyalty would be foremost in Napoleon's mind:

> I will never forget the moment when the double doors of that large bay-windowed room in the town hall opened, and the Emperor Napoleon in his green chasseur uniform approached me with slow steps and, calmly but with his eyebrows drawn together in grim displeasure, addressed me with the laconic question: 'Where is your contingent?'[140]

There followed a torrent of imperial anger as Napoleon vented his convictions and suspicions vis-à-vis Weimar and threatened to punish the duchy for the welcome it gave the Prussians and its widespread anti-French sentiments. He was especially incensed that students from the Jena University had allegedly dressed as Cossacks to spread alarm among Durutte's battered division when it passed through the city. Müller answered as best he could and, finally released from the emperor's wrath, hastened back to Weimar where he persuaded Carl August to travel to Erfurt that very night. The duke's interview with the emperor went well and Napoleon called on Carl August and his wife (whom he admired) as he travelled through Weimar on 28 April. He immediately acceded to the duchess's request that the two officials be released and met a deputation from the Jena University that had come to plead for clemency; although he issued stern warnings to the anxious committeemen, he took no punitive actions against the city or university. Napoleon also used the opportunity to have Carl August write to Saxony's Friedrich August, urging the king to leave Prague and return to Dresden, 'which the Emperor of Russia and the King of Prussia have already left as of this very moment or will leave in a few days'. 'Besides which,' he told the duke, 'it would pain me to have to treat his states as enemy territory.'[141] As described in Chapter 2, this letter would be a key factor in bringing Saxony back into compliance with its Rheinbund obligations. Carl August then accompanied the imperial entourage to Eckartsberga where he dined with Napoleon and Berthier before returning to Weimar that night.

The war then flowed to Lützen, Dresden, Bautzen and beyond, leaving the Saxon Duchies to enjoy a temporary reprieve from direct imperial attention. Napoleon, of course, did not forget either Linker's defection or the contingent the five states owed as members of the Confederation. He also attributed many of the army's rear-area security problems to what he believed to be the permissive attitude of the Saxon Duchies. He thus instructed Maret on 24 May to 'write to Baron Saint-Aignan so that he makes known to the dukes of Gotha and Weimar that they have to re-form their contingent, and that they arm their towns, so that they are safe from the enemy partisans and that they prevent the Prussian raiders from doing any harm to the country and to the French army'. The following day, he added a further injunction: Saint-Aignan was to send notes 'in the strongest terms to the various princes to which he is accredited, to inform them of my discontent that some of the partisans who commit brigandage in the army's rear are supported in their states,' and 'that I hold them responsible' for 'purging the countryside'. 'Should this continue,' he concluded, 'I will eventually come to see ill will in these governments.'[142]

Further prodding came in June – pointedly directed at Weimar – with a public admonishment appearing in the *Journal de l'Empire* in early July and a private message for Saint-Aignan to convey to Carl August concerning Linker's defection: 'that the commander he had chosen has betrayed him, and that nevertheless I do not hear that he has taken action against him, nor has he shown any indignation about his conduct; that he must finally take care of the consequences of all this'.[143] The emperor's desire for a new composite regiment would eventually be fulfilled in August, but his hopes for improvements in the army's rear-area security or more favourable sentiments among the Thuringian populations would be disappointed.

As for Linker, a special military commission in Gotha (because Herzog August held overall direction of military affairs in 1813) duly convicted him in absentia of surrendering his command without offering resistance. He was deprived of his rank, sentenced to twelve years' imprisonment (as soon as he was in custody), and required 'to reimburse all damages and costs caused by his behaviour'. The progress of events, of course, meant that none of these penalties was ever imposed and Linker would retire as a Sachsen-Weimar General-Major.[144]

The Saxon Duchies experienced additional, albeit lesser, military embarrassments between 4 and 6 June during Lützow's foray into Thuringia. As noted above, Napoleon's frustration with the Allied raiders plaguing the army's rear areas led him to order the Thuringian states to establish home guard forces that could deter the roving enemy detachments without detracting from the regular army. The emperor's orders were sent in late May and the microstates seem to have responded rapidly, probably drawing on existing militia ordinances and units. In Gotha's case, the *Herzog* issued his own instructions on the 26th so that by 4 June, Leutnant August Gotthelf von Tümpling was drilling a company of perhaps 120 of these new fencibles outside Roda (now Stadtroda) when a runner rushed up to announce that enemy troops were in the town. Tümpling had sent out patrols, but Lützow's men evaded detection and surprised the militia when the lieutenant, thinking the news a false alarm, marched them back into Roda. Quickly surrounded and intimidated, the militiamen were forced to surrender, many of them agreeing to join Lützow's band. Tümpling, on the other hand, refused Lützow's offers and even managed to obtain reasonable terms in negotiating the capitulation.[145] Details are lacking, but a similar scene played out in Schleiz on the 5th with Lützow capturing approximately 100 men. Though often described as 'Rheinbund contingent troops', these were in fact militia of the rawest variety who were just learning to load their muskets and may not have had live ammunition. Apparently augmented with deserters and other volunteers, they became Lützow's 'infantry' but they had a reputation as ill-disciplined pillagers and, as previously mentioned, they disappeared into the darkness at the first shots during the engagement at Kitzen eleven days later.

Armistice Antics

While the various Thuringian states were establishing their home guards and the military authorities in Gotha were deliberating on Linker's nominal fate during the armistice, Herzog Carl August of Weimar was playing a high-stakes political game. On the one hand, like Ferdinand of Würzburg, he used a month-long habitual visit to the Bohemian spa in Teplitz to meet Austrian Kaiser Franz. This occurred in mid-July before Austria had declared itself and it seems unlikely Franz divulged any secrets regarding his empire's future intentions during this cordial conversation and meal. Nonetheless, the holiday in Bohemia afforded Carl August an opportunity to solidify his personal connection to one of the leading powers of the day and the massive Habsburg military presence on Bohemia's border with Saxony could have left him in no doubt about the imminent renewal of hostilities, with Austria likely on the side of the Coalition. The duke also maintained covert contact with his former confidant Müffling in Blücher's headquarters, including a request that Müffling intercede with the tsar on behalf of Weimar's dynastic interests.[146]

At the same time, Carl August sought to expand his realm and elevate his status through his membership in the Rheinbund. Counting on Napoleon's ability to make drastic changes in Europe's political arrangements with a simple decree, he sent a deputation of several senior officials to imperial headquarters in Dresden in June. Part of their mission was to attain relief from the burdens Weimar suffered for sitting astride one of the Grande Armée's major lines of communication. This was certainly a genuine request, and his ministers pressed it as earnestly as they could, but they also used the duchy's distress as a tool to introduce the idea that enlarging Weimar's territory and granting their monarch a suitably higher rank (such as grand duke) would ease the provision of troops, supplies and other assistance to Napoleon's forces.

In addition to territorial gains, from Carl August's viewpoint, an elevated status would restore his Ernestine branch of the Wettin dynasty to its proper place among Europe's ruling houses after Napoleon had raised Saxony's Friedrich August of the Albertine branch to royal rank in 1806. Carl August could thus bring all of Thuringia under his sceptre as his ministers urged in a memorandum to Maret: 'the former Thuringia, which offers an infinite number of small governments, which, being constantly in unequal struggle with the exigencies of the times, only betray their weakness'. Placing all under Weimar, they argued, would tidy up this political mare's nest and improve administrative efficiency while placing the Ernestine Wettins on the same plane as the Albertines after losing the electoral post (in the Holy Roman Empire) to their Albertine cousins in 1547. Carl August himself appeared in Dresden on his way to Teplitz to make his case to the emperor. In the end, however, the duke was disappointed. Meetings with Napoleon and members of the imperial household did bring some marginal relief as far as French logistical demands were concerned, but the emperor had far more urgent matters to address that summer and Weimar's hopes for expansion and elevation went unfulfilled.[147]

Although Carl August's grandiose desires came to naught, this little episode illuminates several aspects of the quandaries faced by even the smallest states in 1813. First, they sought to straddle the divide between the belligerent powers, maintaining contacts with both sides to secure their futures regardless of the outcome of the war. In Carl August's case, this realpolitik approach was reinforced by his personal affinity for Prussia and his aversion to Napoleon. Second, repugnance towards the emperor and his policies notwithstanding, Carl August turned to Napoleon in the hope of increasing his realm and his rank among German states. Just as Bavaria, Württemberg, Baden and others coveted one another's lands and populations, Weimar endeavoured to enhance its position at the expense of its Thuringian neighbours. The acquisition of additional territory and the assumption of the title *Großherzog*, however, would not come until the Congress of Vienna when the tsar's influence decided the day in favour of at least some of Weimar's aspirations.

Ernst I of Sachsen-Coburg was another errant Confederation monarch playing multiple political games. Pro-Prussian in orientation, he also had connections to the Habsburgs and had quietly offered himself as a covert mediator between Prussia and Austria during the spring in an effort to cajole Vienna into joining the war against the French. He shifted closer to Austria during the summer as Metternich's policies seemed to offer better prospects of retaining his territory and sovereignty, but an open break with France was impossible for such a tiny state and his links to Vienna remained clandestine. Ernst thus continued to supply soldiers to the Grande Armée throughout the autumn campaigns despite his antipathy towards the Rheinbund.[148]

Battle at Hagelberg, Blockade at Magdeburg[149]

Carl August journeyed back to Weimar from Teplitz at the beginning of August as the armistice was coming to a close. While he had been attempting to cajole Napoleon into granting concessions and enlarging his domain, Weimar and the other four duchies were struggling to meet their troop commitments to the Confederation. Despite the losses in Russia and the awkward fact of having Linker and nearly 500 men fighting on the enemy side, they eventually managed to construct a new regiment during the armistice. There seems to have been little difficulty in conscripting new soldiers (there was little of the draft evasion prevalent in Westphalia), but with most of the veteran officers immured in Danzig, leadership was a serious deficiency. There were too few officers overall, many of those present had been recalled from retirement or had only recently been elevated to the officer ranks, and most were too junior for the positions they held. Many of the companies, for instance, were commanded by lieutenants rather than captains.

As one example, on returning from Russia, Oberleutnant Wilhelm Freiherr von Schauroth was astonished to encounter a brand-new lieutenant of the Weimar contingent, 'who a few weeks before had returned with me from Russian captivity as my servant. He had then been a sergeant, and here I found him as commander of a company.' Schauroth's Weimar acquaintance developed into a capable officer, but this was by no means the case with many of the others suddenly thrown forward to lead green recruits into combat. In the company Schauroth was tasked to raise, 'there was a complete dearth of experienced men and recruits were even used to fill leadership positions in the company; the lieutenant assigned to me was a government scribe'.[150]

Regardless of its leadership problems, by 7 August, the regiment was assembled in Jena with 2,417 officers and men divided among three battalions: two 'heavy' battalions (1st and 2nd) composed of men from Gotha, Meiningen and Coburg along with a light battalion (3rd Battalion) from the Weimar and Hildburghausen contingents. All three battalions were supposed to have five companies each, but the 2nd Coburg Company was still missing (this would become Schauroth's), so the 2nd Battalion embarked on the autumn campaign with only four. Commanded by Oberst Friedrich Wilhelm Leberecht von Münch of Gotha, the regiment marched off on 13 August to arrive in Magdeburg via Leipzig on the 19th.[151]

GD Le Marois, the French governor of Magdeburg, reviewed the regiment on the very day of its arrival at the fortress. Although it had lost some men to sickness and desertion,[152] it put on a tolerably good show. Münch reported that Le Marois received him with courteous professionalism and Le Marois told Berthier that the men appeared 'very well disposed'. The French general, however, was troubled by the lack of appropriate officers as the NCOs were all new and the troops were all recruits in need of instruction and supervision. The facile answer that the more senior and experienced officers of the duchies were serving in Danzig was hardly an acceptable explanation as far as Le Marois was concerned.[153] Moreover, he was dissatisfied with the regiment's organisation and immediately instituted two modifications. First, the internal structure of the regiment was altered with the 1st and 2nd Battalions (the 'heavy' or line infantry) being rearranged to align more closely with the French pattern: a grenadier company, a voltigeur company and four fusilier companies each for a total of approximately 600 officers and other ranks per battalion. He also instructed Münch to establish a depot. Second, as with the 9th Westphalian Infantry, Le Marois broke the regiment into two pieces. After deducting a lieutenant and 176 men to form the depot, he assigned the two line battalions to the fortifications on the east bank of the Elbe where they came under the command of GD Lanusse as part of the so-called '1st Magdeburg Division'.

Chart 50: Forces at Magdeburg, 15 September 1813
Governor: *GD Le Marois*

	bns/sqdns	Present under arms
Division *GD Lemoine*		
French infantry	6	4,821
3rd Bns of 11e Léger and 2e, 4e, 37e, 46e, 98e Ligne		
II/Spanish Joseph Napoleon Regiment	1	805
French mixed cavalry detachment	–	151
French artillery/train	–	293
Division *GD Girard (wounded), GD Lanusse*		
French infantry	6	2,823
3rd Bns of 24e Léger, 26e Léger and 18e, 19e, 56e, 72e Ligne		
Det. II/1st Provisional Croat Regiment	–	361
I/9th Westphalian Infantry Regiment	1	472
French artillery/train	–	97
French cavalry depots:	–	3,184
Garrison *GD Laurent*		
4th Provisional Carabinier Regiment	3	525
4th Demi-Brigade of Magdeburg	3	2,117
134e Ligne (III, V, VI)	3	1,959
Det. II/1st Provisional Croat Regiment	–	335
II/9th Westphalian Infantry Regiment	1	499
Saxon Duchies Regiment (4th Rheinbund)	2	1,429
Det. Reuß contingent	–	390
Det. Schwarzburg contingent	–	258
Det. Lippe contingent	–	104
Neapolitans and Italians	–	129
Artillery, artillery artisans and others		
French	–	479
Italian	–	63
Isolated individuals (artillery and artillery artisans)	–	214
Det. Imperial Guard Sailors	–	129
French sappers and miners	–	213
French equipment and artillery train depots	–	483
Convalescents	–	487
Isolated individuals (various units)	–	1,710
French gendarmes	–	10
Westphalian gendarmes	–	6
Total		24,546
Total Rheinbund (included above)		3,158

Note: the second Lippe company had not yet arrived. Lemoine was assigned to Magdeburg from Minden and arrived on 14 September.

Source: SHD, 2C551.

Though part of Le Marois' command, this division was distinct from the fortress garrison proper and was intended to be capable of operations in the field under the overall direction of GD Girard. Le Marois kept the Weimar/Hildburghausen light battalion separate, retaining it in the city as part of the formal garrison. These changes meant that only the two line battalions of the regiment would participate in the disaster at Hagelberg on 27 August.

These two Ducal Saxon battalions had only one day (20 August) to clothe, equip and organise their men and acquaint themselves with their new command before setting off on campaign.[154] As related earlier, GD Girard had been placed in command of Lanusse's Magdeburg Division and Dąbrowski's Polish division from Wittenberg with the task of supporting Oudinot's August thrust towards Berlin. He started east from Magdeburg on 21 August with Lanusse's troops (including the two Ducal Saxon battalions and the Westphalian I/9th Infantry or 'elite battalion'), hoping to link with Dąbrowski as he moved towards Oudinot.[155] This was not to be. With Cossacks swarming the countryside, Girard could neither communicate with his fellow commanders nor gather reliable intelligence on the enemy. With little knowledge of either friend or foe, he thus pushed cautiously eastward to bivouac in the area around Hagelberg just west of Belzig on 26 August, unaware that Oudinot was already retreating after the defeat at Großbeeren on the 23rd. He had already lost several hundred men in skirmishing with Cossacks and Prussian light troops on the 21st and in gruelling marches over the subsequent days. Stragglers were a particular problem as most of those left behind were swept up by ranging Cossack patrols or simply wended their ways homeward once they were sufficiently recovered from fatigue. The two Ducal Saxon battalions may have lost as many as 200 men in this fashion between 22 and 26 August.[156] Fourrier Johann Paul Sauerteig of Meiningen, for instance, turned up in his home duchy with seven others on 4 September and was called before a commission of inquiry to be questioned. Having collapsed from 'exhaustion and hunger' on the night of 21/22 August, he explained, he had met up with other stragglers, some of whom 'had been plundered by the Prussian peasants', crossed the Elbe and eventually returned home despite the danger of being charged with desertion.[157]

Girard's command was still encamped in and north of Hagelberg on the morning of 27 August, but local security was poor, and all attention was turned east towards Belzig where they had skirmished with Chernishev's Cossacks the previous day. The general and his men were thus surprised when GL von Hirschfeld's Prussians advanced to the attack from the north early in the afternoon. Prussian cavalry quickly overran much of the French bivouac and Girard's troops fell back in confusion, struggling to form squares as they did so. The infantry, however, were thrown into disorder when the inexperienced

French cavalry routed through the ranks of the equally inexperienced foot soldiers. 'They pulled back and rode right through the Saxon regiment,' recalled a Meiningen soldier, 'This [the regiment] wanted to defend itself against the attack by forming squares but fell into disorder because the attack was totally unexpected and occurred with great speed. It [the regiment] fell into total disorder.'[158] Cannon balls landing amongst the tightly packed squares heightened the confusion. The 2nd Battalion was especially shaken by the sudden attack and hasty withdrawal.[159]

In pouring rain that rendered muskets almost useless, Girard managed to rally his troops and launched a counterattack that regained lost ground and disorganised part of the Prussian force. It seems to have been at this point that he rode up to a Ducal Saxon square and encouraged the men in broken German: 'Allons, brav Sachs, die Preuß rettirir! En avant, en avant!'[160] His success, however, was temporary. Other elements of Hirschfeld's division resumed the attack, Chernishev's Cossacks appeared in the French rear, and Girard's command began to disintegrate. Throwing away their muskets, packs and other impedimenta, most of the men fled south towards Wittenberg in utter disorder, many falling into enemy hands after collapsing in exhaustion. Sergeant David Wilhelm described the concluding moments of battlefield chaos:

> The riders [French cavalry] pulled back through the Thuringian regiment and assembled behind it. The regiment also wanted to draw back but was shoved into a mass by the riders. Three times the regiment formed itself into square, three times it was broken apart by the enemy cavalry. During the last attack Prussian infantry also came at it from the rear. The entire division was broken up by cannon fire... The Cossacks pursued it and took everything.[161]

Fortunately for Girard and Lanusse, the Prussians were just as weary as their foes. Their fatigue, the rainy weather and approaching night limited the pursuit and allowed the badly wounded Girard and the remains of his ruined command to stumble back to Wittenberg and eventually to return to Magdeburg.

When the two Ducal Saxon battalions reached Magdeburg on 3 September, however, they were grievously diminished. Having started from the fortress with approximately 1,200 officers and men, Oberst von Münch was only able to collect 250 – perhaps as few as 150 – outside Wittenberg on 29 August. Out of about a thousand casualties, some 900 were listed as captured or missing as against 187 killed and wounded combined. Among the missing was the entire complement of drummers who had fled with the drum major early in the combat.[162] The lone Coburg company was also absent; its captain had surrendered his command or allowed it to be taken prisoner and it would soon take its place in the 7th Battalion of the Russo-German Legion.[163] The two battalions had thus been virtually destroyed during the course of Girard's brief expedition. Oberleutnant von Schauroth, who had arrived in Magdeburg with the missing company of Coburg troops in the interim, was reminded of his time as a Prussian officer in 1806 when his regiment had retreated to Magdeburg after the Battle of Jena as 'the fortress was filled to the breaking point in a few days by troops stripped of all weapons and resources'.[164]

The Hagelberg catastrophe necessitated a complete reorganisation of the Ducal Saxon Regiment. On his return to Magdeburg on 3 September, therefore, Münch was instructed to re-form the regiment in two battalions: the Light Battalion became the new 2nd Battalion, while the remnants of the two former line battalions were combined with the depot and Schauroth's newly arrived 2nd Coburg Company to rebuild the 1st. Incorporated into the Rheinbund brigade commanded by Westphalian GB von Langenschwarz, by mid-September the regiment totalled approximately 1,450 officers and men in its two battalions.[165]

With the Allies merely blockading Magdeburg, the Ducal Saxon soldiers saw no further action after Hagelberg, but as September waxed the number of sick began to rise. So too did the number of deserters. As was also the case with the Westphalians, desertion reached epidemic proportions in the wake of Leipzig with a total of 846 men leaving the ranks between 1 October and 12 November despite the best efforts of the officers.[166] Some of the absconders may have joined the Allies like the 1st Coburg Company at Hagelberg, but most simply went home like the soldiers cited above. This massive desertion left a mere 527 behind in Magdeburg, 164 of whom (31 per cent) were in hospital. No longer trusted, the Ducal Saxons and other Germans could only be employed in interior duties (such as preparing ammunition in magazines) or repairing fortifications.[167] These considerations and the regiment's rapidly diminishing numbers led Le Marois to release the remainder rather than deplete his limited stock of rations to feed unreliable formations. As related in Chapter 6, he thus held a review of all the Rheinbund contingents, including the Ducal Saxon troops, on the afternoon of 12 November. The men were to appear on the glacis of the fortress dressed only in their overcoats and ordinary uniforms, all personal items and other gear were to be left in the regiment's quarters. The reason for this unusual order was soon evident. Addressing the men, Le Marois offered them the option of either taking French service or returning to their home countries. Unsurprisingly, the entire body elected to march home and the other ranks were turned out of the fortress at once with the clothes on their backs and a limited supply of food. The officers were granted two days to consider the offer, but they also chose to return to their homelands after pledging not to take up arms against France for a period of one year (a pledge that was violated almost immediately).

Seven years of loyal and competent service thus came to a conclusion in a flurry of defections, desertions and a disgraceful battlefield disaster. With a few exceptions – most notably Major von Linker – the officers had attempted to perform their duties faithfully, but they were too few and too inexperienced to instil in their men the discipline, esprit and professional ethic necessary to meet the demands of this final, stressful campaign.

On the political front, by late November, all the duchies had abandoned the Rheinbund and joined Napoleon's enemies, thus preserving their monarchies into the early twentieth century. Even Napoleon's admirer, August of Gotha, had no choice after Cossacks appeared in his city and captured Napoleon's envoy Saint-Aignan on 22 October. A week later he and his subjects were offering festive displays while Austria's Kaiser transited the duchy heading for Frankfurt.[168] Weimar's Herzog Carl August and Coburg's Ernst I especially welcomed the Coalition victory and Weimar was pleased to host both Tsar Alexander and König Friedrich Wilhelm III when the Allied armies rolled west after Leipzig.[169] Appointed a General of Cavalry in Russian service, Carl August would campaign in the Netherlands in 1814 in command of III German Corps, a composite formation consisting of former Rheinbund troops from Saxony, Anhalt, Weimar, Gotha and Schwarzburg. His chief of staff would be Oberstleutnant Ernst Ludwig von Aster, the former Saxon officer now in Russian service, who had performed the same function for Thielmann in Torgau until May 1813. Similarly, Ernst I of Coburg would be appointed to command V German Corps composed of Berg, Saxon and former Westphalian troops assigned to the blockade of Mainz (Lippe units would later come under his command as well).

The Anhalt Duchies: In Battle for Both Sides

Wedged between the Kingdoms of Westphalia, Prussia and Saxony were the three small duchies of Anhalt-Bernburg, Anhalt-Dessau and Anhalt-Köthen. All three had joined the Rheinbund through the Treaty of Warsaw in April 1807, a step which elevated the rulers of Dessau and Köthen to reigning dukes (in one of his last acts as Holy Roman Emperor, Austria's Kaiser Franz had declared Anhalt-Bernburg a dukedom in 1806). Herzog Leopold III, 73 years old, of Anhalt-Dessau was the head of the house and also served as regent for the 11-year-old Ludwig Augustus of Anhalt-Köthen, but each state was sovereign in its own right and managed its own internal affairs; Anhalt-Köthen, for instance, introduced numerous unique domestic reforms in 1811, including – albeit very briefly – an adaptation of the *Code Napoléon*.

The three duchies combined their Rheinbund contingents to create a single unit, the 1st Battalion of the 5th Rheinbund Regiment (Lippe supplied the 2nd Battalion) with Dessau providing general oversight of joint military affairs. The men were issued a handsome uniform featuring a dark green jacket trimmed in dark rose, dark grey breeches, black gaiters, black shakos and, unusual for the time, black leather cross-belts for their bayonets and cartridge boxes. The battalion had served in the Tyrol during the 1809 war against Austria, had been nearly annihilated in Catalonia in 1810 and was destroyed again when it was among the units called upon to cover the Grande Armée's frozen retreat in late 1812 as part of the French 34th Division. Like the rest of that ill-fated formation, the Anhalt battalion rapidly faded away from combat, desertion and mostly from sickness or cold, with only some 250 shocked survivors making their way to Danzig as the year came to an end (*see* Chapter 8).[170]

These remnants of the old battalion in Danzig were the only Anhalt troops fighting on the French side during the spring campaign, but April saw the Allies making their own demands of the duchies. Wittgenstein's troops had entered Dessau on 2 April to great popular jubilation, but they also delivered a demand for an infantry battalion to join the Allied cause. Leopold III, walking a tight rope between the two belligerents, tried to proclaim himself neutral but was told that neutrality was not an option: failure to provide the troops would result in the duchies being treated as enemy territory by the advancing Allied forces. In response to Wittgenstein's threats, several hundred men were assembled over the following weeks and placed under command of a German major in Russian service as the 'Anhalt Jäger Battalion'. When Napoleon's return to Germany and the Battle of Lützen forced an interruption in its formation and training, this unusual unit was shifted north to become part of Wallmoden's corps for the remainder of the war before being disbanded in early 1814.[171]

Napoleon, absorbed in operational decisions and the affairs of his larger front-line allies such as Saxony, paid little attention to the smaller states during the spring campaign. The armistice, however, allowed him to focus on many things, among them the smaller members of the Rheinbund. In Anhalt's case, this meant the dispatch of an envoy to Dessau as chargé d'affaires to report on the situations of the three duchies and levy new troop requirements, specifically a small infantry battalion (300 men) and a light cavalry regiment (500 men).[172] Leopold III considered this number impossible to fulfil and was able to eliminate the infantry battalion in his negotiations with the French representative, leaving the three duchies to supply a cavalry regiment of 500 men in two squadrons.

The resulting regiment, the Anhalt Jäger-zu-Pferd, was the only unit from the duchies to serve in Saxony during 1813 and was one of the most ephemeral formations of the entire Napoleonic era. Its creation posed seemingly insurmountable challenges, especially since Anhalt had no tradition of supporting mounted troops and the French wanted the regiment ready to take the field in mid-August when the armistice came to an end. Under this pressure, the three duchies moved rapidly to comply. The first troops were called up on 27 June and by 20 July the full complement of men and horses had been assembled, each duchy conscripting men and mounts according to an agreed schedule to make up the required total of 500.[173] Finding enough suitable horses had been difficult, but, as with every other state in this year of emergency mobilisations, locating capable officers was the greatest obstacle. Leopold Friedrich Lebrecht Bürkner, a Dessau native who had served some years as a Prussian hussar, was appointed as major and regimental commander and some men were drawn from the local gendarmerie, but none had commanded at this level, let alone in actual combat. Furthermore, these new officers had to contend with grave deficiencies in equipment and training. Not only was the quality of saddles and harnesses poor, but there were not enough serviceable sabres on hand and no firearms whatsoever. To save money and time, the duchies decided to dress the men in the same outfits as the infantry battalion: dark green jackets with dark rose distinctions, black shakos, black leather gear and dark grey riding trousers with brown leather inserts. Wearing dark yellow coats with rose trim and black bicorne hats, the trumpeters were especially distinctive (and a perennial favourite of uniformologists). As for training, the green recruits had no concept of cavalry tactics – very few even knew how to ride or care for a horse.

The Anhalt Jäger-zu-Pferd was to join the 9th Chevaulegers-Lanciers to form the 21st Light Cavalry Brigade under newly promoted GB Martin Charles Gobrecht as the light cavalry component of GD Vandamme's 1st Corps. Both generals were clearly concerned about the regiment's state of readiness. Gobrecht monitored their preparations carefully and detailed an officer and eight NCOs from the 9th Lancers to assist with training, while Vandamme badgered his chief of staff: 'I wish to know if the Anhalt Jägers are finally armed, this is a pressing matter.'[174] The Anhalters apparently made a good impression during a grand review on 10 August to commemorate Napoleon's birthday and they moved out several days later to arrive in Dresden with the brigade on 19 August. There were so many troops billeted in the overcrowded city that they were forced to bivouac by the roadside, but at least they finally received proper sabres from Saxon arsenals. Another four days would pass, however, before they were issued pistols and carbines from France. The men thus had hardly any time to practice with their new weapons before they found themselves on outpost duty, on patrols and in desperate combat.

The Anhalt troopers had their first sight of the enemy even before the arrival of their firearms. Vandamme's corps was posted between Zittau and the Elbe with Gobrecht's brigade screening along the border with Bohemia supported by the 7ᵉ Léger and three guns. On 23 August, Gobrecht sent a reconnaissance detachment of 100 lancers, 80 Jäger-zu-Pferd and a company of II/7ᵉ Léger to probe into Bohemia where they had a brief skirmish with Austrian *Liechtenstein* Hussars. Simultaneously, a 'good officer' of the Anhalt regiment and 25 troopers conducted a patrol in conjunction with a French infantry platoon. The Anhalters did not cross swords with the enemy in either of these situations, but it is notable that Gobrecht felt secure enough in their abilities to dispatch them on these missions (and he likely saw these expeditions as a way to ease them into field service and promote self-confidence).[175] If the regiment lost neither men nor horses in these minor affairs, it was already eroding as the inexperienced troopers and their mounts succumbed to bad weather, poor food, inept equine care and all the manifold buffets associated with campaigning in 1813. 'These exertions on an extraordinarily bad road,' reported Bürkner, 'the bivouacking in continuous cold rain and the lack of victuals overwhelmed the strength of even the most veteran soldier and were even more destructive for the regiment as it was less used to them.'[176] Desertion was a problem as well (at least one officer slipped away with some troopers), but all these factors combined meant that the Anhalt Jäger-zu-Pferd Regiment was reduced to a single squadron of only 200–250 men fit for duty by late August when it turned west to participate in the fighting south of Dresden.[177]

While Napoleon was assembling the bulk of the Grande Armée to confront the Allied Army of Bohemia at Dresden on 26–27 August, he detached Vandamme to cross the river south of the city and threaten the Allied line of retreat. A lively engagement ensued on the western bank of the Elbe near the Königstein fortress (the Anhalters were present but not engaged in this fighting), and Vandamme's appearance on their distant right flank became a major factor contributing to the Allied decision to withdraw from Dresden and retreat to Bohemia. The subsequent French pursuit, however, ended in disaster when Vandamme, leading the way, became isolated near the town of Kulm. His outnumbered corps resisted stoutly during two days of bitter combat on 29 and 30 August before being surrounded and destroyed when the Prussian II Corps appeared unexpectedly in his rear. Vandamme, 8,000–10,000 of his men and 82 guns were captured and the remaining elements of 1st Corps routed north towards Dresden in confusion.

There were perhaps thirty men of the Anhalt regiment among the 1st Corps fugitives on 30 August in the aftermath of this debacle. Gobrecht's brigade had arrived near Kulm with the corps headquarters on the 29th, skirmished harmlessly with Russian cavalry and suffered artillery fire but was not otherwise engaged on the first day of the battle. Anhalt losses amounted to only three horses killed by Russian shot. Vandamme, however, was sufficiently impressed by the regiment's firm countenance under fire that he called for Major Bürkner, praised the regiment, and donated a cask of wine as a sign of his satisfaction. Food and fodder were still scarce, but the troopers surely welcomed both the symbolism and liquid reality of this gesture.

The following morning, 30 August, Gobrecht's brigade was deployed in reserve behind the centre of the French line, the 9th Lancers and the Anhalt Jägers taking turns to dismount and feed their horses as they waited for orders. While the Jägers were busy caring for their mounts, however, a Russian cavalry attack overran a French battery and broke into Vandamme's line southeast of Kulm. Ordered to counterattack, the 9th Lancers leaped forward while the Anhalters hastened to mount up and follow. They were too late to participate in the hand-to-hand struggle, but they provided Gobrecht with a reserve to threaten the Russians from the front while the lancers struck them in the flank.[178]

Gobrecht's men had withdrawn to their reserve position when cannon fire to the north announced the arrival of the Prussian II Corps in Vandamme's rear. Gobrecht was again ordered into action as part of the frantic charge with which the French tried to force open an escape route up the road to Dresden, but the Anhalt regiment was still re-forming itself after the previous foray when the lancers dashed past to engage the Prussians. The lancers fell back after initial success, but Gobrecht led them forward again, telling Bürkner to hold his men on the main road in reserve.[179] Unfortunately for the Jägers, they came under punishing artillery fire in this position. Seeking some shelter, Bürkner shifted his men to a shallow depression but this afforded little protection. Indeed, the attempt to move the regiment under fire seems to have caused greater disorder as the nervous men, despite the exertions of their officers, crammed together, thus making themselves an even more inviting target for the Russian gunners.

After an hour or so of this anxious agony, Bürkner was ordered to withdraw, but his regiment was charged by Austrian dragoons and Russian cuirassiers as it tried to move.[180] Bunched up and skittish, the regiment shattered on this impact. Bürkner tried to rally his men further to the rear but the pressure of the enemy and chaos of the moment were too great and the Jägers dispersed, some falling into Allied hands, some dragged along in the fleeing mob, some struggling off on their own. 'Soon everything became a confusion,' wrote Gobrecht, as his men 'were also caught up' in the panicked flight.[181] Gobrecht managed to escape by hiding in a forest with a trumpeter, but Bürkner, seven of his officers and at least 80 of the Anhalt troopers were seized and conveyed to a wretched captivity. Bürkner later reported that only 20 men were killed or seriously wounded, but other officers and men were made prisoner in small groups or individually.[182] Trooper Daniel Obermeyer reported that he and a fellow Anhalter were held in Teplitz near the Prussian king's residence but managed to escape. 'I learned from the Prussians who accompanied the king that probably some 100 men of the Anhalt Regiment had been taken prisoner along with the major,' Daniel recorded, 'The Prussians also encouraged me to take service with them, but I refused.'[183] Many others also escaped.

Although the 1st Corps report of 31 August could only note that the Anhalt regiment 'had not yet rallied', by the beginning of September there were five officers and fifty-eight troopers on hand. These seem to have constituted the bulk of the survivors, but some men made their own ways back to Anhalt where they were released from duty and told to merge back into civilian life after turning in their horses and equipment. Of those who had succeeded in locating the remains of the regiment around Dresden, half were incorporated into the 9th Lancers, while the others returned to Anhalt with the regiment's cash box.[184] The Anhalt Jäger-zu-Pferd Regiment thus ceased to exist a little more than a month after it had first been mustered in Dessau.[185]

As the Jäger-zu-Pferd Regiment was preparing itself during the armistice period, the duchies were struggling to navigate between the Coalition and Napoleon. With troops in the ranks on both sides, they sent an envoy to Vienna to sound out Metternich on Austria's intentions. Although the envoy was convinced that Austria would enter the war on the side of the Coalition should the summer negotiations in Prague fail, the three dukes had to respond to Napoleon in the near term. The emperor visited Dessau on 11 July and demanded that Herzog Leopold recall the battalion that Wittgenstein had forced the duchies to provide to the Allies. Napoleon being unwilling to accept any equivocation on this matter, Leopold issued a proclamation ordering the men whom the Russians had removed from Anhalt 'without Our participation or permission' to return within two months; any who failed to comply would be declared rebels and their property would be confiscated 'for the good of the state'. Though realigning the duchies with their Rheinbund obligations, this decree, of course, had no effect on the battalion serving under Wallmoden's command and by November, all three of the little monarchies had changed sides and begun to raise troops to serve alongside the Allied armies.[186]

The Lippe Principalities: Lost in Magdeburg

While the five Anhalt duchies contributed the 1st Battalion of the 5th Rheinbund Regiment, the contingents of Lippe-Detmold and Schaumburg-Lippe formed the 2nd Battalion. Separated by the Weser River and surrounded by

Westphalian territory, these two tiny states were ruled by members of the house of Lippe, a German dynasty with roots in those lands going back to the 12th century. The senior branch of the family was that of Lippe-Detmold but the reigning prince, Leopold I, had died in 1802, leaving his wife, the talented Fürstin (Princess) Pauline, to manage the affairs of the principality's 70,000 inhabitants as regent for her young son Leopold II. Fürst Georg Wilhelm governed the 20,000 residents of Schaumburg-Lippe. Both states joined Napoleon's Confederation in April 1807, thereby preserving their semi-independent existences and elevating their two counties to principalities.[187] Indeed, Pauline had been eager for French protection. Fearing encroachment or absorption by Prussia or Hesse-Kassel, she had approached France in March 1806 even before the establishment of the Rheinbund in order to protect her domain against these large and acquisitive states. Moreover, she was in awe of Napoleon, admired many of his accomplishments and seems to have regarded French hegemony as preferable to that of her more immediate German neighbours. She made personal appeals in this regard to Dalberg, to Napoleon's brother Louis and to Empress Josephine during late 1806 and early 1807.

Once a member of the Rheinbund, Pauline still had to contend with potential infringements by Berg and Westphalia, but the bitterest dispute was between the two Lippe states. In part, the quarrel was a contest of status between the two houses, but it also revolved around possession of several small districts from which both hoped to draw conscripts for the contingents the Rheinbund required them to raise. Pauline thus travelled to Paris in October 1807 on learning that Georg Wilhelm was announcing himself as 'the Sovereign Prince of Schaumburg and of Lippe', that is, the predominant ruler in Lippe. She successfully maintained her family's senior status and her state's independence, but frictions over territory would continue to hamper interactions between these two miniature monarchies for the remainder of the Rheinbund period.[188]

Regardless of their small size, internecine dynastic squabbles, and a strong popular aversion to military service, the two principalities were obligated to provide troops to the Confederation as they had to under the Holy Roman Empire. Lippe's first action under French eagles came with two companies incorporated into the ephemeral *Bataillon des Princes* or Princes' Battalion that served in Catalonia in 1809–10.[189] While this initial tranche of troops was suffering across the Pyrenees, the two principalities had to furnish another complete battalion back in Germany when war with Austria loomed in 1809. Like the first two companies, these men were dressed in a simple but smart uniform of white coats trimmed in dark green with white breeches and black shakos which by 1809 had replaced the former Austrian Jäger-style hats with a turned-up flap on one side (the *Korsenhut*). Combined with the green-clad

Anhalt contingent as the 5th Rheinbund Regiment, the battalion participated on the margins of the war against Austria in 1809, losing heavily to desertion before being sent to Catalonia where it was nearly annihilated during ten months of combat, ambush, disease and privation. Rebuilt, the battalion was assigned to the Danzig garrison during the summer of 1812. It lacked a flag, however, and, at the request of her officers, Pauline had one sewn and sent, but the normal oath-taking ceremony had to be altered because the Schaumburg officers were unwilling to swear a vow to a banner that had come from Detmold. That autumn, the battalion was allocated to the 34th Division and committed to Russia only to be consumed in the final weeks of the retreat before its survivors staggered back into Danzig to be incorporated into the fortress garrison and endure the ensuing siege.[190]

The exigencies of 1813 meant that neither the 5th nor the 6th Rheinbund Regiment was reconstituted: too many officers of these formations were locked up in Danzig, Anhalt was directed to supply cavalry rather than infantry, and everything was in short supply. In place of these two regiments, the French intended to create a new one from the microstate contingents. This was planned to include three battalions, one from Lippe (840 men), one from Reuß and Waldeck (870 men) and a smaller one from the two Schwarzburg principalities (670 men). All these contingents were intended to reinforce the Magdeburg garrison but none of the battalions ever achieved full strength, some of the troops never reached the fortress, and the regiment never came into existence as such. Instead, the various contingents were dispatched in small batches to traverse a countryside rife with Allied raiders before experiencing a brief and largely ignominious tenure inside Magdeburg's walls.[191]

In Lippe's case, the two principalities began to assemble three infantry companies during the armistice. Both governments complained to Reinhard at being required to supply what they viewed as their 'third' contingents (following Spain and Russia). Accredited to the Lippe principalities as well as Westphalia, Reinhard duly relayed their concerns, but no relief was forthcoming.[192] Formation of these new units thus proceeded, albeit with great difficulty, and the 1st Company only departed on 31 August. Hastily thrown together, it numbered 136 officers and men, but it lacked weapons and its uniforms were so poorly manufactured that they shrank to an embarrassing degree on the first washing. The 2nd Company (140 officers and men) marched out on 6 September to join the 1st as part of Westphalian GB Langenschwarz's weak German brigade in Magdeburg. In addition to inadequate equipment and clothing, morale was so poor that the commander of the 2nd Company complained that, 'We continually have serious desertion' even before arriving in the fortress.[193] Losses to desertion, of course, did not cease with the companies' arrival and by the end of September more than one quarter of the men had slipped away, leaving a total of only 150–170 in the ranks.[194] The 3rd Company was not ready until October but given the experience of the first two and the unrelenting news about French defeats, the Lippe authorities decided to keep it for territorial defence and it never left its homeland.

Meanwhile, the situation in Magdeburg continued to deteriorate. The manifold deficiencies of the garrison's Rheinbund troops, especially the rampant desertion that grew during the autumn, had already caused GD Le Marois to restrict their tasks to interior guard duties and repair of the fortifications, but an incident involving Lippe troops on 11 November may have been the final straw that led him to dismiss the German units entirely. A small Lippe detachment overseeing 700–800 civilian workers constructing a new redoubt allowed themselves to be intimidated by the disgruntled labourers. The soldiers fled and the entire workforce dispersed. Two Lippe NCOs likewise deserted on the 11th, part of an exodus of at least 300 (perhaps as high as 500) Rheinbund troops for this single day.[195] As recounted in Chapter 6, therefore, Le Marois ordered all the German units to appear for a review on 12 November, stipulating that they assemble without weapons and equipment, clad only in their ordinary uniforms and coats. He offered the enlisted men the choice of continuing to serve in the garrison or returning home immediately. Although they were not permitted to return to their billets to collect their personal effects, to a man they elected to depart at once. The officers, given two days to decide whether they wanted to take French service or leave, likewise chose to head home. They pledged not to take up arms against France for a year, but their home governments refused to acknowledge this promise, and most would soon be leading rebuilt units against their former French allies.[196]

Lippe-Detmold remained an ally of France until 5 November when Allied troops entered the principality and Pauline issued a declaration dissolving her realm's membership of the Rheinbund. This declaration notwithstanding, her sympathy for Napoleon and her antipathy for Prussia were well known and the Allies – most notably the Prussians – treated her lands as enemy territory, not only imposing severe demands but treating her personally with evident and exaggerated disrespect. She fell into despair, dismayed by her soldiers' lack of discipline, the Allied exactions, and what she regarded as her subjects' ingratitude for her efforts on their behalf. Skilful diplomacy by her agent at Coalition headquarters in Frankfurt, however, rescued her little monarchy. After several weeks of anxiety, he signed treaties with the leading Coalition powers that preserved Pauline's state and restored her to proper dignity in her dealings with the Prussian occupiers. Georg Wilhelm, who had attempted to ingratiate himself by small measures, also signed on the with Allies. By

1 December, therefore, both Lippe states had joined the war against Napoleon, raising twice as many troops as required by the Rheinbund to be incorporated into the V German Corps under Herzog Ernst I of Sachsen-Coburg.[197]

Reuß, Schwarzburg, and Waldeck: Bound for Magdeburg

The remaining Confederation contingents in 1813 came from seven small principalities: four from the House of Reuß (one of the senior line, three of the junior line), Schwarzburg-Rudolstadt, Schwarzburg-Sondershausen, and Waldeck. All seven had become members of the Rheinbund in April 1807 and the experiences of their troops were similar to those of their comrades in the Lippe contingents. They thus contributed four companies, one each from Schwarzburg-Rudolstadt, Schwarzburg-Sondershausen, and Waldeck along with a composite one from Reuß, to join the two Lippe companies in the *Bataillon des Princes* in 1808. Each of these six companies had its own distinctive uniform, making the *Bataillon des Princes* was one of the most colourful as well as one of the most short-lived of the entire era. Committed across the Pyrenees, the battalion soon wasted away, but Napoleon demanded new full-strength contingents from all seven states as he prepared for war with Austria in 1809. These were grouped together as the 6th Rheinbund Regiment with the Schwarzburg troops constituted as the 1st Battalion and the Reuß and Waldeck contingents as the 2nd. The regiment campaigned in Austria and Catalonia in 1809–10 and absorbed the remnants from the *Bataillon des Princes* before returning home in 1811 to be rebuilt for the invasion of Russia. As with the 4th and 5th Regiments, the 6th Rheinbund was allotted to the French 34th Division and was eviscerated during the final weeks of 1812, its survivors retreating to Danzig to be incorporated into the garrison with the sad remainder of the division.[198] The destruction of their units did not spare these states from new demands when the war shifted into Germany in 1813, but they had to contend with all the deficiencies in men, officers, equipment and funds that hampered the other Rheinbund armies.[199] Like the Lippe states, therefore, their new contingents would not approach readiness until the period of the armistice.

Four Princes of Reuß

Membership in the Confederation obligated the four Reuß princes to supply a combined contingent of 450 officers and men. These were dressed in white coats, light blue breeches decorated with yellow Hungarian knots on the thighs, black gaiters and black shakos. From the beginning of its alliance with France, Reuß could only meet its officer requirements by engaging foreigners (such as Saxons) and this problem became more acute in 1813. As with the other small states, many of its officers had been killed or captured in Spain or Russia and most of the remaining servicemen were tied up in Danzig. The princes were thus left to elevate four NCOs to lieutenancies in order to provide a modicum of appropriate leadership for their new contingents in 1813. By such measures, the principalities raised three shaky companies totalling 458 officers and men and marched them off to Magdeburg where they arrived on 25 August.[200] Assigned to construction work and other garrison duties under GB Langenschwarz's brigade, the strength of the companies quickly diminished owing to sickness and desertion. As with all the other German contingents, they appeared in fatigue uniforms without weapons and equipment for Le Marois's 12 November review and all accepted his offer to depart for their homelands rather than continue in French service. The handful of officers followed two days later. By 15 November, therefore, the only Reuß troops still under Napoleon's eagles were the four dozen or so officers and men of the Danzig garrison. The four principalities joined the Coalition at the end of the month, pledging to raise new units for the fight against their former allies.[201]

Though not part of the Reuß troop contingent, Prinz Heinrich LXI zu Reuß-Köstritz (a branch of the family with lands but no ruling authority) participated in the campaigns of 1813 as an individual officer. He had spent several years as a hussar officer in the Austrian army but returned to Germany at some point after 1806 and was expected to take command of the 6th Rheinbund as an *Oberst* in 1812 when it was posted near Hamburg on coastal duty. The serving commander, Oberst Karl August von Heeringen of Waldeck, however, was senior to the prince and the regiment marched off to its grim fate in Russia without Heinrich. He thus remained in northern Germany, first as a supernumerary with GD Carra Saint-Cyr, then entering French service with the rank of *adjutant-commandant* in April 1813. Assigned as chief of staff of the 5th Division in the spring, he was promoted to *général de brigade* in July and given command of the division's 2nd Brigade (46e and 72e Ligne). In this capacity, he fought at Kulm and was mortally wounded on 29 August.[202]

The Two Schwarzburgs

Unlike many of the other Rheinbund states, Schwarzburg-Rudolstadt and Schwarzburg-Sondershausen had been principalities since the early 1700s and did not benefit from elevation in rank by joining the Confederation in April 1807. Although alignment with Napoleon preserved their independence, Günther Friedrich of Sondershausen thus remained a *Fürst* and Caroline of Rudolstadt a *Fürstin*, she serving as regent for her son, Friedrich Günther, who had not yet reached his majority. Concern for their continued existence as sovereign entities also led both to hedge in 1813. Neither Günther Friedrich nor

Caroline fled their states when Allied troops began to appear in Thuringia in April, and Günther Friedrich was careful to entertain Chernishev's officers at a meal when they rode through his lands on the way to Kassel.[203] Both switched to the side of the Coalition in November. Indeed, the young Friedrich Günther of Rudolstadt, eager to embark on a military career, joined the Austrian forces shortly after Leipzig courtesy of relatives in Habsburg service.[204]

Militarily, the involvement of the two Schwarzburg principalities as French allies in 1813 mirrored that of the Reuß monarchies. That is, they scrambled to create new formations at home while the remains of their portion of the 6th Rheinbund endured privation, tedium and combat in Danzig. Each was supposed to contribute 350 men to form their joint battalion as part of the new combined Rheinbund regiment with the Reuß, Lippe and Waldeck contingents. As in the past, these soldiers were dressed in dark green coats sporting red collars, cuffs and turnbacks, accompanied by grey breeches, black leather gear and black shakos. The required strength, however, was never attained. Instead, about half the stipulated number were put into uniform and dispatched to Magdeburg to join the other microstate contingents. Totalling 367 officers and men under arms on 1 September, they were employed in garrison and fortification work but suffered severely from desertion (reduced to 258 two weeks later) until released by GD Le Marois on 12 November.[205]

Waldeck: Dispersed at Braunschweig

Where the other components of the 6th Rheinbund were located in Thuringia, the Principality of Waldeck was a tiny north German state. The largest portion was wedged between Westphalia and Hesse-Darmstadt, but it also included the former Principality of Pyrmont snug against the borders of Lippe-Detmold. Its ruler at the opening of 1813 was Fürst Georg I who had ascended the throne on 24 September 1812 on the death of his brother, Friedrich Carl August. Georg I's reign, however, lasted less than one year.[206] He died on 9 September 1813, leaving his son, Georg II, to be installed as the new *Fürst*. Waldeck had become a member of the Rheinbund in April 1807 and, like the rest of the Confederation, maintained its independent existence by siding with the Allies in November 1813.

Beyond a small number of officers and men trapped in Danzig after the 6th Rheinbund's disastrous foray into Russia, Waldeck formed two new companies in the summer of 1813 for a likely total of 250–300 men. Ordered to Magdeburg in early September, these green recruits marched through Westphalia to reach Braunschweig on the 24th, the day before Prussian Major von der Marwitz's raid on the city. The Waldeckers thus found themselves bundled up in Westphalian GB von Klösterlein's disorderly evacuation of Braunschweig on

25 September. As described in Chapter 6, Prussian audacity and bluff combined with Klösterlein's inept leadership to produce panic among the Westphalian and Waldeck troops, few of whom had any interest in fighting on behalf of the French in the first place. In addition to the significant Westphalian losses, 40 men from the two Waldeck companies were captured (1 officer, 9 NCOs and 30 enlisted soldiers). The rest dispersed, a few taking service with Marwitz's 3rd Kurmark Landwehr Cavalry, but most exploiting the confusion to return home as best they could.[207] Marwitz's swift stroke thus ended Waldeck's participation in the autumn campaign before it even began, though many of the escapees doubtless ended up in the new contingent Georg II's principality formed to fight as part of the Coalition against Napoleon later that year.

*

The participation of the microstate contingents during the 1813 campaigns thus ran the gamut from courage and competence, as exemplified by the Würzburg Chevaulegers and Berg Lancers, to desertion and disrepute as seen in the resurrected 4th Rheinbund Regiment at Hagelberg or the other elements of the Magdeburg garrison. There were instances of individuals or small groups enrolling with Allied units (such as some number of Waldeck troops at Braunschweig), but Major von Linker's battalion was the only case of an entire unit defecting to the other side (possibly the 1st Coburg Company as well). Prompted by a disinclination to fight for the French and a general distaste for military service under any flag, most of the deserters and stragglers simply wanted to return home, even at the risk of being apprehended, tried, and perhaps restored to the ranks or otherwise punished. As always, leadership was a key factor in determining the performance of these contingents, especially as almost all of them were composed of brand-new recruits dragged unwillingly from their homes by local conscription authorities. With few veterans on hand, little training, shoddy uniforms and poor (or no) arms, it is little wonder that so many of these tiny units exhibited low morale and tended to dissolve under stress whether they were assigned to field formations or garrison duties. As will be evident in the next chapter, the contrast between the dubious quality of these new raisings and the steadfast endurance of the experienced troops serving in Danzig is striking.

Chapter 8
The Fortress War: The Iron Yoke of Fate

'Half of these garrisons should be foreign and the other half French.'

Napoleon to Eugène, 4 February 1813[1]

FORTRESSES WERE A CRUCIAL CONSIDERATION for both sides in 1813. Napoleon wanted to exploit their value as pillars of his initial defence, hoping that fortified places would divert enemy troops, threaten Allied supply lines, block key river crossings, and deny the Coalition the resources of major urban areas. More important for him, however, was how such strongholds could support the offensive plans he hoped to launch as soon as his new army was assembled.[2] The Allies certainly considered French-held fortresses to be stumbling blocks, requiring them to create alternative lines of communication to circumvent the blockages, especially over major rivers. Once they had re-routed their supply lines, however, they were content in most cases to establish blockades with second-line troops such as Prussian Landwehr and Russian militia rather than initiate costly formal sieges that would absorb better troops supported by large amounts of artillery and ammunition.

Fortress cities could also have political significance that could override their purely military value. For the Allies, French garrisons deep in their rear areas were galling reminders of Napoleon's reach and potential rallying points for their enemies. The tsar thus pressed his subordinates to reduce Thorn as rapidly as possible not only to eliminate an operational threat but to demonstrate his hold on Poland. Likewise, the Coalition trumpeted the occupation of Saxony's capital Dresden in March as a signal of their inexorable success and Napoleon's ineluctable defeat. On the French side, political concerns seem to have been a key factor in Napoleon's decision to retain his hold on Dresden until late in the autumn.[3] In addition to its undeniable logistical and operational importance, Dresden was the capital of a major Rheinbund state. Although it was vulnerable to real and feigned Allied offensives out of Bohemia, the emperor could not simply abandon the city as this could be construed as betraying his Saxon ally.

He thus tethered himself to Dresden until early October, unwilling to give it up as a base even though an earlier shift to a more northerly location might have been wiser. Moreover, when he finally moved north, he left behind two entire corps (1st and 14th) in addition to the city's small garrison, arguably a grossly over-large force for the outnumbered French under the desperate circumstances at that point in the campaign. Concern for the impact on Saxony and other members of the Rheinbund was certainly not the only consideration on Napoleon's mind that autumn, but neither could he blithely ignore Dresden's political and symbolic significance.

Defence, Defiance, Disease: Rheinbund Fortress Garrisons

The fortresses under threat during the spring campaign included Danzig, Thorn and Modlin on the Vistula; Zamosc deep in Poland; Stettin, Küstrin and Glogau on the Oder; Spandau near Berlin; and Magdeburg, Wittenberg, Torgau and Dresden along the Elbe. Spandau and Thorn fell to the Coalition in April, but the others held out until the last weeks of 1813 or as late as May 1814.[4] More fortresses and fortified cities came under blockade or siege as the war progressed into the autumn: Hamburg, Erfurt and Würzburg east of the Rhine along with Wesel, Mainz-Kastel and Kehl along the great river itself. The numbers of French and French-allied soldiers consigned to these locales fluctuated over time as reinforcements were added or losses deducted, but 140,000 is a reasonable estimate for the total in these numerous garrisons.[5] Conditions within the fortress walls were often poor to horrifying. The men endured bad and insufficient food, inadequate housing, lack of firewood, exhausting work details to build or repair fortifications, fiery bombardments and the strain of constant vigilance against the ever-present danger of enemy raids or assaults. Garrisons also had to conduct their own sorties to gather food, fodder and firewood or to fend off the besiegers' advances. There were also dangers inside the walls as local residents could pressure commandants, undermine garrison morale, collude with the blockading enemy, or incite riots. Most debilitating of all was rampant sickness that preyed on men weakened by enervation, poor nutrition, dubious drinking water and primitive medical care. Places such as Danzig and Torgau became infamous for the nearly unconstrained spread of diseases like typhus that carried off dozens or hundreds of men a day and left garrison commanders with too few fit soldiers to defend their fortresses.[6] The miseries inflicted on the civilian populations were as bad or worse than those suffered by the soldiery. In addition to hunger and illness, local residents could see their homes and livelihoods destroyed by enemy bombardment or their villages and suburbs demolished by the defenders to clear fields of fire outside the walls. In several cases, fortress commanders forced parts of the population out of

Defence, Defiance, Disease: Rheinbund Fortress Garrisons 347

Map 48 The Fortress War Overview: Places Blockaded and/or Besieged

Notes:
- The French abandoned Stralsund in early March (GD Morand's 'division').
- The French never held the Prussian fortresses of Breslau or Graudenz.
- The Warsaw bridgehead of Praga was not defended.
- Rheinbund troops were involved in the blockades/sieges of Danzig, Thorn, Modlin, Küstrin, Glogau, Magdeburg, Torgau and Dresden (a small number may also have been present in Stettin).

★ = fortress
☆ = capital

Capitulation dates, but note that garrisons often remained several weeks longer (e.g., Danzig capitulated on 30 November, but garrison did not depart until early January).
Spring 1813: Pillau (7 Feb), Częstochowa (5 Apr), Thorn (16 Apr), Spandau (26 Apr).
Autumn 1813: Dresden (11 Nov), Zamosc (22 Nov), Danzig (30 Nov), Modlin (1 Dec), Stettin (5 Dec).
1814: Torgau (10 Jan), Wittenberg (13 Jan), Küstrin (20 Mar), Glogau (12 Apr), Magdeburg (14 May), Erfurt (16 May), Würzburg (21 May), Hamburg (28 May).

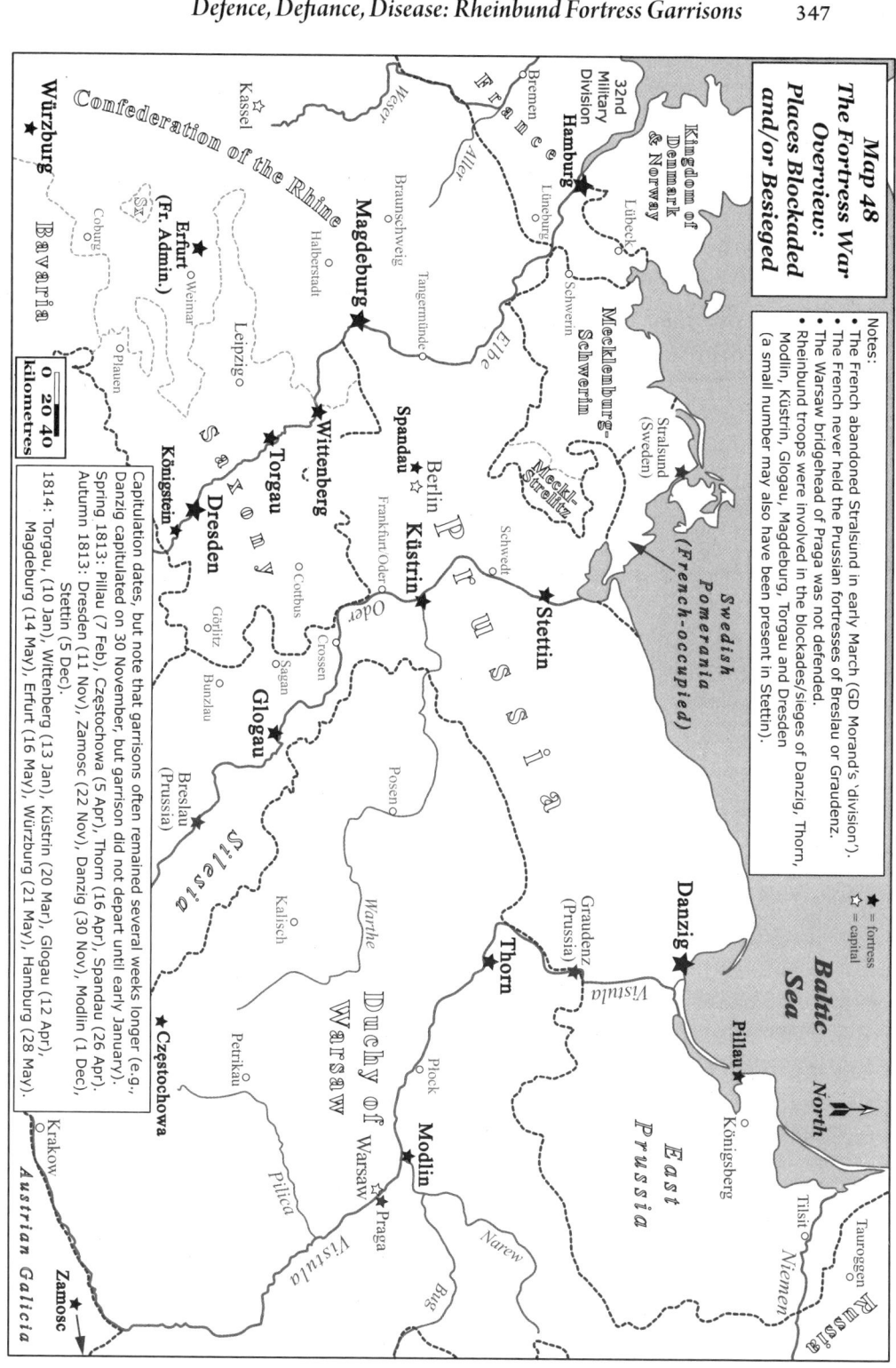

their cities owing to lack of provisions; if the blockading or besieging enemy did not accept these exiles, they could be left in helpless limbo between the warring sides for days. Thus did 'the iron yoke of fate' oppress both garrisons and inhabitants.[7]

The garrisons deposited in the fortresses along the Elbe, Oder and Vistula were of variegated composition and many included Rheinbund units. 'It is necessary that if these places were to be surrounded and the Oder abandoned, half of these garrisons should be foreign and the other half French,' Napoleon had written to Eugène on 4 February. Circumstances, however, did not permit this concept to be implemented in full. As a result, the percentage of German troops was minuscule in some cases, while in others it was sizeable. Indeed, there were virtually no Rheinbund troops in Stettin on the Oder, but the garrison of Thorn on the more distant Vistula was almost entirely Bavarian (*see* Chapter 2). The purpose of the following is not to describe each of the many blockades and sieges that populated the months between January 1813 when the Allies invested Danzig and May 1814 when Hamburg finally surrendered. Nor is it to detail the weeks of drudgery, sickness, deprivation and boredom punctuated by spasms of violence that characterised these varied situations. Rather, the ensuing pages offer summary accounts of only those fortresses east of the Rhine where Rheinbund soldiers were part of the garrison (places such as Hamburg and Erfurt are thus excluded) to paint as complete a picture as possible of the role each Confederation state played across the vast canvas of conflict in 1813.[8] Each section below thus provides an overview of the fortress and a brief synopsis of the blockade and/or siege followed by a more detailed account of the experiences of the Rheinbund troops involved.

Danzig: A Community of Perils and Courage

The struggle for Danzig was one of the most prominent blockades and sieges of 1813 for the size of the fortress and its garrison, the duration of the contest, the port city's political significance and for its location far to the east of the principal theatre of war. There were also more Germans troops in Danzig than in any of the other besieged fortresses: 3,632 present under arms at the start of the blockade in January 1813 as well as an unknown number of sick or wounded in the city's hospitals (*see* Chart 51).[9]

Sitting on the western bank of the Vistula near where the river empties into the Baltic Sea, Danzig was an important commercial centre with a population of 30,000 in 1813. It 'seemed destined to be a fortress,' wrote its governor, GD Jean Rapp, and it had long been protected by formidable fortifications which the French had begun to improve after successfully besieging it in 1807. Though incomplete at the start of 1813, Rapp and his engineers worked tirelessly to rebuild and expand the defences as the year progressed. In addition to manmade walls, ditches and outer works, the city benefited from natural barriers as the river covered its northern side and flooding of the lowlands to the east and south made assault from those directions nearly impossible. The only practicable approaches were therefore from the west in the arc stretching from the suburbs of Ohra to Langfuhr (Orunia to Wrzeszcz). Technically a free city jointly administered by Prussia and Saxony, Danzig was *de facto* under Napoleon's rule after 1807. He devoted considerable attention to its defences and made it a key logistical base for the invasion of Russia in 1812 with numerous Rheinbund units assigned to its garrison at various times starting in 1811. It became a natural refuge for troops retreating from Russia in early 1813 and Napoleon, determined to retain possession, left it with a large garrison even when the rest of his battered army withdrew to the west. In his mind, Danzig would not only be a thorn in the side of the advancing Allies but would also serve as a base of support for the counter-offensives he hoped to launch across northern Germany and into Poland.

Danzig's garrison was a multi-national agglomeration formed around the Grande Armée's 10th Corps, particularly GD Grandjean's 7th Division. Under Marshal MacDonald, 10th Corps had advanced into Russia as the left flank of the grand invasion in June 1812. As such, it withdrew along the Baltic coast when the great retreat began, losing the Prussian division that defected under Yorck's orders at Tauroggen but gaining other formations as it fell back first towards Königsberg and then to Danzig (*see* Chapter 3). These additional formations included the 30th Division of inexperienced French replacement battalions, a composite cavalry division and the 34th Division with its French and Rheinbund brigades. Arriving in Danzig in mid-January, this mix of many nations joined the units already in the fortress: the Neapolitan 33rd Division, a battalion of Spanish sappers, a Saxon artillery company, a small Württemberg detachment and tiny groups of other Rheinbund troops. MacDonald having departed for France, Napoleon selected Rapp as the city's governor over this polyglot force. Rapp, tough, competent and experienced (he had taken his twenty-second wound at Borodino), was one of the emperor's most trusted generals and he knew the city, having served as its governor in 1807. He also had superb motivational skills. Born in Alsace, he brought the additional advantage of speaking German. This combination of leadership and linguistic abilities enabled him quickly to gain the respect and loyalty of his Rheinbund troops as well as the many other nationalities that made up his cosmopolitan command.

Rapp's ability to communicate with his German troops in a variant of their native tongue would be very useful as Germans would play a major role in the

Chart 51: The Danzig Garrison (10th Corps), 21 January 1813
Governor: GD Rapp

		bns/sqdns	Present under arms	Hospital
Staff and gendarmes		–	40	–
Imperial Guard (all arms)		–	328	152
7th Division	*GD Grandjean*	–	11	–
1st Brigade	*GB Bachelu (later GD)*			
1st Westphalian Infantry		2	934	
13th Bavarian Infantry		2	1,001	
2nd Brigade: 5th, 10th, 11th Polish Infantry		6	5,019	
Hospital		–	–	349
30th Division (French)	*GD Heudelet*	18	10,243	2,948
33rd Division (Neapolitan)	*GD Detrès*	c. 5	3,219	386
34th Division	*GD Francheschi (later GD Bachelu)*	–	7	–
French (elements of 22ᵉ Léger, 3ᵉ, 29ᵉ, 105ᵉ, 113ᵉ Ligne)			1,020	
Frankfurt Regiment		2	209	
4th Rheinbund Regiment (Saxon Duchies)		3	307	
5th Rheinbund Regiment (Anhalt, Lippe)		2	568	
6th Rheinbund Regiment (Schwarzburg, Reuß, Waldeck)		2	390	
Saxon *von Rechten* Infantry Regiment (depot)		–	14	
Hospital		–	–	223
French and Polish cavalry	*GB Cavaignac*	c. 14	1,701	57
Artillery and artillery artisans				
French		–	2,145	
Bavarian		–	73	
Württemberg		–	43	
Saxon 10th Company	–		93	
Hospital	–		–	61
French, Polish, Spanish engineers, sappers, miners, pioneers		–	1,000	80
French sailors and naval artisans		–	740	109
French equipment train and artisans		–	262	3
French customs officer organised as infantry		–	168	30
French administrators	–		482	2
French invalids capable of some light duty		–	88	1,519
Total			30,105	5,919
Rheinbund fit for duty (included in total)			3,632	

Notes: Source only gives aggregate hospital totals. The 30th Division included many men from the new French departments in north Germany who would prove prone to desertion. Numbers of battalions for the German troops of 34th Division are nominal, showing the number at their entry into Russia. The 34th Division would be disbanded during the armistice, its men incorporated into the 30th under Heudelet.

Source: chart in d'Artois, *Défense de Danzig* (also in Campredon, *Défense de Danzig*).

city's defence. Indeed, Rheinbund troops made up approximately 10 per cent of the 35,000-man garrison and would be involved in most of the larger actions during the blockade and siege. Rapp considered the Polish, Bavarian and Westphalian regiments of the 7th Division his most reliable assets. He lauded 'the excellent spirit animating the troops of the 7th Division' in a late January report to Berthier: 'It is the soul of the garrison, and it electrifies the other troops numbed by the cold.' Moreover, he repeatedly offered specific praise for the constancy, courage and competence of Bavarian Oberst von Butler and Westphalian Major Bauer.[10] The French held up the Bavarians as examples for other contingents, exciting a degree of jealousy among the other Germans and causing Butler and his officers some embarrassment. Similarly, Rapp held Bauer in high regard. With Oberst von Plessmann dogged by a wound he had received in Spain, Bauer often served as the *de facto* commander of the 1st Westphalian. He thus frequently came to Rapp's attention as this reliable regiment and the 13th Bavarian were routinely engaged in some of the heaviest actions during the siege.[11]

The Germans of the 34th Division would also prove their worth over the course of the garrison's long trial. Unlike the comparatively intact Bavarian and Westphalian regiments, however, the four German regiments of the 34th Division had been nearly destroyed in Russia. They had suffered so heavily, wrote one officer, 'that now it could no longer lay any claim to the name division'.[12] Instead of four regiments with 54 companies, these contingents could only muster ten companies of relatively fit men after struggling into Danzig. They were organised into a thin composite 'brigade' or 'regiment' (the two terms were used interchangeably) of two battalions with fewer than 1,500 men under arms to which the rest of the German soldiers in Danzig, small detachments and groups of individuals alike, were later added. Command was invested in Oberst von Egloffstein of Weimar and Oberst von Heeringen of Waldeck under the overall leadership first of GB Franceschi until his death from typhus in March, then GB Devilliers, and finally newly promoted GD Bachelu (Devilliers took Bachelu's place in 7th Division).[13] The hotchpotch composition of the brigade presented the German officers with daunting leadership challenges, compounded by the sufferings the men had endured in Russia and persistent parochial differences among some of the contingents. Despite having served together for almost two years, despite the shared hardships of 1812, and despite the urgency of their situation as a besieged garrison, small-state sentiments still prevailed in several cases, especially between Lippe-Detmold and Schaumburg-Lippe.[14] Nonetheless, the men would cohere in combat and the brigade, as small as it was, proved a valuable addition to Rapp's command.

> **Chart 52: Rheinbund Troops of the 34th Division at Danzig, early 1813**
>
> **Initial Formation in January**
>
> | Rheinbund state | Number of companies |
> |---|---|
> | Frankfurt Regiment | 1 |
> | 4th Rheinbund Regiment | 2 |
> | 5th Rheinbund Regiment (Anhalt) | 2 |
> | 5th Rheinbund Regiment (Lippe) | 2 |
> | 6th Rheinbund Regiment (Schwarzburg) | 2 |
> | 6th Rheinbund Regiment (Waldeck) | 1 |
> | Total | 10 companies |
>
> Note: the few remaining soldiers from Reuß were likely included in the Waldeck (or Schwarzburg) companies.
> Source: Küster, *Anhaltischen Infanterie-Regiments*, p. 92.
>
> **The 'Europa Battalion' from early February**
>
> | State troops incorporated into the battalion | Original units |
> |---|---|
> | Grand Duchy of Frankfurt | Frankfurt Regiment |
> | Five Saxon Duchies | 4th Rheinbund Regiment |
> | Three Anhalt Duchies | 5th Rheinbund Regiment |
> | Two Lippe Principalities | 5th Rheinbund Regiment |
> | Two Schwarzburg Principalities | 6th Rheinbund Regiment |
> | Four Reuß Principalities | 6th Rheinbund Regiment |
> | Principality of Waldeck | 6th Rheinbund Regiment |
> | Kingdom of Württemberg | 7th Infantry, artillery, individuals |
> | Grand Duchy of Baden | Individuals |
> | Grand Duchy of Hesse-Darmstadt | Individuals |
> | Two Mecklenburg Duchies | Individuals |
>
> Note: all accounts mention a small number of individual soldiers from the Mecklenburg Duchies even though these monarchies had changed sides early in the year.
>
> Sources: Meinhard, *Reuß*, p. 408; Jacobs, *Feldzüge und Schicksale*, p. 272.

Danzig: Spring Blockade

Russian troops had severed Rapp's communications with his emperor by 21 January, but the spring months passed with a blockade rather than a formal siege. This was in large part due to the limited forces the Allies had committed to investing the fortress and to the lacklustre leadership of their commander, Russian Lieutenant General Fedor Fedorovich Löwis von Menar. Things began to change in May with the arrival of a new commander, Herzog Alexander zu Württemberg, an intelligent and energetic if stubborn and egoistic Russian General of Cavalry who was also younger brother to Napoleon's ally König Friedrich. Herzog Alexander, however, had neither the time nor the resources to effect a major change in the blockade before the June armistice put a temporary end to active operations. Nonetheless, there were numerous small but sharp engagements, most occasioned by French sorties beyond the defensive perimeter that Rapp was striving to maintain outside the fortress proper. These forays were limited in scope, designed to collect food from the surrounding countryside, to gain intelligence and to keep the Russians as far as possible from the city's walls, but they sometimes pushed as far as 5–10 kilometres beyond the fortress's gates. The Russians constantly harried the defenders to wear them down, but the only major attack took place on 5 March when the besiegers advanced against the entire circumference of the defence lines. The Russians initially gained some ground but were repelled by Rapp's troops, losing all they had won after heavy fighting. The final engagement of the spring campaign took place on 9 June just before news of the armistice arrived. This was a French attack to the west intended to curtail persistent Russian harassment of the defenders' outpost line and allow the troops to harvest the crops that were ripening just beyond their chain of pickets. Both sides then settled into a welcome armistice until hostilities resumed in mid-August.

The garrison's German troops were involved in many of the actions during the first months of the blockade. Most of these were quite successful, but one on 4 February proved a small-scale disaster. The defenders had noticed increased Russian activity during the first days of the month and Rapp was determined to discover the enemy's intentions and strength. He thus ordered a foray towards Langfuhr at 9 a.m. on the 4th in which the 1st Westphalian, now amalgamated as a single small battalion, played a minor role.[15] The troops along the rest of the defensive line were instructed to stand under arms and observe the enemy without advancing while the Neapolitan 33rd Division conducted this reconnaissance in force. Unfortunately, Waldeck Oberst von Heeringen, commanding in Stolzenberg (Chełm) and Schidlitz (Siedlce), either misunderstood these instructions or decided to act on his own initiative. Known to be brave but also rash, he may have sought to distinguish himself in hopes of earning an award or to redeem his reputation after having been chastised by Murat in Königsberg a month earlier.[16] An alternative but less likely explanation is that he received definitive orders to advance. Whatever the case, he 'imprudently descended into the plain' and set out towards Wonneberg (Ujescisko) around noon with between 280 and 300 officers and men, mostly from the 4th and 6th Regiments of the Rheinbund brigade.[17] He left the remainder of the brigade near Zigankendorf (Suchanino) and ordered it to advance on Pietzkendorf (Piecewo, now Piecki) when the officers saw him engaged with the enemy. Similarly, he directed Hauptmann Wilhelm Georg Eduard Freiherr von Seebach in Wonneberg to accompany his advance with

Seebach's newly formed company of 50 men. Both of these other detachments, however, quickly lost sight of their comrades when Heeringen forged ahead at a rapid pace. Heeringen and his mixed command reached Wonneberg and turned towards Schönfeld (Łostowice), pushing back the Russian outpost line, but were surprised by Cossacks when they struggled back north towards Miggau (Migowo) over the hilly, snow-covered terrain. Heeringen tried to get his ad hoc force onto a hilltop but his men, tired from having been on duty for 48 hours already, were exhausted after stomping through the snow. Moreover, they were not trained as a unit, their march had left them badly dispersed, and the falling snow had rendered many of their muskets unusable. As a result, Heeringen's hasty attempt to form them into a square failed completely. It was all over in minutes. The Cossacks, dashing up from hidden positions in the neighbouring dells, cut the detachment to pieces, killing or capturing all except for Major Georg Friedrich von Horadam of Frankfurt who escaped thanks to the fleetness of his mount. 'I made myself scarce!' he would tell friends later.[18] Heeringen took half a dozen lance wounds and was evacuated to Königsberg where he died several days later.[19]

Hauptmann von Seebach, witnessing this miniature debacle, immediately headed towards Schidlitz with his little company. In addition to the imminent danger of the enemy cavalry, however, his small command threatened to disintegrate from internal dissension when several soldiers from the 6th Rheinbund broke from the ranks and declared that they would prefer to be captured so they could stay with their officers and comrades. Seebach rejected any such notion. Forcing the men back to their posts, he announced that he would personally cut down the first man who left his place or fired without orders. He was soon surrounded by a cloud of Cossacks, but the horsemen withdrew out of range every time he halted and made ready to fire a volley. Many such stops were necessary as they traversed the open rolling hills back to Schidlitz, but thanks to his firm leadership Seebach brought his company to safety without losing a man.[20]

Seebach had given an admirable demonstration of steadfast courage and determination, but this could not compensate for the loss of some 300 men caused by Heeringen's ill-considered advance. Already decimated by disease, the Rheinbund brigade was now reduced to a single battalion whose strength would fluctuate between 500 and 700 officers and men for the remainder of the siege. Rapp was furious. In what would be the only instance of his criticising a German officer during the entire siege, he told Berthier that, 'Colonel Heeringen is guilty of acting without orders, had he not been taken prisoner, I would have referred him to a council of war to be punished according to military law.'[21] The unfortunate affair of 4 February, however, did not destroy the spirit of

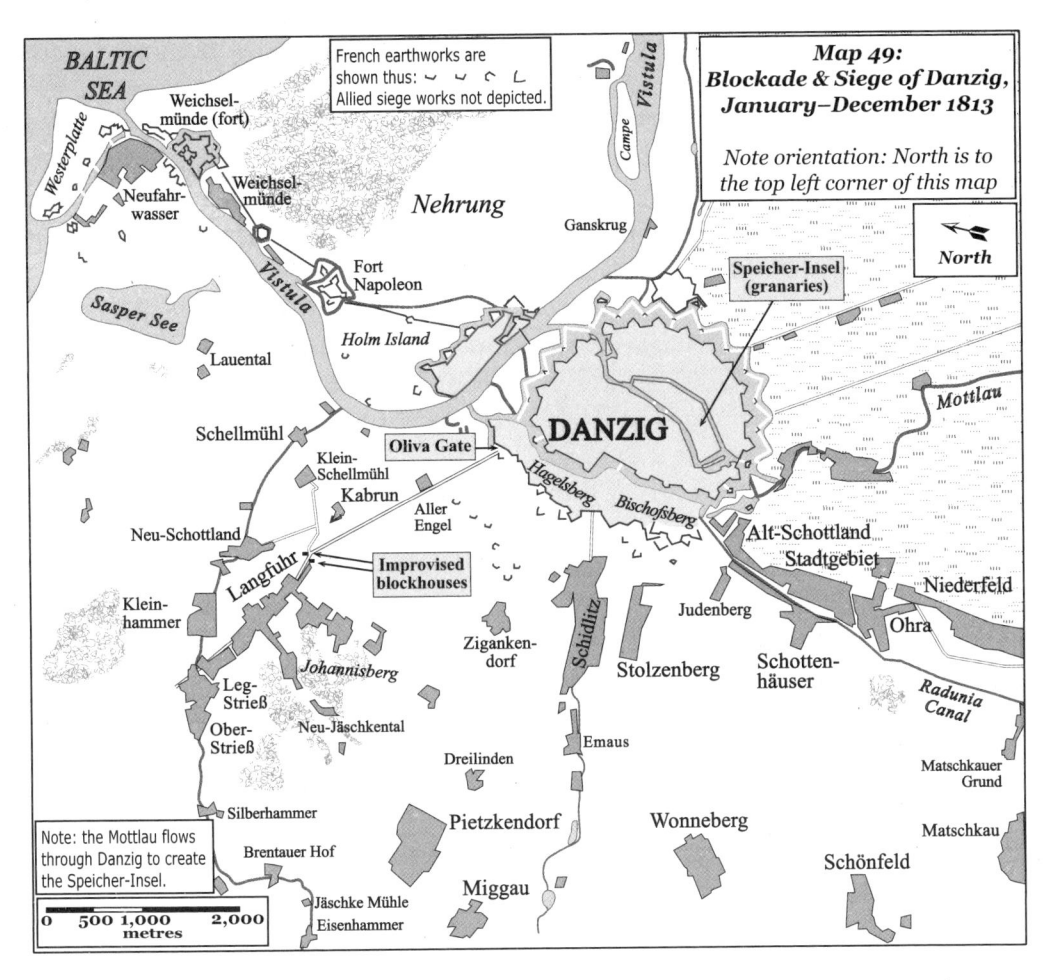

Map 49: Blockade & Siege of Danzig, January–December 1813

the Rheinbund remnants. One month later, they, alongside the Bavarian and Westphalian regiments, would contribute to defeating the Russian assault on 5 March.

The Russians attacked between 4:30 and 5:00 a.m. in the stormy predawn hours of 5 March, striking the entire French defensive line and German troops were heavily engaged on both flanks.[22] On the right, Major Bauer commanded the defence of Langfuhr with the 1st Westphalian (a battalion of perhaps 280 men) and an attached French battalion under his orders. They were initially thrown out of the village but managed to hold on to its eastern end thanks to two homes that had been transformed into improvised blockhouses. Bauer described the tense combat in the village to his brother:

> Imagine for yourself a street, twenty paces wide, two masses opposing each other therein, and how the musket balls flew. As the Russians generally fire

too high, I was in the greatest danger as I was on horseback. It was still so dark that one could not see a pace ahead, add to that the frightful cries of the Cossacks, one can hardly imagine anything more terrible.

With daylight, Bauer counterattacked while reserves rushed up from the rear: 'my men charged with loud cheers and lowered bayonets and threw the enemy out of the village'. By midday, therefore, the garrison had restored the situation in this sector where 'the French and Westphalians rivalled one another in courage,' as GD Étienne Heudelet of the 30th Division recorded in his report. Another French battalion was placed under Bauer's command as he re-established his defences: 'a honour that no officer of the allies had received as according to regulations French officers of similar rank always have command'.[23]

While Bauer was garnering accolades on the right, the combined Rheinbund battalion was embroiled in desperate fighting to counter the assault on the suburbs south of the city. Here the Russians had pushed the French outposts back through Stadtgebiet (Oruńskie Przedmieście) and even entered Alt-Schottland (Stare Szkoty) in their initial rush. The surprise attack caught the Rheinbund men in their quarters in the city so that Lippe Sergeant Dornheim and his compatriots 'were frightened out of sleep by the continuous thunder of the alarm cannons' and hastened to their assembly point in dribs and drabs. 'It was a horrible night,' he remembered, 'pitch black, the storm howled and drove the snow straight into our faces.'[24] Thrown into the fighting in batches as soon as a few were assembled, the Germans and French managed to stem the enemy tide and retake parts of the suburbs but could not evict the tenacious Russians despite vicious combat among the streets and houses. The Bavarian 13th Infantry and the two Bavarian guns were initially committed in this area as well, once again earning plaudits from Rapp, but the battle remained a stalemate.

Late in the day, however, Bachelu changed the equation. The Russians had pressed into Schidlitz and Stolzenberg in the centre during their first onslaught in the early morning hours, but GB Bachelu led a successful counterattack in the afternoon that regained these positions and threw the enemy back beyond Pietzkendorf and Wonneberg. Now, at Rapp's direction, he turned left from his position near Wonneberg to out-flank the Russians in and around the Ohra suburbs and strike them in the rear. The Bavarians, pulled from the suburbs, supported Bachelu's out-flanking attack by holding Wonneberg to mask the French move. Combined with a renewed thrust by the French and Germans in the suburbs, the Russians were forced to evacuate their gains, losing many prisoners in the process. Thanks in no small part to the German elements of the garrison, by nightfall, the Russians had lost almost all their gains and

Rapp was able to re-establish his defences more or less along the line he had previously held.

The combat on 5 March was costly to both sides. Russian casualties numbered more than 1,000 and the garrison probably lost 660 officers and men including 37 Bavarians and 106 from the Rheinbund battalion. 'Rarely has a battle been fought with more bitterness and perseverance than on this day,' wrote Hauptmann Düring of Schaumburg-Lippe.[25] For Rapp, 'This day was one of the most glorious of the siege,' what he called 'a fresh example of what courage and discipline may effect'. 'Under the walls of Danzig, as at the Berezina,' he would write, 'worn out by want or by disease, we were still the same; we appeared on the field of battle with the same ascendancy, the same superiority.'[26]

If perhaps extravagant in his impression of the battle on the 5th, Rapp was unstinting in his praise of the troops after this defensive success. The action at Langfuhr, he reported, 'does the greatest honour to the Westphalian regiment, commanded that day by Major Bauer, a very distinguished officer, who has already proved himself in Spain and in the retreat of the 10th Corps – and to the two French battalions.' Similarly, he recognised the Poles and Bavarians in his report to Berthier and in an order of the day, later telling the men of the 13th Bavarian at a review that they had 'fought like lions'. Additionally, his report on 5 March made specific reference to Weimar Oberst von Egloffstein and Frankfurt Major von Horadam, both of whom had been wounded and both of whom he described as having 'fought valiantly' in the battle.[27]

The men also congratulated themselves on their achievements. The Poles, French, Bavarians, and Germans assembled in Ohra that night and, as Sergeant Dornheim recalled, 'together we marched back to Danzig as victors'. 'Our soldiers', he wrote, 'who looked totally black in the face from biting off cartridges and from powder smoke, our limping wounded, all looked down with a proud feeling on the soldiers and quiet inhabitants who had stayed behind in Danzig.'[28]

The remaining weeks of the spring blockade saw only a few major actions, but Rheinbund troops were involved in several of these. Although losses to sickness meant that the Bavarians and Westphalians had to be formed into a single battalion under Oberst von Butler, they distinguished themselves in a sortie to the south on 24 March, advancing past Niederfeld (Dolnik) with the 10th Polish Infantry and French troops. In addition to pushing back the Russian outposts, gathering food, and collecting intelligence, this action successfully destroyed a levee to expand the flooding on the city's southern flank before returning to friendly lines. Rapp congratulated both contingents, reserving special plaudits for a young Bavarian drummer who had inspired his compatriots and telling Westphalian Major Bauer that 'your people are soldiers who don't fear the devil in hell, each of you has earned the cross [of the Legion of Honour]'.[29]

A month later, the combined Bavarian/Westphalian battalion participated in an extended foray into the Nehrung, advancing up to 10 kilometres and remaining for three days (27–30 April) to forage for supplies and intimidate the enemy.[30] Finally, both the Bavarian/Westphalian battalion and the composite Rheinbund battalion were part of the major French attack on 9 June just before news of the armistice arrived. Herzog Alexander's appearance as commander of the besiegers had produced greater activity on the Russian side and Rapp, weary of the constant annoyances along the outpost line, decided to strike a blow that would chasten the enemy and grant his men some relief. As usual, he hoped the attack would provide an opportunity to acquire food and other supplies for the garrison as well. This 9 June sortie sparked costly combat all along the line from Ohra to Langfuhr.

The Rheinbund battalion stood in the centre that day and Frankfurt Major von Horadam's diary provides an image of the fighting. He and his men were posted in a deep ravine in front of Schidlitz where 'as if by chance a lot of spent balls flew over the hill and clattered against the bayonets so that everyone thought he would soon be hit ... The boys demanded to be led forward at once because they did not want to be shot dead on the spot.' Fortuitously, GB Devilliers rode up a short time later to order an advance. The Germans battled a Prussian Landwehr battalion and threw them back after a tough fight at around one o'clock but 'our men were not to be halted and ran after them for a distance until the aides-de-camp pulled them back to us again'.

> We had all stretched ourselves on the ground and shot into the valley where the Russians were preparing a new attack; then suddenly a roaring cheer sounded from the left. We saw the governor [Rapp] and his staff ride down the entire battle line and, as he came up to us, he shouted 'My dear Germans, I have heard for certain that the emperor has won two great battles in the vicinity of Dresden and has advanced to the Oder; this could bring peace.' Then we all screamed a loud cheer.

The combined Rheinbund battalion and their French comrades engaged in a lengthy firefight through the afternoon in which both sides fired large amounts of ammunition but neither gave way.

> Then, as it wanted to become evening and the barrels of the muskets were so hot that the men could no longer grip them, all of a sudden, a great commotion arose among the enemy and a large number of Bashkirs and Cossacks came bounding down the hill with great cries; they shot off

arrows and pistol balls but did us no harm. We had formed square just like the French next to us. We heard as the old sergeants called out 'hold firm... hold firm!' but this was not necessary with our men. They let the Russians come into good range and gave them three volleys that knocked many of them to the ground. The need was so great on our side, however, that the men immediately sprang out of the ranks and fell upon the horses to slice the best cuts out of them. However, we had to leave behind a lot of blood that day and the battalion is hardly 400 men strong now.[31]

In contrast to Horadam's lively affair, the Bavarian/Westphalian battalion was initially held in reserve behind Schidlitz. Later committed to support the right flank, it helped push back a Russian advance but was not heavily engaged. Though it stood under enemy fire for several hours its losses were few: nine Bavarians wounded along with two Westphalians killed and sixteen wounded.[32]

The 9 June foray did not fulfil Rapp's expectations, but the Rheinbund troops once again emerged with commendations. Johann Pschorr, the corporal charged with the two Bavarian guns, was praised for his skill and calm demeanour (he would soon be raised to the rank of *Unterleutnant*), and a Saxon artillery battery that supported the French advance on the left flank between Ohra and Schönfeld received specific mention. 'The troops of the Confederation displayed a remarkable ardour and bravery', reported Heudelet, 'Majors Horadam [Frankfurt] and Hoppe [Schwarzburg] are to be highly commended.'[33]

This last engagement occurred the day before couriers arrived to announce the armistice. Although the temporary suspension of hostilities was a great relief to the soldiers of both sides, Rapp worried that it would be detrimental to the defence of the city as his garrison would continue to diminish through sickness but would not be able to receive reinforcements, money, or adequate food and fodder. The supply situation eased somewhat with the summer crop season, but the Russians proved recalcitrant in fulfilling the terms of the armistice as far as provisioning the fortress was concerned. The agreement signed at Pläswitz stipulated that the Allies would supply the various French garrisons every five days, but Herzog Alexander made many objections and, on orders from Barclay, halted deliveries entirely for a period in July as retaliation for the attacks on Lützow's and Colomb's bands. New orders from Barclay authorised Alexander to resume supplies to the fortress later in the month, but not before Rapp (who considered Lützow's men 'a band of robbers') had threatened to reopen hostilities and both sides had taken steps to enhance their fortifications.[34]

Worse than enemy action were the ravages of disease, especially typhus, that swept hundreds of soldiers from the ranks and killed 10,000, perhaps more, between January and the beginning of May.[35] Many officers and men recovered when the weather improved in the spring and the overall numbers in the hospitals declined, but with no prospect of reinforcement from the outside, the losses through death could not be replaced. Despite the garrison's forays, food also began to run short early in the blockade, contributing to the length of the sick lists. Fruits and vegetables were luxuries, and Anhalt officers were thrilled to find 'fresh green chives' one day in May 'that tasted as good to us as the finest delicacy'.[36] Fresh and even salted meat were rarities, so that Rapp was forced to issue horse meat to his men, attempting to extol its virtues whenever he reviewed a unit.[37] Supplies of this equine fare, treated with revulsion by many at first despite Rapp's endorsement, also began to diminish and men turned to cats and dogs for sustenance while tallow was used in place of lard and old herring barrels were scraped for salt.[38] As autumn came on, these health and hygiene losses, combined with combat casualties, meant that the garrison was stretched to the limit just to cover its existing defensive requirements and was unable to undertake the extensive sorties Rapp had launched during the spring.

The armistice, while a welcome respite from combat, did not deliver the city from its besiegers or produce the general peace for which most fervently hoped. Nonetheless, the garrison's spirits remained high.[39] Rapp was acutely aware of the importance of good morale within his multi-national command and exerted himself to sustain the garrison's resilience, energy and fealty. Beyond being attentive to the needs of the common soldiers and setting a personal example of resolute courage, he took the unusual step of having Russian proclamations published in the city's gazette and read out to the soldiers at routine formations. This level of openness drained the Russian propaganda of its efficacy and supplemented active measures to arrest and execute enemy agents who sought to suborn the troops.[40] In another extraordinary action, he used the occasion of Easter to hold a full-dress parade on 18 April. Between 6,000 and 7,000 men of the garrison were assembled just beyond the outpost line in full view of the Russians to pass in review before Rapp and his staff with bands playing, banners flying, and loud cries of '*Vive l'Empereur!*' This audacious display of defiance not only served to intimidate the enemy it also bolstered the morale of the garrison. 'There was no mistaking that this peacetime military spectacle, performed in the middle of the war and right under the eyes of the enemy, gave the soldiers of the garrison great self-confidence and raised their courage not a little,' wrote a Gotha officer.[41] 'The spirit of this garrison,' Rapp would tell Napoleon in June, 'rises to such an extent that one can look upon every soldier as a distinguished hero.'[42]

Rapp's leadership and his actions, both routine and unusual, reinforced the ingrained sense of duty among his officers and men. The practical consequence of his efforts was that the garrison experienced almost no desertion and few of the captured Germans accepted the offer to enrol in the Russo-German Legion – and many that did join soon deserted to go home.[43] As August von Blumröder of the Schwarzburg contingent recounted, when Russian officers delivering a surrender demand from Löwis to Rapp attempted to inveigle their German counterparts into defecting, 'Naturally, they received a negative response from both the French governor and the German officers.'[44] Oberst von Butler, writing to Wrede when the armistice allowed communications to resume, was pleased to report on his regiment's attitude: 'Indeed, I also owe the spirit of the regiment the dutiful testimony that it has always, even in the most perilous situations, borne all grievances with a confidence and courageous steadfastness, without expressing the slightest dissatisfaction.'[45] Rapp was likewise content, telling Berthier that, 'The Westphalians and Bavarians are not inferior to the Poles in courage and fidelity, despite all the attempts at seduction the enemy has made, I do not have to deplore the loss of a single man.'[46] Thanks to the armistice, Rapp could present deserving Rheinbund officers and soldiers with crosses of the Legion of Honour and, through special dispensation from the emperor, even promote Corporal Pschorr of the Bavarian artillery to lieutenant as a replacement for the battery commander, who had been killed in the fighting on 5 March, and the only other artillery officer, who had died of typhus.[47]

Morale remained solid, but the garrison's strength had dwindled. The Bavarian 13th Infantry had only 436 men under arms and remained combined with the 1st Westphalian as a single battalion. Commanded by senior Bavarian and Westphalian officers on a rotating basis, its strength varied from 500 to 700 men plus the small Bavarian artillery component of 17 men that often seems to have operated independently of the battalion.[48] The remains of the Rheinbund contingents formerly assigned to the 34th Division also served as a combined battalion. The 34th Division was disbanded during the armistice, however, and its German and French troops were incorporated into Heudelet's 30th Division.[49] To increase its strength, all the other German troops in Danzig were absorbed into its ranks. This odd organisation thus came to include soldiers from 23 of the Rheinbund's states and acquired nicknames such as the '*Landkarte*' (map), '*Musterkarte*' (sample card) or 'the Europa Battalion' (*see* Chart 52). Though some of these sobriquets were regarded as unflattering, the officers managed to mould the battalion into a functional unit. Rheinbund officers and some NCOs also contributed to an ad hoc regiment that Rapp created during the armistice. Heavy losses among enlisted personnel had forced the compression of all the garrison's formations – French as well as Rheinbund – so that regiments were reduced to battalions, battalions were reduced to companies and so forth. This process resulted in a significant number of excess officers (losses to sickness were routinely far higher among the enlisted men than the officers, regardless of national origin). To make use of these extra officers, a smaller number of NCOs and some dismounted cavalrymen, Rapp formed what he called the 'King of Rome Regiment' (named for Napoleon's son whose title was 'Roi de Rome') in July. Colonels commanded its two battalions and majors commanded its companies while other officers and NCOs served as common 'soldiers'. Later expanded to three battalions by adding French officials and some civilians to its ranks, it also included excess German officers and sergeants (apparently on a rotational basis) and served primarily as a police and guard force in the city.[50]

Regardless of their assignments, the officers and men of the garrison greeted the announcement of the armistice with great enthusiasm. Lieutenant Nicholas Louis Planat de la Faye, the courier who had arrived with this news, was thus delighted to write that 'I was received with open arms and like a consoling angel.' One of his messages, however, was less than delightful as the packet of correspondence he brought included a letter from Berthier expressing the hope that Danzig would be able to hold out for another year, that is, until May 1814. Rapp regarded such extended defence as impossible ('good intentions do not create means') and outlined the garrison's many deficiencies in a long letter to Berthier on 16 June. His appraisal was blunt and realistic as far as resources were concerned, but he concluded with a remarkable assessment of his troops:

> I beseech Your Highness, then, to lay before the Emperor the painful situation in which we shall be placed if His Majesty does not come to our assistance. What remains of the garrison is excellent and, by means of a few well applied rewards, one can count on its unbounded devotion. It will do all that the Emperor can expect from his best soldiers, and will justify the confidence which His Majesty has bestowed upon it by placing it among the number of the corps of the Grande Armée.

From his perspective as an outsider, Planat agreed: 'There isn't a soldier in that garrison who doesn't seem like a hero to me.' he would write on 24 June when he returned to imperial headquarters in Dresden.[51]

Danzig: Autumn Siege

Active operations recommenced in August with the Russians, now reinforced by Prussian infantry and artillery as well as British warships and rocket troops, making slow but steady preparations to initiate a formal siege. Herzog Alexander's overall plan was to conduct a feint on his left towards the Oliva Gate, while actually readying his command for an assault on the Bischofsberg. As a first step, the Russians thus launched an assault on Langfuhr in the predawn hours of 29 August with a supporting attack on Ohra. This prompted a swift counterstroke by Rapp with the Bavarian/Westphalian battalion advancing in support of Grandjean's Polish regiments between Langfuhr and Schidlitz to regain much of the ground lost in the morning. The Russians renewed their efforts in this sector on 2 and 3 September, leading to a bitter fight for Langfuhr in which the Bavarians and Westphalians distinguished themselves (*see below*).[52] Thereafter the defenders were subjected to the constant harassment of small attacks and artillery fire, but the besiegers proceeded at a methodical, nearly torpid, pace, digging trenches, establishing siege batteries, and conducting futile shelling of the French shore defences from Russian and British ships in the Baltic. It was not until 10 October that the next major advance took place, this time a partly successful storming of Ohra and Schottenhäuser. To the annoyance of Herzog Alexander's Prussian subordinates (Russo-Prussian frictions were a feature of the siege), another three weeks elapsed before an attack on the night of 1/2 November seized some terrain in the intended principal assault area between Schidlitz and Schottenhäuser in ferocious back-and-forth combat.

In the meantime, the Allies had opened a bombardment of the city itself on 18 October. This proved decisive as shells set fire to Danzig's huge grain magazines on the Speicher-Insel. Flaring out of control in high winds, the flames destroyed most of the city's food reserves. At this point as well, the garrison began to learn of Leipzig and the French retreat to the Rhine. This demoralising news led to fears of desertion among the garrison's soldiers and insurrection in the city's population.[53] The Allied bombardment and the savage fighting in the trenches, blockhouses and redoubts continued, and the defence of the city thus became unsustainable. 'What could we do?' lamented Rapp in his memoirs, 'We had no more provisions.'[54] The next several weeks were marked by a combination of negotiations to surrender and heavy exchanges of artillery fire – the French alone fired 3,000 rounds on 18 November – but the outcome was hardly in doubt. Rapp thus concluded a capitulation on 29 November by which the Poles and Germans would go home while the French and Neapolitans would return to France and Italy respectively, all obligated to pledge not to fight against the Allies for one year. The Coalition monarchs, however, rejected this agreement and, to Rapp's understandable disgust, he and his men left the fortress on 2 January 1814 to be marched off to Russia as prisoners of war.

The remaining Rheinbund troops, though much reduced, participated in many of the small but enervating actions that characterised the autumn campaign at Danzig. On 29 August, for example, the Germans were involved in Rapp's attempt to evict the enemy from the heights the Russians had seized south of Langfuhr the previous night (the Johannisberg). The combined Rheinbund battalion advanced 'under terrible downpours and the heaviest rain of shot and musket balls', losing thirty men as they threw the Russians out of a field entrenchment.[55] The Bavarians and Westphalians, initially in reserve, did not come into action until the end of the day in fighting that cost the Bavarians ten men wounded. The defenders' efforts, however, were only partially successful: they retained the village of Langfuhr but could not regain the heights above it. Though dominated by the heights, Langfuhr, a thin straggle of structures clustered along the road leading to Danzig, was important to the city's defence and could not be abandoned. The Poles, Bavarians and Westphalians were thus directed to hold Langfuhr with outposts in neighbouring Strieß (Strzyża) and reserves in the fortified position at Kabrun. Herzog Alexander, for his part, was intent on mastering Langfuhr and the two improvised blockhouses at the eastern end of the village would be the scene of a heroic stand by the Bavarians and Westphalians when the Allies renewed the struggle several days later.

Bavarian and Westphalian troops had just replaced the Poles on the outpost line on 2 September when the Allies unleashed their assault, hurling the Rheinbund men back towards the eastern fringe of Langfuhr. As Major Bauer recorded: 'On 2 September around 4:00 in the afternoon, after the relief of the Poles, the villages of Strieß and Langfuhr were attacked with such suddenness and strength that the Bavarian and Westphalian garrison of these villages had to throw themselves into the two blockhouses.' While some of the Bavarians and Westphalians from the outpost line fled to Kabrun (also held by Bavarians and Westphalians), Bauer and many others now found themselves trapped in the eastern or left blockhouse with its predominantly Bavarian garrison under Hauptmann Georg von Fahrbeck. Adding the fugitives who had escaped from the village, there were perhaps seventy men in this building as the afternoon waned. The western or right blockhouse, held by approximately forty men (a mix of Westphalians and Bavarians under two Westphalian lieutenants), lay just across the road so the two strongpoints could support each other with fire. Each was surrounded by a makeshift palisade and prepared for emergency defence, but these local homes were far from being solid fortifications (the western one was a massive country house and thus somewhat more defensible). The Russians thus thought to make short work of the defenders and stormed the palisades with great courage, climbing over the corpses of their comrades in their fury, only to be bloodily repulsed. 'Never did I see soldiers fight with greater bravery and determination,' wrote Bauer.[56] Their dead and wounded piled up but they could not dislodge the Rheinbund troops.

Rapp was dining when a Polish officer interrupted to report that the Allies were attacking both Langfuhr and Schellmühl (Młyniska). The garrison was alerted, and two columns were formed to retake the villages. The French successfully ejected the Russians from Schellmühl, but the column dedicated to Langfuhr was brought to a halt. Worse, the leading elements, Neapolitans of the 33rd Division, were cut off and cut down by the numerous Russian cavalry despite a simultaneous sally from the blockhouses in which the survivors now sought refuge. Rapp and his staff could see that the relief effort at Langfuhr had failed but that the blockhouses were still resisting. However, GD Jacques David Martin Campredon, Rapp's chief engineer, watched in horror as the enemy 'set fire to the nearest houses, hoping that it would spread to the latter [the blockhouses], but the brave troops who were trapped there held firm even though the heat became excessive, and the fire had already reached the roof'. The situation looked hopeless, and Rapp called back the counterattack force. With 'many reports assuring that the houses were no longer firing and that the garrisons had been massacred, no further attempts were made' to relieve the blockhouses, noted Campredon.[57]

The defenders in the blockhouses, of course, did not know that they had been given up for lost. They continued to resist stoutly, firing at Russians who tried to set the palisades or their little forts afire and hoping that the main garrison would sortie to relieve them during the night. They were fortunate that the wind was blowing in a favourable direction so that when the Russians put the neighbouring buildings to the torch, most of the flames spread elsewhere in Langfuhr rather than the blockhouses. Much of village was burnt to ruins in a dreadful conflagration but only a few embers reached the blockhouses. Nonetheless, some sparks caught so that the defenders had to fight both the enemy and the fire for much of the night. With no water, they had to use whatever materials were at hand to beat down the flames, and the intense heat forced them to move their ammunition to the interior of the building for fear it would ignite and explode. The night eventually grew quiet, but the trapped men, tormented by heat, smoke and thirst, could not relax their guard. Without food or drink, surrounded by the pitiful cries of the Russian wounded outside, the officers worked hard to maintain morale and the men rested as best they could as they awaited the dawn.

The morning of 3 September brought surprise and new fears. 'To our astonishment', wrote Oberst von Butler in his diary, 'at daybreak the following morning we saw the two aforementioned blockhouses still totally undamaged [this was an understandable error owing to the distance] amidst the ruins and indeed soon realised that a few shots were still coming from them'. As the city's garrison hastened to form a relief force, Bauer experienced 'the most terrifying moment of my life' as he looked out to see 'the Russian cavalry and many columns of infantry and artillery deploying to begin the dance anew'. The Russians focused first on the larger western blockhouse where the tiny garrison resisted until a howitzer shell collapsed the roof around 6:00 a.m. In an attempt to negotiate a surrender, the Westphalians and Bavarians filed out only to be taken under volley fire by the waiting Russians. Bauer and the others watching from the other blockhouse were appalled to see many of their comrades shot down and the officers 'dreadfully abused' by their captors. Only eight soldiers escaped to race the 500 or so metres to safety with their compatriots at Kabrun.

The Russians now turned their guns on the eastern blockhouse. At least seven balls crashed through the structure while exploding howitzer shells landed inside to set the building ablaze and tear apart members of its little garrison. Further defence was impossible. Having witnessed the grim consequences of surrender, Fahrbeck and Bauer quickly concluded that their only hope lay in a life-or-death dash towards friendly lines even though they would have to leave behind the badly wounded. Squeezing through the narrow door and a gap in the palisade, they led their men towards Kabrun at the fastest pace they could manage while assisting the walking wounded. By great good fortune, Rapp and Butler had sent forward French and Bavarian reconnaissance parties to ascertain the state of affairs at the blockhouses. These were instrumental in covering the desperate retreat of their comrades. The men still had to run an agonising gauntlet of Russian fire and cavalry attacks as well as fire from their own men who mistook them for the enemy. About half of them (35–50 officers and men) made it to Kabrun where they were greeted as heroes with cheers, hugs and liquid refreshment. The blockhouse episode thus brought the Bavarians and Westphalians enduring renown at the cost a total of 145 officers and men killed, wounded, or missing (62 Bavarians, 83 Westphalians).

Rapp was profoundly impressed by the resolute defence the blockhouse garrisons had offered and thrilled that some were able to return safely. He issued a special order of the day to honour their valour, citing the defence as 'one of the finest feats of arms' in which 'troops of different nationalities rivalled each other in ardour and devotion'.[58] Additionally, he invited all surviving members to dine with him (a rare privilege for enlisted soldiers) and had the wounded lodged and fed at his residence until they recovered.[59] Colonel Louis Auguste Camus de Richemont, one of the garrison's senior engineers, summed up the view from headquarters: 'This handful of braves defended themselves with such vigour, intelligence and composure that they resisted all attacks and triumphed over all the manifold hazards, even the fire, which they managed to put out while continuing to fight.'[60]

The heroic defence of the blockhouses, of course, did not alter the trajectory of Danzig's fate as the blockade gradually transitioned into a formal siege during the course of the autumn. Rheinbund troops continued to participate in all aspects of the defence: outpost duty, struggles for outer works and fighting fires caused by the Allied bombardment. A Bavarian detachment of eighty-seven men under Hauptmann Fahrbeck, for instance, successfully defended a post east of Schidlitz on the night of 31 October/1 November. It was forced out the following night, but then participated in a sortie to recover the position in a 3:00 a.m. assault on 2 November for the loss of ten men.[61] As the weeks passed, however, rations diminished, sickness increased, the Allied bombardment wreaked havoc on the city and news of Leipzig filtered into the garrison, resulting in discouragement and a degree of desertion. Desertion seems to have afflicted all elements of the garrison, including the French and Poles, but the overall numbers were low despite the hardships and bleak outlook. 'It really is a special honour for my regiment that it has had no more than two cases of desertion during the whole siege', noted Butler proudly, 'as it was subjected to the same privations and the same difficult duties, which are to be regarded as the main cause of this frequent desertion.' Similarly, Leutnant Franz Freiherr von Soden of Schwarzburg-Sondershausen would recall later in life 'the sad feeling ... that gripped me as a German' when he heard Prussian signals horns while on outpost duty. 'Yearning for freedom combined with love of the fatherland flowed through my every fibre,' he would write, 'but duty commanded the noblest feelings to silence.' Closer to the experience, he commented that, 'What can also be said in praise of the garrison is that, after nearly a year of valiant defence of the fortress entrusted to it, it was only forced to surrender by hunger and that even in the hardest times, with few exceptions, no desertions had occurred.'[62] Leutnant Gustav Jacobs of Gotha even noticed the almost perverse manner in which adversity melded units together despite their differences:

> In the final months, desertion among the garrison, of which one had heard nothing at the beginning, became somewhat greater, especially among the German troops, but in total only three men deserted from the Ducal Saxon Regiment; certainly few if one considers the hardships which the soldiers had to endure and weighs the inducements that came to them from the enemy almost daily. These evoked the opposite among the older soldiers, many of them were proud to be part of the Danzig garrison, gladly bore all the privations and were always willing to do the most difficult duties, even voluntarily.[63]

Pressures on the German officers, however, were increasing. Oberst von Butler received a letter from Herzog Alexander on 3 November – the day after the catastrophic destruction of the granaries – asserting that Bavaria had changed sides (which it had) and claiming that he had orders to treat as rebels any Bavarians who remained under French banners. He thus urged Butler to leave the city at once. 'This circumstance placed me in an extremely precarious situation, where compromises of all kinds are so easily possible even with the best will and the choice of the most expedient means which the principles of honour and the inviolability of my incumbent duties dictated to me,' wrote the rather verbose Butler in his diary. On the one hand, the enemy commander had given his word of honour concerning Bavaria's defection; this seemed to validate widespread rumours about the change in Munich's policy. On the other, 'without royal or superior orders from my most gracious King – or his appointed high representative – I could never be allowed to act on my own authority in such a precarious and critical situation'. His solution was to present his dilemma to Rapp and ask to be relieved of outpost duties or other tasks that might compromise him and his men by forcing them to fight the Allies. Rapp, who valued the Bavarian regiment and its colonel, accepted Butler's request even though, as engineer Lieutenant Prosper Honoré d'Artois would later write, 'the garrison was thereby deprived of an elite corps, which had rendered very great services and became even more necessary in those difficult times'.[64] Rapp's generous decision was a great relief to Butler and when Herzog Alexander sent him a second letter two weeks later, the colonel got permission to reply, asking the Russian commander to provide definitive orders from Bavaria. In the meantime, he and his regiment remained within the city's walls.

From the French perspective, 'the Bavarians, natural friends of the French whom they rivalled in glory, had, by their numbers and their discipline, a marked influence on the other German troops; they were, in a sense, the node, the central point of attachment for all the contingents of the Confederation'.[65] The change in the Bavarians' role inside the fortress thus meant that the other Rheinbund troops also had to be relieved of front-line service. The remains of the 1st Westphalian Infantry were an exception. They remained on duty in the outer works until 24 November when Bauer asked for them to be withdrawn from outpost duty.

By the time Bauer made his request, the long siege was coming to an end. The bombardment and close combat finally ceased on 27 November: 'The silence that now fell had something eerie for us,' remembered Schumann of Schwarzburg.[66] Two days later, Rapp signed a capitulation that allowed the French to retain possession of the fortress until 2 January 1814. The terms of the agreement, however, required most of the Germans to be released earlier and the Bavarians marched out of the Oliva Gate with flags flying on 12 December. Rapp had invited Butler and one of his majors to tea with the Russian negotiators on 30 November, introducing him as 'the brave Bavarian colonel who, with his regiment, performed so well during the entire siege'. Similar warm words of respect were exchanged now as the 13th Infantry departed: 'The mutual farewell at this gate', wrote Butler, 'attested to the high degree of respect that my regiment had enjoyed during its entire stay in this city.'[67] With the exception of the Westphalian, Frankfurt and Saxon soldiers, the other Germans left the following day accompanied by 'the most excellent expressions of courtesy' from Rapp. As a sign of the governor's satisfaction, they, like the other contingents, were allowed to draw supplies of clothing and equipment from the city's magazines before departing.[68] 'With melancholy the Germans parted from their brothers in arms with whom they had endured so much,' observed Jacobs, 'but with joy they left the city in which misery had reached an almost unbelievable level.'[69]

Out of an overall garrison strength of 12,900 combatants, there were approximately 1,200 Rheinbund infantrymen plus a handful of artillery and train personnel present for duty in the fortress when it capitulated.[70] As Le Marois had done in Magdeburg, Rapp gave these troops the opportunity to take service in the French army, but only three Westphalian officers chose to accept his offer (to be excoriated by Düring for doing so). The men from Westphalia, Frankfurt and Saxony were initially detained in Danzig as their monarchs had not joined the Coalition. They finally left at the end of December just before the French, in contravention of the agreement Rapp had signed in late November, were escorted to Russia as prisoners of war (the Poles, Neapolitans and Spaniards were released to return home). The Westphalians seem to have been permitted to retain their arms but had to leave their flags behind.[71]

The eleven-month ordeal in Danzig thus came to an end, leaving both Rheinbund and French troops with a sense of accomplishment for having endured so long and successfully. Despite the trials of the siege and the Coalition's refusal to honour his capitulation, Rapp was proud of resisting the investing forces for nearly a year. He thus wrote to a friend from Kyiv on 29 April 1814: 'We ate all the cats and dogs, but I fought glorious battles to the end.'[72] His men, German as well as French, regarded their service in Danzig in similar terms. Indeed, despite their many differences and persistent national biases, a remarkable bond developed between the various elements of the garrison, as Richemont described in a later commentary: '[I]t was not solely a matter of the French here, they were part of a community of perils and courage with the Poles, the Bavarians, the Württembergers, the Saxons, the Hessians, the Neapolitans, the troops of the Grand Duchy of Frankfurt, and those of the Prince of Lippe.'[73]

As for the experiences of the Rheinbund troops during the blockade and siege, Hauptmann von Düring of Schaumburg-Lippe provided an apposite conclusion. Composing his journal of the siege in 1817, Düring captured both the specifics of circumstances in the fortress and more general insights into the situation of German troops in 1813 writ large.

It must strike everyone that a garrison composed of all the nations and peoples allied with the French at that time, throughout the entire ten-month-long period of a protracted and perilous blockade and siege, which moreover struggled with the greatest want and misery ... nevertheless always acted with such energy, vigour and unity on every occasion that arose. In every corps, down to the last soldier, there was a competition to surpass everyone else in courage and perseverance! But where did all this come from? By example alone, by the unwavering sense of the governor, always the same and steadfast. One should not think that I, as a German man, want to give a eulogy to the hereditary enemies and former oppressors of German freedom! Heaven preserve me from such a shameful thought; but what is true can and should be spoken aloud and no one, whoever he may be, should diminish its merit! All those who served under Rapp in this siege will be unanimous in never wishing for a better, braver, and fairer commander; he preferred no troops over others out of bias, the bravest was the dearest to him, he was friendly to the lowest soldier, and possessed, moreover, an excellent and well-known personal bravery. This, together with the feeling of being so completely cut off from the rest of the world, where there was no choice but that between ignominious cowardice despised by everyone of his equal, or perseverance and firm courage, caused such a competition to remain prevalent in the garrison. Desertion was something very rare in the beginning, but increased somewhat towards the end of the siege, yet Hauptmann von Düring boldly dares to claim that in the whole time not 300 men went over to the enemy.[74]

Vistula, Oder and Elbe: The Rheinbund under Siege

In addition to Danzig, Rheinbund troops participated in the defence of six others: Modlin, Küstrin, Glogau, Magdeburg, Torgau and Dresden. Like Danzig, the other fortresses under consideration here were all situated on rivers, each protecting an important bridgehead: Modlin on the Vistula; Küstrin and Glogau on the Oder; Magdeburg, Torgau and Dresden on the Elbe. Regardless of their sizes as a percentage of the various garrisons or the nature of their employment, the Rheinbund contingents in these fortresses each had a role to play in the grinding fortress war of 1813.

Modlin: The Difficulty of Making a Long Defence

The small fortress of Modlin lay 290 kilometres southeast of Danzig at the confluence of the Vistula and Narew Rivers.[75] Although both were washed by the waters of the Vistula, the situations in the two locations were otherwise almost totally different. In the first place, the nature of the fortress itself bore

Marshal Michel Ney (1769–1815): the Baden and Hessian contingents of the 39th Division and the Baden Light Dragoons began the war assigned to Ney's 3rd Corps. He praised the dragoons after Lützen, but his condemnations of the Saxons in the autumn earned him an imperial rebuke.

Marshal Auguste Frédéric Louis Viesse de Marmont (1774–1852): Normann's Württemberg cavalry brigade was assigned to Marmont's 6th Corps and did well. He frequently gave it independent missions with French infantry attached, but later tried to blame the brigade for his defeat at Möckern on 16 October.

GD Henri Gatien Bertrand (1773–1844): his 4th Corps included the Württemberg 38th Division and the Rheinbund cavalry brigade led by Beaumont and Wolff. He was solicitous towards the Rheinbund troops under his command and genuinely respectful and cordial towards his German subordinates.

Marshal Étienne Jacques Joseph Alexandre MacDonald (1765–1840): the only Rheinbund unit in his 11th Corps initially was the Würzburg cavalry squadron, but a Westphalian brigade was assigned to his 31st Division later and the Baden/Hessian 39th Division joined in August and served until Leipzig.

König Friedrich of Württemberg (1754–1816): the corpulent Friedrich was possessed of a keen intellect and iron will. He devoted penetratingly detailed attention to military affairs and demanded absolute obedience from his officers, but his brusque, assertive and autocratic manner won him no friends among his fellow monarchs.

GM Karl Graf von Normann-Ehrenfels (1784–1822): Fellow Württemberg officers thought Normann was a brave leader and good tactician; French generals gave him independent missions with attached French infantry. Allegations of dishonourable behaviour at Kitzen and criticism from his king, however, apparently led to his decision to defect at Leipzig.

GM Ludwig Friedrich von Stockmayer (1779–1837): Assuming command of the contingent's infantry at Bautzen after Franquemont and Neuffer were wounded, he showed skill in leading the division to victory, making the battle a highpoint of his career.

GL Friedrich von Franquemont (1770–1842): An officer of wide experience, Franquemont had distinguished himself at all levels and earned the trust and confidence of his demanding king; he led the Württemberg contingent in the 1814 campaign.

The Battle of Bautzen, second day: Württemberg Jägers and light infantry come under heavy fire as they lead the attack on the Kreckwitz Heights on 21 May in this print by Richard Knötel.

Prinz Emil of Hesse-Darmstadt (1790–1856): Like Wilhelm of Baden, Emil was barely into his twenties in 1813, but he had commanded the Hessian brigade in the Russian campaign, surviving that ordeal to lead the grand duchy's contingent again in 1813. Much admired by his men, he also basked in his father's affection and Napoleon's grace.

GM von Normann's Württemberg cavalry overwhelm Lützow's raiders at Kitzen on 17 June in this Knötel print. Shown here are the *König* Jäger-zu-Pferd (identifiable by their shakos) but the helmeted Leib-Chevaulegers also participated in the attack.

Martens, who participated in the engagement with Lützow's band, painted this watercolour of Württemberg infantry escorting captive raiders on 18 June 1813.

Graf Wilhelm von Hochberg (1792–1859): The youthful Wilhelm served in 1809 as an aide to Marshal Masséna, then led Baden's brigade into Russia, performing a sterling rear-guard action to protect the crossing of the Berezina. He commanded Allied troops besieging French fortresses in 1814.

GD Jean Rapp (1771–1821): An Alsatian who had risen from trooper in the old royal army to general of division under the empire, Rapp proved an excellent choice to lead Danzig's defence. He quickly won the admiration and devotion of the multinational garrison and got the best from them in return.

Jérôme Bonaparte (1784–1860): had Jérôme and his senior officers shown more firmness, they might have repelled Chernishev's raid; instead, he chose to flee, and his brigade commanders made decisions that led to the dissolution of their commands.

GM Karl Freiherr Stockhorner von Starein (1773–1843): The talented Stockhorn entered Baden's army in 1790. He missed the horrors of Russia but was closely involved in forming and leading the new 1st Brigade in 1813.

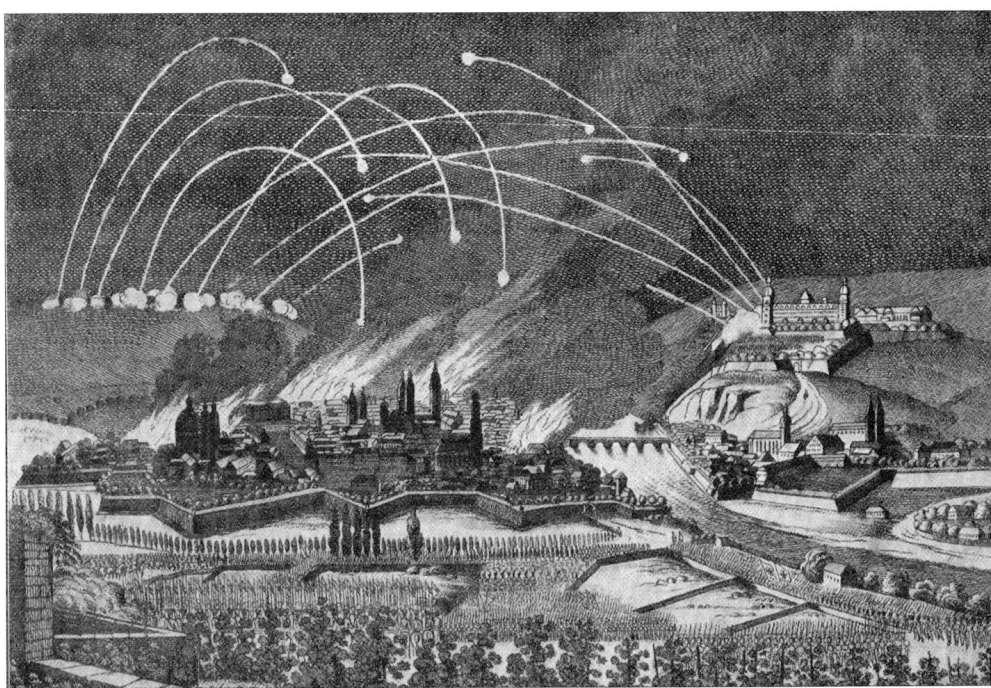

Two views of Würzburg in 1813. At top, Martens shows Württemberg soldiers marching over the old Main Bridge (*alte Mainbrücke*) on 26 May with the Marienberg fortress in the background. Above is a depiction of Bavarian General von Wrede's attack on Würzburg on the night of 24/25 October. Bavarian artillery (*left*) bombard the city causing numerous fires, while French guns reply from the Marienberg high on the south bank of the Main (*far right*). Wrede's appearance forced GD Turreau, the French commandant, to release his Würzburg troops and withdraw his French garrison into the fortress where he would hold out until May 1814.

French and Rheinbund troops in the various garrisons, of course, spent much of their time creating, expanding or repairing fortifications. Here, French soldiers are improving the defences of Dresden in early November 1813. Wooden palisades such as those being emplaced on the right were a common supplement to block streets, gates and other points of access.

As food in blockaded and besieged cities became scarce, soldiers and civilians squabbled for bread and other comestibles. This image depicts starving dogs watching fisticuffs among residents and troops outside a bakery in Dresden in early November 1813.

Shortage of firewood was often among the miseries of besieged cities as winter closed in. In this depiction of Dresden's plight, French soldiers return to their lodgings with scavenged staves while the host family cuts up its furniture to feed their stove for heat.

The final assault on Leipzig, midday, 19 October: the chaos and congestion outside the city's walls are depicted in this contemporary image. Smoke (*centre/right*) shows the advance of the Allied firing line and Cossacks wait on the left, while soldiers and civilians plunder the dead and loot abandoned wagons in the foreground.

Preceded by Cossacks, the tsar and Prussian king ride past the detritus of battle to enter Leipzig in Geißler's painting. Sweden's Crown Prince Bernadotte was already in the city and Austrian Kaiser Franz arrived shortly.

Chart 53: The Modlin Garrison, 1 February 1813
Governor: GD Daendels

	bns/sqdns	Present under arms
Staff and gendarmes	–	27
Brigade		
I/3rd Polish Infantry	1	849
I/17th Polish Infantry	1	418
18th Polish Infantry (Lithuanian) (I, II, III)	3	940
20th Polish Infantry (Lithuanian) (I, II, III)	3	761
21st Polish Infantry (Lithuanian) (I, II)	2	501
Brigade		
I/133ᵉ Ligne	1	358
IV/Würzburg Regiment	1	324
Saxon II/*Prinz Friedrich* Infantry	1	315
Saxon *Niesemeuschel* Infantry Battalion	1	291
Artillery, artillery artisans, train troops, pontooneers		
French	–	185
Polish	–	310
Polish sappers	–	128
Polish 1st Cavalry	–	8
Total		**5,415**
Rheinbund fit for duty (included in total)		930

Note: the 'Livret de Situation' for 15 April (SHD, 2C706) includes small cadres for the 19th and 22nd Polish/Lithuanian Regiments (44 and 65 respectively) and shows the two Saxon battalions combined with 436 officers and men.

Sources: Gembarzewski, *Wojsko Polskie*, pp. 214–5 (strengths); 'Beiträge', *Minerva*, pp. 191–2 (organisation). Charts in Reboul, *Campagne de 1813*, vol. II give slightly higher figures, probably accounting for strengths before the troops arrived in Modlin. Note that Gembarzewski and some other sources erroneously list the Würzburg battalion as 'Württemberg'.

little resemblance to Danzig. Modlin was not a fortified city, rather a minor defensive fortification intended to control access to the Vistula and Narew Rivers along with the connecting Bug River just to the east. Other than a few sutlers, therefore, there was thus no civilian population inside the fortress. Moreover, its condition in early 1813 was poor. Its walls were decrepit and incomplete, there were not enough cannons, food and ammunition stocks were insufficient and the available lodging was inadequate for the proposed garrison. All these factors prompted GB Franciszek Ksawery Kossecki, the acting commander of the fortress, to compose a pessimistic report highlighting the 'extremely worrying details about the difficulty of making a long defence there'.[76] A second difference between Danzig and Modlin was the enemy's behaviour: the Russians outside Modlin's walls made no real effort to seize the little fortress. Although an early assault would likely have succeeded, the enemy – mostly composed of exhausted veterans, untrained recruits or newly conjured militia – were content to blockade the fortress and let time force a surrender. Finally, the multi-national garrison lacked the cohesion and rugged resilience that characterised Danzig's defenders.

This was largely a consequence of the toxic leadership provided by Modlin's governor, GD Herman Willem Daendels, a Dutchman who had become a French general during the wars of the Revolution. Appointed to command the 26th Division in 1812, Daendels collected mistrust, scepticism, and opprobrium from subordinates such as Baden's Graf Wilhelm von Hochberg ('A soldier he was not' concluded Wilhelm) as well as many of those who served under him in Modlin. He seems to have detested the Poles who comprised the majority of the garrison (unlike Rapp who frequently appeared in a Polish uniform) and, eventually convinced that defence was hopeless, he intentionally sowed discord within the garrison in an attempt to justify an early capitulation.[77] Louis Pierre Éduard Bignon, the French representative in Warsaw, summarised the situation in a 30 January report: 'So, above all, the greater or lesser prolongation of the defence will depend very much on the greater or lesser skill of the commander, but there are disadvantages of the position which all imaginable skill cannot remove.'[78] Unfortunately for Napoleon's cause, Daendels would undermine rather than bolster the garrison's resolve and the fact that Modlin held out as long as it did was due to Russian inactivity and the determination of the Polish officers to fight on.

The French intention was to occupy Modlin with two-thirds Poles and one-third French and Saxon troops. Reynier, retreating through Warsaw at the time, was thus directed to detach four battalions to buttress the green Polish units.[79] These were supposed to be two each French and Saxon, but Reynier selected I/133^e Ligne and IV/Würzburg from Durutte's division along with the *Niesemeuschel* Battalion and II/*Prinz Friedrich* from the Saxon contingent (II/*Prinz Friedrich* absorbed most of the remaining enlisted men from I/*Prinz Friedrich* when that battalion's officers and NCOs returned to Saxony to rebuild).[80] These four battalions reached Modlin by the afternoon of 1 February; Daendels arrived on the 4th and the Russians appeared the following day.

The blockade of Modlin featured little fighting as Daendels was not inclined to be aggressive in his defence and the Russians saw no utility in attacking with their generally weak and inexperienced troops. There were occasional artillery exchanges, and the garrison launched a brief sortie on 24 March and several reconnaissance probes during the spring – one of which was an abortive attempt to retrieve 15 milk cows that the Cossacks had nabbed from outside the walls – as well as an innovative but failed riverine attack against the Russian troops on the south bank of the Narew in late August.[81] These small actions were led by GB Kossecki and other Polish officers with Polish troops; no Germans seem to have been involved. Indeed, in May, most of the German enlisted men were seconded to the artillery as fillers to make up for the heavy losses suffered from sickness. The French gunners were 'old, sensible, large and strong men', wrote a common Saxon soldier, 'and we regretted that none of them could speak a word of German. Still, we got along like brothers as one could learn discipline and orderliness from them... We Saxons held it an honour that the French had chosen and designated us for this duty.'[82] The Russians may have threatened an attack on 8 June (the day before a courier arrived with news of the armistice), but nothing came of this beyond artillery fire by both sides in which the fortress apparently came off the best.[83]

Other than these minor episodes, the garrison's existence was characterised by the same problems that plagued the men in other fortresses: disease (especially typhus and scurvy), poor rations, tainted river water, tattered clothing and boredom. The hospital caught fire and burned down in March, killing three of the pathetic inmates in frightful fashion and leaving the survivors to be housed in utterly inadequate stalls and magazines. 'Here we were tormented anew by the evil that the space could not be heated, so that we the sick soon had to freeze terribly,' recalled a Saxon soldier.[84] Quarters for the healthy were seldom better and some were so wretched that a Saxon officer described their circumstances as 'a true troglodyte existence' in earthen huts.[85]

The French and Germans lost many men to disease: 'Sickness and lack of food took most of our soldiers,' as a Würzburg veteran recounted.[86] In the Saxon *Niesemeuschel* Battalion, for example, 133 had died of illness by 12 April and the number reached 170 by 1 May, more than 58 per cent of the battalion. Morale under such conditions was understandably low with some of the discouraged Saxons reportedly getting drunk with Cossacks during the later weeks of the blockade.[87] There was likely some desertion among the Rheinbund units as well, but this scourge was far more prevalent among the Polish units, especially the newly created Lithuanian regiments (18th, 20th and 21st).

Daendels, whose plans to surrender seem to have been interrupted by the armistice, only grew more determined on that course in September when news of Großbeeren and the Katzbach arrived thanks to Prussian newspapers happily delivered by the Russians. October dragged along, but by the end of the month Daendels had set the stage for capitulation. By various devious means, such as cashiering his French chief engineer (who held him in contempt), replacing the Polish fortress commandant with a Saxon officer, promoting disunity within the garrison and excluding most of the Poles from the fortress's Council of Defence, he persuaded enough officers to agree with his conviction that resistance was futile.[88] Having thus crafted a degree of protection against charges of giving in too soon, he agreed to a capitulation on 2 November with a ceasefire beginning the following day. The garrison would turn the fortress over to the Russians on 1 December and be permitted to join the Grande Armée in Germany. As with Danzig, however, the tsar repudiated the initial agreement, and the French were escorted to Russia as prisoners of war while the Poles and Germans were released to return to their respective homelands. Daendels was not present for the surrender ceremony. He left that unpleasant duty to Kossecki and departed for Warsaw where he immediately drafted letters to Tsar Alexander and William of Orange requesting appointment as a general in the Allied forces.[89]

As in Danzig, a counterpart to Hauptmann Düring offers a final word on Modlin, in this case an officer from the Würzburg battalion. He reported back to the grand duchy:

> On 1 December, the fortress was handed over to the Russian General Klein [Andrei Andreevich Kleinmichel] by French General Dutaillis [sic]. The entire garrison laid down its weapons except for the officers who kept their swords. The entire battalion was quartered in some villages along the Vistula... The strength of our contingent shrank from 300 down to 80 men. Oberstleutnant Diez, Oberleutnant von Gemmingen, battalion surgeon Wieth, Leutnant Hauchert, Adjutant Henneberger, staff clerk Strauß and 199 men from sergeant down died from sickness in the fortress. The officers have been without pay since April 1813, the soldiers without salary since 20 December 1812. The state of the uniforms is the worst imaginable.[90]

Küstrin: Dedication and Desertion[91]

This survey of Rheinbund units in the fortress war now shifts west from the Vistula to the Oder where Germans were involved in the blockades and sieges of Stettin, Küstrin and Glogau. The first of these, Stettin, may have harboured a few fugitives of the 6th Rheinbund Regiment after the Russian catastrophe, but, if so, they played no recorded role in the city's defence.[92] The garrisons of Küstrin and Glogau, on the other hand, included substantial numbers of German troops who were active in their respective blockades.

Küstrin, a small city of some 5,700 inhabitants in 1813, sat at the confluence of the Oder and Warthe Rivers. Infamously surrendered to the French in the autumn of 1806 during the pursuit after Jena-Auerstedt, Küstrin, along with Stettin and Glogau, remained under French occupation until it capitulated

Chart 54: The Küstrin Garrison, 21 February 1813
Governor: GB Fornier d'Albe

		bns/sqdns	Present under arms
Staff		–	115
Provisional Regiment	Major Durye	4	2,981
Troops from former 2nd Corps:			
III/128e Ligne			
Detachments of 2e, 19e, 37e, 56e Ligne			
Detachments of 11e and 26e Léger			
Detachments of 1st and 2nd Swiss Regiments			
Elements of the Illyrian Regiment			
Isolated individuals			
Westphalian Brigade	GB Füllgraf		
4th Westphalian Infantry		2	512
5th Westphalian Infantry		2	509
Westphalian artillery		–	38
Württemberg 'Battalion'	Maj. Gaupp	–	c. 29
French artillery, artillery artisans, train troops, sappers		–	371
Total			4,555
Rheinbund fit for duty (included in total)			c. 1,088

Sources: 'La Fortresse de Küstrin', p. 63; 'Belagerung und Wiedereinnahme Küstrins', p. 6; SHD, 2C551 (Situation for 1 August 1813).

to the Allies in March 1814. Commanding the defenders during the 1813–14 blockade was GB Gaspard Hilarion Fornier d'Albe. A veteran officer with nearly three decades of service in arms, Fornier d'Albe knew the city and its surrounding area well, having arrived as governor in 1810 and remaining in that post for the next three years with only a brief interruption in 1811. As in almost all the other fortresses in 1813, the garrison he commanded was multi-national with French, Swiss, Croatian/Illyrian and Rheinbund troops. A key component of the garrison, however, was Westphalian, specifically, GB Füllgraf's brigade consisting of the 4th and 5th Infantry Regiments with two artillery pieces. While the other nationalities were combined into a large provisional regiment composed of units from Oudinot's old 2nd Corps of 1812, Füllgraf's men were considered the remnants of 8th Corps and included Württemberg Major Gaupp's nominal 'battalion' even though Gaupp had only thirty or so men fit for duty.

The story of Küstrin in 1813–14 is one of dogged endurance under sickness and severe privation rather than heavy combat. Although the Russians cut off communications with the Grande Armée in mid-February and had blockaded the fortress fully by early March, there was no reason to risk an assault and they limited their operations to small probes and one or two insignificant bombardments with field guns. Prussian commanders abided by the same calculus when they assumed responsibility for the blockade in August during the armistice. Likewise, the garrison only undertook a few sorties; these were brief affairs lasting no more than a day and limited to spoiling attacks or forays to collect supplies from the local region. The Westphalians were employed in outpost duty and participated in a number of the small sorties, earning particular praise for their role in an action north of the fortress on 22 August under Füllgraf's command. Fornier d'Albe was especially impressed with the Westphalian general, as he reported to Berthier in early June: 'The allied troops are under the orders of Westphalian General Füllgraf who consistently gives proofs of activity and dedication.'[93]

Contrasting with such genuine accolades was the prevalence of desertion. This afflicted the French as well as the foreign units and, combined with rampant sickness – especially an epidemic of scurvy in the autumn – steadily sapped the garrison's strength. Problems with desertion arose early in the blockade such as a Westphalian sergeant, two corporals and twenty-six men who shoved an obstructing sentry into the ditch and dashed away on 9 March. As the trial dragged on, however, officers as well as NCOs and common soldiers sought openings to flee their fortress's fate. Some simply slipped over the walls but by autumn others, even members of Fornier d'Albe's staff, created opportunities for themselves while supposedly checking the outpost line or conducting reconnaissance. Fornier d'Albe tried to curb this evil by executing captured deserters 'with great ceremony'[94] and by mixing foreign troops with Frenchmen on outpost duty and in the fortress's exterior works. With many French also prone to desert, however, these measures had only limited success. The Russians and Prussians, of course, endeavoured to incite desertion and disobedience by smuggling a 'profusion of proclamations' into the fortress.[95] In August, the Prussian commander sought to work on Füllgraf by writing to him directly to encourage defection. Füllgraf shared this letter with Fornier d'Albe, however, and in early December, he returned a second missive unopened. Füllgraf also received praise for leading a 700-man sortie on 22 August that 'succeeded perfectly' in destroying some of the Prussian siege materials and works.[96]

Füllgraf may have demonstrated loyalty, but by October Fornier d'Albe was reluctant to launch sorties owing to doubts about the reliability of his troops, French as well as non-French. 'Desertion had ceased during the armistice,' in the words of the garrison's journal, but now 'it augments in a manner to cause us concern. Even the French desert.'[97] 'The Westphalian officers were despondent,' recorded a resident, 'their soldiers even more so.'[98] Desertion, inadequate victuals and disease remained the garrison's predominant problems, growing in severity and eroding morale as autumn descended into winter. News of French defeats filtered into the garrison while rations decreased, illness increased and remaining food supplies dwindled. 'Crows, magpies, small birds, sometimes partridges and hares were shot with chopped lead – buckshot was not available – and used for barter,' noted the school rector. Indeed, Westphalian Capitaine Gieße cited the lack of decent food as a key factor behind the steady desertion as 1813 turned to 1814. 'Sad situation,' he wrote in his diary, 'Cats and dogs no longer to be seen – eaten!'[99]

The first Westphalian officer to desert was a captain of the 5th Infantry who fled on 2 December along with a corporal, a drummer and eleven men. This incident caused 'a great sensation'[100] and generated understandable mistrust among the French, but it also highlighted the contradictory pressures and sentiments common to such situations. In the first place, a lieutenant and a sergeant of the same regiment refused to join their captain's escape while a lieutenant of the 4th Infantry excited indignation among his compatriots when he asserted that it was ridiculous to go over to the enemy for 'patriotism' (here meaning common German identity and anti-French sentiments). Second, the Westphalian officers felt that their honour had been sullied by this French mistrust and threatened to refuse service on the outer defences if they were to be considered unreliable. Fornier d'Albe found a compromise in mixing French officers with Westphalian units and placing Westphalians among the French, but this little episode illustrates the challenges to leadership experienced by both the French and their allies.[101]

The entire garrison was shocked several days later when Colonel Friedrich Wilhelm von Gröben, commander of the 5th Infantry galloped over to the Prussians while inspecting the outpost line on 7 December. Further desertions occurred in the first months of 1814 as the dreary blockade ground towards its conclusion.[102] By the time the garrison marched out of Küstrin for the last time on 20 March 1814, there were only about 1,200 officers and men fit for duty. Another 1,100 were still in the fortress hospitals and most of the remainder had deserted. For the Westphalians, 393 had deserted during the course of their ordeal, slightly more than 30 per cent of their original strength. Another third had died of illness, leaving only 28 officers and 88 men to march out for the surrender ceremony with 172 remaining behind in their sick beds. Fortunately for the Rheinbund and other non-French survivors, they were allowed to return home while the French were held in Prussia as prisoners of war. The blockade had lasted just over twelve months.[103]

Füllgraf, initially at least, was an exception. He had angered some of his own officers by appearing too pro-French as the blockade progressed, especially when they learned in early March 1814 that he had rejected a letter from the newly restored Kurfürst Wilhelm of Hesse-Kassel urging all Hesse-Kassel subjects to return to the re-established realm. The Kurfürst had sent this note in early January, but Füllgraf had replied that he and his officers had sworn an oath to King Jérôme, and could not change sides while the outcome of the conflict was still undecided. Some of the Westphalian officers were outraged (Gieße now considered Füllgraf a 'criminal') and seventeen of them wrote their own letter to the Kurfürst in hopes of securing places in the new dispensation back in Kassel. When the surrender came, therefore, it was not surprising that Füllgraf elected to remain with the French and be included among the prisoners of war in Prussia. Here he remained a captive for some weeks before being permitted to join Jérôme in Trieste where he later committed suicide.[104]

Major Gaupp and his handful of Württemberg soldiers were also among those heading home after the fall of the fortress. As most of the men in his miniature battalion were sick, they had been sent to Crossen with a handful of relatively hale escorts and never reached Küstrin where the major and 29 men arrived on 21 February with Füllgraf and the Westphalians. Gaupp twice asked permission to leave for Württemberg with his tiny band, only to be denied by Füllgraf. He lost one officer to illness, one to suicide and a third, Hauptmann August von Enzberg, deserted with another Württemberger on 12 January 1814 ('departed without authorisation' reported Gaupp). Leaving nine of his men in Küstrin's hospitals, Gaupp thus turned for home with only ten when the fortress surrendered.[105]

Hauptmann Enzberg would be reminded of his Küstrin experience a year later while serving as a town commandant in Allied-occupied France. A French sentry had tried to stop Enzberg and his comrade when they were making their way over Küstrin's wall that night in January. Pushing the Frenchman into the surrounding ditch, the two Germans escaped into the enfolding darkness with no knowledge of their victim's fate. In the wake of Waterloo in 1815, however, Enzberg, now a major, found himself part of the Allied army of occupation where, as town commandant of Moulins, he had to sign the travel papers of all the French soldiers who had just been released to return to their homes. Hundreds of these men routinely passed through his town and this task, among his many others, was tedious in the extreme. One day, swamped by a flood of these travel papers, Enzberg noticed that one of the waiting French ex-soldiers was examining him closely. '*Commandant*,' said the soldier when his turn came, 'I believe we have seen one another somewhere before.' It soon emerged that the Frenchman was the sentry Enzberg and his compatriot had propelled into the ditch outside Küstrin on that frozen night in January 1814. As was the norm of the age, this unexpected encounter resulted in a hearty meal for the old French soldier, no doubt a glass of local wine, and some coin to see him on his way.[106]

Glogau: The Second Blockade and Siege

Glogau, 143 kilometres southeast of Küstrin, was another of the fortresses the French had occupied since 1806 and it continued to defy the Allies during the autumn of 1813. The blockade of Glogau during the spring campaign has been covered in Chapter 5 since men of the 1st Baden Infantry made up a major portion of the garrison before departing during the armistice to join their brigade in the 39th Division. Left behind were a variety of French, Croatian and Spanish troops along with the 9th Saxon Artillery Company that had participated in the initial blockade. New to the garrison that autumn were the 151^e Ligne (largely Dutch in origin) and the Frankfurt Regiment.

The 1,074 officers and men of the two Frankfurt battalions comprised approximately 12 per cent of Glogau's garrison and seem to have performed adequately in the initial stages of the blockade and siege.[107] GD Laplane, the fortress governor, assigned the regiment important roles in several major sorties in early November, for example, during one of which both the regimental commander and one of the battalion commanders were seriously wounded. Indeed, there seem to have been only seven desertions from the regiment up to the end of September. As 1813 dragged towards its conclusion, however, doubts and dissatisfaction arose among the non-French elements of the garrison. In part this was the result of weakened leadership in the Frankfurt Regiment after those two senior officers were wounded in early November, in part it arose from lack of pay, decreasing rations and the general privations of the siege. The most important factor, however, was the increasing conviction among the soldiers that Napoleon had been defeated and the Rheinbund dissolved. The wildest sorts of rumours had coursed through the garrison during September: the Austrians had occupied Mainz, Napoleon's Empress Marie Louise was herself marching into Austria at the head of an army of 200,000, Marshal Ney's entire army had been captured, Marshal Ney was approaching Glogau with a relief force, and other such tales.[108] Although the French commanders tried to keep news of Leipzig quiet, this proved impossible and from late October the notion of French defeat 'cooled the zeal of the Saxon, Frankfurt and Croatian troops considerably'. The Prussian besiegers, of course, attempted to sap the garrison's morale, especially that of the non-French elements, with persistent propaganda, using rockets to launch pro-Allied newspapers and proclamations into the city and delivering ultimatums to the governor. 'These gazettes', wrote GB Nempde, 'printed and thrown to corrupt the spirits of the garrison, slowly produced their effect.'[109] Laplane, dismissing the news from the Allied side as lies and 'absurd fables', employed his own counter-propaganda measures to sustain the garrison's morale (such as conducting a special religious service to celebrate supposed Napoleonic victories), but for all his energy and imagination, the Allied narratives took hold and there was little he could do to hold off the inevitable.[110]

The Croatian battalions posed the greatest worry for the defence of the fortress, both in regard to desertion and possible mutiny, but by early December the Frankfurt troops and the Saxon artillery company were also becoming increasingly restless. The number of desertions grew and Laplane felt compelled to have his French soldiers guard the exterior ditch to keep desertion in check. Tensions spiked in January. In addition to the widespread suspicion that the French were across the Rhine and the Rheinbund was no more, a message from 'the Military Government in Frankfurt' arrived directing the Frankfurt officers to seek immediate release from the fortress.[111] Whether inspired by this missive or the general state of affairs, the Frankfurt and Saxon officers sent several respectful but forceful letters to Laplane requesting permission to leave. Laplane refused, but he was caught in a dilemma. 'It was impolitic to verify the misfortunes that were said to have overwhelmed our armies; discouragement would have struck the French who were only sustained by hope,' Nempde wrote, but Laplane's efforts to restore the dedication of those 'misled by the alarming reports' arriving daily were unsuccessful. By mid-month, the Frankfurt troops were deserting in dozens – including a captain commanding a battalion – and only the sternest threats prevented a revolt by the Croatians.[112] Laplane felt he had only two options: either 'destroy the city, the population, the rebels and ourselves' by igniting the barrels of power he had ostentatiously placed around the walls and inside the city hall, or 'chase out the mutineers to preserve the fortress'. Fearing that internal mutiny would deliver Glogau to the enemy, he chose the latter course, and, on 24 January, the Frankfurt Regiment and the Saxon company departed without incident. The truculent Croats at first refused to leave until they had been paid, but they marched out on the 26th after receiving partial payment (thanks to an infusion of cash from the city's residents). With the fortress thus 'purged of its most dangerous enemies', Laplane and his remaining troops would hold out until mid-April.[113]

Of the two Rheinbund contingents represented in Glogau that autumn and winter, the Saxon artillerymen were evidently dutiful in the performance of their tasks. Although the veteran gunners who had endured the first blockade had been replaced 'by conscripts who know nothing', they exercised every day and gave little cause for French concern until January. Only six of the hundred or so men in the company deserted and there is no indication that they presented a problem for Laplane. The Frankfurt Regiment likewise conducted itself adequately in the initial two months after the armistice. If not entrusted with independent missions as the Badeners had been, detachments from the two battalions were given normal assignments in the defences and were routinely included in sorties as late as the first ten days of November. This began to change in late October as news of the French disaster in Saxony seeped into the garrison with the active assistance of the besiegers. Much of what the garrison heard was outrageously exaggerated, but the grand duchy's men understandably began to harbour serious doubts despite the steps Laplane took to sustain their fidelity. As 1813 turned into 1814, desertion became rampant and, by the time the regiment left Glogau, it had lost some 330 men in this fashion. Deserters thus accounted for approximately a third of the regiment's strength and included the *Hauptmann* commanding the 3rd Battalion.[114] Though they did not distinguish themselves in the field, therefore, the soldiers of Frankfurt did well enough in defending a fortress under the energetic leadership provided by Laplane and several of their own veteran officers. As with many other contingents, however, adherence to discipline and duty evaporated once the men became convinced of Napoleon's defeat and the Rheinbund's collapse.

Torgau: Endurance on the Elbe[115]

The scene now shifts further west to the banks of the Elbe where Rheinbund troops were incorporated into the garrisons of Magdeburg, Torgau and Dresden. The contingents in Magdeburg have been covered in Chapters 6 and 7, but a brief recapitulation may be in order. The 9th Westphalian Infantry served as part of the city's garrison during the spring and autumn, joined by the Ducal Saxon regiment and the incomplete contingents of Reuß, Schwarzburg and Lippe in late August and early September (the Waldeck companies, also slated for Magdeburg, had been dispersed by Marwitz's raiders in Braunschweig). One of the Westphalian battalions and two from the Ducal Saxon regiment participated in the calamitous engagement at Hagelberg on 27 August, suffering heavy losses in manpower and reputation as a result. Returning to Magdeburg, these three battalions and the other German troops were combined into a brigade under Westphalian GB von Langenschwarz, but all were afflicted by increasing levels of desertion, especially after Leipzig. GD Le Marois, the fortress governor, thus came to regard the Germans as unreliable and released them *en masse* on 12 November. Although Magdeburg would hold out until May 1814 as the last outpost of the Kingdom of Westphalia, it would do so without Rheinbund troops.

Upstream from Magdeburg were the smaller fortresses of Wittenberg and Torgau. Wittenberg was held by French and Polish troops, but the Torgau garrison included substantial numbers of Rheinbund soldiers, most notably

> **Chart 55A: The Torgau Garrison, 21 October 1813**
> **Governor:** *GD Narbonne*
>
> | | *Present under arms* | |
> |---|---:|---:|
> | Fortress staff | 34 | |
> | Fortress administration | 246 | |
> | GB Lauer (garrison) | | |
> | French infantry depots | 7,340 | |
> | Saxon infantry depots | 1,258 | |
> | Artillery | | |
> | French | 358 | |
> | Saxon | 176 | |
> | Engineers/sappers | | |
> | French | 169 | |
> | Saxon | 56 | |
> | 3rd Chasseurs-à-Cheval | 4 | |
> | French Gendarmes | 25 | |
> | Imperial Headquarters troops | | |
> | French | 4,406 | |
> | Hessian (II/Garde-Fusiliers) | 393 | |
> | Administration | 441 | |
> | 3rd Corps troops | | |
> | French | 805 | |
> | Administration | 105 | |
> | 7th Corps troops | | |
> | Saxon | 919 | |
> | Administration | 34 | |
> | V/Würzburg Regiment (and Frankfurt depot) | 771 | |
> | Hessian 2nd Augmentation Battalion | 663 | |
> | In hospital | – | 7,403 |
> | **Total** | **18,203** | **25,612** |
>
> *Note:* The 'Imperial Headquarters troops' heading includes the troops of all services that arrived with Durrieu and the Grande Armée's baggage and parks after their march on the night of 19/20 October. The Frankfurt depot (c. 80 men) had been attached to the Würzburg Battalion. Not listed here is Maillot's Bavarian brigade (Maillot reported a strength of 2,300 on 5 October, but French reports generally credit him with only 1,100–1,200).
>
> *Sources:* 'Situation des Troupes Composant la Garnison de Torgau', 21 October 1813, SHD, 2C168.

Saxons. Torgau, with its population of some 5,000 souls, was a small city with one of the few permanent bridges over the Elbe in 1813. Saxony's government had envisaged enlarging Torgau's defences to create a massive, enduring *Landesfestung* or 'national fortress' that could serve as an arsenal, magazine

Chart 55B: The Torgau Garrison, 11 November 1813
Governor: *GD Dutaillis*

	Present under arms	Sick in quarters	Convalescent
Fortress staff	115	–	
Fortress administration	1,030	–	
Bridgehead Brigade *GB Devaux*			
French	918	74	
Hessian (2nd Augmentation Battalion)	436	52	
Fortress Brigade *GB Brun*			
French	2,529	551	
V/Würzburg (including Frankfurt depot)	451	214	
Exterior Brigade *GB Durrieu*			
French	1,407	196	
Hessian (II/Garde-Fusiliers)	199	54	
Cavalry (Polish 'Cossacks')	101	–	
French depots *GB Lauer*	–	–	1,696
French artillery	1,523	348	
French engineers	690	–	
French equipment train	1,201	–	
In hospital	–	5,910	
Totals	10,600	7,399	1,696

Note: I have translated '*Brigade de Place*' as 'Fortress Brigade' and '*Brigade de Camp*' as 'Exterior Brigade'. The Frankfurt depot (*c.* 80 men) was attached to the Würzburg battalion.

Sources: 'Situation des Troupes Composant la Garnison de Torgau', 11 November 1813, SHD, 2C168.

and shelter for the army at need. Napoleon, on the other hand, saw it more as a temporary field fortification to facilitate operations on either side of the Elbe; it should therefore include a strong bridgehead on the eastern bank and space for an entrenched camp west of the city where an army could defend itself for a short time while preparing for further offensive action. The emperor's conception, combined with lack of time and money, meant that Torgau had not been developed to the extent of major fortresses such as Magdeburg when war came to the Elbe. If it would not withstand a formal siege for long, however, it was proof against sudden assault and, as already seen, figured prominently in all sides' calculations owing to its operational and political importance. After the drama with Thielmann and Saxon vacillation at the beginning of the war, it served as the crossing point for Ney during the spring offensive leading to Bautzen and as the refuge for his broken army in the wake of the Dennewitz disaster. It also functioned as a transport hub and an important link in the French logistical and medical systems throughout the spring and autumn campaigns. One example of the impact of its role was that Torgau was flooded with thousands of sick and wounded transferred from Dresden after Napoleon declared Torgau one of the army's central depots in September.

Torgau's governor as of mid-September was GD Narbonne, an experienced soldier-diplomat known for his probity, clemency and sense of honour. As in many other fortresses, Narbonne oversaw a multi-national garrison whose complexion changed repeatedly, the only constants being the presence of depots for French and Saxon regiments along with numerous French and Saxon artillerymen and engineers. The two Frankfurt battalions, for instance, had been posted in the city during the spring before being reassigned to Glogau, and several Westphalian units served there in the late summer before their transfer to Dresden in September. Two other Rheinbund units associated with Torgau were the Hessian 2nd Augmentation Battalion and the new 5th Battalion of the Würzburg Regiment, both of which arrived in August during or just after the armistice (the latter very much to Durutte's frustration as he wanted it to bolster the Würzburg battalions in his division). Broadly speaking, therefore, the troops allotted to Torgau for most of the war had only been sufficient to defend it against surprise attack (a *coup de main*) and maintain its functions as a stronghold for supplies and replacements. By late September, however, this had changed as 4,500 men from the depots of French infantry, artillery and train units were posted in the fortress in addition to the Hessian and Würzburg battalions, Saxon depots and other oddments. Among the last was a replacement company of Frankfurt troops that arrived in September. Unable to join its regiment in Glogau, the men were designated as the regiment's 'depot' and attached to the Würzburg battalion.[116]

The composition of the garrison altered significantly on 19 October when GB Durrieu appeared from Eilenburg with a large portion of the Grande Armée's parks and trains. After his superb performance during the first blockade of Glogau, Napoleon had promoted Durrieu to *général de brigade* and placed him in charge of the army's vast collection of supply, maintenance and administrative vehicles around Dresden. As the bulk of the Grande Armée shifted away from the Saxon capital in the manoeuvres that would culminate in the Battle of Leipzig, this great mass of vehicles trundled along in its wake, escorted by the remains of the Bavarian brigade under GM Maillot and the Hessian II/Garde-Fusiliers. Given the confused operational situation, however, Durrieu was directed to halt at Eilenburg and await new orders. Here he was joined by parts of the 3rd and 7th Corps baggage trains and their Saxon escort troops (*see* Chapter 2). Durrieu and his men could clearly hear the tremendous thunder of cannon from Leipzig, but new orders never came.

Instead, on 18 October, Russian officers from Bernadotte's headquarters rode up to the Bavarian outposts demanding immediate surrender. Isolated (all efforts to communicate with Berthier having proved fruitless) and fearing the worst, Durrieu contacted Narbonne and the two quickly agreed that the baggage column should seek shelter at Torgau. Narbonne sent out 1,200 men and two guns to help cover Durrieu's withdrawal and, with the Allies focused on Napoleon's destruction, the cumbersome baggage train managed to evade enemy patrols and arrive 'under the guns of Torgau' on 19 October with 6,700 men, 2,560 horses and 540 vehicles of all descriptions.[117]

The arrival of Durrieu's column brought the benefit of experienced soldiers who would buttress Torgau's defence, especially two battalions of naval artisans or artificers (*ouvriers militaires de la marine*) who would perform exceptionally well as infantry and supplementary gunners. At the same time, the addition of so many more men and animals presented Narbonne with an almost insoluble problem as Torgau had only been provisioned to supply a garrison of 4,000 for three months and there were now 18,200 hale and 7,400 sick men to be fed, housed, paid and tended. 'We were very rich in men and above all in fine commanders,' wrote engineer Colonel Simon Bernard in his formal report, but 'We were poor in food.'[118] Many of the horses (for which there was no fodder) were quietly slaughtered at once, but caring for the men was a far greater challenge and one that would be a factor in French decisions concerning their German allies.

For the French, the composition of the garrison was an additional concern owing to the inclusion of so many dubious French depot troops and more than 4,000 Germans. The official journal of the siege described the former as 'malingerers, convalescents, sick, & fugitives, all incapable of active service', while commenting that the Germans were unreliable 'owing to their poor attitude'.[119] The Saxons were objects of particular suspicion. This arose in part from Ney's comments in September about 'the ill will of the Saxons' when he spent several days in Torgau after Dennewitz and in part from what the French officers perceived as recalcitrance, suppressed antipathy and intentional, persistent bureaucratic torpor on the part of Saxon officers and civilian administrators alike. News of the defection at Leipzig only reinforced the existing mistrust. Narbonne, having met with the GM von Mellenthin, the senior Saxon officer, convened his senior officers to address the Saxons' future. He heard varying opinions. GB Brun de Villeret was one of the most distrustful; he and others cited the Saxons as a threat to the fortress and forcefully recommended that they should be disarmed and their units broken up, after which they could be permitted to depart as individuals. Other proposed milder treatment, but all agreed that the Saxons would have to leave the fortress to remove the danger of treason and reduce the strain on the city's food supplies. Narbonne took the less harsh course, informing Mellenthin with diplomatic courtesy that he and his men would have to leave at once, but that they could take their arms and baggage out of consideration for their previous loyalty and the respect due their king as a faithful ally of the emperor. Leaving their sick behind, approximately 1,490 Saxons marched out of Torgau through the bridgehead on the right bank of the Elbe on 24 October.[120] They would soon turn their weapons against their former allies.

The Bavarians were already on their way home. Maillot's little brigade had bivouacked outside the fortress walls with most of Durrieu's column after arriving after their 19/20 October night march; this was a practical measure, but also partly a French precaution against Bavarian defection. Maillot and Narbonne held respectful and frank conversations about Maillot's predicament and agreed that he would send two officers to seek confirmation of Bavaria's status. Even the suspicious Brun recognised that Maillot's 'sense of loyalty did not permit him to take such a step lightly'. When an officer returned with convincing proof that Bavaria had indeed changed sides, however, Maillot dutifully informed the French governor and departed with his few remaining troops on the night of 22/23 October, carrying with them the respect of their French comrades in arms.[121]

The dramatic changes in the garrison's composition – arrival of Durrieu, departure of the Saxons and Bavarians – led Narbonne to reorganise. In hopes of instilling discipline and coherence in the multifarious French depot troops, he assigned them to six provisional 'Torgau battalions' according to their original corps (the 4th Torgau Battalion, for example, consisted of depots from the 5th and 6th Corps) and then placed the new battalions in three 'brigades', one each for inside the fortress, outside the fortress on the left bank and inside the bridgehead on the right bank. As for the Rheinbund units, the small Frankfurt depot was attached to the 5th Würzburg Battalion[122] and placed under Brun's Fortress Brigade ('Brigade de Place'), while the Hessian II/Garde-Fusiliers came under Durrieu in the Exterior Brigade ('Brigade de Camp') and the Hessian 2nd Augmentation Battalion remained on the right bank as part of the Bridgehead Brigade.[123]

However, none of the Germans saw much combat. The Prussians on the right bank were content to blockade the bridgehead, and Durrieu's attempts to sally out in search of food and wood on the left bank were only marginally successful. The Hessian Garde-Fusiliers participated in sorties on 2 and 5 November under Durrieu, fighting against Prussians as well as Saxons under GM Ryssel who had arrived as part of the Coalition force after Leipzig. Although these forays did not provide the supplies the French had hoped to secure, it is notable that the Hessian Schützen did not surrender when suddenly surrounded and attacked by Prussian cavalry. They did not have time to form 'clumps' as was the standard tactic for dispersed infantry facing cavalry, but they maintained a steady skirmishing fire until the rest of their battalion was able to march up to the rescue.[124] These abortive sorties demonstrated to the French commanders that they could not rely on the French depot troops for actions in the open field when they already worried about the Rheinbund units. Durrieu called the French depot soldiers 'malingerers to the last degree' and lamented that he could have defended his sector with vigour 'if the Torgau infantry had been passable and if the fidelity of the Hessians had not been so very doubtful'.[125] Desertion among the Rheinbund units would soon validate French suspicions.

The officers and men of the garrison, however, were discovering that their greatest enemy was not the blockading Prussians and Saxons but rampant disease within the fortress. Typhus and other deadly ailments ravaged soldiers and locals alike, preying on men who were poorly fed, housed and clothed and had little access to clean drinking water. Illness became the principal topic when the defence council met and the chief medical officer provided periodic updates, but remedial efforts proved ineffective. 'The hospitals soon became places of infection, desolation and horror where the slightest ailments were aggravated and became mortal,' wrote a medical officer, 'the spectacle in the rest of the town was no less desolate, no less lugubrious'.[126] The morality rate was terrifying. The report provided to the defence council on 11 November, for instance, listed the death toll in the hospitals between 21 October and 11 November alone as 3,650 with an another 5,910 still in hospital (and, as several officers pointed out, this did not count those who had died outside hospital facilities). 'Typhus developed with a fury difficult to describe', Brun would later write, and as for the hospitals: 'almost no one departed from those corridors of sorrow'.[127] An average of 200–250, sometimes more than 300, died every day and the count of dead totalled an appalling 14,000 from 20 October to 31 December, not including civilians. Of these, only 300–400 were the result of combat; the remainder had succumbed to disease.[128] GD Narbonne was among the victims. Having been injured in a fall from his horse on 7 November, he contracted typhus and died on the 17th to everyone's regret. One-armed GD Adrien Jean-Baptiste Dutaillis took his place as governor.

It was thus Dutaillis who would have to decide on the fate of the Rheinbund troops in Torgau. In the aftermath of Leipzig and with constant encouragement from the Prussian and Saxon outposts, desertion became a major problem among the German units. At least 161 Würzburg soldiers defected during the blockade and Durrieu recorded that 71 Hessians had deserted at one point: 'we cannot count on these troops for anything,' he wrote. The Hessian officers themselves came to the governor on 7 November to report that their troops were deserting despite their best efforts to maintain discipline. According to the official journal of the siege, 'they added that they cannot count on their troops in case they are called upon to fight and they believed it was their duty to so inform the governor'. Narbonne thus allowed them to send an officer to Darmstadt to ascertain their sovereign's wishes. In the meantime, desertion and tension increased. On 23 November, Tauentzien, commanding the Prussian besiegers, provided letters from Darmstadt and Würzburg calling their troops home, the Hessian officer returned with confirmation of that duchy's change of allegiance, and an officer from Würzburg arrived at the same time with similar instructions. The Torgau defence council therefore concluded that, 'The Hessian and Würzburg troops are useless for the defence, desertion is growing among them day by day, retaining them or disarming them would diminish the store of food, hasten as a consequence the rendition and force us to guard inside the fortress men who from one moment to the next could turn against us.'[129] Dutaillis thus decided to release all the remaining Rheinbund contingents. The Würzburg battalion, approximately 400 strong, with its attached Frankfurt depot company (3 officers and 43 men) duly marched out on 24 November with their arms and equipment. The remnants of the two Hessian battalions departed the following day. They were also permitted to take their weapons and baggage, but only after tense negotiations with the French generals and the temporary arrest of the two Hessian battalion commanders.[130]

The Rheinbund troops were thus spared the final harrowing weeks of the siege. Their depleted battalions eagerly headed home while the French hung on, steadily dwindling under the combined scourges of malnutrition, discouragement and disease. Dutaillis finally capitulated at the end of December and turned Torgau over to the Prussians on 10 January 1814. He and his men headed off into captivity, leaving behind a bleak charnel house of a fortress as testament to their endurance and determination.[131]

Dresden: Desertion, Misery and Disease

The blockade of Dresden was similar to the other besieged fortresses discussed here in its physical and psychological aspects, but it was briefer and more central to the outcome of the war. Dresden had served as the Grande Armée's logistical hub and operational pivot until early October when Napoleon belatedly and abruptly decided to abandon it. Aside from its utility as a river crossing and supply base, Dresden was important to the emperor as the capital of his ally Saxony and this political consideration was a crucial factor in his decision to hold on to the city for so long.[132] His failed flailings at the Allied armies in September and Blücher's crossing of the Elbe at Wartenburg, however, left him no alternative but to shift his base of operations away from the Saxon capital. He thus rode out of Dresden on 7 October seeking battle further north. Saxony's Friedrich August followed in his wake. As described in Chapter 2, Napoleon offered the king the option of accompanying him to Leipzig or staying in Dresden. Although his advisors wanted him to take refuge in the Königstein fortress, Friedrich August, cleaving to his sense of duty and believing he had a better chance of influencing events by remaining near the emperor, chose to follow Napoleon. He and his family therefore departed Dresden in a great cavalcade headed for Leipzig and captivity. He would not see his capital again until June 1815.

Left behind in Dresden was a large – indeed, excessively large – force under the overall command of Marshal Gouvion Saint-Cyr consisting of his own 14th Corps, the rebuilt 1st Corps (GD Georges Mouton, Comte de Lobau), and the city's formal garrison. In all, this amounted to 37,531 officers and men more or less fit for duty with another 6,621 sick in the Dresden hospitals or in their quarters. Saint-Cyr faced problems aplenty. Dresden, though surrounded by some fortifications, was not a true fortress and was poorly suited to withstand a formal siege. Additionally, as one of the brigade commanders in 1st Corps pointed out in his memoirs, it would have been necessary to raze Dresden's suburbs to make a proper defence of the city 'and Napoleon could not resolve himself to treat so cruelly the capital of an allied king, the only one who remained loyal to him'.[133] Moreover, food and other essentials, especially firewood, were in short supply from the very beginning and sickness soon began to mount as in almost all the other besieged or blockaded cities.

Dresden was not cut off until mid-October and the blockade was weak initially. Had he moved early, therefore, Saint-Cyr might have been able to break out to join the garrisons of Torgau and Magdeburg by marching north down the Elbe. The marshal, however, seems to have felt constrained by his instructions ('my intention is to retain Dresden' wrote Napoleon on the 7th) and confined himself to holding the city and awaiting new orders.[134] A successful foray was conducted on the left bank on 17 October, but this was only designed to gather supplies and intelligence. News of Leipzig brought a reappraisal, but Saint-Cyr delayed, and the Allies easily repulsed an attempt to break out towards Großenhain on the right bank on 6 November. By this time, the food and ammunition situation had become dire. Hundreds were dying in the 'abominable' hospitals and on the streets.[135] The dreadful scenes prevalent in other besieged cities thus became common in Dresden as well: soldiers squabbling with civilians over scraps of bread, searching refuse piles for edibles, or consuming horses, dogs and cats. 'Here you could see some of these wretches skinning a gaunt dog to make themselves a roast,' as one

Chart 56: The Dresden Garrison, 10–11 October 1813

Overall Commander: *Marshal Gouvion Saint-Cyr*
Governor: *GD Durosnel*

	Present under arms
Garrison — GB Gomez Freyre	
2nd Westphalian Infantry Regiment	823
(Arrived on 18 September with 1,157 officers and men)	
3rd Westphalian Infantry Regiment	822
(Had 1,177 officers and men on 18 September)	
1st Westphalian Light Infantry Battalion	?
(Had 456 officers and men on 18 September)	
Polish infantry depot	645
Saxon cavalry	20
Polish cavalry depot	52
French artillery and artisans	484
French pontooneers	149
Westphalian artillery	58
Westphalian train (see note)	44
Saxon artillery and train	350
Bavarian artillery	25
Polish artillery depot	36
French miners	94
Saxon engineers	45
Total	**3,647**
1st Corps — GD Mouton, comte de Lobau (as of 25 September)	
1st Division	3,316
2nd Division	3,298
23rd Division	3,693
Light Cavalry	704
Artillery, train, engineers	1,211
Total	**12,222**

resident remembered. Another described 'people fighting over bread in front of bakeries', while 'butter, salt and wood were lacking altogether'.[136] Among the victims who succumbed to disease was Baron Serra, the French ambassador to Saxony. 'Our troubles increased from day to day, from hour to hour', wrote the French *intendant* in charge of logistics, and Saint-Cyr would later lament that his troops 'were diminished daily in frightening proportions by desertion, misery and disease'.[137]

Hoping to achieve acceptable surrender terms before supplies ran out, Saint-Cyr therefore opened negotiations with the Allied commander. This was GdK Klenau, whose IV Corps had been detached from the main army after Leipzig to force Dresden's submission. A capitulation was agreed on 11

		Present under arms
14th Corps	Marshal Gouvion Saint-Cyr	
	42nd Division	4,554
	43rd Division	4,508
	44th Division	4,122
	45th Division	6,151
	10th Light Cavalry Division	928
	Artillery, train, engineers	2,443
	Total	21,706
	Total fit for duty	37,575

Notes:

1. The 1st Westphalian Light Infantry Battalion appears on the 2 October 'Situation' with 417 officers/men, but disappears thereafter; though it likely remained in Dresden, its subsequent location is not known with certainty. Additionally, the mid-October entries do not include 44 Westphalian train troops that appear in earlier reports; but they are included here because their absence was likely a clerk's oversight.

2. There were also enormous numbers of sick and wounded: 6,621 listed under the garrison; 6,371 for 1st Corps; and 13,238 for 14th Corps. It is not clear whether there was any overlap between the number of sick listed under the garrison and those entered for each corps; some may have been in hospitals or quarters outside Dresden.

Sources:

'Situations de la Place de Dresde' for 17 September through 11 October 1813 (SHD, 2C546); 1st Corps 'Situation' for 25 September 1813 (SHD, 2C538); 14th Corps 'Situation' for 10 October 1813 (SHD, 2C542).

November and the French, disarmed except for a small escort detachment, were permitted to depart for France over the next several days under the pledge not to take up arms again until exchanged. On receiving Klenau's report of the surrender, however, Schwarzenberg and the Allied monarchs considered the terms too lenient. In another case of Coalition leaders repudiating capitulation agreements, Klenau was ordered to reverse them: the French could either return to Dresden as before or become prisoners of war. With food in the city exhausted and hopes of returning to France crushed, resuming the defence of the city was not a realistic option. Saint-Cyr protested vehemently, but his letters were rejected and he was left with no choice but to surrender his command. Some 29,500 French soldiers thus turned south for captivity in the

Austrian Empire while another 6,000 sick and wounded languished for a time in the captured city.[138]

The only Rheinbund troops in Dresden during the blockade were the Bavarians, Saxons and Westphalians who made up approximately 58 per cent of the 3,647 men in the city's actual garrison. Their numbers were small in comparison to the rest of Saint-Cyr's command, however, and, as part of the garrison, their role was limited to defensive tasks and foraging. The Bavarians were two dozen men and an officer from their division's munitions depot that were somehow left behind when Maillot and the rest of the contingent marched for home. Most of the Saxons were also artillerymen and Saint-Cyr held them in high regard, but after news of Leipzig arrived on 22 October, he summoned the Saxon commander, Oberstleutnant Gustav Gottfried von Hoyer, to ask if he could still count on his men. Hoyer replied that he had had no reason to doubt his men's fidelity up to this point but that he would inform the marshal should that change given the division's defection at Leipzig. Several days later, Hoyer dutifully returned to report that his men had received letters from their comrades urging them to desert 'and told me that his loyalty would not permit him to conceal from me the fact that he had been greatly shaken by this invitation'. Saint-Cyr thus released the Saxons from duty, and they left Dresden at the end of October after depositing their arms in the city's arsenal. Comparing them to the other Confederation troops, Saint-Cyr concluded that 'praise is due to the Saxons who remained in Dresden for their honest conduct'.[139] The Bavarians, who Saint-Cyr described as 'honest and loyal in their conduct', seem to have left with Hoyer's men.[140]

The Westphalians in Dresden were a different story. Major von Brethauer's defection with all or part of his battalion of the 3rd Infantry in September has already been mentioned and desertion only increased as October wore on and the garrison learned of Napoleon's retreat towards the Rhine. 'They could hardly be relied upon', complained a French division commander in 14th Corps, as they 'deserted every day by entire companies'. Saint-Cyr's impression was similar, leading him to write in his memoirs that they 'deserted every day down to the last man'.[141] These were exaggerations, but Leutnant Normann of the Westphalian artillery, whose detachment had been placed under Hoyer's command, discovered at morning roll call that all his men, 'with the exception of a few NCOs and train soldiers', had departed with the Saxon gunners overnight. After reporting this 'very uncomfortable development', Normann found himself with little to do, but his horse still needed to be fed, so he and a fellow lieutenant rode out of the city one morning in search of fodder. They had not planned to defect, but they unexpectedly encountered an Austrian hussar patrol and, seeing no means of safe escape, concluded that giving themselves up was their best course of action. 'We thus quickly decided to ride over to them and declare ourselves as Germans for the German cause to which we had long been devoted and which until now military honour and our oath had kept us from promoting.'[142] Normann's case was but one small instance of the flight from duty among the troops of his command that led Saint-Cyr to report on 28 October that, 'The Poles are deserting and there are no Westphalians left.' Again, this was not quite accurate as most of the Westphalian infantry officers with some number of their men as well as Normann, his train lieutenant and a few soldiers were still with the garrison at the time that Saint-Cyr drafted his report. Indeed, Major von Morgenstern of the 2nd Infantry was indignant because Saint-Cyr had ordered the Westphalians disarmed in late October when he released the Saxons. This 'senseless and fateful step' alone would have been enough to induce him to change sides he would later write, but he was not inclined to join the ranks of the enemy and stayed with his regiment until the surrender on 11 November.

Morgenstern may have been unwilling to betray his oath by signing on with the Allies, but neither he nor any of the other officers accepted the offer when GB Bernard, their brigade commander, tried to persuade them to stay with the army in French service. Bernard, a Frenchman in Westphalian service, was furious at the rejection but his subordinates would not be moved. On Dresden's surrender, they would return to their homes while he headed to Austria as a prisoner of war along with the other French.[143]

Königstein: The Last Outpost

Upstream from Dresden, the ancient Saxon fortress of Königstein sat atop a vertical crag high above the Elbe. Considered nearly impregnable, Königstein served several purposes during 1813. When the king fled Dresden in February, for instance, the Saxon authorities transferred the royal treasury, works of art and other valuables to the fortress for safekeeping along with archives and munitions. Friedrich August named GL von Zeschau as commandant and 371 men of II/Leibgarde were allotted to bolster Königstein's small garrison: 104 artillerymen, a garrison company (40) and the Jägers depot (25). The Jägers marched away for Torgau in mid-May and the Guard battalion departed for Dresden in two groups between the 18th and 25th to be replaced by 202 line troops. Around the same time, Königstein was designated as the assembly point for the Saxon light cavalry that had accompanied the king on his excursion to Prague and the regiments were hastily assembled under its protection before rushing off to join the Grande Armée near Bautzen. It also provided a home for three dozen survivors of the Russian campaign. Suffering from frostbite and exhaustion, they remained under medical care in the fortress until they were sufficiently recovered to be issued new uniforms and returned to their regiments.

As summer and the armistice came to an end, concerns about Austrian incursions from Bohemia led the French to augment the garrison. A battalion of the 27ᵉ Léger (465 officers and men) and 20 French artillerymen thus arrived in the fortress on 21 August. The French wanted to install their own commandant, but GL von Gersdorff successfully insisted that the position remain under Saxon Oberst Heinrich Ernst August von Warnsdorf, who had replaced GL von Zeschau in July when the general was reassigned to command the Saxon division in the field.[144] As the Allies launched their offensive towards Dresden, Warnsdorf used one of his 24-pounders to chase off Russian outposts on 24 August. The Allies were still present (though out of cannon range) the following day, when Vandamme arrived to take advantage of the superb vistas afforded by Königstein's location as he surveyed the region for his thrust across the Elbe. While the fighting raged around Dresden, therefore, Königstein supported Vandamme on 26 August with 61 rounds from its 24-pounders and one from a howitzer. With evening coming on, however, Vandamme found that the fire from the fortress was endangering his own men and instructed Warnsdorf to have the guns continue firing but only with blanks so as to prevent friendly casualties while deceiving his Russian opponents.

The combat associated with Vandamme's attack was the last active engagement for Königstein. The French component of the garrison underwent some changes as IV/40ᵉ Ligne (478 officers and men) replaced the light infantrymen on 2 September and were themselves exchanged for III/27ᵉ Ligne (325 officers and men) on 2 October. All the French departed on 7 October, leaving Königstein entirely in Warnsdorf's hands. He quickly concluded an agreement with FML Bubna, the local Austrian commander, under which the Saxons would grant free passage of the Elbe in exchange for the Coalition treating the fortress as neutral. From the signing of this agreement on 9 October 1813 until the king's return in June 1815, therefore, Königstein was 'an island' technically still under the king's command, a last outpost of Saxon sovereignty.[145]

*

Viewed synoptically, Rheinbund experiences as elements of fortress garrisons featured many commonalities, notably privation, isolation, grinding misery and death by disease. Additionally, the German troops were all subjected to constant, if not always sophisticated, Allied propaganda and all came under increasing pressure to return to their homelands in the wake of Leipzig. Their performances under blockade and siege, however, varied considerably, from those who were reliable, stoic and even heroic, to others who were untrustworthy or incompetent, with the merely adequate in between. Leadership –

from their own officers as well as French generals – and unit cohesion were key to where each regiment, battalion or battery stood on this spectrum of loyalty and competence. Those in Danzig had been training and campaigning together since 1811 and benefited from having the most experienced officers and NCOs their monarchies had to offer. They also had the good fortune to serve under Rapp who genuinely respected them and was solicitous to their needs. They responded to his leadership with admiration and loyalty.[146] As a result, there was no significant desertion among the Rheinbund units (or any others) despite the horrors they had experienced in Russia, despite the numerous opportunities to slip away, and despite the incessant inducements offered by the besiegers.

Similarly, Laplane in Glogau seems to have got the best out of the otherwise dubious Frankfurt troops, at least until several of the regiment's key officers were wounded and news of Napoleon's defeat at Leipzig became widespread. Daendels at Modlin, on the other hand, sowed dissension and defeatism, creating what modern parlance would term a poisonous 'command climate' that compounded the little fortress's many physical deficiencies. The Westphalian regiments locked in Küstrin seem to have performed satisfactorily during the spring and the early weeks of the autumn campaign thanks to GB von Füllgraf and the other officers, but they slipped towards desertion as the situation deteriorated in October. Here again the strategic situation of French setbacks was crucial, as was, if our limited sources are accurate, the sense among the Westphalian officer corps that Füllgraf had become too aligned with French interests.

Desertion among the Westphalian elements of the garrison was also a feature in Dresden with at least part of one battalion and some number of individuals finding ways to escape the city well before it was cut off. Dresden and Torgau were unique, however, in that both, like Magdeburg, only became truly blockaded when the autumn campaign was reaching its climax in mid-October. As a result, the officers and men of the Rheinbund contingents were struggling with issues of duty and loyalty at a time when French fortunes in Germany were on the doorstep of disaster. This broader strategic context incentivised large numbers of enlisted men and some officers to leave the ranks and return to their home hearths. Nonetheless, many of the officers, perhaps most, remained at their posts, even with little or nothing left to command (as Westphalian Lieutenant Normann found in Dresden). The Hessian officers in Torgau and the Saxons in Dresden even felt themselves honour-bound to discuss their predicaments with their French commanders. French governors such as Dutaillis and Saint-Cyr appreciated the candour of their Rheinbund subordinates, but in all three cases – Magdeburg, Torgau, and Dresden – they were content to see the Germans depart once it was clear that their monarchs had changed sides.

The variety of these experiences as fortress garrisons means that the value of the Rheinbund contingents during the fortress war in 1813 has to be assessed not only with regard to location but also over time. In Danzig, Rapp relied on the Germans until nearly the end of the siege and only said farewell to them with regret. In other cases, they were adequate assets during the spring campaign and into the autumn but transformed into potential liabilities in October as French defeats accumulated, especially after Leipzig when their monarchs began to change sides. Unlike Rapp, Le Marois, Narbonne, Dutaillis and Saint-Cyr came to see their Rheinbund units as a burden on scarce food supplies and a potential internal threat to the integrity of their defences. These worries notwithstanding, in no case did a fortress fall because of action or inaction by a German contingent. Rather, the Rheinbund units consigned to fortresses in 1813 played the role that Napoleon had envisaged for them: supplementing French garrisons to hold important locations for extended periods of time.[147] Along with the French, Polish and other troops, they suffered great privation and high mortality rates in maintaining their respective strongholds, most of them for far longer than might have been expected, even beyond the point when their homelands had joined the Coalition or, in Westphalia's case, had ceased to exist.

Epilogue

'We are at a moment when we cannot rely on any foreigner.
They can only be extremely dangerous to us.'

Napoleon to Daru, 15 November 1813[1]

NAPOLEON NEVER DECLARED AN END to the Rheinbund. Indeed, French official proclamations through 1814 still referred to him as the Confederation's 'Protector'. Instead of a formal pronouncement, the institution crumbled bit by bit as the member states either signed agreements with the Coalition powers or, like Westphalia and Berg, simply dissolved. Although his government maintained the fiction of the alliance, Napoleon the realist responded practically to the disturbing fact of the Rheinbund's end. 'We are at a moment when we cannot rely on any foreigner', he told Count Pierre Daru, his Minister of Military Administration, in mid-November, 'They can only be extremely dangerous to us.' He thus issued a decree on 25 November to disarm and intern the remaining Rheinbund troops in France and along the border with Spain.

The dissolution of the Rheinbund turned loose thousands of its former soldiers. Many enlisted men, hoping to return to the civilian life they had enjoyed previously, simply went home as Fourrier Sauerteig of Meiningen who appeared in Chapter 7 had done when he fell out of the ranks on the road to Hagelberg. Questions of desertion from their Rheinbund regiments seem to have been forgotten by local authorities, but these men were soon to be liable for conscription by the new political dispensations. Those who remained in the ranks of units whose states had signed on with the Coalition were almost immediately dispatched to the Rhine to join the new campaign inside France as part of the Allied invasion force. The Bavarians of Maillot's remnant brigade were one example of this phenomenon. Moreover, as the officers of the former Magdeburg garrison soon learned, their home governments dismissed the pledges they had signed not to fight against France for one year, so they too were directed to head west in the new contingents their monarchies were assembling.

The fates of those from the disestablished states, such as Westphalia, were different. Oberst von Pleßmann and most of the 1st Westphalian Infantry from

Danzig became the core of the Reserve Battalion of the Elbe Infantry Regiment organised and outfitted by Prussia, eventually incorporated into the Prussian army as the 2nd Magdeburg Infantry Regiment, Nr. 27.[2] In other cases, former Westphalian, Berg or Frankfurt soldiers found themselves absorbed into new units the Allies were creating in those now vanished states alongside men conscripted by the interim governments. Some individual officers succeeded in gaining employment under newly installed rulers such as the prince-elector of Hesse-Kassel (though often at a reduced rank), but others were turned away, tainted by having served in one of Napoleon's 'model states'.[3] As related in Chapter 7, for example, officers from Berg were treated like traitors when they returned to their homelands. Indeed, former soldiers of Westphalia and their families discovered that the new authorities chose not to acknowledge their service at all. It was as if the kingdom had never existed. Applications for pensions or recognition of awards received from Jérôme's hand were denied or delayed for decades. The situations for the hundreds of families whose menfolk had disappeared in Russia was especially poignant. Nicolas Bourguinat thus describes Westphalia as 'a special case of impossible confrontation with the past' where 'Neither its high officials nor its veterans could be given any particular recognition.'[4] In addition to these men who had once fought under French eagles, thousands of new soldiers were conscripted across the former Rheinbund states with varying degrees of energy and enthusiasm by their home governments. In some cases, these new conscripts were joined by volunteers, but in every case, the number of men demanded by the Coalition – regulars, Landwehr, and home guard – exceeded the number owed to Napoleon under the Rheinbund.

Civilian populations were generally glad to be free from the suffocating presence of French hegemony but what they desired most – peace and stability – did not come and they soon discovered that Coalition demands were as onerous as those imposed by the French. In many places, the Allied armies were initially greeted as liberators, both genuinely out of joy and pragmatically in the hope that local communities could forestall exactions by demonstrating loyalty to the new conquerors. Indeed, the excessive expostulations of the new enthusiasts for the Allied cause aroused accusations of hypocrisy as a young Badener observed:

> Many political conversions took place with inconceivable speed; he who months earlier had prostrated himself at the feet of Napoleon and his satraps, was now the loudest to curse their conduct; he who could not in word and deed praise enough the power, fame and splendour of French arms and statesmanship, now fell upon the overthrown colossus all the more eagerly with defamatory pamphlets and repugnant caricatures.

Or, in the words of the acerbic Saxon veteran, GL von Funck: those who had shown themselves the most subservient to Napoleon were also 'the first to leave his banners' and 'who shouted loudest the empty word freedom'.[5] The liberators, however, quickly became burdensome, the Russians acquiring an especially negative reputation.[6]

The former Rheinbund states raised new armies as directed, but Stein and his subordinates complained that the response was too slow, and that governments were not displaying the requisite level of fervour.[7] Raising Landwehr and Landsturm forces as required by the Coalition proved problematic in southwestern German states, partly for lack of popular enthusiasm and partly because the monarchs were not eager to arm their subjects. Conscription had to be enforced because volunteers did not come forward in the anticipated numbers and desertion among the new German contingents persisted as a serious problem, just as prevalent when fighting against Napoleon as fighting for him.[8] War against Napoleon proved as unpopular as war on the French emperor's behalf and former Rheinbund populations, elites and commoners alike, remained trapped in the web of fear and uncertainty that had been the leitmotif of their lives for the past two decades.

Notably, there were no serious popular uprisings in the Rheinbund states in 1813.[9] The war that year remained one of princes not peoples.[10] Contrary to the hopes and expectations of ardent pan-Germanists or passionate Prussian patriots, the civilians of the Confederation did not take up arms despite the flood of Coalition propaganda and the periodic presence of Allied raiders.[11] The Grande Armée's rear areas were certainly insecure, but the insecurity arose from the actions of the Allied raiding detachments, not from aroused local populations. The slow but steady unravelling of Westphalia created space for passive resistance, joyous receptions for Allied raiding detachments, covert sedition and occasional spurts of local vigilante violence against regime representatives, but the only major problems occurred outside the Rheinbund in areas newly annexed to France such as Hamburg.[12] Although riots, protests and looting had erupted in Frankfurt and Berg early in the year, they were not harbingers of the sort of widespread insurrection the Allies yearned to inspire. Nor were these evanescent disturbances manifestations of some form of nascent pan-German nationalism. Rather, these outbursts were expressions of anti-French sentiment rooted in the deep insecurity felt across German lands after more than twenty years of war and unprecedented socio-political change.[13] While many people understandably blamed Napoleon for the burdens of war and the economic decline stemming from his Continental System, they also attributed the dislocations resulting from reforms and modernisation to the French even when some of the changes might have been beneficial and even when they were instituted by their own monarchs for local regime interests. 'This hatred of forced change, which set the minds of the people in such violent motion, was not combined with an unconditional love for the old ways,' observed the Hanoverian August Wilhelm Rehberg, but the result was widespread resentment of the French as they were seen as having overthrown tradition and imposed incomprehensible and, in some cases undesirable, alterations in peoples' daily lives.[14]

As with German soldiers, personal experiences often shaped German civilian attitudes towards the French. The farmer whose livestock was stolen, the merchant whose shop was looted or the townsman who had to quarter abusive soldiers of the Grande Armée would all have direct, 'concrete' and very individual reasons for anger whereas villagers who encountered courtesy or clemency would be inclined to more forgiving judgments. By 1813, the combination of general and personal factors made antipathy the more common emotion with the result that local people assisted Allied raiding detachments, hid fleeing draft evaders, spread anti-French pamphlets or offered other forms of passive resistance. What common people did not do inside the Confederation was rise up in armed rebellion. Nor did many display the furiously passionate pan-Germanism Stein and his adherents strove to elicit. For the great majority of citizens, subjects and soldiers, being anti-French and longing for peace were not the same as thirsting for a hazily imagined unified German state wrapped in Romantic rhetoric dredged from the past. Nonetheless, the suppressed hum of anti-French sentiment across Germany was unmistakable, a constant murmur in the ears of Rheinbund troops as they fought their last war under Napoleon's eagles. As discussed below, it would pose an additional challenge to Rheinbund officers and their French commanders during the war even in the absence of active insurrection.

Our Situation is Highly Precarious

As the various German armies prepare to turn towards the Rhine as part of the anti-Napoleon Coalition, this study turns to an examination of their records during their last campaigns as French allies. Doing so adds considerable nuance and depth to understanding of the Rheinbund's final year across several dimensions. From the operational military perspective, a more complete picture emerges depicting who fought where and when, under what circumstances and to what effect. This is also an opportunity to dispel some common misperceptions. Moreover, closer investigation locates these forces in the diplomatic and political–military context of their epoch, as instruments of their respective states, interacting with their home governments, their allies and local populations during this year of tremendous turmoil. Such a survey yields some unanticipated conclusions, the most striking of which is that so many of the Rheinbund contingents remained loyal to their oaths and fought alongside their French allies until the bitter end at Leipzig and sometimes beyond. Moreover, they not only fought, but many fought very well indeed, displaying skill and tenacity despite a long list of reasons to expect nothing but desertion, defection and collapse at the first encounter with the enemy. Although some individuals and units, of course, did desert, defect or collapse under pressure, the surprisingly steadfast performance of the majority of the contingents requires some explanation. What kept them fighting for the French despite the host of material deficiencies and psychological disincentives that crowded that desperate year?

The list of disincentives was long. In the first place, as mentioned above, the soldiers were conscripted from and immersed in an atmosphere of increasing anti-French sentiment in their homelands and in their operational areas, predominantly Saxony. The locals who harangued the men of the 39th Division as they marched east through Thuringia in April, the sullenness of Leipzig's inhabitants that Württemberg Leutnant von Martens observed in June, and the Westphalian citizens who attempted to suborn Jérôme's men in September are only three examples of the pressures exerted on the Rheinbund troops once they arrived in the theatre of war. The garrisons of fortress cities were surrounded by similar influences. The dominant concern of such residents was usually the simple desire to spare their homes and families from bombardment, starvation and disease, but their negative attitudes could hardly go unnoticed by the Rheinbund soldiers passing through their districts or assigned to their towns. Indeed, the anti-French sentiments of local populations and passing soldiers, fuelled by rumour and misinformation spread by stragglers and line-crossers, were often mutually reinforcing, facilitating desertion among those who were inclined to ignore their oaths.

The intensity of this growing anti-French attitude across Germany had been deepened by the disaster of 1812. Indeed, many of the problems the Rheinbund contingents faced in 1813 can be attributed directly to the experiences of the Russian debacle the previous year. As historian Paul Holzhausen observes at the opening of his history of the Rheinbund in Russia:

> Anno 1812. No campaign stands so profoundly etched in the souls of the nations and the peoples as this one. Not the war that the great Frederick fought with the Austrians, the French and the Russians, with the finely coiffured Louis XV, with the wild Croats and Pandours that Maria Theresa led, not the year of the Battle of Leipzig, not the campaign of Waterloo, not 1870. None.[15]

The significance of the Russian campaign was not only a matter of memory and historical consciousness as Germans looked back in subsequent decades, it was also an experience that had direct and immediate impact on the Rheinbund armies in 1813, both materially and psychologically. First, as related in the country chapters, each contingent had to contend with manifold deficits in what may be loosely termed the 'material' dimensions. Thousands of men and horses had to be replaced and provided with everything from cannons and bread wagons to muskets, uniforms, horseshoes and harnesses. The requirement to raise new armies from nothing and in haste strained the coffers and bureaucracies of the various Rheinbund states, while simultaneously presenting enormous challenges in the areas of training and leadership. Composed almost entirely of raw conscripts, these new armies seldom had more than the bare minimum of preparation when they were dispatched from their homelands and had to learn the fundamentals of soldiering on the march: drill, discipline, obedience, fieldcraft, foraging and a dozen other skills had to be mastered simply to perform as organised military formations and survive on campaign. The officers and NCOs were often as inexperienced as the common soldiers, recently raised from the ranks or appointed from civilian posts and military academies. Their ability to train their men, form them into functioning units and instil in them what Bavarian GL von Raglovich called 'the spirit of the old days' was hardly guaranteed.

Second, these 'material' lacunae were compounded by the psychological shocks stemming from 1812. The populations of the Rheinbund states were stunned as they gradually learned that the fine armies their monarchs had sent east in 1812 had vanished in the vastness of the tsar's empire. The dreadful losses, the wretched state of the few returnees and the agonising ignorance regarding the fates of friends and family members could hardly be encouraging to the men now being conscripted from those stunned populations. Confidence in Napoleon, his generals and the Grande Armée had been shaken if not shattered by the hideous events across the Niemen and latent frictions – real and imagined – flared after encounters with perceived French arrogance in Russia. Lacking the tradition of victory that had motivated the men lost in Russia and sustained them in adversity, the soldiers in the resurrected Rheinbund regiments were being ordered to war as components of an army that had just suffered one of the ghastliest defeats in military history. Moreover, for those already exasperated by French demands and what they saw as the strictures of the Rheinbund alliance, Napoleon's catastrophe in Russia made resistance seem possible for the first time. The great emperor of battles, the *Schlachtenkaiser*, might not be invincible.[16] There was no certainty that Napoleon would not recover and retaliate for the Russian loss ('What we see, the emperor has certainly foreseen, the man does not err as a general,' commented Saxony's king in August), but detaching themselves from France now became a conceivable option for many Germans at both the state and individual levels. At the same time, the Confederation's soldiers, accustomed 'to pull the chariot of victory', faced the very real possibility of ending up on the losing side in the coming war.[17]

These legacy factors, material and psychological, from 1812 were aggravated during the 1813 campaigns. The images of the French soldiers Germans encountered in early 1813, for example, whether they were pathetic survivors shuffling west or clumsy young conscripts trudging east, did little to renew faith in the Grande Armée or its leaders. There are many favourable accounts of the French army in the German memoir literature as Saxon Oberstleutnant von Odeleben related: 'The military deportment that prevailed in this new army, which had been created and assembled as if by magic, was truly admirable; and even if one had to detest the French soldier for his outrages, the military spirit, the ease of marching and the bravery of the young, so quickly formed troops, who could be compared to the most experienced, nevertheless inspired astonishment.'[18]

Napoleon's legions had clearly changed, however, and not for the better. On the one hand, the wreckage of the 1812 army afforded many Germans direct, visual confirmation of the great defeat. 'The kind of unfortunate people we see in our city is beyond description,' recorded a chronicler in Nuremberg, 'Not a day goes by, often not an hour, without such people coming, frozen hands and feet, full of disease and vermin, ragged and sick, and this began as early as December 1812 and now it is March and there is still no end to it.'[19] On the other hand, German impressions of the new Grande Armée could be equally alarming. Württemberg Foreign Minister Zeppelin passed French columns as he rode to Paris in February and wrote that 'Not one of the soldiers could have been more than 18 years old and these young boys were borne down by the weight of their packs and muskets,' while Franquemont described the marching companies he saw in April as 'all wretched people'.[20] The negative impressions were more common than the favourable in 1813, exciting disgust, disdain or anger owing to the indiscipline, negligence and pillaging that many Germans, soldiers and civilians alike, witnessed on a routine basis. Such sentiments were most acute among Saxons who watched their own country ravaged by the armies of both sides but imagined that affairs were more orderly among the Allied armies as compared to what they saw on the French side. Nor can the plundering and indiscipline prevalent among Rheinbund troops be overlooked; as was evident in reports by their own commanders or in memoirs that often snidely recounted the actions of men from other contingents. The relevant point here, however, is that the nature and behaviour of the French soldiery was an additional reason for Rheinbund soldiers to doubt the alliance after Russia.

The quality of French generalship also came under sceptical scrutiny as 1812 shifted into 1813. Even renowned figures such as Ney in whom many German soldiers invested hopes of success became instead the objects of disappointment and disparagement. The presence of so many Rheinbund contingents in the two failed offensives towards Berlin accentuated the repulse at Großbeeren, the disaster at Dennewitz and the discouraging retreats after both of those defeats in the minds of the German troops. Ney's public and private castigation of the Saxons after Dennewitz, of course, was especially damaging to morale, not only among the Saxon troops but in other Rheinbund contingents: they could easily envisage themselves as future targets of French generals attempting to excuse their own errors. Compounding the seeming French ineptitude on the battlefront was the apparent impunity enjoyed by the various Allied raiding detachments in the French rear areas and the anxiety displayed by many French officers at the thought of being ambushed by Cossacks or other enemy light troops. The raiding parties had practical effects such as intercepting convoys and interrupting communications, but their psychological impact was just as important. Overrunning isolated units, embarrassing local French commanders and spreading Coalition propaganda, these Allied detachments contributed substantially to the impression that Napoleon's subordinates were maladroit and incapable of coping with the growing power of the Allied armies.

The poor to non-existent logistical system and often chaotic administration also contributed to the frustrations and miseries of the Rheinbund soldiers (and to the sufferings of the French troops as well). Wretched medical care became a particular complaint. For Rheinbund troops, the logistical nightmare was sometimes compounded by inadequate support from their own home governments, as was the case with at least the Bavarian, Baden and Württemberg contingents. The Bavarian division's situation was made worse by the lack of replacements or even communication from Munich, a clear indication that Raglovich and his men were considered a regrettable but necessary sacrifice to maintain the French alliance. Frictions with the French also sharpened as the quality of the Grande Armée's soldiery deteriorated. The French often treated their German comrades with courtesy and skill as evidenced by Oudinot and Rapp or even the simple comradeship of French regimental officers hosting meals for German counterparts because they had served together in previous campaigns.[21] More common in German memories, however, were irritations at what they considered routine mistreatment such as French occupying all the quarters in a town or blocking German access to village wells until all French units had drawn water.[22] As noted in the preceding pages, many of these tales likely grew in the telling or were the result of military annoyances common to all armies at all times, but there was clearly a foundation of truth that accumulated over time in the minds of Rheinbund soldiers. As with the German civilian populations, these 'concrete' and 'situationally dependent' personal experiences with the French coloured Rheinbund images of their allies, sometimes sympathetically but more often with an ugly hue.[23]

Allied propaganda attempted to build on all these themes.[24] Just as the Coalition's intensive efforts failed to produce the desired 'patriotic' uprisings among German populations, however, few serving soldiers embraced the pan-German appeals. Indeed, some seem to have quickly dismissed the pamphlets, poems, caricatures and broadsheets for what they were. In fact, some of the early statements undermined Coalition hopes by threatening the legitimacy of the Rheinbund princes, as Saxony's foreign minister wrote to the kingdom's ambassador in Vienna in April: 'In particular the proclamations to the subjects must shake the foundations of every legitimate government and, through their example, disturb the peace of every state.'[25] Nonetheless, the persistent bombardment of materials presented alternatives to the unsustainably rosy public statements from the French side, magnified disaffection with the French, eroded confidence, and fed into the atmosphere of swirling uncertainty in which German soldiers found themselves. Though rarely enough on its own to induce soldiers to desert or defect, the glut of propaganda sometimes contributed where a Rheinbund unit's situation seemed hopeless (as in several garrisons), especially after the defeat at Leipzig.

Finally, and by no means least important, was the grim military situation in 1813. The spring battles of Lützen and Bautzen were clear victories with important political consequences, but it was equally clear that they were incomplete: the unbroken Allied armies remained as tenacious in retreat as they had been in combat. At the same time, the Grande Armée was obviously fraying at the seams and the autumn campaign, though it opened with the grand victory at Dresden, quickly transformed into a concatenation of calamities. Dennewitz was the worst of these from the Rheinbund perspective as the battle decimated the Confederation contingents involved while highlighting the incapacity of the French generals and their troops. Württemberg GL von Franquemont thus told his king that Ney's demoralised army would likely 'disintegrate' in short order if it did not receive a few days of undisturbed rest, while one of his subordinates wrote that the army's situation was 'highly precarious' and 'complete defeat' no longer seemed a distant prospect.[26] This drumbeat of defeats and the evident indecision that hobbled imperial headquarters during September and October – the fruitless marches and countermarches in miserable weather across the devastated Saxon countryside under constant harassment by enemy light troops – raised the spectre of demoralisation among German, French and other soldiers alike, all of which was accentuated by the acute insecurity in the army's rear areas. Considered together, these multiple and overlapping factors prompted professional fears of being on the losing side in a hopeless conflict for a foreign cause and thus created conducive conditions for desertion and defection among the Rheinbund contingents. The surprising aspect is that so many fought on so well for so long.

The Interest of Our King and Fatherland

Although each unit's and indeed each individual officer's or soldier's case was different, a number of general factors help explain the behaviour of the Rheinbund troops in 1813. Chief among these are conceptions of loyalty and identity combined with professional honour and duty, as well as context, unit history, and especially the quality of leadership. As with the disincentives, these factors naturally overlap, but it is useful to discuss each on its own to illuminate its most salient dimensions.

Identity, in terms of the locus of a soldier's loyalty, was one of the most important factors determining how individuals and units would react to the circumstances of the conflict. All Rheinbund officers and men would have considered themselves 'German' in a cultural and linguistic sense, but for most, this 'Germany' was still an abstraction in the early nineteenth century. Men such as the Ryssel brothers in the Saxon army who were instrumental in organising the contingent's defection were rare exceptions, not the norm, and some Rheinbund officers, such as Bavarian Hauptmann Joseph Vögler, scorned the 'schnapps patriotism' of 'weather vane-like' Prussia.[27] 'A distinct German national feeling was only in its nascent stages a hundred years ago,' wrote historian Hans Block in 1913 at the height of Prusso-German nationalist enthusiasm. The number of adherents to a common pan-German destiny in 1813 was small and 'the majority confined what was called national feeling solely to the feeling of belonging to one of the states into which this nebulous Germany was fragmented, and that usually went no further than attachment to the ancestral dynasty'.[28] Furthermore, the states of the Confederation of the Rhine were not Prussia. Though there were many similarities among the elements of the German-speaking world, simply extrapolating from Prussian responses to the pressures of the era in what is now thought of as 'Germany' is likely to deliver erroneous conclusions when considering Rheinbund experiences.[29] Nor were the Rheinbund monarchies a homogeneous bloc. Rather, as Leighton James observes, 'there were plentiful potential state identities' available in the diverse world of German-speaking Europe during the early nineteenth century.[30] Notions of nationalism thus differed from region to region and most

Germans adhered to what a modern historian characterises as 'naïve forms of homey patriotism' that was more powerful, especially in the political sphere, than the vague notions of a larger German cultural community with which it co-existed.[31] The term 'fatherland', for instance sometimes applied to this broad cultural community of German-speakers but more frequently denoted the specific homeland of the individual soldier.

Helmut Walser Smith suggests a useful explanatory model that may be simplified as describing loyalty working along two axes: 'vertical' and 'horizontal', the 'vertical' or 'hierarchical' being attachment to the traditional hierarchy of an individual's monarch, ruling dynasty and homeland, and the 'horizontal' being an 'affinity' for other members of the common German cultural community. In an era when most people still thought of themselves as subjects not citizens, 'hierarchy' determined the loyalty of the majority of Rheinbund soldiers even while they were conscious of their 'affinity' towards Germans from other lands.[32] As Ute Planert notes, therefore, this cultural commonality could not compete with alternative sources of political allegiance, so particularism predominated. That is, Rheinbund soldiers may have developed a stronger feeling of differentiation between French and 'Germans' in a general sense, but their definition of 'German' remained anchored in their attachment to their various native lands: Württembergers thus saw Württemberg as their homeland and gave their loyalty to its monarch and its royal house, likewise Bavarians, Saxons, Hessians and others. These were tangible, experienced 'fatherlands' with centuries of history and tradition rather than airy pan-German abstractions.[33]

Württemberg GM von Stockmayer exemplified this stance: 'I always remained German, mainly, however, in all circumstances a Württemberger in the strictest sense . . . I was always bound by duty and sense of honour towards the interests of my king and fatherland as well as towards my subordinates and the honour of our arms.' Saxon Leutnant von Wolffersdorff summed up the attitude of most officers: 'We believed we had acted in the interest of our king and fatherland . . . we had become accustomed to trusting in the wisdom of our prince all our lives and had often observed that the storms that rose close on our horizon dissipated after a time or were unleashed far away from us.'[34] Napoleon, therefore, though he was exaggerating for public relations purposes, was not entirely wrong when he scorned the Coalition in his proclamation after Lützen: 'The fools! They knew little of the attachment to their sovereigns, the wisdom, the spirit, and the good sense of the Germans.'[35]

Unsurprisingly, the local loyalties of soldiers reflected the particularism of their rulers. None of the Rheinbund monarchs, whether on the thrones of kingdoms or of microstates, wanted to lose what they had gained over eight years of being sheltered under Napoleon's aegis. Their concerns for preservation applied not only to their territories, populations and titles, but also to the domestic reforms that many had instituted to construct what they and their leading ministers considered more coherent, centralised and modern states. These particularist tendencies were closely linked to the suspicion and animosity many of Rheinbund Germany's rulers harboured towards Russia, Prussia and especially toward the anti-monarchical, revolutionary dangers represented by the fiery Stein and his coterie of ardent pan-German enthusiasts. Many certainly chafed under French hegemony and observed anti-French sentiment simmering among their populations, but objecting to French policies, being weary of seemingly endless wars, or even being anti-French was not the same as supporting the hazy pan-German aspirations propagated by a small segment of the educated German elite (who did not even agree among themselves).[36] Despite Napoleon's Russian disaster, therefore, the Rheinbund rulers were motivated to keep their soldiers in the field under French eagles as long as there seemed some chance of the emperor emerging victorious.[37]

Dutiful Prussians found such attitudes and actions abhorrent, as Clausewitz observed during the armistice: 'Unfortunately, there were still German princes who added their battalions to the oppressor's army; unfortunately, the rest of Germany remained in fearful silence, awaiting the moment of liberation with longing, but without the courage to bring it about themselves.'[38] Given the uncertainty of the times, however, these states simultaneously remained alert for the right moment to change sides should fortune turn her face from France. Adamantine determination to retain their lands and sovereignty, of course, did not vanish with Napoleon's defeat as Britain's Robert Stewart, Viscount Castlereagh, was moved to quip at the Congress of Vienna in 1814: 'I witness every day the astonishing tenacity with which all the powers cling to the smallest points of separate interest.'[39]

For the Rheinbund soldiers serving with the French in 1813, especially for the officers, the solemn oaths they swore to their sovereigns were the veritable expression of this prevailing German particularism.[40] The oaths themselves, of course, were integral elements of their conceptions of honour – national, institutional, and personal – as well as their ideas of what it meant to be a military professional in the early nineteenth century. Honour was a central concern for the Rheinbund officers, inherent in the very notion of being an officer.[41] The instructions given to Stockhorn and the correspondence of commanders such as Raglovich and Franquemont are replete with references to their worries that their troops perform with skill and valour on the battlefield, meeting the expectations of the French so as not to tarnish the images of their countries, their monarchs or their armies. At what may be termed the national level, monarchs were determined to preserve the reputations of their realms as was evident in Württemberg's Friedrich cashiering the hapless young lieutenant who meekly allowed his little detachment to be captured by Colomb's raiders in May. If perhaps less draconian, other rulers were equally focused on the preservation of their national honour. Likewise, at the unit level, leaders exhorted their men to uphold the reputations of their homelands and regiments, while proudly reporting the accolades they received from their French superiors and the awards of the Legion of Honour distributed among their units. This history has highlighted numerous examples of this phenomenon: the Hessian battalions that defied demands to surrender when isolated near Haynau and Klix in the autumn, the stalwart defence of Thorn and Danzig, the Württemberg battalions resisting to the last at Dennewitz, the Baden and Hessian brigades surrendering rather than defecting at Leipzig, or Westphalian Lieutenant von Lehsten holding his men to their duty to cite just a few. It is thus important not to project the attitudes of the late nineteenth or early twentieth centuries back on to 1813, just as, from a military perspective, it is important not to judge the Rheinbund armies of 1806–12 by the qualities of their reconstituted successors in 1813.

Honour also operated at the personal level. This was a crucial consideration for men such as Baden Graf Wilhelm and Hessian Prinz Emil at Leipzig. Though their unfaltering dedication to their sense of duty was overshadowed by the Saxon defection, their concern for their own reputations and those of their countries was evident in Wilhelm's assiduous efforts to expunge the spurious claim in the Austrian official account that Baden troops had not done their duty in the final cataclysm. Similar sentiments are apparent in the common fear at falling into what Bavarian Major von Seiboltsdorf termed 'disgraceful captivity'. These notions were also reflected in the sanctity attached to an officer's 'word of honour'. Hence the Allied outrage at Württembergers Kechler and Normann for allegedly violating this cardinal principle at Kitzen in June. This accusation was among the most insulting possible in the common European military culture of the age and Normann strove for the rest of his life to clear his name as a consequence (Kechler, killed at Dennewitz, did not have the opportunity). In this regard, of course, 'artificial' Westphalia was at a disadvantage as it had no hereditary ruling dynasty and many of its citizens looked to their previous monarchs rather than the newly imposed Jérôme. Nonetheless, most Westphalian officers also regarded their oaths to their imported king as sacrosanct and remained loyal to him and his temporary kingdom through the Battle of Leipzig and beyond. Despite the recognition of a common German cultural community distinct from France, being anti-French or simply being frustrated with French dominance east of the Rhine did not, after all, equate to ardour for some Prusso-German or pan-German political solution. Rather, most officers and men found solace and justification in their local loyalties and the oaths they had sworn to their princes.[42]

In a similar fashion, the traditional virtues associated with concepts of military professionalism and duty were also key considerations for soldiers of that era. These notions included obedience to one's legitimate sovereign, faithful allegiance to one's homeland and endurance of travails even if undertaken against one's personal preferences, as Saxon GM von Sahr pronounced so pointedly to Thielmann at Torgau in late April. 'We are soldiers', Leutnant von Soden of Schwarzburg-Sondershausen, would later write, 'we have to do our duty and obey what we are ordered to do.'[43] Professionalism, bolstered by personal ambition and pride in one's country, helps explain the rather unexpected desire for and satisfaction in victory under French banners as evinced by many Rheinbund officers. This attitude towards victory has appeared in Württemberg reports on Bautzen, the Bavarians at Luckau, the fine Württemberg actions during the retreat after Großbeeren, and the Saxon heavy cavalry at Dresden and Leipzig. Even Sergeant Sustermann in collapsing Westphalia dilated dolefully on how Kassel might have been saved. Likewise, some who could write cynical criticisms of serving the French (such as Saxon Major von Hausen or Württemberg cavalry Leutnant von Schlaich) could also express genuinely ferocious elation over battlefield triumph. In other cases, officers anticipated success that was not to be: Baden and Hessian troops were disappointed when their route after Lützen did not take them to Berlin, Saxon officers were optimistic about marching on the Prussian capital with Oudinot before Großbeeren, and prior to the second Berlin offensive under Ney Bavarian Unterleutnant Praun recalled that, 'Everyone stood in the hope that this courageous warrior, still in the best years of his life, would shortly enter the enemy capital at the head of his troops.' 'Idle, useless hope!' he would later lament.[44]

Another major influence on Rheinbund behaviour in 1813 was leadership, both French and German. As stressed repeatedly in this study, the importance of senior commanders and especially of unit officers cannot be over-estimated. Competent, attentive leaders with a firm sense of fealty to their monarchs and oaths could motivate the young Rheinbund troops, hold them to their duties and provide the tactical direction necessary to perform well under fire. The converse, of course, was true when the men were placed under irresolute or unskilled commanders.

Among the senior French officers, Rapp, Laplane and Maurellian stood out as exemplary commanders in blockade/siege situations; while GB Briche led the Württemberg light cavalry with skill and consideration, the able GD

Marchand was attentive to German concerns, and GB Wolff was respected as commander of the Rheinbund brigade in 12th and later 4th Corps. Beaumont, Beurmann and Bruno were less well regarded and Daendels earned a negative reputation for his deleterious handling of the defence of Modlin.

Rheinbund officers also ran the gamut from superb to scoundrel. On the strong side of the ledger were men such as Bauer and Butler in Danzig, royal scions Wilhelm and Emil in the 39th Division, most of the Württemberg generals, Bavarian Oberst Seyssel d'Aix and many others at all levels. Among the timid and inept were the Westphalian officers cited earlier, who lacked the aptitude and resolve to inspire their men and lead them against Chernishev's force outside Kassel when a determined advance might have driven off the Russians. Though he could display bravery at times, Jérôme must be included in this discreditable number in September and October 1813, providing a poor example, succumbing to his fears, and failing to care for his men. GL von Ochs presents an interesting contrast for doing his best to defend his forlorn post at Halberstadt and for refusing appeals to join the Coalition after his capture. At the far end of the spectrum were those such as Linker, Ryssel, Brause, Bünau and Normann who deliberately chose to defect to the Coalition, pulling their men along with them whether the soldiers were so inclined or not.

In addition to sustaining unit cohesion, tactical performance and fidelity to the Rheinbund alliance, good leadership could also ameliorate the growing frictions between the French and their Rheinbund allies. The Bavarians felt valued in Oudinot's corps, Franquemont considered his Württemberg division fairly treated by Bertrand (despite his frictions with Delort), the Badeners appreciated serving under Marchand, and even the coolly distant Reynier maintained his close relationship with the Saxons founded on their common experience in 1812. German opinions of Ney, on the other hand, shifted from admiration during the spring to grave disappointment and disgust in the wake of Dennewitz. Ney heartily returned the disfavour, reserving his special distrust for the Saxon contingent and thereby aggravating the personal enmity between him and Reynier. Of other senior French generals, Ledru in 11th Corps expressed satisfaction with his Westphalian brigade on several occasions even though its ranks apparently thinned badly from desertion. Until Normann's defection at Leipzig, Marmont seems to have held his Württemberg subordinate in good regard, repeatedly sending him on independent missions, usually with French infantry attached under Normann's orders. Indeed, Normann's independent assignments illustrate that French–Rheinbund relations were not always characterised by suspicion and mistrust. Elements of the 39th Division also conducted numerous patrols on their own, often with French troops under Rheinbund command; and there were many examples of such independent German or mixed Franco-German detachments during the sieges of Thorn, Glogau and Danzig. In no case did these missions lead to desertion or defection. Strangely, one of the most common Rheinbund complaints was that they were not trusted by the French. Only rarely was this indignation tempered by the recognition that the French had reason to distrust many of the German units, especially after the defections in the autumn.

These examples of the trust the French officers invested in select Rheinbund units and commanders are one side of the French relationship with their German allies. Indeed, French attitudes ran the gamut from condemnation to admiration. At the senior level, Ney's vocal denunciations stand out whereas Reynier was steadfastly protective of the Saxons under his command. Murat, Rapp, Bertrand and others repeatedly lauded their Rheinbund subordinates. Piré for one, had often served with Baden troops and, though disappointed with the performance of the four Baden companies at Altenburg in September, he thus felt compelled to highlight that the Baden soldiers 'conducted themselves in all circumstances with as much bravery as zeal and loyalty' in his post-war letter. The Saxon defection on the battlefield at Leipzig received universal – and angry – opprobrium, but other units garnered professional praise aplenty in both contemporary reporting and memoirs. The Württemberg division at Bautzen, the Saxon cuirassiers at Dresden and Leipzig, and the Bavarians and Westphalians at Danzig are only a few examples of honest and enduring appreciation for various German contingents from their French allies. The warm farewell offered to the Baden Light Dragoons by Colonel Curély and the French 10th Hussars is a touching instance at the small unit level. At the same time, French suspicion of the German troops was also a frequent theme. This was entirely understandable given the obvious hesitancy displayed by Rheinbund governments such as Bavaria and, later, by unit defections. This persistent suspicion coloured some French memoirs and histories, but where some French veterans expressed doubt about *all* German units, the more thoughtful were careful to describe the differences among the various contingents and judge their actions in the context of time, place and circumstances.

As for Napoleon himself, he needed the Rheinbund for symbolic as well as practical reasons: from being emblematic of his empire in Germany and French hegemony east of the Rhine to mundane but essential military matters such as men, mounts and material. Furthermore, his main lines of communication ran through Rheinbund territories requiring German support in everything from quartering troops and feeding horses to maintaining roads and providing security. Given these considerations, it is hardly surprising that he insisted on adherence to troop commitments from his German allies or that he refused to permit the departure of even the reduced remnants of units such as the Bavarian and Württemberg divisions until after Leipzig; the symbolic cost would have been too high in his estimation, signalling the unravelling of the entire Confederation. He could certainly be imperious in his demands, but he was also conscious of the need for nuance in his dealings with the German states as evident in his admonishments to Bertrand during the contretemps with Raglovich in April or Ney with regard to the Saxons in September. His own perspective is perhaps best illuminated by a frank exchange with Saxon GL von Gersdorff in Dresden on 15 August: 'I must speak freely; my generals no longer have any trust for the Germans, and they may not be wrong even if they exaggerate. The majority [of Germans] follow outward appearances: I win a battle and they come to their senses, I win a second and the Germans are my truest allies. In the meantime, I must give in on some things.'[45]

Associated with leadership, both French and German, are unit history and operational context. The Rheinbund units in Danzig are notable in this respect. Despite having experienced the shocks and miseries of the Russian campaign and despite the seeming wretchedness and hopelessness of their situation, they displayed significantly greater resiliency and tactical competence when compared to their compatriots in the newly raised regiments. This was true of the remnants of the composite 5th and 6th Rheinbund Regiments as well as of the more established 1st Westphalian, 13th Bavarian and 4th Rheinbund. Having been in existence since at least 1811 and having developed the bonds of comradeship that come with surviving horrific trials, even the composite units were cohesive and reliable. In a different manner but with similar results, it is clear that the various contingents in Saxony improved over the course of the war, especially after the intensive training and consolidation conducted during the armistice. As far as operational context is concerned, all the Rheinbund units contended with persistent privations and often with local populations who urged them to abandon their allegiance to the French. All, of course, were also influenced by the military situation as Napoleon had remarked to Gersdorff: they were buoyed by successes such as Bautzen, discouraged by disasters like Dennewitz, and unsettled by the pervasive insecurity in the rear areas. Leipzig naturally loomed largest and finally persuaded many to abandon the Confederation. In Westphalia's case, several daunting factors multiplied the challenges its officers faced trying to lead their units inside the kingdom: all the troops were new, untrained and inexperienced; local people constantly pressed the men to desert; and they were close to home, making desertion a tempting and feasible option, especially when their commanders seemed inept, uncaring and indecisive.

The combination of factors both incentivising German soldiers to stay loyal to the French alliance and discouraging them from doing so created considerable tension for the officers and men of the Rheinbund contingents in 1813. Soldiers' attitudes were often conflicted, and contradictions were common.[46] Painfully awkward situations thus arose, such as Westphalian Lieutenant Lehsten regretting the execution of deserters or Baden's Graf Wilhelm cleverly avoiding instructions to arrest Bavarian GL von Raglovich, but these existed side by side with many instances of battlefield courage and march endurance, or men such as Württemberg Sergeant Buck going to extremes to avoid capture. As noted in the preceding chapters, therefore, in most cases, the Rheinbund's soldiers opted to remain true to their oaths to their own monarchs and only changed sides when they received verified permission from their rulers. There were notable exceptions such as the Saxon division and the Württemberg cavalry at Leipzig, the two Westphalian hussar regiments in August or the many Westphalians who followed Chernishev on his retreat from Kassel; there were also instances of desertion and large-scale draft evasion, especially in Frankfurt and Westphalia (see Appendix 2). Furthermore, two governments, Bavaria and Württemberg, decided against sending replacements and withdrew whatever elements they could while keeping representative contingents in the field. Nonetheless, defections were few, desertion rates remained within the norms of the Grande Armée (at least until after Leipzig), and the great majority of contingents, including those of Bavaria and Württemberg, continued to serve alongside their French allies, frequently with distinction and often to the very bitter end. Most parted from their French comrades-in-arms with honour and mutual respect, and, in most cases, only after receiving formal permission to do so.

Despite widespread disenchantment with or anger towards the French, therefore, Allied appeals to pan-German unity found little traction in the face of tenacious particularist attachments on the part of officers and men to their own separate homelands and dynasties. The service of the Rheinbund contingents under the trying circumstances of 1813 is thus a testament to the power of local identity coupled with contemporary definitions of military professionalism and leadership. Anti-French attitudes co-existed with these factors in many instances, fluctuating over time and ranging from simple disgruntlement to impassioned outrage, but such sentiments seldom had an impact on battlefield performance. If they did not always meet the expectations of the emperor or their French commanders, they endured much, generally served well, and made significant contributions to Napoleon's cause in this final year of the alliance.

*

The Rheinbund was largely unlamented when it vanished from the European political scene. Indeed, the Coalition camp and many former members of the Confederation rejoiced at its demise. In the turmoil that followed, the older monarchies strove to cling to what they had, while the 'model states' such as Westphalia disappeared, their departures cheered by most inhabitants even if few desired an unalloyed return to the 'old ways'[47] (as transpired in Hesse-Kassel where the restored 'prince-elector', 'unrepentant, and uninstructed by calamity', endeavoured to turn the clock back to the mid-eighteenth century).[48] These last were special cases. Westphalia in particular was sentenced to *damnatio memoriae* (condemnation of memory or wiped from memory) and the soldiers of their now-disbanded armies struggled to accommodate themselves to the new circumstances in which their former service was ignored, denigrated or punished.[49] In the majority of states, on the other hand, the regimes managed to transform military service under Napoleon into affirmations of dynastic loyalty and thus fealty to their particularist interests within loose notions of a larger German identity.[50] Furthermore, with the notable exception of Saxony, the other Rheinbund states managed to survive 1813 more or less intact by changing sides in time (albeit at the last minute) and joining the fight against France. Their situations stood in stark contrast to Saxony which was ruthlessly truncated to satisfy Prussian ambitions and whose king was held prisoner for over a year.[51] The storm, exclaimed Wolffersdorff, had broken over his homeland and 'struck us a hard blow with an iron hand!'[52] In contrast, the 'survivor states' could view themselves to a degree as 'winners' coming out of 1813; but even Bavaria, the first to declare for the Allies, had to sacrifice lands to Austria for subsequent compensation west of the Rhine that was not contiguous with the kingdom's heartland – and that only after years of dogged negotiation.

As far as standard 'German' histories were concerned, however, all the former Rheinbund states were indelibly tainted by their membership in the Confederation.[53] Prusso-German interpretations of this nature, instrumentalised, embellished and romanticised over the years, would dominate historical analysis through the First World War and beyond. France would be specifically targeted as the 'hereditary enemy' and the Rheinbund states despised as false Germans who opposed the allegedly inevitable unification of German lands under Prussian leadership. It is thus not a little ironic that post-Napoleonic Germany largely retained the shape given it by the Rheinbund's 'Protector' despite the many assaults on the alliance's legacy after Napoleon's fall.[54]

Fortunately, recent decades have seen a welcome broadening of the historical aperture to include well-researched re-evaluations of the Rheinbund's institutions. Its role as a vehicle to introduce political–social reforms such as the unfulfilled constitutional aspirations of the model states has attracted particular attention and debate. The military dimensions of the Confederation, however, have remained terra incognita in most respects. Combat performance, the differences among contingents, indeed the differences within contingents (such as the solid reliability of the 1st Westphalian Infantry in Danzig as contrasted with the units inside the kingdom), tend to be overlooked and the Rheinbund units all simply treated as an undifferentiated mass: non-French and thus of dubious reliability. A central aim of this work has been to demonstrate that a great deal of historical acuity is lost if the many distinctions and nuances are not observed and assessed, if the Rheinbund armies are not approached with a critical eye and employing updated research. As the Rheinbund continues to be a subject of scholarly study, it is hoped that this survey of the Confederation contingents in their final year will serve as a military adjunct to the ongoing process of reappraisal, offering new data and new insights as a contribution to this larger endeavour.

Notes

Abbreviations Used in Notes

AHGA	*Archiv für hessische Geschichte und Altertumskunde*
AN	Archives Nationales, Paris
BayHStA	Bayerisches Hauptstaatsarchiv, Munich
BayHStA, GHA	" " " Geheimes Haus Archiv
BayHStA, HS	" " " Handschrift
CdN	*Correspondance de Napoléon*, 1858–70
CG	*Correspondance Générale*, 2004–18
CRE	Consortium on the Revolutionary Era (formerly Consortium on Revolutionary Europe)
DBKHG	*Darstellungen aus der Bayerischen Kriegs- und Heeresgeschichte*
Fabry, *Oudinot*	[Fabry, Gabriel]. *Étude sur les Opérations du Maréchal Oudinot du 15 Août au 4 Septembre 1813*, Paris: Chapelot, 1910
Fabry, *MacDonald*	[Fabry, Gabriel]. *Étude sur les Opérations du Maréchal MacDonald du 22 Août au 4 Septembre 1813*, Paris: Chapelot, 1910
Fabry, *Empereur I*	Fabry, Gabriel. *Étude sur les Opérations de l'Empereur du 28 Août au 4 Septembre 1813*, Paris: Chapelot, 1911
Fabry, *Empereur II*	Fabry, Gabriel. *Étude sur les Opérations de l'Empereur du 5 Septembre au 21 Septembre 1813*, Paris: Chapelot, 1913
Fabry, *Empereur III*	Fabry, Gabriel. *Étude sur les Opérations de l'Empereur du 22 Septembre au 3 Octobre 1813*, Paris: Chapelot, 1913
FBPG	*Forschungen zur Brandenburgischen und Preußischen Geschichte*
GLAK	Landesarchiv Baden-Württemberg, Generallandesarchiv, Karlsruhe
HStAD	Hessisches Staatsarchiv, Darmstadt
JdAM	*Jahrbücher für die deutsche Armee und Marine*
LABWHStA	Landesarchiv Baden-Württemberg, Hauptstaatsarchiv, Stuttgart
NASG	*Neues Archiv für sächsische Geschichte*
SHD	Service Historique de la Défense, Vincennes
SHSA	Sächsisches Hauptstaatsarchiv, Dresden
SIRIO	*Sbornik Imperatorskago Russkago Istoricheskago Obschestva*
ZfKWGK	*Zeitschrift für Kunst, Wissenschaft und Geschichte des Krieges*
ZHG	*Zeitschrift des Vereins für hessische Geschichte und Landeskunde*

Chapter 4: Württemberg: Unconditional Obedience

1. Angered by reports of inappropriate remarks from some of his officers during the 1812 campaign in Russia, Friedrich had this read out to the officer corps on 16 April 1813 (in Pfister, *Lager des Rheinbundes*, p. 219). 'Most High' is used to convey the German 'Allerhöchstdieselben'.
2. See Christian Wilhelm von Faber du Faur, *With Napoleon in Russia: The Illustrated Memoirs of Major Faber du Faur, 1812*, ed. and trans. by Jonathan North, London: Greenhill, 2001.
3. Hölzle, *Württemberg im Zeitalter Napoleons*, p. 163.
4. Friedrich to Zeppelin, 23 February 1813, in August von Schloßberger, 'Ein starker Konflikt des Königs Friedrich von Württemberg mit Kaiser Napoleon im Februar 1813 – der Anfang vom Ende der gegenseitigen Freundschaft', *Besondere Beilage des Staats-Anzeigers für Württemberg*, 3 and 14 November 1888.
5. Binder to Metternich, 13 January 1813, in Luckwaldt, *Befreiungskriege*, p. 208.
6. Friedrich to Zeppelin, 23 February 1813, in Schloßberger, 'starker Konflikt', pp. 261–2; Planert, *Mythos*, pp. 578–92. Two brothers in Biberach were tried for high treason after pamphlets appeared at the city's gates on the night of 12/13 February, see *Die Württemberger in den Freiheitskriegen*, Stuttgart: Holland & Josenhans, c. 1915, pp. 24–30.
7. Sauer, *Napoleons Adler*, p. 59. In addition to this work and specific citations, the following sketch of Friedrich and Württemberg's political situation draws on Albert Pfister, *König Friedrich von Württemberg und seine Zeit*, Stuttgart: Kohlhammer, 1888; Pfister, *Lager des Rheinbundes*, pp. 203, 390–1; Erwin Hölzle, *Württemberg im Zeitalter Napoleons und der deutschen Erhebung*, Stuttgart: Kohlhammer, 1937; Paul Sauer, *Der schwäbische Zar: Friedrich, Württembergs erster König*, Stuttgart: Deutsche Verlags-Anstalt, 1984; and Ina Ulrike Paul, 'Die Völkerschlacht bei Leipzig in der Erinnerungskultur Südwestdeutschlands 1813–1913', in Hofbauer/Rink, *Völkerschlacht*, pp. 247–68.
8. Volker Press, 'Südwestdeutschland im Zeitalter der Französischen Revolution und Napoleons' in Christian Väterlein and Axel Burkarth, eds, *Baden und Württemberg im Zeitalter Napoleons*, Stuttgart: Kohlhammer, 1987, vol. 2, p. 13. As Sheehan points out, bureaucrats led reforms in other Rheinbund states with their monarchs' approval, but Friedrich retained the political initiative in Württemberg (Sheehan, *German History*, p. 263). On the army, see Günter Cordes, 'Das württembergische Heerwesen zur Zeit Napoleons', in Väterlein/Burkarth, *Baden und Württemberg im Zeitalter Napoleons*; Joachim Brüser, 'Zwischen Kronprinz Friedrich Wilhelm und Napoleon: Das württembergischen Offizierskorps im Russlandfeldzug 1812', in Wolfgang Mährle und Nicole Bickhoff, eds, *Armee im Untergang*, Stuttgart: Kohlhammer, 2017, pp. 31–45; Paul Sauer, 'Die Neuorganisation des württembergischen Heerwesens unter Herzog, Kurfürst und König Friedrich (1797–1816)', *Zeitschrift für Württembergischen Landesgeschichte*, vol. XXVI, 1967, pp. 395–420; and Karl Pfaff, *Geschichte des Militärwesens in Württemberg von der ältesten bis auf unsere Zeit*, Stuttgart: Schweizerbach, 1842, pp. 106–18.
9. Binder's report of 19 May 1813, in Luckwaldt, *Befreiungskriege*, p. 226.
10. On Wilhelm: Paul Sauer, *Reformer auf dem Königsthron: Wilhelm I. von Württemberg*, Stuttgart: Deutsche Verlags-Anstalt, 1997, pp. 68–76; Luckwaldt, *Befreiungskriege*,

p. 206; quote from Friedrich to Wilhelm, 9 August 1812, Pfister, *Lager des Rheinbundes*, p. 58.
11. Sauer, 'Neuorganisation', p. 410.
12. Friedrich to Wilhelm, 9 August 1812, Pfister, *Lager des Rheinbundes*, p. 58.
13. Eugen Schneider, 'Württembergs Anschluß an die Verbündeten im Jahre 1813', in *Aus der württembergischen Geschichte*, Stuttgart: Kohlhammer, 1926, p. 91.
14. Friedrich to Zeppelin, 4 January 1813, in Hölzle, *Württemberg im Zeitalter Napoleons*, p. 156. Friedrich, like Montgelas, may have believed that Napoleon's empire was a transitory phenomenon (Press, 'Südwestdeutschland', p. 20).
15. Metternich to Binder, 18 February 1813, Oncken, *Oesterreich und Preußen*, vol. I. p. 320.
16. Extract of Binder's 4 April 1813 report, in Luckwaldt, *Befreiungskriege*, p. 206; Schneider, 'Württembergs Anschluß', p. 91.
17. Metternich to Binder, 7 April 1813, Pfister, *Lager des Rheinbundes*, pp. 209–10. See also Hölzle, *Württemberg im Zeitalter Napoleons*, p. 157; and Lefebvre de Béhaine, *Napoléon et les Alliés*, pp. 36–44.
18. Binder's reports of 15 and 19 May 1813, cited in Luckwaldt, *Befreiungskriege*, pp. 211, 226.
19. Stockmayer quoted in Heinz Kraft, *Die Württemberger in den Napoleonischen Kriegen*, Stuttgart: Kohlhammer, 1953, p. 223.
20. The most detailed treatment of this episode, albeit inclined towards the Württembergers, is Pfister, *Lager des Rheinbundes*, pp. 35–61, see also his 'Aus dem Lager des Rheinbundes 1812, eine Abwehr', *Preußische Jahrbücher*, vol. LXXXII, 1895; likewise Kraft, *Württemberger in den Napoleonischen Kriegen*, pp. 196–205 (Kraft perceives an unlikely conspiracy on Napoleon's part to force the crown prince out). Napoleon's letter to Friedrich Wilhelm and other relevant correspondence is in Schloßberger, *Politische und Militärische Correspondenz*, pp. 246–51. Württemberg historian Paul Sauer (*Napoleons Adler*, pp. 263–4) observes that Napoleon did not pull these accusations 'out of the air' and it seems likely that what we would now term the 'command climate' in the contingent was unhealthy, especially if Friedrich Wilhelm, known for his anti-Napoleon views, created or tolerated an atmosphere in which insubordination went unpunished. See also John H. Gill, 'The Rheinbund in Russia 1812: The Württemberg Experience', CRE, *Selected Papers 2013*, Alexander Mikaberidze and Michael V. Leggiere, eds, Shreveport: Louisiana State University, 2016.
21. The following relies primarily on Pfister, *Lager des Rheinbundes*, pp. 179–205, along with the correspondence published in Schloßberger, *Politische und Militärische Correspondenz*, pp. 258–74; and Schloßberger, 'Ein starker Konflikt', p. 266–70.
22. As noted in the Prologue in Vol. 1, Friedrich's view was that 'each public festivity and testimony of joy' would have made a disgraceful display when 'every family in the kingdom has been plunged into such deep grief and sorrow through the loss of fathers, sons and brothers', Friedrich to Wintzingerode, 17 January 1813, in Schloßberger, 'Mutige und treffende Erwiderung', p. 297.
23. Published as 'General-Rescript, die Anordnung einer allgemeinen Vermögens-, Besoldungs- und Pensions-Steuer betr.', in *Königlich-Württembergisches Staats- und Regierungs-Blatt*, no. 1, 2 January 1813.
24. Schloßberger, 'Ein starker Konflikt', p. 254.
25. Napoleon to Friedrich, 18 January 1813 and Friedrich's reply, 26 January 1813, in Schloßberger, *Politische und Militärische Correspondenz*, pp. 258–72. It is impossible to imagine that Friedrich *intended* an insult in using the '800 years' phrase, but it

was certainly read that way in Paris; furthermore, the tone, again almost certainly unintentional, could be construed as condescending.
26. Pfister, *Lager des Rheinbundes*, p. 192.
27. This quote and those in the preceding paragraph are taken from Wintzingerode's lengthy 3 February 1813 report in Schloßberger, 'Ein starker Konflikt', pp. 235–43.
28. Friedrich to Napoleon, 8 February 1813, in Schloßberger, *Politische und Militärische Correspondenz*, pp. 272–4.
29. Zeppelin's 15 February 1813 report, in Schloßberger, 'Ein starker Konflikt', pp. 254–6.
30. Napoleon to Friedrich, 20 February and 18 April 1813, with Friedrich's 20 April reply, Schloßberger, *Politische und Militärische Correspondenz*, pp. 274, 280–4.
31. Moustier is sometimes spelt 'Demoustier' or 'Dumoustier'; this version is taken from the entry in Henri Veyrier, *Dictionnaire des Diplomates de Napoléon*, Paris: Kronos, 1990. It is possible that neither of the ambassadors contributed to smooth relations: Moustier was widely despised in Stuttgart (Friedrich complained to Wintzingerode of Moustier's 'hateful and rude behaviour'); and Wintzingerode held Napoleon in low regard. See Sauer, *Der schwäbische Zar*, p. 316; Schloßberger, 'Ein starker Konflikt', p. 257; Schloßberger, 'Mutige und treffende Erwiderung', p. 297.
32. Report of 9 March 1813, in Pfister, *Lager des Rheinbundes*, p. 204.
33. Friedrich, for example, provided details of the Saxon king's movements and Schwarzenberg's visit to Stuttgart, Friedrich to Napoleon, 23 and 27 April as well as 11 May 1813, Schloßberger, *Politische und Militärische Correspondenz*, pp. 285, 288–90, 296–8.
34. Sauer, 'Neuorganisation', p. 420.
35. Several organisational points are worth noting. (1) Along with the actual Guard troops, those units that had the king as their proprietor (the 1st Jäger Battalion, the Leib-Chevaulegers, the Jäger-zu-Pferd *König*) plus a mounted artillery battery constituted the *Maison du Roi*, but this was an honorary designation rather than a field formation. (2) For a short time, the Garrison infantry carried the title 9th Infantry Regiment, but this number was transferred to the new Jäger Regiment early in 1813. (3) The artillery consisted of three mounted and three foot batteries along with one heavy battery in peace time and a second heavy battery for war, but these small heavy batteries (five pieces each) were administrative in nature and did not operate as such in the field. The kingdom also maintained a depot regiment.
36. Leo Ignaz von Stadlinger, *Geschichte des Württembergischen Kriegswesens von der frühesten bis zur neuesten Zeit*, Stuttgart: Hofbuchdruckerei, 1856, p. 646.
37. Most Württemberg troops fought their last campaigns as French allies in shakos, while the chevaulegers still wore casques as described in the text. On Württemberg uniforms, see Herbert Hahn, *Das Königlich Württembergische Heer 1806–1871*, Beckum: Deutsche Gesellschaft für Heereskunde, 1994; W. J. Rawkins, *The Army of the Kingdom of Württemberg 1806–1814*, e-book edition, 2014; and David Wright's two books: *Württemberg Infantry of the Napoleonic Wars*, and *Württemberg Cavalry, Artillery and Staff of the Napoleonic Wars*, both Huntingdon: Ken Trotman, 2017.
38. *Exerzier-Reglement für die königlich württembergische Infanterie*, Stuttgart, 1809, with thanks to Uwe Ehmke.
39. According to a 14 April 1813 'Tableau général de l'Armée Wurtembergoise', a 'battalion' of 300 'Chasseurs Arquebusiers' composed of forest guards and huntsmen was assembled in Ludwigsburg, a number that could be doubled at need (SHD, 2C542).

Nothing further is known about this organisation; it saw no action and its members likely returned to their arboreal pursuits later in the spring.

40. The planned strengths are from *Standes-Ausweise* of April and May 1813, in LABWHStA, E 270a Bü 224, 'Mobilmachung für den Feldzug gegen Preußen und Rußland und Etats der Truppen'.
41. 'Horse artillery' and 'mounted batteries' are used here for the Württemberg designation '*reitende Artillerie*' (usually spelt '*reutende*' at the time).
42. Faber du Faur/Kausler, *Mit Napoleon in Russland*, p. 106. For grim statistics, see the replacement regimental commander's stark report: 'Abdruck eines Original-Rapports von dem am 28. August 1812 in den Russischen Feldzug nachgesendeten, königl. Ergänzungs-Corps', *Württembergische Jahrbücher*, 1835, pp. 194–7.
43. Scheler to Friedrich, 22 December 1812, in Pfister, *Lager des Rheinbundes*, p. 161; Christian von Martens, *Vor fünfzig Jahren I: Tagebuch meines Feldzuges in Rußland 1812*, Stuttgart: Schaber, 1862, p. 214.
44. Friedrich Notter, *Ludwig Uhland: Sein Leben und seine Dichtungen*, Stuttgart: Metzler, 1863, p. 119.
45. 29th Bulletin, 3 December 1812, in Pascal, *Bulletins de la Grande Armée*, vol. V, pp. 328–43; Pfister, *Lager des Rheinbundes*, pp. 164–5.
46. Pfister, *Lager des Rheinbundes*, pp. 166–7.
47. Some sources refer to this town by an alternative German name: Hohensalza.
48. Starklof, *Zweiten Reiter-Regiments*, pp. 279–80; Richard Starklof, *Geschichte des Königlich Württembergischen vierten Reiterregiments Königin Olga 1805–1866*, Stuttgart: Aue, 1867, pp. 86–7; Reboul, *Campagne de 1813*, vol. I, p. 132.
49. Gaupp reported on 22 February that he had 180 'effectives' but 123 were sick, 27 detached and thus only 30 (including himself) were actually in Küstrin and fit for duty. Most of these men were from the 7th Infantry but the group included soldiers from other infantry regiments as well as a few cavalrymen. His requests to be released to return to Württemberg were denied. His reports are in LABWHStA, E 270a Bü 231, 'Meldungen des Majors und provisorischen Bataillonskommandanten v. Gaupp an den König'. See also Pfister, *Lager des Rheinbundes*, p. 168; Reboul, *Campagne de 1813*, vol. I, p. 155.
50. This was the number as of 1 September 1812, but the total would decline during the siege: LABWHStA, E 270a Bü 227, 'Rapporte über den Stand des württembergischen Armeekorps im Felde'.
51. Pfister, *Lager des Rheinbundes*, p. 217. As in Bavaria, Württemberg's authorities were concerned that conscription would excite unrest in the districts that had been incorporated into the kingdom after 1805 ('neu-Württemberg' or 'new Württemberg'); but the prevailing discontent did not bubble over into violence (Planert, *Mythos*, p. 585).
52. This second column (not to be confused with the 'replacement regiment' that had been destroyed in Russia) consisted of 2,200 men and 140 horses; Walsleben was to purchase an additional 1,200 horses in Leipzig (Theodor Griesinger, *Geschichte des Ulanenregiments „König Karl" (1. Württembergischen) Nr. 19*, Stuttgart: Deutsche Verlags-Anstalt, 1883, p. 89).
53. Hugo Schempp, *Geschichte des 3. Württ. Infanterie-Regiments König Nr. 121*, Stuttgart: Kohlhammer, 1891, pp. 260–1; Albert Pfister, *Denkwürdigkeiten aus der württembergischen Kriegsgeschichte*, Stuttgart: Grüninger, 1868, p. 382.

54. In Dorsch, *Kriegszüge der Württemberger*, p. 206; and Heinrich August Vossler, *With Napoleon in Russia 1812*, Walter Wallich, trans., London: Folio Society, 1969, p. 112. See also Karl Ludwig Geßler, Ulysses Johannes Tognarelli and Theodor Hermann Ströbel, *Geschichte des 2. Württembergischen Feldartillerie-Regiments Nr. 29*, Stuttgart: regimental, 1892, p. 149.
55. Christian Martens, *Vor fünfzig Jahren II., Tagebuch meines Feldzuges in Sachsen 1813*, Stuttgart: Schaber, 1863, vol. II, pp. 1–2.
56. One officer had requested release in January and three more would do so in July and August for a total of nine, see below. Details from 'Anciennete-, National- und Einteilungssliste des württembergischen Offizierskorps (1806–1813)', LABWHStA, E 297 Bü 151.
57. Sauer, *schwäbische Zar*, p. 328; Order to GL von Koch, no. 14, 30 May 1813, LABWHStA, E 270a Bü 238, 'Konzepte königlicher Ordres an das Kommando des württembergischen Armeekorps im preußisch-rußischen Krieg'. Perhaps unsurprisingly, de la Chevallerie was taken into Prussian service in late 1813 (Johannes Melchers, *Stammliste des Offiziers-Korps des Infanterie-Regiments von Horn (3. Rheinisches) Nr. 29*, Trier: Lintz, 1901, p. 155).
58. Martens, *Vor fünfzig Jahren*, vol. II, p. 6. Surgeon Christoph Heinrich Groß of the 2nd Infantry recounted the challenges of simply establishing outposts when the division entered Saxony: *1805–1814: Ganz in der Nähe erweckte Uns Kanonenfeuer*, Dagmar Wuttge, ed., Seeheim-Jugenheim: Tintenfass, 2011, pp. 70–1.
59. See cavalry regimental histories by Griesinger and Starklof; Rudolf Köberle, *Geschichte des 4. Württemb. Infanterie-Regiments Nr. 122*, Ludwigsburg: regimental, 1881, p. 27; Karl Muff and Adolph Wenscher. *Geschichte des Grenadier-Regiments König Karl (5. Württembergischen) Nro. 123*, Stuttgart: Metzler, 1889, p. 28; and Pfister, *Lager des Rheinbundes*, p. 218. Ernst Wilhelm von Baumbach, *Tage-Buch von 1813*, https://baumbach-archiv.net/Seite:Tagebuch.Ernst.von.Baumbach.Napoleons.Russlandfeldzug.1813.djvu [accessed November 2021] with thanks to Herr Uwe Baumbach.
60. Friedrich to Napoleon, 26 January 1813, in Schloßberger, *Politische und Militärische Correspondenz*, pp. 258–72; Napoleon to Friedrich, 2 March 1813, *CG*, no. 32945, vol. XIII, p. 440.
61. See the exchange of letters between 7 March and 23 April 1813, in Schloßberger, *Politische und Militärische Correspondenz*, pp. 274–85.
62. Friedrich to Zeppelin, 18, 20 and 23 February 1813 and 20 February 1813 reply to de Moustier (drafted by Friedrich but signed by his state secretary), in Schloßberger, 'Ein starker Konflikt', pp. 252–61.
63. Pfister, *Lager des Rheinbundes*, p. 218.
64. Planned figures taken from LABWHStA, E 270a Bü 224.
65. Hermann Nübling, *Geschichte des Grenadier-Regiments König Karl (5. Württembergischen) Nr. 123*, Berlin: Eisenschmidt, 1911, p. 169. The special weapons posed ammunition supply problems; during the autumn, GD Bertrand, in whose 4th Corps the Württembergers served, recommended that these troops be issued common French muskets, but this change never occurred (Bertrand to Napoleon, 12 September 1813, Fabry, *Empereur II*, Documents, p. 35). A 16 July French inspection report noted that the soldiers could manufacture their own musket balls but lacked sufficient lead, AN, AF/IV/1661A, Plaquette 1.
66. Martens, *Vor fünfzig Jahren*, vol. II, p. 184.

67. Order of 16 April 1813, in Pfister, *Lager des Rheinbundes*, p. 219.
68. Royal edict, 16 May 1813, in Schloßberger, 'Mutige und treffende Erwiderung', p. 299; Order no. 7 to Franquemont, 16 May 1813, LABWHStA, E 270 a Bü 238; the same was provided to the second detachment on 10 July.
69. 'Ordre an den Divisionaire und General Lieutenant von Franquemont', 16 April 1813, LABWHStA, E 270a Bü 224. Friedrich had given similar secret instructions to Spitzemberg prior to his departure for Würzburg (Pfister, *Lager des Rheinbundes*, p. 218). Franquemont was also provided with routine instructions dated 15 April concerning reporting requirements, discipline and other standard administrative matters.
70. Franquemont to Friedrich, 20 and 29 April, 4, 9 and 14 May 1813, LABWHStA, E 270a Bü 224; and Pfister, *Lager des Rheinbundes*, pp. 221–30.
71. Order no. 2 to Franquemont, 1 May 1813, LABWHStA, E 270 a Bü 238; Franquemont's April reports in Pfister, *Lager des Rheinbundes*, pp. 221–30. Oberst von Spitzemberg had summarily dismissed a junior French commissary who had haughtily announced that he was going to review the 7th Infantry on its arrival in Würzburg (Suckow, 'Feldzug', vol. I, p. 140). Ney's 20 April order of battle from SHD, 2C539.
72. The chronology that follows is drawn from a division journal extract sent to Bangold by Franquemont, 10 August 1816, LABWHStA, E 284 g Bü 69, 'Schriftwechsel des Obersten von Bangold betreffend die Sammlung von Unterlagen zur Abfassung eines Tagebuches über den Feldzug 1813'; Starklof, *Zweiten Reiter-Regiments*, pp. 291–31. Berthier's orders to Ney and Bertrand for the change in assignment are dated 26 April 1813, in *Ordres*, vol. I, pp. 41–2, and Berthier to Franquemont, 4 May 1813, in vol. I, p. 73.
73. Baumbach, *Tage-Buch*, p. 29; Vossler, *With Napoleon*, p. 116.
74. Franquemont to Friedrich, 4 and 9 May 1813, LABWHStA, E 270a Bü 224; and Pfister, *Lager des Rheinbundes*, pp. 221, 229–30.
75. Reports in Pfister, *Lager des Rheinbundes*, pp. 229–30.
76. Suckow, 'Feldzug', vol. I, pp. 231–3.
77. Ibid.
78. Martens, *Vor fünfzig Jahren*, vol. II, p. 7.
79. Baumbach, *Tage-Buch*, p. 25. Though based on his notes from the campaign, Baumbach was writing almost twenty years later and it is not clear that these sentiments about 'Germany' reflected his attitude in 1813. Schlaich's comments from a 2 April 1813 letter in his anonymously published *Interessante Scene aus den Feldzügen 1812 und 1813*, Ludwigsburg: Nast, 1819, p. 108
80. Pfister, *Lager des Rheinbundes*, p. 223.
81. Taken from Buck's diary as published in Starklof, *Zweiten Reiter-Regiments*, pp. 307–12. Franquemont described Buck's actions and recommended awards in his 31 May 1813 report to Friedrich, LABWHStA, E 270a Bü 236, 'Meldungen des Armeekorps aus dem Feld an den König'. Bertrand's reports only address the officer's adventures (18 May 1813 in Foucart, *Bautzen*, vol. I, pp. 201–3).
82. In Nübling, *Grenadier-Regiments König Karl*, p. 171. Note that the slogan '*Hie gut Württemberg alleweg!*' is open to various translations depending on the context.
83. Franquemont to Friedrich, 14 May 1813, LABWHStA, E 270a Bü 224.
84. Vossler, *With Napoleon*, pp. 118–21.
85. Franquemont to Friedrich, 31 May 1813, LABWHStA, E 270a Bü 236; Starklof, *Zweiten Reiter-Regiments*, pp. 302–16; Caemmerer, *Frühjahrsfeldzug*, vol. II, pp. 163–70; Plotho, *Der Krieg in Deutschland*, vol. I, pp. 138–48. Reports on these actions and

the intelligence gathered are in Foucart, *Bautzen*, vol. I, pp. 147–8, 169–74, 187–90. The Russian general is designated Ilovaysky XII to distinguish him from the many others of that name.

86. Starklof, *Zweiten Reiter-Regiments*, pp. 314–18; 'Ancienneteliste des württembergischen Offizierskorps', 1810–1811, LABWHStA, E 297 Bü 160.
87. Franquemont to Friedrich, 31 May 1813, LABWHStA, E 270a Bü 236; Starklof, *Zweiten Reiter-Regiments*, pp. 318–19.
88. Ibid.
89. Suckow, 'Feldzug', vol. II, p. 224; Stockmayer's report to Franquemont, 25 May 1813, LABWHStA, E 270a Bü 237.
90. Some elements of the Württemberg 1st Infantry apparently crossed over the river for a time, and some may have remained on the eastern bank during the night. The Württemberg accounts claim that the French seized the Kiefernberg on the evening of the 20th (Franquemont to Friedrich, 31 May 1813, LABWHStA, E 270a Bü 236, and E 284g Bü 94, 'Schilderung des Generalmajors von Bangold über die Schlacht bei Bautzen am 20. und 21. Mai 1813, insbesondere über die Stellungen und Bewegungen der württembergischen Truppen'), but Caemmerer's detailed history states that Prussian troops held this hill through the night and only departed the following morning (*Frühjahrsfeldzug*, vol. II, p. 215).
91. Groß, *Ganz in der Nähe*, p. 75.
92. Franquemont to Friedrich, 31 May 1813, LABWHStA, E 270a Bü 236. In addition to Franquemont's and Stockmayer's reports, this section on the 20 May actions is drawn from Soult's and Bertrand's reports in Foucart, *Bautzen*, vol. I, pp. 300–2; Caemmerer, *Frühjahrsfeldzug*, vol. II, pp. 207–17; and Württemberg regimental histories.
93. Principal sources for this section are: Franquemont to Friedrich, 22 and 31 May 1813, LABWHStA, E 270a Bü 236; Stockmayer to Franquemont, 25 May 1813, LABWHStA, E 270a Bü 237; Bangold's account, LABWHStA, E 284g Bü 94; [Friedrich von Stockmayer], 'Die Kämpfe der Württemberger im Feldzug 1813. Aus den Aufzeichnungen des Generals v. Stockmayer', *Schwäbische Merkur*, 16 March 1895; and Caemmerer, *Frühjahrsfeldzug*, vol. II, pp. 218–40, including an extract from Neuffer's report on pages 393–5.
94. Franquemont to Friedrich, 31 May 1813, LABWHStA, E 270a Bü 236.
95. Starklof, *Zweiten Reiter-Regiments*, p. 323; and an anecdote related by a trooper named Johann Friedrich Franck in Dorsch, *Kriegszüge der Württemberger*, p. 102.
96. Franquemont to Friedrich, 31 May 1813, LABWHStA, E 270a Bü 236; and Baumbach, *Tage-Buch*, p. 52.
97. Stockmayer, 'Die Kämpfe der Württemberger im Feldzug 1813'.
98. Suckow, 'Feldzug', vol. II, p. 226.
99. Ibid., and Stockmayer's 25 May report, LABWHStA, E 270a Bü 237. 'Deftly' from Leggiere, *Napoleon and the Struggle for Germany*, vol. I, p. 353.
100. Stockmayer's 'Aufzeichnungen', in Oskar Gerhardt, *Die Württemberger im deutschen Befreiungskampf 1813–1815*, Stuttgart: Steinkopf, 1938, p. 56.
101. Johann Gottlob Heere, *Erinnerungen des Schloßaufsehers Heere*, Mergentheim: Thomas, 1847, pp. 21–3.
102. Jules Antoine Paulin, *Les Souvenirs du Général Bon Paulin*, Paris: Plon, 1895, p. 263.
103. Stockmayer, 'Die Kämpfe der Württemberger im Feldzug 1813'; Schlaich, letter of 22 May 1813, *Interessante Scene*, pp. 124–5.

104. Bertrand's report, 5 June 1813, in Foucart, *Bautzen*, vol. I, pp. 323–7.
105. Fourth Corps 'Journal Historique', SHD, 2C448bis.
106. Stockmayer, 'Die Kämpfe der Württemberger im Feldzug 1813'; Franquemont to Friedrich, 22 May 1813, LABWHStA, E 270a Bü 236; Baumbach, *Tage-Buch*, p. 55.
107. Starklof, *Zweiten Reiter-Regiments*, pp. 322–8. The Prussian regimental history is Johann David von Dziengel, *Geschichte des königlichen Zweiten Ulanen-Regiments*, Potsdam: Stein, 1858, pp. 317–20.
108. Heinrich Steffens, *Was ich erlebte*, Breslau: Josef Max, 1843, vol. VII, pp. 185–6. A different English translation is given in *Adventures on the Road to Paris*, London: John Murray, 1848, pp. 100–1. With thanks to Dr Michael Leggiere for calling this to my attention via his unpublished CRE paper 'The Men of the Thirty Years War: Allied Occupation Policy in Saxony 1813'.
109. The official Württemberg reports present slightly different accounts of the orders given to the battalion. Casualties from the 4th Corps 'État des pertes', 29 May 1813, Foucart, *Bautzen*, vol. I, p. 326–7; and Schempp, *Geschichte des 3. Württ. Infanterie-Regiments*, pp. 266–7.
110. From Bismarck's account in his *Ideen-Taktik der Reuterei*, Karlsruhe: Müller, 1829, pp. 332–6; Griesinger, *Geschichte des Ulanenregiments*, p. 94.
111. Groß, *Ganz in der Nähe*, pp. 77–8.
112. Jett to Friedrich, 2 June 1813, LABWHStA, E 270a Bü 236.
113. Sources for Groß-Rosen: Jett to Friedrich, 2 June 1813, LABWHStA, E 270a Bü 236; Bertrand's and Macdonald's reports in Foucart, *Bautzen*, vol. II, pp. 227–30 (MacDonald is notably disparaging towards Bertrand); 4th Corps 'Journal Historique', SHD, 2C448bis; Pfister, *Lager des Rheinbundes*, pp. 247–8; Caemmerer, *Frühjahrsfeldzug*, vol. II, pp. 274–6; Osten-Sacken, *Geschichte des Befreiungskrieges*, vol. IIb, pp. 323–6; Württemberg regimental histories.
114. Schlaich, *Interessante Scene*, pp. 128–30.
115. 'Rapport auf den 1sten Junÿ 1813', LABWHStA, E 270a Bü 227, 'Rapporte über den Stand des württembergischen Armeekorps im Felde'; Jett to Friedrich, 2 June 1813, LABWHStA, E 270a Bü 236.
116. Pfister offered a grim view of Friedrich's attitude: 'once they were posted in the field, he wanted to let the regiments burn out without renewing their exhausted strength' (*Lager des Rheinbundes*, p. 290).
117. Starklof, *Zweiten Reiter-Regiments*, pp. 335–6.
118. Groß, *Ganz in der Nähe*, p. 80.
119. Baumbach, *Tage-Buch*, pp. 78, 109; Martens, *Vor fünfzig Jahren*, vol. II, pp. 31, 42. Baumbach also states that some elements of French drill were incorporated to good effect, but does not elaborate. Quote from a 16 July French inspection report, AN, AF/IV/1661A, Plaquette 1.
120. Bismarck, *Ideen-Taktik*, pp. 363–4. Note that Doering's name is often spelt 'Döring', but he signed his correspondence using the 'oe' spelling and that is retained here.
121. Friedrich to Berthier, 6 June 1813, Schloßberger, *Politische und Militärische Correspondenz*, p. 306.
122. Franquemont to Friedrich, quoted in Griesinger, *Geschichte des Ulanenregiments*, p. 95.
123. Orders to Koch, no. 13, 29 May and no. 17, 9 June 1813, LABWHStA, E 270a Bü 238. Although the relatively small size of Friedrich's army made this meticulous scrutiny possible, his attention to detail in the most minor military matters was remarkable

and is immediately evident in perusing the orders sent to his field forces. It is not uncommon to find his personal emendations in documents that he had almost certainly dictated or drafted in the first place. For Württemberg reports with public praise for the division, see the *Moniteur Westphalien/Westphälischer Moniteur*, no. 153, 3 June 1813.

124. Franquemont was already a 'chevalier' in the Legion of Honour and the order's rules prohibited overleaping a rank as he explained to the king. See Pfister, *Lager des Rheinbundes*, p. 292. Friedrich also sent personal letters to Neuffer and Stockmayer (LABWHStA, E 270a Bü 238).

125. Orders to Franquemont, 10 May 1813, LABWHStA, E 270a Bü 238. In a minor exception to Friedrich's refusal to send replacements to Saxony, the men of this small detachment were to join the 7th Infantry on arrival.

126. Orders to Koch, 29 May and 16 June 1813, LABWHStA, E 270a Bü 238; the notion of sending the little gun with this column seems to have been dropped because the armistice had gone into effect before it departed. Colomb's account is in Colomb, *Tagebuch*, pp. 38–41. See also Gomez-Freyre to Berthier, 26 May 1813, Foucart, *Bautzen*, vol. II, pp. 133–4. The incident was reported in the *Journal de l'Empire* of 19 June 1813.

127. Principal sources for Kitzen are Doering's and Normann's reports to Friedrich (LABWHStA, E 270a Bü 239); 'Rechtfertigung des Generals Grafen v. Normann-Ehrenfels wegen der Affaire bei Kitzen und des Übergangs bei Leipzig', LABWHStA, E 284g Bü 100; Pfister, *Lager des Rheinbundes*, pp. 251–88, and his 'Der Untergang der Lützower bei Kitzen', *Deutsche Revue*, vol. XXI, no. 3, 1896; Starklof, *vierten Reiterregiments*, pp. 104–31, 281–91; 'Der Memoiren des Generals Grafen Karl v. Normann über den Feldzug von 1813', *Schwäbische Kronik*, 1846; Max von Duvernoy, 'Die Württembergischen Kavalleriebrigade Normann im Feldzuge 1813', *Beiheft zum Militär-Wochenblatt*, vol. X, 1907; Albert du Casse, *Le Général Arrighi de Casanova, Duc de Padoue*, Paris: Dentu, 1866, vol. I, pp. 296–352; Jagwitz, *Lützowschen Freikorps*, pp. 6–109; Heinrich Bothe, *Geschichte des Thüringischen Ulanen-Regiments Nr. 6 1813–1913*, Berlin: Mittler & Sohn, 1913, vol. I, pp. 21–40; Adolf Brecher, *Napoleon I. und der Überfall des Lützowschen Freikorps bei Kitzen am 17. Juni 1813*, Berlin: Gaertner, 1897; and Adolph Schlüsser, *Geschichte des Lützowschen Freikorps*, Berlin: Mittler, 1826.

128. *Journal de l'Empire*, 4 July 1813.

129. For simplicity's sake, the term 'Prussian' is used here for all members of Lützow's Freikorps even though many of its volunteers were from other German states, including many from former Prussian territories that Napoleon had allotted to Rheinbund monarchs after 1806. On the composition of Lützow's troops, see Rudolf Ibbeken, *Preußen 1807–1813: Staat und Volk als Idee und in Wirklichkeit*, Cologne: Grote, 1970, pp. 417–26; also Marcel Spivak, 'Aux Origines de "la Legende" du Soulèvement Prussien de 1813: Le Corps Franc du Major Adolph von Lützow', *Revue de l'Institut Napoléon*, no. 130, 1974.

130. Friedrich to Normann and Doering, 29 May 1813, LABWHStA, E 270a Bü 239, 'Konzepte königlicher Ordres an die Brigadiers und Generalmajore Graf v. Döring und Graf v. Normann sowie Meldungen beider an den König'; Napoleon to Durosnel, 3 June 1813, *CG*, no. 34433, vol. XIII, pp. 1088–9.

131. Martens, *Vor fünfzig Jahren*, vol. II, p. 17.

132. Berthier to Arrighi, 3 and 7 June 1813, *Ordres*, vol. I, pp. 158–62, 190–1.

133. Arrighi to Berthier, 16 June 1813, in du Casse, *Arrighi*, vol. I, pp. 315–17; Arrighi's 14 June orders were appended to Doering's report to Friedrich, 15 June 1813, LABWHStA, E 270a Bü 239; printed in Starklof, *vierten Reiterregiments*, pp. 101–4. According to the *Moniteur Westphalien/Westphälischer Moniteur* (no. 170, 21 June 1813), a column of Westphalian troops under GB Jacques Bernard (four squadrons and two battalions with two guns) had also been sent in pursuit of Lützow; we have no details on this force but it did not come into contact with Lützow's band.

134. As Brecher notes, the controversies also involved differences between Prussian and south German conceptions of patriotism (*Überfall*, p. v).

135. Napoleon to Berthier, 19 and 22 June 1813, *CG*, nos. 34858 and 34900, vol. XIII, pp. 1273–4, 1291–2; the French condemned Lützow for 'making war on his own', in other words, not recognising the armistice or properly established national authorities (see for example: *Journal de l'Empire*, 21 June, 28 June, 16 July). The French view was deeply coloured by the experience of Prussian Major von Schill's raid in 1809. For an example of the Prussian view of Napoleon's 'hatred' for Lützow and his alleged secret plot to destroy his band, see Brecher, *Überfall* and Johann August Voigt, ed. *Skizzen aus dem Leben Friedrich David Ferdinand Hoffbauers, weiland Pastor zu Ammendorf: Ein Beitrag zur Geschichte des Lützow'schen Corps*, Halle: Verlag des Waisenhauses, 1869. There is no substantive evidence to support a covert Napoleonic conspiracy. For an especially enraged portrayal of the supposed 'butchery' perpetrated by the French against the 'noble, brave warriors sworn to their banners' see Förster, *Befreiungs-Kriege*, vol. I, p. 406.

136. As related in Chapters 3 and 7, these Rheinbund 'infantrymen' were local militia from Sachsen-Gotha-Altenburg and (presumably) Reuß.

137. Many of Lützow's men expected to head for Bohemia and were surprised when they rode north. The band's attitude is summed up in one of his men telling him 'Don't trust the French dogs!' (Voigt, *Skizzen*, pp. 198–9).

138. From Kechler's detailed report of 5 July 1813, in Pfister, *Lager des Rheinbundes*, pp. 259–63. Unfortunately, Fournier's biography is not helpful on the Kitzen episode and only serves to offer erroneous data (Delpech La Borie, *Fournier-Sarlovèze*, pp. 158–9).

139. Arrighi to Berthier, 18 June 1813, in Du Casse, *Arrighi*, vol. I, pp. 317–20. The III/3rd Naval Artillery (sometimes erroneously translated as 'marines' in English) had been en route to Dresden, but Napoleon authorised Arrighi to detain them temporarily for this miniature crisis (Napoleon to Arrighi, 4 June 1813, *CG*, no. 34438, vol. XIII, pp. 1091–3). Some accounts state that Normann had only two guns, but it seems likely he had two 6-pounders and one howitzer.

140. Normann's 'Rechtfertigung', LABWHStA, E 284g Bü 100. One post-war Württemberg source claims that Normann sent an officer to warn Lützow of his danger and urge the Prussians to depart before the French commander arrived but Normann made no reference to such a warning in any of his writings; so this warning remains unconfirmed. See Wilhelm Zimmermann, *Die Befreiungskämpfe der Deutschen gegen Napoleon*, Stuttgart: Rieger, 1859, pp. 715–18; Brecher, *Überfall*, pp. x–xi, 56–60.

141. Normann to Friedrich, 23 June 1813, LABWHStA, E 270a Bü 239; and Normann's 'Rechtfertigung', LABWHStA, E 284g Bü 100. Prussian participants deny that anyone from the Freikorps opened fire, for example: Pflugk-Harttung, *Befreiungsjahr*, pp. 214–16, and Geßner, *Ein Streifzug der Lützow'schen Reiterschaar und der Ueberfall bei Kitzen*, Berlin: Schlesier, 1863, pp. 47–56; Lützow to Blücher, in Gerhardt, *Württemberger im*

deutschen Befreiungskampf, pp. 66–7. Zimmermann states that the first shot killed a Württemberg cavalryman and that the troopers then attacked without the officers actually ordering them to do so (Zimmermann, *Befreiungskämpfe*, p. 716).

142. Brecher, *Überfall*, pp. 78–80. Brecher concludes that Lützow had 'totally lost his head'.
143. Among those captured from Lützow's corps were three Württemberg deserters who were tried by court martial and executed, orders to Doering, 28 July 1813, LABWHStA, E 270a Bü 239.
144. As mentioned earlier, the infantry component had already withdrawn east of the Elbe after participating in Vorontsov's advance on Leipzig.
145. Funck, *In Russland und Sachsen*, p. 298. Modern historian Michael Hughes is equally dismissive: 'They are better known for poetic celebration of their exploits than their real achievements' (*Nationalism and Society*, p. 43). See also Karl Koberstein, 'Lützow's wilde, verwegene Jagd', *Preußische Jahrbücher*, vol. LI, no. 4, 1883, and, in contrast, Kurt von Lützow, *Adolf Lützow's Freikorps in den Jahren 1813 und 1814*, Berlin: Hertz, 1884. On Körner's escape, see W. Emil Peschel and Eugen Wildenow, *Theodor Körner und die Seinen*, Leipzig: Seeman, 1898, vol. II, pp. 68–80. Krause offers mordantly insightful comments on the patriotic hyperbole associated with the band, *Kampf um Freiheit*, pp. 240–8; and Ute Planert refers to Körner as 'the icon of the liberation struggle' whose verses inspired 'the patriotic fantasies' of later generations ('Das Militär als Zwangsanstalt. Wehrdienst und Rekrutierungsverweigerung zwischen Ancien Regime, napoleonischer Herrschaft und alliierter Kriegsführung', in Jaques-Olivier Boudon, Gabriele B. Clemens and Pierre Horn, eds, *Erbfeinde im Empire?*, Ostfildern: Jan Thorbecke Verlag, 2016, p. 223).
146. Normann later wrote that this claim was 'the most ridiculous'. Neither he nor his men recalled making any such offending cry, but 'What I might have shouted to my men then and there, I no longer know myself, and if I made use of such an expression, I would find it ridiculous to deny it' (his 'Rechtfertigung', LABWHStA, E 284g Bü 100). Leutnant von Oppeln-Bronikowski of Lützow's band seems to be the source of this alleged insult, see his report in Pflugk-Harttung, *Befreiungsjahr*, pp. 214–16.
147. Beroldingen to Friedrich, 12 August 1813, Pfister, *Lager des Rheinbundes*, p. 280–1.
148. Journal accounts in *Berlinische Nachrichten*, nos. 75–80, late June/early July 1813, for example, closely followed a June 1813 Allied propaganda piece entitled *Relation officielle de l'attentat commis le 17 de ce mois contre le corps du major de Lützow extraite des rapports, procès-verbaux et autres pièces originales* (in Jagwitz, *Lützowschen Freikorps*, pp. 93–101, and a slightly different version in Dorow, *Erlebtes*, Anlage A); although Jagwitz asserts that it was not officially published, it appeared in the 20 July 1813 issue of the *Berlinische Nachrichten*; the *Preußische Correspondent*, no. 49, 25 June 1813 was similar; and its main points appeared in press accounts all across northern Germany, sometimes word for word. Beroldingen sent a copy of this 'relation' to Friedrich in his 6 July 1813 report (LABWHStA, E 270a Bü 241). Even the accounts in Munich's *Allgemeine Zeitung* largely echoed the Allied viewpoint (issues 192, 196–201, July 1813). Friedrich had Normann's report published in the Stuttgart paper on 27 June as well as the *Allgemeine Zeitung* (1 July) and *Journal de l'Empire* (6 July). Letter to the king from 'German men of honour': 'Bericht eines Augenzeugen', undated, LABWHStA, E 270a Bü 238. On Friedrich and the state: Pfister, *Lager des Rheinbundes*, p. 283.
149. Friedrich to Beroldingen, 12 July 1813, Pfister, *Lager des Rheinbundes*, pp. 279–80; Friedrich to Doering and Normann, 12 July 1813, LABWHStA, E 270a Bü 239.

150. Beroldingen to Friedrich, 12 August 1813, Pfister, *Lager des Rheinbundes*, p. 281.
151. Napoleon to Arrighi, 12 June 1813, Napoleon to Berthier, 9, 11, 13 and 16 June 1813, *CG*, nos. 34510, 34578, 34612, 34619, 34688, vol. XIII, pp. 1125–7, 1154, 1168, 1171–2, 1196.
152. Bangold's account, LABWHStA, E 284g Bü 102.
153. Normann to Franquemont, 14 August 1813, Pfister, *Lager des Rheinbundes*, pp. 266–7.
154. Fournier's 18 June 1813 report (LABWHStA, E 270a Bü 239), and Beroldingen to Friedrich, 22 June 1813 (LABWHStA, E 270a Bü 241).
155. Normann's 'Rechtfertigung', LABWHStA, E 284g Bü 100. Note that the crucial word 'never' ('*nie*') is missing in Duvernoy's essay (p. 359) whether through oversight or intent, even though it is present in Starklof (which Duvernoy copied), in the archival copy, and in the version printed in the *Schwäbische Kronik*.
156. Martens, *Vor fünfzig Jahren*, vol. II, pp. 22–7; and his 'Tagebuch meines Feldzuges gegen Preußen 1813', LABWHStA, J 56 Bü 21, pp. 50–2. Benedikt Peter, an NCO in the *König* Jägers, participated in the action at Kitzen but made almost no mention of it in his memoirs, leading the editor of the published version to comment: 'The brevity with which Benedikt Peter passes over this fatal episode suggests how the simple soldier regarded the entire affair' (Wilhelm Kohlhaas, editor of *Wachtmeister Peter mit und gegen Napoleon*, Stuttgart: Steinkopf, 1980, p. 89).
157. Order to Franquemont, no. 31, 10 August 1813, LABWHStA, E 270a Bü 238. Normann explained the circumstances of his transfer in his reports of 9 and 14 August 1813, LABWHStA, E 270a Bü 240.
158. Friedrich to Normann, 18 August 1813, and Normann to Friedrich, 26 August 1813, LABWHStA, E 270a Bü 240. The Westphalian complaints are discussed in Berthier to Beroldingen, 24 July 1813, orders to Normann, 10 August 1813, and orders to Franquemont, no. 31, 10 August 1813, all from LABWHStA, E 270a Bü 238.
159. Bangold related his woes in a long letter to the War Ministry, 1 July 1813 (LABWHStA, E 270a Bü 230, 'Berichte des Quartiermeisterleutnants Major v. Bangold über den russisch-preußischen Feldzug sowie Konzepte königlicher Ordres'); see also Pfister, *Lager des Rheinbundes*, p. 292; Baumbach, *Tage-Buch*, p. 78; Suckow, 'Feldzug', vol. II, pp. 304–13; Schlaich, letter of 27 July 1813, *Interessante Scene*, pp. 134–6.
160. Franquemont to Bertrand, 11 August 1813, Pfister, *Lager des Rheinbundes*, pp. 310–11.
161. Baumbach, *Tage-Buch*, p. 80; Schlaich, letter of 22 August 1813, *Interessante Scene*, p. 136.
162. Suckow, 'Feldzug', vol. II, p. 313.
163. Martens, *Vor fünfzig Jahren*, vol. II, p. 59.
164. Starklof, *Zweiten Reiter-Regiments*, p. 352; Fabry, *Oudinot*, Documents, pp. 54, 57–8.
165. Report of Sartis Leopold Bequignol, 10th Infantry, ibid., pp. 70–1.
166. Bertrand to Berthier, 31 August 1813, SHD, 2C154.
167. Key sources for the period up to and including the Jüterbog engagement: Franquemont to Friedrich, 2 September 1813, LABWHStA, E 270a Bü 236; orders to Franquemont, nos. 34 and 35, 7 September 1813, LABWHStA, E 270a Bü 238; Fabry, *Oudinot*, Documents, pp. 54, 57–60, 70–3, 82–4; Quistorp, *Nordarmee*, vol. I, pp. 314–45; Bismarck, *Ideen-Taktik*, pp. 369–72.
168. Baumbach, *Tage-Buch*, p. 108; Suckow, 'Feldzug', vol. II, p. 391; Schlaich offered similar observations in his letter supposedly written on 27 August – but it is difficult to see how news of Dresden could have reached Jüterbog so rapidly (*Interessante Scene*, pp. 139–40).

169. Baumbach, *Tage-Buch*, pp. 109–10; Martens, 'Tagebuch meines Feldzuges gegen Preußen 1813', LABWHStA, J 56 Bü 21, pp. 133–4; Ferdinand Ludwig Fromm, *Geschichte des Infanterie-Regiments König Wilhelm I (6. Württ.) Nr. 124*, Weingarten: regimental, 1901, p. 69.
170. Stockmayer, 'Die Kämpfe der Württemberger im Feldzug 1813'.
171. Martens, *Vor fünfzig Jahren*, vol. II, pp. 73–6.
172. Stockmayer, 'Die Kämpfe der Württemberger im Feldzug 1813'.
173. Suckow, 'Feldzug', vol. II, p. 393.
174. Kechler's 4 September 1813 report, from Köberle, *Infanterie-Regiments Nr. 122*, p. 38. He was the officer, then with the 4th Infantry, who had been involved in the Lützow incident.
175. Suckow, 'Feldzug', vol. II, pp. 393–5. As in many cases with German memoirs, it is not clear that the comments about earning laurels under the French were Suckow's sentiments in September 1813 or thoughts added years later.
176. Stockmayer, 'Die Kämpfe der Württemberger im Feldzug 1813'.
177. Suckow, 'Feldzug', vol. II, p. 395; Stockmayer, 'Die Kämpfe der Württemberger im Feldzug 1813' and his after-action report (Fabry, *Oudinot*, Documents, pp. 98–100); Franquemont reports nos. 13 and 14, 4 and 10 September 1813, LABWHStA, E 270a Bü 236; Rössler, *Tagebücher aus den zehen Feldzügen der Württemberger unter der Regierung Königs Friedrich*, Ludwigsburg: Nast, 1820, vol. II, pp. 336–8; Quistorp, *Nordarmee*, vol. I, pp. 379–81. The history of the 6th Infantry states that the regiment's 2nd Battalion, deployed in a skirmish line, advanced against a Prussian-held wood followed by the 1st Battalion in column and succeeded in capturing the woods without any real fighting; it is not clear where this occurred, perhaps to the left of Stockmayer's brigade (Fromm, *Infanterie-Regiments König Wilhelm I (6. Württ.) Nr. 124*, p. 70).
178. Schlaich, letter of 4 September 1813, *Interessante Scene*, pp. 142–3.
179. Pfister, *Lager des Rheinbundes*, p. 326.
180. Franquemont report no. 13, 4 September 1813, LABWHStA, E 270a Bü 236.
181. The phrase stems from Bernadotte's bulletin of 20 September printed in the *Berlinische Nachrichten von Staats- und gelehrten Sachen*, no. 114, 23 September 1813; and *Proclamations et Bulletins*, pp. 62–7. For other examples of escalating vitriol (but with no attribution), see: Johann Schuster, *Der teutsche Krieg im Jahre 1813 nach Oestreichs Beitritt*, Leipzig: Hartleben, 1814, vol. I, p. 136; Johann Daniel Hensel, *Der Freiheitskrieg in den Jahren 1813 und 1814*, Hirschberg: Krahn, 1815, vol. I, p. 461; Johann Gottfried v. Pahl, *Denkwürdigkeiten aus meinem Leben und aus meiner Zeit*, Wilhelm Pahl, ed., Tübingen: Fues, 1840, p. 725; Zimmermann, *Befreiungskämpfe*, p. 748; Dorsch, *Kriegszüge der Württemberger*, pp. 112–13. Curiously, this episode is often transposed to or implied to have occurred at Dennewitz rather than outside Wittenberg three days earlier; and the Frenchman is sometimes mis-identified as Bertrand.
182. Franquemont's single-word mention of Delort is in an attachment to a letter to Bangold, 10 August 1816, LABWHStA, E 284g Bü 69. His irritation may have been accentuated by personal and professional dislike as he made snide remarks about Morand, characterising the French general as an overweening know-it-all in several of his reports to the king.
183. Fourth Corps 'Journal Historique', SHD, 2C448bis.
184. In addition to Franquemont's two reports of 10 September, general sources for this section include: Friederich, *Herbstfeldzuges*, vol. II, pp. 139–77; Quistorp, *Nordarmee*,

vol. I., pp. 479–535; Pfister, *Lager des Rheinbundes*, pp. 312–35; Starklof, *Zweiten Reiter-Regiments*, pp. 361–73; Rössler, *Tagebücher aus den zehen Feldzügen*, vol. II, pp. 339–49; Robert M. Felder, *Der schwarze Jäger oder Würtembergs Krieger in den Jahren 1805–1816*, Cannstatt: Ruckhäberle, 1839, pp. 68–80.

185. Stadlinger's memoirs in Dorsch, *Kriegszüge der Württemberger*, pp. 106–7; Martens, *Vor fünfzig Jahren*, vol. II, p. 78.
186. This estimate is a compromise between the author's estimate of 6,656 and Quistorp's 6,588 (*Nordarmee*, vol. I, p. 449, adding 347 artillerymen to Quistorp's 6,241 infantry and cavalry). Both derived by subtracting battle losses between 25 August and 4 September from August strength figures.
187. Note that the actions of the 2nd Foot Battery at Dennewitz are unclear; this narrative follows Geßler/Tognarelli/Ströbel, *2. Württembergischen Feldartillerie-Regiments*, p. 161, but although the battery may have advanced with its sister batteries as depicted here, it may have been called forward later or it may have stayed in the rear with Doering until the great retreat. In any case, Doering remained behind with 1st Infantry, I/4th Infantry and 6th Infantry. It is not clear why the 38th Division was organised in this peculiar manner on 6 September. Ney's irritation is from Stockmayer, 'Die Kämpfe der Württemberger im Feldzug 1813'. The 4th Corps 'Journal Historique' claims that Ney took charge of the Württemberg division and shifted it towards Jüterbog (SHD, 2C448bis), but there is no mention of this in Württemberg sources.
188. Spitzemberg's 9 September 1813 report, in Köberle, *Infanterie-Regiments Nr. 122*, pp. 40–1.
189. Ibid. From Spitzemberg's report and the artillery regimental histories, it seems that Spitzemberg had three pieces from the 3rd Foot Battery plus the two howitzers of the horse battery; the whereabouts of the foot battery's other pieces is unclear.
190. Stadlinger in Dorsch, *Kriegszüge der Württemberger*, pp. 108–9; Suckow, 'Feldzug', vol. II, pp. 473–4.
191. Köberle, *Infanterie-Regiments Nr. 122*, p. 41. For a Prussian view that is surprisingly congruent with the Württemberg accounts, see Eduard von Franseky II, *Geschichte des Königlich Preußischen 16ten Infanterie-Regiments*, Münster: Wundermann, 1834, pp. 91–100.
192. Heere, *Erinnerungen* p. 27; Stockmayer, 'Die Kämpfe der Württemberger im Feldzug 1813'; Franquemont private report, 10 September 1813, LABWHStA, E 270a Bü 237. According to Heere, Bertrand also took along a French 8-pounder battery.
193. Martens, *Vor fünfzig Jahren*, vol. II, pp. 80–1. Bismarck, *Ideen-Taktik*, p. 375
194. Stockmayer, 'Die Kämpfe der Württemberger im Feldzug 1813'; Franquemont report no. 14, 10 September 1813, LABWHStA, E 270a Bü 236. Franquemont only mentioned meeting up with I/6th in his report. On the artillery: Geßler/Tognarelli/Ströbel, *2. Württembergischen Feldartillerie-Regiments*, p. 163.
195. Bertrand's after-action report, 9 September 1813, SHD, 2C448bis; Starklof, *Zweiten Reiter-Regiments*, pp. 361–71.
196. Baumbach, *Tage-Buch*, pp. 118–27; Fromm, *Infanterie-Regiments König Wilhelm I*, pp. 72–3. If the 2nd Foot Battery remained with Doering, it is reasonable to assume that it marched with these battalions (whether as an intact entity or in bits and pieces).
197. Dumonceau, *Mémoires*, p. 352.
198. Report of 10 September 1813, LABWHStA, E 270a Bü 236.
199. Schlaich, *Interessante Scene*, p. 143; Pfister, *Lager des Rheinbundes*, p. 331.

200. Casualty figures in this and the preceding paragraph are from the list in Louchet, *Bataille de Dennewitz*, pt. 2, p. 56 (taken from Franquemont's report); these are generally consistent with summary data given in Pfister, *Lager des Rheinbundes*, pp. 330–4. The official '*état des pertes*' (dated 15 September 1813) gives a considerably higher total: 3,309 losses in dead, wounded, prisoners, missing, and 'left on the battlefield, presumed dead, wounded or captured'. This official table covers the period from 1 through 10 September, so some of the losses would have been from the engagements at Thießen and Euper, but even deducting those estimated 500 casualties the total would come to approximately 2,800 (SHD, 2C44bbis). Furthermore, it is likely that some men returned to their units after the data was collected for this table.
201. Orders to Franquemont, no. 38, 18 September 1813, LABWHStA, E 270a Bü 238.
202. Bertrand to Berthier, 10 September 1813 (SHD, 2C448bis); and Franquemont to Friedrich, 10 September 1813 (LABWHStA, E 270a Bü 237, LABWHStA, E 270a Bü 236). Franquemont sent his king a private letter as a well as a formal report on 10 September, neither mentions desertion. The history of the Prussian 4th Reserve Infantry Regiment states that the officers had difficulty restraining their men during the struggle with the Württemberg troops (Franseky, *Preußischen 16ten Infanterie-Regiments*, p. 98).
203. Heere, *Erinnerungen*, pp. 28–34. Heere stated that he was to skirmish with the approaching Prussians but does not indicate that he thought this order in any way unusual.
204. Bismarck, *Ideen-Taktik*, p. 374; Schlaich, letter of 8 September 1813 with 10 September postscript, Schlaich, *Interessante Scene*, p. 143–5.
205. Private report, 10 September 1813, LABWHStA, E 270a Bü 237; his 12 September report in Pfister, *Lager des Rheinbundes*, pp. 342–3.
206. Report of 3 October 1813, LABWHStA, E 270a Bü 237; Bertrand questioned Franquemont on the discrepancy between the barely 1,400 infantrymen he reviewed on 14 September and the Württemberg strength report that gave the total infantry as 1,841 (Bertrand and Delort to Franquemont, 16 September 1813, Fabry, *Empereur II*, Documents, p. 137).
207. Friedrich to Franquemont, 18 October 1813, LABWHStA, E 270a Bü 238. Friedrich's close attention to the details of the war and his firm support to Franquemont provide another contrast with the relationship between Bavaria's king and his army in the field. Note that the date of this brief letter is uncertain; it could be 18 September or 18 October; the thoughtful Pfister opts for the latter, but the references to Dennewitz argue for the former.
208. See Starklof, *Zweiten Reiter-Regiments*, pp. 373–7. The 2,879 figure is for 12 September from the September '*livret*' prepared for Napoleon (Fabry, *Empereur II*, Situations, p. 310); Pfister gives a round number of 2,500 which may be closer to the actual total of those fit for combat (*Lager des Rheinbundes*, p. 340). On the artillery, see Geßler/Tognarelli/Ströbel, *2. Württembergischen Feldartillerie-Regiments*, pp. 164–5.
209. According to one of the artillery histories, the second reduction was per an order from Marshal Ney (Geßler/Tognarelli/Ströbel, *2. Württembergischen Feldartillerie-Regiments*, pp. 164–5).
210. 'Offene ordre', 18 September 1813, and Dillen to Berthier, 18 September 1813, LABWHStA, E 270a Bü 238.

211. See the following on Bieberstein's column: Jerome to Berthier, 17 September 1813, Fabry, *Empereur II*, Documents, p. 298; Berthier to Napoleon, 23 September 1813, *Rapports*, vol. II, p. 166; Napoleon to Berthier, 24 September 1813, *CG*, no. 36441, vol. XIV, p. 631; Berthier to Ney, 24 September 1813, *Ordres*, vol. II, p. 233; Ney–Bertrand exchange, 25 September 1813, and Franquemont's explanation, 29 September 1813, Fabry, *Empereur III*, Documents, pp. 70–1, 158, 188–9.
212. Friedrich to Franquemont, 7 and 18 October 1813, LABWHStA, E 270a Bü 238 (see note 207 above reference the dating of the 18 October missive). Orders to Normann, 7 October 1813, LABWHStA, E 270a Bü 240.
213. Schlaich, letter of 22 September 1813 (mislabelled as 'April'), *Interessante Scene*, p. 146.
214. Normann to Friedrich, 26 September 1813, LABWHStA, E 270a Bü 240.
215. Berthier to Marmont, 24 August 1813, *Ordres*, vol. II, p. 87.
216. Peter, *Wachtmeister Peter*, p. 89.
217. Normann to Friedrich, 11 and 26 September 1813, LABWHStA, E 270a Bü 240. Normann's 3, 5 and 11 September reports to Berthier and Marmont are in Fabry, *MacDonald*, Documents, pp. 63, 71–2, and *Empereur II*, Documents, pp. 53, 58, 66; Peter, *Wachtmeister Peter*, p. 90; see also Starklof, *vierten Reiterregiments*, pp. 143–7; Pfister, *Lager des Rheinbundes*, pp. 336–7; and Quistorp, *Nordarmee*, vol. II, p. 15. Some of Normann's reports mention being attacked by 4,000 enemy troops; he was certainly outnumbered in cavalry, but 4,000 seems a gross exaggeration. He also writes of both Cossacks and Prussian hussars, but the hussar regiment, if present, cannot now be identified (Peter refers to Russian hussars). Normann was correct, however, in reporting that his attackers included elements from both the Army of the North and the Army of Silesia which was beginning its shift northwest to the Elbe.
218. Orders to Normann, 20 September 1813, LABWHStA, E 270a Bü 240. These instructions also reiterated a reproof from a 7 September letter which chastised Normann for failing to apprise the king of a lieutenant's desire to be released from service. The lieutenant, formerly of Mecklenburg, had wounded a fellow officer severely in a duel during the armistice and deserted to the Allies.
219. Oberleutnant von Fleischmann, 'Relation über die Demontirung und Auflösung der Reitender Batterie Maison du Roi', LABWHStA, E 270a Bü 240; Starklof, *vierten Reiterregiments*, pp. 151–3; Plotho, *Der Krieg in Deutschland*, vol. II, pp. 349–57.
220. Peter, *Wachtmeister Peter*, p. 91; and an unpublished account by Hauptmann Fischer cited in Gerhardt, *Württemberger im deutschen Befreiungskampf*, pp. 103–4. Peter gives the wrong date for Leutrum's desertion (13 October), but the other details are congruent. Leutrum defected on 9 October and Stabs-Rittmeister Carl August von Albedyhl disappeared after cowardly behaviour on the 12th. Ironically, a letter awarding Leutrum Württemberg's Military Service Medal for outstanding performance was on the way to Saxony when he defected (Wallerstein to Normann, 14 and 20 October 1813; orders to Normann, 7 October 1813, LABWHStA, E 270a Bü 240). Leutnant Friedrich Hartig of the *König* Jägers requested release but then left without permission on 9 October and was also dismissed for 'dishonourable behaviour'.
221. The numbers are approximate as further research into all these individuals is beyond the scope of this work. However, a total of some eight officers between the ranks of major and lieutenant requested release in September and October, all but one were from the cavalry; almost all had entered Württemberg service from Mecklenburg

or Prussia; and all were with the army in the field. Adding these to the eleven who were granted release between January and August gives a total of nineteen (not all of whom sought release for political reasons). An additional eight left Württemberg service in November and December for various reasons. Only one officer seems to have deserted to the enemy before October (the duelling Mecklenburger). Note that Leutrum came from an old Swabian noble family, but he was born in Piedmont where his father served the Sardinian court, so homegrown Württemberg soldiers may have seen him as a 'foreigner'. Most data from various iterations of the Anciennete-, National- und Einteilungsliste des württembergischen Offizierskorps, LABWHStA, E 297 Bü 146, 147, 148, 149, 150, and 151; Rossler, *Tagebücher aus den zehen Feldzügen*, vol. II, pp. 299–307; letter from two Witzleben brothers, 2 October 1813, 20 September 1813, LABWHStA, E 270a Bü 240; see also Pfister, *Lager des Rheinbundes*, p. 343; and Normann's 'Rechtfertigung', LABWHStA, E 284g Bü 100.

222. For the preceding two paragraphs, see the 29 September–1 October 1813 correspondence among Ney, Bertrand, Franquemont and their subordinates in Fabry, *Empereur III*, Documents, pp. 185–8, 209–12; and Leggiere, *Napoleon and the Struggle for Germany*, vol. II, pp. 451–71.

223. Principal sources for the following: Franquemont's after-action report, 12 October 1813, LABWHStA, E 270a Bü 236; 'Darstellung der Ereignisse bei der schlesischen Armee im Jahre 1813, mit besonderer Berücksichtigung des Antheils der preußischen Truppen', *Beiheft zum Militair-Wochenblatt*, November–December 1844, pp. 303–15; Württemberg Generalstab, 'Bericht über die Theilnahme der Württembergischen Truppen an dem Treffen bei Wartenburg an 3ten Oktober 1813', *Militair-Wochenblatt*, no. 3, 17 January 1847, pp. 10–2; R. Mirus, *Das Treffen bei Wartenburg am 3. Oktober 1813*, Berlin: Mittler & Sohn, 1863; Friederich, *Herbstfeldzuges*, vol. II, pp. 281–98; Pfister, *Lager des Rheinbundes*, pp. 345–55; Quistorp, *Nordarmee*, vol. II, pp. 78–103; Leggiere, *Napoleon and the Struggle for Germany*, vol. II, pp. 471–91. Note that Württemberg accounts often title the battle 'Bleddin' rather than 'Wartenburg'.

224. For example, Mirus, *Wartenburg*, pp. 37–44. Helping to explain Bertrand's decisions is that he did not know the Army of Silesia was across the river (no one on the French side did) nor was he aware that the enemy had built two bridges. He therefore seems to have thought that he would only face a relatively small detachment from Bernadotte's army.

225. Franquemont to Friedrich, 3 October 1813, LABWHStA, E 270a Bü 236. The cavalry had detachments patrolling for many kilometres south along the Elbe, so fewer than a hundred were likely available at Bleddin, perhaps only fifty (Starklof, *Zweiten Reiter-Regiments*, pp. 381–4).

226. Franquemont's after-action report, 12 October 1813, LABWHStA, E 270a Bü 236.

227. Ibid.; 4th Corps 'Journal Historique', SHD, 2C448bis.

228. The units of the 1st and 2nd Prussian Brigades became intermingled as they crossed the river. As a result, Steinmetz (1st Brigade) in front of Wartenburg and Mecklenburg (2nd Brigade) facing Bleddin each commanded a mixed force with units from their two brigades. See Mirus, *Wartenburg*, pp. 111–12.

229. Baumbach, *Tage-Buch*, pp. 139–40.

230. Franquemont's after-action report, 12 October 1813, LABWHStA, E 270a Bü 236; Geßler/Tognarelli/Ströbel, *2. Württembergischen Feldartillerie-Regiments*, pp. 166–9. Interestingly, almost all Württemberg reports and histories refer to and condemn the

ignominious flight of 'French' cavalry at Globig, when in fact the dispersed brigade was composed of Hessian and Westphalian regiments.
231. 'Darstellung der Ereignisse bei der schlesischen Armee', 1844, p. 310.
232. Franquemont's after-action report, 12 October 1813, LABWHStA, E 270a Bü 236; Otto von Bonin, 'Mittheilungen über den Reiter-Angriff bei Globig in dem Treffen bei Wartenburg am 3ten Oktober 1813', *Militair-Wochenblatt*, no. 2. 9 January 1847, p. 7.
233. Pfister, *Lager des Rheinbundes*, pp. 351–2; Bonin, 'Mittheilungen', p. 7; 'Darstellung der Ereignisse bei der schlesischen Armee', p. 310. As Leggiere highlights (*Napoleon and the Struggle for Germany*, vol. II, p. 482), Gneisenau seems to have regarded this act as jolly fun while Yorck was deeply angered at what he considered unsoldierly barbarism (Johann Gustav Droysen, *Das Leben des Feldmarschalls Grafen York von Wartenburg*, Berlin: Veit, 1852, vol. III, pp. 121–2). See also: 'Reminiscenzen aus den Kriegseriegnissen des zweiten Leibhusaren-Regiments in den Feldzügen 1813 und 1814', *ZfKWGK*, vol. 6, 1836, pp. 255–8; August Alexander Ferdinand Milarch, *Denkwürdigkeiten des Meklenburg-Strelitzischen Husaren-Regiments in den Jahren des Befreiungskampfes 1813 bis 1814*, Neubrandenburg: Brünslow, 1854, pp. 97–103; and August Mackensen, *Schwarze Husaren*, Berlin: Mittler & Sohn, 1892, vol. II, pp. 702–4. Some Prussian accounts claim that the shots fired at their comrades by the Württemberg guns prevented the Light Battalion from saving the guns; this seems unlikely. The claim that the Württemberg battalion was nearly wiped out is erroneous.
234. Fromm, *Infanterie-Regiments König Wilhelm I*, p. 76. Pfister states that the percentage of wounded was higher than usual owing to the nature of the much of the combat, suggesting that the extended skirmishing meant men were often behind some kind of cover and thus more likely to be wounded than killed outright, Pfister, *Denkwürdigkeiten*, (pp. 394–6).
235. Schlaich, letter of 8 October 1813, *Interessante Scene*, p. 152.
236. Mirus, *Wartenburg*, p. 58; Ernst Pauly, *Geschichte des 2. Ostpreußischen Grenadier-Regiments Nr. 3*, Berlin: Mittler & Sohn, 1885, vol. II, p. 158.
237. Bertrand to Napoleon, 3 October 1813, AN, AF/IV/1662B Plaquette 3; 4th Corps 'Journal Historique', SHD, 2C448bis; Franquemont's after-action report, 12 October 1813, LABWHStA, E 270a Bü 236. Bertrand to Franquemont, 5 October 1813, Pfister, *Lager des Rheinbundes*, p. 354. The 'Journal Historique' described the Württemberg defence as 'negligent'.
238. Pelet, 'La Campagne de 1813', 6th article, *Spectateur Militaire*, vol. II, 1827, pp. 29–31. Pelet did note that the French and Italian troops 'arrived too late to support the Württembergers'. Given his general anti-Rheinbund bias, Pelet may have been over-reading the statement in Ney's report that 'the Württemberg division could not defend' Bleddin or an exaggerated claim by one of Beaumont's Westphalian officers that 'the Württemberg division has been entirely overthrown with considerable loss' (Fabry, *Empereur III*, Documents, p. 263). Even twenty years later, Pelet's accusation prompted a response in 'Theilnahme der Württembergischen Truppen', p. 12. It also led Bangold to compile notes for a reply: LABWHStA, E 284 g Bü 101, 'Kritische Stellungnahme des Obersten von Bangold an einer Darstellung des "Spectateur militaire", 1826 über den Einsatz württembergischer Truppen beim Übergang der Schlesischen Armee über die Elbe bei Wartenburg am 3. Oktober 1813'. This does not seem to have been published but it is not clear whether the editors rejected it or Bangold never submitted a final version.

239. Friedrich to Franquemont, 7 and 18 October 1813, LABWHStA, E 270a Bü 238.
240. Friedrich to Napoleon, 7 September, 19 September and 3 October 1813, Schloßberger, *Politische und Militärische Correspondenz*, pp. 317–22; Pfister quotes Beroldingen's report of the 5 October audience in *Lager des Rheinbundes*, pp. 357–61. The letter Beroldingen withheld was almost certainly that of 19 September, not 3 October.
241. Friedrich to Napoleon, 3 October 1813, Schloßberger, *Politische und Militärische Correspondenz*, pp. 320–2.
242. Pfister, *Lager des Rheinbundes*, pp. 357–61. Las Cases recorded that Napoleon did receive Friedrich's letter warning of Bavaria's defection (*Napoleon at Saint Helena*, vol. III, pt. 6, pp. 54–5).
243. Schlaich, letter of 13 October 1813, *Interessante Scene*, p. 156; Franquemont to Friedrich, 18 November 1813, LABWHStA, E 270a Bü 236.
244. Hoen, *Leipzig*, vol. V, p. 610.
245. Martens, *Vor fünfzig Jahren*, vol. II, pp. 146–7.
246. Ibid., pp. 158–9.
247. Franquemont to Berthier, 23 October 1813, SHD, 2C158 (with thanks to Bruno Colson). Pelet published an extract of Franquemont's letter in 'La Campagne de 1813', 12th article, *Spectateur Militaire*, vol. III, 1827, pp. 556–7.
248. Pfister, *Lager des Rheinbundes*, p. 374; Bertrand to Franquemont, 24 October 1813, LABWHStA, E 289 a Bü 124, 'Schreiben französischer Militärbehörden an das Kommando der württembergischen Feldtruppen Bemerkung' (printed in Starklof, *Zweiten-Reiter*, pp. 397–8). Franquemont's indignation at what he perceived as French mistrust is understandable but misplaced. First, he cited his assignment as baggage guard as evidence that his command was not trusted, yet in September he had complained that his men were constantly placed in the most dangerous positions. Second, with a small force of barely 1,000 combatants, the Württembergers could not be expected to take on large tasks. Third, the French by this time had every reason to suspect the German troops in general given the defection of the Saxons and Normann's brigade at Leipzig as well as antecedent desertions from other contingents.
249. Martens, *Vor fünfzig Jahren*, vol. II, p. 176; [Amédée Massé], 'Souvenirs de Général Bertrand d'après une Correspondance Inédite', *Le Correspondant*, vol. 238, 1910, p. 558; similar comments on the Württembergers in Chérot, 'Bertrand en 1813 et 1814', *Études*, vol. 91, pp. 51–2.
250. Berthier sent Franquemont's letter to Napoleon on 23 October (*Rapports*, vol. II, p. 225) and replied to Franquemont on the 24th (*Ordres*, vol. II, p. 383). British General Robert Wilson recorded, 'I saw a Würtemberg [sic] officer who was allowed to leave the French army with a thousand men without any impediment'; this was doubtless Franquemont (Robert Wilson, *General Wilson's Journal*, Anthony Brett-James, ed., London: Kimber, 1964, p. 211).
251. From the detailed account in Bangold's notes (LABWHStA, E 284 g Bü 102) there were 1,342 combatants and 77 non-combatants on the division's return. Pfister (*Lager des Rheinbundes*, p. 375), gives a total of 1,198. Note that there were large numbers of sick not included in these lists. Bertrand to Ney, 25 September 1813, Fabry, *Empereur III*, Documents, p. 70.
252. Pfister, *Lager des Rheinbundes*, p. 374; Fritz von Hiller, *Geschichte des Feldzuges 1814 gegen Frankreich*, Stuttgart: Kohlhammer, 1893, pp. 3–14.
253. Franquemont to Friedrich, 23 October 1813, LABWHStA, E 270a Bü 237.

254. Marmont, *Mémoires*, vol. V, p. 282; Starklof, *vierten Reiterregiments*, pp. 156–7; 'Darstellung der Ereignisse bei der schlesischen Armee', July–August 1847, p. 96; Peter, *Wachtmeister Peter*, p. 92; Dumonceau, *Mémoires*, pp. 374–5.
255. Marmont, *Mémoires*, vol. V, pp. 282–7, including his 19 October after-action report (pp. 378–86). Almost identical to the 19 October report is one dated 4 November 1813 in Pelet, 'La Campagne de 1813', 9th article, *Spectateur Militaire*, vol. II, 1827, pp. 538–41. This, too, does not mention the Württemberg brigade.
256. Marmont to Napoleon, midnight, 16 October 1813, SHD, 2C158 (with thanks to Bruno Colson); 'Journal des opérations du 6e Corps depuis le la rupture de l'armistice jusqu'au son retour sur le Rhin', SHD, MR 686.
257. Starklof, *vierten Reiterregiments*, pp. 154–9. Starklof spelt this officer's name 'Troyff', but his personnel file lists him as 'Troyfft' (LABWHStA, E 297 g Bü 141).
258. Ibid. Jean Louis Rieu, an officer of the 1st Naval Artillery, mentions in his memoirs that 'a regiment of chasseurs-à-cheval made a demonstration of charging the enemy, especially his artillery, but they had not gone twenty paces when they turned about and left us to our miserable fate' ('Mémoires de Jean-Louis Rieu', in *Soldats Suisses au Service Étranger*, Geneva: Jullien, 1910, vol. III, p. 185).
259. Other factors contributing to the potential for confusion were the dense battle smoke (that helped the Prussian hussars surprise the French) and the fact that many found it difficult to distinguish friend from foe as both were wearing dark blue overcoats (Rieu, 'Mémoires', vol. III, pp. 185–6).
260. 'Relation über die Schlacht am 16. October auf der Höhe von Leipzig', Pflugk-Hartung, *Leipzig*, pp. 334–6. This is likely the scene Dumonceau describes in his memoirs (p. 375) in which the Prussian cavalry 'rushed headlong at the Württemberg cavalry opposite it'. See also the account of Unterleutnant Carl Friedrich Wilhem von Reyher, the officer who carried the order to the Uhlans, in Förster, *Befreiungs-Kriege*, vol. II, pp. 184–5; Karl Rudolf von Ollech, *Carl Friedrich Wilhem von Reyher*, Berlin: Mittler & Sohn, 1869, vol. II, pp. 73–5; and Maurice-Henri Weil, *Campagne de 1813: La Cavallerie des Armées Alliés*, Paris: Baudoin, 1886, pp. 420–9. The Uhlans' history provides little enlightenment: Georg Friedrich Gottlob Goltz, *Geschichte des Königlich Preußischen dritten Ulanen-Regiments*, Fürstenwalde: Schubert, 1841, pp. 104–5.
261. Peter, *Wachtmeister Peter*, p. 94.
262. In addition to the sources already cited, this discussion draws on: Bangold's notes, LABWHStA, E 284 g Bü 102; Colson, *Leipzig*, pp. 193–201; [Hoepfner], 'Darstellung', 1847, pp. 100–5; Aster, *Leipzig*, vol. I, pp. 538–47; Friederich, *Herbstfeldzuges*, vol. III, pp. 80–100; Leggiere, *Napoleon and the Struggle for Germany*, vol. II, pp. 657–65; Ardenne, *Zieten'schen Husaren-Regiments*, pp. 386–7.
263. Normann apparently met Beroldingen on the battlefield at some point that day and requested guidance, but Beroldingen demurred, protesting that he was not authorised to offer any instructions (Starklof, *vierten Reiterregiments*, p. 162). Normann's 'Rechtfertigung', LABWHStA, E 284g Bü 100; Bangold's papers, LABWHStA, E 284g Bü 102; and J. G. Trefftz, 'Erinnerungen an den Schlachttagen', in Naumann, *Völkerschlacht*, pp. 364–5.
264. Starklof, *vierten Reiterregiments*, pp. 159–60; Fleischmann's after-action report, LABWHStA, E 270a Bü 240. According to the artillery's history, however, four of the pieces were damaged and were captured when Leipzig fell; thus only two pieces

returned to Württemberg with the battery in November (Geßler/Tognarelli/Ströbel, 2. *Württembergischen Feldartillerie-Regiments*, p. 171).

265. Bangold's papers, LABWHStA, E 284g Bü 102; Normann's 'Rechtfertigung', LABWHStA, E 284g Bü 100; Normann to Friedrich, 18 October 1813, LABWHStA, E 270a Bü 240. Note that Bangold's notes on Leipzig were published anonymously as 'Nachricht über die Begebenheiten des Köngl. Württembergischen Truppen-Corps an den Schlacht-Tagen von Leipzig im Feldzuge 1813', *Militair-Wochenblatt*, nos. 5 and 6, 4 and 11 February 1837.
266. Peter, *Wachtmeister Peter*, pp. 94–5. Major Wedel of Bennigsen's staff claims to have been the officer to receive the brigade, *Armee von Polen*, p. 44.
267. Wallerstein to Friedrich, 23 November 1813, LABWHStA, E 270a Bü 258; Normann's 'Rechtfertigung', LABWHStA, E 284g Bü 100; Normann to Friedrich, 18 October 1813, and Fleischmann's after-action report, LABWHStA, E 270a Bü 240. Significant extracts of these materials are published in Pfister, *Lager des Rheinbundes*, and Starklof, *vierten Reiterregiments*.
268. Franquemont to Bangold, 22 July 1826, LABWHStA, E 284g Bü 100; Pfister, *Lager des Rheinbundes*, pp. 375–6.
269. In Duvernoy, 'Kavalleriebrigade Normann', p. 366.
270. Printed in Gerhardt with the king's detailed instructions on the treatment to be meted out to the brigade and other original materials, *Württemberger im deutschen Befreiungskrieg*, pp. 103–12.
271. Peter, *Wachtmeister Peter*, pp. 96–7.
272. Sources for the foregoing: Bangold's papers, LABWHStA, E 284g Bü 102; Duvernoy, 'Kavalleriebrigade Normann', pp. 362–70; Pfister, *Lager des Rheinbundes*, pp. 281–6, 366–78; Starklof, *vierten Reiterregiments*, pp. 151–74; Marmont, *Mémoires*, vol. V, pp. 292–3. Normann's letter to his father was dated 7 December 1813 and is printed in Philipp Christian Friedrich Graf von Normann-Ehrenfels, *Denkwürdigkeiten aus dessen eigenhändigen Aufzeichnungen*, Roth von Schreckenstein, ed., Stuttgart: Kohlhammer, 1891, pp. 252–6. The Prussians regarded Normann with disdain; Gneisenau, for instance, decried the 'disgrace' Normann had incurred at Kitzen and stated that 'neither he nor a single man of his brigade shall have the honour of fighting in the ranks of Prussian warriors' (in Hermann Müller-Bohn, *Die deutschen Befreiungskriege*, Berlin: Kittel, 1901, vol. II, pp. 699–700). It is possible that there were more former Mecklenburgers and Prussians among the officers of Normann's two regiments than in other regiments; further research is required on this point.
273. Marmont, 'Journal des opérations du 6e Corps depuis le la rupture de l'armistice jusqu'au son retour sur le Rhin', SHD MR 686.
274. Marmont's 19 October report, in *Mémoires*, vol. V, pp. 378–86; Las Cases, *Napoleon at Saint Helena*, vol. III, pt. 6, p. 66.
275. Principal sources for the following are: Bezzel, *Studien zur Geschichte Bayerns*, pp. 45–71; Heilmann, *Wrede*, pp. 263–9; Heilmann, *Feldzug von 1813*, pp. 168–79; Junkelmann, *Napoleon und Bayern*, p. 160; Lefebvre de Béhaine, *Napoléon et les Alliés*, pp. 151–79; Lintner, *Kampf*, pp. 224–6; Pfister, *Lager des Rheinbundes*, pp. 378–400; Schneider, 'Württembergs Anschluß', pp. 92–103; Winter, *Wrede*, pp. 67–78.
276. Hölzle, *Württemberg im Zeitalter Napoleons*, p. 159/note 9; Schneider, 'Württembergs Anschluß', pp. 92–3. The banker was most likely Jacob Raphael Kaulla, younger brother to Karoline Kaulla of the family's influential banking house.

277. From a 19 October letter to Montgelas in Heilmann, *Wrede*, p. 306, note 6.
278. Walsleben's command consisted of the 4th and 8th Infantry Regiments, two light infantry companies, a foot artillery battery (four 6-pounders and 2 howitzers), and four light cavalry squadrons that would become the new 3rd Cavalry. The cavalry regiment included 122 men who had been returned from Saxony; likewise, the battery's complement of horses was filled out with animals that had been sent back from Franquemont's division. Starklof, *Zweiten Reiter-Regiments*, pp. 401–4; Wilhelm Strack von Weißenbach, *Geschichte der Königlich Württembergischen Artillerie*, Stuttgart: Kohlhammer, 1882, p. 240. Württemberg unit designations are painfully complicated: this new 4th Infantry, for instance, was cobbled together from depot troops, militia and parts of the 3rd and 5th Regiments; it would acquire the number '8' in 1815, while the 8th Infantry would be renumbered as the 7th in November 1813. See the tangled tables in Cordes, 'württembergische Heerwesen', in Väterlein/Burkarth, *Baden und Württemberg im Zeitalter Napoleons*.
279. Friedrich to Wintzingerode, 22 October 1813, Pfister, *Lager des Rheinbundes*, pp. 392–3.
280. Friedrich to Napoleon, 14 October 1813, Schloßberger, *Politische und Militärische Correspondenz*, pp. 322–4.
281. Las Cases, *Napoleon at Saint Helena*, vol. III, pt. 6, pp. 54–5; Pelet states that Napoleon received warning of Württemberg's shift to the Allies from Kellermann ('La Campagne de 1813', 12th article, *Spectateur Militaire*, vol. III, 1827, pp. 554, 566).
282. Winter, *Wrede*, p. 74.
283. Friedrich to Zeppelin, 24 October 1813, Pfister, *Lager des Rheinbundes*, pp. 396–7.
284. Beroldingen had already seen Metternich and returned to Stuttgart on 26 October with a courteous letter expressing friendly intentions (Heilmann, *Feldzug von 1813*, p. 178).
285. 'Königliches Manifest', printed in Hiller, *Geschichte des Feldzuges 1814*, p. 426. Of course, the 'despotism [*Willkür*] of any single state' could apply to the Coalition powers as well as to Napoleon.
286. Friedrich's situation was complicated by Coalition suspicions that he harboured a secret inclination towards France and hoped for Napoleon's return. Schneider and Sauer convincingly dispose of this spurious claim ('Württembergs Anschluß', pp. 98–103; *schwäbische Zar*, p. 331).
287. Pfister, 'Aus dem Lager des Rheinbundes 1812, eine Abwehr', p. 453.

Chapter 5: Baden and Hesse-Darmstadt: Fighting to the Last

1. Carl to Napoleon, 10 February 1813, in Waller, 'Baden und Frankreich', pp. 162–4.
2. For a short period in late April, Ney thus had the Bavarian 29th and Baden/Hessian/Frankfurt 39th Divisions under his overall command along with the 7th Württemberg Infantry (3rd Corps 'Situation', 25 April 1813, SHD, 2C539).
3. Napoleon's faith in his abilities was shown by his initially placing both the 38th and 39th Divisions under Marchand as a sort of corps-within-a-corps under Ney's 3rd Corps.
4. On the title 'grand duke' and the royal protocol, see Marian Wierichs, *Napoleon und das "Dritte Deutschland" 1805/1806*, Frankfurt am Main: Lang, 1978, pp. 111–28. Regarding efforts to transform Baden into a kingdom: Gustav Steiner, 'Rheinbund und "Königreich Helvetien": 1805–1807', *Baseler Zeitschrift für Geschichte und*

Altertumskunde, vol. 18, 1919; Karlhans Grueninger, 'Warum Baden unter Napoleon nicht Königreich wurde', *Badische Heimat*, vol. 34, 1954; Hansmartin Schwarzmaier, 'Das Epochenjahr 1806 in Baden', *Blick in der Geschichte*, no. 72, 15 September 2006, https://www.karlsruhe.de/b1/stadtgeschichte/blick_geschichte/blick72/grossherzogtum3.de [accessed January 2022].

5. Willy Andreas, *Der Aufbau des Staates im Zusammenhang der allgemeinen Politik*, vol. I of *Geschichte der badischen Verwaltungsorganisation und Verfassung*, Leipzig: Quelle & Meyer, 1913, pp. 24–37; Anneliese Waller, 'Baden und Frankreich in der Rheinbundzeit 1805–1813', dissertation, Albert-Ludwig-Universität, Freiburg im Breisgau, 1935, p. 157; Christian Würtz, *Johann Niklas Friedrich Brauer (1754–1813)*, Stuttgart: Kohlhammer, 2005, pp. 353–7; Friedrich von Weech, *Badische Geschichte*, Karlsruhe: Bielefeld, 1896, p. 504; Alfred Rambaud, *L'Allemagne sous Napoléon Ier (1804–1811)*, Paris: Didier, 1874, pp. 28–9; Schmitt, 'Germany without Prussia', pp. 27–9; Paul, 'Erinnerungskultur Südwestdeutschlands', in Hofbauer/Rink, *Völkerschlacht*, pp. 247–68.

6. Franz Schnabel, *Sigismund von Reitzenstein der Begründer des Badischen Staates*, Heidelberg: Hörning, 1927, pp. 115–26.

7. Among many other sources, good starting points on Baden's bureaucratic development are Loyd E. Lee, 'Baden between Revolutions: State-Building and Citizenship, 1800–1848', *Central European History*, vol. XXIV, no. 3, 1991; and the essays in Anton Schindling and Gerhard Taddey, eds, *1806 – Souveränität für Baden und Württemberg: Beginn der Modernisierung?*, Stuttgart: Kohlhammer, 2007.

8. Curiously, the outdated 'Kompanie-Wirtschaft' or self-administration at the company level was not abolished until the spring of 1813 (Sabina Hermes and Joachim Niemeyer, *Unter dem Greifen: Altbadisches Militär von der Vereinigung der Markgrafschaften bis zur Reichsgründung 1771–1871*, Karlsruhe: Braun, 1984, p. 56; Theophil von Barsewisch, *Geschichte des Großherzoglich Badischen Leib-Grenadier-Regiments 1803–1870*, Karlsruhe: Müller, 1893, p. 137). This was a holdover from an earlier age when each company 'belonged' to its captain, who controlled most of the funds allotted to uniforms, lodgings and upkeep; this naturally fostered a great deal of corruption and neglect of the men (Hochberg, *Denkwürdigkeiten*, p. 135).

9. Losses from Sauzey, *Contingent Badois*, p. 68. Figures vary for exact casualties, but this count is representative. Carl F. C. Pfnor, *Der Krieg, seine Mittel und Wege*, Tübingen: Fues, 1864, pp. 73–4.

10. On Baden uniforms, see W. J. Rawkins, *The Army of the Grand Duchy of Baden*, e-book edition, 2013; Rudolph von Freystedt, *Die Geschichtlichen Uniformen des Bad. Leib-Grenadier Regiments*, Karlsruhe: Albrecht, 1903; and especially Gerhard Söllner, *Für Badens Ehre: Die Geschichte der Badischen Armee*, Karlsruhe: INFO Verlagsgesellschaft, 1995–2001.

11. Wilhelm von Cloßmann, 'Tagebuch von Clossmann 1788–1825', Historisches Museum Schloß Rastatt, n.d., pp. 86–7 (with thanks to Thomas Hemmann).

12. Major Anton Brückner had commanded the column up to its arrival in Glogau. Orders to Brandt and the organisation of the troops are in 'Korrespondenzbuch von dem am 1. Febr. 1812 auf den Feldetat gesetzten großherzoglich-badischen Kontingentcorps./Dez. 1812–Juni 1813', GLAK, 48/4319.

13. Napoleon to Carl, 16 January 1813, *CG*, no. 32300, vol. XIII, p. 100, 18 January 1813, *CG*, no. 32332, vol. XIII, pp. 118–20, and 2 March 1813, *CG*, no. 32927, vol. XIII, p. 433.

14. Carl to Napoleon, 10 February 1813, in Waller, 'Baden und Frankreich', pp. 162–4. In outlining their contributions to the Confederation, the Badeners claimed full strengths for all their units, including the reduced detachment in Spain ('État de Situation de la Force Militaire du Grande Duché de Bade', 8 April 1813, SHD, 2C542).
15. For example: Schäffer to Carl, 7 August 1813, 'Korrespondenz des in das Hauptquartier commandierten GM v. Schaeffer', GLAK, 48/4346. For the troops in Spain: 'Armées en Espagne', 15 March 1813, SHD, 8C470.
16. Carl to Napoleon, 6 March 1813, in Waller, 'Baden und Frankreich', p. 164.
17. Although usually spelt 'Heimrodt' today, he signed his correspondence as 'Heimrod' in 1813.
18. Otto Freiherr Stockhorner von Starein, *Die Stockhorner von Starein*, Vienna: Konegen, 1896, pp. 88–91.
19. Strength report of 19 April 1813, 'Meldungen des GM v. Stockhorn', GLAK, 48/4336; 'Instruktion für den GM v. Stockhorn', 21 March 1813, GLAK, 48/4335.
20. Pappenheim to Ludwig, 12 July 1806, in Hanswerner Ebling, 'Die hessische Politik in der Rheinbundzeit 1806–13', *AHGA*, vol. XXIV, 1952/3, p. 215; Dieterich gives an earlier but thoughtful perspective in 'Politik Landgraf Ludwig'. On reform in Hesse, see Harm Kleuting, 'Nachholung der Absolutismus: Die rheinbündischen Reformern im Herzogtum Westfalen in hessen-darmstädtischer Zeit (1802–1816)', *Westfälische Zeitschrift*, no. 137, 1987; Schmitt, 'Germany without Prussia', pp. 21–2.
21. Börner states that the contingent had been raised to 6,000 after Hesse-Darmstadt had been granted additional territory, but this statement is based on Ebling's now-unavailable 1953 doctoral thesis ('Krise und Ende des Rheinbundes', pp. 8–9) and Börner seems to have misinterpreted it. The published version of Ebling's thesis, albeit abridged, does not state that the contingent's size had been increased, indicating rather that Ludwig had exceeded his commitment (Ebling, 'hessische Politik in der Rheinbundzeit', p. 245); likewise, none of the very detailed regimental histories suggests that Hesse's overall commitment had increased.
22. Karl Wilhelm Heinrich du Bos du Thil, *Denkwürdigkeiten aus dem Dienstleben des Hessen-Darmstädtischen Staatsministers Freiherrn du Thil 1803–1848*, Heinrich Ulmann, ed., Stuttgart: Deutsche Verlags-Anstalt, 1921, p. 150. 'The grand duke always gives me more than I demand,' commented Napoleon (Ebling, 'hessische Politik in der Rheinbundzeit', p. 246).
23. Napoleon to Champagny, 10 December 1810, *CG*, no. 19474, vol. VIII, p. 1312, and Napoleon to Ludwig, 15 January 1809, *CG*, no. 19859, vol. VIII, p. 1500. See also favourable French reports on the Hessian troops as related in the Hessian press, in O. Buchner, 'Die großherzoglich hessischen Truppen in den Kriegen der Rheinbundzeit und die amtliche Presse des Landes', *Hessenland*, vol. X, 1896.
24. Du Thil, *Denkwürdigkeiten*, p. 150; Heinrich Ulmann, 'Hessen-Darmstadt am Scheideweg im Herbst 1813', *AHGA*, IX, 1913, p. 297; Ebling, 'hessische Politik in der Rheinbundzeit', pp. 259–60; Rambaud, *L'Allemagne sous Napoléon*, p. 38. Note that the grand duke's name was spelt 'Ludewig' until the mid-1800s; the modern form is used here.
25. The *Groß- und Erbprinz* Regiment dispatched to Spain was an exception as it was re-formed according to the French organisational model before departing the Rhine.

26. The facings of the Provisional Light Infantry were supposed to be scarlet, but it is possible that poppy-red and light blue distinctions were present or even prevalent given the origins of the two battalions in their previous 'brigades'.
27. On Hessian uniforms, see regimental histories plus W. J. Rawkins, *The Army of the Grand Duchy of Hesse-Darmstadt*, e-book edition, 2014; and especially Klaus Schäfer, Markus Gärtner, Alfred Umhey, Peter Wacker and Edmund Wagner, *Die Achenbach-Bilderhandschrift 1813/14*, Darmstadt: Das Exerzierhaus, 1994.
28. Karl von Zimmermann, *Geschichte des 1. Großherzoglich Hessischen Dragoner-Regiments (Garde-Dragoner-Regiments) Nr. 23.*, Darmstadt: Bergsträsser, 1878, vol. I, pp. 175–7.
29. The preceding paragraphs on the light infantry and artillery are drawn from Wilhelm Bigge, *Geschichte des Infanterie-Regiments Kaiser Wilhelm (2. Großherzoglich Hessisches) Nr. 116*, Berlin: Mittler & Sohn, 1903, pp. 120–47; Fritz Beck, Karl von Hahn and Heinrich von Hahn, *Geschichte des Großherzoglichen Artilleriekorps 1. Großherzoglich Hessischen Feldartillerie-Regiments Nr. 25 und seiner Stämme*, Berlin: Mittler & Sohn, 1912, pp. 178–9; Carl Christian Freiherr von Röder von Diersburg, *Geschichte des 1. Großherzoglich Hessischen Infanterie- (Leibgarde-) Regiments Nr. 115*, Fritz Beck, ed., Berlin: Mittler & Sohn, 1899, pp. 205–11; Friedrich Soldan, *Heinrich Künzels Großherzogtum Hessen: Lebensbilder aus Vergangenheit und Gegenwart*, Gießen: Roth, 1893, pp. 294–5; Alexandre Fursy Guesdon [Mortonval], *Geschichte des Feldzugs in Russland im Jahre 1812*, Darmstadt: Leske, 1831, pp. 204–14 (this segment of the book almost certainly penned by a Hessian veteran of 1812). Sauzey, *Soldats de Hesse et de Nassau*, p. 233 for the remnants from Spain.
30. Ebling, 'hessische Politik in der Rheinbundzeit', p. 250.
31. Friedrich M. Kircheisen, *Fürstenbriefe an Napoleon I.*, Stuttgart: Cotta, 1929, vol. I, pp. 289–90.
32. Heinrich Bergér, 'Hessische Truppen unter Napoleons Fahnen im Jahre 1813', *Wochenbeilage der Darmstadter Zeitung*, no. 2, 11 January 1913.
33. Diersburg/Beck, *1. Großherzoglich Hessischen Infanterie*, pp. 211–12.
34. Details on march dates and mobilisation difficulties from regimental histories. Frey's recollections are in Karl Esselborn, ed., *Neue Erinnerungen hessischer Offiziere, Christian Frey und Franz Schmidt, aus der Zeit der Völkerschlacht bei Leipzig*, Darmstadt: Hessischer Volksschriftenverein, 1913; this is a transcription of his memoir in HStAD Best. G 61 N2. 29/2, Feldzug 1813, Band 4.
35. Hessian accounts mention that Marchand's division also had a French battery of 8 guns at first, but that this was later reassigned (HStAD, Best. G 61 N2. 28/3, Feldzug 1813, Band 2). No such battery appears in the monthly French strength reports ('*livrets*') prepared for Napoleon.
36. Report of 6 April 1813 quoted in Lefebvre de Béhaine, *Napoléon et les Alliés*, p. 53.
37. Additionally, six Hessian gendarmes (*Landdragoner*) were attached to Emil's headquarters to serve as dispatch riders and orderlies (Fritz Beck, *Geschichte des Großherzoglich Hessichen Gendarmeriekorps 1763–1905*, Darmstadt: Hohmann, 1905, p. 43). Figures based on the number of men present on departing the duchy, HStAD Best. G 61 N2. 28/3, Feldzug 1813, Band 2. Slightly different figures are in regimental histories and Ludwig Kattrein, *Ein Jahrhundert deutscher Truppengeschichte dargestellt an derjenigen des Grossh. Hessischen Kontingents 1806–1906*, Darmstadt: Schlapp, 1907, p. 50. The Bavarian envoy in Darmstadt was astonished that the little land could raise troops

Notes to pages xxx

at all, let alone exceed its treaty obligation. On this and Napoleon's offer: Ebling, 'hessische Politik in der Rheinbundzeit', pp. 250–3.

38. Barsewisch, *Badischen Leib-Grenadier-Regiments*, pp. 138–40; Bigge, *2. Großherzoglich Hessisches*, p. 147; Friedrich Klingelhöffer, *Geschichte des 2. Grossherzoglich Hessischen Infanterie-Regiments (Grossherzog) Nr. 116*, Berlin: Mittler & Sohn, 1888, pp. 32–3; Diersburg/Beck, *1. Großherzoglich Hessischen Infanterie*, p. 214.
39. Berthier to Napoleon, 18 March 1813 (relaying Emil's request), *Rapports*, vol. I, p. 50; Berthier to Marchand, Ney and Emil, 19 April 1813, *Ordres*, vol. I, pp. 17–19. Ludwig apparently conveyed this request directly to Napoleon when they met on 18 April in Mainz (Ebling, 'hessische Politik in der Rheinbundzeit', p. 252).
40. Ebling, 'hessische Politik in der Rheinbundzeit', pp. 247–49 (quote dated 17 November 1812); Ulmann, 'Hessen-Darmstadt am Scheideweg', p. 284. At the same time, another of Emil's brothers was serving as a staff officer in the French army. See also Napoleon to Ludwig, 19 April 1813, *CG*, no. 33939, vol. VIII, p. 873.
41. Stockhorn report, 14 April 1813, GLAK, 48/4336. Hessian desertions: HStAD, Best. G 61 N2. 29/1, Feldzug 1813, Band 3; Bergér, 'Hessische Truppen'.
42. Martin C. Ignaz Kösterus, *Die Großherzoglich Hessischen Truppen in dem Feldzug von 1813 in Schlesien*, Darmstadt: Brill, 1840, pp. 4–5.
43. Wilhelm von Bray-Steinburg, *Geschichte des 1. Badischen Leib-Dragoner-Regiments Nr. 20*, Berlin: Mittler & Sohn, 1909, pp. 36–7; Hans Freiherr von Wechmar, *Braune Husaren*, Berlin: Leist, 1893, pp. 27–8.
44. Stockhorn report, 3 May 1813, GLAK, 48/4336.
45. Kösterus, *Großherzoglich Hessischen Truppen*, p. 8.
46. 'Tagebuch des Garde Füsiliers Regiments in der Campagne 1812 u. 1813 von GM Schmidt', HStAD Best. G 61 N2. 26/4, Rußland-Feldzug 1812–1813, Band 3; Bigge, *2. Großherzoglich Hessisches*, pp. 150–1. The strength of Meyer's company is from Hessian sources; the Guard's 'Situation' for 1 April listed the 'Hessian troops' as 116 present under arms and nine sick (SHD, 2C706).
47. Kösterus, *Großherzoglich Hessischen Truppen*, p. 9.
48. Koch, *Journal des Opérations du IIIe Corps*, p. 11; Tournès, *Lützen*, pp. 346–7; Fabry, *Journal des Campagnes*, pp. 48–52; Bogdanovich, *Geschichte des Krieges im Jahre 1813*, vol. I/1, pp. 195–9.
49. 'Tagebuch des provisorischen leichten Gardefusiliers Regiment während der Campagne 1813', HStAD Best. G 61 N2. 31/1, Truppengeschichte 1813, Band 6, emphasis in the original. The distribution of the Baden troops on the left and Hessians on the right is my supposition as the reports of the two commanders, though detailed, are not clear on this point.
50. The Frankfurt battalion and two of the Hessian guns seem to have been held on the division's far left flank throughout the battle.
51. Hauptmann von Beck, 'Relation über den Antheil welchen das Badische Corps an der Schlacht bei Lützen unterem 2ten Maÿ 1813, in so fern ich beobachten konnte, genommen hat', 'Beitrag zur Geschichte des Infanterieregiments von Stockhorn./ Feb.–Juni 1813', GLAK, 48/4339.
52. Kösterus, *Großherzoglich Hessischen Truppen*, pp. 11–12. Kösterus wrote that the regiment soon rallied under Emil's guidance, but this optimistic memory is belied by Emil's bitter report.

53. Emil's report, 3 May 1813, HStAD Best. E 8 B3.10.3, Nr. 128/6, Berichte General-Kommando. Much of this report was published in Diersburg/Beck, *1. Großherzoglich Hessischen Infanterie*, pp. 215–17, but the author omitted the portion quoted here. The enemy force was apparently two squadrons of the Prussian 1st Silesian Hussars, the Lithuanian Uhlans, an unidentified Russian dragoon regiment, a Cossack regiment, and a light battery.
54. 'Auszug aus dem Tagebuch des Vaters des Großherzl. Hess. Hauptmann Schimpf von 9. Februar 1812–27 January 1814', HStAD Best. G 61 N2. 26/4.
55. Beck, GLAK, 48/4339; and Emil's 3 May report, HStAD Best. E 8 B3.10.3, Nr. 128/6.
56. There are several versions of Meyer's escapade with slight variations, but this variant seems most likely as it was reported by Prinz Emil (9 July 1813, HStAD Best. E 8 B3.10.3, Nr. 128/6; and Bigge, *2. Großherzoglich Hessisches*, pp. 150–1). The quote is from Leutnant Georg Franz Schmidt of Meyer's company, who thought his commander's bravado was likely motivated by curiosity ('Tagebuch des Garde Füsiliers Regiments', HStAD Best. G 61 N2. 26/4, Rußland-Feldzug 1812–1813, Band 3).
57. Schmidt, 'Tagebuch', HStAD Best. G 61 N2. 26/4.
58. By this time, parts of Major General Ivan Leontievich Shakhovsky's division had been committed to the fight around Kleingörschen and Kaja.
59. Major Christian Zimmermann, letter of 3 May 1813, 'Auszüge aus Briefen des im Jahr 1832 [illegible] verstorbenen Gr. Generalmajor Zimmermann, geschrieben während den Feldzügen von 1809 bis 1815 usw.', HStAD Best. E 8 B3.10.1, Nr. 124/7.
60. Kösterus, *Großherzoglich Hessischen Truppen*, p. 16. Kösterus, whose account often follows archival reports very closely, likely also benefited from postwar knowledge in granting the Young Guard '10,000 throats', a figure very close to the actual number (Pierre Juhel, 'Napoleon et la Campagne de Saxe – 1813', *Tradition Hors Série* no. 7, 1998, p. 50).
61. This account of the 1st Light Dragoons draws primarily from Heimrodt's 5 May 1813 report ('Meldungen des Dragonerregiments von Freystedt./Apr.–Nov. 1813', GLAK, 48/4342); 'Notizen zur Gefechte des Feldzugs 1813 nach Sachsen und Schlesien, in so fern dieselbe das Dragoner Regiment von Freystedt beruht', 1824 ('Geschichte des Dragonerregiments von Freystedt in Sachsen und Schlesien', GLAK, 48/4341); and Bray, *Badischen Leib-Dragoner-Regiments*, pp. 38–40. See also Chef de Bataillon Roguet, 'Étude sur l'ordre perpendiculaire', *Spectateur Militaire*, no. 107, February 1834, p. 511), who cites Ney's use of the light cavalry to hold off the Allies so his infantry could rally. It is not clear which Prussian battalion was scattered; Bray claims it was the Garde-Füsiliers. A Prussian regimental history that *may* refer to this charge states that its battalion quickly formed square and repelled its attackers (Robert von Gröling II, *Kurze Geschichte des Königl. 1ten Schlesischen Grenadier-Regiments (No. 10)*, Berlin: Blumenthal, 1861, p. 31).
62. Stockhorn's 3 May 1813 report (GLAK, 48/4336) and Heimrodt's reports of 5 and 9 May 1813 (GLAK, 48/4342). The 'Geschichte des Dragonerregiments von Freystedt' (GLAK, 48/4341) gives the missing as 80–90.
63. The number of dead and wounded is from Emil's 3 May report (HStAD Best. E 8 B3.10.3, Nr. 128/6); but the prince did not mention the missing; that figure comes from HStAD Best. G 61 N2. 28/3, Feldzug 1813, Band 2 (this accounting lists only 276 dead or wounded for a grand total of 1,122). The reports sent to the 3rd Corps chief of staff (GB Antoine Henri Jomini) evidently listed the missing as 'wounded' as the corps' report

of losses gave 475 and 1,118 as wounded for the Baden and Hessian infantry respectively with none listed as 'missing' (3rd Corps loss report for Lützen, SHD, 2C167).
64. Stockhorn, report of 9 May 1813, GLAK, 48/4336.
65. Stockhorn, report of 22 May 1813, GLAK, 48/4336.
66. Schimpf, 'Tagebuch', HStAD Best. G 61 N2. 26/4.
67. Letter of 7 May 1813, 'Auszüge aus Briefen', HStAD Best. E 8 B3.10.1, Nr. 124/7. His phrase was *'zum Dienst geschickter zu machen'*.
68. Zimmermann, letter of 3 May 1813, HStAD Best. E 8 B3.10.1, Nr. 124/7.
69. Kösterus, *Großherzoglich Hessischen Truppen*, pp. 11–12 (quote); Bigge, *2. Großherzoglich Hessisches*, pp. 156.
70. Zimmermann, letter of 7 May 1813, HStAD Best. E 8 B3.10.1, Nr. 124/7.
71. Reports of 3 May 1813 by Emil (HStAD Best. E 8 B3.10.3, Nr. 128/6) and Stockhorn (GLAK, 48/4336).
72. Koch, *Journal des Opérations du IIIe Corps*, p. 12. Note that the generally excellent Prussian General Staff history erroneously implies that Emil disparaged *all* his troops. In fact, the prince's report draws a clear distinction between the Leib-Garde and the other components of his command. Equally misleading is the history's averral that the desertions were incontrovertible evidence of south German soldiers seeking the first moment to escape 'the French yoke'. On the other hand, it may be correct in stating that some 200 Hessian prisoners went over to the Prussian side on 3 May near Halle as stated in Caemmerer, *Frühjahrsfeldzug*, vol. II, pp. 78, 337 – note, however, that there is no reference to such defection in Hessian sources.
73. Napoleon's remark in Ebling, 'hessische Politik in der Rheinbundzeit', p. 253; *Journal de l'Empire*, 4 July 1813; Ludwig to Emil, 9 June 1813, HStAD Best. D 4 27.3.4, Nr. 637/1, 'Briefe an Prinz Emil von seinem Vater'.
74. Heimrodt reports of 5 and 9 May 1813, GLAK, 48/4342; 'Geschichte des Dragoner-regiments', GLAK, 48/4341; Bray, *Badischen Leib-Dragoner-Regiments*, pp. 38–41.
75. Kösterus, *Großherzoglich Hessischen Truppen*, p. 25; 'Erinnerungen aus den Feldzügen von 1812 bis 1815 von A. Bieler aus Giessen'; and Schmidt, 'Tagebuch' (both HStAD Best. G 61 N2. 26/40). A few pages later, Schmidt states that those wounded during the Engagement at Haynau on the 26th were transported back to Bunzlau: 'Among the wounded were sutler women who had been slashed in the breast, the Prussians even committed cruelties against the children.' Larrey, the army's senior surgeon, recounts treating some of these injured women: Jean-Dominique Larrey, *Mémoires de Chirurgie Militaire et Campagnes*, Paris: Smith, 1817, vol. IV, pp. 166–7.
76. 'Tagebuch des Gardefusiliers Regiment', HStAD Best. G 61 N2. 31/1; Bieler, 'Erinnerungen', HStAD Best. G 61 N2. 26/40; Bigge, *2. Großherzoglich Hessisches*, p. 158. Anthing had already been wounded at Lützen but continued to serve at Bautzen where he was hit again.
77. The dragoons' role on 22 May is mentioned in 'Geschichte des Dragonerregiments von Freystedt' (GLAK, 48/4341) but not in the regiment's published history.
78. Kösterus, *Großherzoglich Hessischen Truppen*, p. 31.
79. Bigge, *2. Großherzoglich Hessisches*, p. 159; August Keim, *Geschichte des Infanterie-Leibregiments Grossherzogin (3. Grossherzogl. Hessisches) Nr. 117*, Berlin: Bath, 1903, p. 234; 'Journal des GM v. Stockhorn', GLAK, 48/4337; Laboissière to Ney, 6 May 1813, and Marchand to Berthier, 1 June 1813, both in Foucart, *Bautzen*, vol. I, p. 75 and vol. II, p. 215.
80. In Diersburg/Beck, *1. Großherzoglich Hessischen Infanterie*, pp. 219–20.

81. Stockhorn, report of 22 May 1813, GLAK, 48/4336.
82. Kösterus, *Großherzoglich Hessischen Truppen*, pp. 18–19.
83. Bray, *Badischen Leib-Dragoner-Regiments*, pp. 42–4.
84. Zimmermann, *1. Großherzoglich Hessischen Dragoner-Regiments*, vol. I, pp. 177–81. Zimmermann describes a lively cavalry encounter near Hoyerswerda on 27 May, but this is almost certainly an error; his description clearly applies to the Engagement at Hoyerwerda on the 28th (see Prittwitz, *Beiträge zur Geschichte des Jahres 1813*, vol. II, pp. 193–7). Strength from a French mid-May 'Situation', SHD, 2C542.
85. The following draws primarily from 'Journal des Infanterieregiments von Stockhorn Nr. 1 während der Blockade von Glogau', GLAK, 48/4340; Brandt's summary report ('Meldungen des Oberstleutnants von Brand, Kommandeur des 1. Infanterieregiments./Mai–Sept. 1813', GLAK 48/4344) and the reports in SHD 2C168 from Laplane (5 June 1813), Durrieu (29 May 1813), and Nempde (31 May 1813). These are supplemented by overall accounts in Klöffler/Hemmann, *vergessene Befreiungskrieg*, pp. 208–29; Jean-François Brun, *Les Oubliés du Fleuve: Glogau-sur-Oder, un Siège sous le Premier Empire*, Saint-Julien-Chapteuil: Editions du Roure, 1997, pp. 81–145; Gottlob Siegfried Dietrich, *Groß Glogaus Schicksale von 1806 bis 1814*, Glogau: Neue Güntherschen Buchdruckerei, 1815, pp. 81–131; and Ferdinand Minsberg, *Geschichte der Stadt und Festung Groß-Glogau*, Glogau: Gottschalk, 1853. Strength from Hochberg, *Denkwürdigkeiten*, p. 230.
86. Durrieu's 29 May 1813 report, SHD, 2C168.
87. The artillery commander in the fortress formed a mobile battery of four 3-pounders and two howitzers (Nempde's 31 May 1813 report, SHD, 2C168).
88. Details and quotes from 'Journal des Infanterieregiments von Stockhorn', GLAK, 48/4340; as well as Durrieu's 29 May 1813 report and Laplane's 'Journal des Événements' (both SHD 2C168).
89. Durrieu's and Laplane's quotes from Durrieu's 29 May 1813 report and Laplane's 'Journal des Événements' (both SHD GR 2C168). An abridged version of Durrieu's report was published in Issue 13 of the Grande Armeé's *Nouvelles Officielles*, 9 June 1813 and in the *Moniteur Universelle*, no. 161, 10 June 1813. Nempde's remarks from Pierre Michel Nempde-Dupoyet, *Relation des Blocus et Sièges de Glogau*, Paris: n. p., 1827, p. 20. Note that Nempde's published account adds detail to the report he submitted to Berthier on 31 May 1813. See also Georges Bagès, 'Le Siège de Glogau 1813–1814', *Spectateur Militaire*, vol. LX, 1905.
90. Brandt to Carl, 30 May 1813, GLAK 48/4344.
91. 'Journal des Infanterieregiments von Stockhorn', GLAK, 48/4340.
92. Nempde, *Blocus et Sièges de Glogau*, p. 18. This was a curious case as the person executed was a young woman who had disguised her Baden soldier lover in women's clothes and was attempting to smuggle him not out of Glogau, but from the 39th Division's camp at Lüben. As they tried to pass the fortress, they were spotted by a suspicious Baden sentry. The soldier was returned to Lüben, tried, convicted, sentenced to 10 years in prison and escorted back to Karlsruhe (Stockhorn report, 13 August 1813, GLAK 48/4336). The young woman's tale is related sympathetically in the patriotic account by Dietrich in *Groß Glogaus Schicksale*, pp. 130–1.
93. Brandt to Carl, 30 May 1813, GLAK 48/4344.
94. Stockhorn's letters to Carl, 3, 18 and 19 June, GLAK 48/4336; Berthier to Laplane, 17 June 1813, Berthier, *Ordres*, vol. I, pp. 215–16. Strength reports for the eight companies

in early June range from just below 1,000 to slightly more than 1,100 (GLAK 48/4336, SHD 2C168).

95. 'Geschichte der 1. Brigade/Juni–Okt. 1813', GLAK, 48/4338; Kösterus, *Großherzoglich Hessischen Truppen*, p. 34. Fields of crops had to be cleared for the camp and, in one Hessian's words, 'an entire pine forest was used' to build the barracks (Bieler, 'Erinnerungen', HStAD Best. G 61 N2. 26/40).
96. Stockhorn report, 4 August 1813, GLAK 48/4336.
97. Printed in Bergér, 'Hessische Truppen'.
98. Kösterus, *Großherzoglich Hessischen Truppen*, p. 36; Stockhorn reports of 21 June and 4 and 13 August 1813 (GLAK, 48/4336); Emil reports of 11 July and 2 August 1813 (HStAD Best. E 8 B3.10.3, Nr. 128/6); 'Geschichte der 1. Brigade' (GLAK, 48/4338); Hessian regimental histories. Emil's 11 August report does not mention the brawl.
99. Strengths and march details from HStAD Best. G 61 N2. 28/3, Feldzug 1813, Band 2; Emil's remark from his 2 August report (HStAD Best. E 8 B3.10.3, Nr. 128/6); Ludwig to Emil, 9 June 1813, HStAD Best. D 4 27.3.4, Nr. 637/1.
100. Stockhorn's reports of 22 June and 4 August 1813, GLAK, 48/4336.
101. Stockhorn's 4 August 1813 report (GLAK, 48/4336); Kösterus, *Großherzoglich Hessischen Truppen*, p. 37; Schmidt, 'Tagebuch' (HStAD Best. G 61 N2. 26/4).
102. French inspection report, 18 July 1813, AN, AF/IV/1661A, Plaquette 1. A 6th Squadron was formed in mid-August by transferring the 2nd Regiment's 4th Squadron, but this was not sent to Saxony and was instead used later as a source of replacements (Bray, *Badischen Leib-Dragoner-Regiments*, p. p. 56); Söllner, on the other hand, states that the 6th Squadron was dispatched but 'never reached' the regiment in the field (*Badens Ehre*, vol. II, p. 34).
103. Bray, *Badischen Leib-Dragoner-Regiments*, pp. 45–6; 'Beschreibung der Schlacht von Leipzig', GLAK, 48/4345. Heimrodt's brief tenure in this unusual command left few traces. The official French 'Situation' lists the commander as GB Cyrille Simon Picquet (or Piquet) as the report was completed before Heimrodt's appointment, but Picquet seems to have been absent in August. The confusion is compounded by assumptions that Heimrodt commanded the light cavalry of Vandamme's 1st Corps, but this was GB Gobrecht who is discussed in Chapter 7. Heimrodt's posting with the 3rd Brigade under Corbineau is from Ehnl, *Schlacht bei Kulm*, vol. IV, p. 218; and George Nafziger, *Napoleon at Dresden: The Battles of August 1813*, Chicago: Emperor's Press, 1994, p. 340.
104. Zimmermann, *1. Großherzoglich Hessischen Dragoner-Regiments*, vol. I, p. 182.
105. Ludwig to Emil, 9 June 1813, HStAD Best. D 4 27.3.4, Nr. 637/1; Ebling, 'hessische Politik in der Rheinbundzeit', pp. 252–54; Waller, 'Baden und Frankreich', pp. 144–53.
106. Kösterus, *Großherzoglich Hessischen Truppen*, pp. 46–7.
107. 'Geschichte der 1. Brigade', GLAK, 48/4338.
108. Stockhorn's 28 August 1813 report, GLAK, 48/4336; 'Geschichte der 1. Brigade', GLAK, 48/4338.
109. Stockhorn's 28 August 1813 report, GLAK, 48/4336; 'Journal des GM v. Stockhorn', GLAK, 48/4337; Emil's 5 September 1813 report, HStAD Best. E 8 B3.10.3, Nr. 128/6; Kösterus, *Großherzoglich Hessischen Truppen*, pp. 55–61. The Hessians were able to enjoy a gift of plum brandy donated by their grand-duchess and distributed to the troops by Emil. Many of the men doubtless consumed their share at once, but Fourrier Wilhelm Diehl of the Grade-Fusiliers sequestered his flask as a final restorative should

he find himself lying wounded on the battlefield or near death in a hospital (HStAD Best. E 8 B3.10.1, Nr. 126/6, 'Denkwürdigkeiten und Eriegnisse des verabschiedeten Großherzoglich Hessischen Second Lieutenant Wilhelm Diehl, während seine militärische Laufbahn insbesonderen währen den Feldzügen von 1812 u. 1813, aus eigenen Erinnerungen'). 'Desperate straggle' is a paraphrase from a work of fiction: Jack Vance, *The Dragonmasters*, New York: Berkley Books, 1985, p. 97.

110. Details of these three incidents from Kösterus, *Großherzoglich Hessischen Truppen*, pp. 46, 60–2; also Emil's 5 September 1813 report, HStAD Best. E 8 B3.10.3, Nr. 128/6. Note that Wittgenstein's formal title was August Ludwig Prinz von Sayn-Wittgenstein-Berleburg. The Prussian commander's report is in Ardenne, *Zieten'schen Husaren-Regiments*, pp. 404–5.
111. HStAD Best. E 8 B3.10.1, Nr. 124/7.
112. 'Journal des GM v. Stockhorn', GLAK, 48/4337. The Prussian commander's report on 4 October is in Widdern, *Streifkorps*, vol. II, pp. 149–50.
113. 'Journal des GM v. Stockhorn', GLAK, 48/4337; Emil's journal entry for 28 September 1813, HStAD Best. E 8 B3.10.3, Nr. 128/6
114. Kösterus, *Großherzoglich Hessischen Truppen*, pp. 73–5.
115. This paragraph is drawn from 'Geschichte des Dragonerregiments von Freystedt' (GLAK, 48/4341); Bray, *Badischen Leib-Dragoner-Regiments*, pp. 44–83; and Koch, *Journal des Opérations du IIIe Corps*, pp. 44–83. On Dessau, see especially Quistorp, *Nordarmee*, vol. II, pp. 171–7. The splendid success came despite Beurmann's ineptitude according to Colonel Jean Nicolas Curély, commander of the 10th Hussars (*Itineraire d'un Cavalier Léger de la Grande Armée*, Paris: Librairie des Deux Empires, 1999, pp. 352–4).
116. Zimmermann, *1. Großherzoglich Hessischen Dragoner-Regiments*, vol. I, pp. 183–6. Bubna's recollections are quoted extensively in this regimental history.
117. Lehsten, *Am Hofe König Jérômes*, pp. 128–9.
118. 4th Corps summary 'Situation' for 26 September 1813, SHD, 2C539. The next summary situation (6 October) lists the Hessians with only 64 present for duty, so it is possible that the regiment lost two-thirds of its strength at Wartenburg. On the other hand, it is also possible that a substantial portion of the regiment was detached as the summary 'situations' only provide numbers immediately present for duty.
119. Augmentation battalion from HStAD Best. G 61 N2. 28/3, Feldzug 1813, Band 2; and II/Garde-Fusiliers from Bigge, *2. Großherzoglich Hessisches*, pp. 188–95; Napoleon to Durosnel, 18 August 1813, *CG*, no. 35983, vol. XIV, p. 424; Berthier to Margaron, 16 August 1813, *Ordres*, vol. II, pp. 36–7. Each of the regimental replacement groups was considered a 'company' in the Augmentation Battalion and wore the facings of its designated regiment.
120. Hochberg, *Denkwürdigkeiten*, p. 232. The instructions issued to Wilhelm were dated 29 July 1813 and were very similar to those Stockhorn received (GLAK, 'Orders und Erlasse an den Grafen Hochberg', 48/4330).
121. GLAK, 'Aus den Lebenserinnerungen des Obersten Ferdinand Wolff', 65/11381.
122. On 28 August, the Badeners were 2,454 out of a total of 6,640 men in Leipzig (Margaron to Berthier, 28 August 1813, Fabry, *Empereur I*, Documents, pp. 57–8); by 8 September, Baden made up 2,544 of 9,284 men ('Situation de la Place de Leipzig', SHD, 2C546). Over the next several weeks, Wilhelm somehow also ended up with

a small number of Baden light dragoons, perhaps 20–30, whose officers were often assigned to lead foraging parties.
123. Napoleon to Durosnel, 18 August 1813, *CG*, no. 35983, vol. XIV, p. 424; Berthier to Margaron and Dalton, 18 August 1813, *Ordres*, vol. II, pp. 43–7.
124. Although Wilhelm believed many of the young conscripts he saw had intentionally injured themselves, the issue of self-inflicted wounds is complex and the number of cases seems grossly exaggerated in many accounts (including by French generals at the time). See the discussion of the meticulous investigation carried out by Larrey, the army's chief surgeon, during the armistice to refute what he termed these 'odious imputations', in Paul Triaire, *Napoléon et Larrey: Récits Inédits de la Révolution et de l'Empire*, Tours: Mame et Fils, 1902, pp. 422–8; and Larrey, *Mémoires*, vol. IV, pp. 170–8.
125. Hochberg, *Denkwürdigkeiten*, pp. 234–5. The French troops were infantrymen of IV/35e Léger (691) and a detachment from the 138e Ligne (361); the editor of Hochberg's memoirs adds a detachment from the 58e Ligne, but this does not appear in Margaron's reports. Hochberg states that 400 French cavalry recruits were also assigned, but Margaron 'greatly regretted' that they did not march with the Badeners though they arrived safely the next day (Margaron to Berthier, 26 August 1813, Fabry, *Empereur I*, Documents, p. 55).
126. Meier, *Erinnerungen*, p. 102.
127. Hochberg, *Denkwürdigkeiten*, p. 235/Note 1.
128. This column was to help escort a large French baggage train returning west, but the commander, GB Jean-Baptiste Noirot was negligent, and his convoy suffered severe losses at the hands of Allied raiders, leading to his dismissal. GM Brückner, returning to Baden owing to feeble health, barely escaped. Examples of the detachments are in J. D. Haffner, *Geschichtliche Darstellung des Großherzoglich Badischen Armee-Corps*, Karlsruhe: Malsch und Vogel, 1840, pp. 102–3.
129. These were the 1st Voltigeur Company and 1st, 3rd and 7th Fusilier Companies (Haffner, *Darstellung*, p. 102).
130. Margaron to Berthier, 28 August 1813, Fabry, *Empereur I*, Documents, pp. 51–2; Berthier to Lefebvre-Desnouettes, 11 September 1813, *Ordres*, vol. II, p. 179; Hochberg, *Denkwürdigkeiten*, pp. 242–3.
131. Order of the day, 5 October 1813, 'Ordrebuch des Grafen von Hochberg./Juli–Okt. 1813', GLAK, 48/4333; Hochberg, *Denkwürdigkeiten*, p. 243; Wolff, GLAK 65/11381.
132. Wilhelm believed himself spied upon by Bacher, whom he portrays as lurking about in an aggressively inquisitive manner. Wilhelm would thus ostentatiously hide what he was reading when Bacher appeared or loudly make exaggerated statements to his officers if he thought the Frenchman was surreptitiously listening.
133. Hochberg, *Denkwürdigkeiten*, pp. 245–50; Kölle, 'Erlebtes', pp. 222–3. Wilhelm had read Kölle's account and paraphrases him closely. Kölle termed Bacher 'one of Napoleon's most obsequious tools', whom 'we had long known and hated'.
134. The French report only listed Baden losses as 417 captured (Foucart, *Une Division de Cavalerie Légère*, p. 130); Haffner gives the total loss as 473 (*Darstellung*, p. 103).
135. August Friedrich Karl Wagner, *Chronik der Herzoglichen Residenz- und Hauptstadt Altenburg*, Altenburg: Schnuphase, 1827, pp. 163–70. Wagner claims some of the Baden troops fired on the French, but there is no other indication that this occurred and it seems highly unlikely (though there could have been undisciplined random shooting by the frightened green troops).

136. Möller's 29 September 1813 report is in Foucart, *Une Division de Cavalerie Légère*, pp. 119–20; his Legion of Honour file is LH/1891/63 in the Base Léonore. Wilhelm averred, however, that his subsequent actions showed he did not deserve this award (Hochberg, *Denkwürdigkeiten*, p. 242).
137. Principal sources for this summary of the complex action at Altenburg are: Foucart, *Une Division de Cavalerie Légère*; Josef Siebert, 'Über den Streifzug Thielmanns im Feldzuge 1813', *Mitteilungen des K. u. K. Kriegsarchivs*, pp. 180–205; Widdern, *Streifkorps*, vol. II, pp. 310–56; supplemented by Austrian and Prussian regimental histories and Archibald Graf von Keyserling, *Aus der Kriegszeit*, Berlin: Duncker, 1847, pp. 63–9.
138. 'Situation de la Place de Leipzig', 14 October 1813, SHD 2C546. This figure likely included the 20–30 Baden light dragoons.
139. 'Sur la Bataille de Leipzig en 1813, Relativement aux Troupes Badoises', *Spectateur Militaire*, vol. VI, 1828, p. 506; M. D., 'Lettre sur la Bataille de Leipzig', and 'Lettre du Lieutenant-Général Marquis de Piré sur le même sujet', both *Spectateur Militaire*, vol. VII, 1829, pp. 601–4. Dumonceau of the 5th Chasseurs wrote that, 'The Baden battalion laid down its arms after some resistance,' *Mémoires*, p. 361 (whether he was the officer 'D' who submitted the letter to the *Spectateur Militaire* is unknown).
140. Hochberg, *Denkwürdigkeiten*, p. 243.
141. Details from Hochberg, *Denkwürdigkeiten*, p. 247, and 'Notizen über die Theilnahme der Großherzogl. Badischen Truppen an der Schlacht bei Leipzig 1813', *Militair-Wochenblatt*, nos. 714 and 715, February 1830.
142. A half-company of light infantry was also posted in the Reichels-Garten across the river from the Pleißenburg, leaving 4½ in the market square ('Notizen über die Theilnahme', *Militair-Wochenblatt*, 1830). The identity of the Italian battalion is from *Gli Italiani in Germania nel 1813*, Comando del Corpo di Stato Maggiore, Ufficio Storico, Città di Castello: Unione Arti Grafiche, 1914, p. 248; and Quistorp, *Nordarmee*, vol. II, p. 257.
143. Hochberg, *Denkwürdigkeiten*, p. 248–9 (including Schäffer's account of the foray). Wilhelm met Franquemont as he rode to check on his troops prior to this minor affray, but the Württemberg general makes no mention of this encounter in his report.
144. The following draws on the Baden brigade journal (GLAK, 48/4337); Emil's 31 December 1813 summary report (HStAD Best. E 8 B3.10.3, Nr. 128/6); Kösterus, *Großherzoglich Hessischen Truppen*, pp. 83–97; 'Notizen über die Theilnahme', *Militair-Wochenblatt*, 1830; 'Ueber die Schlacht von Leipzig in Beziehung auf die Großhz. Badischen Truppen 1813' (GLAK, 48/4345, published as 'Berichtigung einiger Angaben der Schriftsteller Vaudoncourt, Fain und Norvins über die badische Truppen, in Beziehung auf die Schlacht von Leipzig', *ZfKWGK*, vol. VII, 1826); and regimental histories. For context: Aster, *Leipzig*, vol. II, pp. 89–97, 161–5; Hoen, *Leipzig*, vol. V, pp. 590–6, 618, 639; Friederich, *Herbstfeldzuges*, vol. III, pp. 47–50, 63–4, 149–55.
145. Kösterus, *Großherzoglich Hessischen Truppen*, p. 83.
146. Schmidt in Esselborn, *Neue Erinnerungen*, p. 20 (this is a transcription of extracts from his memoir in HStAD Best. G 61 N2. 26/4).
147. Kösterus, *Großherzoglich Hessischen Truppen*, p. 86; Diehl, HStAD Best. E 8 B3.10.1, Nr. 126/6; Frey in Esselborn, *Neue Erinnerungen*, p. 9.
148. Both quotes from 'Journal des GM v. Stockhorn', GLAK, 48/4337.
149. Ibid.

150. Emil's 31 December 1813 report, HStAD Best. E 8 B3.10.3, Nr. 128/6; Kösterus, *Großherzoglich Hessischen Truppen*, p. 90.
151. Schmidt in Esselborn, *Neue Erinnerungen*, p. 21. Also 'Tagebuch des Gardefusiliers Regiment', HStAD Best. G 61 N2. 31/1, Truppengeschichte 1813, Band 6.
152. Emil's 31 December 1813 report, HStAD Best. E 8 B3.10.3, Nr. 128/6 (first quote); Kösterus, *Großherzoglich Hessischen Truppen*, p. 94; Frey in Esselborn, *Neue Erinnerungen*, p. 10. Unfortunately, Zieten's report is sparse and only notes that 'The brigade's loss in the attack on Zuckelhausen was significant' (Pflugk-Hartung, *Leipzig*, p. 354). Likewise, the relevant Prussian and Austrian regimental histories add little detail regarding the attack on Zuckelhausen: Erzherzog Johann, *Geschichte des K. K. Linien-Infanterie-Regiments Erzherzog Wilhelm no. 12*, Vienna: Seidel & Sohn, 1877, pp. 537–9; Gröling II, *Kurze Geschichte*, pp. 59–61.
153. Schmidt in Esselborn, *Neue Erinnerungen*, p. 22. All the Hessian memoirs remark on the good order, unhurried pace and calm professionalism of the withdrawal; and all contrast this with their impression of the disorderly French retreat from Holzhausen even as they praise French valour in general.
154. The timing of the division reaching Stötteritz is derived from Aster (*Leipzig*, vol. II) and the Prussian and Austrian official histories. Stockhorn gives 11:00, but this is clearly too early; other participants estimate between 1:00 and 2:00 p.m. Frey stated that it took two hours to cover the distance from Zuckelhausen to Stötteritz. The division's exact position is also unclear. This text gives a location from Emil's report and Kösterus; Stockhorn places his brigade with the 3rd Infantry on the right 'in prolongation of the village' of Probstheida with the 1st Infantry on the flank (presumably the left of the brigade).
155. Emil's 31 December 1813 report, HStAD Best. E 8 B3.10.3, Nr. 128/6. Much of this report is printed in Diersburg/Beck, *1. Großherzoglich Hessischen Infanterie*, pp. 227–30. G. Simon, *Die Geschichte des Dynasten und Grafen zu Erbach*, Frankfurt am Main: Brönner, 1858, pp. 471–3.
156. Frey in Esselborn, *Neue Erinnerungen*, pp. 13–16.
157. Rilliet, 'Journal', pp. 140–1.
158. Schmidt in Esselborn, *Neue Erinnerungen*, p. 22 (likely the source for Kösterus, *Großherzoglich Hessischen Truppen*, pp. 96–7); Diehl, HStAD Best. E 8 B3.10.1, Nr. 126/6.
159. Details differ slightly between Emil's report (HStAD Best. E 8 B3.10.3, Nr. 128/6) and the excellent artillery history (Beck/Hahn/Hahn, *Grossherzoglichen Artilleriekorps*, pp. 182–3), but the basics are the same. Additionally, some of the pieces had suffered battle damage such as smashed wheels. The available material does not address the two howitzers specifically, but these also seem to have been saved prior to the retreat.
160. HStAD Best. E 8 B3.10.3, Nr. 128/6.
161. Diehl was proud of having managed to save his papers with these records when he was captured on the 19th, HStAD Best. E 8 B3.10.1, Nr. 126/6. The company had begun the autumn campaign with 164 officers and men, but had lost 85 before Leipzig: 32 sick, 30 missing or left behind on the march, 17 detached, 5 wounded and one captured.
162. GLAK, 48/4337 and 48/4351.
163. 'Relation des Kriegszahlmeisters Koch über die Kriegsereignisse zwischen der kaiserlich-französischen und großen kombinierten Armee./Sept.–Okt. 1813', GLAK, 48/4347.

164. 'Sur la Bataille de Leipzig en 1813, Relativement aux Troupes Badoises', *Spectateur Militaire*, vol. VI, 1828, p. 505. This account was submitted at Wilhelm's behest to rectify false accusations against the Baden contingent and the words were likely his.
165. Emil's 31 December 1813 report, HStAD Best. E 8 B3.10.3, Nr. 128/6. Quistorp (*Nordarmee*, vol. II, p. 270) followed by Friederich (*Herbstfeldzuges*, III, p. 205) places the French 36th Division directly in front of the Grimma Gate between the Hessian and Baden brigades (left and right respectively), but neither Hessian nor Baden accounts mention this arrangement.
166. According to the Saxon postillion who was guiding Napoleon, he led the emperor to the Barfußpförtschen when it became clear that they could not pass through the Ranstädt gate. On arriving at this portal, however, the party learned that the Baden guards did not have a key! There being no time to lose, the guide took the emperor through the Peterstor instead. 'Bericht des ehemaligen Postillions Gabler, der den Kaiser Napoleon während der Leipziger Schlacht geführt hat', in Otto Eduard Schmidt, *Zeitgenössische Berichte über die Leipziger Schlacht vom 16.–19. Oktober 1813*, Leipzig: Reclam, 1918, p. 87. Odeleben, on the other hand, states that he followed the emperor out the Ranstädt gate (*Réclamations*, p. 18).
167. Fleischmann's after-action report, LABWHStA, E 270a Bü 240.
168. Bieler, 'Erinnerungen', HStAD Best. G 61 N2. 26/4.
169. Kösterus, *Großherzoglich Hessischen Truppen*, p. 102.
170. Details of the dispute at the gate are from Bigge, *2. Großherzoglich Hessisches*, p. 185. Kösterus wrote that the Baden light infantrymen 'held themselves entirely passive' (Kösterus, *Großherzoglich Hessischen Truppen*, p. 103).
171. Kösterus, *Großherzoglich Hessischen Truppen*, p. 103. In other words, they elected to dare the odds by escaping rather than join the enemy.
172. Emil's 31 December 1813 report, HStAD Best. E 8 B3.10.3, Nr. 128/6; 'Tagebuch des Gardefusiliers Regiment', HStAD Best. G 61 N2. 31/1, Truppengeschichte 1813, Band 6; Diehl, HStAD Best. E 8 B3.10.1, Nr. 126/6; Hessian regimental histories. Friederich places the Hessian surrender near the Nicolai-Kirche (*Herbstfeldzuges*, III, p. 219). Roller wrote to Emil many years later to recount the episode – and ask for financial help after his family was ruined by a flood, letter of 30 April 1855, HStAD Best. D 4 27.3.2, Nr. 633/5, 'Prinz Emil im russischen Feldzug 1812/13'. See also Paul von Schmidt, *Das 3. Pommersche Infanterie-Regiment Nr. 14 von seiner Gründung bis zum Jahre 1888*, Berlin: Liebel, 1888, p. 21.
173. Both Bieler quotes are from his *Erinnerungen*, HStAD Best. G 61 N2. 26/4; Wolff from GLAK, 65/11381. Hessian Leutnant Schmidt likewise made an adventurous escape from the city (Schmidt in Esselborn, *Neue Erinnerungen*, p. 23–6).
174. 'Tagebuch des Gardefusiliers Regiment', HStAD Best. G 61 N2. 31/1, Truppengeschichte 1813, Band 6; Beck/Hahn/Hahn, *Grossherzoglichen Artilleriekorps*, p. 183. Zimmermann, entries for 20 and 22 October 1813, HStAD Best. E 8 B3.10.1, Nr. 124/7.
175. When ordered to send a division to support Augereau, the annoyed MacDonald claimed he had no troops available, but eventually decided to send a brigade of what he erroneously described as 'the Hessian division' (MacDonald, *Recollections*, vol. II, pp. 73–4).
176. The identity of the cuirassiers is unclear. The Baden account refers to French cuirassiers ('Berichtigung einiger Angaben', p. 285), Quistorp states that they

were Polish. Likewise, some of the remaining Berg lancers and possibly krakus of MacDonald's escort may have been involved (Colson, *Leipzig*, pp. 333–4).
177. Stockhorn's 20 October 1813 report in Hochberg, *Denkwürdigkeiten*, p. 495; 'Notizen über die Theilnahme', *Militair-Wochenblatt*, 1830. According to Quistorp (*Nordarmee*, vol. II, p. 295), one battalion of the 1st Infantry was sent to the Pleißenburg, but Stockhorn makes no mention of this in his report or journal.
178. Wilhelm's 20 October 1813 report, 'Meldung des GL Grafen Hochberg vom 20. Okt. 1813, nebst Verlustliste des bad. Contingents vom 7–19 October usw.', GLAK, 48/4351 (also published in Hochberg, *Denkwürdigkeiten*, pp. 493–5). In his report, Stockhorn states that the regiment crossed the Elster before being captured but this seems unlikely. See also Quistorp, *Nordarmee*, vol. II, p. 297.
179. As Napoleon rode by after farewelling the Saxon Guards, a Baden soldier allegedly called out 'Thank God! Now he can flee!' (As used here, the German verb '*auskratzen*' is colloquial: to escape an unpleasant situation as in 'run off' or 'run away', probably similar to 'skedaddle' as used by soldiers during the American Civil War). From Trefftz, 'Erinnerungen', in Naumann, *Völkerschlacht*, p. 367.
180. Many German writers then and since have complained that Napoleon was sacrificing his allies (especially Germans and Poles) to defend the city so the French troops could escape. This mistaken assertion collapses as soon as the order of battle is examined; numerous French regiments were committed to the defence of the city such as Marmont's 6th Corps which contained no allied units or the all-French 36th Division that fought alongside the Hessians at the Grimma Gate.
181. Hochberg, *Denkwürdigkeiten*, pp. 250–5. The Russian general was likely Karl Wilhelm von Toll. See below for a discussion of the light infantrymen at the Peterstor and Barefoot Portal. Accounts vary on how tenacious the defence inside the Grimma gate was: some report a stalwart effort to hold on, others claim that the Prussian attackers brushed by with ease. Note that Albert du Casse, Arrighi's biographer, (unsurprisingly) presents him in a generally favourable light.
182. Meier, *Erinnerungen*, pp. 113–14.
183. Wilhelm's 20 October 1813 report, GLAK, 48/4351.
184. Hochberg, *Denkwürdigkeiten*, pp. 260–1.
185. Stockhorn's 20 October 1813 report in Hochberg, *Denkwürdigkeiten*, pp. 496–7.
186. Wilhelm's 20 October 1813 report, GLAK, 48/4351. Unfortunately, the Hessian records reviewed for this study do not provide any detail on, or explanation of, the small number who fell into Allied hands on 19 October other than to note the high percentage of officers (45 of approximately 245 prisoners). This is another topic that requires further research.
187. Quote from 'Relation des Kriegszahlmeisters Koch über die Kriegsereignisse zwischen der kaiserlich-französischen und großen kombinierten Armee./Sept.–Okt. 1813', GLAK, 48/4347. Wilhelm believed the Prussians were especially interested in officers to meet the needs of their greatly expanded army (Hochberg, *Denkwürdigkeiten*, p. 269).
188. Hochberg, *Denkwürdigkeiten*, pp. 259–68.
189. For the 19 October 1813 Austrian bulletin, see: *Actenstücke und Materialien zu der Geschichte des großen Kampfes im die Freyheit Europas in den Jahren 1812 und 1813*, Germanien: Hammer, 1814, vol. III, pp. 76–88; among other places, it was published in the *Oesterreichischer Beobachter*, no. 298, 25 October 1813, *Berlinische Nachrichten*,

no. 128, 26 October 1813, and the *Allgemeine Zeitung*, nos. 301 and 302, 28 and 29 October 1813. Schäffer had Wilhelm's 'Berichtigung' placed in *Der Korrespondent von und für Deutschland*, no. 300, 27 October 1813; it also appeared in the *Allgemeine Zeitung*, no. 302, 29 October 1813 as an addendum to the Austrian bulletin. Wilhelm's 22 October 1813 letter to Schwarzenberg and the 30 October 1813 account in the *Badischen Staatszeitung* are in Hochberg, *Denkwürdigkeiten*, pp. 497–9.
190. We can dismiss the claim in MacDonald's sketchy memoirs that the Hessians climbed up to the ramparts and fired on the French in 'fresh treachery'. Curiously, MacDonald repeatedly refers to the 39th Division as 'the Hessian division'. See MacDonald, *Recollections*, vol. II, pp. 74–5 (pp. 217–18 of the 1892 French edition). Also to be dismissed are most of Marbot's comments about the Saxons and Badeners (*Memoirs*, vol. II, pp. 652–9); Marbot can be very useful and it is a mistake to dismiss his memoirs automatically, but these comments are grossly exaggerated. See Colson, *Leipzig*, p. 343.
191. 'Sur la Bataille de Leipzig en 1813', pp. 508–9; Quistorp, *Nordarmee*, vol. II, p. 288; Barsewisch, *Badischen Leib-Grenadier-Regiments*, p. 150; Friederich, *Herbstfeldzuges*, vol. III, p. 212. As an example of the exaggeration induced by confusion, a French officer of the 154^e Ligne wrote that Saxons, Badeners and city residents fired on the French from the windows as he and his men withdrew towards the Grimma Gate, 'or so we believed' (Jacques François Martin, *Souvenirs d'un Ex-Officier (1812–1815)*, Paris: Cherbuliez, 1867, pp. 200–1); it is highly unlikely, of course, that there were any Saxon soldiers in the area on 19 October. Marmont's claim that Bavarians fired on his troops is clearly in error and the likelihood that Saxons did so is also remote (Journal des opérations du 6e Corps depuis le la rupture de l'armistice jusqu'au son retour sur le Rhin', SHD, MR 686).
192. Buturlin, *Tableau de la Campagne d'Automne*, p. 146; Quistorp, *Nordarmee*, vol. II, pp. 294–7; Friederich, *Herbstfeldzuges*, vol. III, pp. 219–23; *Königlich Preußischen Zweiten Infanterie*, pp. 276–84; Aster, *Leipzig*, vol. II, p. 314.
193. The multiplicity of gates, the short time span in which the gates were breached, the contradictory nature of the contending memoirs, and the inherent confusion of combat create an insoluble puzzle concerning the capture or opening of each gate between approximately 11:30 a.m. and 12:30 p.m. on 19 October. The picture is especially complex as regards the Peterstor because the 1st Baden Infantry passed through that gate and most accounts do not differentiate between this line regiment and the light company assigned as the guard force. In what may have been the origin of Buturlin's assertion, for instance, Major Wedel of Bennigsen's staff claimed in his memoir that he led an assault column of eight Russian grenadier battalions to attack the Peterstor, but his task 'was easy to fulfil' because the Baden troops guarding the gate opened it 'as they saw us nearing with cries of "hurrah" and the beating of all our drums' (Wedel, *Lebenserinnerungen*, vol. II, p. 109). As noted in the main text, however, the generally reliable Quistorp and Friederich credit the capture of the Peterstor to Pomeranian troops attacking from *inside* the city; that they could have skewed their accounts so dramatically to satisfy Prussian national sentiment is highly improbable. Furthermore, in his history of the Army of Poland (authored anonymously) Wedel states that he led an assault on the *Grimma Gate* (not the Peterstor), which would coincide with Friederich's mention of one of Bennigsen's divisions entering through the Grimma Gate. Wedel's initial report and Bennigsen's official report also indicate that the Grimma Gate was the main and contested port of entry (Pflugk-Hartung,

Leipzig, pp. 238–42, 403–8). Wedel says British General Wilson was present, but Wilson makes no mention of this event. See: *Herbstfeldzuges*, vol. III, p. 219; Wedel, *Armee von Polen*, p. 52, Wilson, *Journal*, pp. 200–1.
194. Trefftz, 'Erinnerungen', in Naumann, *Völkerschlacht*, p. 368.
195. French histories/memoirs: Fain, *Manuscrit*, vol. II, p. 446; Norvins, *Portefeuille*, vol. II, p. 420; Vaudoncourt, *Histoire de la Guerre*, vol. I, p. 221. See also Pelet, 'La Campagne de 1813', 11th article, *Spectateur Militaire*, vol. III, 1827, pp. 346–7. Wilhelm's response is in the *ZfKWGK*, 1826 ('Berichtigung einiger Angaben', pp. 285–9); and the *Spectateur Militaire*, 1828 ('Sur la Bataille de Leipzig en 1813', pp. 508–10). Colonel Rochechouart, a French émigré serving as a Russian staff officer, also picked up these stories in his memoirs, denouncing 'the infamous treachery' of the Badeners, Saxons, and Württembergers without which 'the victory would have been more hotly disputed', *Souvenirs*, pp. 266–9.
196. Barsewisch, *Badischen Leib-Grenadier-Regiments*, p. 154. See also Colson, *Leipzig*, pp. 334–5.
197. John H. Gill, 'Combat Performance at the End of Alliance: The Baden Army in 1813', paper presented to the CRE, College of Charleston, 2017.
198. Strengths from 4th Corps summary 'Situations' for 6 and 19 October 1813, SHD, 2C539.
199. Key sources for the Hessians at this stage: Beck/Hahn/Hahn, *Grossherzoglichen Artilleriekorps*, pp. 183–5; Bigge, *2. Großherzoglich Hessisches*, pp. 186–8; Kösterus, *Großherzoglich Hessischen Truppen*, pp. 98–113; Zimmermann, *1. Großherzoglich Hessischen Dragoner-Regiments*, vol. I, pp. 198–9. Leutnant Schmidt's memoir is especially useful for the interaction with the Bavarians around Hanau: Schmidt in Esselborn, *Neue Erinnerungen*, pp. 25–33. Note that the Hessian artillery lost a number of men to desertion as it passed near its recruiting districts north of the Main but returned with its six remaining guns, seven other vehicles and 71 officers and men (Heinrich Bergér, 'Hessen-Darmstadts Abfall von Napoleon I.', *Hessenland*, vol. XVI, 1902, p. 156); the number of returning infantry is unknown.
200. Alexander Ferber, *Geschichte des 1. Badischen Feldartillerie-Regiments Nr. 14*, Karlsruhe: Müller, 1906, pp. 100–4. Stockhorn had sent a hundred infantrymen to escort his guns and it is likely Wilhelm did the same, but how many infantry were still with the artillery at this point is unknown. On Mensdorff: 'Tagebuch des Streifkorps', p. 296; Rothauscher, 'Das Wirken des Streif-Corps', p. 25; Gustav Ritter Amon von Treuenfest, *Geschichte des k. k. Huszaren-Regimentes Freiherr von Edelsheim-Gyulai Nr. 4*, Vienna: regimental, 1882, p. 416.
201. 'Geschichte des Dragonerregiments von Freystedt', GLAK, 48/4341; Bray, *Badischen Leib-Dragoner-Regiments*, pp. 52–5.
202. 'Kriegserlebnisse des Georg Klein I. aus Wohnbach 1812/1813', Ferdinand Dreher, ed., *Hessische Chronik*, vol. II, 1913, pp. 152–6.
203. Oberst Josef Friedrich von Sulzer to Max Joseph, 14 October 1813 in Kleinschmidt, *Bayern und Hessen*, pp. 245–6.
204. Principal sources for the following are Wolfgang Windelband, 'Badens Austritt aus dem Rheinbund 1813', *Zeitschrift für Geschichte des Oberrheins*, vol. XXV, 1910; Waller, 'Baden und Frankreich', pp. 147–57; Planert, *Mythos*, pp. 590–613; and Sauer, *Napoleons Adler*, pp. 282–5. These are supplemented by: Maria Glaser, 'Die badische Politik und die deutsche Frage zur Zeit der Befreiungskriege und des Wiener Kongresses',

Zeitschrift für Geschichte des Oberrheins, vol. XLI, 1927, pp. 268–75; Schnabel, *Reitzenstein*, pp. 152–8; Weech, *Badische Geschichte*, pp. 507–9; and Friedrich von Weech, *Baden unter den Großherzogen Carl Friedrich, Carl, Ludwig 1738–1830*, Freiburg: Wagner, 1863, pp. 41–3.

205. This phrase from Willy Andreas ('Baden nach dem Wiener Frieden 1809', *Neujahrsblätter der Badischen Historischen Kommission*, vol. 15, 1912, p. 78) reflects the common sentiment in Baden during 1813.

206. It is not clear which of many possible contemporary definitions of *Meile* or 'mile' is meant here. The actual distance is approx. 225 km in modern units.

207. Carl to Friedrich Wilhelm III, 31 October 1813, in Schäffer, *Denkwürdigkeiten*, p. 256. Reitzenstein had been recalled from semi-retirement to help cope with the existential crisis (Hans Merkle, *Der 'Plus-Forderer' Der badische Staatsmann Sigismund von Reitzenstein und seine Zeit*, Karlsruhe: Braun, 2006, p. 229).

208. Windelband, 'Badens Austritt', pp. 117–19; Wrede to Großherzog Carl, 27 October 1813, in Heilmann, *1813*, p. 226.

209. Andreas, *Aufruf*, p. 34.

210. From one of Reitzenstein's reports in Windelband, 'Badens Austritt', p. 122. Speed was crucial 'to prevent the arrival of Minister Stein', he wrote (Schnabel, *Reitzenstein*, p. 158).

211. Zeppelin's 8 November 1813 report, in Pfister, *Rheinbund*, p. 400.

212. Curiously, Carl demurred when his sister, the tsarina, suggested that he seal his attachment to the Coalition by divorcing Stephanie de Beauharnais (Merkle, *Der 'Plus-Forderer'*, pp. 230–2).

213. Planert, *Mythos*, pp. 468, 609; Hermes/Niemeyer, *Unter dem Greifen*, pp. 73–81.

214. Ute Planert, 'Die Kehrseite der Souveränität. Baden und Württemberg im Krieg', in Anton Schindling and Gerhard Taddey, eds, *1806 – Souveränität für Baden und Württemberg: Beginn der Modernisierung?*, Stuttgart: Kohlhammer, 2007, pp. 145–6.

215. Hermann Meerwarth's phrase in 'Die öffentliche Meinung in Baden von den Freiheitskriegen bis zur Erteilung der Verfassung (1815–1818)', dissertation, Ruprecht-Karls-Universität, 1907, pp. 29–31. Stockhorn's disbelief is from Hochberg, *Denkwürdigkeiten*, p. 266; in general for officers and civil servants: Windelband, 'Badens Austritt', pp. 139–40.

216. The quote is from Waller, 'Baden und Frankreich', p. 153; both items are published in Windelband, 'Badens Austritt', pp. 131–3.

217. Hochberg, *Denkwürdigkeiten*, p. 273. Despite the frostiness of their marriage, Grand Duchess Stephanie, Napoleon's adopted daughter, had elected to stay with her husband and sympathy for her became an additional consideration for state policy and national sentiment.

218. Principal sources for this section: Bergér, 'Hessen-Darmstadts Abfall'; du Thil, *Denkwürdigkeiten*, pp. 149–89; Heilmann, *1813*, pp. 179–3, 222–7; Ebling, 'hessische Politik in der Rheinbundzeit', pp. 254–60; Kleinschmidt, *Bayern und Hessen*, pp. 146–252; Steiner, *Ludwig I., Großherzog von Hessen und bei Rhein*, Offenbach: author, 1842, pp. 165–70; Ulmann, 'Hessen-Darmstadt am Scheideweg'. See also Buchner, 'Die großherzoglich hessischen Truppen', pp. 313–15.

219. Sulzer reports of 25 and 26 October 1813, in Kleinschmidt, *Bayern und Hessen*, pp. 253–4.

220. Du Thil, *Denkwürdigkeiten*, p. 156. Ludwig's wife Louise was sister to Bavaria's queen.

221. Printed in Heilmann, *1813*, pp. 181–2; also Wrede to Walsleben, 28 October 1813, pp. 226–7.

Notes to pages xxx

222. Du Thil, *Denkwürdigkeiten*, pp. 163. One Hessian minister referred to his country being 'under the cannons of Mainz' (Kleinschmidt, *Bayern und Hessen*, p. 251).
223. Du Thil, *Denkwürdigkeiten*, pp. 165; du Thil memorandum in Heilmann, *1813*, pp. 222–3.
224. Bergér, 'Hessen-Darmstadts Abfall', p. 145.
225. Against the advice of his ministers, who feared his letter would be published and would thus excite suspicions among the Allies, Ludwig wrote to Napoleon to inform the emperor of the switch to the Coalition and explain his decision. For this and the audience, see du Thil, *Denkwürdigkeiten*, pp. 164–87.
226. Emil's 31 December 1813 report, HStAD Best. E 8 B3.10.3, Nr. 128/6.
227. *Großherzoglich Hessische Zeitung*, no. 133, 6 November 1813. 'Not a hint of German spirit was to be detected' in the words of historian Ulmann ('Hessen-Darmstadt am Scheideweg', p. 283). Waller makes similar observations about Baden ('Baden und Frankreich', p. 152).
228. As noted in the main text, the Baden Light Infantry Battalion may have been an exception as it listed a large number of missing after Leipzig; this may have simply been a case of confusion in the immediate wake of the battle; the question requires further research (casualty list in Hochberg to Carl, 20 October 1813, GLAK, 48/4351).
229. This conclusion is therefore consistent with what Ute Planert finds in the societal and political domains, see her richly researched, *Mythos vom Befreiungskrieg*.
230. Martin Carl Ignaz Kösterus, *Geschichtliche Darstellung der Entwicklung der Militair-Verfassung der Hessen-Darmstädtischen Truppen*, Darmstadt: Brill, 1840, p. 86. 'Visors' referred to a knight's helmet visor, meaning that the Hessians could take up arms against France openly and unashamedly.
231. Meier, *Erinnerungen*, p. 120.

Chapter 6: Westphalia: Kingdom's End

1. Napoleon to Cambacérès, 9 October 1813, *CG*, no. 36707, vol. XIV, pp. 749–50.
2. Martin Rink, 'Der "Volkskrieg" 1813. Zwischen großer Schlacht und Nebenkriegsschauplätzen', in Hofbauer/Rink, *Völkerschlacht*, pp. 153–5.
3. Oncken, *Oesterreich und Preußen*, vol. I, pp. 126–7, 165, 334–5.
4. Blücher to Amalie, 22 April 1813, in Enno von Colomb, ed., *Blücher in Briefen aus den Feldzügen 1813–1815*, Stuttgart: Cotta, 1876, pp. 26–7; with courteous assistance from Dr Michael V. Leggiere who kindly provided the original text from the archival copy of this letter.
5. Chernishev to Alexander, 17 June 1811, *SIRIO*, vol. XXI, 1877, pp. 110–25;); Pertz, *Stein*, vol. III, pp. 68–74, 604-6. Chernishev's idea became the basis for the formation of the Russo-German Legion in 1812, see Gabriele Venzky, *Die Russisch-Deutsche Legion in den Jahren 1811–1815*, Wiesbaden: Harrassowitz, 1966, pp. 25–8.
6. Details on Scharnhorst's hopes from Jagwitz, *Lützowschen Freikorps*, pp. 8–11; quote from Nicola P. Todorov, '"Le roi appela et ils accourrurent tous": les Provinces Prussiennes Cédées en 1807 dans la Guerre de 1813–1814', *Revue d'Allemagne et des Pays de Langue Allemande*, vol. 47, no. 1, 2015, p. 137. See also Martin Rink, 'Kleinkrieg im Königreich Westphalen: Streifkorps, Patrioten und Kosaken 1809–1813', in Markus Stein, ed., *Das Militär und die Kriege des Königreich Westphalen 1807–13*, May 2021 at http://www.napoleon-online.de/Dokumente/NapoleonOnline_Reader_Symposium_Westphalen_April2008.pdf [accessed May 2022]. On Coalition

employment of press, pamphlets and other public outlets, see Eva Bockholt, 'Der europäische Bund: eine gescheiterte Vision der Freiheitskriege? Studien zur deutschen Publizistik 1813/14', dissertation, Freie Universität Berlin, 2004.

7. See, for example, Leggiere, *Napoleon and the Struggle for Germany*, vol. I, pp. 182–94.

8. Two notes on sources for Westphalia are worth mentioning at the outset. First, this chapter is informed by the two 'traditional' histories of Westphalia: Arthur Kleinschmidt, *Geschichte des Königreichs Westfalen*, Kassel: Horst Hamecher, 1970 (reprint of the original from 1893); and Rudolf Goecke and Theodor Ilgen, *Das Königreich Westphalen*, Düsseldorf: Voß, 1888. Both of these, however, suffer from serious flaws, neither addresses the military in detail and both have been superseded by modern scholarship, especially Mustafa's *Napoleon's Paper Kingdom*, currently the only comprehensive history of the realm. Second, unfortunately, this chapter must rely heavily on secondary sources supplemented by archival material from France as most Westphalian military archives were transported to Russia where, at least as recently as several years ago, they apparently remain uncatalogued. Note also that one ostensible 'primary' source is *not* used: Moritz von Kaisenberg, ed., *König Jérôme Napoleon: Ein Zeit- und Lebensbild*, Leipzig: Schmidt & Günther, 1899. This book has been shown to be a fraud, a combination of lurid invention and shameless plagiarism; see the excoriating but often mordantly funny reviews by August Wolfsteig, 'König Jerome', *Preußische Jahrbücher*, vol. CIII, January–March 1901; August Woringer, book review in *ZHG*, vol. XIV, 1901; and Paul Heidelbach, 'Ein sonderbares Quellenwerk zur Geschichte des Königreiches Westfalen', *Hessenland*, vol. XXI, no. 24, 17 December 1907. For an excellent overview of Westphalian memoir literature, see Thomas Hemmann, 'Westfälische und kurhessische Memoiren', 2002 at http://napoleonzeit.de/ [accessed June 2022].

9. Owzar asks, 'whether there has ever been a non-artificial state' ('Liberty in Times of Occupation', p. 69), but contemporaries certainly considered Westphalia and Berg to be 'artificial', ahistorical and lacking in legitimacy. Michael Rowe's phrase 'legitimacy deficit' may be usefully applied in Westphalia's case ('France, Prussia, or Germany? The Napoleonic Wars and Shifting Allegiances in the Rhineland', *Central European History*, no. 39, 2006, pp. 615–16).

10. In his recent study, Olivier Baustian also highlights Westphalia's role as a commercial 'crossroads' as well as a military march (*Le royaume de Westphalie et le système continental 1807–1813*, Paris: Kronos, 2024, pp. 13–14).

11. The historiography of the 'model states' Westphalia and Berg has been especially contested, with initial emphasis on 'foreign domination' (*Fremdherrschaft*) shifting to greater focus on reform (without ignoring the exploitative and repressive aspects of the Napoleonic era). See Armin Owzar's Introduction, 'Vom Topos der Fremdherrschaft zum Modernisierungsparadigma', in Gerd Dethlefs, Armin Owzar and Gisela Weiß, eds, *Modell und Wirklichkeit: Politik, Kultur und Gesellschaft im Großherzogtum Berg und im Königreich Westphalen*, Paderborn: Schöningh, 2008; Berryman, 'Boundaries of Loyalty', pp. 79–80; Jacques-Olivier Boudon, 'L'Exportation du Modèle Français dans l'Allemagne: l'Exemple de la Westphalie', in Jean-Clément Martin, ed., *Napoléon et l'Europe*, Rennes: Rennes University Press, 2002; and the Preface in Mustafa's *Paper Kingdom*.

12. Terming Westphalia 'a launch pad for French influence in the lands of Germany', Jean Tulard points out that there was also a dynastic angle in the appointment of Jérôme

Bonaparte to rule the kingdom and marrying him to Friedrich of Württemberg's daughter Katherine: 'Siméon et l'Organisation du Royaume de Westphalie (1807–1813)', *Francia*, vol. 1, 1973.

13. Arnulf Siebeneicker, 'Das Königreich Westphalen – Ein Modellstaat und seine Armee', in Stein, ed., *Militär und die Kriege des Königreich Westphalen*. For an overview of the historiography of Westphalia and Berg as 'model states', see Armin Owzar, 'Tagungsbericht: Das Königreich Westphalen und das Großherzogtum Berg. Quellen – Forschungen – Deutungen', *Westfälische Forschungen*, no. 54, 2004. Owzar and others describe part of the problem as reform politics being subordinated to power politics (pp. 409–10).
14. Berding (including 'mosaic of territories' and 'moral conquest'), 'Le Royaume de Westphalie', pp. 346–9. Most of this essay also appears in Jean Tulard's *Dictionnaire Napoléon*, Paris: Fayard, 1987, pp. 1746–50; and *Lippische Mitteilungen*, vol. 54, 1985. An updated, abbreviated essay is his 'Das Königreich Westphalen als napoleonischer Modell- und Satellitenstaat (1807–1813)', in Dethlefs/Owzar/Weiß, *Modell und Wirklichkeit*. See also Bärbel Sunderbrink, 'Das Königreich Westphalen fern seiner Hauptstadt. Symbolische Herrschaftspräsenz in der Provinz', in Jörg Ebeling, Guillaume Nicoud and Thorsten Smidt, eds, *Jérôme Napoléon und die Kunst und Kultur im Königreich Westphalen*, Passages Online vol. 6, Heidelberg: University of Heidelberg, 2021, https://books.ub.uni-heidelberg.de/arthistoricum/catalog/book/730 [accessed May 2022].
15. Napoleon to Jérôme, 15 November 1807, *CG*, no. 16812, vol. VII, p. 1321. As Xavier Abeberry Magescas points out, Napoleon also hoped that the successful introduction of the Napoleonic Code in Westphalia would help overcome the resistance put up by Bavaria and Württemberg to expansion of the Confederation's remit into member states' internal affairs ('Le Royaume de Westphalie Napoléonien, Tentative d'Instauration d'un "État-Modèle"', *Revue du Souvenir Napoléonien*, no. 450, January 2004, pp. 39–48). Boudon describes Westphalia as a 'laboratory' for introducing reforms ('L'Exportation du Modèle Français').
16. The language issue was not unimportant, but H. A. L. Fisher cautioned that 'it was not so great a grievance as might have been expected' (*Studies in Napoleonic Statesmanship: Germany*, Oxford: Clarendon Press, 1903, pp. 247–8); Boudon also offers considerable nuance in his 'L'Exportation du Modèle Français'. Mustafa's *Paper Kingdom* generally grants it more significance.
17. Reinhard, report of 30 January 1812, in du Casse, *Rois Frères*, p. 396; this was in a letter from Princess Pauline of Lippe-Detmold in response to a question from Reinhard (Jean Delinière, *Karl Friedrich Reinhard: Ein deutscher Aufklärer im Dienste Frankreichs (1761–1837)*, Stuttgart: Kohlhammer, 1989, p. 317).
18. Napoleon to Maret, 10 December 1811, *CG*, 29310, vol. XI, p. 1341.
19. Mustafa, *Paper Kingdom*, pp. 53–73. See Jacques-Olivier Boudon for a thorough biography of Jérôme founded on extensive research (*Le Roi Jérôme: Frère Prodigal de Napoléon*, Paris: Fayard, 2008). As Boudon points out (Chapter 21), the historiography of Jérôme as a man and a king has spawned both a 'black legend' and overly generous appraisals. Connelly's effusive praise of the king and his army, for instance, is unwarranted (Owen Connelly, *Napoleon's Satellite Kingdoms*, New York: The Free Press, 1965, pp. 196–7, 221–2, 300).

20. Although Owzar refers to the subordination of reform politics to Napoleon's power politics, he also notes astutely that this was only one of the challenges reform faced in Westphalia and Berg: Owzar, 'Tagungsbericht', pp. 409–14.
21. Fisher, *Napoleonic Statesmanship*, p. 310.
22. Borcke, *Kriegerleben*, p. 277.
23. Berding, 'Royaume de Westphalie', p. 355. There are many detailed studies of Westphalia's political and economic woes. Excellent starting points are Berding's larger work: *Napoleonische Herrschafts- und Gesellschaftspolitik im Königreich Westfalen 1807–1813*, Göttingen: Vandenhoeck & Ruprecht, 1973; and Mustafa's *Paper Kingdom*. Nicola P. Todorov provides a meticulous analysis of the kingdom's Elbe Department in *L'administration du royaume de Westphalie de 1807 à 1813: le département de l'Elbe*, Sarrebruck: Editions universitaires européennes, 2011; and an English version of this analysis is his 'The Napoleonic Administrative System in the Kingdom of Westphalia', in Michael Broers, Peters Hicks and Agustin Guimerá, eds. *The Napoleonic Empire and the New European Political Culture*, London: Palgrave MacMillan, 2012, pp. 173–85. Note that Mustafa and Todorov disagree on many points regarding the end of the kingdom, see the exchange in the *H-France Review*, vol. 19, March 2019 at https://h-france.net/h-france-review-volume-19-2019/ [accessed March 2019]. See also Stefan Brakensiek, 'Die Reichsstände des Königreichs Westphalen', *Westfälische Forschungen*, no. 53, 2003.
24. In addition to the sources cited below, discussion of the army is informed by two papers presented at the Society for Military History annual conference in 2008: Sam A. Mustafa, 'Not Enough Esprit in the Corps: The Failure of the Westphalian Army, 1807–13'; and Michael F. Pavković, 'The Westphalian Army in 1813: Reforming the Palladium of Westphalian Freedom'. My thanks to both scholars for providing copies of these unpublished papers.
25. This was considered the 2nd Westphalian Division at the time (the 1st being the troops left in the kingdom); strength from 'État de Situation des troupes Westphaliennes' for March 1809, SHD, 2C509. The paucity of available Westphalian military archives and the absence of regimental histories forces heavy reliance on secondary sources. As elsewhere in this chapter, therefore, much of the military detail is drawn from Fritz Lünsmann, *Die Armee des Königreichs Westfalen 1807–1813*, Berlin: Leddihn, 1935 (here pp. 281–6). For an overview of the Westphalians in Spain see John H. Gill, 'Vermin, Scorpions and Mosquitos: The Rheinbund in the Peninsula', in *The Peninsular War*, Ian Fletcher, ed., Staplehurst: Spellmount, 1998.
26. On actions in 1809, see Gill, *Eagles*, Chapter 9. Sam A. Mustafa offers a superb study of Schill's escapade in his *The Long Ride of Major von Schill*, Lanham: Rowman & Littlefield, 2008. Rather contrary to expectations and to the opprobrium routinely cast at the Westphalian army, most of the personnel in the early stages were volunteers, not hapless conscripts, see Michael F. Pavković, 'Recruitment and Conscription in the Kingdom of Westphalia: "The Palladium of Westphalian Freedom"', in *Conscription in the Napoleonic Era: A Revolution in Military Affairs?*, Donald Stoker, Frederick C. Schneid and Harold D. Blanton, eds, London: Routledge, 2009.
27. Following the French pattern, Westphalia also had a National Guard but these, unlike their French counterparts, were at best simple ceremonial city guards with no military value (Lünsmann, *Armee des Königreichs Westfalen*, p. 273). They would, however, serve a useful function in Kassel in the period from Chernishev's capture of the city to the return of the French authorities.

28. Although Napoleon worried that the cuirassiers would be too expensive for Westphalia, Dr Mustafa's research shows that they cost less than the hussar regiments (*Paper Kingdom*, p. 114).
29. Meibom, *Aus napoleonischer Zeit*, p. 86.
30. Most uniform data is from the splendid book by Peter Bunde, Markus Gärtner and Thomas Hemmann (*The Westphalian Army in the Napoleonic Wars 1807–1813*, Berlin: Zeughaus, 2019); supplemented by Lünsmann, *Armee des Königreichs Westfalen*, pp. 132–264; and Mustafa, *Paper Kingdom*, Chapter 5.
31. Principal sources for this section on Russia and early 1813 are Gieße, *Kassel–Moskau–Küstrin*, pp. 312–35; Lünsmann, *Armee des Königreichs Westfalen*, pp. 295–310; and Reboul, *Campagne de 1813*, vol. I, pp. 139–43, vol. II, pp. 381–435. Note that unit strengths fluctuated enormously during the period from December 1812 to March 1813; the numbers given here are drawn from Gieße and Reboul, supplemented by Hammerstein's 29 December report and that of the 'mobile column' dated 30 December 1812, SHD, 2C529 (courtesy of Dr Michael F. Pavković). Connelly (*Napoleon's Satellite Kingdoms*, p. 196) stated that Westphalia contributed more soldiers per capita than any other kingdom; this may be accurate, but his fondness for Westphalia, its king and its army often skews his assessments.
32. Bauer, letter to his brother, 15 June 1812, 'Aus dem Leben', p. 110.
33. He recounted his experiences in Friedrich von Bodenhausen, *Tagebuch eines Ordonnanzoffiziers von 1812–1813 und über seine späteren Staatsdienste bis 1848*, Braunschweig: Westermann, 1912, pp. 16–39; his report is in Albert du Casse, *Mémoires et Correspondance Politique et Militaire du Roi Jérôme et de la Reine Catherine*, Paris: Dentu, 1865, vol. VI, p. 17. Strength of the Chevaulegers from 'Armées d'Espagne', 15 March 1813, SHD, 8C470.
34. Mustafa, *Paper Kingdom*, pp. 253–4. In an unpublished paper, he argues that the contingent seemed sluggish and inattentive in Russia ('Not Enough Esprit in the Corps', 2008).
35. Meibom, *Aus napoleonischer Zeit*, p. 154.
36. Gieße, *Kassel–Moskau–Küstrin*, pp. 313–17. Captain Franz von Morgenstern had a similar experience when he reported to Füllgraf: 'The general was shocked by my appearance and immediately had the chief doctor called' (*Kriegserinnerungen des Obersten Franz Morgenstern aus westfälischer Zeit*, Wolfenbüttel: Zwissler, 1912, p. 118). On Hammerstein's roguish past, see August Woringer, 'Westfälische Offiziere IV: Die Freiherrn von Hammerstein', *Hessenland*, vol. XXIII, 1909; and Wilhelm Hartmann, 'Der General Hans Georg Freiherr von Hammerstein-Equord 1771–1841', *Alt-Hildesheim*, no. 40, 1969. With thanks to Dr Sam Mustafa.
37. Gieße, *Kassel–Moskau–Küstrin*, p. 322.
38. Anton Gerdes, *Königlich Westfälische und Großherzoglich Bergischen Truppen im Russischen Feldzug 1812*, Langendreer: Pöppinghaus, 1914, p. 123.
39. Theodor von Papet, 'Tagebuch des Capitains Theodor von Papet über den Feldzug in Russland 1812', Ditmar Haeusler, ed., url: http://amg.hypotheses.org/quellen/papet-1812 [accessed May 2023].
40. Gieße, *Kassel–Moskau–Küstrin*, p. 335. Contrary to the assertion by Carl Friccius (*Geschichte der Blockade Cüstrins in den Jahren 1813 und 1814*, Berlin: Veit, 1854, p. 22), the Westphalians were not made to wait outside the fortress because the governor did not trust them: see Reboul, *Campagne de 1813*, vol. II, pp. 434–5; and the siege journal

published as 'La Fortresse de Küstrin sous l'Occupation Française 1806–1814' in the *Revue du Génie Militaire*, vol. VII, 1893, pp. 24–5 (an abridged version of the original 'Journal des opérations et travaux ordonnés et éxécutés dans la place de Custrin depuis le blocus de cette place par les Russes et les Prussiens', SHD GR 1 VN 83). Oddly, Prussian Oberst Emil Hartmann repeated the Friccius claim while also publishing the French siege journal: 'Die Festung Cüstrin 1806 bis 1814', *Archiv für Artillerie- und Ingenieur-Offiziere des deutschen Reichsheeres*, vol. CIV, 1897, pp. 299–300.

41. Meibom, *Aus napoleonischer Zeit*, p. 155.
42. Constantine Khristoforovich Benckendorff, *The Cossacks. A Memoir*, George Gall, trans, London: Parker, Furnivall and Parker, 1849, pp. 22–3; Lünsmann, *Armee des Königreichs Westfalen*, pp. 309–10; Osten-Sacken, *Geschichte des Befreiungskrieges*, vol. I, pp. 332–3; Plotho, *Der Krieg in Deutschland*, vol. I, p. 40; Prittwitz, *Beiträge*, vol. I, p. 191; Reboul, *Campagne de 1813*, vol. II, pp. 417–19. Osten-Sacken states that the replacement battalion had been redirected to Stettin and gives it a strength of 450, this seems plausible though Lünsmann places it at 600 men. The number of attacking Cossacks varies from 50 to 500 or more depending on the source, several were wounded in the action. Benckendorff, whose Cossacks carried out the attack, credited surprise and determination for his success, but it may have taken two charges to overcome the Westphalian recruits' resistance. Strength from 15 February report submitted when the detachment passed through Küstrin (SHD, 13C83).
43. Bauer, letter to his brother, 1 January 1813, 'Aus dem Leben', p. 113.
44. Bauer, letter to his brother, 23 January 1813, 'Aus dem Leben', pp. 113–15; and Bauer to the Westphalian Minister of War, 12 June 1813, in the Nachtrag to Friedrich Wilhelm von Loßberg, *Briefe des westfälischen Stabsoffiziers Friedrich Wilhelm von Loßberg vom russischen Feldzug des Jahres 1812*, Christian Meyer, ed., Berlin: Eisenschmidt, 1910, p. 194 (this was a new edition of the better-known original: *Briefe in die Heimath*, Kassel: Fischer, 1844).
45. Rapp's 20 January 1813 report, as printed in *Le Moniteur Westphalien/Westfälische Moniteur*, no. 188, 9 July 1813.
46. Bauer, 'Aus dem Leben', p. 114.
47. Napoleon to Jérôme, 23 December 1812, *CG*, 32132, vol. XII, p. 1307; Jérôme's 27 December 1812 reply in du Casse, *Roi Jérôme*, vol. VI, pp. 22–4. The following day, Jérôme sent an official to distribute money to his wounded officers and wrote to Berthier requesting the status of his contingent: Albert du Casse, *Mémoires pour Servir à l'Histoire de la Campagne de 1812 en Russie*, Paris: Dumaine, 1852, pp. 232–3.
48. Leopold von Hohenhausen, *Biographie des Generals von Ochs*, Kassel: Luckhardt, 1827, pp. 288.
49. Napoleon to Narbonne, 26 December 1812, *CdN*, no. 19399, vol. XXIV, p. 352. Baustian notes that many contemporaries referred to Westphalia as France's 'advance guard' or the 'outpost of the French Empire' (*royaume de Westphalie*, pp. 14–15).
50. Jérôme to Napoleon, 16 January 1813, du Casse, *Roi Jérôme*, vol. VI, pp. 105–6. Jérôme several times bemoaned his inability to pay his troops, such as his mid-April letter to Napoleon in du Casse, *Rois Frères*, p. 449 (du Casse, who can be lax with dates, gives this letter the date of 14 April in this work but 18 April in *Roi Jérôme*, vol. VI, p. 312).
51. The 1st Battalion of the 6th Infantry had been destroyed in Russia during an action on 10 October 1812. Jérôme believed this was a case of negligence and thus did not countenance re-establishment of the regiment in 1813 (Borcke, *Kriegerleben*, p. 267).

Lünsmann (pp. 305–6), on the other hand, portrays the battalion as putting up a gallant defence before succumbing to overwhelming odds.
52. Napoleon to Jérôme, 12 March 1813, *CG*, 33171, vol. XIII, pp. 544–5; Jérôme to Napoleon, 10 March 1813, du Casse, *Roi Jérôme*, vol. VI, pp. 131–2.
53. The 3rd Infantry and III/4th were present as early as February and numbered 1,525 and 88 respectively at the end of the month. The 9th Infantry arrived in Magdeburg in the second half of March, but with only its 1st Battalion, numbering 698 officers and men (SHD, 13C85, 'Places en Allemagne'; 2C551, 'Grande Armée, Situations Générale').
54. Napoleon to Jérôme, 11 September 1810, *CG*, 24553, vol. X, pp. 626–7; comment to GB Edouard Legras, in du Casse, *Roi Jérôme*, vol. VI, pp. 10–11. For imperial praise of the Westphalians at Borodino, see Loßberg, *Briefe*, p. 37.
55. Napoleon to Jérôme, 19 April 1813, *CG*, 33931, vol. XIII, pp. 869–70.
56. Delinière, *Karl Friedrich Reinhard*, p. 321.
57. Kleinschmidt, *Westfalen*, p. 551. The troops were 500 infantry and 60 cavalry; commanded by Prinz Salm-Salm, they were likely from the Füsilier-Garde and Chevaulegers-Garde. For the worries of Westphalian officials at this stage, see S. N. Iskul', 'Der Aufstand im Großherzogtum Berg gegen Napoleon im Jahre 1813', *Zeitschrift des Bergischen Geschichtsvereins*, vol. 92, 1986, pp. 63–7.
58. Jérôme to Napoleon, 19 April 1813, and Reinhard to Napoleon, 18 April 1813, du Casse, *Roi Jérôme*, vol. VI, pp. 155–9; see also Jérôme's lengthy 5 December 1811 letter on 'fermentation' across Germany in *Roi Jérôme*, vol. V, pp. 247–9. On the kingdom's very active secret police and espionage services, see Friedrich Thimme, 'Neue Mittheilungen zur Geschichte der hohen Polizei des Königreichs Westfalen', *Zeitschrift des Historischen Vereins für Niedersachsen*, 1898; and Mustafa, *Paper Kingdom*, especially Chapter 6.
59. Hellrung mentions a camp mutiny by NCOs of the 7th Infantry early in 1813 so that the men were redistributed among other regiments but offers neither date nor any further details ('Die Organisation der Westphälischen Armee', *Minerva*, vol. IV, 1840, p. 442). Another incident involved a hussar lieutenant of dubious repute named Wilhelm Kupfermann. On 24 February, he assembled 25 troopers of the 2nd Hussars on parade and rode off, claiming he was leading them to defect to the enemy, but his case seems to have been one of a scoundrel trying to hide financial peculation rather than a genuine patriot of some variety. His men quickly dispersed; he was apprehended hiding in a mill, tried, and executed. See August Woringer, 'Westfälische Offiziere III. Wilhelm Kupfermann', *Hessenland*, vol. XXIII, 1909, pp. 14–16. The French report on this incident is Michaud to Berthier, 3 March 1813, published in Juhel, 'Truppen des Rheinbunds', in *Blutige Romantik*, p. 55. Heinz Heitzer, on the other hand, presents Kuppermann's [sic] action as the heroic forerunner of a new form of resistance (*Insurrectionen zwischen Weser und Elbe*, Berlin: Rütten & Leoning, 1959, p. 242).
60. Du Casse, *Roi Jérôme*, vol. VI, p. 115.
61. Extracts of reports 1–25 April 1813, in Kleinschmidt, *Westfalen*, pp. 572–6; *Kurze Geschichte der Universität und Stadt Halle seit dem Ausbruche des Krieges im Jahr 1806 bis zum dritten August 1814*, Halle: Ruff, 1824, pp. 83–9.
62. Jérôme to Napoleon, 18 April 1813, du Casse, *Jérôme*, vol. VI, p. 154.
63. Johann Ludwig Boedicker, 'Die militärische Laufbahn 1788–1815 des Generallieutenant Ludwig Boedicker', *Beiheft zum Militär-Wochenblatt*, vols. 5 and 6, 1880, p. 277.

64. Borcke, *Kriegerleben*, p. 249; Luxburg to Max Joseph, 26 April 1813, Kleinschmidt, *Bayern und Hessen*, p. 196.
65. Johann Christian Normann, *Aus den Papieren eines alten Offiziers*, Wilhelm Meister, ed., Hannover: Hahn, 1896, p. 6.
66. Du Casse, *Roi Jérôme*, vol. VI, p. 156.
67. Löwenstern, *Mémoires*, vol. II, pp. 24–8; Lehsten, *Am Hofe König Jérômes*, pp. 97–9; du Casse, *Roi Jérôme*, p. 150; Borcke, *Kriegerleben*, p. 251. Göcking's capture is often mistakenly credited to Hellwig at Wanfried, for example: Lippe, *Preuss. 6. Husaren-Regiments*, p. 157/n. 2.
68. The number of prisoners varies, see 'Tagebuch des Hellwigschen Partisan-Corps, von dessen Entstehung bis zu seiner Auflösung, mit einigen Bruchstücken aus dem Leben des Anführers', *Militairische Blätter*, vol. I, Feb. 1820; 'Erinnerungen an den verstorbenen General-Lieutenant v. Hellwig', *Militair-Wochenblatt*, no. 16, 18 April 1846; Fabricius, 'Parteigänger Friedrich von Hellwig', pp. 281–3; du Casse, *Roi Jérôme*, pp. 151–2. The former Hessian officer (who had entered then left Westphalian service) was Carl Friedrich Wilhelm von Bartheld, 'Memoiren des kurhessischen Majors Carl Wilhelm Friedr. v. Bartheld aus Lispenhausen, Ritter des preußischen eisernen Kreuzes und des hessischen eisernen Helms. Aus der Zeit der Fremdherrschaft von 1806 bis 1814', Carl Heiler, ed., *ZHG*, vol. 61, 1936, pp. 183–8. Note that several Prussian sources claim that the captured Westphalian infantrymen became the cadre of the infantry detachment Hellwig formed during the armistice. This is certainly possible, but the case seems overstated: the history of Hellwig's infantry makes no mention whatsoever of Westphalians as the core of the unit (even though Westphalian troops are discussed repeatedly and often favourably in this detailed work), see Hermann Kreuzwendedich von dem Borne, *Geschichte des Infanterie-Regiments Prinz Louis Ferdinand von Preußen (2. Magdeburgischen) Nr. 27 1815–1895 und seiner Stammtruppentheile*, Berlin: Eisenschmidt, 1896, pp. 30–5. There is a brief mention in Wilhelm Lange, 'Kleine Beiträge zur Geschichte der Insurrektionen gegen die westfälische Regierung', *ZHG*, vol. 47, 1914, p. 155. Less useful is the hagiographic Wilhelm Pippart, 'Der Überfall von Wanfried am 18. April 1813', *Hessenland*, vol. 27, no. 6, 1913, pp. 90–92. Two citizens were later executed for allegedly assisting Hellwig's men: Reinhold Strauß, *Chronik der Stadt Wanfried*, Wanfried: Braun, 1908, pp. 153–9.
69. Du Casse, *Roi Jérôme*, vol. VI, p. 165.
70. See Kleinschmidt, *Westfalen*, pp. 548–54; and Heitzer, *Insurrectionen*, pp. 242–8.
71. Jérôme to Napoleon, 18 April 1813, du Casse, *Roi Jérôme*, vol. VI, pp. 152–4.
72. Reinhard to Napoleon, 18 April 1813, du Casse, *Roi Jérôme*, vol. VI, pp. 155–7.
73. Napoleon to Berthier, and to Jérôme (two letters), all 20 April 1813, *CG*, 33943, 33953, 33954, vol. XIII, pp. 875–80; Berthier to Ney, 17 and 19 April, Berthier to Jérôme, 20 April, and Berthier to Teste, 20 April 1813, Berthier, *Ordres*, vol. I, pp. 14–30.
74. Napoleon to Jérôme and to Reinhard, both 20 April 1813, *CG*, 33953, 33960, vol. XIII, pp. 879–82.
75. François Antoine Teste, 'Souvenirs du Général Baron Teste', *Carnet de la Sabretache*, no. 229, January 1912, pp. 22–4.
76. Berthier to Ney, 23 April 1813, Berthier, *Ordres*, vol. I, p. 35.
77. Jacobi, *Hannover's Theilnahme*, pp. 67–70; Zander, *Kriegs an der Nieder-Elbe*, pp. 70–1.
78. Todorov, 'Le roi appela', p. 141.

79. Berthier to Napoleon, 29 April 1813, Berthier, *Rapports*, vol. I, p. 79, summarising a report from Hammerstein. Hammerstein stated that some depot troops had not yet arrived.
80. Du Casse, *Roi Jérôme*, vol. VI, p. 169.
81. Otto Gerland, 'Auszug aus dem letzten Ordrebuch des westfälischen Artillerieregiments von 1813 mit Anmerkungen', *ZHG*, vol. X, 1865, pp. 266–74.
82. Reinhard to Napoleon, 18 April 1813, du Casse, *Roi Jérôme*, vol. VI, p. 163.
83. See the discussion in du Casse, *Roi Jérôme*, Livre XIX (especially pp. 169–70), and Mustafa, *Paper Kingdom*, Chapter 5.
84. This idea is from Connelly, *Napoleon's Satellite Kingdoms*, p. 297. Although this is a logical conclusion, I have not seen any specific reference to such thinking on Napoleon's part.
85. Luxburg to Max Joseph, 20 May 1813, Kleinschmidt, *Bayern und Hessen*, p. 201.
86. Borcke, *Kriegerleben*, p. 251; Lehsten, *Am Hofe König Jérômes*, pp. 99–100.
87. Lehsten, *Am Hofe König Jérômes*, pp. 101–2.
88. Chef d'Escadron Charles Nicholas Fabvier, 13 May 1813, see his and several other reports on this reconnaissance in Foucart, *Bautzen*, vol. I, pp. 149–51, 165–9. Movements and assignments of the Westphalians in May are taken from the correspondence in Foucart, *Bautzen*, vols. I and II; Berthier, *Ordres*, vol. I; and Berthier, *Rapports*, vol. I.
89. 'Campagne de 1813: 1er partie: Historique du 12e Corps, du 4 mai à la rupture de l'armistice le 17 août', prepared by Colonel Ange François Alexandre Blein, SHD, MR 688. The strength of Wolff's brigade is difficult to ascertain. An undated 'situation' (probably around the end of May, SHD, 2C542) lists 682 Westphalians present with 48 detached and 30 sick; while the Hessians are recorded with 160 present, 187 detached and three sick. This gives a total of 842 present for duty in the two contingents with 235 detached; the Bavarians are listed as a separate brigade under Oberst Seyssel d'Aix with 765 officers and men. In addition to lacking a date, this detailed account is problematic in listing the Westphalians as an undifferentiated group and only accounting for six squadrons (rather than eight).
90. The exact locations and strengths of the Westphalian infantry and artillery during this period are murky. Along with two batteries (albeit with only 10 to 12 guns total), there should have been six battalions, but French correspondence sometimes only mentions four or five and their activities and locations are obscure; even Durosnel expressed confusion at one point. Some elements seem to have been utilised along the line of communications west of Dresden for a time, but here too details are missing. See Foucart, *Bautzen*, vol. I, pp. 251–78. As to the foot artillery batteries at Bautzen: Capitaine Karl Ludwig Wille received the Legion of Honour for his role in that battle (*Armee des Königreichs Westfalen*, p. 260) and he was granted a Westphalian award as well (*Moniteur Westphalien/Westphälische Moniteur*, no. 183, 4 July 1813); the other battery was commanded by Capitaine Friedrich Ludwig Shulthes. The two batteries remained with 6th Corps until July (SHD, 2C540).
91. Offering insights into rear-area security, French military procedures and Napoleon's command style, documents relating to this incident are in Foucart, *Bautzen*, vol. II, pp. 49–69. The incident did not harm Lepel's career as he would be promoted to colonel shortly before the dissolution of the kingdom (Friedrich Wilhelm von Mauvillon, 'Skizze über das Militair des ehemaligen Königreichs Westphalen',

Militairische Blätter, vol. IV, no. 1, 1823, p. 455). Some of the Hessians (Leib Regiment) who were escorting Duroc's remains seem to have been involved on the fringes of this incident as well.

92. Principal sources for Halberstadt are Hohenhausen, *Ochs*, pp. 288–98 (drawn from Ochs's papers); 'Relation des Ueberfalls bei Halberstadt am 30. Mai 1813', *Militair-Wochenblatt*, no. 848, 22 September 1832, pp. 4793–6 (reputedly by an anonymous eyewitness); reports and correspondence of Haxo, Teste and the Westphalian High Police, in Foucart, *Bautzen*, vol. II; Bogdanovich, *Geschichte des Krieges im Jahre 1813*, vol. 1/2, pp. 165–7; Weil, *Cavallerie des Armées Alliés*, pp. 67–9; and Widdern, *Streifkorps*, vol. I, pp. 48–56. See also Georg Arndt, *Chronik von Halberstadt von 1801–1850*, Halberstadt: Schimmelburg, 1908; and Günter Maseberg, *Halberstadt zur Zeit der Befreiungskriege*, Halberstadt: Kommission zur Erforschung der Örtlichen Arbeiterbewegung, 1988.

93. Haxo to Berthier, 30 May and 3 June 1813, Foucart, *Bautzen*, vol. II, pp. 208, 337.

94. Bogdanovich may give the best figure with 2,350, but many other sources provide figures that are considerably lower (*Geschichte des Krieges im Jahre 1813*, vol. 1/2, Note 10, p. liv). An anonymous eyewitness wrote that the Russian force numbered 2,500 and that there were also 20 Westphalian foot gendarmes quartered in the town who did not take part in the combat: 'Relation des Ueberfalls bei Halberstadt', *Militair-Wochenblatt*, p. 4794.

95. Hohenhausen, *Generals von Ochs*, p. 294.

96. Ibid., p. 297.

97. First and third quotes from Teste, 'Souvenirs', pp. 25–7; second quote from Teste to Berthier, 4 June 1813, Foucart, *Bautzen*, vol. II, pp. 370–1. The state of Jérôme's morale is evident in his writing to Augereau to ask what troops the marshal could provide because, he claimed, Chernishev was just the advanced guard for Bülow who was supposedly across the Elbe with 18,000 men planning to march on Leipzig (Augereau to Berthier, 3 June 1813, Foucart, *Bautzen*, vol. II, pp. 342–3). It is important to note, however, that Jérôme's assessment, while greatly exaggerated, was not entirely wrong: Vorontsov (not Bülow) and Chernishev were indeed planning to strike across the Elbe aiming at Leipzig with 6,400 men (not 18,000).

98. From a concealed position, Colomb had observed Jérôme pass by with only a small escort (the king was on his way to meet the emperor in Dresden). Colomb claimed that he would have captured the Westphalian king had he known of what was to him the infamous attack on Lützow's band.

99. This account is drawn from Colomb, *Tagebuch*, pp. 66–71; supplemented by Callenius, 'Meine Erlebnisse' (though some details are inconsistent, the basics are the same); and Brecher, *Überfall*, p. 88. This minor incident is not mentioned in any of the Westphalian army histories, and Prussian as well as Russian historians seem to rely exclusively on Colomb's account.

100. Meibom, *Aus napoleonischer Zeit*, pp. 170–1.

101. Jérôme to Dąbrowski, du Casse, *Roi Jérôme*, vol. VI, pp. 184–7; Napoleon to Berthier and Jérôme, 10–16 June 1813 (*CG*, nos. 34550, 34566, 34689, 34722, vol. XIII, pp. 1143–1215); Łukasiewicz, *Armia księcia Józefa*, pp. 217–18. Du Casse (p. 187) speciously suggests that this incident was an indirect cause of the fall of Kassel in September as Marshal Kellermann, fearing Napoleon's ire, would refuse Jérôme's request for help when Chernishev attacked.

Notes to pages xxx 467

102. Napoleon to Berthier and to Durosnel, both 3 June 1813, *CG*, nos. 34413 and 34434, vol. XIII, pp. 1078–89; Berthier to Durosnel, 3 June 1813, Berthier, *Ordres*, vol. I, p. 163.
103. Berthier to Napoleon, 7 and 28 July 1813, Berthier, *Rapports*, vol. I, pp. 369–70, 468–9.
104. An additional impediment was that Jérôme wanted the 9th Infantry released from Magdeburg to guard the kingdom, a shift Napoleon would not countenance given the importance of that fortress in his calculations (Napoleon to Berthier, 1 July 1813, *CG*, no. 35110, vol. XIV, p. 34).
105. 2nd Corps, 'Rapport Détaillé', 31 July 1813, SHD, 2C538.
106. 1st Cavalry Corps, 'Situations' for 15 August and 1 September 1813, SHD, 2C543; Berthier to Napoleon, 28 July 1813, *Rapports*, vol. I, pp. 468–9. The battery and train numbered 132 officers and men present for duty on 1 September, but whether it remained with the corps through the Battle of Leipzig is unknown. Berthier had proposed sending the horse battery to join Wolff's brigade, but that idea was discarded when the Westphalian hussars were detached to 2nd Corps (Berthier to Napoleon, 1 July 1813, *Rapports*, vol. I, p. 341).
107. The Westphalian infantry returned home from Spain in April and provided an experienced cadre to reconstruct the 3rd Light over the summer. The few remaining artillerymen also returned but the 1st Chevaulegers (consolidated into one squadron) stayed along the Pyrenees.
108. Napoleon to Maret, 2 July 1813; to Clarke, 3 July, *CG*, nos. 35156, 35166, vol. XIV, pp. 54–8.
109. Borcke, *Kriegerleben*, p. 266; du Casse, *Roi Jérôme*, vol. VI, pp. 195–200; Wilhelm Grimm, *Kleinere Schriften*, Berlin: Dümmler, 1881, vol. I, p. 530 (first published in *Der Preußische Correspondent*, no. 148, 15 December 1813). For the regiment's horses: Markus Stein, 'Aus dem Archiv: 13. Husarenregiment (Jérôme Napoléon)', *Depesche*, vol. 1, no. 1, 1985/1986. The order forming this unit is dated 24 August 1813, SHD, 2C154.
110. See Friedrich Aster, 'Napoleon in Dresden 1812 und 1813', *Dresdner Geschichtsblätter*, vol. XI, no. 2, 1902.
111. Jérôme to Berthier, 1 June 1813, du Casse, *Roi Jérôme*, vol. VI, pp. 180–92. Berthier to Napoleon, 31 July 1813, *Rapports*, vol. I, pp. 481–3; Tournès, *Lützen*, p. 42.
112. Napoleon to Berthier, 31 July 1813, *CG*, no. 35679, vol. XIV, p. 276; du Casse, *Roi Jérôme*, vol. VI, p. 194.
113. Reinhard to Maret, 10 July 1813, du Casse, *Roi Jérôme*, vol. VI, pp. 200–4. Astonishingly, one of Jérôme's key agenda items with his brother was his desire for a divorce from Katherine to marry one of his mistresses, a suggestion Napoleon rejected out of hand for the offence it would cause Friedrich of Württemberg among other reasons (Delinière, *Karl Friedrich Reinhard*, p. 323). Le Marois is often spelt Lemarois.
114. Intelligence derived from intercepted letters from Magdeburg in early August, AN, IV/1666, Plaquette 1.
115. Heitzer, *Insurrectionen*, pp. 248–52.
116. 'Journal des marches et opérations militaires du 2e Corps d'Armée commandé par S. E. M. le Maréchal duc de Bellune depuis le 14 Août 1813 jusqu'au 13 Octobre de la même année', SHD, MR 683.
117. Woringer, 'Freiherrn von Hammerstein'; Lünsmann, *Armee des Königreichs Westfalen*, p. 316; Kleinschmidt, *Königreich Westphalen*, pp. 599–602; see also Mauvillon, 'Skizze', pp. 442–4; and August Woringer, summary of lecture in *Mitteilungen an die Mitglieder des Vereins für hessische Geschichte und Landeskunde*, 1908/9, pp. 42–6. According to

Lehsten, there were hints during the armistice that Hammerstein planned to desert (*Am Hofe König Jérômes*, p. 120). The number of hussars is estimated from the 2nd Corps strength returns of 16 August and 15 September 1813, SHD, 2C538; see also Hans von Managetta-Lerchenau, 'Die österreichisch-deutsche oder westfälische Legion 1813/14', *Streffleurs Militärische Zeitschift*, vol. I, 1913.

118. Victor to Berthier, 1330, 23 August 1813, SHD, 2C154; and 'Journal des marches et opérations militaires du 2e Corps d'Armée commandé par S. E. M. le Maréchal due de Bellune depuis le 14 Août 1813 jusqu'au 13 Octobre de la même année', SHD, MR683.

119. Napoleon to Jérôme and Maret, 24 August 1813, *CG*, nos. 36067 and 36071, vol. XIV, pp. 463–5. With thanks to Paul L. Dawson for help on clarifying information on the French cavalry depots.

120. Reinhard to Lemoine and Berthier, 27 August, Lemoine's 29 August reply, and Reinhard to Berthier, 6 September 1813, SHD, 2C154 and 2C155; Napoleon to Berthier, 30 August 1813, *CG*, no. 36141, vol. XIV, p. 500; Berthier to Lemoine and Reinhard, 30 August 1813 (*Ordres*, vol. II, pp. 123–7).

121. *Le Moniteur Westphalien/Westphälischer Moniteur*, no. 209 30 July 1813.

122. Lünsmann, *Armee des Königreichs Westfalen*, p. 316; Kleinschmidt, *Königreich Westphalen*, pp. 599–602. With special thanks to Dr Sam Mustafa for background on the rakehellish Hammersteins.

123. *Le Moniteur Westphalien/Westphälischer Moniteur*, nos. 247 and 249, 6 and 8 September 1813.

124. 'Journal des marches et opérations militaires du 2e Corps d'Armée', SHD, MR 683.

125. See correspondence published in Fabry, *Empereur I*, Documents, pp. 46–7, and *Empereur II*, Documents, pp. 104, 123, 143, 155–7, 173–8; especially Bruno's reports of 15, 16 and 17 September 1813. The number of remaining hussars is from the 2nd Corps strength return of 15 September 1813, SHD, 2C538. Victor had ordered reinforcements sent to Freiberg, but unfortunately for Bruno, these were to set out on 18 September and thus had not arrived when he was attacked. See Karworoski to Dufour, 19 September 1813 for a fascinating account of a staff officer who rode into Freiberg unawares after the Austrian success (Fabry, *Empereur II*, p. 191; from SHD, 2C156).

126. Heinrich von Cerrini de Monte Varchi, 'Der Ueberfall von Freyberg am 18. September 1813 durch den österreichischen Generalen Baron Scheither', *Oesterreichische militärische Zeitschrift*, vol. VI, 1833. Note that Lünsmann (and Kleinschmidt following him) claims the hussars allowed themselves to be taken; the Austrian account gives no hint of such perfidy. The entry for Scheither in Jaromir Hirtenfeld (*Der Militär-Maria-Theresien-Orden und seine Mitglieder*, Vienna: Hof- und Staatsdruckerei, 1857, pp. 1137–45) simply abridges Cerrini's account.

127. Berthier to Napoleon, 22 September 1813, *Rapports*, vol. II, p. 163.

128. Napoleon to Berthier, 19 and 21 September 1813, *CG*, nos. 36370 and 36413, vol. XIV, pp. 600–16; Victor to Napoleon, 21 September 1813, Fabry, *Empereur II*, p. 285.

129. *Le Moniteur Westphalien/Westphälischer Moniteur*, no. 247, 6 September 1813; Morgenstern, *Kriegserinnerungen*, pp. 127–8 (emphasis in the original); Gerland, 'Ordrebuch des westfälischen Artillerie-regiments', pp. 287–9.

130. The 31st Division skirmished with Russians of Blücher's army on 30 August at Löwenberg and southeast of Luban, but it is not clear what role if any the Westphalians played in these combats.

131. Ledru to his brother, 4 August 1813 and to his sister, 7 September 1813, in Jean-Louis Bonnéry, *Ledru des Essarts: Un Grand Patriote Sarthois Méconnu*, Le Mans: Imprimerie Maine Libre, 1988, pp. 87–91; MacDonald to Berthier, 4 September 1813, Fabry, *MacDonald*, Documents, p. 67.
132. Normann, *Aus den Papieren*, pp. 14–16.
133. Westphalian loss estimate from 'Darstellung der Ereignisse bei der schlesischen Armee im Jahre 1813, mit besonderer Berücksichtigung des Antheils der preußischen Truppen', *Beiheft zum Militair-Wochenblatt*, September–October 1844, pp. 275–7; and Goltz, *Königlich Preußischen dritten Ulanen-Regiments*, pp. 98–9. MacDonald does not mention the loss of the Westphalians in his reports. This engagement is known as Rothnaußlitz/Göda.
134. MacDonald to Berthier, 2 October 1813, Fabry, *Empereur III*, Documents, pp. 254–5.
135. Aster, *Kriegsereignisse in und vor Dresden*, pp. 60–5, 109–12, 221–41; Aster, 'Darstellung der am 26sten August 1813 stattgefundenen Angriffe'; Horstenau, *Feldzug von Dresden*, vol. III, pp. 216–30. Westphalian dispositions during the battle are murky. Aster gives the garrison of Lunette IV as 100–150 French and Westphalian infantrymen, but most of the Westphalian infantry seem to have been held inside the city walls on both sides of the Elbe. The presence of the Westphalian horse artillery battery is based solely on Normann's memoir, and it is not clear how the six (or possibly eight) guns of the foot battery were distributed. The 1st Light's detachment to Meissen is based on Paul Markus, 'Meißen während der Napoleonischen Kriege', *Mitteilungen des Vereins für Geschichte der Stadt Meissen*, vol. IV, 1897.
136. Normann, *Aus den Papieren*, pp. 8–12; Lünsmann, *Armee des Königreichs Westfalen*, pp. 316–17; *Le Moniteur Westphalien/Westphälischer Moniteur*, nos. 241 and 242, 31 August and 1 September 1813. According to French army records, the Westphalian horse battery had been assigned to 1st Cavalry Corps by this time, but its exact movements are unknown. It may have been in Dresden when the armistice ended and not yet physically co-located with the corps, or perhaps it was detached from the corps during the battle while the rest of the formation operated on the far side of the Weißeritz stream.
137. Lauer to Berthier, 29 August 1813, Fabry, *Empereur I*, Supplement, p. 58; Durosnel to Berthier, 17 and 20 September 1813, Fabry, *Empereur II*, Documents, pp. 159, 218–19.
138. Details of this incident (date, number of men involved, etc.) are missing. See Lünsmann's entry on Brethauer (p. 190); Kleinschmidt (p. 601); and Hellrung (p. 445). If Brethauer indeed led his entire battalion to defect or desert, one may assume the number was as many as 500, but the figure was probably 300–400.
139. Napoleon to Drouot, 3 October 1813, *CG*, no. 36628, vol. XIV, p. 716; Bernard to Durosnel, 2 October 1813, Fabry, *Empereur III*, Documents, p. 251; Juhel, *Automne 1813*, pp. 55–7, for the units attached to the Guard. The 9 October strength report for Dresden (SHD, 2C546) lists the 2nd (823) and 3rd (816) Infantry Regiments and 58 Westphalian artillerymen, to which I have added the 44 train personnel listed in earlier reports (I suspect their absence to be the result of a clerical error). The 1st Light Battalion seems to have been assigned elsewhere, see Bernard's vague reference to it as having departed.
140. According to his well-researched and generally reliable biography, Le Marois reported that 342 of some 1,600 Westphalians had deserted by the beginning of July (Gillot, *Le Marois*, p. 187). Unfortunately, it is not clear which units were included in this

figure. Just the 9th? The 9th and the 3rd Infantry? In any case, enough were on hand to commit a battalion of more than 800 to Girard's August foray and leave another entire battalion in the fortress. Perhaps the deserters were replaced by new conscripts in the interim?

141. Le Marois to Napoleon, 14 August 1813, AN, AF/IV/1661B; Langenschwarz diary (manuscript) courtesy of Dr Michael F. Pavković. Napoleon to Le Marois, 8 August 1813, *CG*, no. 35787, vol. XIV, pp. 323–4. Berthier's orders to Girard (*Ordres*, vol. II, pp. 13–15) stated that the Westphalians assigned to Lanusse's 'Magdeburg Division' would consist of the 9th Infantry's grenadiers and voltigeurs (this is doubtless the reason Quistorp credited the regiment with only four elite companies for perhaps 380 men at Hagelberg in his *Nordarmee*, vol. I, p. 169). The exact composition of the 'battalion' with Girard is not known, but Napoleon granted Le Marois discretion in organising his troops (Napoleon to Berthier, 16 August 1813, *CG*, no. 35939, vol. XIV, p. 398) and the fact that the Westphalians numbered more than 800 officers and men indicates that it was more than four companies.

142. Initial strength and total losses from the report of Lanusse's division (called here the 1st Division), 6 September 1813, SHD, 2C155. Subsequent strength from the report of 1 September 1813, SHD, 2C551 (these reports were routinely backdated); quotes from Le Marois to Napoleon, 5 September 1813, Fabry, *Empereur II*, Documents, p. 246; and Girard to Le Marois, 31 August 1813, SHD, 2C154 (printed in Fabry, *Oudinot*, Documents, pp. 78–9). Girard had reported on 21 August that the Westphalians had performed poorly in the initial engagements on departing Magdeburg (Julius Laumann, 'Der Freiheitskrieg 1813/14 um Magdeburg', *Sachsen und Anhalt*, vol. 15, 1939, p. 291).

143. Gillot, *Le Marois*, p. 203. Note that GD Lemoine was attached to Magdeburg with his division from Minden during September, providing Le Marois with some 6,000 additional French and Spanish troops (no Germans).

144. Langenschwarz composed his memoir in approximately 1821 so his use of the term 'German armies' may be an anachronism. See also Gillot, *Le Marois*, pp. 208–9. Additionally, Le Marois may have learned that Bennigsen, commanding the Russian besiegers had made contact with Rheinbund officers and NCOs of the garrison to persuade them to defect (Laumann, 'Freiheitskrieg 1813/14 um Magdeburg', p. 267). Note that Langenschwarz and Le Marois gave the number of deserters as 500, while other sources give 300. Note also that Langenschwarz incorrectly placed the dismissal from Magdeburg on 11 November, but most others say it occurred on the 12th (e.g., Trefftz citing the report of the Ducal Saxon commander; see citation below).

145. The quotations and much of this depiction are drawn from Langenschwarz's unpublished memoir, supplemented in some details by Johann Trefftz, 'Das 4. Rheinbundsregiment Herzöge von Sachsen im Feldzug 1813', *Zeitschrift des Vereins für Thüringische Geschichte und Altertumskunde*, vol. XVI, 1906, pp. 60–4. Although many other German authors describe this dismissal as demeaning and dishonourable, Langenschwarz portrays Le Marois as courteous and respectful. See also Johann Christian Gotthilf Liebecke, *Magdeburg während der Blokade in den Jahren 1813 und 1814*, Magdeburg: Creutz, 1814, pp. 62–4.

146. Bertrand to Berthier, 31 August 1813, Fabry, *Oudinot*, Documents, pp. 81–2.

147. Lehsten, *Am Hofe König Jérômes*, p. 128.

148. Lehsten, *Am Hofe König Jérômes*, p. 135. It was likely men of the Chevaulegers-Garde that were reported 'without order and without officers' in a village 15 kilometres east of Torgau on 7 September (Lhéritier to Durosnel, 7 September 1813, Fabry, *Empereur II*, Documents, p. 12).
149. Oudinot to Jérôme, 14 September 1813, Fabry, *Empereur II*, Documents, p. 96.
150. Mauvillon, 'Skizze', p. 139; Lehsten, *Am Hofe König Jérômes*, p. 123. Wolff, a Jew from Alsace, transferred to Westphalian service from the French army and had himself baptised once in Kassel.
151. That is: 350 Westphalians and 181 Hessians, 4th Corps summary 'Situation', 26 September 1813, SHD, 2C539.
152. Kleinschmidt, *Königreich Westphalen*, p. 649.
153. Lehsten, *Am Hofe König Jérômes*, pp. 136–42. Curiously, Bertrand remarked in his 3 October report that the 'Generals Beaumont and Wolff, at the head of the Westphalian and Hessian cavalry, made many fine charges' (Fabry, *Empereur III*, Documents, pp. 266–6).
154. This and the previous paragraph from Lehsten, *Am Hofe König Jérômes*, p. 118–35. The lieutenant's father, Ludwig August Detlev von Lehsten, had been a cavalry officer in Hesse-Kassel, took service under Jérôme in 1808, and retired to his estate in Silesia in 1810 ('Lehsten, Ludwig August Detlev von', Hessische Biografie, https://www.lagis-hessen.de/pnd/1147501351 [accessed June 2022]).
155. Mustafa, 'Kassel Has Fallen'.
156. Arthur Kleinschmidt, 'Aus den letzten Tagen des Königreichs Westphalen', *ZHG*, vol. XVI, 1891, p. 246.
157. Friedrich August Karl von Specht, *Das Königreich Westphalen und seine Armee im Jahr 1813, so wie die Auflösung desselben durch das kaiserlich russischen General Graf A. Czernicheff*, Kassel: Luckhardt, 1848, pp. 95–7, 137–9 (erroneously giving a total of 4,202 for the garrison); Meibom, *Aus napoleonischer Zeit*, pp. 174–5. Salm-Salm had commanded this detachment at Celle, but it was transferred to Zandt when it moved to the Harz Mountains.
158. Widdern, *Streifkorps*, vol. II, p. 19.
159. Marwitz, report of 22 September 1813, ibid., vol. II, p. 29.
160. Specht, *Westphalen und seine Armee*, p. 100; Mauvillon, 'Skizze', pp. 449–50.
161. Specht (ibid.) erroneously includes soldiers from Lippe as well as Waldeck in this detachment, but no Lippe troops were present; they were either already in Magdeburg or had been left behind in Lippe.
162. Specht, op. cit., pp. 97–109; Widdern, *Streifkorps*, vol. II, pp. 18–43 (including Marwitz's 26 September 1813 after-action report); Friedrich August Ludwig von der Marwitz, *Aus dem Nachlasse Friedrich August Ludwig's von der Marwitz*, Berlin: Mittler & Sohn, 1852, vol. II, pp. 103–4; Quistorp, *Nordarmee*, vol. II, pp. 73–4.
163. Berthier to Napoleon, 29 September 1813, *Rapports*, vol. II, p. 182. Note that Marshal François Étienne Christophe Kellermann (1735–1820), commanding in Mainz at the age of 78 (!), should not be confused with his son, GD François Étienne Kellermann (1770–1835) who initially served with Ney's 3rd Corps and later commanded 4th Cavalry Corps as shown in Chart 35.
164. In addition to the sources cited specifically, this account of the Chernishev raid draws heavily on Specht (*Westphalen und seine Armee*); Anton Niemeyer, *Casselische Chronik vom acht und zwanzigsten September 1813 bis zum ein und zwanzigsten November desselben*

Jahrs, Cassel: Krieger, 1814; Chernishev's report to Alexander (*SIRIO*, vol. XXI, 1877); an account by Russian General Lachmann, 'Die Eroberung von Kassel am 28. September 1813', published in the *Militair-Wochenblatt*, no. 834, 16 June 1832, and in the *Oesterreichische militärische Zeitschrift*, vol. VIII, 1838; Bogdanovich, *Geschichte des Krieges im Jahre 1813*, vol. 2/2, pp. 7–23; Widdern, *Streifkorps*, vol. II, pp. 55–99; the correspondence published by du Casse (*Roi Jérôme*, vol. VI); and the account published in the *Moniteur Westphalien/Westphälischer Moniteur*, no. 272, 9 October 1813. Supplementary sources include Carl Venturini, *Rußlands und Deutschlands Befreiungskriege von Franzosen-Herrschaft unter Napoleon Buonaparte in den Jahren 1812–1815*, Leipzig: Brockhaus, 1816, vol. II, 387–92; Ludwig Müller, *Aus sturmvoller Zeit: Ein Beitrag zur Geschichte der westfälischen Herrschaft*, Marburg: Eckhardt, 1891, pp. 233–54; Kleinschmidt, 'Aus den letzten Tagen', pp. 244–84; and Falk Urlen, 'Die Vertreibung der Franzosen aus Cassel', Erinnerungen im Netz, 22 September 2013, https://www.erinnerungen-im-netz.de/erinnerungen/erin-artikel/kosaken-kaempfen-1813-im-kasseler-osten/ [accessed June 2022].

165. Reinhard's letter is published in du Casse, *Les Rois Frères*, p. 454; Delinière, *Karl Friedrich Reinhard*, p. 323. See Lieven, *Russia against Napoleon*, pp. 429–30, on Chernishev and Bernadotte.

166. Reinhard to Maret, 29 September 1813, referring to a 24 September letter from Le Marois in Magdeburg, du Casse, *Roi Jérôme*, vol. VI, pp. 345–8.

167. Du Casse, *Roi Jérôme*, vol. VI, pp. 214–15; Delinière, *Karl Friedrich Reinhard*, p. 324/N160. Dalton to Berthier, 29 September 1813 (two letters) and Arrighi to Ney, 2 October 1813, Fabry, *Empereur III*, Documents, pp. 181–2, 237.

168. 'Situation' as of 27 September 1813, SHD, 2C551.

169. Friedrich Karl von Strombeck, *Darstellungen aus meinem Leben und aus meiner Zeit*, Braunschweig: Vieweg, 1833, p. 184.

170. Eduard August Oppermann, in P. von Oppermann, 'Die Artillerie- und Genieschule im Königreich Westfalen. Mitteilungen aus den Papieren eines ihrer früheren Zöglinge', *ZHG*, vol. XXIX, 1905, p. 6.

171. 'Aus den Zeiten der schweren Noth. "Westfälische" Erinnerungen eines Kasselaners', *Die Gartenlaube*, vol. 37, 1879 at https://de.wikisource.org/wiki/%E2%80%9EWestf%C3%A4lische%E2%80%9C_Erinnerungen_eines_Kasselaners [accessed June 2022].

172. Quote from Justus Süstermann, a sergeant in the Grenadier-Garde in 'Aufzeichnungen eines jungen Hildesheimers aus den letzten Tagen des Kgl. Westfälischen Heeres (27. September–5. November 1813)', J. H. Gebauer, ed., *ZHG*, vol. 51, 1917, pp. 6–7; soldiers handing cartridges to boys from Friedrich von Müller, *Kassel seit siebzig Jahren zugleich auch Hessen unter vier Regierungen, die westphälische mit inbegriffen*, Kassel, Hühn, 1876, p. 60.

173. Friedrich M. Kircheisen, *Jovial King: Napoleon's Youngest Brother*, H. J. Stenning, trans., London: Elkin, Mathews & Marrot, 1932, p. 229.

174. Adolf Keysser, 'Oberst Weiß: Ein Bild aus der Kurhessischen Heeresgeschichte', *Hessenland*, vol. 24, no. 1, 1910, p. 2.

175. Chernishev to Alexander, 30 September 1813, *SIRIO*, vol. XXI, 1877, p. 221.

176. Specht, *Westphalen und seine Armee*, pp. 153–5. The guns, apparently forgotten and only guarded by six men, were likely intended for the Guard horse artillery battery Jérôme wanted to raise.

177. Ibid., pp. 155–6.
178. Ibid. This remark is noteworthy because Specht detested the Westphalian regime and had nothing but contempt for the French.
179. Jérôme to Napoleon, 29 September 1813, *Les Rois Frères*, pp. 456–8; du Casse, *Roi Jérôme*, vol. VI, p. 217. Technically, the battery only had six guns, but two others were added from those available in the city.
180. According to Wilhelm Grimm (*Kleinere Schriften*, vol. I, p. 530), the Cossacks stripped some of their captives naked except for their tall blue fatigue caps and laughingly set them loose to run to the Leipzig Gate where they were hidden from public view until some old overcoats could be collected to clothe them. This, however, may have been a colourful invention as it is unlikely Grimm actually witnessed this alleged scene.
181. Grimm, *Kleinere Schriften*, vol. I, p. 531.
182. Müller, *Kassel seit siebzig Jahren*, p. 62. Isolated French soldiers (*isolées*) in the city also joined in the defence (Oppermann, 'Die Artillerie- und Genieschule', p. 7).
183. Kleinschmidt, 'Aus den letzten Tagen', p. 253. The Chevaulegers depot located in Melsungen (approximately 90 men) was quickly evacuated on Chernishev's approach, Dieter Hoppe, 'Die Gedenktafel für den russischen Obersten Bedriaga, gestorben in den Freiheitskriegen am 16/18 September 1813', 'Die Freiheit eine Gasse', part 2, 2009, https://heiligenberg-blog.de/wp-content/uploads/hoppe/A06_Der%20Freiheit%20 eine%20Gasse-Teil2.pdf [accessed June 2022].
184. Jérôme to Napoleon, 29 September 1813, *Les Rois Frères*, pp. 456–8; Jérôme to Napoleon, 1 October 1813, and Jérôme to Clarke, 4 October 1813, du Casse, *Roi Jérôme*, vol. VI, pp. 352–61.
185. Süstermann, 'Aufzeichnungen', pp. 10–11.
186. Jérôme to Napoleon, 29 September 1813, *Les Rois Frères*, pp. 456–8; Jérôme to Napoleon, 1 October 1813, du Casse, *Roi Jérôme*, vol. VI, pp. 352–63; Specht, *Westphalen und seine Armee*, pp. 165–89.
187. Specht, *Westphalen und seine Armee*, pp. 190–200. One those who seems to have been captured at this stage was Major Carl von dem Bussche of the 2nd Cuirassiers; he decided to take Russian service and his letter with this request may be found in Albrecht von dem Bussche, *Auf Pferdesrücken durch Europa*, Mainz: von Hase & Koehler, 1997, pp. 196–7.
188. Specht, *Westphalen und seine Armee*, pp. 200–10; Meibom, *Aus napoleonischer Zeit*, pp. 174–8.
189. Specht, *Westphalen und seine Armee*, p. 204.
190. Jérôme to Napoleon, 1 October, to Clarke, 4 October and to Katherine, 9 October 1813, du Casse, *Roi Jérôme*, vol. VI, pp. 352–63.
191. Napoleon, on the other hand, castigated Jérôme for not having French troops on hand. 'If he had the first notions of good sense, he would have had 8 to 10 thousand French, Swiss and Italians around him,' the emperor wrote to his arch-chancellor, 'I told him this a long time ago' (Napoleon to Cambacérès, 9 October 1813, *CG*, no. 36707, vol. XIV, pp. 749–50).
192. Kellermann to Napoleon, 27, 29 and 30 September 1813, AN, AF/IV/1662B, Plaquette 7; and to Berthier, 29 September 1813, Fabry, *Empereur III*, Documents, pp. 177–80, 206–7.
193. Dalton to Berthier, 29 September 1813 (two letters) Fabry, *Empereur III*, Documents, pp. 181–2; Travers' 'Situation' as of 17 September 1813, SHD, 2C551.

194. Dalton to Berthier, 29 September 1813 (two letters) Fabry, *Empereur III*, Documents, pp. 181–2. Napoleon to Berthier, 27 September 1813, *CG*, no. 36523, vol. XIV, p. 664.
195. Kellermann to Berthier, Clarke and Napoleon, 29 and 30 September 1813, Fabry, *Empereur III*, Documents, pp. 177–80, 206–7. This French force would eventually consist of 7,600 officers and men with eight guns, approximately half of these from Rigau's 54th March Column (parts of the column went elsewhere) and the rest from various garrisons and depots in and around Mainz. These had all left Mainz by 7 October; an additional 228 men (IV/128^e Ligne) departed Mainz on 21 October. None of the elements of the 53rd March Column were involved in Westphalia, nor were any of the troops in the next column (the 55th) which left Mainz on 12 October. Sources: Kellermann to Napoleon, AN, AF/IV/1662B, Plaquette 7; SHD, Lystrac/XP3; and march column 'Situations', SHD, 2C551.
196. Specht, *Westphalen und seine Armee*, pp. 207–12.
197. Boedicker, 'Die militärische Laufbahn', pp. 278–9; Meibom, *Aus napoleonischer Zeit*, pp. 180–1.
198. On the scenes in Kassel on 30 September, see Müller, *Kassel seit siebzig Jahren*, pp. 64–7 (quotes); Oppermann, 'Die Artillerie- und Genieschule', pp. 8–9; Ludwig Völkel, 'Eines hessischen Gelehrten Lebenserinnerungen aus der Zeit des Königs Jérôme', Albert Duncker, ed., *ZHG*, vol. IX, 1882, pp. 291–318; and 'Aus den Zeiten der schweren Noth'.
199. The number of captured guns varies from 32 (Chernishev's report) to 30 (Specht) to 22 (Lachmann). Note that many of the guns were not mounted and thus not available to defend the city when Chernishev attacked.
200. Kleinschmidt, *Westfalen*, pp. 626–32.
201. Quote from a report by Hugot, a member of the French legation (in du Casse, *Roi Jérôme*, vol. VI, pp. 223–33); Stefan Hartmann gives a German translation in 'Kosaken in Kassel: Ein Kapitel aus dem Ende des Königreichs Westfalen', *ZHG*, vol. 99, 1994. Memoirs of this period are full of worry about the 'lower classes' and 'rebellious peasants' sowing chaos, see among others Niemeyer, *Casselische Chronik*, p. 29; Völkel, 'Eines hessischen Gelehrten', pp. 300–5; Borcke, *Kriegerleben*, pp. 274–5. Also: Goecke/Ilgen, *Königreich Westphalen*, pp. 256–7. For an interesting discussion of how the restored regimes treated rioters and vigilantes after Westphalia's disappearance, see Birgit Hoffmann, 'Aufruhrer oder gute Patrioten? Die gerichtliche Verfolgung von Selbstjustiz und Exzessen bei der Auflösung des Königreichs Westphalen im Gebiet des Herzogtums Braunschweig-Wolfenbüttel', *Braunschweigisches Jahrbuch für Landesgeschichte*, vol. 79, 1998, pp. 87–123.
202. Army of the North bulletin, 6 October 1813 (*Recueil des Ordres de Mouvement, Proclamations et Bulletins de S. A. R. le Prince Royal de Suède, Commandant en Chef l'Armée Combinée du Nord de l'Allemagne en 1813 et 1814*, Stockholm: Eckstein, 1839, pp. 334–7); French bulletin, 4 October 1813, Pascal, *Bulletins de la Grande Armée*, vol. VI, p. 158. Although there were incidents of plunder and Kassel's citizens learned to distract their Cossack liberators with drink, the level of theft and violence seems to have been remarkably low.
203. Luxburg to Ringel, 5 October 1813, Kleinschmidt, *Bayern und Hessen*, p. 236.
204. Napoleon to Cambacérès, 9 October 1813, *CG*, no. 36707, vol. XIV, pp. 749–50. Kircheisen states that Jérôme indeed received a letter from his brother on 3 November in Cologne, but that it was 'of such a nature that he caused both the letter and the draft

thereof to be destroyed' (*Jovial King*, p. 231). Chernishev to Alexander, 30 September 1813, *SIRIO*, vol. XXI, 1877, p. 222.
205. Niemeyer, *Casselische Chronik*, p. 34 (his actual comment is that the kingdom's fate would be decided 'on the Elbe', but the sense is the same).
206. It is in this sense that Lieven describes Chernishev as 'the star of a brilliant but largely irrelevant sideshow' as it did not divert any of Napoleon's major forces (*Russia against Napoleon*, p. 430).
207. Du Casse, *Roi Jérôme*, vol. VI, pp. 239–46, including Jérôme to Clarke, 4 October 1813, pp. 354–61. In contrast, his letters to Katherine generally exuded optimism.
208. Borcke, *Kriegerleben*, p. 280. 'Taint of unreality' is from a work of fiction: Jack Vance, *The Green Pearl*, New York: Berkley, 1986, p. 248.
209. Oppermann, 'Die Artillerie- und Genieschule', pp. 9–10; Boedicker, 'Die militärische Laufbahn', pp. 279–83; Borcke, *Kriegerleben*, pp. 268–9; Süstermann, 'Aufzeichnungen', pp. 7–16; Meibom, *Aus napoleonischer Zeit*, pp. 181–90.
210. Du Casse, *Roi Jérôme*, vol. VI, pp. 246–8. Du Casse states that Jérôme now merely saw himself as a French general rather than a king.
211. Heinrich Wilhelm Karl von Harnier, 'Noch einige Worte der Erinnerung an den Grafen Reinhard', *Minerva*, vol. II, April–May–June 1838; G. E. Guhrauer, 'Graf Karl Friedrich Reinhard: Eine Skizze', *Historisches Taschenbuch*, vol. VII, 1846, pp. 261–2; Wilhelm Lang, *Graf Reinhard: Ein deutsch-französisches Lebensbild 1761–1837*, Bamberg: Buchner, 1896, pp. 411–13; Delinière, *Karl Friedrich Reinhard*, p. 324–5.
212. Juhel, 'Automne 1813', p. 64.
213. August Woringer, 'Westfälische Offiziere VII: Die Artillerieoffiziere Schulz und Wille', *Hessenland*, vol. 23, 1909, p. 277; Ochs in Kleinschmidt, *Königreich Westfalen*, p. 649.
214. General Curial, 'Apperçu [sic] des opérations Militaires de la 2eme Division (vielle Garde) Pendant Le Courant de La Campagne de 1813', SHD, MR 682. The battery commander was Capitaine Johann Ludwig Orges.
215. 4th Corps 'Situation', 19 October 1813, SHD, 2C539.
216. Lehsten, *Am Hofe König Jérômes*, pp. 142–4.
217. Ibid., p. 146; Ochs in Kleinschmidt, *Königreich Westfalen*, p. 649.
218. Ibid., pp. 148–9.
219. Ibid., pp. 149–50; Ochs in Kleinschmidt, *Königreich Westfalen*, pp. 650–1.
220. The decree to reconstitute the army was published in the *Moniteur Westphalien/ Westphälischer Moniteur*, no. 277, 14 October 1813. A near-contemporary account observed that, 'Every village in the Kingdom of Westphalia had several deserters and recalcitrant conscripts hiding in it' (Hellrung, 'Organisation der Westphälischen Armee', pp. 448–57).
221. Allix to Kellermann, 7 October 1813, forwarded to Napoleon by Kellermann on 8 October, AN, IV1662B, Plaquette 7.
222. Motivations paraphrased from Stefan Brakensiek, 'Strukturen eines antinapoleonischen Aufstands: Grebenstein 1813', in Ute Planert, ed., *Krieg und Umbruch in Mitteleuropa um 1800*, Paderborn: Schöningh, 2009, pp. 45–61. On the variations among Westphalia's regions, see Todorov, 'Le roi appela', pp. 135–50.
223. Grimm, *Kleinere Schriften*, vol. I, p. 534.
224. Süstermann, 'Aufzeichnungen', p. 21. See also Borcke, *Kriegerleben*, pp. 277–83.
225. War Minister Clarke submitted a list of fourteen officers seeking to enter French service on 7 January 1814 (AN, AF/IV/1152).

226. Reinhard, report of 15 July 1812, Delinière, *Karl Friedrich Reinhard*, p. 320/n. 146. See Baustian's *Le royaume de Westphalie* for an analysis of Westphalia's economy, especially its relationship to the Continental System.
227. From analysis of the tables provided in Venzky, *Russisch-Deutsche Legion*.
228. Further research is needed to identify the numbers of the deserters and defectors and their various fates.
229. Borcke, *Kriegerleben*, p. 248. I have translated Borcke's '*Kreti und Pleti*' as 'anybody and everybody'.
230. Such as Lieutenant von Ochs wondering who would pay him (quoted earlier) or musician Friedrich Klinkhardt who joined the Prussian army after the retreat from Russia (*Feldzugs-Erinnerungen des Königlich Westfälischen Musikmeisters Friedrich Klinkhardt aus den Jahren 1812 bis 1815*, Braunschweig: Scholz, 1908). Berryman assesses that Loßberg's decision to stay with the army was the professional choice of a career soldier ('Boundaries of Loyalty', p. 181).
231. Conrady, *Aus stürmischer Zeit*, p. 378; Heinrich Wesemann, *Kannonier des Kaisers*, Cologne: Verlag Wissenschaft und Politik, 1971, pp. 90–1 (emphasis in the original). Wesemann was later able to escape as was the much-quoted Förster Fleck of the Jäger-Carabiniers (*Erzählung Föster Flecks*). See also Todd B. Berryman, 'Napoleon's German Soldiers: Westphalians in Arms', *Nineteenth Century Studies*, no. 26, 2012. Another who steadfastly sought to return home was an artillery NCO named Jakob Mayer, *Erzählung der Schicksale und Kriegsabenteuer des ehemaligen westfälischen Artillerie-Wachtmeister Jakob Mayer aus Dransfeld während der Feldzüge in Spanien und Rußland*, Engelskirchen: Fachverlag AMon, 2008. See Gerdes, *Königlich Westfälische und Großherzoglich Bergischen Truppen im Russischen Feldzug*, pp. 125–31, on the miseries of the prisoners but note that some Westphalians reported decent treatment by their captors, and some had the good fortune to encounter sympathetic and protective Russian civilians.
232. Despite its good qualities in 1812, Connelly's assessment of the army in 1813 is overly generous (*Napoleon's Satellite Kingdoms*, pp. 294–301).
233. Specht, *Westphalen und seine Armee*, p. 204.
234. Lehsten, *Am Hofe König Jérômes*, pp. 148–9.

Chapter 7: The Miniature Monarchies: A Spectrum of Soldiers

1. Friedrich von Müller, *Erinnerungen aus den Kriegszeiten von 1806–1813*, Braunschweig: Viewig & Sohn, 1851, p. 287.
2. The initial French scheme in 1808–9 was to have seven 'Rheinbund regiments' numbered as follows: 1st (2nd Nassau Infantry), 2nd (1st Nassau Infantry), 3rd (Würzburg), 4th (Saxon Duchies), 5th (Anhalt and Lippe), 6th (Schwarzburg, Reuß and Waldeck), and 7th (Mecklenburg Duchies). In the event, the first three numbers were seldom if ever used and only numbers 4 through 7 had significance in French orders of battle. See Gill, *Eagles*, Chapter 8. (Note that some references designate the Würzburg Regiment as the 1st Rheinbund, with the numbers 2 and 3 assigned to the Nassau regiments.)
3. Johann Otto Georg Wilhelm von Düring describing Kowno (Kaunas), in his *Tagebuch über die Belagerung der Stadt Danzig im Jahre 1813*, Berlin: Enslin, 1817, p. 3.

4. Günter Schumann, 'Die Kontingente der Fürstentümer Schwarzburg, Reuß und Waldeck in den Napoleonischen Kriegen', H. Sterzing, ed., *Montagsblatt, Wissenschaftlicher Beilage der Magdeburgischen Zeitung*, nr. 1, 4 January 1909, p. 7. Similar impressions of Prussian anti-French anger are in Franz Freiherr von Soden, *Beiträge zur Geschichte des Krieges in den Jahren 1812 und 1813, besonders in Bezug des 6ten Regiments der damahligen Fürsten-Division des Rheinbundes*, Arnstadt: Hildebrand, 1821, p. 56.
5. Major Justus Wilhelm von Bose to his wife, 14 January 1813, 'Briefe eines Offiziers an seine Frau aus den Jahren 1807–1813', *Die Grenzboten*, 24, vol. II/IV, 1865, p. 663.
6. Sergeant Johann Friedrich Wilhelm Dornheim (Lippe-Detmold), 'Skizzen aus den Feldzügen des Bataillons Lippe', in Eckhart Kleßmann, ed., *Unter Napoleons Fahnen: Erinnerungen lippischer Soldaten aus den Feldzügen 1809–1814*, Bielefeld: Westfalen Verlag, 1991, pp. 232–3.
7. Ibid., p. 235.
8. Schaumburg-Lippe officer's letter in Wilhelm Wiegmann, *Franzosenzeit und Befreiungskrieg: Zur Geschichte des Fürstentums Schaumburg-Lippe 1807–1815*, Stadthagen: Heine, 1915, pp. 138–9; Wiegmann speculates that the writer was Hauptmann Ernst Heinrich Ludwig Mayer.
9. Schumann, 'Kontingente', p. 7; see also Jacobs, *Feldzüge und Schicksale*, p. 267: 'all at once the soldiers lost all fear of the Cossacks'.
10. Carl Geißler, *Geschichte des Regiments Herzoge zu Sachsen unter Napoleon mit der großen Armee im russischen Feldzuge 1812*, Jena: Mauke, 1840, pp. 322–4.
11. Wiegmann, *Franzosenzeit und Befreiungskrieg*, pp. 138–9.
12. There is no indication that Franceschi, a Corsican, spoke German. He would succumb to typhus in March 1813 to be replaced by GD Bachelu. He should not be confused with Jean-Baptiste Franceschi-Delonne who had died in Spain in 1810.
13. This section draws on Anton Chroust, 'Das Großherzogtum Würzburg (1806–1814)', *Neujahrsblätter*, Würzburg: Stürtz, 1913; Anton Chroust, *Geschichte des Großherzogtums Würzburg (1806–1814): Die äussere Politik des Großherzogtums*, Würzburg: Becker, 1932; Valentin Langmantel, *Die äussere Politik des Grossherzogtums Würzburg*, Munich: Wolf & Sohn, 1878; Dieter Schäfer, *Geschichte Würzburgs*, Munich: Beck, 2003; Dieter Schäfer, *Ferdinand von Österreich*, Graz: Styria Verlag, 1988; and Maximilian Th. L. Rückert, *Politik im Krieg*, Vienna: Böhlau, 2022. See also Ivo Striedinger's review of Chroust's comprehensive work: 'Das Großherzogtum Würzburg', *Zeitschrift für bayerische Landesgeschichte*, no. 6, 1933, pp. 250–6.
14. For a brief period in the first half of 1806, Ferdinand remained a prince-elector as the last vestiges of the old *Reich* drifted away but before his accession to the Rheinbund in September that year. He was thus the last prince-elector of the previous dispensation (not counting Wilhelm of Hesse-Kassel who insisted on retaining the title of elector even after the dissolution of the *Reich*). As a grand duke, he was catalogued with the Confederation kings and his position in the Habsburg dynasty meant that his title was 'imperial and royal' (*kaiserlich und königlich*). In his biography of Ferdinand, Dieter Schäfer notes the decisions about his move from Florence to Salzburg and from thence to Würzburg were all made *for* him by the court in Vienna; he was not consulted (*Ferdinand von Österreich*, p. 226).
15. These were not true 'sappers' per se, rather infantrymen and artillerymen employed as a labour force. Additionally, 25 Würzburg train soldiers served briefly with French rear-area troops under Junot in July 1809. See Gill, *Eagles*, p. 389.

16. Ferdinand to Napoleon, 27 January 1813, Kircheisen, *Fürstenbriefe*, pp. 294–6.
17. Ferdinand to Napoleon, 15 March 1813, Chroust, *Geschichte des Großherzogtums*, pp. 367, 382–4.
18. St Germain to Maret, 17 July 1813, Chroust, *Geschichte des Großherzogtums*, p. 365. Ferdinand's ambivalent stance in 1813 does not submit to easy analysis and may have changed as the fortunes of war shifted from Napoleon gaining victories in May to hopes for peace during the armistice and finally to the increasing likelihood of renewed conflict with Austria on the side of the Coalition. See Chroust, *Geschichte des Großherzogtums*, pp. 382–90, 405–7; Rückert, *Politik im Krieg*, pp. 242–63; Schäfer, *Geschichte Würzburgs*, pp. 246–9.
19. François Armand Édouard Lefebvre de Béhaine, 'L'Attaque de Wurzbourg', *Revue des Études Historiques*, vol. 79, 1913, pp. 504–5. For Ferdinand's role in Vienna's eyes, see Dieter Schäfer, 'Die politische Rolle des Erzherzogs Großherzog Ferdinand, des nächsten Bruders des Kaisers, in seinen Würzburger Jahren', in Wolfgang Altgeld and Matthias Stickler, eds, *'Italien am Main': Großherzog Ferdinand III. der Toskana als Kurfürst und Großherzog von Würzburg*, Rahden: Leidorf, 2007.
20. Strength from the 15 March 1813 'Situation' for the Army of Spain, SHD, 8C470.
21. Durutte to Ferdinand, 27 November 1812, in Fedor Grosch, Eduard Hagen and Albert Schenk, *Geschichte des k. B. 12. Infanterieregiments Prinz Arnulf und seiner Stammabteilungen*, Munich: Lindauer, 1914, pp. 244–8.
22. The little artillery company had remained in the Marienberg. Strength of approximately 120 infantrymen per battalion from a 2 March 1813 report (Chroust, *Geschichte des Großherzogtums*, pp. 352–3; Rückert, *Politik im Krieg*, p. 426).
23. Raising funds and purchasing horses proved far greater problems than conscripting new soldiers. Rückert notes the detachment of the inexperienced IV/Würzburg to Modlin (*Politik im Krieg*, pp. 423–9) as typical of placing the least combat-worthy troops in fortresses.
24. There was some desertion, but its extent is impossible to judge accurately. The two battalions apparently had lost 131 men to desertion by early May, which would have equated to a fairly ordinary 8 to 10 per cent of total strength (Chroust, *Geschichte des Großherzogtums*, p. 364).
25. The emperor noted 'the distinguished conduct' of the Würzburg troops in the 2 July 1813 issue of the *Journal de l'Empire*; Chroust, *Geschichte des Großherzogtums*, pp. 364–5. Strength from the 7th Corps 15 May 1813 'Situation', SHD, 2C541. The two were listed as 1,440 present under arms in mid-April (SHD, 2C706).
26. Napoleon to Berthier and to Maret, both 6 July 1813, nos. 35234, 35254, *CG*, vol. XIV, pp. 87–95; Strength report for 18 September 1813, SHD, 2C156.
27. Some subsequent authors number the newly built battalions as 5th, 6th and 7th according to the sequence of their formation, but this is not how they were designated at the time. An example of the erroneous numeration is Walter Kopp, *Würzburger Wehr: Ein Chronik zur Wehrgeschichte Würzburgs*, Mainfränkische Studien no. 22, Würzburg: Freunde Mainfränkische Kunst und Geschichte, 1979, pp. 131–2.
28. August Eichelsbacher, 'Die Würzburger Truppen in den Kriegen Napoleons I. (1806–1815)', *Frankenland*, vol. I, 1914, pp. 288–9. Strength from the 7th Corps 1 August 1813 'Situation', SHD, 2C541.
29. That is, 40 wounded and 205 missing or capturedcaptured (though no dead were listed in the 7th Corps report, there were doubtless some dead and wounded among

the 'missing'): 4th Corps 'État des Pertes', SHD, 2C154; Grosch/Hagen/Schenk, *Geschichte des k. B. 12. Infanterieregiments*, p. 257; Rückert, *Politik im Krieg*, pp. 446–8.
30. According to Cerrini, a Würzburg battalion was engaged in supporting Ryssel's Saxon brigade on 3 September outside Wittenberg (*Feldzüge der Sachsen*, p. 251).
31. Eichelsbacher, 'Würzburger Truppen', p. 289.
32. Durutte's campaign notes, RAMB, Boite 43. Grosch/Hagen/Schenk, *Geschichte des k. B. 12. Infanterieregiments*, pp. 257–62. Reynier's attempts to have the 5th Battalion withdrawn from Torgau to reinforce the regiment proved ineffective: Reynier to Berthier, 9 and 10 September 1813 and to Ney, 19 September 1813, Fabry, *Empereur II*, Documents, pp. 34–5, 135–6, 308.
33. Chroust, *Geschichte des Großherzogtums*, pp. 365–6; Christian Johann Baptist von Wagner, 'Autobiographie des Staatsrats Christian Johann Baptist von Wagner', *Archiv des Historischen Vereins von Unterfranken und Aschaffenburg*, vol. 74, 1905, pp. 106–7.
34. 7th Corps 'Situation' as of 1 October 1813, SHD, 2C551. An additional 45 men were detached and some 370 were listed in hospital.
35. Rückert, *Politik im Krieg*, p. 451.
36. Grosch/Hagen/Schenk, *Geschichte des k. B. 12. Infanterieregiments*, p. 274; and excellent synoptic charts in Rückert, *Politik im Krieg*, p. 423–4. Although it seems extraordinary that such a small state could have provided so many men, the authors of this regimental history were very meticulous in their research. The paucity of data, however, makes further analysis difficult. This regimental history mentions the detachment going to Dresden, but there is no sign of it in the very detailed reports of the garrison or of the 1st and 14th Corps that remained during the siege (SHD, 2C538, 545, and 546).
37. Chroust, *Geschichte des Großherzogtums*, pp. 356–63, 385–91; Lefebvre de Béhaine, 'L'Attaque de Wurzbourg', pp. 510–15.
38. St Germain to Maret, 15 October 1813, Chroust, *Geschichte des Großherzogtums*, p. 363.
39. This section draws almost exclusively on Hermann Helmes, 'Die Würzburger Chevaulegers im Feldzuge 1812/13', *DBKHG*, no. 11, 1902.
40. Strength from the 11th Corps 'Situation' of 1 April 1813, SHD, 2C541. They were brigaded with the 4th Italian Chasseurs (301 officers and men).
41. Helmes, 'Würzburger Chevaulegers', pp. 20–4, with Fressinet's 19 May and 6 June 1813 letters on pp. 43–4. Fressinet's letters notwithstanding, the French situation reports repeatedly list the chevaulegers with the 35th Division not the 31st (SHD, 2C541).
42. Ibid., pp. 18–24. The company reported that it left on 7 May, but the written order was issued on the 12th (Berthier, *Ordres*, vol. I, p. 97).
43. Ibid., pp. 25–40. Strength from the 11th Corps 'Situation' of 15 May 1813, SHD, 2C541.
44. 'Livret de Situation', 15 August 1813, SHD, 2C708.
45. 11th Corps 'Situation', 15 July 1813, SHD, 2C541.
46. Hermann Helmes, 'Die Würzburger Truppen vor hundert Jahren', *Archiv des historischen Vereins von Unterfranken und Aschaffenburg*, no. 55, 1913, pp. 127–9; Helmes, 'Würzburger Chevaulegers', pp. 40–2; Rückert, *Politik im Krieg*, p. 424. It is possible that some or many of these men were doled out to serve as dispatch riders and orderlies for French generals.
47. Napoleon to Maret, 7 and 13 June 1813, *CG*, nos. 34526 and 34636, vol. XIII, pp. 1134–79.
48. Helmes, 'Würzburger Chevaulegers', pp. 38–42. The infantry battalion in southern France, having been disarmed and interned by the French in December 1813, returned

to Würzburg in May 1814 to become the foundation for the new Bavarian 12th Infantry Regiment.

49. In addition to sources cited previously, see the following for the attack on Würzburg and the shift to the Allies: Georg Adam Ullrich, *Die Blokade der Festung Marienberg und des Mainviertels zu Würzburg in den Jahren 1813 und 1814*, Würzburg: Bonitas, 1819; Wagner, 'Autobiographie', pp. 107–10; and Gilardone, 'Herbstfeldzuge 1813', pp. 70–5. Chroust published Turreau's report to Berthier and a summary account by a Würzburg police official (*Geschichte des Großherzogtums*, pp. 534–42). See also: Franz Eulenhaupt, *Geschichte der Festung Marienberg nebst deren Belagerungen und Blokaden*, Würzburg: author, 1851.

50. Parts of Wrede's menacing first letter (25 October) are in Chroust, *Geschichte des Großherzogtums*, p. 381; his brusque second letter (26 October) is in Heilmann, *1813*, pp. 224–5.

51. Lefebvre de Béhaine, 'L'Attaque de Wurzbourg', pp. 520–1; strength from Hemmann/Klöffler, *vergessene Befreiungskrieg*, p. 505. Approximately 50 Hanseatic German soldiers of the 127e and 128e Ligne also tried to flee only to be bloodily repulsed by loyal members of the garrison (the 'Italian' 113e Ligne and 13th Hussars).

52. Ferdinand's presence created an additional complication for Friedrich of Württemberg just when his representatives were conducting testy negotiations with the bumptious Wrede. The grand duke had taken himself to the former territory of the Hoch und Deutschmeister Order, which was headed by another Habsburg archduke (Anton), and Friedrich feared Ferdinand's arrival would stir unrest similar to the violence the region had experienced in 1809 (Gill, *Thunder*, vol. III, pp. 181–2). He thus invited Ferdinand to move deeper into the kingdom (Lefebvre de Béhaine, *Napoléon et les Alliés*, p. 167).

53. This section on Frankfurt draws heavily on Guillaume Bernays, *Schicksale des Großherzogthums Frankfurt und seiner Truppen*, Berlin: Mittler & Sohn, 1882, Chapter 13. See also Jean Camille Abel Fleuri Sauzey, *Le Régiment de Francfort*, vol. I of *Les Allemands sous les Aigles Françaises*, Paris: Terana, 1987.

54. Bernays (*Schicksale*, pp. 398–400) states that the regiment apparently reached Danzig with only 158 men but returned stragglers increased the figure to 209 by the start of the siege (in addition to some number of senior staff). A 21 April 1813 table submitted by the French representative in Frankfurt (SHD, 2C542), however, gives a total of 27 officers and 444 men based on a 20 January report, but lists none in hospital; it thus seems likely that Bernays gave an accurate account of those physically under arms while the larger figure included those on the sick lists.

55. The regiment is sometimes known as the 'Regiment von Zweyer' for General Franz von Zweyer, the grand duchy's senior military officer.

56. Paul Darmstaedter, *Das Großherzogtum Frankfurt: Ein Kulturbild aus der Rheinbundzeit*, Frankfurt: Baer, 1901, pp. 390–3; Karl Freiherr von Beaulieu-Marconnaÿ, *Karl von Dalberg und seine Zeit*, Weimar: Böhlau, 1879, vol. II, pp. 245–8.

57. Bernays, *Schicksale*, p. 444; depot strength report of 21 April 1813, SHD, 2C542.

58. Strength report of 21 April 1813, SHD, 2C542.

59. Bernays, *Schicksale*, p. 441.

60. Strength report of 21 April 1813, SHD, 2C542.

61. The 3rd Corps loss table for Lützen (SHD, 2C167) does not mention II/Frankfurt at all; either an oversight or because it took no combat losses.

62. Bernays, *Schicksale*, p. 444; battalion report, 15 June 1813, SHD, 2C541.
63. French inspection report, 13 July 1813, AN, AF/IV/1661A, Plaquette 1. Blein, 'Campagne de 1813: 1er partie: Historique du 12e Corps, du 4 mai à la rupture de l'armistice le 17 août', SHD, MR 688.
64. Hermann Ketterer, *Das Fürstentum Aschaffenburg und sein Übergang an die Krone Bayern*, Aschaffenburg: Werbrun, 1914/15, pp. 141–2. As noted in Chapter 8, there may have been as many as 1,300 officers and men present for duty in the regiment, but even so, the number absent was enormous given the arrival of the replacement detachment: 847+713+330= 1,890 total.
65. Bernays, *Schicksale*, pp. 444–9; Ketterer, *Fürstentum Ashschaffenburg*, p. 141. Bernays and Ketterer aver (without giving any detail) that the 3rd Battalion fought at Hoyerswerda and Bautzen, but there is no indication whatsoever in French or Prussian sources that any Frankfurt troops were present at either battle. SHD, 2C551 for the troops in Torgau as the Frankfurt 'depot'; these had arrived via Erfurt (SHD, 2C154).
66. Herbert Hömig, *Carl Theodor von Dalberg: Staatsmann und Kirchenfürst im Schatten Napoleons*, Paderborn: Schöningh, 2011, p. 557; Beaulieu-Marconnaÿ, *Dalberg*, vol. II, pp. 252–62.
67. The Frankfurt troops in the city were issued live ammunition on the evening of 25 October owing to the approach of the Allied armies but 150 of them deserted that night. Shortly thereafter most of the Frankfurt troops were quietly furloughed to return to their homes. See Samuel Gottlieb Finger, 'Auszüge aus S. G. Finger's Tagebüchern von 1795 bis 1818', Lorenz Friedrich Finger, ed., *Archiv für Frankfurts Geschichte und Kunst*, vol. 6, 1877, pp. 305–32; Alexander Kühn, *Erlebnisse eines Soldaten des ehemaligen Großherzogthums Frankfurt und des darauf folgenden General-Gouvernements*, Frankfurt: Wentz, 1862, pp. 5–6.
68. For a comprehensive, deeply researched study of Berg, see Bettina Severin-Barboutie, *Französische Herrschaftspolitik und Modernisierung: Verwaltungs- und Verfassungsreformen im Großherzogtum Berg (1806–1813)*, Munich: Oldenbourg, 2008. This section is also informed by Charles Schmidt's standard work: *Le Grande-Duché de Berg (1806–1813)*, Paris: Alcan, 1905.
69. Hildegard Feldmann, 'Einwohner aus dem Kanton Duisburg im französischen Militärdienst 1806–1813', *Duisburger Forschungen*, vol. 15, 1971, pp. 131–72.
70. Colonel Jean Genty reports of 21 and 26 January 1813, AN, IV/1880. Another 171 officers and men were left behind in hospitals in Prussia. Things did not improve much after their return home: the entire brigade of 3½ regiments only totalled 259 present under arms and 193 sick as of 14 March. Slightly higher but equally grim figures were compiled for a 1 February summary, but this was based on sketchy inputs (AN, IV/1882).
71. Report of 5 January 1813 included as an attachment in Nesselrode to Roederer, 26 January 1813. A report of 9 January 1813 showed only 136 officers and men present for the regiment (both AN, IV/1882) meaning the regiment lost approximately 600 men in Russia (Thomas, *Régiment Rhénan*, p. 62).
72. Reports for II/3rd Infantry (21 January 1813, including 89 sick) and the infantry depot (14 January 1813), AN, IV/1880.
73. Napoleon to Eugène, 15 February 1813, no. 32782, *CG*, vol. XIII, p. 357. The squadron's locations are from Witzleben's reports in AN, IV/1882, where one also finds angry missives from the Berg authorities demanding information from the major.

74. Initially outlined in a Gesetz-Bulletin/Décret Impériale of 29 January 1813. The infantry regiment was to have an artillery 'squad' of two guns, but this was never organised. As evident in Düsseldorf's 8 February 1813 response to Paris, the French Ministry of War and the Berg administration disagreed on details of the gaps in personnel, horses and vehicles to be filled, but there was no doubt that much needed to be done (AN, IV/1880 and IV/1883). A general overview is in Rudolf Goecke, *Das Grossherzogtum Berg unter Joachim Murat, Napoleon I. und Louis Napoleon 1806–1813*, Cologne: DuMont-Schauberg, 1877, p. 45.
75. Latour-Maubourg, report of 15 August 1813, AN, IV/1881. This file also contains Colonel Genty's report and other correspondence from Latour-Maubourg on this issue. Latour-Maubourg was commander of the 14th Military Division at the time.
76. Colonel Genty's reports May to December 1813, AN, IV/1880; also 'Confédération du Rhin, Correspondance Militaire', SHD, 2C65. Genty reported that 78 men deserted as they marched through Belgium, but thereafter the regiment behaved well. Note that the number of 'effectives' included 298 in hospital or convalescing.
77. How the regiment would have performed as part of the Grande Armée in Germany is, of course, a different question.
78. Late November and early December reports in AN, IV/1880. Based on these reports, by 1 December 1813, there were roughly 2,300 Berg infantry and 220 lancers in France (other reports place the number of lancers, many unarmed and unequipped at 380 or so), possibly with a handful of artillery train personnel. The correspondence of Colonel Genty, commander of the 1st Infantry, suggests that some thought was given to taking the Berg units into French pay in November–December, but nothing seems to have come of this idea. For general information on the Berg infantry, see Wilhelm Neff, *Geschichte des Infanterie-Regiments von Goeben (2. Rheinischen) Nr. 28.*, Berlin: Mittler & Sohn, 1890, pp. 12–13; and Richard Wellmann, *Geschichte des Infanterie-Regiments von Horn (3tes Rheinischen) Nr. 29.*, Trier: Lintz, 1894, pp. 5–6.
79. Severin-Barboutie observes that much of the dissatisfaction stemmed from the expansion of state power and the disruptive effects of social change (*Herrschaftspolitik*, p. 295). There would have been discontent and perhaps protest in any case, but the fact that these often-uncomfortable changes occurred owing to an outside power only accentuated popular frustration and provided an easy, external target for anger. Many authors refer to these rapid changes under the broad rubric 'modernisation'.
80. On the '*Knüppelrussen*' phenomenon, see: Schmidt, *Grand-Duché de Berg*, pp. 459–68; Severin-Barboutie, *Herrschaftspolitik*, pp. 287–96; M. Mario Kandil, 'Sozialer Protest gegen das napoleonische Herrschaftssystem im Großherzogtum Berg 1808–1813', Friedrich Ebert Stiftung, Digitale Bibliothek, https://www.fes.de/fulltext/historiker/00671004.htm [accessed August 2022]; W. Meiners, 'Die Knüppelrussen in Elberfeld', *Monatsschrift des Bergischen Geschichtsvereins*, vol. 10, no. 12, December 1903; W. Meiners, 'Noch einmal die Knüppelrussen und Julius (?) Christian Claudius Devaranne', *Monatsschrift des Bergischen Geschichtsvereins*, vol. 11, no. 7, July 1904; and Iskul', 'Der Aufstand im Großherzogtum Berg'. A variant of the term is '*Klöppelrussen*' (clapper-Russians): J. F. Knapp, *Geschichte, Statistik und Topographie der Städte Elberfeld und Barmen im Wupperthale*, Iserlohn: Langwiesche, 1835, p. 22.
81. W. Meiners, 'Die bergische Industrie während der Fremdherrschaft (1806–1813) mit besonderer Berücksichtigung Elberfelds', *Monatsschrift des Bergischen Geschichtsvereins*, vol. 13, no. 1/2, January–February 1906, p. 38. Even the intensely anti-Napoleon

contemporary Johann Joseph Görres described how 'the loose rabble of the whole region…suspicious faces, men and women equipped with empty sacks' gathered to take advantage of the tumult ('Aufruhr im Großherzogthum Berg, 1813', *Rheinischer Merkur*, no. 209, 17 March 1815).

82. Severin-Barboutie, *Herrschaftspolitik*, p. 295.
83. See his correspondence with Le Marois in Gillot, *Le Marois*, pp. 168–73.
84. Beugnot and others suspected a conspiracy instigated by Stein to inflame Prussian passions. On 7 January he wrote: 'I see how Prussians encumber our institutions… they dream of the return of the glories of Frederick II [the Great]' (Schmidt, *Grand-Duché de Berg*, p. 460). These anxieties, however, were exaggerated (Kandil, 'Der Befreiungskrieg in Westfalen und im Rheinland', pp. 201–18).
85. As noted in Chapter 6, the reports of unrest were sufficiently worrying to the authorities in Kassel that Jérôme sent a regiment to the border under Prinz Salm-Salm as a precaution.
86. Napoleon to Le Marois, 30 January 1813, no. 32549; see also his letters to Clarke, 28 and 29 January 1813, nos. 32523 and 32540; all *CG*, vol. XIII, pp. 222–4. Schmidt states that Napoleon was especially irritated because the sole insurrection east of the Rhine was occurring in his own duchy (*Grand-Duché de Berg*, p. 463).
87. Le Marois to Clarke, 4 February 1813 in Gillot, *Le Marois*, p. 159; Chapter V of this biography contains a wealth of data on Le Marois's role in suppressing the disturbances.
88. Le Marois, report of 4 February 1813, Schmidt *Grand-Duché de Berg*, p. 465.
89. Severin-Barboutie, *Herrschaftspolitik*, p. 296.
90. P. Zimmermann, *Erinnerungen aus den Feldzügen der bergischen Truppen in Spanien und Rußland*, Düsseldorf: Stahl, 1840, p. 88.
91. Le Marois had recommended sending the Berg troops to France or Italy, but it is not clear if his suggestion was a prompt for the decision to move the infantry regiment to Cherbourg (report to Berthier, 22 March 1813, Gillot, *Le Marois*, p. 163).
92. Battery commander's reports, 1 June to 1 October 1813, AN, IV/1880 and IV/1883. He complained about expenses and especially about the poor quality of his draft horses, noting that many had been lost during the transit from the Rhine to Dresden even before the depletion in September.
93. August and October strength figures from SHD, 2C708 and Lystrac, XP3. Early November personnel and equipment reports from SHD, 2C542.
94. This account of the Berg Lancer Regiment is drawn primarily from the following sources: Thomas, *Régiment Rhénan*, pp. 63–74; Zimmermann, *Erinnerungen*, pp. 87–131; Armand von Ardenne, *Bergische Lanziers, Westfälische Husaren Nr. 11*, Berlin: Mittler & Sohn, 1877, pp. 118–80; and Hans von Eck, *Geschichte des 2. Westfälischen Husaren-Regiments Nr. 11*, Mainz: Militär-Verlagsanstalt, 1893, pp. 87–118.
95. The complex evolution of the regiment and the even more complex history of its first uniforms are addressed in detail in Guy C. Dempsey Jr, 'The Berg Regiment of Light Horse 1807–1808', Napoleon Series, March 2011, https://www.napoleon-series.org/military-info/organization/Berg/c_BergLancer.html [accessed August 2022]. See also the earlier Guy C. Dempsey Jr and E. Wagner, 'Das Chevauleger-Regiment von Berg 1807–1808', *Depesche*, vol. 7, no. 24.
96. Strength report, 10 March 1813, GB Travers, SHD, 2C542; and the War Ministry's 'Rapport des Situations de la Brigade', 5 April 1813, AN, IV/1881.

97. Napoleon to Clarke, 6 February, and Napoleon to Eugène, 15 February 1813, nos. 32632 and 32782, *CG*, vol. XIII, pp. 287, 357. In addition to the squadron in the field, some 918 officers and men were preparing in the depot as of 1 April 1813 (SHD, 2C542).
98. The exact order of battle of the brigades to which the Berg Lancers were assigned seems to have changed repeatedly, but they were most frequently associated with GD Colbert and the 2nd (Red or Dutch) Lancers of the Guard. Similarly, the numeration of the squadrons changed during the year: at first there were references to a '10th Squadron' in the depot, but these vanish after May and only Squadrons 1 through 6 are listed until November when a '7th Squadron' is mentioned in the depot in France (AN, IV/1881 and 1882).
99. Eck writes that the squadron would have been in peril of being wiped out at one point had not the Guard infantry attacked its pursuers 'with lowered bayonets' and driven them off (*2. Westfälischen Husaren-Regiments*, p. 90). The war ministry had expressed suspicion about Witzleben because he had remained behind initially when his squadron rode off to join the army ('Rapport des Situations de la Brigade', 5 April 1813, AN, IV/1881). He had quarrelled with the ministry in March, apparently dismayed over not being promoted fast enough and later investigation strongly indicates that he was involved in peculation of the regiment's pay and other funds (Witzleben to Roederer, 1 March 1813 and Major von Toll's report of 16 June 1813, AN, IV/1882).
100. Casualty report in Foucart, *Bautzen*, vol. II, p. 5; Toll report of 16 June 1813, AN, IV/1882.
101. 'Rapport des Situations de la Brigade', 22 and 29 May 1813, AN, IV/1881.
102. Reports for 7 March through 2 June 1813, AN, IV/1880 and 1881; Kösterus, *Großherzoglich Hessischen Truppen*, pp. 4–5 (Chapter 5).
103. There were also 7 train personnel. Toll's reports of 16 May, 1 June and 16 June 1813, AN, IV/1882. Strengths noted in the French reports of 1 and 10 May (SHD, 2C542) as well as the army's 15 August 'Situation' (SHD, 2C708) were similar.
104. Eck, *2. Westfälischen Husaren-Regiments*, p. 97. Eck gives the date of the review as 8 August, Ardenne says it was on the 10th.
105. Parade anecdote from Zimmermann, *Erinnerungen*, p. 124. Squadrons and strengths from Berg overall 'Situations' for 1 August, 15 August, and 15 September (AN, IV/1882). Note that these reports do not list a 2nd Squadron at all. On the other hand, Napoleon refers to the 2nd and 6th Squadrons in his correspondence; he also authorised the raising of a seventh if sufficient funds were available (Napoleon to Clarke, 31 July 1813 and to Roederer, 1 August 1813, nos. 35688 and 35718, *CG*, vol. XIV, pp. 280–92). Likewise, Marshal Kellermann reported on 15 September that the 2nd Squadron (250 strong) was to depart from Mainz to Erfurt on 17 September as part of the 53rd March Column; he also listed 160 Berg troops with the 54th March Column. (Kellermann to Napoleon 15, 17 and 27 September 1813, AN, IV/1662B, Plaquette 7).
106. Thoumas, *Grands Cavaliers*, vol. I, p. 217.
107. In addition to the Berg regimental histories, see Dziengel, *Königlichen Zweiten Ulanen-Regiments*, pp. 327–9; and Gustav Ritter Amon von Treuenfest, *Geschichte des k. k. Dragoner-Regimentes Feldmarschall Alfred Fürst zu Windisch-Grätz Nr. 14*, Vienna: Brzezowsky & Söhne, 1886, pp. 446–7. Thomas (*Régiment Rhénan*, p. 69) wonders if the large number of prisoners indicates that many of the men 'allowed' themselves to be taken, but this seems unlikely given the regiment's overall record.
108. Ardenne (*Bergische Lanziers*, pp. 162–5) states that the Berg Lancers took part in the 28 September fight at Altenburg, but Thomas (*Régiment Rhénan*, pp. 70–1), with

reference to Foucart's careful study (*Une Division de Cavalerie Légère*), convincingly disproves this unfounded notion. Thomas, however, errs in recording the regiment being involved in an engagement on 4 October near Altenburg.

109. This was likely the regiment's 6th Squadron, which left Mainz on 17 September as part of the 53rd March Column with 255 officers and men (SHD, 2C551); on the other hand, it may have been a replacement detachment of 172 destined for the army (AN, IV/1882).
110. Reinhard Münch and Irene Eifler, *Lebenslauf der Oberstleutnants Wilhelm Ritgen (1789–1863)*, Leipzig: Engelsdorfer, 2011, pp. 48–51.
111. Draft of a November report to Napoleon on the Berg troops, AN, IV/1881: 'Rapport sur l'esprit du Régiment d'Infanterie de Berg qui est à Cherbourg, et sur celui de la Brigade de Lanciers qui se trouvait à Leipzick'.
112. Ibid.; and report of Chef d'Escadron Joseph The Loosen, 13 November 1813, AN, IV/1882.
113. The Loosen report, 13 November 1813, AN, IV/1882.
114. Travers to Roederer, 20 November 1813; situation report for 8 November 1813; reports of Major Joseph Renard near Mainz, AN, IV/1882. One report refers to the troops at Montmédy as the '7th Squadron'.
115. Zimmermann, *Erinnerungen*, p. 130. Similar sentiments were aired by Nassau, Westphalian and Würzburg officers disarmed and interned along the Pyrenees.
116. Ibid., pp. 89–90 (emphasis in the original).
117. Erich Keerl, 'Herzog Ernst I. von Sachsen-Coburg zwischen Napoleon und Metternich: Ein deutscher Kleinstaat im politischen Kräftespiel der Großmächte 1800–1830', dissertation, Friedrich-Alexander University, Erlangen-Nuremberg, 1973, p. 105.
118. R. Ehwald, 'Gotha im Jahre 1813', *Mitteilungen der Vereinigung für Gothaische Geschichte und Altertumsforschung*, 1912–1913, pp. 1–2.
119. As Franz of Sachsen-Coburg-Saalfeld died in December 1806 and his heir, Ernst I, was serving with the Russo-Prussian forces, the duchy was administered by the French until the Treaty of Tilsit in July 1807 when the tsar prevailed on Napoleon to allow Ernst to return to Coburg and take his place as the reigning duke.
120. Sources for the incident with Linker's battalion: Eduard von Heyne, *Geschichte des 5. Thüringischen Infanterie-Regiments Nr. 94*, Weimar: Böhlau, 1869; Leo von Pfannenberg, *Geschichte des Infanterie-Regiments Großherzog von Sachsen (5. Thüringisches) Nr. 94 und seiner Stammtruppen 1702–1912*, Berlin: Stilke, 1912; 'Ueberfall des Dorfes Ruhla bei Eisenach', *Militair-Wochenblatt*, no. 845, 1 September 1832; 'Gefangennahme der Kontingente der Herzoge v. Sachsen, in Ruhla, Schwarzhausen und Winterstein (am 13. April 1813)', *Beiheft zum Militair-Wochenblatt*, January–February 1847; Robert Kunhardt von Schmidt, 'Aus der Geschichte des 4. Rheinbund-Regiments Herzöge von Sachsen', *Militair-Wochenblatt*, no. 21, 11 March 1903; Widdern, *Streifkorps*, vol. I, pp. 84–91; Wechmar, *Braune Husaren*, pp. 26–7.
121. Voigt to Saint-Aignan, 30 March 1813, in Gustav Emminghaus, 'Das thüringische Bataillon in Ruhla am April 1813', *Zeitschrift des Vereins für thüringische Geschichte und Altertumskunde*, vol. III, 1859, p. 338.
122. Linker's name is presented with various spellings including 'Lincker' and 'Lyncker'.
123. Müller, *Erinnerungen*, p. 274.

124. R. Waitz, *Erinnerungen aus den Kriegsjahren 1813, 1814 und 1815*, Coburg: author, 1847, pp. 17–19; Widdern, *Streifkorps*, vol. I, p. 62.
125. Pinto is sometimes described as a *Rittmeister*, but the regimental history only grants him the rank of *Leutnant* at this stage. Likewise, the size of his detachment is variously given as 15, 20 and 50 riders.
126. The experience of one of these guides, Wilhelm Braun, was published in Adolf Joch, *Teilnehmer an den Napoleonischen Kriegen und den Befreiungskämpfen von 1807–1815 aus dem ehemaligen Herzogtum Sachsen-Meiningen*, Hildburghausen: Gadow & Sohn, 1935, pp. 195–6.
127. Linker report to Carl August, 16 April 1813 from Jena, in Emminghaus, 'Das thüringische Bataillon in Ruhla', pp. 342–3.
128. There is nothing to support the supposition that Linker had prearranged the defection or that it had Herzog Carl August's approval in advance; see Kunhardt von Schmidt, 'Geschichte des 4. Rheinbund-Regiments', pp. 565–6; Hermann Freiherr von Egloffstein, 'Carl August während des Krieges von 1813', *Deutsche Rundschau*, vol. CLVI, July–September, 1913, p. 56; and Heyne, *Geschichte des 5. Thüringischen Infanterie-Regiments*, p. 131. The allegation appears offhandedly in the otherwise reliable history penned by veteran Gustav Jacobs, *Geschichte der Feldzüge und Schicksale der Gotha-Altenburgischen Krieger in den Jahren 1807 bis 1815*, Altenburg: Gleich, 1835, p. 292. See also Max von Eelking, *Geschichte des Herzoglich Sachsen-Meiningenischen Contingents*, Meiningen: Brückner & Renner, 1863, p. 75; and Ehwald, 'Gotha im Jahre 1813', p. 6.
129. Pinto mentioned Carl August because most of the troops captured in Ruhla were from Weimar (Kunhardt von Schmidt, 'Geschichte des 4. Rheinbund-Regiments', p. 564).
130. Gotha investigation report in Emminghaus, 'Das thüringische Bataillon in Ruhla', pp. 340–1.
131. Kunhardt von Schmidt gives the most detailed account of the surprise and capture of Linker's battalion: 'Geschichte des 4. Rheinbund-Regiments', pp. 562–70. The message from Gotha and the Gotha investigation report with Pinto's smug remark are in Emminghaus, 'Das thüringische Bataillon in Ruhla', pp. 339–41.
132. Joch, *Teilnehmer*, p. 31.
133. Eelking, *Herzoglich Sachsen-Meiningenischen Contingents*, p. 76.
134. The Allies would later supply all manner of deserters and prisoners of war to bring the battalion up to a strength of 800 men.
135. As Napoleon asked Württemberg General von Beroldingen in early October: 'Is he still a little bit Prussian?' (Pfister, *Lager des Rheinbundes*, p. 359).
136. Theodor Götze in Robert Krause, 'Weimar in den Jahren 1806 und 1813', *NASG*, vol. IV, 1883, pp. 244–6; Ehwald, 'Gotha im Jahre 1813', p. 4.
137. Weimar record of the meeting, 14 April 1813, in Emminghaus, 'Das thüringische Bataillon in Ruhla', pp. 341–2.
138. Karl von Müffling, *Passages from My Life; together with Memoirs of the Campaign of 1813 and 1814*, Philip Yorcke, ed., London: Bentley, 1853, pp. 29–30. 'Where is your deserter, Mr von Müffling, who has compromised you so badly,' asked one of Napoleon's secretaries in June (Egloffstein, 'Carl August', p. 74). Saint-Aignan termed him 'dangerous' and the cause of delay in raising the duchy's contingent prior to the invasion of Russia (report of 9 March 1812, in Andreas Fischer, *Goethe und Napoleon*, Frauenfeld: Huber, 1900, pp. 189–91).
139. Napoleon to Saint-Aignan, 20 April 1813, no. 33961, *CG*, vol. XIII, p. 882.

140. Müller, *Erinnerungen*, p. 287.
141. Ibid., pp. 287–98. For these several days, see also Egloffstein, 'Carl August', pp. 58–64.
142. Napoleon to Maret, 24 and 25 May 1813, nos. 34313 and 34329, *CG*, vol. XIII, pp. 1032–40.
143. Napoleon to Berthier and Maret, 7 June 1813, nos. 34501 and 34526, *CG*, vol. XIII, pp. 1121, 1135; and Berthier to the rulers of Weimar, Coburg and Gotha as well as to Saint-Aignan, 7 June 1813, *Ordres*, vol. I, pp. 197–8; *Journal de l'Empire*, 4 July 1813. The French faith in Sachsen-Gotha as compared to Weimar and Coburg is evident in these letters. In mid-June, Napoleon wrote to Maret to direct the duchies to provide cavalry instead of infantry because 'The Saxon and German cavalry is good, while the infantry is mediocre'; no serious consideration seems to have been given to this notion (Napoleon to Maret, 13 June 1813, no. 34636, *CG*, vol. XIII, p. 1179).
144. Kunhardt von Schmidt, 'Geschichte des 4. Rheinbund-Regiments', p. 566. The judgment was dated 12 August 1813; it is printed in Heyne, *5. Thüringischen Infanterie-Regiments*, pp. 242–3. The public notice that Linker appear before a court of inquiry was published in the Gotha journal: Hans von Döring, *Geschichte des 7. Thüringischen Infanterie-Regiments Nr. 96*, Berlin: Mittler & Sohn, 1890, vol. I, pp. 233–4.
145. Several points are murky regarding this incident. Sources differ on whether Lützow appeared in Roda on 4 or 5 June and whether his band reached Schleiz on the 5th or 6th (e.g., W. Emil Peschel, *Theodor Körner's Tagebuch und Kriegslieder aus dem Jahre 1813*, Freiburg: Fehsenfeld, 1893, pp. 33–4); I have given the dates in Brecher, *Überfall*, pp. 2–3. Additionally, Tümpling's rank is variously given as *Hauptmann* and *Leutnant*. The basics, however, are clear in his case, see: Wagner, 'Ueber die Aufhebung einer Abtheilung des Altenburgischen Landregiments durch preußische Truppen im Jahre 1813', *Mittheilungen der Geschichts- und Altertumsforschenden Gesellschaft des Osterlandes zu Altenburg*, vol. I, no. IV, 1844, pp. 47–9; and Wolf von Tümpling, *Geschichte des Geschlechtes von Tümpling*, Weimar: Böhlau, 1892, vol. II, pp. 326–31. Förster (*Befreiungs-Kriege*, vol. I, p. 397) claims that Lützow captured 400 men at Roda, but this is an exaggeration. Note that Lützow mentioned 'Saxons' in one of his reports to Blücher (see Jagwitz, *Lützowschen Freikorps*, pp. 70–1, 102–9), but that term was often used for the Saxon Duchies as well as the Kingdom of Saxony – there were certainly no *royal* Saxon troops in either Roda or Schleiz.
146. Egloffstein, 'Carl August', p. 208.
147. On Weimar during the armistice, see Fischer, *Goethe und Napoleon*, pp. 203–9 (including the quote from the memorandum to Maret); and Egloffstein, 'Carl August', pp. 68–75, 200–9. Gerhard Müller points out that Napoleon's principal interest after the intervention in Spain was stability in Germany so that it would be a source of material and political support, not a fount of frictions; he thus had no desire to pursue Carl August's expansive plans of territorial and dynastic rearrangement prior to or after the Russian invasion ('Die sächsische Staaten in der napoleonischen Zeit' in Niedersen, ed., *Sachsen, Preußen und Napoleon*, p. 481).
148. Keerl, 'Herzog Ernst I.', pp. 116–22.
149. The following draws heavily on Trefftz, 'Das 4. Rheinbundsregiment'; supplemented by Jacobs, *Feldzüge und Schicksale*, pp. 291–306. Trefftz made careful use of regional archives and corrects the errors present in some of the regimental accounts.
150. Wilhelm Freiherr von Schauroth, *Im Rheinbund-Regiment der Herzoglich Sächsischen Kontingent Koburg-Hildburghausen-Gotha-Weimar während der Feldzüge in Tirol, Spanien*

und Rußland 1809–1813, Berlin: Mittler & Sohn, 1905, pp. 257–62; Jacobs, *Feldzüge und Schicksale*, p. 297.

151. When the regiment reached Leipzig on 15 August, GB Bertrand ordered it formed into two large battalions, but this change – if it was implemented at all – only lasted until the troops arrived in Magdeburg on the 20th. See Trefftz, 'Das 4. Rheinbundsregiment', pp. 45–7. The initial plan was to deploy the regiment to Dresden (SHD, Lystrac, XP3).
152. There were 62 deserters from the 1,069 men of the Gotha contingent. If this proportion was similar in the other contingents, the desertion rate was only about 5 per cent but Jacobs described it as unusually high with the only other occurrence being when the 4th Rheinbund was ordered to Spain in 1809 (*Feldzüge und Schicksale*, p. 296).
153. Le Marois to Berthier, 23 August 1813, SHD, 2C154. The lack of officers had already come to Napoleon's attention: Napoleon to Berthier, 6 August 1813, no. 35747, *CG*, vol. XIV p. 304. One excuse offered was that the more junior officers could not be promoted ahead of their senior compatriots under siege in Danzig (Eelking, *Herzoglich Sachsen-Meiningenischen Contingents*, p. 84).
154. Jacobs, *Feldzüge und Schicksale*, p. 296.
155. As mentioned in Chapter 6, I/9th Westphalian was actually a composite battalion-size unit, but the French referred to it as the '1st Battalion' or sometimes listed it as an 'elite battalion'.
156. Jacobs, *Feldzüge und Schicksale*, p. 299.
157. For Sauerteig's testimony and that of several other common soldiers, see Joch, *Teilnehmer*, pp. 195–6.
158. Fourrier Zerr's testimony in Joch, *Teilnehmer*, p. 197.
159. Jacobs, *Feldzüge und Schicksale*, p. 300.
160. 'Let's go, brave Saxons, the Prussians are retiring! Forward, forward!' (from Eelking, *Herzoglich Sachsen-Meiningenischen Contingents*, p. 86).
161. Joch, *Teilnehmer*, p. 196. I have translated *zusammengetrieben* here as 'shoved into a mass'.
162. Strength and casualty figures are from Girard's overview report ('*État de Situation de la 1er Division de Magdebourg*', 6 September 1813, SHD, 2C155) and from Trefftz, 'Das 4. Rheinbundsregiment', pp. 52–5. Trefftz used Münch's report, but, unsurprisingly, there are discrepancies. Although both sources give similar starting strengths (1,234 and 1,164 respectively), Girard's report only credits the regiment with 145 officers and men returning to Magdeburg on 3 September, while Trefftz cites Münch stating that he gathered 252 near Wittenberg on 29 August. On the drummers, see Jacobs, *Feldzüge und Schicksale*, p. 302.
163. Quistorp, *Nordarmee*, vol. I, p. 424.
164. Schauroth, *Im Rheinbund-Regiment*, p. 262.
165. These details and figures from Trefftz ('Das 4. Rheinbundsregiment', p. 56) are slightly higher than the 1,429 recorded by the garrison headquarters in its 15 September report (*see* Chart 50); the exact dates of reports or changes in numbers on the sick list or a multitude of other factors could account for this minor difference. Heyne, on the other hand, gives the Coburg company 131 men, but says that an additional company from Gotha and group of Meiningen conscripts had also arrived (*5. Thüringischen Infanterie-Regiments*, p. 147). This explains the regiment's relatively high manpower figures after Hagelberg.

166. Kunhardt von Schmidt, 'Geschichte des 4. Rheinbund-Regiments', p. 567. According to one source, Bennigsen, who was commanding some of the Russian troops outside Magdeburg, contacted the German officers inside the fortress to promote surrender or at least disobedience (Laumann, 'Freiheitskrieg 1813/14 um Magdeburg', p. 267).
167. August Müller, *Geschichtliche Übersicht der Schicksale und Veränderungen des Großherzogl. Sächs. Militairs während der glorreichen Regierung Sr. Königl. Hoheit des Großherzogs Carl August*, Weimar: Landes-Industrie-Comptoir Klassik Stiftung, 1825, p. 9; see also the repeated references to desertion in the courteous note Langenschwarz sent to the Ducal Saxon officers (Beilage 17).
168. Ehwald, 'Gotha im Jahre 1813', pp. 10–14.
169. Carl August seems to have harboured hopes of a royal crown should his cousin Friedrich August be deposed by the Allies in the peace settlement (Keerl, 'Herzog Ernst I.', p. 134/n1).
170. Hans Küster, *Geschichte des Anhaltischen Infanterie-Regiments Nr. 93*, Berlin: Mittler & Sohn, 1893, vol. I, pp. 81–91. For infantry uniforms, see W. J. Rawkins, *The Rheinbund Contingents 1806–1813: Anhalt, Lippe, Schwarzburg, Waldeck, Mecklenburg-Schwerin, Oldenburg & Frankfurt*, e-book edition, 2015.
171. Christian Georg Ackermann, *Darstellung der Kriegsbegebenheiten in Dessau während der Jahre 1806–1815*, Dessau: Ackermann, 1839, pp. 80–103; Karl Hundert, *Anhalt im Jahre 1813*, Dessau: Dünnhaupt, 1913, pp. 34–7; Hermann Wälschke, *Anhaltische Geschichte*, Cöthen: Schulze, 1913, vol. III, pp. 328–38; Daniel Clarke, '"We Endured a Lot, Suffered a Lot": The Anhalt Duchies during the Napoleonic Wars 1804–1814', in Andrew Bamford, ed., *Glory is Fleeting: New Scholarship on the Napoleonic Wars*, Warwick: Helion, 2021, pp. 39–50. The battalion numbered 571 when the autumn campaigns began (Quistorp, *Nordarmee*, vol. III, p. 25).
172. Napoleon to Maret, 17 June 1813, no. 34785, *CG*, vol. XIII, p. 1241. Napoleon did not mention the troop numbers in this note, so it is unclear whether the specifics came from his own instructions delivered orally or were decided by Maret and his envoy.
173. Dessau: 11 officers, 208 men, 226 horses; Bernburg: 7 officers, 143 men, 156 horses; Köthen: 5 officers, 126 men, 131 horses. Dessau and Bernburg also supplied two caissons and 8 horses. Dessau formed the 1st Company, Bernburg the 3rd, and Köthen the 4th, with all three contributing to the 2nd Company and the regimental staff. See Markus Gärtner, 'Le Régiment de Chasseurs des Duchés d'Anhalt en 1813', *Tradition*, no. 221, April 2006, pp. 18–22.
174. Vandamme to Revest, 18 August 1813, Fabry, ed., *Journal des Campagnes*, p. 193.
175. Reports from Gobrecht, the commander of the 9th Lancers and an unnamed Anhalt officer, 23 August 1813, SHD, 2C154; also published in Fabry, ed., *Journal des Campagnes*, pp. 209–12.
176. Bürkner to Herzog Leopold, 15 December 1813, in Hundert, *Anhalt im Jahre 1813*, pp. 108–9 (he was writing from captivity).
177. Clarke, '"We Endured a Lot, Suffered a Lot"', p. 42.
178. The sequence of events in this chaotic battle is confused – in this instance, Corbineau's cavalry division (including the brigade commanded by Baden GM von Heimrodt) also conducted a countercharge against the advancing Russian horse and it is unclear whether this occurred simultaneously with Gobrecht's action or whether Gobrecht merely supported Corbineau.

179. Some Anhalt accounts claim that Gobrecht struck north with the 9th Lancers and abandoned the Jäger-zu-Pferd. For example, Karl-Heinz Wittich, 'Das Anhaltische Chasseur-Regiment 1813', *Salzlandkreis*, https://www.salzlandkreis.de/media/6134/wittich_anhaltisches-chasseur-regiment-1813.pdf [accessed August 2022].
180. Anhalt accounts mention the Austrian *Erzherzog Johann* Dragoons, Nr. 1; the Austrian regimental history lauds the regiment's actions on 30 August but does not refer specifically to the Anhalt regiment (Gustav Ritter Amon von Treuenfest, *Geschichte des k. und k. Bukowina'schen Dragoner-Regimentes*, Vienna: St Norbertus Buch- und Kunstdruckerei, 1892, pp. 257–61).
181. Gobrecht to Frosté, 20 April 1827, Fabry, ed., *Journal des Campagnes*, pp. 251–4. This letter also appears in Georges Bertin, ed., *La Campagne de 1813 d'Après des Témoins Oculaires*, Paris: Flammarion, 1896, pp. 117–22.
182. Bürkner to Herzog Leopold, 15 December 1813, in Hundert, *Anhalt im Jahre 1813*, pp. 108–9 (this figure seems low, and it is possible that the captive Bürkner did not know how many other men of his regiment had been killed or wounded after his capture). He reported himself utterly distraught at the regiment's fate. Ironically, one of the Prussian officers killed in the fighting along the French escape route was Major Christian Friedrich von Anhalt-Köthen-Pleß of the 10th Silesian Landwehr, a relative of the ruling duke in Anhalt-Köthen (Daniel Clarke, 'Officers of the Anhalt Duchies who Fought in the French Revolutionary and Napoleonic Wars, 1789–1815', Napoleon Series, 2017).
183. Testimony in Hundert, *Anhalt im Jahre 1813*, pp. 110–11.
184. 1st Corps 'Situations' for 1 August and 15 September 1813, SHD, 2C538; testimony of trooper Christoph Meyer, in Hundert, *Anhalt im Jahre 1813*, pp. 109–10.
185. There are differing accounts of the Anhalt regiment in the confused combat at Kulm, this narrative is drawn primarily from Ferdinand Siebigk, 'Die Theilnahme Anhaltischer Krieger an den Kriegen für und gegen Napoleon von 1807 bis 1815', unpublished manuscript, courtesy of the Anhaltische Landesbücherei Dessau (now the Stadtbibliothek Dessau-Roßlau). Siebigk's detailed history also informs the rest of this section.
186. Hundert, *Anhalt im Jahre 1813*, pp. 59–61; Clarke, '"We Endured a Lot, Suffered a Lot"', p. 40. Leopold's proclamation can be found in the *Moniteur Westphalien/Westphälischer Moniteur*, no. 204, 25 July 1813. Napoleon directed publication of this recall order 'in all the journals of Saxony and Germany' (Napoleon to Maret, 16 July 1813, no. 35425, *CG*, vol. XIV, p. 173).
187. The former count (*Graf*) of Lippe-Detmold had been granted princely rank in 1789 under the Holy Roman Empire as a personal honour, but entry into the Rheinbund raised both Lippe counties to permanent status as principalities (Hans Kiewning, *Fürstin Pauline zur Lippe 1769–1820*, Detmold: Meyer, 1930, p. 285).
188. Sadly, space does not permit further exploration of the remarkable Fürstin Pauline and her accomplishments, but see the following for her history and general background to this introduction: Kiewning, *Fürstin Pauline*, pp. 285–399; Erich Kittel, *Geschichte des Landes Lippe*, Cologne: Archiv für deutsche Heimatpflege, 1957, pp. 165–84; Johannes Arndt, *Das Fürstentum Lippe im Zeitalter der Französischen Revolution 1770–1820*, Münster: Waxmann, 1992, pp. 41–4; Stefan Meyer, 'Georg Wilhelm Fürst zu Schaumburg-Lippe (1784–1860)', dissertation, Universität Hannover, 2005, pp. 62–73.

189. For a tidy summary of this odd battalion, see D. Fiebig, 'Das Bataillon des Princes', *Zeitschrift für Heeres- und Uniformkunde*, Heft 63/64, January 1934.
190. Hans von Dewall, 'Kurzer Abriss der lippischen Militärgeschichte', *Lippische Mitteilungen*, vol. 31, 1962, pp. 85–93 (he gives the Lippe troops as the 1st Battalion); Gerd Stolz, 'Das Bataillon Lippe in Danzig in den Jahren 1812–13', *Heimatland Lippe*, vol. 62, no. 6, November 1969, pp. 226–8; Kiewning, *Fürstin Pauline*, p. 388.
191. Berthier's orders to Girard (*Ordres*, vol. II, pp. 13–15) reflect both the exaggerated hopes for this regiment entertained in imperial headquarters and the imprecision so often evident in French reporting on Rheinbund troops, especially the tiny contingents; in this case, Berthier told Girard that the Magdeburg Division under Lanusse would include 'an elite battalion drawn from the Lippe regiment' when Lippe was only providing a battalion in total. Le Marois and Girard adjusted Lanusse's order of battle to accommodate the actual troops available.
192. Reinhard to Berthier, 21 August 1813, SHD, 2C154.
193. Hauptmann Karl Wilhelm Friedrich von Campe, report of 15 September 1813, in Wiegmann, *Franzosenzeit und Befreiungskrieg*, p. 163.
194. This figure is from Lippe secondary sources (*see below*); apparently through an oversight, the French 1 September 1813 report for Magdeburg does not list any Lippe troops (SHD, 2C551).
195. The number of deserters is unclear: as noted in Chapter 6, Westphalian GB Langenschwartz recorded the number as 500; the city's history states that the total was 300 men (Friedrich Wilhelm Hoffmann, *Geschichte der Stadt Magdeburg*, Magdeburg: Baensch, 1850, pp. 474–5). Magdeburg's citizens detested the *corvée* labour and were outraged that even well-to-do residents were supposed to participate (Rudolph Holzapfel, *Das Konigreich Westfalen: mit besonderer Berücksichtigung der Stadt Magdeburg*, Magdeburg: Lichtenberg, 1895, pp. 186–8).
196. In addition to Wiegmann, *Franzosenzeit und Befreiungskrieg*, pp. 153–64; this account draws on Dewall, 'Kurzer Abriss', pp. 93–4; Kiewning, *Fürstin Pauline*, pp. 396–7; and Wilhelm Oesterhaus, *Geschichte der Fürstlich Lippischen Truppen in den Jahren 1807–1815*, Detmold: Meyer, 1907, pp. 70–2.
197. Kiewning, *Fürstin Pauline*, pp. 399–415; Meyer, 'Georg Wilhelm', pp. 72–3; Dewall, 'Kurzer Abriss', p. 94–5.
198. J. M. Meinhard, *Geschichte des Reußischen Militairs bis zum Jahre 1815*, Gera: Blachman & Bornheim, 1842, pp. 391–412; Michael Reichstädter, 'Napoleons langer Schatten: Das Fürstentum Reuß älterer Linie vom Rheinbund bis zur Julirevolution', in Werner Greiling and Hagen Rüster, eds, *Reuß älterer Linie im 19. Jahrhundert: Das widerspenstigste Fürstentum?*, Jena: Vopelius, 2013, p. 94.
199. See, for example, a 10 April 1813 letter from the Waldeck finance minister outlining his tiny state's woes: in Juhel, 'Truppen des Rheinbunds', in *Blutige Romantik*, Juhel, p. 54.
200. Strength from the 1 September 1813 report for Magdeburg, SHD, 2C551. The August dates are from Döring, *Geschichte des 7. Thüringischen Infanterie-Regiments*, vol. I, p. 252 (who gives a strength of 414 men); Meinhard (*Reußischen Militairs*, p. 410) states that the companies (no strength given) departed in early July to arrive in the middle of that month.
201. Hans Stahlberg, 'Reußisches Militär bis zum Ende der Befreiungskriege', *Zeitschrift für Heeres- und Uniformkunde*, Heft 269, January 1977; Friedrich Herrmann, 'Uniformen des reußischen Kontingents 1809–1813', *Zeitschrift für Heeres- und Uniformkunde*, Heft

281, January 1979; Sigismund Stucke, *Die Reußen und ihr Land*, St Michael: Bläschke, 1984, pp. 164–7; Reichstädter, 'Napoleons langer Schatten', pp. 93–4.
202. Reinhard Münch, *Als die Schwarzburger und Reußen für Napoleon fochten*, Leipzig: Engelsdorfer, 2018, pp. 105–11.
203. Bogdanovich, *Geschichte des Krieges im Jahre 1813*, vol. 2/2, p. 11.
204. FML Philipp zu Hessen-Homburg and GdK Friedrich von Hessen-Homburg, Caroline's father. Friedrich Günther's father, Ludwig Friedrich II, had died in 1807.
205. Döring, *Geschichte des 7. Thüringischen Infanterie-Regiments*, vol. I, pp. 250–4; Bernhard Schüser, *Geschichte des schwarzburg-rudolstädtischen Contingents in den Kriegsjahren von 1807 bis 1815*, Rudolstadt: Stroh, 1874, pp. 57–8; Georg Ortenburg, 'Das Militär in Schwarzburg-Rudolstadt', in *Das Schwarzburger Militär*, Rudolstadt: Thüringer Landesmuseum Heidecksburg, 1994, pp. 42–56. Strengths from SHD, 2C551, reports for 1 and 15 September 1813; also Lystrac, XP3.
206. As with the other Rheinbund states, the convoluted history of Waldeck and Pyrmont is beyond the scope of this study except to note that Pyrmont was raised from a *Grafschaft* (county) to a principality through adherence to the Rheinbund and that Georg I united the two under one rule (Karl Theodor Menke, *Pyrmont und seine Umgebungen*, Hameln & Pyrmont: Weichelt, 1840, pp. 65–7).
207. Friedrich Ludwig Freiherr von Dalwigk zu Lichtenfels, *Geschichte der waldeckischen und kurhessischen Stammtruppen des Infanterie-Regiments v. Wittich (3. Kurhess.) Nr. 83 1681–1866*, Oldenburg: Littmann, 1909, pp. 109–11. Specht (*Westphalen und seine Armee*, p. 100) erroneously states that Lippe troops were also present at Braunschweig; as noted above, however, of Lippe's three companies, two were already in Magdeburg and the other never left Lippe.

Chapter 8: The Fortress War: The Iron Yoke of Fate

1. Napoleon to Eugène, 4 February 1813, no. 32607, *CG*, vol. XII, p. 269.
2. On Napoleon and fortresses during 1813, see Frédéric Reboul, 'Napoléon et les Places d'Allemagne en 1813', *Revue d'Histoire*, vol. 42, April–June 1911.
3. Technically, Dresden was not considered a 'fortress' by early nineteenth century standards but is included here owing to its functions during these campaigns.
4. The beginning and ending dates of the various blockades and sieges are the subject of controversy, particularly as active operations halted during the summer armistice. Questions such as whether or not the months of the armistice 'count' as part a particular blockade period are beyond the scope of this study. For a discussion of this issue as it relates to Danzig, see Gustav Köhler, *Geschichte der Festungen Danzig und Weichselmünde bis zum Jahre 1814 in Verbindung mit der Kriegsgeschichte der freien Stadt Danzig*, Breslau: Koebner, 1893, vol. II, pp. 496–8.
5. Friederich, *Herbstfeldzuges*, vol. III, pp. 351–2.
6. Nearly 10,000 died in Danzig alone between January and the end of April, Prosper Honoré d'Artois, *Relation de la Défense de Danzig en 1813, par le 10e Corps de l'Armée Française, contre l'Armée Combinée Russe et Prussienne*, Paris: Ladrange, 1820, pp. 59–61.
7. 'Mittheilungen über die Vertheidigung von Danzig im Jahre 1813. Aus dem Tagebuch des königl. bayer. Obersten Kajetan Grafen von Buttler, des 13. Infanterie-Regiments', *Archiv für Offiziere aller Waffen*, vol. V, no. 3, 1848, p. 44.

8. This is a good opportunity to mention once again the invaluable study of the fortress war of 1813–14 that informs much of the following: Thomas Hemmann and Martin Klöffler, *Der Vergessene Befreiungskrieg*, 2018. Readers seeking additional information, especially regarding the instances where German troops were not involved, will benefit from consulting this work.
9. Strength report of 21 January 1813 in d'Artois, *Relation*. This chart is also published in Jacques David Martin Campredon, *Défense de Danzig en 1813*, Charles Auriol, ed., Paris: Plon, 1888. Note that Campredon, d'Artois and Richemont were all engineer officers who participated in the siege.
10. Rapp to Napoleon, 17 June 1813, in Campredon/Auriol, *Défense de Danzig*, p. 101. Quote from Rapp to Berthier, 29 January 1813 in *Gli Italiani*, pp. 576–8; this report was also printed in the *Moniteur Westphalien/Westfälische Moniteur*, no. 188, 9 July 1813. Note that the 1st Westphalian Regiment incorporated four officers and some 30 Westphalian enlisted men who happened to be in Danzig when it arrived.
11. 'Mittheilungen über die Vertheidigung von Danzig', p. 60; Bauer, letter to his brother, 23 January 1813, 'Aus dem Leben', p. 115. It is not clear how or when Bauer's letters were sent to his brother as there is no indication that such communications were permitted during the siege. Those written in the first half of the year may have been dispatched during the armistice, but the later missives likely had to await his release in December.
12. Soden, *Beiträge*, p. 62. Although a 12 March decree disbanded the 34th Division and assigned its remaining elements to the 30th Division, it is likely Rapp did not learn of this change until the armistice. It is thus convenient to use the designation '34th Division' (including the Rheinbund components) during the spring blockade. The decree is in *CdN*, no. 19698, vol. XXV, pp. 63–5.
13. The terminology used to describe the remaining Germans of the 34th Division was imprecise; it was called both a 'brigade' and a 'regiment', initially with two 'regiments' or two 'battalions' regardless of the number of soldiers (e.g., Jacobs, *Feldzüge und Schicksale*, p. 272; Meinhard, *Reußischen Militairs*, p. 408). Similarly, command arrangements were murky and the exact roles of Egloffstein and Heeringen at different times are unclear.
14. Oesterhaus, *Fürstlich Lippischen Truppen*, p. 61.
15. Bauer, letter to his brother, 5 February 1813, 'Aus dem Leben', pp. 119–20. The Bavarians do not seem to have been engaged.
16. Bernays, *Schicksale*, pp. 403–4.
17. Jean Rapp, *Memoirs of General Count Rapp*, London: Colburn & Co., 1823 (Ken Trotman reprint, Cambridge, 1985), p. 264.
18. Franz Freiherr von Soden, *Leben und Schicksale des fürstlich Schwarzburgischen Kammerherrn und Oberstlieutents Freiherrn Franz von Soden*, Nördlingen: Beck, 1871, p. 79.
19. This incident is recounted in many of the sources cited for Danzig (e.g., Köhler, *Danzig*, vol. II, pp. 257–8). From Rapp's official report to Berthier (15 February 1813 in *Gli Italiani*, pp. 579–84), his memoirs, and d'Artois's history, it is clear that 'the posts had orders to stand under arms without taking themselves forward' (*Relation*, pp. 54–6; *Memoirs*, pp. 263–4). Similarly, several contemporary German veterans specify that Heeringen acted on his own either out of a desire to cleanse his reputation from Murat's criticism, or to gain an award, or simply because of his own impulsive nature (August von Blumröder, *Meine Erlebnisse im Krieg und Frieden in der großen*

Welt und in der kleinen Welt meines Gemüths, Sondershausen: Eupel, 1857, pp. 84–5; Dornheim/Kleßmann, 'Skizzen aus den Feldzügen', p. 240; Soden, *Beiträge*, pp. 66–8). Others assert that Heeringen received an order to attack (Lichtenfels, *Stammtruppen*, pp. 103–4; Meinhard, *Reußischen Militairs*, pp. 405–7). Düring writes that Heeringen was only to make a demonstration but that the orders arrived 'inexcusably' late (*Tagebuch*, pp. 27–30). Meinhard and Schumann ('Kontingente', p. 7) also note that the Germans and Russians had been occupying Wonneberg sequentially for several days, the Russians at night and the Germans during the day as more or less a matter of routine.

20. Jacobs, *Feldzüge und Schicksale*, pp. 268–71.
21. Rapp to Berthier, 15 February 1813, in *Gli Italiani*, pp. 579–84.
22. In addition to the sources cited below, see d'Artois, *Relation*, pp. 72–80; and Köhler, vol. II, pp. 266–73 for the 5 March assault.
23. Bauer, letters to his brother, 4 and 7 March 1813, 'Aus dem Leben', pp. 120–3; and Heudelet's journal published in Louis Antoine François de Marchangy, *Le Siège de Danzig en 1813*, Paris: Chaumerot, 1814, p. 105. The French battalion under Bauer's orders seems to have been IV/21e Léger or possibly IV/28e Léger.
24. Dornheim/Kleßmann, 'Skizzen aus den Feldzügen', p. 252.
25. Düring, *Tagebuch*, pp. 34–5. German losses from 'Mittheilungen über die Vertheidigung von Danzig', p. 28; and Bernays, *Schicksale*, p. 406.
26. Rapp, *Memoirs*, pp. 270–1.
27. 'Mittheilungen über die Vertheidigung von Danzig', p. 28; Rapp to Berthier, 10 March 1813, in *Gli Italiani*, pp. 584–9; printed in *Moniteur Westphalien/Westfälische Moniteur*, no. 190, 11 July 1813. Rapp's memoirs also contain references to 'the brave Colonel Butler' of the 13th Bavarian Infantry (p. 267).
28. Dornheim/Kleßmann, 'Skizzen aus den Feldzügen', p. 247. Almost all French and German accounts remark on the prevalence of drunkenness among the Russian soldiers, especially in this battle because Ohra and the nearby suburbs were home to a number of brandy distilleries which the Russian troops plundered to such a degree that 'they became so intoxicated that they were unable to fight any more and some even fell into our hands unconscious' (Düring, *Tagebuch*, p. 35).
29. Bauer, letter to his brother, 27 March 1813, 'Aus dem Leben', p. 124; Rapp, *Memoirs*, pp. 272–6; 'Mittheilungen über die Vertheidigung von Danzig', pp. 29–30; Schubert/Vara, *K. B. 13. Infanterie-Regiments*, vol. I, pp. 298–300.
30. Rapp, *Memoirs*, pp. 272–85; Campredon/Auriol, *Défense de Danzig*, pp. 70–1. Rapp commended Bachelu and his men for the foray in a 1 May order of the day, 'Mittheilungen über die Belagerung von Danzig im Jahre 1813 nach Dokumenten, welche im Archiv des Russischen Kriegsministeriums niedergelegt sind', *Archiv für die Offiziere des Königlich Preußischen Artillerie- und Ingenieur-Korps*, vol. X, no. 20, 1846, pp. 115–16.
31. Horadam's diary in Bernays, *Schicksale*, pp. 413–15. Wiegmann (*Franzosenzeit und Befreiungskrieg*, p. 144) and Bauer (letter to his brother, 10 June 1813, 'Aus dem Leben', pp. 124–5) are among many others who note the cheering that accompanied Rapp's announcement of Napoleon's victories and the Grande Armée's progress. Soden is the only memoirist who claims not to have been encouraged by this news (*Beiträge*, pp. 106–7) but perhaps that was a subsequent adjustment.

32. Bauer, letter to his brother, 10 June 1813, 'Aus dem Leben', pp. 124–5; 'Mittheilungen über die Vertheidigung von Danzig', pp. 38–9.
33. In Marchangy, *Siège de Danzig*, p. 117; d'Artois, *Relation*, pp. 150–2; Köhler, *Danzig*, vol. II, pp. 299–305.
34. The relevant correspondance is in [Alexander of Württemberg], *Aperçu des Opérations des Troupes Alliées devant Danzig en 1813*, Leipzig: n.p., 1821, pp. 111–44; Rapp, *Memoirs*, p. 293; see also Köhler, *Danzig*, vol. II, pp. 322–7; d'Artois, *Relation*, pp. 472–5.
35. Siméon Bernard Tort, one of the garrison's medical officers during the siege, described the health problems from a contemporary medical perspective in his *Dissertation sur le typhus contagieux, qui a régné épidémiquement à Dantzick pendant le blocus et le siège de cette place dans l'année 1813*, Paris: Faculté de Médecine de Paris, 1817; Campredon/Auriol, *Défense de Danzig*, p. 82.
36. Diary of an anonymous Anhalt officer in *Die ersten Kriegszüge des Anhaltischen Regiments 1807–1814*, Dessau: Dünnhaupt, 1907, p. 90.
37. Dornheim/Kleßmann, 'Skizzen aus den Feldzügen', p. 248.
38. A former Schaumburg-Lippe voltigeur would later regale his friends with an anecdote of how he and his squad-mates captured a cat and presented it to their hostess as a 'rabbit', at which the sceptical woman replied: 'As long as it is not a roof rabbit ['*Dachhase*', German slang for a house cat].' He claimed that he and his comrades enjoyed the resulting stew (Oesterhaus, *Fürstlich Lippischen Truppen*, p. 62).
39. 'Mittheilungen über die Vertheidigung von Danzig', p. 34.
40. See, for example, Düring, *Tagebuch*, pp. 42–3. Some members of the garrison thought it meet to demonstrate to the Russians their disdain towards these proclamations, so a colonel led a detachment out to the forward pickets, had the men pull out copies of the proclamations, lay them on the ground and deface them, apparently by urination in full view of the Russian outposts. Very pleased with this bit of mischief, the detachment then returned to the city (Nicholas Louis Planat de la Faye, *Vie de Planat de la Faye, Aide-de-Camp des Généraux Lariboisière et Drouot, Officier d'Ordonnance de Napoléon Ier*, Paris: Ollendoff, 1895, p. 154).
41. Jacobs, *Feldzüge und Schicksale*, p. 276. See Campredon/Auriol, *Défense de Danzig*, pp. 79–80; Rapp, *Memoirs*, pp. 281–2. Soden cynically disparaged the Easter parade, *Beiträge*, pp. 91–3, but acknowledged Rapp's efforts: 'it must be said to the general's credit that he used every effort to keep his troops in good spirits' (p. 144).
42. Rapp to Napoleon, 17 June 1813 in Campredon/Auriol, *Défense de Danzig*, pp. 96–103.
43. Blumröder, *Erlebnisse*, p. 85; Soden, *Beiträge*, p. 75; Bernays, *Schicksale*, p. 404.
44. Blumröder, *Erlebnisse*, p. 83. Butler reported similar dismissal of Russian entreaties, Uebe, *Stimmungsumschwung*, p. 121.
45. Butler to Wrede, 14 June 1813, in Schubert/Vara, *K. B. 13. Infanterie-Regiments*, vol. I, p. 306.
46. Rapp to Berthier, 15 February 1813 in *Gli Italiani*, pp. 579–84.
47. Xylander, *Geschichte des 1. Feldartillerie-Regiments*, vol. II, pp. 391–5. Even the meticulous Xylander could only find a few details on the Bavarian artillery at Danzig.
48. Bauer, letter to his brother, 10 June 1813, 'Aus dem Leben', p. 124; Schubert/Vara, *K. B. 13. Infanterie-Regiments*, vol. I, p. 310.
49. SHD, 2C708 and Lystrac, XP3. This explains why Heudelet's after-action report mentions the combined Rheinbund battalion. Although the amalgamation of the 30th and 34th Divisions was dictated by Napoleon's 12 March decree, it is likely that

Rapp only learned of this decision when Planat de la Faye arrived with his packet of dispatches in June to announce the armistice.
50. Rapp to Berthier, 4 August 1813 in Campredon/Auriol, *Défense de Danzig*, pp. 115–16.
51. Berthier to Rapp, 5 June 1813, *Ordres*, vol. I, p. 170; Rapp to Berthier, 16 June 1813, from the English translation of his *Memoirs*, pp. 294–301, with adjustments based on the original French version (*Mémoires du Général Rapp, Premier Aide-de-Camp de Napoléon*, Paris: Bossange, 1823, pp. 296–302). See also the courier's account in Planat de la Faye, *Vie de Planat*, pp. 145–58; and his *Correspondance Intime de Planat de la Faye*, Paris: Ollendorff, 1895, pp. 66–7. Rapp's reports to Napoleon made similar points but in less detail (Campredon/Auriol, *Défense de Danzig*, pp. 96–103).
52. Köhler, *Danzig*, vol. II, pp. 348–54.
53. Jules Marnier, *Souvenirs de Guerre en Temps de Paix*, Paris: Faure, 1867, pp. 308–10 (Marnier, a *capitaine* at the time, was one of Rapp's most trusted staff officers); Campredon/Auriol, *Défense de Danzig*, pp. 188–90, 229–36 (see especially the minutes of the defence council Rapp convened on 26 November); d'Artois, *Relation*, pp. 410–12.
54. Rapp, *Memoirs*, p. 336.
55. Soden, *Beiträge*, pp. 119–20.
56. Bauer's diary published in Johann Karl Plümicke, *Skizzierte Geschichte der russisch-preußischen Blockade und Belagerung von Danzig im Jahr 1813*, Berlin: Maurer, 1817, pp. 193–4.
57. Campredon/Auriol, *Défense de Danzig*, pp. 135–6.
58. Special order of the day, 4 September 1813 in *Gli Italiani*, pp. 589–90.
59. This section on the 2–3 September actions around the 'blockhouses' is drawn from 'Mittheilungen über die Vertheidigung von Danzig', pp. 50–2; Bauer, letter to his brother, 4 September 1813, 'Aus dem Leben', p. 126–31; Bauer/Plümicke, pp. 193–8; Düring, *Tagebuch*, pp. 79–82; Campredon/Auriol, *Défense de Danzig*, pp. 134–41 (including personal notes by Rapp's aide-de-camp Marnier); Rapp, *Memoirs*, pp. 311–16; Schubert/Vara, *K. B. 13. Infanterie-Regiments*, vol. I, pp. 317–23; Baptist Schrettinger, *Das Königlich Bayerische Militär-Max-Joseph-Orden und seine Mitglieder*, Munich: Oldenbourg, 1882, pp. 213–19; Köhler, *Danzig*, vol. I, pp. 355–66.
60. Louis Auguste Camus de Richemont, *Capitulation de Danzig, Traduit d'Allemand de Plotho avec Observations Critiques*, Philippe Himly, trans., Paris: Corréard, 1841, pp. 9–10.
61. Schubert/Vara, *K. B. 13. Infanterie-Regiments*, vol. I, pp. 332–3.
62. 'Mittheilungen über die Vertheidigung von Danzig', pp. 59–60; Soden, *Leben und Schicksale*, p. 89; Soden, *Beiträge*, p. 144.
63. Jacobs, *Feldzüge und Schicksale*, p. 285.
64. 'Mittheilungen über die Vertheidigung von Danzig', pp. 65–7; d'Artois, *Relation*, pp. 411–12. Düring gives a slightly different rendition: that Rapp informed Butler of Bavaria's defection and told him that he and his regiment were free to depart; Butler would not go without specific orders from home, but also believed he could no longer fight against the Allies (Düring, *Tagebuch*, p. 132).
65. D'Artois, *Relation*, p. 412.
66. Schumann, 'Kontingente', pp. 7–8.
67. 'Mittheilungen über die Vertheidigung von Danzig', pp. 68–9. On the regard the French had for Butler, see also the comments by Rapp's aide-de-camp Marnier in his *Souvenirs*, pp. 308–12; and Casimir Stanislas d'Arpentigny, *Voyage en Pologne*

et en Russie par un Prisonnier de Guerre de la garnison de Dantzick en 1813 et 1814, Paris: Dupont, 1828, p. 4.
68. Soden, *Beiträge*, p. 147.
69. Jacobs, *Feldzüge und Schicksale*, p. 286.
70. D'Artois, *Relation*, p. 381. There were more than 4,000 of all nationalities in hospital as well, but it is not clear how many were from Rheinbund units.
71. Düring, *Tagebuch*, pp. 139–45; Soden, *Beiträge*, pp. 147–53.
72. Rapp to Michael Paira, 29 April 1814 from Kyiv, in Gaston Paira, ed., 'Lettres Inédites du Général Rapp à M. Michael Paira à Paris', *Revue d'Alsace*, vol. XII, 1883, p. 28.
73. Richemont/Himly, *Capitulation*, p. 23.
74. Düring, *Tagebuch*, pp. 36–8. See also: Soden, *Leben und Schicksale*, pp. 93–4. Auriol, editing Campredon's papers, noted (p. 78): 'The fidelity of the numerous foreigners who made up the garrison seemed a veritable phenomenon to the enemy. The sentiment of military honour, particularly lively in that epoch, sufficed to attach the officers to our banners, their dedication did not waver for an instant. But the constancy of the troops is more difficult to explain and greatly astonished the enemy, who did everything in their power to suborn them. It is to the personal attachment which the Governor knew how to inspire, it is to the breath of heroism which he made, by his example, circulate in the ranks of his small army, that was due the excellent spirit which has astonished the Russian and German writers ever since.'
75. Modlin has largely been incorporated into the modern community of Nowy Dwór Mazowiecki and the airport now covers part of the old fortress. Principal sources for this section are: 'Beiträge zur Geschichte der Blocade von Modlin vom 5. Februar 1813, bis zu deren Uebergabe den 1. December 1813; nebst Bemerkungen, Anecdoten, u.', *Minerva*, February 1835, pp. 177–269 (written by an anonymous Saxon officer of the *Niesemeuschel* Battalion based on his diary of the blockade); Richard Belostyk, 'Modlin en 1813', *Francja-Polska XVIII–XIX w.* Warsaw, Państwowe Wydawnictwo Naukowe, 1983; Hemmann/Klöffler, *vergessene Befreiungskrieg*, pp. 170–91; Piotr Oleńczak, *Napoleońskie Dziedzictwo na Mazowszu: Twierdza Modlin a Latach 1806–1830*, Warsaw: Mazowieckie Centrum Kultury, 2008, pp. 69–84. On French plans to improve the fortress in 1811–12, see Richard (Ryszard) Belostyk, 'Fortifikacja Wzorcowa Napoleona', *Przeglad Historyczny*, 71/1, 1980, pp. 91–111.
76. Bignon to Maret, 25 and 30 January 1813, Marcel Handelsman, *Instructions et Dépêches des Residents de France à Varsovie*, Krakow: Académie des Sciences de Cracovie, 1914, vol. II, pp. 346–58; Kossecki to Poniatowski, 25 January 1813, Bronisław Gembarzewski, *Wojsko Polskie: Księstwo Warszawskie 1807–1814*, Warsaw: Wolff, 1905, pp. 212–14. See also Reynier to Murat, 19 January 1813, and Schwarzenberg to Eugène, 22 January 1813, in Reboul, *Campagne de 1813*, vol. II, pp. 464–71; Louis Pierre Édouard Bignon, *Souvenirs d'un Diplomate: la Pologne (1811–1813)*, Paris: Dentu, 1864, pp. 278–9.
77. 'Beiträge', *Minerva*, pp. 183–91; extracts of Kossecki's reports and those of the French chief engineer in Belostyk, 'Modlin en 1813'; Hochberg, *Denkwürdigkeiten*, p. 214; as well as J. D., *Notice sur le Général de Division Prévost de Vernois*, Paris: Dumaine, 1860, pp. 85–97.
78. Handelsman, *Instructions et Dépêches*, vol. II, p. 358.
79. Eugène to Reynier, 19 January 1813, Reboul, *Campagne de 1813*, vol. II, pp. 461–2; Łukasiewicz, *Armia księcia Józefa*, pp. 100–2.
80. Cerrini, *Feldzüge der Sachsen*, pp. 116–17; Larraß, *6. Infanterie-Regiments*, pp. 52–3.

81. Russian accounts of the blockade claim another sortie took place on 27 April (Hemmann/Klöffler, *vergessene Befreiungskrieg*, pp. 179–80).
82. 'Die Leiden der sächsischen Besatzung der Festung Modlin: Kriegsgefangenschaft und Rückmarsch 1813–14', *Der Kamerad*, 1863, p. 262. The writer states that the Würzburg soldiers were not selected.
83. Belostyk, 'Modlin en 1813', pp. 282–3. The *Moniteur* printed a brief missive from Daendels highlighting this episode but presenting an overly cheery image of the garrison's condition (no. 189, 8 July 1813).
84. 'Leiden der sächsischen Besatzung', p. 254. This unnamed Saxon soldier recalled being forced to rely on the 'black, swampy water of the Narew or even the disgusting, filthy water of the Vistula' when the fortress's only well failed (p. 261).
85. 'Beiträge', *Minerva*, p. 202.
86. Johann Michael Zimmermann, 'Aufzeichnungen eines Veteranen aus der Zeit 1806–1814', *Das Bayernland*, vol. 22, no. 6, 1911, p. 61.
87. 'Beiträge', *Minerva*, p. 197; Belostyk, 'Modlin en 1813', p. 289.
88. The French engineer, Colonel Simon Pierre Nicolas Prévost de Vernois, at one point tried to convince Kossecki and the other Polish officers to lock the fortress gates when Daendels went to confer with the Russians; the Poles, however, demurred (D., *Prévost de Vernois*, p. 91).
89. Daendels to King William, 4 December 1813, Isidore Mendels, *Herman Willem Daendels, voor zijne Benoeming tot Gouverneur-General van Oost-Indië (1762–1807)*, 's-Gravenhage: Nijhoff, 1890, Bejlage LVI/E, pp. 202–3. The officer who maintained the fortress's journal opined that, 'this was the end of the Modlin fortress, which could still have held out for some time or which could at least have gained a more favourable surrender...' (Łukasiewicz, *Armia księcia Józefa*, pp. 326–7).
90. Eichelsbacher, 'Würzburger Truppen', p. 290.
91. This section on Küstrin relies on 'Fortresse de Küstrin', pp. 21–61; the German translation and commentary in Hartmann, 'Festung Cüstrin', pp. 294–340; [Johann Friedrich Gieße], 'Belagerung und Wiedereinnahme Küstrins 1813/14', Thoma, ed., *Schriften des Vereins für Geschichte der Neumark*, vol. 41, 1923, (attribution to Gieße courtesy of Thomas Hemmann); Hemmann/Klöffler, *vergessene Befreiungskrieg*, pp. 230–7; and K. W. Kutschbach, *Chronik der Stadt Küstrin*, Küstrin, Enslin, 1849, pp. 228–43.
92. The 15 April and 15 August 'Livrets de Situation' (SHD, 2C706 and 2C708) prepared for Napoleon listed 77 men of the 6th Rheinbund, but a 'Recapitulation' dated 5 August (SHD, 2C551) shows no Rheinbund troops at all and there is no indication in any other source (such as the spring siege journals in SHD, 2C168) that they were a factor in the blockade or that they were even present. On the blockade of Stettin in general, see Hemmann/Klöffler, *vergessene Befreiungskrieg*, pp. 250–61.
93. 'Fortresse de Küstrin', p. 41; Fornier d'Albe to Berthier, 12 June 1813 in *Le Moniteur Universel*, no. 178, 27 June 1813 (this issue also contains a 10 June report from the chief engineer, Major Blanc); [Gieße], 'Belagerung und Wiedereinnahme Küstrins', p. 14.
94. Schrader in Berg, 'Erfahrungen und Schicksale', p. 35.
95. Fornier d'Albe to Berthier, 12 June 1813, in *Le Moniteur Universel*, no. 178, 27 June 1813.
96. 'Journal des opérations et travaux', SHD GR 1 VN 83.
97. Journal entry for 23 October, 'Journal des opérations et travaux ordonnés et éxécutés dans la place de Custrin', SHD GR 1 VN 83; 'Fortresse de Küstrin', p. 46.

98. Schrader, in Berg, 'Erfahrungen und Schicksale', p. 40.
99. Schrader, in Berg, 'Erfahrungen und Schicksale', p. 52; and [Gieße], 'Belagerung und Wiedereinnahme Küstrins', p. 19.
100. Schrader, in Berg, 'Erfahrungen und Schicksale', p. 50. According to Schrader, the French officers feared that desertion would increase when winter brought the freezing of the Oder and Warthe (pp. 51–2).
101. Journal entry for 2 December, 'Journal des opérations et travaux', SHD GR 1 VN 83; [Gieße], 'Belagerung und Wiedereinnahme Küstrins', pp. 18–27; 'Fortresse de Küstrin', p. 63.
102. The garrison's journal claimed that sickness rates were much higher among the non-French troops as compared to the French and regarded the numbers hospitalised as a sign of the poor morale among the non-French contingents (Journal entry for 3 January, 'Journal des opérations et travaux', SHD GR 1 VN 83).
103. ‚Situation de la garnison de Custrin au 18 mars 1814', in 'Journal des opérations et travaux', SHD GR 1 VN 83; [Gieße], 'Belagerung und Wiedereinnahme Küstrins', pp. 18–27; 'Fortresse de Küstrin', p. 63.
104. [Gieße], 'Belagerung und Wiedereinnahme Küstrins', pp. 20–7; 'Fortresse de Küstrin', p. 52; Friccius, *Blockade Cüstrins*, p. 43; Hartmann, 'Festung Cüstrin', p. 331.
105. Gaupp's reports from 22 February 1813 to 24 March 1814, in LABWHStA, E 270a Bü 231.
106. Suckow, *Soldatenleben*, pp. 341–6.
107. This is the figure given in the emperor's 15 August 'Livret de Situation' (SHD, 2C708); Bagès lists 1,034 ('Le Siège de Glogau', p. 275). The published version of Nempde's report, on the other hand, gives a figure of 1,304 (*Blocus et Sièges de Glogau*, p. 36) and this appears in most other sources.
108. Bernays, *Schicksale*, p. 449–51. These are taken from a diary kept by an unidentified Frankfurt officer, probably one of the battalion commanders.
109. Nempde, *Blocus et Sièges de Glogau*, p. 46; Bagès, 'Le Siège de Glogau', pp. 278–83; Bernays, *Schicksale*, pp. 449–63. On the rockets, see, Dietrich, *Groß Glogaus Schicksale*, p. 204.
110. Quoted in Brun, *Oubliés*, pp. 189. Much of the correspondence between Laplane and the besiegers as well as Laplane's orders of the day can be found in Dietrich, *Groß Glogaus Schicksale*, pp. 206–35.
111. Dietrich, *Groß Glogaus Schicksale*, pp. 167–8, 225–6 (the letter was undated). Bernays gives 7 January 1814 as the date for the letter from the Frankfurt officers to Laplane (*Schicksale*, pp. 460–1); it is not clear when or how this letter was delivered.
112. Nempde wrote that Laplane decided 'to facilitate desertion by a new disposition of duties' (*Blocus et Sièges de Glogau*, p. 57) at this perilous point in mid-January, presumably by leaving gaps in the guard posts or placing foreign troops in areas from which they could easily slip away.
113. Quotes from Nempde, *Blocus et Sièges de Glogau*, pp. 45–62; general course of events from Brun, *Oubliés*, pp. 173–97; and Bagès, 'Le Siège de Glogau', pp. 277–89, 381–9. See also extracts from Laplane's report in Joseph Auguste Constant Schmitt, *Historique du 151ᵉ Régiment d'Infanterie*, n. p,: n. p., 1901, pp. 62–77.
114. Or a quarter if we grant the regiment a strength of 1,304. See the charts in Brun, *Oubliés*, pp. 258–9. For the conscript Saxon gunners: French inspection report, 13 July 1813, AN, AF/IV/1661A, Plaquette 1.

115. This section draws heavily on the official reports in the French archives (SHD, 2C168) along with Antoine Marie Augoyat, *Relation de la Défense de Torgau par les Troupes Françaises en 1813 sous les Généraux de Division Comte de Narbonne et Comte Du Taillis*, Paris: Leneveu, 1840. Augoyat follows the siege journals very closely and a German translation with some commentary is available as 'Die Belagerung von Torgau 1813', *Archiv für die Offiziere der Königlich Preußischen Artillerie- und Ingenieur-Korps*, vol. VI, no. 12, 1841. See also Hemmann/Klöffler, *vergessene Befreiungskrieg*, pp. 366–81; and various essays in Niedersen, *Sachsen, Preußen und Napoleon*.
116. Torgau 'Situation', 25 September 1813, SHD, 2C551 and Lystrac, XP3.
117. Durrieu to Berthier, 24 October 1813 and other correspondence, Le Ploge, *Torgau*, pp. 6–13; 'Journal du Siège de Torgau', SHD, 2C168.
118. Colonel Bernard, report of 9 January 1814; and 'Journal du Siège de Torgau', SHD, 2C168.
119. 'Journal du Siège de Torgau'; and Colonel Claude Pierre Ferdinand Girod de Novilars, 'Journal Historique', 9 January 1814; both SHD, 2C168.
120. 'Journal du Siège de Torgau'; GB François Louis Bouchu, 'Journal abrigé du blocus et siège de Torgau', 31 December 1813; and 'Rapport de Monsieur le Général Brun de Villeret Baron de l'Empire sur la Défense de la Place Torgau', 11 January 1814; all SHD, 2C168.
121. 'Journal du Siège de Torgau'; Girod de Novilars, 'Journal Historique'; Brun, 'Rapport'; all SHD, 2C168. Note that Maillot reported a strength of 2,300 on 5 October, but French reports generally credit him with only 1,100– 1,200, *see* Chart 26.
122. The Würzburg Battalion had also been employed to man blockhouses between Torgau and Meissen during part of September with 70 men per blockhouse (Reiset to Marmont, 29 September 1813, Fabry, *Empereur II*, Documents, p. 164).
123. 'Journal du Siège de Torgau', SHD, 2C168. On 1 November, five of these battalions would be combined into three provisional 'Torgau Regiments' (the 1st Torgau Battalion, composed of Imperial Guardsmen, remained independent), but the results were far below what the French generals had hoped to achieve; German troops were not included in these regiments (details in SHD, 23YC251).
124. Bigge, *2. Großherzoglich Hessisches*, pp. 191–2. A Prussian source states that Prussian troops overthrew Hessian defenders on the left bank north of Torgau on 5 October, well before the fortress was truly blockaded; but no such action appears in the Hessian regimental histories: J. L. Vogel, *Belagerungen von Torgau und Wittenberg 1813 und 1814*, Berlin: Nauck, 1844, p. 15.
125. Durrieu, 'Rapport de Général Durrieu sur ce qui s'est passé dans la brigade dite du Camp depuis la fin d'Octobre jusqu'au 27 Décembre 1813'; and 'Journal du Siège de Torgau', SHD, 2C168.
126. Joseph Antoine Auguste Masnou, 'Histoire Médicale du Siège de Torgau, en Saxe', *Journal de Médicine, Chirurgie, Pharmacie, etc.*, vols. XXXV–XXXVI, June–July 1816, p. 98.
127. Brun, *Cahiers*, pp. 162–7.
128. Dutaillis to Berthier, 10 January 1814, SHD, 2C168. The later medical staff calculation was 15,448 (Masnou, 'Histoire Médicale', vol. XXXVI, July 1816, pp. 204–5). See also Georg August Richter, *Medizinische Geschichte der Belagerung und Einnahme der Festung Torgau und Beschreibung der Epidemie welche daselbst in den Jahren 1813 und 1814 herrscht*, Berlin: Nicolai, 1814. For a modern medical analysis that includes many of the

frightening statistics, see Dr Karsten Dohm, *Die Typhusepidemie in der Festung Torgau 1813–1814*, Düsseldorf: Triltsch, 1987.
129. 'Journal du Siège de Torgau', SHD, 2C168; 'Tagebuch des Gardefusiliers Regiment', HStAD Best. G 61 N2. 31/1.
130. Augoyat, *Défense de Torgau*, pp. 65–6; 'Tagebuch des Gardefusiliers Regiment', HStAD Best. G 61 N2. 31/1; Bigge, *2. Großherzoglich Hessisches*, pp. 192–5; Chroust, *Geschichte des Großherzogtums*, p. 367; Eichelbacher, 'Würzburger Truppen', p. 273; Bernays, *Schicksale*, p. 462. The two battalion commanders were released three days later on 28 November; the French siege journals, however, make no mention of such an incident. Cerrini remarks that German troops 'came over to us' almost daily after the 2 November sortie, but he erroneously places the date of the Saxon release from Torgau as 4 November rather than 24 October (*Feldzüge der Sachsen*, p. 340). On 20 November, the Hessians had 314 men fit for duty in the 2nd Augmentation Battalion and 134 in the II/Garde-Fusiliers plus 79 and 50 sick respectively; the Würzburg/Frankfurt battalion had 349 under arms and 317 sick (SHD, 13C85).
131. The French also left behind a legend of hidden treasure. When Durrieu arrived with the Grande Armée's administrative and baggage train, rumours immediately appeared claiming that the French had hidden the army's cash reserves somewhere in Torgau. After the city's fall, Prussian soldiers who had not been paid apparently cited this supposed treasure in an effort to demand their backpay from their officers; Durrieu, now a Prussian prisoner, even felt it necessary to debunk this myth in a 4 May 1814 report back to Paris from Berlin (SHD, 2C168): See K. H. Petri, *Vor 65 Jahren in und um Torgau*, Torgau: Fügner, 1879, pp. 28–9.
132. Juhel, 'Dresden 1813', in *Blutige Romantik*, pp. 99–100.
133. Raymond-Aimery-Philippe-Joseph de Montesquiou Fezensac, *Souvenirs Militaires de 1804 à 1814*, Paris: Dumaine, 1870, p. 504.
134. Napoleon to Gouvion Saint-Cyr, 7 October 1813, no. 36687, *CG*, vol. XIV, p. 740.
135. Carl August Weinhold, *Dresden und seine Schicksale, im Jahre 1813*, Dresden: Arnold, 1814, p. 56. On illness and wretched medical care, see Anton Friedrich Fischer, 'Geschichtliche Darstellung der im Herbst 1813 in Dresden ausgebrochenen und bis gegen Ende Januars 1814 angedauerten Epidemie', *Annalen der Heilkunst des Jahres 1814*, pp. 81–94. Conditions in the hospitals had been frightful even in September, see Praun's observations in Chapter 3.
136. Lindau, *Darstellung*, p. 177; Taggesell, *Tagebuch eines Dresdner Bürgers*, p. 177.
137. Mathieu Dumas, *Souvenirs du Lieutenant Général Mathieu Dumas de 1770 à 1836*, Paris: Gosselin, 1839, p. 535; Gouvion Saint-Cyr, *Mémoires*, vol. IV, p. 245; Brandt, *Dresden*, p. 380.
138. See Moritz Edlen von Angeli, 'Die Capitulation von Dresden 1813', *Mittheilungen des K. K. Kriegsarchivs*, 1881. The Prussian official history notes that the Allied refusal to accept the capitulation, if not technically a violation of the 'norms of warfare' common to the era, 'must at least be described and deplored as unchivalrous' (Friederich, *Herbstfeldzuges*, vol. III, p. 358).
139. Gouvion Saint-Cyr, *Mémoires*, vol. IV, pp. 245–7. The exact date of the Saxon departure is not clear: it was some time between 29 October and 1 November. Saint-Cyr apparently offered the Saxons the opportunity to take service with France, but none accepted (Lindau, *Darstellung*, pp. 168–9).

140. Gouvion Saint-Cyr, *Mémoires*, vol. IV, p. 245; Xylander, *Geschichte des 1. Feldartillerie-Regiments*, vol. II, p. 391. Saint-Cyr wrote that they were released on request when they learned that Bavaria had changed sides.
141. Gouvion Saint-Cyr, *Mémoires*, vol. IV, p. 245; Pierre Berthezène, *Souvenirs Militaires de la République et de l'Empire*, Paris: Dumaine, 1855, p. 291.
142. Normann, *Aus den Papieren*, pp. 16–17. The alleged '*Tagebuch*' (diary) of a supposed Westphalian lieutenant named F. L. Wagner must also be mentioned in relation to Dresden. 'Wagner' claims that he was assigned to the Dresden garrison as part of the '2nd Leib-Garde Regiment', pithily writing 'Much duty, frequent desertion' and stating that the dearth of food increased desertion. According to this 'diary', he and three other lieutenants led a detachment of 170 men to defect on 15 October during a sortie by the garrison. Unfortunately, this piece must be treated with great caution as it is replete with discrepancies even though parts seem consistent with known history. For example, Lünsmann's lists of officers (*Ranglisten*) do not give a 'Wagner' for any of the units stationed in Dresden (1st Light Battalion, 2nd and 3rd Infantry) nor for the Garde-Fusiliers (assuming this is the unit meant by '2nd Leib-Garde' and assuming that 'Wagner' somehow remained in the city when that regiment departed). Similarly, the other three lieutenants he mentions by name do not appear in Lünsmann for any of the relevant regiments. Wagner's biographic sketch mentions service with the Austrian *Deutschmeister* Infantry Regiment, no. 4 as an ensign (*Fähnrich*) in 1809, but he is not in either the 1808 or 1810 official Austrian 'Schematismus' of serving officers, nor does he appear in the regimental history. It is possible that his name was Riquet/Riquette and that he was using 'Wagner' as an alias for some reason: Lünsmann does give a 'Riquet' with the Garde-Fusiliers who seems to match some of Wagner's profile and a 'Riquette' appears as a lieutenant in the Prussian 12th Infantry in 1815 as stated in 'Wagner's' biographic sketch. In any event, the piece is worth consulting with these caveats in mind: 'Tagebuch des Königlich Westfälischen Leutnants F. L. Wagner aus den Jahren 1809 bis 1813', H. Heimke-Duderstadt, ed., *JdAM*, vol. 111, 1899.
143. Gouvion Saint-Cyr to Napoleon, 28 October 1813, *Mémoires*, vol. IV, pp. 466–7; Morgenstern, *Kriegserinnerungen*, pp. 128–9. Bernard's harsh words and insults when his offer was rejected almost led to a duel between him and one of the Westphalian officers. Although many early histories state that the Westphalians and Saxons were disarmed at the same time, the evidence of Morgenstern's and Normann's memoirs shows that the Westphalians, at least most of the officers, remained in the city after the Saxons had departed and indeed until the very end. See, for example, Lindau, *Darstellung*, pp. 168–9; and Friedrich Richter, *Geschichte des Deutschen Freiheitskrieges vom Jahre 1813 bis zum Jahre 1815*, Berlin: self-published, 1838, p. 544.
144. Napoleon was well aware that sending French troops to Königstein was a sensitive issue for the Saxons and he approached it most delicately with GL von Gersdorff; they were able to resolve it without generating new recriminations (Falkenstein, 'Gersdorff', pp. 41–3).
145. Ingo Busse, 'Die Festung Königstein als "Rheinbundfestung"', in Niedersen, *Sachsen, Preußen und Napoleon*, pp. 335–42; and extensive personal communication from Herr Busse (qualified museologist and research associate at Festung Königstein), who generously provided otherwise inaccessible information.
146. As with Maurellian in Thorn, the experiences outlined here reaffirmed the observations of an anonymous officer writing in 1822: '...*the commandant and his staff*

are the heart of every fortress defence' ('Gedanken über die Belagerung der Festung Thorn', p. 365, italics in the original).
147. The wisdom of Napoleon's fortress strategy writ large is a separate question beyond the scope of this study. As recounted earlier, the Coalition temporarily suspended food supplies to the fortresses during the armistice in retaliation for the attack on Lützow's band at Kitzen in June. This has led to claims that the suspension hastened the surrender of the fortresses (e.g., Brecher, *Überfall*, p. 100), but this is a canard given that many of the garrisons held out until Napoleon's abdication.

Epilogue

1. Napoleon to Daru, 15 November 1813, no. 37601, *CG*, vol. XIV, p. 908.
2. Kreuzwendedich, *Geschichte des Infanterie-Regiments Prinz Louis*, pp. 41–51.
3. Among these was Capitaine Theodor von Papet, formerly of the 3rd Westphalian Line, who by late September had found a slot among the Coalition forces in the newly created Hanoverian Landwehr in his old rank. Sadly, Papet's diary skips over the first half of 1813, so we do not know how he came to join the Allies, that is, whether he defected (assuming he stayed with his old regiment, he may have been one of those who slipped away while assigned to the Dresden garrison) or changed sides after being captured. Papet, 'Tagebuch', http://amg.hypotheses.org/quellen/papet-1813-14 [accessed May 2023].
4. Nicolas Bourguinat, 'Présentation', and Anika Bethan, 'La Réception Mémorielle de la Campagne de Russie des Soldats Westphaliennes après 1813', pp. 111–16, 177–84.
5. Franz Freiherr von Andlaw, *Mein Tagebuch: Auszüge aus Aufschreibungen der Jahre 1811 bis 1861*, Frankfurt: Sauerländer's Verlag, 1862, vol. I, p. 41; Funck, *In Russland und Sachsen*, pp. 247–9. 'The looming fall of the conqueror evoked an irresistible feeling of relief mixed with malicious glee,' writes Junkelmann (*Napoleon und Bayern*, pp. 158–9).
6. Andlaw is but one of many examples (*Mein Tagebuch*, vol. I, pp. 32–7); see Poßelt, *Grande Armée*, pp. 274–8. An official in Berg wrote to Stein to protest the 'incalculable misfortune' inflicted on the populace by 'the innumerable hordes of Cossacks' (quoted in Kandil, 'Befreiungskrieg in Westfalen', pp. 207–8); and a Nassau official referred to the Coalition as 'the new tyrants' (Ulmann, 'Hessen-Darmstadt am Scheideweg', p. 294).
7. Stein and other pan-Germanist zealots were acidic in their scorn for governments that did not display what they considered sufficient zeal and alacrity in raising new troops (Wilhelm Just, *Verwaltung und Bewaffnung im westlichen Deutschland nach der Leipziger Schlacht 1813 und 1814*, Göttingen: Vandehoeck & Ruprecht, 1911, pp. 82–5).
8. Planert, 'Kehrseite', pp. 145–51; and her 'Das Militär als Zwangsanstalt', p. 224–40. She notes, for instance, that villagers in Baden mocked the 'festival foolishness' of the local Landwehr. See also Hagemann, 'Männlicher Muth', p. 401; James, *Witnessing*, p. 81.
9. Roger Dufraisse, 'À Propos des Guerres de Délivrance Allemandes de 1813: Problèmes et Faux Problèmes', in *L'Allemagne à l'Époque Napoléonienne*, p. 475; Kitchen, *Modern Germany*, p. 22; Echternkamp, *Aufstieg*, pp. 219–20; Ibbeken, *Preußen*, pp. 401–2.
10. For H. W. Smith, the idea of 1813 as a German war of liberation fought by and for the people 'belongs to the realm of nationalist myth-making' ('Nation and Nationalism', p. 237). In addition to the sources cited in the Prologue, see the Einleitung by Hofbauer and Rink in their *Völkerschlacht*, pp. 1–24; Sheehan *German History*, p. 386;

Echternkamp, *Aufstieg*, pp. 222–4; Nipperdey, *Germany*, pp. 69–70; Peter Brandt, 'Die Befreiungskriege von 1813 bis 1815 in der deutschen Geschichte', in Michael Güttner, Rüdiger Hachtmann and Heinz-Gerhard Haupt, eds, *Geschichte und Emanzipation*, Frankfurt: Primus, 1999, p. 41; and Bernhard Struck and Claire Gantet, *Revolution, Krieg und Verflechtung 1789–1815*, Darmstadt: Wissenschaftliche Buchgesellschaft, 2008, p. 116.

11. See among others: Nipperdey, *Germany*, pp. 19, 69–70; Ibbeken, *Preußen*, pp. 413–14; Börner, 'Krise und Ende des Rheinbundes', pp. 14–19; Echternkamp, *Aufstieg*, pp. 14, 216–19; Breuilly, 'Response to Napoleon and German Nationalism', pp. 271–5; Planert, 'Dichtung und Wahrheit', in Hofbauer/Rink, *Völkerschlacht*, p. 276; and H. W. Smith, *Germany*, pp. 171–87 (with interesting nuances). Hughes notes that there was no 'national dynasty' around which pan-German sentiment could coalesce (*Nationalism and Society*, pp. 1–7, 31); the Hohenzollerns of Prussia clearly did not qualify. See also the Prologue of this study.

12. Roger Dufraisse, 'Le Grand Soulèvement de 1813', *Historia Spécial*, no. 12, July–August 1991.

13. On modernisation as a source for insecurity and protest, see sources cited in the Prologue.

14. August Wilhelm Rehberg, *Zur Geschichte des Königreichs Hannover in den ersten Jahren nach der Befreiung von der westphälischen und französischen Herrschaft*, Göttingen: Bandenhoeck & Ruprecht, 1826, pp. 7–8. This came to my attention owing to Mustafa, *Paper Kingdom*, pp. 307–8.

15. Holzhausen, *Deutschen in Rußland*, p. XI. With thanks to Leighton James for calling this to my attention in his 'German Soldiers in Russia 1812', Introductory Text to the Exhibition of www.mwme.eu (2015), http://www.mwme.eu/essays/index.html [accessed January 2023].

16. Karen Hagemann, 'Occupation, Mobilization, and Politics: The Anti-Napoleonic Wars in Prussian Experience, Memory, and Historiography', *Central European History*, vol. 39, 2006, p. 594; Poßelt, *Auf gegen Napoleon*, pp. 198–9.

17. Falkenstein, 'Gersdorff', p. 44; Meier, *Erinnerungen*, p. 120.

18. Odeleben, *Napoleons Feldzug*, pp. 59–60.

19. From the 'Genealogischer Staatskalendar auf das Jahr 1813', in Rieger, 'Stimmung und Haltung', p. 34.

20. Zeppelin to Friedrich, 14 February 1813, Schloßberger, 'starker Konflikt'; Franquemont, 21 April 1813, in Pfister, *Lager des Rheinbundes*, p. 221.

21. Such as the Hessians joking with French gunners at Bautzen or as happened when officers of the 12[e] and 75[e] Ligne in Magdeburg hosted Hessian officers whose unit was en route to Danzig in 1811 (Keim, *Geschichte des Infanterie-Leibregiments Grossherzogin*, p. 202).

22. As Rheinbund stragglers related to Westphalian appellate judge Gottfried Philipp von Bülow as they made their way west after Dennewitz; see his *Rückblicke auf mein Leben*, Helmstedt: Flackeisen, 1844, pp. 89–90.

23. See, for example, Lintner, *Im Kampf*, p. 91.

24. It is useful to remember that the Coalition could indulge in propaganda and deception as well as the French, such as initially portraying Lützen as a battlefield success, a fallacy that contributed to delay in Saxony returning to the French alliance (Chapter 2, and Taggesell, *Tagebuch eines Dresdner Bürgers*, pp. 102–4).

25. Senfft to Watzdorf, 4 April 1813, in Oncken, *Oesterreich und Preußen*, vol. II, p. 260.
26. Franquemont, private report, 10 September 1813, LABWHStA, E 270a Bü 237; and Schlaich, letter of 8 September 1813 with 10 September postscript, *Interessante Scene*, p. 143–5.
27. Diary note of 13 May 1813, quoted in James, *Witnessing*, pp. 76–7.
28. Block, *Sachsen im Zeitalter der Völkerschlacht*, p. 64; 'abstraction' from Gretschel/Bülau, *Sächsischen Volkes*, p. 452.
29. As Hagemann points out and as is evident in this survey, the loyalties of the various Rheinbund states and their populations could oppose as well as promote the ideas of a federal pan-German political configuration ('Männlicher Muth', pp. 29–30); Arnold, 'Westphalian Soldiers', p. 3.
30. James, *Witnessing*, p. 9. He describes German-speaking Europe as 'polycratic' at the time. See also Pierre Branda's Preface to Baustian, *Le royaume de Westphalie*, pp. 11–12.
31. Brandt, 'Die Befreiungskriege', in Grüttner/Hachtmann/Haupt, eds, *Geschichte und Emanzipation*, p. 34; Echternkamp, *Aufstieg*, pp. 178–83. H. W. Smith notes the regional variations, arguing cogently that the 'starkest hues and deepest grounding' of German nationalism 'remained Prussian in origin and aspiration' ('Nation and Nationalism', p. 237).
32. H. W. Smith, 'Nation and Nationalism', pp. 234–6. He concludes that 'The birth of German nationalism, *as an ideology widely shared*, cannot be deduced from the raw experience of the Wars of Revolution and the subsequent Napoleonic invasion' (emphasis added).
33. Planert, 'Collaboration to Resistance', pp. 694–705; Aaslestad/Hagemann, 'Collaboration, Resistance, and Reform', pp. 569–70; Hippler, 'Problematicher Nationalismus', p. 115. See also: Berryman, 'Boundaries of Loyalty', pp. 5–18; Bleyer, *Auf gegen Napoleon*, pp. 134–5; and Schuck/Gantet, *Revolution, Krieg und Verflechtung*, pp. 115–17. Shanahan goes so far as to argue that 'a strong sense of state identity' developed in south Germany 'as a result of the Rheinbund' ('Neglected Source', p. 122).
34. Wolffersdorff, 'Meine Erlebnisse', pp. 23–4.
35. Proclamation to the Army, 3 May 1813, *CdN*, no. 19952, vol. XXV, p. 262.
36. John Breuilly, *Austria, Prussia and the Making of Germany 1806–1871*, Harlow: Pearson, 2011, Chapter 2.
37. Sheehan observes that even Napoleon's Russian defeat did not produce 'clear convictions about the future' (*German History*, p. 313).
38. Clausewitz, *Hinterlassene Werke*, vol. VII, p. 283.
39. Quoted in Sheehan, *German History*, p. 401. Ute Planert highlights how monarchs of the small German states used post-war memorialisation activities to legitimate their continued rule ('Auf dem Weg zum Befreiungskrieg: Das Jubiläum als Mythenstifter. Die Reinterpretation der Napoleonischen Zeit in den Rheinbundstaaten', in Winfried Müller, ed., *Das historische Jubiläum: Genese, Ordnungsleistung und Inszenierungsgeschichte eines institutionellen Mechanismus*, Münster: Lit, 2004, pp. 195–219).
40. Józef Grabowski, a staff officer with imperial headquarters, recalled listening to the conversations of Rheinbund officers who believed that 'their honour and their conscience no longer permitted them to fight against their compatriots and to support French domination of Germany' (*Mémoires Militaires 1812–1813–1814*, Paris: La Vouivre, 1997, p. 63). Grabowski's memory is likely correct, but his experience stands in contrast

to the majority of Rheinbund officers and men who saw their honour tied to obedience to their monarchs and thus to the French alliance.
41. Leighton James remarks on 'the continued relevance of aristocratic warfare' in this era with 'the traditional aristocratic emphasis on honour' and the importance of 'occupational pride and sense of status' among officers (*Witnessing*, pp. 192–3).
42. Bernays (hardly a Napoleon-apologist), thus wrote regarding the Rheinbund troops in Danzig: 'It deserves to be stated that from the numerous diaries of that time which are available to us, not a single one dares to make political observations of any kind, so that it is impossible to assert that any great German ideas had found an entrance into the minds of the German troops' (*Schicksale*, p. 418).
43. Soden, *Beiträge*, p. 75.
44. See Chapters 2, 3, 4 and 5; Praun, 'Tagebücher', BayHStA, HS 743.
45. Falkenstein, 'Gersdorff', p. 41.
46. As Mustafa points out, conflicted emotions also applied to civilians (*Paper Kingdom*, p. 311).
47. Mustafa, *Paper Kingdom*, pp. 307–8, paraphrasing justice Rehberg.
48. Fisher, *Napoleonic Statesmanship*, p. 378.
49. Owzar, 'L'Historiographie Allemande', pp. 124–6; and Bethan, 'Réception Mémorielle', p. 179.
50. See Planert, 'Auf dem Weg' for a discussion of post-war use of the Napoleonic experience.
51. At the Congress of Vienna, the smaller German states were keen to see Saxony preserved as a counterbalance to Prussia (Siegel/Janke, 'Sachsen und Napoleon 1806 bis 1813', in Hofbauer/Rink, *Völkerschlacht*, p. 242).
52. Wolffersdorff, 'Meine Erlebnisse', p. 24.
53. Winfried Müller, 'Das Ende des Alten Reiches und die deutschen Territorien: Sachsens Weg in den Rheinbund und zur Königskrone', in Martin/Vötsch/Wiegand, eds, *200 Jahre Königreich Sachsen*, pp. 56–7.
54. Sheehan writes that 'Napoleonic Germany would survive the defeat of its creator' (*German History*, p. 322); or in Driault's tart phrasing: 'The Germany of 1806 remained, the Germany born at Jena, the Germany of Napoleon' (*Chute de l'Empire*, p. 191). One of the best and tidiest summaries is Schmitt, 'Germany without Prussia', pp. 38–9. See also Tim Blanning, 'Napoleon and German Identity', *History Today*, April 1998, p. 38.

Appendix 1
Synoptic Tables of Battles and Sieges/Blockades

(overleaf)

Rheinbund Participation in Major Battles of 1813

	Möckern 3–5 Apr.	Lützen 2 May	Bautzen 20–21 May	Großbeeren 23 Aug.	Dresden 25–26 Aug.	Katzbach 26 Aug.	Hagelberg 27 Aug.	Kulm 29–30 Aug.	Dennewitz 6 Sept.	Wartenburg 3 Oct.	Leipzig 16–19 Oct.
Saxony			•	•	•				•		•
Bavaria			•						•		•
Württemberg			•		•				•	•	•
Baden		•	•			•					•
Hesse		•	•							•	•
Westphalia		•	•	•	•	•			•	•	•
Frankfurt		•									
Würzburg	•	•			•		•		•		
Saxon Duchies											
Anhalt								•			•
Berg		•	•								

Note: • simply indicates the presence of elements from the contingent on the battlefield. In some cases, the number of troops was very small, and those present were not always engaged in active combat (e.g., the tiny Hessian remnant with the Imperial Guard at Möckern in April or the lone Bavarian battalion in the rear at Leipzig). Some Westphalian artillery were likely present at Bautzen (with 6th Corps).

Synoptic Tables of Battles and Sieges/Blockades 509

Rheinbund Participation in Sieges/Blockades (1813–14)

	Danzig Jan. 1813–Jan. 1814	Thorn Feb.–Apr. 1813	Glogau 1 Feb.–May 1813	Glogau 2 Aug. 1813–May 1814	Küstrin Mar. 1813–Mar. 1814	Torgau Nov. 1813–Jan. 1814	Magdeburg Nov. 1813–May 1814	Dresden Oct.–Nov. 1813	Modlin Feb.–Dec. 1813
Saxony	•		•					•	•
Bavaria	•	•						•	
Württemberg	•								
Baden			•						
Hesse									
Westphalia	•					•		•	•
Würzburg					•	•			
Frankfurt	•			•		•			
Saxon Duchies	•						•		
Anhalt	•								
Lippe	•						•		
Reuß	•						•		
Schwarzburg	•						•		
Waldeck	•								

Note: end dates of the sieges/blockades indicate when the last French forces left each fortress. In some cases, the Rheinbund troops departed before the French (e.g., Magdeburg). Isolated individuals (*isolées* to the French) are not noted.

Appendix 2
Draft Evasion, Desertion and Defection

ONE OF THE MOST DIFFICULT PROBLEMS associated with the Rheinbund experience in 1813 is untangling the claims and assumptions regarding draft evasion, desertion and defection among the various contingents. Draft evasion and desertion were vexing challenges for governmental authorities in all countries during the Revolutionary and Napoleonic eras. They remain vexing challenges for historians today. The relevant data are often hard to locate, imprecise, inconsistent over time, or absent altogether. Moreover, the source material may be misleading. Civil officials, for instance, might under-report draft evasion so as not to appear incompetent for failing to meet their conscription quotas. Similarly, commanders and staffs might conceal their losses to desertion by disguising them under anodyne labels or might highlight the desertion rates of other units in order to stand in a comparatively favourable light or to blame others for battlefield setbacks. As noted repeatedly, this last phenomenon was common in 1813 with French officers disparaging Rheinbund troops and Germans deriding their French and Italian comrades in arms. The metrics to use in gauging desertion present an additional challenge as different contemporary accounts or different historians might apply varying definitions of what constituted high or low desertion rates.

This preamble is to highlight the complexity of the issue from the historian's perspective and the need for much more research, especially at the local district level and within individual unit records. Even more diligent investigation, however, may not produce data sets with the requisite degree of granularity across all contingents and comparative figures for French and other elements of the Grande Armée during its final year in Germany. Despite the absence of more detailed data, several broad observations may be made drawing on the materials examined for this study.

First of all, it is important to distinguish among the three categories mentioned in the title of this appendix: draft evasion, desertion and defection. For the purposes of this analysis, the first, draft evasion, denotes efforts by young men to avoid being conscripted in the first place or to escape service if they are chosen by whatever process their local authorities employed. This could involve everything from claiming an exemption (such as a disability or congenital illness) to self-mutilation (such as rendering a hand incapable of firing a musket), to bribery, to flight with or without the assistance of family and friends.[1] Motivations were many: simple fear of death or wounding seeming most prominent, combined with dislocation anxiety based on attachment to the familiarity of native village, family and circumstances. Individuals or communities might question the legitimacy of conscription or object to service under the French, but 'patriotic or pan-German attitudes' were seldom if ever the cause to avoid military service.[2] For most people, notes Helmut Walser Smith, 'conscription remained a plague not a calling' regardless of the cause.[3]

Just as in France, all the German states experienced problems with men seeking to circumvent their conscription systems and, just as the level of evasion varied from department to department in France, the severity of the problem varied from state to state and often within different districts of a state.[4] As noted in Chapter 3, for instance, Bavarian authorities encountered far greater difficulties collecting the allotted number of conscripts in former Prussian territories such as Franconia as compared to the traditional districts of 'Old Bavaria' (Altbayern) – though these traditional regions also presented greater challenges in 1813 than they had in earlier years. Draft evasion was most prevalent in the 'artificial state' of Westphalia, forcing local authorities to adopt extreme measures to fill their quotas. Saxon newspapers contained repeated admonitions to turn in draft evaders and reported hundreds of young men who had fled when called.[5] Widespread hatred of conscription compounded the difficulties faced by local officials as villagers and townspeople were often willing to hide or otherwise abet draft evaders. Manifold obstacles notwithstanding, in almost all cases the Rheinbund states managed to raise and equip their contingents to the numbers stipulated in the Confederation's treaties; Hesse-Darmstadt and Würzburg even exceeded their commitments. Troop quality was certainly a concern, but Rheinbund requirements were generally met in terms of numbers.

The second category of absence from duty is desertion. For this study that means men who were already in uniform and had undergone some basic training but who chose to absent themselves while en route to their units or after they had arrived in the theatre of war. Unfortunately, where usable data for draft evasion is available in published sources for some select cases (especially certain French departments), reliable figures for desertion in the field are much more elusive. Research on the French army for the period 1803 to 1814, however, yields a desertion rate of approximately 10 per cent over the period 1803 to 1814.[6]

Taking this figure as a benchmark, the Rheinbund contingents in 1813 compare quite favourably to their French allies. Although some units suffered higher losses to desertion, most seem to have fallen in the 5–10 per cent bracket for the bulk of the conflict. There were, of course significant exceptions such as the raw Rheinbund battalions at Hagelberg and especially the truly massive desertion among Westphalian units inside the kingdom in late September (although it bears repeating that these occurred under extraordinary circumstances and that more determined leadership by Jérôme and his generals likely would have stemmed much of the flight). The Frankfurt contingent was also notorious for desertion. In other words, with some notable exceptions most German units were no more prone to desert than the French. During the retreat from Dennewitz, for instance, the German regiments lost heavily to straggling and apparent desertion as well as combat, but Oudinot's two French divisions were so badly depleted that they had to be consolidated into one even though they had hardly been involved in the battle. As another example, the Rheinbund fortress garrisons proved remarkably steadfast. Despite innumerable opportunities and deluges of Allied inducements, there were almost no desertions from Thorn, Danzig, Glogau or other locales until after Leipzig when German officers began to request release and individuals started slipping away in large numbers.

The question of desertion clearly requires much more research, but the limited data examined for this study suggest several additional conclusions. First, the Rheinbund armies regarded desertion as a stain on their reputations and strove to curtail it as best they could. The humiliating penalties inflicted on the returning Baden and Hessian deserters afford one example of this attitude, but it was common throughout the Confederation. Second, it seems that most of the men who deserted did not do so to defect to the Allies, but rather out of a desire simply to go home, to escape the rigours and dangers of campaigning and to return to the family fold. The desertion drain on the Grande Armée, therefore, did not result in a corresponding gain for the Allies in any substantial sense. Third, it is worth considering whether or not the newly recruited Rheinbund units suffered most from desertion on the march from their home countries to the theatre of war but solidified after what Kösterus disparaged as 'those despicables who had deserted out of fear' and other malingerers sneaked away from the ranks. In addition to this anecdote, the experiences of the Berg Lancers and 1st Berg Infantry seem to point in this direction, as does Stockhorn's confident assertion that desertion would decline and cohesion grow as his brigade headed east.[7] The evidence is thin, but this is another aspect of the desertion problem that would benefit from further analysis.

Additionally, there seem to have been only a very few cases of men 'allowing' themselves to be captured and thus freeing themselves from their duties without the stigma of desertion. On the contrary, memoirs, unit histories and contemporary reports are full of stories describing men evading or escaping the enemy and travelling across country on foot for days to regain their regiments rather than submit to capture. Detailed statistics are regrettably lacking, but there were clearly many instances of this phenomenon. Württemberg Sergeant Buck was an extraordinary example, but there were many others such as Hessian Fourrier Diehl who pretended to be a Saxon seeking his family in order to elude the Prussians in Leipzig, Bavarian troops firing on a fleeing NCO after Dennewitz, the Saxon units at Kalisch forging through the enemy's cavalry to safety across the ice-bound Prosna River, or Saxon Corporal Buhle who slipped away from the Russians after being taken at that battle and made his way home through Bohemia while refusing Russian and Austrian offers to enrol in their ranks.[8] Similarly, more than a hundred men returned to the Würzburg Regiment after the Dennewitz disaster and the Württemberg division experienced a similar surge of returnees who had been jarred loose during the battle or eluded their captors afterwards. Reynier too commented on numerous troops returning to the ranks when submitting his list of 7th Corps losses after Dennewitz. Perhaps the most dramatic illustration of the preference for escape over capture or desertion is provided by the hundreds, perhaps thousands, of German troops who chose to risk swimming the rivers west of Leipzig under fire during the final hours of that city's agony. Only a small percentage of these men, some of whom were already wounded, would have known how to swim and even those who did were not guaranteed escape. These incidents and the many others cited in this study suggest the need for closer examination of German desertion in 1813. It was certainly a significant concern for all Rheinbund armies – as it was for the French and the Coalition forces – but, with the exception of a few cases of large-scale flight, its extent seems overstated when compared with the thousands of men who did *not* desert and who indeed risked their lives to avoid capture even when surrender or desertion were available as easy and immediate alternatives.

Finally, the foregoing reminds us that levels of desertion cannot be deduced by simply subtracting the number of men 'present under arms' from one point in the campaign to the next. Close scrutiny is required because large numbers of troops were usually detached or in hospital. As noted earlier, all these men, along with the missing and prisoners of war, were recorded as 'effectives' in the French system of personnel accounting. As a result, simply tracking the fluctuations in numbers 'present under arms' can lead to misleading conclusions regarding desertion. The Württemberg 38th Division in September provides a good example. According to the 4th Corps 1 September strength return, the division had 9,673 'effectives' prior to Dennewitz, of whom 7,022 were 'present under arms', 716 detached, 1,269 in hospital, 255 'in the rear' and 411 prisoners of war; 'in the rear' ('*en arrière*') was sometimes used as a euphemism for stragglers or deserters, meaning that the division's loss to desertion at this point was at most only some 3 per cent (assuming that term even applied in this case). In other words, approximately three-quarters of the division's 'effectives' were 'present under arms' even if the prisoners and possible deserters are deducted. The post-Dennewitz report of 14 September lists only 3,051 'present under arms', but this is deceptive as 1,356 were detached, 1,328 wounded and 1,694 either missing or captured for a total of 7,429 'effectives'.

The fact that many contingents sent excess officers and NCOs home as cadres along with sick and wounded presents an additional complication. Continuing with the Württemberg case, Oberst von Bieberstein was leading a column of approximately 1,000 such sick, wounded and excess men back to the kingdom in mid-September; they were not deserters but would not have been counted as part of the division's 'effectives' and thus might be mistaken for soldiers who had left the ranks without permission.[9] While reasonable estimates of the number of men available for combat at any particular time can be achieved in most cases, this brief excursion is to suggest the importance of much deeper research in unit records to develop reliable figures for deserters from armies in the field.[10]

The third aspect to consider is defection, going over to the enemy. As with desertion, the image of extensive defection among the Rheinbund troops is misleading. Counting the units that intentionally defected to join the Allied armies, rather than men who defected as individuals or in small groups and not including those who might have changed sides after being captured, the total comes to approximately 6,400.[11] Several hundred more may be added to avoid underestimation and to account for small units that may have 'allowed' themselves to be captured, (such as the 1st Coburg Company at Hagelberg). This brings the total to roughly 7,000, or 10 per cent of the 70,000 Rheinbund troops present under arms in the late August–early September timeframe.[12] Even adding Westphalians who might have switched sides *after* being captured during the Allied raids in September, the total number of men in defecting units would not exceed 10,000, or 14 per cent of those under arms. Moreover, the total drops to between 8 and 9 percent if the 20,000 or so Rheinbund sick and wounded in hospitals across Germany are added to the calculation. Any defection or desertion, of course, is anathema to an army, bringing deleterious psychological, material and tactical consequences, but these were not debilitating percentages. Furthermore, the major unit defections were those of the Saxon division and Normann's Württemberg cavalry brigade. These two incidents accounted for 65 to 70 per cent of the total number of men estimated in unit defections (assuming 6,400 to 7,000 as the total), but they did not occur until Leipzig when the Grande Armée was surrounded by superior numbers and crushing defeat seemed imminent. Viewing the number of soldiers involved in unit defections in this manner thus places these incidents in context and helps compensate for the distortion created by the sensational nature of the major defections at Leipzig.

In addition to what might be termed 'self-generated' actions such as desertion and defection, the Allies employed several methods to encourage Rheinbund troops to change sides: demanding a battalion from Anhalt, incorporating the men Linker surrendered as the cadre of an independent battalion, and pressuring individual captives to take Prussian service. These methods seldom produced the desired results, but a formation called the Russo-German Legion was created from prisoners of war during the armistice and took the field as part of Wallmoden's corps in the autumn. The Legion had been established in early 1812 under Russian auspices to receive an anticipated flood of German defectors. Justus Gruner, a former Prussian official and one of the Legion's most ardent advocates, envisaged it as 'the seed of hatred and revenge against the enemy of the fatherland'.[13] Inspired by such sentiments, the tsar and Stein's Committee of German Affairs hoped that it would form the vanguard of a Russian invasion of Germany, arousing the German populace to mass insurrection in line with Chernishev's expectations from 1811. Few defectors appeared, however, and subsequent appeals to prisoners of war likewise failed to generate many volunteers. A captive Hessian officer gave a typically earnest reply when a Russian general scornfully asked why he and his comrades had come to Russia in the service of the 'bandit Napoleon': 'it was as much part of our duty to prince and fatherland to follow the designated banner as Your Excellency would fulfil your duty to your emperor if you now march with him to Germany'.[14] Some 5,500 were finally assembled in Königsberg by late May 1813 but many of these were Prussians or Baltic Germans rather than Rheinbund troops and few displayed the pan-German patriotism that Stein and Gruner had anticipated. Oberstleutnant Wilhelm G. F. Wardenburg, one of the battalion commanders, noted sourly that the men who had joined 'did not do so because they were concerned about the liberation of their fatherland, rather because Napoleon's situation was becoming worse daily and because good rations seemed preferable to a meagre existence in captivity'.[15] Rather than engaging in 'the good cause', some Rheinbund soldiers viewed joining the Legion as a vehicle to get them closer to their homelands so they could then desert the Legion and return to their families. Others were little more than military adventurers. 'It turned out', observes historian Gabriele Venzky, 'that the Legion was not the result of some general patriotic enthusiasm, rather that we are dealing here with a foreign legion, that was mostly composed of "*Landsknechten*",' in other words, mercenaries or soldiers of fortune.[16] Harsh measures, including salutary executions and frequent resort to corporal punishment, were necessary to instil and maintain discipline.

Although intended as a formation of German defectors, deserters and rebranded prisoners of war, it is not clear how many Rheinbund soldiers served in the Russo-German Legion. From the limited data available, there were very few former Rheinbund men in the artillery or in the two hussar regiments; almost all were distributed among the Legion's seven infantry battalions. The 1st Battalion was entirely Prussian and the 2nd largely Prussian with some Bavarians and Dutch. In the 3rd Battalion, roughly 50–60 per cent came from the Rheinbund as did slightly more than 70 per cent in the 4th Battalion. The largest 'contributions' seem to have come from Westphalia, followed by Saxony and Bavaria. The 6th Battalion, as noted (*see* Chapter 2), was founded on some 500 men from the Saxon *Prinz Max* Regiment, while the cadre of the 7th came from 273 mostly Saxon deserters and prisoners of war collected during the spring campaign and joined by the 1st Coburg Company after Hagelberg.[17] The rest of the enlisted men and NCOs originated from every corner of Europe: Dutch, Poles, Italians, Austrians, Illyrians and even a few Frenchmen. The officer corps was also a colourful mix with approximately 25–30 per cent having been in the service of a Rheinbund state as compared to a nearly equal percentage of Prussians.[18] The sixteen junior former Rheinbund officers who signed a declaration in Berlin in March to explain their enrolment in the Legion were thus not the harbingers of an outpouring of patriotic pan-German sentiment, rather representatives of an enthusiastic but very small minority.[19] Committed to the side-lines of the war along the lower Elbe and later sent to seize Denmark on Sweden's behalf, the Legion had only marginal impact on the outcome of the conflict, neither serving as a vanguard for the Allied cause nor as a powerful magnet to draw Rheinbund soldiers away from their duties.

Notes to Appendix

1. One of the few German conscripts to relate his experiences as a draft evader (in 1809) was Johann Friedrich Ruthe in his *Leben, Leiden und Widerwärtigkeiten eines Niedersachsen von ihm selbst beschrieben*, Berlin: self-published, 1841. In Bavaria, some young men knocked out their own front teeth as this would render them incapable of biting off the ends of cartridges and thus, they hoped, ineligible for conscription. The army accepted them anyway and assigned them to the artillery where musketry was not an important skill.
2. Michael Sikora, 'Desertion und nationale Mobilmachung: Militärische Verweigerung 1792–1813', in Ulrich Bröckling and Michael Sikora, eds, *Armeen und ihre Deserteure: Vernachlässigte Kapitel einer Militärgeschichte der Neuzeit*, Göttingen: Vandenhoeck und Ruprecht, 1998, pp. 122, 134–5.

Draft Evasion, Desertion and Defection

3. H. W. Smith, 'Nation and Nationalism', p. 237.
4. The classic study for France is Alan Forrest, *Conscripts and Deserters: The Army and French Society during the Revolution and Empire*, Oxford: Oxford University Press, 1989; but see also Alain Pigeard, *La Conscription au Temps de Napoléon*, Clamecy: Laballery, 2003, especially Chapter V. On Westphalia's problems with conscription, see Mustafa, *Paper Kingdom*, Chapter 5.
5. Donath/Engelberg/Füßler/Uhlmann, *Leipzig 1813*, pp. 119–20.
6. Sikora, 'Desertion und nationale Mobilmachung', p. 116; Lünsmann estimated Westphalian desertion rates at 7–9 per cent prior to 1813 (*Armee des Königreichs Westfalen*, pp. 38–9).
7. Kösterus, *Großherzoglich Hessischen Truppen*, pp. 4–5; Stockhorn's 14 April 1813 report, GLAK 48/4336. Commentators often draw this conclusion from the history of the Confederate Army of Northern Virginia during the 1862 invasion of Maryland when it suffered heavily from straggling.
8. Diehl, HStAD Best. E 8 B3.10.1, Nr. 126/6; *see* Chapters 2 and 5.
9. The lack of replacements for many Rheinbund contingents can also skew the picture of desertion as contrasted with detachments, battle losses and especially sickness as causes for declines in strength. The French army, on the other hand, received more than fifty replacement detachments during the war averaging roughly 3,000 to as many as 5,000 per column.
10. Figures from the 4th Corps 'Situations' for 1 and 14 September 1813, SHD, 2C539.
11. In approximate numbers: Linker's Saxon Duchies battalion (430), Westphalian Hussars (400–600), Saxon *König* Infantry (360), Westphalian battalion at Dresden (300–400), Saxon division at Leipzig (3,800), and Normann's Württemberg brigade at Leipzig (800 assuming some losses from the 1,000 men on hand on 1 October). Excluding the dubious case of Linker's men, all these defections occurred during the autumn and the great majority (4,600) only during the denouement at Leipzig.
12. Figures based on the mid-August 'Livret de Situation' (SHD, 2C708) combined with mid-September to mid-October data for fortresses and Specht for Westphalia – *see* Chapter 1.
13. Gruner memorandum of March 1812, quoted in Venzky, *Russisch-Deutsche Legion*, p. 29.
14. Friedrich Peppler, *Schilderung meiner Gefangenschaft in Rußland vom Jahre 1812 bis 1814*, Worms: Kranzbühler, 1832, pp. 25–6. Peppler's experience is echoed in many other German memoirs, officers and privates alike. Although not a Rheinbund officer, Carl Anton Wilhelm Graf von Wedel, a German officer in the French/German 30th Chevaulegers, offered similar thoughts: *Geschichte eines Offiziers im Kriege gegen Rußland 1812, in russischer Gefangenschaft 1813 bis 1814, im Feldzuge gegen Napoleon 1815*, Berlin: Asher, 1897.
15. Wardenburg's diary in Venzky, *Russisch-Deutsche Legion*, p. 79.
16. Venzky, *Russisch-Deutsche Legion*, p. 18.
17. The composition of the 5th Battalion is unclear.
18. The national origin and former service of many officers is unknown. Percentages calculated from tables in Venzky's *Russisch-Deutsche Legion* and Quistorp's *Russisch-Deutsche Legion*.
19. 'Erklärung' signed by sixteen junior officers to explain their decisions to join the Russo-German Legion in *Berlinische Nachrichten von Staats- und gelehrten Sachen*, no. 35, 23 March 1813.

Bibliography

Archival Material

Note: I have used the American military term 'after-action report' for several German and French phrases, most commonly *'Relation'*.

Belgium
Royal Army Museum Archives, Brussels (RAMB)

France
Archives Nationales (AN)
Service Historique de la Défense (SHD), Archives de la Guerre et de l'Armée de Terre, Vincennes. Most are from Série GR C², Premier Empire, especially the files of 'Situations' and 'Correspondance de l'Armée'. Note: one of the files from the Service Historique de la Défense is a helpful collection of order of battle data compiled by Lieutenant Colonel de Lystrac (apparently just prior to World War I) and catalogued as XP3. Although the finding guide warns that Lystrac drew all his data from published sources, this is inaccurate as he also referred – at least as far as 1813 is concerned – to many reports in the French archives.

Germany
Baden: Landesarchiv Baden-Württemberg, Generallandesarchiv, Karlsruhe (GLAK)
Bavaria: Bayerisches Hauptstaatsarchiv, Munich (BayHStA)
Hesse-Darmstadt: Hessisches Staatsarchiv, Darmstadt (HStAD)
Saxony: Sächsisches Hauptstaatsarchiv, Dresden (SHSA)
Württemberg: Landesarchiv Baden-Württemberg, Hauptstaatsarchiv, Stuttgart (LABWHStA)

United States
Morgan Library and Museum, Manuscripts, New York City

Dictionaries, Encyclopedias and Other Compilations

Clerq, Jules de. *Recueil des Traités de la France*, Paris: Amyot, 1864–86
Haering, Hermann and Otto Hohenstatt. *Schwäbische Lebensbilder*, Stuttgart: Kohlhammer, 1940
Hirtenfeld, Jaromir. *Der Militär-Maria-Theresien-Orden und seine Mitglieder*, Vienna: Hof- und Staatsdruckerei, 1857
Martens, Fedor Fedorovich. *Recueil des Traités et Conventions conclus par la Russie avec les Puisssances Étrangères*, St Petersburg: Devrient, 1874–1902
Martinien, Aristide. *Tableaux par Corps et par Batailles des Officiers Tués et Blessés pendant les Guerres de l'Empire (1805–1815)*, Paris: Editions Militaires Européennes, 1984
Pénichon, Christophe. *La Cavalerie Française à l'Automne 1813*, Lille: Pénichon, 2018

Bibliography

Pigeard, Alain. *Les Etoiles de Napoléon*, Entremont-le-Vieux: Quatuor, 1996
—— *Les Campagnes Napoléoniennes*, Entremont-le-Vieux: Quator, 1998
Quintin, Danielle and Bernard. *Dictionnaire des Colonels de Napoléon*, Paris: SPM, 1996
Schröder, Bernd Philipp. *Die Generalität der Deutschen Mittelstaaten 1815–1870*, Osnabrück: Biblio Verlag, 1984
Six, Georges. *Dictionnaire Biographique des Généraux & Amiraux Français de la Révolution et de l'Empire*, Paris: Manutention à Mayenne, 1989
Tulard, Jean. *Dictionnaire Napoléon*, Paris: Fayard, 1987
Veyrier, Henri. *Dictionnaire des Diplomates de Napoléon*, Paris: Kronos, 1990
Weech, Friedrich von. *Badische Biographieen*, Heidelberg: Bassermann, 1875

Memoirs, Correspondence, Biographies and Published Documents

Note: in almost all cases, I have listed these works by the names of the memoirist rather than the editor (thus 'Hochberg' for Wilhelm von Hochberg's *Denkwürdigkeiten* ed. Karl Obser).

'Abdruck eines Original-Rapports von dem am 28. August 1812 in den Russischen Feldzug nachgesendeten, königl. Ergänzungs-Corps', *Würtembergische Jahrbücher*, 1835
Ackermann, Christian Georg. *Darstellung der Kriegsbegebenheiten in Dessau während der Jahre 1806–1815*, Dessau: Ackermann, 1839
Actenstücke und Materialien zu der Geschichte des großen Kampfes um die Freyheit Europas in den Jahren 1812 und 1813, Germanien: Hammer, 1814
Adalbert, Prinz von Bayern. *Eugen Beauharnais der Stiefsohn Napoleons*, Berlin: Propyläen Verlag, 1940
—— *Max I. Joseph von Bayern: Pfalzgraf, Kurfürst und König*, Munich: Bruckmann, 1957
Ainval, Christiane d'. *Gouvion Saint-Cyr*, Paris: Copernic, 1981
Andlaw, Franz Freiherr von. *Mein Tagebuch: Auszüge aus Aufschreibungen der Jahre 1811 bis 1861*, Frankfurt: Sauerländer's Verlag, 1862
Arpentigny, Casimir Stanislas d'. *Voyage en Pologne et en Russie par un Prisonnier de Guerre de la garnison de Dantzick en 1813 et 1814*, Paris: Dupont, 1828
Artois, Prosper Honoré d'. *Relation de la Défense de Danzig en 1813, par le 10e Corps de l'Armée Française, contre l'Armée Combinée Russe et Prussienne*, Paris: Ladrange, 1820
Aster, Eduard von, ed. *Kurzer Lebens-Abriss des weil. Königlich Preussischen General's Ernst Ludwig von Aster*, Berlin: Voss, 1878
Atteridge, Andrew Hilliard. *Marshal Murat King of Naples*, Felling Tyne & Wear: Worley, 1992 (reprint of 1911 edition)
'Aufruf an die Deutschen', in *Das neue Deutschland*, vol. I, no. 3, Berlin 1813
'Aus den Zeiten der schweren Noth. "Westfälische" Erinnerungen eines Kasselaners', *Die Gartenlaube*, vol. 37, 1879
Barrès, Jean-Baptiste. *Memoirs of a French Napoleonic Officer*, London: Greenhill, 1988
Bartheld, Carl Friedrich Wilhelm von. 'Memoiren des kurhessischen Majors Carl Wilhelm Friedr. v. Bartheld aus Lispenhausen, Ritter des preußischen eisernen Kreuzes und des hessischen eisernen Helms. Aus der Zeit der Fremdherrschaft von 1806 bis 1814', Carl Heiler, ed., *Zeitschrift des Vereins für hessische Geschichte und Landeskunde*, vol. 61, 1936
Bauer, Johann Philip. 'Aus dem Leben des Kurhessischen Generallieutenants Bauer', *Beihefte zum Militärwochenblatt*, Hefte 3–4, 1887
Baumgarten-Crusius, Artur. *Die Sachsen 1812 in Rußland*, Leipzig: Wigand, 1912
Beaulieu-Marconnaÿ, Karl Freiherr von. *Karl von Dalberg und seine Zeit*, Weimar: Böhlau, 1879

'Beiträge zur Geschichte der Blocade von Modlin vom 5. Februar 1813, bis zu deren Uebergabe den 1. December 1813; nebst Bemerkungen, Anecdoten, u.', *Minerva*, Feb. 1835

Benckendorff, Constantine Khristoforovich. *The Cossacks. A Memoir*, George Gall, trans., London: Parker, Furnivall & Parker, 1849

Berg, nfn. 'Die Erfahrungen und Schicksale Cüstrins in den Jahren 1813–1814', *Schriften des Vereins für Geschichte der Neumark*, vol. XXVI, 1911

Bernhardi, Theodor von. *Denkwürdigkeiten aus dem Leben des kaiserl. Russ. Generals der Infanterie Carl Friedrich Grafen von Toll*, Leipzig: Wigand, 1866

Berthezène, Pierre. *Souvenirs Militaires de la République et de l'Empire*, Paris: Dumaine, 1855

[Berthier, Alexander]. *Registre d'Ordres du Maréchal Berthier pendant la Campagne de 1813*, Paris: Chapelot, 1909

—— *Rapports du Maréchal Berthier à l'Empereur pendant la Campagne de 1813*, Paris: Chapelot, 1909

Bertin, Georges, ed. *La Campagne de 1813 d'après des Témoins Oculaires*, Paris: Flammarion, 1896

Bignon, Louis Pierre Édouard. *Souvenirs d'un Diplomate: la Pologne (1811–1813)*, Paris: Dentu, 1864

Bismarck, Friedrich Wilhelm. *Vorlesungen über die Taktik der Reuterey*, Karlsruhe: Müller, 1826

—— *Ideen-Taktik der Reuterei*, Karlsruhe: Müller, 1829

Note that his name appears as both 'Bismarck' and 'Bismark'.

Bitterauf, Theodor. 'Napoleon I. und Kronprinz Ludwig von Bayern', *Schriften des Vereins für Geschichte des Bodensees und seiner Umgebung*, vol. XXXIX, 1910

Blücher, Gebhard Lebrecht von. *Blücher in Briefen aus den Feldzügen 1813–1815*, Enno von Colomb, ed., Stuttgart: Cotta, 1876

Blumröder, August von. *Meine Erlebnisse im Krieg und Frieden in der großen Welt und in der kleinen Welt meines Gemüths*, Sondershausen: Eupel, 1857

Bodenhausen, Friedrich von. *Tagebuch eines Ordonnanzoffiziers von 1812–1813 und über seine späteren Staatsdienste bis 1848*, Braunschweig: Westermann, 1912

Boedicker, Johann Ludwig. 'Die militärische Laufbahn 1788–1815 des Generallieutenant Ludwig Boedicker', *Beiheft zum Militär-Wochenblatt*, vols. 5 and 6, 1880

Boehm, Gottfried von. 'Ein angeblicher Abdankungsantrag Napoleons an König Max Joseph von Bayern', *Forschungen zur Geschichte Bayerns*, vol. XI, 1903

Böhme, Carl Friedrich Ferdinand. *Tagebuch 2te Periode (II)*, Jörg Titze, ed., Norderstedt: Books on Demand, 2017

Bonin, Otto von. 'Mittheilungen über den Reiter-Angriff bei Globig in dem Treffen bei Wartenburg am 3ten Oktober 1813', *Militair-Wochenblatt*, no. 2, 9 January 1847

Bonnefons, André. *Un Allié de Napoléon: Frédéric Auguste*, Paris: Perrin, 1902

Bonnéry, Jean-Louis. *Ledru des Essarts: Un Grand Patriote Sarthois Méconnu*, Le Mans: Imprimerie Maine Libre, 1988

Borcke, Johann von. *Kriegerleben*, Stanislaus von Leszczynski, ed., Berlin: Mittler & Sohn, 1888

Bose, Justus Wilhelm von. 'Briefe eines Offiziers an seine Frau aus den Jahren 1807–1813', *Die Grenzboten*, 24, vol. II/IV, 1865

Bossuroy, Emilien. 'Le général Durutte: parcours de la carrière d'un officier au service de la France 1792–1815', dissertation, University of Louvain, 2019

Boudon, Jacques-Olivier. *Le Roi Jérôme: Frère Prodigal de Napoléon*, Paris: Fayard, 2008

Boulart, Jean François. *Mémoires Militaires*, Paris: Librarie Illustrée, 1892 (reprinted Tallandier, 1992)

Boyen, Hermann von. *Denkwürdigkeiten und Erinnerungen*, Stuttgart: Lutz, 1899

Bibliography

Brun de Villeret, Louis Bertrand Pierre. *Les Cahiers du Général Brun*, Paris: Plon, 1953
Buhle, Carl. *Erinnerungen aus den Feldzügen von 1809 bis 1816*, Bautzen: Schlüssel, 1844
Bülau, Friedrich. 'General Thielmann', in *Geheime Geschichten und Räthselhafte Menschen*, vol. X, Leipzig: Brockhaus, 1858
—— 'Noch einmal über General Thielmann', in *Geheime Geschichten und Räthselhafte Menschen*, vol. XII, Leipzig: Brockhaus, 1860
Bülow, Gottfried Philipp von. *Rückblicke auf mein Leben*, Helmstedt: Flackeisen, 1844
Bussche, Albrecht von dem. *Auf Pferdesrücken durch Europa*, Mainz: von Hase & Koehler, 1997
Callenius, Gustav. 'Meine Erlebnisse bei dem Streifzuge der v. Colomb'schen Reiterschaar im Frühjahr 1813', *Der Beobachter an der Saale, Schwarza und Ilm*, nos. 27–29, 7, 14 and 21 July 1863
Campredon, Jacques David Martin. *Défense de Danzig en 1813*, Charles Auriol, ed., Paris: Plon, 1888
Camus de Richemont, Louis Auguste. *Capitulation de Danzig, Traduit d'Allemand de Plotho avec Observations Critiques*, Philippe Himly, trans., Paris: Corréard, 1841
Chérot, Henri. 'Le Général Bertrand en 1813 et 1814', *Études de théologie, de philosophie et d'histoire*, vols. 90–91, 1902
Cloßmann, Wilhelm von. 'Tagebuch von Clossmann 1788–1825', Historisches Museum Schloß Rastatt, n.d.
Coignet, Jean-Roche. *The Note-Books of Captain Coignet*, London: Greenhill, 1989
Colomb, Friedrich August Peter von. *Aus dem Tagebuch des Rittmeisters v. Colomb*, Berlin: Mittler & Sohn, 1854
Colson, Bruno. *Le Général Rogniat: Ingénieur et Critique de Napoléon*, Paris: Economica, 2006
Combier, A. *Mémoires de Général Radet*, Saint-Cloud: Belin, 1982
Conrady, Ludwig Wilhelm von. *Aus stürmischer Zeit: Ein Soldatenleben vor hundert Jahren*, Wilhelm von Conrady, ed., Berlin: Schwetschke & Sohn, 1907
Copies des Lettres Originales et Dépêches des Généraux, Ministres, Grand Officiers d'État, etc., Écrites de Paris à Buonaparte pendant son séjour à Dresde, ainsi qu'une Correspondance de divers personnages de cette même famille entr'eux' Interceptées par les avant-postes des Alliés dans le Nord de l'Allemange, Paris: Galignani, 1815
Curély, Jean Nicolas. *Itineraire d'un Cavalier Léger de la Grande Armée*, Paris: Librairie des Deux Empires, 1999

D., J. *Notice sur le Général de Division Prévost de Vernois*, Paris: Dumaine, 1860
D., M. 'Lettre sur la Bataille de Leipzig', *Spectateur Militaire*, vol. VII, 1829
Danneil, Johann Friedrich. *Das Geschlecht der von der Schulenburg*, Salzwedel: Schmidt, 1847
Darnay, Antoine. *Notices Historiques sur Son Altesse Royale le Prince Eugène, Vice-Roi d'Italie*, Paris: David, 1830
Davidov [Davydov], Denis. *In the Service of the Tsar against Napoleon*, Gregory Troubetzkoy, ed. and trans., London: Greenhill, 1999
Davout, Marshal Louis-Nicolas. *Correspondance de Maréchal Davout*, Charles de Mazade, ed., Paris: Plon, 1885
Deifl, Josef. *Infanterist Deifl*, Eugen von Frauenholz, ed., Munich: Beck, 1939
Delinière, Jean. *Karl Friedrich Reinhard: Ein deutscher Aufklärer im Dienste Frankreichs (1761–1837)*, Stuttgart: Kohlhammer, 1989
Delvaux, Steven L. 'Witness to Glory: Lieutenant-Général Henri-Gatien Bertrand, 1791–1815', dissertation, Florida State University, 2005

Derrécagaix, Victor Bernhard. *Maréchal Berthier*, Paris: Chapelot, 1905
'Der Untergang der Lützower bei Kitzen' (review), *Württembergische Vierteljahrshefte für Landesgeschichte*, vol. V, 1896
'Die Leiden der sächsischen Besatzung der Festung Modlin: Kriegsgefangenschaft und Rückmarsch 1813–14', *Der Kamerad*, 1863
'Die sächsischen Truppen in der Schlacht bei Leipzig, den 18. Oktober 1813', *Der europäische Aufseher*, nos. 2 and 6 November 1821
Dörnberg, Hugo Freiherr von. *Wilhelm von Dörnberg: Ein Kämpfer für Deutschlands Freiheit*, Marburg: Elwert, 1936
Dormann, Hasso. *Feldmarschall Fürst Wrede*, Munich: Süddeutscher Verlag, 1982
Dornheim, Johann Friedrich Wilhelm. 'Skizzen aus den Feldzügen des Bataillons Lippe', in Eckhart Kleßmann, ed., *Unter Napoleons Fahnen: Erinnerungen lippischer Soldaten aus den Feldzügen 1809–1814*, Bielefeld: Westfalen Verlag, 1991. Originally published anonymously in the *Lippisches Magazin für vaterländische Cultur und Gemeinwohl*, 1837–9.
Dorow, Wilhelm. *Erlebtes aus den Jahren 1813–1820*, Leipzig: Hinrichs, 1843
Dreßler und Scharffenstein, Franciscus Xaver (Franz) von. *Darstellung der Begebenheiten in Torgau, vor, während und nach dem Rückzuge der Franzosen aus Sachsen, in den Monaten Februar, März und April 1813*, Dresden: Arnold, n.d. (1813 or 1814)
Dreßler und Scharffenstein, Friedrich von. *Bericht eines Augenzeugen von den Operationen des 4ten, 7ten und 12ten französischen Armeecorps unter Anführung der Generale Bertrand, Reynier und Oudinot, von Ankündigung des Pleischwitzer Waffenstillstand, bis nach der Schlacht bei Jüterbogk, vom 14 August bis 6 September 1813*, Dresden: Arnold, 1814
—— 'Das sächsische Gardebataillon unter Commando des Capitains nachherigen Majors von Dreßler vom 14. August bis 5. November 1813', in Reinhard Münch, ed., *Des Königs Butterkrebse*, Leipzig: Pro Leipzig, 2011
Droysen, Johann Gustav. *Das Leben des Feldmarschalls Grafen York von Wartenburg*, Berlin: Veit, 1852
Du Casse, Albert. *Mémoires pour Servir à l'Histoire de la Campagne de 1812 en Russie*, Paris: Dumaine, 1852
—— *Mémoires et correspondance politique et militaire du Prince Eugène*, Paris: Lévy, 1858–60
—— *Mémoires et Correspondance Politique et Militaire du Roi Jérôme et de la Reine Catherine*, Paris: Dentu, 1861–66
—— *Le Général Arrighi de Casanova, Duc de Padoue*, Paris: Dentu, 1866
—— *Le Général Vandamme et sa Correspondance*, Paris: Didier, 1870
Dumas, Mathieu. *Souvenirs du Lieutenant Général Mathieu Dumas de 1770 à 1836*, Paris: Gosselin, 1839
Dumonceau, François. *Mémoires*, Brussels: Brepols, 1958–63
Dunan, Marcel. 'Nouveaux documents sur l'Allemagne Napoléonienne: Lettres du roi de Bavière au Maréchal Berthier (1806–1813)', *Revue Historique*, vol. CLXXXVI, July–December 1939
Dupont, Marcel. *Murat*, Paris: Hachette, 1934
Düring, Johann Otto Georg Wilhelm von. *Tagebuch über die Belagerung der Stadt Danzig im Jahre 1813*, Berlin: Enslin, 1817
Du Thil, Karl Wilhelm Heinrich du Bos. *Denkwürdigkeiten aus dem Dienstleben des Hessen-Darmstädtischen Staatsministers Freiherrn du Thil 1803–1848*, Heinrich Ulmann, ed., Stuttgart: Deutsche Verlags-Anstalt, 1921

Eckhardt, M. 'Briefe aus den Märztagen 1813', *Leipziger Zeitung*, no. 41, 5 April 1904

'Erinnerungen an den verstorbenen General-Lieutenant v. Hellwig', *Militair-Wochenblatt*, no. 16, 18 April 1846

Erinnerungen an Heinrich Wilhelm v. Zeschau, Dresden: Ramming, 1866

'Die Erinnerungen des Generallieutenants von Funck', *Militärische Mittheilungen*, vol. IV, 1830

'Erinnerungen von funfzig Jahren her aus einem abgelegenen Dorfe', *Hessenzeitung*, January–October 1863

Espitalier, Albert. *Napoléon et le Roi Murat*, Paris, Perrin, 1910

Esselborn, Karl, ed., *Neue Erinnerungen hessischer Offiziere, Christian Frey und Franz Schmidt, aus der Zeit der Völkerschlacht bei Leipzig*, Darmstadt: Hessischer Volksschriftenverein, 1913

Eugene of Württemberg, *Journal des Campagnes*, Gabriel Fabry, ed., Paris: Chapelot, 1907

Faber du Faur, Christian, and Franz G. F. Kausler, *Mit Napoleon in Russland*, Stuttgart: Steinkopf, 1987

Faber du Faur, Christian Wilhelm von. *With Napoleon in Russia: The Illustrated Memoirs of Major Faber du Faur, 1812*, Jonathan North, ed. and trans., London: Greenhill, 2001

Fabricius, Hans. 'Der Parteigänger Friedrich von Hellwig und seine Streifzüge', *Jahrbücher für die deutsche Armee und Marine*, vol. 94, 1895

[Fabry, Gabriel]. *Lettres de l'Empereur Napoléon non Insérées dans la Correspondance*, Paris: Levrault, 1909

Fain, Agathon Jean François. *Manuscrit de Mil Huit Cent Treize*, Paris: Delaunay, 1825

—— *Manuscrit de Mil Huit Cent Quatorze* in *Mémoires des Contemporains*, Paris: Bossange, 1824

Falk, Johannes. *Johannes Falk's Kriegsbüchlein: No. I, Darstellung der Kriegsdrangsale Weimar's in dem Zeitraum von 1806 bis 1813*, Weimar: Hoffmann, 1815

Falkenstein, Karl. 'Karl Friedrich Wilhelm von Gersdorff', *Zeitgenossen. Ein biografisches Magazin für die Geschichte unserer Zeit*, Series 3, vol. 5, nos. XXXIII–XL, 1836

Fane, John (Lord Burghersh). *Memoir of the Allied Armies under Prince Schwarzenberg and Marshal Blucher*, London: John Murray, 1822

Favier, Franck. *Berthier: L'Ombre de Napoléon*, Paris: Perrin, 2015

Felkel, Alain. *Louis Nicolas Davout*, Hamburg: Osburg Verlag, 2013

Fezensac, Raymond-Aimery-Philippe-Joseph de Montesquiou. *Souvenirs Militaires de 1804 à 1814*, Paris: Dumaine, 1870

Finger, Samuel Gottlieb. 'Auszüge aus S. G. Finger's Tagebüchern von 1795 bis 1818', Lorenz Friedrich Finger, ed., *Archiv für Frankfurts Geschichte und Kunst*, vol. 6, 1877

Fischer, Andreas. *Goethe und Napoleon*, Frauenfeld: Huber, 1900

Fischer, Anton Friedrich. 'Geschichtliche Darstellung der im Herbst 1813 in Dresden ausgebrochenen und bis gegen Ende Januars 1814 angedauerten Epidemie', *Annalen der Heilkunst des Jahres 1814*

Fleck, Förster. *Erzählung Förster Flecks von seinen Schicksalen auf dem Zuge Napoleons nach Rußland und von seiner Gefangenschaft 1812–1814*, Cologne: Schaffstein, 1912 (2008 reprint)

Frenzel, Christian Friedrich. *Erinnerungen eines sächsischen Infanteristen an die napoleonischen Kriege*, Sebastian Schaar, ed., Dresden: Thelem, 2008

Friesen, Hermann Freiherr von. 'Napoleon in Dresden (8. Mai 1813)', *Neues Archiv für Sächsische Geschichte*, vol. II, 1881

Funck, Ferdinand von. *Erinnerungen aus dem des sächsischen Corps, unter dem General Grafen Reynier, im Jahr 1812*, Dresden: Arnold, 1829

—— *In Russland und in Sachsen 1812–1815*, Artur Brabant, ed., Dresden: Heinrich, 1930

Furtenbach, Friedrich von. 'Die Generale des Bayerischen Heeres im Feldzuge gegen Rußland 1812/13', *Darstellungen aus der Bayerischen Kriegs- und Heeresgeschichte*, Heft 21, 1912

Gallaher, John G. *The Iron Marshal,* Carbondale & Evansville: Southern Illinois University Press, 1976
—— *Napoleon's Enfant Terrible: General Dominique Vandamme,* Norman, OK: University of Oklahoma Press, 2008
Garden, Guillaume de. *Histoire Générale des Traités de Paix,* Paris: Amyot, 1848–87
Geißler, Carl. *Geschichte des Regiments Herzoge zu Sachsen unter Napoleon mit der großen Armee im russischen Feldzuge 1812,* Jena: Mauke, 1840
Georges de Leuchtenberg. *Le Prince Eugène de Beauharnais à la Tête de la Grande Armée (16 janvier–15 avril 1813),* Paris: Chapelot, 1915
Geßner, nfn. *Ein Streifzug der Lützow'schen Reiterschaar und der Ueberfall bei Kitzen,* Berlin: Schlesier, 1863
Gielissen, P., and F. A. Koens. *Herman Willem Daendels 1762–1818,* den Haag: Matrijs, 1991
Gieße, Johann Friedrich. *Kassel–Moskau–Küstrin 1812–1813: Tagebuch während des russischen Feldzuges geführt,* Leipzig: Dyk, 1912
[Gieße, Johann Friedrich]. 'Belagerung und Wiedereinnahme Küstrins 1813/14', Thoma, ed., *Schriften des Vereins für Geschichte der Neumark,* vol. 41, 1923
Gillot, Gaston. *Le Général Le Marois: Un Aide de Camp de Napoléon,* Paris: Conquistador, 1957
Glitzcke, Gottfried Nathanael. 'Tagebuch', Arthur Semrau, ed., *Mitteilungen des Coppernicus-Vereins für Wissenschaft und Kunst zu Thorn,* vol. 16, 1908
[Globig, Hans August Fürchtegott von] 'Miscellen', *Archiv für die Sächsische Geschichte,* vol. IV, 1878
Goebel, Eduard Rudolf. *Zwei Ritter der Ehrenlegion,* Radeberg: Pfeil, 1906
Gollwitzer, Heinz. *Ludwig I. von Bayern,* Munich: Ludwig, 1997
Gouttes, Jean François de. 'Un Revélois dans la Grande Armée 1804–1815', Maurice de Poitevin, ed. at http://www.lauragais-patrimoine.fr/HISTOIRE/DE-GOUTTES/Jean-de-Gouttes.html
Gouvion Saint-Cyr, Laurent. *Mémoires pour servir a l'Histoire Militaire sous le Directoire, le Consulat et l'Empire,* Paris: Anselin, 1831
Grabowski, Józef. *Mémoires Militaires 1812–1813–1814,* Paris: La Vouivre, 1997
Grautoff, Ferdinand. *In Leipzig während der Völkerschlacht,* Leipzig: Dieterich, 1913
Grimm, Wilhelm. *Kleinere Schriften,* Gustav Hinrichs, ed., Berlin: Dümmler, 1881
Griois, Charles Pierre Lubin. *Mémoires du Général Griois 1792–1822,* Paris: Plon, 1909
Groß, Christoph Heinrich. *1805–1814: Ganz in der Nähe erweckte Uns Kanonenfeuer,* Dagmar Wuttge, ed., Seeheim-Jugenheim: Tintenfass, 2011
Gross, Johann Carl. *Erinnerungen aus den Kriegsjahren,* Leipzig: Voß, 1850
Guhrauer, G. E. 'Graf Karl Friedrich Reinhard: Eine Skizze', *Historisches Taschenbuch,* vol. VII, 1846

[Haars, Johann Gottleib]. *Ein Braunschweiger im Russischen Feldzuge von 1812,* Braunschweig: Scholz, 1897
Haebler, K. 'Neue Beiträge zur Characteristik des Generals von Thielmann', *Neues Archiv für Sächsische Geschichte und Altertumskunde,* vol. XV, 1904
Handelsman, Marcel. *Instructions et Dépêches des Residents de France à Varsovie,* Krakow: Académie des Sciences de Cracovie, 1914
Harnier, Heinrich Wilhelm Karl von. 'Noch einige Worte der Erinnerung an den Grafen Reinhard', *Minerva,* vol. II, April–May–June 1838
Hartmann, Stefan. 'Kosaken in Kassel: Ein Kapitel aus dem Ende des Königreichs Westfalen', *Zeitschrift für hessische Geschichte und Landeskunde,* vol. 99, 1994

Bibliography

Hartmann, Wilhelm. 'Der General Hans Georg Freiherr von Hammerstein-Equord 1771–1841', *Alt-Hildesheim*, no. 40, 1969

Hausen, Heinrich Carl Friedrich Ferdinand von. *Tagebuch und Briefe, 01.01.1812–02.02.1814*, Jörg Titze, ed., Norderstedt: Books on Demand, 2019

Hausmann, Cynthia Joy, and John H. Gill, eds. *A Soldier for Napoleon: The Campaigns of Franz Joseph Hausmann, 7th Bavarian Infantry*, London: Greenhill, 1998

Heere, Johann Gottlob. *Erinnerungen des Schloßaufsehers Heere*, Mergentheim: Thomas, 1847

Heidelbach, Paul. 'Ein sonderbares Quellenwerk zur Geschichte des Königreiches Westfalen', *Hessenland*, vol. XXI, no. 24, 17 December 1907

Heigel, Karl Theodor. *König Ludwig von Bayern*, Leipzig: Duncker & Humblot, 1872

—— 'Strasbourg, die Vaterstadt Ludwigs I. von Bayern', *Historische Vorträge und Studien*, vol. III, Munich: Rieger, 1887

—— 'Kronprinz Ludwig im Befreiungsjahr 1813', *Quellen und Abhandlungen zur neueren Geschichte Bayerns*, Munich: Rieger, 1890

Heilmann, Johann. *Feldmarschall Fürst Wrede*, Leipzig: Duncker & Humblot, 1881

Heller von Hellwald, Friedrich. *Der k. k. österreichische Feldmarschall Graf Radetzky*, Stuttgart: Cotta, 1858

—— ed. *Erinnerungen aus den Freiheitskriegen*, Stuttgart: Cotta, 1864.

Herrmann, August Leberecht. *Friedrich August König von Sachsen*, Dresden: Walther, 1827

[Herzog, Christian Gottlob]. *Sieben Jahre aus dem Leben eines sächsischen Artilleristen*, Dresden: Arnold, 1845

Hohenhausen, Leopold von. *Biographie des Generals von Ochs*, Kassel: Luckhardt, 1827

Holtzendorff, Albrecht Graf von. *Beiträge zu der Biographie des Generals Freiherrn von Thielmann*, Leipzig: Nauck, 1830

—— *Berichtigung der Schrift: 'Erinnerungen aus dem Feldzuge des sächsischen Corps im Jahre 1812'*, Dresden: Walther, 1831

Holzing, Karl Franz von. *Unter Napoleon in Spanien*, Berlin: Hugo, 1937

Hömig, Herbert. *Carl Theodor von Dalberg: Staatsmann und Kirchenfürst im Schatten Napoleons*, Paderborn: Schöningh, 2011

Hormayr zu Hortenburg, Joseph. *Lebensbilder aus dem Befreiungskriege*, Jena: Frommann, 1841

Hourtoulle, F. G. *Davout le Terrible*, Paris: Copernic, 1975

Hulot, Frédéric. *Le Maréchal Davout*, Paris: Pygmalion, 2003

Hussell, Christoph Heinrich Ludwig. *Leipzig während der Schreckenstage der Schlacht im Monat October 1813 als Beytrag zur Geschichte dieser Stadt*, Gerhard Graf, ed., Leipzig: Zentralantiquariat der DDR, 1987

Hüttel, K. von. *Der General der Kavallerie Freiherr v. Thielmann*, Berlin: Laue, 1828

J., M. 'Zur Erinnerung an den Königl. bayerischen General der Infanterie und General-Quartiermeister der Armee, Clemens von Raglovich', *Jahrbücher für die Deutsche Armee und Marine*, vol. 36, 1887

Jacob, Johann Gotthelf. *Lebenslauf eines alten Soldaten*, Dresden: Jacob, 1844

Jenak, Rudolf, ed. *'Mein Herr Bruder': Napoleon und Friedrich August I. Der Briefwechsel des Kaisers der Franzosen mit dem König von Sachsen 1806–1813*, Beucha: Sax-Verlag, 2010

Johann Georg, Herzog zu Sachsen. 'Karl von Watzdorf, 1759–1840', *Neues Archiv für Sächsische Geschichte*, vol. XXXIX, 1918

—— 'König Friedrich August der Gerechte vom 14. Dezember 1812 bis 7. Juni 1815', *Neues Archiv für Sächsische Geschichte*, vol. XL, 1919

Junkelmann, Marcus. *Montgelas*, Regensburg: Pustet, 2015

Kaisenberg, Moritz von, ed. *König Jérome Napoleon: Ein Zeit- und Lebensbild*, Leipzig: Schmidt & Günther, 1899

Keyserling, Archibald Graf von. *Aus der Kriegszeit*, Berlin: Duncker, 1847

Keysser, Adolf. 'Oberst Weiß: Ein Bild aus der Kurhessischen Heeresgeschichte', *Hessenland*, vol. 24, no. 1, 1910

Kiewning, Hans. *Fürstin Pauline zur Lippe (1769–1820)*, Detmold: Meyer, 1930

Kircheisen, Friedrich M. *Gespräche Napoleons*, Stuttgart: Lutz, 1912

—— *Fürstenbriefe an Napoleon I.*, Stuttgart: Cotta, 1929

—— *Jovial King: Napoleon's Youngest Brother*, H. J. Stenning, trans., London: Elkin, Mathews & Marrot, 1932

Kirchmayer, Georg. *Veteranen-Huldigung oder Erinnerungen an die Feldzugsjahre 1813, 1814 und 1815*, Munich: Wild, 1846

Klein, Georg. 'Kriegserlebnisse des Georg Klein I. aus Wohnbach 1812/1813', Ferdinand Dreher, ed., *Hessische Chronik*, vol. II, 1913

Klinkhardt, Friedrich. *Feldzugs-Erinnerungen des Königlich Westfälischen Musikmeisters Friedrich Klinkhardt aus den Jahren 1812 bis 1815*, Braunschweig: Scholz, 1908

Kluckhohn, August. 'Aus dem handschriftlichen Nachlasse L. Westenrieders', *Abhandlungen der historischen Classe der Königlich Bayerischen Akademie der Wissenschaften*, vol. XVI, Part II, 1883

Koch, Frédéric. *Journal des Opérations du IIIe Corps en 1813*, Gabriel Fabry, ed., Paris: Teissedre, 1999; reprint, originally published Paris:Chapelot, 1902

Kohlschütter, Karl Christian von. *Akten- und thatmäßige Widerlegung einiger der gröbsten Unwahrheiten und Verläumdungen, welche in der Schrift Blicke auf Sachsen, seinen König und sein Volk, enthalten sind*, n.p., 1815

Kölle, Christoph Friedrich Karl. 'Erlebtes vom Jahr 1813', *Deutsche Pandora*, vol. I, Stuttgart: Literatur-Comptoir, 1840

Kösterus, Martin Carl Ignaz. *Die Großherzoglich Hessischen Truppen in dem Feldzug von 1813 in Schlesien*, Darmstadt: Brill, 1840

—— *Geschichtliche Darstellung der Entwicklung der Militair-Verfassung der Hessen-Darmstädtischen Truppen*, Darmstadt: Brill, 1840

Krause, Robert. 'Weimar in den Jahren 1806 und 1813', *Neues Archiv für Sächsische Geschichte und Altertumskunde*, vol. IV, 1883

Kühn, Alexander. *Erlebnisse eines Soldaten des ehemaligen Großherzogthums Frankfurt und des darauf folgenden General-Gouvernements*, Frankfurt: Wentz, 1862

Kummer, August. *Erinnerungen aus dem Leben eines Veteranen der Königlich Sächsischen Armee*, Dresden: Meinhold & Söhne, 1870

Lachmann. 'Die Eroberung von Kassel am 28. September 1813', *Militair-Wochenblatt*, no. 834, 16 June 1832; and *Oesterreichische militärische Zeitschrift*, vol. VIII, 1838

Lamby, Jean. 'Itinéraire d'un Brigadier du 2e Régiment des Gardes d'Honneur pendant la Campagne de 1813, en Saxe', Albert Dépréaux, ed., *Carnet de la Sabretache*, no. 287, January–February 1924

La Motte Fouqué, Friedrich de. *Lebensgeschichte des Baron Friedrich de la Motte Fouqué*, Halle: Schwetschke, 1840

Lang, Wilhelm. *Graf Reinhard: Ein deutsch-französisches Lebensbild 1761–1837*, Bamberg: Buchner, 1896

Langeron, Louis Alexander Andrault. *Mémoires de Langeron*, Gabriel Fabry, ed., Paris: Picard et Fils, 1902

Larisch, August von. *Oberst von Larisch: Ein Zeit- und Lebensbild*, Dresden: Baensch, 1888
Larrey, Jean-Dominique. *Mémoires de Chirurgie Militaire et Campagnes*, Paris: Smith, 1817
Las Cases, Emmanuel Augustin Dieudonné Joseph. *Journal of the Private Life and Conversations of the Emperor Napoleon at Saint Helena*, London: Colburn, 1823
Laun, Friedrich. *Memoiren*, Bunzlau: Appun, 1837
Lauterbach, Werner. 'Ernst Gottfried Freiherr von Odeleben (1774–1828)', *Mitteilungen des Freiberger Altertumsverein*, vol. 100, 2007
[LeCoq, Carl Christian Erdmann Edler von]. *Beleuchtung des zweiten Theils der Schrift: Mittheilungen aus dem russischen Feldzuge an einen Offizier des Generalstabs*, Dresden: Walther, 1818
Lehsten, Karl August Unico von. *Am Hofe König Jérômes*, Otto von Boltenstern, ed., Berlin: Mittler & Sohn, 1905
Liess, Albrecht. 'Kronprinz Ludwig von Bayern und Napoleon', 2006, at www.france-bayern.info
Lejeune, Louis-François. *Memoirs of Baron Lejeune*, London: Longmans, Green & Co., 1897 (Felling: Worley reprint, 1987)
Leonhardt, Kurt. 'Denkschrift Dietrichs von Miltitz über seine Wirksamkeit in den Kriegsjahren 1806–1814', *Mitteilungen des Vereins für Geschichte der Stadt Meißen*, vol. IX, no. 1, 1913
Lindau, Wilhelm Adolf. *Darstellung der Ereignisse in Dresden im Jahr 1813*, Dresden: Arnold, 1816
Loßberg, Friedrich Wilhelm von. *Briefe des westfälischen Stabsoffiziers Friedrich Wilhelm von Loßberg vom russischen Feldzug des Jahres 1812*, Christian Meyer, ed., Berlin: Eisenschmidt, 1910 (new edition of: *Briefe in die Heimath*, Kassel: Fischer, 1844)
Löwenstern, Vladimir Ivanovich. *Mémoires du Général-Major Russe Baron de Löwenstern*, M. H. Weil, ed., Paris: Fontemoing, 1903
Lüders, Ludwig, and Karl Heinrich Ludwig Pölitz, *Diplomatisches Archiv für Europa*, Leipzig: Baumgarten, 1823

MacDonald, Étienne Jacques. *Souvenirs du Maréchal MacDonald, Duc de Tarente*, Camille Rousset, ed., Paris: Plon, 1892; also published as *Recollections of Marshal MacDonald, Duke of Tarentum*, London: Bentley & Son, 1892, (reprinted Felling: Worley, 1987)
Maillinger, Joseph. 'Tagebuch des Hauptmanns Joseph Maillinger im Feldzuge nach Rußland 1812', Paul Holzhausen, ed., *Darstellungen aus der Bayerischen Kriegs- und Heeresgeschichte*, no. 21, 1912
Mändler, Friedrich. *Erinnerungen aus meinen Feldzügen*, Nürnberg: Lotzbeck, 1854
Mandelsloh, Friedrich Maximilian von. *Erinnerungen 1803–1812 (I)* and *Erinnerungen 1812–1814 (II)*, Jörg Titze, ed., Norderstedt: Books on Demand, 2021
Marbot, Jean-Baptiste-Antoine-Marcelin. *The Memoirs of Baron de Marbot*, Arthur J. Butler, trans., London: Longmans, Green, & Co., 1905
Marmont, Marshal Auguste-Frédéric-Louis Viesse de. *Mémoires du Maréchal Duc de Raguse de 1792 a 1832*, Paris: Perrotin, 1857
Marnier, Jules. *Souvenirs de Guerre en Temps de Paix*, Paris: Faure, 1867
Martens, Christian von. *Vor fünfzig Jahren I., Tagebuch meines Feldzuges in Rußland 1812*, Stuttgart: Schaber, 1863
—— *Vor fünfzig Jahren II., Tagebuch meines Feldzuges in Sachsen 1813*, Stuttgart: Schaber, 1863
Martin, Jacques François. *Souvenirs d'un Ex-Officier (1812–1815)*, Paris: Cherbuliez, 1867
Marwitz, Friedrich August Ludwig von der. *Aus dem Nachlasse Friedrich August Ludwig's von der Marwitz*, Berlin: Mittler & Sohn, 1852

[Massé, Amédée]. 'Souvenirs de Général Bertrand d'après une Correspondance Inédite', Eugène de Budé, ed., *Le Correspondant*, vol. 238, 1910

Mayer, Jakob. *Erzählung der Schicksale und Kriegsabenteuer des ehemaligen westfälischen Artillerie-Wachtmeister Jakob Mayer aus während der Feldzüge in Spanien und Rußland*, Engelskirchen: Fachverlag AMon, 2008

Meerheim, Franz Ludwig August von. *Erlebnisse eines Veteranen der großen Armee während des Feldzugs in Russland 1812*, Dresden: Meinhold, 1860

Meibom, Heinrich Friedrich von. *Aus napoleonischer Zeit*, Leipzig: Koehler & Amelang, 1943

Meier, Wilhelm. *Erinnerungen aus den Feldzügen 1806 bis 1815*, Karlsruhe: Müller, 1854

Meissner, Johann Carl. *Leipzig 1813: Tagebuch und Erinnerungen an die Völkerschlacht*, Kassel: Hamecher, 2001

Mendels, Isidore. *Herman Willem Daendels, voor zijne Benoeming tot Gouverneur-General van Oost-Indië (1762–1807)*, 's-Gravenhage: Nijhoff, 1890

Mercy d'Argenteau, François Joseph Charles Marie, comte de. 'La Bavière en 1812 & 1813', *Revue Contemporaine*, vol. LXIX, 1869

Merkle, Hans. *Der 'Plus-Forderer' Der badische Staatsmann Sigismund von Reitzenstein und seine Zeit*, Karlsruhe: Braun, 2006

Metternich-Winneburg, Prince Clemens Lothar Wenzel von. *Aus Metternich's nachgelassenen Papieren*, Vienna: Braumüller, 1880

Meyer, Stefan. 'Georg Wilhelm Fürst zu Schaumburg-Lippe (1784–1860)', dissertation, Universität Hannover, 2005

Mikhailovsky-Danilevsky, Alexander Ivanovich. *Denkwürdigkeiten aus dem Feldzuge vom Jahre 1813*, Dorpat: Kluge, 1837

'Mittheilungen über die Vertheidigung von Danzig im Jahre 1813. Aus dem Tagebuch des königl. bayer. Obersten Kajetan Grafen von Buttler, des 13. Infanterie-Regiments', *Archiv für Offiziere aller Waffen*, vol. V, no. 3, 1848

Montgelas, Maximilian Graf von. *Denkwürdigkeiten*, Stuttgart: Cotta, 1887

Morgenstern, Franz. *Kriegserinnerungen des Obersten Franz Morgenstern aus westfälischer Zeit*, Wolfenbüttel: Zwissler, 1912

Mouthon, V. E. *Précis de la Vie Militaire du Lieutenant-Général Comte François Durutte*, Douai: Contrejean-Campion, 1836

Müffling, Karl von. *Passages from My Life; together with Memoirs of the Campaign of 1813 and 1814*, Philip Yorcke, ed., London: Bentley, 1853

Müller, Eduard, ed. 'Die Abenteuer eines sächsischen Chevauxlegers während der Leipziger Völkerschlacht', *Der Leipziger*, vol. 2, no. 15, 1907

Müller, Friedrich von. *Erinnerungen aus den Kriegszeiten von 1806–1813*, Braunschweig: Viewig & Sohn, 1851

Müller, Friedrich von. *Kassel seit siebzig Jahren zugleich auch Hessen unter vier Regierungen, die westphälische mit inbegriffen*, Kassel, Hühn, 1876

Müller, Ludwig. *Aus sturmvoller Zeit: Ein Beitrag zur Geschichte der westfälischen Herrschaft*, Marburg: Eckhardt, 1891

Münch, Reinhard, ed. *An der Seite Napoleons: Augenzeugen der Völkerschlacht*, Leipzig: Tauchaer Verlag, 2013

Münch, Reinhard, and Irene Eifler, eds. *Lebenslauf des Oberstleutnants Wilhelm Ritgen (1789–1863)*, Leipzig: Engelsdorfer, 2011

Napoléon I. *Correspondance de Napoléon Ier publiée par ordre de l'Empereur Napoléon III*, Paris: Plon, 1858–1870

—— *Correspondance Générale*, vols. XIII and XIV, Paris: Fayard, 2016–17

Natzmer, Gneomar Ernst von. *Aus dem Leben des Generals Oldwig von Natzmer*, Berlin: Mittler & Sohn, 1876

Nempde-Dupoyet, Pierre Michel. *Relation des Blocus et Sièges de Glogau*, Paris: n.p., 1827

Niemeyer, Anton. *Casselische Chronik vom acht und zwanzigsten September 1813 bis zum ein und zwanzigsten November desselben Jahrs*, Cassel: Krieger, 1814

Noël, Jean Nicole Auguste. *Souvenirs Militaires d'un Officier du Premier Empire*, Paris: Rolin, 1895; also published as *With Napoleon's Guns*, London: Greenhill, 2005

Nollet, Jules. *Histoire de Nicolas-Charles Oudinot*, Bar-le-Duc: Rolin, 1850

Normann, Christian. *Aus den Papieren eines alten Offiziers*, Wilhelm Meister, ed., Hannover: Hahn, 1896

Normann-Ehrenfels, Carl Graf von. 'Der Memoiren des Generals Grafen Karl v. Normann über den Feldzug von 1813', *Schwäbische Kronik*, 1846

Normann-Ehrenfels, Philipp Christian Friedrich Graf von. *Denkwürdigkeiten aus dessen eigenhändigen Aufzeichnungen*, Roth von Schreckenstein, ed., Stuttgart: Kohlhammer, 1891

'Notice historique sur la conduite du général saxon Thielmann en 1813', *Spectateur Militaire*, vol. VII, 15 April–15 September 1829

Notter, Friedrich. *Ludwig Uhland: Sein Leben und seine Dichtungen*, Stuttgart: Metzler, 1863

Oberreit, Hermann. *Beitrag zur Biographie und Characteristik des Generals Freiherrn v. Thielmann*, Dresden: Hilscher, 1829

Odeleben, Ernst Otto Innozenz Freiherr von. *Napoleons Feldzug in Sachsen, im Jahr 1813*, 2nd edition, Dresden: Arnold, 1816

—— *Relation Circonstanciée de la Campagne de 1813, en Saxe*, Paris: Plancer, 1817

—— *Die Umgegend von Bautzen mit Beziehung auf die Schlacht vom 20. und 21. May 1813*, Dresden: Arnold, 1820

—— *Réclamations du Colonel Baron d'Odeleben au Sujet 1° de la Traduction qu'on Publiée de son Ouvrage sur la Campagne de 1813; 2° de quelques Passages contenu dans l'Ouvrage de M. le Baron Fain, Manuscrit de Mil Huit Cent Treize pour Servir à l'Histoire de Napoléon*, Paris: Delaunay, 1825

Ô'Bÿrn, Friedrich August Freiherr. *Camillo Graf Marcolini*, Dresden: Schilling, 1877

Ollech, Karl Rudolf von. *Carl Friedrich Wilhem von Reyher*, Berlin: Mittler & Sohn, 1869

Oman, Carola. *Napoleon's Viceroy: Eugène de Beauharnais*, New York: Funk & Wagnalls, 1966

Oppermann, P. von. 'Die Artillerie- und Genieschule im Königreich Westfalen. Mitteilungen aus den Papieren eines ihrer früheren Zöglinge', *Zeitschrift für hessische Geschichte und Landeskunde*, vol. XXIX, 1905

Pahl, Johann Gottfried von. *Denkwürdigkeiten aus meinem Leben und aus meiner Zeit*, Tübingen, 1840

Paira, Gaston, ed. 'Lettres Inédites du Général Rapp à M. Michael Paira à Paris', *Revue d'Alsace*, vol. XII, 1883

Papet, Theodor von. 'Tagebuch des Capitains Theodor von Papet über den Feldzug in Russland 1812', Ditmar Haeusler, ed., http://amg.hypotheses.org/quellen/papet-1812

Parquin, Charles Denis. *Souvenirs et Campagnes d'un Vieux Soldat de l'Empire*, A. Aubier, ed., Paris: Berger-Levrault, 1903; also published as *Napoleon's Army: The Military Memoirs of Charles Parquin*, London: Greenhill, 1987

Paulin, Jules Antoine. *Les Souvenirs du Général Bon Paulin*, Paris: Plon, 1895

Peppler, Friedrich. *Schilderung meiner Gefangenschaft in Rußland vom Jahre 1812 bis 1814*, Worms: Kranzbühler, 1832

Pertz, Georg Heinrich. *Das Leben des Ministers Freiherrn vom Stein*, Berlin: Reimer, 1851
—— *Das Leben des Feldmarschalls Grafen Neithardt von Gneisenau*, Berlin: Reimer, 1869
Peschel, W. Emil. *Theodor Körner's Tagebuch und Kriegslieder aus dem Jahre 1813*, Freiburg: Fehsenfeld, 1893
Peschel, W. Emil, and Eugen Wildenow. *Theodor Körner und die Seinen*, Leipzig: Seeman, 1898
Peter, Benedikt. *Wachtmeiter Peter mit und gegen Napoleon*, Wilhelm Kohlhaas, ed., Stuttgart: Steinkopf, 1980
Petersdorff, Herman von. *General Johann Adolph Freiherr von Thielmann ein Charakterbild aus napoleonischen Zeit*, Leipzig: Hirzel, 1894
Petri, K. H. *Vor 65 Jahren in und um Torgau*, Torgau: Fügner, 1879
Pfister, Albert. *König Friedrich von Württembergs und seine Zeit*, Stuttgart: Kohlhammer, 1888
Pfnor, Carl F. C. *Der Krieg, seine Mittel und Wege*, Tübingen: Fues, 1864
Piré, Hippolyte Marie Guillaume de Rosnyvinen, comte de. 'Lettre du Lieutenant-Général Marquis de Piré sur le même sujet', *Spectateur Militaire*, vol. VII, 1829
Planat de la Faye, Nicholas Louis. *Vie de Planat de la Faye, Aide-de-Camp des Généraux Lariboisière et Drouot, Officier d'Ordonnance de Napoléon Ier*, Paris: Ollendoff, 1895
—— *Correspondance Intime de Planat de la Faye*, Paris: Ollendorff, 1895
Poppe, Maximilian. *Chronologische Uebersicht der wichtigsten Begebenheiten aus den Kriegsjahren 1806–1815*, Dresden: Thomas, 1848
Poteau, Gérard. *Le Général Comte Le Marois: Aide de Camp de l'Empereur*, Cherbourg-Octeville: Éditions Isoète, 2011
Probsthayn, Friedrich Gottlob. *Tagebuch vom 14.05.1813 bis 29.09.1814*, Konrad Probsthain and Jörg Titze, eds, Norderstedt: Books on Demand, 2016
Proclamations de S. A. R. le Prince-Royal de Suède et Bulletins publiés au Quartier-Général de l'Armée combinée du Nord de l'Allemagne, Stockholm: Sohm, 1815

Querengässer, Alexander. *LeCoq: Ein sächsisches Soldatenleben*, Berlin: Zeughaus Verlag, 2017

Rapp, Jean. *Memoirs of General Count Rapp*, London: Colburn, 1823 (Ken Trotman reprint, Cambridge, 1985); also published as *Mémoires du Général Rapp, Premier Aide-de-Camp de Napoléon*, Paris: Bossange, 1823
Redlich, August. *Clemens Franziscus Xavierus von Cerrini di Monte Varchi*, Dresden: Expedition der Freimüthigen Sachsen-Zeitung, 1852
Réfi, Attila. 'A Career with an Unfair Ending: The Life and Military Activity of the Austrian Lieutenant General Baron Joseph Meskó de Felsőkubin (1762–1815)', *Napoleonic Scholarship*, no. 9, December 2018
Rehberg, August Wilhelm. *Zur Geschichte des Königreichs Hannover in den ersten Jahren nach der Befreiung von der westphälischen und französischen Herrschaft*, Göttingen: Bandenhoeck & Ruprecht, 1826
Reichold, N. *Soldaten-Sohn und das Kriegsleben von 1805 bis 1815*, Munich, 1851
Reiset, Marc-Antoine de. *Souvenirs*, Paris: Calmann Lévy, 1904
'Reminiscenzen aus den Kriegseriegnissen des zweiten Leibhusaren-Regiments in den Feldzügen 1813 und 1814', *Zeitschrift für Kunst, Wissenschaft und Geschichte des Krieges*, vol. 6. 1836
Rieu, Jean Louis. 'Mémoires de Jean-Louis Rieu', *Soldats Suisses au Service Étranger*, vol. III, Geneva: Jullien, 1910
Rilliet, Frédéric Jacques Louis. 'Journal d'un Sous-Lieutenant de Cuirassiers', *Soldats Suisses au Service Étranger*, vol. I, Geneva: Jullien, 1908

Rochechouart, Louis Victor Léon, comte de. *Souvenirs sur la Révolution, l'Empire et la Restauration*, Paris: Plon, 1892

Röder von Bomsburg, Otto Wilhelm Karl. *Mittheilungen aus dem russischen Feldzuge an einen Offizier des Generalstabs*, Leipzig: Engelmann, 1818

Roos, Heinrich U. L. von. *Ein Jahr aus meinem Leben*, St Petersburg: Kray, 1832

Ruthe, Johann Friedrich. *Leben, Leiden und Widerwärtigkeiten eines Niedersachsen von ihm selbst beschrieben*, Berlin: self-published, 1841

Sauer, Paul. *Der schwäbische Zar: Friedrich, Württembergs erster König*, Stuttgart: Deutsche Verlags-Anstalt, 1984

Schäfer, Dieter. *Ferdinand von Österreich*, Graz: Styria, 1988

Schäffer, Conrad Rudolph von. *Denkwürdigkeiten aus dem Leben des Freiherrn C. R. von Schäffer*, Georg Muhl, ed., Pforzheim: Dennig, 1840

Schauroth, Wilhelm Freiherr von. *Im Rheinbund-Regiment der Herzoglich Sächsischen Kontingent Koburg-Hildburghausen-Gotha-Weimar während der Feldzüge in Tirol, Spanien und Rußland 1809–1813*, Berlin: Mittler & Sohn, 1905

Schiemann, Theodor. 'Ein Brief Napoleons an König Maximilian Joseph von Bayern', *Historische Zeitschrift*, Neue Folge vol. 54, 1903

Schlaich, Ludwig von. *Interessante Scene aus den Feldzügen 1812 und 1813*, Ludwigsburg: Nast, 1819 (also published as *Briefe eines deutschen Offiziers während der Feldzüge in den Jahren 1812 und 1813*, Ludwigsburg: Nast, 1819)

Schloßberger, August von, ed. *Politische und Militärische Correspondenz König Friedrichs von Württemberg mit Kaiser Napoleon I., 1805–1813*, Stuttgart: Kohlhammer, 1889

—— 'Ein starker Konflikt des Königs Friedrich von Württemberg mit Kaiser Napoleon im Februar 1813 – der Anfang vom Ende der gegenseitigen Freundschaft', *Besondere Beilage des Staats-Anzeigers für Württemberg*, 3 and 14 November 1888

—— 'Mutige und treffende Erwiderung des Königs Friedrich von Württemberg auf einen ungerechtfertigten Vorwurf des Kaisers Napoleon, d.d. 17. Januar 1813', *Besondere Beilage des Staats-Anzeigers für Württemberg*, 1889

Schlosser, Ludwig. *Erlebnisse eines sächsischen Landpredigers in den Kriegsjahren 1806–1815*, Wiesbaden: Staadt, 1914

Schmidt, Otto Eduard. 'Carl Adolf von Carlowitz und Ferdinand Funck', *Neues Archiv für sächsische Geschichte und Altertumskunde*, vol. LX, 1934

Schmidt, Otto Eduard, ed. *Zeitgenössische Berichte über die Leipziger Schlacht*, Leipzig: Reclam, 1918

Schnabel, Franz. *Sigismund von Reitzenstein der Begründer des Badischen Staates*, Heidelberg: Hörning, 1927

Schreibershofen, Maximilian. *Maximilian von Schreibershofen: Erinnerungen 1805–1815*, Jörg Titze, ed., Norderstedt: Books on Demand, 2021

[Schulenburg, Carl Rudolf von]. 'Die Gefangennahme König Friedrich Augusts am 19. Oktober 1813', *Leipziger Kalendar*, 1912

Sepp, Johann Nepomuk. *Ludwig Augustus, König von Bayern und das Zeitalter der Wiedergeburt der Künste*, Regensburg: Manz, 1903

Seibt, nfn. 'Der König Friedrich August von Sachsen in den Tagen vom 7–26. October 1813', in Robert Naumann, *Aus dem Jahre 1813*, Leipzig: Wiegel, 1869

Senfft von Pilsach, Friedrich Christian Ludwig Graf. *Mémoires*, Leipzig: Veit, 1863

Simon, G. *Die Geschichte des Dynasten und Grafen zu Erbach und ihres Landes*, Frankfurt am Main: Brönner, 1858

'Skizze: Der französische Divisionsgeneral Graf Reynier, Oberbefehlshaber des königlich sächsischen Armee-Korps im Jahr 1812', *Zeitschrift für Kunst, Wissenschaft und Geschichte des Krieges*, vol. LXVIII, 1840

Soden, Franz Freiherr von. *Beiträge zur Geschichte des Krieges in den Jahren 1812 und 1813, besonders in Bezug des 6ten Regiments der damahligen Fürsten-Division des Rheinbundes*, Arnstadt: Hildebrand, 1821

—— *Leben und Schicksale des fürstlich Schwarzburgischen Kammerherrn und Oberstlieutenants Freiherrn Franz von Soden*, Nördlingen: Beck, 1871

Steffens, Heinrich. *Was ich erlebte*, Breslau: Josef Max, 1843

—— *Adventures on the Road to Paris*, London: John Murray, 1848

Stockhorner von Starein, Otto Freiherr. *Die Stockhorner von Starein*, Vienna: Konegen, 1896

[Stockmayer, Ludwig Friedrich von]. 'Die Kämpfe der Württemberger im Feldzug 1813. Aus den Aufzeichnungen des Generals v. Stockmayer', *Schwäbische Merkur*, 16 and 20 March 1895

Strantz, Karl Friedrich Ferdinand von. 'Marsch der Herzoglich Warschauischen Truppen (8. französische Armeekorps) under dem Fürsten Poniatowsky, und einer Brigade Sachsen unter dem General von Gablenz, 1813 von Krakau durch die östreichischen Staaten nach Zittau in Sachsen', *Zeitschrift für Kunst, Wissenschaft und Geschichte des Krieges*, vol. 7, 1832

Strombeck, Friedrich Karl von. *Darstellungen aus meinem Leben und aus meiner Zeit*, Braunschweig: Vieweg, 1833

Streit, Arnold. *Für Napoleon im Felde*, Dresden: Militärhistorische Schriften des Arbeitskreises Sächsische Militärgeschichte, 2012

Suckow, Karl von. 'Mein Feldzug im Jahre 1813', *Hausblätter*, vols. I and II, Stuttgart, 1863

—— *D'Iéna à Moscou: Fragments de ma Vie*, Paris: Plon, 1901

Süstermann, Justus. 'Aufzeichnungen eines jungen Hildesheimers aus den letzten Tagen des Kgl. Westfälischen Heeres (27. September–5. November 1813)', J. H. Gebauer, ed., *Zeitschrift des Vereins für hessische Geschichte und Landeskunde*, vol. 51, 1917

'Tagebuch des Hellwigschen Partisan-Corps, von dessen Entstehung bis zu seiner Auflösung, mit einigen Bruchstücken aus dem Leben des Anführers', *Militairische Blätter*, vol. I, February 1820

'Tagebuch des Königlich Westfälischen Leutnants F. L. Wagner aus den Jahren 1809 bis 1813', H. Heimke-Duderstadt, ed., *Jahrbücher für die deutsche Armee und Marine*, vol. 111, 1899

Taggesell, David August. *Tagebuch eines Dresdner Bürgers oder Niederschreibung der Ereignisse eines jeden Tages soweit solche vom Jahre 1806 bis 1851 für Dresden und dessen Bewohner von geschichtlichem, gewerblichem oder örtlichem Interesse waren*, Dresden: Kuntze, 1854

Teste, François Antoine. 'Souvenirs du Général Baron Teste', *Carnet de la Sabretache*, no. 229, January 1912

Thielmann, Johann Adolph. 'Ueber den General Thielmann und seinen Uebertritt in russische Dienste', *Deutsche Blätter*, no. 3, 19 October 1813

Thirion, Auguste Jean Michel Isidore. *Souvenirs Militaires*, Paris: Berger-Levrault, 1892

Thoumas, Charles. *Les Grands Cavaliers du Premier Empire*, Paris: Levrault, 1890

Thurn und Taxis, August Prinz von. 'Tagebuch eines Officiers im Generalstabe der bayerischen Armee im Feldzuge 1812', *Mittheilungen des K. und K. Kriegs-Archivs*, vol. VII, 1893

—— *Aus drei Feldzügen 1812 bis 1815*, Leipzig: Insel-Verlag, 1912

Titze, Jörg, ed. *Die Tagebücher von Johann Carl von Dallwitz (1812–1815) und Adolf Georg von Göphardt (1813)*, Norderstedt: Books on Demand, 2015

Töppel, Roman. 'Watzdorf, Karl Friedrich Ludwig von', in: *Sächsische Biografie*, herausgegeben vom Institut für Sächsische Geschichte und Volkskunde e.V., wissenschaftliche Leitung: Martina Schattkowsky, Online-Ausgabe: http://www.isgv.de/saebi

Triaire, Paul. *Napoléon et Larrey: Récits Inédits de la Révolution et de l'Empire*, Tours: Mame & Fils, 1902

Tümpling, Wolf von. *Geschichte des Geschlechtes von Tümpling*, Weimar: Böhlau, 1892

Vasson, Jacques de. *Bertrand: Le Grande-Maréchal de Sainte-Hélène*, Issoudun: Laboureur, 1935

Vaudoncourt, Frédéric Guillaume de. *Histoire politique et militaire du Prince Eugène Napoléon*, Paris: Mongie, 1828

Venturini, Carl. *Geschichte unserer Zeit*, Leipzig: Steinacker, 1811

— *Rußlands und Deutschlands Befreiungskriege von Franzosen-Herrschaft unter Napoleon Buonaparte in den Jahren 1812–1815*, Leipzig: Brockhaus, 1816

Viennet, Jean. 'Souvenirs de la vie militaire', *Carnet de la Sabretache*, 1929

Vieth, Johann Justus von. *Auszüge aus den Papieren eines Sachsen: Anekdoten und Ereignisse als Beiträge zur Geschichte des Königreichs Sachsen in den Jahren 1812 bis 1815*, Meißen: Klinkicht, 1843; republished: Heinrich Freiherr von Welck, ed., 'Auszüge aus den Papieren eines Sachsen (Justus Vieth von Golßenau, kgl. Sächs. Generalmajor) 1812–1815', *Mitteilungen des Vereins für Geschichte der Stadt Meißen*, vol. 8, no. 2, 1911

Voigt, Johann August, ed. *Skizzen aus dem Leben Friedrich David Ferdinand Hoffbauers, weiland Pastor zu Ammendorf: Ein Beitrag zur Geschichte des Lützow'schen Corps*, Halle: Verlag des Waisenhauses, 1869

Völkel, Ludwig. 'Eines hessischen Gelehrten Lebenserinnerungen aus der Zeit des Königs Jérôme', Albert Duncker, ed., *Zeitschrift des Vereins für hessische Geschichte und Landeskunde*, vol. IX, 1882

Vollborn, Friedrich. *Erlebtes (III)*, Jörg Titze, ed., Norderstedt: Books on Demand, 2013

— *Erlebtes (I & II)*, Jörg Titze, ed., Norderstedt: Books on Demand, 2016

Vossler, Heinrich August. *With Napoleon in Russia 1812*, Walter Wallich, trans., London: Folio Society, 1969

Wagner, Christian Johann Baptist von. 'Autobiographie des Staatsrats Christian Johann Baptist von Wagner', *Archiv des Historischen Vereins von Unterfranken und Aschaffenburg*, vol. 74, 1905

Waitz, R. *Erinnerungen aus den Kriegsjahren 1813, 1814 und 1815*, Coburg: author, 1847

Wartensleben, Julius Graf von. *Nachrichten von dem Geschlechte der Grafen von Wartensleben*, Berlin: Nauck, 1858

Watson, S. J. *By Command of the Emperor: A Life of Marshal Berthier*, Cambridge: Ken Trotman, 1988 (reprint of 1957 edition)

Weber, Karl von. 'Detlev Graf von Einsiedel, Königl. Sächsischer Cabinets-Minister', *Archiv für Sächsische Geschichte*, vol. I, 1863

Wedel, Carl Anton Wilhelm Graf von. *Geschichte eines Offiziers im Kriege gegen Rußland 1812, in russischer Gefangenschaft 1813 bis 1814, im Feldzuge gegen Napoleon 1815*, Berlin: Asher, 1897

Wedel, Carl Anton Wilhelm Graf von. *Lebenserinnerungen*, Curt Troeger, ed., Berlin: Mittler & Sohn, 1913

Weil, Maurice-Henri. *Le Prince Eugène et Murat*, Paris: Fontemoing, 1902

Weinhold, Carl August. *Die Elbbrücke zu Dresden, historisch und malerisch dargestellt*, Dresden: Arnold, 1813

— *Dresden und seine Schicksale, im Jahre 1813*, Dresden: Arnold, 1814

Wesemann, Heinrich. *Kannonier des Kaisers*, Cologne: Verlag Wissenschaft und Politik, 1971
Wilhelm von Baden, Markgraf. *Denkwürdigkeiten des Markgrafen Wilhelm von Baden*, Karl Obser, ed., Heidelberg: Winter, 1906
Winter, Alexander. *Karl Philipp Fürst von Wrede als Berater des Königs Max Joseph und des Kronprinzen Ludwig von Bayern (1813–1825)*, Neue Schriftenreihe des Stadtarchivs München, Heft 7, Munich: Stadtarchiv, 1968
Wintzingerode, Wilhelm Clothar Ferdinand von. *General der Kavallerie Ferdinand Freiherr von Wintzingerode: Ein Lebensbild aus den napoleonischen Kriegen*, Arolsen: Loewié, 1902
Wolffersdorff, Eduard Franz von. 'Meine Erlebnisse in und nach der Schlacht bei Leipzig, während des 17., 18. und 19. Octobers 1813', in Robert Naumann, *Zum 19. October 1864*, Leipzig: Weigel, 1864
Wolfsteig, August. 'König Jerome', *Preußische Jahrbücher*, vol. CIII, January–March 1901
Woringer, August. Review of *König Jérôme Napoleon* in *Zeitschrift für hessische Geschichte und Landeskunde*, vol. XIV, 1901
—— Lecture in *Mitteilungen an die Mitglieder des Vereins für hessische Geschichte und Landeskunde*, 1908/9
—— 'Westfälische Offiziere III: Wilhelm Kupfermann', *Hessenland*, vol. XXIII, 1909
—— 'Westfälische Offiziere IV: Die Freiherrn von Hammerstein', *Hessenland*, vol. XXIII, 1909
—— 'Westfälische Offiziere VII: Die Artillerieoffiziere Schulz und Wille', *Hessenland*, vol. XXIII, 1909
Würtz, Christian. *Johann Niklas Friedrich Brauer (1754–1813)*, Stuttgart: Kohlhammer, 2005
Yelin, Christoph Ludwig von. '1812: Aus dem Tagebuch eines württembergischen Offiziers', *Süddeutsche Monatshefte*, vol. II, 1908
—— *Merkwürdige Tage meines Lebens*, Stuttgart: Sattler, 1817
Zezschwitz, Johann Adolf von, and Jean Baptiste Honoré Raymond. *Capefigue 1814 und 1815. Der Wiener Congreß und das heutige Europa. Nebst actenmäßiger Darstellung der Königl. Preuß. Decimation des, seinem Eide treugebliebenen Sächsischen Heeres*, Grimma: Verlag-Comptoir, 1847
Zezschwitz, Joseph Woldemar von. *Mittheilungen aus den Papieren eines sächsischen Staatsmannes*, Dresden: Zeh, 1864
Zimmermann, Johann Michael. 'Aufzeichnungen eines Veteranen aus der Zeit 1806–1814', *Das Bayernland*, vol. 22, no. 6, 1911
'Züge zur Geschichte Dresdens und des Krieges in Sachsen im Jahre 1813', *Europäische Annalen*, vol. IV, 1817
'Zur Schlacht von Dennewitz', *Militair-Wochenblatt*, no. 265, 21 July 1821

Official Histories

Just before World War I, the Prussian and Austrian General Staffs each published two series of detailed studies of the 'Befreiungskriege' written by respected military historians. These are listed by their authors in the endnotes (e.g., Caemmerer, *Geschichte des Frühjahrsfeldzuges*, vol. II), but sorting them in a bibliography can be confusing, so they are compiled below for ease of reference. The French staff did not compose an official history per se, but a wealth of documents were assembled and published by Gabriel Fabry (some anonymously, some under his name).

Austria

A. Series title: *Befreiungskrieg 1813 und 1814*, 5 vols. Individual volumes used:

Criste, Oskar. *Österreichs Beitritt zur Koalition*, vol. I, Vienna: Seidel & Sohn, 1913
Wlaschütz, Wilhelm. *Österreichs entscheidenes Machtaufgebot 1813*, vol. II, Vienna: Seidel & Sohn, 1913
Horstenau, Edmund Glaise von. *Feldzug von Dresden*, vol. III, Vienna: Seidel & Sohn, 1913
Ehnl, Maximilian. *Schlacht bei Kulm*, vol. IV, Vienna: Seidel & Sohn, 1913
Hoen, Maximilian Ritter von. *Feldzug von Leipzig*, vol. V, Vienna: Seidel & Sohn, 1913

B. Series title: *Österreich in den Befreiungskriegen 1813–1815*, 10 vols. Individual volumes used:

Veltzé, Alois. *Die Politik Metternichs*, vol. I, Vienna: Edlinger, 1911
Horstenau, Edmund Glaise von. *Die Tage von Dresden 1813*, vol. II, Vienna: Edlinger, 1911
Woinovich, Emil von. *Kulm, Leipzig, Hanau 1813*, vol. III, Vienna: Edlinger, 1911
Holtz, Georg Freiherr von. *Die innerösterreichische Armee 1813 und 1814*, vol. IV, Vienna: Edlinger, 1912
Horstenau, Edmund Glaise von. *Die Heimkehr Tirols*, vol. X, Vienna: Verlag für vaterländische Gesellschaft, 1914

Prussia

A. Series title: *Geschichte der Befreiungskriege 1813–1815*. Individual volumes used:

Holleben, Albert von. *Geschichte des Frühjahrsfeldzuges 1813 und seine Vorgeschichte*, vol. I, *Vorgeschichte und Geschichte des Feldzuges bis zum 26. April 1813*, Berlin: Mittler & Sohn, 1904
Caemmerer, Rudolf von. *Geschichte des Frühjahrsfeldzuges 1813 und seine Vorgeschichte*, vol. II, *Die Ereignisse von Ende April bis zum Waffenstillstand*, Berlin: Mittler & Sohn, 1909
Friederich, Rudolf. *Geschichte des Herbstfeldzuges 1813*, vol. I, *Vom Abschluß des Waffenstillstandes bis zur Schlacht bei Kulm*, Berlin: Mittler & Sohn, 1903
Friederich, Rudolf. *Geschichte des Herbstfeldzuges 1813*, vol. II, *Von der Schlacht bei Kulm bis zu den Kämpfen bei Leipzig*, Berlin: Mittler & Sohn, 1904
Friederich, Rudolf. *Geschichte des Herbstfeldzuges 1813*, vol. III, *Von der Völkerschlacht bei Leipzig bis zum Schluße des Feldzuges*, Berlin: Mittler & Sohn, 1906

B. Friederich, Rudolf. *Die Befreiungskriege 1813–1815*, 4 vols., Berlin: Mittler & Sohn, 1912–13. Used for this work: vol. I, *Der Frühjahrsfeldzug 1813* (1913) and vol. II, *Der Herbstfeldzug 1813* (1912)

France

[Fabry, Gabriel]. *Étude sur les Opérations du Maréchal Oudinot du 15 Août au 4 Septembre 1813*, Paris, Chapelot, 1910
—— *Étude sur les Opérations du Maréchal MacDonald du 22 Août au 4 Septembre 1813*, Paris, Chapelot, 1910
Fabry, Gabriel. *Étude sur les Opérations de l'Empereur du 28 Août au 4 Septembre 1813*, Paris, Chapelot, 1911
—— *Étude sur les Opérations de l'Empereur du 5 Septembre au 21 Septembre 1813*, Paris, Chapelot, 1913
—— ed. *Étude sur les Opérations de l'Empereur du 22 Septembre au 3 Octobre 1813*, Paris: Chapelot, 1913

General Works

Note that many of these histories (e.g., Aster, Buturlin, Pelet and Völerndorff) were written by participants in the campaign or other contemporaries.

Aaslestad, Katherine, and Karen Hagemenn, 'Collaboration, Resistance, and Reform: Experiences and Historiographies of the Napoleonic Wars in Central Europe', *Central European History*, no. 39, 2006

[Alexander, Herzog zu Württemberg]. *Aperçu des Opérations des Troupes Alliées devant Danzig en 1813*, Leipzig: n.p., 1821

Andreas, Willy. 'Baden nach dem Wiener Frieden 1809', *Neujahrsblätter der Badischen Historischen Kommission*, vol. 15, 1912

—— *Der Aufbau des Staates im Zusammenhang der allgemeinen Politik*, vol. I of *Geschichte der badischen Verwaltungsorganisation und Verfassung*, Leipzig: Quelle & Meyer, 1913

Angelelli, Jean, and Alain Pigeard. *La Confédération du Rhin*, Paris: Quator, 2002

Angeli, Moritz Edlen von. 'Die Capitulation von Dresden 1813', *Mittheilungen des K. K. Kriegsarchivs*, 1881

—— 'Die Theilnahme des k. k. österreichischen Auxiliar-Corps unter Commando des G. d. C. (später Feldmarschalls) Fürsten Carl zu Schwarzenberg im Feldzuge Napoleon I. gegen Russland', *Mittheilungen des K. K. Kriegsarchivs*, Vienna, 1884

Arndt, Georg. *Chronik von Halberstadt von 1801–1850*, Halberstadt: Schimmelburg, 1908

Arndt, Johannes. *Das Fürstentum Lippe im Zeitalter der Französischen Revolution 1770–1820*, Münster: Waxmann, 1992

Arnold, Christopher. 'Westphalian Soldiers and the Myth of the War of Liberation – Evolving Notions of Identity, Francophobia, and Soldier-Masculinity in Napoleonic Germany', masters thesis, Texas Tech University, 2014

Arnold, James R. *Napoleon 1813: The Battle of Bautzen*, Lexington, VA: Napoleon Books, 2015

Arvind, T. T., and Lindsay Stirton. 'Explaining the reception of the Code Napoleon in Germany: a fuzzy-set qualitative comparative analysis', *Legal Studies*, vol. 30, no. 1, 2010

Aster, Friedrich. 'Napoleon in Dresden 1812 und 1813', *Dresdner Geschichtsblätter*, vol. XI, no. 2, 1902

Aster, Karl Heinrich. 'Nachrichten über die Sprengung der Dresdener Elb-Brücke', *Archiv für die Officiere der Königlich Preußischen Artillerie- und Ingenieur-Korps*, vol. IV, no. 7, 1838

—— 'Darstellung der am 26sten August 1813 stattgefundenen Angriffe der alliirten Armee auf die vor der Altstadt Dresden erbauten französischen Feldschanzen Nr. III. und IV. und die dazwischen liegende Seevorstadt', *Archiv für die Officiere der Königlich Preußischen Artillerie- und Ingenieur-Korps*, vol. V, no. 10, 1840

—— *Die Kriegsereignisse zwischen Peterswalde, Pirna, Königstein und Priesten im August 1813 und die Schlacht bei Kulm*, Dresden: Adler & Dietze, 1843

—— *Die Gefechte und Schlachten bei Leipzig im Oktober 1813*, Dresden: Arnold, 1852

—— *Schilderung der Kriegsereignisse in und vor Dresden vom 7. März bis 28. August 1813*, Dresden: Arnold, 1856

'Der Aufstand der Sachsen in Lüttich (2. Mai 1815)', *Preußische Jahrbücher*, vol 16, 1865

Augoyat, Antoine Marie. *Relation de la Défense de Torgau par les Troupes Françaises en 1813 sous Les Généraux de Division Comte de Narbonne et Comte Du Taillis*, Paris: Leneveu, 1840

Auriol, Charles. 'Retraite du 10e Corps de la Grande-Armée de la Dwina sur Dantzig (1812)', *Spectateur Militaire*, no. 42, July–August–September 1888

B., A. 'Theodor Körner's Leier und Schwert', *Die Gartenlaube*, no. 8, 1863

Bagès, Georges. 'Le Siège de Glogau 1813–1814', *Spectateur Militaire*, vol. LX, 1905

[Bangold, Joseph Konrad von]. 'Nachricht über die Begebenheiten des Königl. Würtembergischen Truppen-Corps an den Schlacht-Tagen von Leipzig im Feldzuge 1813', *Militair-Wochenblatt*, nos. 5 and 6, 4 and 11 February 1837

Baranowski, Marcin. *Bitwa pod Kaliszem 13 lutego 1813*, Zabrze: Inforteditions, 2006
Bauer, Gerhard, Gorch Pieken, and Matthias Roggs, eds. *Blutige Romantik: 200 Jahre Befreiungskriege*, Dresden: Militärhistorisches Museum der Bundeswehr, 2014
Baustian, Olivier. *Le royaume de Westphalie et le système continental 1807–1813*, Paris: Kronos, 2024
Bayern 1813, Munich: Bayerland-Verlag, 1913
Beck, Karl. 'Zur Vorgeschichte des Rheinbunds', dissertation, Universität Giessen, 1890
Becker, Gottfried Wilhelm. *Der Krieg der Franzosen und ihrer Alliirten gegen Rußland, Preußen, und seine Verbündeten*, Leipzig: Engelmann, 1814
Behm, Werner. *Die Mecklenburger 1813 bis 15 in den Befreiungskriegen*, Hamburg: Hermes, 1913
Belostyk, Richard (Ryszard). 'Fortifikacja Wzorcowa Napoleona', *Przeglad Historyczny*, 71/1, 1980
—— 'Modlin en 1813', *Francja-Polska XVIII–XIX w.*', Warsaw: Państwowe Wydawnictwo Naukowe, 1983
Berding, Helmut. *Napoleonische Herrschafts- und Gesellschaftspolitik im Königreich Westfalen 1807–1813*, Göttingen: Vandenhoeck & Ruprecht, 1973
—— 'Le Royaume de Westphalie, État-Modèle', *Francia*, vol. 10, 1982
Bergér, Heinrich. 'Hessen-Darmstadts Abfall von Napoleon I.', *Hessenland*, vol. XVI, 1902
'Berichtigung eine Stelle im 1ten Theile von Plothos Krieg in Deutschland und Frankreich', *Kriegs-Schriften herausgegeben von baierischen Officieren*, vol. IV, 1820
Berryman, Todd B. 'Boundaries of Loyalty: Territorial Consolidation and Public Allegiance in Northwest Germany, 1797–1817', dissertation, University of North Carolina at Chapel Hill, 2004
—— 'Napoleon's German Soldiers: Westphalians in Arms', *Nineteenth Century Studies*, no. 26, 2012
Bethan, Anika. ' La Réception Mémorielle de la Campagne de Russie des Soldats Westphaliennes après 1813', in *Revue d'Allemagne et des Pays de Langue Allemande*, vol. 47, no. 1, January–June 2015
Bezzel, Oskar. *Studien zur Geschichte Bayerns in der Zeit der Befreiungskriege*, Munich: Bayerisches Kriegsarchiv, 1926
Bignon, Louis Pierre Édouard, and Alfred Auguste Ernouf. *Histoire de France depuis le Commencement de la Guerre de Russie jusqu'à la Deuxième Restauration*, Brussels: Meline, Can & Compagnie, 1846
Billinger, Robert D. Jr. 'Good and True Germans: The "Nationalism" of the Rheinbund Princes, 1806–1814', in Heinz Durchhardt and Andreas Krug, *Reich oder Nation? Mitteleuropa 1780–1815*, Mainz: Zabern: 1998
Bilz, Wolfram. 'Die Grossherzogtümer Würzburg und Frankfurt: Ein Vergleich', dissertation, Julius-Maximilian-Universität, Würzburg, 1968
Bippen, Wilhelm von. *Geschichte der Stadt Bremen*, Halle: Müller, 1904
Bitterauf, Theodor. 'Zur Geschichte der Öffentlichen Meinung im Königreich Bayern im Jahre 1813 bis zum Abschluss des Vertrages von Ried', *Archiv für Kulturgeschichte*, vol. XI, 1910
Blank, Isabella. 'Der bestrafte König? Die sächsische Frage 1813–1815', dissertation, Ruprecht-Karl University Heidelberg, 2013
Blanning, Tim. 'Napoleon and German Identity', *History Today*, April 1998
Bleibtreu, Karl. *Ein Lied von der deutschen Treue*, Leipzig: Deutscher Kampf-Verlag, 1906
Bleyer, Alexandra. *Auf gegen Napoleon! Mythos Volkskriege*, Darmstadt: Primus, 2013

Block, Hans. *Sachsen im Zeitalter der Völkerschlacht*, Leipzig: Leipziger Buchdruckerei, 1913
Bockholt, Eva. 'Der europäische Bund: eine gescheiterte Vision der Freiheitskriege? Studien zur deutschen Publizistik 1813/14', dissertation, Freie Universität Berlin, 2004
Bogdanovich, Modest Ivanovich. *Geschichte des Feldzuges im Jahre 1812*, Leipzig: Schlicke, 1863
—— *Geschichte des Krieges im Jahre 1813 für Deutschlands Unabhängigkeit*, St Petersburg: Hässel, 1865
Boll, Ernst. *Geschichte Meklenburgs*, Neubrandenburg: author, 1856
Börner, Karl-Heinz. *Vor Leipzig 1813*, Berlin: Verlag der Nation, 1988
—— 'Krise und Ende des Rheinbundes – hauptsächlich unter militärpolitischem Aspekt', *Jahrbuch der Geschichte*, vol. 38, 1989
Bothmer, Felix Graf von. 'Anteil des K.B. 13. Infanterie-Regiments an der Belagerung Danzigs im Jahre 1813', *Jahrbuch der Militärischen Gesellschaft*, 1896/97
Böttinger, Carl Wilhelm. *Geschichte des Kurstaates und Königreiches Sachsens*, Hamburg: Perthes, 1831
Böttinger, Carl Wilhelm, and Theodor Flathe. *Geschichte des Kurstaates und Königreiches Sachsens*, Gotha: Perthes, 1870
Boudon, Jacques-Olivier. 'Napoléon et la Bavière', 2006, at www.france-bayern.info
—— 'L'Exportation du Modèle Français dans l'Allemagne' in *Napoléon et l'Europe: Colloque de La Roche-sur-Yon*, Jean-Clément Martin, ed., Rennes: Presses universitaires de Rennes, 2002
Boué, Gilles. *Leipzig 1813*, Paris: Histoire & Collections, 2012
Bourguinat, Nicolas. 'Présentation', in *Revue d'Allemagne et des Pays de Langue Allemande*, vol. 47, no. 1, January–June 2015
Brabant, Arthur. *In und Um Dresden 1813*, Dresden: Köhler, 1913
Brakensiek, Stefan. 'Die Reichsstände des Königreichs Westphalen', *Westfälische Forschungen*, no. 53, 2003
—— 'Strukturen eines antinapoleonischen Aufstands: Grebenstein 1813', in Ute Planert, ed., *Krieg und Umbruch in Mitteleuropa um 1800*, Paderborn: Schöningh, 2009
Brandt, Peter. 'Die Befreiungskriege 1813 bis 1815 in der deutschen Geschichte', in Peter Brandt, ed., *An der Schwelle zur Moderne: Deutschland um 1800*, Bonn: Forschungsinstitut der Friedrich-Ebert-Stiftung, 1999
—— 'Die Befreiungskriege von 1813 bis 1815 in der deutschen Geschichte', in Michael Güttner, Rüdiger Hachtmann, and Heinz-Gerhard Haupt, eds, *Geschichte und Emanzipation*, Frankfurt: Campus, 1999
Brandt, Peter, Martin Kirsch, and Arthur Schlegelmilch, eds. *Handbuch der europäischen Verfassungsgeschichte im 19. Jahrhundert. Institutionen und Rechtspraxis im gesellschaftlichen Wandel*, Bonn: Dietz, 2006
Brecher, Adolf. *Napoleon I. und der Überfall des Lützowschen Freikorps bei Kitzen am 17. Juni 1813*, Berlin: Gaertner, 1897
Breuilly, John. 'The Response to Napoleon and German Nationalism', in Alan Forrest and Peter H. Wilson, eds, *The Bee and the Eagle: Napoleonic France and the End of the Holy Roman Empire, 1806*, London: Palgrave Macmillan, 2009
—— *Austria, Prussia and the Making of Germany 1806–1871*, Harlow: Pearson, 2011
Bröckling, Ulrich, and Michael Sikora, eds. *Armeen und ihre Deserteure: Vernachlässigte Kapitel einer Militärgeschichte der Neuzeit*, Göttingen: Vandenhoeck & Ruprecht, 1998
Broers, Michael, Peters Hicks, and Agustin Guimerá, eds. *The Napoleonic Empire and the New European Political Culture*, London: Palgrave MacMillan, 2012

Brun, Jean-François. *Oubliés du Fleuve: Glogau-sur-Oder, un Siège sous le Premier Empire*, Saint-Julien-Chapteuil: Editions du Roure, 1997
—— 'Les Unités Étrangères dans les Armées Napoléoniennes: un Élement de la Stratégie Globale du Grand Empire', *Revue Historique des Armées*, no. 255, 2009
—— 'Du Niéman à l'Elbe: la Manoeuvre Retardatrice de la Grande Armée', *Revue Historique des Armées*, 2012
Bruyère-Ostells, Walter. *Leipzig 16–19 octobre 1813*, Paris: Tallandier, 2013
—— 'Les Troupes Allemandes de la Grande Armée à Leipzig (1813): Depasser les Lectures Idéologiques d'une Défection', in Franck Mercier, Yann Lagadec, and Ariane Boltanski, eds, *La Bataille: Du Fait d'Armes au Combat Idéologique, XIe–XIXe Siècle*, Rennes: Presses Universitaires Rennes, 2015
Buchner, O. 'Die großherzoglich hessischen Truppen in den Kriegen der Rheinbundzeit und die amtliche Presse des Landes', *Hessenland*, vol. X, 1896
Bürger, Johann Christian August. *Nachrichten über die Blokade und Belagerung der Elb- und Landesfestung Torgau im Jahre 1813*, Torgau: Wideburg, 1838
Buturlin, Dmitri Petrovich. *Tableau de la Campagne d'Automne de 1813 en Allemagne*, Paris: Bertrand, 1818

Caemmerer, Rudolf von. *Die Befreiungskriege 1813–1815: Ein strategischer Überblick*, Berlin: Mittler & Sohn, 1907
Calvet, Stéphane. *Leipzig, 1813: La Guerre des Peuples*, Paris: Vendémiaire, 2013
Camon, Hubert. *La Guerre Napoléonienne: Les Systèmes d'Opérations, Théorie et Technique*, Paris: Chapelot, 1907
Carl, Horst. 'Der Mythos des Befreiungskrieges. Die "martialische Nation" im Zeitalter der Revolutions- und Befreiungskriege 1792–1815', in Dieter Langewiesche and Georg Schmidt, eds, *Föderative Nation: Deutschlandkonzepte von der Reformation bis zum ersten Weltkrieg*, Munich: Oldenbourg, 2000
Cazalas, Jean Jules André Marie Eutrope. *De Stralsund à Lunebourg: Épisode de la Campagne de 1813*, Paris: Fournier: 1911
Cerrini de Monte Varchi, Heinrich von. 'Der Ueberfall von Freyberg am 18. September 1813 durch den östereichischen Generalen Baron Scheither', *Oestereichische militärische Zeitschrift*, vol. VI, 1833
Chambray, Georges de. *Histoire de l'Expédition de Russie*, Paris: Chez Pillet Ainé, 1838
Chandler, David G. *The Campaigns of Napoleon*, New York: Macmillan, 1966
Charras, Jean-Baptiste-Adolphe. *Histoire de la Guerre de 1813 en Allemagne*, Leipzig: Brockhaus, 1866
Chroust, Anton. 'Das Großherzogtum Würzburg (1806–1814)', *Neujahrsblätter*, Würzburg: Stürtz, 1913
—— *Geschichte des Großherzogtums Würzburg (1806–1814): Die äussere Politik des Großherzogtums*, Würzburg: Becker, 1932
Citino, Robert M. *The German Way of War*, Lawrence: University of Kansas, 2005
Clarke, Christopher. *Iron Kingdom: The Rise and Downfall of Prussia 1600–1947*, Cambridge: Harvard University Press, 2006
Clausewitz, Carl von. *Hinterlassene Werke*, Berlin: Dümmler, 1862
—— *On War*, Michael Howard and Peter Paret, ed. and trans., Princeton: Princeton University Press, 1984
—— *The Campaign of 1812 in Russia*, New York: Da Capo Press, 1995
Clercq, M. de. *Recueil des Traités de la France*, Paris: Amyot, 1864

Colson, Bruno. *Leipzig: La Bataille des Nations*, Paris: Perrin, 2013
Comando del Corpo di Stato Maggiore, Foucartio Storico. *Gli Italiani in Germania nel 1813*, Città di Castello: Unione Arti Grafiche, 1914
Connelly, Owen. *Napoleon's Satellite Kingdoms*, New York: The Free Press, 1965
Curtze, Ludwig Ferdinand Christian. *Geschichte und Beschreibung des Fürstentums Waldeck*, Arolsen: Speyer, 1850
Czubaty, Jaroslaw. *The Duchy of Warsaw 1807–1815*, London: Bloomsbury, 2011

Darmstaedter, Paul. *Das Großherzogtum Frankfurt: Ein Kulturbild aus der Rheinbundzeit*, Frankfurt: Baer, 1901
'Darstellung der Ereignisse bei der schlesischen Armee im Jahre 1813, mit besonderer Berücksichtigung des Antheils der preußischen Truppen', *Beiheft zum Militair-Wochenblatt*, 1843–5
Dawson, Paul Lindsay. *Napoleon's German Artillery*, Raleigh: Lulu, 2010
Delau, Reinhard. *Brüder, es brennt, es brennt: Napoleonzeit in Sachsen*, Dresden: Dresdener Verlagshaus Technik, 2012
Delbrück, Hans. *Erinnerungen, Aufsätze und Reden*, Berlin: Stilke, 1902
—— *Das Leben des Feldmarschalls Grafen Neidhardt von Gneisenau*, Berlin: Stilke, 1908
Demmler, Heinrich. 'Die Neubildung der bayerischen Heeresabteilung nach dem Rückzuge aus Rußland 1812 und die Ereignisse bis zur Rückkehr in die Heimat 1813', *Darstellungen aus der Bayerischen Kriegs- und Heeresgeschichte*, no. 15, 1906
—— 'Anteil der Bayerischen Division Raglovich am Frühjahrsfeldzug 1813', *Darstellungen aus der Bayerischen Kriegs- und Heeresgeschichte*, no. 16, 1907
Dethlefs, Gerd, Armin Owzar, and Gisela Weiß, eds. *Modell und Wirklichkeit: Politik, Kultur und Gesellschaft im Großherzogtum Berg und im Königreich Westphalen*, Paderborn: Schöningh, 2008
'Die Belagerung von Torgau 1813', *Archiv für die Offiziere der Königlich Preußischen Artillerie- und Ingenieur-Korps*, vol. VI, no. 12, 1841
'Die grosse Chronik' (review), *Militair-Literaturzeitung*, vol. IV, July–August 1841
Die Württemberger in den Freiheitskriegen, Stuttgart: Holland & Josenhans, c. 1915
Dietlein, H. Rudolph. *Die Schlacht bei Wartenburg*, Wittenberg: Herrosé, 1863
Dieterich, J. R. 'Die Politik Landgraf Ludwig X. von Hessen-Darmstadt von 1790–1806', *Archiv für hessische Geschichte und Altertumskunde*, vol. VII, 1910
Dietrich, Gottlob Siegfried. *Groß Glogaus Schicksale von 1806 bis 1814*, Glogau: Neue Güntherschen Buchdruckerei, 1815
Doeberl, Michael. *Bayern und die deutsche Erhebung wider Napoleon I.*, Munich: Akademie der Wissenschaften, 1907
—— *Entwicklungsgeschichte Bayerns*, Munich: Oldenbourg, 1912
Dohm, Karsten. *Die Typhusepidemie in der Festung Torgau 1813–1814*, Düsseldorf: Triltsch, 1987
Donath, Fritz, Ernst Engelberg, Heinz Füßler, and A. M. Uhlmann, *Leipzig 1813: Die Völkerschlacht im nationalen Befreiungskampf des deutschen Volkes*, Leipzig: Veb, 1953
Dorsch, Paul. *Kriegszüge der Württemberger im 19. Jahrhundert*, Stuttgart: Vereinsbuchhandlung, 1913
Driault, Édouard. *La Chute de l'Empire: La Légende Napoléon (1812–1815)*, Paris: Félix Alcan, 1927
Dufraisse, Roger. 'Le Grand Soulèvement de 1813', *Histoiria Special*, no. 12, July–August 1991
—— *L'Allemagne à l'Époque Napoléonienne*, Bonn: Bouvier, 1992

—— 'Politique Douanière Française, Blocus et Système Continental en Allemagne', *Revue du Souvenir Napoléonien*, no. 389, June–July 1993

Dunan, Marcel. *Napoléon et l'Allemagne: la Système Continental et les Débuts du Royaume de Bavière*, Paris: Plon, 1942

Duval, Jules. 'Napoléon, Bülow et Bernadotte', *Spectateur Militaire*, vol. LXI, 1905

Duvernoy, Max von. 'Die Württembergischen Kavalleriebrigade Normann im Feldzuge 1813', *Beiheft zum Militär-Wochenblatt*, vol. X, 1907

Ebling, Hanswerner. 'Die hessische Politik in der Rheinbundzeit 1806–13', *Archiv für hessische Geschichte und Altertumskunde*, XXIV, 1952/3

Echternkamp, Jörg. *Der Aufstieg des deutschen Nationalismus (1770–1840)*, Frankfurt: Campus, 1996

Egloffstein, Hermann Freiherr von. 'Carl August während des Krieges von 1813', *Deutsche Rundschau*, vol. CLVI, July–September, 1913

Ehwald, R. 'Gotha im Jahre 1813', *Mitteilungen der Vereinigung für Gothaische Geschichte und Altertumsforschung*, 1912–1913

Eidahl, Kyle O. 'Napoleon's Faulty Strategy: Oudinot's Operations against Berlin, 1813', The Consortium on Revolutionary Europe 1750–1850, *Selected Papers 1995*, Bernard A. Cook, Kyle O. Eidahl, Donald D. Horward,, and Karl Roider, eds, Tallahassee: Florida State University 1995

—— 'He "Deliberately Obeyed Ney's Order": Oudinot at Dennewitz', The Consortium on Revolutionary Europe 1750–1850, *Selected Papers 1999*, Owen Connelly, Charles Crouch, Donald D. Horward, William Olejniczak, and Michael F. Pavkovic, eds, Tallahassee: Florida State University 1999

'Einschließung und Belagerung von Thorn im Jahre 1813', *Kriegs-Schriften herausgegeben von baierischen Offizieren*, vol. III, 1821

Elting, John R. *Swords Around a Throne*, New York: The Free Press, 1988

Emminghaus, Gustav. 'Das thüringische Bataillon in Ruhla im April 1813', *Zeitschrift des Vereins für thüringische Geschichte und Altertumskunde*, vol. III, 1859

Esposito, Vincent J., and John R. Elting. *A Military History and Atlas of the Napoleonic Wars*, New York: Praeger, 1968

Eulenhaupt, Franz. *Geschichte der Festung Marienberg nebst deren Belagerungen und Blokaden*, Würzburg: author, 1851

Fehrenbach, Elisabeth. *Traditionelle Gesellschaft und revolutionäres Recht: Die Einführung des Code Napoléon in den Rheinbundstaaten*, Göttingen: Vandenhoeck & Rupprecht, 1978

—— 'Verfassungs- und Sozialpolitische Reformen und Reformprojekte in Deutschland unter dem Einfluss des Napoleonischen Frankreich', *Historische Zeitschrift*, vol. 228, 1979

—— *Vom Ancien Regime zum Wiener Kongress*, 4th edn, Munich: Oldenbourg, 2001

Feldmann, Hildegard. 'Einwohner aus dem Kanton Duisburg im französischen Militärdienst 1806–1813', *Duisburger Forschungen*, vol. 15, 1971

Feldzug der Kaiserlich Russischen Armee von Polen in den Jahren 1813 und 1814, Friedrich Karl Ferdinand Müffling, ed., Hamburg: Hoffmann & Campe, 1843.

Finley, Milton. '"They Will Turn Their Guns on Us": Reynier, the Saxons and Großbeeren', The Consortium on Revolutionary Europe 1750–1850, *Selected Papers 1999*, Owen Connelly, Charles Crouch, Donald D. Horward, William Olejniczak, and Michael F. Pavković, eds, Tallahassee: Florida State University 1999

Fisher, H. A. L. *Studies in Napoleonic Statesmanship: Germany*, Oxford: Clarendon Press, 1903

Flathe, Theodor. *Neuere Geschichte Sachsens*, Gotha: Perthes, 1873

Foerster, Max. *Die Geschichte der Dresdner Augustus-Brücke*, Dresden: Dressel, 1902
Forrest, Alan. *Conscripts and Deserters: The Army and French Society during the Revolution and Empire*, Oxford: Oxford University Press, 1989
Förster, Friedrich. *Geschichte der Befreiungs-Kriege 1813, 1814, 1815*, Berlin: Hempel, 1862
Fortescue, John W. *A History of the British Army*, London: Macmillan, 1920
'La Fortresse de Küstrin sous l'Occupation Française 1806–1814', *Revue du Génie Militaire*, vol. VII, 1893
Foucart, Paul-Jean. *Une Division de Cavalerie Légère en 1813*, Paris: Berger-Levrault, 1891
—— *Bautzen*, Paris: Berger-Levrault, 1897
Francke, Heinrich. *Mecklenburgs Noth und Kampf vor und in dem Befreiungskriege*, Wismar: Schmidt & Cossel, 183
Frauenholz, Eugen von. 'Die Eingliederung von Heer und Volk in den Staat in Bayern 1597–1815', *Münchener Historische Abhandlungen*, no. 14, 1940
Fremont-Barnes, Gregory, ed. *Armies of the Napoleonic Wars*, Barnsley: Pen & Sword, 2011
Freytag-Loringhoven, Hugo Freiherr von. *Aufklärung und Armeeführung dargestellt an den Ereignissen bei der Schlesischen Armee im Herbst 1813*, Berlin: Mittler & Sohn, 1900
Friccius, Carl. *Geschichte der Blockade Cüstrins in den Jahren 1813 und 1814*, Berlin: Veit, 1854
Fröhlich, Michael. 'Die Konvention von Tauroggen und die Instrumentalisierung eines Mythos', in Portal Militärgeschichte, 13 August 2014, http://portal-militaergeschichte.de/froehlich_konvention

Garden, Guillaume de. *Histoire Générale des Traités de Paix*, Paris: Poultel, n.d.
Garnier, Hermann. 'Wo wurde der Waffenstillstand vom 4. Juni 1813 abgeschlossen?', *Zeitschrift des Vereins für Geschichte und Alterthum Schlesiens*, vol. 38, 1904
Garnier, Herman, ed., *Hohenzollernbriefe aus den Freiheitskriegen 1813–1815*, Leipzig: Hirzel, 1913
Gebler, Wilhelm Edlen von. *Das k. k. Österreichische Auxiliar Corps im russischen Feldzuge 1812*, Vienna: Braumüller, 1863
'Gedanken über die Belagerung der Festung Thorn im Jahre 1813, und die Festung selbst', *Militairische Blätter*, vol. II, 1822
Gerhardt, Oskar. *Die Württemberger im deutschen Befreiungskampf 1813–1815*, Stuttgart: Steinkopf, 1938
Germiny, Marc le Bégue de. 'La Bataille de Dresde', *Revue des Questions Historiques*, vol. XXVI, 1901
—— 'Frédéric-Auguste devant Napoléon', *Revue des Questions Historiques*, vols. XXXIII & XXXIV, 1905
Gill, John H. *With Eagles to Glory: Napoleon and His German Allies in the 1809 Campaign*, London: Greenhill, 1992; revised paperback edition, 2018
—— 'Vermin, Scorpions and Mosquitos: The Rheinbund in the Peninsula', in *The Peninsular War*, Ian Fletcher, ed., Staplehurst: Spellmount, 1998
—— 'Wrede in Russia: Alliance and Independence in 1812', The Consortium on Revolutionary Europe 1750–1850, *Selected Papers 1999*, Owen Connelly, Charles Crouch, Donald D. Horward, William Olejniczak, and Michael F. Pavkovic, eds, Tallahassee: Florida State University, 1999
—— 'The Bavarian Army in 1813: Military Performance at the End of Alliance', paper presented to the Society for Military History, 1999
—— 'Conscripts and Deception: Napoleon's Rear Area Security Strategy: 1809 and 1813', paper presented to the Society for Military History, 2000

—— '1809: Year of Emergence for the Rheinbund Armies', paper presented to the German Studies Association, 2005

—— 'The Rheinbund in Russia 1812: The Württemberg Experience', The Consortium on the Revolutionary Era 1750–1850, *Selected Papers 2013*, Alexander Mikaberidze and Michael V. Leggiere, eds, Shreveport: Louisina State University, 2016

—— 'Combat Performance at the End of Alliance: The Baden Army in 1813', paper presented to The Consortium on the Revolutionary Era 1750–1850, College of Chareleston, 2017

—— 'Combat Performance at the End of Alliance: The Hesse-Darmstadt Contingent in 1813', paper presented to The Consortium on the Revolutionary Era 1750–1850, West Chester University of Pennsylvania, 2018; published in *Napoleonic Scholarship*, no. 10, 2019–20

—— 'Battle of Leipzig', Oxford bibliographies, March 2017, updated February 2022, https://www.oxfordbibliographies.com/view/document/obo-9780199791279/obo-9780199791279-0126.xml

Gilli, Marita. Review of Nicola P. Todorov, *L'administration du royaume de Westphalie de 1807 à 1813*, in *Annales Historiques de la Révoultion Française*, no. 1, 2016

Glaser, Hubert, ed., *Krone und Verfassung: König Max I. Joseph und der neue Staat*, Munich: Hirmer, 1980

Glaser, Maria. 'Die badische Politik und die deutsche Frage zur Zeit der Befreiungskriege und des Wiener Kongresses', *Zeitschrift für Geschichte des Oberrheins*, vol. XLI, 1927

'Gefangennahme der Kontingente der Herzoge v. Sachsen, in Ruhla, Schwarzhausen und Winterstein (am 13. April 1813)', *Beiheft zum Militair-Wochenblatt*, January–February 1847

Goecke, Rudolf. *Das Grossherzogtum Berg unter Joachim Murat, Napoleon I. und Louis Napoleon 1806–1813*, Cologne: DuMont-Schauberg, 1877

Goecke, Rudolf, and Theodor Ilgen. *Das Königreich Westphalen*, Düsseldorf: Voß, 1888

Görges, W. *Lüneburg vor hundert Jahren. Das Treffen am 2. April 1813, der erste Sieg in den Befreiungskriegen*, Lüneburg: Herold & Wahlstab, 1913

Görres, Johann Joseph. 'Aufruhr im Großherzogthum Berg, 1813', *Rheinischer Merkur*, no. 209, 17 March 1815

Grautoff, Ferdinand. *Leipzig während der Völkerschlacht*, Leipzig: Dieterisch, 1913

Gretschel, Karl, Christian Kanis, and Friedrich Bülau. *Geschichte des Sächsischen Volkes und Staates*, Leipzig: Hinrichs, 1853

Große, Karl. *Geschichte der Stadt Leipzig*, Leipzig: Schmidt, 1898

Grueninger, Karlhans. 'Warum Baden unter Napoleon nicht Königreich wurde', *Badische Heimat*, vol. 34, 1954

Guesdon, Alexandre Fursy [Mortonval]. *Geschichte des Feldzugs in Russland im Jahre 1812*, Darmstadt: Leske, 1831

Guillaume de Vaudoncourt, Frédéric François. *Histoire de la Guerre soutenue par les Français en Allemagne en 1813*, Paris: Barrois, 1819

Guttenberg, Erich Freiherr von. 'Die bayerische Nationalgarde II. Klasse in den Befreiungskriegen', *Darstellungen aus der Bayerischen Kriegs- und Heeresgeschichte*, no. 22, 1913

Hagemann, Karen. *'Mannlicher Muth und Teutsche Ehre': Nation, Militär und Geschlecht zur Zeit der Antinapoleonischen Kriege Preußens*, Paderborn: Schöningh, 2002

—— 'Francophobia and Patriotism: Anti-French Images and Sentiments in Prussia and Northern Germany during the Anti-Napoleonic Wars', *French History*, vol. 18, no. 4, 2004

—— 'Occupation, Mobilization, and Politics: The Anti-Napoleonic Wars in Prussian Experience, Memory, and Historiography', *Central European History*, vol. 39, 2006

—— '"Unimaginable Horror and Misery": The Battle of Leipzig in October 1813 in Civilian Experience and Perception', in Alan Forrest, Karen Hagemann, and Jane Rendell, eds, *Soldiers, Citizens and Civilians: Experiences and Perceptions of the Revolutionary and Napoleonic Wars, 1790–1820*, London: Palgrave Macmillan, 2009

Hartmann, Emil. 'Die Festung Cüstrin 1806 bis 1814', *Archiv für Artillerie- und Ingenieur-Offiziere des deutschen Reichsheeres*, vol. CIV, 1897

Häuser, Ludwig. *Deutsche Geschichte vom Tode Friedrichs des Großen bis zur Gründung des deutschen Bundes*, Berlin: Weidmann, 1862

Hegner, Willi. *Die politische Rolle des Grafen Senfft und seine Memoiren*, Greifswald: Abel, 1910

Heilmann, Johann. *Feldzug von 1813: Antheil der Bayern seit dem Rieder Vertrag*, Munich: Deschler, 1857

—— 'Das Ende des Bayerischen Heeres im Jahre 1812', *Jahrbücher für die Deutsche Armee und Marine*, vol. XIII, 1874

Heine, Gerhard. *Geschichte des Landes Anhalt und seiner Fürsten*, Köthen: Heine, 1866

Heitzer, Heinz. *Insurrectionen zwischen Weser und Elbe*, Berlin: Rütten & Leoning, 1959

Hemmann, Thomas. 'Westfälische und kurhessische Memoiren', 2002 at http://napoleonzeit.de/

Hemmann, Thomas,, and Martin Klöffler, *Der vergessene Befreiungskrieg*, Norderstedt: Books on Demand, 2018

Hensel, Johann Daniel. *Der Freiheitskrieg in den Jahren 1813 und 1814*, Hirschberg: Krahn, 1815

Hessen im Rheinbund: Die napoleonischen Jahre 1806–1813, Darmstadt: Hessisches Staatsarchiv, 2007.

Heuser, Beatrice. 'Small Wars in the Age of Clausewitz: The Watershed Between Partisan War and People's War', *Journal of Strategic Studies*, vol. XXXIII, no. 1, February 2010

Heusinger, Edmund. *Geschichte der Residenzstadt Braunschweig von 1806 bis 1831*, Braunschweig: Bock, 1861

Hewiston, Mark. *Absolute War: Violence and Mass Warfare in the German Lands, 1792–1820*, Oxford: Oxford University Press, 2017

Hiller, Fritz von. *Geschichte des Feldzuges 1814 gegen Frankreich*, Stuttgart: Kohlhammer, 1893

Hippler, Thomas. 'Les Soldats Allemands dans l'Armée Napoléonienne d'après leurs Autobiographies: Micro-Républicanisme et Décivilisation', *Annales Historiques de la Révolution Française*, no. 348, April–June 2007

—— 'Problematicher Nationalismus: Kaiserkult und Volkssouveränität in Selbstzeugnissen deutscher Soldaten unter Napoleon', in Andreas Gestrich and Bernhard Schmitt, eds, *Militär und Gesellschaft in der Frühen Neuzeit, Themenheft Militär und Gesellschaft in Herrschaftswechseln*, Potsdam: Universitätsverlag, 2013

Hoburg, K. *Die Belagerungen der Stadt und Festung Thorn seit dem 17. Jahrhundert*, Thorn: Lambeck, 1844

Hofbauer, Martin, and Martin Rink, eds, *Die Völkerschlacht bei Leipzig*, Oldenburg: De Gruyter, 2017

Hoffmann, Birgit. 'Aufruhrer oder gute Patrioten? Die gerichtliche Verfolgung von Selbstjustiz und Exzessen bei der Auflösung des Königreichs Westphalen im Gebiet des Herzogtums Braunschweig-Wolfenbüttel', *Braunschweigisches Jahrbuch für Landesgeschichte*, vol. 79, 1998

Hoffmann, Friedrich Wilhelm. *Geschichte der Stadt Magdeburg*, Magdeburg: Baensch, 1850

Holzapfel, Rudolph. *Das Konigreich Westfalen: mit besonderer Berücksichtigung der Stadt Magdeburg*, Magdeburg: Lichtenberg, 1895

Holzhausen, Paul. *Die Deutschen in Russland 1812*, Berlin: Morawe & Scheffelt, 1912

Hölzle, Erwin. 'Das Napoleonischen Staatssytem in Deutschland', *Historische Zeitschrift*, vol. 148, no. 2, 1933

—— *Württemberg im Zeitalter Napoleons und der deutschen Erhebung*, Stuttgart: Kohlhammer, 1937

Hoppe, Dieter. 'Die Gedenktafel für den russischen Obersten Bedriaga, gestorben in den Freiheitskriegen am 16/18 September 1813', 'Die Freiheit eine Gasse', part 2, 2009, https://heiligenberg-blog.de/wp-content/uploads/hoppe/A06_Der%20Freiheit%20eine%20Gasse-Teil2.pdf

Horstenau, Edmund Glaise von. 'Die Division Mesko bei Dresden 1813', *Steffleurs Militärische Zeitschrift*, vol. I, no. 2, 1911

Hößlin, R. von, and E. Hagen, 'Die Verteidigung von Thorn vom 20. Januar bis 16. April 1813', *Darstellungen aus der Bayerischen Kriegs- und Heeresgeschichte*, no. 3, 1894

Hughes, Michael. *Nationalism and Society: Germany 1800–1945*, London: Edward Arnold, 1988

Hundert, Karl. *Anhalt im Jahre 1813*, Dessau: Dünnhaupt, 1913

Ibbeken, Rudolf. *Preußen 1807–1813: Staat und Volk als Idee und in Wirklichkeit*, Cologne: Grote, 1970

Iskul', S. N. 'Der Aufstand im Großherzogtum Berg gegen Napoleon im Jahre 1813', *Zeitschrift des Bergischen Geschichtsvereins*, vol. 92, 1986

Jacobi, Bernhard von. *Hannover's Theilnahme an der deutschen Erhebung im Frühjahre 1813*, Hannover: Helwing, 1863

Jagwitz, Fritz von. *Geschichte des Lützowschen Freikorps*, Berlin: Mittler & Sohn, 1892

Jahr, Anton. 'Das Drama von Torgau', in *Der Praktische Schulmann*, Leipzig: Brandstetter, 1898

James, Leighton S. *Witnessing the Revolutionary and Napoleonic Wars in German Central Europe*, New York: Palgrave Macmillan, 2013

—— 'German Soldiers in Russia 1812', Introductory Text to the Exhibition of www.mwme.eu (2015), URL: http://www.mwme.eu/essays/index.html

Jenak, Rudolf. 'Sächsische Territorialwünsche im Sommer 1813', *Mitteilungen der Vereins für sächsische Landesgeschichte*, vol. I, 2004

—— *Sachsen, der Rheinbund und die Exekution der Sachsen betreffenden Entscheidungen des Wiener Kongresses (1803–1816)*, Neustadt an der Aisch: Schmidt, 2005

—— 'Die Realität der Österreichisch-sächsischen Konvention vom 20. April 1813', *Mitteilungen des Vereins für sächsische Landesgeschichte*, vol. V, 2007

—— *Die Teilung Sachsens*, Dresden: Hellerau, 2007

—— 'Die politische Rolle der Festung Torgau im Frühjahr 1813: Die Errichtung der Landesfestung Torgau als Bestandteil der sächsischen Militärreform', *Sächsische Heimatsblätter*, vol. 57, no. 1, 2011

—— 'Die Note des Barons von Serra vom 8. Mai 1813 an den sächsischen König', *Neues Archiv für sächsische Geschichte*, vol. LXXXIII, 2012

—— 'Der königlich-sächsische Generalleutnant Johann Adolph von Thielmann als Kommandant der Landesfestung Torgau', *Mitteilungen des Vereins für Sächsische Landesgeschichte*, vol. 10, 2012

—— 'Siegesmeldungen nach der Schlacht bei Lützen vom 2. Mai 1813', Dresden: n.p., 2018.

Juhel, Pierre. 'Napoleon et la Campagne de Saxe – 1813', *Tradition Hors Série*, no. 7, 1998

—— 'Août 1813: Napoléon Face à l'Europe Coalisée', *Tradition Hors Série*, no. 10, 1999

—— 'Automne 1813: Napoléon et la Bataille des Nations', *Tradition Hors Série*, no. 15, 2000

—— 'Kalisch: La Dernière Bataille de la Retraite de Russie', *Tradition*, nos. 196, 199 and 201, January, April and June 2004
Junkelmann, Marcus. *Napoleon und Bayern*, Regensburg: Pustet, 2014
Just, Wilhelm. *Verwaltung und Bewaffnung im westlichen Deutschland nach der Leipziger Schlacht 1813 und 1814*, Göttingen: Vandenhoeck & Ruprecht, 1911

Kandil, M. Mario. 'Sozialer Protest gegen das napoleonische Herrschaftssystem im Großherzogtum Berg 1808–1813', Friedrich Ebert Stiftung, Digitale Bibliothek, https://www.fes.de/fulltext/historiker/00671004.htm
—— 'Der Befreiungskrieg in Westfalen und im Rheinland 1813/14 und die Wirksamkeit des neuen Konzeptes vom Nationalkrieg', in Veit Veltzke, ed., *Für die Freiheit – gegen Napoleon: Ferdinand von Schill, Preußen und die deutsche Nation*, Cologne: Böhlau, 2009
—— *Die deutsche Erhebung 1812–1815*, Stegen am Ammersee: Druffel & Vowinkel, 2011
Keerl, Erich. 'Herzog Ernst I. von Sachsen-Coburg zwischen Napoleon und Metternich: Ein deutscher Kleinstaat im politischen Kräftespiel der Großmächte 1800–1830', dissertation, Friedrich-Alexander Universität, Erlangen-Nuremberg, 1973
Keferstein, Karl Wilhelm. *Die Belagerung und Einnahme der Stadt und Festung Thorn im Jahre 1813*, Thorn: Lehmann, 1826
Kerchnawe, Hugo. 'Von Leipzig bis Erfurt', *Mitteilungen des k. und k. Kriegsarchivs*, vol. IV, 1906
Ketterer, Hermann. *Das Fürstentum Aschaffenburg und sein Übergang an die Krone Bayern*, Aschaffenburg: Werbrun, 1914/15
Keubke, Klaus-Ulrike, and Uwe Poblenz, *Die Mecklenburger in den Napoleonischen Kriegen 1806–1815*, Schwerin: Förderkries für Festung Dömitz, 2011
Kitchen, Martin. *A History of Modern Germany*, Chichester: Wiley-Blackwell, 2012
Kittel, Erich. *Geschichte des Landes Lippe*, Cologne: Archiv für deutsche Heimatpflege, 1957
Kleuting, Harm. 'Nachholung der Absolutismus: Die rheinbündischen Reformen im Herzogtum Westfalen in hessen-darmstädtischer Zeit (1802–1816)', *Westfälische Zeitschrift*, no. 137, 1987
Klang, Daniel. 'Bavaria and the War of Liberation, 1813–1814', *French Historical Studies*, vol. 4, no. 1, Spring 1965
Kleinschmidt, Arthur. 'Aus den letzten Tagen des Königreichs Westphalen', *Zeitschrift des Vereins für hessische Geschichte und Landeskunde*, vol. XVI, 1891
—— *Geschichte des Königreichs Westfalen*, Kassel: Horst Hamecher, 1970 (reprint of the original from 1893)
—— *Bayern und Hessen 1799–1815*, Berlin: Räde, 1902
Klobuczyński, Christian Bruno von. 'Die letzten Monate der westphälischen Herrschaft in Kassel', Institute für angewandte Biografie- und Familienforschung, 19 October 2013
Klüber, Johann Ludwig. *Acten des Wiener Congresses in den Jahren 1814 und 1815*, Erlangen: Palm & Enke, 1817
Klug, Karl. *Geschichte Lübecks während der Vereinigung mit dem französischen Kaiserreiche 1811–1813*, Lübeck: Rahtgens, 1856
Knapp, J. F. *Geschichte, Statistik und Topographie der Städte Elberfeld und Barmen im Wupperthale*, Iserlohn: Langwiesche, 1835
Koberstein, Karl. 'Lützow's wilde, verwegene Jagd', *Preußische Jahrbücher*, vol. LI, no. 4, 1883
Köhler, Gustav. *Geschichte der Festungen Danzig und Weichselmünde bis zum Jahre 1814 in Verbindung mit der Kriegsgeschichte der freien Stadt Danzig*, Breslau: Koebner, 1893
Koischwitz, Otto. 'Poischwitz oder Pläswitz?', *Forschungen zur Brandenburgischen und Preußischen Geschichte*, vol. 17, 1904

Kolditz, Gerald. 'Von der Schlacht bei Dresden am 26./27. August 1813 bis zur Kapitulation der Franzosen in der Stadt am 11. November', *Dresdener Hefte*, no. 37, 1994

Koppen, Wilhelm. *Deutsche gegen Deutschland: Geschichte des Rheinbundes*, Hamburg: Hanseatische Verlagsanstalt, 1936

Kosen, F. von. *Journal der Kriegsoperationen der Kaiserlich-Russischen und der verbündeten Armeen von der Eroberung Thorns bis zur Einnahme von Paris*, Riga: Meinshausen, 1815

Kraft, Heinz. *Die Württemberger in den Napoleonischen Kriegen*, Stuttgart: Kohlhammer, 1953

Krause, Arnulf. *Der Kampf um Freiheit: Die Napoleonischen Befreiungskriege in Deutschland*, Stuttgart: Theiss, 2013

Krebs, Kurt. *Sächsische Kriegsnot in den Jahren 1806 bis 1815*, Leipzig: Teutonia-Verlag, 1908

Kroeger, Tobias Friedrich. *Zwischen eigenstaatlicher Souveränität und napoleonischem Imperialismus: Das bayerische Offizierskorps 1799–1815*, Munich: AVM, 2013

Kurze Geschichte der Universität und Stadt Halle seit dem Ausbruche des Krieges im Jahr 1806 bis zum dritten August 1814, Halle: Ruff, 1824

Kutschbach, K. W. *Chronik der Stadt Küstrin*, Küstrin, Enslin, 1849

Lange, Bernhard. 'Die öffentliche Meinung in Sachsen von 1813 bis zur Rückkehr des Königs 1815', *Geschichtliche Studien*, Gotha: Perthes, 1912

Lange, Wilhelm. 'Kleine Beiträge zur Geschichte der Insurrektionen gegen die westfälische Regierung', *Zeitschrift für hessische Geschichte und Landeskunde*, vol. 47, 1914

Langmantel, Valentin. *Die äussere Politik des Grossherzogtums Würzburg*, Munich: Wolf & Sohn, 1878

Lanrezac, Charles Louis Marie. *La Manoeuvre de Lützen 1813*, Paris: Berger-Levrault, 1904

Larraß, Anton. 'Zur Beurteilung der Schlacht bei Dresden', *Dresdner Geschichtsblätter*, vol. XIV, no. 3, 1905

Laumann, Julius. 'Der Freiheitskrieg 1813/14 um Magdeburg', *Sachsen und Anhalt*, vol. 15, 1939

Lee, Loyd E. 'Baden between Revolutions: State-Building and Citizenship, 1800–1848', *Central European History*, vol. XXIV, no. 3, 1991

Lefebvre de Béhaine, François Armand Édouard. *Napoléon et les Alliés sur le Rhin*, Paris: Perrin, 1913

—— 'L'Attaque de Wurzbourg', *Revue des Études Historiques*, vol. 79, 1913

Leggiere, Michael V. *Napoleon and Berlin*, Norman: University of Oklahoma Press, 2002

—— *Napoleon and the Struggle for Germany*, Cambridge: Cambridge University Press, 2015

—— 'The Men of the Thirty Years War: Allied Occupation Policy in Saxony 1813', unpublished paper presented to the Consortium on the Revolutionary Era

Lentz, Thierry. *Nouvelle Histoire du Premier Empire*, vol. II *L'Effondrement du Système Napoléonien 1810–1814*, Paris: Fayard, 2003

Le Ploge, Fernand. *La Défense de Torgau en 1813*, Paris: Berger-Levrault, 1896

Leth, Ehrhardt. *Annalen des Königreichs Westphalen*, Göttingen: Dieter, 1809

Lettow-Vorbeck, Oscar von. 'Die Meuterei des sächsischen Grenadier-Regiments Anfang Mai 1815 und die vorangegangenen Ereignisse, die hierzu Veranlassung gegeben haben', *Napoleons Untergang 1815*, Berlin: Mittler & Sohn, 1904

Liebecke, Johann Christian Gotthilf. *Magdeburg während der Blokade in den Jahren 1813 und 1814*, Magdeburg: Creutz, 1814

Lieven, Dominic. *Russia against Napoleon*, London: Allen Lane, 2009

Lindau, Martin B. *Geschichte der Haupt- und Residenzstadt Dresden*, Dresden: Kuntze, 1860

Lintner, Philipp. *Im Kampf an der Seite Napoleons: Erfahrungen bayerischer Soldaten in den Napoleonischen Kriegen*, Munich: Beck, 2021

Luckwaldt, Friedrich. *Oesterreich und die Anfänge des Befreiungskrieges von 1813*, Berlin: Ebering, 1898

Lüdtke, Franz. 'Die strategische Bedeutung der Schlacht bei Dresden 1813', dissertation, University of Berlin, 1904.

—— 'Die Überlieferung und Legende der Schlacht bei Dresden 1813', *Dresdner Geschichtsblätter*, vol. XIII, no. 4, 1904.

Łukasiewicz, Mariusz. *Armia księcia Józefa 1813*, Warsaw: Mon, 1986

Lützow, Kurt von. *Adolf Lützow's Freikorps in den Jahren 1813 und 1814*, Berlin: Hertz, 1884

Malecki, Zdzislaw Jan, and Pawel Golebiak. 'Bitwa pod Kaliszem 13 Lutego 1813 r.', *Zeszyty naukowe – inżynieria lądowa i wodna w kształtowaniu środowiska*, nr. 13, 2015

Marcowitz, Reiner. 'Finis Saxoniae? Frankreich und die sächsische-polnische Frage auf dem Wiener Kongreß 1814/15', *Neues Archiv für sächsische Geschichte*, vol. 68, 1998

Magescas, Xavier Abeberry. 'Le Royaume de Westphalie Napoléonien, Tentative d'Instauration d'un "État-Modèle"', *Revue du Souvenir Napoléonien*, no. 450, January 2004

Mährle, Wolfgang, and Nicole Bickhoff, eds. *Armee im Untergang*, Stuttgart: Kohlhammer, 2017

Marchangy, Louis Antoine François de. *Le Siège de Danzig en 1813*, Paris: Chaumerot, 1814

Martin, Guntram, Jochen Vötsch, and Peter Wiegand, eds. *200 Jahre Königreich Sachsen*, Beucha: Sax-Verlag, 2008.

Markus, Paul. 'Die alte Elbbrücke zu Meißen', *Mitteilungen des Vereins für Geschichte der Stadt Meissen*, vol. II, 1891

—— 'Meißen während der Napoleonischen Kriege', *Mitteilungen des Vereins für Geschichte der Stadt Meissen*, vol. IV, 1897

Martin, Jean-Clément, ed., *Napoléon et l'Europe*, Rennes: Rennes University Press, 2002

Maseberg, Günter. *Halberstadt zur Zeit der Befreiungskriege*, Halberstadt: Kommission zur Erforschung der Örtlichen Arbeitersbewegung, 1988

Masnou, Joseph Antoine Auguste. 'Histoire Médicale du Siège de Torgau, en Saxe', *Journal de Médicine, Chirurgie, Pharmacie, etc.*, vols. XXXV–XXXVI, June–July 1816

Maude, Frederic Natusch. *The Leipzig Campaign*, London: Sonnenschein, 1908

Meerwarth, Hermann. 'Die öffentliche Meinung in Baden von den Freiheitskriegen bis zur Erteilung der Verfassung (1815–1818)', dissertation, Ruprecht-Karls-Universität, 1907

Meinecke, Friedrich. 'Zur Beurteiling Bernadottes im Herbstfeldzuge 1813', *Forschungen zur Brandenburgischen und Preußischen Geschichte*, vol. VII, 1894

Meiners, W. 'Die Knüppelrussen in Elberfeld', *Monatsschrift des Bergischen Geschichtsvereins*, vol. 10, no. 12, December 1903

—— 'Noch einmal die Knüppelrussen und Julius (?) Christian Claudius Devaranne', *Monatsschrift des Bergischen Geschichtsvereins*, vol. 11, no. 7, July 1904

—— 'Die bergische Industrie während der Fremdherrschaft (1806–1813) mit besonderer Berücksichtigung Elberfelds', *Monatsschrift des Bergischen Geschichtsvereins*, vol. 13, no. 1/2, January–February 1906

Menke, Karl Theodor. *Pyrmont und seine Umgebungen*, Hameln & Pyrmont: Weichelt, 1840

Mikaberidze, Alexander. *Kutuzov: A Life in War and Peace*, Oxford: Oxford University Press, 2022

Minsberg, Ferdinand. *Geschichte der Stadt und Festung Groß-Glogau*, Glogau: Gottschalk, 1853

Mirus, R. *Das Treffen bei Wartenburg am 3. Oktober 1813*, Berlin: Mittler & Sohn, 1863

'Mittheilungen über die Belagerung von Danzig im Jahre 1813 nach Dokumenten, welche im Archiv des Russischen Kriegsministeriums niedergelegt sind', *Archiv für die Offiziere des Königlich Preußischen Artillerie- und Ingenieur-Korps*, vol. X, no. 20, 1846

Müller, Wilhelm. 'Der Ueberfall bei Kitzen', *Hausblätter*, vol. II, 1863

Müller-Bohn, Hermann. *Die deutschen Befreiungskriege*, Berlin: Kittel, 1901

Münich, Friedrich. *Geschichte der Entwickelung der bayerischen Armee seit zwei Jahrhunderten*, Munich: Lindau, 1864

Murken, Julia. *Bayerische Soldaten im Russlandfeldzug 1812*, Munich: Beck, 2006

Mußgnug, Reinhard. 'Der Rheinbund', *Der Staat*, vol. 46, no. 2, 2007

Mustafa, Sam A. *The Long Ride of Major von Schill*, Lanham, MD: Rowman & Littlefield, 2008

—— 'Not Enough *Esprit* in the *Corps*: The Failure of the Westphalian Army, 1807–13', paper presented at the Society for Military History annual conference, 2008

—— 'Kassel Has Fallen: The Disintegration of the Westphalian State and Army, Autumn 1813', paper presented at the Consortium on the Revoutionary Era annual conference, 2017

—— *Napoleon's Paper Kingdom: The Life and Death of Westphalia, 1807–1813*, Lanham, MD: Rowman & Littlefield, 2017

Nafziger, George. *Lützen & Bautzen: Napoleon's Spring Campaign of 1813*, Chicago: Emperor's Press, 1992

—— *Napoleon at Dresden: The Battles of August 1813*, Chicago: Emperor's Press, 1994

—— *Napoleon at Leipzig: The Battle of Nations 1813*, Chicago: Emperor's Press, 1996

Nafziger, George F., Mariusz T. Wesolowski, and Tom Devoe, *Poles and Saxons of the Napoleonic Wars*, Chicago: Emperor's Press, 1991

'Napoléon à Dresde (1812–1813)', *Nouvelle Revue Rétrospective*, vol. II, July–December 1900

Naulet, Frédéric. 'La Trahison des Saxons', *Gloire & Empire*, no. 51, November–December 2013

—— *Leipzig (16–19 Octobre 1813): La Fin du Rêve de Napoléon et de l'Empire Français*, Paris: Economica, 2014

Naumann, Robert. *Die Völkerschlacht bei Leipzig*, Leipzig: Weigel, 1863

—— *Aus dem Jahre 1813*, Leipzig: Weigel, 1869

Niedersen, Uwe, ed. *Sachsen, Preußen und Napoleon*, Dresden: Sächsische Landeszentrale für politische Bildung, 2013

Niemetz, Gustav, *Napoleon in Sachsen*, Berlin: Amadis, 1997

Nipperdey, Thomas. *Deutsche Geschichte 1800–1866*, Munich: Beck 1983; also published as *Germany from Napoleon to Bismarck 1800–1866*, Daniel Nolan, trans., Princeton: Princeton University Press, 1996

Nieuważny, Andrzej. *Kampania 1813 r. na Północnym Zachodzie Księstwa Warzawskiego: Napoleońska Twierdza Toruń i jej Obrona*, Torun: Universytetu Mikołaja Kopernika, 2017

Norvins, Jacques de Montbreton de. *Portefueille de Mil Huit Cent Treize*, Paris: Mongie, 1825

—— 'Réponse à l'article anonyme, inséré dans la 11e Livraison du deuxième volume du Spectateur Militaire, sous ce Titre: Dispositions Relatives aux Opérations de l'Armée d'Italie, en 1814', *Journal des Sciences Militaires*, 1827

Oleńczak, Piotr. *Napoleońskie Dziedzictwo na Mazowszu: Twierdza Modlin a Latach 1806–1830*, Warsaw: Mazowieckie Centrum Kultury, 2008

Oncken, Wilhelm. *Oesterreich und Preussen im Befreiungskriege*, Berlin: Grote, 1879

Osten-Sacken und von Rhein, Julius Ottomar Hermann Freiherr von der. *Militärisch-politische Geschichte des Befreiungskriges im Jahre 1813*, Berlin: Voss, 1906

Owzar, Armin. 'Tagungsbericht: Das Königreich Westphalen und das Großherzogtum Berg. Quellen – Forschungen – Deutungen', *Westfälische Forschungen*, no. 54, 2004
—— 'Liberty in Times of Occupation: The Napoleonic Era in German Central Europe', in *Napoleon's Empire: European Politics in Global Perspective*, Ute Planert, ed., New York: Palgrave Macmillan, 2015
—— 'L'Historiographie Allemande et le Mythe d'une "Guerre de Libération" en 1813. Le Cas du Royaume de Westphalie', in *Revue d'Allemagne et des Pays de Langue Allemande*, vol. 47, no. 1, January–June 2015

Pascal, Adrien. *Les Bulletins de la Grande Armée*, Paris: Prieur/Dumaine, 1844
Pavković, Michael F. 'The Westphalian Army in 1813: Reforming the Palladium of Westphalian Freedom', paper presented at the Society for Military History annual conference, 2008
—— 'Recruitment and Conscription in the Kingdom of Westphalia: "The Palladium of Westphalian Freedom"', in *Conscription in the Napoleonic Era: A Revolution in Military Affairs?*, Donald Stoker, Frederick C. Schneid, and Harold D. Blanton, eds, London: Routledge, 2009
Pelet, Jean-Jacques. 'Des Principales Opérations de la Campagne de 1813', *Spectateur Militaire*, 1826–8
Petre, Francis Loraine. *Napoleon's Last Campaign in Germany – 1813*, London: John Lane, 1912
Pfaff, Karl. *Geschichte des Militärwesens in Württemberg von der ältesten bis auf unsere Zeit*, Stuttgart: Schweizerbach, 1842
Pfister, Albert. 'Aus dem Lager des Rheinbundes 1812, eine Abwehr', *Preußische Jahrbücher*, vol. LXXXII, 1895
—— 'Der Untergang der Lützower bei Kitzen', *Deutsche Revue*, vol. XXI, no. 3, 1896
—— *Aus dem Lager des Rheinbundes 1812 und 1813*, Stuttgart: Deutsche Verlags-Anstalt, 1897
Pflugk-Harttung, Julius von. 'Bernadotte im Herbstfeldzuge 1813', *Jahrbücher für die deutsche Armee und Marine*, January–June 1905
—— 'Bülows Bericht über die Schlacht bei Groß-Beeren und die preußische Zensur', *Forschungen zur Brandenburgischen und Preußischen Geschichte*, vol. XXIII, 1910
—— *Das Befreiungsjahr 1813*, Berlin: Union Deutsche Verlagsanstalt, 1913
—— 'Zur Beurteilung Bernadottes 1813', *Forschungen zur Brandenburgischen und Preußischen Geschichte*, vol. XXV, 1913
—— *Leipzig 1813*, Gotha: Perthes, 1913
Pigeard, Alain. *L'Armée Napoléonienne*, Apremont: Editions Curandera, 1993
—— *La Conscription au Temps de Napoléon*, Clamecy: Laballery, 2003
—— *Leipzig*, Napoléon 1er Editions, 2009
Pigeard, Alain, Frédéric Naulet, Stéphane Calvet, and Pierre Gérard. 'Leipzig – 1813', *Gloire & Empire*, no. 51, November–December 2013
Pippart, Wilhelm. 'Der Überfall von Wanfried am 18. April 1813', *Hessenland*, vol. 27, no. 6, 1913
Planert, Ute. 'Auf dem Weg zum Befreiungskrieg: Das Jubiläum als Mythenstifter. Die Reinterpretation der Napoleonischen Zeit in den Rheinbundstaaten', in Winfried Müller, ed., *Das historische Jubiläum: Genese, Ordnungsleistung und Inszenierungsgeschichte eines institutionellen Mechanismus*, Münster: Lit, 2004
—— 'From Collaboration to Resistance: Politics, Experience, and Memory of the Revolutionary and Napoleonic Wars in Southern Germany', *Central European History*, no. 39, 2006
—— *Der Mythos vom Befreiungskrieg*, Paderborn: Schöningh, 2007

—— 'Die Kehrseite der Souveranität. Baden und Württemberg im Krieg', in Anton Schindling and Gerhard Taddey, eds, *1806 – Souveranität für Baden und Württemberg: Beginn der Modernisierung?*, Stuttgart: Kohlhammer, 2007

—— 'Das Militär als Zwangsanstalt. Wehrdienst und Rekrutierungsverweigerung zwischen Ancien Regime, napoleonischer Herrschaft und alliierter Kriegsführung', in Jaques-Olivier Boudon, Gabriele B. Clemens, and Pierre Horn, eds, *Erbfeinde im Empire?*, Ostfildern: Jan Thorbecke Verlag, 2016

Platthaus, Andreas. *1813: Die Völkerschlacht und das Ende der alten Welt*, Berlin: Rowohlt, 2013

Plotho, Carl von. *Der Krieg in Deutschland und Frankreich in den Jahren 1813 und 1814*, Berlin: Amelang, 1817

Pölitz, Karl Heinrich Ludwig. *Die Regierung Friedrich Augusts Königs von Sachsen*, Leipzig: Hinrich, 1830

Plümicke, Johann Karl. *Skizzierte Geschichte der russisch-preußischen Blockade und Belagerung von Danzig im Jahr 1813*, Berlin: Maurer, 1817

Popov, Andreï. 'Les Bavarois pendant la Campagne de Russie', *Tradition*, no. 253, January–February 2011

Poppe, Maximilian. *Chronologische Uebersicht der wichtigsten Begebenheiten aus den Kriegsjahren 1806–1815*, Dresden: Thomas, 1848

Poser, Steffen. *Hiob 38,11. Bis hierher sollst du kommen und nicht weiter; hier sollen sich legen deine stolzen Wellen: Denkmale erzählen über die Leipziger Völkerschlacht*, Beucha: Sax-Verlag, 1998

—— 'Zur Meuterei der sächsischen Truppen in Lüttich im Jahre 1815', 2004 Workshop in Leipzig, 'Armeen des Rheinbundes: Königreich Sachsen'

—— *Die Völkerschlacht bei Leipzig: 'In Schutt und Graus begraben'*, Leipzig: Stadtgeschichtliches Museum Leipzig, 2013

Poßelt, Stephanie. *Die Grande Armée in Deutschland 1805 bis 1814*, Frankfurt: Lang, 2013

Price, Munro. 'Napoleon and Metternich in 1813: Some New and Some Neglected Evidence', *French History*, vol. 26, no. 4, 2012

Prittwitz, Karl Heinrich. *Beiträge zur Geschichte des Jahres 1813*, Potsdam: Riegel, 1843

Prussian Great General Staff. *Das Preußische Heer im Jahre 1813*, Berlin: Mittler & Sohn, 1914

Quistorp, Barthold. *Geschichte der Nordarmee im Jahre 1813*, Berlin: Mittler & Sohn, 1894

Rambaud, Alfred. *L'Allemagne sous Napoléon Ier (1804–1811)*, Paris: Didier, 1874

Reboul, Frédéric. *Campagne de 1813: Les Préliminaires*, Paris: Chapelot, 1910

—— 'Napoléon et les Places d'Allemagne en 1813', *Revue d'Histoire*, vol. 42, April–June 1911

Recueil des Ordres de Mouvement, Proclamations et Bulletins de S. A. R. le Prince Royal de Suède, Commandant en Chef l'Armée Combinée du Nord de l'Allemagne en 1813 et 1814, Stockholm: Eckstein, 1839

Reichstädter, Michael. 'Napoleons langer Schatten: Das Fürstentum Reuß älterer Linie vom Rheinbund bis zur Julirevolution', in Werner Greiling and Hagen Rüster, eds, *Reuß älterer Linie im 19. Jahrhundert: Das widerspenstigste Fürstenetum?*, Jena: Vopelius, 2013

'Relation des Ueberfalls bei Halberstadt am 30. Mai 1813', *Militair-Wochenblatt*, no. 848, 22 September 1832

Richter, Friedrich. *Geschichte des Deutschen Freiheitskrieges vom Jahre 1813 bis zum Jahre 1815*, Berlin: self-published, 1838

Richter, Georg August. *Medizinische Geschichte der Belagerung und Einnahme der Festung Torgau und Beschreibung der Epidemie welche daselbst in den Jahren 1813 und 1814 herrscht*, Berlin: Nicolai, 1814

Rieger, Leonhard. 'Die Stimmung und Haltung der fränkischen Provinzen im Jahre 1813', dissertation, Ludwig-Maximilian University, Munich, 1921

Riezler, Sigmund. 'Ebbe und Fluth deutscher Gesinnung in Bayern', *Beilage zur Allgemeine Zeitung*, no. 57, 9 March 1901

Roguet, Chef de Bataillon. 'Étude sur l'ordre perpendiculaire', *Spectateur Militaire*, no. 107, February 1834

Rothauscher, F. J. C. 'Das Wirken des Streif-Corps unter dem k. k. Oberst Emanuel Grafen Mensdorf-Pouilly im Feldzuge 1813 in Deutschland', *Österreichische militärische Zeitschrift*, vol. XVII, no. 1, 1876

Rousset, Camille. *La Grande Armée de 1813*, Paris: Perrin, 1892

Rowe, Michael. 'France, Prussia, or Germany? The Napoleonic Wars and Shifting Allegiances in the Rhineland', *Central European History*, no. 39, 2006

Rückert, Maximilian Th. L. *Politik im Krieg: Ferdinand III. von Toskana und das Großherzogtum Würzburg*, Vienna: Böhlau, 2022

Rühle von Lilienstern, Johann Jakob Otto August. 'Aufstand der Sächsischen Truppen in Lüttich', *Jahrbücher für wissenschaftliche Kritik*, nos. 211 and 212, November 1827

'Sachsen heute vor fünfzig Jahren', *Die Grenzboten*, vol. XXIV, 1865

Sachsens Verwüstung durch die Franzosen 1813, Leipzig: Engelmann, 1814

Sauer, Paul. 'Die Neuorganisation des württembergischen Heerwesens unter Herzog, Kurfürst und König Friedrich (1797–1816)', *Zeitschrift für Württembergischen Landesgeschichte*, vol. XXVI, 1967

—— *Napoleons Adler über Württemberg, Baden und Hohenzollern*, Stuttgart: Deutsche Verlags-Anstalt, 1987

Schäfer, Dieter. *Geschichte Würzburgs*, Munich: Beck, 2003

—— 'Die politische Rolle des Erzherzogs Großherzog Ferdinand, des nächsten Bruders des Kaisers, in seinen Würzburger Jahren', in Wolfgang Altgeld and Matthias Stickler, eds, *'Italien am Main': Großherzog Ferdinand III. der Toskana als Kurfürst und Großherzog von Würzburg*, Rahden: Leidorf, 2007

Schäfer, Klaus, Markus Gärtner, Alfred Umhey, Peter Wacker, and Edmund Wagner. *Die Achenbach-Bilderhandschrift 1813/14*, Darmstadt: Das Exerzierhaus, 1994

Schäfer, Wilhelm. *Chronik der Dresdner Elbbrücke*, Dresden: Adler & Dietze, 1848

Scheibeck, Ludwig. 'Die Deutschnationale Bewegung in Bayern 1806–1813', Munich: Hueber, 1914

Schimpff, Georg von. *1813. Napoleon in Sachsen*, Dresden: Baensch, 1894

Schindling, Anton, and Gerhard Taddey, eds. *1806 – Souveränität für Baden und Württemberg: Beginn der Modernisierung?*, Stuttgart: Kohlhammer, 2007

Schirmer, Uwe, ed. *Sachsen 1763–1832: Zwischen Rétablissement und bürgerlichen Reform*, Beucha: Sax-Verlag, 2000

'Die Schlachten von Großbeeren und Dennewitz', *Denkwürdigkeiten für Kriegskunst und Kriegsgeschichte*, vol. V, 1819, and vol. VI, 1820

Schlenkrich, Elke, and Ira Spieker, 'Ausgeplündert und abgebrannt. Alltag in der ländlichen Gesellschaft Sachsens im Kriegsjahr 1813', *Neues Archiv für sächsische Geschichte*, vol. 78, 2007

Schlüsser, Adolph. *Geschichte des Lützowschen Freikorps*, Berlin: Mittler, 1826

—— 'Replik', *Militair-Literaturzeitung*, vol. II, March–April 1842

Schmeidler, Bernhard. 'Bernadotte vor Großbeeren', *Forschungen zur Brandenburgischen und Preußischen Geschichte*, vol. XXIX, 1916

Schmidt, Charles. *Le Grande-Duché de Berg (1806–1813)*, Paris: Alcan, 1905

Schmidt, Georg. 'Der napoleonische Rheinbund – ein erneutes Altes Reich?', in Volker Press and Dieter Stievermann, *Alternativen zur Reichsverfassung in der frühen Neuzeit?*, Munich: Oldenburg, 1995
—— 'Friedrich Meineckes Kulturnation: Zum historischen Kontext nationaler Ideen in Weimar-Jena um 1800', *Historische Zeitschrift*, vol. 284, no. 1, 2007
Schmidt, Otto Eduard. *Zeitgenössische Berichte über die Leipziger Schlacht vom 16.–19. Oktober 1813*, Leipzig: Reclam, 1918
Schmitt, Hans A. 'Germany without Prussia: A Closer Look at the Confederation of the Rhine', *German Studies Review*, vol. 6, no. 1, February 1983
Schneid, Frederick C. 'The Dynamics of Defeat: French Army Leadership, December 1812– March 1813', *Journal of Military History*, vol. 63, no. 1, January 1999
—— 'Kings, Clients and Satellites in the Napoleonic Imperium', *Journal of Strategic Studies*, vol. 31, no. 4, August 2008
Schneider, Eugen. 'General Normann und der Überfall bei Kitzen', *Beilage zur Allgemeine Zeitung*, no. 87, 28 March 1887
—— 'Württembergs Anschluß an die Verbündeten im Jahre 1813', in *Aus der württembergischen Geschichte*, Stuttgart: Kohlhammer, 1926
Schroeder, Paul W. *The Transformation of European Politics*, Oxford: Clarendon Press, 1994
Schuck, Gerhard. *Rheinbund Patriotismus und politische Öffentlichkeit zwischen Aufklärung und Frühliberalismus*, Stuttgart: Steiner, 1994
Schuler, Thomas. *'Wir sind auf einem Vulkan': Napoleon und Bayern*, Munich: Beck, 2015
Schuster, Johann. *Der teutsche Krieg im Jahre 1813 nach Oestreichs Beitritt*, Leipzig: Hartleben, 1814
Schwarz, Hans Wolf. *Die Vorgeschichte des Vertrages von Ried*, Munich: C. H. Beck, 1933
Schwarzmaier, Hansmartin. 'Das Epochenjahr 1806 in Baden', *Blick in der Geschichte*, no. 72, 15 September 2006, https://www.karlsruhe.de/b1/stadtgeschichte/blick_geschichte/blick72/grossherzogtum3.de
Schweitzer, Jérôme. 'Mémoires, mythes et relectures de la bataille de Leipzig en Allemagne de 1813 à 1871', *Revue d'Allemagne et des Pays de Langue Allemande*, vol. 47, no. 1, January–June 2015
Schwenk, Rudolf. *Die Lützower vor Hof*, Hof: Kleinschmidt, 1897
Seeley, John Robert. *Life and Times of Stein*, Cambridge: Cambridge University Press, 1878
Seidel, Friedrich von. 'Die Mitwirkung des k. k. dritten, von dem Feldzeugmeister Grafen Ignaz Gyulai befehligten Armeekorps während der Schlacht von Leipzig, bis zur Uebergang der Saale', *Österreichische militärische Zeitschrift*, vol. III, no. 8, 1836
Severin-Barboutie, Bettina. *Französische Herrschaftspolitik und Modernisierung: Verwaltungs- und Verfassungsreformen im Großherzogtum Berg (1806–1813)*, Munich: Oldenbourg, 2008
Shanahan, William O. 'A Neglected Source of German Nationalism: The Confederation of the Rhine', in Michael Palumbo and William O. Shanahan, eds, *Nationalism: Essays in Honor of Louis L. Snyder*, Westport, Greenwood, 1981
Sheehan, James J. *German History 1770–1866*, Oxford: Clarendon, 1989
Showalter, Dennis. *The Wars of German Unification*, London: Bloomsbury, 2015
Siebert, Edouard. *Über den Streifzug Thielmanns im Feldzuge 1813*, Vienna: Seidel & Sohn, 1895
Siemann, Wolfram. *Metternich: Strategist and Visionary*, Cambridge, Massachusetts: Harvard University Press, 2019
Smith, Helmut Walser. *Germany: A Nation in Its Time*, New York: Liveright, 2020

—— 'Nation and Nationalism', in Jonathan Sperber, ed., *Germany: 1800–1870*, Oxford: Oxford University Press, 2004

Soldan, George. *Die Eröffnung des Herbstfeldzuges 1813 durch die verbündete Hauptarmee*, Berlin: Mittler & Sohn, 1914

—— 'Die strategische Bedeutung der Schlacht bei Dresden 1813', *Jahrbücher für die deutsche Armee und Marine*, July–December 1908

Soldan, Friedrich. *Heinrich Künzels Großherzogtum Hessen: Lebensbilder aus Vergangenheit und Gegenwart*, Gießen: Roth, 1893

Spivak, Marcel. 'Aux Origines de "la Legende" du Soulèvement Prussien de 1813: Le Corps Franc du Major Adolph von Lützow', *Revue de l'Institut Napoléon*, no. 130, 1974

Sporschil, Johann. *Der große Chronik*, Braunschweig: Westermann, 1841

—— 'Verrätherischer ueberfall des Lützow'schen Freicorps durch die Franzosen bei Kitzen', in *Neues Heldenbuch für die Deutsche Jugend, enthaltend die Großthaten der Deutschen in den Befreiungskriegen von 1813, 1814 und 1815*, Braunschweig: Westermann, 1844

Staszewski, Janusz. *Kaliski Wysiłek Zbrojny 1806–1813*, Kalisch: Towarzystwo Przyjaciół Książki, 1931

—— *Dywizja Gdanska w Latach 1812–1813*, Gdansk: Society of Friends of Science and Art in Gdansk, 1937

Stein, Markus, ed. *Das Militär und die Kriege des Königreich Westphalen 1807–13*, May 2021 at http://www.napoleon-online.de/Dokumente/NapoleonOnline_Reader_Symposium_ Westphalen_April2008.pdf

Stein, Otto. 'Die strategische Bedeutung der Schlacht bei Dresden 1813', dissertation, University of Berlin, 1911

Steiner, Gustav. 'Rheinbund und "Königreich Helvetien": 1805–1807', *Baseler Zeitschrift für Geschichte und Altertumskunde*, vol. 18, 1919

Steinmann, Paul. 'Zum 30. März 1813', and 'Chronik der Stadt Burg Stargard und ihrer Gemarkung im Rahmen der Landesgeschichte', *Das Carolinum*, vol. 29, no. 3, 1963

Strauß, Reinhold. *Chronik der Stadt Wanfried*, Wanfried: Braun, 1908

Stricker, Wilhelm F. C. 'Die Auflösung des Grossherzogthums Frankfurt', *Archiv für Frankfurts Geschichte und Kunst*, vol. 3, 1865

—— *Neuere Geschichte von Frankfurt am Main*, Frankfurt: Auffarth, 1874

Striedinger, Ivo. 'Das Großherzogtum Würzburg', *Zeitschrift für bayerische Landesgeschichte*, no. 6, 1933

Streisand, Joachim. 'Wirkungen und Beurteilungen der Befreiungskriege', in Fritz Straube, ed., *Das Jahr 1813: Studien zur Geschichte und Wirkung der Befreiungskriege*, Berlin: Akademie-Verlag, 1963

Struck, Bernhard, and Claire Gantet. *Revolution, Krieg und Verflechtung 1789–1815*, Darmstadt: Wissenschaftliche Buchgesellschaft, 2008

Stucke, Sigismund. *Die Reußen und ihr Land*, St Michael: Bläschke, 1984

Sunderbrink, Bärbel. 'Das Königreich Westphalen fern seiner Hauptstadt. Symbolische Herrschaftspräsenz in der Provinz', in Jörg Ebeling, Guillaume Nicoud, and Thorsten Smidt, eds, *Jérôme Napoléon und die Kunst und Kultur im Königreich Westphalen*, Passages Online vol. 6, Heidelberg: University of Heidelberg, 2021, https://books.ub.uni-heidelberg.de/arthistoricum/catalog/book/730

'Tagebuch des Streifkorps unter Führung des k. k. Oberst Emanuel Grafen Mensdorf-Pouilly', *Mitteilungen des K. und K. Kriegsarchivs*, vol. III, 1904

Thamer, Hans-Ulrich. *Die Völkerschlacht bei Leipzig: Europas Kampf gegen Napoleon*, Munich: Beck, 2013
Thimme, Friedrich. 'Neue Mittheilungen zur Geschichte der hohen Polizei des Königreichs Westfalen', *Zeitschrift des Historischen Vereins für Niedersachsen*, 1898
Thiry, Jean. *Leipzig*, Paris: Berger-Levrault, 1972
Thürauf, Ulrich. 'Die öffentliche Meinung im Fürstentum Ansbach-Bayreuth zur Zeit der französischen Revolution und der Freiheitskriege', Munich: Beck, 1918
Todorov, Nicola P. *L'administration du royaume de Westphalie de 1807 à 1813: le département de l'Elbe*, Sarrebruck: Editions universitaires européennes, 2011
—— '"Le roi appela et ils accoururent tous": les Provinces Prussiennes Cédées en 1807 dans la Guerre de 1813–1814', *Revue d'Allemagne et des Pays de Langue Allemande*, vol. 47, no. 1, 2015
Töppel, Roman. *Die Sachsen und Napoleon: Ein Stimmungsbild 1806–1813*, Cologne: Böhlau, 2008
—— 'Die Stimmung in Sachsen während der Befreiungskriege 1813–1815', in *Helden nach Mass*, Leipzig: Stadtgeschichtliches Museum Leipzig, 2013
Tort, Siméon Bernard. *Dissertation sur le typhus contagieux, qui a régné épidémiquement à Dantzick pendant le blocus et le siège de cette place dans l'année 1813*, Paris: Faculté de Médecine de Paris, 1817
Tournès, René. *Lützen: Étude d'une Manoeuvre Napoléonienne*, Paris: Charles-Lavauzelle, 1931
Treitschke, Heinrich von. *Deutsche Geschichte im Neunzehnten Jahrhundert*, Leipzig: Hirzel, 1879
Troschke, Paul von. 'Das Gefecht in und bei Lüneburg am 2 April 1813', *Beiheft zum Militär-Wochenblatt*, 1903
Tulard, Jean. 'Siméon et l'Organisation du Royaume de Westphalie (1807–1813)', *Francia*, vol. 1, 1973
—— 'Napoléon et la Confédération du Rhin', in Eberhard Weis and Elisabeth Müller-Luckner, eds, *Reformen im rheinbündischen Deutschland*, Munich: Oldenbourg, 1984

Uebe, Kurt. *Der Stimmungsumschwung in der Bayerischen Armee gegenüber den Franzosen 1806–1812*, Munich: Beck, 1939
'Überfall bei Langensalza in der Nacht vom 12–13 April 1813', *Archiv für Offiziere aller Waffen*, vol. I, 1848
'Ueberfall des Dorfes Ruhla bei Eisenach', *Militair-Wochenblatt*, no. 845, 1 September 1832
Ullrich, Georg Adam. *Die Blokade der Festung Marienberg und des Mainviertels zu Würzburg in den Jahren 1813 und 1814*, Würzburg: Bonitas, 1819
Ulmann, Heinrich. 'Hessen-Darmstadt am Scheideweg im Herbst 1813', *Archiv für hessische Geschichte und Altertumskunde*, IX, 1913
—— *Geschichte der Befreiungskriege 1813 u. 1814*, Munich: Oldenbourg, 1915
Urlen, Falk. 'Die Vertreibung der Franzosen aus Cassel', Erinnerungen im Netz, 22 September 2013, https://www.erinnerungen-im-netz.de/erinnerungen/erin-artikel/kosaken-kaempfen-1813–im-kasseler-osten/
Ussel, Jean d'. *La Défection de la Prusse*, Paris: Plon, 1907
—— *L'Intervention de l'Autriche: dècembre 1812– mai 1813*, Paris: Plon, 1912

Väterlein, Christian, and Axel Burkarth, eds, *Baden und Württemberg im Zeitalter Napoleons*, Stuttgart: Kohlhammer, 1987
Venturini, Carl. *Rußlands und Deutschlands Befreiungskriege von Franzosen-Herrschaft unter Napoleon Buonaparte in den Jahren 1812–1815*, Leipzig: Brockhaus, 1816

Vetter, Julius. *Chronik der Stadt Luckau*, Luckau: Meißner, 1904
Vogel, J. L. *Belagerungen von Torgau und Wittenberg 1813 und 1814*, Berlin: Nauck, 1844
Völderndorff und Waradein, Eduard von. *Kriegsgeschichte von Bayern unter König Maximilian Joseph I.*, Munich: n.p., 1826
Volger, Wilhelm Friedrich, ed. *Die merkwürdigsten Begebenheiten in Lüneburg während der Jahre 1813 und 1814*, Lüneburg: Herold & Wahlstab, 1839
Wagner, nfn. 'Ueber die Aufhebung einer Abtheilung des Altenburgischen Landregiments durch preußische Truppen im Jahre 1813', *Mittheilungen der Geschichts- und Altertumsforschenden Gesellschaft des Osterlandes zu Altenburg*, vol. I, no. IV, 1844
Wagner, August. *Plane der Schlachten und Treffen welche von der preußischen Armee in den Feldzügen der Jahre 1813, 14 und 15 geliefert worden*, Berlin: 1821
Waller, Anneliese. 'Baden und Frankreich in der Rheinbundzeit 1805–1813', dissertation, Albert-Ludwig-Universität, Freiburg im Breisgau, 1935
Wälschke, Hermann. *Anhaltische Geschichte*, Cöthen: Schulze, 1913
Walz, Dieter. *Sachsenland war abgebrannt*, Leipzig: Sächsenbuch, 1996
[Wedel, Karl von]. *Feldzug der Kaiserlich Russischen Armee von Polen in den Jahren 1813 und 1814*, Hamburg: Hoffmann & Campe, 1843
Weech, Friedrich von. *Baden unter den Großherzogen Carl Friedrich, Carl, Ludwig 1738–1830*, Freiburg: Wagner, 1863
—— *Karlsruhe. Geschichte der Stadt und ihrer Verwaltung*, Karlsruhe: Macklot, 1895
—— *Badische Geschichte*, Karlsruhe: Bielefeld, 1896
Weil, Maurice-Henri. *Campagne de 1813: La Cavallerie des Armées Alliés*, Paris: Baudoin, 1886
Weis, Eberhard. 'Der Einfluss der französischen Revolution und des Empire auf die Reformen in den Süddeutschen Staaten', *Francia*, vol. 1, 1973
—— 'Napoleon und der Rheinbund', in *Deutschland und Italien im Zeitalter Napoleons*, Armgard von Reden-Dohna, Wiesbaden: Steiner, 1979
—— *Deutschland und Frankreich um 1800: Aufklärung, Revolution, Reform*, Walther Demel and Bernd Roeck, eds, Munich: C. H. Beck, 1990
—— 'Die Grundlegung des modernen bayerischen Staates in der Ära Montgelas', *Zeitschrift für bayerische Landesgeschichte*, vol. 66, no. 2, 2003
—— *Montgelas: Eine Biographie*, Munich: C. H. Beck, 2008
Welden, Ludwig Freiherr von. *Der Feldzug der Oesterreicher gegen Russland im Jahre 1812*, Vienna: Gerold, 1870
Welk, Stephan Freiherr von. 'Der Aufstand sächsischer Grenadiere gegen Feldmarschall Blücher im Mai 1815', *Sächsische Heimatsblätter*, no. 2, 2016
Wernicke, Julius Emil. *Geschichte Thorns aus Urkunden, Dokumenten und Handschriften*, Thorn: Lambeck, 1842
Wertheimer, Eduard. 'Die Revolutionierung Tirols im Jahre 1813', *Deutsche Rundschau*, vol. CXX, July–August–September 1904
Widdern, Georg Cardinal von. *Die Streifkorps im Deutschen Befreiungskriege 1813*, Berlin: Eisenschmidt, 1894
Wiehr, Ernst. *Napoleon und Bernadotte*, Berlin: Cronbach, 1893
Wierichs, Marion. *Napoleon und das 'Dritte Deutschland' 1805/1806*, Frankfurt am Main: Lang, 1978
Wilson, Peter H. *Iron and Blood: A Military History of the German-Speaking Peoples since 1500*, Cambridge: Belknap Press, 2023
Wilson, Robert. *General Wilson's Journal*, Anthony Brett-James, ed., London: Kimber, 1964

Windelband, Wolfgang. 'Badens Austritt aus dem Rheinbund 1813', *Zeitschrift für Geschichte des Oberrheins*, vol. XXV, 1910

Zander, Christian Ludwig Enoch. *Geschichte des Kriegs an der Nieder-Elbe im Jahre 1813*, Lüneburg: Herold & Wahlstab, 1839

Zimmermann, Wilhelm. *Die Befreiungskämpfe der Deutschen gegen Napoleon*, Stuttgart: Rieger, 1859

Zirges, Wilhelm. *Sachsen in den Jahren 1813 und 1815 oder wie das so gekommen ist*, Leipzig: Zirges, 1839

Zwehl, K. J. von. 'Die Befreiung Bremens von französischer Herrschaft durch Tettenborn im Jahre 1813', *Bremisches Jahrbuch*, vol. XX, 1902

Saxon Contingent Histories (7th Corps)

Bauer, Gerhard. 'Geblendet vom Glanz der Goldenen Adler – Das sächsische Heer an der Seite der Großen Armee 1806–1813', in Guntram Martin, Jochen Vötsch, and Peter Wiegand, eds, *200 Jahre Königreich Sachsen*, Beucha: Sax-Verlag, 2008

Berger, Otto von, and Arndt von Kirchbach. *Geschichte des Königl. Sächs. Schützen-Regiments 'Prinz Georg' Nr. 108*, Leipzig: Jacobsen, 1909

'Bewegungen und Gefechte des Königl. Sächsischen Corps, im Feldzuge von 1812', *Militärisches Taschenbuch*, 1819

Bunde, Peter, Markus Gärtner, and Markus Stein. *Die Sächsische Armee 1810–1813*, Berlin: Zeughaus Verlag, 2009

Cerrini de Monte Varchi, Clemens Franz Xaver von. *Die Feldzüge der Sachsen in den Jahren 1812 und 1813*, Dresden: Arnold, 1821

Exner, Moritz. *Der Antheil der Königlich Sächsischen Armee am Feldzuge gegen Russland 1812*, Leipzig: Duncker & Humblot, 1896

Friedel, Paul. *Geschichte des 7. Infanterie-Regiments 'König Georg' Nr. 106*, Leipzig: Jacobsen, n.d.

Geschichte des Königl. Sächs. Königs-Husaren-Regiments Nr. 18, Leipzig: Baumert & Ronge, 1901

Gülich, Wolfgang. *Die Sächsische Armee zur Zeit Napoleons: Die Reorganisation von 1810*, Beucha: Sax-Verlag, 2008

Hansch, Friedrich Wilhelm. *Geschichte des Königlich Sächsischen Ingenieur- und Pionier-Korps*, Dresden: battalion publication, 1898

Hodenberg, Gottlob Freiherr von. *Das Königlich Sächsische 1. (Leib-) Grenadier-Regiment Nr. 100*, Dresden: Heinrich, 1883

Holtzendorff, Albrecht Graf von. *Geschichte des Königlich Sächsischen Leichten Infanterie*, Leipzig: Giesecke & Devrient, 1860

Kretschmar, Alfred von. *Geschichte der kurfürstlich und königlich Sächsischen Artillerie*, Berlin: Mittler & Sohn, 1876

Larraß, Johannes Anton. *Geschichte des Königlich Sächsischen 6. Infanterie-Regiments Nr. 105 und seine Vorgeschichte 1701 bis 1887*, Straßburg: Kayser: 1887

Nagel, Jürg. *Sächsische Soldaten 1810 bis 1815*, Leipzig: Engelsdorfer, 2015

[Odeleben, Ernst Otto Innosenz von]. *Sachsen und seine Krieger in den Jahren 1812 und 1813*, Leipzig: Hinrich, 1829

Oppell, Karl von. *Sammlung von Beiträgen zur Geschichte des Königl. Sächs. 1. Leichten Reiter-Regiments vacant Prinz Clemens*, Freiberg: Gerlach, 1857

Pigeard, Alain. 'Les Cuirassiers de Zastrow', *Tradition*, no. 229, January–February 2007

Pivka, Otto von [Digby Smith]. *Napoleon's German Allies (3): Saxony*, London: Osprey, 1979

Popov, Andreï. 'Les Cuirassiers Saxons pendant la Campagne de 1813', *Tradition*, no. 234, November–December 2007

Salisch, Markus von. 'Das Beispiel Sachsens: Militärreform in deutschen Mittelstaaten', in Karl-Heinz Lutz, Martin Rink, and Marcus von Salisch, eds, *Reform-Reorganisation-Transformation: Zum Wandel in deutschen Streitkräften von den preußischen Heeresreformen bis zu Transfomation der Bundeswehr*, Munich: Oldenbourg, 2010

Sauzey, Jean Camille Abel Fleuri. *Les Saxons dans nos rangs*, Paris: Terana, 1987

Schimpff, Georg von. *Geschichte des Kgl. Sächs. Garde-Reiter-Regiments*, Dresden: Baensch, 1880

Schimpff, Hans von. *Geschichte der beiden Königlich Sächsischen Grenadier-Regimenter: Erstes (Leib-) Grenadier-Regiment Nr. 100 und Zweites Grenadier-Regiment Nr. 101*, Dresden: Höckner, 1877

Schönberg, Georg von. *Geschichte des Königl. Sächsischen 7. Infanterie-Regiments 'Prinz Georg' Nr. 106*, Leipzig: Brockhaus, 1890

Schuster, Oskar W., and Friedrich A. Francke. *Geschichte der Sächsischen Armee*, Leipzig: Duncker & Humblot, 1885

Summerfield, Stephen. *Saxon Artillery 1733–1827*, Nottingham: Partizan Press, 2009

Süßmilch gen. Hörnig, Moritz von. *Geschichte des 2. Königl. Sächs. Husaren-Regiments Nr. 19*, Leipzig: Brockhaus, 1882

Titze, Jörg. 'Der Übergang der Sachsen am 18.10.1813', Sprotta: self-published, 2002

—— *1812: Die Sachsen in Rußland*, Norderstedt: Books on Demand, 2012

—— *Das Regiment Artillerie zu Fuß, die reitende Artillerie-Brigade und Handwerker-Kompanie 1810–1813*, Norderstedt: Books on Demand, 2012

—— *Das sächsische Ingenieur-Korps und die Pontonierkompanie 1810–1813*, Norderstedt: Books on Demand, 2012

—— *Die königlich sächsische Infanterie (I): Die leichten Regimenter, die Regimentsschützen und das Jägerkorps 1810–1813*, Norderstedt: Books on Demand, 2013

—— *1813: Die Sachsen im eigenen Land*, Norderstedt: Books on Demand, 2013

—— *Das Sächsische Artilleriekorps: Die Regimentsartillerie 1806–1815*, Norderstedt: Books on Demand, 2017

—— *Zur Geschichte der Sächsischen Leib-Grenadier-Garde (I)*, Norderstedt: Books on Demand, 2017

—— *Die königlich sächsische Kavallerie (II): Die Chevauxlegers-Regimenter 1810–1815*, Norderstedt: Books on Demand, 2020

—— *Journale, Tagebücher, Befehle (II): Journale und Rapporte 01.01.1813–09.03.1813*, Norderstedt: Books on Demand, 2020

—— *Die Königlich sächsische Kavallerie (III): Das Husaren-Regiment 1810–1815*, Norderstedt: Books on Demand, 2022

Titze, Jörg, ed. *Reglement für die Königlich Sächsische leichte Infanterie zu den Uebungen außer der geschlossenen Ordnung*, Norderstedt: Books on Demand, 2011

Verlohren, Heinrich August. *Stammregister und Chronik der Kur- und Königlich Sächsischen Armee*, Leipzig: Beck, 1910

Bavarian Unit Histories (12th Corps)

Allegemeine Verordnungen über das Aufgebot der mobilen Legionen und die Errichtung eines National-Chevaulegers-Regiment, Munich: Hubschmann, 1813

Auvera, Alfred. *Geschichte des Kgl. Bayer. 7. Infanterie-Regiments Prinz Leopold von Bayern*, Bayreuth: Ellwanger, 1898

Berg, Franz. *Geschichte des Königl. Bayer. 4. Jäger-Bataillons*, Landshut: Rietsch, 1887

Bezzel, Oskar. *Das K. B. 4. Infanterie-Regiment König Wilhelm von Württemberg vom Jahre 1806–1906*, Munich: Lindau, 1906

—— *Geschichte des Königlich Bayerischen Heeres unter König Max I. Joseph von 1806 (1804) bis 1825*, Munich: Schick, 1933

Bunde, Peter, Markus Gärtner, and Markus Stein, *Die bayerische Armee 1806–1813*, Berlin: Zeughaus Verlag, 2011

Buxbaum, Emil. *Das königlich Bayerische 3. Chevaulegers-Regiment 'Herzog Maximilian' 1724 bis 1884*, Munich: Oldenbourg, 1884.

Dauer, Joseph. *Das königlich Bayerische 10. Infanterie-Regiments*, Ingolstadt: Ganghofer, 1906

'Die Bayern im Jahre 1813', *Neue Militär-Zeitung*, no. 31, 1 August 1857

Döderlein, Alfred. *Geschichte des Königlich Bayerischen 8. Infanterie-Regiments*, Landshut: Rietsch, 1898

Erhard, A. 'Die Bayern in der Schlacht bei Dennewitz am 6. September 1813', *Jahrbücher für die Deutsche Armee und Marine*, vol. XX, 1876

Fabrice, Friedrich von. *Das Königlich Bayerischen 6. Infanterie-Regiment Kaiser Wilhelm, König von Preussen*, Munich: Oldenbourg, 1896

Gerneth, Hans, and Bernhard Kießling, *Die Geschichte des königlich Bayerischen 5. Infanterie-Regiments*, Berlin: Mittler & Sohn, 1893

Geschichte des Königl. Bayer. 2ten Lin. Inf. Regiments Kronprinz von seiner Entstehung Anno 1682 bis 1826, manuscript, n.p., n.d.

Geschichte und Thaten des Königlich Bayerischen 2. Chevaulegers-Regiments Fürst von Thurn und Taxis, Ansbach: Brügel, 1847

Grosch, Feodor, Eduard Hagen, and Albert Schenk. *Geschichte des K. B. 12. Infanterie-Regiments Prinz Arnulf und seiner Stammabteilungen*, Munich, 1914

H., M. *Kurze Darstellung der Geschichte des Königlich Bayerischen 4. Chevaulegers-Regiments 'König' von 1744 bis zur Gegenwart*, Berlin: Mittler & Sohn, 1895

Heinze, Emil. *Geschichte des Kgl. Bayer. 6. Chevaulegers-Regiments 'Prinz Albrecht von Preussen'*, Leipzig: Klinkhardt, 1898

Hutter, Hermann. *Das Königlich Bayerische 1. Chevaulegers-Regiment*, Munich: Oldenbourg, 1885

Kneußl, Paul. *Geschichte des k. bayer. 2. (vormals 3.) Jäger-Bataillons*, Würzburg: Stürz, 1899

Leyh, Max. *Die Feldzüge des Königlich Bayerischen Heeres unter Max I. Joseph von 1805 bis 1815*, volume VI/2 of *Geschichte des Bayerischen Heeres*, Munich: Schick, 1935

Obpacher, Josef. *Das k. b. 2. Chevaulegers-Regiment Taxis*, Munich: Bayerisches Kriegsarchiv, 1926

Pivka, Otto von [Digby Smith]. *Napoleon's German Allies (4): Bavaria*, London: Osprey, 1980

Rang-Liste für die Königlich-baierischen Armee für das Jahr 1811, Munich: Hübschmann, 1811

Ruith, Maximilian. *Königlich Bayerisches 3. Infanterie-Regiment Prinz Carl von Bayern 1698–1900*, Ingolstadt: Ganghofer, 1900

Sauzey, Jean Camille Abel Fleuri. *Nos Alliés des Bavarois*, Paris: Terana, 1988

Schrettinger, Baptist. *Das Königlich Bayerische Militär-Max-Joseph-Orden und seine Mitglieder*, Munich: Oldenbourg, 1882

Schubert, Franz, and Hans Vara. *Geschichte des K. B. 13. Infanterie-Regiments Kaiser Franz Joseph von Österreich*, Munich: Lindau, 1906

Sichlern, Oskar von. *Geschichte des königlich bayerischen 5. Chevaulegers-Regiments 'Prinz Otto'*, Munich: regimental, 1876.

'Skizzen einer Geschichte des 11ten k. baierischen Linien-Infanterie-Regiments', *Kriegs-Schriften, herausgegeben von baierischen Offizieren*, vol. I, Munich, 1820

Ulrich, Maximilian. *Die Königs-Chevaulagers*, Vienna: self-published, 1892

Xylander, Rudolf Ritter von. *Geschichte des 1. Feldartillerie-Regiments Prinz-Regent Luitpold*, Berlin: Mittler & Sohn, 1909

Zoellner, Eugen. *Geschichte des K. B. 11. Infanterie-Regiments 'von der Tann' 1805–1905*, Munich: Lindauer, 1905

Württemberg Unit Histories (4th Corps)

Felder, Robert M. *Der schwarze Jäger oder Würtembergs Krieger in den Jahren 1805–1816*, Cannstatt: Ruckhäberle, 1839

Fromm, Ferdinand Ludwig. *Geschichte des Infanterie-Regiments König Wilhelm I (6. Württ.) Nr. 124*, Weingarten: regimental, 1901

Geßler, Karl Ludwig, Ulysses Johannes Tognarelli, and Theodor Hermann Ströbel. *Geschichte des 2. Württembergischen Feldartillerie-Regiments Nr. 29*, Stuttgart: regimental, 1892

Griesinger, Theodor. *Geschichte des Ulanenregiments 'König Karl' (1. Württembergischen) Nr. 19*, Stuttgart: Deutsche Verlags-Anstalt, 1883

Hahn, Herbert. *Feldzeichen des Königlich Württembergischen Heeres. Handbuch der Fahnen und Standarten 1806 bis 1918*, Stuttgart: Spemann, 1985

—— *Das Königlich Württembergische Heer 1806–1871*, Beckum: Deutsche Gessellschaft für Heereskunde, 1994

Köberle, Rudolf. *Geschichte des 4. Württemb. Infanterie-Regiments Nr. 122*, Ludwigsburg: regimental, 1881

Marx, Karl. *Geschichte des Infanterie-Regiments Kaiser Friedrich, König von Preußen (7. Württembergischen) Nr. 125*, Berlin: Mittler & Sohn, 1895

Menzel, Rudolf. *Geschichte des Infanterie-Regiments Kaiser Wilhelm König von Preußen (2. Württembergischen) Nr. 120*, Stuttgart: Uhland, 1909

Muff, Karl, and Adolph Wenscher. *Geschichte des Grenadier-Regiments König Karl (5. Württembergischen) Nr. 123*, Stuttgart: Metzler, 1889

Müller, Herbert. *Geschichte des 4. Württembergischen. Infanterie-Regiments Nr. 122*, Heilbronn: Scheuerlen, 1906

Neubronner, Karl Georg Konstantin von. *Geschichte des Dragoner-Regiments König (2. Württ.) Nr. 26*, Stuttgart: regimental, 1905

Niethammer, Georg von. *Geschichte des Grenadierregiments Königin Olga*, Stuttgart: Kohlhammer, 1886

Niethammer, Hermann. *Festschrift für die Hundertjahrfeier des Infanterie-Regiments Kaiser Friedrich von Preussen (7. Württemb) Nr. 125*, Stuttgart: Belser, 1909

Nübling, Hermann. *Geschichte des Grenadier-Regiments König Karl (5. Württembergischen) Nr. 123*, Berlin: Eisenschmidt, 1911

Peterman, Hermann. *Gehorsam, furchtlos und treu! Geschichte des Infanterieregiments Kaiser Wilhelm König von Preußen (2. Württ.) Nr. 120*, Stuttgart: Kohlhammer, 1890

Pfister, Albert. *Denkwürdigkeiten aus der württembergischen Kriegsgeschichte*, Stuttgart: Grüninger, 1868

—— *Geschichte des Infanterieregiments Kaiser Wilhelm König von Preußen (2. Württ.) Nr. 120*, Stuttgart: Metzler, 1881

Rawkins, W. J. *The Army of the Kingdom of Württemberg 1806–1814*, e-book edition, 2014

Rössler, nfn. *Tagebücher aus den zehen Feldzügen der Württemberger unter der Regierung Königs Friedrich*, Ludwigsburg: Nast, 1820

Schempp, Hugo. *Geschichte des 3. Württ. Infanterie-Regiments König Nr. 121*, Stuttgart: Kohlhammer, 1891

Schmahl, Julius, and Gottfried Speemann. *Geschichte des 2. Württembergischen Feld-Artillerie Regiments*, Stuttgart: regimental, 1892

Stadlinger, Leo Ignaz von. *Geschichte des Württembergischen Kriegswesens von der frühesten bis zur neuesten Zeit*, Stuttgart: Hofbuchdruckerei, 1856

Starklof, Richard. *Geschichte des Königlich Württembergischen Zweiten Reiter-Regiments, ehemaligen Jäger-Regiments zu Pferde Herzog Louis*, Darmstadt: Zernin, 1862

—— *Geschichte des Königlich Württembergischen vierten Reiterregiments Königin Olga 1805–1866*, Stuttgart: Aue, 1867

Strack von Weißenbach, Wilhelm. *Geschichte der Königlich Württembergischen Artillerie*, Stuttgart: Kohlhammer, 1882

Wright, David. *Württemberg Infantry of the Napoleonic Wars*, Huntingdon: Ken Trotman, 2017

—— *Württemberg Cavalry, Artillery and Staff of the Napoleonic Wars*, Huntingdon: Ken Trotman, 2017

Württemberg Generalstab. 'Bericht über die Theilnahme der Württembergischen Truppen an dem Treffen bei Wartenburg an 3ten Oktober 1813', *Militair-Wochenblatt*, no. 3, 17 January 1847

Baden & Hessian Unit Histories (3rd Corps, 11th Corps)

Barsewisch, Theophil von. *Geschichte des Grossherzoglich Badischen Leib-Grenadier-Regiments 1803–1870*, Karlsruhe: Müller, 1893

Beck, Fritz. *Geschichte des 1. Großherzoglich Hessischen Infanterie-(Leibgarde)-Regiments Nr. 115*, Berlin: Mittler & Sohn, 1899

—— *Geschichte des Großherzoglich Hessichen Gendarmeriekorps 1763–1905*, Darmstadt: Hohmann, 1905

Beck, Fritz, Karl von Hahn, and Heinrich von Hahn. *Geschichte des Grossherzoglichen Artilleriekorps 1. Grossherzoglich Hessischen Feldartillerie-Regiments Nr. 25 und seiner Stämme*, Berlin: Mittler & Sohn, 1912

Bergér, Heinrich. 'Hessische Truppen under Napoleons Fahnen im Jahre 1813', *Wochenbeilage der Darmstadter Zeitung*, no. 2, 11 January 1913

Bibliography

'Berichtigung einiger Angaben der Schriftsteller Vaudoncourt, Fain und Norvins über die badische Truppen, in Beziehung auf die Schlacht von Leipzig', *Zeitschrift für Kunst, Wissenschaft und Geschichte des Krieges*, vol. VII, 1826

Bigge, Wilhelm. *Geschichte des Infanterie-Regiments Kaiser Wilhelm (2. Grossherzoglich Hessisches) Nr. 116*, Berlin: Mittler & Sohn, 1903

Blankenhorn, Erich. *1808–1814: Badische Truppen in Spanien*, Karlsruhe: Armeemusuem, 1939

Bray-Steinburg, Wilhelm von. *Geschichte des 1. Badischen Leib-Dragoner-Regiments Nr. 20 und dessen Stammregiments des Badischen Dragoner-Regiments von Freystedt von 1803 bis zur Gegenwart*, Berlin: Mittler & Sohn, 1909

Caspary, Ernst. *Geschichte des dritten Grossherzoglich Hessischen Infanterie-Regiments (Leib-Regiments) Nr. 117*, Darmstadt: Lange, 1877

Ferber, Alexander. *Geschichte des 1. Badischen Feldartillerie-Regiments Nr. 14*, Karlsruhe: Müller, 1906

Haffner, J. D. *Geschichtliche Darstellung des Großherzoglich Badischen Armee-Corps*, Karlsruhe: Malsch & Vogel, 1840

Hermes, Sabina, and Joachim Niemeyer. *Unter dem Greifen: Altbadisches Militär von der Vereinigung der Markgrafschaften bis zur Reichsgründung 1771–1871*, Karlsruhe: Braun, 1984

Historische Notizen über das Großherzoglich Hessische Leibgarde-Regiment seit dessen Errichtung, Darmstadt: n.p., 1821

Kattrein, Ludwig. *Ein Jahrhundert deutscher Truppengeschichte dargestellt an derjenigen des Grossh. Hessischen Kontingents 1806–1906*, Darmstadt: Schlapp, 1907

Keim, August. *Geschichte des Infanterie-Leibregiments Grossherzogin (3. Grossherzogl. Hessisches) Nr. 117*, Berlin: Bath, 1903

Klingelhöffer, Friedrich. *Geschichte des 2. Grossherzoglich Hessischen Infanterie-Regiments (Grossherzog) Nr. 116*, Berlin: Mittler & Sohn, 1888

'Notizen über die Theilnahme der Großherzogl. Badischen Truppen an der Schlacht bei Leipzig 1813', *Militair-Wochenblatt*, nos. 714 and 715, February 1830

Pivka, Otto von [Digby Smith]. *Napoleon's German Allies (5): Hessen-Darmstadt & Hessen-Kassel*, London: Osprey, 1982

Rau, Ferdinand. *Geschichte des 1. Badischen Leib-Dragoner Regiments Nr. 20 und dessen Stamm-Regiments von Freystedt von 1803 bis zur Gegenwart*, Berlin: Mittler & Sohn, 1878

Rawkins, W. J. *The Army of the Grand Duchy of Baden*, e-book edition, 2013

—— *The Army of the Grand Duchy of Hesse-Darmstadt*, e-book edition, 2014

Röder von Diersburg, Carl Christian Freiherr von. *Geschichte des 1. Großherzoglich Hessischen Infanterie- (Leibgarde-) Regiments Nr. 115*, Fritz Beck, ed., Berlin: Mittler & Sohn, 1899

Sauzey, Jean Camille Abel Fleuri. *Le Contingent Badois*, Paris: Terana, 1987

—— *Les Soldats de Hesse et de Nassau*, Paris: Terana, 1988

Söllner, Gerhard. *Für Badens Ehre: Die Geschichte der Badischen Armee*, Karlsruhe: Info Verlagsgesellschaft, 1995–2001

'Sur la Bataille de Leipzig en 1813, Relativement aux Troupes Badoises', *Spectateur Militaire*, vol. VI, 1828

Wenz zu Niederlahnstein, Rolf von, Heinrich Hentz, and Otto Abt. *Dreihundert Jahre Leibgarde Regiment (1. grossherzoglich Hessisches) Nr. 115*, Darmstadt: Kichler, 1929

Zimmermann, Karl von. *Geschichte des 1. Großherzoglich Hessischen Dragoner-Regiments (Garde-Dragoner-Regiments) Nr. 23.*, Darmstadt: Bergsträsser, 1878

Westphalian Contingent Histories (11th Corps)

Bunde, Peter, Markus Gärtner, and Thomas Hemmann. *The Westphalian Army in the Napoleonic Wars 1807–1813*, Berlin: Zeughaus, 2019

Gärtner, Markus, and Edmund Wagner. *Westphälisches Militär*, Beckum: Gesellschaft für Heereskunde, 1990

Gerdes, Anton. *Königlich Westfälische und Großherzoglich Bergischen Truppen im Russischen Feldzug 1812*, Langendreer: Pöppinghaus, 1914

Gerland, Otto. 'Auszug aus dem letzten Ordrebuch des westfälischen Artillerie-Regiments von 1813 mit Anmerkungen', *Zeitschrift des Vereins für hessische Geschichte und Landeskunde*, vol. X, 1865

Hewig, Wilhelm. 'Die Armee des Königreichs Westfalen 1808–1813', *Zeitschrift für Heeres- und Uniformkunde*, nos. 142/143–146/147, Mai/July 1955–January/March 1956

Hellrung, nfn. 'Die Organisation der Westphälischen Armee', *Minerva*, vol. IV, 1840

Köhler, H. 'Ueberblick des Kriegswesens im gewesenen Königreiche Westphalen und gedrängte Uebersicht der Geschichte der Westphälischen truppen', *Braunschweigisches Magazin*, nos. 29–30, July 1845

Lünsmann, Fritz. *Die Armee des Königreichs Westfalen 1807–1813*, Berlin: Leddihn, 1935

Mauvillon, Friedrich Wilhelm von. 'Skizze über das Militair des ehemaligen Königreichs Westphalen', *Militairische Blätter*, vol. IV, 1823

Pivka, Otto von [Digby Smith]. *Napoleon's German Allies (1): Westfalia and Kleve-Berg*, London: Osprey, 1975

Specht, Friedrich August Karl von. *Das Königreich Westphalen und seine Armee im Jahr 1813, so wie die Auflösung desselben durch das kaiserlich russischen General Graf A. Czernicheff*, Kassel: Luckhardt, 1848

Stein, Markus. 'Aus dem Archiv...13. Husarenregiment (Jérôme Napoléon)', *Depesche*, vol. 1, nr. 1, 1985/1986

Tenge, Torsten. 'Das Bataillon der westphälischen Grenadier-Garde', *Depesche*, vol. 8, nr. 26, April 1994

—— 'Das Regiment der Husaren der Garde des Königreichs Westphalen', *Depesche*, vol. 9, nr. 27, January 1995

—— 'Das Regiment "Königin" (Füsilier-Garde) 1812–1813', *Depesche*, vol. 9, nr. 28, December 1996

Tohsche, Klaus. 'Die Leichte Infanterie des Kgr. Westfalen 1808–1813', *Depesche*, vol. 3, nr. 11, 1985/1986

Note: all issues of *Depesche* may be accessed at http://www.napoleon-online.de/quellen_depesche.html

Wiebe. 'Die Armee des Königreichs Westfalen in den Jahren 1808 bis 1813', *Beiheft zum Militär-Wochenblatt*, vol. VI, 1887

Histories of Other Contingents

[Anon.] *Die ersten Kriegszüge des Anhaltischen Regiments 1807–1814*, Dessau: Dünnhaupt, 1907

'Aperçu Historique: Des Modifications que la Force Armé du Grand Duché de Saxe-Weimar à subies pendant le Règne de Son Altesse Royale le Grand Duc Charles Auguste', *Spectateur Militaire*, vol. II, 1827

Ardenne, Armand von. *Bergische Lanziers, Westfälische Husaren Nr. 11*, Berlin: Mittler & Sohn, 1877

Bernays, Guillaume. *Schicksale des Großherzogthums Frankfurt und seiner Truppen*, Berlin: Mittler & Sohn, 1882

Clarke, Daniel. 'Officers of the Anhalt Duchies who Fought in the French Revolutionary and Napoleonic Wars, 1789–1815', Napoleon Series, 2017

—— '"We Endured a Lot, Suffered a Lot": The Anhalt Duchies during the Napoleonic Wars 1804–1814', in Andrew Bamford, ed., *Glory is Fleeting: New Scholarship on the Napoleonic Wars*, Warwick: Helion, 2021

Dalwigk zu Lichtenfels, Friedrich Ludwig Freiherr von. *Geschichte der waldeckischen und kurhessischen Stammtruppen des Infanterie-Regiments v. Wittich (3. Kurhess.) Nr. 83, 1681–1866*, Oldenburg: Littmann, 1909

Darbou, René. 'Die Infanterie des Großherzogtums Berg (1806–1813)', *Zeitschrift für Heeres- und Uniformkunde*, no. 128, January 1953

Dempsey, Guy C. Jr. 'The Berg Regiment of Light Horse 1807–1808', Napoleon Series, March 2011

Dempsey, Guy C. Jr.,, and E. Wagner, 'Das Chevauleger-Regiment von Berg 1807–1808', *Depesche*, vol. 7, no. 24

Dewall, Hans von. 'Kurzer Abriss der lippischen Militärgeschichte', *Lippische Mitteilungen*, vol. 31, 1962

Döring, Hans von. *Geschichte des 7. Thüringischen Infanterie-Regiments Nr. 96*, Berlin: Mittler & Sohn, 1890

Eck, Hans von. *Geschichte des 2. Westfälischen Husaren-Regiments Nr. 11*, Mainz: Militär-Verlagsanstalt, 1893

Eelking, Max von. *Geschichte des Herzoglich Sachsen-Meiningenischen Contingents*, Meiningen: Brückner & Renner, 1863

Eichelsbacher, August. 'Die Würzburger Truppen in den Kriegen Napoleons I. (1806–1815)', *Frankenland*, vol. I, 1914

Fiebig, D. 'Das Bataillon des Princes', *Zeitschrift für Heeres- und Uniformkunde*, Heft 63/64, January 1934

—— 'Das 4., 5. und 6. Rheinbund-Regiment', *Zeitschrift für Heeres- und Uniformkunde*, Heft 64/65, April 1934

Gärtner, Markus. 'Le Régiment de Chasseurs des Duchés d'Anhalt en 1813', *Tradition*, no. 221, April 2006

Grosch, Fedor, Eduard Hagen, and Albert Schenk. *Geschichte des k. B. 12. Infanterieregiments Prinz Arnulf und seiner Stammabteilungen*, Munich: Lindauer, 1914

Helmes, Hermann. 'Die Würzburger Chevaulegers im Feldzuge 1812/13', *Darstellungen aus der Bayerischen Kriegs- und Heeresgeschichte*, vol. 11, 1902

—— 'Die Würzburger Truppen vor hundert Jahren', *Archiv des historischen Vereins von Unterfranken und Aschaffenburg*, no. 55, 1913

Herrmann, Friedrich. 'Uniformen des reußischen Kontingents 1809–1813', *Zeitschrift für Heeres- und Uniformkunde*, Heft 281, January 1979

Heyden, Hermann von. 'Der Concordien-Orden, die Ehren-Medaillen, sowie die Feldzugs- und Dienstalterzeichen des Grossherzogtums, des General-Gouvernements und der Freien Stadt Frankfurt', *Archiv für Franksfurts Geschichte und Kunst*, vol. 3, 1891

Heyne, Eduard von. *Geschichte des 5. Thüringischen Infanterie-Regiments Nr. 94*, Weimar: Böhlau, 1869

Jacobs, Gustav. *Geschichte der Feldzüge und Schicksale der Gotha-Altenburgischen Krieger in den Jahren 1807 bis 1815*, Altenburg: Gleich, 1835

Jacobsen, Carl. *Geschichte des 8. Thüringischen Infanterie-Regiments Nr. 153 und seiner Stammtruppen*, Leipzig: Jacobsen, (c. 1907)

Joch, Adolf. *Teilnehmer an den Napoleonischen Kriegen und den Befreiungskämpfen von 1807–1815 aus dem ehemaligen Herzogtum Sachsen-Meiningen*, Hildburghausen: Gadow & Sohn, 1935

Kopp, Walter. *Würzburger Wehr: Ein Chronik zur Wehgeschichte Würzburgs*, Mainfränkische Studien no. 22, Würzburg: Freunde Mainfränkische Kunst und Geschichte, 1979

Kunhardt von Schmidt, Robert. 'Aus der Geschichte des 4. Rheinbund-Regiments Herzöge von Sachsen', *Militair-Wochenblatt*, no. 21, 11 March 1903

Küster, Hans. *Geschichte des Anhaltischen Infanterie-Regiments Nr. 93*, Berlin: Mittler & Sohn, 1893

Lantz, Georg. *Geschichte der Stammtruppen des 6. Thüringischen Infanterie-Regiments Nr. 95 als Deutsche Bundes-Kontingente von 1814–1867*, Braunschweig: Sattler, 1897

Meinhard, J. M. *Geschichte des Reußischen Militairs bis zum Jahre 1815*, Gera: Blachman & Bornheim, 1842

Müller, August. *Geschichtliche Übersicht der Schicksale und Veränderungen des Großherzogl. Sächs. Militairs während der glorreichen Regierung Sr. Königl. Hoheit des Großherzogs Carl August*, Weimar: Landes-Industrie-Comptoir Klassik Stiftung, 1825

Münch, Reinhard. *Napoleons Völkerschlachtsoldaten aus Sachsen-Anhalt*, Taucha: Tauchaer, 2013

—— *Napoleons Völkerschlachtsoldaten aus Thüringen*, Taucha: Tauchaer, 2013

—— *Als die Ernestiner, Anhalter und Lipper für Napoleon fochten*, Leipzig: Engelsdorfer, 2017

—— *Als die Schwarzburger und Reußen für Napoleon fochten*, Leipzig: Engelsdorfer, 2018

Neff, Wilhelm. *Geschichte des Infanterie-Regiments von Goeben (2. Rheinischen) Nr. 28.*, Berlin: Mittler & Sohn, 1890

Oesterhaus, Wilhelm. *Geschichte der Fürstlich Lippischen Truppen in den Jahren 1807–1815*, Detmold: Meyer, 1907

Ohl, Manfred. *Das Fürstentum Schwarzburg-Sondershausen: Ein Beitrag zur Militärgeschichte*, Sondershausen: Starke Druck und Werbeerzeugenisse, 1997

Ortenburg, Georg. 'Das Militär in Schwarzburg-Rudolstadt', in *Das Schwarzburger Militär*, Rudolstadt: Thüringer Landesmuseum Heidecksburg, 1994

Pfannenberg, Leo von. *Geschichte des Infanterie-Regiments Großherzog von Sachsen (5. Thüringisches) Nr. 94 und seiner Stammtruppen 1702–1912*, Berlin: Stilke, 1912

Pigeard, Alain. 'Le Régiment de Würzburg', *Tradition*, no. 272, March–April 2014

Rawkins, W. J. *The Rheinbund Contingents 1806–1813: The Duchy of Nassau, the Grand Duchy of Würzburg & the Saxon Duchies*, e-book edition, 2015

—— *The Rheinbund Contingents 1806–1813: Anhalt, Lippe, Schwarzburg, Waldeck, Mecklenburg-Schwerin, Oldenburg & Frankfurt*, e-book edition, 2015

Reuter, Claus. *Das weimarische Militärwesen bis 1815*, Cospeda: Gedenkstätte Jena 1806, n.d.

Ruith, Maximilian. *Das K. Bayer. 12. Infanterie-Regiment 'Prinz Arnulf'*, Ulm: Ebner, 1902

Sauzey, Jean Camille Abel Fleuri. *Le Régiment de Francfort*, vol. I of *Les Allemands sous les Aigles Françaises*, Paris: Terana, 1987

Schumann, Günter. 'Die Kontingente der Fürstentümer Schwarzburg, Reuß und Waldeck in den Napoleonischen Kriegen', H. Sterzing, ed., *Montagsblatt, Wissenschaftlicher Beilage der Magdeburgischen Zeitung*, 1908–9

Schüser, Bernhard. *Geschichte des schwarzburg-rudolstädtischen Contingents in den Kriegsjahren von 1807 bis 1815*, Rudolstadt: Stroh, 1874

Siebigk, Ferdinand. 'Die Theilnahme Anhaltischer Krieger an den Kriegen für und gegen Napoleon von 1807 bis 1815', unpublished manuscript, Stadtbibliothek Dessau-Roßlau

Stahlberg, Hans. 'Reußisches Militär bis zum Ende der Befreiungskriege', *Zeitschrift für Heeres- und Uniformkunde*, Heft 269, January 1977

Stolz, Gerd. 'Das Bataillon Lippe in Danzig in den Jahren 1812–13', *Heimatland Lippe*, vol. 62, no. 6, November 1969

Thomas, J. *Un Régiment Rhénan sous Napoléon Premier*, Liège: Vaillant-Carmanie, 1928

Trefftz, Johann. 'Das 4. Rheinbundsregiment Herzöge von Sachsen im Feldzug 1813', *Zeitschrift des Vereins für Thüringische Geschichte und Altertumskunde*, vol. XVI, 1906

Wellmann, Richard. *Geschichte des Infanterie-Regiments von Horn (3tes Rheinischen) Nr. 29.*, Trier: Lintz, 1894

Wiegmann, Wilhelm. *Franzosenzeit und Befreiungskrieg: Zur Geschichte des Fürstentums Schaumburg-Lippe 1807–1815*, Stadthagen: Heine, 1915

Wittich, Karl-Heinz. 'Das Anhaltische Chasseur-Regiment 1813', *Salzlandkreis*, https://www.salzlandkreis.de/media/6134/wittich_anhaltisches-chasseur-regiment-1813.pdf

Zimmermann, P. *Erinnerungen aus den Feldzügen der bergischen Truppen in Spanien und Rußland*, Düsseldorf: Stahl, 1840

French Unit Histories

Duroisel, Georges. *93e Régiment d'Infanterie, Ancien Enghien & 18e Léger*, Roche-sur-Yon: Ivonnet, 1893

Histoire du 23e Régiment d'Infanterie de Ligne, Paris: Dondey-Dupré, 1841

Maindreville, M. de. *Historique du 132e Régiment d'Infanterie*, Reims: Michaud, 1890

Paimblant du Rouil, Adrien. *La Division Durutte*, Paris: Charles-Lavauzelle, 1896

Pigeard, Alain. 'Les Régiments de Réfractaires 1810–1814', *Tradition*, no. 167, May 2001

Schmeißer, Georg. 'Die Refraktärregimenter unter Napoleon I. und die aus ihnen hervorgegangene Division Durutte', *Beiheft zum Militär-Wochenblatt*, no. 23, 1890

Schmitt, Joseph Auguste Constant. *Historique du 151e Régiment d'Infanterie*, np: np, 1901

Simond, Émile. *Historique des Nouveaux Régiments Créés par la Loi du 25 Juillet 1887*, Paris: Baudoin, 1889

Allied Unit Histories

Ardenne, Armand Freiherr von. *Geschichte des Zieten'schen Husaren-Regiments*, Berlin: Mittler & Sohn, 1874

Bibliography

Bagensky, Karl von. *Geschichte des 9ten Infanterie-Regiments gennant Colbergsches*, Colberg: Post, 1842

Bichmann, Wilhelm. *Chronik des k. k. Infanterie-Regiments Nr. 62*, Vienna: Mayer, 1880

Bothe, Heinrich. *Geschichte des Thüringischen Ulanen-Regiments Nr. 6, 1813–1913*, Berlin: Mittler & Sohn, 1913

Dziengel, Johann David von. *Geschichte des königlichen Zweiten Ulanen-Regiments*, Potsdam: Stein, 1838

Franseky II, Eduard von. *Geschichte des Königlich Preußischen 16ten Infanterie-Regiments*, Münster: Wundermann, 1834

Goltz, G. F. G. *Geschichte des Königlich Preußischen dritten Ulanen-Regiments*, Fürstenwalde: Schubert, 1841

Gottschalck, Max. *Geschichte des 1. Thüringischen Infanterie-Regiments Nr. 31*, Berlin: Mittler & Sohn, 1894

Gröling II, Robert von. *Kurze Geschichte des Königl. 1ten Schlesischen Grenadier-Regiments (Nr. 10)*, Berlin: Blumenthal, 1861

Hagen, Eduard von. *Geschichte des Neumärkischen Dragoner-Regiments Nr. 3*, Berlin: Mittler & Sohn, 1885

Hülsemann, Bernhard. *Geschichte des Königlich-Hannoverschen vierten Infanterie-Regiments*, Hannover: Helwing, 1863

Johann, Erzherzog of Austria. *Geschichte des K. K. Linien-Infanterie-Regiments Erzherzog Wilhelm Nr. 12*, Vienna: Seidel & Sohn, 1877

Kopka von Lossow, Rudolph. *Geschichte des Grenadier-Regiments König Friedrich I. (4. Ostpreußischen) Nr. 5.*, Berlin: Mittler & Sohn, 1901

Kreuzwendedich von dem Borne, Hermann. *Geschichte des Infanterie-Regiments Prinz Louis Ferdinand von Preußen (2. Magdeburgischen) Nr. 27, 1815–1895, und seiner Stammtruppentheile*, Berlin: Eisenschmidt, 1896

Lippe-Weißenfeld, Ernst Graf zur. *Geschichte des Königl. Preuss. 6. Husaren-Regiments*, Berlin: Königlichen Geheimen Ober-Hofbuchdruckerei, 1860

Mach, Anton von. *Geschichte des Königlich Preußischen Zweiten Infanterie – genannt Königs-Regiments*, Berlin: Mittler, 1843

Mackensen, August. *Schwarze Husaren*, Berlin: Mittler & Sohn, 1892

Malinowsky I., Louis von, and Robert von Bonin. *Geschichte der brandenburgisch-preußischen Artillerie*, Berlin: Duncker & Humblot, 1846

Managetta-Lerchenau, Hans von. 'Die österreichisch-deutsche oder westfälische Legion 1813/14', *Streffleurs Militärische Zeitschift*, vol. I, 1913

Melchers, Johannes. *Stammliste des Offiziers-Korps des Infanterie-Regiments von Horn (3. Rheinisches) Nr. 29*, Trier: Lintz, 1901

Milarch, August Alexander Ferdinand. *Denkwürdigkeiten des Meklenburg-Strelitzischen Husaren-Regiments in den Jahren des Befreiungskampfes 1813 bis 1814*, Neubrandenburg: Brünslow, 1854

Mueller, Hugo von. *Geschichte des Grenadier-Regiments Prinz Carl von Preußen (2. Brandenburgisches) Nr. 12*, Berlin: Mittler & Sohn, 1875

Pauly, Ernst. *Geschichte des 2. Ostpreußischen Grenadier-Regiments Nr. 3*, Berlin: Mittler & Sohn, 1885

Pizzighelli, Cajetan. *Geschichte des K. u. K. Dragoner-Regimentes Johannes Josef Fürst von und zu Liechtenstein Nr. 10*, Vienna: regimental, 1903

Pohlmann. *Geschichte des Infanterie-Regiments Graf Barfuß (4. Westfälischen) Nr. 17*, Berlin: Mittler & Sohn, 1906

Quistorp, Barthold von. *Die Kaiserlich Russisch-Deutsche Legion*, Berlin: Heymann, 1860

Schmidt, Paul von. *Das 3. Pommersche Infanterie-Regiment Nr. 14 von seiner Gründung bis zum Jahre 1888*, Berlin: Liebel, 1888

Schöning, Kurd Wolfgang von. *Geschichte des Königlich Preußischen Fünften Husaren-Regiments*, Berlin: Lüderitz, 1843

Schwertfeger, Bernhard. *Geschichte der Königlich Deutschen Legion 1803–1816*, Hannover: Hahn, 1907

Treuenfest, Gustav Ritter Amon von. *Geschichte des k. k. 12. Huszaren-Regimentes*, Vienna: Mayer, 1876

—— *Geschichte des k. k. Husaren-Regimentes Alexander Freiherr von Koller Nr. 8*, Vienna: Mayer, 1880

—— *Geschichte des k. k. Huszaren-Regimentes Freiherr von Edelsheim-Gyulai Nr. 4*, Vienna: regimental, 1882

—— *Geschichte des k. k. Dragoner-Regimentes Feldmarschall Alfred Fürst zu Windisch-Grätz Nr. 14*, Vienna: Brzezowsky & Söhne, 1886

—— *Geschichte des k. und k. Bukowina'schen Dragoner-Regimentes*, Vienna: St Norbertus Buch- und Kunstdruckerei, 1892

Venzky, Gabriele. *Die Russisch-Deutsche Legion in den Jahren 1811–1815*, Veröffentlichungen des Osteuropa-Institutes München no. 30, Wiesbaden: Harrassowitz, 1966

Wechmar, Hans Freiherr von. *Braune Husaren: Geschichte des braunen Husaren-Regiments*, Berlin: Leist, 1893

Ziegler, Gustav von. *Erinnerungen aus den Jahren 1813/14*, Cologne: Greven, 1853

Newspapers and Journals for 1813

Allgemeine Zeitung
Baierische National-Zeitung
Berlinische Nachrichten
Europaisiche Annalen
Gazette Nationale ou Moniteur Universel
Journal de l'Empire
Korrespondent von und für Deutschland
Moniteur Westphalien/Westphälischer Moniteur
Oesterreichischer Beobachter
Preußische Correspondent
Regensburger Zeitung

Index

'>' indicates a promotion during 1813

Alexander I, Tsar: 8, 13, 110, 117, 189, 191, 198, 206, 278–9, 310, 321, 325–6, 332, 345, 374, 402
Allied/Coalition military formations:
  Army of Bohemia (Main Army): 85, 164, 249, 345, 390
  Army of the North: 66, 260, 262, 278
  Army of Silesia: 85, 89, 91, 105, 164, 232
  raiding detachments: 5, 50, 52, 57, 77, 81, 88, 99, 149, 168–9, 172, 193, 197, 203, 206, 212, 225–8, 231–6, 241, 243–4, 258, 260, 262–3, 274, 286, 300, 323–3, 339, 381, 399–400, 404, 409, 514
Allix de Vaux, GD Jacques Alexandre François: 259, 263, 268, 275–7, 280–1, 284–5
Altenburg, Engagement at (28 September): 172–3, 225, 412
Anhalt duchies and military units (*see also* Danzig): 332–7, 339–40, 350, 352, 360, 515
Arrighi de Casanova, GD Jean Toussaint: 52–7, 61, 66, 68, 168, 170–1, 185, 187, 236,
Augereau, Marshal Pierre (Duke of Castiglione): 173, 186, 188, 300
Austria: 3–4, 8–11, 16, 54, 113–16, 121, 127, 168, 190–1, 198, 201, 207, 210, 295–6, 300, 304, 325–6, 332, 333, 337, 338–9, 341, 342, 343, 391–3, 401, 409, 415
Austrian military formations: 101–2, 172, 174–9, 188, 191, 193, 210, 242, 244, 249, 282, 288, 304, 315–16, 335–6, 379, 392, 394

Bachelu, GD Gilbert Désiré Joseph: 218, 350–1, 356
Baden: 4–5, 10, 28, 109, 119–29, 132–204, 326, 372, 398
Baden military units: 352, 379, 381, 404, 409–12, 414

1st Brigade (39th Division): 5, 28, 119, 126, 132–88, 239, 306, 379, 401, 411
2nd Brigade (Leipzig): 121, 123, 166–75, 183, 186–7
1st Light Dragoons: 121–5, 132, 136–7, 141–7, 153, 157, 159, 163–4, 174, 178–9, 194, 322, 412
Barclay de Tolly, General of Infantry Mikhail Bogdanovich (Russia): 35, 359
Bastineller, GB Karl Gottlob von (Westphalia): 236–7, 258–9, 262–4, 268–9, 271–2, 275, 288
Bautzen, Battle of (20–21 May): 4, 25, 32–43, 47, 63, 72, 115, 117–18, 146–7, 149, 151, 161–2, 195, 232, 238, 297, 302, 306, 314, 323, 383, 393, 405, 410, 412–13
Bavaria: 4, 7–11, 84, 99, 109, 113–17, 119–21, 193, 196–202, 207, 210, 224, 279, 295, 303–4, 307, 308, 326, 406–7, 409–15, 511
Bavarian military units: 3, 5–6, 18, 28, 33, 79, 80, 98–9, 104, 122, 127, 134, 150, 151, 155, 193, 225, 230–2, 293, 320, 321, 348, 390, 392, 513, 516
  29th Division: 28, 38, 72, 77, 172, 382, 384–6, 397, 402, 404
  13th Infantry Regiment: 18, 218–19, 292, 350–1, 355–69, 413
  Chevaulegers Regiment: 158, 164, 166, 239, 246, 254
Beaumont, GD Louis Chrétien Carrière de: 49, 91, 93, 95–6, 149, 158
Benckendorff, Maj. Gen. (Russia): 229, 263–8, 277, 286, 300
Berg: 221, 290, 308–17, 397–9
Berg military units: 332
  Lancers: 293, 309–10, 312–17, 344, 512
  1st Infantry Regiment: 293, 309–10, 312, 314, 317, 512

Bernadotte, Marshal Jean-Baptiste, Crown Prince of Sweden: 66, 71, 90–1, 188–9, 190, 260, 262, 278, 385

Beroldingen, GM Joseph Ignaz von (Württemberg): 49–50, 57–8, 99–100, 116

Berthier, Marshal Alexander (Prince of Wagram): 31, 34, 52, 56, 58, 66, 83–4, 86, 98–9, 102–4, 116, 134, 153, 168, 218, 227–9, 238, 240–1, 243, 250, 261, 274–5, 279, 299, 303, 323, 327, 351, 354, 357, 361–2, 376, 385

Bertrand, GD Henri Gatien: 28, 30–31, 35–6, 41–8, 62–8, 70–80, 81, 84, 90–8, 100–1, 103–4, 165–6, 174, 193, 225, 254, 281–2, 411–13

Blücher, Maj. Franz von (Prussia): 136, 320, 322

Blücher, GdK Gebhard Leberecht (Prussia): 43, 85, 88–9, 91, 100, 105, 138, 160, 163–4, 174, 205, 226, 248, 320–2, 325, 388

Brause, Oberst Friedrich Wilhelm August von (Saxony): 411

Briche, GB André Louis: 30–1, 36, 39, 43, 47, 49, 63, 66, 68, 72, 82–3, 92, 410

Bülow, GL Friedrich Wilhelm von (Prussia): 90, 96

Carl August, Duke of Saxon-Weimar: 317–26, 332

Carra Saint-Cyr, GD Jean: 342

Chernishev, Maj. Gen. Alexander Ivanovich (Russia): 53, 206, 232–6, 251, 262–81, 282, 286, 329–30, 343, 411, 414, 515

civilian experiences: 28, 31, 32, 48, 53–4, 56, 61, 123, 126, 130, 136, 147–8, 153–4, 171, 191, 195, 199, 207, 212, 222, 229, 231, 236, 260, 267, 269, 272–3, 276–8, 282, 284, 299, 311, 317, 321, 337, 340, 346, 362, 371, 387, 389, 397, 398–401, 403, 405, 413

Colomb, Rittmeister Friedrich August Peter von (Prussia): 50–1, 57, 236–7, 359, 409

Cossacks: 30–5, 45, 49, 53, 56, 64–6, 78, 80, 86, 89, 102, 105, 109–10, 130, 136, 138, 147, 149–50, 160–2, 165, 169–70, 193–5, 217–18, 222, 225–6, 231–5, 242, 251, 254, 258, 262–81, 283, 292–4, 299–302, 306–7, 316, 320, 322–3, 329–30, 332, 354, 356, 358–9, 373, 404

Croatian troops: 34, 124, 150–3, 251–2, 328, 375, 379–80

Dąbrowski, GD Jan Henryk (Duchy of Warsaw): 66, 68, 100–1, 237, 251–2, 329

Daendels, GD Herman Willem: 371–4, 395, 411

Dalberg, Carl Theodor von, Grand Duke of Frankfurt and Prince-Primate of the Confederation: 304–8, 338

Danloup-Verdun, GD Louis (Westphalia): 238, 239, 265–6, 280

Danzig, Siege of: 5–6, 18, 20, 24, 113, 129–30, 211, 215, 218–19, 222, 224, 238, 239, 291–4, 305, 319, 326–7, 333, 339, 341–4, 346–72, 374, 395–6, 398, 409, 411–13, 416

Davout, Marshal Louis Nicholas (Prince of Eggmühl): 216, 229, 251, 260

Denmark: 516

Dennewitz, Battle of (6 September): 3–4, 71–82, 96, 104, 117–18, 165–6, 239, 254, 257, 298–9, 385, 404–5, 409, 411, 413, 512, 513, 514

Doering, GM Christoph Friedrich David von (Württemberg): 29, 38–62, 63–6, 69–70, 73, 77, 82, 90–7, 98, 118

Dörnberg, Maj. Gen. Wilhelm Freiherr von (Coalition): 210, 212, 225, 227, 229

Dresden: 3, 30–2, 52, 147, 149, 155–6, 162–4, 166, 168, 195, 219, 224, 231–2, 237–40, 244, 247, 287, 297, 299, 302, 312–15, 321, 323, 325, 334–7, 345–6, 358, 362, 413; Battle of (26–27 August): 66, 85, 99, 160, 243, 248, 405, 410, 412; Bridge: 31; Siege of: 211, 248–50, 251, 288–9, 370, 381, 384–95

Duchy of Warsaw: see Poland

Durosnel, GD Antoine Jean Auguste Henri: 231–2, 237, 244, 250, 390

Durrieu, Adjutant-Commandant > GB Antoine-Simon: 150–2, 156, 167, 382–7

Durutte, GD Pierre: 68, 296–8, 321, 372, 384

Dutaillis, GD Adrien Jean-Baptiste: 383, 387–8, 395–6

Emil, GL Prince of Hesse-Darmstadt: 127, 132, 134, 136–7, 139–40, 145, 154–5, 158–62, 167, 178–89, 192–3, 202–3, 409, 411

Erfurt: 102, 116, 168–70, 193–4, 225, 263, 273–4, 283, 297, 299, 321–3, 346, 348

Index

Eugène de Beauharnais, Viceroy of Italy: 123, 130, 138, 140, 217, 220–1, 25, 300–1, 305, 307, 309, 313, 345, 348
Euper/Thießen, Battle of (3–4 September): 64–71, 84, 139

Ferdinand von Habsburg, Grand Duke of Würzburg: 294–6, 299–301, 303–4, 325
Fornier d'Albe, GD Gaspard Hilarion: 375–7
Fournier-Sarvlovèse, GD François: 54–9
Frankfurt military units: 28, 126, 132, 134, 138, 146, 153, 155, 290–1, 293, 304–8, 350, 352, 354, 358–9, 369, 379–81, 382–4, 395, 398, 512
Frankfurt, unrest: 399, 414
Franquemont, GL Friedrich von (Württemberg): 25–44, 48–52, 57–78, 79–84, 88–104, 107–10, 113, 116, 117–18, 126, 134, 145, 193, 257, 282, 403, 405, 408, 411
Franz I, Kaiser of Austria: 110, 112, 188, 242, 295–6, 304, 325, 332
French military formations.
  Army of Berlin: 62–7, 72, 78, 164, 251, 329, 404, 410
  Army of the Bober: 160–2
  Imperial Guard: 5, 36, 129–31, 133–8, 141, 160, 162, 166–7, 170–1, 211, 225, 242, 248–50, 281–2, 293, 312–17, 328, 350
  1st Corps: 293, 334–7, 346, 389–91
  2nd Corps: 146, 211, 238–9, 241–6; in 1812: 129, 375
  3rd Corps: 11, 119, 125–6, 132–3, 136–41, 145–9, 155, 157–60, 164, 174, 178, 225, 293, 382, 384
  4th Corps: 30, 34–6, 39, 42, 44, 47, 49, 62–6, 70, 72, 76–8, 81–4, 90–5, 97, 100–1, 151–2, 165–6, 174, 179, 193, 211, 239, 257, 281–3, 411, 513
  5th Corps: 146, 252, 386
  6th Corps: 29, 36, 60, 63, 83, 85–6, 88–9, 104–7, 113, 133, 138, 149, 230–1, 238, 297, 386; 1812: 291
  7th Corps: 64, 66, 72, 90, 146, 152, 291, 293, 296–8, 382, 384, 513
  8th Corps/1812: 20, 211, 215–17, 221, 375
  9th Corps: 230
  10th Corps: 20, 29, 211, 350; 1809: 210, 212; in 1812: 215, 218, 349, 357

  11th Corps: 36, 44–5, 49, 138, 140, 159–50, 162–3, 174–80, 195, 211, 237–8, 245, 246–50, 281, 293, 300–2, 411; in 1812: 291
  12th Corps: 36, 49, 64, 66–7, 70, 72, 149, 158, 164–6, 211, 231, 238, 245–6, 307, 338, 411
  14th Corps: 346, 389, 391–2
  1st Cavalry Corps: 138, 157, 163, 239, 245, 246, 248
Friedrich, King of Württemberg: 4–5, 7–33, 43, 47, 49–52, 55–8, 60–1, 66, 70, 78, 80, 83–4, 87, 92, 98–100, 103–4, 109–17, 144, 303, 352, 409
Friedrich August, King of Saxony: 3, 187, 317, 323, 325, 389, 393
Friedrich Wilhelm III, King of Prussia: 189, 196, 260, 321, 332,
Füllgraf, GB Friedrich Wilhelm von (Westphalia): 217, 245, 288, 275–8, 385

Gablenz, GM Heinrich Adolf von (Saxony): 68
Gersdorff, GL Karl Friedrich von (Saxony): 54, 394, 413
German nationalism: 59, 117, 143–4, 198, 202, 204, 206, 311, 399–400, 406–8, 410, 414, 511, 515–16
Girard, GD Jean-Baptiste: 217–18, 246, 251–3, 328–31
Glogau, Blockades/Sieges of: 5, 123–6, 150–3, 155–6, 293, 306–7, 321, 346, 370, 374, 379–81, 384, 395, 412, 512
Gouvion Saint-Cyr, Marshal Laurent: 389–93, 395–6
Great Britain: 14, 189, 207, 210, 229, 308, 362–3, 408
Großbeeren, Battle of (23 August): 4, 64, 72, 251, 298, 329, 373, 404, 410
Groß-Rosen, Battle of (31 May): 45–6, 72, 302

Hagelberg, Battle of (27 August): 5, 239, 250–4, 326, 329–32, 344, 381, 397, 512, 514, 516
Halberstadt, Engagement at (29 May): 212, 232–7, 240, 411
Hamburg: 211, 216, 225, 229, 251, 260, 291, 342, 346, 348, 399
Hammerstein, GD Hans Georg von (Westphalia): 216, 222, 224–32, 238, 239, 243

Hammerstein, Col. William von (Westphalia): 238–9, 241–6
Hanau, Battle of (30–31 October): 4, 193, 201, 307, 316
Hellwig, Maj. Friedrich von (Prussia): 225–6, 229, 286, 320
Hesse-Darmstadt: 4–5, 28, 119, 126–7, 199–204, 222, 511
Hessian military units: 28, 80, 108, 127–33, 192–6, 231, 291, 314, 369, 407, 409–10, 512, 513, 515
  39th Division: 5, 28, 119, 126, 132–49, 153–74, 175–82, 186–92, 411–12
  2nd Augmentation Battalion (Torgau): 166, 193, 382–8, 395
  Garde-Chevaulegers: 127–9, 130, 132–3, 149, 158–9, 163–6, 174, 179, 193, 246, 254, 256, 283
Hesse-Kassel: 207, 226, 257–8, 270, 278, 284–5, 308, 338, 378, 398
Hochberg, GL Graf Wilhelm von (Baden): 167–75, 179, 182, 186–93, 196, 199, 203–4, 372, 409, 411, 414
Hruby, Carl Eduard von Löwenberg-Hruby und Geleny (Austrian diplomat): 201

Italian troops: 24, 28, 34–6, 41, 66, 72–4, 79, 91–6, 103, 118, 124, 150–2, 157, 166, 174, 301–2, 328, 515

Jérôme Bonaparte, King of Westphalia: 5, 84, 119, 205–16, 219–28, 230, 233, 235–41, 243, 249, 256, 258–89, 309, 378, 398, 401, 409, 411
Jett, GM Karl August Maximilian von (Württemberg): 25, 27, 30, 44–5, 47, 49, 63, 66, 68, 77, 82, 83, 92, 98, 118

Kalisch, Battle of (13 February): 4, 166, 297, 513
Kassel: Chernishev's attack on: 5, 205, 206, 262–81, 284–5, 288, 410–11, 414
Katzbach, Battle of the (26 August): 159–60, 164, 247, 302, 321, 373
Kechler, Oberstleutnant Johann Karl Christoph von (Württemberg): 53–4, 59, 69, 74–5, 409
Kellermann, Marshal François (Duke of Valmy): 261, 263, 273–5, 280
Kitzen, Engagement at (17 June): 51–8, 112, 118, 324, 409
Klösterlein, GB Karl Friedrich Adolph von (Westphalia): 259–61, 288, 343–4
Königstein Fortress: 335, 389, 393–4
Kulm, Battle of (29–30 August): 85, 163, 335–7, 342
Küstrin, Blockade/Siege of: 20, 24, 113, 211, 217, 222, 224, 239, 245, 346, 370, 374–9, 395

Langeron, General of Infantry Louis Alexander Andrault (Russia): 105
Lanusse, GD Pierre: 246, 251–2, 327–30
Laplane, GB > GD Jean Grégoire Barthélmy Rouger, comte de: 150–3, 379–81, 395, 410
Latour-Maubourg, GD Marie Victor Nicholas de Fay, marquis de: 248, 310
LeCoq, GL Carl Christian Erdmann Edler von (Saxony): 68
Leipzig, Battle of (Battle of Nations): 3–6, 83, 84, 89–90, 99–102, 105–10, 112, 113, 116, 120, 121, 123, 130, 158–9, 174–96, 198, 199–200, 202–4, 248, 250, 253, 257–8, 281–5, 299, 302, 303, 315–16, 331, 332, 343, 363, 367, 379, 381, 384–7, 389, 390, 392, 394, 395, 396, 401, 405, 409–14, 513, 515
Le Marois, GD Jean Léonor François: 241, 251–3, 311, 327–9, 331, 340, 342, 343, 369, 381, 396
Lemoine, GD Louis: 243, 328
Linker, Major Johann August Ludwig von (Weimar): 28, 293, 320–6, 332, 344, 411, 515
Lippe military units: 251, 291–4, 328, 332–3, 337–41, 343, 350–2, 356–7, 369–70, 381
Lüneburg, Battle of (2 April): 210, 225, 229
Lützen, Battle of (2 May): 30, 48, 130, 131, 135–46, 149, 155–7, 164, 180, 195, 230–1, 301–2, 311, 313, 323, 333, 405, 407, 410
Lützow, Major Ludwig Adolph Wilhelm von (Prussia): 53–60, 112, 206, 236, 324, 359

MacDonald, GD Étienne Jacques (Duke of Taranto): 44–7, 49, 80, 140, 160–2, 174, 175, 215, 218, 237–8, 247–8, 281, 301–2, 349

Index

Magdeburg: 5, 52, 131, 205, 207, 210–11, 219–21, 222, 224–5, 232–6, 239, 241, 243, 245–6, 250–4, 260, 262, 280, 285, 293, 301, 311, 326–31, 337–44, 346, 369, 370, 381, 383, 389, 395, 397
Maillot de la Treille, Oberst > GM Nikolaus Hubert von (Bavaria): 382, 384, 386, 392, 397
Marchand, GD Jean Gabriel: 28, 119, 126, 132–8, 142–3, 161–3, 175–9, 186–8, 292, 294, 306, 411
Maret, Hughes Bernard (Duke of Bassano): 14–15, 134, 147, 172, 279, 302, 323, 325
Margaron, GD Pierre: 168–70, 174
Marmont, Marshal Auguste (Duke of Raguse): 38, 60, 85–8, 100, 105–9, 113, 118, 133, 138, 149, 174, 225, 230–2, 238, 297, 301, 316, 411
Marwitz, Oberstleutnant Friedrich August Ludwig von der (Prussia): 260–3, 286, 343–4, 381
Maureillan, GB Jean Poitevin Baron de: 410
Maximilian I. Joseph, King of Bavaria: 4, 7–9, 14, 114–17, 200, 224, 290–1, 307
Metternich, Clemens von (Austria): 11, 104, 113, 116–17, 205, 326, 337
Möckern, Battle of (2–5 April): 131, 300–1 (see 'Leipzig' for the sub-battle at Möckern in October)
Modlin, Blockade of: 293, 296, 298, 346–7, 370–4, 395, 411
Montgelas, Maximilian Graf von (Bavaria): 9–10, 114, 116, 120
Morand, GD Charles Antoine: 36, 42, 44, 47, 66–8, 71–4, 90–6, 112
Morand, GD Joseph: 290–1, 347
Murat, Marshal Joachim, King of Naples: 88, 221, 308, 312, 353, 412

Napoleon: 3–6, 26, 28–9, 52–3, 57, 67, 106, 109, 111, 114, 172, 173, 196, 210, 235, 277, 362, 372, 400; birthday commemorations: 61–2, 155, 334; relations with Württemberg: 8–16, 22–4, 50, 58, 83–4, 99–100, 115–17, 352; relations with Baden: 119–25, 169, 187–90, 197–9; relations with Hesse-Darmstadt: 126–33, 134, 145, 158, 199–204; and Westphalia/Jérôme: 205–9, 213, 215–16, 218, 219–24, 226–8, 230–2, 236–8, 240–1, 243, 248, 249–50, 268, 270, 273–4, 278–8, 281, 282, 284–5, 287–9; relations with the smaller states: 290, 294–9, 301–2, 304–6, 308–15, 317–26, 332, 333, 337, 338, 340–1, 342–4; relations with Saxony: 388–9; and the Rheinbund/German troops: 31, 44, 51, 66, 71–2, 86, 90, 97–8, 102, 113, 157, 163, 166, 183, 185, 194, 230, 360, 379–81, 392, 395–6, 397–99, 402–4, 407–8; and Russia/1812: 11–12, 104, 291, 408, 412–15; strategy, plans & operations: 34–8, 85, 88–9, 136, 137, 146, 147, 150, 151, 162, 164, 168, 182, 225, 229, 232, 244–5, 247, 256, 301, 303, 307, 335, 345–6, 348–9, 383–5, 388
Narbonne-Lara, GD Louis Marie Jacques Amalric de: 219, 382, 384–8, 410
Nassau duchies and troops, 271, 294, 308
Neuffer, GM Carl von (Württemberg): 25, 40–1, 44, 115,
Ney, Marshal Michel (Prince of the Moscow): 11, 28, 30–9, 67–81, 90–1, 100, 118–19, 133, 137–49, 154–7, 165, 178, 219, 225, 228–9, 287, 298, 306, 379, 385, 404–5, 410–13
Normann, GM Karl Friedrich Leberecht Graf von (Württemberg): 29, 51–61, 63, 83–90, 98, 100, 102–4, 105–13, 117–18, 183, 409, 411–12, 514

Oudinot, Marshal Nicholas Charles (Duke of Reggio): 62–8, 85, 149, 164–5, 231–2, 251–4, 256, 306–7, 329, 375, 404, 410–11, 512

Pauline, Princess of Lippe-Detmold: 338–40,
Piré, GB Hippolyte Marie Guillaume de Rosnyvinen, Comte de: 173, 412
Poland (Duchy of Warsaw): 4, 11–12, 18, 21, 119, 148, 296, 345–6, 349
Polish troops: 66, 186, 217–18, 237, 251–2, 257, 314, 329, 350–1, 357, 363–4, 371–2, 373–4, 381, 383, 390, 396, 516
Poniatowski, GD > Marshal Prince Joseph: 173, 188, 316
Prussia: 3, 5, 8–10, 16, 21–2, 27–8, 30, 34, 38–44, 50, 52–60, 62, 66–8, 70, 73–7, 86, 90–6, 105–7, 117–18, 120, 121, 123, 127, 136, 139–42, 146, 149, 150, 153, 161–2, 165–6, 172, 177, 179–96, 198, 201–4, 205–7, 210, 218, 222, 225–6, 231, 236–7, 240, 243, 248, 251, 254–8,

260–1, 263, 278, 280, 286, 292, 296, 300–1, 308, 311, 315, 316, 317, 318, 320–3, 326, 329–31, 332, 334, 335–7, 338, 340, 343–4, 345, 347, 349, 358, 362–3, 367, 373, 376–9, 386–8, 398–9, 406, 408, 410, 415, 511–16

Raglovich zum Rosenhof, GL Clemens von (Bavaria): 38, 68, 98, 172, 402, 404, 408, 413–14
Rapp, GD Jean: 29, 218, 348–70, 372, 395 6, 404, 410, 412
Rechberg und Rothenlöwen, GM > GL Joseph Graf von (Bavaria): 28, 193, 320
Reuß military units units (see also Danzig): 251, 291, 293, 328, 339, 341–3, 350, 352, 381
Reynier, GD Jean: 64, 66, 68, 72, 90, 152, 297, 372, 411–12, 513
Rheinbund (Combined) Regiments (see also Danzig): 291–4, 318–19, 328, 333, 339, 341, 343, 344, 349–61, 366–70, 374
Rigau, GB Antoine: 261–3, 268–9, 273–5, 285
Russia and Russian troops: 3, 8, 10–16, 24, 27, 32–9, 45–7, 64–6, 78, 91, 93, 105, 109, 130, 138–41, 146–7, 153, 156, 164, 174, 181, 187, 198, 201–3, 217, 218, 226, 230, 233–6, 248, 262–81, 285–8, 294, 297, 310, 323, 332, 333, 336, 345, 352–69, 372–4, 375–6, 385, 394, 399, 408, 411
Russian campaign (1812): 7, 10–16, 18, 24, 26–8, 43, 49, 68, 104, 119, 121–4, 127–9, 131, 133, 134, 137, 145, 147, 151, 167, 206, 211–21, 224, 230, 233, 241, 286, 290–3, 296–7, 300, 305, 309–10, 313, 319, 327, 333, 339, 341, 343, 349–51, 372, 374, 375, 393, 395, 401–4, 411, 413, 515
Russo-German Legion: 189, 287–8. 331, 361, 515–16
Ryssel, Oberst > GM Xaver Gustav Reinhold von (Saxony): 68, 386, 408, 411

Sahr, GM Carl Ludwig Sahrer von (Saxony): 410
Saxon duchies and military units (see also Danzig): 225, 251–3, 291, 293, 317–32, 350, 352, 367, 381, 514, 516
Linker's battalion: see Linker
Saxony, Kingdom of: 3–4, 22, 32, 50–1, 54, 59, 78, 81, 84, 98, 110, 114, 116, 121, 124, 136,

148, 149, 159, 187, 196, 198, 210, 224, 228, 231, 236–8, 241, 279, 286, 288, 296, 297, 314, 332–4, 345–6, 349, 388–9, 401, 403, 405, 511
Saxon military units (see also Danzig, Glogau, Modlin, 7th Corps): 3, 44, 56, 60, 77, 79–80, 109, 113, 133, 150–2, 156, 170, 174, 181, 186, 190, 232, 249, 290–1, 297, 341, 349–50, 359, 369, 371–4, 379–87, 392, 393–4, 395, 399, 404, 406–8, 410–15, 511, 513–14, 516
Schwarzburg principalities and military units units (see also Danzig): 291, 293–4, 318, 328, 332, 339, 341–3, 350, 352, 359, 361, 367, 368, 410
Schwarzenberg, Feldmarschall Carl Phillip Fürst zu (Austria): 11, 14, 110, 114, 190, 391
Sebastiani, GD Horace François Bastien: 151, 164, 229
Serra, Charles François Joseph: 390
Spain: 8, 119, 121, 122, 125, 127–9, 203, 210–15, 220–1, 224, 230, 269, 293–4, 296, 298, 305, 309–17, 318, 339, 342, 351, 357, 397
Stein, Baron Heinrich Friedrich Karl von und zum (Coalition): 14, 117, 125, 197–8, 206, 304, 307, 399–400, 408, 515
Stettin, Blockade/Siege of: 346, 348, 374–5
Stockhorn, i.e., GM Karl Freiherr Stockhorner von Starein (Baden): 125–6, 134–7, 143, 145, 148, 150, 153–6, 159, 161–3, 176, 178, 180, 182, 183, 185–6, 188, 191–3, 199, 202–3, 408, 512
Stockmayer, GM Ludwig Friedrich von (Württemberg): 25, 33, 36, 39–44, 46–7, 49, 63, 64, 67–70, 73–7, 82, 93, 94–5, 98, 118, 407

Tauentzien, GL Bogislav Friedrich Emanuel Graf (Prussia): 74, 388
Tettenborn, Maj. Gen. Friedrich Carl Freiherr (Russia): 208, 225
Thielmann, GL Johann Adolf Freiherr von (Saxony > Russia): 146, 172–3, 243, 258, 278, 332, 383, 410
Thorn, Blockade/Siege of: 6, 20, 151, 216, 345–9, 409, 412, 512
Tilsit, Treaties of: 205, 207
Torgau: 77–8, 84, 100, 130, 165, 232, 239, 245, 250, 254, 257, 299, 306, 307, 393; under Thielmann's command: 146, 332, 410;

Index

blockade of: 159, 160, 166–7, 193, 293, 297, 298, 346, 370, 381–8, 389, 395–6
Travers, GB Étienne Jacques: 273–4, 313, 315–17
Tyrol: 8, 99, 304, 318, 333

Vandamme, GD Dominique René (Count of Unebourg): 80, 85, 215–16, 229, 334–5, 336–7, 394
Victor, Marshal Claude (Duke of Belluno): 238–9, 242–5

Waldeck and military units (*see also* Danzig): 259–61, 291, 293, 339, 341, 343–4, 350–3, 381
Wallmoden-Gimborn, Lt. Gen. Ludwig Graf von (Coalition): 208, 258, 274, 277, 333, 337, 515
Warsaw, Duchy of: *see* Poland
Wartenburg, Battle of (3 October): 4–5, 81–3, 90–8, 100, 117, 159, 163, 164, 166, 256, 282, 321, 388
Westphalia: 5–6, 52, 56, 60, 83–4, 205–7, 219–22, 284–9, 326, 338, 343, 397–9, 400; as a 'model state': 207–9, 308–11, 398, 415–16
Westphalian military units (in general): 20, 24, 80, 149, 209–18, 222–37, 238–41, 242–8, 281–4, 290–2, 300, 320, 339–40, 344, 375–8, 395–6, 409–14, 511–13, 514, 516; in Dresden: 248–50, 384, 390–3; in defence of the kingdom: 225–38, 239–40, 258–81, 284–5
1st Infantry Regiment: 5–6, 211, 215, 218–19, 222–3, 224, 238, 245, 350–69, 397–8, 413, 416
31st Division (11th Corps): 175, 177, 238–9, 245–8, 250, 281
9th Infantry Regiment: 211, 220–1, 222, 224, 239, 245, 246, 249–54, 259, 327, 328–30, 381
Chevaulegers-Garde: 149, 158, 164–6, 179, 193, 211, 213–14, 220, 222–3, 224–7, 230–1, 239–40, 243, 245–6, 254–8, 259, 282–4, 288
Wintzingerode, Carl Friedrich Heinrich Levin (Württemberg): 14–15, 118
Wittenberg: 60, 64, 66, 71, 96, 146, 163, 165, 175, 195, 251–2, 300, 329–30, 346, 381

Wittgenstein, General of Cavalry Peter Khristianovich (Russia): 320, 333, 337
Wolff, GB Marc François Jérôme (Westphalia): 49, 67, 68, 91, 93, 149, 158, 164–6, 179, 193, 222, 224, 231, 239, 246, 254, 256–7, 284, 288, 411
Wrede, GL Carl Philipp Freiherr von (Bavaria): 4, 104, 113–17, 196–201, 291, 295, 299, 303–4, 361
Württemberg: 4–5, 7–16, 113–17, 119, 121–2, 126, 144, 172, 196, 198–201, 207, 208, 303–4, 326, 403
Württemberg military units: 16–33, 117–18, 139, 155, 217, 231, 298, 350, 352, 369, 375, 378, 401, 405, 407, 409, 411, 413, 414, 513–14
38th Division: 25, 28, 31, 34–51, 62–72, 98–104, 166, 193, 257, 513; at Dennewitz: 72–84; at Wartenburg: 90–8
Doering's Infantry Brigade: 29, 38–62, 63–6, 69–70, 73, 77, 82, 90–7, 98, 118
Normann's Cavalry Brigade: 29, 51–61, 63, 83–90, 98, 100, 102–4, 105–13, 117–18, 183, 409, 411–12, 514
Würzburg, Grand Duchy: 294–6, 303–4, 325; military units (*see also* Modlin): xii, 5, 290–1, 293, 370–4, 381–8, 511
Infantry Regiment in 7th Corps: 296–300
Chevaulegers: 293, 295–6, 300–3, 344

Yorck, GL Hans David Ludwig von (Prussia): 13–14, 27, 91–6, 105–7, 218, 321, 349

Zahna, Battle of (5 September): 70, 165, 254, 257
Zamosc, Blockade/Siege of: 346
Zandt, GB Friedrich von (Westphalia): 258–9, 263, 267, 269, 271–2, 275, 288–9
Zeppelin, Ferdinand Ludwig Graf von (Württemberg): 15, 24, 104, 110, 114–16, 198, 403
Zeschau, GL v Heinrich Wilhelm on (Saxony): 393–4
Żółtowski, GB Edward (Duchy of Warsaw): 252

Gazetteer

Numbers indicate maps

Modern/alternative names given in parentheses.

Aller River: 33, 41, 46, 48
Alt-Schottland (Stare Szkoty): 49
Annaburg: 36, 38

Baruth: 33, 36, 38, 41, 44
Basankwitz: 34
Bautzen (Budyšin): 33, 34, 38, 41, 44
Berlin: 33, 36, 41, 44, 46, 48
Bernburg: 46
Bettelbrücke (Beggar's Bridge): 47
Bettenhausen: 47
Bischofswerda: 38
Bleddin: 36, 39
Blockhouses (Langfuhr/Danzig): 49
Bober River: 33, 41, 44
Bölauberg (Bautzen): 34
Braunschweig (Brunswick): 33, 41, 44, 46, 48
Breitendorf: 44
Bremen: 33, 41, 44, 46, 48
Breslau (Wrocław): 33, 41, 44, 48
Bunzlau (Bolesławice): 33, 41, 44, 48

Chemnitz: 44, 46
Coburg: 41, 48
Cölln: 34

Cottbus: 33, 38, 48
Crossen (Krosno Odrzańskie): 48
Częstochowa: 48

Dahme: 33, 36, 38
Danzig (Gdańsk): 33, 41, 44, 48, 49
Delitzsch: 38, 40, 45
Dennewitz: 36, 38, 41, 44
Dessau: 33, 38, 41, 44, 46
Dirschau (Tczew): 41
Dresden: 33, 38, 41, 44, 46, 48
Düben: 36, 38, 40
Düsseldorf: 46

Eilenburg: 38, 40
Eisdorf: 42
Elbe River: 33, 36, 37, 38, 39, 41, 42, 44, 46, 48
Elster (town): 39
Elster (Weiße) River: 38, 40, 43
Erfurt: 33, 41, 44, 45, 46, 48
Euper: 33, 36, 37

Flossgraben: 42
Frankfurt am Main: 46
Frankfurt-an-der-Oder: 41, 48
Freiberg: 33, 38, 41, 44, 46
Freyburg: 38, 45
Friedberg: 45
Fulda: 41, 46
Fulda River: 44, 45, 46, 47

Gadegast: 36
Gera: 33, 38, 45
Gießen: 41, 46
Globig: 36, 39
Glogau (Glogow): 33, 41, 44, 48
Gohlis: 40, 43
Görlitz: 33, 41, 48
Gotha: 33, 41, 44, 45, 46
Gottlobsberg: 34
Graudenz (Grudziądz): 33, 41, 44, 48
Grimma: 38, 43
Großbeeren: 33, 41, 44
Großenhain: 41
Großgörschen: 42
Groß-Rosen (Rogoźnica): 35
Großwelka: 34
Gutschdorf (Goczałków): 35

Hagelberg: 38, 44
Halberstadt: 33, 41, 44, 46, 48
Halle: 38, 40, 45
Hamburg: 33, 41, 44, 46, 48
Hanover: 33, 41, 44, 46
Harz Mountains: 33, 41, 44, 45
Haynau (Chojnów): 41
Heiligenstadt: 44, 45
Heiterer Blick farmstead: 40
Helsa: 45, 47
Hersfeld (Bad Hersfeld): 45
Herzberg: 36, 38
Herzogswaldau (Niedaszów): 35

Gazetteer

Hof: 33, 41, 44
Hoyerswerda: 33, 38, 41, 44

Ilmenau: 41, 45

Jauer (Jawor): 33, 35
Jena: 33, 41, 44, 45
Jeschütz: 34
Johannisberg: 49
Jüterbog: 33, 36, 38

Kabrun: 49
Kaja (Caja): 42
Kalisch (Kalisz): 33, 41, 44, 48
Kamenz: 38
Kassel: 33, 41, 44, 45, 46, 47, 48
Katzbach River: 41
Kaufungen: 45, 46, 47
Kemlitz: 36
Kiefernberg (Bautzen): 34
Kitzen: 33, 42
Kleingörschen: 42
Kleinzschocher: 40
Kleinwelka: 34
Klix: 34
Koblenz: 46
Kolberg: 33, 41, 44
Königsberg (Kaliningrad): 48
Königsbrück: 38
Königshofen (Bad Königshofen): 41
Königstein: 48
Königswartha: 33, 34, 41
Kopatschberg (Kopatche, Bautzen): 34
Köthen: 38
Krakow (Kraków): 48
Kreckwitz/Kreckwitz Heights: 34
Kropstädt: 36
Kupferhammer: 47
Kurzlipsdorf: 38
Küstrin (Kostrzyn): 33, 41, 44, 48

Langfuhr (Wrzeszcz): 49
Langensalza (Bad Langensalza): 45, 46
Lauban (Lubań): 33
Leipzig: 33, 40, 41, 43, 44, 45, 46, 48; Leipzig gates: 43
Leipzig Gate (Kassel): 47
Lichtenau: 45
Liegnitz (Legnica): 41
Lindenau: 40
Lindenthal: 40
Lüben (Lubin): 41, 44
Lübben: 38, 41, 44
Lübeck: 33, 41, 44, 48
Luckau: 36, 38, 41, 44
Luckenwalde: 36, 38
Luga: 34
Lüneburg: 33, 41, 48
Lützen: 33, 38, 40, 41, 42, 45

Magdeburg: 33, 38, 41, 44, 46, 48
Mainz (Mayence): 46
Marienberg fortress: see Würzburg
Marzahna: 36, 38
Meissen: 38
Melsungen: 45, 47
Merseburg: 38, 45, 46
Meuchen: 42
Miggau (Migowo): 49
Minden: 44, 46
Mittenwalde: 36
Möckern (Elbe): 41
Möckern (Leipzig): 40
Modlin: 48
Morschen: 45
Mühlhausen: 45
Mulde River: 36, 38, 41, 44
Münden: 45, 47

Narew River: 48
Naumburg: 38, 45
Nehrung: 49
Niederfeld (Dolnik): 49
Niederzwehren: 47

Niemen River (Nieman, Neman, Memel): 48
Nordhausen: 45
Nuthe River: 38

Ochsenfurt: 33, 41, 44
Oder River: 33, 41, 44, 48
Oehna (Bautzen): 34
Oehna (Dennewitz): 36, 38
Ohra (Orunia): 49
Oliva Gate (Danzig): 49
Ortrand: 38

Parthe River: 38, 43
Pegau: 38
Petrikau (Piotrków Trybunalksi): 48
Pietzkendorf (Piecewo, now Piecki): 49
Pilica River: 48
Pillau: 48
Pirna: 38
Plauen: 33, 41, 44, 48
Pleiße River: 38, 43
Pließkowitz: 34
Płock: 48
Posen (Poznań): 33, 41, 44, 48
Possendorf: 38
Prague (Praha): 41
Primkenau (Przemków): 33, 36
Profen (Mściwojów): 35
Purschwitz: 34

Quatitz: 34
Queiss River (Kwisa): 33, 41, 44

Radefeld: 38, 40, 45
Rahna: 42
Reichelsgarten: 43
Richtersgarten: 43
Rietzschke stream: 40
Rochlitz: 33
Roda (Stadtroda): 45
Rosslau: 38

Rudolstadt: 45
Ruhla: 45

Saale River: 33, 38, 41, 44, 45
Sagan: 48
Schildau: 38
Schidlitz (Siedlce): 49
Schleiz: 45
Schleusingen: 45
Schlieben: 38
Schellmühl (Młyniska): 49
Schönewalde: 36
Schönfeld/Leipzig: 40
Schönfeld (Łostowice): 49
Schottenhäuser: 49
Schmilkendorf: 37
Schwarze Elster River: 36, 38
Schwedt: 33, 41, 44, 48
Schwerin: 33, 41, 44, 48
Silesia: 33, 41, 44, 48
Sondershausen: 45
Spandau: 33, 41, 44, 48
Speicher-Insel (Danzig): 49
Spree River: 34, 38
Sprottau: 33
Stadtgebiet (Oruńskie Przedmieście): 49
Starsiedel: 42
Stettin (Szczecin): 33, 41, 44, 48

Stolzenberg (Chełm): 49
Stralsund: 33, 41, 44, 48
Striegau (Strzegom): 33
Strieß (Strzyża): 49

Tangermünde: 33, 41, 48
Taucha: 38
Tauroggen (Tauragė): 48
Thießen (Coswig): 36, 37
Thorn (Toruń): 33, 41, 44, 48
Thuringia: 45
Tilsit: 48
Trebbin: 36, 38
Torgau: 33, 36, 38, 41, 44, 46, 48

Unstrut River: 38, 45

Vacha: 41
Vistula River: 33, 41, 44, 48, 49

Wabern: 45, 46
Wanfried: 45
Warsaw: 48
Warthe (Warta) River: 33, 41, 44, 48
Weimar: 33, 41, 44, 45, 48
Weinberg (Bautzen): 34
Weiße Elster River, *see* Elster

Weiße Steine (Bautzen): 34
Weißenfels: 38, 45
Werben: 36
Wesel: 46
Weser River: 33, 41, 44, 45, 46, 48
Wetzlar: 46
Wiederitzsch: 38, 40
Wittenberg: 33, 36, 37, 38, 41, 44, 46, 48
Witzenhausen: 45
Wolfenbüttel: 46
Wolfsanger: 47
Wölkau: 38
Wonneberg (Ujescisko): 49
Würzburg: 33, 41, 44, 46, 48
Wurzen: 38, 41
Wütende Neisse River: 35

Zahna: 36, 37, 38
Zamosc: 48
Zeitz: 33, 41, 44, 45
Zesch (Zesch am See): 36, 41, 44
Zigankendorf (Suchanino): 49
Zittau: 44
Zwethau: 36, 38